Proceedings in Parliament 1625

The preparation of this volume was made possible in part by a grant from the Texts Program of the National Endowment for the Humanities, an independent federal agency.

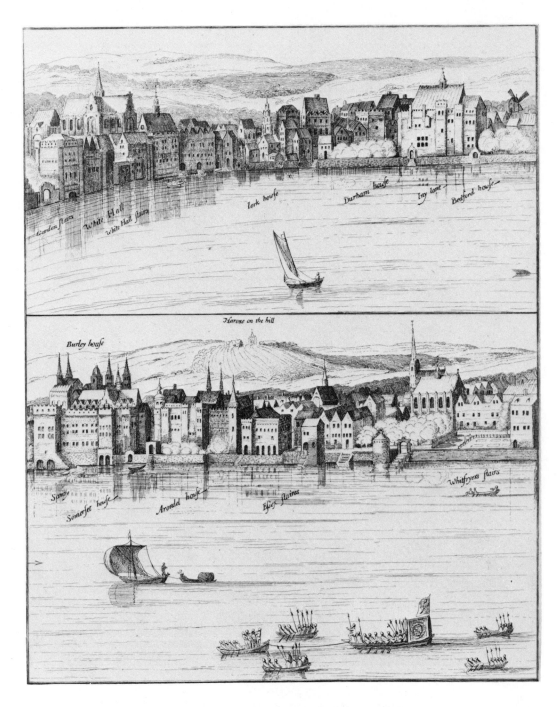

Prospect of London from Whitehall to Whitefriars,
engraving by Richard Sawyer after Visscher

Proceedings in Parliament

1625

Edited by
Maija Jansson and William B. Bidwell

The Yale Center for Parliamentary History
J. H. Hexter, Director

New Haven and London   Yale University Press

Library of Congress catalog card number: 86–50026
International Standard Book Number: 0–300–03544–6

Set in Baskerville Roman types.
Printed in the United States of America by
Halliday Lithograph, West Hanover, Mass.

*The paper in this book meets the guidelines for
permanence and durability of the Committee on
Production Guidelines for Book Longevity of the
Council on Library Resources.*

Permission to reproduce Richard Sawyer's engraving of
the prospect of London from Whitehall to Whitefriars
Stairs during the reign of James I (frontispiece) was
granted by the Yale Center for British Art, Paul Mellon
Collection.
Permission to reproduce the engravings of William
Fiennes, Viscount Saye and Sele, and Thomas Howard,
Earl of Arundel and Surrey (see below, p. 26), and Sir
Thomas Edmondes (see below, p. 188) from the
Graham collection was granted by the Beinecke Rare
Book and Manuscript Library, Yale University.

The Yale Center for Parliamentary History

CONTENTS

DIRECTORIAL ACKNOWLEDGMENTS

As always to cover the cost of its work the Yale Center for Parliamentary History has relied on the help of three organizations. For its home headquarters it has enjoyed the hospitality of Yale University along with indispensable access to the treasures of Yale's book collections and the accessibility of its president, A. Bartlett Giamatti, to the Director's more anguished howls of administrative suffering. For the expenses of publication the Center has received the aid of The John Ben Snow Memorial Trust. And, as for more years than the Director would care to acknowledge, the largest share of the Center's costs has come from grants from the Division of Research Programs of the National Endowment for the Humanities. There the Director of the Center has benefitted from the good sense and good advice of Kathy Fuller and Helen Aguera of the Division staff and from the endless patience of the Division's Director, Harold Cannon.

The Center has also had the help of a new benefactor, The Leverhulme Trust (London). The Director is most grateful to the Trust for that help and for the time and undivided attention he received from the Director, Dr. Ronald Tress, on a visit to London four years ago.

Here the Director wishes for the first time to attempt adequate acknowledgment of the two people on whom for years he has relied for the devotion and the quality of work that has made the editorial performance of the Center the best ever—Dr. William Bidwell and Dr. Maija Cole. Responsibility for that quality rests on them. A recent reviewer refers with awe to the index of *Proceedings in Parliament 1628* which, he said, "must have taxed the capacities of the finest word-processor". The capacities were actually supplied by the hands and eyes of Dr. Bidwell. This time round on *Proceedings in Parliament 1625* we were able to bring the computer to the Center's assistance.

At this moment the Director wishes to single out Dr. Cole for particular congratulations and thanks. While carrying a full-time load of editorial and administrative work at the Center Maija Cole also edited *Proceedings in Parliament 1614 (House of Commons)* and finished her work on *Two Diaries of the Long Parliament* recently published (under her maiden name, Maija Jansson) by Alan Sutton, Ltd. and St. Martin's Press. Finally, she has found time to shed light and truth on undergraduate Yalies in her seminar at Davenport College on early modern palaeography and at the same time to replenish the till at the Center with her seminar stipend, and thus to provide it with that saving bit of income for which it does not have to account.

What would the Director do without both of them? God knows!

J. H. Hexter

EDITORIAL ACKNOWLEDGMENTS

The editors of *Proceedings in Parliament 1625* wish first to thank those individuals who helped prepare the volume for press. In the early stage of the editorial work, Myra Rifkin, for two years a member of the staff, assisted in transcribing and organizing the sources used. Professor Paul Bushkovitch of Yale University identified and translated many of the Latin passages in the texts. Professor Paul Slack of Exeter College, Oxford, supplied us with references regarding the spread of the plague. Professor Robert Ruigh of the University of Missouri allowed us to print his transcript of Richard Dyott's diary, and supplied us with a full description of that manuscript. He has also answered our queries about events in the parliament of 1624. During the preparation of *Proceedings in Parliament 1625* Professor Conrad Russell, Editorial Consultant to the Center, has answered numerous technical and substantive questions on that parliament for us. He also made many useful suggestions after reading our final transcripts. Professor John Gruenfelder of the University of Wyoming generously shared with us all of the materials on the parliament of 1625 that he collected while writing his book on early Stuart elections. Those materials expanded and enriched the Appendix to this volume. On procedure in the House of Lords the editors have relied on the expertise of Professor Elizabeth Read Foster of Bryn Mawr College. Vernon F. Snow of Syracuse University has given us suggestions and ideas that grew out of his deep interest in parliament and its procedures. As Consultant to the Center, Professor Mary Frear Keeler has provided invaluable perceptive judgments on the text as she did on the Center's previous set of volumes, *Proceedings in Parliament 1628*. For the generosity with which

all these scholars have given their time and effort we are most grateful.

Our typist, Richard Philibert, became an essential part of the production of our book. We thank him for the invaluable service he performed in typing text, footnotes, and the front and back materials replete with complex tables and index numbers.

We also want to thank our editors at Yale University Press for their counsel and advice regarding the production of the book. Charles Grench, history editor, and Mary Alice Galligan, editions editor, patiently answered questions about design and copy editing as well as about distribution and financing.

During our work on this volume the Yale Center has incurred numerous debts to many archives and libraries, to many archivists and librarians. Most of all, of course, to the Yale University Library. All of the editorial work on *Proceedings in Parliament 1625* was carried out in the Center for Parliamentary History, Sterling Memorial Library, Yale University. Rutherford Rogers, University Librarian, and Donald Engley, Associate University Librarian, emeritus, have helped us find our way through administrative mine fields through which a small enterprise in a great university must make its way. From the staffs of Sterling Library, the Yale University Law Library, and the Beinecke Rare Book and Manuscript Library we have always received courteous assistance. Mr. Stephen R. Parks, Curator of the Osborn Collection (Beinecke Library) has generously allowed us to examine seventeenth-century manuscripts in that collection and granted us permission to print selections from John Brown's Commonplace Book. Alexandra Mason, Archivist of the Department of Special Collections, Spencer Research Library, University of Kansas, and her staff have kept the Center abreast of their parliamentary holdings and allowed us to print selections from the manuscript of parliamentary notes—MS E237—in that library. For help in our researches in England we owe thanks to M. P. G. Draper, Archivist at the Bedford Estate Office, and to the staffs of the British Library and the House of Lords Record Office. Maurice F. Bond, recently retired Clerk of the Records at the H.L.R.O., Harry S. Cobb, present Clerk of the Records, and David Johnson, Assistant Clerk, have not only aided our researches on this volume but have also been staunch supporters of the Center itself as the place where research in Tudor and Stuart parliamentary history can best be carried out in the United States. Ruth F. Vyse, Oxford University Assistant Archivist, helped us to uncover the materials in the University archives that relate to the parliament of 1625. We would also like to thank for their help the staffs of the Hampshire Record Office, the Institute of Historical Research, and the Public Record Office, in London, and the staff of the Northamptonshire Record Office.

For permission to publish manuscripts in this volume the editors wish to thank the following persons and libraries: the trustees of the Bedford Estates for Bedford MS. 197 (Woburn MSS., H.M.C., 197); the British Library for sections of B.L. Add. MSS. 26,239 and 48,091, Harleian MSS. 161 and 5007, and excerpts from the Stowe and Egerton MSS.; Lt. Col. P. T. Clifton, for his permission to print MS. cl/c/360, on deposit in the University of Nottingham, Department of Manuscripts; Captain P. Davies-Cooke for his permission to print an election letter deposited on loan at the Clwyd Record Office, Hawarden (D/GW/2109); Mr. Richard Dyott of Freeford Manor for his permission to print Richard Dyott's diary of 1625 on deposit at the Staffordshire Record Office; the East Sussex Record Office and the Rye Town Council for permission to print documents from the Rye Corporation manuscripts; the Essex Record Office, Chelmsford, Essex, for permission to publish selections from the Morant MSS., volume 43; the Great Yarmouth Bor-

ough Council for permission to publish extracts from the Assembly Book in the appendix to this volume. We also wish to thank A. R. I. Hill, for permission to publish several letters from Downshire MSS. vols. 17, 18, and 29; and Amanda Arrowsmith, County Archivist, Berkshire Record Office, for her attention to our inquiries about this collection; the House of Lords Record Office, for permission to reprint the Journals for both Houses, Sir Nathaniel Rich's notes (Historical Collections 143 and 204), and selections from the Main Papers and Braye MSS.; the Huntingdon Library, San Marino, for permission to print a letter from the Hastings collection (HA. 5499); the Masters of the Bench of the Inner Temple for permission to print Petyt MS. 538/8; Mr. J. L. Jervoise for permission to print a letter to Henry Sherfield on deposit at the Hampshire Record Office (H.R.O. 44/M/69); the National Library of Wales for permission to print letters from the Wynn collection and the Chirk Castle MSS.; the Keeper of the Archives, University of Oxford, for permission to print a part of the Chancellor's Court Register, 1625–1628 (c.c. Reg., 1625–8, hyp./A/36); the Kent Archives Office for permission to print materials relating to the Sandys/Scott election controversy; the Leicestershire Record Office for permission to print materials in the Leicester Borough Records; the Norfolk and Norwich Record Office and the Great Yarmouth Borough Council for permission to print materials from the Yarmouth Corporation MSS.; the Northamptonshire Record Office and His Grace the Duke of Buccleuch and Queensberry for permission to print Lord Montagu's Journal, Montagu MSS., vol. 30; and to Mr. P. I. King, Archivist, and the Trustees of the Duke of Sutherland for permission to print a letter from the Ellesmere (Brackley) collection (E.B. 585/1); the Public Record Office, London, for permission to print documents from State Papers, Foreign and Domestic;

the Queen's College, Oxford, for permission to cite from Q.C. 449; the Scarborough Borough Council for permission to print letters on the parliamentary elections of 1625 in the borough records; the Warwick Town Council, for permission to print extracts from the Warwick Borough Muniments Minute Book; and the York City Archives for permission to print selections from the House Book, 1613–1635.

Last, we wish especially to thank Lord Eliot for permission to reprint Sir John Eliot's *Negotium Posterorum*.

Maija Jansson
William B. Bidwell

ABBREVIATIONS AND SHORT TITLES

A.C.	*Alumni Cantabrigienses.* Cambridge, 1922–1927.
A.O.	*Alumni Oxonienses.* Oxford, 1891–1892.
A.P.C.	*Acts of the Privy Council of England.* London, 1921–.
Appeal	Montagu, Richard, *Appello Caesarem. A just appeale from two unjust informers.* London, 1625. *S.T.C.,* no. 18030.
Archbp.	Archbishop.
Ashton, *Crown and the Money Market*	Ashton, Robert, *The Crown and the Money Market 1603–1640.* Oxford, 1960.
A.T.	Attendance Table. The compiled table indicating attendance and excuse of the members of the Upper House in the parliament of 1625, pp. 592–597 in the present volume.
Aylmer, *King's Servants*	Aylmer, G. E., *The King's Servants.* London, 1974 (Revised ed.).
Bibliotheca Lindesiana	*Bibliotheca Lindesiana, A Bibliography of Royal Proclamations of the Tudor and Stuart Sovereigns.* Oxford, 1910.
Birch, *Court and Times of Chas. I*	Birch, Thomas, *The Court and Times of Charles the First. . . .* 2 vols., London, 1848.
Black's *Law Dict.*	Black, Henry Campbell, *Black's Law Dictionary,* 3rd ed. St. Paul, Minn., 1933.
B.L.	British Library.
Bowyer	*The Parliamentary Diary of Robert Bowyer 1606–1607,* ed. by David Harris Willson. Minneapolis, 1931.
Bp.	Bishop.
Brook, *Lives of the Puritans*	Brook, Benjamin, *The Lives of the Puritans.* 3 vols., London, 1813.
c.	*capitulum.*
Cal. Pat. Rolls	*Calendar of the Patent Rolls preserved in the Public Record Office.* London, 1893–.
Cal. S.P. Dom.	*Calendar of State Papers: Domestic Series.* London, 1857–.
Cal. S.P. Venetian	*Calendar of State Papers and Manuscripts Relating to English Affairs, Existing in the Archives and Collections of Venice and in the Other Libraries of Northern Italy.* London, 1900–.
C.C.C.	Corpus Christi College.
C.D. 1621	*Commons Debates 1621,* ed. by Wallace Notestein, Frances Helen Relf, and Hartley Simpson. 7 vols., New Haven, 1935.
C.D. 1625 (Knightley MS.)	*Debates in the House of Commons in 1625,* ed. by Samuel Rawson Gardiner. London: Camden Society, 1873. An account of proceedings in the 1625 parliament in the possession of Sir Rainald Knightley at the end of the nineteenth century but now lost. The account is sometimes referred to as the "Fawsley" manuscript after the ancestral home of the Knightley family.
C.D. 1628	*Commons Debates 1628,* ed. by Robert C. Johnson, *et al.,* volumes 1–4 of the 6 volume set of *Proceedings in Parliament 1628,* New Haven, 1977–1983.

Chamberlain, *Letters*

Chamberlain, John, *The Letters of John Chamberlain*, ed. by N. E. McClure. 2 vols., Philadelphia: The American Philosophical Society, 1939.

Chron. Angliae

Chronicon Angliae . . . , ed. by Edward Maunde Thompson. London: Rolls Series, 1874.

C.J.

Journals of the House of Commons. London, 1742–.

Cobbett, *Parl. Hist.*

Cobbett, William, *The Parliamentary History of England. From the Norman Conquest, in 1066, to the year, 1803.* 36 vols., London, 1806–1820.

Coke, *First Inst.*

The First Part of the Institutes of the Laws of England; or A Commentary upon Littleton. 3 vols., London, 1794.

Coke, *Second Inst.*

The Second Part of the Institutes of the Laws of England. 2 vols., London, 1797.

Coke, *Third Inst.*

The Third Part of the Institutes of the Laws of England. London, 1797.

Coke, *Fourth Inst.*

The Fourth Part of the Institutes of the Laws of England. London, 1797.

Coke, *Reports*

The Reports of Sir Edward Coke in Thirteen Parts. 6 vols., London, 1826.

D'Ewes, *Journal . . . Elizabeth*

D'Ewes, Sir Simonds, *A Compleat Journal of the Votes, Speeches and Debates, both of the House of Lords and House of Commons throughout the whole Reign of Queen Elizabeth.* London, 1693.

Dietz, *Public Finance*

Dietz, F. C., *English Public Finance 1558–1641.* New York, 1932.

D.N.B.

The Dictionary of National Biography Founded in 1882 by George Smith, ed. by Sir Leslie Stephen and Sir Sidney Lee. New York, 1885–1904.

Dyer, *Reports*

Reports of Cases in the Reigns of Hen. VIII, Edw. VI, Q. Mary, and Q. Eliz., taken and collected by Sir James Dyer, Knt. 3 vols., Dublin, 1794.

E.H.R.

English Historical Review.

Eliot, *Negotium*

An Apology for Socrates and Negotium Posterorum: by Sir John Eliot, ed. by Rev. A. B. Grosart. 2 vols., London, 1881. The text of *Negotium Posterorum* is printed in the present volume, pp. 487–569, from the original manuscript at Port Eliot.

Elsynge, *Parliaments*

Elsynge, Henry, *The Manner of Holding Parliaments in England.* London, 1768.

E.R.

[The] English Reports, full reprints. London, 1907.

Fleta

Fleta, ed. by H. G. Richardson and G. O. Sayles. 2 vols., London: Selden Society, 1955.

Forster, *Eliot*

Forster, John, *Sir John Eliot: A Biography, 1590–1632.* 2 vols., London, 1864.

Fortescue, *De Laudibus Legum Anglie*

Fortescue, Sir John, *De Laudibus Legum Anglie,* ed. and trans. by S. B. Chrimes. Cambridge, England, 1942.

Foss, *Judges*

Foss, Edward, *The Judges of England.* 7 vols., London, 1848–1864.

Foster, *Elsyng*

Foster, Elizabeth Read, *The Painful Labour of Mr. Elsyng.* Philadelphia: The American Philosophical Society, 1972.

Gagg	Montagu, Richard, *A Gagg for the new Gospel? No: A New Gagg for an old Goose.* London, 1624. *S.T.C.,* no. 18038.
Gardiner, *History of England*	Gardiner, S. R., *History of England from the Accession of James I to the Outbreak of the Civil War 1603–1642.* 10 vols., London, 1886.
Gascoigne, *Loci e Libro*	*Loci e Libro Veritatum,* passages selected from Gascoigne's Theological Dictionary, ed. by James E. Thorold Rogers. Oxford, 1881.
G.E.C.	G. E. C[okayne], *The Complete Peerage.* . . . 12 vols., London, 1910.
Gl.	Glossary of Foreign Words and Phrases.
Glanville, *Reports*	*Reports of Certain Cases Determined and Adjudged by the Commons in Parliament . . . collected by John Glanville.* London, 1775.
Grafton, *Chronicle*	Grafton's *Chronicle; or, History of England.* 2 vols., London, 1809.
H. of C.	House of Commons.
H. of L.	House of Lords.
Hacket, *Scrinia Reserata*	Hacket, John, *Scrinia Reserata: a Memorial Offer'd to the Great Deservings of John Williams, D.D.* London, 1693. Wing, *S.T.C.,* no. H 171.
Hall, *Chronicle*	Edward Hall's *Chronicle.* London, 1809.
Hatsell, *Precedents*	Hatsell, John, *Precedents of Proceedings in the House of Commons.* 4 vols., London, 1818 ed.
Hil.	Hilary term.
H.L.R.O.	House of Lords Record Office, London.
H.M.C.	Historical Manuscripts Commission.
Holinshed, *Chronicles*	Holinshed's *Chronicles of England, Scotland, and Ireland.* 6 vols., London, 1807.
Howell, *S.T.*	*A Complete Collection of State Trials and Proceedings for High Treason. . .,* compiled by T. B. Howell. 21 vols., London, 1816.
Jacob's *Law Dict.*	Jacob, Giles, *A New Law Dictionary.* London, 1732.
K.S.R.L.	Kenneth Spencer Research Library, University of Kansas.
Keeler, *L.P.*	Keeler, Mary Frear, *The Long Parliament, 1640–1641.* Philadelphia: The American Philosophical Society, 1954.
Knighton, *Chronicle*	*Chronicon Henrici Knighton,* ed. by Joseph Rawson Lumby. London: Rolls Series, 1889.
L. 1ᵃ; L. 2ᵃ	*Lectio prima* (first reading); *Lectio secunda* (second reading).
Leg. Cit.	Legal Citations, list of.
Le Neve's *Fasti*	*Le Neve's Fasti Ecclesiae Anglicanae . . . ,* compiled by John Le Neve and ed. by T. Duffus Hardy. 3 vols., Oxford, 1854.
Letters and Papers H. VIII	*Calendar of Letters and Papers, Foreign and Domestic, of H. VIII,* ed. by J. S. Brewer, J. Gairdner, and J. Gairdner, LL.D., and R. H. Brodie. 21 vols., London: Rolls Series, 1870–.
Levack, *Civil Lawyers*	Levack, Brian P., *The Civil Lawyers in England, 1603–1641.* Oxford, 1973.
L.J.	*Journals of the House of Lords.* London, 1767–.

Lords Debates 1624 and 1626	*Notes of the Debates in the House of Lords officially taken by Henry Elsyng, Clerk of the Parliaments, A.D. 1624 and 1626,* ed. by Samuel Rawson Gardiner. London: Camden Society, 1879.
L.P. 1628	*Lords Proceedings 1628,* ed. by Mary Frear Keeler, Maija Jansson Cole, William B. Bidwell, volume 5 of the 6 volume set of *Proceedings in Parliament 1628,* New Haven, 1977–1983.
m. (mbs.)	Membrane(s).
McGrath, *Papists and Puritans*	McGrath, Patrick, *Papists and Puritans under Elizabeth I.* London, 1967.
Matthew Paris, *Chronica*	Matthaei Parisiensis, *Chronica Majora,* ed. by Henry Richards Luard. London: Rolls Series, 1872–1880.
Mich.	Michaelmas term.
M.P.	Member of Parliament.
MS.; MSS.	Manuscript; manuscripts.
MS. Cal. Pat. Rolls	Manuscript calendars of the patent rolls, preserved in the Public Record Office, London. (Unprinted.)
Neale, *Elizabeth I and her Parliaments*	Neale, J. E., *Elizabeth I and her Parliaments 1584–1601.* New York, 1966 (Norton Library edition).
Nicholas, *Proceedings and Debates in 1621*	Nicholas, Edward, *Proceedings and Debates of the House of Commons in 1620 and 1621,* ed. by Thomas Tyrwhitt. 2 vols., Oxford, 1766.
O.B.	Orders of Business.
O.R.	*Return of the Name of Every Member of the Lower House of Parliament.* 2 vols., Accounts and Papers, Session of 1878 [London], 1878. The Official Return.
Pasch.	Paschae, Easter term.
pl.	*placita.*
Pollard and Redgrave, *S.T.C.*	Pollard, A. W., and G. R. Redgrave, *A Short-Title Catalogue of Books printed in England, Scotland, and Ireland and of English Books printed Abroad, 1475–1640.* London, 1926.
Privileges and Practice of Parliaments	*The Privileges and Practice of Parliaments in England.* London, 1640 (Reprinted 1979, Garland Publishing, Inc., New York).
P.R.O.	Public Record Office, London.
Proceedings in Parliament 1610	*Proceedings in Parliament 1610,* ed. by Elizabeth Read Foster. 2 vols., New Haven, 1966.
Q.C. 449	Queens College Manuscript 449 (see Introduction, below).
R.O.	Record Office.
Roll of Standing Orders	Roll of Standing Orders of the House of Lords, *The Manuscripts of the House of Lords.* Vol. X, New Series, ed. by Maurice F. Bond. London, 1953.
Rot. Parl.	*Rotuli Parliamentorum ut et Petitiones, et Placita in Parliamento.* 6 vols. [n.d., n.p.].
rot. pat.	Patent rolls, preserved in the Public Record Office, London. (Unprinted.)
Ruigh, *Parliament of 1624*	Ruigh, Robert E., *The Parliament of 1624.* Cambridge, Mass., 1971.

Rushworth, *Hist. Collections*

Rushworth, John, *Historical Collections of Private Passages of State, Weighty Matters in Law, Remarkable Proceedings in Five Parliaments.* London, 1659.

Russell, *Parliaments*

Russell, Conrad, *Parliaments and English Politics 1621–1629.* Oxford, 1979.

Rymer, *Foedera*

Rymer, Thomas (ed.), *Foedera Conventiones, Literae, et cujuscunque generis Acta Publica inter Reges Angliae.* 10 vols. [n.p.], Joannem Neaulme, 1739–1745.

Salvetti dispatch(es)

Manuscripts of Henry Duncan Skrine, Esq., dispatches of Amerigo Salvetti to the Grand Duke at Florence, Historical Manuscripts Commission, *Eleventh Report, Appendix, Part I.* London, 1887.

Shaw, *Knights*

Shaw, William A., *The Knights of England.* 2 vols., London, 1906 (Reprinted, Baltimore, 1971).

S.P.

State Papers. Public Record Office, London.

S.R.

The Statutes of the Realm. 11 vols., London, 1810–1828.

S.T.C.

See Pollard and Redgrave (above), and Wing (below).

Stuart Proclamations

Stuart Royal Proclamations, vol. I, ed. by James F. Larkin and Paul L. Hughes. Oxford, 1973. Vol. II, ed. by James F. Larkin. Oxford, 1983.

Stubbs, *Select Charters*

Stubbs, William, *Select Charters and Other Illustrations of English Constitutional History from the Earliest Times to the Reign of Edward the First.* Oxford, 1895.

Trin.

Trinity term.

Wing, *S. T. C.*

Wing, D. G., *Short-Title Catalogue . . . 1641–1700.* New York, 1945–1951.

Y.C.P.H.

Yale Center for Parliamentary History.

Introduction

INTRODUCTION

Proceedings in Parliament 1625 is the second major editorial effort of the Yale Center for Parliamentary History. The Center has already produced *Proceedings in Parliament 1628* in six volumes. It is now engaged in editing *Proceedings in Parliament 1626*. When that work is finished inquirers will have available in modern editions, properly annotated, all the known accounts of the first three parliaments of Charles I.[1]

Of all the parliaments of the 1620s that of 1625 is least fully dealt with in the surviving sources. For the House of Commons in 1621, 1624, 1626, and 1628 there are notes on proceedings taken by members as business went forward day by day for the whole or most of a session. Of this sort of account no exemplar survives for 1625. Perhaps there never was such an account to survive. Besides the standard big-city diversions of London, in 1625 a major distraction took the minds of country members, ordinarily the most assiduous recorders of parliamentary proceedings,[2] off parliamentary matters. Before the parliament of 1625 assembled in London, one of the worst plague epidemics of the century had begun to ravage the City. Despite the onset of the disease, during the latter half of May and the first half of June the members were held in London by a series of prorogations.[3] The summer months were killing ones. The death toll in thirty-one London parishes, nearly a hundred and sixty-five during the week when the parliament at last opened, had increased by about 150 percent in the next fortnight. Recent estimates put the mortality in town from plague during 1625 at between one-eighth and one-fifth of the population. As of mid-August 4,500 Londoners were dying each week.

By then, however, the parliament of 1625 had been adjourned from London to Oxford. But pestilence preceded the members to the university city. The Oxford session lasted only ten days. With the plague loose in the land circumstances were not propitious for the conduct of parliamentary business, much less for assiduous daily note taking. In any case, although the plague did not at the outset markedly restrict attendance in parliament,[4] it may have done so when the deaths in London

---

1. Except for the proceedings of the House of Lords in 1629. The first modern edition of the accounts of a session of parliament, *Commons Debates for 1629*, ed. W. Notestein and F. Relf (Minneapolis, 1921), did not include the surviving accounts of proceedings in the House of Lords.

2. Singularly, none of the eminent lawyers, who always played a major role and sometimes a dominant one in the debates in Commons under the early Stuarts, appears to have taken regular notes on the proceedings of the House. Bulstrode Whitelocke, who kept a major journal of the parliament of 1626, attained eminence at law a generation later. No account of any parliament of the 1620s, however, can confidently be ascribed to the galaxy of legal lights that shone in the House of Commons during that decade.

3. Charles had to delay assembling the members waiting in London until the snarls in the marriage treaty with France were straightened out and his bride, Henrietta Maria, was delivered to England.

4. In terms of maximum numbers recorded in divisions between 1604 and 1629, the 1625 House of Commons, in its first division of 22 June, was of precisely middle rank. For that division the C.J. records 367 voting members and 4 tellers. The House was anxious for good attendance at Charles's first parliament and out of respect for the new King many were willing to take the risk of coming to plague-infested London for the opening of the session. On 5 July, ten business days later, the C.J. records a second division which indicates the presence of only 227 members and 4 tellers. Between the occurrence of the first and second divisions 140 fewer members were in attendance. The attendance figures for the Upper House also sharply decline between 22 June and 5 July: 17 bishops and 32 peers attended on 22 June; 14 bishops and 23 peers were present on 5 July. The decline in attendance in parliament can be correlated with the increase in plague deaths for the same period. During the week ending 7 July there were 428 more plague burials in London than there had been in the week ending 16 June as shown in the following table.

climbed precipitously between mid-June and early July and when the Houses reassembled in Oxford in August. In 1625 the generally shared expectation that the parliament would be a short one and would have little chance to do anything of consequence also may have inhibited the pens of the considerable number of members who had made extensive notes on business in prior parliaments or were to make them in future ones. Of the twenty-one men of the Lower House who kept extensive diaries in 1621 and/or 1624 and the eleven men who kept them in 1621 and/or 1628 only one—John Pym—kept such a diary in 1625.[5]

Paradoxically, although the parliament of 1625 was the least reported of its decade, up to the 1920s it was proportionally the most published one. Before 1921 only one contemporary account of the complete proceedings of any other parliament of the 1620s that a present day historian would feel comfortable to cite as an authority had appeared in print.[6] The two fullest narratives of the sitting of the House of Commons in 1625, those of Pym and Eliot, had been published in the nineteenth century, and, of course, the journals of both Houses in the eighteenth. Subsequently the only private journal of proceedings in the House

of Lords discovered up to now was published by the Historical Manuscripts Commission in its report on the manuscripts of the Duke of Buccleuch.

There remain some manuscripts on sittings of the Commons in 1625 not edited before now. More important, the two main contemporary private accounts of the proceedings in Commons, Eliot's and Pym's, are not available outside large libraries. Pym's narrative is hardly accessible except in those libraries, not all that numerous even in England, and less so elsewhere, which subscribed to Camden Society Publications in the 1870s, when the society issued it (Samuel Rawson Gardiner, ed., *Debates in the House of Commons in 1625* [London, 1873]). The initial restricted accessibility of Eliot's *Negotium Posterorum* was achieved by the human decision to publish but one hundred copies "for private circulation only" (Alexander B. Grosart, ed., *An Apology for Socrates and Negotium Posterorum: by Sir John Eliot* [London, 1881]). The effect of human decision has been accentuated by chemical reaction. The deterioration of the acidic paper on which the limited edition was published has by now reduced many of the few initial copies to dust. Finally, the previously published material on the parliament of

Week ending	All burials	Plague burials
2 June	395	69
9 June	434	91
16 June	510	165
23 June	640	239
30 June	942	390
7 July	1222	593
14 July	1741	1004
21 July	2850	1819
28 July	3583	2471
4 Aug.	4517	3659
11 Aug.	4855	4115
18 Aug.	5205	4463
25 Aug.	4841	4218
1 Sept.	3897	3344

Source note: Table reprinted from F. P. Wilson, *The Plague in Shakespeare's London* (Oxford, 1927), pp. 132, 136.

5. Sir Nathaniel Rich kept brief notes of proceedings on several days in 1625, as did Richard Dyott, but neither of these collections of fragmentary notes constitutes a full diary. See below for a description of the Rich and Dyott notes.

6. Except for the official journals of the two Houses and the assistant clerks' official notes of proceedings in the Upper House, only Edward Nicholas's *Proceedings and Debates in 1621* and the brief and fragmented notes of John Lowther (H.M.C., *13th Report*) had appeared before the 1920s.

1625 has by and large been simply transcribed rather than edited. Even S. R. Gardiner's transcription of the Knightley copy of Pym's diary is very lightly annotated. Inevitably, given the piecemeal publication of the various accounts, cross-referencing is practically nonexistent. No scholarly aids have been provided in the publication of any of the sources for the parliament of 1625 now in print.

The editors became acutely aware of the difference between having a uniformly and fully edited collection of sources and having the scatter of printed and manuscript material previously available for 1625 when they compared that scatter with the efficient and manageable arrangement of sources, annotated and cross-referenced and provided with aids to scholars in *Proceedings in Parliament 1628*. We[7] have used those volumes as our model. This does not mean that we have adhered slavishly to all the procedures we adopted in them. Since, however, those procedures seem on the whole to have pleased the scholars who have used the volumes, we have only adapted, amended, or abandoned them when such modifications seemed called for by the nature of the sources, by the discovery of a better way of presenting the sources, or by significant external constraints.

The last ominous phrase points to one change. The thumb indexes that make it easy to turn at once to the beginning of any day's proceedings in the volumes on debates in the House of Commons in 1628, a surviving touch of handicraft in a machine age, turned out to be an exorbitant luxury. We have to do without them in *Proceedings in Parliament 1625*. Because of the thumb indexes it did not matter that in the 1628 volumes of debates in Commons we put the dates in the running heads on the inside rather than the outside of the pages. By reversing the elements in the running

heads, placing the dates on the outside of the page (as we have already done in *Lords Proceedings 1628*), we have minimized the inconvenience to the readers of the loss of the thumb indexes.

We have also deviated somewhat from the editorial policy followed in *Proceedings in Parliament 1628* of presenting all major accounts of parliament in a consolidated day-by-day format rather than text-by-text. (For the rationale of that procedure, see *Commons Debates 1628*, I, Introduction, II C, p. 40.) No accounts of the proceedings in either House in 1628 were so personal, so disengaged from the minute-by-minute progress of the proceedings of the Houses, so engaged in eliciting the meaning or significance of those proceedings, as was Sir John Eliot's *Negotium Posterorum* for 1625. That work is about the parliament of 1625, but some of its most important passages describe events that did not take place on the floor of either House, although they help render intelligible events that did take place there. While Pym's accounts of parliaments tell something about the form of his mind—its tidiness, precision, sense of order—Eliot's *Negotium* reveals directly the substantive inclination of its author's mind—how he felt about the events he describes. Of all the accounts of parliaments by members, it alone aims at literary effectiveness. For that reason, to arrange it with the other accounts day-by-day would seem a repudiation of Eliot's own literary intention.[8] We did not, however, want to make it hard to use the materials in the *Negotium* in conjunction with that material in other sources to flesh out a day's proceedings. We have tried, as near as can be, to give users of this volume the best of both worlds. We have printed the *Negotium Posterorum* continuously from beginning to end separate from the day-by-day proceedings. We have, however, included in the daily

7. The "we" here and hereafter is neither regal nor editorial. It refers to the collectivity comprising the Director of the Yale Center for Parliamentary History and the co-editors of this volume.

8. As such an arrangement does not repudiate the (non-existent) literary intention of the other diarists.

Orders of Business references to the relevant passages from the *Negotium* at the chronologically appropriate points.

Because we did not make the editorial decision to publish the proceedings in the House of Lords for 1628 until *Commons Debates 1628* was already in press, we could not cross-reference from Commons debates to the Lords proceedings, but only the other way about. For 1625, however, we were able to cross-reference both ways.

With regard to the problem of identifying M.P.s who had surnames identical or similar to that of other members, we have followed the policy described in *Commons Debates 1628*, I, 37–39. Because of differences in membership a number of the 1628 identification problems do not occur with respect to the 1625 materials, however new ones arise. For example, the election of Edward Moore in addition to John and Poynings More makes it impossible to determine which one—or more—of the three spoke several times in the debates concerning religion; and it is equally hopeless to attempt to distinguish between Mr. (Edward) Clarke and Mr. (Henry) Clerke in the case of various committee appointments.

The rest of the Introduction to the *Proceedings in Parliament 1625* will concern itself first with the manuscripts recording those proceedings and second with the principles, practices, and procedures we have followed in editing those manuscripts, but only insofar as they deviate from the general editorial policy of the Yale Center fully described in *Commons Debates 1628,* I, Introduction, pp. 35–48, to which we refer the reader.

I. Manuscript Sources for the House of Lords

A. Official Sources

MS. Journal of the House of Lords

The manuscript Journal of the House of Lords, H.L.R.O., Vol. 11, for the parliament of 1625 comprises 118 pages; pages 1–102 are a record of the business of the Upper House, pages 104–118 an alphabetical index which was added to the MS. in the eighteenth century. The pages measure $17'' \times 11\frac{1}{2}''$, bound in rough calf, with two steel clasps. In the upper left-hand corner of page 1 of the MS. is the signature "H. Elsynge, *Cler. parliamentorum*". Henry Elsynge, Clerk of the Parliaments, also signed his name at the end of the last page of the account of the last day (12 August) of the second and last session of the parliament of 1625. On pp. 3–8 are the Latin writs of prorogation of 17 and 31 May, and 13 June. The daily accounts of proceedings for the London session (18 June–11 July) extend from p. 9 through p. 59. There is a list of members with annotations showing attendance before the record of each day's business. Pages 60 through 62 are blank. The account of proceedings for the Oxford session (1–12 August) extends from page 63 through page 99. The blank page 100 is followed on pp. 101–102 by a list giving the status of bills at the dissolution of the parliament; page 103 is blank, followed by the index of proceedings of both sessions (pp. 104–118).

The compilation of the fair copy of the Lords Journals was the responsibility of Elsynge. He drew on his own rough notes and probably on those of his two underclerks.[9] However, for 1625 little of this material has survived (see below: H.L.R.O., Manuscript Minutes, H.L., 1625).

As Clerk of the Parliaments Elsynge oversaw the preparation of the 1625 Parliament Roll (P.R.O., C G5/189). The Roll, a permanent, public and legal record of significant activity in the session includes memoranda relating to the postponement of the opening of the session, a list of receivers and triers of petitions, the prolocutor's speech in Convocation, the King's speech, and the six acts other than the subsidy bill passed during the session.

In 1625 Elsynge apparently did not, as he

9. Foster, *Elsyng*, p. 12.

did in subsequent sessions, prepare additional lists of the actions on bills in the Lords during the session.[10] The only surviving record of business in select committees and of the debate on legislation in committee in the Upper House in 1625 is the Committee Book compiled by one of the Clerk's assistants (see below). We have collated the MS. Journal of the House of Lords with the printed *Lords Journal*, III, 435–489.

H.L.R.O., Manuscript Minutes, H.L., 1625

The House of Lords Manuscript Minute Book for 1625 is a foliated paper book, 12″ × 7⅞″, originally bound in parchment but now covered by a composition binding. The leaves seem to have been inadvertently scrambled on some occasion when the volume was rebound, and the folio numbers must be used as a guide to reconstruct the original order. As now bound, the folio numbers run consecutively from 1 through 38v, then skip to f. 57, run through f. 73v, and then revert to f. 39 and run to f. 56v, the blank final folio. Folio 1 includes lists of names of the peers who paid fees of entrance in 21 *Jac.* and in 1 *Car.*; f. 2 contains notes on writs of summons for the 1625 session, and ff. 3–4 notes on the prorogations of 1625. The account of proceedings begins on f. 5 with a report of the business of 18 June, preceded by a list of Lords present. All subsequent daily accounts maintain the same regular format of attendance list followed by a report of business. F. 38v contains part of the day's account for 9 July. The misplaced folios numbered 57–72 are blank; f. 72v contains a list of the names of the Lords spiritual and temporal summoned to attend the 1625 session, f. 73 a list of judges and learned counsel that were appointed to attend the Lords for the session, and f. 73v an order regarding the case of the John Edwardses, Sr. and Jr. Following f. 73v, on f. 39, is the end of the day's account for 9 July. The entry for 11 July begins on f. 39v; ff. 42–42v are blank; and the proceedings at the Oxford session begin on f. 43 and continue through f. 56.

The hand of the 1625 Minute Book is the same as that of the second assistant clerk who kept a comparable book in 1624 and 1628 (see *Lords Proceedings 1628*, pp. 5–6).

The Manuscript Minutes are particularly important for this session because of the scarcity of accounts. Professor E. R. Foster points out that these minutes are "the one set of running notes" on the activity in the Upper House in 1625 which has survived.[11] (*Notes of the Debates in the House of Lords officially taken by Robert Bowyer and Henry Elsynge, Clerks of the Parliaments, AD 1621, 1625, 1628*, ed. by F. H. Relf, Camden, 3rd series, vol. 42, prints extracts from H.L.R.O., Manuscript Minutes, H.L., 1625.)

H.L.R.O., Main Papers, H. L., 10 August, 1625 (Committee Book)

The Committee Book of the House of Lords for 1625 is a small paper book bound in with other materials and foliated by the House of Lords Record Office. It contains only eleven folios, numbered 149–159, and is preceded by an index at f. 147. The book is a record of proceedings in several select committees that met between 23 June and 11 August 1625. There are entries only for 23, 25, 27, and 30 June, 1, 5, and 6 July, and 2, 5, 8, and 10 August. They consist of a dated heading, sometimes a breviate of a bill, a list of committee members, and notice of when a committee was to meet. The manuscript is in the hand of an assistant clerk. Henry Elsynge added marginal notes to several of the entries. Thus on 23 June he writes in the margin the names of Lords added to a committee after the initial appointments were made.

B. Private Account
Journal of Edward, Lord Montagu of Boughton

The journal of proceedings in the House of Lords kept by Lord Montagu of

---

10. Foster, *Elsyng*, p. 14.

11. Foster, *Elsyng*, p. 24.

Boughton is bound in Montagu MSS., vol. 30, a volume of several manuscript parliamentary diaries or journals deposited in the Northamptonshire Record Office by his Grace the Duke of Buccleuch and Queensberry. It is a paper book, 12″ × 8″, of nine pages written in ink. The first, fifth, and last pages are numbered respectively 1, 2, 3; in order to distinguish the intervening unnumbered pages, we have assigned them consecutive letters so that the second page of the MS. is referred to as p. 1a, the third as p. 1b, the sixth as p. 2a, etc. This journal of proceedings in the House of Lords is for the Oxford session only. Edward, Lord Montagu, did not attend the London session. According to the H.L.R.O., M.M. (23 June), he was granted license to be absent from parliament.[12] Within the bound volume the account of the proceedings for 1625 follows the journal for 1626 and precedes the journal for 1624. It is entitled: *Some notes of the passages at the parliament held and begun at Oxford the first of August 1625.* The journal is endorsed: *Parliament at Oxford the first of August 1625, the first of King Charles, which proved very discontent.* For each leaf of the journal Montagu lists days of the week vertically in chronological order down the left-hand margin, and on the right side of the page he gives very brief notes of the proceedings for the days so listed.

As M.P. for Northamptonshire Montagu kept a journal of proceedings in the Lower House for 1604, 1606–1607, and the spring session of the 1621 parliament. In June 1621 he was elevated to the peerage as Edward Montagu, first Baron Montagu of Boughton. In the second session of the parliament of 1621 he took his seat in the Upper House for the first time and began keeping a journal of proceedings in the House of Lords. He subsequently kept a journal of that House in 1624, 1625, 1626,

1629, and both the Short and Long Parliaments.

Besides writing his journal, Montagu collected separates and fair copies of parliamentary materials. From the 1625 session he kept the report of the King's message of 8 August and an abbreviated copy of the King's answers to the petition against recusants.[13] Montagu's journal for 1625 exemplifies his interest in parliamentary practice and procedure. Thus on 4 August, after Sir John Coke's speech, Montagu records the concern of members at the King's unprecedented use of a commoner to act as his porte-parole to both Houses.

(Montagu's diary for 1625 is published in H.M.C., *Buccleuch MSS.*, III, 247–252.)

II. MANUSCRIPT SOURCES FOR THE HOUSE OF COMMONS

A. Official Sources

MS. Journal of the House of Commons

The manuscript Commons Journal for the parliament of 1625, MS. Vol. 15, in the House of Lords Record Office, is a paper book, 14½″ × 9″, originally bound in parchment and now additionally covered by a black composition binding. The parchment cover is stamped "N° 8" and bears the inscription: "*Parliamentum incipiend. 21° Junii apud Westm. anno primo Caroli Regis*". Below that inscription is written: "*Desinit hic liber Veneris 11° Augusti Caroli 1mi*". All entries in this journal are in the hand of John Wright, Clerk of the House of Commons.

Parliament was in session in London from 18 June to 11 July. Adjourned to reassemble at Oxford, it met there from 1 August through 12 August. Pages 1–35 of the MS. Journal record proceedings of the London session, pp. 36–60 business of the Oxford session. The MS. Journal contains an occasional minor error of commission,

---

12. See also, Esther S. Cope, *The Life of a Public Man; Edward, First Baron Montagu of Boughton, 1562–1644*

(Philadelphia, 1981), pp. 105–106.

13. H.M.C., *Buccleuch*, III, 252–253, 260.

e.g., on 21 June Sir William Erle for Sir Walter Erle.

The MS. Journal for 1625 is singularly incomplete. There are entries in it for less than half the days during which parliament was sitting in London:[14] none for the first two days (18 and 20 June), entries for 21 and 22 June (misdated 23 June in the Journal itself), then no entries until 4 July. Thereafter until the cessation of the meetings in London and for the whole of the brief renewal of sittings in Oxford the MS. Journal records the proceeding for each day's sitting.

We are unable to account for the gaps in the Journal. There are a few peculiarities about one gap to which we would call attention. All the sittings missing from the MS. Journal between 23 June and 4 July, inclusive, are reported in the Draft Journal of the House of Commons (see below), kept from 21 June through 5 July, inclusive, by John Wright's son. The single day overlap on both ends between the two accounts and the otherwise precise fit between the son's account and the gap in the father's account has the appearance of significance, but we are at a loss to say what that significance is. Even more unusual is the lack in the MS. Journal of an account of the proceedings of the first sitting of the House, when the members elected a Speaker. There is no such lack in the official journal of any other parliament of the early Stuarts, nor of any parliament of Elizabeth for which the Clerk's journal survives. We have no evidence that an account by the Clerk for the missing days ever existed, and we have strong grounds for the inference that no such account existed at least as early as 1630. The copy of the Commons Journal that Sir John Eliot used in writing his *Negotium Posterorum* (see below) around that time also had no entries for the days on which they are now absent from the MS. Journal. Lacking any more specific expla-

nation one is inclined to associate this peculiar situation with the universal confusion with which the epidemic of the plague seemed to suffuse the parliament of 1625.

One other matter may be related to the incompleteness of the Journal. There is no evidence that the committee of privileges appointed a subcommittee to "peruse" the Journal in 1625 as it had done in other early Stuart parliaments. So beyond the confusion engendered by the plague and the remove to Oxford, the lack of a committee to keep the Clerk up to the mark increased the likelihood of poor record-keeping.

Draft Journal of the House of Commons

House of Lords Record Office, Main Papers, Addenda Series, MS. 3409, Draft Journal of the House of Commons, is a paper book, $14\frac{1}{2}'' \times 9''$, bound in with other Addenda manuscripts, and foliated by the archivist of the Record Office. The book was kept by John Wright's son, who worked as an assistant clerk to his father. The first leaf of the book bears the inscription: "My son's journal of the parliament; *21° Junii Caroli R[egis]*". Below that inscription is the name "Jo." followed by "Wright", written twice and lined through. The book contains 28 folios. They are numbered f. 126 (the cover sheet) through f. 154v. They record the proceedings of the House from 21 June through 5 July. Folio 127 is blank, the proceedings of 21 June begin on f. 128, and the entries for 5 July end on f. 153v. Folio 154 is headed *Veneris 8 Julii*, but no entries follow; f. 154v is blank.

Fortunately the Draft Journal provides accounts of the proceedings in the House between 23 June and 4 July which are lacking in the MS. Journal of the House of Commons (see above). (For a further description of the Draft Journal, see Maurice F. Bond, *The Manuscripts of the House of Lords*, XI [New Series], London, 1962, pp.

---

14. Nine days out of twenty.

xi–xiii. The Draft Journal itself is printed in the same volume on pp. 177–203.)

Committee Book

The Committee Book, House of Lords Record Office, Main Papers, Addenda Series, MS. 3410, was also kept by John Wright's son. The foliation, ff. 155–161, was added by the Record Office. The outside leaf (f. 155) contains the following inscription in John Wright's hand: "Committee Book *21° Junii, 1° Caroli Regis;* Book: [Illegible, possibly *Harry*] Wright; Jo. Wright". Between folios 156 and 159v are brief entries of proceedings in the committee of the Whole House in the London session—24 June (morning and afternoon), 28 June (morning and afternoon), 30 June (afternoon), and 1 July (afternoon). On f. 160 is the following heading in John Wright's hand: "*8° Aug., 1° Caroli Regis.* A committee of the Whole House". Folio 160v is blank and on f. 161, the last leaf in the book, is the signature "Thomas Cromwell, 1719" and the note, "calf 01, dog 03, beaver 07". Folio 161v is blank. (For a further description of the Committee Book, see Maurice F. Bond, *The Manuscripts of the House of Lords,* XI [New Series], London, 1962, pp. xi–xiii. The Committee Book itself is printed in the same volume on pp. 204–207.)

B. Private Accounts

The Pym Diary

The most accurate, detailed account of the proceedings of the House of Commons in 1625 at present survives in three forms: a copy of a complete manuscript diary, Bedford MS. 197 (Woburn MSS., H.M.C. 197); *Debates in the House of Commons in 1625,* ed. Samuel Rawson Gardiner, transcribed and published in 1873 from a manuscript then in the library of Sir Rainald Knightley at Fawsley, Northamptonshire, a manuscript that appears not to have survived; and B.L. Add. MS. 26,639, a collection of excerpts from the same parliamentary diary. We will

here describe the three exemplars or forms in which the diary at present exists, and then deal briefly with the questions of by whom and when the diary was first set down.

The exemplars:

1. *Bedford MS. 197*

This MS. is a paper book, $13\frac{1}{2}'' \times 8\frac{3}{4}''$, bound in parchment with "4" written on the spine and the Bedford crest stamped on the front and back of the binding. A paper sheet attached to the inside front binding bears the shelf mark "Az4.4"; four unfoliated leaves of index of the manuscript and five blank leaves follow. The journal of proceedings in the 1625 session begins on the first numbered folio with the entry for 18 June and continues through f. 74 to the final entry for 12 August. It is followed by an account of the 1629 session, unfoliated. That account is the True Relation (see *Commons Debates 1628,* I, 9–11; Wallace Notestein and Frances Helen Relf, eds., *Commons Debates for 1629* [Minneapolis, 1921], pp. xv–xix) of which many copies survive. Interspersed throughout the manuscript in the left margin are triangular clusters of three dots. The manuscript has been annotated. The annotator's hand is that of Francis Russell who in 1625 was Lord Russell of Thornhaugh, and in 1627 became 4th Earl of Bedford.

2. *British Library, Add. MS. 26,639*

Add. MS. 26,639, in the British Library, is a paper book containing excerpts of proceedings in the parliaments of 1624 and 1625. Although bound together in sequence, the excerpts from the proceedings in the two parliaments seem originally to have been separate manuscripts. The first folio for 1625, f. 38, is dirtier and shows more wear than f. 37, the last leaf of the 1624 section, suggesting that it had once served as a cover sheet. Furthermore, the leaves of the 1625 section, measuring $14\frac{1}{2}'' \times 8\frac{5}{8}''$, are slightly larger than those containing the 1624 notes. The heading on f. 38 written in black ink in law French says: *"Plmt. sumon May 1° Car. prorogue al 18th de June"*. The notes following are in English and in brown ink. B.L. Add. MS. 26,639 is one of a group of manuscripts once belonging to Oliver St. John.

3. *Debates in the House of Commons in 1625*

The principal manuscript which is transcribed for this book printed by the Camden Society was examined by John Bruce. His opinion of it appears in the Third Report of the Historical Manuscripts Commission in 1872:

It contains notes taken *de die in diem* by a member of the House. From the handwriting, which is that of a transcriber, from various mistakes and from blanks in it, I deem it to be a copy. That the original notes were taken by a member seems clear from the language throughout. . . . I conclude that the writer was a person known in the House to be interested in the religious questions of the day and probably on the puritan side.

Samuel Rawson Gardiner transcribed the manuscript for publication in 1873 by the Camden Society as the sixth volume in its new series. At the time of transcription the manuscript was in the library of Sir Rainald Knightley, Bart., at Fawsley, Northamptonshire. If the manuscript still survives, its present whereabouts is unknown.

As to the relation among these three accounts, it is evident on examination that Bedford MS. 197 and the Knightley MS. which Gardiner copied are substantially identical. Between them the discrepancies are few. Aside from the occasional word variant, the more extensive differences where a whole line is included in one manuscript but omitted from the other (for examples, see below, H. of C., 23 June, n. 43, and 28 June, n. 26) are very rare.

Gardiner believed incorrectly that the folios relating to 1625 in B.L. Add. MS. 26,639 were "taken from a report of which the Knightley MS. is a copy". The evidence suggests rather that the source of B.L. Add. MS. 26,639 is Bedford MS. 197, and that the latter is a collateral rather than an ancestor of the Knightley MS. which Gardiner transcribed. The probable dependence of B.L. Add. MS. 26,639 on Bedford MS. 197 is shown by the relation of the foliation of the former to the location of the previously mentioned three-dot clusters in the latter. Each passage in the 1625 segment of B.L. Add. MS. 26,639 coincides with sections set off by dots in Bedford MS. 197, and there is no passage in the former whose content is not to be found following the three-dot clusters of the latter. The correspondence strongly suggests that the Bedford MS. was the source from which the copyist chose the passages for the British Library MS. This inference is further confirmed by numbers in the margin of the latter. For example, on the right-hand margin of f. 38 of B.L. MS. 26,639 is the notation "6b". The material on folio 38 coincides with that on the verso of folio 6 of the Bedford MS. Thirty-nine of the passages in B.L. Add. MS. 26,639 have numberings that correspond to the foliation of Bedford MS. 197.

The relation between the Bedford and the Knightley copies of the account is less certain. Gardiner did not incorporate folio numeration in his edition of the Knightley MS. Therefore we cannot check for correspondence. We do know, however, that in the late 1630s the author of the account, John Pym, lived at Fawsley, the home of his friend Richard Knightley. He may have left his copy of the 1625 diary there.

As indicated above, the author of the diary that was copied for Bedford MS. 197, B.L. Add. MS. 26,639, and the Knightley MS. was John Pym. In 1625 Pym stood in the second rank among leaders in the House, behind a half dozen to a dozen more eminent veterans. In the Long Parliament he held front rank. It was he who ultimately led the English parliament into confrontation and civil war with England's king, Charles I. When he transcribed the diary for the Camden Society, Gardiner may have suspected that Pym was its author. He did not, however, try to establish the authorship. Six decades later, the editors of the *Commons Debates 1621* concluded that Pym was the author of the 1625 diary as well as of one for 1621 and one for 1624. Nowhere in any of the accounts themselves does Pym's name appear as author, nor does any contemporary source state that he ever kept a parliamentary diary. Nevertheless in a superb piece of historical detective work the editors of *Commons Debates 1621* demonstrated Pym's authorship of all three manuscripts beyond reasonable doubt. The combined weight of the circumstantial evidence brought to bear on this point is of such force that, if there existed—as there does not—direct testimony that Pym did not write one or all of the accounts, a reader of the edition's argument might be inclined to query the *bona fides* of the direct rather than of the circumstantial evidence. This being the case, it makes no sense to attempt again in our introduction what the editors of *Commons Debates 1621* have done so well and so exhaustively. We refer users of this book to that work.[15] Here we will only describe the kinds of evidence those editors brought to bear.

(A.) Evidence that all three manuscripts— those for 1621, for 1624, and for 1625—are the work of the same person.

(1.) The macrorhetorical evidence. The macrorhetorical structures of the three accounts are markedly similar one to the other and wholly divergent from that of any other parliamentary diary of the 1620s. None of the three manuscripts is a series of notes taken as debate proceeded in the House. All three are organized accounts of the course of debate. Unlike other such accounts they feature individual speeches less than they do the course and structure of an argument. They do this by presenting the positions of both collective parties to an issue.

(2.) The microrhetorical evidence. The accounts all share a whole congeries of tricks of language and preferences of phrasing that are not the common or immutable choice of contemporary writers in context, but mark consistent and repeated verbal mannerisms.

(3.) The evidence of interlinking references. The diaries of 1621 and 1624 cross-refer to each other. The diaries of 1624 and 1625 both contain references to a collection of separates for speeches omitted from the diaries themselves.

(B.) Evidence that John Pym was the writer of the diary from which the manuscripts were copied.

(1.) The rhetorical evidence. Both in the way he structures his argument (macrorhetoric) and in his phraseology as evidenced in records of his speeches in other sources, Pym's mode of discourse is remarkably similar to that of the author of the three accounts.

(2.) If we can surely identify the author of one diary, we will have identified the author of all three. We can identify the author of the 1625 diary. He says he was a member of a particular subcommittee of six members. These members are named in another source. For persuasive reasons we can eliminate the names of five of the six as possible authors of the diary.[16] The one left uneliminated is John Pym. The same process of elimination can be carried on with respect to the members of a committee of 1621 of which the diarist says he was a member, and with the same result. So the author of all the diaries is Pym. Most important for the purposes of the editors of *Proceedings in Parliament 1625*, clearly the author of Bedford MS. 197 must be Pym.

---

15. *C.D. 1621*, I, 26–62.
16. See *C.D. 1621*, I, 40–42, and see below, H. of C.,

28 June, n. 50.

(3.) There are a series of peculiarities about the way in which the author of the three accounts deals with speeches which, on the evidence of others, Pym made. The diarist throws a blanket of anonymity or uncertain identity over Pym's known speeches in the House that he does not systematically grant to those of anyone else.

To the powerful argument made by the editors of *Commons Debates 1621* we may add a slender additional prop. In the 1620s, Francis Russell, Lord Thornhaugh, saw to it that he had accounts of parliaments to study and annotate. He annotated copies of diaries from 1621, 1624, 1625, and 1629. The author of these diaries at one time referred to himself as "Mr. P."; William Drake in his commonplace book (Historical Collection no. 49, H.L.R.O.) includes speeches delivered by Pym in the Long Parliament which he attributes to "Mr. P.".[17] Francis Russell, later Earl of Bedford, was an early patron of John Pym to whom he made available a seat in parliament for Tavistock which was at his disposal. These connections support the other evidence of Pym's authorship.

Pym's Russell connection does not enable us to fix the exact time at which he set down his diary for 1625, but it does give us a *terminus ad quem* for the process. Lord Russell annotated a speech of 5 August in which Sir Richard Weston commented on the contempt for England which the coldness between James I and his people had produced in France. In the margin Russell wrote, "So now in France when my Lo. of Holland and Carleton went about Rochelle". Those emissaries had gone to France about La Rochelle in December 1625. The "now" suggests that the mission was recent or in process when Russell wrote his marginal note. Therefore the latest plausible date for Pym's completion of his diary for 1625 is December of that year. Unfortunately there is no internal evidence as to the earliest possible date of the entries later than the date headings themselves.

The diary we are concerned with then is an account of the parliament of 1625 by John Pym, probably based on notes he took of the day-to-day business in the House, notes that no longer exist. Pym probably prepared his finished account between the dissolution of 12 August and the following December. As was his wont he imparted to his account of the proceeding a level of coherence and clarity of direction such as the actual exchanges on the floor of the House almost certainly failed to achieve.

An Anonymous Diary

Four surviving manuscripts present in part or in its entirety an anonymous diary of the parliament of 1625. They are as follows:

1. *Inner Temple Library, Petyt MS. 538/8*

The manuscript of proceedings in the House of Commons in 1625 is ff. 106–156v of a volume of 168 folios, 12″ × 7¾″, containing parliamentary journals, abstracts, and separates. Folios 106 through 156v contain an account of the proceedings in both the London and Oxford sessions of the parliament of 1625, followed by (ff. 158–163) "the report of the message delivered unto the Houses of Parliament from H.M.'s Lord Keeper, the Duke of Buckingham, and the Lord Treasurer, 8 August 1625". The folios, catalogued as "extracts from the journals of the House of Commons",[18] contain rather a fair-copied narrative of the

---

17. *C.D. 1621,* I, 59–60. A number of William Drake's other commonplace books (Ogden MSS., University College London) also contain references to "Mr. P.". For a calendar of the books, see Stuart Clark, "Wisdom Literature of the Seventeenth Century: A Guide to the Contents of the Bacon-Tottel Commonplace Books", pts. I and II, *Transactions of the Cambridge Bibliographical Society* (Cambridge), VI (1976), 291–305, and VII(1977), 46–73.

18. J. Conway Davies, ed., *Catalogue of Manuscripts in the Library of the Honourable Society of the Inner Temple* (Oxford, 1972), II, 708–710.

parliament, compiled after the fact (see below).

2. *The Queen's College (Oxford) MS. 449*

MS. 449 is approximately 12″ × 7⅘″; the account of proceedings in the parliament of 1625 begins on a folio numbered f. 231. It continues through f. 300, every fifth leaf bearing a folio number which is a fairly frequent archivist's procedure for foliation. Sittings are designated not by date but by Latin headings indicating the day of the week—*Die Lunae, Die Martis*, etc. This manuscript lacks a title page but includes the following heading at the beginning of the account: "The first parliament of King Charles was prorogued from *xvii Maii* to *18ᵛᵒ Junii existente die Sabb[at]hi. 1625 primo Caroli Regis* and then it began at Westminster". To the right above the heading is written, "Sir William Walter".

We do not know why Sir William Walter's name is written at the beginning of the manuscript. The manuscript may have been at one time part of Walter's library. There is no evidence to indicate that the account was compiled at his order. Sir William Walter of Wimbledon, Surrey, sat for Peterborough in 1614, Lugershall in 1626, and Lichfield in 1628. In 1624, as an unsuccessful candidate in a contested election for Stafford, he petitioned against Richard Dyott, Recorder of Stafford, who had carried the election. The House declared the election void, but Walter was not returned in the by-election. He was knighted in May 1603 and served as sheriff of Surrey and Sussex in 1631.[19]

3. *British Library, Add. MS. 48,091*

Bound in parchment and measuring 11″ × 7¾″, this MS. is marked "100" on the outside spine. The unfoliated title page bears the inscription: "Oxford parliament in the first yeare of Kinge Charles", and the shelf mark "MSS. Yelverton N. 100". This indi-

cates that the volume was part of the collection of Yelverton papers acquired by the British Library in 1953 from Brigadier R. H. Anstruther-Gough-Calthorpe. The manuscript has 64 leaves; the foliation begins on the first leaf which contains a heading that reads: "The first Parliament of Kinge Charles was prorogued from *decimo septimo Maii* to *18ᵛᵒ Junii existente die Sabb[ath]i. 1625 primo Caroli Regis*, and then it began at Westminster". The narrative of the opening of the parliament follows. Folios 1–25v describe proceedings at Westminster (18 June–11 July) and include a list of nine bills that received royal assent in the London session; folios 26–64 describe the Oxford session.

4. *British Library, Harl. 5007*

This is a bound volume of 92 leaves of parliamentary materials followed by several blank unfoliated leaves. Folios 1 through 74 contain reports and speeches connected with the 1626 parliament. An account of the Oxford session of the parliament of 1625 begins on f. 75 and continues through f. 86v. The journal itself is written only on the recto side of paper sheets which measure 14½″ × 12″, somewhat larger than the paper in the beginning of the volume, indicating that the contents of the two sections were originally separate, bound together after they were written. The foliation of the account is erratic. The account itself has no title page or heading, but is endorsed: "N. 3 Parliament begun at Oxford 1° August 1625". Samuel Rawson Gardiner edited Harl. 5007 and included it as the first Appendix in his volume of *Debates in the House of Commons in 1625*, pp. 129–163.

All four accounts appear to have been copied from an original that does not survive. They share a confused chronology, which indicates that the original was neither written during the course of business

---

19. *Collections for a History of Staffordshire*, ed. by Josiah C. Wedgwood for The William Salt Archaeo-   logical Society (London, 1920), II, 28, 56–57.

of the day being narrated nor during the adjournment at the end of that day's business. Entries concerning the fast which we have printed under 24 June 1625 actually deal with events which occurred from 21 June through 3 July (see below, H. of C., 24 June, n. 25). The chronology of the journal is thrown off by the attempt to cluster in one place a particular piece of business actually carried through in the course of several days' proceedings. Thus the House debated about Richard Montagu on several occasions between 24 June and 9 July. All business concerned with Montagu in the London session, however, is gathered at one place in the journal. (In the present volume the editors have included the material in its correct chronological place and annotated it accordingly; see below, H. of C., 1 July, n. 47.) It is also possible that the writer of the account failed to indicate clearly in his notes the day when the events he recorded took place, and that when he came to writing out what was in his notes he relied on his own defective memory for the chronology of events.

Notes of Sir Nathaniel Rich

Two sets of notes in Sir Nathaniel Rich's combination of shorthand and longhand are printed in *Proceedings in Parliament 1625*. Although the notes themselves are undated, the earliest ones are those on the debate on recusancy and the petition concerning religion which occurred over a week's time toward the end of June 1625. We have placed Rich's notes with the accounts of 25 June (see below, H. of C., 25 June, n. 28). The striking similarity between the speeches recorded by Rich and those included in the other 1625 accounts (particularly the committee book entry for 23 June) is apparent. Formerly the Rich notes on recusancy were on deposit in the P.R.O. (30/15/168) among the papers of the Duke of Manchester. They were sold at Sotheby's in June 1975 and purchased by the House of Lords Record Office where

they are now part of the Historical Collection, shelf number 204. The notes are on a single folded sheet of paper measuring approximately 12″ × 8″; they are written in ink by Rich, presumably during the session itself and not afterwards. They are undated and include no heading, but are endorsed: "Notes concerning the petition against recusants".

The second set of Rich notes comprises the debate on a single day, 11 August. They are the first three folios of an MS. (H.L.R.O., Historical Collection, 143; purchased by the H.L.R.O. at Sotheby's in 1973) the remainder of which is Rich's diary of the parliament of 1626. A small paper book, $5\frac{5}{8}″ \times 3\frac{1}{2}″$, bound in parchment, it contains the following heading on the second leaf: "Notes of the first parliament of King Charles which was prorogued from Westminster after it had sat there, to Oxford 1° August 1625. As also notes of the second parliament of King Charles which began at Westminster 6 Feb. 1625". The verso of the title page is blank and the notes of 11 August begin on the third leaf with the heading: "11 Aug. At the committee for giving answer to the King's message", and end on the verso side of the fourth leaf. Two blank folios precede the 1626 notes which begin on folio 7 and continue through f. 97.

Diary of Richard Dyott

The diary of Richard Dyott, MS. D661/11/1/2, Staffordshire Record Office, is in an unbound book of 181 leaves, each leaf measuring $5\frac{13}{16}″ \times 3\frac{3}{4}″$. The manuscript contains several pages of notes pertaining to business in the 1625 session on 5, 11, and 12 August as well as a diary of proceedings in the parliament of 1624. It is neither foliated nor paginated. While preparing the texts for his edition of the parliamentary proceedings of 1624 Professor Robert Ruigh worked out logical foliation for the diary, which for the 1625 notes runs backward from the end of the volume. Regarding the Dyott volume Professor Ruigh writes:

While I was in England the manuscript was never officially foliated or paginated by the archivists. My foliation is due to my counting and collating the manuscript with the photographs I obtained. The first folios in the diary are blank although it appears that some vestiges of writing remain. The first decipherable words occur on folio 5 in connection with the use of affidavits in the Cambridgeshire election case. From folio 9v (possibly earlier) Dyott stopped writing on the reverse side of each folio so all the versos from 9v to 41v are blank. Folios 42v and 43 are written on but it is not clear that there are entries on folio 43v. Folios 44 and 45 detail the action on the Stafford election (folio 44v is blank). All succeeding folios are blank until folios 50 and 51 which on their recto sides record proceedings on 15 March [1624]. Folios 51v and 52v appear to be blank.

The 1625 diary ends on folio 52v. It begins on folio 68 and is written on both sides of each folio and the volume turned upside down.

The 1624 diary resumes on folio 69. All versos from folios 68v to and including 80v are blank. From 81v to and including 90v each verso is written on lengthwise. Folio 90v is dated 29 May [1624] and ostensibly these notes in reverse order relate business for the last day of parliament, but there is little correlation with other accounts. Many of the entries seem to have relation to other events in the parliament. Midway on folio 91 begins the King's speech on 23 April [1624] in answer to the petition against recusants. Thereafter the diary continues on both recto and verso sides in chronological sequence virtually to the end of the volume.

The Dyott diary is exceedingly difficult to read because of damage done to the manuscript during the Second World War. Although the Dyott family had placed it in a bank vault in London for safekeeping the vault itself was flooded in the attempts to put out the fires during the blitz, and water leeched the text. The Staffordshire Record Office made photocopies of the diary under ultraviolet light in the hope that some of the passages spoiled by damp might be clarified but the project was not entirely successful. We are grateful to Professor Ruigh for allowing us to print the transcript of the diary he made from the original manuscript.

British Library, Harl. 161

Harleian MS. 161, as described in *Catalogus Librorum Bibliothecae Harleianae*, p. 57, is "a collection of small tracts and loose papers . . . relating chiefly to parliamentary affairs". In the calendar provided in the catalog under the above description is an entry listing the "fragment of a journal of the House of Commons for Tuesday, 21 June, f. 59". The fragment, which begins on f. 67 rather than f. 59, is a fair copy of an account of the proceedings that day in parliament written in the distinctive italic hand of Sir Simonds D'Ewes. The account covers both sides of the same leaf and is bound in with the other "tracts and loose papers" with no indication given that it may have at one time been part of a larger compilation. This fragment is the most complete record we have of the debates of 21 June, fuller and more detailed than the Journal for that day and than the accounts in Bedford 197 or Petyt 538/8.

Many of the papers compiled in Harleian 161 are in the hand of D'Ewes and the bulk of them relate directly to parliamentary affairs, as described in the Harleian catalog. The papers in Harleian MS. 161 clearly are related to D'Ewes's plan to record and preserve for posterity accounts of the proceedings in the parliaments of Elizabeth and the early Stuarts. The early folios of Harl. 161 are copies of lists of peers and debates in the Upper House in 1621. On f. 17 is D'Ewes's chart of "The several days on which every parliament or session of parliament during the reign of Queen Elizabeth began, as also the several days of the dissolution or prorogation of the same, together with the number-folios of their beginnings and endings in these three ensuing volumes", followed by indices of the dates of proceedings in the Elizabethan sessions and the folio numbers of the manuscripts in which those proceedings occur. The remainder of the volume contains separates and notes on the parliaments of 1626 and 1628.

Kenneth Spencer Research Library, MS E237

Manuscript MS E237 in the Kenneth Spencer Research Library at the University of Kansas is a parchment bound volume, 12″ × 10″, containing a lengthy diary of the 1614 session, a somewhat briefer diary of both the 1621 and 1624 sessions, and a few notes and a separate of the King's speech from the parliament of 1625. The diaries are fair copied in one hand throughout. The identity of the author is unknown.

The material for 1625, comprising folios 116–117v, consists of entries of proceedings on 18, 21, 23, 24, 25, and 28 June and a separate of the opening speech delivered by Charles I on 18 June; it is not preceded in the manuscript by a title page.

MS. Negotium Posterorum

The Manuscript. *Negotium Posterorum* is a paper book, 13″ × 8½″, which was bound in brown leather in the nineteenth century. The spine of the volume is stamped in gilt, "Negotium Posterorum by Sir John Eliot with Preface; First Parliament of Charles I, Westminster and Oxford 1625, MS.", and the outside of the front and back covers are stamped with the Eliot coat of arms. The volume begins with seven unfoliated leaves. On the recto of the first leaf is pasted the title from the original paper or thin parchment covering of the manuscript: "Negotium Posterorum, Charles ye 1st". On the second leaf is a brief description of the manuscript, probably written in the nineteenth century by John Forster, Eliot's biographer, and a more recent reference to "H.M.C. Vol. III". The remaining five unfoliated leaves are blank.

Following these first seven unfoliated leaves are five numbered and a sixth unnumbered leaf. These six leaves contain an incomplete draft, written and extensively altered in his own hand, of what Eliot apparently planned as the preface to the *Nego-*

tium. The leaves are one quarter of an inch shorter than, and bear a different watermark from, the other leaves of the volume. Unlike the other leaves, they are creased in such a way as to suggest that at one time they were folded in half and then in half again. On the verso side of the unfoliated sixth leaf is the endorsement: "An Introduction to *Negotium Posterorum* 1628". This, too, is written in Eliot's hand and appears to use the same ink as the preceding five foliated leaves. These six leaves were discovered among the papers at Port Eliot by John Forster and were not joined to the main body of the *Negotium* until this manuscript was bound in the nineteenth century.

Immediately following the endorsed leaf of the Introduction is a single unnumbered leaf bearing the title: "*Negotium Posterorum, Tomus Secundus, Liber Primus*". The text of the *Negotium*, a fair copy in Eliot's handwriting, follows on pages numbered 1 through 276, with a second title, "*Negotium Posterorum, Tomus Secundus, Liber Secundus*", inserted on page 127 prior to the account of the Oxford session of the 1625 parliament. At the end of the volume are nine blank leaves.

The Narrative. *Negotium Posterorum* tells the story of the parliament of 1625 as the writer remembered experiencing it. This differentiates it from all other surviving accounts by members of that parliament or of any other parliament of the early Stuarts. All other such narratives focus wholly on the business of one House or the other as it unfolded on the floor of that House and occasionally on business of the committees of the House. Judgments by the narrator on the performance of speakers are rare in these narratives. Information about preliminary political maneuvers are even rarer. The author of *Negotium Posterorum*, however, offers a connoisseur's view of the oratorical effect and effectiveness of the speakers he reports on, and with an orator's instinct he caressingly picks up their oratorical flourishes.

The author of the *Negotium* is also what in the political jargon of a little while back was called an "inside dopester", one who had access to "the news behind the news". As no other narrator of the 1620s did and as few perhaps were in a position to do, he writes about how men who were trying to manipulate the House of Commons for their own particular ends went about doing it. In 1625 the author of the *Negotium* knows from the inside, as only an intimate of the Duke of Buckingham would know, how through unpreparedness the "King's friends" let a bill for only two subsidies be the first motion on supply of the King's needs to come before the House of Commons. The *Negotium* offers a detailed account of the bullheaded persistence of the King and the Duke and of the courtiers who marched to their music in their unprecedented attempt to get a second bill for supply in the same session out of a House of Commons that had already passed one such bill.

The Composition. When did Eliot write the *Negotium*? It has been usually assumed that he composed it in prison after his arrest for being involved in the unseemly ruckus with which the 1629 session of parliament came to an end. Several passages in the *Negotium* itself seem to refer to events subsequent to the adjournment of the session of 1628. One says "seem" in deference to Eliot's penchant for baroquely convoluted prose that often conceals rather than reveals his meaning. For 5 August 1625 Eliot records a debate in the House of Commons on the second subsidy bill which Buckingham had sponsored. After describing the support of that proposal by several privy councillors Eliot continues:

So hard it is, where public wrongs are done, to keep them from vindication or complaint. . . . That meeting [at Oxford] might have been prevented with much safety but, being met, that crime was thought unpardonable. He that was the occasion of that trouble must have his share

therein . . . and then vengeance must surprise him like a whirlwind, and no favor or greatness may deliver him; but, as his merit, such must be his reward.

On 6 August, according to the *Negotium*, despite the sound counsel of his friends, the Duke, a man "moveable by every air of flattery", as usual chose the worse rather than the better course, this time with respect to leaving the Arminian Montagu to the punishment due him:

He had once determined to be guided by his friends but his parasites were more powerful to distract him from their principles, which then increased his troubles and after proved his ruin.

Buckingham's ruin did not come until 23 August 1628, when Lieutenant Felton stabbed him with a dagger, an experience not only ruinous but fatal. The relatively crisp inexactness of the second passage dispels the murkiness of the first sufficiently to warrant our judgment that both refer to the Duke's untimely end in August of 1628.

In discussing the debates of 9 August 1625 stemming from the Duke of Buckingham's speech at the meeting of both Houses the previous day, Eliot makes reference to Gustavus (II) Adolphus, King of Sweden, as one "who was then scarcely heard of (so envious was time unto the honor of that person whom fortune and virtue had reserved for the wonder of the world)". It seems unlikely that Gustavus would be considered the "wonder of the world" by the English prior to his spectacular campaign in Germany in 1631. We know that news of Gustavus's success was a heartening topic in the correspondence of Eliot and his friends in the fall of 1631, Eliot himself exulting to Sir Oliver Luke in his letter of 3 October 1631: "if at once the whole world be not deluded, fortune and hope are met".

If these interpretations of Eliot's allusions are correct, it would mean that the writing of the above-quoted passages—and hence of the final draft of the *Negotium*—

took place between the time of the Duke's assassination in August 1628 and Eliot's death in the Tower in November 1632, the same period during which Eliot was working on his treatises, *The Monarchy of Man* and *De Jure Majestatis,* and his essay, *Apology for Socrates.* John Forster and Harold Hulme, Eliot's biographers, concluded that Eliot's references to his working on "things more serious"—in his letter of 26 April 1631 to John Hampden and in his dedication "To the Reader" for his *Monarchy of Man*—were to the *Negotium.*[20] That may well be so. However, such a conclusion must be based on conjecture, for the surviving correspondence contains no titles of the various manuscripts which were sent back and forth between Eliot in the Tower and Hampden, Richard Knightley, and some of Eliot's other friends, and the correspondence contains sufficiently specific comments to identify with certainty only one of those manuscripts: *The Monarchy of Man.*

Of course, even if it could be indisputably established that the surviving fair copy of the *Negotium* was written during Eliot's years of imprisonment, we would still not have an answer to the question of when he first began work on the tract. Undoubtedly Eliot wrote at least one rough draft from which the fair copy was derived, though no rough draft appears to have survived. The date "1628" is included in Eliot's endorsement to the Introduction (see above, p. 17), and there seems to be no reason to doubt that the draft introduction was composed during that year, perhaps at Port Eliot before Eliot left for London to attend the second session of the 1628–1629 parliament, never to return to Cornwall. The remainder of Eliot's introduction has not survived. Perhaps it was planned as a broad study of earlier parliaments, a first volume, *Tomus Primus,* to preface the two parts of the *Negotium* which are headed *Tomus Se-*

cundus, Liber Primus and *Tomus Secundus, Liber Secundus.*

The Sources. Supposing that Sir John Eliot wrote the *Negotium Posterorum* at least three years after the events of the parliament of 1625 which it describes, from what sources did he draw his narrative? The most immediate and perhaps the most important source was his memory. He was a member of the House for Newport, Cornwall, in 1625. He is recorded as having spoken or as having been appointed to committees on ten of the nineteen days that the House sat.

Yet, the coincidence of the order in which Eliot places the speakers with the order in which they appear in other accounts suggests either that he had a phenomenal memory for details of events three years or more past, or that he had access to notes or a narrative of the 1625 proceedings to put him in mind of the order of business. The only such notes which are known to survive among the Eliot papers at Port Eliot, however, are copies of entries from the 1625 Commons Journal and the Committee Book (MS. 3410, H.L.R.O., see above) which do not include reports of many of the speeches recorded in the *Negotium* and could not have served as the principal foundation for Eliot's work.

Nevertheless, there is reason to suspect that when composing the *Negotium* Eliot had access to one or more of the still-surviving narratives of the 1625 proceedings. There are passages in Eliot's *Negotium* and John Pym's 1625 diary (see above, p. 10) in which their selection of speakers (both often including speeches not noted in any other extant account) and their versions of the speeches themselves converge with each other and diverge from other versions in such a way as to suggest that one of them had used the other's version, or that they

20. John Forster, *Sir John Eliot: A Biography* (London, 1864), II, 612 and 666; Harold Hulme, *The Life of*

Sir John Eliot (London, 1957), p. 359.

both had access to a third source, perhaps a compilation of separates. For example, their accounts of Sir Benjamin Rudyard's speech of 22 June (see below, pp. 219 and 502) are nearly verbatim copies of one another, yet their version of the speech is far different from the highly abbreviated account given in the Commons Journal (below, p. 215), the only other version of Rudyard's speech that we have found.

The degree of word-for-word congruity between the Eliot and Pym accounts of

Rudyard's speech is unusually high, for in most cases Eliot placed his indelible stylistic embellishments upon the speeches he included in the *Negotium*. Yet, the Eliot and Pym accounts of other 1625 speeches show striking similarities in content, structure, and phrasing. The record of Sir John Coke's delivery of a message from the King on 8 July 1625 provides a more usual sample than the Rudyard speech of the kinds of parallels that exist between the *Negotium* and Pym's 1625 diary.

Pym (Bedford MS. 197, below, p. 350)

By commandment from the King, to give the House true information of his Majesty's estate, as he doubts not but that we came together with true affections; and that his Majesty graciously accepts the gift which is already resolved of as a welcome and pledge of the love not only of this representative body, but of the whole kingdom. Yet he takes notice of our anticipation of that business, and that we fall into it without intervention of any ministers of state, which he imputes to our forwardness in his service, and confidence in his favor and correspondency with us. . . .

And because from that last business had grown some doubts, he was commanded to give a more particular account of it. His late Majesty, loving peace and hating war, when he saw how ill he had been used, that the power of the contrary party had almost overspread Christendom, and his own people discontented at his seeming backwardness in this cause, yet considering the three subsidies we had given (though a royal gift) would only enable him for a while to secure his own, and that in the end he should grow from a lingering ague to a burning fever, and by suffering the enemy to enjoy that which they had gotten, and by degrees to fret upon the other princes of Germany, this only would ensue, that (like Ulysses with Polyphemus) he should be last devoured, he negotiated and concluded a strong confederacy with the King of France and Denmark, the state of Venice, Duke of Savoy, and Low Countries. This first appeared in the army beyond the Alps, and in Mansfeld's army. . . .

Eliot (*Negotium Posterorum*, below, p. 521)

That the King not doubting their affections in that meeting, and taking graciously for a testimony thereof the gift which was resolved on as a welcome pledge of the love not only of that representative body of the kingdom but of the whole (though he took notice of their anticipation in that business and that they fell into it without the intervention of any ministers of state, which he did impute to their forwardness in his service and confidence in his favor), in correspondence thereof had commanded him to give the House a true information of his estate. . . .

And because from that last business had grown some doubts, he was to give a more particular account therein. His late Majesty, loving peace and hating war, when he saw how ill he had been used, that the power of the contrary party had almost overspread Christendom, and his own people discontented at his seeming backwardness in this cause, considering the three subsidies and fifteenths that were granted him (though a royal gift) would only enable him for a while to secure his own, and that in the end he should grow from a lingering ague to a burning fever, and by suffering his enemies to enjoy that which they had gotten make them more able by degrees to fret upon the other German princes, whence it would ensue that, like Ulysses with Polypheme, he should only have the favor to be the last devoured, he negotiated and concluded a strong confederacy with the kings of France and Denmark, the state of Venice, the Duke of Savoy, and the Low Countries, which first appeared in the army beyond the Alps and with Count Mansfeld. . . .

Of course Pym and Eliot may have been independently producing an accurate quasi-verbatim report of a speech they both had heard. This possibility, however, is attenuated by the fact that the version of this speech written in Sir John Coke's own hand (printed in the Appendix, below, pp. 654–656), while similar in substance to the version given by Pym and Eliot, is quite different in wording; and the brief accounts in the Commons Journal and in Petyt 538/8 — the only other versions of Coke's speech which we have found — are far different from that in Pym and Eliot. The possibility that the close parallels between the works of Eliot and Pym result from the two M.P.s independently producing word-for-word reports of the same speeches is further diminished by Pym's well-known habit of *not* producing quasi-verbatim accounts, but at a later date writing coherent summaries of transactions in the House (see above, p. 12). Verbal turns in a parliamentary account of John Pym that occur in the account of some other member are therefore more than ordinarily likely to be the consequence of some cross-fertilization. If we are correct in suggesting that Pym wrote his diary by the end of 1625 (see above, p. 13) and that Eliot did not compose the *Negotium* before 1628, then clearly it must have been Eliot who made use of Pym's work rather than the other way around. This conclusion is supported by textual evidence. Given the fact that Eliot nearly always overlaid his own rhetorical flourishes onto the speeches he was recording — flourishes which do not surface in Pym's diary — and the fact that the *Negotium* often only summarizes speeches given more extensively by Pym, it is highly unlikely that Pym could have based his diary upon Eliot's work.

While we have no evidence of personal contact between these two parliamentary leaders outside the walls of the House — indeed, their temperaments and political styles were so antithetical as to make such contact unlikely—there were numerous opportunities for Eliot to have gotten hold of a copy of Pym's diary secondhand. Eliot was a close friend of a number of members of what has come to be known as the Hampden-Barrington connection of parliamentary families, most notably John Hampden, Richard Knightley, and Sir Oliver Luke, with each of whom Eliot carried on a rather extensive correspondence and exchange of manuscripts during the time of his imprisonment in the Tower.[21] This group was in turn, particularly through the person of Oliver St. John, linked to the ramifying western connection of the Earl of Bedford, of which John Pym was a part. As noted above (see pp. 10–11), copies of the Pym diary for 1625 found their way into the papers of Knightley, the Earl of Bedford, and Oliver St. John.

However close the relationship between the Pym diary and the *Negotium,* it seems clear that Pym was not the exclusive source from which Eliot worked.[22] The *Negotium* contains passages which are not covered by Pym's diary and which are not likely to have been recalled in their entirety from Eliot's memory of the 1625 events. The peculiarities and perplexities of the relation between the *Negotium* and other accounts of transactions in the House in 1625 may be illustrated but not resolved by considering the peculiarities of the reporting of Christopher Sherland's speech of 12 August, the day the King dismissed parliament. Of this speech four versions survive, in order of increasing length: Dyott, Pym (Bedford MS. 197), Petyt MS. 538/8, and *Negotium Posterorum.* Dyott's version, the shortest, has no notable peculiarities. It is a succinct ver-

21. See Alexander B. Grosart, ed., *De Jure Majestatis or Political Treatise of Government (1628–30) and The Letter Book of Sir John Eliot (1625–1632)* (London, 1882), vol. II.

22. For example, the Speaker's speech, 20 June, is entirely omitted in the Pym diary but the versions in Petyt 538/8 and the *Negotium* are very similar.

sion of what appears in one or two other of the remaining three versions and the sequence of points in the account is also identical with that followed in one or another of those versions.

Let us consider the other three versions.

Two — Petyt and the *Negotium* — are long, the former three times the length of Pym's version, the latter three and two-thirds as long. Length, however, is not all that is worth attention. The phrasings of the *Negotium* and Petyt reflect each other:

Petyt 538/8 (see below, p. 477)

The question now in debate is whether to give or not to give. [He thinks it not fit to give,] but before he gives his reasons he will speak something in answer to those reasons that have been passed for giving, and first there has been an objection made against insisting on precedents and that we should not make them our gods. And though he loves precedents well, yet he will not idolize them. But precedents were the life of the parliament and therefore should be constant and certain.

For as in other courts difference of precedents had been badges of worse times and of the weaker [judges], much more would it be in this great court which makes laws for other courts.

But those that speak most against them have most magnified them. For when they have deserted reason, how have they strained precedents to give some strength to their argument. . . .

Eliot (*Negotium Posterorum*, see below, p. 565)

Mr. Speaker, the question in debate is whether to give or no, and therein my opinion is absolute: not to give. For which before I declare my reasons I will make some answers to the arguments on the contrary, whereby the worth of both may more easily appear.

First, there has been an objection made against insisting on old precedents, and that we should not make them gods, which in part was answered—that they were venerable, though not idols. But further, precedents are the life and rule of parliaments, no other warrant being for the parliament itself for the authorities it pretends to than the ancient use and practice which is drawn out by precedents. And should not then parliaments be careful to preserve that rule inviolable to make it constant like itself? In other courts difference of precedents are badges of distemper and weakness in those times, much more it would be in this great court of parliament, which being the rectifier of others, should this way do itself; and if that stray or wander by which the rest are guided, who shall then rectify and reduce it? But even those that speak against them do most magnify and endear them when they think them useful to themselves. For when reason has forsaken them, as in the agitation of this question, how have they strained for precedents to be assistant to their arguments. . . .

Although Petyt is more compact than the *Negotium,* and so briefer, where it substantively corresponds, the two speeches correspond in content item by item. However, after maintaining close parallelism for more than a thousand words, Petyt abruptly stops while the *Negotium* goes on for an additional three hundred words. More peculiarly still, at almost exactly the point in Sherland's speech where Petyt stops, Pym starts — that is, in terms of con-

tent and some phrasing, his account picks up the parallelism with the *Negotium* where Petyt's account of the speech ends.

That is odd, but no more odd than the whole of the *Negotium*'s report on the speech. That report is incongruously crisp and clear. Crispness and clarity are not Sir John Eliot's natural style of discourse. How it happened that writing three to six years after the speech he is describing, Eliot declines from his ordinary high flown cloud-covered mode of discourse in which the rest of the *Negotium* is written into mere lucidity is itself a puzzle.

Indeed it is fair to say that the oddities in the relation between the three versions of Sherland's speech may simply be the result of accident. Before stretching the long arm of coincidence that near to the breaking point, however, we should like to propose a highly conjectural explanation which assumes that all the oddities we have noted did not just happen to happen that way.

We have earlier suggested that for his running story of what happened in the House of Commons in 1625 Eliot may well have relied on John Pym's narrative, or parts of it, using it as a means for refreshing his memory of events and things said rather than following its line slavishly. When it came to Sherland's speech, however, the Pym version let Eliot down. The speech is the first major recorded address that we have found in the parliamentary career of a young lawyer who, as Eliot knew when he wrote the *Negotium,* was to play an active part in the impeachment proceedings against the Duke of Buckingham in 1626 and was several times to intervene decisively in debate during the crucial parliament of 1628. More than that, it stated in more general terms, and yet more precisely than any other speech of which we have record by any member in 1625, the position on the freedoms of Englishmen that by 1628 the House of Commons had firmly entrenched itself in, the grounds on which the theory rested, and the sources of those freedoms.[23] But most of this is missing from the Pym version of Sherland's speech. Yet Eliot remembered Sherland's speech as especially important, indeed necessary from a rhetorical point of view to round off the *Negotium Posterorum* in the dramatic way

that in the future would impress its readers with the deep significance of what was in process in those days in 1625, a significance of which by 1629 or 1630 Eliot himself already had some consciousness. So he turned to a more satisfactory version of Sherland's speech, one which he may have had at hand in the form of a separate or as part of a copy of the anonymous diary of 1625 of which Petyt 538/8 is an exemplar. Thus Eliot was able to do justice to Sherland's concise and careful argument as he could not have done from Pym's account alone and as his own stylistic propensities unrestrained by a present model would not have permitted him to do.

The Title. If this conjectural reconstruction of what happened to impart a certain oddity to three versions of Sherland's speech of 12 August and their relations to each other is correct it may offer a clue to account for a conspicuous oddity of the *Negotium Posterorum* itself, its title — the Affairs (or Business or Doings) of Posterity (or Our Successors). But the book is not about the doings of the successors of Sir John Eliot's generation, either the biological successors of the persons or the political successors of the members of parliament of his day. It is in fact about the doings of just those members of parliament. Why is Eliot telling about their business? He is telling it *for* posterity. And the story he is telling is that of the insistence of the House on the sanctity of custom, tradition, and law which are the inheritance of free subjects. The House insists on those things against claims of courtiers that they should be set aside in the face of alleged emergencies and necessities. In short the business of the recent past that stands as a lesson *for* posterity is the political business of preserving the

---

23. There is a sign that the importance of Sherland's topic and his way of addressing it was widely recognized at the time. In the ill-reported parliament of 1625, the number of speeches that appear in two accounts is relatively few, the number that appear in four is derisory. There are, however, four accounts of Sherland's speech.

princely commonwealth by keeping the royal prerogative and the royal exercise of it within the bounds of law, of reining in the prerogative at the points where it threatens to bring the rights of Englishmen into subjection to the whim of the prince and appetites of his misadvisers.

What all this suggests is that the *Negotium Posterorum* may be more than the offering of one man to posterity. It may in fact have been viewed by Eliot as a kind of collaborative work in which he used the records of several men who sat in several parliaments to narrate the actions of those men and their colleagues. In intention it may have been the bequest of a whole generation of those men to men who were to sit in parliament in the future, a witness to that earlier generation's devotion to freedom, the testimony to posterity that in the chain which linked the generations of free Englishmen from the immemorial past to the unfathomable future the Englishmen of the 1620s had held their place firmly and faithfully.

This at least seems a possible way to read the meaning of that unique parliamentary account, the *Negotium Posterorum*. For evidence effectively to confirm this way of reading it we would be as grateful as for evidence decisively to disconfirm it.

III. EDITORIAL AIDS AND CONVENTIONS

In *Proceedings in Parliament 1625* we have with few exceptions provided the same scholarly aids and employed the same editorial conventions as appeared in *Proceed-*

ings in Parliament 1628. As to scholarly aids this is true with respect to the attendance table for the Upper House, the lists of members returned, the lists of officials, the list of abbreviations and short titles, the glossary of foreign words and phrases, the legal citations, and the tables of bills. As to editorial conventions it is true with respect to spelling, capitalization, punctuation, abbreviations, italics, quotation marks, and brackets, and folio and page numbers. Our procedure in all these matters is described in *Commons Debates 1628*, I, 42–136, with explanation and justification of the scholarly aids preceding the aids themselves where it seemed necessary or useful. It seems unlikely that any library having *Proceedings 1625* will lack *Proceedings 1628*, so in the interest of economy we will not repeat here what is said fully there, but will refer users to the appropriate section of *Proceedings 1628*. For the convenience of users where the treatment of the aids and conventions is identical as between *Proceedings 1625* and *Proceedings 1628* we have indexed the relevant sections of *Proceedings 1628* in the footnote below.[24]

The editors have made minor changes in a few of their procedures because of differences in editorial policy between *Proceedings 1625* and *Proceedings 1628*. The ways in which we have modified our editorial procedure on thumb indexing, the arrangement of sources, and cross-references have been described earlier and the grounds for the modification explained.[25]

---

24. On the Attendance Table, see *Lords Proceedings 1628*, V, 28–45; the lists of members returned, *Commons Debates 1628*, I, 52–74; the lists of officials, ibid., 75–80; the list of abbreviations and short titles, ibid.,

81–87; the glossary of foreign words and phrases, ibid., 88–103; the legal citations, ibid., 104–136; tables of bills, *Proceedings in Parliament 1628*, VI, 3–25.

25. See above, pp. 5–6.

House of Lords

Thomas Howard, Earl of Arundel and Surrey,
Earl Marshal of England

William Fiennes, Viscount Saye and Sele

SATURDAY, 18 JUNE 1625

I. JOURNAL OF THE HOUSE OF LORDS

[L.J. 435]

[p. 9] *Die Sabbathi, viz., decimo octavo die Junii 1625*[1]

[*List of Lords; see A.T.*][2]

The King's Majesty being placed in his royal throne, the Lords in their robes, and the Commons present below the bar, his Majesty commanded prayers to be said.[3] And, during the time of prayers, his Majesty put off his crown and kneeled by the chair of estate.[4]

Then it pleased his Majesty to declare the cause of the summons of this parliament in manner following, *vizt.:*

My Lords spiritual and temporal, and you gentlemen of the House of Commons in this present parliament assembled, I thank God that the business that is to be treated of at this time is of such a nature that it needs no eloquence for to set it forth; for I am neither able to do it, nor does it stand with my nature to spend much time in words. It is no new business (being already happily begun by my father, of blessed memory, that is with God), therefore it needs no narrative.[5] **[L.J. 436]** I hope in

1. The parliament had been summoned to meet on 17 May but the opening of the session was postponed three times because of the delayed arrival in England of Henrietta Maria (Charles I's bride-to-be). On 17 May the parliament was prorogued until the 31st; on 31 May it was prorogued to meet on 13 June, at which time it was again prorogued until the 18th of the same month. For accounts of the prorogations, see Appendix, below, pp. 642–644. Concerning the delay in the opening of the session, see S.P. 16/2:27, 55, and 80 (printed in Chamberlain, *Letters,* II, 614–619); S.P. 16/3:16, 17, printed in the Appendix, below, p. 640; and *Negotium,* below, p. 492. See also, *Cal. S.P. Venetian, 1625–1626,* pp. 62, 70, 83; and Salvetti dispatches, pp. 5, 7–8, 22. In the end the new Queen did not attend the opening of the session, having not yet recovered from the voyage from France; see Salvetti dispatch, p. 22.

2. In the MS. L.J. at the beginning of the record of each session (morning and afternoon) there is a list of members organized by benches (i.e., bishops', earls', and barons' benches) and, within each bench, by precedency. Beside the name of each member present a "pr" is included in the list. Instead of printing these lists, we have compiled the information into an Attendance Table (A.T.). See the introduction to the A.T. below, Appendix, p. 592.

3. The prayer is printed in the Appendix to this volume, below, pp. 645–646. Several of the French lords who had accompanied Henrietta Maria to England were the King's guests at this ceremony (see H. of C., 18 June, p. 190 and n. 4). A letter of 24 June to Sir M. Stuteville notices their uncertainty about conduct during the prayers: "[the King] caused a bishop to say prayers before the beginning, whereof he made the door suddenly to be shut and so enforced the popish lords to be present; some whereof kneeled down, some stood upright, and one did nothing but cross himself" (Harl. MS. 389, f. 464v).

4. Charles sat on the chair of state and wore the royal crown for the opening of parliament although the official coronation did not take place until 2 February 1626. Zuane Pesaro, Venetian ambassador in England, wrote to the Doge and Senate on 4 July that: "Parliament opened on the 18/28th, the appointed day, the King having entered it privately without the usual pomp because he has not been crowned, although on his royal throne he put on the robe and wore the King's crown" (*Cal. S.P. Venetian, 1625–1626,* p. 96). And see Salvetti dispatch, p. 23. See also the letter of 24 June to Sir M. Stuteville (Harl. MS. 389, f. 464v), and the questions raised by Lord Keeper Williams in S.P. 16/3:44, printed in the Appendix, below, pp. 640–641.

5. James I died on 27 March 1625. For background concerning the proceedings in the previous parliament (1624), the broken Spanish treaties, and the legacy of foreign commitments, see the speech of James I to both Houses of parliament in answer to their address to him, 23 March 1624 (Nicholas diary, S.P. 14/166, f. 107; and S.P. 14/161:24); and also Gardiner, *History of England,* V, 43–214; Ruigh, *Parliament of 1624,* pp. 16–42, 382–397; and Russell, *Parliaments,* pp. 145–203. See also Sir John Coke's speech of 4 August in the Oxford session of this parliament (H. of C., 4 August, O.B.); the account of public affairs in England from the entry into the treaties with Spain until early 1626 (S.P. 16/21:86) printed in the Appendix to *C.D. 1625,* pp. 164–178; and below, p. 394, n. 39. On the Spanish marriage treaty generally, see *Narrative of the Spanish Marriage Treaty,* edited and translated by Samuel Rawson Gardiner (London: Camden Society, 1869), and see also *Considerations Upon the Treaty of Marriage Between England and Spain* (n.p., 1623) (*S.T.C.,* no. 10003).

There are several extant versions of the King's speech included with collections of materials relating to proceedings in the Lower House. See H. of C., 18

God that you will go on to maintain it[6] as freely as you were willing to advise my father to it. It's true that it may seem to some that he was too slack to begin so just and so glorious a work, but it was his wisdom that made him loath to begin a work until he might find means to maintain it; but, after he saw how much he was abused in the confidence he had in other states, and was confirmed by your advices to run the course we are in, with your engagements to the maintaining of it, I need not press to prove how willingly he took your advice, for the preparations [p. 10] that are made are better able to declare it than I can speak it. The assistance of those in Germany, the fleet that is ready for action, with the rest of the preparations, which I have only followed my father in, do sufficiently prove that he entered not superficially but really and heartily into this action.

My Lords and gentlemen, I hope that you do remember that you were pleased to employ me to advise my father to break both those treaties that were then on foot, so that I cannot say that I came hither a free unengaged man.[7] It's true that I came into this business willingly, freely, like a young man, and consequently rashly; but it was by your entreaties, your engagements, so that though it were done like a young man, yet I cannot repent me of it. And I think none can blame me for it, knowing the love and the fidelity you have ever borne to your kings; I having had likewise some little experience of your affections. I pray you remember that this being my first action, and begun by your advice and entreaty, what a great dishonor it were both to you and me if this action, so begun, should fail for that assistance you are able to give me. Yet, knowing the constancy of your loves both to me and this business I needed not to have said this, but only to show what care and sense I have of your honors and mine own.

I must entreat you likewise to consider of the times we are in, how that I must venture your lives, which I would be loath to do, if I should continue you here long;[8] and you must venture the business if you be slow in your resolutions, wherefore I hope you will take such grave and wise counsel as you will expedite what you have now in hand to do, which will do me and yourselves an infinite deal of honor—you, in showing your loves to me, and me, that I may perfect a work which my father has so happily begun.

Last of all, because some malicious men may and as I hear have given out that I am not so true a keeper and maintainer of the true religion that I profess, I assure you that as I may say with Saint Paul that I have been bred up at Gamaliel's feet[9] (although I shall never be so arrogant as to assume to myself the rest), so I shall so far show the effects of it that all the world may see that no man has or shall be ever more desirous to maintain the religion that I now profess than I shall be.

Now, because I am unfit for much speaking,[10] I mean to bring up the fashion of my predecessors to have my Lord Keeper to

---

June, n. 6. Apparently the copies of the speech which circulated in London were known to be "imperfect and very short". Birch, *Court and Times of Chas. I*, I, 37.

6. I.e., the war for the recovery of the Palatinate and the defeat of the Spanish.

7. Concerning the part played by Charles, then Prince of Wales, in the dissolution of the Spanish treaties, see Gardiner, *History of England*, V, 172–214; Ruigh, *Parliament of 1624*, pp. 392–395; and Russell, *Parliaments*, pp. 145–203.

8. The plague had broken out in London in April. During the week of parliament's opening in June the number of deaths was 165 in 31 parishes; see Mead's letter to Sir M. Stuteville, 18 June (Harl. MS. 398, f. 462), and below, p. 212. Regular accounts of the number of dead, taken from the weekly death lists, are given in the newsletters in Birch, *Court and Times of Chas. I*, I, 32–91, *passim*. See also, Salvetti dispatches, pp. 21, 25, 26–27, 28; Russell, *Parliaments*, pp. 213–214; and the Introduction to the present volume, above, pp. 3–4, n. 4.

9. Acts 22:3.

10. Charles was referring to "a defect or impediment of his tongue" as well as a "want of experience"; see Salvetti dispatch, p. 23.

speak for me in most things. Therefore I commanded him to speak something to you at this time, which is more for formality than any great matter he has to say unto you.

The Lord Keeper, according to his Majesty's commandment, declared:

That the King's main reason of calling the parliament (besides the looking on the faces of his subjects) is to let them understand the great engagements for the recovery of the Palatinate imposed on his Majesty by the late King, his father, and by themselves, and that the two late treaties with Spain were broken off by the last parliament.

That the many treaties and alliances since, the arms sent into the Low Countries, the reparations of the forts, and the fortifying of Ireland meet all in one center, the Palatinate, and that herein are already spent all the subsidies granted the last parliament (whereof the account is ready) and as much more of the revenues of the crown.[11] His Lordship commended three circumstances to their considerations. First, the time—all Europe being at this day as the pool of Bethesda, the first stirring of the waters is to be laid hold on,[12] wherefore his Majesty desires them to bestow this meeting on him, or rather on these actions; and the next shall be theirs, as long and as soon as they will, for domestic business. Secondly, the supply of this great action—if subsidies be thought too long and backward, his Majesty desires to hear, and not to propound the manner thereof. Thirdly, the issue of

this action which so highly concerns the honor and reputation of his Majesty, being his first, for which he relies very much upon their loves, with the greatest confidence that ever King had in his subjects—witness his royal poesy, *amor civium regis munimentum;*[13] and he doubts not but that as soon as he shall be known in Europe to be their king, they shall be as soon known to be a loving and loyal nation to their king.

Then his Lordship willed the Commons to choose their Speaker, and to present him on Monday next.[14]

The Clerk read the names of the receivers and triers of petitions, in French:[15]

[p. 11] *Les receavors des peticions d'Engleterre, d'Ecoce, d'Irelande:*
    Messire Randall Chrew, Chr. et Chiefe Justicier
    Messire Johan Dodderidge, Chr. et Justicier
    Messire Jaques Whittlocke, Chr. et Justicier
    Messire Edward Salter, Chr.
    Messire Roble. Rich, Chr.

    Les Receavors des peticions de Gascoigne, et des autres terres et pais de per la mere et des Isles:
    Messire Henry Hobert, Chr. et Baronet, et Chiefe Justicier de banc. comun.
    Messire Edward Bromley, Chr. et Baron de Excheqr.
    Messire Wyll. Jones, Chr. et Justicier
    Messire Charles Caesar, Chr. et Docteur au Droit Civil
    Messire Peter Mutton, Chr.

    Trieurs des peticions d'Engleterre, d'Escoce, et d'Irelande:
    L'Achievesque de Canterbury
    Le Baron Ley, Grande Tresorier

11. See the message concerning the King's estate delivered by Sir John Coke to the Commons on 8 July (below, H. of C., 8 July, O.B.) and the Lord Treasurer's account of the King's estate delivered on 8 August and reported to both Houses on 9 August (below, H. of L., 9 August, p. 166 and n.74). For an account of the disbursements of the 1624 subsidy monies, entitled "A Collection of all the Warrants directed to be paid by the Treasurers of the Subsidy moneys", dated 28 June 1625, see *Cal. S.P. Dom., 1625–1649, Addenda*, pp. 23–27.

12. John 5:2–4.
13. For the translation of foreign words and phrases of less than fifteen words, see Glossary, below, pp. 622–626.
14. The Lower House chose Sir Thomas Crew. See below, H. of C., 20 June, O.B.
15. The old French from the MS. L.J., below, has been kept exactly as it appears in the manuscript. The editors have not modernized or translated the French because of the number of changes that would result not only in spelling but also in dealing with elisions.

Le Vicount Maundevill, President de Councell le
    Roy
Le Duc de Buckingham, grande Admirall
    d'Engleterre
Le Count de Arundell, grande Marescal
Le Count de Pembroc, Senesc du Maison le Roy
Le Count de Northton
Le Count de Warwic
Le Count de Carlile
Le Count de Clare
L'Evesque de Duresme
L'Evesque de Ely
Le Baron Willoughby de Er.
Le Baron Sheffeild
Le Baron Carew

Touts ceux ensemble ou quatre des prelats et
snrs. avantditz appellants as eux les Sergaunts
quant serra besoigne tiendront leur place en le
Chamber du Tresorier.

[L.J. 437] Trieurs des peticions de Gascoign et
des autres terres et pais de per la mere et des Isles:
    Le Count de Worcestere, Gardein de Privie Seale
    Le Count de Essex
    Le Count de Dorsett
    Le Count de Mountgomery
    Le Count de Bridgwater
    Le Count de Leistre
    Le Count de Holland
    [p. 12] L'Evesque de Londres
    L'Evesque de Worcestre
    L'Evesque de Coventree et Lich.
    Le Baron Wentworth
    Le Baron Russell
    Le Baron Mountague

Touts ceux ensemble ou quatre des prelats et
Seigneurs avantditz appellants as eux les Ser-
jaunts le Roy et ainsi l'attourney du Roy quant
serra besoigne tiendront leur place en Chamber
du Chamberleyne.

Dominus custos magni sigilli ex jussu domini
regis continuavit praesens parliamentum usque

in diem Lunae, 20ᵐ diem instantis Junii, hora 2ᵃ
post meridiem.[16]

II. MINUTE BOOK, H.L.R.O., M.M., 1625

[f. 5] Die Sabbathi 18 Junii 1625.
[List of Lords Present; see A.T.][17]

[f. 5v] Prayers.

[f. 6] L. Keeper. My Lords and gentlemen, you have heard the King's speech
which might seem short, but it was not so.

His Majesty has expressed the substance,
the circumstance I shall show unto you.
The main reason of this parliament, besides
looking upon his [subjects],[18] was to recover the Palatinate of forces both by sea
and land.

For the dissolving of the two treaties with
a promise of your enterprises. The late
King that is with God[19] had no greater
thoughts to his dying thought of the recovery of the Palatinate. The great navy for the
recovery of the Palatinate and not as the /

That the King had rather go to the grave
than to cease from the recovery of the Palatinate. Actions do not command time but
time commands actions, be they never so
great.[20]

[f. 7v] The state of Christendom stands
like the pool of Bethesda and this kingdom.
The King expects this session for him, or
this action, the first circumstance.

If in your judgments you find subsidies to
be too slow for this action he desires to hear
from you how you will supply his occasions.
He desires to hear it from you.

I may say of the King as the orator said of
himself, so may I say of the King.[21] The
King has put upon your loves that his honor
consists upon your care. The King does not
doubt but by that time that his Majesty is

16. "The Lord Keeper of the Great Seal, by command of the King, has continued the present parliament until Monday, the 20th day of this June, at 2
o'clock in the afternoon".
17. In H.L.R.O., M.M., 1625, at the beginning of
the record of each session (morning and afternoon) is
a list of Lords present, organized by benches. Instead
of printing these lists, we have compiled the information into an A[ttendance] T[able]. See the introduction
to the A.T. below, Appendix, p. 592.
18. See L.J., above.
19. MS.: good.
20. See above, n. 5.
21. Cf. H. of C., 18 June, p. 191.

known to be a king his resolutions may be known by your furtherance.

The receivers and[22] triers of petitions read by the Clerk.

22. MS.: *of the.*

Adjourned, 2 Monday next.

HOUSE OF LORDS
ORDER OF BUSINESS   MONDAY, 20 JUNE 1625

[*Afternoon*]
Prayers

MONDAY, 20 JUNE 1625

I. JOURNAL OF THE HOUSE OF LORDS

[L. J. 437]

[p. 13] *Die Lunae, vicesimo die Junii 1625, post meridiem*
[*List of Lords; see A.T.*][1]

Prayers being said (as on the first day of the parliament), the Commons were admitted who presented Sir Thomas Crew, Knight, Serjeant at Law, for their Speaker, who made his excuse as the manner is.[2] But his Majesty approving their election as was declared by the Lord Keeper, he[3] made an eloquent speech unto his Majesty wherein, having first protested that he undertook the office of Speaker in obedience only to his Majesty, he remembered the proceedings of **[L.J. 438]** the last most happy parliament in which it pleased the late King of famous memory to ask the advice of his people, and expressed their joy that God, who has the power of the hearts of kings, directed his Majesty (that now is) to proceed in the like parliamentary course. That as a woman forgets her sorrow at the birth of a man child,[4] so they when his Majesty was placed in his father's throne. And showed their hopes that, as good King Hezekiah was five and twenty years of age when he began his reign,[5] and at his first entrance showed his zeal to God and his care of re-

ligion, so his Majesty, being of the same age and having a wise and a great council and a faithful people to advise him, will maintain true religion and the ancient laws so much esteemed in all ages; and their hopes are the greater for that his Majesty begins with a parliament. And remembered his father's charge to maintain our religion, and God's merciful power to bring his Majesty back out of danger when he was in a strange land, and their sorrow for his then absence, and exceeding great joy at his safe return.[6] And humbly besought [p. 14] his Majesty that, now God had put the sword into his hand, he would extend it for recovery of the Palatinate, so dishonorably gotten and kept by hostile arms,[7] which was anciently a refuge for religion, and not to suffer those locusts, the Jesuits, to eat up the good fruits of this land.[8] He acknowledged his Majesty's stem to be lineally descended from Lucius, the first British king that embraced the Gospel,[9] and concluded with the accustomed petitions for freedom from arrests during the parliament, *eundo, sedendo, et redeundo,* for freedom of speech in their consultations, not doubting but to confine themselves within the limits of duty and modesty, [for] access unto his Majesty upon all needful occasions, and [for] a benign interpretation of all their actions and of this his speech.[10]

1. See H. of L., 18 June, n. 2.

2. For the Speaker's speech of excuse and the Lord Keeper's approbation of the election on the behalf of the King, see the accounts in H.L.R.O., M.M. and Osborn fb 155, below.

3. I.e., Serjeant Crew. For other accounts of the Speaker's acceptance speech, see H. of C., 20 June, pp. 198–201 and n. 11; *Negotium*, below, pp. 494–497; and the copy from Osborn fb 155 in the Appendix, below, pp. 651–652.

4. John 16:21.

5. 2 Kgs. 18:2; 2 Chr. 29:1.

6. A reference to the journey made by Charles to Spain in 1623. See H. of C., 18 June, n. 28.

7. Spanish troops invaded the Palatinate in the summer of 1620 during the time that the English and Spanish were negotiating the Spanish marriage treaty. Gardiner, *History of England*, III, 325–369.

8. Ps. 105:34–35; Deut. 28:38.

9. According to early legend, transmitted by Bede, Lucius was a second-century king of the Britons who converted to Christianity. Geoffrey of Monmouth describes him as the only son of Coilus who was crowned king at the time of his father's death. *The Venerable Bede's Ecclesiastical History of England . . .* , ed. J. A. Giles (London, 1849; reprinted, AMS Press, N.Y., 1971), p. 10; Geoffrey of Monmouth, *The History of the Kings of Britain*, ed. Lewis Thorpe (Baltimore, 1966), p. 124.

10. These were the four customary petitions to the king at the opening of a session: freedom from arrest during the session, liberty of speech, access to the King, and a request that the monarch overlook mistakes on the part of the members and Speaker. See Hatsell, *Precedents*, I, 75–76; Elsynge, *Parliaments*, 175–192.

The Lord Keeper, having first conference with his Majesty, answered to this effect, *vizt.:*[11]

That his Majesty has amply accepted Mr. Speaker's obedience, though he refused his sacrifice. And, as the Speaker remembers the last parliament to be happy, that it was so accounted by our late King, so esteemed of by his Majesty, and so it proved by the event, wherein the two treaties with Spain were dissolved, and so many gracious laws enacted, it became the late King so to close his government, in which parliament our King, being a principal actor,[12] he can never forget the desires of the Commons nor the wishes of the Lords.

That his Majesty takes in good part Mr. Speaker's observation of the five circumstances of his entrance to the crown: as that he began with a parliament; that he came to us with the blood of nobles, being lineally descended from the ancient British kings;[13] that his succession sweetened the loss of his glorious father; that God was with him in the strange land and delivered him from thence (even as God was with Moses, so be he always with his Majesty, to which let all say Amen);[14] and lastly, that his Majesty professes the true religion, it being the last blessing his father gave him to have a special care thereof.[15]

As Mr. Speaker commends to his Majesty the laws of this land, so he recommends the same to the lawyers, that they study the ancient laws themselves and not the Abridgements.

And whereas you represent unto his Majesty that unjust acquisition of the Palatinate (the dishonor of our nation), no man can but be sensible of his Majesty's care for the recovery thereof, he having given a lively representation of his affection to it himself the other day in this place.[16] He now hopes that you who first drew him into this action will give him such supplies as shall enable him to perform it.

And as touching the banishment of those locusts (the priests and Jesuits), his Majesty commends that of St. Ambrose:[17] that the poorest man has interest in religion. Yet, he desires you to trust him with the manner thereof, and he will be careful to give you good satisfaction of his zeal herein.

And as touching Mr. Speaker's petitions for your privileges, his Majesty grants them all without any limits, knowing well that yourselves will punish the abusers thereof.

Dominus custos magni sigilli ex jussu domini regis continuavit praesens parliamentum usque in diem Mercurii, 22ᵐ instantis Junii, hora nona.[18]

II. MINUTE BOOK, H.L.R.O., M.M., 1625

[f. 8] *Die Lunae 20 die Junii 1625, post meridiem.*
[*List of Lords Present; see A.T.*][19]

[f. 8v] The Speaker brought to the bar by

---

11. For other versions of the Lord Keeper's speech, see H. of C., 20 June, pp. 196–197; *Negotium,* below, pp. 497–499; and the copy from Osborn fb 155 in the Appendix, below, pp. 652–653.

12. See H. of L., 18 June, n. 7; and H. of C., 18 June, n. 29.

13. See above, n. 9.

14. Josh. 1:5.

15. King James's last wish was that: "when he [Charles] was married he should so respect religion here that he should marry her person and not her religion". See the report of the Duke's speech upon presenting the King's answers to the petition concerning religion, H. of C., 9 August, p. 430.

16. See the King's speech to both Houses, 18 June, above, pp. 28–30.

17. *St. Augustine* in *Negotium,* below, p. 499. We are unable to find the reference.

18. "The Lord Keeper of the Great Seal, by command of the King, has continued the present parliament until Wednesday, the 22nd of this June, at 9 o'clock". The Lower House met on Tuesday the 21st to resolve on the fast and appoint a committee of privileges, etc. See below, H. of C., 21 June. Members of the Upper House may have attended the declaration of the King's marriage held in the Banqueting House on the 21st; see the letter of 22 June from Locke to Carleton, printed in the Appendix, below, p. 706.

19. Following the attendance list this day in the MS. is the note: *Proxy to Denny.* A proxy list is printed in the Appendix, below, p. 590.

Sir Thomas Edmondes and Mr. Chancellor of the Duchy.

Speaker.[20] Most gracious Sovereign, the k[nights], c[itizens], and b[urgesses] of the Commons House of parliament have cast their eyes upon me. I put them in mind of my inabilities which, when not having license, I am constrained to appeal to Caesar [*illegible*] to your Majesty that your Majesty would be pleased to command them to choose another Speaker.

L. Keeper. Mr. by [*sic*] Speaker, that you were not to be released if you speak.

Your rhetoric has spoiled the rhetoric [*sic*][21] and his Majesty has confirmed their choice.

[f. 9] Speaker.[22] Since it is your pleasure to command I must command [*sic*]. I am the more enabled because of the concordancy of the House last session. Your royal father was pleased to/

Your readiness to further all means we desired. Solomon, the wisest of kings, called that kingdom happy/

It is God's course to mix joys with sorrows, but as a woman with child when the[y] strive to take away/

Our late King to set your[23] Majesty upon the throne/

The ark[24] of true religion is flourishing in your kingdom, that will bring you to happiness. It was David's command to his son of [*sic*] Solomon, and your loving and dying father['s], to keep the Gospel professed.

[f. 9v] It is your Majesty's desire to recover the Palatinate and it is a great dishonor to us to have his ancient patrimony taken away.

I will present unto us our ancient privileges: 1, from arrests; 2, of free speeches, that truth may be discerned and ambiguities fully discovered; 3, that you would be pleased we may have access unto your Majesty upon occasions at your Majesty's own convenient time; 4, that your Majesty would make a benign and favorable construction of all our actions and enterprises; that he who is a Speaker for others may desire your Majesty's favor for himself.

L. Keeper. His Majesty has heard with approbation; has command[ed] me to answer some part. Though your speech be round, yet must give me leave/
Somewhat of yourself/
[f. 10] his entrance, 5 things/
of religion
1. Of yourself you said little but do much/ You the/
2. The last parliament it was happy, so thought by the Commons. The treaties were dissolved, statutes were enacted, and more bill[s] of grace were a Magna Carta.
3. The late King was the very body, soul of that invention of parliament some time which the committees soon/
4. Of his Majesty's entries in this kingdom. It is a sign of his love that he begins with a parliament. He was no sooner proclaimed than the writs went out.[25]
[f. 10v] That he does in some sort sweeten the death of his father.
Lastly, his great delivery of his late arrival, it filled our hearts with joy and tongues with laughter. He was God's child and they could take no hold of him.
The last care that his father gave him was to keep the people in the same religion that is now professed.

---

20. For another account of this speech, see Osborn fb 155, below. See also the first paragraph of the Speaker's acceptance speech in Petyt 538/8, below, p. 198.

21. I.e., spoiled the logic, see the Lord Keeper's speech in Osborn fb 155, below.

22. For references to Biblical citations and other matters in the speeches of the Speaker and the Lord

Keeper, below, see the annotation to the fuller accounts in the L.J., above, and in H. of C., 20 June, pp. 196–201.

23. MS.: *with*.

24. Possibly *state*.

25. Charles was proclaimed King on 27 March and writs went out for the parliament on 2 April; see Appendix, below, p. 642.

For the laws of his kingdom he has privately, and now publicly, that the judges and practicers the[y] go forward with the old course of law.

Touching the Palatinate you, Mr. Speaker, you cannot imagine how much the King [*illegible*] your care of the Palatinate.

His Majesty has fully expressed himself the last meeting. His Majesty desires not to live but gloriously. That you that drew him to his business/

[f. 11] For the abounding of the priests and Jesuits, he does commend your care and zeal. He desires you to trust him, he desires you to trust him in the manner.

His Majesty desires you to remember what his father said for the particular managing—he will be as careful/[26]

For the 4 petitions,[27] he grants them all without any bounds, assuming that you will be as careful yourselves if any commit any incivility to reprehend it as he would do.

Adjourned. 9 Wednesday morning next.

III. SPEECH OF SIR THOMAS CREW, SERJEANT AT LAW, TO THE KING. OSBORN FB 155, P. 96.[28]

Most gracious Sovereign, the knights, citizens, and burgesses of the Lower House of parliament assembled according to your Majesty's direction and their ancient privileges have here presented a Speaker, passing over many abler men, and have cast their eyes upon me, your humble servant, who have desired them to alter their choice in regard of my weakness whereof myself have greatest cause to be sensible. And having put them in mind of their particular [knowledge] of my insufficiency to perform this service but not prevailing, am forced to appeal to Caesar, my gracious Sovereign, and to fly to your throne to the which I am an humble suitor as to be so gracious as to command them to reconsult and advise of a second and a better choice.

IV. SPEECH OF LORD KEEPER WILLIAMS, BISHOP OF LINCOLN, ON BEHALF OF THE KING, APPROVING THE ELECTION OF SIR THOMAS CREW AS SPEAKER. OSBORN FB 155, PP. 96–97.

Mr. Serjeant, his Majesty likes very well their choice yet, though you are in the same case as Gilbertus,[29] to plead ill or well, for if you had pleaded ill (which you were not wont to do) that could not remove his opinion from you in regard of your former service; but you have pleaded worthily like yourself (for not one that hears your speech can believe your insufficiency), for your rhetoric has spoiled your logic and his Majesty applauds the election of the House in their choice of you.

26. Concerning the reference to the words of James I, see H. of C., 20 June, n. 7.

27. See above, n. 10.

28. Both Sir Thomas Crew's disabling speech and the King's response delivered by the Lord Keeper are printed from John Browne's Commonplace Book, Osborn fb 155. Formerly a Braye manuscript, the book is now part of the Osborn collection in the Beinecke Rare Book and Manuscript Library, Yale University. The speeches are not included in most of the collections of separates for the 1625 parliament. The only other copy of them we have found is in Braye MSS. 1, f. 82.

29. St. Gilbert of Sempringham who, in 1165, was accused by the crown of having assisted Archbishop Thomas Becket. Gilbert, affirming ecclesiastical law, refused to deny the charges. *John Capgrave's Lives of St. Augustine and St. Gilbert of Sempringham* . . . , ed. J. J. Munro, Early English Text Society, vol. 140 (London, 1910), pp. 93–96. *D.N.B.* The version of the Lord Keeper's speech printed in Hacket, *Scrinia Reserata* (pt. II, p. 11) makes the reference to Gellius's account of Euathlus (Aulus Gellius, *The Attic Nights*, 5, 10) rather than to Gilbertus.

I.   Journal of the House of Lords,   39–40
II.   Minute Book, H.L.R.O., M.M., 1625,   40–41

WEDNESDAY, 22 JUNE 1625

I. JOURNAL OF THE HOUSE OF LORDS

[L.J. 438]
[p. 15] *Die Mercurii, viz., vicesimo secundo die Junii 1625*
[*List of Lords; see A.T.*]
[L.J. 439]

For that divers Lords do this day attend the King's Majesty, the calling of the House is deferred upon the Lord Keeper's motion.

Memorandum: That these Lords underwritten were this day brought into the House, in their parliament robes in manner following, *vizt.:*
John, Earl of Clare, between the Earl of Salisbury and the Earl of Northampton; Edward, Earl of Dorset, supplying the Earl Marshal's place, all in their parliament robes; Garter King of Arms, in his Herald's coat, going before the Earl of Dorset. Garter carried the patent of the Earl of Clare's creation and delivered it to the Lord Keeper, and his Lordship to the Clerk;[1] then the Earls of Salisbury and Northampton presented the Earl of Clare unto his Lordship and afterwards conducted him to his due place.

Oliver, Earl of Bolingbroke, and Francis, Earl of Westmorland, were brought in in the like manner.[2]

William, Lord Viscount Saye and Sele,[3] was brought in in like manner between the Lord Viscount Rochford and the Lord Russell.

So were James, Lord Ley (Lord High Treasurer of England),[4] between the Lord Sheffield and the Lord Walden, and placed on the barons' bench next the Lord Grey of Warke.

Francis, Lord Deincourt,[5] between the Lord Wentworth and the Lord Paget, and placed next the Lord Ley.

[p. 16] And Richard, Lord Robartes of Truro,[6] between the Lord Paget and the Lord Russell, and placed next the Lord Deincourt.

The LORD KEEPER signified his Majesty's pleasure that such Lords as have not taken the oath of allegiance in this House do now take the same.[7]

And agreed, that all the Lords of this House do take the oath of allegiance as well those Lords who have heretofore taken that oath in the House as those who have not; and that the order is for the same oath to be taken always after the adjournment of the House.

Memorandum: That the Roll of Remembrances for Order and Decency to be Kept in the Upper House of Parliament, etc., was this day read, and one clause therein, *vizt.,* that bishops are only Lords of parliament but not peers, is referred to be considered of by the Lords committees of the privileges, etc.[8]

---

1. The Garter King at Arms was Sir William Segar and Henry Elsynge, Sr., was the Clerk of the Parliaments. John Holles was created Earl of Clare on 2 November 1624.
2. Oliver St. John was created Earl of Bolingbroke on 28 December 1624 and Francis Fane, Earl of Westmorland, on 29 December of the same year. *G.E.C.* Concerning their entrance into the House, see the account in H.L.R.O., M.M., below.
3. William Fiennes was created Lord Viscount Saye and Sele on 7 July 1624. *G.E.C.*
4. James Ley was created Baron Ley of Ley on 31 December 1624. *G.E.C.*

5. Francis Leke was created Lord Deincourt of Sutton on 26 October 1624. *G.E.C.*
6. Richard Robartes was created Lord Robartes of Truro on 26 January 1625. *G.E.C.*
7. Concerning the oath of allegiance, see *S.R.,* 7 *Jac.* I, c. 6. Section 10 of the Roll of Standing Orders of the House of Lords indicates that new members must take the oath before sitting.
8. Although according to *S.R.,* 25 *E.* III, stat. 6, c. 6, bishops at one time claimed to be peers of the realm, section 34 of the Roll of Standing Orders states that, "It would be resolved what privilege noble men and peers have, betwixt which this difference is to be ob-

Their Lordships renewed their former order for absence from prayers, *vizt.*, each earl to pay two shillings, and each bishop and baron one shilling, that came after prayers.[9]

[*Notice of Adjournment*]

The names of the Lords who took the oath of allegiance this day, after the adjournment of the House:

Imprimis, the Lord Keeper took the said oath alone by himself, kneeling at his woolsack.

Then, in the same place, these Lords following took the said oath, *vizt.*:

The Lord Archbishop of Canterbury
The Lord Ley, Lord Treasurer
Viscount Mandeville, Lord President of the King's Council
The E. of Worcester, Lord Privy Seal
The E. of Kent
The E. of Sussex
The E. of Lincoln
The E. of Nottingham
The E. of Dorset
The E. of Salisbury
The E. of Leicester
The E. of Northampton
The E. of Clare
The E. of Bolingbroke
The E. of Westmorland
The Lo. Vic. Rochford
The Lo. Vic. Saye and Sele

The Lord Bp. of London
The Lord Bp. of Winchester
The Lord Bp. of Norwich
The Lord Bp. of Rochester
The Lord Bp. of Bath and Wells
The Lord Bp. of Bangor
The Lord Bp. of Ely
The Lord Bp. of Llandaff
The Lord Bp. of Salisbury

The Lord Bp. of Exeter
[**L.J. 440**]
The Lord Bp. of St. Davids
The Lord Bp. of Bristol
The Lord Bp. of Carlisle
The Lord Bp. of Gloucester

The Lord Wentworth
The Lord Sheffield
The Lord Walden
The Lord Russell
The Lord Spencer
The Lord Carey of Leppington
The Lord Robartes of Truro

II. MINUTE BOOK, H.L.R.O., M.M., 1625

[f. 12] *Die Mercurii 22 die Junii 1625.*
[*List of Lords Present; see A.T.*]

Prayers.

L. KEEPER. Whether their Lordships would put off the calling of the House in regard the King has employed many of the Lords.

L. SHEFFIELD. To put it off till tomorrow.

Agreed by the House.

[f. 12v] L. KEEPER. Whether their Lordships will rectify[10] the former order for such Lords as come late to pay as formerly.

LORD SHEFFIELD. That the orders of the House be read.[11]

E. of Dorset, having authority from the E. Marshal, brought in the [Earl of Clare], between the [Earls of] Salisbury and Northampton; the E. of Clare [and] the Herald,[12] going between the E. of Dorset and the other Lords.

E. of Bolingbroke brought in by the E. of Rutland and the E. of Kent.

---

served, that bishops are only Lords of parliament, but not peers, for they are not of trial (i.e., triable) by nobility". We have found no record of a later report on this matter from the committee of privileges in 1625.

9. See section 15 of the Roll of Standing Orders. The matter of fines for Lords who were absent without leave from an entire day's session, rather than simply

absent from prayers, was raised on 25 June; see below, p. 53.

10. Possibly *ratify.*

11. See L.J., above.

12. Sir William Segar, see above, n. 1. The bracketed words are taken from the L.J.

E. of Westmorland brought in by the E. of Rutland and the E. of Salisbury.

L. Viscount Saye and Sele brought in between the Lord Rochford and the Lord Russell.

Lord Ley, Lord Treasurer, brought in between my Lord Sheffield [and] Lord Walden, who took his place according to his creation and after removed to his place as Lord Treasurer.

Lord Deincourt brought in by the Lord Wentworth and the Lord Paget.

L. KEEPER. That their Lordships by the way of conveniency would suffer some French gentlemen to see the manner of the House sitting.[13]

L. Robartes of Truro brought in by the Lord Paget and Lord Russell.

[f. 13] LORD KEEPER. That those Lords that have not received the oath may now take it, and so he has been appointed by the King.

Agreed that all the Lords, as they are Lords of parliament, may take the oath of allegiance.

The orders of the House read by the Clerk.

L. BISHOP OF COVENTRY AND LICHFIELD. That his Lordship was of the committee; that they were certified from the Tower that the bishops were peers of parliament.

L. PRESIDENT. That the question be referred to the committees for privileges.

Adjourned. 9 tomorrow morning.

Several of the Lords took the oath of allegiance according to the motion made by the Lord Keeper.
[f. 13v] These Lords subscribed took the oath of allegiance and supremacy:

[col. 1]	[col. 2]
Bishop of Exeter	E. of Kent
Bishop of Carlisle	E. of Clare
Bishop of Gloucester	L. Spencer
	L. Walden
	L. Sheffield
	L. Vic. Saye and S[ele]

[col. 3]
L. Russell
L. V. Rochford

---

13. Customarily, private persons were not allowed to be present while the House was in session; see sec-tions 18 and 30 of the Roll of Standing Orders.

Prayers
Message from the Commons
   desiring a **conference**
   regarding the **general fast**
   (Sir Richard Weston, Sir
   Thomas Edmondes, and
   others) [*see below*]   43, 46; *25/6;
                                          28/6(2)
The messengers withdraw   43
ARCHBISHOP OF CANTERBURY   46
The Lords agree to a conference
   by committee   43, 46
The messengers from Commons
   called in again   43
Answer given to the Commons'
   message: the Lords have
   appointed a committee for a
   present conference (LORD
   KEEPER, Bp. of Lincoln)   43, 46
Committee for the conference on
   the general fast: appointed
   [*see below*]   43, 46, 48
LORD KEEPER (Bp. of Lincoln)   47
Report of the conference with the
   Commons: on the petition
   for a general fast
   (ARCHBISHOP OF
   CANTERBURY)   43, 47
The petition for the general fast:
   read   43, 47
   [*The petition for the general fast is
   printed on p. 44*]
Words added and the petition
   read again and agreed to   44, 47
Messengers for desiring access to

the King for presenting the
   petition for the general fast:
   appointed [*see below*]   44
Committee for the conference:
   sent to inform the Commons'
   committee of Lords' decisions
   concerning the petition [*see
   above and below*]   44
Report from the committee for
   the conference (ARCHBISHOP
   OF CANTERBURY)   44, 47
The House **called**: list of Lords
   excused   44, 47
Committee of **privileges**:
   appointed   45, 48, 49
Report of the King's answer
   concerning presenting the
   petition for the **general fast**
   (EARL OF PEMBROKE, L.
   Steward) [*see above*]   44, 48
Message to the Commons on
   presenting the petition for
   the general fast to the King
   (Sir Thomas Coventry, Att.
   General, and Sir Thomas
   Richardson)   44, 48
House adjourned during pleasure   48
Report of the Commons' answer
   to the message: the
   Commons will be ready for
   presenting the petition   44, 48
Committee for the conference: to
   receive the engrossed petition   48
House adjourned   46, 48
Lords take the **oath of allegiance**   46

THURSDAY, 23 JUNE 1625

I. JOURNAL OF THE HOUSE OF LORDS

[L.J. 440]

[p. 17] *Die Jovis, vizt., vicesimo tertio die Junii 1625*

[*List of Lords; see A.T.*]

Message from the House of Commons by Sir Richard Weston, Chancellor of the Exchequer, and others: The knights, citizens, and burgesses of the Commons House of parliament do congratulate with your Lordships the happy assembly of this parliament, and, to express their earnest affection to continue the union and good understanding between both Houses, they desire a conference with your Lordships for joining in petition unto the King's Majesty for a general fast throughout the whole kingdom.[1] The time and place and number of committees they humbly leave unto your Lordships.

The messengers were withdrawn and, the House having considered of this message and agreed on a committee for that conference, they were called in again, and this answer was delivered by the Lord Keeper, *vizt.*: **[L.J. 441]** That the Lords have taken this message into consideration and return thanks for the congratulation. Their Lordships promise all good union and understanding, for their parts, between the two Houses and, for a taste thereof, they have appointed a committee of four and twenty to confer with the committee of the Commons about this petition to be made unto the King. To meet presently, in the Painted Chamber, so as the business of that House will then permit it.

The names of the Lords committees appointed for the said conference, *vizt.*:[2]

[p. 18]

[col. 1]	[col. 2]
Lo. Archbp. of Canterbury	E. Marshal
Lo. Treasurer	L. Steward
Lo. President	E. of Dorset
Lo. Privy Seal	E. of Clare

[col. 3]	[col. 4]
L. Bp. of Rochester	L. Willoughby
L. Bp. of Coventry and Lichfield	L. Scrope
	L. Stourton
L. Bp. of Bath and Wells	L. Darcy
	L. Wentworth
L. Bp. of St. Davids	L. Sheffield
L. Bp. of Carlisle	

[col. 5]

L. Russell
L. Grey of Groby
L. Spencer
L. Carey of L[eppington]
L. Robartes of Truro

To meet in the Painted Chamber presently.

The Lords being returned from the conference, the LORD ARCHBISHOP OF CANTERBURY reported: That the committee for the Commons presented unto their Lordships a petition to be made unto the King, wherein they had left a blank for your Lordships to be joined with them, if you please.

The which petition was presently read; and the blank being filled with these words, viz.: "Lords spiritual and temporal", and was again, the second time, read, and generally assented unto by the whole House.

The tenor of the said petition follows, *in haec verba, vizt.*:

1. Upon a division in the Lower House on whether to consult with the Lords regarding the petition for a fast, the Commons had resolved on 22 June to request a conference with the Upper House. See H. of C., 22 June, p. 217.

2. The list of committee members included in the Committee Book (below, p. 49) varies somewhat from that in the Lords Journal and the H.L.R.O., M.M. The editors have not annotated such differences. Using the page numbers listed in the Orders of Business readers can conveniently make their own comparisons of the membership lists for each of the 1625 committees. For members of the conference committee appointed by the Lower House, see H. of C., 23 June, p. 228.

Most gracious Sovereign,[3]

We your Majesty's most loyal and dutiful subjects, the Lords spiritual and temporal and Commons, now assembled in parliament to consult and advise of the great and weighty affairs of Church and state, knowing that all human counsels and helps without God's divine assistance are of no force and, observing that God has already laid His hand upon us by pestilence and unseasonable weather, threatening a famine, for these and many other important reasons do, as in duty we conceive ourselves bound, and, as a thing most suitable to the present times and occasions, humbly beseech your Majesty that you will be pleased to command a general fast throughout your whole kingdom. That so, humbling ourselves by fasting and prayer, we may upon our true repentance make our peace with God and thereby both divert His heavy judgments inflicted and deserved, and draw down a blessing upon our consultations and counsels and upon your Majesty's sacred person, your kingdoms, and all your royal designs and enterprises.

The House, having thus generally assented to join in the delivery of this petition, first, their Lordships agreed to send two Lords, members of this House, unto the King to know what time it will please his Majesty to appoint for the committees of both Houses to attend him for delivery of the same, and then to send the Commons notice thereof, and also that the Lords committees shall intimate this, together with their Lordships' general assent unto this petition, unto the committee of the Com-

mons who attended their Lordships' return, in the Painted Chamber, and that they should redeliver them the said petition again to be engrossed.

The said Lords committees being returned again, the LORD ARCHBISHOP OF CANTERBURY reported the same unto the House.

Whereupon the Lord Steward and Lord Conway were sent unto the King as aforesaid, who, being returned, reported the time appointed by his Majesty for delivery of the said petition.

Message sent unto the Commons by Mr. Attorney General and Mr. Serjeant Richardson, *vizt.*: That the King's Majesty will admit the committees of both Houses to deliver their petition for a general fast tomorrow morning between nine and ten, at the Banqueting House in Whitehall.

Answered: That the committee of the Commons shall be ready to accompany the committee of the Lords at the time and place appointed. That they have sent back the very copy of that petition which they formerly sent and received again of their Lordships, and will send the said petition when it is engrossed unto the Lord Archbishop of Canterbury his Grace.

[p. 19] *Memorandum:* That this day the House was called. The Clerk read first the names of the barons and so ascending upwards, and the absence of these Lords following were excused on this manner, *vizt.*:[4] The Lord Montagu excused for want of health.[5]

---

3. The petition, with slight word variants, is also included in the H.L.R.O., Main Papers, H.L., 23 June 1625, and in Petyt 538/8 (see H. of C., 22 June).

4. The list that follows is composed of the names of the Lords excused from attendance for this day and/or the entire session. The list varies somewhat from the one included in the H.L.R.O., M.M. (see below). For information concerning the attendance of all members of the Upper House, see the Attendance Table, below, pp. 592–597. Where additional information on attendance is available we have included it in the following footnotes. For proxies, see the Proxy List, be-

low, p. 590.

5. In a letter received by Edward, Lord Montagu, on 2 July, his brother, Henry, Viscount Mandeville, reported that the King had granted Edward's request for leave of absence from parliament because of his poor health. H.M.C., *Buccleuch MSS.*, I, 261. Despite this license to be absent, Edward chose to attend the Oxford session and kept a journal of those proceedings. See above, p. 8; and see Esther S. Cope, *The Life of a Public Man* (Philadelphia: The American Philosophical Society, 1981), pp. 105–107.

The Lord Stanhope of Shelford had sent his proxy.

The Lord Arundell of Wardour had leave of the King to be absent and intends to send his proxy.[6]

Lord Carew in town but sick.

Lord Denny had sent his proxy.[7]

Lord Danvers in town but sick.

Lord Petre had leave of the King to be absent being hurt by a fall from his horse.[8]

Lord Wotton had sent his proxy.

Lord North excused for want of health.[9]

Lord Cromwell *extra regnum* and intends to send his proxy.

Lord Windsor *extra regnum.*

Lord Stafford has leave of the King to be absent.

Lord Dacre of Hurstmonceaux excused for want of health.

Lord Zouch sent his proxy.

Lord Abergavenny sick of the gout.

Lo. Bp. of St. Asaph has leave to be absent.

Lo. Bp. of Exeter in town but not well.

Lo. Bp. of Chester sent his proxy.

Lo. Bp of Worcester sick but intends to come.

Lo. Bp. of Hereford sent his proxy.[10]

Lo. Bp. of Peterborough has leave to be absent.

Lo. Vic. Wallingford sick, intends to send his proxy.

Lo. Vic. Montagu has leave to be absent.[11]

Earl of Anglesey not well.

Earl of Bristol sent his proxy.[12]

Earl of Bridgewater sick.

Earl of Salisbury not well.

Earl of Essex *extra regnum.*

Earl of Hertford has leave to be absent and intends to send his proxy.

Earl of Bedford has leave to be absent and intends to send his proxy.

Earl of Bath has sent his proxy.

Earl of Cumberland has leave to be absent.

Earl of Rutland not well.[13]

Earl of Derby has sent his proxy.

Earl of Shrewsbury has leave to be absent.[14]

Earl of Oxford *extra regnum.*

The Marquis of Winchester has leave to be absent.[15]

Lord Archbishop of York has sent his proxy.[16]

[**L.J. 442**] The names of the Lords committees appointed this day by the House to take consideration of the customs and orders of this House and the privileges of the peers of the kingdom or Lords of parliament, *vizt.*:

L. Archbp. of Canterbury	L. Conway
L. President	L. Willoughby
E. Marshal	L. Berkeley
E. of Dorset	L. Stourton
E. of Leicester	L. Darcy and Meinill
E. of Warwick	L. Wentworth
E. of Clare	L. Sheffield
L. Vic. Saye and Sele	L. Russell
	L. Grey of Groby
L. Bp. of Durham	L. Spencer
L. Bp. of Norwich	L. Carey of Leppington
L. Bp. of Coventry and Lichfield	L. Robartes of Truro
L. Bp. of Bath and Wells	
L. Bp. of Bristol	
L. Bp. of Carlisle	

6. The letter excusing Lord Arundell was dated 24 June. *Cal. S.P. Dom., 1625–1626,* p. 541.

7. Dispensation was granted to Edward, Lord Denny, on 19 July. *Cal. S.P. Dom., 1625–1626,* p. 545.

8. Dispensation was granted to William, Lord Petre, on 27 June. *Cal. S.P. Dom., 1625–1626,* p. 542.

9. Dudley, Lord North, was absent for the first week and a half of the 1625 parliament but subsequently attended both the London and Oxford sessions.

10. Dispensation was granted to Francis Godwin, Bp. of Hereford, on 14 June. *Cal. S.P. Dom., 1625–1626,* p. 540.

11. Anthony Maria Browne, Viscount Montagu, attended only the opening day of the session (18 June).

12. The letter excusing John, E. of Bristol, was dated 11 June. *Cal. S.P. Dom., 1625–1626,* p. 540.

13. Dispensation was granted to Francis, E. of Rutland, on 25 June. *Cal. S.P. Dom., 1625–1626,* p. 542. He attended 18, 20, and 22 June.

14. Dispensation was granted to George, E. of Shrewsbury, on 21 May. *Cal. S.P. Dom., 1625–1626,* p. 537. See also, H.M.C., *Various Collections,* II (1903), p. 312.

15. Dispensation was granted to William, Marquis of Winchester, on 14 June. *Cal. S.P. Dom., 1625–1626,* p. 540.

16. Dispensation was granted to Tobias Matthew, Archbp. of York, on 21 May. *Cal. S.P. Dom., 1625–1626,* p. 537.

To attend the Lords: L. Chief Justice, L. Chief Justice of the Common Pleas, Mr. Justice Jones, Mr. Justice Whitelocke, Mr. Justice Yelverton, Mr. Serjeant Davies, Mr. Attorney General.

To meet every Thursday, at two after dinner, in the Little Committee Chamber.

[p. 20] And *memorandum:* That their Lordships are to meet on Saturday next, at two in the afternoon, in the Painted Chamber, to name a subcommittee; and the said subcommittee, from time to time, to peruse and perfect the Journal Book.

[Notice of Adjournment][17]

The names of those Lords who took the oath of allegiance this day in the House after the adjournment, *vizt.:*
The Earl Marshal
L. Steward
E. of Warwick
E. of Devonshire
E. of Cambridge
E. of Holderness
E. of Denbigh

L. Vic. Mansfield
L. Vic. Andover

Lo. Bp. of Durham
Lo. Bp. of Coventry and Lichfield
Lo. Bp. of Chichester

Lo. Conway
Lo. Willoughby
Lo. De La Warr
Lo. Berkeley
Lo. Darcy

II. MINUTE BOOK, H.L.R.O., M.M., 1625

[f. 14] *Die Jovis 23 die Junii 1625*
[List of Lords Present; see A.T.]

Sir Richard Weston, accompanied by Sir Thomas Edmondes and others: desire that the k[nights], c[itizens], and b[urgesses] of the Commons do congratulate very much with the states of this time; for a happy entrance unto the same [they] desire a conference with your Lordships; the number, time, and place the[y] leave to your Lordships.

L. CANTERBURY. I need not say much; there needs a general petition both in respect of war, etc.

Concluded to have a conference.
6 of a bench.[18] To meet presently in the P[ainted] Chamber.

L. KEEPER. That the Lords have taken consideration, etc., give thanks for the union and for a taste of their respects have appointed a committee of 24 to meet presently in the Painted Chamber.

The Lords committees that are to meet and confer with a committee of the Commons House touching a petition to his Majesty for a general fast, viz.:[19]

2. L. Treasurer	1. Willoughby
4. L. Privy Seal	3. Stourton
6. L. Steward[20]	2. Scrope
5. L. Marshal	4. Darcy of M[einill]
7. L. Dorset	5. Wentworth
3. L. President	6. Sheffield

17. The Lower House met on 24 June although the Upper House did not reconvene until the 25th. The committees of both Houses presented the petition for the general fast to the King on the morning of the 24th.

18. I.e., six members from each of the earls' and bishops' benches, twelve from the barons' bench, a total of twenty-four. The number of barons named to a committee was generally equal to the combined number of bishops and earls. According to Henry Elsynge's tract, "The Method of Passing Bills in Parliament", *Harleian Miscellany*, V (London, 1810), p. 227, "in the naming of committees . . . if there be five earls, then five bishops, and ten barons; the reason whereof I

know not". In the 1628 parliament a subcommittee was ordered to search "whether there be any order or ancient custom to double the number of barons in committees". See *L.P. 1628*, p. 115.

19. See above, n. 2. The names of the committee members were set down in the Minute Book by the assistant clerk in the order which he heard them. *Harleian Miscellany*, V (London, 1810), p. 228. The numbers to the left of the names indicate the order of precedence which is the order in which the names are recorded in the finished Journal, see *L.J.*, above.

20. *Chamberlain* is crossed out in the MS. following *L. Steward.*

8. E. of Clare
1. L. Canterbury[21]

9. Spencer
7. Russell
8. Grey of G[roby]

2. Coventry and
L[ichfield]
5. Carlisle
3. Bath and W[ells]
4. Davids
1. Rochester[22]

11. Robartes of
T[ruro]
10. Carey of
Leppington

To meet presently in the Painted Chamber.

[f. 15] L. KEEPER. That the Commons have appointed a fast on Saturday next, that your Lordships will talk with them to know.

Report, L. ARCHBISHOP OF CANTERBURY: That their Lordships would join with them, the Commons, in a general fast, for in regard of the sickness by the plague, the last unseasonable weather that may bring a death, and the war that is intended, that instead of a visitation we may draw a blessing on us.

The petition was read first with a blank for the words "Lords spiritual and temporal"; after being put in, it was the second time read again.

L. ARCHBISHOP OF CANTERBURY. That their Lordships have added the words "Lords spiritual and temporal", that the

House intends to send some one Lord or more to wait of the King to know when his Majesty would be attended and a/

The House called and those that were absent excused, some by proxies and some by license, etc.[23]

Bishop of Exeter
excused by/

Deincourt[24]
[Grey of] Warke
Montagu, *ex*
Mandeville[26]
Brooke
Noel, E. of Clare[28]

Carew
Stanhope
Denny, proxy[30]

[f. 15v]
Herbert, proxy
Dudley
Stafford, leave of/
Dacre, sick
Morley
Zouch
Audley, proxy

Oxford
Worcester, sick
Hereford, proxy[35]

Danvers, sick
Petre, *ex* Privy Seal[25]
Wotton
[Howard of] Walden
North, sick, Keeper[27]
Paget
Eure
Cromwell, proxy
St. John Basing[29]
Mordaunt
Windsor, beyond sea
Vaux, proxy
[f. 15v]
Bath, proxy
Huntingdon[31]
Sussex[32]
Cumberland, license
Rutland, sick[33]
Derby, proxy
Shrewsbury, license[34]
Oxford, *extra*
[*regnum*]
M. Winchester,
license[36]
Duke[37]

---

21. *Durham* is crossed out in the MS. following *Canterbury*.

22. *L. Keeper* is crossed out in the MS. following *Rochester*.

23. See the list in the L.J., above, which omits a number of names that appear on this H.L.R.O., M.M., list but includes the following names omitted here: Lord Arundell, Lord Abergavenny, and the bishops of St. Asaph and Chester.

24. Francis Leke, Lord Deincourt, had been introduced into the House the previous day (see above, p. 39) but apparently was absent for the remainder of the session.

25. See above, n. 8. The Lord Privy Seal was Edward Somerset, Earl of Worcester.

26. See above, n. 5.

27. See above, n. 9.

28. John Holles, E. of Clare, may have proffered the excuse for Edward, Lord Noel.

29. Dispensation was granted to John, Lord St. John of Basing, on 24 June. *Cal. S.P. Dom., 1625–1626*, p. 541.

30. See above, n. 7.

31. Henry Hastings, E. of Huntingdon, requested that William Herbert, E. of Pembroke, be his proxy. See Hastings MS. 5501 in the Appendix, below, p. 670.

32. Dispensation was granted to Robert, E. of Sussex, on 25 June. *Cal. S.P. Dom., 1625–1626*, p. 542.

33. See above, n. 13.

34. See above, n. 14.

35. See above, n. 10.

36. See above, n. 15.

37. George Villiers, Duke of Buckingham, attended the parliament only sporadically.

Peterborough, leave   York, proxy[38]
Winchester
London[39]

Visc. Tunbridge
Colchester
Purbeck
Wallingford
Montagu, license[40]

Earl Holland
Anglesey
Bristol, proxy[41]
Bridgewater, sick
Montgomery
Exeter
Salisbury, sick
Suffolk, proxy
Essex, beyond seas
Hertford, license
Bedford, license

[f. 16] The grand committee for privileges to take consideration of the customs and orders of the House, and privileges of the peers of parliament, viz.:[42]

3. Marshal	2. Willoughby
4. Dorset	8. Sheffield
2. President	11. Spencer
6. Warwick	9. Russell
8. Saye	7. Wentworth
7. Clare	12. Carey of
5. Leicester	Leppington
1. Bp. Canterbury	3. De La Warr
	4. Berkeley
1. Durham	6. Darcy
3. Coventry and	5. Stourton
L[ichfield]	1. Conway
4. B[ath] and W[ells]	10. Grey of G[roby]
5. Bristol	13. Robartes
2. Norwich	
6. Carlisle	

[To attend:] 1. L[ord] Chief Justice, 2. Jones, 3. Whitelocke, 4. Yelverton, 6. Attorney, 5. Davies.[43]

To meet Saturday, 2 [o'clock] next, Painted Chamber.[44]

L. STEWARD. That the King will give an audience tomorrow between 9 and 10 in the morning.

Serjeant Richardson and Mr. Attorney to the Commons: That the King will give audience between 9 and 10 tomorrow morning, and that the Attorney call for the petition to enter upon record.

Adjourned during pleasure.

[f. 16v] Returned: 1. Attorney, 2. Serjeant Richardson. The message was delivered. That they will wait, at the time and place appointed, on his Majesty; and the Commons sent the copy of the petition touching the general fast, and the engrossed [petition] they will also return to the committee.

That the committees shall have power to receive the engrossed petition.

Adjourned. 9 Saturday.

III. COMMITTEE BOOK, H.L.R.O., MAIN PAPERS, H.L., 1625

[f. 1] *Die Jovis 23° Junii a° Domini 1625*[45]

Lords committees to meet with a committee of the Commons about a petition to be delivered unto the King's Majesty for a general fast. *Vizt.*:

38. See above, n. 16.
39. *Archbp.* is crossed out in the MS. following *London.* George Monteigne, Bp. of London, attended both sessions.
40. See above, n. 11.
41. See above, n. 12.
42. On the order of names, see above, n. 19.
43. *Finch* is crossed out in the MS. and replaced with *Davies.*
44. Apparently there was some confusion in appointing the meeting time and place of this committee. The line, *To meet at 2 every Thursday hereafter* is crossed out in the MS., and the word *stet* then inserted. Cf. the orders concerning this committee in the L.J., above, and in the Committee Book, below.
45. For a description of the Committee Book, see the Introduction, above, p. 7. Also, cf. above, L.J., where the lists vary somewhat and do not include the later additions and alterations indicated in the Committee Book.

[col. 1]

1° *Julii* X⁴⁶ Lo. Archbp. of
L. Keeper   Canterbury
added.   Lo. Treasurer
              L. President
              L. Privy Seal
              E. Marshal
Montgomery   L. Steward
           X E. of Dorset
L. Saye   E. of Clare

Winchester
Ely   L. Bp. of Rochester
              L. Bp. of Coventry and
                 Lichfield
              L. Bp. of Bath and W[ells]
              L. Bp. of St. Davids
              L. Bp. of Carlisle

[col. 2]

L. Willoughby of Eresby
L. Scrope
L. Stourton
L. Darcy of Meinill
L. Wentworth
L. Sheffield
X L. Russell   L. North *1° Julii*
L. Grey of Groby
L. Danvers, added *28°*
   Junii
L. Spencer
L. Carey of Leppington   L. Grey of W[arke]
X L. Robartes of Truro   *1 Julii*

To meet presently in the Painted Chamber.

Expedited.⁴⁷

[f. 1v] *Die Jovis 23 die Junii 1625.*

The Lords committees named to take consideration of the customs and orders of the House, and privileges of the peers of the kingdom, or Lords of parliament. *Vizt.*:

25 *Junii* 1625
This committee is to meet presently after the adjournment of the House, to name a subcommittee and to go on with the business besides.

1 *Julii* 1625
This committee to consider of Ralph Brooke, York Herald, his petition, on Tuesday next by [*illegible*] in the afternoon in the Painted Chamber.⁴⁸
6 *Julii* 1625
York's petition to be considered of on Friday next by 8.

[col. 1]

L. Archbp. of Canterbury
L. President
E. Marshal
E. of Dorset
E. of Leicester
E. of Warwick
E. of Clare

L. Vic. Saye and Sele

L. Bp. of Durham
L. Bp. of Norwich
L. Bp. of Coventry
   and Lichfield
L. Bp. of Bath and
   W[ells]
L. Bp. of Bristol
L. Bp. of Carlisle

[col. 2]

L. Conway
L. Willoughby of E[resby]
L. De La Warr
L. Berkeley
L. Stourton
L. Darcy and Meinill
L. Wentworth
L. Sheffield
L. Russell
L. Grey of Groby
L. Spencer
L. Carey of Leppington
L. Robartes of Truro

To attend the Lords: the two Lords Chief Justices, Mr. Justice Jones, Mr. Justice Whitelocke, Mr. Justice Yelverton, Mr. Serjeant Davies, Mr. Attorney General.

---

46. An *X* beside the name in the MS. indicates the removal of that Lord from the committee membership; occasionally the name is also struck through in the manuscript. In order for the reader to follow the changes made in the committee, the editors have transcribed the *X*'s where they occur in the MS. list but have not deleted the names struck through in the MS. Names of new members added as replacements and the dates of their appointments are entered in the margins of the MS. in the hand of Henry Elsynge, Sr.

47. Where "Exped." is entered in the margins of the Committee Book we have extended the term to "Expedited" and inserted it into the text at the end of the entries for the committee to which it applies. Concerning the use of the term in reference to the passage of bills, see below, H. of L., 30 June, n.5.

48. The petition of Ralph Brooke and the warrant committing him to the Marshalsea are printed below, H. of L., 1 July.

[To meet on Saturday the 25th of this instant month by 2 in the afternoon in the Painted Chamber.

And after this first meeting their Lordships are constantly to meet every Thursday in the afternoon by 2 of the clock in the Painted Chamber; and have power to appoint a subcommittee of themselves to look to the entry of the Journal.]⁴⁹

To meet every Thursday at 2 after dinner in the Little Committee Chamber.

And *memorandum,* that their Lordships are to meet on Saturday next at 2 in the afternoon in the Painted Chamber to name a subcommittee [and to go on with the business besides] and there to peruse and perfect the Journal Book from time to time.

49. The passages within brackets here and below are crossed out in the MS. See above, n. 44.

HOUSE OF LORDS
ORDER OF BUSINESS   SATURDAY, 25 JUNE 1625

Prayers

EARL OF PEMBROKE (L. Steward): presents the following petitions   52, 53

Petition of **Augustine Coles**: read   52, 53, 55
[*Cole's petition is printed on p. 55*]

Ordered: the parties complained of by Coles to be sent for   52, 53,*4/7

Petition of **Robert Browne**: read   52, 53, 55
[*Browne's petition is printed on p. 55*]

Ordered: the parties complained of by Browne to be sent for [*see below*]   52, 53,* 28/6

LORD KEEPER (Bp. of Lincoln): concerning case of **Samuel Markham**, servant to the Earl of Sussex   52

Ordered: a *habeas corpus* to be granted for Markham   52, 54,* 28/6

Ordered: a *habeas corpus* to be granted for Robert Browne [*see above*]   52

L. 1a. An act for confirming of the copyhold estates and customs of the tenants of the manor of **Cheltenham** [*see below*]   52, 54,* 28/6; 30/6; 9/7

EARL OF CLARE: concerning **fines** for Lords who are **absent** without leave   54, *28/6

The matter of fines for absent Lords: referred to the committee of **privileges**   53, 54

Lords excused   53, 54

LORD SHEFFIELD: concerning fines for proxies held by absent Lords   54

This business referred to the committee of **privileges**   53, 54

Lord excused   54

Report on presentation of the petition for the **general fast** to the King (VISCOUNT MANDEVILLE, L. President)   53, 54, *23/6

L. 2a. An act for confirming of the copyhold estates and customs of the tenants of the manor of **Cheltenham**: committed [*see above*]   52, 54(2)

Committee of **privileges** to meet after the adjournment of the House to name a **subcommittee** to consider **bills** not dispatched last session and **disorders of pages**, footmen, etc.   53, *27/6; 28/6

SATURDAY, 25 JUNE 1625

I. JOURNAL OF THE HOUSE OF LORDS

[L.J. 442]
[p. 21] *Die Sabbathi, vizt., vicesimo quinto die Junii 1625*
[*List of Lords; see A.T.*]
[L.J. 443]

Hodie prima vice lecta est billa, An act for the settling and confirmation of the copyhold estates and customs of the tenants in base tenure of the manor of Cheltenham, in the county of Gloucester, and of the manor of Ashley, otherwise called Charlton Kings, in the said county, being holden of the said manor of Cheltenham according to an agreement thereof made between the King's most excellent Majesty, being then Prince of Wales, Duke of Cornwall and of York, and Earl of Chester, lord of the said manor of Cheltenham, and Giles Greville, Esquire, lord of the said manor of Ashley, and the said copyholders of the said several manors.

Et 2ᵈᵃ vice lecta est eadem billa, et commissa

L. Treasurer	L. Conway
L. President	L. Berkeley
L. Privy Seal	L. Scrope
L. Bp. of Durham	L. Russell
L. Bp. of St. Davids	L. Danvers
L. Bp. of Gloucester	L. Spencer

To attend the Lords: Mr. Justice Jones, Mr. Justice Whitelocke, Mr. Baron Trevor, Mr. Attorney General, Mr. Serjeant Richardson.

To meet on Monday next, at eight in the morning, in the Painted Chamber.

[p. 22] The LORD STEWARD presented unto the House two petitions: The one of Augustine Coles, one of the yeomen of his Majesty's Chamber in ordinary, complaining that while he was in his Majesty's service at Dover, William Swetname, John Birde, and Thomas Bartlette, bailiffs, entered his house and carried away goods to the value of thirty pounds at the suit of Michael Harrison for a debt (wherein he was surety for Richard Cotle) of ten pounds, whereof four pounds is paid.[1]

Which petition being read, it is ordered that the said William Swetname, John Birde, and Michael Harrison be brought before their Lordships on Tuesday, the 28th of this June, in the morning, to answer their contempt and breach of privilege of parliament.

The other of Robert Browne, his Majesty's servant, arrested by Henry Fetch, Serjeant, and Hugh Povey, his yeoman, at the suit of Henry Shawe, in contempt of the privileges of this high court.

Ordered, that the said Henry Fetch, Hugh Povey, and Henry Shawe be brought before their Lordships on Tuesday next, the 28th of this June, by eight in the morning.[2]

The LORD KEEPER signified unto the House that one Samuel Markham, servant to the Right Honorable the Earl of Sussex, was lately arrested in London, contrary to the privilege of parliament.[3]

Ordered that a *habeas corpus, etc.,* be awarded unto the sheriffs of London to bring the body of the said Samuel Markham before their Lordships on Tuesday next, at nine in the morning.

The like *habeas corpus, etc.,* is awarded to bring Robert Browne before their Lordships.

---

1. The petition of Augustine Coles is printed below, p. 55. The bailiff (Swetname) and underbailiffs (Birde and Bartlette) and Michael Harrison were brought in to the bar on 4 July, see H. of L., 4 July, O.B.

2. Robert Browne's petition is printed below, p. 55.

3. For a letter from the E. of Sussex to the L. Keeper describing the circumstances of Markham's arrest and asking for his discharge, see H.L.R.O., Main Papers, H.L., 25 June 1625.

The House being moved that whereas those Lords that came late to prayers do pay to the poor man's box, *vizt.*, each earl two shillings, and each bishop and baron one shilling; and yet those Lords who are absent altogether that day without leave pay nothing, that it would please their Lordships to conceive some order against the willful neglect of those that be absent.[4] And that such might not only pay for themselves after the said rate, but also for all those whose proxies they have; for that the House does not only lose the votes of such absent Lords, but of their proxies also. The which is referred to be considered of by the Lords committees for privileges, etc.

The LORD PRESIDENT reported to the House that yesterday the Lords committees of both Houses delivered unto his Majesty the petition (agreed on) for a general fast, and that his Majesty's answer was to this effect, *vizt.*:

That the message pleased him very well, and this their beginning with God promised celerity in their actions. That he liked of the petition, required time to consider of the form and manner of a fast, and would appoint the same to be done speedily and effectually.[5]

The Lords committees for privileges, etc., are to meet in the Painted Chamber presently, after the adjournment of the House, and to name a subcommittee.[6]

And those Lords subcommittees are to consider of the bills begun and not dispatched the last session, and to order which of them shall be presented to the House. And to consider of some order to be made against the misdemeanors of pages and footmen, etc.[7]

These Lords are this day excused for not coming to the House, *vizt.*:[8]
The Lord Archbp. of Canterbury
The Earl of Northampton
The Lo. Bp. of Oxford
The Lo. Bp. of Bangor
Lo. Danvers
Lo. North
Lo. Deincourt
Lo. Brooke
E. of Bridgewater

[*Notice of Adjournment*]

II. MINUTE BOOK, H.L.R.O., M.M., 1625

[f. 17] *Die Sabbathi 25 die Maii [sic] 1625.* [*List of Lords Present; see A.T.*]

L. STEWARD certified the House that 2 of the King's servants were arrested.[9]

The petitions read:

The petition of Augustine Coles.
Ordered that the party that caused him to be arrested and the bailiffs be sent for against Monday next, 9 in the morning.

The petition of Robert Browne.
Ordered that the party and serjeants be in the court by 9 on Tuesday next.

---

4. The motion was made by the E. of Clare, see H.L.R.O., M.M., below. For the order concerning Lords coming into the House after prayers, see above, 22 June, p. 40.

5. A full answer from the King to the petition for the fast, presented on 24 June, was delivered by L. Conway on 28 June; see below, p. 66. See also the Solicitor's report, H. of C., 28 June, O.B.

6. For the members appointed to the subcommittee, see below, 27 June, p. 59. According to the order of 23 June (see above, p. 46) the subcommittee to be named this afternoon (25 June) was to peruse and perfect the Journal Book.

7. For the subcommittee's report on the disorders of pages and the commitment of George Whitchar, keeper of a tavern near the Parliament House, see H. of L., 28 June, p. 64.

8. The daily lists of the Lords excused which appear in the L.J. and in H.L.R.O., M.M., frequently differ. The editors have not annotated such differences. For those readers who wish to make their own comparisons, the page numbers of the lists of excused members are given in the Orders of Business. Information concerning attendance is readily accessible in the Attendance Table.

9. I.e., Augustine Coles and Robert Browne. See above, nn. 1 and 2.

[f. 17v] Samuel Markham, the E[arl] of Sussex's man, [to] be brought by a *habeas corpus* on Monday, [and] the delinquents.[10]

Hodie 1ª vice lecta est billa, An act for his Majesty's tenants of Cheltenham, in Gloucestershire, etc.

E. OF CLARE. That those Lords that are willfully absent might have some course taken for them.[11]

This referred to the committees of privileges.

Excused:[12]
Exeter
Lincoln
Canterbury
Northampton
Oxford
Bangor
North
Deincourt

L. SHEFFIELD. That those that have proxies might answer for their absence.

Referred to the committees.

E[arl] of Lincoln excused by the E. of Westmorland.

Report, L. PRESIDENT, in the absence of the Lord Archbishop of Canterbury, to present the petition to his Majesty: that he liked the form and method but desired that the time might be considered and the business speedily expedited.

Hodie 2ª vice lecta est billa, An act for his Majesty's tenants of Cheltenham, in the county of Gloucester, etc.

L. President	4. Russell
Treasurer	2. Berkeley
Privy Seal	5. Danvers
	3. Scrope
Gloucester	1. Conway

| Durham | 6. Spencer |
| Davids | |

[To attend:] Baron Trevor, Attorney, Whitelocke,[13] Jones, Richardson.

Monday next by 8, P[ainted] Chamber.

Adjourned. 9 Monday.

III. COMMITTEE BOOK, H.L.R.O., MAIN PAPERS, H.L., 1625

[f. 2] *Die Sabbathi 25 Junii 1625.*

An act for the settling and confirmation of the copyhold estates and customs of the tenants in base tenure of the manor of Cheltenham, in the county of Gloucester, and of the manor of Ashley, otherwise called Charlton Kings, in the said county, being holden of the said manor of Cheltenham, according to an agreement thereof made between the King's most excellent Majesty, being then Prince of Wales, Duke of Cornwall and of York, and Earl of Chester, lord of the said manor of Cheltenham, and Giles Greville, Esquire, lord of the said manor of Ashley, and the said copyholders of the said several manors. Committed unto:

L. Treasurer	L. Conway
L. President	L. Berkeley
L. Privy Seal	L. Scrope
	L. Russell
L. Bp. of Durham	L. Danvers
L. Bp. of St. Davids	L. Spencer
L. Bp. of Gloucester	

To attend the Lords: Mr. Justice Jones, Mr. Justice Whitelocke, Mr. Baron Trevor, Mr. Attorney General, Mr. Serjeant Richardson.

To meet on Monday the 27th of this instant month by eight in the morning in the Painted Chamber.

Expedited.[14]

---

10. See above, n. 3.
11. See above, n. 4.
12. See above, n. 8.
13. *Herbert* is crossed out in the MS. and *Whitelocke* is inserted.

14. Concerning the use of "expedited" in the Committee Book, see above, 23 June, n. 47.

IV. PETITION OF AUGUSTINE COLES, ONE OF
THE YEOMEN OF HIS MAJESTY'S CHAMBER IN
ORDINARY. H.L.R.O., MAIN PAPERS, H.L., 25
JUNE 1625.

To the Right Honorable the Lords Spiritual and Temporal of the Upper House of Parliament assembled.

The humble petition of Augustine Coles, one of the yeomen of his Majesty's Chamber in ordinary, most humbly showing,

That where your petitioner with another surety became engaged only for the appearance of one Richard Cotle, at the suit of Michael Harrison, for a debt of 10 *l.*, since which there has been 4 *l.* of the said debt paid. So it is, Right Honorable, that William Swetname, John Birde, and Thomas Bartlette, bailiffs, entered your petitioner's house (he being then employed in his Majesty's service at Dover) and carried away goods to the value of 30 *l.* for the said 6 *l.* behind, and still detain the same, to the discrediting of your petitioner, he being a widower and upon his preferment in marriage, and of estate sufficient (and willing) to give every man satisfaction.

In regard whereof and for that the same was done in spleen purposely to disgrace your supplicant (then discharging his service to his Majesty), the debt being none of his nor he never having notice of any prosecution since the payment of the said 4 *l.*, and his brother, then in town, being [of] a very sufficient means, offering to engage himself for what could be demanded, so the goods might remain till your petitioner return, and offering also 2*s.* 6*d.* a day for one to stay in the house with the goods in the plaintiff's behalf till your supplicant came home; but nothing would serve their turn but your supplicant's disgrace, they no way molesting either him that owed the debt or the other surety, being both sufficient.

Wherefore he humbly beseeches your

honors to grant warrant for the said Michael Harrison and the bailiffs to appear before your Lordships to answer this their abuse, and thereupon such order taken for repairing your petitioner's credit and the restitution of his goods as to your honorable wisdoms shall seem fit. And he, as by duty bound, will ever pray for your honors' healths and happiness.[15]

[*Endorsed*] Augustine Coles, petitioner.
Per dominum Steward
25 *Junii* 1625
Read and ordered

V. PETITION OF ROBERT BROWNE, HIS
MAJESTY'S SERVANT. H.L.R.O., MAIN PAPERS,
H.L., 25 JUNE 1625.

To the Right Honorable the Lords Spiritual and Temporal assembled in the High Court of Parliament.

The humble petition of Robert Browne, his Majesty's servant, humbly showing,

That whereas your petitioner (lately traveling into London about his affairs) was, by Henry Fetch, Serjeant, and Hugh Povey, his yeoman, arrested without leave at the suit of one Henry Shawe, and in contempt of the privileges of the High Court of Parliament whereby his Majesty's servants are protected [they] violently hauled him away and carried him to the Counter in Wood Street and there imprisoned him, where he still remains.

In consideration whereof, and of the disgrace done your petitioner, the debt being not his but having been cunningly gotten thereunto, he most humbly beseeches your honors to take such order as well for your petitioner's liberty as the punishment of the said persons for their contempt as in your honorable and grave wisdoms shall be thought meet.

And he shall daily pray for a blessing to

---

15. At the bottom of the MS. petition Henry Elsynge, Clerk of the Parliaments, added the order to send for the bailiff and underbailiffs. See above, n. 1.

be procured on your honors and all your
proceedings from above.[16]

[*Endorsed*] Robert Browne, his Majesty's
servant, arrested without leave and now imprisoned in the Counter.
Per dominum Steward
25 *Junii* 1625
Read and ordered

16. Following the MS. petition Henry Elsynge added the order to send for Fetch, Povey, and Shawe. On
28 June Elsynge added a second note: *28 Junii, Povey
and Shawe committed; Browne discharged. H.E.*

HOUSE OF LORDS
ORDER OF BUSINESS   MONDAY, 27 JUNE 1625

I.   Journal of the House of Lords,   58–60
II.   Minute Book, H.L.R.O., M.M., 1625,   60
III. Committee Book, H.L.R.O., Main
      Papers, H.L., 1625 (10 August),   60–61

Prayers

Lords excused — 58, 60

LORD KEEPER (Bp. of Lincoln): concerning the case of **Toby Horton**, servant to the E. of Rutland — 58, 60

Horton brought in; the *habeas corpus* read — 59, 60

Ordered: Horton to be discharged from prison — 59, 60

L. 1a and *L. 2a*. An act to enable the King's Majesty to make leases of lands parcel of his Highness's **Duchy of Cornwall**: committed — 58, 60(2), *28/6; 30/6; 9/7

Report from the committee of privileges concerning the subcommittee (VISCOUNT MANDEVILLE, L. President) — 59, 60, 61, *25/6

Message from the Commons bringing the bill for the Lord's day (Sir Edward Coke and others) — 58, 60

L. 1a. An act for punishing abuses committed on the **Lord's day** — 58, 60, *30/6; 1/7

L. 1a. An act for the making of the **arms** of the kingdom more serviceable — 58, 60, *30/6

L. 1a. An act for the better maintenance of **hospitals and almshouses** — 58, 60, *6/7

L. 1a. An act for the better preserving of his Majesty's **revenue** — 58, 60, *2/8

Edward, Lord Conway, brought into the House — 59, 60

House adjourned — 60(2)

MONDAY, 27 JUNE 1625

I. JOURNAL OF THE HOUSE OF LORDS

[L.J. 444]
[p. 23] *Die Lunae, vizt., vicesimo septimo die Junii 1625*
[*List of Lords; see A.T.*]

Hodie 1ª et 2ᵈᵃ¹ vice lecta est billa, An act to enable the King's Majesty to make leases of lands parcel of his Highness's Duchy of Cornwall or annexed to the same.
    Committed unto the

L. Treasurer	L. Danvers
L. President	L. Darcy and M[einill]
	L. Wentworth
L. Bp. of Bath and W[ells]	L. Carey of Leppington
L. Bp. of Exeter	

    To attend the Lords: Mr. Justice Hutton, Mr. Baron Trevor, Mr. Serjeant Davenport.
    To meet tomorrow at eight in the Painted Chamber.

Hodie allata est a domo communi una billa, vizt., An act for punishing divers abuses committed on the Lord's day, called Sunday.
    The which bill was presently once read.²

Hodie 1ª vice lecta est billa, An act for the making of the arms of the kingdom more serviceable in time to come.³

Hodie 1ª vice lecta est billa, An act for the better maintenance of hospitals and alms-houses.⁴

Hodie 1ª vice lecta est billa, An act for the better preserving of his Majesty's revenues.⁵

    The absence of these Lords were⁶ excused:
The Lo. Steward
The E. of Exeter
The Lo. Russell⁷
Lo. Brooke
Lo. Noel

    [L.J. 445] The LORD KEEPER related unto the House that he, being trusted with the redress of breach of privileges of parliament due unto their Lordships [p. 24] after the adjournments, had granted out divers and several writs of *habeas corpus, etc.,* to bring before his Lordship such of their Lordships' servants as were arrested contrary to the said privilege, and discharged them accordingly, causing the Clerk to attend him and to make orders thereupon.⁸

---

1. *et 2ᵈᵃ* is omitted in the printed edition.
2. The bill is included in the H.L.R.O., Main Papers, H.L., 27 June. See also the act printed in *S.R.,* V, 1.
3. This bill and the two following, initiated in the Upper House in the previous session (1624), were presented this day, 27 June 1625, by the subcommittee of privileges; see the L. President's report, below. The bill concerning arms had been read first on 6 April 1624 (*L.J.,* III, 291) and read a second time and committed on 7 April (ibid., 293).
4. The bill concerning hospitals and almshouses had been read first on 13 March 1624 (*L. J.,* III, 260) and read a second time and committed on 18 March (ibid., 267).
5. The bill for the preservation of the King's revenue was read first on 17 April 1624 (*L.J.,* III, 312), read a second time and committed on 24 May (ibid., 403), and read the third time and assented to by the Lords on 25 May (ibid., 407). It was sent to the Lower House on 26 May (ibid., 408).
6. *was.* Printed edition. Concerning the lists of excused members, see above, 25 June, n. 8.
7. Lord Russell's absence from parliament was directly related to the spread of the plague in London. See H.L.R.O., M.M., below. According to the account in Joseph Mead's letter of 2 July to Sir Martin Stuteville, "my Lord Russell being to go to parliament had his shoemaker to pull on his boots, who fell down dead of the plague in his presence; whereupon he abstains from that honorable assembly and has sent the Lords word of this accident". Birch, *Court and Times of Chas. I,* I, 39.
8. The standard form of protection given by Lords for their servants, as printed in *Privileges and Practice of Parliaments* (pp. 20–21), stated that, "the Lords spiritual and temporal, the knights, citizens and burgesses of the parliaments have always had their servants and followers privileged and free from any molestation, trouble, arrest or imprisonment for some certain days, both before the beginning and after the ending of the same . . . ".
On 28 May 1624, the Lords had ordered that the privilege of parliament for Lords and their servants was "to begin with the date of the writ of summons; and to continue twenty days after every session of par-

That now he had granted the like writ of *habeas corpus, etc.*, to bring before his Lordship the body of one Toby Horton who is servant to the Right Honorable the Earl of Rutland and arrested within the time of privilege by one Robert Robotham, and detained in prison in the King's Bench; and moved their Lordships that the said Toby Horton may be brought before their Lordships by virtue of the said writ, which was assented unto.

And thereupon the said Toby Horton being brought before their Lordships, and it appearing that he was arrested on the fourteenth day of June, *Anno Domini* 1624, which was within the time of twenty days limited for continuance of the privilege of parliament after every session, the last session ending on[9] the 29th of May before, and the said writ of *habeas corpus, etc.*, with the return thereof being read: It is this day ordered by the Lords spiritual and temporal in this High Court of Parliament assembled that Tobias Horton, servant to the Right Honorable the Earl of Rutland, being arrested in execution at the suit of Robert Robotham and others within the time of privilege of parliament and detained in prison in the Marshalsea in the King's Bench, shall be discharged out of the said prison, and that the Marshal shall be discharged for delivering him out of his custody, saving nevertheless unto the said Robert Robotham and to all those at whose suit he was arrested or detained in prison their due and lawful remedy hereafter against him, the said Toby Horton, according to the intent and true meaning of one act of parliament in that case made and provided.[10]

The LORD PRESIDENT reported to the House that, according to the order of 25th of June,[11] the grand committee for privileges, etc., met and named these Lords for the subcommittee, *vizt.:*

[col. 1]	[col. 2]
E. of Warwick	L. Bp. of Norwich
E. of Clare	L. Bp. of Coventry and
L. Vic. Saye and Sele	Lichfield
	L. Bp. of Bristol

[col. 3]	[col. 4]
L. De La Warr	L. Sheffield
L. Darcy et M[einill]	L. Russell
L. Wentworth	L. Spencer

They or any four of them, at their own conveniency, to perform the service imposed on them; which was agreed unto by the House.

He reported also that they had considered of the bills begun and not dispatched the last session, and had agreed to present unto their Lordships three bills which had their first beginning in this House, *vizt.:*[12]

The bill for making the arms of the kingdom more serviceable in time to come.

The bill for better maintenance of hospitals and almshouses.

And the bill for better preserving of his Majesty's revenues.

The which bills were presently once read as before is declared.

Memorandum: That this day Edward, Lord Conway, was brought into the Parliament House between the Lord Willoughby and the Lord Wentworth (the Earl of Montgomery supplying the Earl Marshal's place), all in their parliament robes; Garter going before in his Herald's coat, and having the patent of the Lord Conway his creation[13] in his hand, which he delivered to

---

liament". *L.J.*, III, 417–418. For some of the Lord Keeper's writs and orders for discharge of men imprisoned contrary to the privileges of parliament following the 1624 session, see *L.J.*, III, 425.

9. *on* is omitted in the printed edition.

10. According to an act of 1 *Jac.* l, writs of execution could be renewed against persons discharged by privilege of parliament when they ceased to be privileged.

S.R., 1 *Jac.* I, c. 13.

11. *of the 25th June.* Printed edition. Concerning the functions of the subcommittee, see above, 25 June, p. 53 and n. 6.

12. See above, nn. 3, 4, and 5.

13. *Conway's creation.* Printed edition. Edward Conway was created Lord Conway of Ragley on 24 March 1625. *G.E.C.*

the Lord Keeper. Then they presented the Lord Conway unto his Lordship and afterwards conducted him to his due place next to the Lord Robartes of Truro.

[*Notice of Adjournment*]

II. MINUTE BOOK, H.L.R.O., M.M., 1625

[f. 18] *Die Lunae 27 Junii 1625.*
[*List of Lords Present; see A.T.*]

Excused:
L. Steward
E. of Exeter
L. Robartes
L. Russell, his shoemaker dead of the sickness[14]
L. Brooke

L. KEEPER moved that my E[arl] of Rutland's man might be brought in,[15] who had a *habeas corpus, etc.,* to bring him before me; but being but the Speaker and the House sitting, that he might be freed in court.

The party brought in; the *habeas corpus* read, with the returns, and the prisoner freed.

This order to be drawn up against 4 *post meridiem.*

[f. 18v] *Hodie 1ª vice lecta est billa,* An act to enable his Majesty to make leases of lands parcel of his Highness's Duchy of Cornwall.
Hodie 2ª vice lecta est billa, An act to enable his Majesty to make leases of lands parcel of his Highness's Duchy of Cornwall.
2 of a bench[16]

L. Treasurer	3. L. Danvers
President	2. L. Wentworth
Exeter	4. L. Carey of L[eppington]
Bath and W[ells]	1. L. Darcy of M[einill]

[To attend:] Trevor, Hutton, Davenport. Tomorrow at 8, Painted Chamber.

L. PRESIDENT, the first of the grand committee for privileges, reported to the House the subcommittee that the grand committee had nominated.[17] They considered of such bills as had been read the last session, that they might now be expedited.

A message from the Commons by Sir Edward Coke and others. They presented to the Lords the bill of Sunday, etc.
[f. 19] [From] Commons:
Hodie 1ª vice lecta est billa, An act for the punishing of divers offenses committed on the Lord's day, called Sunday.

Hodie 1ª vice lecta est billa, An act to make the arms of the kingdom more serviceable in time to come.

Hodie 1ª vice lecta est billa, An act for the better maintenance of hospitals and almshouses.

Hodie 1ª vice lecta est billa, An act for the better preserving of his Majesty's revenue.

L. Conway brought in by the Lords Willoughby and Wentworth, the E. of Montgomery supplying the Marshal's place.

Adjourned. 9 tomorrow.

A proxy, a bishop.
A proxy, E. of Sussex.[18]

III. COMMITTEE BOOK, H.L.R.O., MAIN PAPERS, H.L., 1625

[f. 2v] *Die Lunae 27° die Junii 1625.*

An act to enable the King's Majesty to make leases of lands parcel of his High-

14. See above, n. 7.
15. I.e., Toby Horton, see L.J., above.
16. Concerning the number of members to be appointed from each bench, see above, 23 June, n. 18.
17. *with the attendants* is crossed out in the manuscript following *nominated.* For the subcommittee members, see the list in the L.J., above, and the Committee Book, below.
18. The proxy list at the beginning of the L.J. for 1625 does not include Robert, Earl of Sussex, as either a sender or a receiver of a proxy. Cf. the Proxy List, below, p. 590.

ness's Duchy of Cornwall, or annexed to the same. Committed unto:

Lo. Treasurer
Lo. President
Lo. Bp. of Bath and W[ells]
Lo. Bp. of Exeter

L. Darcy of Meinill
L. Wentworth
L. Danvers
L. Carey of Leppington

To attend the Lords: Mr. Justice Hutton, Mr. Baron Trevor, Mr. Serjeant Davenport.

To meet on Tuesday the 28th of this instant month by eight of the clock in the morning in the Painted Chamber.

Expedited.

[f. 3] *Die Lunae 27° Junii 1625.*

Lords subcommittees nominated to take consideration of the customs and orders of the House, and privileges of the peers of the kingdom, or Lords of parliament. *Vizt.:*[19]

[col. 1]
1. Hertford
5. Mulgrave
3. Westmorland
4. Cleveland

[col. 2]
2. E. of Warwick
E. of Clare
6. L. Vic. Saye and Sele

L. Bp. of Norwich
L. Bp. of Coventry and Lichfield
L. Bp. of Bristol

[col. 3]
L. De La Warr
L. Darcy of Meinill
L. Wentworth
L. Sheffield
2. L. Russell
3. L. Spencer

[col. 4]
1. Dacre
5. Montagu
4. Denny

Their Lordships, or any four of them, at their own conveniency, are to perform the service imposed upon them.

19. For the correct 1625 subcommittee list, see L.J., above. In the Committee Book list, below, the names of the Lords De La Warr, Darcy, Wentworth, and Sheffield are crossed out in the manuscript and the names in columns one and four of this list have been added in the hand of Henry Elsynge, Sr. Apparently the Clerk made these changes in recording those nominated on 15 February 1626 for the subcommittee of the 1626 session (see *L.J.*, III, 499–500). For a similar case of changes made to a 1625 Committee Book list during the 1626 session, see below, H. of L., 30 June, n. 15.

TUESDAY, 28 JUNE 1625

I. JOURNAL OF THE HOUSE OF LORDS

[L.J. 445]
[p. 25] *Die Martis, vizt., vicesimo octavo die Junii 1625*
[*List of Lords; see A.T.*]
[L.J. 446]

The LORD TREASURER reported the bill touching the copyhold tenants of Cheltenham, in the county of Gloucester, etc., fit to pass, with some small amendments.

The which amendments were presently twice read and assented unto, and the bill is to be engrossed accordingly.

The LORD TREASURER also reported the bill touching leases to be made by the King's Majesty of lands parcel of the Duchy of Cornwall, etc., fit to pass, with a small amendment.

The which was twice read and assented unto, and the bill ordered to be engrossed accordingly.

Hodie allatae sunt a domo communi duae billae:

1. An act for the explanation of a branch of the statute made in the third year of the reign of our late sovereign lord King James entitled, An act for the better discovering of popish recusants.

2. An act for the enabling and confirmation of an agreement or composition made between the King's Majesty's commissioners of revenue (his Majesty then being Prince of Wales, Duke of Cornwall and of York, and Earl of Chester), on his Majesty's behalf, and his Majesty's copyholders of his Highness's manor of Macclesfield, in the county of Chester, and of a decree made in the Court of Exchequer at Chester for the perfect creation and confirmation of certain lands and tenements parcel of the said manor to be copyhold and customary lands according to the tenor of the same decree.

[p. 26] The EARL OF WARWICK reported to the House that the Lords subcommittees for privileges, etc., had considered of certain orders for the suppressing of disorders by coachmen and pages, etc.

And that their Lordships had convented before them George Whitchar for keeping a tavern in the Old Palace, contrary to the order of the last session of parliament,[1] and committed him to an officer of this House to be brought hither this morning to the bar.

His Lordship reported also that one Lionell Farington had exhibited a petition touching privilege of parliament claimed by one Androwes in a suit commenced against him upon the statute of recusancy,[2] and that their Lordships' opinion is that the said Androwes shall remain liable to the said actions, the privilege of parliament by him claimed notwithstanding. All which their Lordships did humbly leave to the House.

Hereupon, first the said orders against the pages, etc., were read *in haec verba, vizt.*:[3]

Orders made by the Lords spiritual and temporal assembled in the High Court of Parliament for the suppressing of disorders, as follows:

All companies of coachmen, pages, and footmen by what name soever they call themselves, to be forthwith dissolved and broken and, if they shall meet again in such companies, or labor to erect the same again, they are to be punished severely for public example.

---

1. On 16 March 1624, the Lords had agreed to a set of orders for preventing and punishing disorders by their servants and for suppressing George Whitchar's tavern. *L.J.*, III, 264. For the record of the examination of Whitchar on 16 March 1624 (erroneously placed with the materials for 28 June 1625 in the Main Papers), see H.L.R.O., Main Papers, H.L.,

28 June 1625.
2. For Farington's petition, see below.
3. Aside from some alterations of the wording in the order concerning Whitchar's tavern, the following orders are the same as those agreed to by the Lords on 16 March 1624 (see above, n. 1).

That no tavern keeper, victualer, or any other that may invite disorder of this kind shall from henceforth receive any pawns for satisfaction of any money spent or gathered in or for any such disorderly meetings; neither shall they permit any such disorderly meetings in their houses if they can resist the same and, if they cannot, then to inform some of the Lords of parliament both of the fact and the names of the offenders.

That the tavern now kept by George Whitchar near the back stairs going up to the higher House of parliament shall be suppressed and no more kept as a tavern during any session of parliament; and that from henceforth no other tavern be erected or permitted in that court.

And the House approved the said orders.

The said George Whitchar being brought to the bar, at first pleading ignorance of the said order made the last session of parliament, but it being affirmed by divers Lords that he had warning given him thereof, as also that he confessed so much yesterday before the Lords subcommittees, he confessed his fault and humbly craved pardon for the same.

Ordered to be committed to the Gatehouse for his contempt of the said former order of parliament, but to pay no fees, and to enjoy the privilege of parliament against his creditors during the time of his commitment.[4]

Then the petition of Lionell Farington was read, *in haec verba, vizt.:*[5]

To the Right Honorable the Lords Spiritual and Temporal in the High Court of Parliament assembled, the humble petition of Lionell Farington, Gentleman, showing,

That your petitioner does sue one William Androwes, Gentleman, a popish recusant, *tam* [**L.J. 447**] *pro domino rege quam pro seipso,* for 220*l.* in the Court of Common Pleas upon the statute of *23° Eliz.* for popish recusancy,[6] and upon the statute of *3° Jacobi* for 1,200*l.* for practicing the common law as a common solicitor being a convicted popish recusant.[7]

The said Androwes, in contempt of the court, would not appear, whereupon your petitioner caused him to be arrested upon an attachment at the suit of his Majesty upon the 18th day of this instant June and, being arrested, he showed forth a protection dated *9° Maii* last,[8] subscribed by the Right Honorable the Lord Eure; whereupon your petitioner, in obedience to this honorable court of parliament, caused the serjeants to set him at liberty.

He humbly craves your honors would be pleased to give direction whether your petitioner may proceed against the said Androwes upon the said suits and arrests (he being a convicted recusant), notwithstanding his protection.

[p. 27] The which petition being read, after serious debate of the privilege of parliament, it is ordered and declared: That none are to be privileged against any statute of recusancy; and it was then also agreed that the said Lionell Farington may proceed in his suits against the said William Androwes touching recusancy, any privilege of parliament claimed by the said Androwes notwithstanding.

Message sent from the Commons by Sir Edward Coke and others: That they have received a pious message from the King concerning a public and general fast. For

---

4. For Whitchar's petition for release from the Gatehouse, see H. of L., 30 June, below.

5. A similar copy of Lionell Farington's petition is included in the H.L.R.O., Main Papers, H.L., 28 June.

6. *S.R.*, 23 *Eliz.* I, c. 1, *An act to retain the Queen's Majesty's subjects in their due obedience.* On 1 July 1625 one William Androwes of Denton, Northamptonshire, was given the King's pardon for recusancy. See Rymer,

Foedera, VIII, pt. 1, p. 103.

7. *S.R.*, 3 *Jac.* I, c. 5, pt. 7.

8. We have been unable to find Lord Eure's protection for Androwes. Concerning protections generally, see above, 27 June, n. 8; and for a particular protection given during the 1625 session, see below, H. of L., 30 June, n. 2.

the public, if it could be so soon, the King would have it on Thursday come seven-night.[9]

Concerning the private, for their own House, he left it to themselves and their own way.

They humbly desire a conference for appointing a time for the fast of both Houses.

Answered: That the Lords, being now engaged in some business, will return answer by messengers of their own very speedily.

The reason why no other answer was given is for that this House had not as yet received any message from his Majesty of his pleasure touching the said fast, which their Lordships expected to receive first from the King himself, considering that the petition was offered as well from themselves as from the Commons.[10]

The EARL OF WARWICK also reported to the House an order conceived by the said Lords subcommittees touching those that shall be absent from the House without leave or lawful excuse; which was read *in haec verba, vizt.:*

If any Lord of parliament shall be absent from the House and shall not by some other Lord make such an excuse for his absence as the House shall allow of, he shall pay to the poor man's box five shillings for every such absence. If any Lord of parliament that has a proxy be absent as aforesaid, he shall pay for every proxy five shillings.

The which order, being twice read, was generally approved and assented unto as touching those that shall be absent to begin after Monday next. Yet it [was] put to the

question whether by this order the bishops and barons shall pay equal with the earls or no, and agreed unto *per plures* to pay equal with the earls; and so the said order was fully concluded.

Robert Browne, his Majesty's servant, was brought to the House by a *habeas corpus, etc.* (according to the order of the 25th of this June), and it appearing to their Lordships that he was arrested and detained in prison contrary to the privilege of parliament, he was set at liberty and the sheriffs of London discharged for the same. And Hugh Povey, the serjeant's yeoman who arrested him, and Henry Shawe, at whose suit he was arrested, were committed to the Fleet for their willful breach of the privileges of parliament.

Samuel Markham, servant to the Right Honorable the Earl of Sussex, was also brought before their Lordships by *habeas corpus, etc.,* according to an order of the said 25th of this June, and the writ and return being read, and it appearing to their Lordships that he was arrested and detained contrary to the said privileges he, the said Samuel, was set at liberty, and the Marshal of the King's Bench (whose prisoner he was) discharged for the same, saving to his creditors their several actions against him hereafter.

The LORD CONWAY signified to the Lords that he had been commanded by the King to deliver unto the House his Majesty's pleasure concerning the fast, acknowledging his error that he had not delivered it sooner unto them, which was occasioned by businesses with the ambassadors from the

---

9. I.e., Thursday, 7 July. The Lords decided that this would not give the kingdom enough time to prepare and therefore proposed that the public fast be held on Saturday, 16 July, to which the Commons agreed. See below, p. 68 and n. 15.

10. The petition having been preferred by both Houses, each expected to receive a message of re-

sponse from the King; however, the Lower House was the first recipient of the message. The Lords chose not to reply to the Commons until they themselves had heard directly from the crown. Their delay in receiving the message was the fault of Lord Conway, who had been appointed to deliver it and was detained, see below.

States, who detained him longer than he expected.

[p. 28] And his Lordship delivered the King's pleasure to their Lordships to the same effect as it was delivered to the Commons.

Whereupon a message was sent to the Commons by Mr. Attorney General and Mr. Serjeant Davenport: That the Lords have received his Majesty's pleasure touching the petition for a general fast and therefore have appointed the conference by them desired to be presently, in the Painted Chamber, with the former committee that delivered the said petition.

Answered: That they have appointed their former committee to meet their Lordships presently.

The Lords being returned from the conference the LORD TREASURER reported: That the Commons did refer the time and place for the fast of both Houses unto their Lordships; that they had made choice of four preachers when they had appointed a private fast for themselves, and had ordered that every member of their House should be present.[11] And intimated their desire that the private fast of both Houses may precede the general fast.

The report ended, their Lordships agreed to defer their answer until the afternoon, for that the day was far spent.

Notice thereof was given to the Commons accordingly.

[*Notice of Adjournment*]

[**L.J. 448**; p. 29] *Die Martis vicesimo octavo die Junii, post meridiem, 1625*
[*List of Lords; see A.T.*]

Their Lordships being put in mind of their conference to be had this afternoon touching the general fast, the House was adjourned *ad libitum* to the end it might be the more freely discussed what should be propounded to the Commons concerning the same.

The House being resumed again, it was agreed by their Lordships as follows:

1. The fast of the Lords and Commons to precede the general fast.

2. And this to be on Saturday next.

3. To be kept after the same manner which is prescribed by the King's Majesty in a book now in printing,[12] the time of meeting to be at nine in the morning.

4. This House to keep the fast in the collegiate church of Westminster by itself.

5. Two bishops appointed to preach there, *vizt.*, the Lord Bishop of Bath and Wells and the Lord Bishop of Salisbury.[13]

6. A collection to be then made for the poor.

And this to be intimated to the Commons with this reservation, if the Commons can attend[14] the fast on that day.

Then their Lordships took into their considerations on what day the general fast should be appointed, for that Thursday come sevennight (the day propounded for

---

11. The private fast for the Commons was originally scheduled for 25 June (see H. of C., 21 June, p. 204) but, in conjunction with the Lords' plans, was subsequently altered to the following Saturday, 2 July (see H. of C., 24 June, p. 239, and 28 June, p. 259); concerning the preachers chosen by the Lower House, see below, H. of C., 21 June, nn. 8 and 32.

12. The book prescribing the manner of prayers and fasting, printed by the King's authority, was entitled *A Forme of Common Prayer, Together with an Order of Fasting* (S.T.C., no. 16540). According to Bedford MS. 197, four hundred copies of the book were sent down to the Commons by the Lord Chamberlain, see

below, H. of C., 28 June, p. 265. The book directed that prayers and fasting be held every Wednesday, and a proclamation to this effect was issued by Charles I on 3 July 1625 (S.T.C., no. 8787). The proclamation is printed in *Stuart Proclamations*, II, 46–48.

13. I.e., Arthur Lake and John Davenant; Lake was to preach first, see H.L.R.O., M.M., 1625, below. For Lake's sermon, see *Sermons with some Religious and Divine Meditations by the Right Reverend Father in God, Arthur Lake. . .* (London, 1629), pp. 200–220 (S.T.C., no. 15134). Davenant's sermon apparently was not printed.

14. MS.: *intend*.

it) is too short a time for the whole kingdom to take notice thereof and to prepare themselves for it.

In the end, their Lordships agreed on Saturday next for the City of London to keep their fast, [p. 30] on Monday following for the city of Westminster, and on Saturday come fortnight for the whole kingdom.[15]

Message sent to the Commons by Mr. Serjeant Finch and Mr. Serjeant Richardson, *vizt.:* [**L.J. 449**] That the Lords are now ready for the conference desired in the morning with the former committees in the Painted Chamber.

Answered: They will give their Lordships a present meeting for the same at the place appointed.

The Lords committees being returned from the conference the LORD TREASURER reported that the Commons agree in all circumstances with this House touching the said fast.

Memorandum: That the Earl of Clare, the Lord Bishop of Bangor, and the Lord Spencer are appointed by the House to take the names of those Lords who shall be present at the fast.

[Notice of Adjournment][16]

II. MINUTE BOOK, H.L.R.O., M.M., 1625

[f. 19v] *Die Martis 28 Junii 1625.*
[*List of Lords Present; see A.T.*]

L. TREASURER, first of the committee, touching the King and his tenants of Cheltenham; with some amendments fit to pass.

L. TREASURER, first of the committee, touching the King and his tenants of Cornwall.

The amendments of both bills read *1ª et 2ª* [*illegible*].

The widow Lowe['s] man in Bullhead alley, in the Greene in Clerkenwell.[17]

[f. 20] A message from the Commons by Sir Edward Coke and others, with two bills: 1, touching recusants; 2, between the King and the tenants of [Macclesfield] in Chester.

E. OF WARWICK, the first of the subcommittee for privileges: 1, that the orders touching coachmen and pages might be ratified; 2, that Whitchar, a vintner near the parliament, be suppressed.

Whitchar at the bar: That he be committed but freed from other actions to be entered against him during his imprisonment; and to pay no fees.

The petition of Farington against Androwes, a popish recusant.[18]

Sir Edward Coke and others with a message from the House of Commons: That they of that House have received a pious and religious answer touching the fast. That it is to be a public and private fast, the public to be on Thursday come sennight,[19] the private left to their consideration when they shall think fit.

[f. 20v][20] That Androwes being a recusant/
It is declared that none be privileged against any statute of recusancy.

---

15. I.e., 2 July for the City of London, 4 July for the City of Westminster, and 16 July for the whole kingdom.

16. The Lower House met on Wednesday, 29 June, although the Upper House did not reconvene until 30 June.

17. This line is entered in the margin at the bottom of the page in the MS. The activity of the widow Lowe's man may relate to the consideration this day of the misdemeanors of pages and footmen.

18. Farington's petition is printed in the L.J., above.

19. See above, n. 9.

20. *That the King be attended to know the King's business. E. Marshal, E. of Montgomery* is crossed out in the MS. at the top of f. 20v. The note may relate to the matter of the fast or to the case of Androwes who was arrested on an attachment at the suit of the King; see L.J., above.

An order conceived by the subcommittees touching absent Lords: If any Lord be absent without leave of the House, to pay 5 *s.*, and those that have proxies to pay both for himself and the rest that grant proxies.

Shawe and Povey that arrested Mr. Browne/[21]

L. CONWAY. That the public fast be kept on Thursday come sennight and the private to be when the Lords think good.

Mr. Attorney General, Mr. Serjeant Davenport with a message to the Commons: That their Lordships desire a present conference with the Commons, touching the fast, in the Painted Chamber.

[f. 21] Answer returned: That the committee of the Commons will attend, at the time and place will attend.

E. MARSHAL. That we take no notice of sending to the King, and that the Lord Treasurer speak at the committee.

L. TREASURER reported the conference with the committees of the Commons.

L. TREASURER. That they have certified the Commons that the House sit this afternoon.

Adjourned, 3 *post meridiem.*

[f. 22v] *Die Martis 28 Junii 1625 post meridiem*
[*List of Lords Present; see A.T.*]

E. MARSHAL. That their Lordships would consider of the business which caused this mee/

The LORD KEEPER/

The [House] adjourned during pleasure.

The fast. Concluded the fast to be on Saturday, the place to be the Abbey church.

The preachers: 1, L. Bishop of Bath and Wells; 2, L. Bishop of Salisbury. The Bishop of Bath and W[ells] to preach first.

[f. 23] The fasts to be several, to begin at 9 in the morning and 2 *post meridiem.* And a collection for the poor in the same [*illegible*] and the same day. The private fast to precede the public.

Mr. Serjeant Finch and Mr. Serjeant Richardson with a message to the Commons.

L. BISHOP OF LONDON. Whether in the fasts the sacrament should not be ministered, and whether the City of London might not keep a fast at the time that the two Houses do fast.

Concluded that London fast on Saturday when the Lords fast, and Saturday as soon after as is thought fit.

Answer: That the message was delivered; that they will attend at the time and place appointed.

BISHOP OF BANGOR. That those Lords that are voluntarily absent from the fast pay somewhat.

To observe that the Lords are present, all: E. of Clare, Bishop of Bangor, L. Spencer.

That the assistants be present at the fast.

Adjourned. Thursday 9.

21. See L.J., above. Shawe and Povey were committed to the Fleet for the arrest of Robert Browne.

Prayers

Lords excused — 71

L. 3a. An act to enable the King's Majesty to make leases of lands parcel of his Highness's **Duchy of Cornwall**: assented to — 71, 72, *27/6

BISHOP OF COVENTRY AND LICHFIELD — 72

L. 3a. An act for confirming of the copyhold estates and customs of the tenants of the manor of **Cheltenham**: assented to — 71, 72, *25/6

Message to the Commons sending down the above two bills (Sir Thomas Trevor and Sir Humphrey Davenport) — 73

Petition of Charles, **Lord Lambart**: read and referred to the **committee of privileges** — 71, 73, *1/7

Petition of Rowland Heylyn, *et al.,* concerning Lambart's arrest: read and referred to the committee of privileges — 71, 73

Petition of George **Whitchar** for his release from the Gatehouse: read — 72, 73, 74, *28/6

[Whitchar's petition is printed on p. 74]

Ordered: Whitchar to be enlarged; other issues of his petition referred to the **subcommittee of privileges** — 72, 73

Petitions of Henry Shawe and Hugh Povey, committed for their arrest of Robert **Browne**, for their release — 73, *28/6

L. 2a. An act for punishing abuses committed on the **Lord's day**: committed — 72, 73(2), *27/6

L. 2a. An act for the making of the **arms** of the kingdom more serviceable: committed — 72, 73, 74, *27/6

House adjourned — 72

THURSDAY, 30 JUNE 1625

I. JOURNAL OF THE HOUSE OF LORDS

[L.J. 449]

[p. 31] *Die Jovis, vizt., tricesimo die Junii 1625*

[*List of Lords; see A.T.*]

Excused: the Lord Steward, the Earl of Exeter, the Lo. Vic. Andover.

Hodie 3ª vice lecta est billa, An act to enable the King's Majesty to make leases of lands parcel of his Highness's Duchy of Cornwall or annexed to the same.

And put to the question and generally assented unto.

Hodie 3ª vice lecta est billa, An act for the settling and confirmation of the copyhold estates and customs of the tenants in base tenure of the manor of Cheltenham, in the county of Gloucester, and of the manor [L.J. 450] of Ashley, otherwise called Charlton Kings, in the said county, being holden of the said manor of Cheltenham according to an agreement thereof made between the King's most excellent Majesty, being then Prince of Wales, Duke of Cornwall and of York, and Earl of Chester, lord of the said manor of Cheltenham, and Giles Greville, Esquire, lord of the said manor of Ashley, and the said copyholders of the said several manors.

Put to the question and generally assented unto.

This day was read the petition of Charles,

Lord Lambart, Baron of Cavan in the realm of Ireland, showing:[1]

That having a writ of privilege granted unto him by the Right Honorable the Lord Keeper, not expired until the twelfth of July, and being son-in-law unto Richard, Lord Robartes, and one [p. 32] of his family, and daily appointed to give his personal attendance upon his Lordship and to be employed by him for divers special occasions during the time of this parliament, ready to be showed under his seal at arms and registered in the sheriff's office of Middlesex,[2] and thereby, according to the ancient liberties and privileges of the peers of this realm, ought to have his body freed from arrests; yet, notwithstanding, upon the seven and twentieth day of this instant June he was arrested upon mesne process and yet remains in the custody of the sheriff of Middlesex.

He humbly prays that he may have his liberty restored and such satisfaction for the abuses offered unto him as to their Lordships shall seem meet.

The which petition being read it was referred to the Lords committees for privileges, etc.

And one other petition also of Rowland Heylyn and Robert Parckhurst, aldermen of London and high sheriffs of Middlesex, and of Nathaniel Sampson, Gentleman, their undersheriff, there was read,[3] showing the manner of the said arrest, etc., and referred to the said Lords committees for

1. A similar copy of the petition of Charles, Lord Lambart, is included in the H.L.R.O., Main Papers, H.L., 30 June.

2. The letter of protection for Lord Lambart from Richard, Lord Robartes, dated 27 June 1625, reads: "Whereas I have appointed Charles, Lord Lambart, the bearer hereof, to give his personal attendance upon me and otherwise to be employed by me for divers causes and special occasions during the time of this parliament and the continuance thereof. These are therefore to require you and every of you whom it may concern quietly to permit and suffer him to pass and repass, abide and remain without any of your ar-

rests, restraints, imprisonments or molestations whatsoever that may tend to the breach or infringing of any of the ancient liberties or privileges belonging to the High Court of Parliament and to every peer of this realm, as you will answer the contrary at your uttermost peril. Given under my hand and seal this seven and twentieth day of June *Anno Domini* 1625". H.L.R.O., Main Papers, H.L., 27 June 1625. Concerning protections generally, see above, 27 June, n. 8.

3. The two aldermen of London were sheriffs of London and Middlesex. We have been unable to find their petition.

privileges, etc., and their Lordships are to meet thereon this afternoon.

George Whitchar, vintner, who was committed on the 28th of this June unto the Gatehouse in Westminster for keeping of a tavern near the Parliament House in contempt of an order made the last session of parliament to the contrary, did this day petition the Lords to be released out of his said imprisonment, and that he may be privileged by their Lordships for his safe and free return with his goods and household stuff to his former dwelling.[4]

Their Lordships, considering of this petition, did readily condescend unto his enlargement but referred the rest unto the Lords subcommittees for privileges, etc.

Hodie 2da vice lecta est billa, An act for the punishing of divers abuses committed on the Lord's day, called Sunday.
Committed unto the

[col. 1]	[col. 2]
L. President	L. Bp. of Bangor
E. of Lincoln	L. Bp. of Rochester
E. of Bolingbroke	L. Bp. of Ely
L. Vic. Saye and Sele	L. Bp. of St. Davids

[col. 3]	[col. 4]
L. De La Warr	L. Sheffield
L. Scrope	L. North
L. Darcy and M[einill]	L. Danvers
L. Wentworth	L. Spencer

To attend the Lords: Lord Chief Baron, Mr. Justice Yelverton, Mr. Serjeant Finch.

To meet tomorrow morning at eight in the Painted Chamber.

Hodie 2da vice lecta est billa, An act to make the arms of the kingdom more serviceable in time to come.

Committed unto

[col. 1]	[col. 2]
L. Privy Seal	L. Bp. of Norwich
E. of Montgomery	L. Bp. of Rochester
E. of Leicester	L. Bp. of Coventry and
E. of Northampton	Lichfield
E. of Westmorland	L. Bp. of St. Davids
L. Vic. Rochford	L. Bp. of Bristol
	L. Bp. of Carlisle

[col. 3]	[col. 4]
L. De La Warr	L. North
L. Scrope	L. Walden
L. Stourton	L. Spencer
L. Wentworth	L. Grey of Groby
L. Sheffield	L. Grey of W[arke]

To attend the Lords: Mr. Justice Jones, Mr. Justice Croke, Mr. Serjeant Richardson. To meet on Monday next at eight in the Painted Chamber.

[*Notice of Adjournment*]

II. MINUTE BOOK, H.L.R.O., M.M., 1625

[f. 24] *Die Jovis 30 die Junii 1625*
[*List of Lords Present; see A.T.*]

Hodie 3^a vice lecta est billa, An act to enable the King's Majesty's most excellent Majesty to make leases of lands parcel of the Duchy of Cornwall or annexed to the same.

Put to the question and passed. Expedited.[5]

L. BISHOP OF COVENTRY AND LICHFIELD. The Lord of Canterbury does commend his service and deliver[s] a message that the Commons had sent a former book of Mr. Montagu's and desired his answer, who desired 2 days respite. He desires your Lordships' direction.[6]

Hodie 3^a vice lecta est billa, An act for the tenants of Cheltenham, in Gloucestershire.

---

4. For Whitchar's petition, see below, p. 74.
5. Where "Exped." or "Expedited" is entered in the margins of H.L.R.O., M.M., 1625, we have inserted "Expedited" into the text. In this session the term was generally employed in reference to those bills which eventually received the assent of both Houses.
6. On 29 June the Lower House appointed four members to attend the Archbishop of Canterbury to

determine what action had been taken with regard to Montagu's book, the *Gagg*, which had been complained about in 1624. See H. of C., below, 29 June, O.B. According to the report of the Archbishop's answer to the Lower House he desired respite because of ill health, although he dictated an answer to Sir Dudley Digges which was read in that House on 1 July. See H. of C., 1 July, O.B.

And the b[ill] put to the question and passed. Expedited.

[f. 24v] Baron Trevor and Mr. Serjeant Davenport sent to the Commons with 2 bills, *vizt.:* the King's bill for Cornwall, the other for Cheltenham tenants.

The petition of George [*sic*], Lord Lambart, Baron of Lambart in Ireland, servant [to] the Lord Robartes of Truro, that was arrested, desired the privilege of the parliament.[7]

The petition of the two sheriffs of London and the sheriff of the same county; that the Lord Lambart was arreste[d] for great sums of money.[8]

The petition of George Whitchar for his release and freeing him from arrests for the space of a month.[9]
Order.

The petition of Henry Shawe for a release out of prison.
Release.

The petition of Hugh Povey for a release out of imprisonment.[10]
Release.

Hodie 2ª vice lecta est billa, An act for punishing of divers abuses committed of the Lord's day, called Sunday.

[col. 1]	[col. 2]
President	4. Davids
Bolingbroke	2. Bangor[11]
Lincoln	3. Ely
Saye	1. Rochester

[col. 3]
5. Sheffield
4. Wentworth

7. Lambart's petition is printed in the L.J., above. He was denied privilege. See the Lord President's report, below, 1 July, p. 81.
8. See above, n. 3.
9. For Whitchar's petition, see below, p. 74.
10. On 28 June the Lords had ordered that Shawe and Povey be committed for their breach of the privileges of parliament in arresting Robert Browne (see above, p. 66). We have been unable to find the petitions of Shawe and Povey.

8. Spencer
6. North
7. Danvers
3. Darcy
2. Scrope
1. La Warr
[To attend:] 2. Yelverton,[12] 3. Finch, 1. Chief Baron.
Tomorrow by 8, Painted Chamber.

[f. 25] *Hodie 2ª vice lecta est billa,* An act for the making of the arms of the kingdom more serviceable in time to come.

5. Westmorland	2. Scrope
4. Northampton	4. Wentworth
6. Rochford	9. Spencer
3. Leicester	7. Walden
2. Montgomery	10. Grey of W[arke]
1. Privy Seal	8. Grey of G[roby]
	6. North
5. Bristol[13]	1. De La Warr
6. Carlisle	5. Sheffield
1. Norwich[14]	3. Stourton
3. Coventry and L[ichfield]	
4. Davids	
2. Rochester	

To attend: Croke, Richardson, Jones.
To meet on Monday next by 8, Painted Chamber.

III. COMMITTEE BOOK, H.L.R.O., MAIN PAPERS, H.L., 1625

[f. 3v] *Die Jovis 30 Junii 1625.*

An act for punishing of divers abuses committed on the Lord's day, called Sunday. Committed unto

L. President	L. De La Warr
E. of Lincoln	L. Scrope
E. of Bolingbroke	L. Darcy of Meinill
L. Vic. Saye and Sele	L. Wentworth
	L. Sheffield

11. *Canterbury* and *Winchester* are crossed out in the MS. following *Bangor.*
12. *Attorney* is crossed out in the MS. at the beginning of this list. *Hutton* and *Jones* are crossed out following *Yelverton.*
13. *London* is crossed out in the MS. following *Bristol.*
14. *Rochester* and *Durham* are crossed out in the MS. following *Norwich; Rochester* is re-entered below.

L. Bp. of Rochester   L. North
L. Bp. of Bangor   L. Danvers
L. Bp. of Ely   L. Spencer
L. Bp. of St. Davids

To attend the Lords: L. Chief Baron, Mr. Justice Yelverton, Mr. Serjeant Finch.

To meet tomorrow morning being the first of July by 8 of the clock in the Painted Chamber.

Expedited.

[f. 4] *Die Jovis 30 Junii 1625.*

An act for the making of the arms of the kingdom more serviceable in time to come. Committed unto

[col. 1]
    L. Privy Seal
    E. of Montgomery
X E. of Leicester
Essex E. of Northampton
    E. of Westmorland
Totnes L. Vic. Rochford

Durham
    L. Bp. of Norwich
    L. Bp. of Rochester
    L. Bp. of Coventry and Lichfield
    L. Bp. of St. Davids
    L. Bp. of Bristol
X L. Bp. of Carlisle

[col. 2]
X L. De La Warr   Willoughby
X L. Scrope   Cromwell
    L. Stourton
    L. Wentworth
    L. Sheffield
    L. North
    L. Walden
    L. Grey of Groby
    L. Spencer
    L. Grey of Warke   Vere

To attend the Lords: Mr. Justice Jones, Mr. Justice Croke, Mr. Serjeant Richardson, Mr. Serjeant Davies.

Sine die. To meet on Monday the fourth of July by eight of the clock in the morning in the Painted Chamber.

16 Febr.: All lieutenants of the shires. To meet on Saturday next at 2.[15]

IV. PETITION OF GEORGE WHITCHAR, VINTNER, FOR RELEASE FROM THE GATEHOUSE. H.L.R.O., MAIN PAPERS, H.L., 30 JUNE 1625.

To the Right Honorable the Lords Spiritual and Temporal of the Upper House of Parliament.

The humble petition of George Whitchar, vintner, most humbly showing,

That whereas he now remains prisoner in the Gatehouse, upon your Lordships' command for a contempt concerning the house wherein he now dwells. For as much as he first placed himself there as well for others' good convenience as his own profit, and has thereupon exhausted the most part of his own former estate and utterly undone himself and his poor family (upon hope of future times) by paying of a long dead rent and by running into divers great debts, and is now (in his old age) hopeless of any recovery if your Lordships' displeasure should long continue upon him.

May it therefore please your good Lordships to accept this his unfeigned sorrow for his offense (which, upon his knees, he acknowledges without extenuation or excuse) and out of a tender feeling of his misery not only to extend your present pity in his release but your honorable protection for his free and safe return to his former dwelling with such goods and household stuff as is left in this his unfortunate house, which he shall not else be able to do without the interruption, arrests, and perpetual imprisonment of the landlord and other cred-

---

15. The "X"ing out of the names in the above list, together with the additions of the names in the margins, the name of the Bishop of Durham within column one, and the final lines beginning "16 Febr.", all in the hand of Henry Elsynge, Sr., appear to have been alterations made on 16 February 1626, upon the commitment of the bill for arms in the 1626 session (*L.J.,* III, 501–502). For a similar case of changes made to a 1625 Committee Book list during the 1626 session, see above, 27 June, n. 19.

itors, who (upon notice of this disaster) begin already to be very harsh towards him, and whom he may the better satisfy if by this, your Lordships' goodness, he may gain a convenient time for the same. And he shall be forever bound to pray for your Lordships' preservation in all honor and happiness.

Prayers

Message from the Commons (Sir
  Edward Coke and others)
  desiring: 78, 80
a **conference** touching a
  petition concerning religion
  [*see below*];
expedition of the bill
  concerning the **Lord's day**
  [*see below*];
and expedition of the bill
  concerning a **statute of 3 Jac.**
  for repressing popish
  recusants [*see below*];
and bringing:
(1) a bill for the ease in
  obtaining licenses of
  alienation   *5/7
(2) a bill for the further
  restraint of **tippling** in inns,
  alehouses, etc.   *5/7
(3) a bill for the increase of
  shipping and for free liberty
  of **fishing**   *7/7
Answer given to the Commons'
  message: Lords agree to a
  present **conference** by
  committee and promise
  expedition of the two bills [*see
  above and below*]   78
Names of members of the former
  committee for the conference
  on the **general fast**: read, and
  members added for the
  conference on the **petition
  concerning religion** [*see above
  and below*]   78, 80, *23/6
Report from the committee on
  the bill concerning the **Lord's
  day** (Viscount Mandeville,
  L. President) [*see above*]   78, 80, *27/6
L. 3a. An act for punishing abuses
  committed on the **Lord's**

day: assented to and
  expedited   78, 80
L. 1a. An act for explanation of a
  statute of 3 Jac. for
  repressing popish recusants
  [*see above*]   78, 80, *28/6;
                                           10/8
House adjourned during pleasure
  so that the committee could
  attend the **conference**   78
House resumed   78
Report of the conference with the
  Commons: on the **petition
  concerning religion** (Lord
  Keeper, Bp. of Lincoln) [*see
  above*]   78, 80
The draft petition concerning
  religion: read   79, 80, *4/7;
                                           5/7; 6/7; 8/7;
                                           9/7; 11/7; 8/8

[*The completed petition concerning
  religion is printed on pp. 155–
  160*]
Message to the Commons that the
  Lords will send them answer
  by messengers of their own   79
The petition concerning religion
  to be considered on Monday
  next [4 July]   79, 80
Earl of Arundel and Surrey (E.
  Marshal): moves that the
  petition of Ralph **Brooke** be
  read   80
Petition of Ralph Brooke, York
  Herald: read   79, 81(2), *23/6;
                                          6/7; 9/7

[*Brooke's petition is printed on pp.
  81–82*]
Earl of Arundel and Surrey (E.
  Marshal)   81
Brooke's petition referred to the
  committee of privileges   79, 81
Earl of Clare: moves that some

FRIDAY, 1 JULY 1625

I. JOURNAL OF THE HOUSE OF LORDS

[L.J. 450]

[p. 33] *Die Veneris, viz., primo die Julii 1625*
[List of Lords; see A.T.]

[L.J. 451]

Message from the Commons by Sir Edward Coke and others: That the Commons desire a conference with their Lordships touching a petition to be exhibited unto the King's Majesty for the maintenance of true religion and for abolishing of popery and superstition.[1]

That they have sent up to their Lordships three bills:

1. An act for the ease in obtaining of licenses of alienation, and in the pleading of alienations with license, or of pardons of alienations without license in the Court of Exchequer and elsewhere.

2. An act for the further restraint of tippling in inns, alehouses, and other victualling houses.

3. An act for the maintenance and increase of shipping and navigation and for the free liberty of fishing and fishing voyages to be made and performed in and upon the seas, seacoasts, and places of Newfoundland, Virginia, New England, and other the seas, seacoasts, and parts of America.

And that the Commons desired expedition in the bill for punishing abuses committed on the Lord's day, called Sunday, and in the bill touching popish recusants.

Answered: That their Lordships have taken their message into consideration and have appointed their former committee touching the petition of the general fast to meet with the like committee of that House [p. 34] presently, in the Painted Chamber, touching the petition now desired, and their Lordships do promise all possible expedition of the two bills as is required.

The names of the former committee being read and divers of them found to be absent these Lords were added, *vizt.*:

[col. 1]	[col. 2]
L. Keeper	L. Vic. Saye and Sele
E. of Montgomery	L. Bp. of Winchester

[col. 3]	[col. 4]
L. Bp. of Ely	L. Grey of W[arke]
L. North	

The bill for Sunday reported by the LORD PRESIDENT fit to pass without any amendment.

Hodie 3ª vice lecta est billa, An act for the punishing of divers abuses committed on the Lord's day, called Sunday.

Put to the question and generally assented unto.

Hodie 1ª vice lecta est billa, An act for the explanation of a branch of the statute made in the third year of the reign of our late sovereign lord King James, entitled, An act for the better discovering and repressing of popish recusants.

The House was adjourned *ad libitum* for that the Lords committees were to go to the conference with the Commons (*ut supra*), and the Lord Keeper was one of the said committee.

The Lords committees being returned and the House resumed, the LORD KEEPER reported: That the Commons declared how that the last session of parliament the Lords and they, in their zeal to true religion and detestation of popery and superstition, did join in a petition to the King of famous memory, deceased, touching recusants,

---

1. On 30 June the draft of the petition concerning religion had been brought from committee into the Lower House, read, and, with one amendment, was assented to by the Commons. See H. of C., 30 June, p. 274 and n. 2. For a summary of both Houses' action on the petition concerning religion, see H. of L., 9 August, n. 12.

which petition proceeded originally from them, they being the general inquisitors of the kingdom.[2] They have now framed another petition which is in part a repetition of the former, with some addition, for that there is a great and apparent increase of popery and superstition, the answer of our late Sovereign not taking that good success which was expected.[3]

That they humbly desire the Lords to join with them in this petition also.

The petition being delivered to the Clerk to be read, and the Lords intending to advise on each particular thereof with the more deliberation, their Lordships thought fit to let the Commons understand that they will send them answer by messengers of their own; which was done accordingly, and then the petition being read, the Lords agreed to consider thereof on Monday next, in the morning.[4]

The petition of Ralph Brooke, York Herald, touching his imprisonment, etc., by the Earl Marshal,[5] was read and referred to be examined by the committees of privileges, etc., who are appointed to meet upon it on Thursday next, at two, in the Painted Chamber; and York is to have notice of it and to be there present.

The House being moved that some good order might be made touching those that are infected with the plague, vizt., to have some mark on their doors as others may be warned thereof, and to have watchmen appointed (as heretofore has been used) not to permit the infected to go abroad, and some maintenance to be provided for the poor that are infected.

It was referred to these Lords undernamed to draw up an order concerning the same, vizt.:

E. Marshal	L. Bp. of Durham
E. of Warwick	L. Bp. of Rochester
E. of Clare	L. Sheffield
L. Vic. Saye and Sele	L. Spencer

To meet in the Council Chamber at Whitehall at two this afternoon.

[p. 35] It is agreed that each earl shall pay twenty shillings and each bishop and baron ten shillings to the poor at the collection for the fast appointed tomorrow.

And that the Lords shall meet here in the House tomorrow morning and go from hence to the collegiate church of Westminster.[6]

[Notice of Adjournment]

[p. 36] The order made by the Lords committees this first of July, *post meridiem*, touching the infected in London and the places adjoining:

The Lords of the higher House of parliament taking notice of the great abuse generally committed in and about the liberties of London and Westminster by not keeping the ancient and laudable orders for the preventing the spreading of the infection of

2. The 1624 petition concerning religion was drafted by the Commons and was delivered to the Lords at a conference on 3 April 1624. After major revisions by the Upper House, the petition was presented to the King on 23 April. The Commons' draft of the petition is printed in *L.J.*, III, 289–290, and in Rushworth, *Hist. Collections*, I, 141–143; the petition in its final form is printed in *L.J.*, III, 298. For references to other petitions concerning religion, presented to James I in earlier parliaments, see below, H. of C., 23 June, n. 27.

3. In his answer to the 1624 petition, James I promised "not only [to] grant the substance of what you crave but add something more of my own. . . . It needs no more but that I declare by proclamation,

which I am ready to do, that the Jesuits and priests do depart by a day. . . . This I will do, and more: I will command all my judges, when they go their circuits, to take the same course for putting all the laws against recusants in execution". The answer is printed in *L.J.*, III, 317–318, and in Rushworth, *Hist. Collections*, I, 143–144.

4. The 1625 petition in its final form, with the King's answers, is printed on 9 August. See below, pp. 155–160.

5. Brooke's petition against the Earl of Arundel, Earl Marshal, is printed below, p. 81.

6. It was customary for the members to attend services collectively as a House of Parliament rather than separately as individuals.

the plague, as the marking of the places infected upon the door by which other persons have notice given of the danger of that place, as likewise a watchman continually to attend at the door to the end that none may come in or out, and that necessary sustenance and provision may be supplied to the persons within, have resolved that, first, their strict commandment be entered in this House for the exact performance of these good orders above mentioned and all other which may conduce to the suppressing of the infection from further increasing, and that, after, if all whom it may concern do not, in their several jurisdictions and precincts in and near the cities of London and Westminster, after notice use all possible endeavors with care and diligence to that good end, that then exemplary punishment shall be inflicted upon the superior officers, to the terror of others.

And for this purpose the Clerk of this great council has commandment to send forth copies of this order, examined by him, to the Lord Mayor of the City of London; the Lord Wentworth, for his precincts in Stepney and Hackney; the Dean of Westminster and justices of Westminster, for Westminster; the Chancellor of the Duchy, for that liberty; the justices of the peace of Surrey, for their precincts adjacent to the City of London; and the justices of the peace of Middlesex in their precincts adjacent to the City of London and Westminster.

II. MINUTE BOOK, H.L.R.O., M.M., 1625

[f. 25v] *Die Veneris, 1° Junii [sic] 1625.*
[*List of Lords Present; see A.T.*]

A message by Sir Edward Coke and others from the Commons: That they proceed in a petition with their Lordships to the King touching a petition against recusants;[7] to expedite three bills brought up by them.

Added to the committee that are to meet with the Commons: E. of Montgomery, L. Saye, North, Keeper.[8]

L. Keeper.[9]

[f. 26] LORD PRESIDENT reported the bill for the Lord's day, called Sunday, fit to pass and to have a third reading.

Hodie 3ª vice lecta est billa, An act for the punishing of divers abuses committed on the Lord's day, called Sunday.
Put to the question and passed.
Expedited. Co[mmons].

Hodie 1ª vice lecta est billa, An act against popish recusants, etc.

LORD KEEPER reported from the Commons that he has little to say but much to read, so the gentleman said that delivered the matter at the conference. The narrative that your Lordships joined with them to the late King, touching religion, in a petition which is the ground of this petition with some additions, and that the gracious answer which the last King made touching religion has not taken that effect as he desired and therefore they now move in the same behalf.[10]

The petition of the Commons to the King touching recusancy, *1ª vice lecta.*
This petition to be considered on Monday next by 8 of the clock in the morning.[11]

[f. 26v] The E. OF ARUNDEL moved the House that whereas there is one [petition] in the behalf of a Herald of Arms which is delivered to some Lords, his Lordship desired that the petition might be read, and

---

7. See above, n. 1.
8. Cf. the longer list in the L.J., above.
9. The meaning of the entry "L. Keeper" in this place is unclear. We have no other indication that he

spoke before the Lord President.
10. See above, nn. 2 and 3.
11. *Adjourned to Monday* is crossed out in the MS. following *morning.*

delivered one to the Clerk himself, which was read.

The petition of Ralph Brooke, York Herald, read.[12]

E. MARSHAL desired that the petitioner might be heard at large.

This petition referred to the Lords committees on Thursday[13] in the afternoon. He to have notice.

E. OF CLARE. That in regard this dangerous time of the sickness there is no care for the dispersing the sickness,[14] that some course may be taken. That all orders in this kind may be kept.

The earls to give at the fast 20s., the barons 10s.

The L. PRESIDENT reported that the Lord Lambart is not to have the privilege.[15]

The Lords, before they go to the fast, to meet at this House first.[16]

[f. 27] That these Lords consider that the orders touching the plague may be/
Marshal
Clare
Warwick
Saye and S[ele]
Sheffield
Spencer
Durham
Rochester
[To attend:] L[ord] Chief Justice.
To meet at 2, in Whitehall.
That the justices attend at the committee.

Bishop of Exeter excused by the B[ishop] of Norwich.

Adjourned. 8 Monday next.

12. Brooke's petition is printed below.
13. *Tuesday* is interlined in the MS. above *Thursday.*
14. I.e., no care to prevent the dispersing of the sickness.
15. No notice of the Lord President's report on Lambart is included in the L.J. Concerning Lambart's petition for release from imprisonment, see above, 30 June, O.B.

III. COMMITTEE BOOK, H.L.R.O., MAIN PAPERS, H.L., 1625

[f. 4v] *Die Veneris 1° Julii 1625.*

Lords committees appointed by the House to draw up an order to prevent the dispersing of the sickness in and about London and Westminster. *Vizt.:*

E. Marshal	L. Bp. of Durham
E. of Warwick	L. Bp. of Rochester
E. of Clare	L. Sheffield
L. Vic. Saye and S[ele]	L. Spencer
L./	

To attend the Lords: L. Chief Justice.
To meet at Whitehall this afternoon by two of the clock.
Expedited.

IV. PETITION OF RALPH BROOKE, YORK HERALD. H.L.R.O., MAIN PAPERS, H.L., 1 JULY 1625.

To the King's most excellent Majesty and the Right Honorable the Lords Spiritual and Temporal assembled in the High Court of Parliament.

The humble petition of Ralph Brooke, York Herald, most humbly showing,

That your poor supplicant and servant for coming to Whitehall gate on the 27th day of March last and there attending with other his fellows the heralds in their coats of arms, to do their duty and office to proclaim your Majesty King, was suddenly, without knowing any cause, arrested and carried by the Knight Marshal to prison by warrant of the Right Honorable the Earl Marshal (the copy whereof is hereunto annexed),[17] where he has continued ever since and there is like to lie without the favor and relief of your most gracious Maj-

16. See above, n. 6.
17. The copy of the Earl Marshal's warrant, annexed to Brooke's petition in H.L.R.O., Main Papers, reads: Whereas there is cause to commit Ralph Brooke to your custody to remain prisoner in the Marshalsea, these shall be to will and require you to receive him into your charge and to keep him safe prisoner there until further order.

esty and this honorable House of parliament.

For the said Earl has formerly caused your supplicant (having served your Highness's father and the late Queen Elizabeth 45 years and being now almost fourscore years of age) to be sequestered from his office and profits thereof, which he holds by letters patent under the Great Seal of England as his freehold during his life,[18] never showing any just cause for the same (contrary to the statute of 25 E. 3),[19] and for these five years has caused all his fees and profits of his said office to be detained from him.[20]

For which your petitioner did prefer a bill in your Highness's Court of Chancery (as he conceives was lawful for him to do) against those his Lordship had caused to detain his said fees; for which only cause the said Earl caused him to be committed to the Marshalsea, where he remained 17 months without bail or mainprize, and had lain there still had not the right honorable lords of the Privy Council delivered him.[21]

Which done, his Lordship, within less than two hours after, caused his servant Hagget, with others, to break into your supplicant's lodgings and to seize upon all his goods, books, writings, and evidence of his lands to the value of 3,000 l., who, locking up all his inner doors, mured up his outward door with brick (as though he had committed felony or treason), which he keeps so shut up still and will not show any just cause for the same. In which time of your supplicant's first imprisonment the said Earl also imprisoned your supplicant's son and two servants 4 days in the Gatehouse, whereof one of them was 3 days close prisoner.

And not herewith contented, his Lordship has by letters and other means stayed all his legal proceedings in the common law for the recovery of his right, pretending that all your supplicant's suits ought to be tried in his Court Marshal (where he is both judge and party), contrary to the acts of parliament of the 8 R. 2; 13 R. 2; and 2 H. 4,[22] which forbid the Constable and Marshal to hold plea of anything in their court but only of matters of arms and war, which may not be determined at the common law of this realm.

Your poor, aged, and distressed petitioner and servant therefore most humbly beseeches your Majesty and this honorable House of parliament to take into consideration the premises and to give order for his enlargement. And that these hard proceedings and extreme wrongs done unto your petitioner by the said Earl may be examined and your petitioner and servant (according to the equity of his cause) relieved. And he, according to his bound duty and service, shall ever pray for your Majesty, etc.

18. MS. Cal. Pat. Rolls, f. 32v, 34 *Eliz.* I, pt. 15.

19. *S.R.*, 25 *E*. III, st. 5, c. 4.

20. Trouble had broken out between Brooke, York Herald, and Robert Treswell, Somerset Herald, on one side, and other officers of the College of Arms and Court of Chivalry and the Earl of Arundel, the future Earl Marshal, on the other side, over Brooke's publishing of *A Catalogue and Succession of the Kings, Princes, Dukes, Marquesses, Earles, and Viscounts of this Realme*, in 1619 (*S.T.C.*, no. 3832). See *A.P.C., 1617–1619*, pp. 338–339; *Cal. S.P. Dom., 1619–1623*, p. 110. For more details concerning the detaining of Brooke's fees, see the committee report on a similar petition which Brooke submitted to the Commons in 1624, *C.J.*, I, 701. See also the report on Brooke's cause in the Court of Chivalry, 24 November 1623, *Cal. S.P. Dom., 1623–1625*, p. 118.

21. Following the reading of a letter from the King expressing concern over the actions of Brooke and Robert Treswell with regard to the Earl Marshal and the Marshal's Court, the Privy Council, on 12 December 1621, ordered Brooke and Treswell to appear at the Board, and on 14 December the Council issued a warrant to commit the two men to the Marshalsea. Treswell was released on 3 January 1622 but, despite a declaration of his offenses by the Council in December 1622, Brooke remained recalcitrant until 25 March 1623 when, upon acknowledging his errors and offenses, he was discharged from the Marshalsea by order of the Council. See *A.P.C., 1621–1623*, pp. 99, 364–365, 450.

22. *S.R.*, 8 *R*. II, c. 5; *S.R.*, 13 *R*. II, cc. 2 & 3; *S.R.*, 2 *H*. IV, c. 23. Concerning Brooke's suits in the Court of Common Pleas and in Chancery, see *A.P.C., 1621–1623*, pp. 99, 267–268, 364–365; *Cal. S.P. Dom., 1619–1623*, pp. 321, 399.

MONDAY, 4 JULY 1625

I. JOURNAL OF THE HOUSE OF LORDS

[L.J. 452]
[p. 37] *Die Lunae, vizt., quarto die Julii 1625*
[List of Lords; see A.T.]
[L.J. 453]

Swetname, the bailiff of Westminster, and his underbailiff were brought to the bar for attaching the goods of Augustine Coles (a yeoman of the guard), contrary to the privileges of parliament,[1] who pleaded ignorance: that he knew not that the privileges extended unto goods, and that the warrant was brought unto him to attach the goods of Augustine Coles, bricklayer.

Michael Harrison, at whose suit the goods were attached, pleaded ignorance also.

Ordered that the goods be redelivered unto Coles, saving unto Michael Harrison his execution after the expiration of the privileges.[2] And that the said Swetname and the underbailiff and the said Michael Harrison be discharged of all contempts but commanded to take better notice of the privileges hereafter.

The House was moved to give thanks unto the two reverend and learned prelates that preached at the fast on Saturday last, which was done.[3]

And that at the next session *lex sumptuaria* may be made according to their admonition given in their sermons to restrain the excess of riot and apparel and, in the meantime, this House to be a rule unto themselves therein.

The care whereof is referred to the committee for privileges, etc.[4]

[p. 38] The LORD KEEPER remembered the House of the great business now in hand, *vizt.*, the petition touching religion.

Whereupon the House was adjourned *ad libitum* and the said petition was read in parts and each part fully discussed by itself.[5]

The House being resumed, these Lords were appointed to set down the alterations and amendments agreed on in the petition, *vizt.*:

The L. Keeper	L. Bp. of Norwich
L. President	L. Bp. of Bath and
Earl Marshal	W[ells]
E. of Clare	L. Bp. of Coventry and
L. Vic. Saye and Sele	Lichfield
	L. Wentworth
	L. Sheffield
	L. Spencer

Mr. Attorney General to attend the Lords. To meet presently in the Painted Chamber.

The LORD KEEPER signified unto the Lords that he had a message to deliver them from the King, *vizt.*: That his Majesty, considering the great danger of the infection at this time (whereof he is more sensible in respect of this assembly than of his own particular), will put an end to this session so soon as he shall understand of their readiness for the same; and that this be signified unto the Commons.

Agreed to be signified unto them at the conference touching the petition.

Message sent to the Commons by Mr. Serjeant Davies and Mr. Attorney General: That the Lords desire a conference at five this afternoon touching the petition to be delivered unto the King, with the former

1. For the petition of Coles against Swetname, *et al.*, see above, 25 June, p. 55.
2. See above, 27 June, n. 10.
3. For the two Upper House preachers, see above, 28 June, n. 13.
4. No report concerning excess of apparel was made during the remainder of the 1625 parliament.

However, during the 1626 session a bill concerning apparel was introduced and eventually assented to by the Lords. See *L.J.*, III, 542, 545, 549, 554, 556.
5. For a brief account of the discussion in the committee of the whole House, see H.L.R.O., M.M., 1625, below, pp. 85–86.

committee appointed for the fast; and that this House will sit this afternoon.

Answered: They will attend accordingly.

[*Notice of Adjournment*]

[**L.J. 453**; p. 39] *Die Lunae, vizt., quarto die Julii 1625. Post meridiem*
[*List of Lords; see A.T.*]
[**L.J. 454**]

Excused for their absence: The Lord Bp. of London, the Lord Bp. of Ely, the Lord Bp. of Durham.

Report made by the LORD KEEPER: That the committee appointed to set down the amendments (agreed on this morning) of the petition touching religion have accordingly written down the said amendments in such form as their Lordships conceive fit to be delivered to the Commons at the conference together with the reasons of each amendment.
The which his Lordship read out of a paper and the House did generally approve of the said amendments and reasons.[6]

The House being adjourned *ad libitum* the Lords committees went to the conference, the Lord Keeper being of the said committee.

Being returned, and the House resumed, the LORD KEEPER reported: That first he delivered unto the Commons the message from the King touching his Majesty's sorrow for the great danger they were in by reason of the sickness, and that his Majesty is ready to make an end of the session when he shall understand that they are ready to have an end.
Then, that their Lordships did generally allow of the petition touching religion, with the alterations here agreed, and delivered

the same unto them together with their Lordships' reasons for the said alterations.
[p. 40] That the Commons did express unto their Lordships the wonderful and inward rejoicing not only of his own subjects but of all foreign Protestants also for his Majesty's accompanying the Lords in that pious fast, which they humbly desire may be intimated unto his Majesty by one way or other.

[*House Adjourned*]

II. MINUTE BOOK, H.L.R.O., M.M., 1625

[f. 27v] *Die Lunae 4to die Julii 1625*
[*List of Lords Present; see A.T.*]

Swetname, Harrison, Bartlette brought to the bar for the attaching the goods of a yeoman of the guard.[7]

Ordered, the goods to be restored and the offenders released upon their present humble submission.

E. MARSHAL. That there be some course to [*sic*] taken touching luxury and excess of apparel.

Agreed that the Lords committees for privileges do consider of this matter by 2 this afternoon.[8]

[f. 28] House adjourned during pleasure to consider of the popish recusants.

[*Committee of the Whole House*]

Nota. Lord Bishop of Chichester. That in my diocese there was a bishop of the Roman church did act the parts of a bishop in a nobleman's house, and I thought it my duty to inform the House.

The petition of the Commons against the recusants was read a part and considered

---

6. The completed petition concerning religion is printed on 9 August, below, pp. 155–160, with those sentences and words italicized or footnoted which at the Lords' request were resolved to be added or altered by the House of Commons. See below, H. of L., 9

August, n. 12. For the Lords' alterations to the petition, see also H. of C., 4 July, below, pp. 298–299, 305–306.
   7. See above, n. 1.
   8. See above, n. 4.

particularly of every branch therein by the Lords of parliament.[9]

Nota. L. Steward. That the King has certified him and others that such servants as she[10] had when she was princess, of papists, only to wait on her, and that she shall have no subjects of his to serve her without they go to church.

Nota. Lord Steward. The King has given a strict command to his porter at St. James, his house where the Queen's chapel is to be erected,[11] that no one subject whatsoever should be suffered to come to the mass.

L. Bishop of Bangor. That there is a great concourse of people to St. Winifred's well and another well, an old chapel new mended, and public mass said continually.[12]

[f. 28v]

L. Keeper	President
L. Saye	Marshal
L. Dorset	Durham
Clare	Norwich
Wentworth	Bath and Wells
Spencer	Coventry and Lichfield
Sheffield	

[To attend:] Attorney.

L. KEEPER. A message from the King: That there was a meeting of both Houses touching a petition; that his Majesty was very sorry for the sickness, more in regard of them than he would for himself; and he wished that they had dispatched that; he would be ready to give [*illegible*] a royal assent.

Serjeants Davies and Finch with a message: That the Lords desire a conference in the Painted Chamber,[13] the former committee touching recusants; and desire them to meet with their former committee.

Answer: That the Commons will meet at the time and place appointed.

Adjourned. 4 *post meridiem.*

[f. 29] *Die Lunae 4to die Julii 1625 post meridiem.*
[*List of Lords Present; see A.T.*]

Excused by L. Bishop of Llandaff: L. Bishops of London and Ely.

L. KEEPER, first of the committee to prepare a conference with the Commons, read the amendments of the Commons [*sic*] and the reasons at the conference.

L. Bishop of Durham excused by Bishop of Rochester.

L. KEEPER certified the Commons that his Majesty should be ready to make a session upon the intimation of this House and the Lower [House] of the dispatch of business. Some amendments in the petition. A desire of the Commons that there might be some expression of great joy that is not only here in this kingdom but also of the Protestants in all Christendom for his Majesty [*illegible*] at this great business, the fast.

Adjourned. 8 tomorrow.

9. *The causes of the increase of popish recusants, nothing said; the interposing of foreign ambassadors, nothing said; that the papists are not sufficiently taxed* is crossed out in the MS. following *parliament.* Concerning the petition and the Lords' amendments, see above, n. 6.

10. I.e., Henrietta Maria, the new Queen.

11. The Queen's chapel at St. James palace, completed in 1627, had been authorized originally in 1623 in anticipation of a Spanish marriage (*Cal. S.P. Dom., 1619–1623*, p. 593) and was provided for again

in the French marriage articles which assured the future Queen "a chapel within all the houses royal" (Lansdowne MS. 93, no. 37).

12. St. Winifred's well at Holywell, Flintshire, Wales, was a popular place of pilgrimage for English Catholics. See D. Thomas, "St. Winifred's Well and Chapel, Holywell", *Historical Society of the Church in Wales, Journal*, VIII (1958), 15–31.

13. *by five in the p.m. with* is crossed out in the MS. following *Chamber.*

Prayers

Lords excused   88, 89

L. 1a and *L. 2a*. An act for the
  Earl of Dorset touching lands
  appointed to be sold by
  Richard, late Earl of Dorset,
  to pay his debts, etc.:
  committed   88, 89, 90, *6/7;
                                            8/7

Message from the Commons
  regarding the alterations to
  the **petition concerning
  religion** and desiring
  dispatch of all **bills** sent up to
  the Lords (Sir Edward Coke
  and others)   88, 89, *1/7

Answer given to the Commons'
  message: Lords agree to a
  present meeting by
  subcommittee of both Houses
  for penning the alterations,
  and promise expedition of
  bills   88

Subcommittee for penning the
  alterations to the petition:
  appointed   88, 89

L. 1a. An act for the ease in
  obtaining licenses of
  alienation   88, 89, *1/7;
                                            6/7; 11/7

L. 1a. An act for the further
  restraint of **tippling** in inns,
  alehouses, etc. [*see below*]   88, 89, *1/7;
                                            6/7; 7/7; 9/7;
                                            11/7

Lords excused   88, 89

L. 1a and *L. 2a*. An act to confirm
  an agreement between the
  King and his tenants of
  Macclesfield: committed   88, 90, 91,
                                            *28/6; 6/7;
                                            11/7

Lord excused   90

Petition of the **Earl of Sussex**:
  read   90, 91
  [*Sussex's petition is printed on pp.
  91–92*]

Petition of Tobias **Anderson**,
  servant to the Earl of
  Rutland: read   89, 90

Tobias Anderson brought to the
  bar and set at liberty   89, 90

L. 2a. An act for the further
  restraint of **tippling** in inns,
  alehouses, etc.: committed
  [*see above*]   88, 90, 91

House adjourned   89, 90

TUESDAY, 5 JULY 1625

I. JOURNAL OF THE HOUSE OF LORDS

[L.J. 454]

[p. 41] *Die Martis, vizt., quinto die Julii 1625*
[*List of Lords; see A.T.*]

[L.J. 455]

Excused: the Lo. Paget, L. Bp. of London, L. Vic. Andover, L. Stourton, E. of Salisbury, L. Bp. of Bristol, E. of Warwick, L. Sheffield, L. Brooke, E. of Bolingbroke, L. Willoughby, E. of Leicester, E. of Sussex.

Hodie 1ᵃ et 2ᵃ vice lecta est billa Edwardi comitis Dorset touching lands appointed to be sold by Richard, late Earl of Dorset, to pay his debts and raise portions for his daughters and to settle divers lands on himself and his son and his heirs.[1]

Committed unto the

L. President	L. De La Warr
E. of Nottingham	L. Berkeley
L. Vic. Rochford	L. Scrope
	L. Wentworth
L. Bp. of Winchester	L. North
L. Bp. of Chichester	L. Grey of Groby

To attend the Lords: Mr. Justice Yelverton, Mr. Serjeant Finch. To meet tomorrow at eight in the Painted Chamber.

[p. 42] *Hodie 1ᵃ et 2ᵈᵃ vice lecta est billa,* An act for the further restraint of tippling in inns, alehouses, and other victualling houses.

Committed unto the

E. of Clare	L. De La Warr
L. Vic. Rochford	L. North
L. Bp. of Llandaff	L. Grey of Groby
L. Bp. of St. Davids	L. Grey of Warke

To attend the Lords: Mr. Justice Hutton, Mr. Serjeant Davies. To meet presently.

Hodie 1ᵃ et 2ᵈᵃ vice lecta est billa, An act to confirm an agreement between the King's Majesty and his tenants of Macclesfield, in the county of Chester, etc.[2]

Committed unto the

L. Treasurer	L. De La Warr
E. of Northampton	L. Scrope
L. Bp. of Durham	L. Grey of Groby
L. Bp. of Bangor	L. Carey of Leppington

To attend the Lords: The Lord Chief Baron, Mr. Serjeant Davenport. To meet tomorrow morning at eight near the parliament presence.[3]

Hodie 1ᵃ vice lecta est billa, An act for the ease in obtaining of licenses of alienation, and in the pleading of alienations without license in the Court of Exchequer and elsewhere.

Message from the Commons by Sir Edward Coke and others: That their committee had delivered them divers alterations to be made in that pious petition to the King touching the establishing of religion which (being eleven in number) were put to the question and generally agreed unto by that House.[4]

They desire a subcommittee to be appointed to amend the said petition accordingly, and they do think (if their Lordships please) that six of their House will be a competent number; but they humbly leave the number, time, and place unto their Lordships. And do likewise desire expedition of all those bills which they have sent, or hereafter shall send, to their Lordships.

Answered: That the Lords return all thanks for their fair acceptance of those accommodations of that petition; their Lordships have appointed a subcommittee of

---

1. For a brief of Dorset's bill, see below, Committee Book, p. 90.

2. The private act concerning the tenants of Macclesfield is engrossed on the 1625 Parliament Roll. See *Rot. Parl.*, 1 *Car.* I, no. 8.

3. The H.L.R.O., M.M., and the Committee Book, below, indicate that the committee was to meet in the Lord Treasurer's Chamber.

4. For the Lords' alterations to the petition concerning religion, see H. of C., 4 July, below, pp. 298–299, 305–306, and the petition printed on 9 August, below, pp. 155–160.

four to meet presently,[5] and do promise expedition of the bills sent, and to be sent, unto their Lordships.

The petition of Tobias Anderson, servant to the Right Honorable the Earl of Rutland, was read, humbly desiring to be freed of his imprisonment according to the privilege of parliament.[6]

And *memorandum:* That the said Tobias Anderson was brought up by the sheriff of Lincolnshire by virtue of a *habeas corpus cum causa, etc., coram domino rege in Cancellaria,* and was brought before their Lordships upon the said petition.

Ordered to be set at liberty, the execution to be saved to the plaintiff, and the sheriff to be discharged.

[*Notice of Adjournment*]

II. MINUTE BOOK, H.L.R.O., M.M., 1625

[f. 30] *Die Martis 5to die Julii 1625.*
[*List of Lords Present; see A.T.*]

Excused:
L. Paget left his proxy with the Lord Keeper.
Bishop of London by the Bishop of Llandaff.
L. Denny, proxy with the Lord Danvers.
L. Viscount Andover by Lord Danvers.
E. of Salisbury excused by Viscount Rochford.
Bishop of Bristol by Bishop Bangor.
E. of Warwick, L. Sheffield, L. Brooke, E. of Bolingbroke by the Viscount Saye.

[f. 30v] *Hodie 1^a vice lecta est billa,* An act for the Earl of Dorset, etc.[7]
Hodie 2^a vice lecta est billa, An act for the Earl of Dorset, etc.

Committed unto
President	4.	L. Wentworth
Nottingham	2.	L. Berkeley
Rochford	3.	L. Scrope
	5.	L. North
Winchester	6.	L. Grey [of] Groby
Chichester	1.	L. De La Warr

To attend: J[ustice] Yelverton, Serjeant Finch.

To meet tomorrow morning by 8, Painted Chamber.

A message from the Commons by Sir Edward Coke and others: 1, that they desire an accomplishment of the petition against recusants; 2, they desire a dispatch of those bills that have been sent up and such as shall be sent up. That those amendments that the Lords made, being severally put to the vote, were generally assented, *nemine contradicente;* that a subcommittee to consider of the petition, etc., to meet with the Commons.[8]

President
Darcy and M[einill][9]
Coventry and Lichfield
Wentworth

To meet presently in Painted Chamber.

[f. 31] *Hodie 1^a vice lecta est billa,* An act for the pleading of alienations with license or without license, etc.

Hodie 1^a vice lecta est billa, An act for the further restraint of tippling in inns, alehouses, etc.

L. Willoughby excused by L. Viscount Rochford.

E. of Leicester excused by the E. of Clare.

---

5. I.e., a subcommittee of the Lords' conference committee originally appointed on 23 June (see above, p. 43). For the names of the four Lords appointed to the subcommittee for penning the Lords' alterations to the petition, see below, H.L.R.O., M.M., 1625; for the names of the eight members of the Lower House appointed to meet with them, see H. of C., 4 July, p. 299.

6. We have been unable to find Tobias Anderson's petition.

7. For a brief of Dorset's bill, see below, Committee Book, p. 90.

8. Concerning the subcommittee, see above, n. 5; with regard to the alterations, see above, n. 4.

9. *Durham* is crossed out in the MS. following *Darcy and M.*

Hodie 1ᵃ vice lecta est billa, An act for the manor of Macclesfield, etc.[10]

Hodie 2ᵃ vice lecta est billa eadem et commissa est.

Treasurer	L. Scrope
Northampton	L. Carey of
Durham	Leppington
Bangor	L. De La Warr
	L. Grey of Groby

To attend: Chief Baron, Serjeant Davenport.

To meet tomorrow by 8 in the Lord Treasurer's Chamber.

E. of Sussex excused by the E. of Clare.

The petition of the E. of Sussex read.[11]

[f. 31v] E. of Rutland's man: the petition of Tobias Anderson;[12] being arrested, was brought to the bar and set at liberty. To be set at liberty and the execution saved.

Hodie 2ᵃ vice lecta est billa, An act to restrain the inordinate haunting of inns, alehouses, etc.

Committed:

Viscount Rochford[13]	De La Warr[14]
E. of Clare	North
	L. Grey of W[arke]
Bp. of Llandaff	L. Grey of G[roby]
B. of St. Davids	

To attend: J[ustice] Hutton, S[erjeant] Davies, J/

To meet presently.

Adjourned. 9 tomorrow morning.

III. COMMITTEE BOOK, H.L.R.O., MAIN PAPERS, H.L., 1625

[f. 5] *Die Martis 5ᵗᵒ die Julii.*

An act for the better enabling of Sir George Rivers, Knight, Richard Amherst, Serjeant at Law, and Edward Lindsey, Es-quire, to sell certain manors, lands, tenements, and hereditaments mentioned to be conveyed to them and to the Right Honorable the Lord William Howard of Naworth, in the county of Cumberland, or some of them, by the late Right Honorable Richard, Earl of Dorset, for and towards the payment of the debts of the said Earl and to raise portions to his daughters, according to his will in writing, and for the confirmation of the sales, by them already made, of part thereof for that purpose. And for the better settling and establishing of divers manors, lands, tenements, and hereditaments of the said late Earl, upon the Right Honorable Edward, Earl of Dorset, of the most noble order of the Garter, Knight, and his sons and the heirs male of the several bodies of the said sons to be begotten. And upon the Right Honorable Anne, Countess Dowager of Dorset, for term of her life for her jointure. And upon the Lady Margaret and the Lady Isabella Sackville, daughters of the said Richard, Earl of Dorset, and upon the heirs of their several bodies respectively, according to the purport of certain conveyances, hereafter in this act mentioned to be made by the said late Earl of Dorset, deceased. And to enable the said Edward, Earl of Dorset, to make sale of some part of his lands, assuring other lands of as much yearly value or more to his sons in lieu thereof.

Committed unto

L. President	L. De La Warr
E. of Nottingham	L. Berkeley
L. Vic. Rochford	L. Scrope
	L. Wentworth
L. Bp. of Winchester	L. North
L. Bp. of Chichester	L. Grey of Groby

To attend the Lords: Mr. Justice Yelverton, Mr. Serjeant Finch.

10. See above, n. 2.
11. For the petition of Robert, Earl of Sussex, see below, p. 91.
12. We have been unable to find Tobias Anderson's petition.

13. The name *Rochester* is crossed out in the MS. and *Rochford* inserted.
14. *Carey of Leppington* is crossed out in the MS. preceding *De La Warr*.

To meet tomorrow morning by 8 in the Painted Chamber.

Sent to the Commons.[15]

[f. 5v] *Die Martis 5to die Julii 1625.*

An act for the enabling and confirmation of an agreement or composition made between the King's Majesty's commissioners of revenue (his Majesty then being Prince of Wales, Duke of Cornwall, and Earl of Chester) on his Majesty's behalf, and his Majesty's copyholders of his Highness's manor of Macclesfield, in the county of Chester, and of a decree made in the Court of Exchequer, at Chester, for the perfect creation and confirmation of certain lands and tenements, parcel of the said manor, to be copyhold and customary lands according to the tenor of the same decree.

Committed unto

L. Treasurer   L. De La Warr
E. of Northampton   L. Scrope
    L. Grey of Groby
L. Bp. of Durham   L. Carey of
L. Bp. of Bangor   Leppington

To attend the Lords: L. Chief Baron, Mr. Serjeant Davenport.

To meet tomorrow morning by eight of the clock, near the parliament, in the Lord Treasurer his chamber.

Expedited.

[f. 6] *Die Martis 5 Julii 1625.*

An Act for the further restraint of tippling in inns, alehouses, and other victualling houses. Committed unto

E. of Clare
L. Vic. Rochford   L. De La Warr
    L. North
L. Bp. of Llandaff   L. Grey of Groby
L. Bp. of St. Davids   L. Grey of Warke

To attend the Lords: Mr. Justice Hutton, Mr. Serjeant Davies.

---

15. This note appears in the margin of the manuscript. Dorset's bill was sent to the Commons on 8 July and was assented to by the Lower House on 9 August but was not returned to the Lords.

To meet presently near the parliament presence.

Expedited.

IV. PETITION OF ROBERT, EARL OF SUSSEX.
H.L.R.O., MAIN PAPERS, H.L., 5 JULY 1625.

To the Right Honorable the Lords Spiritual and Temporal in the Upper House of parliament assembled.

The humble petition of Robert, Earl of Sussex, showing unto your good Lordships,

That about 4 years since one Lawrence Poulton, a person of a defected life and wandering condition, happened to come into the parish of Yateley, in the county of Southampton and, within a short time after, with some materials he did take from a copyhold tenement of your petitioner's wife[16] (adjacent to her dwelling house called Minley in the said county of Southampton, upon the very confines of the two commons or wastes of Yateley and Minley), he built him a cabin or cottage, and covered it with turf and thatch, and made thereof a habitation for himself and family, and there entertained all manner of all disordered persons who lived upon the ruin and spoil of the inhabitants there, insomuch that your petitioner's wife could not keep in safety from them neither warren, poultry, nor any other household provision. After many admonitions and no hope of reformation and having made her complaint to the steward of the Dean of Winchester, being lord of that manor, it being by him thought fit to be removed, the truth is your petitioner's wife, taking a constable with her, and first laying apart such goods or lumber as was within the said house (most part whereof had formerly been purloined from her), did cause her servants to pull the said cabin down. And in the night after, it

---

16. I.e., Frances, the daughter of Hercules Meautys and widow of Francis Shute, who was the second wife of Robert Radcliffe, Earl of Sussex.

happened that some sparks of the hearth crept along the heath where the lumber lay and burned part of an old bed. For this the said Poulton, being thereunto incited by certain evil[ly] disposed persons, preferred a scandalous petition against your petitioner's wife to his late Majesty, thereby endeavoring to draw her within compass of felonious burning of a house. Thereupon his Majesty was graciously pleased to refer the examination thereof to the assize, viz., the Lord Chief Baron deceased[17] and Mr. Justice Hutton. They for their better information referred the examination and final determination thereof to 4 justices of the peace of that county, viz., Sir Henry Wallop, Sir Edward More, Sir James Wolveridge, and Sir Walter Tichborne, Knights, or to any 2 of them. The said Sir Henry Wallop and Sir James Wolveridge at large heard what could be said on both sides and demanded of Poulton what his house and the materials in the setting up stood him in, who confessed that all, both erecting and materials, cost him but 15s.

Whereupon the justices persuaded your petitioner's wife to give him some recompense, at whose entreaty she gave him 40s. which (with the confession of his faults acknowledging that it was more than he had sustained in loss) he took very thankfully, as by their annexed certificate will more plainly appear to your Lordships.

Thus (may it please your Lordships) it rested by the space of 2 years and then again, by instigation of some ill affected to your petitioner's wife, the said Poulton was gotten to be admitted *in forma pauperis*, and a bill in Star Chamber in the name of the said Poulton was exhibited against your petitioner's wife, her daughter, and 7 or 8 of her servants. Which bill is prosecuted not by the said Poulton as a complaint *in forma pauperis,* but by others in his name with great continuance and plenty of money. And now also the said malicious prosecutors do publish that they will insert your petitioner's name as a defendant in the said bill.

Now whether your petitioner being a peer of this realm shall be thus vexed by a bill in Star Chamber preferred in the name of a person of so mean condition, and for a matter of so small value already doubly recompensed and more, and ended by the justices as appears by their certificate, and whether the said malicious prosecutors shall be suffered unlawfully to maintain the said bill against your petitioner, your petitioner appeals to this most honorable House for justice.

17. Sir Lawrence Tanfield, Chief Baron of the Exchequer, died on 30 April 1625. *D.N.B.*

Prayers
Lord excused   95
L.2a. An act for the ease in
   obtaining licenses of
   alienation: committed [*see
   below*]   95, 97, 99, *5/7
Sir Ranulphe Crew (L. Chief
   Justice) brings in the record
   touching the writ of error of
   Edward **Hayne**   95, 97, *8/7
Report from the committee on
   the bill for the further
   restraint of **tippling** in inns,
   alehouses, etc. (EARL OF
   CLARE) [*see below*]   95, 97, *5/7
Addition to the above bill: put to
   the question and agreed; bill
   to be engrossed   95, 97
Report from the committee on
   the bill for the ease in
   obtaining licenses of
   alienation (LORD LEY, L.
   Treasurer) [*see above*]   95, 97
L. 3a. An act for the ease in
   obtaining licenses of
   alienation: assented to and
   expedited   95, 97
Report from the committee on
   the bill to confirm an
   agreement between the King
   and his tenants of
   Macclesfield (EARL OF
   NORTHAMPTON)   95, *5/7
L. 3a. An act to confirm an
   agreement between the King
   and his tenants of
   Macclesfield: assented to and
   expedited   95, 97
L. 2a. An act for the better
   maintenance of **hospitals and
   almshouses**: committed   95, 97, 98, *27/6
Report from the subcommittee
   for penning alterations to the
   petition concerning religion

(VISCOUNT MANDEVILLE, L.
   President)   96, *1/7
Message from the Commons
   desiring the Lords to sit this
   afternoon for receiving the
   engrossed petition
   concerning religion and
   other matters (Sir Edward
   Coke and others) [*see below*]   96, 98
Answer given to the Commons'
   message: the Lords will sit
   this afternoon   96, 98
L. 3a. An act for the further
   restraint of **tippling** in inns,
   alehouses, etc.: assented to
   and expedited   95, 98
Report from the committee on
   the bill for the **Earl of Dorset**
   (VISCOUNT MANDEVILLE, L.
   President)   95, 98, *5/7
Mr. Lindsey testifies at the bar
   that the Countess Dowager of
   Dorset gave her consent to
   the bill for the Earl of Dorset   98
Amendment to Dorset's bill: read
   twice; bill to be engrossed   95
House adjourned   96, 98
   [*Afternoon*]
Lords excused   96, 98
Message from the Commons
   bringing the **petition
   concerning religion** and
   report touching **ending the
   session** (Sir Edward Coke
   and others) [*see below*]   96, 98, *4/7
Committee to join with Commons
   in delivering the petition
   concerning religion to the
   King: appointed   96, 98, 99
Lord Keeper (Bp. of Lincoln) to
   write to the Earl of Pembroke
   (L. Steward) desiring access
   to the King for presenting
   the petition   97

WEDNESDAY, 6 JULY 1625

I. JOURNAL OF THE HOUSE OF LORDS

[**L.J. 456**]
[p. 43] *Die Mercurii, vizt., sexto die Julii 1625*
[*List of Lords; see A.T.*]
[**L.J. 457**]

Lord Steward excused.

Hodie 2ª vice lecta est billa, An act for the ease in the obtaining of licenses of alienation, and in the pleading of alienations without license in the Court of Exchequer or elsewhere.
Committed unto the

L. Treasurer	L. Bp. of Bath and
L. President	W[ells]
L. Privy Seal	L. Bp. of Salisbury
L. Vic. Saye and Sele	
	L. Sheffield
L. Bp of Durham	L. Grey
L. Bp. of Rochester	

To attend the Lords: Mr. Justice Yelverton, Mr. Serjeant Finch. To meet presently.

The bill being reported by the LORD TREASURER, *hodie 3ª vice lecta est billa praedicta.*
Put to the question and generally assented unto.

Hodie 3ª vice lecta est billa, An act to confirm an agreement between the King's Majesty and his tenants of Macclesfield, in the county of Chester, etc.
Put to the question and assented unto.
Memorandum: It was first reported by the EARL OF NORTHAMPTON.

The EARL OF CLARE reported the bill against tippling fit to pass, with an addition touching taverns.

1ª et 2ᵈᵃ lecta est the addition, put to the question, agreed, and ordered to be engrossed.

[p. 44]·*Hodie 3ª vice lecta est billa praedicta,* An act for the further restraint of tippling in inns, alehouses, and other victualling houses.
Put to the question and assented unto together with the schedule annexed.

Hodie 2ª vice lecta est billa, An act for the better maintenance of hospitals.
Committed unto the

L. Treasurer	L. Willoughby
E. of Leicester	L. Darcy and M[einill]
E. of Clare	L. Sheffield
	L. Grey of Groby
L. Vic. Saye and Sele	L. Carey
L. Bp. of Durham	L. Grey of Warke
L. Bp. of Winchester	
L. Bp. of Bath and	
W[ells]	
L. Bp. of Bangor	

To attend the Lords: Mr. Justice Jones, Mr. Baron Trevor, Mr. Attorney General.
But no time was appointed for their meeting.

Report made by the LORD PRESIDENT of the Earl of Dorset's bill, fit to pass with one amendment.

1ª et 2ᵈᵃ vice lecta est, amended accordingly and ordered to be engrossed.

Hodie Sir Ranulphe Crew, Knight, Lord Chief Justice of the King's Bench, returned into this court his Majesty's writ of error granted unto Edward Hayne, and brought in the record and process between the said Hayne and Thomas Crouch, and delivered the said writ of error and a transcript of the said record unto the Lord Keeper.

Memorandum: That at the rising of the House the record was carried back again, and the transcript left with the Clerk, together with Hayne his[1] petition to the King, signed by his Majesty.

---

1. *Haines's petition.* Printed edition. For a copy of Hayne's petition to the King, see S.P. 16/1:110. We are unable to find the transcript of the record of the case

which was presumably left with the Clerk. Under normal circumstances such a record would have become part of the collection of the H.L.R.O., Main Papers,

The LORD PRESIDENT reported that the subcommittees of both Houses had agreed and perfected the alterations in the petition for religion.[2]

Message from the Commons by Sir Edward Coke and others: That the House of Commons desire their Lordships would be pleased to sit this afternoon, that they may present the petition touching religion (which will be by that time fair engrossed with the amendment), and impart some other matters of importance concerning the commonwealth unto their Lordships.[3]

Answered: The Lords are resolved to sit this afternoon and to receive anything that shall be presented unto them from that House.

[*Notice of Adjournment*]

[**L.J. 457**; p. 45] *Die Mercurii, vizt., sexto die Julii, post meridiem, 1625.*
[*List of Lords; see A.T.*]

[**L.J. 458**] Excused: E. of Sussex, E. of Holderness, L. Howard of Walden, L. Robartes, L. Grey of Warke, L. Carey, L. Brooke.

Message from the Commons by Sir Edward Coke and others: That the House of Commons have sent unto their Lordships the petition for advancement of true religion and suppressing of superstition and idolatry as it is accommodated and agreed by both Houses, humbly desiring their Lordships to appoint a committee to join with a committee of their House for delivery thereof unto his Majesty, the number they leave unto their Lordships. As touching the message delivered from his Majesty touching the session of parliament, they can say nothing to it as yet.[4]

Answered: That the Lords have appointed a committee of eight to join in the delivery of this petition at such time as it shall please his Majesty to appoint.[5] And that they have ordered the Lord Keeper to write unto the Lord Steward to know his Majesty's pleasure when he will be pleased to admit them to his presence, which they hope to understand tomorrow.

[p. 46] *Memorandum:* That before this answer was given the Lords did appoint these lords to deliver the said petition, *vizt.:*

---

but because of the dislocation of the session many petitions and other records of the parliament were apparently lost. On 8 July it was agreed that Hayne and his attorney would be heard at the next sitting of parliament; see below, H. of L., 8 July, O.B. A related petition from Thomas Hayne was read in the Upper House on 11 July; see H. of L., 11 July, O.B.

2. The petition concerning religion is printed on 9 August, below, pp. 155–160, with those sentences and words italicized which at the Lords' request were resolved to be altered by the House of Commons.

3. The "other matters" apparently refers to the question of ending the session. See the message from the Commons this afternoon and n. 4, below.

4. The King's message concerning ending the session was communicated to the Commons at the conference of 4 July. See above, H. L., 4 July, O.B. Fearing that the King's assent to some acts would signal the end of the session rather than simply an adjournment, the Commons, on 5 July, read and committed a bill stipulating that the present session should not be determined by the King's assent to one or more acts of par-

liament. See below, H. of C., 5 July, O.B.

Traditionally, royal assent to bills was granted at the end of a parliament. The assent assured that the bills which had passed both Houses became acts and that the parliament was a session rather than a convention in which by definition no legislation passed. Coke, *Fourth Inst.*, ff. 27–28. However, in 1621, Coke, Noy, and others had argued that a session was not determined by the royal assent to legislation. See particularly, *C.D. 1621*, III, 332; IV, 132, 386–388; V, 182, 279; VI, 358 (and ibid., I, Index, *sub* Parliament, Adjournment of, June). Also, see below, H. of C., 7 July, n. 88.

On this day (6 July), the bill concerning the ending of the session was reported, considered, and received its third reading in the Lower House but, upon some exceptions, was recommitted rather than assented to. See below, H. of C., 6 July, O.B. The bill passed the Lower House and was sent to the Lords on 8 July.

5. For the committee appointed by the Lower House to attend the King, see H. of C., 8 July, p. 349 and n. 22.

L. President   L. Darcy and M[einill]
L. Privy Seal   L. Wentworth
L. Bp. of Durham   L. Sheffield
L. Bp. of Winchester   L. North

And their Lordships appointed the Lord Keeper to write, *ut supra*.

The said petition was read, *vide postea 9no Augusti*.[6]

The petition of the prisoners of the Fleet exhibited to this House whereby they humbly desired to have the benefit of his Majesty's writ of *habeas corpus*, etc. (heretofore used but now denied) in this time of infection.[7]

Read and committed unto the

L. President   L. Scrope
E. of Northampton   L. Wentworth
E. of Clare   L. Sheffield
L. Bp. of Durham   L. North
L. Bp. of Bangor

To meet tomorrow at eight in the Painted Chamber, and to consider of the petition and to consider what answer or order shall be made thereon.

The Lords committees for privileges, etc., are to meet on Friday next, at eight in the morning, touching the petition of Ralph Brooke, York Herald.[8]

[*Notice of Adjournment*]

II. MINUTE BOOK, H.L.R.O., M.M., 1625

[f. 32] *Die Mercurii 6 die Julii 1625.*
[*List of Lords Present; see A.T.*]

Hodie 2ª vice lecta est billa, An act for the ease in obtaining of licenses of alienations.

[col. 1]	[col. 2]
L. Treasurer	Durham
Privy Seal	Salisbury
Saye and S[ele]	Chichester
President	Bath and W[ells]
	Rochester

[col. 3]
Sheffield
Grey of G[roby]
Grey of W[arke]

[To attend:] J[ustice] Yelverton,[9] S[erjeant] Finch.

To meet presently near the parliament presence.

[f. 32v] L. Chief Justice brought in the record touching the writ of error of Mr. Hayne.

E. OF CLARE reported the bill touching [haunting] of inns and tippling houses with an addition, was read *1ª et 2ª vice.*

The additions put to the questions and passed. To be engrossed.

L. PRESIDENT reported the bill of alienations as fit to pass.

Hodie 3ª vice lecta est billa, An act for the ease in obtaining of licenses of alienations, etc.

Expedited.

Hodie 3ª vice lecta est billa, An act between the King and the tenants of Macclesfield.

Put to the question and passed. Expedited.

Hodie 2ª vice lecta est billa, An act for hospitals, etc.

[col. 1]	[col. 2]
L. Treasurer	Winchester
E. of Leicester	Durham
E. of Clare	Bath and W[ells]
L. Viscount Saye and S[ele]	Bangor

[col. 3]
Willoughby
Darcy and M[einill]
Sheffield
2 Lords Grey
Carey of Leppington

---

6. See above, n. 2.

7. The prisoners' petition is printed below, p. 99. A joint conference with the Commons concerning this petition was held on 9 July and was reported on the same day in both Houses. For debate on this issue in the Lower House following the conference report, see below, H. of C., 9 July, pp. 360–361, 363–364.

8. For Brooke's petition, see 1 July, p. 81. For the report on his case, see below, H. of L., 9 July, O.B.

9. *Chief Justice* is crossed out in the MS. preceding *J. Yelverton.*

To attend the Lords: J[ustice] Jones,[10] Trevor, Attorney.

To meet tomorrow.

[f. 33] A message from the Commons by Sir Edward Coke and others: That their Lordships would sit this afternoon both for the returning up of the petition touching recusants as also touching other business that might be considered of.

Answer: That the Lords will sit this afternoon.

Hodie 3ª vice lecta est billa, An act against tippling in inns, alehouses, etc., with the additions.
Put to the question and passed. Expedited.

L. PRESIDENT reported the bill of the E. of Dorset as fit to pass with amendments.

It was doubted by the Lords whether the Countess Dowager of Dorset gave consent to the bill.

Mr. Lindsey, a feoffee in trust touching the E. of Dorset, sworn at the bar, testifies that the Countess Dowager of Dorset gave her consent to the passing of the bill; that the Lord Russell, who was trusted by the Lady, had seen the bill and that his Lordship had sent a letter to the E. of Dorset testifying the Lady's consent.[11]

Adjourned. 4 *post meridiem.*

[p. 33v] *Die Mercurii, 6ᵗᵒ Julii, post meridiem 1625.*
[*List of Lords Present; see A.T.*]

[Excused:] E. of Sussex, Lord Walden, Lord Robartes.

A message from the Commons: Sir Edward Coke, with others, brought up the petition against recusants; that they cannot yet give any consent for the ending of the session.

[f. 34] Lords committees appointed to confer with a proportionable number of the Commons:

L. President	L. Darcy and M[einill]
L. P[rivy] Seal	Wentworth
	Sheffield
Bp. Durham	North
Winchester	L. Willoughby added instead of the Lord Sheffield[12]
	L. Grey of Warke

The petition against recusants read.

The petition of the prisoners of the Fleet read.[13]

L. President	Scrope
L. Sheffield	Northampton
Durham	
Bangor	
Wentworth	
North	

To meet on this petition tomorrow morning by [*blank*] and to conceive an order.

Adjourned. 9 tomorrow.

III. COMMITTEE BOOK, H.L.R.O., MAIN PAPERS, H.L., 1625

[f. 6v] *Die Mercurii 6ᵗᵒ die Julii 1625.*

An act for the better maintenance of hospitals and almshouses.
Committed unto

Lo. Treasurer	L. Willoughby of
E. of Leicester	Eresby
E. of Clare	L. Darcy and Meinill
L. Vic. Saye and S[ele]	L. Sheffield
	L. Grey of Groby
2. L. Bp. of	L. Carey of
Winchester	Leppington

---

10. *Master of Rolls* is crossed out in the MS. preceding *J. Jones.*

11. Francis, Lord Russell, was a cousin of Anne, Countess Dowager of Dorset. On 8 July the Lord Keeper certified to the House that he had received a letter from Lord Russell confirming the Countess Dowager of Dorset's consent to the act. See below, p. 105.

12. Lord Willoughby and Lord Grey of Warke were added to this committee on 8 July. See below, pp. 99 and 104.

13. See above, n. 7.

1. L. Bp. of Durham L. Grey of Warke
   L. Bp. of Bath and
      W[ells]
   L. Bp. of Bangor

To attend the Lords: Mr. Justice Jones, Mr. Baron Trevor, Mr. Attorney General. *Sine die.* To meet/

[f. 7] *Die Mercurii 6to die Julii 1625.*

An act for the ease in the obtaining of licenses of alienation and in the pleading of alienations with license or of pardons of alienations without license in the Court of Exchequer and elsewhere.
Committed unto

L. Treasurer	L. Sheffield
L. President	L. Grey of Groby
L. Privy Seal	L. Grey of Warke
L. Saye and Sele	

L. Bp. of Durham
L. Bp. of Rochester
L. Bp. of Bath and
   W[ells]
L. Bp. of Salisbury

To attend the Lords: Mr. Justice Yelverton, Mr. Serjeant Finch.

To meet presently near the parliament presence.

Expedited.

[f. 7v] *Die Mercurii 6to die Julii post meridiem 1625.*

Lords committees appointed by the House to confer with a committee of the Commons touching a petition to be offered to his Majesty against popish recusants:

L. President	L. Darcy and Meinill
L. Privy Seal	L. Wentworth
	L. Sheffield
L. Bp. of Durham	L. North
L. Bp. of Winchester	

L. Willoughby
L. Grey of W[arke] } added 8 July

Expedited.

14. See above, n. 7.

[f. 8] *Die Mercurii 6 Julii post meridiem 1625.*

The petition of the prisoners of the Fleet touching *habeas corpus.*
Committed unto

L. President	L. Scrope
E. of Northampton	L. Wentworth
	L. Sheffield
L. Bp. of Durham	L. North
L. Bp. of Bangor	

To attend the Lords: The two Lords Chief Justices, Mr. Justice Hutton, Mr. Justice Croke, Mr. Baron Trevor.

Expedited.

IV. PETITION OF THE PRISONERS IN THE FLEET. H.L.R.O., MAIN PAPERS, H.L., 6 JULY 1625.[14]

To the most reverend and most honorable assembly of Lords in parliament.

The most humble petition of the distressed prisoners for debt in the prison of the Fleet, showing,

That that prison not being removable at the pleasure of the warden thereof (as other common jails are by the sheriffs of the counties) and so the prisoners therein more subject to any local inconvenience which by contagion or other accident may befall that place, remediable only by writs of *habeas corpus* heretofore, now and then, with much difficulty and very sparingly granted to some few prisoners for some time suitable to the weight and urgency of their then necessary occasions.

That by reason of a complaint of the abuse of some persons having had the benefit of the said writ, all the prisoners now there for debt are most unseasonably thereof restrained, to the imminent hazard of their lives, the sickness so reigning in and about the City of London.

That in so much as the just and moderate use of the said writs has been and is duly found to have enabled divers debtors to pay or compound their debts, to the great benefit of the creditors themselves and saving of many debtors' estates which else had been irrecoverably ruined; and for that this time of humiliation, under the heavy hand of God, begs at the hand of man the duties of mercy and compassion.

Their most humble suit to this great council is that it (in imitation of that great God of mercy who forgets not his prisoners and who has hitherto preserved this prison and the others in this city from the infection) would favorably be pleased mercifully to visit the said prison by moving the honorable and venerable judges who have his Majesty's delegated power in the fitting dispensation of those writs, out of the consideration of the present necessity which is the law of time, to give now a more free and liberal way to the most needful and pressing use of the same for the likely preserving of many persons who lie pestered in this prison, whose lives the petitioners hope will be held precious in the eyes of so religious and honorable a senate. The rather for that so pious an act, besides the opportunity thereof being now truly *opus diei in die suo*, cannot be but a most acceptable and expiatory service to that good God, who prefers such deeds of mercy and compassion far above and before all sacrifice, and will forever bind the petitioners with many hundreds depending on them to pray for a rich blessing upon your persons and consultations.

Miserationem perdere miseris ultimu est.

Prayers

Lords excused   102(2)

L. 1a. An act for the increase of
   shipping and for free liberty
   of **fishing**   102(2), *1/7;
                                           11/8

L. 1a. An act against forging and
   counterfeiting of the **seals** of
   the King's courts   102, *11/8

EARL OF NORTHAMPTON: reports
   his answer to the petition
   exhibited last session by
   Henry **Williams**   102

Petition of Henry Williams: read   102(2)

Report from the committee on
   the petition of the **prisoners
   in the Fleet** concerning *habeas*

corpus (VISCOUNT
   MANDEVILLE, L. President)   102, *6/7

Message to the Commons desiring
   a conference on the petition
   of the **prisoners in the Fleet**
   and returning the bill for the
   further restraint of **tippling**
   in inns, alehouses, etc. (Sir
   Thomas Coventry, Att.
   General, and Sir Humphrey
   Davenport)   102(2), *5/7

Report of the Commons' answer
   to the message: they will send
   answer by messengers of
   their own   102(2)

House adjourned   102(2)

THURSDAY, 7 JULY 1625

I. JOURNAL OF THE HOUSE OF LORDS

[L.J. 459]

[p. 47] *Die Jovis, vizt., septimo die Julii 1625*
[*List of Lords; see A.T.*]

Excused: E. of Lincoln, E. of Leicester, E. of Devonshire, L. Bp. of Ely, L. De La Warr.

Hodie 1ª vice lecta est billa, An act for the maintenance and increase of shipping and navigation, and for the free liberty of fishing and fishing voyages to be made and performed in and upon the seas, seacoasts, and places of Newfoundland, Virginia, New England, and other the seas, seacoasts, and parts of America.

The Lord President of Wales (the EARL OF NORTHAMPTON) reported to the House his answer to the reference of the petition exhibited the last session by Henry Williams against Sir Thomas Middleton, Knight, *vizt.,* That the complaint consisted of a riot, pardoned by the late King's general pardon, and of a title to land which will not hold plea before his Lordship.[1]

Whereupon the second petition of the said Henry Williams was read (exhibited this session), and answered: The petitioner is to take his course by law and to trouble this House no more, otherwise he is to be committed.

The LORD PRESIDENT reported the opinion of the Lords committees of the petition of the prisoners of the Fleet to be that a conference be prayed with the Commons therein.

[p. 48] Message sent to the Commons accordingly by Mr. Attorney General and Mr. Serjeant Davenport.

[L.J. 460] And the bill for the further restraint of tippling in inns, alehouses, and other victualling houses was returned by them to the Commons with a schedule thereunto annexed by the Lords.

Answered: They are now employed in business of great weight and importance which will hold them long;[2] and they will send answer touching the conference required by messengers of their own.

[*Notice of Adjournment*]

II. MINUTE BOOK, H.L.R.O., M.M., 1625

[f. 34v] *Die Jovis 7° die Julii 1625.*
[*List of Lords Present; see A.T.*]

Excused:
Bishop Ely by Bishop of Llandaff.
E. Devonshire by Lord Grey of G[roby].
L. De La Warr by Lord Darcy.
E. of Exeter by E. of Clare.
E. of Lincoln by Northampton.

Hodie 1ª vice lecta est billa, An act concerning fishing and increase of shipping, etc.

Hodie 1ª vice lecta est billa, An act against the counterfeiting of the King's courts in Westminster, etc.[3]

[f. 35] The petition of Henry Williams read.

Mr. Attorney and Mr. Davenport with a message to the Commons to consider of a petition of the prisoners of the Fleet touching *habeas corpus,* etc., to meet presently near the Painted Chamber.

Answer: the message delivered; that they are in serious business now; that/

Adjourned. 9 tomorrow.

---

1. Upon the report from the committee for petitions on 28 May 1624 (*L.J.,* III, 416), the petition of Henry Williams complaining against Sir Thomas Middleton, the younger, was referred to the Lord President and Council of Wales. The report of the Earl of Northampton's response to the petition is included in the H.L.R.O., Main Papers, H.L., 7 July 1625. We are unable to find either the 1624 or 1625 petition of Hen-

ry Williams.
2. The Lower House was engaged in a discussion of Richard Montagu this day. See below, H. of C., 7 July, O.B.
3. The first reading of the bill against forging and counterfeiting of the seals of the King's courts was not entered in the L.J. It was read for the second time and committed by the Lords on 11 August.

Prayers

LORD KEEPER (Bp. of Lincoln):
concerning the bill for the
Earl of Dorset   105, *5/7

L. 3a. An act for the Earl of
Dorset touching lands
appointed to be sold by
Richard, late Earl of Dorset,
to pay his debts, etc.:
assented to   104, 105

The Earl of Dorset's bill sent
down to the Commons (Sir
Henry Finch and Sir
Humphrey Davenport)   104, 105

LORD KEEPER (Bp. of Lincoln):
the King will receive the
petition concerning religion
this afternoon   104, *1/7

Committee to join with Commons
in delivering the petition
concerning religion: member
added [see below]   104

Message from the Commons
bringing a bill for the grant
of two entire **subsidies** by the
temporalty (Sir Thomas
Edmondes and others)   104

L. 1a. The above bill for the
subsidies [see below]   104, 105, *11/7

Message from the Commons
(Lord Cavendish and others)
concerning: 104, 105
    a conference on the
    petition of the **prisoners in
    the Fleet**;   *6/7
    the delivery of the
    **petition concerning
    religion** [see above and
    below];
and bringing:
    A bill that this **session** of
    parliament shall not
    determine by royal assent
    to one or more acts [see
    below]

L. 2a and L. 3a. An act for the

grant of two entire **subsidies**
by the temporalty [see above
and below]   104, 105

Edward **Hayne** and his attorney
brought in: Hayne's case to
be heard at the next sitting of
parliament   104, 105, *6/7

Message to the Commons
concerning the delivery of
the **petition concerning
religion** (Sir Thomas
Coventry, Att. General, and
Sir Humphrey Davenport)
[see above]   105

Report of the Commons' answer
to the message: their
committee shall be ready for
delivering the petition   105

L. 1a and L. 2a. An act that this
session of parliament shall
not determine by royal assent
to one or more acts:
committed [see above and
below]   105(2), *9/7;
                                            11/7

Bill for the grant of two entire
subsidies by the temporalty:
put to the question and
assented to [see above]   104, 106

Report from the committee on
the bill that this **session** of
parliament shall not
determine by royal assent to
one or more acts   105

Amendment to the above bill:
read twice and allowed   105

L. 3a. An act that this session of
parliament shall not
determine by royal assent to
one or more acts: assented to   105, 106

Message to the Commons sending
down the above bill (Sir
Henry Finch and Sir
Humphrey Davenport)   105, 106

House adjourned   105, 106

FRIDAY, 8 JULY 1625

I. JOURNAL OF THE HOUSE OF LORDS

[**L.J.** 460]
[p. 49] *Die Veneris, vizt., octavo die Julii
1625*
[*List of Lords; see A.T.*]

Hodie 3ª vice lecta est billa, concerning the
lands of the Earl of Dorset.

Put to the question and assented unto.

And sent down to the Commons by Mr.
Serjeant Finch and Mr. Serjeant Davenport.

The LORD KEEPER related to the House
that the Lord Steward signified unto him
late last night that his Majesty will admit the
committees of both Houses to deliver the
petition touching religion this day, at
Hampton Court, at three in the afternoon;
and that his Lordship did presently take
order with the Clerk to give their Lordships[1] notice thereof, craved pardon that
he did it without direction of the House.

The names of the Lords committees for
delivery of the said petition being read, the
Lord Grey of Warke is added, for that the
Lord Sheffield is absent and sent his
excuse.[2]

[**L.J.** 461] *Hodie allata est a domo communi
per Thomam Edmonds, Chr. et alios, billa,* An

act for the grant of two entire subsidies
granted by the temporalty.

*Hodie 1ª, 2ᵈᵃ, et 3ª vice lecta est billa praedic-
ta,* and put to the question and generally
assented unto.

*Memorandum: Quod hodie Edwardus Hayne,
Generosus, executor testamenti Thomae Hayne,
nuper de Upway in comitatu Dorset, senioris,
Generosi ponit Thomam Ventris attornatum
suum in breve de errore versus Thomam Crouch,
Generosum, de placito transgressionis et ejectione
firmae.*

*Et superinde venit praedictus Thomas Ventris,
et assignavit errores in judicio dato in curia regis,
pro dicto Thoma Crouch, versus dictum Edwar-
dum Hayne in placito praedicto.*

*Super quod ordinatum est, quod exeat breve de
scire facias pro dicto Edwardo Hayne, vicecomiti
Dorset directum ad praemuniendum praedictum
Thomam Crouch, etc., retornatum immediate
coram magnatibus in parliamento domini regis.*

*Errores praedicti patent in faleaciis hujus
parliamenti.*[3]

Message from the House of Commons by
the Lord Cavendish and others: That the
House of Commons had sent up to the
Lords a bill entitled An act that this session
of parliament shall not determine by his
Majesty's royal assent to this and some
other acts.

---

1. I.e., the Lords appointed on 6 July to the committee for delivering the petition concerning religion to
the King. According to the Roll of Standing Orders,
no. 2, the Lord Keeper "is not to adjourn the House or
do any thing else, as mouth of the House, without the
consent of the Lords first had".

2. For the committee of eight originally appointed
by the Lords to deliver the petition, see L. J., above, 6
July, pp. 96–97; for the changes in the committee, see
above, 6 July, n. 12.

3. The record concerning Hayne's case had been
brought into the House by Sir Ranulphe Crew on 6
July. See above, p. 95 and n. 1. It was agreed this day (8
July) by the House that Hayne and his attorney should
be heard at the next sitting of parliament. See below,
H.L.R.O., M.M., 1625.

The above memorandum concerning Hayne reads:

That today Edward Hayne, Gentleman, by testament executor of Thomas Hayne, the elder, Gentleman, lately of Upway, county Dorset, makes
Thomas Ventris his attorney in a writ of error
against Thomas Crouch, Gentleman, of a plea of
trespass and *ejectione firmae.*

And besides, the aforesaid Thomas Ventris comes
and assigns errors in the judgment made in the
King's Bench for the said Thomas Crouch against
the said Edward Hayne in the aforesaid plea.

Upon which order issues a writ of *scire facias* for
the said Edward Hayne directed to the sheriff of
Dorset to warn the aforesaid Thomas Crouch, etc.,
returnable immediately into the great court in the
parliament of the lord King.

The abovesaid errors are obvious in their fallacy
at this parliament.

With this message, *vizt.*, that they are now ready for the conference required by the Lords touching the petition for *habeas corpus*, etc.[4]

And with this intimation, that whereas the Lords and they have appointed committees to deliver a petition to his Majesty at such time as his Majesty shall be pleased to admit them to his presence, they do expect to hear from this House what time it has pleased his Majesty to appoint for the same, as was promised by their Lordships.

Answered: That the Lords have appointed the conference touching the petition for *habeas corpus*, etc., tomorrow morning, at eight, in the Painted Chamber.

That they will send answer as touching the time appointed by his Majesty for delivery of the petition touching religion by messengers of their own.

Message sent to the Commons by Mr. Attorney General and Mr. Serjeant Davenport: That his Majesty has signified his pleasure to this House that the committees of both Houses attend him at Hampton Court at three this afternoon for delivery of the said petition.

Answered: That their committee shall be ready to attend accordingly.

Hodie 1ª et 2ᵈᵃ vice lecta est billa, An act that this session of parliament shall not determine by his Majesty's royal assent to this and some other acts.

Committed to the Lo. Treasurer [and] L. President, to consider of it presently; who reported one amendment to be necessary. The said amendment was twice read and allowed of.

Hodie 3ⁱᵃ vice lecta est billa praedicta; put to the question and generally assented unto, with the said amendment.

And the said bill was returned to the

Commons by Mr. Serjeant Finch and Mr. Serjeant Davenport.

[Notice of Adjournment]

II. MINUTE BOOK, H.L.R.O., M.M., 1625

[f. 35v] *Die Veneris 8 Julii 1625.*
[*List of Lords Present; see A.T.*]

LORD KEEPER certified the House that the Lord Keeper received a letter from the Lord Russell who averred the consent of the Lady.[5]

Hodie 3ª vice lecta est billa, An act for the Earl of Dorset, etc.
Put to the question and passed.

This bill was presently sent down to the Commons.

[f. 36] *Hodie 1ª vice lecta est billa*, An act for the subsidy of the temporalty, etc.

A message from the Commons, L. Cavendish and others: That though they were not ready yesterday to confer touching the petition of *habeas corpus*, etc.; and whereas there is a present petition to be offered to the King by both Houses, they have received no direction from his Majesty and therefore cannot go with their Lordships.

Hodie 2ª vice lecta est billa, An act for the subsidy of the temporalty, etc.
Hodie 3ª vice lecta est billa, An act for the subsidy of the temporalty.

Hayne and his attorney brought in and he to have audience *ad audiendum errores* at the next sitting in parliament.

Hodie 1ª vice lecta est billa, An act that this session of parliament may not determine business depending in court.

[f. 36v] *Hodie 2ª vice lecta est billa*, An act that this session of parliament shall not de-

---

4. I.e., the conference on the petition of prisoners in the Fleet, requested by the Lords on 7 July.

5. See above, p. 98 and n. 11.

termine by his Majesty's royal assent to some special acts.

The bill of the subsidy put to the question and passed.[6]

6. It is unclear why the voting on the subsidy bill did not occur immediately after the third reading of the bill earlier this day. The names of the Lord Treasurer and Lord President, below this entry in the H.L.R.O.,

L. Treasurer
L. President

Billa eadem 3ª vice lecta et missa communibus.

Adjourned. 9 tomorrow.

M.M., 1625, refer to the committee appointed to consider the bill concerning the end of this session of parliament (see above, L.J.).

SATURDAY, 9 JULY 1625

I. JOURNAL OF THE HOUSE OF LORDS

[L.J. 461]
[p. 51] *Die Sabbati, vizt., nono die Julii 1625*
[*List of Lords; see A.T.*]
[L.J. 462]

The Lord Bishop of Winchester (in absence of the Lord Archbishop of Canterbury), being the eldest bishop now present of the province of Canterbury,[1] presented to the House the subsidies granted unto the King by the clergy of that diocese.

The Lord Bishop of Rochester excused.

Mr. Serjeant Finch and Mr. Serjeant Davenport returned answer that they had delivered to the Commons the bill touching the adjournment of the parliament.[2]

Message from the Commons by Sir Thomas Edmondes and others:[3] They presented to the Lords the bill of subsidy of tonnage and poundage. That they are now ready for the conference required by their Lordships touching the petition of the prisoners of the Fleet for *habeas corpus,* etc., and do desire another conference also with their Lordships touching the recess of this parliament to be by the same committee, if it shall so please their Lordships.

Answered: The Lords are ready for both the conferences desired to be presently in the Painted Chamber.

The LORD PRESIDENT reported to the House: That the committee of both Houses yesterday delivered[4] the petition touching religion unto the King and that his Majesty promised a speedy answer thereunto.

His Lordship added that the King takes notice of the thinness of this House and that his pleasure is that they which are present do not depart.

[p. 52] The LORD PRESIDENT also reported: That the committees for privileges, etc., had considered of the petition exhibited by Ralph Brooke, York Herald, at large, which petition has these five particular points, *vizt.:*

1.[5] That the Earl Marshal committed him to prison for that on the 27th of March last he attended in his Herald's coat to perform his office to proclaim the King.

2ly. That the Earl Marshal had sequestered him from his office and the profits thereof.

3ly. That, he preferring a bill into the Chancery for his fees, the Earl Marshal committed him to the Marshalsea.

4ly. That the Earl Marshal caused his study of books to be locked up.

5ly. That the Earl Marshal stayed all his proceedings at common law for recovery of his right.

These particulars their Lordships examined and found that York had gone through all courts with it. They heard York and his counsel at full and it appeared to their Lordships to be a very sharp invective petition against the Earl Marshal, but very false and untrue in all points.

Wherefore they are of opinion that the petitioner deserves to be severely punished for exhibiting such a false and scandalous petition against a member of this House.

Their Lordships thought it fit also that York's lawyer suffer rebuke,[6] for that he could not but know these particulars to be

---

1. I.e., Lancelot Andrewes, born in 1555. *D.N.B.*

2. I.e., An act that this session of parliament shall not determine by his Majesty's royal assent to any act or acts of parliament.

3. According to the H.L.R.O., M.M., 1625, below, the message was delivered by Lord Cavendish, not Edmondes. Cavendish reported the answer to the Lower

House. See H. of C., 9 July, p. 359.

4. MS.: *did yesterday delivered.*

5. *1.* is omitted in the printed edition. Brooke's petition is printed above, 1 July, p. 81.

6. The accounts of Brooke's case do not reveal the identity of his lawyer.

false and yet, from time to time, he gave him his advice and was of his counsel to speak for him.

The House taking this into consideration agreed that the lawyer shall receive a public reproof.

And York having been at the bar and heard what he could speak for himself, the Lords agreed on their censure.

And then, York being brought to the bar again, the LORD KEEPER pronounced the same against him, *in haec verba, vizt.:*

That he shall make his submission to the Earl Marshal here at the bar.

That he shall be imprisoned in the Tower during pleasure.

That he shall be fined at a thousand marks.

York being withdrawn, and having considered of the submission he was to make, and subscribed the same with his hand, he was again brought to the bar and read it *in haec verba, vizt.:*[7]

My Lords, I am very sorry that I have offended this honorable House in general and the Earl Marshal in particular by the delivery of this scandalous petition which I acknowledge to be untrue in the particulars which this most honorable House has so adjudged, and I acknowledge your Lordships' censure against me for the same to be most honorable and just. Ralph Brooke, York Herald.

York being withdrawn, the EARL MARSHAL gave the House all hearty thanks

for clearing his honor of this false aspersion. And he often and earnestly besought their Lordships that the rest of the sentence against York might be pardoned.

[**L.J.** 463] Which being granted, and York brought to the bar again, the LORD KEEPER told him that the Lords are pleased (at the earnest entreaty of the Earl Marshal) to pardon the rest of the sentence against him, both for the imprisonment and fine.

For which York humbly thanked all their Lordships, and the Earl Marshal in particular.

Hodie 1ᵃ vice lecta est billa, An act for a subsidy of tonnage and poundage.

Moved by the EARL OF CLARE, and agreed, that if any servant of the nobility be imprisoned (contrary to the privileges) after the recess of this parliament, that the Lord Keeper shall deliver him out of prison upon a *habeas corpus,* etc., as if the parliament were sitting.[8]

[p. 53] The petition of John Evelyn was read, desiring to be paid one thousand seven hundred pounds arrear unto him for his monthly provision of powder and for the constant payment of his monthly provision of gunpowder hereafter, for else he shall not be able to provide the same.[9]

Answered: The Lords do recommend the petitioner unto the care of the Lord Treasurer to see him paid, and withal do wish the Council of War that if any money of the last subsidy be undisposed, this petitioner may be remembered.[10]

---

7. *vizt.* is omitted in the printed edition.

8. Sections 41 and 42 of the Roll of Standing Orders define the nature of privilege. See also, above, 27 June, n. 8. An order was to be drawn and signed by the Clerk to assure the continuance of the privileges during the time of adjournment. See H.L.R.O., M.M., 1625, below.

9. We are unable to find Evelyn's petition. John Evelyn held a special license for the collecting and processing of saltpeter. 2 *Jac.* I, pt. 7, MS. Cal. Pat. Rolls, f. 117. In April 1624 Prince Charles and a committee of the Upper House for viewing and supplying stores of arms and munitions had prepared a contract to be

made with Evelyn whereby he was to furnish the King's ordnance with twenty lasts of gunpowder per month for three years. Following the prorogation of the 1624 parliament, the Privy Council gave authority to the Duke of Buckingham, Lord Admiral, and others to conclude the contract with Evelyn. *A.P.C., 1623–1625,* pp. 229–230. According to the account of the disbursement of the subsidy monies, 1,700*l.* per month had been regularly paid to Evelyn for the gunpowder through May 1625. *Cal. S.P. Dom., Addenda, 1625–1649,* pp. 24–25.

10. The debt to Evelyn remained unpaid at the end of August 1625 and Evelyn refused to supply further

The petition thus answered, was re-delivered unto him.

The LORD PRESIDENT reported the conference with the Commons touching the petition of the prisoners for *habeas corpus,* etc., *vizt.:* That they render unto the Lords all hearty thanks, that they are pleased to confer with them herein; that they conceive the prisoner's liberty upon *habeas corpus,* etc., without the assent of all his creditors, to be against law; and has been much abused by many prisoners insomuch that they have prepared a bill to be presented to their Lordships against it; and that they had concluded nothing upon the petition.[11]

He reported also that the Commons do humbly desire the Lords that the recess may be on Monday next.

Agreed, that the Lord President do move his Majesty herein, and to express the earnest desire of the Lords and Commons that the recess may be on that day.

Whereas in the last session of parliament there was a bill exhibited by John Edwards, the younger, against John Edwards, the elder, to reverse a decree obtained in the Court of Requests, the which bill was read and committed but, by reason of the shortness of time, it could not be any further proceeded in and therefore the Lords spiritual and temporal in the Upper House of parliament assembled did then refer the consideration thereof to the Lord Bishop of Bangor, Mr. Baron Bromley, Mr. Justice Hutton, and Mr. Justice Chamberlain, or any three of them, whereof the Bishop of Bangor to be one, to mediate an end and determine the differences between them, if they could, or else to certify the House of their opinion the next session. The LORD BISHOP OF BANGOR did this day report unto the House how far they had proceeded herein as by the said report appears.[12]

Whereupon it is this day ordered that in respect of the adjournment of this session which now draws to an end, the committees shall have further time and power unto the next access of parliament to hear this matter again if they be requested thereunto by either of the said parties and to alter or otherwise order any thing therein as they shall think fit upon the rehearing of both parties.

The Earl of Clare, the Lord Bishop of Bangor, and the Lord Wentworth are appointed to dispose of the money in the poor's box and of the money collected at the fast.

The petition of Richard Culpeper, servant to the Lord Cromwell, was read, desiring to be released of his imprisonment in execution for three hundred pounds odd money recovered against him upon a *nihil dicit* for a battery.[13]

Referred to be considered by the Lords

---

powder until he received payment of the arrears. In a letter to Secretary Conway, 26 August, Sir John Coke reports that: "Another thing whereof I gave notice to the Lord Admiral is the want of powder, there being (as some of the officers tell me) not above 80 lasts in the Tower for all occasions that may fall out, and Mr. Evelyn ceasing to make further provision for want of due payment for the proportions he had delivered heretofore. . . . that the King is already in his debt 2,550*l.* for powder and that the Lord Treasurer, howsoever he has been pressed by the Council of War, by the Lord Admiral, by the Upper House of Parliament, and by the King himself, yet has directly answered that there be no monies for him". S.P. 16/5:85.

11. For debate in the Commons on the petition of the prisoners in the Fleet following the report of this conference, see H. of C., 9 July, pp. 360–361, 363–364.

12. The bill concerning the Edwardses, father and son, had been brought up from the Lower House on 20 May 1624, first read on 22 May, and second read and committed on 26 May (*L.J.,* III, 393, 402, 408). Upon the report from the committee on the bill, finding that "right is in the son, equity in the father", the House referred the bill to the consideration of the Bishop of Bangor and the three judges (ibid., 414). For a brief account of the Bishop of Bangor's report, see H.L.R.O., M.M., 1625, below. See also, below, n. 17.

13. We are unable to find Culpeper's petition. The same or a very similar petition from Culpeper was read in the Upper House at the end of the Oxford session (12 August 1625) and was referred to the Lord Keeper. See below, p. 183 and n. 1.

subcommittees for privileges, etc., and their Lordships to certify whether his case be within the privilege or no.

[*Notice of Adjournment*]

Retornatae sunt a domo communi quattuor billae. Exped.
1. To enable the King to make leases of the duchy land of Cornwall.
2. For the further restraint of tippling.
3. That this session shall not determine by the royal assent unto this and some other acts.
4. Confirmation of the customs, etc., of the King's tenants of Cheltenham.

These bills were brought after the House was up and the Clerk received them, being to carry them and other bills to the King next morning.

II. MINUTE BOOK, H.L.R.O., M.M., 1625

[f. 37] *Die Sabbathi 9° die Julii 1625*
[*List of Lords Present; see A.T.*]

L. Bishop of Winchester delivered the subsidy of the clergy to the L. Keeper.

These Lords subscribed were added to the Lords committees touching the petition of the prisoners of the Fleet.
E. Marshal
Viscount Rochford
L. Darcy
L. Grey, both
L. Robartes

Rochester excused by the Bishop of St. Davids.

Serjeant Finch and Serjeant Davenport delivered the bill of continuing the acts.

[f. 37v] A message by the Lord Cavendish: That the Commons have sent the bill of tonnage and poundage; and desire a conference touching the petition of the prisoners of the Fleet; and lastly, they de-

sire a conference touching the recess of this present parliament.

L. PRESIDENT. That the Lords committees attended the King's Majesty; that they were presently admitted to his presence and the petition was presently read quite through by Mr. Attorney General.

L. PRESIDENT, the report of [the] York [Herald]: That he has waded through many courts in this cause; that there are many scandalous words against the E. Marshal and not any one word true. The opinion of the committees: that he be imprisoned during the pleasure of the House, a fine, and a satisfaction by submission. They reproved the counsel, and for York to have punishment they thought, if it fit.

[f. 38] York's censure.
The opinion of the Lords committees:
To be imprisoned in the Tower during the pleasure of the House.
Put to the question and passed.
To be fined in the sum of 1,000 marks.
Put to the question and passed.
To make his submission here at the bar to the E. Marshal and to the House, which he did in writing under his hand.

Hodie 1ª vice lecta est billa, An act for the subsidy of tonnage and poundage.

Nota. The petition of George Mathew to be privileged in regard of a writ of error depending in court.[14] And was to be privileged from this rising to the next meeting.

Order. An order to be drawn up and signed by the Clerk to certify the continuance of the privileges from this rising to the next meeting.[15]

The petition of John Evelyn, his Majesty's gunpowder maker, to have a direction here to have 1,700 *l.* already due and for such other sums as may be due hereafter.[16]

14. We are unable to find Mathew's petition.
15. See above, n. 8.

16. See above, nn. 9 and 10.

Order. Ordered that the petitioner and petition be recommended to the Lord Treasurer.

[f. 38v] L. BISHOP OF BANGOR reported the business between Edwards and Edwards. That he and the lord judges that were to consider of the cause jointly with him have, with much pains, drawn up a report. But since that time we were desired to rehear the cause but never heard of any of them since and therefore desire that report may be cer[tified] into the court and read.[17]

Order. That the parties have leave between this and the next meeting to be heard further, if any party desire it.

York brought to the bar.

L. KEEPER. That you have exhibited a scandalous petition against the E. Marshal. That in the petition you have insisted upon five several points where you have laid much aspersion upon the E. Marshal.

And for his offense he is to be censured.

The censure pronounced as afore it is entered.

That he is sorry for his fault and does in general acknowledge it to the House and, in particular, to the E. Marshal, a member of this House.

Upon the E. Marshal's petition to the House on the behalf of York, the fine and imprisonment was released after his submission made at the bar.

L. PRESIDENT to wait on the King to desire the King earnestly that the Houses rise on Monday next.

[f. 39] The petition of Richard Culpeper, servant [to] the Lord Cromwell.

This petition referred to the Lords committees for privileges.[18]

Adjourned. 7 Monday next.

17. The original report on the Edwardses' cause drawn up by Bangor and the judges on 12 June 1624 and presented to the House this day (9 July 1625) is in the H.L.R.O., Main Papers, H.L., 9 July 1625. The following copy of a decision by Bangor and his committee of judges on 2 June 1625 to rehear the cause is inserted in the H.L.R.O., M.M., 1625, as f. 73v:

Inter Johannem Edwards, Jun., et Johannem Edwards, Sr., sen deftem.

Upon the solicitation of Mr. Edwards, the elder, we are to [sic] content to rehear what can be said against our former order. And do therefore appoint both parties, with their counsel or solicitors, to at-

tend us upon the 25th day of this instant June, at Serjeants' Inn Hall, in Chancery Lane, about two of the clock in the afternoon. 2° Junii 1625.

Lewis, Bangor
Edward Bromley
Richard Hutton

This was written out of the original brought me by Mr. Hutton, who keeps it.

18. According to the L.J., above, Culpeper's petition was referred to a subcommittee of the committee of privileges for them to certify whether the case "be within the privilege or no".

HOUSE OF LORDS
ORDER OF BUSINESS   MONDAY, 11 JULY 1625

Prayers

L. 1a, 2a, and *3a.* An act for confirmation of **subsidies** granted by the **clergy**: assented to [*see below*]   116, 121

Message to the Commons sending down the above bill (Sir George Croke and Sir Henry Yelverton)   116, 121

Message from the Commons bringing the above bill (Sir Edward Coke and others)   116, 121

LORD KEEPER (Bp. of Lincoln): whether Lords pleased to have a report concerning the **recess**   121, *9/7

Granted by the House that the report on the recess be given   121

Report that the King has granted the recess to begin this day (VISCOUNT MANDEVILLE, L. President)   116, 121

Message to the Commons desiring a conference by committees concerning the King's answer touching the recess (Sir Thomas Coventry, Att. General, and Sir Humphrey Davenport)   116, 121

LORD CONWAY: on the recess and the King's necessities   116, 121

Report of the Commons' answer to the message: the Commons' committee will attend the conference presently   116

Committee for conference concerning the recess: appointed   116, 121

EARL OF WARWICK   121

Petition of Thomas **Hayne**, servant of the Earl of Suffolk: read   116, 121, 122, *10/8; 11/8

[*Hayne's petition is printed on pp. 122–123*]

Hayne's petition referred to a subcommittee of the committee of **privileges**   116, 122

EARL OF ARUNDEL AND SURREY (E. Marshal): concerning **attendance** at the next session   122

Ordered: the House to be fully attended at the next session   117

Viscount Mandeville (L. President) and Earl of Arundel and Surrey (E. Marshal) to move the King not to grant license unto any to be absent   122

Message to the Commons: that the King has sent his **royal assent** to the bills passed this session and has sent a **commission for the adjournment** of parliament, and desire Commons to come up to hear them read (Sir Thomas Coventry, Att. General, and Sir Humphrey Davenport) [*see below*]   117, 122

Report of the Commons' answer to the message: they will return an answer presently by messengers of their own   117, 122

Message from the Commons: they will attend to hear the letters patent for the royal assent but will not stay to hear the commission for the adjournment read (Sir Edward Coke and others)   117, 122

Lords agree that the Commons may depart after hearing the letters patent for the royal assent   117

Commons come up to the Lords House   117

Sir Thomas Crew (Speaker): presents the bill for the grant of two entire **subsidies** and divers other bills unto which they desire the King's assent [*see below*]   117, 122, *8/7

Message from the King: on the answer to the **petition concerning religion** and on the **adjournment** of the

MONDAY, 11 JULY 1625

I. JOURNAL OF THE HOUSE OF LORDS

[L.J. 463]

[p. 55] *Die Lunae, viz., undecimo die Julii 1625*
[*List of Lords; see A.T.*]

[L.J. 464]

Hodie 1ᵃ, 2ᵃ, et 3ᵃ vice lecta est billa, An act for confirmation of the subsidies granted by the clergy.

Put to the question and assented unto generally.

Sent to the Commons by Mr. Justice Croke and Mr. Justice Yelverton. Returned from the Commons.

The LORD PRESIDENT reported: That his Majesty according to the earnest desires of both Houses has grant[ed] the recess from parliament to be on this day.

Message sent to the Commons by Mr. Attorney General and Mr. Serjeant Davenport: That the Lords have received his Majesty's answer touching the recess from parliament which they are willing to impart unto them by a committee of four if the Commons shall think fit to appoint a committee of their House to meet for that purpose in the Painted Chamber presently.[1]

Answered: Their committee shall attend their Lordships presently.

Lords appointed for the committee:

L. President	L. Wentworth
L. Bp. of London	L. Carey of Leppington

Upon the reading of the petition of Thomas Hayne, servant to the Right Honorable the Earl of Suffolk, desiring to be relieved against John Parham, Esquire, for putting him out of the possession [p. 56] of his house and lands (at Martin's town, in the county of Dorset) during the time of privilege of parliament, a great part of the said land being then sown by him with corn, it is ordered that the examination of breach of privilege be referred to the Lords subcommittees for privileges, etc., at the next access; and that the Lord Keeper of the Great Seal do write unto two of the next justices of the peace to sequester the crop of corn sown by the petitioner; and that the said Parham and Hayne do appear before the said Lords subcommittees at the next access; and the Clerk to write unto the said Parham to appear accordingly.[2]

The LORD CONWAY signified unto the Lords: That his Majesty takes knowledge of the two subsidies now granted unto him, which he does most graciously accept of, but the necessities of the present affairs are such that they cannot rest there, but their further counsels are to be had therein.[3] The late King, of famous memory, was provoked beyond his nature to undertake a war by breaking of the two treaties of the Match and the Palatinate.[4] It appeared then by computation that the war to recover the Palatinate would cost seven hundred thousand pounds per annum. Wherefore his Majesty, considering the necessities to

---

1. For the committee of eight appointed by the Commons, see H. of C., 11 July, p. 368.

2. Hayne's petition is printed below, p. 122. For the subcommittee's membership, see below, 10 August, p. 177. And for the subcommittee's report on Hayne's case, see below, H. of L., 11 August, O.B. The case came up again on 22 May and 12 June 1626 (*L.J.,* III, 648, 675) and on 30 May, 17 and 25 June 1628, when it was still not resolved (ibid., 831, 860, 875). Concerning a related petition from Edward Hayne, see above, 6 July, p. 95 and n. 1, and 8 July, n. 3. A draft of a letter from the Lord Keeper to the justices of the peace concerning sequestering the corn is annexed to Thomas Hayne's petition in H.L.R.O., Main Papers, H.L., 11 July 1625.

3. A similar message from the King requesting further counsels and more subsidy was delivered by Conway to Sir John Coke and presented by Coke to the Lower House later this day. See H. of C., 11 July, O.B. Details of the war expenditures are included in the reports given to both Houses on 9 August of the speeches of the Duke of Buckingham and Lord Ley, L. Treasurer, delivered at Christ Church Hall the previous day. See below, H. of L., 9 August, O.B., and H. of C., 9 August, O.B. For the account of the disbursements of the 1624 subsidy monies, see *Cal. S.P. Dom., Addenda, 1625–1649,* pp. 23–27.

4. For background concerning the broken treaties and England's foreign affairs, see above, 18 June, n. 5.

uphold the Low Countries, and to prevent the enterprise of the Emperor from concluding with the princes of Germany utterly to exclude his son-in-law,[5] levied an army under Count Mansfeld in which France, Savoy, and Venice joined for a war of diversion. This procured the kings of Denmark and Sweden and the princes of Germany to levy another army wherein his Majesty joins. Much more money has been spent in these, and in preparing the fleet, than the subsidies now and formerly granted came to. And yet the charges of Mansfeld's and Denmark's armies for the upholding of the Low Countries and setting out of the fleet must be continued. Wherefore his Majesty, considering the danger of this place, has granted a recess at their requests, but his necessities require their further counsels herein.

[L. J. 465] The Lords, considering that his Majesty's necessities (as was delivered by the Lord Conway) required so sudden an access to parliament again, for their further counsels and assistance therein, did order that the House be fully attended by all the Lords in general at the next access, and agreed that the King be moved not to grant license unto any to be absent, and declared their opinion that his Majesty's proclamation touching the access, commanding the personal appearance of the Lords at the day and place prefixed, determines all former licenses to be absent, and their proxies.[6]

Message to the Commons by Mr. Attorney General and Mr. Serjeant Davenport: That his Majesty has sent his letters patent of his royal assent unto the acts passed this parliament, and a commission for the adjournment of the parliament to a further time.[7] That the Commons be pleased to come with their Speaker to hear them read.

Answered: They will send an answer by messengers of their own.

Message from the Commons by the Lord Cavendish and others:[8] That whereas the Lords have sent them word of his Majesty's letters patent for the royal assent, and of his commission to adjourn the parliament, and required them to come to hear them read, they will most willingly attend to hear the letters patent for the royal assent, and humbly desire that they may not stay to hear the commission read for the adjournment, [p. 57] but that they may (without offense unto their Lordships) depart to adjourn themselves according to their use and the privilege of their House.[9]

This said, the messengers departed, and the Lords agreed that the Commons might freely depart after the letters patent for the royal assent is read.

The Commons being come and their Speaker at the bar, he said: May it please your Lordships, the knights, citizens, and burgesses of the Commons House of parliament, as the first fruits of their love, do humbly present two subsidies granted unto his Majesty (whereof they crave acceptance), together with divers bills unto which they desire his Majesty's royal assent.[10]

Then the Lord Keeper declared that he had a short message from his Majesty to deliver unto the Lords and Commons:

5. Frederick, Elector Palatine. See below, H. of C., 20 June, n. 5.

6. Both the King's commission (see below, p. 120) and his proclamation for the adjournment (printed in *Stuart Proclamations*, II, 48–49) called for the personal appearance at the Oxford session of all Lords spiritual and temporal and all M.P.s.

7. The royal assent by letters patent and the commission are printed below.

8. According to the H.L.R.O., M.M., 1625, and the H. of C. accounts, below, Sir Edward Coke carried the message.

9. Concerning the Commons' power to adjourn themselves, see the debate and action on this issue in 1621. *C.D. 1621*, IV, 384–385, 402–404; V, 202–203, 398; *C.J.*, I, 634–635, 639. See also, Coke, *Fourth Inst.*, pp. 27–28.

10. Concerning the presentation of the subsidy bill, see H. of C., 11 July, n. 8.

That whereas a petition was lately delivered him from both Houses, touching religion, unto which he gave a present gracious answer, he is now pleased to return a more particular answer, *vizt.*, an assurance of his Majesty's real performance of every part of that petition.[11]

His Lordship also declared: That the parliament is to be adjourned this day unto Oxford, on the first of August next.

The Clerk read his Majesty's letters patent directed unto the Lords and Commons for his royal assent unto the bills now passed, *in haec verba, vizt.:*[12]

Charles R.

Charles, by the grace of God, King of England, Scotland, France, and Ireland, defender of the faith, etc. To our right trusty and right well-beloved the Lords spiritual and temporal, and to our trusty and well-beloved our knights, citizens, and burgesses, the Commons in this present parliament assembled, greeting:

We have seen and perfectly understood divers and sundry acts and ordinances annexed and affixed to these presents agreed and accorded on by you our loving subjects the Lords spiritual and temporal and Commons in this our present parliament assembled, and severally endorsed by you as has been accustomed, the titles and names of which acts hereafter do particularly ensue, that is to say:

An act for punishing divers abuses committed on the Lord's day, called Sunday.

An act to enable the King's Majesty to make leases of lands parcel of his Highness's Duchy of Cornwall or annexed to the same.

An act for the ease of the obtaining of licenses of alienation, and in the pleading of alienations with license or of pardons of alienations without license in the Court of Exchequer or elsewhere.

An act for the further restraint of tippling in inns, alehouses, or other victualling houses.

An act for settling and confirmation of copyhold estates and customs of the tenants in base tenure of the manor of Cheltenham, in the county of Gloucester, and of the manor of Ashley, otherwise called Charlton Kings, in the said county, being holden of the said manor of Cheltenham according to an agreement thereof made between the King's most excellent Majesty, being then Prince of Wales, Duke of Cornwall and of York, and Earl of Chester, lord of the said manor of Cheltenham, and Giles Greville, Esquire, lord of the said manor of Ashley, and the said copyholders of the said several manors.

An act for the enabling and confirmation of an agreement or composition made between the King's Majesty's commissioners of revenue, his Majesty being then Prince of Wales, Duke of Cornwall, and Earl of Chester, on his Majesty's behalf, and his Majesty's copyholders of his Highness's manor of Macclesfield, in the county of Chester, and of a decree made in the Court of Exchequer at Chester for the perfect creation and confirmation of certain lands and tenements parcel of the said manor to be copyhold and customary lands according to the tenor of the same decree.

An act for the grant of two entire subsidies granted by the temporalty.

An act for the confirmation of the subsidies granted by the clergy.

An act that this session of parliament

11. The King's full answer to the petition concerning religion was delivered by the Duke of Buckingham to a meeting of both Houses on 8 August and was reported to the Lords on 9 August. See below, pp. 155–160.

12. The King's letters patent was a device to assure royal assent to the bills without the King being present in person at the closing of the session. Because of the spread of the plague the court had moved outside of London. For precedents on the use of the royal letters patent in parliament, see below, H. of C., 9 July, n. 10. On the acts, see Leg. Cit., below, pp. 631–632.

shall not determine by his Majesty's royal assent to this and some other acts.[13]

And, albeit the said several acts and ordinances, by you our said subjects, the Lords and Commons in this our present parliament assembled, be fully agreed and consented unto, yet, nevertheless, the same be not of force and effect in law without our royal assent given and put to the same acts and ordinances. And, forasmuch as for divers great and urgent causes [p. 58] and considerations we cannot conveniently at this present be personally, in our royal person, in the higher House of our said parliament, being the place accustomed to give our royal assent unto such acts and ordinances as have been agreed upon by our said subjects the Lords and Commons; we have therefore caused these our letters patent to be made, and have signed the same and, by the same, do[14] give and put our royal assent to all and singular the said acts and ordinances, and to all articles, clauses, and provisions in them contained. And be it fully agreed and assented to all and singular the said acts, willing that the said acts, and every article, clause, sentence, and provision in them contained, from henceforth shall be of the same strength, force, and effect as if we had been personally present in the said higher House and had openly and publicly, in the presence of you all, assented to the same. And we do, by these presents, [declare][15] and notify the same our royal assent as well to you [**L.J. 466**] the said Lords spiritual and temporal and the Commons aforesaid, as to all others whom it may concern, commanding also, by these presents, our Lord Keeper of our

Great Seal of England to seal these our letters patent with our Great Seal, and to declare and notify this our royal assent in our absence in the said higher House in the presence of you the said Lords spiritual and temporal and the Commons in our parliament there to be assembled for that purpose. And the Clerk of our parliament to endorse the said acts with such terms and words in our name as is requisite and has been accustomed for the same. And also to enroll these our letters patent and all and every the said acts in the parliament roll. And these our letters patent shall be to either of them sufficient warrants in that behalf. And finally, we declare and will that after this our royal assent given and passed by these presents, and declared and notified as aforesaid, that then immediately the said acts and every of them shall be taken, accepted, and admitted good, sufficient, and perfect acts of parliament and laws to all intents, constructions,[16] and purposes, and to be put in due execution accordingly, the continuance or dissolution of this our parliament or any other use, custom, thing, or things, to the contrary thereof notwithstanding.

In witness whereof, we have caused these our letters to be made patent. Witness ourself, at Westminster, the eleventh day of July, in the first year of our reign.

                                        Edmondes.

Then, the Commons being gone, the commission for the adjournment was read, *in haec verba:*[17]

[King Charles,

Charles, by the grace of God, King of En-

---

13. By 8 July the act that the session should not be determined by his Majesty's royal assent to any act or acts of parliament had passed both Houses. The King's assent to this bill guaranteed that although legislation had passed and the London meeting was constituted a session yet the bills in progress could nevertheless be continued over the adjournment and did not have to be begun anew at Oxford. See Coke, *Fourth Inst.*, pp. 26–27.

14. MS.: *go.*

15. *declare* is omitted in the MS. but included in the printed edition within brackets.

16. MS.: *instructions.* In keeping with modern usage the printed edition uses the word *constructions.*

17. The entire commission is in Latin in the MS. L.J. For the convenience of readers, we have given a translation of the Latin commission below, within brackets. For the Latin, see *L.J.*, III, 466.

gland, Scotland, France, and Ireland, defender of the faith, etc. To the most reverend father in Christ and our faithful counsellor George, Archbishop of Canterbury, primate and metropolitan of all England; and to the reverend father in Christ and our faithful counsellor John, Bishop of Lincoln, Lord Keeper of our Great Seal of England; and also to the most reverend father in Christ Tobias, Archbishop of York, primate and metropolitan of England; and also to our well-beloved and faithful counsellor James, Lord Ley, our Lord Treasurer of England; and to our most dear cousins and counsellors Henry, Viscount Mandeville, Lord President of our Council; Edward, Earl of Worcester, Lord Keeper of our Privy Seal; George, Duke of Buckingham, our Lord Admiral of England; Thomas, Earl of Arundel and Surrey, our Earl Marshal of England; William, Earl of Pembroke, Lord Steward of our Household; and also to our most dear cousin Edward, Earl of Dorset; as well as to our most dear cousin and counsellor Philip, Earl of Montgomery; and to our most dear cousin William, Earl of Northampton, President of our Council of the Principality and Marches of Wales; and to our most dear cousin and counsellor James, Earl of Carlisle; as well as to our most dear cousins John, Earl of Clare and Henry, Viscount Rochford, and also to the reverend fathers in Christ, George, Bishop of London, and Richard, Bishop of Durham, and to the reverend father in Christ and our faithful counsellor Lancelot, Bishop of Winchester; and also to the reverend fathers in Christ Samuel, Bishop of Norwich, and William, Bishop of St. Davids; and to our well-beloved and faithful counsellors Edward, Lord Conway, one of our principal secretaries [of state] and Edward, Lord Zouch, and also to our well-beloved and faithful

Emanuel, Lord Scrope, President of our Council in the Northern Parts; Thomas, Lord Wentworth; Edmund, Lord Sheffield; and to our well-beloved and faithful counsellors George, Lord Carew, and Fulke, Lord Brooke, greeting:

Since we have lately ordained this our present parliament to commence and be held at our city of Westminster on the eighteenth day of June last for certain difficult and pressing business concerning us, the state and defense of our kingdom of England and the English Church; from which day the same our parliament was held and continued then and there until the present eleventh day of July. Know ye that we have thought fit to adjourn the same our parliament as well as all the cases and matters begun and not yet finished for divers pressing causes and considerations especially moving us. Therefore we, confiding very much in your fidelity, prudence, and circumspection, have with the advice and consent of our Council assigned you our commissioners giving full power and authority to you and any three or more of you by the tenor of these presents from this present Monday in our name to adjourn and continue our present parliament and all business and aforementioned matters yet (as stated) not finished to the first day of August now next following at our city of Oxford there then to be held and continued.[18] And therefore we command you to attend diligently to the premises and effectually fulfill them in the manner aforesaid. Moreover, we strictly command all and singular archbishops, dukes, marquises, earls, viscounts, bishops, barons, knights, citizens, and burgesses and all others whom it concerns, by the tenor of these presents, to meet at this our said parliament, that they observe, obey, and assist you as is proper in the execution of the premises. In witness

18. For the King's proclamation concerning the adjournment of the parliament, issued on 12 July, see *Stuart Proclamations,* II, 48–49. With regard to preparations for the parliament at Oxford, see the materials printed in the Appendix, below, pp. 660–664.

whereof we have caused these our letters to be made patent. Witness ourself, at Westminster, the eleventh day of July, in the first year of our reign.

Edmondes.
Ex. per J. Bendbo.[19]

Which being read, the LORD KEEPER declared that, according to this commission, this session is adjourned from this eleventh of July to the first of August next, unto Oxford.

And the commission was sent down to the Commons by Mr. Justice Croke and Mr. Baron Trevor.[20]

II. MINUTE BOOK, H.L.R.O., M.M., 1625

[f. 39v] *Die Lunae 11 die Julii 1625*
[*List of Lords Present; see A.T.*]

Hodie 1ª vice lecta est billa, An act for the confirmation of three subsidies granted by the clergy.

Hodie eadem billa 2ª et 3ª vice lecta est et missa communibus.[21]

The confirmation of the subsidies being only read, not the body of the act once read.

Sir Edward Coke and others brought up the subsidy of the clergy.

L. KEEPER. Whether their Lordships pleased to have a report from his Majesty touching the recess.

Granted by the House.

[f. 40] L. PRESIDENT. Report. Yesterday he moved the King for a recess. His Majesty was pleased there might be a recess; and on this day. That the Commons be acquainted with it if the House please.

A message by Mr. Attorney and Mr. Serjeant Davenport, to the Commons:

That the Lords have received a message from the King for a recess, and desire to meet a small committee of the Commons touching the same, with a proportionable [number] of theirs.[22]

L. CONWAY. That his Majesty had commanded him to certify that he well contented with the recess of the parliament at this present in regard of the danger of the sickness, for nothing was more precious to him than your persons. Yet, in regard of the occasions and present state of this kingdom he must speedily call them again. It is a business that his late father and our sovereign was drawn into by your advices, by the breaking up of the two treaties and consequently a war must needs ensue. He declared the charge that his Majesty had been at with the war touching the Palatinate by land, and since by sea; that his charge by sea had been double to that money which the last three subsidies brought into the Exchequer; and that if he were not assisted in this fleet, it would give occasion to his allies to think that he were both weak in ability and affection. And lastly, that he must come to them for their assistance and continued advice.[23]

[f. 40v] Lords appointed to confer with a proportionable committee of the Commons touching the recess of the parliament:
L. President
L. Bp. of London
L. Wentworth
L. Carey

E. OF WARWICK moved the House in the/

The petition of Thomas Hayne. Has had his lands, goods discharged,[24] having a writ

---

19. John Bendbo was deputy to Sir Thomas Edmondes, Clerk of the Crown in Chancery. See *C.D. 1628*, IV, 177, n. 4.
20. As was customary, the Lower House adjourned itself. See above, n. 9.

21. MS.: *comissa comitibus.*
22. See above, n. 1.
23. See above, nn. 3–5.
24. MS.: *goods and discharged.* Concerning Hayne's petition, see above, n. 2.

of error depending in parliament and waiting of his Lord[ship], the E. of Suffolk. Desires relief herein.

This petition and petitioner to be referred to the Lords subcommittees for privileges at the next meeting; that the Lord Keeper write to some of the justices to sequester the corn till the House meet; that Parham and Hayne do both attend the committees.

E. MARSHAL. An order to be drawn that when and where the parliament shall meet next the Houses may be well attended.

L. President and E. Marshal do desire the King to be sparing to grant any license for more Lords to be absent from the parliament.

A message by Mr. Attorney and Serjeant Davenport: That the King has given assent to the bills passed, and that their Lordships are ready to adjourn the parliament by commission and desire them to come up.

[f. 41] Answer from Commons: That they will return an answer presently by messengers of their own.

A message from the Commons by Sir Edward Coke: That whereas they had received a message touching 2 commissions, the one declaring the King's assent to the acts passed, the other for the adjournment of the/

Mr. Speaker. The knights/

The Commons, as their first fruits, have given two entire subsidies, the one to be paid the [blank], the other [blank];[25] and also do wait to know his Majesty's royal consent to such bills as in this short time could be passed.

The Speaker delivered the acts, being fixed to the commission.

Lord Keeper. That the bills to which the royal assent was passed should be read, but

25. See above, n. 10.

first I have a message to deliver: That he intends to give a full and direct answer to all those particulars in the said petition against recusants not in words [but] by act[s]. That this parliament is to be put off to the city of Oxford about the first [of] August next, as by a commission that [we] will leave in your House shall appear.

[f. 41v] The commission for the royal assent was read by the Clerk with a loud voice, the Commons being below the bar with their Speaker.

The commission for the proroguing of the parliament was read by the Clerk to the Lords only and after sent down to the Commons and was likewise read by them in their own House.

For the proroguing of this present parliament from this instant 11th of July to the first of August next at the city of Oxford.

L. KEEPER adjourned this session of parliament from this day to the first of August, and from Westminster to the city of Oxford.

III. PETITION OF THOMAS HAYNE. H.L.R.O., MAIN PAPERS, H.L., 11 JULY 1625.

To the King's most excellent Majesty and to the Right Honorable the Lords Spiritual and Temporal of the Upper House of Parliament assembled.

The humble petition of Thomas Hayne, Gentleman, showing,

That whereas, John Parham, Esquire (an unconscionable usurer), had of late a suit in the name of Thomas Crouch against Robert Angell and others your petitioner's servants in an *ejectione firmae* for the petitioner's house and lands in Dorsetshire, and thereon obtained an erroneous judgment at the common law. Whereupon your petitioner brought a writ of error into this most high and honorable House, signed by his late Majesty deceased, which depended here until his Highness's death, by which the same abated; his said adversaries in Easter term last, taking sudden advantage hereby, did, before the sitting of this right honorable House, take forth a writ of execution and by force thereof caused your petitioner's wife, children, and goods, in a cruel and barbarous manner, to be cast out of his dwelling house, while your petitioner was here at Westminster attending certain affairs for the Right Honorable the Earl of Suffolk, his lord and master (the high sheriff and undersheriff being before acquainted therewith notwithstanding). Forasmuch therefore as the said writ of error abated, not by default of your petitioner but by the act of God, and your petitioner having procured a new writ of error, signed by your Majesty's hand, and is here depending with the record of the said former judgment, and for that your petitioner, by his adversaries' practices and extreme dealings, is dispossessed of his house (being his only habitation), together with all his lands and goods, being obtained against the privilege of this honorable House (as your petitioner conceives), your petitioner likewise having much corn growing upon the same lands which they also intend to convert to their own use. Most humbly beseeches this most honorable court to give order for the restitution of your petitioner's possessions, of his said house and lands, until this cause be heard and determined in this most high and honorable court. And he shall according to his bounden duty ever pray, etc.

Prayers
Lords excused   125(2)
House adjourned   125(2)

.

MONDAY, 1 AUGUST 1625

I. JOURNAL OF THE HOUSE OF LORDS

[**L.J. 467**]
[p. 63] *Die Lunae, vizt., primo die Augusti 1625 Oxonia*
[*List of Lords; see A.T.*]

The Lords bishops of Rochester and Salisbury excused by the Lord Keeper for a few days, for want of health.

The Lord Bishop of Norwich excused in like manner by the Lord Bishop of Coventry and Lichfield.

[*Notice of Adjournment*]

II. MINUTE BOOK, H.L.R.O., M.M., 1625

[f. 43] Oxford. *Die Lunae primo die Augusti*
[*List of Lords Present; see A.T.*]

Prayers.

Excused by the Lord Keeper: L. Viscount Rochford, Bishop of Salisbury.
L. B[ishop] of Norwich excused by the Bishop of Coventry and Lichfield.

Adjourned. 9 tomorrow morning.

III. JOURNAL OF EDWARD, LORD MONTAGU, MONTAGU MSS., VOL. 30, NORTHAMPTON-SHIRE RECORD OFFICE

[p. 1] Some notes of the passages at the parliament held and begun at Oxford, the first of August, 1625.

Monday, 1 August

On Monday the first, the parliament began at Oxford.

TUESDAY, 2 AUGUST 1625

I. JOURNAL OF THE HOUSE OF LORDS

[L.J. 468]

[p. 64] *Die Martis, vizt., secundo die Augusti 1625 Oxonia*
[*List of Lords; see A.T.*]

Excused: the Earl of Bridgewater, the Lord Bishop of Exeter, the Lord Bishop of Gloucester.

Hodie secunda vice lecta est billa, An act for the better preservation of his Majesty's revenue.

Committed unto the

L. Archbp. of Canterbury	L. Conway
L. Treasurer	L. Willoughby
L. President	L. De La Warr
E. Marshal	L. Stourton
L. Bp. of London	L. Danvers
L. Bp. of Rochester	L. Spencer

To attend the Lords: Lord Chief Baron, Mr. Justice Croke, Mr. Attorney General.

To meet in the Painted Chamber,[1] tomorrow, at eight.

[*Notice of Adjournment*]

II. MINUTE BOOK, H.L.R.O., M.M., 1625

[f. 43v] *Die Martis 2da die Augusti 1625.*
[*List of Lords Present; see A.T.*]

Excused by the Lord Keeper: E. of Bridgewater, L. Bishop of Exeter.

Excused by the Bishop of Bristol: L. Bishop of Gloucester.

Hodie 2^a vice lecta est billa, An act for the better preserving of his Majesty's revenue.

Committed unto

Ex.[2]   Lds.

L. Treasurer	1. Conway
President	3. De La Warr
Marshal	6. Spencer
	2. Willoughby
Bps.	5. Danvers
Rochester	4. Stourton
London	
Canterbury	

To attend: Chief Baron, Attorney, J. Croke.

To meet in the Painted Chamber tomorrow by 8.

Adjourned. 10 tomorrow.

III. JOURNAL OF EDWARD, LORD MONTAGU, MONTAGU MSS., VOL. 30, NORTHAMPTONSHIRE RECORD OFFICE

[p. 1]   Tuesday, 2 August

The second, I came to the town and lay in Trinity College.

IV. COMMITTEE BOOK, H.L.R.O., MAIN PAPERS, H.L., 1625

[f. 8v] *Oxon. Die Martis 2° die Augusti 1625.*

An act for the better preserving of his Majesty's revenue.

Committed unto

Lo. Archbp. of Canterbury	L. Conway
L. Treasurer	L. Willoughby of Eresby
L. President	L. De La Warr
E. Marshal	L. Stourton
	L. Danvers
L. Bp. of London	L. Spencer
L. Bp. of Rochester	

---

1. The Painted Chamber adjacent to the Lords House in Westminster Palace was a regular meeting place for Lords' committees and for conferences held between the Houses when the parliament was meeting in London. In Oxford there were several buildings with painted ceilings in the proximity of the north wing of the Picture Gallery where the Lords were meeting; of these, it seems probable that the room being referred to as the "Painted Chamber" was the south wing of the Gallery which a contemporary account described as appointed for the use of the "grand committee" (see Appendix, below, p. 662) and which, according to Anthony à Wood, was used for a walkway by the Lords (see Anthony à Wood, *The History and Antiquities of the University of Oxford* [Oxford, 1796], II, 355, 789–790, 954).

2. The *Ex.* may indicate that the list had been examined by the Clerk. Cf. Foster, *Elsyng*, p. 28.

To attend the Lords: Lo. Chief Baron,
Mr. Justice Croke, Mr. Attorney General.

To meet on Wednesday the third of this
instant August by 8 in the Painted Chamber.

HOUSE OF LORDS
ORDER OF BUSINESS   WEDNESDAY, 3 AUGUST 1625

WEDNESDAY, 3 AUGUST 1625

I. JOURNAL OF THE HOUSE OF LORDS

[L.J. 469]
[p. 65] *Die Mercurii, vizt., tertio die Augusti 1625*
[*List of Lords; see A.T.*]

The Earl of Clare excused, for that one lately died in his house.

Lord Bishop of Llandaff [and] Lord Paget excused for want of health.

Lord Bishop of Durham [and] Lord Bishop of Exeter excused, and that they had sent their several proxies.

[*Notice of Adjournment*]

II. MINUTE BOOK, H.L.R.O., M.M., 1625

[f. 44] *Die Mercurii 3° die Augusti 1625.*
[*List of Lords Present; see A.T.*]

Excused by the Lord Keeper: the E. of Clare, L. Bishop of Llandaff.

1. Concerning the King's proclamation for prayers and fasting every Wednesday, see above, H. of L., 28 June, n. 12. On 19 July the Oxford Council had arranged for Alexander Harry of Exeter College and Mr. Smith of Queen's College to be the regular preachers at the Wednesday services and had made plans for the use of St. Martin's church for the services, including the removal of its windows to let in fresh air. H. E. Salter, ed., *Oxford Council Acts, 1583–1626* (Oxford, 1928), p. 331.

None of the parliamentary accounts other than Montagu indicates where the 3 August fast services were held, however C.C.C. MS. E257 (see below, p.

Excused by the E. of Dorset: L. Paget.

L. Bishop of Durham, proxy to Bishop of Rochester.

L. Bishop of Exeter, proxy to the Bishop of London.

Adjourned. 9 tomorrow.

III. JOURNAL OF EDWARD, LORD MONTAGU, MONTAGU MSS., VOL. 30, NORTHAMPTON- SHIRE RECORD OFFICE

[p. 1]   Wednesday, 3 August

The third the fast was held, and prayers and sermons, one in the forenoon, the other in the afternoon, at St. Mary's, where many of the Lords were and most of the Commons;[1] but because of the plague, which was begun before the parliament began, and some increase thereof, there was no other assemblies kept in the town.[2]

662) agrees with Montagu in stating that the services were held at St. Mary's.

On 2 August the Commons had insisted that Dr. Thomas Anyan be prevented from preaching before the House at the fast services of 3 August. See below, H. of C., 2 August, O.B.; see also, Thomas Fowler, *The History of Corpus Christi College* (Oxford, 1893), p. 180.

2. Regarding the increase of the plague in Oxford, see below, H. of L., 4 August, n. 8. Concerning the prohibition of public assemblies for celebration of the fast in parishes affected by the plague, see the Privy Council's letter to the Archbishops of Canterbury and York, *A.P.C., 1625–1626*, p. 125.

HOUSE OF LORDS
ORDER OF BUSINESS   THURSDAY, 4 AUGUST 1625

Prayers
LORD KEEPER (Bp. of Lincoln):
    declares the King's pleasure
    that both Houses attend him
    presently   132, 135, 136
House adjourned   132, 136(2)
King's speech to both Houses   132, 136; **C**,
                                              386, 388
Lord Conway (Secretary of State):
    on the state of Christendom   133, 136, 137;
                                              C, 386, 389
Sir John Coke   133, 136, 137;
                                              C, 387, 389
    [*Afternoon*]
Prayers
LORD KEEPER (Bp. of Lincoln):
    moves for an adjournment   135
Lords excused   135, 136(2)
House adjourned   135, 136(2)

THURSDAY, 4 AUGUST 1625

I. JOURNAL OF THE HOUSE OF LORDS

[L.J. 469]

[p. 67] *Die Jovis, vizt., quarto die Augusti 1625*

[*List of Lords; see A.T.*]

[L.J. 470]

LORD KEEPER declared that his Majesty expects their Lordships' attendance presently in Christ Church Hall,[1] where his Majesty intends to speak somewhat unto their Lordships and the Commons.

[*Notice of Adjournment*]

Memorandum: That this day the Lords and Commons were commanded to attend his Majesty in Christ Church Hall, in Oxford, where his Majesty spoke unto them in manner following, *vizt.:*[2]

My Lords and you of the Commons well all remember that from your desires and advice my father (now with God) broke off those two treaties with Spain that were then in hand; well you then foresaw that as well for regaining my dispossessed brother's inheritance as home defense a war was likely to succeed.[3] And that as your counsels had led my father into it, so your assistances in a parliamentary way to pursue it should not be wanting. The aid you gave him by [p. 68] advice was for succor of his allies, guarding

Ireland and the home parts, supply of munition, preparing and setting forth of his navy. A council you thought on and appointed for the war, and treasurers for issuing of your monies. And, to begin this work of your advice, you gave three subsidies and as many fifteens, which with speed were levied, and by direction of that Council of War (in which the preparation of this navy was not the least) disbursed.[4] It pleased God at the entrance of this preparation (by your advice begun) to call my father to His mercy, whereby I entered as well to the care of your designs as his crown. I did not then, as princes of custom do, and for formality, reassemble you; but that by your further advice and aid I might be able to proceed in that which, by your counsels, my father was now engaged in. Your love to me and forwardness to further those affairs you expressed by a grant of two subsidies, yet ungathered, although I must assure you by myself and others, upon credit, taken up and aforehand disbursed, all far too short as yet to set forth that navy now preparing, as I have lately found by estimate of those of care and skill employed about it.[5] Before you could be acquainted fully with those necessities of further aid, it pleased God to visit the place of your assembly then with a grievous plague.[6] To stay you in that danger had been a neglect of my just care. To

---

1. The rooms at Christ Church had been reserved for the use of the Privy Council and King's officers during the Oxford session. See the materials printed in the Appendix, below, pp. 660–662.

2. A similar version of the King's speech is in Petyt 538/8, printed below, H. of C., 4 August. The Petyt version is essentially the same as a copy of the speech included in John Brown's Commonplace Book (Osborn fb 155). With regard to the Lower House's concern about wearing hats at this meeting, see H. of C., 4 August, p. 386 and n. 10. Sir Francis Nethersole reports the speeches of this day in his letter of 9 August to Sir Dudley Carleton, S.P. 16/5:30, see Appendix, below, p. 710. For general reports on the events of this day as well as the rest of the Oxford session, see Zuane Pesaro's letter of $\frac{11}{21}$ August to the Doge and the Senate of Venice, *Cal. S.P. Venetian, 1625–1626*, pp. 141–

143; and Salvetti's dispatch of $\frac{9}{19}$ August, Salvetti dispatch, pp. 29–30.

3. With regard to the Spanish treaties, see above, H. of L., 18 June, nn. 5 and 7. Concerning Frederick V, brother-in-law of Charles I, see below, H. of C., 20 June, n. 5.

4. The Council of War and the treasurers were named in the 1624 subsidy act. See *S.R.*, 21 *Jac.* I, c. 33. For the account of the disbursement of 1624 subsidy monies, see *Cal. S.P. Dom., Addenda, 1625–1649*, pp. 23–27.

5. For an estimate of the monies eventually brought in by the act for two subsidies which had received the royal assent on 11 July 1625, see below, H. of C., 8 July, n. 9.

6. Concerning the plague in London, see above, H. of L., 18 June, n. 8.

prorogue the parliament had destroyed the enterprise.[7] I therefore adjourned you to this place, a place then free of that [**L.J. 471**] infection, which since it has pleased God to visit also.[8] Here then to hold you long against your own desires were to express in me little care of your safeties, and to adjourn it without your further helps were to destroy the preparations already made. I therefore leave the care of both to your elections, resolutions, and answers, only acquainting you with my own opinion, which is, that better far it were both for your honors and mine that with hazard of half the fleet it were set forth than with assured loss of so much provision stayed at home.

When you shall be pleased the whole[9] particular of all expenses about this preparation to take an account, my Lord Trea-

surer there and other the ministers employed shall acquaint you.[10]

And his Majesty promised an answer within two days unto the petition delivered him touching religion.[11]

His Majesty's speech being ended he commanded the Lord Conway and afterwards Sir John Coke to declare the state of his Majesty's affairs more particularly;[12] the effect whereof was:

That our sovereign lord King James, of famous memory, at the suit of both Houses of parliament, and by the powerful operation of his Majesty (that now is), gave consent to break off the two treaties with Spain touching the match and Palatinate.[13] That is was then foreseen a war would ensue, there being no other means to recover the

---

7. Concerning the matter of adjourning rather than proroguing the parliament, see above, 6 July, n. 4.

8. In a letter of 27 July, John Prideaux, Vice-chancellor of Oxford, informed the Earl of Pembroke that three houses in the city were infected. S.P. 16/4: 130. And on 28 July the Oxford Council made a series of orders for dealing with cases of plague in the city and for reducing the influx of strangers other than parliament men into the city. See H. E. Salter, ed., *Oxford Council Acts, 1583–1626* (Oxford, 1928), p. 331. Also, see the Salvetti dispatch of $\frac{9}{19}$ August, p. 29, and the Earl of Westmorland's letter of 7 August to Sir George Manners, H.M.C., *12th Report, App., Pt. IV* (Rutland MSS.), 473–474.

9. *of the whole.* Printed edition.

10. On 8 August, at a meeting of a committee of both Houses, the Duke of Buckingham, Lord Admiral, delivered an account of the preparations of the fleet, and the Lord Ley, Lord Treasurer, delivered an account of the state of the King's finances. These speeches of the Duke and the Lord Treasurer were reported in both Houses on 9 August. See H. of L., 9 August, O.B.; and H. of C., 9 August, O.B.

11. For the King's answer to the petition concerning religion, see below, H. of L., 9 August, O.B.

12. Judging from the account of the speeches of Lord Conway and Sir John Coke given in Elsynge's notes, below, p. 137, and in Bedford MS. 197, below, pp. 386–388, the report which follows in the MS. L.J. is of Coke's speech alone. There was concern expressed by members of both Houses that Sir John Coke, a member of the Commons, should be asked to

speak in parliament "at his Majesty's pleasure" as a mouthpiece of the crown. See the Montagu journal, below, p. 136, and *Negotium,* below, p. 534. See also, Coke's letter of 4 August to Lord Brooke, printed in H.M.C., *12th Report, App., Pt. III,* 134–135; and Lord Keeper Williams's comment concerning Coke in his letter to the King, 14 August 1625, printed in Hacket, *Scrinia Reserata,* pt. II, p. 18. Coke had been a Commissioner of the Navy since 1618 but was not appointed Secretary of State until after the death of Sir Albertus Morton in September 1625. See *Cal. S.P. Dom., 1625–1626,* p. 100.

The version of Coke's speech which is included as a separate in several MS. collections of 1625 speeches and is printed in Cobbett, *Parl. Hist.,* II, 9–11, and Rushworth, *Hist. Collections,* I, 178–179, is essentially the same as that in the MS. L.J., below. A draft of this speech, written in Coke's hand and with a note that it was originally appointed to be delivered in the Lower House, is in S.P. 16/5:14, printed in the Appendix, below, pp. 648–651. A similar speech on foreign policy and preparations of the fleet had been delivered by Coke, at the King's command, in the Lower House on 8 July. See H. of C., 8 July, O.B.

For Lord Conway's speech which preceded Coke's, see below p. 137, and H. of C., 4 August, pp. 386–387. On 11 July the Lord Conway had delivered in the Upper House a speech containing much of the same material included in his 4 August remarks. See H. of L., 11 July, O.B.

13. Concerning background on the European situation and the treaties with Spain, see above, H. of L., 18 June, nn. 5 and 7.

Palatinate, nor to vindicate the many wrongs and scorns done unto his Majesty and his royal children.

Besides, if the King of Spain had been suffered to proceed in his conquests he would, under pretence of the Catholic cause, have been the Catholic monarch, which he so much affects.

With these necessities, our late Sovereign considered also the dangers that might ensue: first, that he should run a hazard with his people by their indisposition unto war, being so long inured unto peace. And secondly, what opinion his neighbor princes might have if he should suddenly run into a war, wherefore he suffered himself to be wrought upon by new treaties for the restitution of the Palatinate, which were nourished by the friends and agents of Spain. And herein his Majesty proceeded so far as the wisest prince could, and suffered himself to be won unto that which otherwise was impossible for his royal nature to endure.

Our late Sovereign also considered the many difficulties abroad. The King of Spain, by force and contract, was fully possessed of the Palatinate and most of the electors and princes of Germany were joined with him, some having the electoral dignity, and others part of the land; and the estates of other princes there, who were most likely to join in a war for the recovery thereof, seized on and all secured by a great army. Besides, the emperor had called a diet in which he would take away all possibility hereafter for recovery of the honor or the inheritance of the Palatinate. Thus it

stood in Germany. And in France, the King there chose to sheath his sword in the bowels of his own subjects rather than to declare himself against the Catholic cause.

In the Low Countries the sect of the Arminians prevailed much, who inclined to the papists rather than their own safety, notwithstanding that the enemy had a great and a powerful army there at that time, so that his Majesty was enforced to protect and [p. 69] to countenance them with an army of six thousand from hence; but with caution of repayment of the charges, and of the like supply from hence, if required. And he sought alliance with France by a match for his royal Majesty that now is, thereby to get an interest in that King, and to win him to be a party.

The last consideration was his Majesty's own honor. He had labored the two king's of Denmark and Sweden and the German princes, from whom he received cold answers, they refusing to join unless they did first see his Majesty in the field. Of this his Majesty was very tender unless the League were broken or he first warred upon. The forces of an army were considered and whether to proceed by way of invasion or diversion. The charges thereof appeared in parliament to be seven hundred thousand pounds per annum,[14] besides, Ireland was to be fortified, the forts here repaired, and a navy prepared. Whereupon he thought it more feasible to enter into league with the French King, the Dukes of Savoy and Venice.[15] And hereupon an army was committed to Count Mansfeld, the charge whereof came but to twenty thousand pounds a

14. We have not found any entry in the acounts of the parliament of 1624 which gives the figure of 700,000 *l.* as the expected annual cost of such an army. During debates in the House of Commons on 11 and 19 March 1624, several M.P.s moved that a committee draw up projected costs of a war before the House vote on a figure for supply (see *C.J.*, I, 732–733, 740–744), but on 20 March the House proceeded, without the projected cost figures, to resolve on a year's supply of three subsidies and three fifteens (an anticipated total of 360,000 *l.*) for the war effort (see *C.J.*, I, 744). The amount voted was considerably below the King's origi-

nal request for five subsidies and ten fifteens (for an anticipated total of 750,000 *l.*) and his second request for six subsidies and twelve fifteens (or 900,000 *l.*) (see *L.J.*, III, 266).

15. On 26 August 1624, France, Venice, and Savoy had entered a league for the recovery of the Valtellina. To facilitate the recovery, the Duke of Savoy, with the aid of a French force, was to attack Genoa, and Count Mansfeld was to attack Alsace and the Austrian possessions in Swabia. Gardiner, *History of England*, V, 265.

month for his Majesty's part, and commanded this great fleet also to be prepared.[16] All which so heartened the princes of Germany that they sent ambassadors to the kings of Denmark and Sweden, and those two kings offered a greater army, *vizt.*, of [blank] foot and [blank] horse, towards which his Majesty is to pay [blank] per mensem.[17] The army of Count Mansfeld, though disastrous, yet brought forth these happy effects:

1. It prevented the diet intended by the Emperor.
2. The German princes gathered new courage to defend themselves and oppose the enemy.
3. The King of Denmark raised an army with which he is marched in person as far as Minden.
4. The confederates of France and Italy have prosecuted a war in Milan.
5. War is denounced to the King of Spain in Milan and peace is now made by the French King with his subjects.

So by this army breath is given to our affairs.

The[18] parliament is not called for any formality upon his now Majesty's first coming to the crown, but upon these real occasions to consult with the Lords and Commons; wherein two subsidies are already given and very graciously accepted, but the money thereof (and more) already disbursed. The fleet is now at the sea and hastening to be at the rendezvous at the time appointed; the army ready at Plymouth expecting their commanders.

Here is engaged the honor of his Majesty and religion and the safety of the kingdom; besides, the King is most certainly advised of undertakings to infest his Majesty's dominions in Ireland and our coasts, and of the enemy's increase of shipping in all parts for that purpose.

These call you hither (the Lords and Commons) again. The charge of all this amounts to above four hundred thousand pounds, and the King is not able to bear the further prosecution thereof. All which his Majesty has left to your considerations. His Majesty is verily persuaded that there is no king better loves his subjects, religion, and laws of the land than himself. And likewise that there is no people better loves their king, which he will cherish to the uttermost.

It was thought this place had been safe and secure for this assembly, and that it might here continue. And, since the sickness has brought some fear thereof, his Majesty wills the Lords and Commons to put into the balance the fear of the sickness, and these his and their great and weighty occasions.

[**L. J. 472**; p. 70] *Die Jovis, vizt., quarto die Augusti 1625. Post meridiem* [List of Lords; see A.T.]

The LORD KEEPER moved that, in respect that there was no such occasion of sitting this afternoon as was expected, the House might be adjourned.

The Lord Brooke excused by the Lord Viscount Saye and Sele, for want of health.
The Lord Morley excused for a time.
The Earl of Westmorland excused, and that he had sent his proxy.
The Lord Bishop of Worcester excused for want of health.

[*Notice of Adjournment*]

II. MINUTE BOOK, H.L.R.O., M.M., 1625

[f. 44v] *Die Jovis 4to Augusti 1625* [List of Lords Present; see A.T.]

The LORD KEEPER told the Lords that the King expected their Lordships presently in Christ Church Hall, where his Majesty

16. See H. of C., 8 July, nn. 36 and 38.
17. For figures where the L.J. account has been left blank, see the account of Coke's speech in Bedford MS. 197, below, p. 388. Regarding the agreement with

Christian IV, King of Denmark, see Gardiner, *History of England*, V, 299, 323.
18. *This.* Printed edition.

intends to speak somewhat to their Lordships and the Commons.

Adjourned to 3 *post meridiem.*

[f. 45] *Die Jovis 4to Augusti 1625, post
meridiem*
[*List of Lords Present; see A.T.*]

L. Brooke excused by Saye.
L. Morley excused by the E. Marshal.
E. of Westmorland, proxy.
L. Bishop of Worcester excused by the
Bishop of St. Davids.

Adjourned. 9 tomorrow.

III. JOURNAL OF EDWARD, LORD MONTAGU,
MONTAGU MSS., VOL. 30, NORTHAMPTON-
SHIRE RECORD OFFICE

[p. 1]   Thursday, 4 August

On Thursday the 4th the King, lying at
Woodstock, came in the morning to Christ
Church, to the Dean's lodging.[19] Commandment was sent both to the Lords and
Commons that they should attend his Majesty at Christ Church Hall, which was prepared accordingly. Between 10 and a [*sic*]
11 of the clock the King came; and after he
was set he had a little private speech with
the Lord Conway and Sir John Coke, a
member of the Commons House, who went
and stood at the nether end of the room.

The King made a short speech of the calling us to this parliament, etc.[20] [p. 1a] And
for our further satisfaction he had appointed some to relate unto us the carriages of
the businesses; whereupon the Lord Conway, standing at the foot of the stairs going
up to his Majesty's chair, made his speech,
etc.

Then Sir John Coke related what was in
charge to him;[21] which being ended, the
King arose and went to dinner.

19. See above, n. 1.
20. See above, L.J., and n. 2.
21. See above, n. 12.
22. See above, n. 12.

But there arose a great murmuring of the
Commons, with some dislike also of the
Lords, that Sir John Coke, being a member
of the Commons House, should deliver in
that presence his Majesty's pleasure, being,
as all thought, without precedent.

After the Lords had dined, myself with
other Lords went to the King, who was
walking in the Dean's garden. Coming up
one of the alleys, I standing there, he
looked graciously upon me, and after he
was a little passed by me, he turned himself,
"Come on, my Lord Montagu, you are an
old parliament Lower House man". And so
[I] going up to him, he said, the Duke and
the Earl of Hertford being by, "I hear that
the Lower House, some of the youn[g]
men, find fault that Sir John Coke spoke
today; what say you to it?"[22] [p. 1b] I besought his Majesty to give me leave to deal
faithfully with him: "I never saw it before".
Which, said his Majesty, "It was by my commandment". I answered, that was above all,
but I hope[d] his Majesty would bear with
me for dealing faithfully with him; and so
he went forward up the alley. And after he
had sat awhile in an arbor, he went back
again to Woodstock to meet the Queen,
who that day came thither to him.

The Lords had adjourned their House to
3 in the afternoon that if there might be an
occasion they might debate of it, otherwise
adjourn the court; where we met, and after
prayers ended, some Lords being excused
for their absence, the House was adjourned
till 9 the next day.

IV. NOTES OF HENRY ELSYNGE, OSBORN FB
161, FF. 16–17.[23]

Oxon, 4 August 1625

Rex called hither.

23. Henry Elsynge's notes of the 1625 speeches of
Lord Conway and Sir John Coke are bound together
with papers from the early part of the Long Parliament, 1641, in Osborn fb 161.

Conway.[24] How the King came into these actions you know. What the King has done since by prosecution you shall know now.

1. By examination of the state abroad. Germany almost subjected. Palatine all lost. Remedy by the sword only.

Friends confederated abroad; the expenses of the war so great. Alliances. Germany cold; [*illegible*] you be first in the field, now them first. Defense of Ireland.

Prevailed so much that the princes of Germany began to be warm. But not able to do the war himself. His friends weakened. A diet propounded by the Emperor.

To pay this. Mansfeld 20,000 *l.* per month.

Embassages. Denmark came on.

The King's charges in Ireland. The navy prepared.

Examine the charges. If Mansfeld, Denmark, or the fleet quail, or the Low Countries, all will be lost. The charges so great that contrary to his expect[ations] he cannot proceed. Want of credit for money. All the subsidy being spent also.

Honor, surety of this nation and of religion throughout the world.

All friends engaged in hope of the King's actions. If this fail the rest will make their peace with Spain and the Emperor. His Majesty resorts only to the parliament.

Coke.[25] Most sacred Majesty, etc., being commanded to acquaint the parliament with the present state of your Majesty's affairs, he will begin, etc.

Called to memory that K[ing] J[ames] at suit of both Houses and your Majesty gave consent to break the 2 treaties.[26]

A war to ensue. No other means to recover the Palatin[ate] nor vindicate the wrongs and scorns. Besides, if Spain had been suffered to proceed, he a Catholic monarch.

The danger considered: the hazards by indisposition of his people to war; the opinion of his neighbor princes if suddenly into a war. Suffered himself to be wrought upon by new treaties for restitution nourished by Spain.

Proceeded as far as the wisest. Suffered himself to be won to that which otherwise impossible.

The difficulties many. How he stood abroad. Spain fully possessed of the Palatinate. Most of the electors and princes joined with him. The estates of other princes seized. All secured by a great army. A diet to take away all possibility hereafter for inheritance or for passage for the King thither.

How stood it in France. The King there sheathed his sword in the bowels of his own rather than against the Catholic cause.

Low Countries. Arminians there inclined to the papists rather/

The King protected them and countenanced them.

24. For another account of Secretary Conway's speech, see H. of C., 4 August, p. 386.

25. Concerning other accounts of Coke's speech, see above, n. 12.

26. See above, n. 13.

Prayers

Petition of Mary **Broccas**: read   139, 140, 141
  [*Broccas's petition is printed on p.*
  141]

Former order concerning
  Broccas: confirmed   140(2)

Complaint that Rowland **Pitt** had
  taken the horse of Justice
  George Croke to ride post   139, *12/8

Ordered: the Serjeant at Arms to
  bring Rowland Pitt before
  their Lordships   139

ARCHBISHOP OF CANTERBURY:
  concerning money collected
  for the **captives at Algiers**   139, 140, *10/8

Committee to take account of the
  money collected for the
  captives at Algiers: appointed   139, 140, 141

EARL OF ARUNDEL AND SURREY (E.
  Marshal): concerning the
  plague in London   139, 140, *10/8

DUKE OF BUCKINGHAM   140(2)

Committee concerning a
  collection for the **distressed
  people of London** and
  Westminster: appointed   139, 140,
                             141(2), *6/8;
                             8/8; 10/8;
                             12/8

House adjourned   140(2)

Friday, 5 August 1625

I. JOURNAL OF THE HOUSE OF LORDS

[L.J. 473]

[p. 71] *Die Veneris, quinto die Augusti 1625*
[*List of Lords; see A.T.*]

Complaint was made to the House that one Rowland Pitt, a fishmonger, had taken the horse of Mr. Justice Croke to ride post, knowing it was the judge's horse.

Ordered that the Serjeant at Arms do cause the said Rowland Pitt to be brought before their Lordships to answer his contempt and breach of privilege of this House, for that the said judge does now attend this parliament, being thereunto summoned by his Majesty's writ.[1]

Upon the Lord ARCHBISHOP OF CANTERBURY's motion these Lords undernamed are appointed to take the account of the money collected for the captives of Algiers, etc., *vizt.*:[2]

L. President	L. North
E. of Dorset	L. Russell
L. Bp. of London	L. Carey of
L. Bp. of Rochester	Leppington

The House, being moved to consider the lamentable estate of the cities of London and Westminster and the parishes adjoining,[3] appointed these Lords to conceive an order for their relief, *vizt.*:

L. Duke of	L. Willoughby
Buckingham	L. Wentworth

L. President	L. Cromwell
E. of Dorset	L. North
	L. Russell
L. Bp. of London	L. Carey of
L. Bp. of Rochester	Leppington
L. Bp. of Norwich	

Mr. Attorney General to attend the Lords. To meet presently.

[**L. J. 474**; p. 72] Whereas, upon the petition of Mary Broccas, exhibited in parliament *anno 21° Jacobi,*[4] it was ordered 28 *Maii* 1625 [*sic*] that the Muscovy Company should bring in to the treasurer of the said Company, by Midsummer Day then next coming, their several and respective leviations and assessments lastly made by the said Company for and towards the payment of such debts as were then owing by their said Company upon their common seal for monies borrowed at interest of strangers not free of the said Company, whereof she, the said Mary Broccas, to be first paid her debt with interest of five pounds in the hundred since the time they forebore to pay her eight in the hundred (as by the said order, among other things concerning these merchants of that Company, may appear). All which was, by the said order, referred to the Court of Chancery to be put in execution accordingly.

And whereas the said Mary Broccas has exhibited a second petition in parliament here at Oxford, complaining that she had (notwithstanding the said order) received

---

1. Sir George Croke's name is included with the list of "judges and learned counsel that were appointed to attend in the parliament held *1° Caroli Rgs.*", f. 73, H.L.R.O., M.M., 1625. He became justice of Common Pleas in February, 1625. *D.N.B.* Rowland Pitt was discharged on 12 August; see below, p. 183.

2. Following the reading of a petition from English captives of the Turks, the Lords, on 27 May 1624, had agreed to a general collection to be made for the redemption of English captives at Algiers, the money to be sent to the Archbishop of Canterbury. *L.J.*, III, 411, 413. The committee appointed this day (5 August) was to take account of the money received and disbursed by the Archbishop. Another committee was appointed 23 March 1626 (ibid., 538) to take further account of

the money collected.

3. The Duke of Buckingham motioned for relief of the poor in London and Westminster; see below, H.L.R.O., M.M., 1625. Concerning the plague in London, see above, H. of L., 18 June, n. 8.

4. The 1624 petition of Mary Broccas is included in H.L.R.O., Main Papers, H.L., 27 May 1624. The order concerning that petition was made in the Upper House on 27 May 1624 and on the same day the case was referred to the Court of Chancery (*L.J.*, III, 412–413). The 1625 petition of Broccas is printed below, p. 141. The case was not settled by 1628 when Mary Broccas again petitioned the Upper House. See *L.P. 1628*, p. 109 and see also ibid., pp. 667–671, 673.

but seven hundred pounds of her interest and principal money, the principal being a thousand pounds lent many years since at eight pounds *pro centum,* and that the governor and merchants of the said Company did seek delays to defraud her of the residue, making divers interpretations of the said order, for which she prayed relief, and that the said governor and merchants might be called before their Lordships to set down their exceptions to the said order.

The Lords, considering the danger of the time, thought it not fit to draw the governor and merchants of that Company to this place. Wherefore they did, on this fifth day of August, order the said petitioner's cause to be referred to the Chancery, to be executed according to the former order with as much conveniency as may be in respect of the sickness at this time.

[*Notice of Adjournment*]

II. MINUTE BOOK, H.L.R.O., M.M., 1625

[f. 45v] *Die Veneris 5to Augusti 1625.*
[*List of Lords Present; see A.T.*]

The petition of Mrs. Broccas read, and the order made *a° 21 Jac. Regis.*

The Lords do ratify and confirm the former order, and the petitioner be relieved by the Chancery.
The Lord Keeper has promised to see the order performed.

L. ARCHBISHOP OF CANTERBURY desired that whereas there had been money gathered for the prisoners of Algiers, etc., and brought to him, that there be a committee appointed to take an account from his Grace.[5]

L. President	Rochester
E. of Dorset[6]	London

North
Russell
L. Carey of
    Leppington

[f. 46] E. MARSHAL. That whereas there is a proclamation to prohibit Londoners from[7] coming to court, that there might be an order drawn up, entered, and published that thereby such might avoid the coming to court or parliament, as it is reported they now do, in countrymen's apparel.

L. D[UKE] OF BUCKINGHAM. That whereas the sickness is now in London and many poor people there in a manner imprisoned by reason of the contagion and want of commerce are in a miserable case; that, for want of means, very many perish. Therefore that this court take some course for their relief.

Lords committees to consider of a collection for the distressed people of London and Westminster:

L. Duke	North
L. President	Wentworth
E. of Dorset	Carey of Leppington
	Willoughby
London[8]	Russell
Rochester	Cromwell
Norwich	

Mr. Attorney to attend.
To meet presently in the Painted Chamber.

Adjourned. 9 tomorrow morning.

III. JOURNAL OF EDWARD, LORD MONTAGU, MONTAGU MSS., VOL. 30, NORTHAMPTON-SHIRE RECORD OFFICE

[p. 1b]   Friday, 5 August

Friday, the fifth. Nothing done, but only a motion made by the LORD DUKE for relief

---

5. See above, n. 2.
6. *Wentworth* is crossed out in the MS. following *Dorset.*
7. MS.: *for.* The proclamation, issued on 26 June 1625, is printed in *Stuart Proclamations,* II, 45–46. Re-

garding orders by the Oxford Council restricting entry of strangers into the city, see above, H. of L., 4 August, n. 8.
8. *Canterbury* is crossed out in the MS. preceding *London.*

for London; whereupon a small committee was chosen to frame an order in writing.

It seems the Commons House had much debate about the proposition for more money, but concluded not anything.[9]

IV. COMMITTEE BOOK, H.L.R.O., MAIN PAPERS, H.L., 1625

[f. 9] *Die Veneris 5to die Augusti 1625.*

Lords committees to take an account from my Lord's Grace of Canterbury touching such monies as have been collected for the prisoners in Algiers, etc., *vizt.:*

L. President	L. North
E. of Dorset	L. Russell
	L. Carey of
L. Bp. of London	Leppington
L. Bp. of Rochester	

[f. 9v] *Die Veneris 5[t]o die Augusti 1625.*

Lords committees to consider of a collection to be made for the distressed people in the cities and suburbs of London and Westminster, *vizt.:*

L. Duke of	L. Willoughby
Buckingham	L. Wentworth
L. President	L. Cromwell
E. of Dorset	L. North
	L. Russell
L. Bp. of London	L. Carey of
L. Bp. of Norwich	Leppington
L. Bp. of Rochester	

To attend the Lords: Mr. Attorney General.

To meet presently in the Painted Chamber.

V. PETITION OF MARY BROCCAS, H.L.R.O., MAIN PAPERS, H.L., 5 AUGUST 1625.

To the Right Honorable the Lords Spiritual and Temporal of the High Court of Parliament assembled.

The humble petition of Mary Broccas, humbly showing,

That whereas by your Lordship's honorable order, made the last parliament (the copy whereof is hereunto annexed),[10] your petitioner was to receive of the Company of Muscovy Merchants the sum of 1,000 *l.*, which she had formerly lent them at 8 *l.* per centum, and 5 *l.* in the hundred for the interest of the said 1,000 *l.* which then amounted unto the sum of 175 *l.*, the same to be delivered in such manner as by the said order is expressed.

Now so it is, that your petitioner has received of her principal but 700 *l.* and no more, and she has spent to obtain the same 120 *l.* or thereabouts. And the governor merchants of the said Company seek by delays to defraud your petitioner of the residue, making divers interpretations of your said order, contrary to the true meaning thereof.

May it therefore please your good Lordships to call the said governor before you and command him to set down the exceptions to the said order. And to show cause why your petitioner is not paid the remainder of the said debt and her interest.

And thereupon may it also please your good Lordships so to explain your Lordships' said order and to cause the same to be executed, so as your petitioner may speedily receive the remainder of the debt and her interest, and such recompense for her charges as to your Lordships shall seem meet.

And your petitioner shall duly pray, etc.
[*Endorsed*]
5 August 1625
Mary Broccas

O.B.

9. The Lower House was this day debating the matter of giving further subsidies; see H. of C., 5 August,

10. See above, n. 4.

HOUSE OF LORDS
ORDER OF BUSINESS   SATURDAY, 6 AUGUST 1625

Prayers
Report from the committee
  concerning a **collection** for
  the **distressed people of
  London** and Westminster
  (VISCOUNT MANDEVILLE, L.
  President)   143, 144, *5/8
Order concerning a tax and
  collection for the distressed
  people: read and approved   143, 144
  [*The order is printed on pp. 143–
  144*]
Ordered: Lord Keeper (Bp. of
  Lincoln) to move his Majesty
  that briefs be granted for a
  general collection   143
House adjourned   144(2)

SATURDAY, 6 AUGUST 1625

I. JOURNAL OF THE HOUSE OF LORDS

[L.J. 474]

[p. 73] *Die Sabbathi, vizt., sexto die Augusti 1625*

[*List of Lords; see A.T.*]

[L.J. 475]

The LORD PRESIDENT reported the order conceived by the Lords committees for relief of the poor at London, Westminster, etc., which, being read, and an addition to the same by the House, their Lordships approved thereof.

And the Lord Keeper is appointed to move his Majesty that briefs be granted for a general collection through the kingdom, as is mentioned in the said order.[1]

The which order follows, *in haec verba:*

The Lords, having this day taken into their charitable consideration the lamentable distress of the poor people inhabiting in the cities and suburbs of London and Westminster, and in the out-parishes adjoining, and in the parish of Stepney, who, in this time of the plague now reigning in those parts, are less subject to good orders, being left destitute of convenient relief, in respect that the rich and able citizens, and other inhabitants of all sorts, being departed thence for avoiding the infection, have not taken sufficient order for relief of the poor people remaining behind, have thought fit, and do now order, advise, and direct that, over and besides all provision already made, there be this further added for their better relief, *vizt.:* That all persons taxed or taxable in the limits and places aforesaid,

either for houses, lands, goods, or otherwise, towards the relief of the poor (being not so impoverished themselves by this visitation as they shall be forborne to [p. 74] be taxed), shall, by the proper officers, be taxed to bear a double proportion of tax, at the least, during the time of this visitation, and more if it shall be found requisite by the magistrates, justices of peace, or other officers there abiding for the time. And, after notice given to any person so taxed or left at his house, wheresoever he shall be remaining, he is hereby ordered to make due payment, weekly or monthly, as shall be required. And, because it is conceived that very many are removed so far from London as that notice cannot be conveniently given with such speed as may presently supply the necessity of the poor, their Lordships do desire the Chamber or Bridge House[2] of London to lend and disburse one thousand pounds at the least for this purpose. And it is ordered that they, or any charitable and able inhabitants, laying out that sum or any further sums which shall be wanting, shall be surely repaid whatsoever they shall disburse out of the sums so taxed, so soon as they may be levied, and out of a general collection which his Majesty (at their Lordships' humble suit) has declared his pleasure to recommend throughout the whole kingdom for relief of the said poor, wherein their Lordships now assembled will themselves set an example for encouragement of others.[3] And, to the intent that the monies to be raised by way of taxation as is abovementioned may be the more certainly and speedily levied, their Lordships, during the time while they shall sit, will be

---

1. The King's brief for a general collection was issued on 11 August. See *Bibliotheca Lindesiana*, V, no. 1444; *S.T.C.*, no. 8794.

2. I.e., the Bridge House Estate, which managed income from property held by the City which was set aside for the maintenance of London Bridge. In November 1625, in response to a letter from the Mayor and aldermen of London, the Privy Council directed the Bishop of London to reimburse the City,

out of the money collected in accordance with the King's brief, for the 1,000 *l.* which the Chamber had issued for the relief of the poor. See *Cal. S.P. Dom., 1625–1626*, p. 155; *A.P.C., 1625–1626*, pp. 250–251.

3. The amount decided on by the Lords as a gift from their own House was 20*s.* apiece for members of the barons' bench and 40*s.* for members of the earls' bench. See Montagu journal, 8 August, below, p. 149.

pleased to take knowledge of all complaints against such as shall refuse to pay the said taxation, and to punish them so exemplarily as shall be a terror unto others. And they do further order that, after the sitting shall end, the Lords of his Majesty's Privy Council, upon complaint to them, and the Lord Keeper of the Great Seal of England, upon complaint to him, shall do the like.

And their Lordships, having been informed of the good and charitable course held by some companies and others within the City in forbearing their companies' and hall dinners and turning them unto the relief of the poor, do highly commend those that have so done; and do wish their example may be followed by the Lord Mayor, sheriffs, and the rest, as a thing much pleasing to God and agreeable to [the] time.

Copies of this order were sent to London, Westminster, Duchy, justices of peace for Middlesex, justices of the peace for Surrey, and to Stepney.[4]

But those copies did not directly agree with this order here entered, for that the same received some small additions afterwards, *10 Augusti*, and therefore the Clerk has entered it as it is in the printed brief.[5]

[*Notice of Adjournment*]

II. MINUTE BOOK, H.L.R.O., M.M., 1625

[f. 46v] *Die Sabbathi 6 Augusti 1625*
[*List of Lords Present; see A.T.*]

L. PRESIDENT, first of the committee for collecting of money for the distressed people in the cities and suburbs of London and Westminster, certified the House that the Lords committees had conceived an answer and desired it should be read, which was accordingly.[6]

Adjourned. 9 Monday next.

III. JOURNAL OF EDWARD, LORD MONTAGU, MONTAGU MSS., VOL. 30, NORTHAMPTONSHIRE RECORD OFFICE

[p. 1b]   Saturday, 6 August

Nothing done but only the order for relief of London, which was assented. It was expected the King would have been in the town this morning, but altered his mind, commanding all the Council to be with him in the afternoon; who went accordingly.

It was said one Clarke was committed by the Commons for some distasteful words of those that spoke the day before.[7]

---

4. Henry Elsynge's draft of a letter which accompanied the order when it was sent out is included in H.L.R.O., Main Papers, H.L., 6 August 1625.

5. For the Earl Marshal's report concerning the alterations, see H. of L., 10 August, p. 175. A draft of the order, partially amended by the Lords, is in the

H.L.R.O., Main Papers, H.L., 6 August 1625.

6. See the order printed in the L.J., above.

7. On this day (6 August) the Commons committed Edward Clarke, M.P., to the Serjeant for his offense in criticizing other members for speeches made in the House on 5 August, See H. of C., 6 August, O.B.

Prayers

Message from the Commons
desiring a **conference on
religion** (Lord Cavendish
and others) [*see below*]   146, 147, 148,
                                        *9/8

Answer given to the Commons'
message: the Lords have
appointed a committee for a
conference tomorrow (LORD
KEEPER, Bp. of Lincoln)   146, 147, 148

LORD KEEPER (Bp. of Lincoln):
that the King's answer to the
petition concerning religion
is ready to be delivered to
both Houses [*see below*]   147, 148, *1/7

Message to the Commons desiring
a present **meeting of both
Houses** to receive the King's
answer to the petition
concerning religion (Sir
Thomas Coventry, Att.
General, and Sir Ranulphe
Crew, L. Chief Justice) [*see
below*]   146, 147, 149

Committee for the **conference on
religion**: appointed [*see above*] 146, 147, 150

Report of the Commons' answer
to the message desiring a
meeting of both Houses:
they will send answer by
messengers of their own (Sir
Thomas Coventry, Att.
General, and Sir Ranulphe
Crew, L. Chief Justice) [*see
above and below*]   146, 148

Agreed: that any Lord may
explain the King's message at
the meeting of both Houses   146

LORD KEEPER (Bp. of Lincoln):
reports King's response to
Lords' action concerning the
distressed people of London
[*see below*]   148, *5/8

Message from the Commons
concerning arrangements for
the **meeting of both Houses**
(Sir Edward Coke and others)
[*see above*]   146, 148, 149

Answer given to the Commons'
message (LORD KEEPER, Bp.
of Lincoln)   147, 148, 149

Message from the Commons: they
will give meeting at the time
and place appointed (Sir
Edward Coke and others)   147, 148, 149

Lords agree on their contribution
for relief of the **distressed
people of London** [*see above*]   149

House adjourned   147, 148, 149
[*Afternoon*]

Meeting of both Houses at Christ
Church Hall   149

Lord Keeper, Bp. of Lincoln   149

Duke of Buckingham: delivers
the King's answers to the
petition concerning religion
[*see above*]   150

Sir Thomas Coventry (Att.
General): reads the petition
and the King's answers   150
[*The petition concerning religion
and the King's answers are
printed on pp. 155–160*]

Duke of Buckingham   150

Sir John Coke   150

Lord Ley (L. Treasurer)   150

MONDAY, 8 AUGUST 1625

I. JOURNAL OF THE HOUSE OF LORDS

[**L. J. 475**]
[p. 75] *Die Lunae, vizt., octavo die Augusti 1625*
[*List of Lords; see A.T.*]
[**L.J. 476**]

Message from the Commons by the Lord Cavendish and others: That the knights, citizens, and burgesses of the House of Commons desire a conference with their Lordships touching matters of religion, humbly leaving to their Lordships the time, place, and number of committees.[1]

Answered: The Lords have appointed a committee of theirs, of sixteen, to meet a proportionable number of the Commons tomorrow, at eight, in the Painted Chamber.[2]

The names of the said Lords committees:

L. Archbp. of Canterbury	L. Willoughby
L. Treasurer	L. De La Warr
L. President	L. Berkeley
E. Marshal	L. Wentworth
L. Steward	L. North
L. Bp. of London	L. Walden
L. Bp. of Norwich	L. Danvers
L. Bp. of Coventry and Lichfield	L. Russell
	L. Montagu

L. Bp. of Bath and W[ells]

Message sent to the Commons by Mr. Attorney General and Mr. Doctor Eden:[3] That the Lords have received a message from the King which is to be delivered unto the Lords and Commons together by the Lord Keeper and the Duke of Buckingham. And that his Majesty has commanded the Lord Keeper to require the Lord Treasurer, the Lord Conway, and Sir John [p. 76] Coke to assist his Grace therein; wherefore the Lords require a present meeting with their whole House, presently in the Painted Chamber, if it may so stand with their occasions.[4]

Answered: That the Commons have taken this message into their consideration and will return a speedy answer by messengers of their own.

Agreed, that any of the Lords of this House may explain the King's message at this conference, or anything else that shall concern them.

Answer to this message by Sir Edward Coke and others of the House of Commons: That in the message sent to them by the Lords they consider three circumstances, *vizt.*, the time, the persons, and the

1. The conference was with regard to the petition drafted by the Commons to be presented to the King complaining of the pardon of Alexander Baker and ten other papists, and concerning a letter from Secretary Conway excusing Mary Estmond's refusal to take the oath of allegiance. See H. of C., 6 August, nn. 9 and 10; see also, the Archbishop's report of the conference, below, H. of L., 9 August, O.B.
2. For the names of the Lower House committee members, see H. of C., 8 August, p. 422. The L.J., the Minute Book, and the Committee Book lists of the Lords' conference committee include the names of eighteen rather than sixteen Lords. According to Elsynge's tract, "The Method of Passing Bills in Parliament", *Harleian Miscellany*, V (London, 1810), p. 228, "if the Clerk happen to set down more [names for a committee] than the number agreed on, it is in the liberty of the House to take out the latter, and so to

leave the just number, or to admit them".
The House of Commons requested that the meeting be held in St. Mary's church rather than the Painted Chamber. See n. 6, below.
3. The Minute Book, below, and the accounts in H. of C., 8 August, indicate that it was Chief Justice Crew, not Dr. Thomas Eden, who accompanied the Attorney General as messenger.
4. The meeting was held in the afternoon this day; the speeches were reported the following day (9 August). Members of both Houses had earlier expressed disapproval of Sir John Coke as a spokesman of the King; see above, H. of L., 4 August, n. 12. On 8 August Coke was given leave by the Lower House to speak at the meeting as the King's servant but not as a member of the Lower House; see below, H. of C., 8 August, p. 423.

place. That they have assented unto the time. For the persons, they desire (for clearing of all doubts, and keeping afoot the good correspondency between them) to understand whether their Speaker be to come also with them.[5] The place,[6] they think it too weak to bear so great a multitude and therefore have, at this time, presumed underhand to intimate St. Mary's church for the meeting, if it so please their Lordships.

Answered by the Lords: That the meeting of both Houses is to be understood of a committee of both Houses, and not otherwise. That nothing has been omitted by their Lordships' care, nor their servants, touching the strength of the place appointed, yet, with thanks for their care herein also, their Lordships have changed the place to the hall in Christ Church. And, it being now late, they have appointed the meeting to be at two this afternoon, if the occasions of the Commons will then permit it; whereof they desire a speedy answer.

The messengers returned answer: That the Commons will meet at the time and new place appointed. And whereas intimation is given that there might be some use of a worthy member of that House in the delivering of this message from his Majesty, though it be against the very fundamental privileges of the House of Commons, yet they have given way unto it, with this: That he speak as the King's servant and commissioner,[7] and not as a member of their House.

[Notice of Adjournment]

II. MINUTE BOOK, H.L.R.O., M.M., 1625

[f. 47] *Die Lunae 8 die Augusti 1625.*
[*List of Lords Present; see A.T.*]

A message from the Commons House by the Lord Cavendish and others: The k[nights], c[itizens], and b[urgesses] of the Commons House of parliament desire a conference with your Lordships touching religion; the time, place, and number left to your Lordships.

A committee of 16 to meet the Commons tomorrow morning touching religion.

[f. 47v] Answer, L. KEEPER: That the Lords have considered of the message and will meet with a committee of theirs with a committee of 16 in the Painted Chamber tomorrow morning by 8 of the clock.[8]

L. KEEPER. The King has called the Council together and with deliberate advice resolving of remedies particularly to every question in the petition against recusants, and appointed the D[uke] of Buckingham this day to certify both Houses, in the Painted Chamber,[9] this answer of his Majesty.

A message to the Commons by the Lord Chief Justice and Mr. Attorney: That the Commons [*sic*] desire a present meeting in the Painted Chamber to receive an answer from his Majesty touching their petition against recusants, as also concerning another great business.

Lords committees named to meet with a committee of the Commons at the conference for religion.

5. The Lower House was concerned about proper protocol: if they went as a committee they would go without their Speaker and "uncovered" (i.e., without hats); if they went as a House, accompanied by their Speaker, they would go covered. See H. of C., 4 August, n. 10, and 8 August, pp. 423 and n. 12, 425, 426.
6. For the identification of the "Painted Chamber", suggested by the Lords as the place of meeting, see above, 2 August, n. 1. Concerning the weakness of

the timberwork for the third-story Gallery, see Charles Edward Mallet, *A History of the University of Oxford* (London, 1924), II, 228, n. 1. With regard to St. Mary's church, see below, n. 16.
7. See above, n. 4.
8. See above, n. 2.
9. Here and in the message to Commons, below, the Clerk has crossed out *Christ Church Hall* and inserted *Painted Chamber.*

Ex.

1. L. Treasurer	5. L. North
2. L. President	8. Danvers
4. L. Steward	1. Willoughby
3. L. Marshal	4. Wentworth
	2. De La Warr
1. Canterbury[10]	3. Berkeley
3. Norwich	6. Walden
4. Coventry and	7. Russell
Lichfield[11]	9. Montagu
2. London	
5. Bath and Wells	

To meet tomorrow at 8 in the Painted Chamber.

[f. 48] Answer by the Lord Chief Justice and Mr. Attorney General: That they will take it into their consideration and return a speedy answer by messengers of their own.

L. KEEPER. That he had acquainted his Majesty with that course that your Lordships took touching the poor distressed people of London and Westminster. His [Majesty] much rejoiced and will give largely out of his own private purse and the brief is gone out.[12]

Answer from the Commons by Sir Edward Coke and others. That the Commons have conceived three parts in this answer, *vizt.*, time, persons, and place. The time they assent unto; they desire to know whether your Lordships mean to have the whole House with their Speaker or only a committee; that the place called the P[ainted] Chamber is somewhat dangerous and therefore wish another of meeting for so great a company.[13]

Answer to the Commons, being called in, LORD KEEPER: That the Lords have taken into their consideration the 3 circumstances of your message and return this answer— that a committee of both Houses meet with-

out their Speaker, that the place of meeting be Christ Church Hall, and the time of meeting 2 *post meridiem* this present day.

[f. 48v] Message from the Commons by Sir Edward Coke and others: That the Commons will give a meeting at the time and place now appointed. That whereas there was an intimation that there would be some occasion of a member of theirs [to speak], namely Sir John Coke, though it be contrary to the privileges of their House, yet to satisfy his Majesty they will give way to it, but as a Commissioner of the Navy or as a servant of the King.[14]

Adjourned. 9 tomorrow.

III. JOURNAL OF EDWARD, LORD MONTAGU, MONTAGU MSS., VOL. 30, NORTHAMPTON-SHIRE RECORD OFFICE

[p. 2]   Monday, [8] August

The 8th. The Commons sent us a message wherein they desired a conference with us of some things concerning religion. We returned them answer to confer with them tomorrow morning in the Painted Chamber, with the number of 16 Lords, whereof I was one.

Afterwards the LORD KEEPER told us that he was to deliver a message to both Houses, and that afterwards that the Duke's Grace was to deliver some things to both, with asking of leave he might do so, and that he might have the Lord Treasurer and the Lord Conway to assist him, and that for some things he might have Sir John Coke to deliver them.

The Earl of Pembroke, Lord Steward, being also Lord Chamberlain, was added to be an assistant to the Duke.

---

10. *Bristol* is crossed out in the MS. following *Canterbury.*

11. *Carlisle* is crossed out in the MS. following *Coventry and Lichfield.*

12. Concerning the order and brief for relief of the poor of London and Westminster, see above, 6 Au-

gust, p. 143 and n. 1. According to the Montagu journal (see below), the Lords agreed this day (8 August) on their contribution for the relief of the poor.

13. See above, n. 6.

14. See above, n. 4.

Hereupon a message was sent to the Commons. That the Lord Keeper had a message to deliver to both Houses and that afterward the Lord Duke was to deliver some things by special direction from his Majesty to be assisted with the Lord Treasurer and the Lord Conway and Sir John Coke, a member of the Commons. The place to be the Painted Chamber, presently.

The nomination to both Houses bred some debate in the Commons House whether the Speaker was to be included in that message. And after we had tarried an hour, musing what should be the stay, some of the Lower House having speech whether we intended by the House the Speaker, or else but a committee of both Houses.

This be[ing] made known to some[15] of the Lower House, and they intimating to the rest that our meaning was but to a committee of both Houses, [p. 2a] they presently returned answer, which they divided into 3 parts: the time, person, and place.

The time they assented to. For the person, which being to the House includes the Speaker, whether we meant he should come, or else to be but to a committee of the House.

For the place, though it was to the usual place, the Painted Chamber, yet because they heard of the weakness of the floors of that House which, when it should be loaded with so many, might be dangerous, they desired that we would look unto our own safety, and to have care of the poor Commons their lives, and therefore desired it might be in Saint Mary's; and because it might not be thought to be any profanation to that

place they told how the acts and many school disputations were kept there.[16]

They withdrawing and coming in again we delivered this answer: For the person, it was intended to be but a committee. For the place, we gave them great thanks for the[ir] care; though there had been provision to prevent those fears, yet we were contented it should be at Christ Church Hall, where formerly we had been. For the time, the day was now so far spent, and if their leisures served, we desired [it] to be at two of the clock that afternoon.

The[y] returned answer of their being ready accordingly. And for Sir John Coke to speak, though it touched one of the fundamental privileges, yet they gave way to it, so that he spoke as a commissioner or being the King's servant, but not as a parliament man.

We agreed that morning the Lords should give for the present relief of London as they did for Algiers, which was, for the barons' bench 20s. a piece, and 40s. for the earls' bench.[17]

The[y] adjourned till 9 tomorrow.

At two a clock the Lords and Commons met. But this I noted: that the Lords came in scatteringly by themselves, and not together, which was a breach of the order.[18]

[p. 2b] When we were met, the Lord Keeper told us that his Majesty's pleasure was that his answer to the petition should be delivered, which the Duke had in charge to do from the King, and to acquaint us further matters.[19]

---

15. MS.: *to the same.*

16. Concerning university meetings in St. Mary's, the university church, see Andrew Clark, ed., *Survey of the Antiquities of the City of Oxford . . . by Anthony Wood,* vol. II, "Churches and Religious Houses" (Oxford, 1890), p. 30. The Oxford University Chancellor's records (O.U.A. W.P.B./21/4) list the costs of renovating St. Mary's in preparation for the parliament.

17. On 27 May 1624, the Lords had agreed to contribute these same amounts toward the general collec-

tion for the redemption of English captives at Algiers, etc. *L.J.,* III, 413.

18. According to section 26 of the Roll of Standing Orders, at conferences the Lords were "to come in thither in a whole body, and not some Lords scattering before the rest, which both takes from the gravity of the Lords, and besides prevents the places".

19. All of the speeches delivered at the meeting of both Houses this afternoon were reported to the Houses the following day and consequently are in-

The Duke rose up and delivered them to the Lords, who commanded Mr. Attorney [to read] them; who read the petition through; but when he came to the remedies, he first read the remedy, and then the answer particularly to every remedy. They are of record; *ergo vide*.

Then the Duke began his speech, which for his better memory he had drawn what he would say into questions and answers, which were about some 14: *vide* the copy of that, as is reported.

Sir John Coke spoke after him, and then the Lord Treasurer; [for] which I refer to the report. And so we rose.

IV. COMMITTEE BOOK, H.L.R.O., MAIN PAPERS, H.L., 1625

[f. 10] *Die Lunae 8° die Augusti 1625.*

Lords committees named to meet with a committee of the Commons at the conference for religion. *Vizt.:*

L. Archbp. of Canterbury	L. Willoughby
	L. De La Warr
L. Treasurer	L. Berkeley
L. President	L. Wentworth
E. Marshal	L. North
L. Steward	L. Walden
	L. Russell
L. Bp. of London	L. Danvers
L. Bp. of Norwich	L. Montagu
L. Bp. of Coventry and Lichfield	
L. Bp. of Bath and W[ells]	

To meet on Tuesday the ninth of this instant by 8 in the morning in the Painted Chamber.

To meet at 3 *post meridiem* the 9th of August in Painted Chamber, 1625.[20]

cluded in the MS. accounts for 9 August. See below, H. of L., 9 August, O.B.; H. of C., 9 August, O.B.

20. This note is entered in the margin of the MS., beside the columns of names.

C: Proceedings in House of Commons, below

TUESDAY, 9 AUGUST 1625

I. JOURNAL OF THE HOUSE OF LORDS

[L.J. 477]
[p. 77] *Die Martis, vizt., nono die Augusti 1625*
[*List of Lords; see A.T.*]

The Earl of Warwick excused for want of health.

The LORD ARCHBISHOP OF CANTERBURY reported the conference with the Commons this morning touching religion, to this effect, *vizt.*:

That they presented a petition directed to his Majesty desiring this House to join therein with them, the effect whereof is— That whereas the Lords and Commons did, at their last meeting this session, petition his Majesty for advancement of God's true religion and suppressing the contrary, unto which his Majesty vouchsafed as well by his own mouth as by the Lord Keeper, on the eleventh of July last, to return such an answer as gave them assurance of royal performance thereof; yet, at this meeting they find that, on the twelfth of July last, his Majesty has granted a pardon unto Alexander Baker, a Jesuit, and ten other papists which (as they are informed) was upon the importunity of some foreign ambassador, and that it passed by immediate warrant, and

was recommended from the Principal Secretary of State without paying the ordinary fees.[1]

And divers copes, altars, chalices, etc., being found in the house of one Mary Estmond, of Dorsetshire, by 2 justices of the peace, who thereupon tendered her the oath of allegiance and, upon refusal, committed her to the constable from whom she made an escape and complained to his Majesty, the said Principal Secretary did write unto those justices in her favor.[2]

All which they humbly desire his Majesty to take into consideration and to give a due, effectual, and speedy redress therein.

[p. 78] The said petition, pardon, and letter were read.[3]

[L.J. 478] The LORD ARCHBISHOP further reported: That as touching the pardon, the Commons insisted much upon three points:

First, the date of the pardon, being the next day after the King's answer delivered to both Houses by the King's commandment.

2. That the pardon dispenses with so many laws, *vizt.*, with the statutes of 23 *et* 27 *Eliz.*, and 3 *Jac.* provided to keep his Majesty's subjects in their due obedience, and with the statute of 10 *E.* III,[4] which directs

---

1. The matter of Alexander Baker's pardon was first raised in the House of Commons on 1 August when it became apparent that a pardon to Baker and other Catholics was dated 12 July, the day after Charles had promised a "real and not verbal" answer to the petition concerning religion. See H. of C., 1 August, nn. 3–4.

According to Montagu's account (below, p. 172), in light of the King's full answer to the petition concerning religion, delivered on 8 August, the Upper House felt that the petition proposed by the Commons regarding the pardon of Baker and other papists was no longer fit to be presented. In a conference on 10 August the Lords suggested that the substance of the petition now proposed should be intimated to the King when both Houses gave their thanks for his answer to the petition concerning religion. See Sir Edward

Coke's report of the 10 August conference, below, H. of C., 11 August, p. 458.

2. Mary Estmond's case was first debated in the Lower House on 6 August (see below, H. of C., 6 August, n. 10). For Secretary Conway's letter to the two Dorsetshire J.P.s, and their response, see Appendix, below, p. 665. The primary grievance regarding the Estmond case was the leniency in the exercise of laws against recusants as a result of the intercession of foreign ambassadors.

3. The proposed petition is printed below, pp. 154–155; a copy of the pardon for Baker, *et al.*, in Latin, is included in the H.L.R.O., Main Papers, H.L,, 9 August 1625; and a copy of Conway's letter concerning Mary Estmond is printed in the Appendix, below, p. 665.

4. *S.R.*, 23 *Eliz.* I, c. 1; *S.R.*, 27 *Eliz.* I, c. 2; *S.R.*, 3 *Jac.* I, c. 5; *S.R.*, 10 *E.* III, st. 1.

that every felon, upon pardon obtained, should be bound to the good behavior.

The third, that it was solicited by the Principal Secretary, the Lord Conway.

And that they added these circumstances: That this Jesuit was formerly imprisoned and, being now set at liberty, his conversation will be very dangerous to the perverting of many of his Majesty's subjects.

That heretofore, in the time of Queen Elizabeth, if any such were convicted and pardoned (for she pardoned none before conviction, as their fault might be first known), they were banished also, not to return upon pain of death, which is prevented by this pardon.

They concluded that this pardon and letter were both procured at the importunity of foreign ambassadors, which is of dangerous consequence to give the subject any dependency upon them.

The Lord Archbishop of Canterbury, having ended, the LORD CONWAY affirmed: That this pardon, though dated the next day after the King's promise to the parliament, yet it is no breach thereof, for it was granted long before.[5]

And his Lordship showed how that at Christmas last his late Majesty promised unto Ville-aux-clercs, the French ambassador, certain graces and privileges to the papists. Marquis de Effiat did afterwards obtain the like, to the end that the Queen might come the more easily hither. And the

Duke of Chevreuse, his Majesty's kinsman who brought the Queen over, importuned him that he might carry home the like graces also.[6]

The pardon passed by immediate warrant to take off the ambassador's continual importunity to the King. And he, being Secretary of State, solicited it himself (but at his Majesty's absolute command) to take off all imputation from his Majesty, and not out of any affection of his to that religion, which he ever hated.

As touching the not paying of the fees, Mr. Bendbo[7] demanded fifty pounds for the fees, and the ambassador complaining thereof unto his Majesty, he commanded him to see that no fees should be taken. That the Duke of Chevreuse importuned the King to write that letter himself in favor of Mrs. Estmond so that he, as Secretary, was enforced and commanded by the King to do it rather than that his Majesty should. The said Duke complained much of the justices' hard carriage unto her, but he never heard any thing of her obstinate behavior to them, nor of any copes or altars found in her house. Wherefore he wrote also to be advertised of her offense by them, but was not until within these few days.[8]

His Lordship protested his sincerity to the true religion here established, whereof he had formerly given good testimony, and wherein he will persevere; and that what he did in these matters was only to take away all scandal from his Majesty, though it lighted upon himself, and that he did nothing

5. The pardon was sealed and dated 12 June, the day following the King's brief answer to the petition concerning religion and the adjournment of the London session. Concerning the date of the original warrant for granting the pardon, see the Lord Keeper's speech, below.

6. The recusancy laws were suspended in December 1624 following ratification of the French marriage articles and as a result of the private engagement with the French signed by Prince Charles and Secretary Conway. See Gardiner, *History of England*, V, 277–279; see S.P. 14/177:23–29, 36–39; and see also, Salvetti dispatches, pp. 4–5. A policy of leniency was con-

firmed in May 1625 by Charles I, shortly before his marriage. See S.P. 16/2:1–6; Salvetti dispatch, pp. 12–13.

As recently as 12 March 1625 Secretary Conway had sent to the Attorney General a list of Roman Catholics for whom the French ambassador sought grace. See *Cal. S.P. Dom., 1623–1625*, p. 496, and S.P. 14/185:54; S.P. 16/521:8. See also, Gardiner, *History of England*, V, 377.

7. MS.: *Benbowe*. On Bendbo, see above, H. of L., 11 July, n. 19.

8. See above, n. 2.

but what he was first commanded to do expressly by his Majesty.

The LORD KEEPER also affirmed: That his Lordship received the said pardon long before the date thereof. If he had made a *recepi* upon the warrant, as is usual in other cases, it had borne date with it, though sealed afterwards, but his Lordship deferred the sealing thereof in hope that the ambassadors would have been gone first, as they were often upon going; but they staying and daily urging the King for the pardon he (being again commanded) sealed it at the next general seal, and so it had date with the time of the seal and not of the grant, his Lordship well hoping upon the departure of [the] ambassadors to have stayed it with his Majesty, [p. 79] otherwise it had been sealed before the King's promise to the parliament, and therefore this can be no breach of the King's promise.

And his Lordship showed that the ambassador urged his Majesty very much to give a general dispensation to the papists, but the King was advised rather to pardon some few of them what was passed, which counsel, though to be commended, yet none gave way unto it but much against their wills, and his Lordship wished that a petition might be presented unto his Majesty to stay the like pardons hereafter.

The petition:
Most gracious Sovereign:
We your Majesty's most loyal subjects, the [*blank*] and Commons, in this present parliament assembled having at our last meeting in this session, out of our duty to God and to your Majesty, our zeal to religion and our country, presented our humble petition to your sacred Majesty for advancement of God's true religion and suppress-

ing the contrary, unto which your Majesty vouchsafed, as well by your own mouth, as after, on the eleventh of July, by the mouth of the Lord Keeper, to return such an[9] answer as gave unto us not a hope only, but an assurance of real performance of those things for which we humbly petitioned; yet, at our present meeting we find that, on the twelfth of July last, your Majesty has granted a pardon to one Alexander Baker, a known and notorious Jesuit (who had been formerly released for the like offenses), and also to ten others of the popish religion which, we are informed, was drawn from your Majesty by the importunity of some foreign ambassador, a course of late so frequently practiced by your ill-affected subjects, of dangerous consequence, inducing a dependency upon foreign princes. In which pardon we further observe: That it extends to all treasons, felonies, *praemunires*, and penalties mentioned by the statute 23 and 27 *Eliz.* and 3 *Jacobi*,[10] with great judgment provided to keep your Majesty's subjects in their due obedience.

That it dispenses with the statute 10 *E.* III[11] which directs that every felon, upon pardon obtained, should be bound to the good behavior. That it was passed by immediate warrant, which is not used but for your own immediate service. That it came recommended from your Principal Secretary of State, and solicited by one of his servants. That it was passed without paying the ordinary fees, that they might be more bound to their patrons for it.

And whereas divers copes, altars, chalices, and other stuff pertaining to the exercise of the popish religion were lately found in the house of one Mary Estmond by two justices of the peace in the county of Dorset, who thereupon did tender unto her the oath of allegiance, which she refused, and

9. *an* is omitted in the printed edition. The King had made a brief response to the petition concerning religion when it was presented to him on 8 July (see Solicitor Heath's report to the Commons on 9 July, below, p. 361) which was reiterated in the King's message delivered to both Houses on 11 July by Lord Keeper Williams (see below, p. 371).

10. *S.R.*, 23 *Eliz.* I, c. 1; *S.R.*, 27 *Eliz.* I, c. 2; *S.R.*, 3 *Jac.* I, c. 5.

11. *S.R.*, 10 *E.* III, st. 1.

being for that refusal committed to the constable, she made an escape and complained to your Majesty. We find that a letter was written by the [**L.J. 479**] same Secretary to those justices, bearing date the seventeenth day of July last, in her favor. All which tending, as we conceive, to the prejudice of true religion, to your Majesty's dishonor, to the discouragement of the High Court of Parliament, the discountenancing of your ministers of justice, the grief of your good people, and the animating of the popish party who, by such example, daily grow more proud and insolent, we, in all humility, beseech your Majesty to take the same into your most wise, religious, and gracious consideration, and to give a due, effectual, and speedy redress herein.

[p. 80] The LORD KEEPER reported the message delivered from his Majesty unto both Houses, yesterday in the afternoon, in Christ Church Hall, in Oxford, to this effect, *vizt.*:

First, that his Lordship told them that his Majesty had graciously, fully, and parliamentarily answered the petition touching religion delivered him by both Houses at Hampton Court, the eighth day of July last, and had commanded his Lordship to signify unto the Lords and Commons that his Majesty had commanded the Lord Admiral

to deliver his said answer thereunto to both Houses to be by them disposed as the answers of kings unto petitions exhibited in this kind are wont to be. And withal to deliver unto them a message from his Majesty concerning those great affairs of his Majesty's now in hand and agitation in the House of Commons.

That then the Lord Admiral said his Majesty had laid upon him such a charge as, when he did consider his own weakness, might utterly discourage him, were it not that, reflecting again upon that plainness and sincerity wherewith a king should deal with his people, he found himself the fitter for the employment, in that he was sure to deliver it without rhetoric or art. As concerning the petition, he could dispatch that in two words, that is, by giving us full assurance that all was granted which was desired, but held it fitter for our satisfaction to read the petition with the answers annexed.

Which was read accordingly by Mr. Attorney, *in haec verba:*
The petition.[12]
To the King's most excellent Majesty.
Most gracious Sovereign,
It being infallibly true that nothing can *more* establish your throne and assure the peace and prosperity of your people than the unity and sincerity of religion, we your

---

12. The petition concerning religion was drafted by the Lower House on the basis of articles drawn up by the subcommittee of religion and presented to the Commons committee of the whole House on 28 June (H. of C., pp. 260–264). The petition was sent to the Lords on 1 July. It was discussed in the Upper House on 4 July and alterations in the Commons' draft were then proposed. The changes propounded by the Lords were discussed in Commons later on 4 July (H. of C., pp. 298–299 and 305–306) and eleven alterations were accepted (see Sir Edward Coke's message, above, H. of L., 5 July, O.B.). By 6 July the petition was "fair engrossed with the amendment" (H. of L., 6 July, p. 96). Printed below is the authoritative text of the completed petition entered on the parliament roll (*Rot. Parl.*, 1 *Car.* I, P.R.O., c 65/189), which contains only a few word variants from the copy in the MS. L.J. Collated with the parliament roll text is the Commons'

draft version of the petition from B.L. Add. 48,091, ff. 45v–54. The editors have italicized those words and phrases which were added to the Commons' draft version by the Upper House and have footnoted those words which were altered before the petition was completed. The petition and the King's answers are printed in Cobbett, *Parl. Hist.*, II, 21–25, and Rushworth, *Hist. Collections*, I, 181–186. Versions of it are also included in various manuscript collections for the parliament, such as Petyt 538/8, ff. 161–163; Q.C. 449, ff. 278v–287v; Osborn fb 155, ff. 104–109; Cornell Univ. MSS. +H83, ff. 5–7; Braye MSS. 1, ff. 85–87v; Peniarth 410D, pt. 2, Nat. Lib. Wales; and S.P. 16/5:25; a report of the answers only is in S.P. 16/4:68. The *Negotium* includes a copy of the completed petition in the account of 4 July and the King's answers on 9 August.

Majesty's most humble and loyal subjects, *the Lords spiritual and temporal* and Commons in this present parliament assembled, observing that of late there is an apparent mischievous increase of papists in your dominions, hold ourselves bound in conscience and duty to *re*present the same to your sacred Majesty together with the dangerous consequence, and what we conceive to be the principal causes *thereof*, and what may be the remedies.

The dangers appear in these particulars:

1. Their desperate ends, being the subversion both of church and state, and the restlessness of their spirits to attain those ends, the doctrine of their teachers and leaders persuading them that therein they shall do God good service.

2. Their evident and strict dependency upon such foreign princes as no way affect the good of your Majesty and this state.

3. The opening a way of popularity to the ambition of any who shall adventure to make himself head of so great a party.

The principal causes of the increase of papists:

1. The want of the due execution of the laws against Jesuits, seminary priests, and popish recusants, occasioned partly by connivancy of the state, partly by *some defects in the laws themselves, and partly by the manifold*[13] abuses of officers.

2. The interposing of foreign princes by their ambassadors and agents in favor of them.

3. Their great concourse to the City and their frequent conventicles and conferences there.

4. *Their open and usual resort to the houses and chapels of foreign ambassadors.*

5. The education of their children in seminaries and houses of their religion in foreign parts which of late have been greatly multiplied and enlarged for entertaining of the English.

6. That in some[14] places of this your realm, your people are not sufficiently instructed in the knowledge of true religion.

7. The licentious printing and dispersing of popish and seditious books.

8. The employment of men ill-affected in religion in places of government who *do, shall, or may* countenance the popish party.

The remedies against this contagious and dangerous disease we conceive to be these ensuing (*whereunto his Majesty's answers are set down severally, as they follow in order*):

1. That the youth of this realm be carefully educated by able and religious schoolmasters, and they to be enjoined diligently to catechize and instruct their scholars in the grounds and principles of true religion. And whereas, by many complaints from divers parts of the[15] kingdom, it does plainly appear that sundry popish schoolmasters, dissembling their religion, have craftily crept in and obtained the places of teaching in divers counties and thereby infected and perverted their scholars and so fitted them to be transported to the popish seminaries beyond the seas.[16]

That therefore there be[17] great care in the choice and admitting of schoolmasters and that the ordinaries make diligent inquiry of their demeanors, and proceed to the removing of such as shall be faulty or justly suspected.

[Answer] This is well allowed of and, for the better performance of what is desired, letters shall be written to the two archbishops and from them letters to go to all the ordinaries in their several provinces to see this done, and the several ordinaries to give account of their doings herein to the

---

13. *many.* B.L. Add. 48,091.

14. *many.* B.L. Add. 48,091.

15. *your.* B.L. Add. 48,091.

16. B.L. Add. 48,091 includes: *In which there has been a special complaint against one Conyers at York.* The Lords

had requested that the reference to Conyers be deleted because he had already been punished. See H. of C., 4 July, p. 298 and n. 28.

17. *be a.* B.L. Add. 48,091.

archbishops respectively, and they to give account to his Majesty of their proceeding herein.

2. That the ancient discipline of the two universities be restored, being the famous nurseries of literature and virtue.

[Answer] This is approved by his Majesty, and the Chancellor of each university shall be required to cause due execution of it.

3. That special care be taken to enlarge the preaching of the word of God through all parts of your Majesty's dominions, as being the most powerful means for the planting of true religion and rooting out of the contrary, to which end, among other things, may it please your Majesty to advise the bishops by fatherly entreatment and tender usage to reduce to the peaceable and orderly service of the Church such able ministers as have been formerly silenced, that there may be a profitable use of their ministry in these needful and dangerous times, and that nonresidency, pluralities, and commendams may be moderated, where we cannot forbear *most humbly* to thank your Majesty for diminishing the number of your own chaplains, nothing doubting of your[18] like princely care for the well-bestowing of your benefices both to the comfort of your people and *for* the encouragement of the universities, being full of grave and able ministers unfurnished of[19] livings.

[Answer] This his Majesty likes well, so as it be applied only to such ministers as are peaceable, orderly, and conformable to the Church government. For pluralities, nonresidency, and commendams, these are so *now* moderated that the archbishop affirms there be now no dispensations for pluralities granted, nor no man *now* has above two benefices, and those not above thirty miles distant. And for avoiding nonresidency, the canon in that case provided shall

be duly put in execution. For commendams, they shall be but sparingly granted, only in cases where the exility and smallness of the bishopric requires it. Also, his Majesty will cause that the benefices belonging to him shall be well bestowed and, for the *better* propagating of religion, his Majesty recommends to the House of Parliament that care may be taken and provision made that every parish shall allow competent maintenance for an able minister, and that the owners of parsonages impropriate would allow to the vicars, curates, and ministers in villages and places belonging to their parsonages sufficient stipends and allowances for preaching ministers.

4. That there may be straight provision against the transporting of English children to the seminaries beyond the seas, for recalling *of* them who are there already placed, and for the punishing of such of your subjects as are maintainers of those seminaries, or of the scholars there, considering that besides the seducing of your people[20] great sums of money are yearly expended upon them to the impoverishing of this kingdom.

[Answer] The law in this case shall be put in execution and, further, there shall be letters written to the Lord Treasurer as[21] also to the Lord Admiral, that all the ports of the realm and the creeks and members thereof be straightly kept, and strict searches made to this end, and proclamation shall be to recall both the children of noblemen and the children of any other men, and they to return by a day. Also the maintenance of seminaries and scholars there shall be punished according to law.

5. That no popish recusant be permitted to come within the court unless your Majesty be pleased to call him upon special occasion agreeable to the statute of *3° Jac., cap. 5°*. And whereas your Majesty, for the preventing of many apparent mischiefs both to

---

18. *the.* B.L. Add. 48,091.
19. *with.* B.L. Add. 48,091.

20. *subjects.* B.L. Add. 48,091.
21. *and.* B.L. Add. 48,091.

your Majesty and the state, have [*sic*], in your princely wisdom, taken order that none of your natural-born subjects, not professing the true religion by law established, be admitted into the service of your most royal consort the Queen, we give your Majesty most humble thanks and desire that your order therein may constantly be observed.[22]

[Answer] If his Majesty shall find or be informed of any concourse of recusants to the court, the law shall be strictly followed. And his Majesty is pleased that by proclamation the British and Irish subjects shall be put in the same case. And as his Majesty has provided in the treaty with France, so his purpose is to keep it that none of his subjects shall *be* admitted into his[23] service, *or into the service* of his royal consort the Queen that are popish recusants.

6. That all the laws now standing in force against Jesuits, seminary priests, and others having taken orders *by authority* derived from the see of Rome, be put in due execution. And, to the intent they may not pretend to be surprised, that a speedy and certain day be prefixed by your Majesty's proclamation for their departure out of this realm and all other your dominions, and not to return upon the severest penalties[24] of the law now in force against them. And that all your Majesty's subjects may be thereby also admonished not to receive, entertain, comfort, or conceal any of them upon the penalties which may be lawfully inflicted. And that all such priests,[25] Jesuits, and recusants convicted which are or shall be imprisoned for recusancy, or any other

cause, may be so strictly restrained as that none shall have conference with them, thereby to avoid the contagion of their corrupt religion. And that no man who shall be justly suspected of popery be suffered to be keeper of any your Majesty's prisons.

[Answer] The law in this case provided shall be put in execution and a proclamation shall be to the effect desired, and such restraint shall be made as is desired. And no man that is justly suspected of popery shall be suffered to be keeper of any his Majesty's prisons.

7. That your Majesty be pleased to take such order, as to your princely wisdom shall be expedient, that no *natural-born subject, or* stranger, bishop, nor any other by authority from[26] the see of Rome confer ecclesiastical orders or exercise any ecclesiastical function whatsoever towards or upon any[27] your Majesty's natural subjects within any of your dominions.

[Answer] This is fit to be ordered accordingly as it is prayed, and it shall be so published by proclamation.

8. That your Majesty's learned counsel may receive order and commandment to consider of[28] all former grants of recusants' lands, that such of them may be avoided[29] as are made to the recusant's use or trust, or out of which the recusant[30] receives benefit, which are either void or voidable by law.

[Answer] The King will give order to his learned counsel to consider of the grants, and will do accordingly as is desired.

9. That your Majesty be[31] likewise pleased straightly to command all judges

---

22. The Lords had proposed revisions in article 5, see H. of C., 4 July, p. 298. The B.L. Add. 48,091 draft petition reads as follows: *According to which statute we also most humbly pray your Majesty that none of your natural born subjects not professing the true religion by law established be admitted into the service of your most royal consort the Queen, for the preventing of many apparent mischiefs both to your Majesty and the state where the contrary must needs ensue.*

23. *the.* B.L. Add. 48,091.

24. *punishment.* B.L. Add. 48,091.

25. *papists and Jesuits as shall be imprisoned be kept close prisoners to avoid the contagion of their corrupt religion.* B.L. Add. 48,091.

26. *derived from.* B.L. Add. 48,091.

27. *any of.* B.L. Add. 48,091.

28. *to look into.* B.L. Add. 48,091.

29. *and to avoid such of them.* B.L. Add. 48,091.

30. *recusants receive any benefit if by law they can.* B.L. Add. 48,091.

31. *will be.* B.L. Add. 48,091.

and ministers of justice, both ecclesiastical and temporal, to see the laws of this realm against popish recusants to be duly executed and, namely, that the censure of excommunication be declared and certified[32] against them, and that they be not absolved but upon public satisfaction by yielding to conformity.

[Answer] His Majesty leaves the laws to their course and will give order in the point of excommunication as is desired.[33]

10. That your Majesty be pleased to remove from all places of authority and government all such persons as are either popish recusants or (according to direction of former acts of state) justly to be suspected.

[Answer] This his Majesty thinks fit, and will give order for it.[34]

11. That present order be taken for the disarming of all popish recusants legally convicted or justly suspected according to the laws in that behalf and the orders taken by his late Majesty's Privy Council upon reason of state.

[Answer] The laws and acts of state in this case provided shall be followed and put in execution.[35]

12. That your[36] Majesty be also pleased in regard of the great resort of recusants to[37] and about London to command that forthwith, upon pain of your indignation and severe execution of *the* laws, they retire themselves to their several countries, there to remain *confined* within five miles of their dwelling places.

[Answer] For this the laws in force shall be forthwith executed.[38]

13. And whereas your[39] Majesty *has* straightly command*ed* and take*n* order that none of your natural-born subjects repair to *the hearing of* mass *or other susperstitious services* at the chapels or houses of foreign ambassadors, or in[40] any other place wheresoever,[41] *we give your Majesty most humble thanks and desire that your commandment and order therein may be continued and observed*, and that the offenders herein be punished according to the laws.

[Answer] The King gives assent hereunto and will see that observed which herein has been commanded by him.[42]

14. That all such[43] insolences as any popishly affected have lately committed, or shall hereafter commit, to the dishonor of *our* religion, or to the wrong of the true professors thereof, be exemplarily punished.[44]

[Answer] This shall be done as is desired.[45]

---

32. *pronounced.* B.L. Add. 48,091. Sir Henry Marten had objected to the word "pronounced" and proposed "certified" in its place. See H. of C., 30 June, p. 277.

33. *That his Majesty's judges and justices shall be forthwith commanded to see the laws put in execution against popish recusants and that they shall be excommunicated and not absolved but according to law.* B.L. Add. 48,091.

34. The answer to article 10 is omitted in B.L. Add. 48,091. Apparently the copyist erred in his placement of the King's answers within the B.L. Add. 48,091 text of the petition; they are frequently out of order from this point on.

35. *That they shall be disarmed accordingly.* B.L. Add. 48,091.

36. *his.* B.L. Add. 48,091.

37. *in.* B.L. Add. 48,091.

38. *The restraint of popish recusants from resorting to London shall be done as is desired according to the law.* B.L. Add. 48,091.

39. *That your.* B.L. Add. 48,091.

40. *to.* B.L. Add. 48,091.

41. *whatsoever.* B.L. Add. 48,091.

42. For article 13, B.L. Add. 48,091 includes the King's answer for article 12.

43. *public Jesuits' insolencies by them committed as any.* B.L. Add. 48,091.

44. *And namely that heinous act of one Foster openly tearing the Bible in the Cathedral Church of Canterbury.* B.L. Add. 48,091. In view of the fact that Foster had already been partially punished, the Lords proposed omitting the clause pertaining to him. See H. of C., 4 July, p. 299.

45. *All public insolencies and offenses by them committed shall be punished according to the law as is desired.* B.L. Add. 48,091. In the draft petition the answer to article 14 is followed by an article for a commission which was removed at the Lords' request (see H. of C., 4 July, p. 299). The article was as follows:

That a general commission be granted to choose able persons to direct and oversee the execution of the laws against popish recusants, and to prevent the fraud now ordinarily

15. That the statute of *primo Eliz.* for the paying of twelve pence every Sunday by such as shall be absent from divine service in the church without lawful excuse may be put in due execution,[46] the rather for that the penalty is by *the* law given to the poor, and therefore not to be dispensed with.

[Answer] It is fit this statute be executed and the penalty shall not be dispensed with.

16. Lastly, that your Majesty be pleased to extend your princely care also over the kingdom of Ireland that the like courses may be there taken for the restoring and establishing of true religion.

[Answer] His Majesty's cares are and shall be extended over that kingdom of Ireland and will do all that a religious king should do for the restoring and establishing of true religion there.

And thus, most gracious Sovereign, according to our duty and zeal to God and religion, to your Majesty, and your safety, to the Church and commonwealth and their peace and prosperity, we have made a plain and faithful declaration of the present estate, the causes and remedies of this increasing disease of popery, humbly offering the same to your Majesty's princely care and wisdom. The answer of your Majesty's father, our late Sovereign of famous memory, upon the like petition did give us great

comfort and expectation of a reformation in these things.[47] But your Majesty's many gracious promises made in that kind do give us confidence and assurance of the continual performance thereof; in which comfort and confidence reposing ourselves, we most humbly pray for your Majesty's long continuance in all princely felicity.[48]

[**L.J. 481**; p. 84] The petition and answers being read, the Lord Admiral said: That as his Majesty took well your putting him in mind of this care of religion, so he would have done all this granted at this time, though he never had been petitioned unto. Neither does his Majesty place this petition in this order as a wheel to draw on other affairs and designs, but leaves them to move upon their own spheres, as being of sufficient poise and weight within themselves. What is done in this petition comes from these two fountains: conscience and duty to his father who, in his last speech, recommended unto him the person, not the religion, of his Queen.[49]

Then his Grace signified that by the King's commandment he was to give unto both Houses an account of the fleet and all the preparations thereof, which his Grace began in this manner, *vizt.:*[50]

---

used to defeat your Majesty of the penalties and to save the offenders from punishment. And that the particular commissions into the several counties for execution of these laws may extend to all counties, cities, and towns and other liberties within the precincts of the same shire.

46. *S.R.*, 1 *Eliz.* I, c. 2.

47. On James I's answer to the 1624 petition concerning religion, see above, H. of L., 1 July, n. 3.

48. *But your Majesty's own gracious promises at the last parliament which (with much joy and thankfulness) we do remember, that you would never by any treaty with foreign princes be engaged to do anything in prejudice of our religion or to the slacking of the due execution of the laws against popish recusants, do give us confidence; reposing ourselves, we most humbly pray for your Majesty's long continuance in all princely fidelity.* B.L. Add. 48,091. On 6 April 1624, following a conference with the Lords on the draft of the petition against recusants, Solicitor Heath reported to the Commons that the Lords informed them that the Prince "professed and bound it with an oath

that whensoever it should please God to bestow upon him any lady that were popish, she should have no further liberty but for her family, and no advantage to the recusants at home". *C.J.*, I, 756. See also, *Lords Debates 1624 and 1626*, pp. 53–59; and Ruigh, *Parliament of 1624*, pp. 243–244.

49. See H. of L., 20 June, n. 15.

50. The Duke of Buckingham's account of the fleet is printed in Cobbett, *Parl. Hist.*, II, 26–31. The speech apparently circulated as a separate and is included in various manuscript collections: Tanner 276, ff. 154–158; Osborn fb 57, pp. 179–182; Braye MSS. 1, ff. 92v–95v. See also the Lower House accounts, H. of C., 9 August, O.B.

Buckingham, as Lord Admiral, and others, had been granted a special commission on 15 April 1625 "to take into their considerations all such particulars as shall concern the security of all the King's dominions and for furnishing and preparing the navy". 1 *Car.* I, pt. 3, MS. Cal. Pat. Rolls, f. 10.

[p. 85] That the first and last time he had the honor to speak in this auditory was of the same business, and then he was so happy as to be honored and applauded by both Houses.[51] And he made no question but, speaking with the same heart, and of the same business, he should be so now; for, if you look upon the change of the estate in Christendom, you cannot think it less than a miracle. Then the King of Spain was sought and courted by all the world. He was become master of the Valtellina, had broken all Germany in pieces and was possessed of the Palatinate. The princes of Germany were weak and not able to resist and by reason of my master's neutrality caused by a treaty he kept all other kings and princes in awe. Now, on the contrary side, the Valtellina is at liberty. The war is proclaimed beyond the Alps. The King of Denmark is in arms with seventeen thousand foot and six thousand horse, besides commissions to make them up thirty thousand. The King of Sweden is also interested. The princes of the union are revived and the King of France engaged against Spain and, for that purpose, has made peace with his own subjects and joined and confederated himself with Savoy and Venice.[52] Why should not he therefore hope for the same success, considering that, since that time of his last speech to both Houses, there was not one action or a thought of his that leveled at any other than the same object, that is, to please your desire? If he should credit all rumors (which he will not do), he should speak with some confusion of fear, to hold the same place he formerly

had in your affections but, having still the same virtuous ambition and, considering his own heart to the King and state, he could find no cause of alteration but of all courage and confidence.

Here he made a request to the House of Commons that if any man has spoken or shall speak anything in discharge of his conscience, zeal of reformation, or love to his country which may seem to reflect upon some particular persons, he may be the last that shall apply it to himself because he is confidently assured of two things: first, that they are just not to fall upon him without cause, so lately approved by them; and secondly, that himself shall deserve nothing that shall unbecome a faithful Englishman.

For the method of his ensuing speech his Grace chose rather to proceed by way of questions and answers rather than in one continued speech, as being the speedier way and means to yield satisfaction.

He would take his rise, he said, from the breach of the treaties and alliance, and put questions upon [**L.J. 482**] himself, yet none but such as should be material to the business in hand.

Here his Grace did move some twelve, which the Lord Keeper said he would dissolve, for clearness and perspicuity['s] sake, into fourteen questions.

1. The first question: By what counsel these designs and actions of war were carried and enterprised?

The answer: First, by the counsel of the parliament; and this his Grace proved by the act of both Houses, *23° Martii 1623*, which was read.[53] And then his Grace pro-

51. As a prelude to the breaking of the Spanish treaties, Buckingham had delivered his narrative concerning the Spanish negotiations to both Houses at Whitehall on 24 February 1624. *L.J.*, III, 220–232. And on 17 April 1624 Buckingham informed a conference committee of both Houses of the King's letter to Spain concerning the dissolution of the treaties, of the King's intentions to appoint a Council of War, of troubles in Ireland, and of the need for supply. *C.J.*, I, 769–770.

52. For background on the European situation prior to the breaking of the Spanish treaties, see above, H.

of L., 18 June, n. 5. Concerning the changes since the breaking of those treaties, see Gardiner, *History of England*, V, 246–306.

53. On Tuesday 23 March 1624 a committee of both Houses presented a written "Proposition" to James I declaring that, upon his dissolution of the Spanish treaties, parliament would grant three subsidies and three fifteens towards "the defense of this realm, the securing of Ireland, the assistance of your neighbors the States of the United Provinces, and others your Majesty's friends and allies, and for the setting forth of your royal navy". *L.J.*, III, 275. In his response

ceeded and said: Here you see, my Lords and Gentlemen, that his Majesty, moved by this counsel, applied himself accordingly for the defense.of the realm, the securing of Ireland, the assisting of our neighbors, the States of the United Provinces, and other our friends and allies, and for the setting forth of the navy royal.

His Majesty, looking into his purse, saw enough to do all the former actions, but not this latter; for, when he came to consider the navy there was neither money nor preparations. Yet, looking upon the affairs of Christendom, he found that of most necessity. Hereupon his Majesty, of famous memory, did his Grace that honor as to write from Newmarket unto him at London a letter to this effect: That, looking into the affairs of Christendom, he found it necessary that a royal fleet should be prepared and set in readiness, but that he had no money. Wherefore his Lordship and his friends must begin to lay out, and no doubt but others would follow, and by [p. 86] this means the King might the longer lie concealed and undiscovered in the enterprise, as bearing the name of the subjects only,

and other princes, in hope to draw him on, would sooner come to the business.[54]

Upon this letter his Grace leaped into the action with all alacrity and, having received all that he had from his Majesty, was most desirous and held it a happiness to pour it out upon his service and occasions. But this he did not upon his own head, but fortified with the advice and counsel of these worthy persons: the Lord Conway, Lord Chichester, Lord Grandison, Lord Carew, Lord Brooke, Lord Hervey, Sir Robert Mansell, and Sir John Coke.[55]

Their first consultation was of the war; the next, of the means; but both the one and the other was justified by more than himself. He never did any thing but by them. Nothing was ever resolved on or altered but in their company; for either he repaired to them, or else they did him that honor (as his Grace termed it) to resort to his chamber. When all was thus digested and prepared and that they came to proportion time and levies, then, with the King's leave, the business was imparted to all the lords of the Council and the account was made unto them and allowed by them,

---

to the committee of both Houses, the King declared that he would break the treaties with Spain regarding the Palatinate and the marriage of Charles, then Prince of Wales, to the Infanta. This was reported to the Upper House by the Duke of Buckingham on 24 March. *L.J.*, III, 279. The same day (24 March) a conference was called with a committee of the Lower House wherein it was agreed that a subcommittee of each House would together draw up the King's declaration of 23 March (*L.J.*, III, 280; *C.J.*, I, 749) which was then read in each House respectively on 25 March and is printed in full in the *L.J.* with the proceedings of that day. *L.J.*, III, 282–283. See also S.P. 14/161:18–24, 36, 46. On the dissolution of the Spanish treaties, see also Gardiner, *History of England*, V, 172–248; Ruigh, *Parliament of 1624*, pp. 230, 236, 241–242, 246–247, 248; and Russell, *Parliaments*, pp. 145–203.

54. We have been unable to find the letter. The naval preparations were in anticipation of the expedition to Cadiz which sailed in October 1625. According to the account presented by Sir John Coke to the Commons on 8 July, and reiterated by Coke in reference to Buckingham's answer to his third question (below, p.

163), Buckingham had furnished above 44,000 *l.* toward the costs of the navy, and other officers had contributed over 50,000 *l.* See H. of C., 8 July, below, p. 348. By 18 April 1624 a warrant had been issued to Buckingham to equip twelve ships with ordnance, provisions, and men ready to sail. S.P.14/163:4. See also the copy of a warrant of December 1624 from the King to the Council of War concerning repayment of the sums advanced by Buckingham for setting forth the twelve ships and giving further orders for the repair and furnishing of more ships. S.P.14/176:58.

55. With the exception of Lord Hervey and Sir John Coke, these men were all members of the original Council of War appointed by the King on 21 April 1624 and later named in the 1624 subsidy act. The other members of the Council of War were: Sir Edward Cecil, Sir Horace Vere, Sir John Ogle, and Sir Thomas Button. S.P. 14/163:18; *S.R.*, 21 *Jac.* I, c. 33; and see 22 *Jac.* I, pt. 1, MS. Cal. Pat. Rolls, f. 147. William, Lord Hervey, was added to the Council of War when it was reappointed on 14 April 1625. Rymer, *Foedera*, VIII, pt. 1, pp. 18–19.

who said there openly (his Majesty being present), that if this were put in execution it would do well, and gave some attributes unto it.[56]

Here Sir John Coke justified the showing and approving of these accounts at the Council Table: That the accounts consisted of long particulars of soldiers to be levied, mariners to be pressed, forwardness of the ships and provision, and that nothing wanted[57] but money, and that he had all these particulars ready to be shown to the House of Commons if they should require it.

His Grace proceeded and showed that he was so religious to guide these great affairs by counsel that, at his journey into France (which fell out about this time),[58] he desired his Majesty to recommend the business to a select council, as his Majesty did, to the Lord Treasurer, the Lord Chamberlain, the Lord Conway, and the Lord Brooke, who in his absence took care of the same.[59] This his Grace thought fit to tell your Lordships, that you may see by what counsel this great business was carried and that, in all the managing thereof, he stepped no step but by their approbation.

2. The second question: Why did not his Majesty declare the enemy presently upon the granting of those three subsidies?[60]

The answer: His Majesty considered the estate of Christendom at that season and found it full of danger to declare the enemy for three reasons: first, because that great enemy would be more prepared; secondly, Spain being the enemy, our merchants would be embargoed who are now drawn home; thirdly, our friends, finding us so long unprepared after our declaration, had despaired and never believed any reality of our intendments.

3. The third question: Whether this vast sum of forty [sic] thousand pounds bestowed upon the navy, together with forty thousand pounds more to be now employed, and threescore thousand pounds at the return, be so frugally husbanded as is fit?

The answer: This his Grace refers to Sir John Coke's accounts, which the House of Commons may peruse and, when Sir John Coke has done, the particular officers also shall be ready to justify it with their accounts.[61]

Here Sir John Coke interposed that he had already showed his account and that his Grace had laid out of his own four and forty thousand pounds, and the Treasurer of the Navy (at his request) above fifty thousand pounds; and his Grace added that all this borrowed money was managed by the proper officers as if it had issued out of the Exchequer, and had not been borrowed elsewhere.

[p. 87] 4. The fourth question: Whether a

---

56. A list of proportions for the levying of troops, etc., was presented to the Privy Council on 13 October 1624 and by 31 October the Council was preparing letters to be sent out to the counties for the levying of 12,000 men. See *A.P.C., 1623–1625*, pp. 338, 351–353.

57. *was wanted.* Printed edition.

58. Buckingham left England for France on 12 May 1625 in command of the fleet which was to bring Henrietta Maria across to England. During his several weeks in France, he attempted unsuccessfully to negotiate an alliance with the French against Spain and to arrange for a peaceful settlement of the civil strife between the French government and the Huguenots. Gardiner, *History of England*, V, 326–333.

59. This is the "selected or cabinet council" referred to by John Chamberlain in his letter of 23 April 1625 to Sir Dudley Carleton. Chamberlain, *Letters*, II, 611.

60. The question is omitted in the Petyt 538/8 version of the Duke's speech (H. of C., 9 August, below, p. 436). The three subsidies referred to are those granted in the previous parliament: *S.R., 21 Jac.* I, c. 33.

61. On 8 July Sir John Coke, at the King's command, had presented to the House of Commons an account of the King's estate. See H. of C., 8 July, O.B. On money advanced by Sir William Russell, Treasurer of the Navy (below), see S.P. 14/182:28. On war expenditures, 1624–1628, see Dietz, *Public Finance*, pp. 216–222.

considerable sum of money be yet required?

The answer: Forty thousand pounds is yet necessary, but that our master is exhausted, his treasure anticipated, his lands pawned, his plate offered to be pawned but not accepted, and yet his Majesty must be maintained.

5. The fifth question: Whether this fleet was ever intended to go out or not?[62]

The answer: There have been some flying rumors to that effect. But what policy were it in the King with the charge of four hundred thousand pounds to amaze the world, cozen his people, and put you to such a hazard? What should he gain by an act that should make him blush when he met with you again? Certainly the King would never employ such a sum, but for a necessity in the affairs of Christendom to do it. And it was done with an intention to set it out with all the speed that might be.

[**L.J. 483**] 6. The sixth question: Why was not this want of money foreseen in the first project of the whole service, but now only thought upon unexpectedly and dangerously considering the sickness? Why not before the last adjournment, whereby we are cast upon so unseasonable a time?

The answer: It was foreseen before, but interrupted by unfortunate accidents: 1, the death of the late King; 2, the funeral, which for decency could follow no sooner; 3, the journey into France and the marriage, which procured more delays than was expected, but necessary.

Since the opening of the parliament his Majesty declared this necessity and told you plainly that this sitting must be not for counsel but resolution. And when he understood the grant of the two subsidies he conceived that money to be but a matter of

custom to welcome him to the crown, and intended, when you should present them unto him, to dilate of the business more at large, as afterwards he did by Sir John Coke.[63]

7. The seventh question: Who gave counsel to meet so suddenly when the sickness was so dangerously spread?

The answer: His Majesty commanded him to say that it was the business itself which gave the counsel and the necessity of it, else his Majesty would not have hazarded the two Houses, nor the rest of the kingdom by the spreading of it. If he had been able any way, without your help, to have set out the navy he would have done it and trusted upon you for a supply afterward.

If it be a fault (as I see none, said his Grace), why should the realm, the action, and the state of Christendom suffer for it? If it be undertaken for your good and the King's honor (now budding), and the state of Christendom, why should a particular man's fault make it miscarry? I hope your wisdoms shall so pierce through it, as to set it forward.

8. The eighth question: Why should not the King help this action with his own estate?

The answer: Judge you whether he does; for, observing the great gift you gave the [p. 88] sessions before,[64] he was unwilling to take any more from you and laid all his estate upon the enterprise, and will do so again as soon as he shall be enabled.

9. The ninth question: Is not the time of the year too far spent for the navy to go forth?

The answer: The King answered this the last day. Better half the navy should perish than the going forth thereof should be stayed.[65] It would show such want of coun-

---

62. The plan for the expedition to Cadiz was kept secret, but because of the levies of mariners and provisioning of ships rumors concerning the expedition were rampant. See H. of C., 12 August, n. 11.

63. I.e., on 4 August. For Sir John Coke's speech, see above, pp. 133–135.

64. This is presumably a reference to the three subsidies and three fifteens granted in 1624 (*S.R.*, 21 *Jac.* I, c. 33) rather than to the 1625 grant (see H. of C., 8 July, n. 9).

65. This is a reiteration of a point made in the King's speech of 4 August. See above, p. 133.

sel and experience in the design, want of courage, weakness, and beggarliness in being not able to go through with it. And for the time: there was not one only, but three ends proposed of this service, and the time of year is yet seasonable for either of them. I could demonstrate the same if the design might be published, which your wisdoms will not think fit.[66]

Here his Grace said he would satisfy the Houses in some other things.

10. The tenth question: Whether those eight ships lent to the French King were paid with the subsidy money, or to be employed against the Rochellers?[67]

The answer: To the first, those eight ships were employed at the charge of the French King; to the second, it is not always fit for kings to give account of their counsels. Judge the King by the event.

11. The eleventh question: Whether, having been our servant to break with Spain, his Grace made not a worse match with France, and upon harsher conditions?

The answer: I hope the contrary will appear by the answers to your petition.[68]

And he assured us that his Majesty had broken no public faith in giving the same answers.

12. The twelfth question: Did not his Grace serve us in breaking the treaties with Spain out of particular spleen and malice to Count Olivares?[69]

The answer: There was no cause for him to hate Olivares; he was the means to make his Grace happy, for out of his hands came those papers by which his Grace gained the love of a nation which before thought not so well of him. He is not vindictive in his nature; he can forgive those which had no such natural respects to that country as Olivares had, neither does his Grace love that any man should be an instrument by ill means to do a good action, as Olivares intended to serve his master and kingdom by indirect means.

And his Grace can make a further proof that he is not vindictive; he can forgive one of his own nation that concurred with Olivares,[70] but he was pleased to leave that business asleep which, if it should wake, would prove a lion to devour him which was the author of it, meaning one of our own nation who cooperated with Olivares.

---

66. See above, n. 62.

67. On 8 May 1625 the Duke of Buckingham had ordered Captain John Pennington and the fleet of eight English ships contracted for by the French King to proceed to France. S.P. 16/2:37. Initially the agreement with France stated that the ships be used "against whomsoever except the King of Great Britain", which left open the possibility that the ships might be employed against the Huguenots. Sir John Coke clarified the orders after they were given, stating that the ships be used to serve against the "foreign enemies" of France and England, not "in the civil wars of the French". S.P. 16/2:74. See also S.P.16/3:71, 99, 120, and Gardiner, *History of England*, V, 328–329. However, Pennington resisted turning the ships over to the French until on 28 July he was commanded by the crown to deliver his ship or answer at his "uttermost peril". Eliot Papers, Vol. 9, ff. 62, 65; see also, S.P. 16/4:78–85, 100, 105, 114–122 passim, 132–138, and Salvetti dispatch, p. 28. Section G of the Appendix, below, contains a selection of correspondence relating to the loan of ships to France, including many of the State Paper documents referred to above. The matter of Buckingham's contracting to make available En-

glish ships to the French became article seven in the impeachment proceedings brought against him in 1626. See *L.J.*, III, 621, 661.

68. I.e., the King's answers to the petition concerning religion, reported earlier this day. See above, pp. 155–160.

69. While in Madrid in 1623 negotiating the Spanish marriage the Duke of Buckingham and Count Olivares (Gaspar de Guzman, Duke of San Lucar) had often argued over the treaty arrangements. See *Cal. S.P. Venetian, 1623–1625*, pp. 20–21, 25, 37–38, 40, 50, 53, 114, 117. See also, Gardiner, *History of England*, V, 38, 111–112, 116; and Ruigh, *Parliament of 1624*, pp. 349–352.

70. I.e., John Digby, Earl of Bristol, who was adamantly hostile to Buckingham's handling of the Spanish negotiations in 1623. See Ruigh, *Parliament of 1624*, pp. 345–381; Russell, *Parliaments*, p. 216. Bristol was charged and examined in the 1626 parliament regarding his part in the negotiations with Spain, but the session was dissolved before the investigation was completed. See *L.J.*, III, 587, 588, 591, 594, 631–645, 648, 655, 669, 670–671, 672, 673, 676, 680–681.

[p. 89] 13. The thirteenth question: It will be objected in the thirteenth place that hitherto his Grace speaks of nothing but immense charges, which the kingdom is not able to bear, as, the King of Denmark, thirty thousand pounds per mensem; to Count Mansfeld, twenty thousand pounds a month; to the Low Countries, eight thousand pounds a month; to Ireland, two thousand six hundred pounds a month; besides the seconding of the fleet with a supply for the which twelve of his Majesty's ships are now in preparing?[71]

The answer: Make the King chief of the war by a diversion in this kind and he will give a greater advantage to all his allies than by allowing them fifty thousand pounds, nay, a hundred thousand pounds a month. [L.J. 484] What is it for his allies to snatch with the King of Spain? To win a town today and lose it tomorrow? To get or lose a town by snatching?[72] It is almost impossible to hope for a conquest in this kind, the King of Spain being so able by land. But let the King (our sovereign) be master of the wars elsewhere and make a diversion, and let the enemy be compelled to spend his money and men in other places, and our allies in these parts will be suddenly and unperceivedly strengthened and enabled. And by this kind of war you send no coin out of the land, you issue nothing but beef, mutton, and powder, and the kingdom is not impoverished but may make good returns.

14. The fourteenth question: Where is the enemy?

The answer: Make the fleet ready to go out and the King has given him[73] commandment to bid you name the enemy yourselves. Put the sword into his Majesty's hands and he will employ it to your honor, and the good of the true religion.

As you issue nothing that is lost, so will you bring home somewhat again, and henceforward maintain the war by the perquisites thereof; make but once an entrance, it may afterward be maintained with profit.

When the enemy is declared you may have letters of marque, none shall be denied. I have not been (said his Grace) so idle, but I shall make propositions of venturing whither you yourselves may go and shall have the honey of the business.

Lastly, his Grace told us that the King commanded him to admonish the assembly to take care of the season and their own health, for if you lose time, no money can purchase it. And he ended with this apology: If, in this relation, through my weakness, I have injured the affairs, the King, the estate of Christendom, I crave your pardon; my intentions were good.

The LORD KEEPER further reported: That the message which the Lord Treasurer was to deliver from his Majesty at that time also was to let them know his Majesty's estate.

His Lordship[74] produced a paper wherein he had set the same down according as his memory and the time would permit him on the sudden. He divided the same into three parts: 1, the estate the late King left; 2, the estate the King now stands in; 3, and how it will be in the future.

1. The first his Lordship divided into three parts: the late King's debts, anticipations, and engagements.

His debts are to London and other gen-

---

71. On these military expenditures, see the accounts presented by Sir John Coke on 8 July and 4 August, below, pp. 347–348, 350–352, 387–388; and see the following report of the Lord Treasurer's speech, below. On war expenditures, 1624–1628, see Dietz, *Public Finance*, pp. 216–222.

72. *scratching.* Printed edition.

73. I.e., the Duke of Buckingham.

74. I.e., James, Lord Ley, Lord Treasurer. For Pym's report to the Commons of the Lord Treasurer's speech, see H. of C., 9 August, pp. 431–432. See also the brief report included on 8 August at the end of the Petyt 538/8 account of the afternoon proceedings, below, p. 427.

tlemen, borrowed upon the Great Seal, [p. 90] and the lords' bonds, six score thousand pounds, besides growing interest.[75]

To the wardrobe, forty thousand pounds at the least, part whereof is due to poor people.[76]

To the King of Denmark, seventy-five thousand pounds and the interest, which was borrowed for the Palatinate.[77]

Arrearages for pensions, a large sum but not cast up.

To his household, a great sum, which his Lordship left to the officers thereof to relate unto the Commons.

The anticipations made by the late King of his rents before they were due come to fifty thousand pounds, which was presently bestowed on this action.

His engagements are for the pay of six thousand foot in the Low Countries, of ten thousand foot under Count Mansfeld, the rigging, victualling, and providing this great navy, not the like in our memory.

2. As touching the state of the King as now it stands, his Lordship divided the same into debts and disbursements which he defrays out of his coffers; that his fa-

ther's debts, anticipations, and engagements lie all upon him.

His own debts as Prince came to seventy thousand pounds at the least, feared to be ninety thousand pounds, for payment whereof his Majesty has engaged those lands he then had and those commissioners' bonds. This great action brought his Majesty (when he was Prince) thus in debt; for he then gave twenty thousand pounds to the navy[78] and twenty thousand pounds to Count Mansfeld,[79] besides other great gifts that way, whereas before he did owe very little or nothing, to his Lordship's own knowledge.

His Majesty's disbursements defrayed out of his own coffers:

To the King of Denmark, six and forty thousand pounds.[80]

To the soldiers at Plymouth and Hull, sixteen thousand pounds.[81]

For mourning and funeral, twelve thousand pounds paid, and sixteen thousand pounds to pay.[82]

Expenses of the Queen, entertainment of ambassadors in diet and gifts, forty thousand pounds.[83]

75. In 1617 James I had requested a loan of 100,000 *l.* from the City for one year at ten percent interest. The Corporation of London assessed some 280 citizens and by June of that year raised 96,466 *l.* for the crown. Before he died James I privately repaid part of the loan but at the accession of Charles I the debt to those who had lent on Corporation bonds was 86,066 *l.* 13*s.* 4*d.* The Treasurer reports the total figure as debts to London and other gentlemen. See Ashton, *Crown and the Money Market*, pp. 122–126. See also, S.P. 16/3:9.

76. We have been unable to verify the figure of this debt. For a general discussion of the wardrobe finances during the early Stuart period, see Dietz, *Public Finance*, pp. 398–406.

77. James I had borrowed 50,000 *l.* from Christian IV in the summer of 1620 and another 25,000 *l.* the following year. See Gardiner, *History of England*, III, 386; IV, 180. At the same time that England was paying interest on the money borrowed from Denmark by James it was supplying funds agreed to by Charles for

furnishing Danish troops. See below, H. of C., 8 July, n. 8.

78. See H. of C., 8 July, p. 348.

79. See H. of C., 8 July, n. 36.

80. See H. of C., 8 July, n. 8.

81. Concerning costs and disbursements for soldiers at Plymouth and Hull, see S.P. 16/3:22, 52, 74; 4:50, 109.

82. The funeral expenses were estimated by John Chamberlain to be 50,000 *l.* (S.P. 16/2:55) and by the Tuscan ambassador to be 200,000 crowns (Salvetti dispatches, pp. 4, 17). For a list of persons receiving funeral blacks, the costs, and yardage, see K.S.R.L., MS E205, ff. 514v–552.

83. Between 1 April 1625 and 1 July 1626 a little over 9,000 *l.* was expended on the diet and expenses of the French ambassadors alone. S.P. 16/31:8. According to a letter, 9 July 1625, from Thomas Locke to Sir Dudley Carleton, S.P. 16/4:29 (see Appendix, below, p. 707), "All the money that is put in the Exchequer will not serve to feed the French".

Advanced to the Queen, fifty thousand pounds.[84]

The King and Queen of Bohemia, eleven thousand pounds.[85]

The navy, three hundred thousand pounds. And one hundred thousand pounds to be disbursed, *vizt.*, forty thousand pounds now and sixty thousand pounds at the return.[86]

3. The King's state in the future, as in charges of continuance, consist of these ten particulars:

1. Debts unpaid and interest.

2. Anticipations of old, of fifty thousand pounds.

3. Anticipations of new, of two hundred thousand pounds anticipated by himself to the emptying of all his coffers, even of that which should maintain him with bread and drink from this day forward.

4. To the King of Denmark, thirty thousand pounds per mensem.[87]

5. To Count Mansfeld, twenty thousand pounds per mensem.[88]

6. To the Low Countries, eight thousand five hundred pounds per mensem.[89]

7. To Ireland, two thousand six hundred pounds per mensem.[90]

8. The Queen's allowance and diet, thirty-seven thousand pounds per annum.[91]

9. To the King and Queen of Bohemia, twenty thousand pounds per annum.[92]

10. Preparations for defense of the realm, and seconding the navy.

[p. 91] His Lordship alleged that some sums are omitted because they are uncertain, and were before his Lordship's time. [**L.J. 485**] That no total is cast up because his Lordship had no auditor here. And promised that himself or his subordinate officers will be ready to give satisfaction of all or any of these particulars.

The Lord Keeper having ended these reports, the same were approved by the Lords.

The House was put in mind of the request of the Commons to join with them in a petition to the King, as was reported this morning by the Lord Archbishop of Canterbury, and moved to send a message to the Commons for a conference at three this afternoon touching the same, for that it may be they will not sit tomorrow.[93]

The message was sent accordingly by Mr.

---

84. The report of this account in Bedford MS. 197 (below, p. 432) gives the figure as 5,000 *l.* On 20 July 1625 a warrant was issued to pay to the cofferers of the King's household, Sir Henry Vane and Sir Marmaduke Darrell, 1,666 *l.* 13*s.* 4*d.* monthly for the expenses of the Queen's household. *Cal. S.P. Dom., 1625–1626*, p. 66. The allowance of money for the Queen's use was set at 15,000 *l.* per annum. *Cal. S.P. Dom., 1625–1626*, p. 157. For an unfinished list of the estimated yearly charges for diet and household allowances given to the Queen, dated 21 November 1625, see S.P. 16/10:11.

85. The report in Bedford MS. 197 (below, p. 432) gives the figure as 10,000 *l.* for the last half year. A monthly allowance of 500 *l.* for Frederick, King of Bohemia and Elector Palatine, and 1,000 *l.* for Elizabeth, Queen of Bohemia and Electress Palatine, a total of 18,000 *l.* per annum, was paid by England in 1623 and 1624. *Cal. S.P. Dom., 1623–1625*, p. 153; S.P. 14/150:44. By the end of 1624 the prince and princess Palatine requested an allowance increase of 500 *l.* a month (S.P. 14/177:53) which we have no evidence was granted. Money for the defense of the Palatinate

was derived primarily from the imposition on wines (see H. of C., 29 June, nn. 11–12).

86. See above, p. 163 and n. 61.

87. Concerning the English King's commitments to Christian IV of Denmark, see H. of C., 8 July, n. 8.

88. See H. of C., 8 July, n. 36.

89. On 5 June 1624 a treaty had been signed with the States General by which England was to supply six thousand soldiers to the Low Countries for two years. Gardiner, *History of England*, V, 244. Three months' pay for this force amounted to 25,932 *l.* (*Cal. S.P. Dom., Addenda, 1625–1649*, p. 24), a cost of 8,644 *l.* per month.

90. In August 1624 James I decided to send 2,250 foot and 230 horse to Ireland. S.P. 14/171:24. The accounts of the 1624 subsidy money indicate that a total of 12,443 *l.* was disbursed for the first six months' pay of this force. *Cal. S.P. Dom., Addenda, 1625–1649*, p. 26.

91. See above, n. 84.

92. See above, n. 85.

93. See above, p. 152 and nn. 1–3.

Attorney General and Mr. Doctor Eden, but the Commons were risen before.

[*Notice of Adjournment*]

II. MINUTE BOOK, H.L.R.O., M.M., 1625

[f. 49] *Die Martis 9° Augusti 1625.*
[*List of Lords Present; see A.T.*]

E. of Warwick excused by the Lord Keeper.

L. ARCHBISHOP OF CANTERBURY, first of the committee touching a conference with the Commons about religion, reported that the Commons desired the Lords to join in a petition with them to his Majesty.

The former part of the petition read.

L. ARCHBISHOP. That whereas there was a promise from his Majesty granted the 11 of July, the pardon was granted on the [*blank*] day of that month, passed,[94] by Secretary Conway and followed by one [f. 49v] of his Lordship's servants, and that they might be the more beholding to their patron the pardon was passed without paying the ordinary fees.

The copy of [the] pardon was read.

L. ARCHBISHOP OF CANTERBURY. That this Baker, one of the Jesuits pardoned, had been imprisoned and after his pardon that he had liberty to go whither he would to infect the people; not formerly allowed [in] the Q[ueen's] time.

The second, there was a woman in Dorsetshire, one Mary Estmond, a recusant who received priests, etc. Two justices of the peace came unto her house, being a noted receptacle of priests, etc., found in a private place in her house a cope[95] and several vestments for Jesuits, etc. The justices offered her to take the oath of allegiance and upon her refusal she was committed to the constable from whom she made an escape and came to London and procured a letter from his Majesty; the contents: that the gentle[woman] was driven from her house by some hard measure of offering the oath to her, that they would permit her to [*illegible*] to in her harvest, etc., and that they certify in what measure they have proceeded against her.

L. CONWAY. I shall give an account of his Majesty and myself; the Lord Conway has done nothing, the Secretary has done it.[96] There is a charge of the King to have broken his word because he pardoned some persons after his answer to the petition against recusants; this was granted long before the answer of the petition was made. The seal was only put to the parchment after the answer.[97]

[f. 50] As for the letter, I confess I did it, but by the direction of his Majesty, solicited by the D[uke] of Chevreuse or some other. That my man was a solicitor. I confess I caused it to ease the King and so commanded by him. Touching the fees, I was commanded that they should be taken off. They complained that Mr. Bendbo demanded 50 *l.* which the King commanded should be taken off in the passing of the business.

L. KEEPER. I did stay it and therefore I put not a *recepi* upon it; and I stayed it because it was procured by the ambassadors, thinking if they had gone it might have been quite taken off. The importunity of the ambassadors procured it, though much against all officers' wills. Yet such were the necessities of the time that the granting of

---

94. *procured* is crossed out in the MS. and replaced with *passed.* Concerning the pardon and the proposed petition, see above, nn. 1 and 3.

95. MS.: *pape* or *pope.* Concerning Mary Estmond's case and Secretary Conway's letter, see above, n. 2.

96. I.e., Conway did none of these things in a personal capacity, but acted only in his official capacity as Secretary of State upon command from the King. See the account of Conway's speech in the L.J., above, pp. 153–154.

97. See above, n. 5.

this pardon to some particular persons was a good service for the King and commonwealth and deserved no blame considering the Q[ueen's] coming. In the end our King had for the settling quiet with the King of France and his people.

E. MARSHAL. That we both might join to give thanks to his Majesty for his gracious answer touching the petition and also then we may intimate unto his Majesty our desire that foreign ambassadors do not undertake anything of the like nature hereafter, that the ill-affected subjects may not rely on[98] foreign princes or their agents.

L. KEEPER. I had an intent to have the report should have been short, but it so fell out that I shall not do it, and therefore shall desire excuse if it prove long.

The first was of the Lord Keeper his speech and so short it was that indeed it was nothing at all, nor to be thought or esteemed any speech.

[f. 50v] The Lord Duke said [he] was able to answer them in one word that was, that his Majesty had answered the petition in one word granting all [that] was desired, which was particularly read with the remedies.

His Majesty's answer consisted upon these things: the first, his Majesty's own conscience, the charge of his late father.[99] That the Duke was to give an account touching the fleet, that it must be considered the charge of Christendom, the power of the K[ing] of Spain and his power, the alteration/[100]

1 question the D[uke] made to himself was that some men might ask him by what men the business was carried. The advice first was the parliament, and so proceeded on.

His Majesty so looking into his purse he found ability enough for all but for the navy. And considering the necessity of Christendom, and found it to be most necessary, the King sent a letter to the Duke that he would of his strength and his friends to set out a navy royal; yet he did nothing without the advice of many understanding and able men, and of himself did nothing.[101]

[f. 51] 2 question: Why his Majesty did not declare the enemy at the receiving the money of the three subsidies?

Reasons: 1, the King of Spain would have strengthened himself; 2, would have surprised our ships; 3/

3 question: Whether this great sums received be husbanded as[102] it should?

Duke of Buckingham referred them to the disbursements passed his hands. Sir John Coke told them that the Duke had disbursed for himself/

4. Whether any considerable sum be required for the sending out the fleet?

The D[uke] answered: 40,000 *l.*

5. Whether the fleet were intended or no?

He referred your Lordships to consider of it because he has disbursed 40,000 *l.* [*sic*].

6. Why this want of money was not thought upon?

His Grace answered, it was seen before but omitted for many reasons: first, the death of the King, the funeral, the voyage into France.

[f. 51v] 7. Who gave counsel to meet so suddenly, seeing the danger of the time?

His Majesty commanded his Grace to certify the House that the necessity required it.

8. Why should not the King help out with this action with his own estate?

That his Majesty has disbursed all he may and will be ready to do the like hereafter.

98. MS.: *of.*
99. See above, H. of L., 20 June, n. 15.
100. For a fuller report of Buckingham's account concerning the fleet, see L.J., above, pp. 160–166.

101. See above, nn. 53–55.
102. MS.: *at.* Concerning the disbursements for the navy, see above, n. 61.

9. Whether the time of the year be not too far spent to effect that good we desire?

Answer: That they had declared what the King had said, that it were better to lose half the fleet than to stay here and enterprise nothing.[103]

10. [*Blank*]

11. Whether it might not be objected by some that the D[uke] had been our servant to break off with Spain?

12. Whether the Duke did not break off the match for some spleen against particulars, as against Olivares?

That he has no such cause because out of his hands he received that act of his hands as made him well though[t] of by his nation.

[f. 52] 13. That he, the D[uke], speaks of nothing but immense charges which this kingdom could not support.

That if they would suffer the King [to] become master of the war he would give 50,000 *l.* a month, nay 100,000 *l.*

14. His Grace supposed this will be the end.

His answer: That if the fleet be sent out let them name the enemy and the/

That the time must be considered that money would nor could relieve[104] it. And in excuse of himself, that if through him the state of this kingdom and Christendom/

Lord Treasurer his report, as the L. Keeper reported unto the House, that he was far remote from his papers and must trust to his memory.[105]

That the late King owed to the City of London and some private gentlemen/

[f. 52v] Debts of his father lie on him as his own. His debts as they were owing when he was Prince, viz., 700,000 [*sic*], but being

looked to would be ninety thousand pounds.[106]

To the navy: 20,000 *l.*
To Mansfeld: 20,000 *l.*
Mourning: 120,000 *l.* [*sic*], hereafter 160,000 *l.* [*sic*].
The King and Queen of Bohemia: 20,000 *l.* per annum.

VISCOUNT SAYE. That they would send to the Commons that the conference might be this afternoon.

Mr. Attorney and Dr. Eden sent to the Commons: That the Lords desire to meet with the Commons this afternoon with the former committee touching recusants.

Adjourned. 8 tomorrow morning.

Bp. of Bath and W[ells]
E. of Northampton
L. Morley and M[onteagle][107]

III. JOURNAL OF EDWARD, LORD MONTAGU, MONTAGU MSS., VOL. 30, NORTHAMPTONSHIRE RECORD OFFICE

[p. 2b]   Tuesday, 9 August

The Lords and Commons for the conference met: but note, the Lords were set in the room before the Commons came, which is not according to the ancient order, for the Commons should be come before the Lords sit down;[108] but being at Oxford, there is no precedent to be made of these small errors. But to the matter.

Sir Edward Coke, in the name of the rest of the committees, told us he would be short. Their desire of conference was that we would join with them in a petition to his

---

103. See above, n. 65.

104. Possibly *redeem.*

105. For fuller reports of the Lord Treasurer's account, see L.J., above, pp. 166–168, and Bedford MS. 197, below, pp. 431–432.

106. Concerning the amounts listed here and below, see above, pp. 167–168 and nn. 78–88.

107. It is unclear why the above three names are listed here in the MS.

108. Concerning procedure at conferences, see section 26 of the Roll of Standing Orders. Montagu, as a member of the Lords' conference committee (see above, p. 148), is here recording the actual meeting of the committees of both Houses. For a full account of the report of this conference and the subsequent discussion by the Lords of the matter concerning the pardon of papists, see L.J., above, pp. 152–154 and nn. 1–6.

Majesty, which consisted of two parts: one, against a pardon granted to a seminary priest, one Alexander Baker, and ten more papists, where divers circumstances were considerable. First, to be gotten by the importunity of ambassadors; secondly, the time, after the King had promised to the House that his answer should not be verbal but real—now the date of this pardon was just the day after this promise, which was the 12 July; 2 [*sic*], it was gotten by an immediate warrant, followed by the Principal Secretary[109] and his man, and without any fees.

The petition was first read, then the pardon.

The second part was about a letter of the same Secretary [p. 2c] to two justices of peace of Dorsetshire, for the redelivery of certain relics which they had found and taken in a gentlewoman's house in that country, and to suffer the gentle[woman] to abide quietly to follow her hay and corn business; which gentlewoman was formerly committed by them to a constable for refusing of the oath of allegiance; from whom she escaped, and so petitioned the King; who by the ambassadors procured this letter, which with the petition and pardon was delivered to us. And so we parted.

The LORD ARCHBISHOP, after prayers, made the report to the Lords, where the petition, pardon, and letters were read.

The Lords thought not this petition, so penned, fit to be presented; neither did they think the Commons would have presented it if this conference had not been appointed before his Majesty's answer yesterday was delivered, which for the future gives satisfaction in this.

But because it was told us by Sir Edward Coke that their chief end was that the importunity of foreign ambassadors might be hereafter stopped, we thought fit that first we should give thanks to his Majesty for his gracious answer, and then to add to it this further suit as also desire that no pardons might be granted to any such persons before they were convicted.

Hereupon we sent messengers to the Commons for another meeting this afternoon about this business, but they were risen before we sent.

The LORD KEEPER made report of the Duke's speech yesterday; who did it excellently well; as also the declaration of the King's estate delivered by the Lord Treasurer. See those notes.

The LORD ARCHBISHOP put us in mind what [was] fit to be done tomorrow about the fast, which by his Majesty was not thought fit to hold in infected places.

And so we hearing the Lower House had appointed to sit tomorrow at 8 a clock, we adjourned to the same hour.

109. Marginal note: "The Lord Conway".

HOUSE OF LORDS
ORDER OF BUSINESS   WEDNESDAY, 10 AUGUST 1625

Prayers
Message to the Commons desiring
  a conference by committees
  concerning the petition
  regarding **pardon of papists**,
  etc. (Sir Thomas Coventry,
  Att. General, and Thomas
  Eden) [*see below*]   174, 175, *9/8
Report of the Commons' answer
  to the message: the
  Commons' committee will
  attend the conference   174
L. 2a. An act for explanation of a
  statute of 3 *Jac.* for
  repressing popish recusants:
  committed   174, 175,
                                           176(2), *1/7
BISHOP OF COVENTRY AND
  LICHFIELD: concerning the
  petition of Thomas **Hayne**   174, 175, *11/7
Subcommittee of the **committee
  of privileges** for considering
  Hayne's petition: members
  added [*see below*]   174, 175, 177
The report on Hayne's petition to
  be made to the House rather
  than to the committee of
  privileges   175
VISCOUNT SAYE AND SELE:
  concerning the **collection** for
  the **distressed people of
  London** and Westminster   175, *5/8
BISHOP OF LONDON   174
Committee to review the former
  order concerning the
  collection for the distressed
  people: appointed [*see below*]   174, 175, 176

Message to the Commons desiring
  that their committee at the
  afternoon conference be
  empowered to confer
  concerning the collection (Sir
  Thomas Coventry, Att.
  General, and Thomas Eden)
  [*see above and below*]   175
Report of the Commons' answer
  to the message: the
  Commons' conference
  committee will be so
  empowered   175
Ordered: Lords absent from the 2
  July **fast** to pay double for
  collection for the poor   175, *28/6
Ordered: absent Lords who sent
  proxies shall pay to any
  collection made in the House   175
Report from the committee to
  review the former order
  concerning the **collection** for
  the **distressed people** (EARL
  OF ARUNDEL AND SURREY, E.
  Marshal) [*see above*]   175
Subcommittee of the **committee
  of privileges** for considering
  Hayne's petition to meet this
  afternoon [*see above*]   176, 177
House adjourned   175, 176
Lords take the **oath of allegiance**   175, 176
  [*Afternoon*]
Conference concerning the
  petition regarding **pardon of
  papists**, etc. [*see above*]   176

WEDNESDAY, 10 AUGUST 1625

I. JOURNAL OF THE HOUSE OF LORDS

[L.J. 485]
[p. 93] *Die Mercurii, viz., decimo die Augusti 1625*
[*List of Lords; see A.T.*]

Message sent to the Commons by Mr. Attorney General and Mr. Doctor Eden: That the Lords desire a conference between the former committees touching the petition for religion which they sent up yesterday; the conference to be at three this afternoon in the Painted Chamber.[1]

Answered: The Commons will meet accordingly.

Hodie 2ª vice lecta est billa, An act for the explanation of the statute made in the third year of the [**L.J. 486**] reign of our late sovereign lord King James entitled, An act for the better discovering and repressing of popish recusants.

Committed unto the

Lo. Archbp. of	L. Conway
Canterbury	L. Willoughby
L. Treasurer	L. De La Warr
L. President	L. Berkeley
E. Marshal	L. Stourton
L. Steward	L. Wentworth
E. of Essex	L. North
E. of Dorset	L. Russell
E. of Montgomery	L. Howard of Walden
L. Vic. Saye and Sele	L. Danvers
L. Bp. of London	L. Grey of Groby
L. Bp. of Norwich	L. Montagu
L. Bp. of Bath and	L. Grey of Warke
Wells	L. Robartes
L. Bp. of Coventry and	
Lichfield	
L. Bp. of Ely	

To attend the Lords: Lord Chief Justice, Lord Chief Baron, Mr. Justice Croke, Mr. Attorney General.
[p. 94] To meet tomorrow, at two, in the Painted Chamber.

The Lord BISHOP OF COVENTRY AND LICHFIELD remembered the petition of Thomas Hayne, which, on the eleventh of July last, was referred to the examination of the Lords' subcommittees for privileges, etc., at this access.

And, for that some of those Lords were absent,[2] these were added, *vizt.*, the Earl of Essex and the E. of Dorset.

And their Lordships agreed to meet thereon this afternoon.

The Lord BISHOP OF LONDON moved that those Lords who were appointed the fifth of this August to take the account of the money collected for Algiers may take the account likewise of the money to be collected for London and the out-parishes.[3]

Whereupon a committee was appointed to review the order made the sixth of this August for the said collection,[4] for that the same is to be inserted in the brief, and to see that it provides specially for a distribution for the out-parishes.

The names of the said committee:

E. Marshal	L. Wentworth
L. Vic. Saye and Sele	L. North
L. Bp. of London	L. Russell
L. Bp. of Rochester	L. Danvers

Mr. Attorney General to attend the Lords.

To meet presently in the Little Committee Chamber, and agreed that the Commons be acquainted with this collection.

---

1. I.e., a second conference with regard to the petition concerning Mary Estmond and the pardon of the Jesuits. The Lords had proposed the conference on 9 August but their messengers had arrived after the Commons had adjourned for the day (see Montagu journal, above, p. 172). See Sir Edward Coke's report of the conference, below, H. of C., 11 August, O.B., and the Archbishop of Canterbury's report to the Upper House, below, H. of L., 11 August, p. 179.

2. The list of members of this subcommittee included in the H.L.R.O. Main Papers (see below, p. 177 and n. 13) indicates that the E. of Clare and the E. of Warwick were the absent members.

3. For the committee to take account of the money collected for the captives at Algiers, see above, p. 139.

4. The order is printed above, pp. 143–144.

Message sent to the Commons by Mr. Attorney General and Mr. Doctor Eden: To enable their committee this afternoon at the meeting to confer with the Lords touching a collection to be made for the poor of London and the out-parishes.[5]

Answered: Their committee will meet, enabled, as is desired.

It is this day ordered that those Lords that were absent at the general fast in Westminster (the second of July) and then paid nothing to the poor, that now they shall pay double.

It is ordered that all Lords who are absent by the King's license and sent their proxies shall pay to any collection here in this House according as the other Lords present do pay.

The EARL MARSHAL reported that the Lords committees had perused the brief and order for collection for London, etc., and had in some points altered and amended the same.

[*Notice of Adjournment*]

This day, after the rising of the court, these Lords took the oath of allegiance, *vizt.*:

The Lo. Bp. of Oxford.
The Lo. Grey of Groby.
The Lo. Montagu.

II. MINUTE BOOK, H.L.R.O., M.M., 1625

[f. 53] *Die Mercurii 9° [sic] die Augusti 1625.*
[*List of Lords Present; see A.T.*]

A message to the Commons by Mr. Attorney and Dr. Eden for a conference concerning the petition lately sent up from them.[6]

Hodie 2ᵃ vice lecta est billa, An act against popish recusants.
Committed:
Ex.[7]

[col. 1]	[col. 2]
E. Marshal	1. Canterbury
4. L. Essex	3. Coventry and
2. L. President	Lichfield
3. Steward	4. B[ath] and W[ells]
5. E. of Dorset	5. Ely
1. Treasurer	2. Norwich
6. Montgomery	1. London
7. Saye and S[ele]	

[col. 3]	[col. 4]
2. Willoughby	9. Russell
11. Danvers	14. Robartes of
12. Montagu	T[ruro]
3. De La Warr	5. Stourton
4. Berkeley	10. Grey of Groby
8. Walden	6. Wentworth
1. Conway	
13. Grey of W[arke]	
7. North	

[To attend:] Chief Baron, Chief Justice, J. Croke, Mr. Attorney.
2 tomorrow in Painted Chamber.

[f. 53v] L. BISHOP OF COVENTRY AND LICHFIELD. That whereas the subcommittees for privileges have a matter of one Hayne referred to them and not full enough to hear the cause, desire they may be augmented.

And there were added, viz.: E. of Essex, E. of Dorset.

The report to be made to the House and not to the grand committee.

L. SAYE. That a committee be appointed for the distributing and collection of the money for the distressed people in London and Westminster.

L. Marshal	North
L. Saye	Wentworth

---

5. I.e., desiring the Commons to empower their conference committee to confer concerning the collection as well as the petition regarding pardon of papists, etc., as earlier arranged. On 12 August the Commons also resolved to take up a collection for the poor. See below, H. of C., 12 August, p. 472 and n. 1.

6. See above, n. 1.

7. See above, H. of L., 2 August, n. 2.

L. London   Russell
Rochester   Danvers
    Mr. Attorney to attend.
    To meet presently, Painted Chamber.

    To meet on[8] Hayne's business, to meet at
4 *post meridiem* this day.

    Adjourned. 9 tomorrow.

III. JOURNAL OF EDWARD, LORD MONTAGU,
MONTAGU MSS., VOL. 30, NORTHAMPTON-
SHIRE RECORD OFFICE

[p. 3]   Wednesday, 10 August

    This day the Lord Bishop of Oxford, the
Lord Grey of Groby, and myself took the
oath of supremacy and oath of allegiance,
divers other Lords having done the same
before at the beginning of the parliament.[9]

    The bill concerning the recusants' grants
of their land was secondly read, which was
the same bill passed both the Houses before, and stayed when it came to be assented by King James.[10] It was committed,
whereof I was one, and to be sit on tomorrow at 3 a clock.

    The afternoon we had conference with
the Commons about the petition formerly
mentioned, where we declared our opinions of the alteration and the taking of another way which liked them well, but had no
power but declare it to the House.
    The Lords acquainted them what we had
done for the relief of London.[11]

    The King sent to the Commons a mes-
sage that morning that they should present-

ly enter into the consideration of his
supply.[12]

    The court adjourned till 9 the next day.

IV. COMMITTEE BOOK, H.L.R.O., MAIN
PAPERS, H.L., 1625

[f. 10v] *Die Mercurii 10ᵐᵒ die Augusti 1625.*

    Lords committees named to review and
alter an order formerly made by other
Lords committees concerning the dis-
tressed people in the cities and suburbs of
London and Westminister, *vizt.:*
E. Marshal   L. Wentworth
L. Vic. Saye and S[ele]   L. North
                          L. Russell
L. Bp. of London   L. Danvers
L. Bp. of Rochester
    To attend the Lords: Mr. Attorney
General.
    To meet presently in the Little Commit-
tee Chamber.

[f. 11] *Die Mercurii 10ᵐᵒ die Augusti 1625.*

    An act for the explanation of a branch of
the statute made in the third year of the
reign of our late sovereign lord King James
entitled, An act for the better discovering of
popish recusants.
    Committed unto
L. Archbp. of   L. Conway
    Canterbury   L. Willoughby
L. Treasurer   L. De La Warr
L. President   L. Berkeley
E. Marshal   L. Stourton
L. Steward   L. Wentworth
E. of Essex   L. North
E. of Dorset   L. Walden
E. of Montgomery   L. Russell

8. MS.: *of.*
9. See above, H. of L., 22 June, p. 39 and n. 7.
10. In 1624 both Houses had passed the bill for
explanation of the statute of 3 *Jac.* for repressing
popish recusants (*C.J.*, I, 730; *L.J.*, III, 278). But when
the bill was presented to the King at the end of the
parliament James, expressing concern about the ill will
its passage might produce among prospective foreign
allies, stated that it was "best to be left till next session"
and refused to give it his assent. Harl. MS. 159, ff.

132v–133.
11. In the afternoon conference the Lords acquainted the Lower House committee with their activities for the relief of the London poor. See Sir Edward Coke's report of that conference to the Lower
House, H. of C., 11 August, O.B., and the Archbishop
of Canterbury's report to the Upper House, below, H.
of L., 11 August, p. 179.
12. For the King's message, see H. of C., 10 August,
O.B.

L. Vic. Saye and S[ele] L. Grey of Groby
                         L. Danvers
L. Bp. of London   L. Montagu
L. Bp. of Norwich   L. Grey of W[arke]
L. Bp. of Coventry   L. Robartes of Truro
  and Lichfield
L. Bp. of Bath and
  W[ells]
L. Bp. of Ely

To attend the Lords: L. Chief Justice, Lo. Chief Baron, Mr. Justice Croke, Mr. Attorney General.

To meet on Thursday the 11th of this instant August by 3 in the afternoon in the Painted Chamber.

Decimo Augusti 1625.[13]

Lords subcommittees for privileges, etc., to consider of the petition of Thomas Hayne, etc., *vizt.:*

	E. of Essex	L. De La Warr
	E. of Dorset	L. Darcy and
absent {	E. of Warwick	M[einill]
	E. of Clare	L. Wentworth
	L. Vic. Saye and	L. Sheffield
	Sele	L. Russell
		L. Spencer

L. Bp. of Norwich
L. Bp. of Coventry
  and Lichfield
L. Bp. of Bristol

To attend the Lords: L. Chief Justice, L. Chief Baron.

To meet presently near the parliament presence.

At 4 this afternoon in the former place, *vizt.,* in the Little Committee Chamber.

13. The following list of members of this subcommittee of the committee of privileges is not included in the Committee Book. It is an unfoliated leaf of H.L.R.O., Main Papers, H.L., 11 August 1625. The final sentence, scheduling a meeting of the subcommittee in the Little Committee Chamber, has been added in the hand of Henry Elsynge, Sr.

Prayers
L. 2a. An act for the increase of
   shipping and for free liberty
   of **fishing**: committed   .   179, 180, *7/7
L. 2a. An act against **forging** and
   counterfeiting of the **seals** of
   the King's courts: committed   179, 180, *7/7
Report from the subcommittee of
   the **committee of privileges**
   on the petition of Thomas
   Hayne (EARL OF DORSET)   179, 180, *11/7
Orders concerning Hayne's
   petition   179
Report of the **conference**
   yesterday with the Commons
   on the petition regarding
   pardon of papists, etc.
   (ARCHBISHOP OF
   CANTERBURY)   179, 180, *9/8
Report of the second part of
   yesterday's conference,
   concerning the **collection** for
   the **distressed people of**
   London (LORD LEY, L.
   Treasurer)   180
House adjourned   180

THURSDAY, 11 AUGUST 1625

I. JOURNAL OF THE HOUSE OF LORDS

[L.J. 486]

[p. 95] *Die Jovis, vizt., undecimo die Augusti 1625*

[*List of Lords; see A.T.*]

[L.J. 487]

Hodie 2ª vice lecta est billa, An act for the maintenance and increase of shipping and navigation, and for the freer liberty of fishing and fishing voyages to be made and performed in and upon the seas, seacoasts, and places of Newfoundland, Virginia, New England and other the seas, seacoasts, and parts of America.

Committed unto the

L. Archbp. of Canterbury	L. Willoughby
	L. De La Warr
L. Treasurer	L. Berkeley
E. Marshal	L. Stourton
L. Steward	L. Wentworth
E. of Montgomery	L. North
E. of Northampton	L. Howard of W[alden]
E. of Warwick	L. Russell
	L. Danvers
L. Bp. of London	L. Grey of Groby
L. Bp. of Coventry and Lichfield	L. Montagu
	L. Robartes
L. Bp. of Bath and W[ells]	
L. Bp. of Ely	
L. Bp. of Bristol	

To attend the Lords: Lord Chief Justice, Lord Chief Baron, Mr. Attorney General.

To meet on Saturday next, at three *post meridiem,* in the Painted Chamber.

Hodie 2ª vice lecta est billa, An act against the forging, falsifying, and counterfeiting of the King's Majesty's seals of his Highness's courts of King's Bench, Common Pleas, the Exchequer, and Duchy.

[p. 96] Committed unto the

L. President	L. Wentworth
E. of Dorset	L. North

L. Vic. Andover	L. Walden
L. Bp. of London	L. Russell
L. Bp. of Norwich	L. Danvers
L. Bp. of Chichester	L. Grey

To attend the Lords: Lord Chief Justice, Lord Chief Baron, Mr. Baron Denham, Mr. Justice Croke.

To meet on Monday next, at eight, in the Painted Chamber.

The EARL OF DORSET reported: That the petition of Thomas Hayne versus John Parham being referred to a select committee, their Lordships are of opinion that the differences touching the land in question between them be referred to the arbitrament of the Lord Chief Justice and the Lord Chief Baron. That Thomas Hayne shall have his goods and the corn sown by him; that Thomas Hayne and his son shall enjoy the privilege of parliament; and that the possession of the land in question shall remain where the law has settled it until it be determined by the writ of error depending here, or by the arbitrament of the said judges.[1]

All which is ordered by the House accordingly.

The Lord ARCHBISHOP OF CANTERBURY reported the conference had with the Commons yesterday in the afternoon touching the petition for religion, wherein they desired the Lords to join with them unto the King, *vizt.:*[2]

That his Grace first related unto them upon what grounds the pardon mentioned in that petition was granted, and the reason of the date thereof, and the King's commandment both for the pardon and for the letter written by the Principal Secretary, and how that all was done at the great importunity of foreign ambassadors (*prout antea,* in the former report, *nono Augusti*),[3] and further, that his Grace signified unto

---

1. Concerning Hayne's petition and the House's action, see above, 11 July, n. 2.

2. See also Sir Edward Coke's report of the conference to the Lower House, below, H. of C., 11 August, O.B.

3. On the petition, the pardon, and Secretary Conway's letter, see above, pp. 152–155.

the Commons their Lordships' motion to join together in humble thanks to his Majesty for his gracious answer to their former petition,[4] and to beseech his Majesty not to be importuned hereafter by any foreign ambassadors to grant anything contrary to the said answers.

And lastly, his Grace signified unto the Lords that they of the Commons seemed to be satisfied touching the said pardon, and the date thereof, and the said letter; and seemed to approve of their Lordships' motion to join in the thanks and petition unto the King. All which they promised to relate to their own House.

[**L.J.** 488] The LORD TREASURER also reported: That at the said conference the Commons were acquainted with the order made here for the collection for London, etc., and how that the Lords had left it unto them whether the Commons would do any thing therein or no. Whereupon they of the Commons required a copy of the said order, and had it, and promised to acquaint their House therewith.[5]

[*Notice of Adjournment*]

II. MINUTE BOOK, H.L.R.O., M.M., 1625

[f. 54] *Die Jovis 11ᵐᵒ die Augusti 1625.*
[*List of Lords Present; see A.T.*]

Hodie 2ᵃ vice lecta est billa, An act for the free trade of fishing in America, etc.

E. Marshal	Russell
E. of Montgomery	Robartes of [Truro]
E. of Warwick	Willoughby
L. Steward	Danvers
L. Treasurer	Montagu
E. Northampton	Berkeley
	Walden
Bp. London	Stourton

Coventry and	Wentworth
L[ichfield]	North
Bath and W[ells]	De La Warr
Canterbury	Grey of G[roby]
Bristol	
Ely	

To attend the Lords: Chief Justice, Chief Baron, Mr. Attorney.

To meet on Saturday next by 3 *post meridiem,* Painted Chamber.

[f. 54v] *Hodie vice lecta est billa,* An act against the forging and counterfeiting, etc., of the King's seals of the King's Bench, Exchequer, etc.

President	Russell
Dorset	North
Andover	Wentworth
	Walden
Bps. Canterbury	Danvers
Oxford	Grey
Norwich	
London	
Chichester	

To attend the Lords: Chief Justice, Chief Baron, Baron Denham, J. Croke.

To meet on Monday next by 8, in the Painted Chamber.

E. OF DORSET. That he that was in possession should remain in it; the person privileges [*sic*] from any arrests; the corn reserved for Hayne; the cause touching the writ of error left to the lords the judges, viz., Chief J[ustice], Chief Baron.

[f. 55] L. ARCHBISHOP OF CANTERBURY/

III. JOURNAL OF EDWARD, LORD MONTAGU, MONTAGU MSS., VOL. 30, NORTHAMPTONSHIRE RECORD OFFICE

[p. 3]   Thursday, 11 August

We had little to do, only read one bill, which was committed.[6]

---

4. I.e., the petition concerning religion presented to Charles on 8 July and answered article by article on 8 August. See the report of the King's answer, 9 August, above, pp. 155–160.

5. The order for the collection, approved by the Lords on 6 August and slightly altered by a committee

on 10 August (above, p. 175), is printed above, pp. 143–144. Concerning the collection in the Lower House, see H. of C., 12 August, p. 472 and n. 1.

6. Two bills were committed this day; see L.J., above.

It was told us the Commons House bent much against the supply, and had some speeches which trenched upon a great man.[7]

As soon as we had dined my nephew,

Walter Montagu, came in all haste from the King to command the lords of Council to attend his Majesty presently, which drove us all into a maze.[8] And they went presently away.

7. For speeches in the Commons' committee of the whole House on the King's message of 10 August concerning supply and on the question of whether the Duke of Buckingham was at fault for the present state of necessity, see below, H. of C., 11 August, O.B.

8. There is no record in *A.P.C., 1625–1626*, of a Council meeting on 11 August. According to Zuane Pesaro's dispatch to Venice the King called his Council for advice concerning the manner of dissolution. See *Cal. S.P. Venetian, 1625–1626*, p. 147.

Prayers

Rowland **Pitt** is discharged   183, 184, *5/8

LORD KEEPER (Bp. of Lincoln): concerning the **distressed people of London**   184, *5/8

LORD KEEPER (Bp. of Lincoln): declares he has received his Majesty's **commission for dissolving the parliament**   183, 185

Message to the Commons: that the King has sent a commission for dissolving the parliament, and desire the Commons with their Speaker to come up to hear the commission read (James Maxwell, Gentleman Usher of the Black Rod) [*see below*]   183, 185

Petition of Richard **Culpeper**, servant to Lord Cromwell: read   183, 185, *9/7

Culpeper's petition referred to the Lord Keeper   183, 185

Lord Keeper (Bp. of Lincoln): delivers the **commission for dissolution** to the Clerk [*see above*]   183, 185

Henry Elsynge, Clerk of the Parliaments: reads the commission for dissolution   183, 185 [*The commission is printed on pp. 183–184*]

LORD KEEPER (Bp. of Lincoln): declares the parliament dissolved   185

FRIDAY, 12 AUGUST 1625

I. JOURNAL OF THE HOUSE OF LORDS

[L.J. 488]
[p. 97] *Die Veneris, vizt., duodecimo die Augusti 1625*
[*List of Lords; see A.T.*]

Rowland Pitt, who took Mr. Justice Croke his horse to ride post (*prout antea 5to Augusti*) is this day upon this petition to the House discharged, paying the ordinary fees.

Richard Culpeper, Gentleman, servant to the Lord Cromwell, exhibited his petition showing: That he was arrested in execution for three hundred thirteen pounds, six shillings, and eight pence, at the suit of William Galthropp, brewer, for a battery, the plaintiff being alive without any maim or loss of limb, humbly praying to be released of his imprisonment according to the privilege of parliament.

The which petition being read, the Lords referred the same unto the Lord Keeper of the Great Seal to do therein as unto his Lordship shall seem good.[1]

The LORD KEEPER signified that he had received his Majesty's commission directed unto divers Lords for dissolution of the parliament, whereupon the Gentleman Usher[2] was commanded to signify unto the Speaker of the House of Commons that their Lordships have received **[L.J. 489]** his Majesty's commission which is to be read unto both Houses; and do therefore desire the Commons, with their Speaker, to come up presently and to hear the same read.

Memorandum: That the Lords ought to be in their robes at the reading of this commission, but their Lordships agreed to dispense with that ceremony at this time, for that many of their Lordships had not their robes in town. And [p. 98] the sitting of the commissioners upon forms overthwart the House (as the manner is) was also agreed to be dispensed with, for that the House was thin and most of the Lords then present were in the commission.[3]

The Commons, with the Speaker, being come, the Lord Keeper delivered the said commission to the Clerk of the Parliament, who read the same, and then the parliament was dissolved accordingly.[4]

The tenor of the said commission, *vizt.:*[5]
[King Charles,

Charles, by the grace of God, King of England, Scotland, France, and Ireland, defender of the faith, etc. To the most reverend father in Christ and our faithful counsellor George, Archbishop of Canterbury, primate and metropolitan of all England; and to the reverend father in Christ and our faithful counsellor John, Bishop of Lincoln, Lord Keeper of our Great Seal of England; and also to the most reverend father in Christ, Tobias, Archbishop of York, primate and metropolitan of England; and also to our well-beloved and faithful counsellor James, Lord Ley, our Lord Treasurer of England; and to our most dear cousins and counsellors Henry, Viscount Mandeville, Lord President of our Council; Edward, Earl of Worcester, Lord Keeper of our Privy Seal; George,

1. Culpeper's petition is not among the extant parliamentary papers for this session. A petition from Culpeper had been read in the Upper House at the end of the London session and had been referred to a committee. See above, H. of L., 9 July, O.B. The Lord Keeper ordered Culpeper discharged on 17 August 1625. A record of the discharge is included in H.L.R.O., Main Papers, H.L., 6 May 1626.
2. According to the Montagu journal, below, the Serjeant at Arms accompanied the Gentleman Usher to the Lower House.

3. For the customary procedure at the reading of a commission of dissolution, see the account of the dissolution of the 1614 parliament in *L.J.*, II, 716.
4. Before the dissolution the Lower House this day passed a protestation to the King. See H. of C., 12 August, p. 475 and n. 21.
5. The entire commission is in Latin in the MS. L.J. For the convenience of readers, we have given a translation of the Latin commission below, within brackets. For the Latin, see *L.J.*, III, 489.

Duke of Buckingham, our Lord Admiral of England; Thomas, Earl of Arundel and Surrey, our Earl Marshal of England; William, Earl of Pembroke, Lord Steward of our Household; and also to our most dear cousin Edward, Earl of Dorset; as well as to our most dear cousin and counsellor, Philip, Earl of Montgomery; and to our most dear cousin William, Earl of Northampton, President of our Council of the Principality and Marches of Wales; and to our most dear cousin and counsellor James, Earl of Carlisle; as well as to our most dear cousins John, Earl of Clare, and Henry, Viscount Rochford, and also to the reverend fathers in Christ, George, Bishop of London, and Richard, Bishop of Durham, and to the reverend father in Christ and our faithful counsellor Lancelot, Bishop of Winchester; and also to the reverend fathers in Christ, Samuel, Bishop of Norwich, and William, Bishop of St. Davids; and to our well-beloved and faithful counsellors Edward, Lord Conway, one of our Principal Secretaries [of State] and Edward, Lord Zouch, and also to our well-beloved and faithful Emanuel, Lord Scrope, President of our Council in the Northern Parts; Thomas, Lord Wentworth; Edmund, Lord Sheffield; and to our well-beloved and faithful counsellors George, Lord Carew, and Fulke, Lord Brooke, greeting:

Since we have lately ordained this our present parliament to commence and be held at our city of Westminster on the eighteenth day of June last for certain difficult and pressing business concerning us, the state and defense of our kingdom of England and the English Church; from which day the same our parliament was held and continued until the eleventh day of July last; and on that same day the same our parliament and all cases and matters begun and not finished was adjourned to the first day of the present month of August at our city of Oxford and there at that time was held and continued until the pres-

ent twelfth day of August. Know ye that we have thought fit that same parliament on this present twelfth day of August be dissolved for divers pressing causes and considerations especially moving us. Therefore we, confiding very much in your fidelity, prudence, and circumspection, have, with advice and consent of our Council, assigned you our commissioners giving to you and any three or more of you by the tenor of these presents full power and authority on the present twelfth day of August to dissolve fully this our parliament in our name. And therefore we command you, that you or any three or more of you fully dissolve and terminate this our parliament on this twelfth day of August in our name by virtue of these our letters patent. And therefore we command that you attend diligently to these premises and effectually fulfill them in the manner aforesaid. Moreover, we strictly command all and singular archbishops, dukes, marquises, earls, viscounts, bishops, barons, knights, citizens, and burgesses and all others whom it concerns, by the tenor of these presents, to meet at this our said parliament, that they observe, obey, and assist you as is proper in the execution of the premises. In witness whereof we have caused these our letters to be made patent. Witness ourself, at our city of Oxford, the twelfth day of August, in the first year of our reign.

Edmondes
H. Elsynge, Clerk of the Parliaments]

II. MINUTE BOOK, H.L.R.O., M.M., 1625

[f. 55v] *Die Veneris 12mo Augusti 1625.*
[*List of Lords Present; see A.T.*]

Pitt to be released paying all fees, who attached the horse of Mr. Serjeant Croke.

L. KEEPER. That he has received a note from the recorder of London that their poor in the City might be left out of the general relief that is to go through the kingdom, for that the City is able to relieve their poor.

[f. 56] LORD KEEPER declared that he had received his Majesty's commission for dissolving of this parliament and desired the Lords to consider of it that notice might be given to the Speaker and Commons that they might come up to hear.

The petition of Richard Culpeper, servant to the Right Honorable L[ord] Cromwell.
Referred to the Lord Keeper.

L. Keeper, the Commons being at the bar with their Speaker: I have received his Majesty's commission for the dissolving of this parliament, which is to be read to both Houses as they are now assembled; and therefore if you please to give [*illegible*] to have it read.

The which commission was delivered to the Clerk by the L. Keeper and read with a loud voice by him in the presence of the said Houses then assembled, according to the course in that case accustomed.[6]

LORD KEEPER. My Lords and Gentlemen, according to his[7] present commission this present parliament is dissolved.

III. JOURNAL OF EDWARD, LORD MONTAGU, MONTAGU MSS., VOL. 30, NORTHAMPTON-SHIRE RECORD OFFICE

[p. 3]   Friday, 12 August

The parliament was dissolved by commission. We should have been in our robes, but because many Lords wanted them, we sat as at other times. When the Lower House was to be sent for, it grew into some debate what the precedent was who should be the messengers, and found it was by the Gentleman Usher and Serjeant at Arms; and so it was done accordingly.

---

6. For the commission, see above, L.J.

7. Possibly *this*.

House of Commons

Sir Thomas Edmondes, Treasurer of the Household,
Clerk of the Crown in Chancery

HOUSE OF COMMONS
ORDER OF BUSINESS   SATURDAY, 18 JUNE 1625

L: Proceedings in House of Lords, above
N: *Negotium,* below

M.P.s are sworn	191
[*Afternoon*]	
Prayers	
King's speech to both Houses	190, 191, 192; **L**, 28; **N**, 492
Lord Keeper (Bp. of Lincoln): paraphrases the King's speech	190, 192, 193; **L**, 30, 31; **N**, 493
Commons withdraw to their own House	191, 192; **N**, 494
SIR THOMAS EDMONDES: nominates Sir Thomas Crew for **Speaker**	193
Sir Thomas Crew elected Speaker of the Lower House	191, 192; **N**, 494

*The page numbers of clearly definable set speeches recorded in the *Negotium* (printed below, pp. 491–569) are included in the daily Orders of Business.

SATURDAY, 18 JUNE 1625

I. MS. 197, BEDFORD ESTATES, LONDON[1]

[f. 1]   18 *Junii* 1625.

At the parliament summoned at Westminster the 17th[2] day of May in the first year of King Charles, and held by prorogation upon the eighteenth of June following.[3]

[*Afternoon*]

A place was made in the Upper House for the Duke of Chevreuse,[4] the French ambassador, who with his Lady and divers others French[5] lords and ladies were present to see the solemnity of the first day.

His Majesty began with a profession of his own want of ability to speak,[6] but that the business of this meeting needed it not, being begun in his father's time when both he (as an intercessor) was engaged by us and we, by a liberal declaration, engaged ourselves, so that it would be a dishonor to him and to us not to perfect it by yielding such supply as the greatness of the work and variety of provision did require. This he spoke not out of diffidence but to show his sense of the public interest, for he knew our zeal to religion and[7] matchless fidelity

and love to our King, which is the ancient honor of this nation; and that he for his part would be as forward to dispose all his means to the common good and defense of this realm as he doubted not but we would be forward to aid him.

The Lord Keeper. That the King had left him little to speak, having abundantly declared the substance of all in showing that engagement which his father left to him, and which was laid upon them both by the kingdom in the advice given by the parliament for breaking the treaties, for recovery of the Palatinate, and of his Highness's marriage with Spain.[8]

Since that time our late Sovereign had no other object but the Palatinate and, to make way to that, supplies the Low Countries, raises an army for Mansfeld, prepares (by God's blessing) an invincible navy to scatter the forces of his opposites in the circumference [f. lv] of their own large dominions, which are now united in the Low Countries and Germany.[9] In which preparations the King that now is is so engaged that he had rather go to his grave than not to go on in this design.

In these businesses all the subsidies are

1. There is no entry in the Commons Journal for 18 June. In the present text Bedford MS. 197 is collated with the extracts in B.L. Add. 26,639 and the printed edition of the Knightley manuscript (Samuel Rawson Gardiner, ed., *Debates in the House of Commons in 1625*, Camden Society, 1873), the original of which is no longer extant; the substantive variants are noted. For a full description of these manuscripts, see the Introduction, above, pp. 10–13.

2. The date is omitted in the manuscript.

3. *18 Junii 1625. Parliament summoned May 1° Car., prorogued al 18th de June.* Add. 26,639. Concerning the prorogations, see above, H. of L., 18 June, n. 1.

4. Claude de Lorraine, Duke of Chevreuse, had been the proxy for Charles I at his marriage to Henrietta Maria in Paris, 1 May 1625, and accompanied the new bride to England as "the chief and ambassador of the convoy". *Cal. S.P. Venetian, 1625–1626*, pp. 81–82; Salvetti dispatches, p. 23; and *Negotium*, below, p. 492.

5. *friends. C.D. 1625* (Knightley MS.).

6. See above, H. of L., 18 June, n. 10. For a more complete version of the King's speech, see *L.J.*, above, pp. 28–30. For a second version, see K.S.R.L. MS E237, below, p. 192; a third version is in *Negotium*, pp. 492–493, below. A fourth version from S.P. 16/3:88 (1) and a fifth from Braye MSS. 1, f. 80v and Osborn MS. fb 155, pp. 93–94 are in the Appendix, below, pp. 647–648. According to one report, circulated copies of speeches from the opening of this parliament were of poor quality. Birch, *Court and Times of Chas. I*, I, 37.

7. *our. C.D. 1625* (Knightley MS.).

8. On England's foreign commitments at the time of the death of James I, see above, H. of L., 18 June, n. 5.

9. For accounts of the expenditures on these military activities, see the reports of the speeches of the Duke of Buckingham and the Lord Treasurer at the 8 August meeting of both Houses, above, H. of L., 9 August, O.B. and below, H. of C., 9 August, O.B.

spent, and as much more of the revenue, for which his Majesty now desires a supply. This is the substance; he would add only 3 circumstances.

First, for the time, which is the greatest commander of all actions. A supply too late is none. Europe is now stirred like the pool of Bethesda by a good angel[10] for the recovery of the honor and happiness of England, if we slip not our opportunity; wherefore we should bestow this meeting upon him and this action, the next upon domestical business.

Second, for the manner. If we find the usual ways of contribution too slack, not to fear in an occasion of such consequence to advise some other that may be more proper.

Third, to regard, as the end of this action, the reputation of our sweet King. As princes sow their actions in the beginning, so shall they reap[11] glory afterward. His Majesty puts his fame, his reputation (which is all he has of a king) upon us, not in desperation, as Caesar amongst the Romans, *jacta est alea,*[12] but with the greatest confidence according to his poesy, *amor civium regis munimentum.* Kings and subjects are *relata simul natura;* as soon as he shall be known for a valiant prince, you shall be esteemed a faithful people.

He concluded with an admonition to choose a Speaker, and to present him the next sitting day.

The Commons withdrew themselves into their own House and made choice of Serjeant Crew, who had been Speaker the last parliament.[13]

II. PETYT 538/8, INNER TEMPLE LIBRARY[14]

[f. 106] 18 *Junii* 1625 at Westminster

The first parliament of King Charles begun at Westminster and ended at Oxford.

The knights, citizens, and burgesses of parliament sworn in the morning.

[Afternoon]

And in the afternoon they all attended the King in the Upper House where the Duke of Chevreuse and his Duchess, with other French ladies and divers French men, were placed in the House near the upper end, on the right hand of the King. And the King put on his crown and robes in the lobby (where the earls do use to robe themselves) and thence came up to his chair of state;[15] a straight and narrow search being by the Lord Chamberlain and Earl Marshal to exclude all that were not of the House. And about four of the clock he entered into his speech, which was short and to this purpose.

His Majesty's speech. Lords and gentlemen, the occasion of my calling of you together at this time is not unknown to many of you that are here. You have heretofore engaged my father (who is with God) in a war for the recovery of the Palatinate, so that by succession I am not only involved therein, but can challenge a particular promise of your loves and affections to that purpose the last parliament when I labored [f. 106v] all I could to bring my father to assent thereto.[16] It has been begun in his time, but not received so good

---

10. John 5:2–4.

11. *raise. C.D. 1625* (Knightley MS.).

12. Suetonius, *De Vita Caesarum,* 1, 32.

13. For Sir Thomas Edmondes's speech nominating Sir Thomas Crew, who had been Speaker in 1624, see below, pp. 193–194. Concerning Crew, see *Negotium,* below, p. 494 and n. 10.

14. Petyt 538/8 is collated with B.L. Add. 48,091

and Q.C. 449 and the substantive variants are noted. For a full description of these manuscripts, see the Introduction, above, pp. 13–15.

15. Although the coronation did not take place until winter, Charles wore the crown for the opening of this session. See above, H. of L., 18 June, n. 4.

16. See H. of L., 18 June, n. 7.

effect in some particular as I could wish and I know you all desire. Yet such is my affection to pursue that action that I would do all I can to settle them[17] in their ancient patrimony. And for that purpose, besides those land forces which are prepared, and the reuniting of the princes, our allies, it pleased the King, my father, in his life, not long before his death, to think of this course of preparing of a fleet which I have accordingly pursued, wherein there has been more money laid out than he [sic] have already given and much more must be or else that charge will be lost and the fleet that is now in such forwardness must stand still with our help and supply.[18] Besides, this being my first action, all the eyes of Christendom will be on me; and as I do in this, so it will get me credit and repute abroad and honor at home. The time of the year yet serves; but if you slack or delay it longer it will be too late. Besides, I would have you think upon your own danger that you are in here by reason of the infection, which requires expedition.[19] Now for my own religion, [f. 107] I hope none here makes doubt of it.[20] I have been bred up at the feet of Gamaliel (without ostentation be it spoken) not assuming to myself the graces[21] of St. Paul.[22] For my government, I say unto you that I will do as much therein as my father did, and when I have said so, I hope I have said enough.

The King's speech being ended, after a little pause, the Lord Keeper declared how the King had said *multum in parvo,* and therefore he could not call it a short speech. And, enlarging the same with eloquence

and reason, he told them that his Majesty would be ready on Monday, in the afternoon, to receive their Speaker, which then they would present unto.

And from thence they returned to the House and elected the Speaker, and then chose Sir Thomas Crew, Serjeant at the Law, and his Majesty's serjeant, who had been Speaker in the former parliament; and then the House rose.[23]

III. MS E237, KENNETH SPENCER RESEARCH LIBRARY

[18 June 1625]

[Afternoon]

[f. 116] Upon the 18 day of June 1625 the King came to the Parliament House and before he sat down in his chair he took off his cap and crown and kneeled down and heard prayers.[24] That done, and his Majesty sitting, he told the House the cause of calling this parliament was for supply of those actions which we, in the former parliament by our advice and counsels, had engaged his father and him in, in which both his honor and ours was far engaged to bring something to effect; and that which we would do must be done speedily, for that the businesses in hand and this infectious time would endure no delays. And therefore willed us speedily to resolve of that business only at this time, and at Michaelmas we should have as long a session as we would to effect other businesses. And for his religion, which he was bred and born in, his Majesty professed he would as constantly maintain as ever his father did.

---

17. I.e., Frederick, Elector Palatine, and Elizabeth, his wife. See below, H. of C., 20 June, n. 5.

18. *without your help and supply.* B.L. Add. 48,091 and Q.C. 449.

19. See H. of L., 18 June, n. 8.

20. *I think here is none here that makes doubt of it.* Q.C. 449.

21. *speech.* B.L. Add. 48,091 and Q.C. 449.

22. Acts 22:3.

23. For Sir Thomas Edmondes's speech nominating Sir Thomas Crew, see below, pp. 193–194.

24. For the prayers at the opening of the session, see Appendix, below, pp. 645–646. Concerning the conduct of the French during the prayers, see above, H. of L., 18 June, n. 3.

[f. 116v] King Charles his speech to the parliament.[25]

My Lords spiritual and temporal and you gentlemen of the Commons, I am fit neither by nature nor ability to speak long, and need to be the shorter because that which I am to speak of is not new, concerning the recovery of the Palatinate, but was begun in my father['s] time who is now with God. Touching which I can not call myself a free man being engaged by you, when it pleased you to do me the favor to use me as an intercessor to him, which was undertaken by him not in words but really as is expressed by the supply to the Low Countries, Count Mansfeld's army, the provision of the forts, and the preparation of the fleet.[26] This I commend to you as a matter that concludes your honor and mine deeply. You ever have been a nation famous for your love to your king, so that what I speak is not out of diffidence but to show the sense I have both of your honor and my own. For religion, I may say with St. Paul, I have been brought up at the feet of Gamaliel,[27] though I will not be so arrogant as to say I have been as good a scholar as he was, but I shall never give occasion of doubt of my love to maintain that religion wherein I have been bred but will show it as much as ever my father did, and in that I have said enough. This is the substance of that I have to say, yet something I have commended to my Lord Keeper, rather for formality than of any importance.

The Lord Keeper only amplified what the King had spoken and concluded that if we gave unto the King now, the King would give unto us next.

IV. SPEECH OF SIR THOMAS EDMONDES NOMINATING SIR THOMAS CREW TO BE SPEAKER. S.P. 16/3:84.

May it please this honorable House,

By the sad unexpected accident of our late Sovereign's death, King James of glorious memory, we are now called together by new summons from the rightful heir and most worthy successor, King Charles, a prince peerless for the care, qualifications, and endowments both in respect of the breeding in the cabinet council of the wise father and in the great councils of the kingdom; as also with the experience which he acquired by his dangerous journey into foreign parts which miraculously brought him to our true understanding of nations and thereby enabled him to discover the deep mysteries of foul dissimulations and dangerous practices.[28] (And only the fearful adventure and sufferances were capable to redeem both him and us from those great perils which otherwise we were falling into.)

Now great blessings we may expect in him both for the maintaining of the true religion and preserving the honor, justice, and prosperity of the kingdom; the zealous undertakings in parliaments past when he [illegible] as a peer of the realm may give us all ample assurance. For he gave full proof hereof in the exigencies of the former parliament, when as it did manifestly appear to us all that he did not only become a continual advocate to his deceased father for the favorable granting and happy speeding of our petitions, but also did carefully and dexterously interpose his mediation for the pacifying and removing of all misunder-

25. This separate of the King's speech is in K.S.R.L. MS E237, f. 116v, following the description of the opening of parliament. Concerning other accounts of the speech, see above, n. 6.

26. See above, n. 9.

27. Acts 22:3.

28. For the journey taken by Charles, then Prince of

Wales, and George Villiers, Duke of Buckingham, to Spain in 1623 to negotiate the proposed marriage treaty, see Gardiner, *History of England*, V, 1–129; S. R. Gardiner, ed. and trans., *Narrative of the Spanish Marriage Treaty* (London: Camden Society, 1869), pp. 198–270.

standings which casually fell out between him and us, laboring in the service of the kingdom as much (I dare say) as any member in the whole body, which gave evident testimony that it was not want of will but of power if he did not in every particular satisfy our just desire.[29]

God, having now added the *posse* to his *velle*, the princely power to his willing mind, and thereby enabled him to execute what before he could but will; if then we should not be confident that he will put into execution that love of which he has made so large expression, we should much wrong both him and ourselves.

Upon these undoubted premises it then follows to be necessarily resolved by us, that we likewise for our parts do express how much our hearts do abound in joy and love towards him, and that in his beginning of his trial of our dutiful affections we may give him such a pledge thereof as may more and more endear us to him and him to us, and give him comfort and encouragement to pursue those noble designs with all alacrity which his Majesty has projected for the reviving and recovery of the lost power of the state.

But this is not now the time further to prosecute this agreement than by way of preparing our affections, the proper work of this day being to choose a Speaker, which I suppose will be an easy work because I shall presume to name him of whom I assure myself every member of this House has made choice in his heart in respect of the trial we gave God of the singular abilities and most remarkable service in the last parliament. That is Sir Thomas Crew, whose worth every man knows that knows his name. I confess he has just reason to plead his excuse in respect of the weak estate of his body, and that he has already served in the place. But because there is so necessary a use of his employment in so important a service, I hope God will redouble all necessary [*illegible*] abilities upon him. And therefore, in that confidence we humbly propose that he intend to undergo Jacob's task to serve a double apprenticeship.[30]

[*Endorsed*] Copy of my speech in the Parliament House at the election of Sir Thomas Crew to be the second time Speaker.

---

29. Both Charles and Buckingham were active in "managing" the business of the 1624 session. See Ruigh, *Parliament of 1624*, pp. 392–395; Russell, *Parliaments*, pp. 145–203.

30. Cf. Gen. 27, 29.

[*Afternoon*]

Sir Thomas Crew: disabling
   speech to the King 196, 197; **L**, 34,
     36, 37

Lord Keeper (Bp. of Lincoln): the
   King's **approbation** of the
   Speaker 196, 198; **L**, 34,
     36, 37; **N**, 497

Sir Thomas Crew: **acceptance**
   speech and **petition for**
   privileges 196, 198; **L**, 34,
     36; **N**, 494

Lord Keeper (Bp. of Lincoln): the
   King's response 196; **L**, 35, 36;
     N, 497

Mr. Speaker and the Commons
   return to the Lower House 201
[*L. 1a.*] An act against
   depopulation and **decay of**
   farms 201, *1/8

MONDAY, 20 JUNE 1625

I. MS. 197, BEDFORD ESTATES, LONDON

[f. 2]   20 *Junii* 1625.

[*Afternoon*]

The Speaker was presented to his Majesty and, according to the usual formality, desired to be excused, which by his Majesty's direction was answered by the Lord Keeper, and the election confirmed.[1]

His[2] speech was not long but effectual, propounded without any division of parts, but reduced by the Lord Keeper's answer to 7 points:[3]

First, concerning himself, his submission to the King's pleasure. Encouragement by God's blessing upon the last parliament in the many good laws then passed, and the special furtherance which they received from his Majesty being then Prince.

To which was replied, that he spoke little of himself but did much. Before he offered the sacrifice of his lips which was refused but now he offered his obedience which, being accepted, was declared to be the better sacrifice. The last parliament was justly accounted happy. It made a kind of reconciliation between the King and his people. *Foedera infida dissolubilia;* the respects between a king and his people are bound by such mutal interest that they cannot long be severed. There passed then more flowers of the crown, more bills of grace than in Magna Carta; and the part his Majesty bore in that parliament may assure us that he will hereafter be to parliament as a soul in the body, and can never pretend himself a stranger to the customs or forgetful of the wishes and desires of parliaments.

Second, concerning the King, wherein he observed five circumstances: [1,] his first action; 2, his noble descent; 3, his succession; 4, his hopes; 5, his great deliverance.

To which was replied, that those actions are most sincere which are most natural. [1.] By beginning with a parliament his Majesty does express what delight he shall take in this conference with his people. [f. 2v] 2. That nobility of blood was in him more eminent than in any prince in Christendom. He had *deus in utroque parente,* being derived both by father and mother from a long succession of kings. 3. His succession had sweetened the loss of his father, which could not have been done by any but himself, nor by himself if he had been the son of his body alone. 4. The experience we had of his abilities and virtues gave us great hope. 5. Those hopes are confirmed by the great deliveries which he received in his late journey, declaring him to be the child of King James, a *noli me tangere,* and that God will never leave nor forsake his.

Third, concerning religion, which he called the fundamental wall, whereby the safety both of King and kingdom were preserved, the maintenance whereof was left unto him as the last charge of his dear and dying father.[4]

The answer consisted in an acknowledgment of the many blessings which the true religion had brought upon this nation for the space of seventy years continuance; and that the King's own zeal was quickened to the defense thereof by the last admonition

---

1. There is no entry in the C.J. for 20 June. Full copies of the Speaker's disabling speech and of the Lord Keeper's approbation of the Speaker's election on the behalf of the King are included in none of the narrative accounts for this day. We have printed them from Osborn MS. fb 155 in H. of L., 20 June, above, p. 37. For a copy of the Speaker's disabling speech, see also below, p. 198 and n. 11.

2. Marginal note in the Earl of Bedford's hand: "Sir Thomas Crew". For several versions of Crew's speech

of acceptance and petition for privileges for the Commons, see above, H. of L., 20 June, pp. 36–37; below, pp. 198–201; *Negotium,* below, pp. 494–497; and the account from Osborn fb 155 in the Appendix, below, pp. 651–652.

3. An account of the King's response delivered by the Lord Keeper is also included in the L.J. See above, H. of L., 20 June, p. 35 and n. 11.

4. See H. of L., 20 June, n. 15.

of his father, so that he would omit nothing in his government whereby our joy might be perpetual of seeing Jerusalem to flourish.

Fourth, touching the common law, which was commended as affording the fittest principles of government both for the King and subject.

In the answer it was acknowledged that by a long continuance of time the common law is fitted to the temper of this nation, and that his Majesty would observe it as the most proper rule of government. But withal the students of the laws were admonished to bend their studies to the ancient maxims and not to rest upon new cases or statutes framed upon special occasion. They should find the ancient grounds of the laws founded in reason proceeding from God himself, the latter issuing [f. 3] only from the invention of men. In the former times, always strong premises though sometimes weak conclusions; in these later, weak premises but peremptory conclusions.

Fifthly, touching the Palatinate, the distressed estate whereof was remembered with grief, in that it had been heretofore a sanctuary for those of our nation persecuted for religion [and] was the inheritance of a confederate[5] prince of our own religion, so near allied to us, of which he was deprived in time of peace, when our ships were as a wall about their country by whose forces it were effected; and in this case if we withhold our succor we shall be liable to that curse of Egypt and Meroz for not for helping the Lord.[6]

The answer: Now his Majesty found himself head of this body, having both the same sympathy, he will show himself to be neither Meroz nor Egypt; he has expressed

himself sufficiently that he desires not to live but in glory, and this you shall see performed by the supplies which from time to time he will provide for this enterprise.

Sixth, for the restraint of priests and Jesuits by proclamation.

It was answered, his Majesty did absolutely grant the matter but desired to be trusted with the way. He was *custos utriusque tabulae*, and in a fit time would either grant the manner or improve it to better; and did remember what his father said, that he would be as careful of this as he prayed God to be merciful unto him.[7]

Seventhly, the united and accustomed petitions of the Commons for freedom from arrests, free speech, access upon occasion, favor and acceptance of their proceedings. And one particular suit for himself: that all his defects might be covered[8] with a veil of a gracious construction.

[f. 3v] In the repetition my Lord Keeper called these 4 petitions the four cornerstones of the Commons House and answered that his Majesty did grant them all without any other limitation but of our modesty and wisdom, not doubting but if any abuse were committed we would be more ready to punish than he should be to take exception.

II. PETYT 538/8, INNER TEMPLE LIBRARY

[f. 107]   *Die Lunae*, 20th of *Junii*

[*Afternoon*]

The House met in the afternoon and attended their Speaker to the Upper House where the King was sat and, after [f. 107v] three conges solemnly made, he came to the bar. And the Speaker first showed how he had made his just excuse to the Commons

---

5. *considerate. C.D. 1625* (Knightley MS.). Frederick V (1596–1632), Elector Palatine (1610–1623), elected King of Bohemia in 1619, was defeated at the battle of White Mountain in 1620, and deprived of the Electorate by the Emperor in 1623. A Protestant, Frederick was married to Elizabeth, sister of King Charles I.

6. Ezek. 29:1–12; Judg. 5:23.

7. See James I's answers to the petitions concerning religion in 1621 and 1624. *C.D. 1621*, IV, 70–75; *L.J.*, III, 317–318.

8. *bound. C.D. 1625* (Knightley MS.).

House, which they had rejected; and therefore he appealed from them to his Majesty, and most humbly besought him, considering his infirmities and insufficiency, to excuse and command the House of Commons[9] to make choice of some other more worthy member of their House.

And thereupon, standing with a great pause, the Lord Keeper, in the name of his Majesty, recommended the discretion of the House in their choice of him; and in showing his disability he did the more enable himself, and so gave approbation and allowance of their choice.

And then the Speaker proceeded:[10]

Most gracious Sovereign, the knights, citizens, and burgesses of the Commons House of parliament assembled by your royal writ, according to your Majesty's commandment and their ancient privilege, have proceeded to the choice of their Speaker who, passing over many of great ability and judgment, have cast the eye of their favor on me your unworthy servant. Too weak [f. 108] to undergo so heavy a burden, and unable to wield so weighty a charge, I endeavored with them to make a choice of some other and presented to their second thoughts my known wants and weakness, my declining years, my personal infirmities, whereof I myself am and have cause to be sensible. I put such in mind as were before of the House of their particular knowledge of my former defects and dis-

abilities, and of the disadvantage that might now thereby redound to the public service. But not prevailing with them, I am enforced to appeal to Caesar, my sovereign lord and King, and to fly to the sanctuary and refuge of your royal person, sitting in your imperial throne, to whom I am a most humble suitor for my relaxation and discharge, that your Majesty would so far extend your grace, as to acquit me of this weighty charge and to command the House to reconsult and advise of a second and better choice.[11]

Dear and dread Sovereign, since it is your Majesty's royal pleasure to command it [f. 108v], it is my duty to obey; *tuus o rex magne quid optes explorare labor mihi jussa capessere fas est.*

I know a sparrow falls not to the ground without God's providence.[12] And as the divisions of matters, so the hearts of kings are in His hands, *impellit quo voluerit.* And I am the more encouraged by former experience of the goodness and mercy of God who, at our last meeting, made [*illegible*] of one House of one mind, and united the head and members of one body in one heart, which produced *parliamentum felix,* crowning with honor the memory of the public acts of your dear father to all posterity, who then was pleased to ask and follow the advice of his great council in dissolving the two treaties,[13] parting with some fruitful leaves from the flowering garland of his crown for the ease and benefit of his sub-

9. *to excuse him and to cause the House of Commons.* Q.C. 449.

10. Marginal note: "Taken out of his own original". Of the three similar accounts (Petyt 538/8; B.L. Add. 48,091; and Q.C. 449) only Petyt 538/8 includes the Speaker's speech. Both B.L. Add. 48,091 and Q.C. 449 give the identical paraphrase of the speech as follows:

And then the Speaker proceeded to show the great hope that the whole kingdom had of his gracious and good government, and the happy instrument he had been in producing those good effects of the last parliament: his noble birth, his great deliverance from his rare voyage; the great joy that the people had in his desire to recover the Palatinate; and a

request from them to expel the priests, Jesuits, and seminaries, and to maintain true religion, with a desire of the continuance of their ancient liberties and craving pardon for his own infirmities.

11. The contents of the above paragraph are recorded in other accounts as the Speaker's disabling speech rather than as the introduction to his acceptance speech. See H. of L., 20 June, pp. 36 and 37. The following version of the Speaker's acceptance speech is nearly identical to that in the *Negotium,* below, pp. 494–497.

12. Matt. 10:29.

13. See above, H. of L., 18 June, nn. 5 and 7.

jects, and gave his royal assent to as many good laws as passed at any one time since the Great [Charter].[14] In which we then discerned your princely care of the public, your readiness be [sic] removed all rubs that might hinder, and your hand always at hand to help [f. 109] and further our desires, *beneficium postulat officium.* And now that God has put into your heart in your happy entrance to tread the true path of a parliamentary way, in comparison whereof all other courses are out of the way, you have to your own honor and our comfort shaken hands with your subjects and made your face shine in the eyes of your people. Solomon, the wisest of kings, calls that land blessed whose king is the son of nobles; and blessed are those subjects whose sovereign, trained up in true religion and by lineal descent of inheritance the undoubted heir of the crown, in the prime of his strength is invested in his royal birthright by an immediate patent from God, with the applauses of all his people.[15]

It is God's method with his dearest children to mix crosses with comforts, but as a woman with travail forgets her sorrow for joy a man child is born,[16] so our grief, occasioned by the departure of our late Sovereign, is swallowed up with joy to see upon his sunset his own son to succeed, of whose rare [f. 109v] and religious reign and government we have a great expectation. God in his eternal counsel had set the bounds of your father's days, which he could not pass, and the great husbandman best knew the time when his corn was ripe and ready to gather into his own government.

It is He which has made you (which were as yesterday our hopeful prince and pledge of our future peace) to become now our sovereign lord and King and set you in your father's throne to judge the Israel of God.

The good Hezekiah was 25 years old when he began his reign; your Majesty is passed 24.[17] He did uprightly in His sight, sanctified the House of God, had in his heart to make a covenant with the Lord; God magnified him in the sight of all nations and in every danger gave him deliverance. And your Majesty shall become mighty with Jotham while you direct your way before the Lord your God.[18]

You have a faithful and loyal people that fear and love you—*amor civium regis munimentum*—understanding council to advise you.

[f. 110] Your imperial diadem shines bright in it, that it is enameled and compassed with a beautiful border of the ancient fundamental laws of this kingdom which, as sinews, hold the body of the commonwealth and are suitable to the nature of the people and safest for the sovereign. The ark of true religion is with you to waft you over the waves of all dangers of this life and, when you are old and full of days, to land you in the safe harbor of heaven. David (being to go the way of all the world) gave a charge to Solomon his son to walk in the ways of God, that he might prosper in all he did,[19] and it is our singular comforts to hear that it was the advice of your dear and dying father to maintain the religion professed in this kingdom.[20] We have long enjoyed the blessing of peace and gone forth in the dance of them that be joyful. In this is the truth and power of God; the other a mist of man's invention, a mystery of iniquity.[21] God (whom we worship according to His word), bowing down His ears to our earnest prayers, brought you

---

14. MS.: *Chiere.* The bracketed word is supplied from the copy of the speech included in *Negotium*, below, p. 494.

15. Cf. Eccles. 10:16–17; 1 Kgs. 8 and 9; Prov. 22:6.

16. John 16:21.

17. 2 Kgs. 18:2; 2 Chr. 29:1. Charles was in his

twenty-fifth year in 1625.

18. 2 Chr. 27:6.

19. 1 Kgs. 2:1–3.

20. See H. of L., 20 June, n. 15.

21. 2 Thess. 2:7.

back from foreign parts in a rare [f. 110v] adventure full of peril, delivered you from the dangers of the deep, covered you under the wings of His immediate protection, suffered no man to do you harm, and wrought a marvelous light out of a fearful darkness, worthy to be written with a pen of iron and a point of diamond in all true English hearts.[22] We then for sorrow hanged our harps on the willows and could not sing the song of Zion while you were in a strange land.[23] It is lodged in the register of God's special mercies to this nation, and your Majesty may hereafter say to all and it *forsan et haec olim meminisse juvabit*. Your Majesty has revived the memory of the distressed [Palatinate];[24] in the times of persecution [it] was a sanctuary. And every good heart is sensible of the dishonor to our nation to see and suffer a confederate prince [of] our own religion,[25] matched with an immediate branch of the royal blood, invaded and defeated of his ancient patrimony and inheritance in that time when there was treaty of peace and when our royal navy floated on foreign seas and was [f. 111] to others a wall of brass and tower of defense.[26] Now that the scepter and sword is come into your own hand, extend it to hold up them that are helpless that so you may be a happy instrument to close up the breaches and raise up the ruins of that desolate country. *Qui non propellit injuriam cum possit facit.*

It was said to Caesar that his fortune had nothing greater than that he could, nor his nature better than he would, *conservare quam plurimus.* Egypt was destroyed for being a staff of reed to the house of Israel,[27] and Meroz was cursed for not coming to help the Lord in battle against the mighty.[28]

Lucius, a Britain king,[29] was the first of all Europe whose royal diadem was lightened with the heavenly beams of Christianity. And you that are *rex totius Brittaniae*, lineally descended from the stem of both roses, and in whose person is a union of both kingdoms, shall add happiness to your crown and state by pulling down the pride of that antichristian [f. 111v] hierarchy, and in abandoning by public edict really executed that wicked generation of Jesuits and seminary priests who are the sons of bitchery that blow the coals of contention, incendiaries that lie in wait to set combustion, and blood and powder the badges of their wicked profession. Your Majesty no doubt in your deep wisdom does discern them and in due time will curb them and suffer such locusts no longer to eat up the good fruit of the land and to abuse the simple,[30] lest the Church and commonwealth suffer, but send them home to their own cells, not to return again.

But that I may not take away time (that is so precious, especially at this time) from your Majesty's so many and weighty affairs, nor hinder public business, I hasten to conclusion. And, according to the duty of my place, by special charge and commission from the Commons House, with the warrant of ancient approved precedents, I humbly present to your Majesty our wonted and accustomed petitions:[31]

1. That you would graciously give allowance [f. 112] to our ancient immunities for ourselves, and such servants and attendants as are capable of this privilege, both in *eundo et redeundo* and during the time of our sitting to be free from arrest and troubles, whereby we may the better attend the public service.

---

22. Cf. Ps. 107.
23. Ps. 137:2–4.
24. The bracketed word is supplied from *Negotium*, below, p. 496.
25. I.e., Frederick V; see above, n. 5.
26. See H. of L., 20 June, n. 7.

27. Ezek. 29:6.
28. Judg. 5:23.
29. Concerning Lucius, see above, H. of L., 20 June, n. 9.
30. Cf. Ps. 105:34–35; and Joel 2:25.
31. See H. of L., 20 June, n. 10.

2. That your Majesty would vouchsafe unto us liberty of free speech according to our ancient privilege, that by a free debate of reasons on both sides truth may the better be discerned and matters at last by common consent happily concluded; and I doubt not but we shall confine ourselves within the limits and compass of duty and obedience.

3. In regard the subject may be such and so great a moment and consequence as shall minister just cause of an immediate resort for advice or redress to the oracle of your own mouth, that your Majesty would be graciously pleased upon all needful occasions upon our humble suits and at your fit time to permit us access to your royal presence.

4. Lastly, that your Majesty would be graciously pleased to entertain us in your gracious [f. 112v] and good opinion and of all our proceedings to make a benign interpretation.

There only remains that I, which by free choice of the House and your Majesty's gracious approbation am, though unworthy, a Speaker for others, may be permitted to become an humble suitor for myself to your excellent Majesty, that you would be pleased to cover my errors and defects with a veil of gracious construction and so extend to me, your most humble servant, the first of all others that in public needs it, craves it, your free and gracious pardon.

And then the Speaker had the mace delivered unto him and the Serjeant returned in with him, carrying it before him into the House. And when they came into the House a bill was read against depopulation and converting of tillage into pasture; and the House rose.

L. 1a. An act for punishing abuses committed on the **Lord's day**	204, 208, 210, 212, 213, *22/6; 23/6; 24/6; 27/6; 11/7	SIR EDWARD WARDOUR	204
		SIR FRANCIS GOODWIN	204
		THOMAS WENTWORTH	204
		WILLIAM CAGE	204
L. 1a. An act to confirm an agreement between the King and his tenants of **Macclesfield**	204, 208, 213(2), *23/6; 24/6; 27/6; 28/6; 11/7	Ordered: a private fast for the House to be held on Saturday next [25 July]; preachers appointed	204, 208, 210, 211, 212, 213; **N**, 500, *22/6; 24/6; 28/6; 29/6
SIR EDWARD GILES: moves for a **communion**	204, 208, 210; **N**, 499	Members to give notice to the preachers for the fast: appointed	205, 208
		SIR JOHN JEPHSON	210
		SIR DUDLEY NORTON	210
SIR MILES FLEETWOOD: for a **communion** and a **fast**	204, 208, 210, 212; **N**, 499, *22/6; 23/6; 28/6	SIR BENJAMIN RUDYARD	210
		Upon question: to petition the King for a **general fast**	205, 208, 211, 212; **N**, 500, *22/6; 23/6; 24/6; 28/6
Ordered: members to receive the communion on Sunday next [26 June]	204, 208, 210, 211, 212, 213; **N**, 500		
		Committee for drawing a petition to the King for a general fast: appointed	205, 208, 210
SIR WILLIAM STRODE	204		
The 1624 order for a communion: read	204	SIR THOMAS JERMYN: moves that the Lords be moved to join in the petition	205, 208
Committee for seeing the order for the communion performed: appointed	204, 208	Agreed: as Jermyn moved	205
		SIR GEORGE MORE	205
Upon question: John Hacket to preach at the communion	204, 208, 210, 211, 212	Agreed: the Speaker to have authority to make warrants for **new elections** when necessary	205, 208, 210
WILLIAM CORYTON: for a **private fast** day for the House	204, 208	SIR GEORGE MORE: moves for a **committee of privileges**	205, 208
JOHN PYM	204	NICHOLAS HYDE: elects to serve for Bristol	205, 208
JOHN WHITSON	204		

TUESDAY, 21 JUNE 1625

I. JOURNAL OF THE HOUSE OF COMMONS

[C.J. 799]
[p. 1] *Martis, 21° Junii, 1° Caroli*

L. 1*ᵃ*. An act for punishing of divers abuses committed on *the* Lord's day, called Sunday.

L. 1*ᵃ*. Macclesfield.[1]

SIR EDWARD GILES renews[2] the motion for all the members of this House to receive a communion.

SIR MILES FLEETWOOD seconds the motion and moves a public fast before: 1, for a blessing from God upon the King; 2ly, for the miseries of the Christian churches beyond seas; 3ly, for a blessing upon our navy; 4ly, in respect of the grievous visitation now upon us by the plague. To have a day before the communion for a private fast among ourselves. To have an order for this among ourselves, not general as last time.[3]

1. Upon question, a communion by all the members of the House; without one negative. Upon Sunday next.[4]

SIR WILLIAM STRODE moves for a general fast, and that the King may be moved in it by some special persons.

The place: St. Margaret's in Westminster.
The last order read.[5]

Sir Francis Barrington, Sir Edward Giles, Sir Francis Goodwin, Sir William Pitt, Sir Edward Wardour, and the Clerk of the House to see the order performed, which now read and allowed.
Mr. Hacket to be the preacher.[6]

MR. CORYTON moves for a certain day for a fast among ourselves.

MR. PYM, *accordant;* yet moves to have it general and to send to the Lords to join with us in petition to the King for his direction in it. A committee to draw a petition and then to send to the Lords to join in it.

MR. WHITSON, SIR EDWARD WARDOUR, *accordant*; for no such cause for a fast last parliament as now, in respect of the plague and other occasions.

SIR FRANCIS GOODWIN, *contra*; for our doing it a means to draw on the general. We may now order it for ourselves; the insisting upon the general may lose the particular.

MR. WENTWORTH, *contra;* to have it general.

MR. CAGE. To settle the particular first, and then to petition for the general.

Upon question, a general fast among ourselves upon Saturday next.[7] Three

---

1. I.e., a bill for confirming an agreement between the King and his tenants of Macclesfield in the County Palatine, Chester. The private act passed this session is engrossed on the Parliament Roll. See *Rot. Parl.*, 1 *Car.* I, no. 8.

2. We have no record of an earlier motion in this session for the communion. Sir Edward Giles is requesting the continuation of the separate communion of Lower House members begun in 1614. Since then, in the sessions of 1614, 1621, and 1624, the Commons communed in St. Margaret's and the peers met in Westminster Abbey. John F. Wilson, *Pulpit in Parliament* (Princeton, 1969), pp. 23–28; *C.J.*, I, 671.

3. In 1624 the proposal had been for a general fast throughout the kingdom, which required the King's approbation. *C.J.*, I, 671. James agreed to consider the

matter but never returned an answer. Unlike a general fast, a private fast for the Commons was within the power of the House to order.

4. On 24 June the House resolved to defer the private communion, and on 28 June it resolved to hold the communion service on the following Sunday, 3 July.

5. I.e., the order for the communion read in the two previous parliaments (1624 and 1621) which was that drawn in 1614. See *C.J.*, I, 671, 508, 457.

6. John Hacket, incumbent of St. Andrew's, Holborn. *D.N.B.*

7. I.e., a private fast for the Commons. On 24 June the House resolved to defer the private fast, and on 28 June it resolved to hold the fast on the following Saturday, 2 July.

preachers: Mr. Shute, Lombard Street; Dr. Preston; Dr. Westfield.[8] Sir A. Ingram, Sir M. Fleetwood, Sir Richard Newport to move them from the House. The place: St. Margaret's Church; to begin [at] *nine of*[9] the clock.

[p. 2] Upon question, a petition to his Majesty for a general fast.

Mr. Solicitor	Serjeant Ashley
Sir Nathaniel Rich	Mr. [John] Pym
Sir Francis Seymour	Sir Francis Goodwin
Sir James Fullerton	Sir Robert Phelips
Sir Benjamin Rudyard	Sir Robert Carr

to draw this petition, this afternoon, two clock, Exchequer Chamber.

SIR THOMAS JERMYN. To move the Lords to join with us in this petition after it is framed and agreed upon.

Agreed.

SIR GEORGE MORE moves that this petition may not be delivered to the King, nor any motion to the Lords, till our fast past.

A general warrant to Mr. Speaker to make warrants for new elections, during all this parliament, upon double returns, deaths, or remove, etc.

Agreed.

SIR GEORGE MORE moves also for a committee for privileges. All petitions about elections past to be brought in within one week, and so a week after for such as shall be made hereafter.

Not resolved.

MR. NICHOLAS HYDE, returned for Bristol and Bath, elects for Bristol.

MR. WHISTLER. To take the elections as now, without questioning them, because the time so short.

SIR A. HERRIS, elected for a knight for Essex and for Maldon, elects for Essex.

SIR JOHN HOTHAM, elected for Appleby, Westmorland, elects for Beverley in Yorkshire.

SIR WILLIAM HERBERT, for Wilton in Wiltshire, elects for Montgomeryshire.

MR. LITTLETON elects for Leominster.

SIR THOMAS WILFORD, for Christchurch in Southampton, etc., elects for Canterbury.

Sir George More	Mr. [Christopher]
Sir Edward Giles	Wandesford
Mr. [John] Glanville	Sir Walter Erle[10]
Sir William Herbert	Sir Thomas Went-
[William] Lord	worth
Cavendish	Mr. [Edward] Kirton
Sir Dudley Digges	Sir Francis Seymour
Sir Miles Fleetwood	Sir Robert Hatton
Mr. [William]	Sir Benjamin Rud-
Mallory	yard
Mr. [Christopher]	Sir Arthur Ingram
Brooke	Sir William Strode
Sir Thomas Cheeke	Sir George Manners
Sir Guy Palmes	Sir Henry Anderson

8. Josiah Shute was rector of St. Mary Woolnoth, Lombard Street. *D.N.B.* John Preston, formerly chaplain in ordinary to Prince Charles, was master of Emmanuel College, Cambridge, lecturer at Trinity Church, Cambridge, and preacher at Lincoln's Inn. Brook, *Lives of the Puritans*, II, 352–361; *D.N.B.* Thomas Westfield (who later declined and was replaced by Holdsworth, see below, n. 32) was rector of Hornsey and of St. Bartholomew, Smithfield. *D.N.B.* The only sermon of this group to have been published is that of Preston, which is printed as an appendix to *The Saints Qualification* (London, 1633), pp. 246–305 (*S.T.C.*, no. 20262). On Preston, see also John F. Wilson, *Pulpit in Parliament*, pp. 29–31; and Irvonwy Morgan, *Prince*

Charles's Puritan Chaplain (London, 1957). The sermons continued for nine hours but "not any one man fainted". George Roberts, ed., *Diary of Walter Yonge, Esq.* (London: Camden Society, 1848), p. 86.

Following *Dr. Westfield* the words *the Serjeant to move them from the House* are crossed out in the MS.; *Mr. Strode* is crossed out following *Ingram*.

9. The corners and edges of the manuscript for this day are torn and frayed. The words that appear within brackets in the printed *C.J.* are italicized here without brackets.

10. *Sir William Erle.* Printed edition. The list is of members appointed to the committee of privileges.

Attorney Wards

[p. 3]
Secretary[11]
   Cottington
Sir Clement Throck-
   morton
Sir John Eliot
Sir Thomas Hatton
Sir Talbot Bowes
Mr. [John] Pym
Sir Francis Goodwin
Sir Nathaniel Rich
Sir Robert Phelips
Sir Francis Barring-
   ton
Sir A. St. John
Mr. Charles Price
Serjeant Hitcham
Mr. [Edward] Alford
Sir Oliver Luke
Mr. Lawrence
   Whitaker
Serjeant Ashley
Sir John Danvers
Mr. Spencer
Sir William Morgan
Sir Gervase Clifton
Sir Ferdinando Fair-
   fax
Mr. John Drake
Sir Thomas Gran-
   tham
Mr. [Nicholas] Hyde
Mr. [William] Cage
Sir Francis Popham
Mr. Edward Herbert
Sir Andrew Corbet
Sir John Stradling
Sir Richard Wenman
Sir Robert Pye

Mr. [William] Cory-
   ton
Sir Edmund Sawyer
[p. 3]
Sir Robert Crane
Mr. Solicitor
Sir Francis
   Fulforde
Mr. [Thomas]
   Wentworth
Sir Edward Peyton
Mr. Chancellor
   Duchy
Sir Robert Cotton
Mr. [John] Del-
   bridge

To begin this afternoon, and so every Thursday, Saturday, and Tuesday, Star Chamber.

[p. 4] SIR EDWARD GILES tenders a petition from Yorkshire about the election of Sir John Savile.

Referred to the committee for privileges, and to be 1st this afternoon.[12] The rest, in order, as presented.

[C.J. 800] MR. DRAKE prefers another, concerning Sir J. Perrot.

Referred, as the other.

SIR THOMAS PUCKERING tenders a petition from the borough of Warwick.[13]

SIR JOHN DANVERS, another from Westminster.

SIR W. TICHBORNE elects for Wootton Bassett, in Wiltshire.

SIR A. INGRAM and MR. ALFORD move for a law to prevent these questions.[14]

SIR JOHN DANVERS moves Mr. Noy may deliver to the House a bill for the poor.[15]

MR. BROOKE to move/

Moved and resolved, that the committee of privileges shall hear counsel and witnesses and send for any records.

MR. SAUNDERS tenders a petition against Sir William Cope by the Lady Coppin and her son.

---

11. Sir Francis Cottington had served as secretary to Charles when he was Prince of Wales but did not continue in that office after Charles became King. S.P. 16/1:8; *D.N.B.*

12. Concerning the Yorkshire election, see the O.B. references and *Negotium*, below, pp. 500, 511–516. The case was discussed at length on 4 July and resolved on 5 July. See also Appendix, below, p. 704.

13. Concerning the dispute between Sir Thomas Puckering and the corporation of Warwick and for the resolutions in the committee of privileges regarding the borough election, see the Appendix, below, p. 703.

14. It is unclear to what questions Ingram and Alford refer. No other manuscript records their speeches.

15. We are unable to determine the title of the bill.

Which, by direction of the House, was read in the House.[16]

SIR WILLIAM COPE moves this may be referred to the committee of privileges.

MR. BROOKE. The only point, whether one in execution before the summons of parliament be eligible here, or not.

SERJEANT ASHLEY. The questions, 2: 1, whether Sir William Cope in execution before the summons of parliament; 2ly, whether he come hither by *habeas corpus* or not. For now some plead by *habeas corpus*, others preach so; and now, if they would sit here so, all the prisons of England may be emptied thus.

MR. MALLORY moves to petition the King to adjourn till Michaelmas, in respect of the plague.[17]

SIR WILLIAM STRODE moves for a committee for petitions.

Not to have them delivered to one man, but publicly, and notes presently to be taken of them, and change to be made of him that sits in the chair; one, one day; one, another.

SIR ROBERT PHELIPS seconds the motion, yet considerable whether this time fit to receive petitions against courts of justice, etc.

[p. 5] For Mr. Mallory his motion—rare

at the beginning of a parliament to petition to be put off, but consider now of the danger of the plague, with other circumstances, and it will be very considerable whether not fit to petition the King to defer the parliament to some other time or place.

MR. ALFORD moves for a committee of the whole House, to consider of the course fit to be held both for King and kingdom.

Mr. Serjeant Ashley
Mr. Solicitor
Mr. Serjeant Hitcham
Mr. [Edward] Alford
Mr. Brooke
And all the lawyers of the House

Tomorrow, at two of the clock in the afternoon, in the Court of Wards. The petition against Sir William Cope referred to them, and they to report to the House.

SIR GEORGE MORE moves the former motions may be considered of till tomorrow, and then be further debated.

MR. SOLICITOR. Of two evils, the less to be chosen: better to fall into the hands of God than into the hands of men.[18] Moves a committee to consider of the best course for guiding all our proceedings this parliament.

MR. WANDESFORD moves for an adjournment to another place.

16. Lady Coppin's petition against Cope is not extant in the manuscript materials for this parliament. Lady Coppin had begun suit against Cope in 1621 over debts she claimed he still owed for lands in Essex purchased from her late husband, Sir George Coppin, Clerk of the Crown in Chancery (see Edward Nicholas, *Proceedings and Debates . . . 1620 and 1621* [Oxford, 1766], I, 306; *C.J.*, I, 595). At issue in 1625 was the matter of Cope's election to parliament and concomitant privilege from arrest during his service (see the committee report and debate in the House on 23 June, below, p. 227). For a fuller description of the case, see below, this day, Harl. 161, p. 212; and *Negotium*, below, p. 516.
Cope answered Lady Coppin's petition on 22 June with a petition of his own which the House rejected.

See below, 22 June, O.B. And on 23 June, following a committee report on the case, it was ordered that Cope be discharged from the House and a warrant be issued for a new election. See below, 23 June, O.B.
17. *The petition concerning Sir William Cope referred to the committee of privileges concerning the privilege of the House and report of the matter in fact to be made from them* is crossed out in the MS. following Mallory's speech. The Draft Journal, below, has a similar order which is not crossed out. This order was apparently superseded by an order later in the day, recorded in both the C.J. and Draft Journal, referring Cope's case to a newly named select committee which was to meet the next day (Wednesday, 22 June).
18. 2 Sam. 24:14.

Upon question, the proposition made concerning a petition for adjournment of the parliament not now to be put to the question.

II. DRAFT JOURNAL, MS. 3409, H.L.R.O.

[f. 128]   *Martis 21 Junii 1625.*

Lectia 1ᵃ. An act for the enabling and confirmation of an agreement or composition made between the King's Majesty/[19]

Lectia 1ᵃ. An act for punishing divers abuses committed on the Lord's day called Sunday.

SIR EDWARD GILES moves to have a time and place assigned for receiving the communion.

SIR MILES FLEETWOOD seconds the motion and moves for a public fast; for 4 reasons: 1, for a blessing of God upon our new king; 2, in regard of the miseries of Christian churches; 3ly, for a blessing upon our navy; 4ly, in regard of the grievous visitation of sickness among us.

Resolved upon question that all the members of the House shall receive the communion on Sunday next at St. Margaret's Church in Westminster, according to the former order of the last parliament.[20]
Sir Francis Barrington, Sir Edward Giles, Sir Francis Goodwin, Sir William Pitt, Sir Edward Wardour, and the Clerk of the House to see the order performed.
Resolved upon a 2d question, Mr. Hacket to be the preacher.[21]

MR. CORYTON moves to have a certain day for a fast among ourselves.

Resolved upon question that there shall be a fast amongst ourselves on Saturday next, by 3 preachers. Mr. Shute, Doctor Preston, and Doctor Westfield to be the

men.[22] Sir Miles Fleetwood, [Sir Arthur] Ingram, and Sir Richard Newport to give them [*torn*]. St. Margaret's Church to be the place; to be [*torn*] 9 of the clock.

[f. 128v] Resolved upon question that a petition shall be drawn by a committee to his Majesty for a general fast.
Mr. Solicitor   Serjeant Ashley
Sir Nathaniel Rich   Mr. [John] Pym
Sir Francis Seymour   Sir Francis Goodwin
Sir James Fullerton   Sir Robert Phelips
Sir Benjamin Rudyard Sir Robert Carr
This afternoon, 2 clock, Exchequer Chamber.

SIR THOMAS JERMYN. To move the Lords to join with us before we send the petition to the King.

A general warrant to Mr. Speaker from the House to grant warrants for new writs during all this session of parliament upon double returns, deaths, or removes, etc.

SIR GEORGE MORE moves to have all petitions about elections past brought in to the committee of privileges within a week.

MR. HYDE elects to serve for Bristol, being also returned for Bath.

SIR ARTHUR HERRIS, double returned for the county of Essex and the town of Maldon, elects to serve for the county of Essex.

SIR JOHN HOTHAM elects to serve for Beverley.

SIR WILLIAM HERBERT elects to serve for the county of Montgomeryshire.

MR. LITTLETON.

SIR THOMAS WILFORD elects to serve for Canterbury.

[f. 129] [*Blank.*] To begin this afternoon and so every Tuesday, Thursday, and Saturday, in the Star Chamber;[23] with power

19. See above, n. 1.
20. See above, nn. 4 and 5.
21. See above, n. 6.

22. See above, nn. 7 and 8.
23. This order refers to the committee of privileges. For the list of members, see C.J., above.

to hear counsel, examine, and send for witnesses. The petitions to be heard as they come in in priority.

[f. 129v] SIR EDWARD GILES tenders a petition from the freeholders of Yorkshire.[24]

Referred to the committee of privileges; to be the first cause this afternoon.

MR. DRAKE tenders another petition, from Sir James Perrot.

Read, and referred to the committees. To be the 2d cause.

SIR THOMAS PUCKERING tenders another, from the county of Warwick.[25]

SIR JOHN DANVERS another, from Westminster.

SIR WALTER TICHBORNE elects to serve for Wootton Bassett in Wiltshire.

MR. SAUNDERS tenders a petition from the Lady Coppin and her son against Sir William Cope, a member of this House.[26]

The petition read.

MR. BROOKE. The question is whether this House shall admit a man to sit as a member of this House that was in execution 6 weeks before the summons of this parliament. Fit to be considered of with all expedition.

This business referred to the committee of privileges; concerning matter of privilege.[27]

MR. MALLORY moves to petition the King to adjourn the parliament until Michaelmas in respect of the increase of the sickness.

SIR ROBERT PHELIPS. This day of parliament like the 1st day of a term, assigned for motions. We have made a good beginning with God. Other propositions are likewise fallen in concerning the privileges and liberties of this House and concerning the courts of justice. Thinks we shall have no time now to deal with any of these. Unusual and extraordinary at the beginning of a parliament to petition for an adjournment; yet now considerable in regard of the fearful increase of the sickness, at least to the putting it off to another place.

[f. 130] SIR THOMAS WENTWORTH seconds this motion. To have a committee appointed to draw a petition to his Majesty to this purpose.

MR. ALFORD. To have a committee of the whole House to take consideration of all the weighty business concerning the King and kingdom.

Serjeant Ashley   And all the lawyers of
Serjeant Hitcham   the House
Mr. Solicitor
To take consideration of the petition against Sir William Cope. To meet tomorrow, 2 clock, Court of Wards. And to report to the House.

SIR GEORGE MORE moves to put off the consideration of the former weighty proposition until tomorrow, the day being now far spent.

MR. SOLICITOR. David was in a great strait, so are we; better to fall into the hands of God than men.[28] Of dangers, the least is to be chosen. The eyes of all Christendom are upon the first and greatest actions of our King, and upon the affections of his subjects. Will not persuade a long continuance together. To name a committee to consider of things of weight in this House. Thinks there is now priority of business. To determine first the most necessary.

SIR HENRY ANDERSON. To decline this

24. See above, n. 12.
25. This concerned the borough election; see above, n. 13.

26. See above, n. 16.
27. See above, n. 17.
28. 2 Sam. 24:14.

question now, and to let it rest for some 2 days more.

Upon question, resolved to have no question at this time made of the proposition of consideration of adjournment of the parliament.

III. MS. 197, BEDFORD ESTATES, LONDON

[f. 3v] 21 *Junii* 1625.

The first bill read was for preventing abuses upon the sabbath day.

SIR EDWARD GILES moved for a communion.

SIR MILES FLEETWOOD. To petition the King for a public fast, and by our own order to enjoin a fast to our own members. For which he gave these reasons: 1, in thanksgiving for God's preservation of the King; 2, for relief of the distressed churches beyond seas; 3, for a blessing upon the preparation of our own (which he called invincible) navy; 4, for appeasing God's anger showed in the great mortality now begun.

The communion was ordered by question. Mr. Hacket appointed for preacher.

The fast of our own House ordered to be upon Saturday, being the day preceding the communion. 3 preachers appointed: Dr. Preston, Dr. Westfield, and Mr. Shute.

Some question was made of the place. It was propounded by SIR JOHN JEPHSON, seconded by SIR DUDLEY NORTON, to be in our own House; and thus [refused][29] by SIR BENJAMIN RUDYARD: I beseech you not to refuse the church, remember it is God's house, lest we make this a conventicle which should be a council.

So it was agreed to be kept in St. Margaret's, Westminster.

A committee appointed to draw the petition for a public fast.

By order, the Speaker was authorized to make warrants for new elections in cases of double returns.

[f. 4] A committee for privilege was named, and Sir John Savile's and Sir James Perrot's petitions to have precedence.

A complaint was exhibited on the behalf of the Lady Coppin and her son against Sir William Cope, reciting divers frauds and delays in some suits between them for debt, and that he being in prison upon execution, but abroad by *habeas corpus,* was elected in Banbury above six months after his imprisonment.

Divers lawyers spoke against the validity of this election and the dangerous consequences if it should be admitted, whereupon it was specially referred to a committee.

MR. MALLORY. To petition the King that we may be adjourned till Michaelmas.

This motion SIR WILLIAM STRODE thought to divert by another for a committee for petitions, and that one man might not be employed in the chair for that service, but divers.

But the former was seconded by SIR ROBERT PHELIPS. That it was no time, considering the sickness, to take upon us such business. A supply was propounded, but we ought rather to consider how we may supply the commonwealth. In the first place to look to the law of God. Then was matter of fear in sundry parts of the state. Before we think of giving now, we ought likewise to take an account of that which was last given, and because our time cannot possibly extend to all, we should rather desire his Majesty to be referred to some other place.

The same opinion was confirmed by MR. WHISTLER.[30]

---

29. The bracketed word is printed here as it appears in *C.D. 1625* (Knightley MS.); there is a blank

space in both Bedford MS. 197 and B.L. Add. 26,639.

30. *Solicitor. C.D. 1625* (Knightley MS.).

Prosecuted by SIR THOMAS WENTWORTH that a committee might be named to draw a petition for that purpose. Somewhat moderated by MR. ALFORD and SIR GEORGE MORE, that the committee should consider of it as a matter propounded, not concluded. But directly opposed by MR. SOLICITOR as [f. 4v] different from our former order for a fast. There is danger on all sides, but David in a strait chose rather to fall into God's hands than into the hands of men. This is our case. If we advise not maturely all at this time for the public defense we are like to fall into the hands of men. All Christendom are upon the eyes of this action and herein do most specially observe the affection of his Majesty's subjects, which must be his strength. If we part now without doing anything it will weaken his reputation more than can be restored by the grant of many subsidies. He concluded, because our time could not be long we should name a committee to consider what was most necessary for the present and to bend ourselves to that.

MR. WANDESFORD, seeing the House uncapable of the way,[31] willing to get as near it as might be, altered the motion a little from a petition for an adjournment to a new time, to a petition for removal to another place.

But this, which indeed included the former, was opposed by SIR FRANCIS NETHERSOLE and MR. MALET, and the whole matter suppressed by order.

IV. PETYT 538/8, INNER TEMPLE LIBRARY

[f. 112v]   *Die Martis. 21mo Junii*

A *Jove principium:* first, the House re-

solved to receive the communion on Sunday following, in respect of the shortness of the time that they had to sit. The place: St. Margaret's in Westminster; the preacher: Mr. Hacket. [f. 113] And then upon debate, in respect of the great action which they had in hand, which was for a war, and the great affliction like to fall on them by the pestilence which was in the City, and the immoderate wet weather threatening a dearth, thought fit to have a fast to humble themselves by prayer and fasting. The fast to be observed the day before their receiving of the communion. To have three sermons, Mr. Shute of Lombard Street, Doctor Preston, preacher of Lincoln's Inn, and Mr. Holdsworth,[32] endeavoring by unfeigned repentance to appease God's wrath that was gone out against us by plague, unreasonable [sic] weather, and the unprofitableness of our wars.

And upon further debate, it was moved and agreed on that a petition should be made unto his Majesty for [a] general fast throughout the kingdom; and resolved to move the Lords to join with us in [it], and thereupon the former determination of fasting by our House only, and receiving of the sacrament, deferred.

The petition for the fast.[33]

[f. 113v] MR. MALLORY[34] moved to have a petition preferred to his Majesty for an adjournment to another place by reason of the sickness [f. 114] and the important affairs,[35] requiring some long time, which this place will not afford to be done with any safety.

SIR ROBERT PHELIPS accorded.

31. *true way.* C.D. 1625 (Knightley MS.).
32. The other accounts for this day list Thomas Westfield (see above, n. 8) rather than Holdsworth. Richard Holdsworth, rector of St. Peter the Poor, Broad Street, London (*D.N.B.*) was chosen on 22 June to replace Westfield. See below, 22 June, O.B.
33. The petition for the fast is omitted in B.L. Add. 48,091 and Q.C. 449. Petyt 538/8 includes the petition with this day's proceedings (21 June); however we

have moved the text to 22 June when it was reported by the committee appointed this day (21 June; see C.J., above) and read in the House. The petition is also printed in the L.J. See above, H. of L., 23 June, p. 44.
Concerning the deferring of the private fast and communion, see above, nn. 4 and 7.
34. *Mr. Waller.* B.L. Add. 48,091; *Mr. Walter.* Q.C. 449.
35. *officers.* Q.C. 449.

But the House generally disliked this motion and rejected it upon MR. SOLICITOR's motion.

The petition preferred unto the House by the Lady Coppin against Sir William Cope, for that he, being in execution at her suit for 3,000 *l.*, was chosen a burgess of parliament and admitted into that House; which was referred to a special committee of lawyers and others, in the Court of Wards, tomorrow afternoon.

And a committee made for privileges.

V. NOTES OF PROCEEDINGS, 21 JUNE, COMPILED BY SIR SIMONDS D'EWES. HARL. MS. 161, FF. 67–67v.

June [21]

A bill for the due observation and keeping of the sabbath in restraining unlawful games upon it. This was a bill which had passed both the Houses last session.[36] The first reading.

A long dispute whether by reason of the sickness and plague (of which there had died 165 the last week)[37] and other important occasions, it were not fit to join with the Lords in a petition to the King for a general fast. Some thought it fit not to join because they were a body of themselves and might have immediate access by petition to his Majesty, but chiefly because the Lords had refused them in like occasions in former times. But at length agreed by all that a petition should be drawn for the Lords to join with them and if they refused that then they should petition the King alone. Yet it was not yet resolved whether the Lords should be motioned to join with them or no.

Before this dispute on the fast, Sunday following was appointed for a communion to be received by the whole assembly of the Lower House [at] the church of St. Margaret's, Westminster; the preacher, Dr. Hacket.

SIR MILES FLEETWOOD moved that a particular fast might be appointed. This lay in their own power to accomplish, the general fast did not; and by this the willingness of the whole kingdom was represented in them.

This motion was seconded by divers and at length Saturday following appointed for day. The hour, to begin at 9 in the morning; the church where to assemble, St. Margaret's. The preachers nominated to perform the several succeeding sermons for that day were Dr. Westfield, Dr. Preston, and Mr. Shute.[38] Mr. Shute was to begin, Dr. Preston to follow, and Dr. Westfield to end.

A committee for privileges of the number of 60 appointed; to sit Tuesdays, Thursdays, and Saturdays.

A petition preferred by the Lady Coppin against Sir William Cope, chosen burgess for Banbury in Oxfordshire, which sends but one burgess. Because having a long time sued him upon some debt, and now at length with much trouble having gotten him in execution,[39] he procured himself to be chosen a member of that House so to avoid the due and just process of the law.

SIR WILLIAM COPE, then present in the House, spoke for himself: that he was in the service of the last parliament for collection of the subsidies when he was taken, and that

36. A bill for punishing abuses committed on the Lord's day had been passed by the Commons on 6 March 1624 (*C.J.*, I, 678) and by the Lords on 9 March 1624 (*L.J.*, III, 252).
37. See above, H. of L., 18 June, n. 8.
38. See above, n. 8.

39. Cope was imprisoned in the castle of Oxford on 6 July 1624 and shortly after was removed by *habeas corpus* to the Fleet. See Chamberlain, *Letters*, II, 571, 574; and see the committee report on the case, below, 23 June, pp. 227, 233, 234.

he went abroad by *habeas corpus* and would come sit in the House by the same *habeas corpus.*

SIR FRANCIS ASHLEY upon that said he disliked that most of all, for to his grief he saw men plead at bar by *habeas corpus* and others to preach in the pulpit by *habeas corpus,* but he would be most troubled to see men come and sit in that House to make laws by *habeas corpus.*

Divers upon this moved that Sir William Cope should withdraw himself while his own cause in agitation. But the greater part overruled it, that he should be present, upon this difference: in all criminal causes laid to any man's charge being a member of the House he ought to withdraw himself; but this being a matter that only concerned his election as touching the privilege of the House, it was reason he should sit still and defend his own cause.

Upon this followed an order which was made that no man of the [f. 67v] committee of privileges should assist or be present as one of the committee at the hearing of his own cause.

A bill for the confirmation of a decree made by his Highness, now King, while he was Prince of Wales, etc., and Earl of Chester concerning certain lands within the earldom of Chester.[40]

MR. MALLORY moved that the House would petition the King to have the parliament adjourned presently by reason of the pestilence still increasing.

But this motion was suddenly dashed for many reasons:
1. The state of Christendom depended somewhat upon that assembly, and if the opportunity were now lost perhaps it would never again be regained.

2. It would be inconvenient that, many members of that House coming from the remotest parts of the kingdom and for the most part all of them having lain in town since the first summons more or less time for this meeting, [they] should presently upon it dissolve to no purpose without doing anything.
3. This overthrew all this morning's work, for then all the matters already agitated of the public and private fast were like to come to no effect.
4. The King's present necessities.

SIR ROBERT HEATH added that this sickness at home was the hand of God, but to break off without anything done were to give advantage to the enemy abroad and the malcontent and evilhearted at home. He had rather, therefore, in the words of David, to fall into the hands of God than men.

VI. MS E237, KENNETH SPENCER RESEARCH LIBRARY

[21 June 1625]

[f. 116] The 20 [*sic*] day of June. First we read a bill for the sabbath, then another concerning the King about his lands in the County Palatine of Chester.

After, upon motion, we resolved that on the 25 of June we would keep a solemn fast in the church of St. Margaret's at Westminster, and have 3 preachers for that day. The next day, being the 26, we would have the general communion.

Then we had an untimely motion that we might petition the King that in respect of this dangerous time for the plague the parliament might be adjourned till Michaelmas, which, after long debate how and when to consult further of it, it was resolved by question [th]at the motion should die.

40. See above, n. 1.

L. 2a. An act for punishing abuses committed on the **Lord's day**   215, 217, 218, 221; **N**, 501, *21/6

NICHOLAS DUCK   218

The above bill: committed   215, 217, 218, 221; **N**, 501

SIR HENRY WALLOP: presents Thomas Westfield's excuse from preaching at the **fast**   218, *21/6

Westfield's excuse accepted; Richard Holdsworth appointed to preach in Westfield's place; order of sermons arranged   215, 218

SIR WILLIAM COPE: delivers in a petition   218

Petition of Sir William **Cope** concerning his cause with Lady **Coppin**: read and rejected   215, 218, 222, *21/6

[*Cope's petition is printed on pp. 222–223*]

JOHN CARVILL: offers a bill for reversing erroneous sentences and judgments in **courts of equity**   215, *23/6

SIR THOMAS HOBY: moves for a **committee of grievances**   215, 218, 219; **N**, 501

EDWARD ALFORD: moves for a committee to consider what **course** to take this parliament   215

SIR BENJAMIN RUDYARD   215, 218, 219; **N**, 502

SIR EDWARD COKE   215, 220
SIR JOHN ELIOT   216
SIR GEORGE MORE   220
SIR FRANCIS SEYMOUR   216, 220
JOHN DELBRIDGE   220
HENRY BULSTRODE   216
SIR THOMAS WENTWORTH   216

THOMAS MALET   216
SIR GEORGE MORE   216
SIR ROBERT PHELIPS   216, 220
SIR EDWARD GILES   216
JOHN DELBRIDGE   216
SIR EDWARD COKE   216, 220

Resolved: a committee of the whole House to meet tomorrow morning   216, 221

Sir Edward Coke given longer time to elect for which place he will serve   216

SIR ROBERT HEATH (Solicitor)   216

Report from the committee for drawing a petition to the King for a **general fast** (SIR ROBERT HEATH, Solicitor)   217, 218, *21/6

The petition for the general fast: read by the Clerk   217, 218, 221, *21/6

[*The petition for the general fast is printed on pp. 221–222*]

SIR EDWARD COKE   217, 221

Upon question: the draft of the petition for the general fast allowed   217, 218

Upon a division: resolved to send to the Lords for a conference tomorrow morning   217, 218, 221

Report from the **committee of privileges**: concerning the **Yorkshire election** (SIR GEORGE MORE)   217, 218, 221, *21/6

Upon question: the sheriff of Yorkshire, Sir Richard Cholmley, to be heard at committee of privileges tomorrow; resolution concerning time for hearing Wentworth and Fairfax respited   217, 218, 221

WEDNESDAY, 22 JUNE 1625

I. JOURNAL OF THE HOUSE OF COMMONS

[C.J. 800]
[p. 5] *Mercurii, 23° [sic] Junii, 1° Caroli*

L. 2ª. An act for punishing of divers abuses committed on the Lord's day, called Sunday.
Committed to

Sir Edward Coke[1]	Mr. William Whitaker
Mr. [Nicholas] Duck	Mr. Recorder
Sir George More	Sir William Strode
Sir Walter Erle	Mr. [John] Pym
Sir Roger North	Mr. [Richard] Taylor
Mr. Serjeant Ashley	Sir Edward Giles
Mr. John Drake	Mr. [Thomas]
Mr. [Thomas] Sherwill	Wentworth
Sir Thomas Hoby	Mr. [Henry] Rolle
Mr. [Henry] Bulstrode	Sir Francis Goodwin
Sir Nicholas Sanderson	
Mr. Francis Drake	

Exchequer Chamber,[2] two clock.

[p. 6] Dr. Westfield excuses his preaching upon Saturday. His excuse accepted, and Mr. Holdsworth appointed in his room.[3] Mr. Shute to preach first, Mr. Holdsworth 2nd, and Dr. Preston.

A petition from Sir William Cope read, which, by a general voice, rejected.[4]

MR. CARVILL, with a preface, offers in a bill for reversing or correcting of erroneous sentences, judgments, decrees, or orders in courts of equity.

SIR THOMAS HOBY moves for a committee for grievances.

MR. ALFORD. To have a committee to consider of what course we shall take in all business this parliament.

SIR BENJAMIN RUDYARD.[5] The late distastes between the late King and parliament the chief cause of all the miseries of the kingdom. The first turn whereof given by the now King, then Prince, wherein more benefit to the subject than in any parliament these many 100 years, and his subjects expressed their duty to the King. What may we then now expect from him being King and having power? His good natural disposition, his freedom from vice, his travels abroad, his breeding in parliament.

Moves, to take course now to sweeten all things between King[6] and people.

SIR EDWARD COKE. Not now to have any committee of grievances or courts of justice: 1st, in respect of the plague; 2ly, because this the 1st beginning of the now King's reign, wherein no grievances as yet; 3ly, because grievances preferred last parliament to the late King, whereof no answer, which preferred too late.[7] To petition

1. Sir Edward Coke's name is omitted from the list in the Draft Journal, below. Hereafter the editors will not generally note the variations in committee lists as readers can easily compare the lists using the page numbers supplied in the Orders of Business.
2. *Court of Wards* is crossed out in the MS. following *Exchequer Chamber.*
3. See above, H. of C., 21 June, nn. 8 and 32.
4. Cope's petition of 22 June (see below, p. 222) was in answer to a petition tendered against him the previous day by John Saunders on the behalf of Lady Coppin; see above, H. of C., 21 June, n. 16.
5. The version of Rudyard's speech in Bedford MS. 197 (below, pp. 219–220), identical to that in *Negotium* (below, pp. 502–503), is considerably longer than this version from the C.J.
6. *the King.* Printed edition.
7. James I prorogued the 1624 parliament before giving a complete answer to the grievances of the Lower House. Consideration of the general grievances began with the appointment of the committee of the whole for grievances on 23 February 1624, and consideration of the trade grievances began with the appointment of the committee of the whole for trade on 24 February (*C.J.*, I, 671–672). On 22 May (ibid., 709) the draft of the list of grievances was ordered to be brought into the House where it was read on 25 and 26 May (ibid., 711–712). The grievances were presented to James on 28 May (ibid., 714). He responded that he must first advise with the judges and Council before giving answer. The parliament was prorogued the following afternoon (29 May) and James died before a new session met, leaving the House without a full reply from the King. The list of grievances and James's response are included in the Nicholas diary, S.P. 14/166, ff. 242–244 (Y.C.P.H. transcripts); full copies of the

the King now for an answer to those grievances; for, though the prince gone, the King lives: no interregnum.

SIR JOHN ELIOT. No particular or private business to be entertained; a special committee to regulate the business of the House.

SIR FRANCIS SEYMOUR. 1st, our duty to God; 2ly, King and kingdom, which cannot be severed, no more than head and body.

To petition the King the laws against Jesuits, priests, etc., may be put in execution,[8] and to restrain the resort to ambassadors' houses and other places to mass.

That fit to supply the King. To have a committee to consider of religion and of this supply.

MR. BULSTRODE. More cause to fear the plague of our souls than of our bodies. The best preservative and cure, the execution of the laws against Jesuits, etc.

[p. 7] To supply the King amply and quickly for the wars. [To] petition the King for execution of the laws against Jesuits: we punish them but in their purses.

SIR THOMAS WENTWORTH. Not to alter the ancient form of parliaments. To proceed *more majorum*. To have a committee for grievances and leave it to their discretion to entertain nothing unfitting.

MR. MALET, *contra*, for Sir Edward Coke's reasons. Would have the laws against Jesuits, etc., executed, but knows no cause to petition for it, there being (so far as he knows) no bar to it. The King's supply now, *hoc unum necessarium*.

SIR GEORGE MORE. To take care to see the laws put in execution against Jesuits, etc.

SIR ROBERT PHELIPS. Not yet timely for a committee for religion and supply. To think of the propositions made till tomorrow; then to have a committee of the whole House to debate and resolve of a fitting course to be held in our consultations and resolutions for religion and for the King and kingdom.

SIR EDWARD GILES furthers the motion for execution of the laws against Jesuits, etc.

MR. DELBRIDGE seconds Sir Robert Phelips's motion.

SIR EDWARD COKE remembers Queen Elizabeth's great actions, and how God prospered her. The reason was because she cleaved to God. Moves a committee of the whole House, tomorrow morning, Mr. Speaker sitting by: 1, to begin with God; 2ly, tonnage and [**C.J. 801**] poundage, not now meddling with other impositions; to establish a settled book of rates.

Moves a committee of the whole House tomorrow morning.

Resolved, a committee of the whole House, tomorrow morning, Mr. Speaker sitting by, to consider of all the foresaid propositions, and of whatsoever else shall be offered.

Liberty given to Sir Edward Coke for a time before he elect for which place he will serve.

MR. SOLICITOR. That his Majesty has taken care of our grievances preferred the last parliament, and at any day, when this

first group—the general grievances (#1–13)—and James's comments upon them in his speech at the prorogation are printed in Cobbett, *Parl. Hist.*, I, 1489–1502; full copies of the second group—the trade grievances (#14–22)—compiled by John Holles, are in Harl. MS. 4289, ff. 180v–191 (Y.C.P.H. transcripts). Charles I's answers to the 1624 grievances were delivered to the House on 4 July 1625. See below,

H. of C., 4 July, O.B.

8. A subcommittee for framing heads for a petition concerning religion was appointed by the committee of the whole House on 24 June. See below, pp. 240–241, 242. For a summary of both Houses' action on the petition concerning religion, see above, H. of L., 9 August, n. 12.

House will assign, satisfaction shall be given therein to this House.[9]

MR. SOLICITOR tenders also a draft of a petition, which thrice[10] read by the Clerk.

SIR EDWARD COKE. That *17° E. III* the Commons petitioned the King to have prayers generally made of thanksgiving.[11]

The draft of the petition upon question allowed, without 1 negative.

Mr. Chancellor of the Exchequer, Sir James Fullerton, Sir Robert Carr/[12]

Upon the question whether a conference to be desired with the Lords concerning joining in a petition to his Majesty for a general fast, the House divided. The yea went out.

[p. 8] Tellers for yea:[13]	Sir Thomas Cheeke
	Sir Charles Montagu
For the no:	Sir Francis Seymour
	Sir George More
With the no:	172
	23 odds.
With yea:	195

Agreed, to send to the Lords to desire a conference tomorrow morning, if the Lords sit, else at the next sitting. Mr. Chancellor of the Exchequer to be the messenger.

SIR GEORGE MORE reports from the committee for privileges, the case about the election of the knights for the county of York.[14]

That the sheriff, having read the writ, pronounced Sir Thomas Wentworth and Sir Thomas Fairfax, knights; where, Sir John Savile/

That the poll required in time and the sheriff granting it and polling about 35,[15] left the polling.

That this the substance of the petition subscribed by 1,050[16] freeholders. That the petition also fortified by 7 witnesses, *viva voce; vizt.*, that Sir John Savile had the greater number of freeholders; and the poll was in due time demanded, granted, begun, and broken off, as contained in the petition.

That Sir Thomas Wentworth agreed not to any of those things alleged. That his witnesses in the country far off. Desired to be heard by his counsel, and time to send for his witnesses.

Agreed, by a general consent of the committee, that the sheriff should be forthwith sent for, and that Sir Thomas Wentworth and Sir Thomas Fairfax may be heard by their counsel upon Tuesday come sevennight, which now Sir Thomas Wentworth and Sir Thomas Fairfax also desired.

Upon question resolved, the sheriff of Yorkshire shall be heard tomorrow, at two of the clock, before the committee for privileges; and to respite the resolution for giving time for hearing Sir Thomas Wentworth and Sir Thomas Fairfax with their counsel and witnesses till report from the committee.

II. DRAFT JOURNAL, MS. 3409, H.L.R.O.

[f. 130v] *Mercurii 22 Junii 1625.*

Lectio 2ᵃ. An act for punishing divers abuses committed on the Lord's day, commonly called Sunday.

     Committed to

---

9. See above, n. 7.
10. MS.: *3.* This is the petition for the general fast.
11. The citation is incorrect. The Clerk may have this precedent confused with Coke's reference to rates in 17 *E.* III. See Coke's speeches, below, pp. 220–221. We have been unable to find such a petition in the time of E. III.
12. It is unclear why the three names are included here.

13. *the yea.* Printed edition.
14. Concerning further reports on the Yorkshire election, see above, H. of C., 21 June, n. 12.
15. The Draft Journal, below, states that *some 30* were polled; Eliot's figure (*Negotium*, below, p. 513) agrees with the C.J.
16. The Draft Journal, below, gives the figure as 1,400; and Bedford MS. 197, below, states that 1,450 persons subscribed.

Mr. [Nicholas] Duck
Sir George More
Sir Walter Erle
Mr. Recorder
Mr. [Thomas] Sherwill
Mr. John Drake
Sir Thomas Hoby
Mr. [Henry] Bulstrode
Sir Nicholas Sanderson

Sir Roger North
Serjeant Ashley
Mr. William Whitaker
Sir William Strode
Mr. [John] Pym
Mr. [Richard] Taylor
Sir Edward Giles
Mr. [Thomas] Wentworth
Mr. [Henry] Rolle
Sir Francis Goodwin

Exchequer Chamber, 2 clock this afternoon.

SIR HENRY WALLOP. Doctor Westfield desires to be excused from preaching at the fast; has occasion to be out of town.

Resolved to have Mr. Holdsworth in his place. To be in the 2d place.[17]

SIR WILLIAM COPE delivers in a petition. Which was read and rejected.[18]

SIR THOMAS HOBY. To have a committee for grievances appointed.

SIR BENJAMIN RUDYARD.

[f. 131v] MR. SOLICITOR reports from the committee appointed to draw a petition to his Majesty for a general fast.

The petition read and upon question allowed.

Upon question of joining with the Lords in this petition, the House divided and the yeas went out.

Sir Thomas Cheeke
Sir Charles Montagu
tellers for the yea.
195 for the yea.

Sir George More
Sir Francis Seymour
tellers for the no.
172 for the no.

Resolved to send to the Lords tomorrow morning by the Chancellor of the Exchequer.

SIR GEORGE MORE reports from the committee of privileges. The 1st cause they took into consideration was that of Yorkshire. The petition subscribed by 1,400 freeholders.[19] Sir Richard Cholmley, the sheriff, upon view of the freeholders pronounced Sir Thomas Wentworth and Sir Thomas Fairfax knights. The freeholders desired the poll. The sheriff said he need not use it; but after began it at the back gate of the castle. After he had polled some 30 he desisted and went away and returned Sir Thomas Wentworth and Sir Thomas Fairfax. Besides this petition, Sir John Savile produced 7 witnesses which all averred that the writ was read and the poll demanded and begun but given over. Moved at committee that Sir Thomas Wentworth and Sir Thomas Fairfax might be heard. Sir Thomas Wentworth denied all they had said and desired to be heard by counsel and to have his witnesses heard; to have time to send for them up; no indirect means used by Sir Thomas Wentworth or Sir Thomas Fairfax.

In the committee, agreed to send for the sheriff and to have Sir Thomas Wentworth's witnesses and counsel heard and to have a fortnight's time to bring up their witnesses.

[f. 132] Resolved upon question by the House that the sheriff of Yorkshire being now in town shall be heard at the committee of privileges tomorrow in the afternoon, without prejudice to these gentlemen whom it concerns.

Upon a 2d question, the time to be given to the parties to send for witnesses respited.

III. MS. 197, BEDFORD ESTATES, LONDON

[f. 4v]   22 Junii 1625.

The bill of the sabbath the second time read. And committed upon an exception by MR. DUCK that the law extended not to any provision for the levying of the penalties [for offenses][20] committed by country men

---

17. See above, H. of C., 21 June, nn. 8 and 32.
18. See above, n. 4.
19. See the C.J., above, and n. 16.

20. The bracketed words are supplied from *C.D. 1625* (Knightley MS.).

within towns corporate, unless they had goods in the same place.

A motion was made for a committee of grievances. But the House thought it unfit in respect of the short and dangerous time.

[f. 5] SIR BENJAMIN RUDYARD. Mr. Speaker, to say this is the first parliament of the King is no great matter, but that the first parliament of the King should have a temperate proceeding and prosperous success is[21] a matter[22] of extraordinary consideration and consequence. For it is commonly seen that the same influence which governs in the beginning of an action infuses itself throughout and continues to the end, as in this particular of parliaments we have had too dear experience.

Certainly, Mr. Speaker, the disagreement between the King (who is with God)[23] and his people, begun and continued by mutual distastes in parliament, have been the cause almost of all that we can call amiss in this state. It was the King who is now who first gave the happy turn in the last, wherein I may truly say there descended more grace from the crown to the subject than in any parliament some hundred years before; and I may rehearse, though not object, that we also did our duties. If his Majesty when he was Prince and had but a mediating interest did us so many good offices, so many gracious favors, what may we expect now that he is King and has absolute power in his own hands? We may well trust him whom we have so well tried, especially seeing he gives us daily new[24] arguments of his goodness, of his wisdom.

How publicly and frequently he avows and justifies his own, the true religion, with discountenance to the false; how effectually this devotion of his works upon his life. Insomuch as I may strictly say there can hardly be found a private man of his years so free from all ill which, as it is more rare and difficult in [f. 5v] the person of a king, so it is more exemplary and extensive in the operation and, no doubt, being a blessing, will call down more blessings from heaven upon this kingdom for his sake.

For his wisdom, we see that in his particular actions he is naturally regular and orderly which howsoever some retired abstruse spirits may account but a formality, yet wise men know how much it conduces to wealth, to greatness, to government, order being indeed the very soul of outward things. Besides, his breeding has given him an advantage above all the kings in Christendom. For he has been abroad and has treated with a wise and subtle nation in a business so great that himself was the subject of it, which has not only opened and enlarged but quickened and sharpened his natural abilities and made him understand his own kingdom the better. For to know a man's own country alone is but a solitary kind of knowledge in respect of knowing it by comparison with others.

But that which is of most use and application to us is that he has been bred in parliaments, which has made him not only to know but to favor the ways of his own subjects, whereof it becomes us always to have a grateful remembrance.

Upon these foundations, Mr. Speaker, I will humbly move this honorable House in that wherein I hope we all come hither prepared and moved in ourselves, that is to carry ourselves in this first session with sweetness, with duty, with confidence in and towards his Majesty; for which no doubt we shall respectively receive such grace, such favor, such satisfaction as the dangerousness of this time and therefore the shortness of it can possibly allow. Towards the happy effecting whereof I do further move that we may fall upon such

21. MS.: *as.*
22. *great matter. C.D. 1625* (Knightley MS.).
23. I.e., James I. Concerning the "happy turn"
given by Charles to the previous session, see above, H. of C., 18 June, n. 29.
24. *more. C.D. 1625* (Knightley MS.).

things only as are necessary, clear, and of dispatch. And that those businesses which have in them either perplexity, difficulty, or asperity, if the House be pleased[25] [f. 6] altogether to omit them, yet that they may be but only touched by way of claim or grievance and so remitted to the next session when we shall have fitter opportunity and better leisure to debate and settle them.[26]

Last of all, to take off the least scruple of prejudice which misinterpretation may cast upon me, I do solemnly protest that as heretofore I did never speak with the King, Prince, or favorite of parliament businesses, so with our present King I never had the honor to speak forty words of any purpose whatsoever. Insomuch as what I have said I have spoken it out of the sincerity of my own heart, without any other end but the good of the commonwealth, whereof this assembly is the a-bridgement.

The rest of the morning[27] was spent in considering what to do rather than in doing anything.

SIR EDWARD COKE gave 3 reasons against making committees for grievances and courts of justice: first, the danger of infection by drawing the meaner sort of people about us, which was the judicial reason of the adjourning of the term; 2, there have

been no grievance[s] since the King came to the crown; 3, we have yet received no answer of our last grievances,[28] therefore we are first to begin to petition his Majesty for that; and hereafter let us be careful to present our grievances in such time that we may have an answer before the breaking up of the parliament.

Others were unwilling to depart from the custom of the House by relinquishing those committees. But SIR GEORGE MORE affirmed that this is a custom of late beginning, and that in Queen Elizabeth's time no such committees were appointed but upon particular occasions.[29]

[f. 6v] SIR FRANCIS SEYMOUR and MR. DELBRIDGE. For a bold but manifold[30] petition concerning the toleration of papists, by which both their number and insolency was increased.

SIR ROBERT PHELIPS added the consideration of the new impositions and some fit propositions[31] in this respect in the act of tonnage and poundage, and how the revenue of this crown might be supplied, being so wasted as was unable to support public charges. Not to neglect the account of the last subsidies, in provision for which there was so much time spent the last parliament.[32]

SIR EDWARD COKE. For a book of rates to

25. Marginal note in the Earl of Bedford's hand: "No".
26. Marginal note in the Earl of Bedford's hand: "No".
27. *forenoon*. C.D. 1625 (Knightley MS.).
28. See above, n. 7.
29. Marginal note in the Earl of Bedford's hand: "No". Although appointment of a standing select committee of privileges at the beginning of a session dated from Elizabeth's time, the practice of establishing standing "grand" committees of the whole House to meet regularly during a session in order to deal with three or four areas of major concern (grievances, courts of justice, trade, and/or religion) originated during the parliaments of James I and was still not

fully developed by 1625. In 1614, eleven years before the meeting of the present parliament, only the standing committees of privileges and petitions (grievances) were organized (C.J., I, 456, 457). In 1621 and again in 1624, standing committees of privileges, grievances, courts of justice, and trade were set up early in each parliament (C.J., I, 507, 510, 514, 523, 528, 671–672). See also, Eliot's comments concerning the grand committees, below, *Negotium*, p. 501.
30. *mournful*. C.D. 1625 (Knightley MS.).
31. *provisos*. C.D. 1625 (Knightley MS.).
32. An account of the disbursements from the 1624 subsidy monies was included as the first part of Sir John Coke's 8 July report on the King's estate. See below, H. of C., 8 July, O.B.

be established by parliament according to a precedent, 17 E. 3.[33]

It fell into question whether we should join with the Lords in our petition for a public fast.

SIR EDWARD COKE vouched a precedent in E. 3 time wherein the like petition was by the Commons alone.[34]

But divers reasons were given for joining: that it would be more to God's honor, more suitable to the occasion, which was a fear of a public calamity. So, upon the question and dividing of the House, it was ordered that we should go to the Lords, and for that purpose a message was appointed tomorrow morning.

SIR GEORGE MORE reported from the committee of privileges, first reciting Sir John Savile's petition, subscribed by 1,450 persons,[35] charging Sir Richard Cholmley, sheriff of Yorkshire, to have returned Sir Thomas Wentworth and Sir Thomas Fairfax, notwithstanding he had double so many voices as they, without polling, though the poll were demanded in due time. And this was proved at the committee by seven witnesses.

Sir Thomas Wentworth, not confessing the demand of the poll, desired time to send for his witnesses and to be heard by his counsel. The committee had agreed upon a fortnight's time.

[f. 7] Against this opinion of the committee[36] was objected that there needed no time, nor further examination of witnesses, when the affirmative was so well proved. But it being informed that the sheriff was in town, it was ordered that he should be heard tomorrow, and thereupon the House to proceed as they should see cause.

IV. PETYT 538/8, INNER TEMPLE LIBRARY

[f. 114]   *Die Mercurii 22° Junii*

A bill for better keeping of the Lord's day, commonly called Sunday, and for avoiding of unlawful sports and games on that day. Once read and committed because it formerly passed both Houses.[37]

And afterwards the whole day spent in debate what was fit to be done in respect of the shortness of time and the necessity of supply and, for satisfaction of the commonwealth, who were to give the same.

And thereupon a committee to be of the whole House, tomorrow, to debate wholly[38] what things are fit to be done either for grievances, laws, or supply.

[f. 113] The petition for the fast.[39]

We your Majesty's most loyal and dutiful subjects, the Lords spiritual and temporal [f. 113v] and Commons, now assembled in parliament to consult and advise of the great and weighty affairs of Church and state, knowing that all human counsel and helps without God's divine assistance are of no force and, observing that God has already laid His hand upon the pestilence and unseasonable weather, threatening a famine, for these and many other important reasons do, as in duty we conceive ourselves bound, and, as a thing most suitable to the present times and occasions, humbly beseech your Majesty that you will be pleased to command a general fast throughout the whole kingdom. That, we humbling ourselves by fasting and prayer, we may upon our true repentance make our peace with God and thereby both divert

---

33. *Rot. Parl.,* 17 *E.* III, no. 17.
34. We have been unable to find the petition.
35. See the C.J., above, and n. 16.
36. *Against that of the committees. C.D. 1625* (Knight-

ley MS.).
37. See above, H. of C., 21 June, n. 36.
38. *to resolve.* B.L. Add. 48,091.
39. See above, H. of C., 21 June, n. 33.

His heavy judgments inflicted and deserved, and drawn down a blessing upon our consultations and counsels and upon your Majesty's sacred person, your kingdom, and all your royal designs and enterprises.

V. PETITION OF WILLIAM COPE, KNIGHT AND BARONET. H.L.R.O., MAIN PAPERS, H.L., 22 JUNE 1625.

To the honorable assembly of the House of Commons in this present parliament assembled.

The humble petition of Sir William Cope, Knight and Baronet, humbly shows,

Whereas the petition yesterday preferred by the Lady Coppin[40] was filled with much reviling and untruths, which the petitioner hopes to clear, intending to run a contrary course, and will set down nothing but the truth in fair language. For about 7 years since, the petitioner having done great courtesies for Sir George Coppin, Knight, deceased, in requital whereof the said Sir George promised to gratify the petitioner in selling unto him the manors of Great and Little Wakering, which he agreed to sell at the rates of 16 years purchase for the lands in possession and nine years purchase for the lands in reversion; that, being cast up according to the rate of a false particular warranted to be true under the hands of the said Sir George, amounted to 20,000 l., in payment of which money the petitioner paid 12,000 l. (as the Lady Coppin confesses) and 3,000 l. more she has received out of the profits of the land, which is more than the land comes to according to the rates agreed upon.

For relief whereof the petitioner preferred his bill in the honorable Court of Chancery, the certainty whereof could not be proved in respect the petitioner's writings warranted by Sir George were then wanting, being now, with great labor found, ready to be showed to this honorable assembly, being the proper place for such causes as cannot be remedied by any ordinary course of justice (your petitioner having been deceived of, at the least, 6,000 l. by the said Sir George Coppin). Yet, since his death, his executors, hoping by cruelty to suppress the petitioner from seeking relief in this his great distress, having received 15,000 l. of the purchase money and the quietly possessing the said land for which he paid the same, have nevertheless laid execution of 3,000 l. upon the petitioner's person, who can make it appear that Sir George Coppin did [with] many deep protestations assure the petitioner that the land better worth by 200 l. per annum than the values he did warrant by his handwriting, whereas in truth those grounds which the said Sir George had in his own occupation were worth but half the rent he warranted them at. As for example, one ground called Lambgore warranted to be worth 60 l. per annum, was not worth above 30 l. per annum. Another ground called Potting, warranted by Sir George after the expiration of an old lease to be worth 300 l. per annum, which in truth neither was nor is worth 180 l. A mill warranted by Sir George to be worth 20 l. more by the year than it is or ever was worth. A jointure of Mrs. Moores warranted to be worth 1,400 l., which neither was nor is worth 160 l. per annum. Now divers others of the like nature.

For the ground[s] which were demised, they were let to such tenants who were men unable to pay their rents, which they covenanted to do at a far higher value than the lands were worth and they paid no rent unto Sir George, which was only done by Sir George unduly to draw in a purchaser. Whereupon the petitioner was not only deceived but likewise compelled to buy out the said tenants or else he should neither have received rent nor enjoyed land.

When discovery was made of all this de-

40. See above, H. of C., 21 June, n. 16.

ceit, and the petitioner preferred his bill in Chancery against Sir G., one Mr. Lassells came to Mr. Wright of the Inner Temple and undertook to help the petitioner to a chapman that should give present money for the said lands, so that the said Mr. Lassells might have a note to view the same, which was presently granted. And the petitioner, expecting a chapman for the said lands, instead thereof the next new[s] was that the said Mr. Lassells was examined in Chancery as the petitioner's surveyor by Sir George Coppin.

And the Lady Coppin set down upon her oath the petitioner bought not the said lands so much upon Sir George's warranty as upon the survey of Mr. Lassells. Whereas, in truth, the petitioner has yet no acquaintance at all with the said Lassells. Neither did he ever hear of or see the said Lassells to his knowledge until two years after the petitioner had bought the said lands.

Wherefore, in regard the said Sir George is now dead and the petitioner without remedy in Star Chamber against the practice of Sir George and Mr. Lassells, and likewise the other tenants not to be found, who did so indirectly agree with Sir George for taking their lands at over values, and in respect actions at law will not lie against the executors of the said Sir George and this court therefore is the proper place to relieve those who are helpless in other courts, may it therefore please this most honorable assembly to refer the examination of all these allegations to the committee for the Lady Coppin.

L. 2a. An act to confirm an agreement between the King and his tenants of **Macclesfield**: committed — 226, *21/6

SIR THOMAS MIDDLETON: elects to serve for Denbighshire — 226

SIR JOHN STRADLING: moves for a committee concerning **former monies** given — 226

Report from the committee on the bill for punishing abuses committed on the **Lord's day** (SIR THOMAS HOBY) — 226, 232, *21/6

Ordered: the above bill to be engrossed — 226

SIR TALBOT BOWES: moves that the **committee of privileges** have power to send for the sheriff in the **Yorkshire election** case — 226

Power given to committee of privileges to send for sheriffs — 226

Ordered: **public bills** to be proceeded with after the business of religion and supply — 226

L. 1a and *L. 2a.* An act for explanation of a **statute of 3 Jac.** for repressing popish recusants — 226, 232, *24/6; 27/6; 28/6

SIR HENRY WHITEHEAD — 226, 232

SIR JOHN STRADLING — 226

The above bill: committed — 226, 233

Report from the committee to consider Lady **Coppin's** petition against Sir William **Cope** (ROBERT HITCHAM) — 227, 233, 234, *21/6

THOMAS WENTWORTH — 227

HENRY ROLLE — 227

SIR EDWARD COKE — 227

Resolved: Sir William Cope to be discharged the House and a warrant to be issued for a new election — 228, 235; **N**, 516

Message to Lords desiring a **conference** regarding the petition for a **general fast** (Sir Richard Weston, Chancellor of the Exchequer) [*see below*] — 228, 235, *21/6

L. 1a. An act for the quiet of **ecclesiastical persons** (SIR EDWARD COKE) — 228, *24/6; 2/8; 4/8; 6/8; 9/8

Bill of **simony** to be looked up — 228, *28/6

L. 1a. An act for the further restraint of **tippling** in inns, alehouses, etc. — 228, *24/6; 28/6; 1/7; 7/7; 9/7; 11/7

L. 1a. An act for mitigation of the sentence of the greater **excommunication** (SIR EDWARD COKE) — 228, *27/6

Report of the Lords' answer to the message: the Lords have appointed a committee for a present **conference** (SIR RICHARD WESTON, Chancellor Exchequer) [*see above and below*] — 228

Committee for the conference on the **general fast**: appointed — 228

L. 1a. An act for reversing erroneous sentences and judgments in **courts of equity** — 228, *22/6

L. 1a. An act concerning **petty larceny** — 228, *25/6; 9/7; 6/8

Bill concerning **Michaelmas term** to be looked up — 229, *28/6

L. 1a. An act for ease in obtaining licenses of **alienation** — 229, *25/6; 30/6; 1/7; 11/7

THURSDAY, 23 JUNE 1625

I. DRAFT JOURNAL, MS. 3409, H.L.R.O.

[f. 132]   *Jovis 23 Junii.*

L. 2ª. An act for the tenants of Macclesfield. Upon question, committed.
Sir James Fullerton
Sir Henry Vane
Sir Walter Erle
Knights, burgesses [of] Cheshire and Lancashire and Derbyshire
Sir Edward Giles
Sir Thomas Hoby
Mr. [Francis] Downes
Mr. Nicholas Hyde
Mr. Clarke
Sir Arthur Ingram
Mr. Solicitor
Sir Miles Fleetwood
Mr. [John] Lowther
Sir Oliver Cromwell
This afternoon, 2 clock, Exchequer Chamber.

SIR THOMAS MIDDLETON elects to serve for the county [of] Denbigh.

SIR JOHN STRADLING. To appoint a committee to take examination of the bestowing the former monies given.[1]

SIR THOMAS HOBY reports the bill of the sabbath without any amendments.[2]

Ordered to be engrossed.

SIR TALBOT BOWES. To have the committee of privileges [have] power to send for the sheriff in Sir Thomas [Fairfax of][3] Denton's case.

Power given to the committees of privileges to send for sheriffs if they see cause.

[f. 132v] Ordered upon question that after the great business of religion and supply is over, the best public bills shall be proceeded with.

L. 1ª. Recusants.[4]
L. 2ª. Recusants.

SIR HENRY WHITEHEAD. To have some course taken in this bill for licenses granted to recusants to travel, that the state may always know where to have their bodies.

SIR JOHN STRADLING. To have those that are parties have benefit by discovering these fraudulent estates.

Committed to

Sir Edward Coke	Sir George More
Sir Henry Whitehead	Serjeant Hitcham
Mr. [John] Glanville	Mr. Recorder
Sir John Stradling	Sir Robert
Sir Francis Goodwin	Cholmondeley
Sir Francis Seymour	Sir Edwin Sandys
Sir Miles Fleetwood	Sir Clement
Sir Francis Barrington	Throckmorton
Sir Thomas Hoby	Mr. [Thomas]
Mr. Solicitor	Wentworth
Sir James Fullerton	Sir Edward Giles
Mr. [William] Coryton	Mr. [Robert] Bateman
Sir Edward Peyton	Mr. Drake

1. Stradling may be reiterating the concern voiced by Sir Robert Phelips on the previous day (see above, H. of C., 22 June, p. 220 and n. 32) for an accounting of the disbursements of the 1624 subsidy monies.
2. I.e., the bill concerning abuses on the Lord's day. For a report on reasons against amending the bill, see Bedford MS. 197, below, p. 232.
3. The edge of the MS. is torn following *Thomas*. Bowes's motion probably concerned the Yorkshire election case involving Sir Thomas Fairfax of Denton, which was under consideration in the House at the end of the previous day (see above, H. of C., 22 June, O.B.), rather than having anything to do with Sir Thomas Denton, who was returned for Buckinghamshire in 1624 and again in 1626 but who, as far as we can determine, was not connected with any contested election in 1625. The editors thank Mary F. Keeler for suggesting this interpretation of the entry in the Draft Journal.
4. I.e., An act for explanation of a statute of 3 *Jac.* for repressing popish recusants. For a draft bill for explanation of the 3 *Jac.* statute, see *C.D. 1621*, VII, 61–65. Many of the bills preferred in 1625 had been introduced in previous parliaments. The drafts of those bills considered by the Lower House in 1621 that are contained in the H.L.R.O. Main Papers are printed, without date, in Appendix A of *C.D. 1621*. The wording of the 1621 draft bills is probably very similar, if not identical, to the wording of the 1625 bills on the same subjects.

Sir Thomas Middleton   Sir Roger North
Mr. [Richard]   Sir Warwick Hele
    Knightley   Mr. [Henry] Bulstrode
                      Sir Guy Palmes
                      Sir Daniel Norton

Tomorrow, 2 clock, Court of Wards.

SERJEANT HITCHAM reports from the committee to examine the Lady Coppin's case. The case this: the end of the last parliament, Sir W. Cope was taken in execution 33 days after; a week after committed to the Fleet by a *habeas corpus* from the L. Keeper. Privilege of parliament [f. 133] 16 days before and 16 after; his time longer.[5] Resolved by the committee that a person thus taken in execution so long after the parliament cannot serve in parliament; and there[fore] to have a warrant for a new writ.

For the other collateral matter, they meddled not with it.

MR. WENTWORTH. To make now a good precedent for hereafter. The case this: the parliament not dissolved at the prorogation at end of a session. Sir William Cope a member of the House in the first session. Question whethe[r], if that parliament had held, Sir W. Cope should not have had privilege at the next session. Thinks for his part he should not. Privilege holds during an adjournment but not after a prorogation.[6]

MR. ROLLE. *Contra.* Thinks if the former parliament had held Sir William Cope should have been delivered, though taken in execution so long after the parliament, because his election at the first was due and there[fore] no writ can go for a new election.

SIR EDWARD COKE. The liberty of parliament the heartstring of parliament. 2 questions: Whether Sir William Cope shall have his privilege for the last parliament or this.

14 H. 4, the knights could have no wages because the parliament dissolved and the King's death.[7]

Privilege holds as well upon prorogation as adjournment. 31 H. 6, the parliament prorogued. The Duke of York, regent, sued the Speaker in the vacation and had a judgment. The Commons desired their Speaker.[8]

---

5. Concerning Cope's imprisonment after the 1624 parliament, see above, H. of C., 21 June, n. 39. The fact that Cope was "in the service of the last parliament" as a subsidy collector when he was taken (see H. of C., 21 June, p. 212) was not considered an extenuating factor in his arrest. The period of privilege from arrest for a member going to or returning from parliament was established by the Lower House in Sir Vincent Skinner's case, October 1610, at sixteen days before and after each session. *Proceedings in Parliament 1610*, II, 306–308, 387; and cf. *Bowyer*, pp. 35–36.

6. The 1624 parliament was prorogued on 29 May and was not reassembled prior to its dissolution by the King's death on 27 March 1625. In 1621 the House had established that privilege holds during an adjournment but is extended for a limited time only following a prorogation. See Hatsell, *Precedents*, I, 40, 100–101, 163–164, 168, 180–182. With regard to what constitutes a prorogation, what an adjournment, see Coke, *Fourth Inst.*, ff. 27–28; *C.D. 1628*, IV, 16 n. 14 and 199 n. 9.

7. Henry IV died on 20 March 1413, thereby dissolving the parliament which met on 3 February 1413. The first session of his son's first parliament, which opened in May of the same year, petitioned that the knights and burgesses of the previous parliament should receive the usual recompense for their expenses despite the fact that nothing passed in that parliament. Henry V answered the petition by stating that the decision must follow precedent, and records were ordered to be searched accordingly. *Rot. Parl.*, 1 *H. V*, no. 26. See also, Coke, *Fourth Inst.*, p. 46; Cobbett, *Parl. Hist.*, I, 318–319.

8. During the period of prorogation of parliament between 2 July 1453 and 14 February 1454 the Duke of York had brought an action of trespass in the Exchequer against the Speaker of the Lower House, Thomas Thorpe, for Thorpe's having removed goods from Durham House. Upon the verdict in the Exchequer, Thorpe was imprisoned in the Fleet and when parliament reassembled on 14 February 1454 the Commons requested of the King and the Upper House that Thorpe be given his liberty according to the privileges of parliament. Having consulted with the judges, the Lords decided that, according to law, Thorpe should remain in prison notwithstanding his privilege, and in the King's name commanded the Commons to choose a new Speaker, which order they

Being 33 days he ought not to have the privilege of parliament.

Resolved upon question that Sir William Cope shall be discharged the House, and a warrant issued for a new election.

Mr. Chancellor Exchequer sent up to the Lords to desire a conference about the petition for a fast.

[f. 133v] Sir Edward Coke prefers a bill to quiet the estates of ecclesiastical persons.

Read.
Lectia 1ª. An act to quiet/

Bill of simony to be looked up.[9]

L. 1ª. An act for the further restraint of tippling.

Sir Edward Coke prefers another bill, to mitigate the sentence of excommunication.

L. 1ª. An act for mitigation of the sentence of the greater excommunication.

Mr. Chancellor Exchequer reports from the Lords. The Lords return all thanks and entreat us to be assured they will use all care to hold good correspondence with this House. Have appointed 24 of their House to meet our committee presently in the Painted Chamber.

Mr. Treasurer	Sir Roger North
Chancellor Exchequer	Mr. Solicitor
Sir Edward Coke	Mr. Recorder
Sir Francis Seymour	Sir Thomas Hoby
Sir Henry Wotton	Sir Edwin Sandys

Sir Miles Fleetwood	Sir Thomas Wentworth
Lord St. John	Sir Francis Barrington
Mr. [Edward] Wraye	Sir Walter Erle
Sir Robert Carr	Sir Nathaniel Rich
Sir James Fullerton	Sir William Strode
Sir John Coke	Sir Robert Hatton
Sir Thomas Cheeke	Sir Benjamin Rudyard
Lord Burghersh	Sir Dudley Digges
L. Strange	Mr. [Richard] Knightley
L. Percy	Sir Robert Cholmondeley
L. Holles[10]	Mr. Richard Spencer

[f. 134]

Sir Edward Rodney	Sir Edward Villiers
Sir Henry Mildmay	Sir Edward Giles
Sir Thomas Hatton	Sir Henry Vane[11]
Sir George More	
L. Cavendish	
Sir William Herbert	
Sir Oliver Luke	
Sir John Eliot	
Sir Rowland St. John	
Mr. Francis Drake	
Mr. John Drake	
Chancellor Duchy	
Mr. [John] Pym	

Sent up to confer with the Lords about the petition to the King for a general fast.

Chancellor Exchequer to make the report.

L. 1ª. An act for reversing erroneous sentences and judgments in courts of equity.

L. 1. An act concerning petty larceny and

complied with, naming Sir Thomas Charleton. *Rot. Parl.*, 31 & 32 *H.* VI, nos. 25–29; see also, Hatsell, *Precedents*, I, 28–34, and Cobbett, *Parl. Hist.*, I, 392–393.

9. There is an *X* in the margin of the MS. next to this entry on the simony bill, and similar marks appear in the Draft Journal and the Committee Book before other entries concerning matters of business (see below, n. 13). The *X* is apparently the Clerk's reminder of future activity which may or may not require his attention. The marks on the entries for this day serve as the Clerk's reminder to collect and bring to the House the bills listed that were introduced but not completed in

the previous session. The simony bill had passed the Lower House on 15 May 1624 (*C.J.*, I, 789) but had only one reading in the Upper House, 20 May 1624 (*L.J.*, III, 393).

10. I.e., John Holles, styled Lord Houghton after his father was created Earl of Clare in November 1624.

11. *Sir Nicholas Sanderson* and two illegible names are crossed out in the MS. following *Vane* (MS.: *Fane*). Disregarding the crossed-out entries the list contains 48 names of M.P.s, which constitutes the customary double number of Commoners to meet with the Lords' 24 committee appointees.

the manner of punishing the offenders therein.[12]

Michaelmas term to be looked up.[13]

L. 1[a]. An act for the ease in obtaining licenses of alienations.

SIR HENRY VANE elects to serve for Carlisle.

Bill of fishing to be brought tomorrow.

L. 1[a]. An act to abolish all trials by battel.

Transportation of wools to be looked up.

Secret offices tomorrow.

L. 1[a]. An act for restraint of assignment of debt.

CHANCELLOR EXCHEQUER reports from the Lords. They presented the model of the petition,[14] heard it read, and approved the form. L. Canterbury in the [torn] of the Lords told them that they returned [torn] [f. 134v] possible thanks to this House for their desire of good correspondence. They had taken into consideration the matter of our petition; thought it very necessary at this time. The Lords thought we had taken the right way to petition the King, for public fasts always from him. Cited the fast spo-

ken of in Joel proclaimed by a trumpet.[15] Approved all. But told them they could not approve the form till they had acquainted the House with it. Went back to their House, and returned with this answer: they approved the form without any alteration; only filled up the blank with the names of the Lords spiritual and temporal;[16] did presently purpose to attend the King, and thought we should have an answer this day. To have it presently engrossed.

L. 2[a]. Assignment of debts.

MR. WHISTLER. A new trick found in the Exchequer for debts. To have this bill meet with that.

Committed

Mr. Treasurer	Sir Thomas Fanshawe
Sir Edward Coke	Sir Robert Pye
Chancellor	Sir John Stradling
Exchequer[17]	Sir Guy Palmes
Chancellor Duchy	Sir William Pitt
Serjeant Ashley	Sir Thomas
All the lawyers of the	Wentworth
House	Mr. Charles Price
Sir Anthony Forest	Sir Edwin Sandys
Sir John Coke	Sir Robert Killigrew
Sir George More	Mr. Cholmley
Mr. [Edward]	Mr. Thomas Fanshawe
Hungerford	

12. For a draft bill on petty larceny, see *C.D. 1621*, VII, 265–267 (concerning the 1621 draft bills, see above, n. 4).

13. Marginal note: "X". See above, n. 9. There are similar *X*'s next to the entries on fishing, wool, and secret offices, below. A bill for abbreviation of Michaelmas term had passed the Lower House on 3 May 1624 (*C.J.*, I, 782), was read twice in the Upper House, committed and reported (*L.J.*, III, 342, 384, 397), but not passed. A draft of the 1625 bill is in H.L.R.O., Main Papers, H.L., 28 June; see also *C.D. 1621*, VII, 294–298. A bill for alienations (see below) was passed by the Commons on 28 May 1624 (*C.J.*, I, 715) and passed by the Lords on 29 May (*L.J.*, III, 421), but did not receive the King's assent (Harl. MS. 159, f. 135v). For a draft bill on alienations, see *C.D. 1621*, VII, 185–187. A bill for free fishing upon the coast of America passed the Lower House on 3 May 1624 (*C.J.*, I, 782) and was sent up to the Lords the following day (*L.J.*, III, 340) but was never read there. For a draft bill on fishing upon the coast of America,

see *C.D. 1621*, VII, 202–204. A bill against exportation of wool and woolfells passed the Commons on 26 April 1624 (*C.J.*, I, 775), was twice read and committed in the Upper House (*L.J.*, III, 322, 337, 403), but was not passed there. For arguments concerning a bill against exporting wool, see *C.D. 1621*, VII, 250–254; a draft bill against exportation of wool is included in H.L.R.O., Main Papers, H.L., 27 April 1624. A bill concerning secret offices had been read and committed by the Commons on 8 March 1624 (*C.J.*, I, 731), but it never passed the Lower House. See Russell, *Parliaments*, pp. 43–44. For a draft bill against secret offices, see *C.D. 1621*, VII, 193–197.

14. I.e., the petition for a general fast.

15. Joel 2:12–15.

16. The Commons had left a blank for the words "Lords spiritual and temporal" to be filled in by the Upper House. See H. of L., 23 June, O.B.

17. The name *Sir Edward Coke*, placed above the Chancellor here, appears in the MS. on the same line and to the left of the *Chancellor Exchequer*.

Sir Walter Erle
Sir [*sic*] Anthony
 Langston
Mr. [John] Pym
Sir William Herbert
Sir Henry Spiller
Sir Henry Mildmay
Mr. [Thomas] Bancroft
Sir Thomas Cheeke
 Monday, 2 clock, Exchequer Chamber.

[f. 135] MR. PYM. To have an alteration of our day for our fast, for some reasons: 1, in regard of the Lords conformity with us; 2ly, it will be pleasing to his Majesty.

A message from the Lords by Mr. Attorney and Serjeant Richardson. The Lords signify to this House that they have caused my L. Steward and my L. Conway to attend the King to know his pleasure when the committee of both Houses should attend him about the petition. He is pleased that the committee of both Houses attend him tomorrow at 9 of the clock in Whitehall at the Banqueting House. And [the Lords] desire a copy of the petition to be sent to them to remain in that House with them.
 Answer: The committee of this House shall attend the committee of their Lordships to the King at the time and place appointed by his Majesty. And have also sent their Lordships a copy of the petition as was desired.

SIR EDWARD COKE. *Sapiens incipit a fine.* A deferring of the fast has been moved. There must be some cause for it. Precedent cited suits not with this. We shall tomorrow attend the King, and doubts not but he shall have a gracious answer. There[fore] not to stir this question.

The engrossed petition read and allowed.[18] To be delivered tomorrow morn-

ing by Mr. Chancellor Exchequer to my L. of Canterbury.

Resolved upon question, a committee of the whole House to sit this afternoon at 2 of the clock to debate the great business, and the Speaker to sit by.[19] And all other committees to cease this afternoon and hold tomorrow in the afternoon.

[f. 135v] *Jovis 23 Junii 1625*
    post meridiem.

The Speaker taking the chair, MR. SOLICITOR reported from the grand committee.[20] They have adjourned the debate of the great business of religion until tomorrow morning, 7 clock.

The House ordered to sit tomorrow, being Midsummer Day, in regard of the great business in hand and the shortness of time they have to sit.

II. COMMITTEE BOOK, MS. 3410, H.L.R.O.

[f. 156] *Jovis 23 Junii 1625.*
    Post meridiem.

Mr. Solicitor had the chair.

Sir John Eliot.[21] Matter of religion falls first. Propo[sitions], 2 considerable: unity and purity. This kingdom now suffers many divisions and fractions in religion. The cause lies in the laws or execution. Here must be the remedy: to take a review of the laws, if any defect in them to have it supplied; if any fail in the execution/

Mr. Bulstrode. If convictions had been duly pursued, this evil far less. To look into that why convictions are not followed. To see where this stop is. Next to see how to recover those parts of the body that are not yet decayed. To establish a good and learned ministry to teach the people.

---

18. *And sent up to the Clerk of the Lords House by our Serjeant* is crossed out in the MS.
 19. Marginal note: "X".
 20. For the speeches at the committee of the whole

House, see the account in the Committee Book, below.
 21. A fuller version of Eliot's speech is included in *Negotium,* below, p. 504.

Sir Thomas Hoby. In the place that he serves for this rule observed since 9 of the King.[22] 2,400 recusants certified into the Exchequer in 2 years. Connivancy the occasion of this. A new course taken of late of sending *certiorari* to remove the indictment which hinders the proceeding of the indictment. This one cause of the hindrance of convictions. Another cause is procuring of pardons. A 3d cause is letters coming down that prohibit the proceeding against them, even the taking of 12*d.* upon a Sunday,[23] which goes to the poor.

Sir Thomas Wilford. Will acquaint the House with the insolency of the recusants in the place for which he serves.[24] 12 March last, in Christ Church in Canterbury, some papists assembled. One went to the Bible and opened it in Job; takes 2 leaves, rends them out, and puts them in pocket. Complaint was made to the dean; he pursued it. The party conveyed out of the town and means made to stop all proceedings against him. This man a priest, and belongs to the Lord Teynham.[25]

[f. 156v] [Sir] Nicholas Sanderson. Will

note 3 devices the papists have to avoid the law: 1 is changing of names; 2, conveying away their goods into privileged places; 3, *certioraries*.[26] To have some additions to former laws to prevent these abuses, or else to devise a new law.

Sir Thomas Fanshawe. *Certioraries* very sparingly granted out of the King's Bench. Some have come of late out of the Chancery under the Great Seal.

Serjeant Hitcham. A great abuse in informations against recusants; procure informations against themselves to prevent others.

Mr. Moore.

Sir Robert Phelips. To have those petitions that were presented to the late King touching recusants reviewed that so we may resolve of such a course of declaration to his Majesty as may advantage our religion and discountenance our enemies.[27]

Sir Clement Throckmorton. The infinite confluence of priests and Jesuits into this kingdom a great cause of the increase of

---

22. Sir Thomas Hoby sat for Ripon, Yorkshire. It is difficult to date precisely the beginning of leniency in English recusant laws. The marriage treaties negotiated first with Spain and then with France necessitated a less stringent enforcement of those laws. Regarding the provisions of the Spanish marriage treaty (subsequently dissolved in 1624), see the private articles in favor of Roman Catholics, sworn to by James I, printed in Rushworth, *Hist. Collections,* I, 89. Concerning the French marriage articles, see above, H. of L., 9 August, n. 6. On stays of proceedings in the Exchequer against recusants, see S.P. 14/177:24. Concerning the use of *certioraries* to move the indictments into Chancery, see below, H. of C., 25 June, p. 247. And on the matter of pardons, see the pardon granted on 4 May to twenty men for their offenses against the statutes concerning recusancy. S.P. 16/2:22. See also, below, H. of C., 1 August, when a pardon for recusants, apparently solicited by the French ambassador, was complained of in the House. The pardon became the subject of a petition to the King and a conference with the Lords. See below, H. of C., 6 August, O.B.; and above, H. of L., 9 August, O.B.

23. According to *S.R.,* 1 *Eliz.* I, c. 2, and 3 *Jac.* I, c. 4, pt. 18, the fine of 12*d.* was charged on Protestants and papists alike for absence from divine service on Sundays, with the money so collected to be employed for the use of the poor. See also, S.P. 14/185:54. The matter of the fine was incorporated into the petition concerning religion. See above, H. of L., 9 August, p. 160.

24. Sir Thomas Wilford sat for Canterbury. His complaint was against one Foster. See below, 28 June, p. 264 and n. 39.

25. John Roper, Lord Teynham, was included on the recusant list compiled by the Upper House in 1624 as a commissioner of the peace in Kent and was known "by common report" to be a popish recusant. *L.J.,* III, 394.

26. Concerning *certioraries,* see below, 25 June, p. 247.

27. Petitions or articles against recusants had been prepared and/or presented to James I in 1607 (*C.J.,* I, 384–385), 1610 (*Proceedings in Parliament 1610,* II, 118–125, 254–257), 1621 (*C.D. 1621,* IV, 69–75; *C.J.,* I, 655–661, and Rushworth, *Hist. Collections,* I, 40–46), and 1624 (*L.J.,* III, 297–298).

popery among us. To have a petition preferred to the King for sending away these locusts.

Mr. Whitaker. Much nearer hand than York or Lancaster these do swarm. God not the same to us that he has been formerly; goes not out with our armies. The heathen observed this to be cause of it when they had ill success in their affairs, suffering false religions.

[f. 157] Mr. Littleton.[28] To pass some sharp law.

Sir Edwin Sandys. To bend to three particulars. 1, to give the King a true information of the state in point of religion. In the latter end of Queen Elizabeth's reign, 400 priests and 60 Jesuits. Has received late information from some of that side that there are now 1,064 priests and Jesuits. To have the knights and burgesses of every county meet and bring in the number of all the recusants in their countries, that so we may know the whole number of them. 2, the causes of this great increase; to search out those exactly. And then, 3ly, to proceed to the remedies.

Sir Edward Coke. *Non intellecti nulla est curatio morbi.* Diseases kill not men for the most part, but the neglect of cure in due time. So in the politic body, 4 causes of the swarming of these locusts: [1,] suffering of them in the land with impunity; 2, begging of recusants; 3, dependence upon landlords and great men. To appoint a committee to look over the former petitions and answers.

Sir Henry Whitehead.

Mr. Whitson. Will propound a way whereby the King may be righted upon recusants without making any further law against them.

To have the King seize all the lands of recusants into his hands, and to allow them a 3d out of it. They are exceedingly undervalued; a 1,000 *l.* per annum valued at a 100 *l.*

Resolved by the committee to put off the further debate of this business until tomorrow morning, 7 clock.[29]

III. MS. 197, BEDFORD ESTATES, LONDON

[f. 7] 23 *Junii* 1625.

Upon the report from the committee for the bill of the sabbath. The exception was thought material,[30] yet they did not think good to alter the bill for 3 reasons:

First, because it passed both Houses the last parliament in this manner and the King, being then a member of the Upper House, gave his voice to it and therefore is not likely to deny his assent now, unless it receive alteration.[31]

[2.] It is a probationer and may be amended at the next meeting.[32]

3. The justices will be more careful to apprehend the offenders before they go out of the liberties.

An act for explanation of a branch of 3 *Jac.* concerning the discovering and repressing of popish recusants was twice read together. And thereupon was moved by SIR HENRY WHITEHEAD that the clause concerning licenses to travel from the place of their confinement may be so explained that it be sufficiently provided that the state may always know where to find the recusants.[33]

---

28. *Sir W. Strode* is crossed out in the MS. preceding *Mr. Littleton.*

29. Marginal note: "X". See above, n. 9.

30. For the exception, made by Nicholas Duck on 22 June, see above, p. 218.

31. See above, H. of C., 21 June, n. 36.

32. A probationary period was sometimes used in order to test the effects of legislation before it was

made permanent. In this case the act was to continue to the end of the first session of the next parliament (*S.R.,* V, 1).

33. The clause concerning license to travel is included in *S.R., 3 Jac.* I, c. 5, pt. 5. For a draft bill for explanation of the 3 *Jac.* statute, see *C.D. 1621,* VII, 61–65.

Some other small alterations were desired, and the bill committed.

[f. 7v] Sir William Cope's case was reported. The last parliament was prorogued, and he, being a member of the same and after the session ended and the time of privilege expired, was arrested upon an execution and so brought to the Fleet, went abroad by *habeas corpus*, and was chosen again this parliament.

The questions were two: [1.] Whether he ought to have privilege of the last parliament? 2. If not of the last, whether of this? The opinion of the committee was that no privilege at all did belong unto him, but that a warrant of course to issue[34] for a new election. The reason[s] of which are these:

First, the privilege is in respect of the service, but in the time of prorogation there is no service and so no privilege; but he remained still a member, and if that House had met again they might have called for him; but that parliament being dissolved by the King's death the privilege is likewise taken away. The cases vouched were 36 *H.* 8, Trewynard's case;[35] 31 H. 6, the Duke of York's case, wherein the Speaker was taken in execution;[36] 14 H. 4, the King died during the parliament, the knights sued for wages, resolved they should have none.[37]

[2.] A man in execution is not eligible, for though he come out by *habeas corpus* the law intends him to be a prisoner and not able to serve, and therefore, although he should have paid the debt and been discharged before the appearance, yet must there be a new election, for that which was void at first cannot be made good by any post fact.

Right to privilege and eligibility are convertible; whosoever may be chosen ought to have privilege; that law gives no privilege where the creditor is deprived of all further remedy, as in this case, which is not provided for by the act *1° Jac.*[38]

[f. 8] The committees of both Houses met in a conference concerning the petition for a fast. The Lord Archbishop, in the name of that House, approved our good intention and the motives, being only sorry he had not begun. Declared the use and necessity of fasts out of Joel, in which the authority of the King was necessary, and the advice of the priests (not the Levites, but only the sons of Aaron).[39]

The Lords appointed the Lord Steward and the Lord Conway to know the King's pleasure.

It was apprehended by some members of the House, as well by the Archbishop's speech as by other private information, that exception was taken by his Majesty that we should by our own order enjoin a fast for ourselves. To avoid a contestation with his Majesty, and disavowing of our own power, it was moved that the day of our fast should be put off till Sunday sennight, for which was alleged only the expectation we had that the Lords would determine the like fast for themselves, and so both Houses might perform it upon one day with more solemnity.

The order respited till tomorrow after we should hear the King's answer.

34. *but that a warrant must be drawn.* C.D. 1625 (Knightley MS.). Concerning Cope's case, see above, n. 5.

35. Of the three cases cited, Trewynard's is the only one to have been heard in King's Bench; 1 Dyer, *Reports*, ff. 59b–61b, Executors of Skewys against Chamond, Pasch., 36 and 37 *H.* VIII. See also, Hatsell, *Precedents*, I, 59–65. For nonpayment of rent Trewynard (a burgess) was placed in custody during a prorogation of parliament on 12 November 1543. Parliament reconvened 14 January 1544, a writ of privilege was granted 22 February, and Trewynard was released from custody on 20 March.

36. See above, n. 8.

37. See above, n. 7.

38. *S.R.,* 1 *Jac.* I, c. 13, *An act for new executions to be sued against any which shall hereafter be delivered out of execution by privilege of parliament, and for discharge of them out of whose custody such persons shall be delivered.*

39. Joel 2:12–17.

To the bill against assignment of debts.[40]

CHANCELLOR OF THE DUCHY. That we should first seek to prevent the shifts of debtors before we shut up the ways which, by reason of these shifts, were invented for recovery of debts.

[*Afternoon*]

Eodem die at the great committee concerning religion and supply.

[*Committee of the Whole House*]

[f. 8v] The matter of religion and the question for supply stood committed to the whole House, wherein religion was to have the first place.

The Solicitor [being] named to the chair, exception was taken by Mr. Alford because he was sworn to the King and of his fee.

The Chancellor of the Duchy disliked that exception, as tending to division by setting marks of distrust upon the King's servants.

Sir George More. Popham being Solicitor, and Puckering being the King's Serjeant, were chosen Speakers.[41]

The House remaining distracted between him and Sir E. Sandys, it was moved that the Speaker might go to the chair and determine it by question in the House.

Sir Francis Popham. It is against precedent that he that sits in the chair at a committee should be named by the House.[42] Whomsoever we employ, we are too many witnesses to suffer wrong.

So they agreed upon Mr. Solicitor.

[There were divers propositions but nothing concluded, wherefore they shall be entered together with the other proceedings.][43]

IV. PETYT 538/8, INNER TEMPLE LIBRARY

[f. 114v]   *Die Jovis* 24th [*sic*] of June

MR. SERJEANT HITCHAM reported the opinion of the committee touching Sir William Cope for matter of privilege, whose cause was as follows:

The session of parliament ending the 29th day of May, 22 *Jacobi* was, by his Majesty's writs, adjourned to 2*do* of November. 6*to* July[44] next after *Maii*, and before November, he was taken in execution at the suit of the Lady Coppin and by *habeas corpus* removed himself to the Fleet. And King James, dying in March last, a new summons of parliament issued out by King Charles and Sir William, going abroad by *habeas corpus,* is chosen a burgess of parliament for Banbury in Oxfordshire and now sits in the House.

---

40. The bill for restraint of assignment of debts had been read twice and committed earlier this day. In order to keep all of the entries concerning the fast together (see above), the author of the Bedford MS. 197 account may have placed the Chancellor's comment concerning the bill out of proper chronological sequence. It may have occurred at the time of that of John Whistler prior to the commitment of the bill. See the O.B. for this day, above.

41. Sir John Popham, Solicitor General, was elected Speaker of the House of Commons in 1580. Sir John Puckering, Serjeant at Law, was Speaker in 1584–1585 and in 1586–1587; during the latter parliament he was made Queen's Serjeant. *D.N.B.*

42. It appears that customarily the chairman of a committee was selected by that committee and not by

the House itself, although there is little clear evidence on this matter in the records of the early Stuart parliaments. For some debate and a resolution in the House on this matter, 19 April 1621, see *C.D. 1621*, II, 22; IV, 237–238; *C.J.*, I, 582; and Edward Nicholas, *Proceedings and Debates . . . 1620 and 1621* (Oxford, 1766), I, 279. See also, C. S. Sims, "'Policies in Parliaments' An Early Seventeenth-Century Tractate on House of Commons Procedure", *Huntington Library Quarterly*, XV (1951–1952), pp. 52–53.

43. The passage in brackets is in *C.D. 1625* (Knightley MS.) but not in Bedford MS. 197.

44. *Junii.* B.L. Add. 48,091. July is correct; Cope was taken in execution 33 days after the prorogation of 29 May. See above, p. 227. See also, above, H. of C., 21 June, n. 39.

And upon debate it was resolved by the whole committee that he ought not to have a privilege, but to be dismissed.

And thereupon, the Speaker putting it to the question, the House resolved it so, and that a warrant for a new election should be made by the Speaker accordingly unto the mayor and company of Banbury. And in this case it was resolved that if he were in execution and had escaped, for that he was at liberty, and then elected, he should have privilege of parliament. And that if a man be in execution at the time of election [f. 115] he is then uncapable and not eligible. And some conceived that if one were at liberty at the time of summons of parliament and afterwards, and before election he is taken in execution, that he should have the privilege of parliament. But not resolved *ideoque die hoc.*

But resolved that the privilege of parliament is [16] days before the sitting and 16 days after the end of it.[45] But if a man be in prison upon mesne process at the time of election, where he is bailable, for want of bail, whether he should be uncapable as in prison upon an execution was not[46] resolved.

But afterwards, *vide* the next week, in Mr. Arthur Basset of Devonshire his case (who was in prison upon mesne process in the King's Bench, for that he could not find bail the debts were so great, at the suit of his father, and elected a burgess), upon debate

in the House it was resolved that he should have the privilege of parliament and a warrant to be made by the Speaker to the keeper of that prison or his deputy, to bring him to the House who, the next day accordingly, brought him [f. 115v] to the House, and the keeper of the prison discharged of him.[47] And the principal reason was that he was bailable and therefore eligible.

V. MS E237, KENNETH SPENCER RESEARCH LIBRARY

[Thursday, 23 June 1625]

[f. 117] The Lower House having resolved to keep a solemn fast at St. Margaret's Church in Westminster on the 25 of June 1625, they afterwards sent to the Lords that they would join with them in a petition to the King for a general fast throughout the kingdom. To one the 22 of June the Lords, upon conference,[48] consented to join with us and approved of the petition we had drawn without altering any word, and their Lordships sent to the King to know his pleasure when his Majesty would give leave for both the Houses to attend him.

His Majesty appointed they should attend him in the Banqueting Chamber on the 24 day between 9 and 10 in the morning.

---

45. The Draft Journal, above, suggests that this was a resolution of the committee but does not indicate that it was so resolved by the House. See above, n. 6.

46. *not* is omitted in Q.C. 449.

47. The reference here to Basset's case, which was referred to the committee of privileges on 4 July (see below, 4 July, O.B.), indicates that the original version from which Petyt 538/8 was copied was probably not written on a day-to-day basis but was compiled at least a week and a half after the fact. Concerning the legal

points of Basset's case, see below, O.B., 4 and 8 July.

48. The resolution of the Commons for their private fast in St. Margaret's was made 21 June. See H. of C., 21 June, O.B. The conference with the Lords regarding the petition for a general fast was held on this day, 23 June. See above, p. 228, for the names of the Commons' committee appointed. For the accounts of the Chancellor of the Exchequer's report from the conference, see O.B., above.

HOUSE OF COMMONS
ORDER OF BUSINESS   FRIDAY, 24 JUNE 1625

Prayers — 238, 239

[*Committee of the Whole House*]

Former petitions of **religion**: read
[*see below*] — 239

[*End: Committee of the Whole House*]

The committee sent to present the petition for a **general fast** to the King — 238, *21/6

[*The petition for a general fast is printed on pp. 221–222*]

L. 1a. An act against **secret offices** and inquisitions [*see below*] — 238, *23/6; 2/8

L. 1a. An act for the increase of **shipping** and for free liberty of **fishing** — 238, *23/6; 27/6; 30/6; 1/7

L. 1a. An act for the quiet of the subject against pretences of **concealments** — 238, *25/6; 1/7

L. 1a. An act for **subscription** — 238, *27/6

L. 1a. An act for repressing **houses of bawdry** (THOMAS WENTWORTH) — 238

L. 1a. An act concerning the granting of **administrations** (HENRY ROLLE) — 238

SIR EDWARD COKE: concerning the report on the presentation of the petition for a **general fast** [*see above and below*] — 238

L. 2a. An act for the quiet of **ecclesiastical persons** — 238, 241, *23/6

SIR EDWARD COKE — 241

Bill for the quiet of ecclesiastical persons: committed — 238

Bill of the **Lord's day** (sabbath) to be put to the question this afternoon [*see below*] — 238

L. 2a. An act against **secret offices** and inquisitions [*see above*] — 238, 241

THOMAS SHERWILL — 241

SIR EDWARD COKE — 241

Bill against secret offices: committed — 238, 241

Report from the committee on the presentation of the petition for a **general fast** (SIR RICHARD WESTON, Chancellor Exchequer) — 238, 241, 242, 243; **N**, 506

SIR EDWARD COKE: to postpone the **private fast** for the House — 239

SIR FRANCIS ASHLEY — 239

Resolved: to defer the time of the private fast and communion — 239, 241, 243

Resolved: a committee of the whole House to sit this afternoon; no other committee to sit — 239

Committee of **privileges** to meet tomorrow — 239

Ordered: the House rising, whosoever shall depart the House before the Speaker shall pay a fine — 239, 241

[*Afternoon*]

Committee on the bill to confirm an agreement between the King and his tenants of **Macclesfield** to meet tomorrow — 239, *21/6

Committee on the bill for explanation of a **statute of 3 Jac.** for repressing popish recusants to meet tomorrow — 239, *23/6

L. 1a. An act to take away the **benefit of clergy** in some cases — 239, *25/6

L. 1a. An act for more speedy suffering of **common recoveries** — 239

L. 2a. An act for the further

FRIDAY, 24 JUNE 1625

I. DRAFT JOURNAL, MS. 3409, H.L.R.O.

[f. 135v]   *Veneris 24 Junii 1625.*

After prayers the Speaker went out of his chair and the House fell into a committee.[1]

The Speaker took his chair again. And the committees appointed to attend the King about the petition for a general fast sent away; Mr. Chancellor Exchequer to make the report.

L. 1ª. An act against secret offices and inquisitions.[2]

L. 1ª. An act for the increase of navigation, and for liberty of free fishing.

L. 1ª. An act for the future general quiet of the subject against all pretence of concealments.

L. 1ª. An act for subscription.

L. 1ª. An act for repressing of houses of bawdry and common uncleanness.[3]
Preferred by MR. WENTWORTH.

MR. ROLLE prefers a bill concerning administrations.
Read.

L. 1ª. An act concerning the granting of administrations.

[f. 136] SIR EDWARD COKE. The King has commanded his counsel to attend him at 10 of the clock. There[fore] Mr. Chancellor Exchequer desires to be excused from making the report[4] until the afternoon. Could not deliver the petition to my L. of Canterbury, for he sick, but to his gentleman who delivered to my L. President.

L. 2ª. An act for the quiet of ecclesiastical persons.
Committed to

Sir Edward Coke	Sir Francis Barrington
Serjeant Ashley	Sir George More
Sir John Stradling	Mr. John Drake
Mr. [John] Glanville	Sir Nathaniel Rich
Sir Henry Marten	Sir Arthur Mainwaring
Sir Francis Knollys	Sir Francis Glanville
All the lawyers of the	Sir Francis Fulforde
House	Mr. [William] Coryton
Mr. Solicitor	Mr. Francis Drake
Sir William Strode	

Court of Wards, 7 clock, Monday morning.

Bill of the sabbath to be put to the question this afternoon.

L. 2ª. An act against secret offices and inquisitions to be taken on his Majesty's behalf.
Committed to

Mr. Chancellor	Sir William Pitt
Exchequer	Sir George More
Sir Edward Coke	Sir William Strode
Serjeant Ashley	Sir Thomas Fanshawe
All the lawyers of the	Auditor Sawyer
House	All the officers of the
Sir Edwin Sandys[5]	Exchequer and
Sir Miles Fleetwood	Court of Wards
Sir Benjamin Rudyard	Sir Thomas Lucy
Sir John Stradling	Sir Robert
Sir James Fullerton	Cholmondeley
Sir Robert Phelips	Sir Nathaniel Rich

Monday, 2 clock, Court of Wards.

[f. 136v] CHANCELLOR EXCHEQUER reports from the King. L. President delivered the petition with these words: that according to the golden rule of his father, a *Jove principium*, they presented him with a petition for a general fast.

Made this answer: He liked our method

---

1. The committee heard read the former petitions on religion and then adjourned until the afternoon; see below, Committee Book.

2. Concerning action on the bill against secret offices and the bill for shipping and fishing (below) in the 1624 parliament, see above, H. of C., 23 June, n. 13.

3. For a draft of the bill for repressing houses of

bawdry, see below, Appendix, p. 638.

4. I.e., the report on the presentation to the King of the petition for a general fast. See the report, given later in the morning by Chancellor Weston, below.

5. *Chancellor Duchy* is crossed out in the MS. following *Sir Edwin Sandys.*

well in beginning from God. Liked our petition well; would grant it, speedily and effectually. Would consider of the manner of it.

SIR EDWARD COKE. To have now our private fast put off, in regard his Majesty has given way to a public; that so we may all join in it.[6]

SERJEANT ASHLEY. This an act of extraordinary humiliation which requires extraordinary preparation. The warning very short to those that are appointed to preach. Will be more acceptable to join with the Lords. Public fasts always come from warrant from the King. Seeing we may have warrant without question, to defer ours.

Resolved to defer the time of the fast and of the communion for this time, and notice to be given to those that were appointed to preach.[7]

Resolved, a committee of the whole House to sit this afternoon, and the Speaker to sit by. All other committees to cease this afternoon.

Ordered, the committee of privileges to sit tomorrow in the afternoon.

Ordered, that whosoever at the time of rising of the House shall rise before the Speaker and go out of the House shall forfeit 12[d.][8] to the Serjeant.

Veneris 24 Junii, post meridiem.

Tenants of Macclesfield, tomorrow afternoon, Exchequer Chamber.

Recusants the like.

L. 1ª. An act to take away the benefit of clergy in some cases.

L. 1ª. An act for more speedy suffering of common recoveries.

[f. 137] *L. 2ª.* An act to prevent tippling in inns and alehouses.
Committed to

Sir Henry Whitehead	Sir Francis Barrington
Mr. [William] Cage	Sir Francis Knollys
Sir Henry Anderson	Mr. [John] Glanville
Sir Edward Rodney	Mr. [William] Coryton
Sir Walter Erle	Sir Charles Howard
Sir Thomas Hoby	Sir Nathaniel
Sir Henry Mildmay	Barnardiston
Mr. [Thomas]	Sir Francis Glanville
Cornwallis	Sir Edward Peyton

Tomorrow morning, 7 clock, Committee Chamber.

L. 3. An act to punish abuses committed on the Lord's day called Sunday.
Upon question, passed for a law.[9]

MR. COTTON elects to serve for Marlow.

II. COMMITTEE BOOK, MS. 3410, H.L.R.O.

[f. 157v] *Veneris 24 Junii 1625*

[After prayers were ended, the Speaker went out of his chair and the House fell into a committee.][10]

[Committee of the Whole House]

The former petitions about religion, read.[11]

The committee adjourned till the afternoon.

Veneris 24 Junii 1625, post meridiem

Mr. Moore.

---

6. On the changes of dates for the fast and communion, see H. of C., 21 June, p. 204 and nn. 4 and 7.

7. Marginal note: "X". See H. of C., 23 June, n. 9.

8. An illegible mark follows the *12*. The Bedford MS. 197, below, cites 12*d.*

9. The bill passed only the Lower House this day and was not read in the Lords House until 27 June. See above, H. of L., 27 June, O.B.

10. The words in brackets are crossed out in the MS.

11. It is unclear exactly which petitions were read on the morning of 24 June. According to Bedford MS. 197, below, those petitions drawn in 1621 and 1624 (see H. of C., 23 June, n. 27) were read in the afternoon along with the "Prince's protestation" of 1624. Presumably the reference to the Prince's protestation is to Charles's oath upon an article of the 1624 petition. Concerning the oath, see above, H. of L., 9 August, n. 48.

Sir Robert Phelips. Thinks we are not yet fallen upon the true causes of the increase of recusants and their insolency. The unfortunate treaty with Spain a great cause of it.[12]

To have some lawyers of the House to make a supply of the defect of those laws that are in force against them. Then to select a committee to take consideration of the former petitions and their answers, and the sequel of them, and then to draw an humble remonstrance to his Majesty.

Chancellor Duchy. Times and counsels must alter as things alter. The treaties with foreign princes of contrary religion have cast a slumber upon the laws.[13] The King's heart as right towards religion as we would desire it. Affairs of Christendom have enforced him to do as he has; has guided his counsels upon great reason.

Sir Francis Seymour. Priests and Jesuits may now be made in this kingdom. They shall not need to go over to fetch orders.

[f. 158] Sir Edwin Sandys. To have a select committee to take into consideration all former laws and acts of state and petitions, and to proceed by way of article, how to strengthen our own religion and weaken theirs, and present this to the grand committee.

The estate of France not to be compared with ours, though they have 2 religions. The Protestants there have no dependence upon any foreign state; the recusants with us have.[14] They depend upon Rome for the spirituality and upon Spain to be feared for the temporalty.

Sir Edward Coke. We have not yet touched the center point of the decay of religion. Where prophecy ceases, the people perish. A great part of the realm without teaching. To petition the King to have this in some sort remedied. A precedent for this in the midnight of popery: *quinquagesimo* of E. 3, n. 96,[15] the Commons complained of this to the King, this long before Luther. To desire the King that he would call his bishops to him and advise with them.

Mr. Sherfield. To have Mr. Montagu's book considered of, which he thinks to be a very dangerous and seditious book.[16]

[col. 1]	[col. 2]
Sir Edward Coke[17]	Sir Thomas Cheeke
Sir Francis Seymour	Sir John Coke
Sir Edwin Sandys	Sir George More
Sir Robert Phelips	Mr. Recorder
Sir Thomas	Mr. [Christopher]
Wentworth	Brooke
Sir Thomas Hoby	Mr. [Thomas]
Sir Benjamin Rudyard	Wentworth
Sir Francis Barrington	Sir [*sic*] [Henry]
Sir Nathaniel Rich	Sherfield
Sir William Strode	Mr. [John] Glanville
Mr. [John] Pym	Sir Edward Giles
Sir John Eliot	Mr. [Richard]
Sir James Fullerton	Knightley
Sir Henry Wotton	Mr. [William] Coryton

---

12. I.e., the marriage treaty dissolved in 1624. See H. of C., 23 June, n. 22.

13. Concerning the effects of the Spanish and French marriage treaties, see H. of C., 23 June, n. 22.

14. Sandys spoke with authority as the author of a study of European religion, *Europae Speculum, or a view or survey of the state of religion in the western parts of the world* (The Hague, 1629) (*S.T.C.*, no. 21718). The work was compiled in Paris in 1599 and circulated in manuscript before appearing in print in 1629 after Sandys's death. (Sandys had earlier procured an order from the High Commission for burning an unauthorized edition printed in England in 1605 from a stolen manuscript.) *D.N.B.*

15. *Rot. Parl.*, 50 E. III, no. 96; see also, *Rot. Parl.*, 50 E. III, no. 90.

16. Richard Montagu, *Appello Caesarem. A just appeale from two unjust informers* (London, 1625) (*S.T.C.*, no. 18030). This record of Sherfield's motion is added in the margin of the MS.; Sherfield's speech may have been made at a later date. See below, 1 July, p. 287 and n. 48. For further debate on Montagu, see H. of C., 1 July, O.B.

17. The names listed below constitute the subcommittee which, according to Bedford MS. 197, below, met on 25 and 27 June. The names of Marten, Drake, and Ashley (below) are inserted in the margin of the MS.

Sir Walter Erle

Sir Miles Fleetwood

Sir Dudley Digges

Sir Guy Palmes

Mr. Solicitor

Sir Oliver Luke

Mr. Richard Spencer

Sir Henry Whitehead

Mr. Nicholas Hyde

L. Cavendish

Mr. Moore

Sir Rowland St. John

[col. 3]

Sir Henry Marten

Mr. Francis Drake

Serjeant Ashley

[f. 158v] To meet tomorrow morning at 7 of the clock in the Court of Wards. To digest and frame certain articles and heads by petition or otherwise to be presented to his Majesty concerning religion, and to report to the grand committee.

III. MS. 197, BEDFORD ESTATES, LONDON

[f. 8v]   25 [sic]¹⁸ *Junii* 1625.

An act to prevent lapses in the case of qualifications.¹⁹

This bill was very much commended by SIR EDWARD COKE.

An act against secret offices.

MR. SHERWILL. The bill not like to prevent the mischiefs. Here is no new provision which is not in practice already; warning by a privy [f. 9] seal, proclamation, and entry at the county court. Only the bill gives a fee where there was none before, and by these orders the grievance is six times increased.²⁰ The ancient course was to give notice at the land 20 days before. If we enjoin the like by a short bill it will do much more good, and it may be found and certified into the office that such warning was given.

SIR EDWARD COKE. By the course of the Court of Wards after an office found no traverse is allowed but by bill, which is a restraint to the common law and was one of the offenses of Empson and Dudley.²¹

If a better bill be preferred, we may make our choice of both; in the meantime to go on with this.

Committed.

MR. CHANCELLOR OF THE EXCHEQUER reported the King's answer in the Banqueting House at Whitehall to the petition delivered by the committees of both Houses concerning a fast. A short introduction in the delivery thereof was made by my Lord President (for the Archbishop of Canterbury, who was appointed to that service, was sick). That according to the golden rule of his father, a *Jove principium*, his humble subjects the Lords and Commons presented his Majesty with that petition.

The petition was read by my Lord Keeper. The King told us that he liked our method well, to begin with devotion, and hoped we would proceed the better and with more speed after so good a beginning. He approved our petition, both for the matter [f. 9v] and the form, and did fully grant our desires; and for the time and the manner would very speedily advise with the bishops and put it into execution.

After some small debate it was now ordered that both the fast and communion should be put off till Sunday sennight.

The ancient custom of the House was revived by an order that, the House rising, the Speaker should go first out, and every man to keep his place till he were passed, under the penalty of 12*d*.

18. In Bedford MS. 197 the 24 June account appears erroneously in the MS. under the heading for 25 June.

19. This is the bill for the quiet of ecclesiastical persons, preferred by Sir Edward Coke and first read on 23 June. Concerning the content of the bill, see the committee report on 4 August, below, pp. 385–386.

20. *worse increased. C.D. 1625* (Knightley MS.).

21. Sir Richard Empson and Edmund Dudley were tried for treason and beheaded in 1510. See Howell, *S.T.*, I, 283–288.

[Afternoon]

Eodem die post meridiem.

The bill of the sabbath was passed,[22] and the House turned into the great committee.

[Committee of the Whole House]

The petitions in former parliaments 18 and 21, and the Prince's protestation the last parliament, were now read.[23]

Divers matters were propounded and debated and then a subcommittee appointed. That subcommittee sat the 25 of June and then adjourned to the 27th when they appointed Sir Edwin Sandys and Mr. Pym to reduce all that had been propounded to certain heads, distinguishing the matters fit for our petition to his Majesty from other points which could not be redressed but by bill.[24]

IV. PETYT 538/8, INNER TEMPLE LIBRARY

[f. 119v]   *Die Sabbati. 25to Junii [sic]*[25]

A committee was made to draw a petition to present unto his Majesty to have a general fast, and the Lords to join with us in it, which they assented unto.[26]

And the petition being preferred, his Majesty's answer was, that he would consent unto it but he would advise with his bishops for the manner of it, and we should [have] a speedy answer.

And the House proceeded to the nomination of Mr. Shute, Dr. Preston, and Mr. Holdsworth to be their preachers for their fast, and that to be on Saturday next, and the communion on Sunday following, and Mr. Hacket their preacher at St. Margaret's in Westminster, who all had warnings according[ly] and, in respect of Sir [sic] Preston's weakness, it was moved that he might begin, and it was assented unto.[27] The offering that day was 55 *l.*, and the preachers had each of them a ring of 40*s.* apiece given out of it, [f. 120] and the officers and necessary attendants discharged. The rest was given to the infected parishes for the relief of the houses shut up. And we were in

---

22. *quest[ioned].* C.D. 1625 (Knightley MS.).

23. See above, n. 11.

24. In the Bedford MS. 197 and *C.D. 1625* (Knightley MS.) this paragraph is followed by the articles concerning religion which were debated in the subcommittee on 25 and 27 June and then put into writing for the subcommittee by Sandys and Pym on 27 June and the morning of 28 June (see below, p. 260). The articles were reported from the subcommittee and read in the committee of the whole House on 28 June, and we have placed the Bedford MS. 197 text of them with the materials for that day (see below, H. of C., 28 June, n. 23).

Immediately following the entry of the articles concerning religion in Bedford MS. 197 and *C.D. 1625* (Knightley MS.) is a statement that "Divers other things were promiscuously uttered at the committee, not particularly inserted into these articles", which is followed by notes of debate on various issues touched on in the articles. These notes may represent a compilation of debate which occurred over several days' time. A number of the points included in these notes had been discussed in the committee of the whole House on the afternoon of 23 June (see above, pp. 230–232). However, combining evidence from the Committee Book, Bedford MS. 197 (above), and K.S.R.L. MS E237 (below, p. 249), it appears that the longest debate of these matters occurred on 25 June

and so we have placed the notes on that day along with some undated notes on the same subject taken by Sir Nathaniel Rich (see below, H. of C., 25 June, n. 28).

25. We have placed this section of Petyt 538/8 on 24 June, the day that the petition for a fast was presented to the King, rather than 25 June as indicated in the MS. The account covers events from 21 June (see below, n. 26) through 3 July, the day of the communion service for the House. It is apparent that the Petyt entry is a report compiled after the fact rather than an account made at the time of these proceedings in the House (see H. of C., 23 June, n. 47).

26. Marginal note: "Vide the petition before". The text of the petition is included in Petyt 538/8, above, p. 221. The committee had been appointed on 21 June to draw the petition for a general fast. The Lords assented to the petition on 23 June, and it was presented to the King on this day (24 June). Charles responded that he would consult with the bishops concerning the time and manner of the fast. The King's message after his consultation with the bishops was delivered by the Solicitor on 28 June. See H. of C., 28 June, O.B.

27. On the appointment of the preachers for the Commons' private fast and communion, see H. of C., 21 June, nn. 6, 8, and 32. On the scheduling of the fast and communion, see H. of C., 21 June, nn. 4 and 7. On Preston's poor health, see *D.N.B.*

church from half an hour after 8 until half an hour past six; and the Lords had that day two sermons in the Abbey, and the King was at the first.

V. MS E237, KENNETH SPENCER RESEARCH LIBRARY

[Friday, 24 June 1625]

[f. 117] When his Majesty had heard the petition read, he said he liked well both of the method and matter, that we did begin first with God; that he granted our desires and would give order that it should be done speedily and effectually, only desired to take a short time to advise of the best manner to have it done.

Upon his Majesty's gracious answer we deferred our fast and communion till we heard further from the King.

SATURDAY, 25 JUNE 1625

I. DRAFT JOURNAL, MS. 3409, H.L.R.O.

[f. 137] *Sabbati 25 Junii 1625.*

L. 1ᵃ. An act for the passing of sheriffs' accounts.[1]

L. 1. An act against exportation of wool and woolfells.[2]

SIR NICHOLAS SANDERSON, defendant in a *quare impedit,* desires to have a stay of all proceedings.[3]

Ordered, a warrant shall go to the party plaintiff against Sir Nicholas Sanderson, in a *quare impedit,* for stay of all proceedings against himself.

L. 1ᵃ. An act touching benefices appropriate.

L. 1ᵃ. An act for avoiding delay in writs of partition.

L. 1ᵃ. An act against scandalous and unworthy ministers.

MR. SPEAKER moves the House for the reading and entertaining of private bills such as are without any opposition.

Assented to by the House.

[f. 137v] Inns and hostelries to be looked up.[4]

Bill to enable ministers to take leases.[5]

L. 1. An act for ease of freeholders in the county of York.

L. 2. An act concerning petty larceny and the manner of punishing of offenders therein.

SIR JOHN STRADLING. Against the body of the bill. A very dangerous bill. It erects a new court of justice in the justice of peace house. Great offenses will pass under color of this. Better these persons be kept in the jail than run up and down the country and do more mischief.

Committed to

Serjeant Ashley	Sir Nicholas Sanderson
Mr. [John] Glanville	Mr. Nicholas Hyde
Mr. [William] Denny	Sir John Jephson
Mr. [Christopher] Brooke	Sir Charles Morrison
	Mr. [Rowland] Pugh
Sir Francis Glanville	Mr. John Drake
Mr. [John] Whistler[6]	Sir Thomas Middleton
Mr. [William] Cage	Sir Francis Fulforde
Mr. [John] Carvill	Sir John Danvers
Sir Thomas Morgan	Sir Thomas Puckering
Sir Robert Crane	Mr. Francis Courtenay
Sir Clement Throckmorton	Sir Robert Cholmondeley
Sir Samuel Rolle	Mr. [Edward] Alford
Sir Warwick Hele	Sir Edward Peyton
Sir Thomas Grantham	Sir Thomas Lucy
Mr. [John] Delbridge	Mr. Price
Sir John Cowper	Mr. [John] Lowther
Mr. [Richard] Vaughan	
Sir George Rivers	

Monday, 2 clock, Court of Wards.

[f. 138] *L. 2.* An act for the future general quiet of the subjects against all pretences of concealments.

Committed to

Lord Strange	Sir John Hippisley
Master Wards	Sir John Cowper
Sir Francis Cottington	All the lawyers of the
Serjeant Ashley	House
Sir Arthur Ingram	
Sir John Strangways	

---

1. For a draft bill on passing of sheriffs' accounts, see *C.D. 1621,* VII, 170–171 (concerning the 1621 draft bills, see above, H. of C., 23 June, n. 4).

2. For activity on this bill in the 1624 session, see above, H. of C., 23 June, n. 13.

3. I.e., desires privilege of parliament. As a member of parliament Sanderson was immune from legal prosecution during time of parliament except in cases of treason, felony, and breach of peace.

4. A bill concerning the new erecting and ordering of inns passed the Lower House on 3 May 1624 (*C.J.,* I, 782) and was later read twice but rejected by the Upper House (*L.J.,* III, 372, 414, 418).

5. A bill to make ministers capable of leases of lands, etc., received a second reading and was committed by Commons on 22 March 1624 (*C.J.,* I, 746).

6. *All the lawyers of the House except Mr. Rolle* is crossed out in the MS. following *Mr. Whistler.*

Mr. [Walter] Steward
Sir Thomas Cheeke
Mr. [Christopher]
  Brooke
Sir William Pitt

All that will come to have voice. Monday, 2 clock, Star Chamber.

L. 2. An act for ease in pleading of alienations.

SIR PETER OSBORNE. To have the officers of the Exchequer heard at this committee by counsel, and time given for them to instruct their counsel. To have some court in Westminster Hall appointed for the place that so the records may be brought.

Committed to

Sir Francis Cottington
Sir Robert Phelips
Sir Nicholas Sanderson
Sir Francis Fulforde
Sir Warwick Hele
Serjeant Ashley
Sir Thomas Hatton
Sir Arthur Ingram
Mr. Charles Price
Sir George Rivers
Sir Henry Mildmay
Sir John Franklin
Sir Thomas Cheeke
Mr. John Drake
Sir John Strangways
Mr. [Francis] Downes
All the lawyers of the
  House
Mr. [Edward] Alford
Sir Robert Hatton
Mr. Herbert
Sir Edward Peyton
Sir Robert Carr

All to have voice. Tuesday, 2 clock, Exchequer Chamber; and counsel to be heard for the officers of the Exchequer.

[f. 138v] MR. MALLORY delivers in a bill concerning the clerk of the market.[7]

L. 2. An act to take away the benefit of clergy in some cases.

Committed to

Sir John Stradling
Mr. [Thomas]
  Cornwallis
Sir William Strode
Sir Francis Glanville
Sir John Strangways
Sir Henry Whitehead
Mr. John Drake
Sir Thomas Grantham
Mr. [Richard] Taylor
Mr. [John] Glanville
Sir Francis Knollys
Sir Roger North
Sir Nicholas Sanderson
Sir Edward Peyton
Mr. Charles Price
Sir John Cowper
Mr. [Thomas]
  Wentworth
Mr. [Christopher]
  Brooke
Sir Nathaniel Napier
Sir Samuel Rolle
Sir Thomas Fanshawe
Sir Francis Fulforde
Sir Robert Crane

Wednesday, 2 clock, Exchequer Chamber.

II. MS. 197, BEDFORD ESTATES, LONDON

[f. 13v]   [25 June 1625][8]

Concerning the increase of papists and their insolencies.

Sir Thomas Hoby. In Yorkshire they are doubled, if not trebled, since this connivancy. In the North Riding there were 1,200 convicted five years since, now 2,400.[9]

Mr. Moore.[10] In one parish of Lancashire 533 presented, and in four parishes 400 reformed by the 12*d.* a Sunday, and 80 *l.* collected for the poor.

Sir Edwin Sandys. In the end of the Queen's time in all the kingdom but 400 priests and 60 Jesuits; about three years since there were known to be 1,000.[11]

[f. 14] Mr. Moore.[12] In Lancashire 60 of them joined together and beat the sheriff

---

7. Mallory was a member of the committee to which the bill for better ordering of the office of the clerk of the market had been committed on 14 April 1624 (*C.J.,* I, 766). For a letter from Nottingham, a market town, concerning the 1625 bill, see below, Appendix, p. 639.

8. Concerning the placing of the following notes on this day (25 June), see above, H. of C., 24 June, n. 24.

9. The subjects of this speech by Hoby and the following speech by Moore are similar to those covered in a speech made by Hoby at the committee of the whole

House on 23 June. See above, p. 231.

10. Probably Edward Moore, who sat for Liverpool, Lancashire. Concerning the fine of 12*d.*, see above, H. of C., 23 June, n. 23.

11. *1,060. C.D. 1625* (Knightley MS.). These figures were also cited by Sandys in his speech at the committee of the whole on 23 June. See above, p. 232.

12. As the subject matter is again Lancashire this may be Edward Moore speaking a second time, which was permissible in committee though not in the House.

coming to levy the 12*d.* for absence from church. They have built a church yard, carry up and down an altar publicly, have certain places where none but recusants come; one Tarren a priest used to ride up and down with six men, and, when their armor has been taken, letters have been procured to deliver it again.

Touching the favor showed to papists and other causes of this increase by the manifold shifts and devices on their behalf.

Divers pardons procured[13] and warrants for priests taken, whereof one was vouched in Exeter.

Letters sent into Yorkshire not to levy the 12*d.* according to the statute.

Misnaming men in process and commission for execution.

Certioraries to remove the indictments out the country with a *retorne immediate* into the Chancery, whither no man will come up to prosecute because of the charge, and then if they appear they are acquitted for want of evidence.

Sir Thomas Fanshawe. This is a new cause, and under the Great Seal there is no such return in the King's Bench.[14]

Selling their goods and removing their dwellings out of the county into privileged places.

Informers licensed to compound before conviction and other informations by collusions.

[f. 14v] Popish schoolmasters: One in York had 56 scholars, of which there were 36 papists.[15] This schoolmaster was licensed by the official of York, who has the keeping of the seal during his life, without the privity of the Archbishop. The like schoolmaster in Buckinghamshire, another at St. Clether in Cornwall, another in Lancashire.

By printing books of mediation to reconcile us and the papists, such as Mr. Montagu's,[16] where, of 47 questions, he defends but 7 or 8 to be matters in difference between us and the papists. Another book printed of the conversion of the late Bishop of London and dispersed, wherein Sir Edwin Sandys is likewise touched.[17]

Concerning the enlarging of preaching.

That silenced[18] ministers may be allowed to preach in all points agreeable to the doctrine and discipline of the Church of England (this was moved by Sir Nathaniel Rich). The like petition has been almost in every parliament. They refuse not to sub-

---

13. *procured* is omitted in *C.D. 1625* (Knightley MS.). Concerning pardons and leniency in the English recusant laws, see above, H. of C., 23 June, n. 22. Concerning a pardon for Alexander Baker and ten other Catholics imprisoned at Exeter, the warrant for which was not sealed until 12 July 1625, see below, H. of C., 1 August, n. 3.

14. Fanshawe, Clerk of the Crown in King's Bench, had spoken concerning *certioraries* in the committee of the whole on 23 June. See above, p. 231.

15. Concerning one Conyers, a popish schoolmaster in York, see above, H. of L., 9 August, n. 16, and below, H. of C., 4 July, n. 28.

16. I.e., *A Gagg for the New Gospell? No: A New Gagg for an Old Goose* (London, 1624) (*S.T.C.*, no. 18038). See the report from the Archbishop of Canterbury regarding Montagu, below, H. of C., 1 July, O.B. Many of the articles in the *Gagg* were subsequently debated in the 1628 parliament. See *C.D. 1628*, III, 112–113; IV, 238–240.

17. John King, Bishop of London, 1611–1621, was rumored to have converted to Roman Catholicism on his deathbed. *D.N.B.* His conversion was alleged in a pamphlet printed in 1621, entitled, *English Protestants Plea and Petition for English Priests and Papists* (*S.T.C.*, no. 10415), p. 19. George Musket included the story in his book entitled, *The Bishop of London his Legacy* (1623) (*S.T.C.*, no. 18305). There (p. 124) Musket referred to Sandys as "a great Master in Israel" and quoted from the 1605 edition of Sandys's *A Relation of the State of Religion*, which had been printed without Sandys's approval (see above, H. of C., 24 June, n. 14).

18. MS.: *silent*. A marginal note on Rich's motion, in the Earl of Bedford's hand, reads: "No".

scribe to the Articles according to the statute, but another subscription is required by canon;[19] and no canon can compel any man under a penalty to lose his freehold.

Sir B. Rudyard thought good to leave out this article, because moderate bishops would do it of themselves.

Mr. Solicitor. To mitigate it. That we desire the King to propound it by way of advice to the bishops, not by way of injunction.

For the lessening of nonresidencies and pluralities, there are three sorts of petitions: [1,] of grace; 2, of right; 3, of provision. Of this nature the [f. 15] Commons delivered a petition 50 E. 3[20] that the people might not be those means be deprived of their spiritual food; since that, in 17 R. 2; 2[d], 4[to], 6[to], 11° H. 4; 10 H. 6; 1, 4[to], 6[to], 7 H. 8.[21] Then Cardinal Wolsey disgraced parliaments to the King, so there was but one between this and 21[22] in which, and all the former recited time [since][23] 50 E. 3, there have been perpetual complaints against nonresidency.

For the admittance of none but sufficient persons; *idonea* persons not to be tried by jury but by the metropolitan. If the patron be lay, he must have notice if he be insufficient, but not if he be spiritual. This idoneity in respect of learning is interpreted to extend only to be able to give account of his faith in Latin; yet if the clerk die before trial, then it shall be inquired by jury, because he cannot answer. It does likewise extend to manors. If the exception be *malum prohibitum,* and not *malum per se,* no cause of refusal, as a haunter of taverns in a case of my Lord Dyer;[24] *scismaticus inveteratus* no cause unless the heresy be assigned in special.

The increase of maintenance. Before 31 H. 8[25] ordinaries might have increased the maintenance by charging the impropriations; it is otherwise now. The whole charge not to be put upon the impropriations, because they are all confirmed by law; nor to meddle with *modus decimandi.* There are freed grounds anciently belonging to the four great orders of friars,[26] which by exemption were to pay no tithes *dum in manibus suis excoluntur.* These were now desired to be made in some measure chargeable with this increase; the rest to be raised

19. *S.R.,* 13 *Eliz.* I, c. 12, required that ministers subscribe to the thirty-nine Articles of Religion agreed upon by the Convocation of 1562. Canon 36 of the *Constitutions and Canons Ecclesiastical* of 1 *Jac.* contained three articles which were to be subscribed to in a specific manner by all ministers (see *Sermons, or Homilies, appointed to be read in Churches in the time of Queen Elizabeth . . . to which are added, the Articles of Religion; the Constitutions and Canons Ecclesiastical* [London, 1817], pp. 603–604).

20. Cf. *Rot. Parl.,* 50 *E.* III, nos. 90 and 96–97.

21. For petitions from parliament concerning residency of the clergy, see: *Rot. Parl.,* 7 *R.* II, no. 54; *Rot. Parl.,* 17 *R.* II, no. 43; *Rot. Parl.,* 2 *H.* IV, no. 50; *Rot. Parl.,* 4 *H.* IV, no. 58; *Rot. Parl.,* 7 & 8 *H.* IV, no. 114; *Rot. Parl.,* 11 *H.* IV, no. 70; *Rot. Parl.,* 3 *H.* VI, no. 38; *Rot. Parl.,* 4 *H.* VI, no. 31; *Rot. Parl.,* 10 *H.* VI, no. 40. We have found no petition or statute from the early parliaments of Henry VIII concerning nonresidency.

22. I.e., between 7 *H.* VIII (1515) and 21 *H.* VIII (1530). From the time that Thomas Wolsey was made Lord Chancellor in 1515 until his fall from power in

1529 parliament was summoned only once, in 1523. Despite personal appeals from Wolsey for money to support the crown's foreign policy, the 1523 parliament refused to grant the full amount requested. See Edward Hall, *Chronicle* (London, 1809), pp. 652–657. The next parliament, which met in 1530, passed a bill which provided for a fine to be levied on spiritual persons who did not reside in their benefices. *S.R.,* 21 *H.* VIII, c. 13.

23. The bracketed word is supplied from *C.D. 1625* (Knightley MS.). For complaints against nonresidency, see above, nn. 20–22.

24. 3 Dyer, *Reports,* Bell against the Bishop of Norwich, 8 & 9 *Eliz.* I, Mich., *pl.* 2.

25. *S.R.,* 31 *H.* VIII, c. 13. Marginal note in the Earl of Bedford's hand: "No".

26. Friars minors (Grey friars or Franciscans), Friars preachers (Black friars or Dominicans), Augustins, and Carmelites (White friars). Jacobs, *Law Dict.* Concerning the friars' exemption from payment of tithes, see *S.R.,* 31 *H.* VIII, c. 13, pt. 17.

upon the parish, so as every living might be worth 50 *l.* per annum at the least.

III. MS E237, KENNETH SPENCER RESEARCH LIBRARY

[Saturday, 25 June 1625]

[f. 117] The 25 was spent how to frame a petition to his Majesty to have the laws executed against the priests and papists.[27]

IV. NOTES TAKEN BY SIR NATHANIEL RICH. H.L.R.O., HISTORICAL COLLECTION 204

Notes concerning the petition against recusants.[28]

1. Safety of the state consists in the safety of religion.
2. That this religion is the ground of sedition.
3. Now the fittest time because preparation abroad, we shall be engaged abroad and therefore dangerous to have a party at home to take part with them.[29]

Sir N. R[ich]. 1. The petition to be first for the execution of the laws in general.
2. That the laws may not be silenced or dispensed with by mediation of foreign princes or treaty of marriage.[30]
3. That commissioners may be appointed to see to the execution of the laws.
4. That the Lords may take an oath this parliament to observe the laws.

Sir T. Ho[by]. 5. That all known papists may be in the state of convict recusants to such as have their wives recusants and their eldest sons recusants.

Mr. Whitaker. The 2 politic ends: 1, to secure ourselves from domestic treachery as from foreign invasion; 2ly, to give content to the country who will be satisfied in 2 things: 1, that they may not be discouraged as heretofore by being bearded while others go in greater frequency to mass than they to church; 2ly, that the people may be eased from bearing of public charge. It costs every good subject a subsidy every year by collection in churches, also paying of all the parish charges; the papists have called them rogues, dogs, heretics, and that they hope to have a day.

Mr. Knightley. The fruit of the sleeping of the laws is nothing but spreading of ruse and sowing of faction.
A game of all example for the good has been disheartened and the bad discouraged.

The silencing of the laws have proceeded from relation to the treaty.
Reason: the dependen/

Sir E. Sandys. 1,064 priests in England now, whereas but 400 priests and 60 Jesuits in Q[ueen] Elizabeth's time.[31]

---

27. For debate on the petition concerning religion and the recusancy laws, see the notes in Bedford MS. 197, above, and those of Sir Nathaniel Rich, below.
28. Sir Nathaniel Rich's notes are undated. We have placed them on 25 June 1625 because they deal with the framing of the petition concerning religion and, according to K.S.R.L. MS E237, much of this day was taken up with that debate. A petition had not been decided on as the means to carry these grievances to the King until 24 June and by 28 June the points noted by Rich were formulated into articles on which to frame the petition. Therefore, it seems likely that because Rich's notes relate specifically to points to be included in a petition they constitute a record of debate that occurred sometime between the 24th and the 28th. The House did not meet on the 26th (Sunday). The subcommittee appointed on 24 June to frame the

heads of the petition met on the 25th and the 27th (see above, p. 242). Of the speakers recorded by Rich, Sir Thomas Hoby, Mr. Whitaker, and Sir Edwin Sandys had all made speeches on this subject in the debate in the committee of the whole House on 23 June (see above, pp. 231–232). Concerning the placing of the Rich notes on 25 June, see also, above, H. of C., 24 June, n. 24.

Rich's undated notes are written in his own unique combination of longhand and shorthand on both sides of a 12″ by 8″ sheet of paper and are endorsed in Rich's hand as "Notes concerning the petition against recusants".

29. *Reason of profit to the King* is crossed out in the MS. following *them.*
30. See above, H. of C., 23 June, n. 22.
31. See above, n. 11.

1. The sending of the Jesuits and priests and commanding of the subjects not to receive them, and if they depart not by such a time then the law to be executed against them, i.e., that they die as traitors. These men are called locusts; let there be an [2 signs illegible] to [illegible sign] themselves.

The priests and regulars write one against another hotly contending who deserve most for their good service in converting the people in England.

2 laws in particular to be executed: the statute of 5° Eliz. [and] 35° Eliz.[32] 5° Eliz., 1°, against those that by printing, etc. This statute is appointed to be read in all sessions. 35° [Eliz.] against such as shall persuade or

(to that end or purpose) these words to be left out for this tends to faction.

2ly. To disarm all popish recusants convict (and all known papists).

3. To confine them.

4. Against those that hear mass, the laws/[33]

The recusants' lands came the last year but to 400 l. Moved the profit may be to the war, but not liked, but that it may go to the payment of the King's debts.

That commissioners should be appointed to see to the execution of these laws. But to this the objection: we close the King's hand from mercy.

---

32. *S.R., 5 Eliz.* I, c. 1; *S.R., 35 Eliz.* I, c. 2.
33. *Moved that the ambassadors be restrained* is crossed

out in the MS. following *laws.*

MONDAY, 27 JUNE 1625

I. DRAFT JOURNAL, MS. 3409, H.L.R.O.

[f. 138v]   *Lunae 27 Junii 1625.*

L. 1ª. Erith and Plumstead.[1]

L. 1. An act for the free and quiet elections of knights and burgesses.

SIR GEORGE MORE.[2]

Ordered that the committee of privileges shall hear and determine those petitions that were presented in the House on the first day in order as they came in; for the rest, left to their discretion to do as they shall think fit.[3]

MR. LOWTHER reports the bill for the tenants of Macclesfield.[4]

The amendments 2 read. Ordered to be engrossed.

[f. 139] *L. 1ª.* An act to prevent the granting of writs of *habeas corpus.*

L. 2. An act against exportation of wool and woolfells.

Committed to

Sir Edward Coke	Burgesses[5] of clothing
Attorney Ward[s]	towns and shires
Sir Arthur Ingram	Mr. [John] Glanville
Mr. [Edward] Alford	Sir Nicholas Sanderson
Sir Robert Crane	Sir John Brooke
Mr. Recorder	Sir Thomas
Serjeant Ashley	Barrington
Mr. John Drake	Sir Clipsby Crew
Sir John Oglander	Sir Maurice Berkeley

Mr. John Crew	Mr. [Thomas]
Sir Thomas Jermyn	Cornwallis
Mr. [Christopher]	Sir William Pitt
Wandesford	Burgesses of port
Sir John Stradling	towns
Sir Robert Brooke	Sir George Dalston
Sir Francis Popham	

All that will come to have voice. Tomorrow, 2 clock, Court of Wards.

Sir Edward Coke sent up to the Lords with the bill of the sabbath alone for honor sake.[6]

L. 1ª. An act for the better execution of the office of the clerks of the market.

SIR MILES FLEETWOOD reports the bill of recusants.[7]

The amendments 2 read. Ordered to be engrossed with speed.

L. 2. An act for the freer liberty of fishing and fishing voyages.

[f. 139v] MR. SNELLING. To have the bill made more general, for free fishing in all parts.

Committed to

Sir Edward Coke	Knights of maritime
Mr. Recorder	shires
Serjeant Ashley	Burgesses of port
Sir Walter Erle	towns
Mr. [*Illegible*]	Sir William Strode
Sir Guy Palmes	Mr. John Drake
Sir Francis Glanville	Sir John Stradling
Sir Warwick Hele	Mr. [John] Glanville

---

1. Cf. the bill which was read in the 1626 parliament as "An act for the settling and dividing of certain marshlands lately surrounded and now recovered and inned from the inundation of the river of Thames lying in the parishes of Erith and Plumstead, etc.". *C.J.,* I, 820.

2. Sir George More, as chairman of the committee of privileges, may have asked for directions concerning the order in which the committee should consider petitions, or he may have planned to report on the first petition referred to it, on Yorkshire. For some reason that report seems to have been delayed. Petyt 528/8 (and B.L. Add. 48,091 and Q.C. 449) includes the report for Yorkshire on this day, but following the chronology of the C.J. we have moved the Petyt entry (ff. 120–121) to 4 July, when More made the Yorkshire report.

3. Marginal note: "X". See above, H. of C., 23 June, n. 9.

4. Marginal note: "X".

5. *Knights and* is crossed out in the MS. preceding *Burgesses.*

6. *Sir Nicholas Sanderson* is crossed out in the MS. after the entry regarding the bill for the sabbath and before the reading of the bill concerning the clerk of the market.

7. I.e., An act for explanation of a statute of 3 *Jac.* for repressing popish recusants.

Sir Robert Crane   Sir Thomas Morgan
Sir John Rowse   Sir Dudley Digges
Sir Thomas Cheeke   Sir John Strangways
                 Sir Edward Giles

Wednesday, 2 clock, Exchequer Court.[8]

L. 2. An act to restrain the granting of writs of *habeas corpus.*

Committed to

Sir Edward Coke	Sir Guy Palmes
Attorney Wards	Mr. [William] Cage
Mr. Recorder	Mr. [John] Carvill
Serjeant Ashley	Sir Edward Wardour
Serjeant Towse	All the lawyers of the
Mr. [Christopher]	House
Brooke	Sir Nicholas Sanderson
Mr. [John] Glanville	Sir Baptist Hicks
Mr. Solicitor	Sir John Stradling
Sir Anthony Forest	Sir Thomas Jermyn
	Mr. Charles Price

Tomorrow, 7 clock, Court of Wards.

L. 2. An act/[9]

[f. 140] Committed to

Sir Edward Coke	All the lawyers of the
Attorney Wards	House
Mr. Recorder	
Mr. [Edward] Alford	
Mr. [Henry] Rolle	
Sir Warwick Hele	
Serjeant Ashley	
Serjeant Towse	

Wednesday, 7 clock, Court of Wards.

L. 2. An act for mitigation of the sentence of the greater excommunication of and preservation of the ecclesiastical jurisdiction.

MR. LANGSTON. To have 2 other things inserted in this bill: 1, the process of, *coram nomine;*[10] 2, to have a man know his accuser.

Committed to

Sir Edward Coke	Sir Thomas Hoby
Sir Henry Marten	Sir Anthony Drury
Sir Anthony Forest	Sir George More

Mr. [Anthony]   All the civil lawyers of
   Langston   the House

Sir Alexander St. John	Sir Francis Barrington
Lord Strange	Sir Thomas
Sir Guy Palmes	Wentworth
Sir Walter Erle	Sir Francis Glanville
Mr. [Walter] Steward	Sir Nicholas Sanderson
Sir George Goring	Sir Oliver Luke
Lord St. John	Mr. Francis Drake
Sir Henry Mildmay	Sir Dudley Digges
Mr. Richard Spencer	Sir Robert Hatton
Mr. Edward Spencer	Sir Nathaniel Rich
Sir Edwin Sandys	Mr. [Christopher]
Mr. [Robert] Snelling	Brooke
Mr. [Ignatius] Jordan	Sir Thomas Jermyn

Wednesday, 8 clock, Court of Wards.

L. 2. An act for subscription.

[f. 140v] Committed to

Sir Edward Coke	Sir Henry Mildmay
Mr. Recorder	Sir Nathaniel Rich
Mr. Solicitor	Sir Francis Seymour
Sir Edwin Sandys	Sir Thomas Hoby
Mr. [Robert] Snelling	Mr. [Christopher]
Serjeant Ashley	Wandesford
Sir Benjamin Rudyard	Sir Robert Hatton
Sir Miles Fleetwood	Mr. [Christopher]
Sir Thomas Cheeke	Sherland
Sir Ferdinando Fairfax	Sir John Stradling
Sir Francis Glanville	Sir Thomas
Mr. [Thomas] Bowyer	Wentworth
Sir Dudley Digges	Sir Francis Barrington
Sir Francis Goodwin	Sir Maurice Berkeley
Sir Henry Marten	Sir Richard Newport
Mr. [John] Pym	Sir Clement
Mr. [William] Cage	Throckmorton
Mr. Francis Drake	Sir Gerrard Fleetwood
Sir Nathaniel	All the civil lawyers of
Barnardiston	the House
Sir Thomas Jermyn	Mr. [Edward] Alford
Sir Robert	
Cholmondeley	
Mr. Clarke	
Sir Thomas Barrington	
Sir Robert More	
Sir Rowland St. John	

---

8. *Court of Wards* is crossed out in the MS. preceding *Exchequer Court.*

9. Marginal note: "Partition"; this was the second reading of An act for avoiding delay in writs of partition.

10. Langston is referring to the judicial process and jurisdiction of excommunication. *Coram nomine* is part of the writ removing the case into King's Bench. See *S.R., 5 Eliz.* I, c. 23.

Sir Guy Palmes
Sir Thomas Lucy
Sir William Strode
Sir Edward Peyton
Mr. [John] St. Amand
   Wednesday, 2 clock, Court of Wards.

L. 1a. An act for restraint of the
transportation of **iron
ordnance** (SIR EDWARD
PEYTON)   257
SIR JOHN ELIOT: delivers in the
petition of Arthur **Basset**,
M.P.   257
Petition of Arthur Basset: read
and referred to the
committee of privileges   257, *4/7; 8/7;
                                   9/7
L. 1a. An act for the breeding and
bringing up of **recusants'
children** (SIR JOHN STRODE)   257
EDWARD ALFORD: moves for a
**committee of the whole
House** to meet tomorrow   257
L. 2a. An act for **Erith and
Plumstead**: committed   257, *27/6
L. 1a. An act concerning the
privileges of the Commons
House of parliament (HENRY
BELASYSE)   257
L. 3a. An act for explanation of a
statute of 3 *Jac.* for
repressing popish recusants:
passed [*see below*]   257, *23/6
L. 3a. An act to confirm an
agreement between the King
and his tenants of
Macclesfield: passed   257, *21/6
Sir Edward Coke sent up to Lords
with: 257
  (1) bill for the explanation of a
  statute of 3 *Jac.* [*see above*]
  (2) bill to confirm an agreement
  between the King and his
  tenants of **Macclesfield** [*see
  above*]
L. 1a. An act for abbreviation and
limitation of **Michaelmas term**   257, *23/6
Message from the King regarding
the petition for the **general
fast**, leaving matter of the

private fast to parliament
(SIR ROBERT HEATH,
Solicitor)   257, 260, 266,
                                   *21/6
Message to the Lords concerning
King's response to the
petition for the general fast
and desiring a **conference**
(Sir Edward Coke) [*see below*]   258
L. 1a. An act against the
procuring of **judicial places**
for money   258, *29/6; 1/7;
                                   4/8
Report of the Lords' response to
the message: Lords will
return answer by messengers
of their own (SIR EDWARD
COKE) [*see above and below*]   258
SIR ROBERT MANSELL: concerning
the **Council of War's account**   258, *30/6
[*Committee of the Whole House*]
Report from the subcommittee
for framing heads for a
petition concerning religion
(Sir Edwin Sandys)   260, *24/6
Articles concerning religion
conceived by the
subcommittee as heads for
the petition: read   260(2)
[*The articles are printed on pp.
261–264*]
Upon question: the articles to be
debated at a committee of the
whole this afternoon   260
[*End: Committee of the Whole
House*]
Report from the committee of the
whole House concerning the
articles (SIR ROBERT HEATH,
Solicitor)   258
Ordered: a committee of the
whole House to meet this
afternoon to debate the
articles [*see below*]   258

TUESDAY, 28 JUNE 1625

I. DRAFT JOURNAL, MS. 3409, H.L.R.O.

[f. 141]   *Martis 28 Junii 1625.*

SIR EDWARD PEYTON delivers in the bill against the transportation of iron ordnance.

L. 1. An act for restraint of the transportation of iron ordnance.

SIR JOHN ELIOT. A gentleman of this House of good worth arrested at the suit of his father. Delivers in a petition from him, Mr. Arthur Basset.[1]

The petition read, and referred to the committee of privileges to be heard with all convenient speed.[2]

SIR JOHN STRODE delivers in a bill for the educating of the children of popish recusants.

L. 1ᵃ. An act for the breeding and bringing up of recusants' children.

MR. ALFORD. To have a committee of the whole House sit tomorrow in the afternoon to take into consideration these 3 things: [1,] to have a view of the grievances last parliament; 2, to have an account of the subsidies given last parliament; 3, to consider of the bill of tonnage and poundage.

L. 2. Erith and Plumstead.
Committed to

Sir Edward Coke	Sir Francis Fulforde
Sir Thomas Fanshawe	Knights, burgesses of
Sir [*sic*] Charles	Kent and Essex
Glemham	Barons of the ports
Sir Thomas Hoby	Sir Robert Brooke
Sir John Danvers	Lord Burghersh
Sir Edmund Verney	Sir Thomas Cheeke

Sir Charles Montagu	Mr. Clarke
Mr. [Henry] Sherfield	Sir Oliver Luke
Mr. [Nicholas] Duck	Sir Oliver Cromwell
Mr. [Edward] Bysshe	Sir Francis Popham
	Sir Edward Peyton

[f. 141v]
Mr. [John] Middleton
Sir John Cutts
Sir Thomas Morgan

Thursday, 2 clock, Court of Wards.

MR. BELASYSE delivers in a bill to preserve the liberties of the Commons House of parliament.

L. 1. An act concerning the privileges of the Commons House of parliament.

L. 3. An act for explanation/[3]
Upon question, passed for a law.

L. 3. An act for the enabling and confirmation of an agreement or composition made between the King's Majesty's commissioners of revenue and his Majesty's copyholders of the manor of Macclesfield.
Upon question, passed.

Sir Edward Coke sent up to the Lords with these 2 bills.

L. 1ᵃ. An act for abbreviation and limitation of Michaelmas term.[4]

MR. SOLICITOR. A message from the King. This morning he attended his Majesty. Bade him signify to the House that he had taken our last petition into consideration; advised with his bishops. Willing that we and the Lords take our own time as soon as we will, and our own way; for the public fast to begin on Thursday 7-night.[5] Resolved to have solemn public prayers every Wednesday throughout the kingdom.

---

1. Arthur Basset (M.P. for Fowey, Cornwall), in prison on charges of debt pressed by his father, Sir Robert Basset, was petitioning for release on grounds of parliamentary privilege. For the report on this case, see H. of C., 8 July, O.B. We have been unable to find Basset's petition.

2. Marginal note: "X". See above, H. of C., 23 June, n. 9.

3. I.e., An act for explanation of a statute of 3 *Jac.* for repressing popish recusants.

4. See above, H. of C., 23 June, n. 13.

5. I.e., 7 July. The date was later changed to 16 July; see below, n. 14. Concerning the resolution to have public prayers every Wednesday, see above, H. of L., 28 June, n. 12.

Besides, he takes knowledge of our care concerning religion, well our zeal. Only desire is to take consideration of the present state of Christendom and our own [*illegible*]; that were it not for urgent occasions he would not hold us together at this time. To dispatch this as soon as may be.

[f. 142] Sir Edward Coke sent up to the Lords to let them understand that we have received a gracious answer this morning from his Majesty about our petition. That he is pleased to leave the time and way of our own fast to ourselves. To desire a conference with their Lordships about it.

L. 1ª. An act against the procuring of judicial places for money.

Sir Edward Coke reports from the Lords. The Lords now in hand with earnest business; with convenient speed they will send an answer by their own messengers.[6]

Sir Robert Mansell. The Council of War have appointed to meet this afternoon to perfect their account. Shall be ready to bring it in on Thursday.

Mr. Speaker went out of his chair, and the House fell to a committee.[7]

Mr. Speaker took his chair again.

And Mr. Solicitor reports from the grand committee. The articles have been read at the committee and have adjourned the debate of them until the afternoon.

Ordered, a committee of the whole House to sit this afternoon at 2 of the clock to debate these articles; the Speaker to be here and sit by.

All committees appointed this day to hold tomorrow in the afternoon.

A message from the Lords by Mr. Attorney and Serjeant Davenport: [f. 142v] The Lords signify to us that they have [*illegible*] the King's pleasure touching the fast much to that effect they received from us. They are very willing to have the committee appointed to attend his Majesty to meet their committee presently in the Painted Chamber, if it may stand with the leisure of this House.

Answer: This House has taken into consideration the message. The committees of this House shall give a present meeting to the Lords as is desired.

The committees sent up to the Lords;[8] Sir Edward Coke to make the report.

L. 1ª. An act for accounting upon oath for monies received to general and public uses.

Bill of tippling in alehouses, presently, in the Committee Chamber, and all to have voice.

L. 1ª. Bill of simony.[9]

Sir Edward Coke reports from the Lords: Their House sits this afternoon; desire us to do the like.

Martis 28 Junii, post meridiem.

Mr. Solicitor reports from the grand committee the articles allowed by them.[10]

---

6. The Lords chose not to reply to the Commons until they themselves had heard directly from the crown. See above, H. of L., 28 June, n. 10.

7. The committee of the whole House on religion was convened this morning for hearing read the articles for the petition concerning religion drafted by the subcommittee which had been appointed on 24 June. See Committee Book, below. The reading of the articles in the morning provided opportunity for thought about them preceding debate in the afternoon meeting of the committee of the whole.

8. I.e., the committee that the Commons originally appointed on 23 June to confer with the Lords' committee on the petition for the general fast and then to attend the Lords in presenting the petition to the King (see above, H. of C., 23 June, O.B.).

9. Concerning activity on the bill against simony in the 1624 session, see above, H. of C., 23 June, n. 9. Concerning the second reading of this bill in the 1625 parliament, see below, H. of C., 6 July, n. 5.

10. The Solicitor reported the articles concerning religion, but debate on them was interrupted by the

[f. 143] A message from the Lords by Serjeant Finch and Serjeant Richardson:

The Lords in this pious business of the fast are ready to perfect the conference, in the same place and with the same persons, and presently if it please this House.

Answer: The committees of this House shall presently give meeting as is desired.

The committee sent up to the Lords;[11] Sir Edward Coke to make report.

SIR EDWARD COKE reports from the Lords. L. Treasurer said that the Lords had considered of our proposition and that resolved.[12] For time, they resolved to have it precede the general, at 9 clock Saturday next; the place, as near us as might be at the collegiate church at Westminster; for the persons they would have 2 bishops,[13] left our persons to ourselves. Had appointed an earl, bishop, and baron to observe who do perform that duty.

The King prescribed the manner of it. That form to be unanimously observed by both Houses. This shortly to come out in print. Intimated the time of the general fast to be short. Thought his Majesty would defer that till Saturday fortnight if we did like it. Thought fit that the City of London should begin this fast before it went down into the country, because the sickness there

first began.[14] Moved at last to have some collection made for the poor by our company, as they intended by theirs.

Resolved, our fast to hold on Saturday next at 9 of the clock in St. Margaret's Church in Westminster. To be performed by the same men that were formerly named,[15] and in the same manner that shall be prescribed by the King.

[f. 143v] Resolved likewise that the communion shall hold on Sunday next in the same place and the same man that was first appointed to preach.[16]

Care to be taken that none shall be admitted to the fast or communion but the members of the House.[17]

Every man to bring his name and place for which he serves and to deliver it to those gentlemen who are deputed to that purpose by the House to receive them and these men to gather the collection.

SIR HENRY MARTEN labors to reconcile the difference about one article to be presented to his Majesty concerning silenced ministers.[18] Sets it down in writing.

Approved by the House.

SIR FRANCIS NETHERSOLE. To have that particular instance of Doctor Anyan struck out. A petition against him in these griev-

---

message from the Lords, the subsequent conference, and the resolutions passed concerning the private fast for parliament. After the interruption the House returned to the debate of the questionable articles, eventually voted on them, and appointed a committee to draw up a petition concerning religion based on the articles. See below.

11. See above, n. 8.

12. I.e., of a fast and communion for parliament members.

13. I.e., the Bishops of Bath and Wells and Salisbury; see above, H. of L., 28 June, p. 67. For the preachers appointed by Commons, see above, H. of C., 21 and 22 June, O.B.s.

14. The Lords suggested that the fast for the city of London be held on 2 July, that for the city of Westminster to be 4 July, and that for the whole kingdom to be 16 July (see H. of L., 28 June, p. 68 and n. 15). Concerning the book, printed by the King's authority, pre-

scribing the manner of the prayers and fasting, see H. of L., 28 June, n. 12.

15. Marginal note: "Dr. Preston to begin". For the preachers, see above, H. of C., 21 June, nn. 8 and 32. There is an X beside this entry in the MS.

16. Marginal note: "X". John Hacket was appointed to preach at the communion. See above, H. of C., 21 June, n. 6.

17. Marginal note: "X". The same marginal note also appears in the MS. next to the following entry regarding delivery of names and gathering the collection at the fast.

18. The business of the fast and communion being resolved, the House returned to the business of those articles of religion to which exceptions were taken. See above, n. 10. Marten refers to article 3 in the section concerning the remedies of the "dangerous disease . . . in strengthening our own religion" (see below, p. 262).

ances were presented the last parliament; to which we expect our answer now.[19]

Resolved upon question, that article to stand.

All the articles allowed by the House upon question.

Sir Edward Coke   Mr. [John] Pym
Sir Edwin Sandys
Mr. Solicitor
Sir Francis Seymour
Sir Nathaniel Rich

These 6 appointed by the House to draw this petition. To meet tomorrow morning, 7 clock, Court of Wards.

II. COMMITTEE BOOK, MS. 3410, H.L.R.O.

[f. 158v]   *Martis 28 Junii 1625*

Sir Edwin Sandys reports to the grand committee from the subcommittee. They have met divers times about it. They have reduced into articles the heads that they think fit to be presented. Into 3 main heads: 1, the increase; 2, the causes; 3, the remedies. Divided into branches, to strengthen our and weaken ours [*sic*].

The articles read.[20]

Upon question, these articles to be debated at a committee of the whole House this afternoon.

Martis 28 Junii, post meridiem.

The articles read severally.

Sir Francis Seymour. To put the King in mind of his gracious promise made the last parliament when he was prince.[21]

This, upon question, added to the 2d article, and the articles upon question allowed to be reported to the House.

III. MS. 197, BEDFORD ESTATES, LONDON

[f. 15v]   28 *Junii* 1625.

About ten a clock that day, Sir Edwin Sandys and Mr. P[ym] who had been absent all the morning and the most part of the day before in framing the articles, brought them ready, whereupon the subcommittee was presently appointed to sit in the Court of Wards, to whom they were delivered; and the great committee was appointed to sit in the afternoon to receive the report of the subcommittee,[22] that so they might be examined and debated.

MR. SOLICITOR, in a message from the King, declared that his Majesty had, according to our petition, given direction for a public fast, wherein he had appointed one day weekly throughout the kingdom to be observed, but for the Houses of parliament he left it to themselves, when they would begin, and to make choice of their own day.

[Committee of the Whole House]

[f. 9v][23] Articles concerning religion conceived by the subcommittee as fit heads whereon to frame a petition to be presented

---

19. Nethersole is referring to article 2 concerning remedies by strengthening religion (see below, p. 262). Dr. Anyan, president of Corpus Christi College, Oxford, had been petitioned against in the Commons on 28 April 1624 on four counts of misconduct (*C.J.*, I, 692, 707, 777, 791). After a conference with the Lords on the matter of Anyan's behavior it was resolved by the Lower House to petition the King to remove him from office (ibid., 796). This petition was included in the list of grievances presented to James I on 28 May 1624 (see above, H. of C., 22 June, n. 7) and, along with the other 1624 grievances, received an answer from Charles I on 4 July 1625 (see below, H. of C., 4 July, p. 303). On Anyan, see also Thomas Fowler, *The History of Corpus Christi College* (Oxford, 1893), pp. 175–181, and below, H. of C., 2 August, pp. 380, 383.

20. For the articles, see Bedford MS. 197, below.
21. Concerning the promise, see above, H. of C., 24 June, n. 11. In the preceding parliament Charles, then Prince, had also voted for the passage of an act reinforcing penal statutes against recusants. See S.P. 14/161: 36; and Ruigh, *Parliament of 1624*, pp. 240–242.
22. According to the Draft Journal and the Committee Book, above, the committee of the whole House received and read the articles in the morning, reserving debate of them for the afternoon session of the same committee. The Solicitor's report of the King's message (below) was given before the morning meeting of the committee of the whole (see O.B.).
23. In Bedford MS. 197 and *C.D. 1625* (Knightley MS.) the following articles concerning religion are in-

to his Majesty, or otherwise to be proceeded upon by bill, and now offered to the consideration of the grand committee.

[f. 10] First, to make a true representation to his Majesty of the late great increase of papists in this realm and of the dangerous consequences thereof unless timely remedy be provided. The danger is first in their ends and in the restlessness of their spirits for the attaining of them; they aiming not only at the utter extirpation of our religion but also at the possessing themselves of the whole power of the state. And such is the restlessness of their spirit that if they gain but a connivancy, they will press for a toleration, then strive for an equality, and lastly aspire to such a superiority as may work the extermination both of us and our religion; in all which they still think they do God's good service, such being the doctrine both of their teachers and leaders.

The danger of effecting whereof is much increased by their known strict dependency upon foreign princes, such as no way affect the good of his Majesty and this state, and by opening a way of popularity to the ambition of any who shall adventure to make himself head of so great a party.

The causes of this great and dangerous increase we conceive to be many, whereof we will touch only the principal.

1. First, the late suspension of the execution of the laws against the Jesuits, seminary priests, and popish recusants and while they live, in some sort executed, the manifold abuses of officers to the defrauding of his Majesty and protecting and encouraging the ill-affected subjects.[24]

[f. 10v] 2. The interposing of foreign princes by their ambassadors and agents in favor of them, whereto his Majesty has already given a gracious promise not to harken to the prejudice of our religion or to the slacking of the due execution of the laws against them, which promise his Majesty's subjects do with much joy, comfort, and thankfulness remember and thereon with great confidence and assurance do rely.[25]

3. Their great concourse to this City and their frequent conventicles and conferences there. Their open and usual resort also to the houses and chapels of foreign ambassadors.

4. The education of their children in seminaries and houses of their religion in foreign parts, the number of which seminaries have been greatly multiplied in this later time, whence has issued the great swarm of priests and Jesuits, seducers of his Majesty's subjects, dispersed over all parts of this kingdom.

5. The licentious printing and dispersing of popish and seditious books, whereas contrariwise they are restrained[26] from reading our books by the rules of their religion, and thereby kept in a perpetual ignorance of the truth.

6. The distressed estate of the professors of our religion in foreign parts. The unfortunate accidents to the princes nearest in blood to his Majesty caused by the strong confederacy of some princes of the Romish religion banding their counsels and means[27] to the advancing their own and suppressing our religion.

[f. 11] The remedies against this con-

---

cluded under the date of 25 June (see above, H. of C., 24 June, nn. 18 and 24). However, since the finished articles were not reported and read in the committee of the whole until the morning of 28 June (see the Committee Book, above), we have inserted the Bedford MS. 197 text of them here. This text contains a section which was not actually added to the articles until the afternoon's meeting of the committee of the whole this day (see below, n. 25). For the text of the petition concerning religion which was derived from these articles, see above, H. of L., 9 August,

pp. 155–160.

24. See above, H. of C., 23 June, n. 22.

25. On the interposing of foreign princes and ambassadors, see H. of C., 23 June, n. 22. On the King's promise, see H. of C., 24 June, n. 11, and above, n. 21. The section of this article referring to the King's promise was not added until this afternoon's meeting of the committee of the whole House. See above, p. 260.

26. *whereas contrariwise they are restrained* is omitted in *C.D. 1625* (Knightley MS.).

27. *power. C.D. 1625* (Knightley MS.).

tagious and dangerous disease we conceive to be of two kinds: the first to consist in strengthening our own religion, the second to the weakening and abating of theirs.

1. In the first part does first offer itself to serious consideration the well educating of the youth of this realm; and forasmuch as by many particular complaints it does appear that sundry popish schoolmasters dissembling their religion have craftily crept in and obtained the places of teaching in divers counties, and thereby infected and perverted their scholars, and so fitted them to be transported to the popish seminaries beyond the seas;[28] it is therefore desired to petition his Majesty that provision be made for greater care in the choice and admitting of schoolmasters, and that they be enjoined to catechize and instruct their scholars in the grounds and principles of true religion, and that the ordinary make diligent inquiry thereof, and proceed to the removing of such as shall be faulty or justly suspected.

[2.] It is also to be petitioned that his Majesty be pleased to take into his princely care the restoring of the ancient discipline of the two universities, being the famous nurseries of good literature and virtue. And forasmuch as Dr. Anyan, president of Corpus Christi College in Oxford, after three days public hearing at a committee in the last session of parliament, was found to be a man criminous and unworthy of that place, it is desired he may be proceeded against in a course of justice.[29]

3. To oppose against the multitude of priests abounding in this realm; that his Majesty be petitioned out of his princely wisdom to advise the bishops [f. 11v] to restore such learned and painful [sic][30] ministers to the liberty of preaching the word of God and catechizing of children as have been formerly silenced, provided that they demean themselves peaceably and orderly without impugning the government of the Church or the ecclesiastical rites and ceremonies by law established.

4. Forasmuch as nonresidency, pluralities, and commendams are great hindrances to the instructing of the people in the true knowledge and service of God, and consequently to[31] give way to the entrance of false religion, being [persons][32] which in all ages have been complained of; and forasmuch as the qualifications by law permitted have been of late years greatly increased by the increase of the nobility, that therefore a bill be prepared against the next session for the moderating and regulating thereof, seeing the same cannot be proceeded in without conference with the Lords who are interested therein, which the shortness of this session will not permit. And that his Majesty may be thanked for diminishing the number of his chaplains, nothing doubting of his princely care for the well bestowing of his own benefices both to the comfort of his people and for the encouragement of the universities, being full of grave and able ministers unfurnished of livings.

5. To the end that learned ministers able to instruct the people[33] may be planted over all the realm in the several parishes thereof, which cannot be without raising the livings to a convenient proportion, it is desired that the House be pleased to take the same into special consideration, and (if they think fit) to pray a conference with the Lords for the better effecting thereof, and that a bill be drawn to enable every man that is owner of an impropriation by deed en-

---

28. On popish schoolmasters, see above, p. 247.
29. See above, n. 19.
30. The final version of the petition concerning religion reads: *such able ministers.* See H. of L., 9 August, p. 157.
31. *do. C.D. 1625* (Knightley MS.).

32. The bracketed word is from *C.D. 1625* (Knightley MS.); Bedford MS. 197 is blank in this place.
33. MS.: *children people.* Apparently one of the words was meant to be crossed out.

rolled to make the same presentative as to charge it with an annuity for the maintenance of the minister, and that the bill against simony be speedily proceeded with.[34]

[f. 12] 6. The House to be moved to take order that information be brought against the next session of parliament[35] of all such churches in every shire where there is no usual preaching, as also of all such benefices or stipends of ministers as are under the value of 50*l.* per annum.

Now to come to the second kind of remedies addressed to the weakening and abating of the popish religion in this realm.

1. It is first desired, that no recusant or person popishly affected be admitted to have any schoolmaster in his private family, to the end his children may have the public and lawful education of this realm, and this to be proceeded in by bill.[36]

2. That a bill [be] preferred to the House as well to prevent the transporting of English children to the seminaries beyond the seas, as also for recalling them home which are there already placed, and for the severe punishment of the maintainers of those seminaries, or of the scholars there; and that his Majesty be also petitioned for his princely care therein, considering that, besides the seducing of his subjects, great sums of money are yearly expended upon them, to the impoverishing of the kingdom.

3. To petition his Majesty that no popish recusant be permitted to come within the court unless his Majesty be pleased to call him upon special occasion agreeable to the statute of *3° Jac.*, c. 5.[37] And accordingly that it be most humbly prayed of his Majesty that none of his subjects not professing the true religion, by law established, be ad-

mitted into the service of his most royal consort the Queen, for the preventing of many apparent [f. 12v] mischiefs both to his Majesty and the state, which by the contrary must needs ensue.

4. That his Majesty be petitioned, by some such course as he shall think fit, to give present order that all the laws now standing in force against Jesuits, seminary priests, and all others having taken orders by authority derived from the see of Rome, be put in due execution; and to the intent they may not pretend to be surprised, that a speedy and certain day be prefixed by his Majesty's proclamation for their departure out of this realm and all other his dominions, and not to return upon the severest penalties now in force against them; and that all his Majesty's subjects may thereby also be admonished not to receive, entertain, comfort, or conceal any of them, upon the penalties and forfeitures which may be lawfully inflicted; and that all such priests and Jesuits as shall be imprisoned be kept close prisoners, to avoid the contagion of their corrupt religion, and that no man who shall be justly suspected of popery be suffered to be keeper of any his Majesty's prisons.

5. That his Majesty be likewise petitioned to take such order as to his princely wisdom shall seem expedient that no bishop, stranger, nor any other by authority derived from the see of Rome confer ecclesiastical orders, or exercise any ecclesiastical function whatsoever towards or upon any of his Majesty's natural subjects, within any of his Majesty's dominions.

[6.] That petition be made to his Majesty, that he be pleased straightly to command all judges and ministers of justice, both eccle-

---

34. The former bill of simony had been ordered to be looked up on 23 June (see above, H. of C., 23 June, p. 228 and n. 9) and received its first reading of the 1625 session on this day, 28 June (see above, p. 258).

35. *of parliament* is omitted in *C.D. 1625* (Knightley MS.).

36. A bill for the breeding and bringing up of recusants' children was introduced into the House and received its first reading on this day, 28 June (see above, p. 257).

37. *S.R., 3 Jac.* I, c. 5.

siastical and temporal, to see the laws of this realm against popish recusants to be duly executed and, namely, that the censure of excommunication be pronounced against [f. 13] them, and that they be not absolved but upon public satisfaction by their conformity; and that a general commission be granted to choice and able persons to oversee the execution of those laws, and to prevent the frauds now ordinarily used to defeat his Majesty of the penalties and to save the offenders from punishment. And that the particular commissions into the several counties for the execution of the laws may extend to all counties of cities and towns and other liberties within the precincts of the same shires.

7. That his Majesty be likewise petitioned that his learned counsel may receive order and commandment to look into all former grants of recusants' lands, and to void them if by law they can. And the bill now in the House to that effect to be proceeded with.[38]

8. That his Majesty be petitioned to remove all such persons from place of authority and government as are popishly affected.

9. The like petition, that present order may be taken for disarming of all popish recusants legally convicted or justly suspected, according to the laws in that behalf and the orders taken by his late Majesty's Privy Council upon reason of state.

10. That his Majesty be also pleased, in regard of the great resort of recusants in and about London, to command that forthwith, upon pain of his indignation and severe execution of the laws, they retire themselves to their several counties, there to remain confined within five miles of their dwelling places.

11. That it may likewise please his Majesty straightly to command and take order that none of his natural-born subjects repair to the hearing of mass at the chapels or houses of foreign ambassadors or of any other privileged persons whatsoever, and that the offenders may be punished according to the laws.

[f. 13v] 12. That all such insolencies as any popishly affected have lately committed or shall hereafter commit to the dishonor of our religion, or to the wrong of the true professors thereof, may be exemplarily punished, and namely that heinous fact of one Foster, in openly tearing the Bible in the cathedral church of Canterbury.[39]

13. That his Majesty be petitioned, that the statute of *primo Eliz.* for the paying of 12*d.* every Sunday by such as shall be absent from divine service in the church without lawful excuse may be put in due execution, the rather for that the penalty is given by law to the poor, and therefore not to be dispensed with.[40]

14. Lastly, that his Majesty be pleased[41] to extend his princely care also over the kingdom of Ireland, that the like course may be there taken for the restoring and establishing of true religion.

Divers other things were promiscuously uttered at the committee, not particularly inserted into these articles.[42]

[f. 15v] A message came from the Lords desiring a present conference, which was granted; and the effect of it was that both

38. I.e., the bill for explanation of a statute of 3 *Jac.* for repressing popish recusants, which received its third reading and was passed by the Lower House and sent up to the Lords this day, 28 June (see above, p. 257).

39. The incident concerning Foster was related at the committee meeting, 23 June, by Sir Thomas Wilford. See above, p. 231. The Upper House objected to the inclusion of the particular concerning Foster and it was omitted from the final petition concerning religion. See Coke's report, below, H. of C., 4 July, p. 299.

40. See above, H. of C., 23 June, n. 23.

41. *petitioned. C.D. 1625* (Knightley MS.).

42. Concerning the notes of debate which follow this statement in the MS., see above, H. of C., 24 June, n. 24.

Houses might agree upon a time and place for the solemnity of the fast, and whether to be together or asunder.

400 copies of his Majesty's orders[43] for the fast were sent down by my Lord Chamberlain for the members of the Commons House.

Eodem die post meridiem.

[*Committee of the Whole House*]

The great committee examined the articles concerning religion, the Speaker sitting by, and these exceptions were taken:

[f. 16] [1.] Against the article for deprived ministers. Exception was taken by Sir Robert Hatton and Sir Dudley Digges.

Which yet was maintained by Sir Thomas Hoby upon reason of law, that no penalty can be extended to the loss of a freehold but by act of parliament.[44] And very well by Mr. Crew, the Speaker's son, by reasons of equity and conscience. 1. The fame of those men who had been of the same opinions, Mr. Hooper a martyr, Doctor Rainolds, [and] Mr. Bright[man].[45] 2. The excess of the punishment; it being without precedent in Christendom that men united to the Church in fundamental points should suffer in so high a measure.

[*End: Committee of the Whole House*]

In this variety the House being like to be divided, SIR HENRY MARTEN propounded a form of entry for that article which for the present settled the debate.[46] And he was commanded to write it down in paper for direction of the committee who, notwithstanding, apprehended such exceptions to it that it was altered in the petition.

[2.] Against the article for reformation of the universities and the complaint of Dr. Anyan.

But both were ordered to stand.

The Speaker being called to the chair,[47] a report was made of the conference with the Lords concerning the fast, wherein the time propounded was Saturday, the place for them the collegiate church, 2 bishops appointed to preach; three Lords to observe such as were absent. The manner according to the King's direction in print, and a collection for the poor.

[f. 16v] The same day was by us appointed for ourselves, St. Margaret's, Westminster, the place; three preachers: Dr. Preston, Mr. Shute, Mr. Holdsworth; Dr. Westfield, who was first named, being excused;[48] and likewise a gathering for the poor.

A select committee was appointed out of the former article[49] to frame a petition to the King in the matter of religion; and to present by themselves to the House such other points as were to be reformed by bill.

Q. What was done the 29 June when I was out of the House about framing the petition.[50]

43. *proclamation. C.D. 1625* (Knightley MS.). On the printed book of orders concerning prayers and fasting, see H. of L., 28 June, n. 12.

44. Marginal note in the Earl of Bedford's hand: "No".

45. John Hooper, Dr. John Rainolds, and Thomas Brightman. *D.N.B.*

46. There is no indication given in Bedford MS. 197 at this point that the Speaker had resumed the chair. See below, n. 47. We have followed the Draft Journal in constructing the order of business for this day.

47. The resumption of the chair by the Speaker signaled the adjournment of the committee and the return to the House. Either the House and committee had adjourned and resumed several times in the course of the reading of the articles without the diarists having noted it, or this entry regarding the Speaker is in error in its placement. See n. 46, above. We have recorded in the O.B. what seems to us to be the actual order of the day's proceedings.

48. Concerning the preachers for both Houses, see above, n. 13.

49. *articles. C.D. 1625* (Knightley MS.).

50. According to this statement the author of the diary of which Bedford MS. 197 is a copy was a mem-

IV. MS E237, KENNETH SPENCER RESEARCH
LIBRARY

[Tuesday, 28 June 1625][51]

[f. 117] We received a message from his
Majesty, that he had given order to have a
book made which should be published in
print for the manner of the fast;[52] that his
Majesty gave liberty to the Lords and us to
go our own way for the time and place
where we would keep our fast, yet wished it
might be before the general fast, which his
Majesty had appointed to be kept throughout England on the 16 day of July;[53] and
our fast ended, London to precede all other
places for their fast.

Whereupon the Lords and we met, and
the Lords and we agreed that the manner
of the fast should be as his Majesty did pre-
scribe. For the time and place, the Lords
appointed to keep theirs in the cathedral
church at Westminster, and to have two
bishop[s] to preach, and desired our place
might be as near theirs as might be and to
be kept on the second day of July 1625. The
Lords appointed an earl, a baron, and
bishop to take notice of the Lords absent.

We appointed [f. 117v] to have ours on
the same day in St. Margaret's Church in
Westminster; to have 3 preachers: Doctor
Preston, Doctor Westfield, and Mr. Shute
in Lombard street; to begin at 9 of the clock
in the morning and to hold till six at night; 6
gentlemen of the House were appointed to
take the names of all that were present and
to note the absent, and to collect the benevolence for the poor. We likewise appointed
to have our communion on the next day,
which was the 3 of July.

Afterwards we appointed a committee to
draw our petition to the King against the
priests and papists.

---

ber of the select committee appointed this day (28
June) to draw the petition concerning religion from
the articles passed in the House. For the names of the
six M.P.s appointed to the committee, see above, p.
260. Coke's name can safely be omitted from the list of
possible diarists because he was in the House and
spoke on the 29th. Rich can also be ruled out on the
assumption that as the known author of notes from the
session (see Introduction, above, p. 15) it is unlikely
that he also kept a diary which shows no correspondence with those notes. For additional reasons to eliminate Coke and Rich as well as grounds to reject all of

the other members of this committee except John Pym
as possible authors of the diary, see *C.D. 1621*, I, 41–
42. For further discussion of the evidence for attributing the authorship of this diary to John Pym, see the
Introduction, above, pp. 11–13.

51. Marginal note: "27 June".
52. Concerning the book, see above, H. of L., 28
June, n. 12.
53. The King's message proposed that the general
fast be held on Thursday, 7 July. However, at the
Lords' suggestion, the date was changed to Saturday
fortnight, i.e., 16 July. See above, nn. 5 and 14.

WEDNESDAY, 29 JUNE 1625

I. DRAFT JOURNAL, MS. 3409, H.L.R.O.

[f. 144] *Mercurii 29 Junii 1625*

L. 1ª. An act for planting and increasing of timber and wood.[1]

MR. DELBRIDGE. A petition from certain merchants against the imposition on wines.

The petition read.[2]

SIR ROBERT PHELIPS. To have that part of the Lord Treasurer's charge which concerns this particular to be reviewed.[3]

SIR EDWARD COKE. This will fall aptly into consideration when the bill of tonnage and poundage comes in.[4]

SIR THOMAS WENTWORTH. To have this petition taken into consideration and presented to the King among the rest of the grievances.

Resolved upon question, a select committee to take consideration of this petition.

Master Wards	Mr. Recorder
Sir Edward Coke	Mr. [William] Mallory
L. Strange[5]	Mr. [Edward] Alford
Sir Robert Phelips	Sir Edwin Sandys
Sir Thomas	Sir Clement
Wentworth	Throckmorton

Sir Dudley Digges	Mr. [Nicholas] Duck
Mr. Richard Spencer	Mr. [Robert] Bateman
Mr. [John] Delbridge	Mr. [Christopher]
Mr. [Thomas] Sherwill	Wandesford
Sir Walter Erle	Mr. [Roger] Matthew

This committee is appointed by the House to take into consideration this petition, tomorrow, 2 clock, Exchequer Chamber.

SIR THOMAS HOBY. Mr. Montagu's book the last parliament referred to my L. of Canterbury; to have an account what done in that.[6]

[f. 144v] Sir Henry Marten, Sir Robert Hatton, Sir Dudley Digges, and Sir Thomas Hoby to attend presently my L. of Canterbury to desire his Grace to acquaint this House what has been done concerning that book of Mr. Montagu's which was complained of the last parliament.

MR. MALLORY. To have a committee of grievances appointed. The alnager's office very grievous to the subject in Yorkshire.[7]

Resolved to let this particular rest till the general come to be handled.

MR. BATEMAN.[8] Mr. Shute desires that he may be the first preacher at the fast, according to the 1 appointment.[9]

---

1. For a fragment of the draft of this bill (H.L.R.O., Main Papers, H.L., 29 June), see Appendix, below, pp. 638–639.

2. The petition is printed below, pp. 269–271.

3. I.e., the charge in the 1624 impeachment proceedings against Lord Treasurer, Lionel Cranfield, Earl of Middlesex, concerning the customs farms for wines. See *L.J.*, III, 307–310, 351–358. See also, below, H. of C., 1 July, n. 26. On 30 June George Lowe wrote to the Earl of Middlesex reporting on the wine merchants' petition and other business of the House this day. See H.M.C., *4th Report, App.*, p. 289.

4. Concerning the bill for tonnage and poundage, see below, H. of C., 5 and 7 July, O.B.s.

5. I.e., James Stanley, styled Lord Strange.

6. On 13 May 1624 John Pym reported to the House from the committee on corruption in learning and religion that a petition complaining against Richard Montagu's book, the *Gagg*, had been submitted to that committee. Following Pym's report the House appointed a committee to acquaint the Archbishop of Canterbury (George Abbot) with both the petition and Montagu's book. *C.J.*, I, 704, 788.

7. Complaints against the alnager's office had been considered by the committee of trade in 1624 and, upon the committee report, the House had resolved that a bill concerning the office should be prepared for consideration by the next parliament and that the King should be petitioned to redress the abuses of the office. *C.J.*, I, 689, 709, 774, 793. See also, S.P. 14/165: 26, 27. The complaint against abuses of the office constituted one of the grievances concerning trade presented to James I in 1624 and answered by Charles I on 4 July 1625. See below, p. 309.

8. *Mr. Riddell* is crossed out in the MS. preceding *Mr. Bateman.*

9. The House had resolved on 22 June that Shute was to preach first, Holdsworth second, and Preston last. See above, p. 215. However, on 24 June it was moved and assented that Dr. Preston, in respect of his weakness, was to begin. See above, p. 242.

Resolved, Mr. Shute to be 2d.

SIR THOMAS JERVOISE delivers in a bill for maintenance of justice and right.

L. 1ª. An act for the maintenance of justice and right.

L. 1. An act to relieve creditors and to reform the abuses of sheriffs.

SIR THOMAS HOBY reports from my Lord of Canterbury. They attended his Grace and desired his Grace to signify to this House what/

He desired to have remembered his respective thanks to this House. Was at this time very ill disposed in health. Desires a day or 2 respite and then hopes to give good satisfaction to this House.[10]

L. 2ª. An act against the procuring of judicial places for, and against giving and receiving of bribes.
Committed to
[f. 145]

Mr. Treasurer	Lord Cavendish
Mr. Chancellor	Sir Benjamin Rudyard
Exchequer	Sir Guy Palmes
Master Wards	Sir Dudley Digges
Sir Edward Coke	Mr. [Christopher]
Mr. Recorder	Wandesford
Sir Robert Phelips	Mr. [Thomas]
Serjeant Ashley	Wentworth
Mr. [Christopher]	Mr. [Thomas] Lane
Brooke	Mr. [John] Whistler
Mr. [Edward] Littleton	Sir Francis Fulforde
Mr. Charles Price	Sir John Eliot
Sir Nicholas Sanderson	Sir John Danvers
Sir Francis Cottington	

Sir Thomas
  Wentworth
Sir Henry Mildmay
Mr. [Henry] Rolle
Sir George More
Sir Thomas Fanshawe
L. Percy
Sir James Fullerton
Sir Henry Marten
Sir Charles Morrison
All that will come to have voice. Tomorrow, 2 clock, Court of Wards.

MR. GLANVILLE reports the bill of tippling in inns and alehouses.
The amendments 2 read, ordered to be engrossed.

MR. CLARKE, double returned, elects to serve for Hythe.

II. PETITION OF THE ENGLISH MERCHANTS TRADING IN WINES. HARLEIAN MS. 6803, F. 21.[11]

To the honorable assembly of the Commons House of Parliament.

The humble petition of the English merchants trading in wines, showing,

That in January 1621 the petitioners having brought about 2,700 tuns of wines into the river of Thames there was order given by the then Lord Treasurer that the farmers should not suffer any wines to be landed without further warrant from his Lordship. And shortly after by his procurement, and without any notice given the petitioners, there was a new impost of 3 *l.* a tun laid upon wine over and above all former

---

10. A new committee was appointed on 1 July to attend the Archbishop that day. For the report of Canterbury's response to that committee, see below, H. of C., 1 July, O.B.

11. This copy of the wine merchants' petition included in the Alford papers is undated. Similar complaints from the wine merchants were considered by the Lower House in 1624 (see *C.J.*, I, 759–760, 763) and a petition from the merchants was referred by the Upper House to the Privy Council on 27 May 1624 (*L.J.*, III, 411). The reference in the petition below to the recent "privy seal from his Majesty that now is for the continuance of the said new impost of 20*s.*", is

evidence that this is a copy of the 1625 petition. Subscribed to this copy, in a different hand, is the note: "King Charles's answer was that this was for the maintenance of the Q. of Bohemia and marvelled that we would desire that it should be taken away". This was the King's answer to the 1625 petition from the House, reported on 9 July. See below, p. 359. The petition to the King from the House, derived from the wine merchants' petition below, is printed below, H. of C., 6 July, pp. 326–327. See also S.P. 16/3:111 for undated notes on the inconveniences caused by the new impositions on wines.

customs and impositions which were 50 percent.[12]

This unsufferable burden being laid on them on the sudden and after their wines were come into the river they were often humble suitors that this imposition might be removed and that they might have liberty to land their wines, paying the ancient customs and impost,[13] yet could they find no relief nor be suffered to discharge their wines which otherwise would have perished till they had given bond to pay that 3 l. upon a tun. By reason whereof, and freight being far dearer that year than other[s], and the petitioners being also compelled to pay unto the Rochellers 30s. upon every tun of wine toward maintenance of their wars,[14] they sold their wines to great loss. Besides, they lost that year about 20,000 l. by bad vintners,[15] which losses and unsufferable charges swallowed some of the petitioners' whole estates, others it disabled to exercise future trade or to pay the bonds given for the said new imposition.

Notwithstanding being threatened with extents, and some by order from the Lord Treasurer taken and carried away by pursuivants, they were at last, to avoid imprisonment, compelled to borrow money to pay the first bonds, being the moiety of the said new impost. And not being able to pay the other moiety they were induced by Mr. William Cooper,[16] collector of the said new impost, to deliver a petition to the then Lord Treasurer, drawn by Cooper himself: That if his Lordship would get that moiety remitted they would pay 20s. a tun in the future, which their meaning was (as they have deposed), should continue no longer till the other moiety were collected and then to cease.[17] But his Lordship otherwise wrested it, and taking advantage of this their pretended voluntary act, the petitioners have ever since been constrained to give bonds for the said 20s. of which they have paid part, to their irrecoverable damage, many of them having lately paid yearly in custom double their estates,[18] and they have not only been great losers by wines, but have lost their principal stock whereby they should have bought cloth and other manufactures of this kingdom to be vented into other countries.

And in further oppression of the petitioners and the ruin and decay of trade, there has been lately procured a new privy seal from his Majesty that now is for the continuance of the said new impost of 20s.,[19] for which divers of the petitioners were enforced to give bond rather than to suffer their wines to perish and others that refused so to do had their wines seized by

12. MS.: *50 l. per cent.* In January 1622, in order to raise money for the defense of the Palatinate, Lionel Cranfield, the Lord Treasurer, arranged for the imposts on wine to be doubled for a year's time from 3 l. to 6 l. per tun, an amount equal to the original cost of the wine purchased from foreign suppliers. *A.P.C., 1621–1623*, pp. 114–115.

13. For the merchants' complaints, see *A.P.C., 1621–1623*, p. 122; see also, *Cal. S.P. Dom., 1619–1623*, pp. 342–343.

14. I.e., an export duty on wines brought from La Rochelle.

15. On the actions of the vintners, see *A.P.C., 1621–1623*, pp. 306, 512.

16. Concerning Cooper, see *A.P.C., 1621–1623*, p. 362, and *Cal. S.P. Dom., 1623–1625*, pp. 337–338.

17. In response to the merchants' complaints, the King agreed toward the end of 1622 to abate the new impositions from 3 l. to 20s. See *A.P.C., 1621–1623*, p.

306; *Cal. S.P. Dom., 1619–1623*, p. 440; see also, *A.P.C., 1623–1625*, p. 50; *Cal. S.P. Dom., 1623–1625*, pp. 337–338.

18. Although the original increase of 3 l. per tun was to have been assessed for only one year (see above, n. 12), following its abatement to 20s. per tun the new imposition on wine continued to be collected into 1624, causing further concern on the part of the wine merchants. This issue was considered in the Lower House and its committee of trade in 1624. *C.J.*, I, 759–760, 763. In June 1624 the King declared that bonds taken for the payment of the 3 l. imposition should be remitted only to those who pay the new 20s. imposition. See *A.P.C., 1623–1625*, p. 295.

19. Following the death of James I, Charles confirmed the imposition of 20s. the tun in the port of London and 13s. 14d. in the outports "until further order be herein taken". *A.P.C., 1625–1626*, p. 28.

his Majesty's officers who still detain them in their custody whereby the petitioners are very much damnified.

Now, forasmuch as trade groans under the burden of this new imposition, and the petitioners are no ways able to pay the same, and for that many of their bonds are returned into the Exchequer and process of extent made out thereupon and prosecuted with much violence, for stay whereof the petitioners have appeared to some and pleaded to others and his Majesty's Attorney General has demurred to their pleas and intends to procure judgment upon some nice point in law. And for that the petitioners are likewise threatened with extents speedily to be awarded against them upon the residue of their bonds, which evil if it be not prevented by some timely remedy will be the present ruin of the petitioners and in short time be the consumption of all merchants trading in wines.

May it therefore please this honorable assembly (where all grievances have ever found redress) to take this important affair into your wise considerations and to give the petitioners such relief therein as in grievances of this high nature have ever been accustomed, and so to provide that all proceedings at the common law may stay upon their bonds already returned into the Exchequer. And those and the rest in Cooper's hand to be brought into this honorable House and there to be cancelled and made void and the said new impositions to be absolutely damned by the censure and judgment of this honorable assembly, and that the petitioners may have reimbursement of the monies so unjustly exacted from them by the violent courses aforesaid. And they shall pray, etc.

Report from the committee on the bill for ease in obtaining licenses of **alienation** (SIR EDWARD COKE)   274, *23/6

Ordered: the above bill to be engrossed   274

Report from the committee on the bill for the increase of **shipping** and for free liberty of **fishing** (JOHN GLANVILLE)   274, *24/6

Amendments to the above bill: read twice; bill to be engrossed   274

Engrossed bills to be put to the question tomorrow morning   274

CHRISTOPHER WANDESFORD: concerning privilege for Sir John **Stradling**, M.P.   274

Ordered: Stradling to have the privilege of the House   274

Report from the committee for drawing the **petition concerning religion** (JOHN PYM)   274, 277, *24/6

The draft of the petition concerning religion: read   274, 277

[*The completed petition concerning religion is printed on pp. 155–160*]

SIR HENRY MARTEN: offers an amendment to the draft   277

The petition with the amendment: allowed by the House   274, 277

SIR THOMAS WENTWORTH   274, 277

Resolved: to send a message to the Lords requesting a **conference** concerning the **petition**   274, 277

Report from the committee for drawing the petition concerning religion: delivering in a remembrance of those things that the committee thinks fit to be proceeded in by bill (SIR EDWIN SANDYS)   274, 277

SIR FRANCIS SEYMOUR: concerning the **subsidy** [*see below*]   274, 277, 279; **N**, 507, *1/7; 4/7; 5/7; 6/7; 8/7; 11/7

SIR BENJAMIN RUDYARD   274, 277; **N**, 507

SIR ROBERT KILLIGREW   274

SIR EDWARD GILES   274

SIR GEORGE MORE   275

SIR ROBERT CRANE   275

EDWARD BYSSHE   275

SIR ROGER NORTH   275

SIR FRANCIS ASHLEY   275

SIR HENRY WHITEHEAD   275, 278

SIR NICHOLAS SANDERSON   275

SIR JOHN WRAY   275

JOHN MAYNARD   275

Message from the Lords (Sir Thomas Trevor and Sir Humphrey Davenport) bringing: 275

(1) bill to enable the King to make leases of lands parcel of his Highness's **Duchy of Cornwall**   *1/7

(2) bill for confirming of the copyhold estates and customs of the tenants of the manor of **Cheltenham**   *1/7

SIR ROBERT PHELIPS: concerning the **subsidy** [*see above*]   275, 278; **N**, 507

SIR THOMAS FAIRFAX   275

SIR EDWIN SANDYS   275, 278

EDWARD ALFORD   275

SIR WILLIAM STRODE   276

SIR THOMAS WENTWORTH   276, 278

SIR EDWARD COKE   276, 279

SIR FRANCIS SEYMOUR   276

CHARLES PRICE   276

273

THURSDAY, 30 JUNE 1625

I. DRAFT JOURNAL, MS. 3409, H.L.R.O.

[f. 145]   *Jovis 30 Junii 1625*

SIR EDWARD COKE reports the bill of pleading alienations.

Counsel heard at the committee for the officers. The fee advanced from 4 nobles to 30*s*.

Ordered to be engrossed.

MR. GLANVILLE reports the bill of free fishing.

The amendments 2 read. Ordered to be engrossed.

Those engrossed bills that are ready to be put to the question to tomorrow morning, 9 clock.

[f. 145v] MR. WANDESFORD. Sir John Stradling desires to have the privilege of the House. An action between him and the dean and chapter of Exeter.[1]

Ordered, he shall have the privilege of the House. A warrant to the parties for stay of proceedings and a letter to the judge where it depends.

MR. PYM delivers in the petition from the committee that is to go to the King concerning recusants.[2]

The petition read; and with some little alteration allowed by the House.

SIR THOMAS WENTWORTH. Thinks we shall have no time now to go to the Lords to join in this petition.

Resolved upon question, a message to the Lords for a conference about this petition.

SIR EDWIN SANDYS delivers in a remembrance of those things that the committee think fit to have proceeded in by bills.[3]

SIR FRANCIS SEYMOUR. Matter of religion being now in this good forward, to apply ourselves to supply his Majesty. To give for the present one subsidy and one fifteen.

SIR BENJAMIN RUDYARD. The King's domestical charges exceeding great; for funeral, entertainment of ambassadors, and coronation.[4] The charge of the navy like to be 3 hundred thousand pounds. To have that we give be in some proportion to this great charge.

SIR ROBERT KILLIGREW. Fears we shall not meet at Michaelmas in regard of the infection. To give 2 subsidies and 2 fifteens.

[f. 146] SIR EDWARD GILES. King and commonwealth not to be severed. Lately given 3 subsidies and 3 fifteens to be paid within a year.[5] In some places the poor subjects enforced to sell their necessaries to pay that. If we give more than 1 subsidy and fifteen now, in what time can it be paid? To give one subsidy and 1 fifteen for the present to be paid as soon as may be.

1. We have been unable to find further details of Stradling's case.
2. Pym's report is from the select committee appointed on 28 June to draw the petition concerning religion from the articles considered in the Lower House on that day. The petition, in its corrected and amended form, is printed above, H. of L., 9 August, pp. 155–160.
3. On 28 June (see above, p. 260) when the articles were reported from the subcommittee to the committee of the whole they were described as "fit heads whereon to frame a petition . . . or otherwise to be proceeded upon by bill". According to the entry in Bedford MS. 197 (above, p. 265) the same committee

appointed to draw the petition was also to present to the House "such other points as were to be reformed by bill".
4. For the expenses of James I's funeral, the entertainment of the French ambassadors, and the charge of the navy, see the report of the Lord Treasurer's account of the King's estate, above, H. of L., 9 August, p. 167 and nn. 82 and 83. Although the coronation was not to take place until 2 February 1626, the costs were already being estimated. The coronation of James I in 1603 had cost nearly 20,000 *l.* (see Dietz, *Public Finance*, p. 402).
5. I.e., the subsidy passed in 1624. *S.R.*, 21 *Jac.* I, c. 33.

SIR GEORGE MORE. This complaint of poverty *vetus querela*. The 3 *l.* men and 40*s.* that make up the subsidy.[6] To offer 2 subsidies and 2 fifteens; to be paid in a convenient time.

SIR ROBERT CRANE. We have heard of the King's great charges. To walk therefore a middle way to give 2 subsidies and no fifteens, they fall upon the poorer sort. This will give good content to the country.

MR. BYSSHE.[7] Thinks this motion of supply now very seasonable. To have this and our petition of religion go hand in hand. To give no fifteens at all.

SIR ROGER NORTH. Cannot give less than 2 subsidies at this time, being the first gift we ever gave our King.

SERJEANT ASHLEY. The bells toll and the bills[8] tell of great mortality. *Quod uni accidit alteri potest.* Time therefore for us to think of that which must be done. Let us cast our eye upon that great and royal navy that is ready now to ready [*sic*] to weigh anchor. To give 2 subsidies and 2 fifteens.

SIR HENRY WHITEHEAD. Thinks fit to grant some fifteens as well as subsidies. The last fifteens came in very easily.[9] To give 2 subsidies and 2 fifteens.

[f. 146v] SIR NICHOLAS SANDERSON. We have now *regnum dei* in hand. Expected to have had that in some better forwardness before *regnum Angliae* had come in; but being relatives, let them go together. It has pleased his Majesty to acquaint us with his wants. We have engaged him in a war which

must be established by counsel, which is nothing worth without money which is the sinews of war. To give this in a proper measure. *Aquila non capit muscas.* Would not have the King a borrower. The King's charge now 2,000 *l.* a day. Not to protract the time of our gift. Lincolnshire willing to contribute as much as may be; the most the House shall agree of.[10]

SIR JOHN WRAY. To give 2 subsidies without fifteens.

MR. JOHN MAYNARD. To give 3 subsidies; one to welcome him to the kingdom and 2 for the affairs of the commonwealth.

A message from the Lords by Baron Trevor and Serjeant Davenport.

The Lords have sent down 2 bills: one to enable his Majesty to make leases of lands parcel of his Duchy of Cornwall; the other/[11]

SIR ROBERT PHELIPS.[12] To declare our affection at this time, but not to exclude reason and judgment. This work ever wont to be the last work of a parliament. To give at this time 2 subsidies without any fifteens. To have this levied with as much speed as may be. To put this to the question without any more dispute or debate.

SIR THOMAS FAIRFAX. Agrees to give 2 subsidies.

SIR EDWIN SANDYS. To consider the manner, measure, and time. For the manner, to have it wholly by [f. 147] subsidy without fifteens. For the measure, 2 subsidies but a small proportion, considering how much

---

6. The subsidy was assessed only upon those who owned property worth at least 3 *l.* or land yielding 20*s.* or more per annum. Fifteenths, on the other hand, were assessed on all subjects as a percentage of their personal property. See *S.R.*, 21 *Jac.* I, c. 33.

7. *Mr. Coryton* is crossed out in the MS. preceding *Mr. Bysshe.*

8. I.e., the lists of the dead. See above, H. of L., 18 June, n. 8.

9. See below, n. 23.

10. Sanderson sat for Lincolnshire.

11. An act for confirming of the copyhold estates and customs of the tenants of the manor of Cheltenham. See above, H. of L., 30 June, p. 73.

12. Bedford MS. 197, below, includes a longer version of Phelips's speech. Eliot, in his *Negotium*, below, p. 508, says "there was in this gentleman a natural grace of oratory, a moving and Nestorian way of rhetoric".

we owe his Majesty. Yet, considering we shall have another session shortly, to give but 2 subsidies for the time; the 1 to be paid in September next; the next to be respited till Candlemas.

MR. ALFORD. Hopes these 2 reasons will satisfy the country: the King's extraordinary occasions, and the great infection of the plague. To give 2 subsidies, the first to be paid in the 10th of October, the other the 10 of March.

SIR WILLIAM STRODE. Thinks this motion of supply very seasonable, before we go to the King with our petition like to have never the worse answer for giving 2 subsidies. To give 2 subsidies to be paid as last was moved.

SIR THOMAS WENTWORTH. To give 2 subsidies freely and cheerfully without relation to his present occasions but only as a testimony of the duty of the subject towards his Majesty. To have recusants pay double subsidy. Agrees for the time of payment.

SIR EDWARD COKE. The King's ordinary charges always borne by his ordinary revenue. *Commune periculum commune auxilium.* 27 E. 3, the King had war 14 years and yet no help from the subjects because he had good officers.[13] Before 31 Eliz. never above one subsidy granted.[14] 35 [Eliz.], 3 subsidies and 3 fifteens granted. 39 [Eliz.], 4 subsidies and 6 fifteens.[15] We gave the last King 3 subsidies and 3 fifteens, which is 300,000 *l.* of English money.[16] The tonnage and poundage every year 100 and 60 thousand pounds, besides 4 subsidies of the clergy.[17] Concurs to give 2 subsidies to be paid in October and April; before the last of either.

SIR FRANCIS SEYMOUR. Likes well of that time of payment. To have recusants pay double subsidy.

[f. 147v] MR. CHARLES PRICE. Although we give now no fifteens, yet not to waive them forever hereafter. Likes well of the proportion of 2 subsidies.

MR. SPENCER. Agrees to give 2 subsidies at the time before propounded: October and April. To have the arrearages of recusants go to this.

SIR THOMAS HOBY. To send to the Lords about our petition, which is[18] a thing forgotten.

Resolved upon question without any one negative voice to give the King at this meeting a free gift of 2 entire subsidies.

Resolved upon a 2 question without a negative, that the first of these subsidies shall be paid in the end of October next; the other at end of April next.

Resolved upon a 3d question without a negative that those which now stand recusants convict, or shall stand recusants convict before the time of the assessment of these subsidies, shall pay double subsidy.

Sir Edward Coke
Serjeant Ashley
Mr. Solicitor
Sir Robert Phelips
Mr. Recorder
Sir Nathaniel Rich
Sir Thomas Wentworth
Sir Benjamin Rudyard

---

13. See below, n. 27.

14. In 31 *Eliz.* I two subsidies and four fifteenths and tenths were granted. *S.R.,* 31 *Eliz.* I, c. 15. See also, Coke, *Fourth Inst.,* p. 33.

15. The figures are incorrectly recorded for 35 and 39 *Eliz.* I. In each of those years three subsidies and six fifteenths and tenths were granted. *S.R.,* 35 *Eliz.* I, c. 13; *S.R.,* 39 *Eliz.* I, c. 27. See also, Coke's speech in

Bedford MS. 197, below, p. 279.

16. *S.R.,* 21 *Jac.* I, c. 33.

17. Concerning tonnage and poundage, see Coke, *Fourth Inst.,* p. 32. For the four subsidies granted by the clergy in 1624, see *S.R.,* 21 *Jac.* I, c. 34.

18. MS.: *in.* Hoby is apparently referring to the petition concerning religion.

Sir Francis Seymour
Sir Edwin Sandys
Mr. [John] Pym
Sir Dudley Digges

This committee is appointed by the House to draw a preamble for the bill of subsidy. Tomorrow, 2 clock, Exchequer Chamber.

[f. 148] Resolved, a committee of the whole House to sit this afternoon to receive the account of the Council of War.

Mr. Solicitor to give an account of the grievances of the last parliament to the House tomorrow morning.

II. COMMITTEE BOOK, MS. 3410, H.L.R.O.

[f. 159] *Jovis 30 Junii, post meridiem*

Sir Robert Mansell. Appointed to attend the Council of War this afternoon. They have no order to bring in their account. The account ready.

Upon reading of the last bill of subsidy, it appears that the account must be demanded by warrant, under the Speaker's hand, from the Council of War.
The House to be moved for a warrant to this purpose.[19]

Sir Thomas Middleton. The treasurers can give an account of what they have received. Have paid it all out by warrants.
200 hundred 50 one thousand, 100 *l.* and 14 *l.*

III. MS. 197, BEDFORD ESTATES, LONDON

[f. 17]   30 *Junii* 1625.

A draft of a petition was presented by the committee and read, only one exception being taken by SIR HENRY MARTEN. In the 9

article it was desired that the censure of excommunication might be "pronounced" against recusants. He alleged that in the canon law there was *excomunicatio juris* and *excomunicatio hominis.* By the statute[20] it was enacted that all recusants should be *ipso facto* excommunicated; and this, which is *excomunicatio juris,* is in reputation of law greater than the other which is *hominis.* So that he did not think fit there should be a new sentence pronounced; therefore to leave out that word, and to alter it thus: "the censure of excommunication might be declared and certified against recusants".

With this amendment the draft of the petition was allowed. And, notwithstanding our joining with the Lords was opposed by SIR THOMAS WENTWORTH, a message was sent to their House to desire a conference to that effect.

The articles concerning these points which were to pass by bill was delivered to the Clerk.[21]

SIR FRANCIS SEYMOUR (the business of religion being settled), moved that we might go to the next point of supply and propounded a subsidy and one fifteen.

SIR BENJAMIN RUDYARD declared the necessity of the King's estate, his great charges in domestical occasions, the funeral, entertainment of ambassadors, coronation, foreign preparations of the navy, Low Countries, Mansfeld, Denmark.[22] He concluded the sum propounded to be too little both in respect of his want and of his reputation.

[f. 17v] Debate wavered a great while: some would have one, others two subsidies with the addition of one, others two, others

<hr>

19. Concerning demanding the account of the 1624 subsidies from the Council of War by warrant, see section 39 of *S.R.,* 21 *Jac.* I, c. 33. See also, Sir Thomas Crew's letter to Secretary Conway, S.P. 16/4:10, printed in the Appendix, below, p. 717. The warrant was read in the House on the following morning and the account was presented to the committee of the

whole House in the afternoon. See H. of C., 1 July, O.B.
20. *S.R.,* 3 *Jac.* I, c. 5.
21. See above, n. 3.
22. On these charges, see the report of the Lord Treasurer's account of the King's estate, above, H. of L., 9 August, pp. 166–168. See also, above, n. 4.

four fifteens. But the most were inclinable
to no fifteens at all, being very burdensome
to the poorer sort, especially in towns and
ancient boroughs (though SIR HENRY
WHITEHEAD affirmed when he was collector
of the fifteens in Hampshire then payments
came in easily and without grievance),[23]
and pitched upon two entire subsidies.

SIR ROBERT PHELIPS.[24] Divers circumstances in this gift will express the affections
of the subjects more than the value, and
wished we should so make it an act of affection as not to exclude judgment. 1. We
made it the first work of a parliament which
was wont to be the last. 2. Not four kings of
England that ever had so great a supply.[25]
3. Though we cannot so give up the sense of
our state as not to say that never king found
a state so out of order, the privileges of the
kingdom, the privileges of this House, have
been so broken, such burdens laid upon the
people, that no time can come in comparison with this. These things considered,
there cannot be a greater argument of our
love than that we are at this time contented
to lay aside the right of the subject. 4. There
is no engagement; the promises and declarations of the last parliament were in respect of a war. We know yet of no war nor of
any enemy.[26] 5. We have yet no account of
the money which they say is ready; but what
account is to be given of 20,000 men, of
many hundred thousands of treasure,
which have been expended without any
success of honor or profit? It was not wont
to be so when God and we held together;

witness that glorious Queen who with less
supplies defended herself, consumed
Spain, assisted the Low [f. 18] Countries,
relieved France, preserved Ireland.

He concluded that we should be suitors
to the King to take these things into his consideration and to proceed in this government by a grave and wise counsel. And, for
supply, he fixed upon the proposition of 2
subsidies without fifteens. There is no cause
for more, and hopes no man will press for
more. They diminish the King that think
money can give him reputation. The hearts
of his subjects are his greatest treasure and
reputation. His example I hope will amend
us towards God. His government will cause
a reformation amongst ourselves. There
was never any king upon whom there were
fewer notes of vice, and we shall ever be
thankful subjects. But it will be most for his
honor that what we do come freely from us.
If any press his merit to extend us farther,
they miss the way. For other argument we
know what can be said, and hope that at the
return of the navy there will be better
inducements.

SIR EDWIN SANDYS agreed to the same
sum. Added the times of payment: September next and Candlemas.

SIR THOMAS WENTWORTH. So far from
consenting that he would not have any man
heard that should speak for a greater proportion. This was given to his Majesty freely
and cheerfully as the first fruits of the
springing love of his subjects. Yet, to en-

23. Fifteenths were granted in both 1610 (*S.R.*, 7
Jac. I, c. 23) and 1624 (*S.R.*, 21 *Jac.* I, c. 33). Sir Henry
Whitehead was a collector of the free gift in 1614 (*Sir
Henry Whithed's Letter Book* [Hampshire, 1976], I, 121–
122), but the archives in the Hampshire Record Office
do not reveal what year he was a collector of the fifteenths. His speech recorded in the Draft Journal,
above, suggests it was 1624.
24. See above, n. 12.
25. Concerning supply granted to former monarchs, see Sir Edward Coke's speech, above, p. 276. See
also, Coke, *Fourth Inst.*, p. 33.

26. In their declaration delivered to King James on
14 March 1624 (*L.J.*, III, 259), their proposition delivered on 23 March (*L.J.*, III, 275), and in the 1624
subsidy act itself (*S.R.*, 21 *Jac.* I, c. 33), the two Houses
had made it clear that their offers of assistance were
contingent upon the King's dissolution of the two treaties and engagement in the war with Spain which was
expected to ensue. For the Duke of Buckingham's response to the objection that the enemy is not declared,
see his answers to the second and fourteenth questions
in his speech to both Houses on 8 August (H. of L., 9
August, pp. 163, 166).

large our gift thus far: that these subsidies may be doubly charged upon recusants. He added by way of motion that at our next meeting we should remember to go soundly on so to regulate the revenues of the crown that they might hereafter bear some part of the public charge.

[f. 18v] SIR EDWARD COKE. Ordinary charges the King should bear alone; but *ubi, commune periculum commune auxilium.* In extraordinary he may require relief. 27 E. 3, the King told his subjects he demanded no aid because he had good officers.[27] The King's revenue as it is, is able to supply his ordinary. Ancient parliaments did so limit their gifts, that they might meet again. Till 31 Eliz. never but one subsidy granted, and Sir Walter Mildmay, though he were a great officer, spoke against it then.[28] But since that time there has been no such thing.[29] *35to*, 3 subsidies, 6 15[s]; *39to*, 3 subsidies, 6 15[s]; *43to*, 4 subsidies, 8 15[s]; etc.[30] And it is not to be forgotten that the tonnage and poundage which yields 160,000 *l.* per annum, and the subsidies of the clergy 20,000 *l.* per annum, are all by gifts of parliament.[31] The time for these two subsidies he would have October and April.

The House began now to settle both upon this proportion and upon the times, when divers courtiers came in who were most of them absent in the beginning of this motion, as not expecting this would have fallen out a day for that business. So, though divers were provided to have spoken and meant to have urged for a larger proportion, yet not knowing how the debate had passed, and seeing no likelihood of prevailing, they held their peace.

Three reasons were given against the double subsidies upon recusants. 1. Not suitable to mix punishment with gratulation, which was spoken not to spare the recusants, but to burden them in an ordinary way. 2. It would make the bill in penning, and the taxation, more intricate. 3. The advantage to his Majesty would be very small, for if it be limited to recusants convict [f. 19] there are few of those; if left at large, some new way must be devised to direct to the commissioners for trying of them.

But it was moved to extend to recusants indicted without conformity, or else to all such as had not received within a year.

IV. PETYT 538/8, INNER TEMPLE LIBRARY

[f. 121] [Thursday, 30 June 1625]

SIR FRANCIS SEYMOUR moved, that in respect of things[32] necessity and the [f. 121v] danger we sat in there, to give unto the King one subsidy.

Which motion once being on foot was concluded on the same morning to give unto the King two subsidies: the one payable at the end of October, the other at the end of April next; none of the King's Council or servants speaking in it then.

---

27. Concerning Edward III and money for preparations for war with France in 1353, see *Rot. Parl.*, 27 E. III, no. 32. We have been unable to find a more direct statement issued in that year by Edward III regarding aid. In 27 E. III a subsidy on cloth was granted to the King in addition to the regular customs. *S.R.*, 27 E. III, st. 1, c. 4; and see Coke, *Fourth Inst.*, p. 30.

28. See above, n. 14. On 11 February 1589, following a speech by Sir Walter Mildmay, Chancellor of the Exchequer, a committee was appointed to consider a bill of subsidy (D'Ewes, *Journal . . . Elizabeth*, p. 431). Several days later Mildmay reported the committee's recognition of the need for extraordinary supply that year, but also stated its concern that the high amount not become a precedent (ibid., p. 433).

29. *stint. C.D. 1625* (Knightley MS.). Marginal note in the E. of Bedford's hand: "No".

30. See above, n. 15. *S.R., 43 Eliz.* I, c. 16.

31. See above, n. 17.

32. *the King's.* B.L. Add. 48,091. In the MS., Seymour's motion follows the narrative concerning the Yorkshire election. See below, H. of C., 4 July, p. 307 and n. 89.

L. 1a. An act for confirming of
the copyhold estates and
customs of the tenants of the
manor of **Cheltenham** [*see
below*]   282, *30/6; 4/7;
                                             9/7; 11/7
L. 1a. An act to enable the King to
make leases of lands parcel of
his Highness's **Duchy of
Cornwall**   282, *30/6; 4/7;
                                             7/7; 9/7; 11/7
Motions concerning pressing of
soldiers, etc,   285
Committee for drawing a bill
concerning the **muster
masters** and **pressing of
soldiers**, and to consider a
bill for arms: appointed   282
RICHARD YARWOOD: delivers in a
bill concerning the **poor**   282
SIR THOMAS PUCKERING: moves to
have the cause concerning
the **Warwick** election heard
at the committee of
privileges this afternoon   282, *21/6
Ordered: as Puckering moved   282
Committee for attending the
Archbishop of Canterbury
concerning **Montagu's** book:
appointed [*see below*]   282, 285, 287,
                                             *29/6; 7/7;
                                             6/8
The warrant to the treasurers and
Council of War to bring in
their **accounts**: read [*see
below*]   282, *30/6
The Serjeant sent away with the
warrants   282
L. 3a. An act for ease in obtaining
licenses of **alienation**: passed
[*see below*]   282, *23/6
L. 3a. An act for the further

restraint of **tippling** in inns,
alehouses, etc.: passed [*see
below*]   282, *23/6
L. 3a. An act for the increase of
shipping and for free liberty
of fishing: passed [*see below*]   282, *24/6
SIR FRANCIS BARRINGTON: delivers
in a **petition** from one
wishing to inform the House   282
Ordered: the person complained
of in the petition delivered by
Barrington to be sent for and
kept in the custody of the
Serjeant   282
Petition from the **constables of
Yorkshire**: read   282
Message to the Lords (Sir Edward
Coke) sending up: 282
  (1) bill for ease in obtaining
  licenses of **alienation** [*see
  above*]
  (2) bill for the further restraint
  of **tippling** in inns, alehouses,
  etc. [*see above*]
  (3) bill for the increase of
  shipping and for free liberty
  of **fishing** [*see above*]
and desiring a **conference** on
the **petition concerning
religion** [*see below*]   *24/6
SIR THOMAS WENTWORTH:
concerning **subsidy** and the
account of the **Council of
War** [*see above and below*]   283
SIR ROBERT MANSELL   283
SIR FRANCIS SEYMOUR   283
EDWARD ALFORD   283
SIR EDWIN SANDYS   283
CHRISTOPHER WANDESFORD   283
Report of the Lords' response to
the message: Lords'
committee will attend a

FRIDAY, 1 JULY 1625

I. DRAFT JOURNAL, MS. 3409, H.L.R.O.

[f. 148]   *Veneris 1 July 1625*

L. 1. An act for confirming of the copyhold estates and customs of the tenants in base tenure of the manor of Cheltenham in the county of Gloucester.

L. 1. An act to enable the King's Majesty to make leases of his Highness's Duchy of Cornwall.

Serjeant Digges
Mr. [Henry] Sherfield
Mr. [Nicholas] Hyde
Mr. [Nicholas] Duck
These 4 are appointed by the House to draw a bill against the next meeting concerning the pressing of soldiers and the muster masters and to consider of a bill for arms.

MR. YARWOOD delivers in the bill concerning the poor.[1]

MR. THOMAS PUCKERING. To have the cause of Warwick heard at the committee of privileges this afternoon.[2]

Ordered.[3]

Sir Henry Marten
Sir Robert Hatton

Sir Thomas Hoby
Mr. John] Pym
To attend my L. of Canterbury concerning Montagu's book.[4]

[f. 148v] The warrant read to the treasurers and Council of War for bringing in their account this afternoon, and the committee of the whole House to sit to take the accounts.[5]

Serjeant sent away with these warrants.

L. 3. An act for pleading/[6]
Upon question, passed.

L. 3. An act for the further restraint of tippling in inns.
Upon question, passed.

L. 3. An act for maintenance and increase of shipping and navigation and for the freer liberty of fishing and fishing voyages.
Upon question, passed.

SIR FRANCIS BARRINGTON delivers in a petition from one that offers to inform the House.

Ordered, he shall be sent for presently and be kept in the custody of the Serjeant.[7]

A petition read from the constables of Yorkshire.[8]

Sir Edward Coke sent up to the Lords with these 3 bills;[9] and to desire their Lord-

1. Apparently the bill was not read in the House this session. A bill for the relief of the poor had been considered in the 1624 parliament, and on 28 May 1624, prior to the prorogation of that parliament, the bill was committed to the care of William Noy "to be framed against next session" (*C.J.*, I, 699, 701, 714). Noy was not returned to the 1625 parliament.

2. Puckering had submitted the petition concerning the Warwick election on 21 June. See above, H. of C., 21 June, p. 206 and n. 13.

3. Marginal note: "X". See above, H. of C., 23 June, n.9.

4. Sir Dudley Digges was also on the committee to attend the Archbishop of Canterbury and made the report to the House at the committee's return (see O.B.). Digges had been one of the four members sent to the Archbishop of Canterbury on 29 June. See above, H. of C., 29 June, p. 268 and n. 6.

5. Concerning the warrant, see above, H. of C., 30 June, p. 277 and n. 19, and see the letter from Speaker

Crew to Lord Conway, S.P. 16/4:10, which, from internal evidence, should be dated 1 July.

6. I.e., an act for ease in obtaining licenses of alienation.

7. The petition is not identified in the proceedings. The case may be related to that of Foreman who was in the custody of the Serjeant on 4 July. See below, H. of C., 4 July, p. 298 and n. 17.

8. We are unable to find a copy of the petition. Judging by the remarks of Sir Thomas Wentworth, below, and the resolutions in the committees of the whole this afternoon (see below, p. 285), the constables may have been petitioning to receive allowances out of the 1624 subsidy monies for charges connected with military preparations. See also, the order of the House following the report from the committee of the whole on this matter, 6 July, below, p. 325.

9. I.e., the three bills passed in the House this day. See above.

ships to speed them; and to desire a conference with their Lordships concerning the petition of religion.

SIR THOMAS WENTWORTH. This the case of the whole kingdom. This quite contrary to the last act of subsidy. When the Council of War come in the afternoon to know of them why these [*illegible*] are not satisfied.[10]

[f. 149] SIR ROBERT MANSELL. This received much debate at the Council of War. Thought they could not allow it, unless by special order at this House. Will be ready to give their reasons to the House.

SIR FRANCIS SEYMOUR. The very direct words of the act that these monies shall be allowed. In some places justices of peace have sent out their warrants for levying this money.

MR. ALFORD. When we enter into the bill of subsidy, to take all these things into consideration.

SIR EDWIN SANDYS. In the county of Kent has been levied half a subsidy for these things. It will be proper for the House to demand the reason of the not allowance of this when the Council of War comes to the House.
Deferred till then.

MR. WANDESFORD. To enter a protestation against this act of the justices of peace.

SIR EDWARD COKE reports from the Lords. They will give conference presently by the same committee.[11]
They had the former bills in hand and would/[12]

SIR EDWIN SANDYS reports from the grand committee yesterday to receive the account of the Council of War.

Mr. [William] Ravenscroft
Mr. [Robert] Caesar
To see whether the oath of the treasurers and Council of War be enrolled in the Chancery.

The committee[13] sent up to the Lords to confer about the petition. Sir Edward Coke to make the report.

[f. 149v] Judicial places, Monday, 2 clock.

Transportation of wools, Monday, 2 clock, Court of Wards.

Habeas corpus, Monday, 2 clock. And all other bills that are *sine die* to hold on Monday.

L. 2. An act for confirmation/[14]
Upon question, not to be committed.
To be put to the passage on Monday next.

Concealments,[15] Monday morning, 7 clock, Court of Wards.

SIR DUDLEY DIGGES. They have attended my L. of Canterbury. The last parliament Mr. Montagu's book complained of, transferred over to the Archbishop. Returned.
Set it down in writing; which he read.[16]

Referred to the former committee for the petition of religion to take consideration of this answer of my L. of Canterbury.[17] They to report their opinion to the House what they think fit to be done in it.

---

10. Wentworth is probably referring to the petition from the constables of Yorkshire. See above, n. 8.

11. I.e., the Lords agreed that their committee originally appointed on 23 June for the conference on the general fast and this day augmented with seven new members to replace absentees would meet with the Commons on the petition concerning religion. See above, H. of L., 1 July, p. 78.

12. The Lords promised expedition of the bills concerning the Lord's day and the statute of 3 *Jac.* for repressing popish recusants. See above, H. of L., 1

July, O.B.

13. I.e., the conference committee of forty-eight appointed by the House on 23 June. See above, p. 228.

14. Marginal note: "Cheltenham".

15. *Sir Clement Throckmorton* is crossed out in the MS. preceding *Concealments*.

16. For the Archbishop's answer to the committee, taken in writing by Sir Dudley Digges, see below, pp. 286–287.

17. The "former committee" intended by this reference is not entirely clear since there were several

Sir Dudley Digges,[18] Sir Henry Marten, Mr. Francis Drake, Serjeant Ashley added to the committee.

This committee likewise is to take consideration of Mr. Montagu's last book.[19]

Monday morning, 7 clock, Star Chamber.

[f. 150] L. Carew and L. Grandison cannot attend this afternoon;[20] the one out of town, the other sick.

Mr. Francis Morris, Mr. Dowlich, clerks to the Council of War, to be warned to be here this afternoon, 2 clock.

SIR EDWARD COKE reports from the Lords. They will send an answer by messengers of their own. Left the petition with them.[21]

SIR EDWIN SANDYS reports from the committee appointed to examine the impost on wines. The merchants being in great extremity, having paid one half of the impost, and given bond for the rest, urged to pay an addition of 20s. on a tun for ever.[22]

They say they gave no consent; justified it upon their oaths.[23] 2nd exception: the outports gave no consent although the merchants of London did. 3rd exception, of parliament. 17 E. 3, the merchants yielded an imposition, which the parliament disavowed;[24] 2, 22 E. 1, the merchants agreed an imposition on the wools, the merchants desire to be excepted out of the pardon for this.[25] No petition of grievance presented to the King about this the last parliament; went up only to the Lords in the Lord Treasurer's charge.[26] This imposition of 20s. laid down for a time in London; but not in the outports. This now taken up again.[27] They must enter bond for payment of it. If they refuse, their wines are seized. The committee advised the merchants to complain of this in the Exchequer and to come to a trial by law. The committee thought fit to have a complaint from all the Commons. This concerns all the commonwealth. To entertain it as a grievance; and to have a course taken for the penning of it.

---

committees which dealt with the petition concerning religion. Most recently appointed was the committee of six members named on 28 June to draw up the petition following the House's approval of the articles (see above, H. of C., 28 June, p. 260). And on 24 June a subcommittee for framing heads for the petition had been appointed (see above, H. of C., 24 June, pp. 240–241). The fact that Recorder Finch was not appointed to the committee of six on 28 June and yet he served as the reporter from the committee concerning Montagu on 7 July (see below, H. of C., 7 July, O.B.) suggests that the "former committee" referred to here may be the 24 June committee.

The committee concerning Montagu was further augmented on 4 July and possibly on 2 August (see below, pp. 298 and 380).

18. *Mr. Recorder and some others* is crossed out in the MS. following *Digges*, and the names of Marten, Drake, and Ashley are added in the margin of the MS., as they are on the Committee Book subcommittee list of 24 June (see above, H. of C., 24 June, p. 240 and n. 17).

19. I.e., the *Appeal*. See above, H. of C., 24 June, n. 16.

20. I.e., George, Baron Carew of Clopton, and Oliver St. John, Viscount Grandison, members of the Council of War, would be unable to attend the commit-

tee of the whole this afternoon for the delivery of the Council's account. See the letter from Speaker Crew to Lord Conway cited in n. 5, above.

21. I.e., the petition concerning religion.

22. See the petition from the wine merchants, above, H. of C., 29 June, pp. 269–271 and nn. 11–19.

23. See above, p. 270.

24. *Rot. Parl.*, 17 E. III, no. 28.

25. *Rot. Parl.*, 22 E. III, no. 4.

26. The grievances of the wine merchants, though considered by the committee of trade (see *C.J.*, I, 759–760), were not included in the petition of grievances drawn up in 1624 (see above, H. of C., 22 June, n. 7). However, the complaints against new impositions on wines were coupled with accusations of bribery regarding customs and were formulated as one of the charges against the Lord Treasurer, Lionel Cranfield, Earl of Middlesex. The charges against Cranfield were reported to the Lower House on 15 April (*C.J.*, I, 767) and were transmitted to the Upper House later that day (*L.J.*, III, 307). For the proceedings against and the sentencing of Cranfield, see *L.J.*, III, 344–383. The charges are printed in Cobbett, *Parl. Hist.*, I, 1411–1477. See also Ruigh, *Parliament of 1624*, pp. 313–341.

27. See H. of C., 29 June, nn. 17 and 18.

SIR EDWARD WARDOUR.[28] To have the collectors of this imposition called to give an account, for nothing has come to the King.

[f. 150v] Sir Edwin Sandys and the same committees[29] required by the House to draw this into a petition of grievance to be presented to his Majesty; and are to meet on Monday morning, 7 clock, Exchequer Chamber.

Mr. Solicitor to give an account of the grievances of the last parliament on Monday morning.

II. COMMITTEE BOOK, MS. 3410, H.L.R.O.

[f. 159]   *Veneris 1 Julii,*
             post meridiem

Question whether Sir Robert Mansell, that is one of the Council of War, shall stand as an accountant or sit as a member of this House.

Resolved by the committee, the Lords to have stools and sit.[30]

The Council of War: L. Grandison, Sir Edward Cecil, Sir Robert Mansell, Sir Thomas Button.[31]

The account read.

[f. 159v] Sir Thomas Middleton delivers

in the account of the treasurers, which was read.[32]

Sir Thomas Middleton. To appoint some to compare these 2 accounts.

Resolved as the opinion of the committee that the charge of 8d. the day after such time as the Council's letters came to the lieutenants ought to be allowed to the country according to the act of parliament.

The like for the constables' necessary charges for impress money and attendance.[33]

The House to be moved to deliver their opinion to the Council of War that these charges ought to be allowed.

III. MS. 197, BEDFORD ESTATES, LONDON

[f. 19]   *Primo Julii.*

Divers motions were made concerning arms and soldiers, that the authority of pressing, of taxing wages for the muster master, imposing arms, and punishing those that, being pressed, shall run from their captains, may be reduced to some certainty, and not left arbitrary or by commission.[34]

Sir Dudley Digges and four others were sent to my Lord of Canterbury to know what his Grace had done upon the reference made to him by the House of Commons the last

28. Sir Edward Wardour was the Clerk of the Pells.
29. I.e., the select committee appointed on 29 June, see above, p. 268.
30. The question here concerned the custom that witnesses should stand when testifying to a committee. Lords had been permitted to sit, however, when they came into the Lower House on 17 May 1614 (K.S.L.R., MS E237, f. 30; *C.J.*, I, 487; see also, Hatsell, *Precedents*, II, 145; III, 1–3), and apparently the single Lord among those on the Council of War who came now was seated. As to Mansell, whether he was permitted to sit, as was his right as an M.P., or required to stand, as a witness, the record does not show.
31. This entry suggests that only four of the nine current members of the original ten-member Council of War (Arthur, Lord Chichester, had died in February 1625) attended the committee meeting. According to the Draft Journal, above, and Speaker Crew's letter to Lord Conway (S.P. 16/4:10), apparently written on

the morning of 1 July, Viscount Grandison was at Battersea and was not expected to receive notice of the meeting in time to attend.
32. Middleton was one of the treasurers for the 1624 subsidy monies. An account of the treasurers' receipts is printed below, pp. 289–292. For an account of the treasurers' disbursements, see *Cal. S.P. Dom., Addenda, 1625–1649*, pp. 23–27. We have not located a copy of the account of the Council of War.
33. On 6 July (see below, p. 324) upon the report from the committee of the whole, the House ordered that "all charges disbursed for the uses mentioned in that act [21 *Jac.* I, c. 33] are to be disbursed out of the subsidies and 15eens, and to be paid according to the act". Concerning the constables' charges, see above, n. 8.
34. For those members appointed to draw a bill concerning muster masters and the pressing of soldiers, see above, p. 282.

parliament concerning Montagu's book.[35] They found him sick and upon his couch; but after they had delivered the message, the rest of the committee entreated Sir D. Digges to take his Grace's answer in writing as he spoke it, and the report thereof was now read out of that paper:

When it pleased that wise and judicious House the last session of parliament to recommend unto me the consideration of Mr. Montagu's book, I saw I was with care and caution to deal in that matter because it carried with it divers difficulties. For albeit it intended a great trust and confidence which that worthy assembly had in me, yet I found that it came unto me without touching on the Lords spiritual and temporal, or either of them, but directly to myself as Archbishop of [f. 19v] Canterbury.[36] 2ly, I could not tell how everywhere it was tasted that the book should be handled or questioned in the High Court of Parliament. 3ly, I had reason to foresee that it might be objected: By what authority will my Lord of Canterbury censure this book without the Convocation, or without the Commission Ecclesiastical?

Yet, finding that it was fit that truth should be supported, scandal should be removed, the peace of the Church continued, and that great assembly receive convenient satisfaction, I addressed myself to do my duty, finding that, albeit divers things excepted against might receive some favorable interpretation, yet there were some others of another nature. I with my best advice fell on this resolution: First, to acquaint the King of blessed memory what had been directed to me, and to move his Majesty that I might send for Mr. Montagu to speak with him concerning that book; whereunto his Majesty graciously assenting, I sent for Mr. Montagu by a letter, to which he returned this answer.

The answer was read, which expressed a general sorrow that he should be thus questioned, a profession of his clearness from popery, a promise of repairing to the Archbishop as soon as he should be able, being then sick of a fever.

His Grace proceeded: 2ly, when I had received this letter, thinking there had been modesty and ingenuity in the man, I acquainted the King with it, and told him in what course I did purpose to hold with him, which his Majesty very well approved.

There passed divers days before his coming to me, and by that time that I saw him I was fallen into a strong fit of the gout, so that it was much pain unto me to speak unto him; but the words I used were to this purpose:

[f. 20] Mr. Montagu, you profess that you hate popery, and no way to incline to Arminianism; you see what disturbance is grown in the Church and in the Parliament House by the book by you lately put forth.[37] Be occasion of no scandal or offense, and therefore this is my advice unto you: go home; review over your book. It may be divers things have slipped you which upon better advice you will reform. If anything be said too much, take it away; if anything be too little, add unto it; if anything be obscure, explain it; but do not wed yourself to your own opinion, and remember we must give an account of our ministry unto Christ.

He seemed to embrace this counsel, and took it kindly at my hands that I had dealt so fatherly with him. But being gone from me (saving fames and rumors) I never heard word of him till May day last in the morning at what time, being in my rochet going to my barge to wait upon the King at court, Mr. Montagu in my great chamber presented me with his second book;[38] whereabout when I had expostulated with him (not having read one word of it) what the cause should be that I should be so slighted and the book published without the least notice of mine, he gave me a cold answer: That since his departure from me

35. See above, H. of C., 29 June, n. 6.

36. I.e., the Commons had submitted the petition of complaint directly to the Archbishop and not first to the Upper House or to Convocation.

37. I.e., the *Gagg.*

38. I.e., the *Appeal.*

he had not been at London till the week before Easter last; in that time he was busy in printing of his book.

Now, whether I or[39] others whom it may concern have been fairly used, I leave to other men's opinions; for this second book itself I shall, God willing, freely give my judgment of it when and where I shall be orderly directed to it.

The business was referred to the committee appointed for matters of religion, as well touching the first as the second book.[40]

[f. 20v] SIR EDWIN SANDYS made a report concerning a petition delivered by divers merchants touching 20s. per tun newly imposed upon wines.[41] My Lord of Middlesex had laid 3l. a tun upon wines, whereof there was a complaint the last parliament, hereof the merchants were enforced to pay one half in hand, and to give bond for the rest. It was mediated by Mr. Cooper that if they would pay 20s., they should have a longer day and take up their bonds.[42] This was now urged upon them in perpetuity upon pretense of a consent; yet they offer to prove by oath they never gave consent. 2ly, if the merchants of London had consented, that would not bind the outports. 3ly, no consent of merchants can conclude the par-

liament or prejudice the kingdom. 17 E. 3 and 22 E. 1, there was an agreement made for an imposition upon wools; the Commons desire the merchants may be excepted out of the pardon.[43]

The reason why the merchants renewed their complaint now was because this particular was left out of the petition the last time, and so they are without remedy.[44]

It was ordered to be drawn by Sir Edwin Sandys into the form of a petition.[45]

Oxford ordered to be placed before Cambridge in the bill of subsidy.[46]

IV. PETYT 538/8, INNER TEMPLE LIBRARY

[f. 121v]   *Die Martis.* 28th
                        Junii [sic][47]

Mr. Sherfield[48] moved that there was a book lately set out, entitled *Appello Caesarem*, by one Mr. Montagu, which had many dangerous positions tending to popery. And that he justified his book which was questioned the last parliament, and abused the petitioners[49] who were grave divines and complained against it, which was formerly [referred][50] to the Lord of Canterbury.

And thereupon it was ordered that Sir

---

39. *and. C.D. 1625* (Knightley MS.).

40. See above, n. 17.

41. See the petition from the wine merchants, above, H. of C., 29 June, pp. 269–271 and nn. 11–19.

42. See above, H. of C., 29 June, p. 270 and nn. 16 and 17.

43. Marginal note in the E. of Bedford's hand: "No". For the precedents, see above, nn. 24 and 25.

44. See above, n. 26.

45. For the petition from the House to the King regarding the wine merchants' complaint, see below, H. of C., 6 July, pp. 326–327.

46. No other account indicates that such an order was made this day (1 July). The subsidy bill was not read in the House until 4 July and not passed until 8 July.

47. The author of the original MS. of which Petyt 538/8, B.L. Add. 48,091, and Q.C. 449 are copies compiled most of the Montagu material from the June and July 1625 proceedings into a single narrative. We have separated the Montagu material from Petyt 538/8 into two main entries and, following the chronology of the

Draft Journal, have placed the two sections under 1 July and 7 July respectively, the days on which the main action recounted in each section occurred.

48. Because the record of proceedings concerning Montagu is compiled into a single narrative in Petyt 538/8 (see above, n. 47), it is difficult to establish the date on which Sherfield made this motion. Record of the same or a similar motion by Sherfield is entered in the margin of the Committee Book entries for 24 June (see above, H. of C., 24 June, p. 240 and n. 16), but it may have been added there at some date after 24 June. Such a motion might well have been made on 29 June prior to the appointment of the committee sent to the Archbishop of Canterbury, which is referred to below (see below, n. 51).

49. *commoners* or *commissioners.* Q.C. 449. The 1624 petitioners were John Yates and Samuel Ward. Concerning the petition against Montagu in 1624, see below, H. of C., 7 July, n.3.

50. The bracketed word here and the single words within brackets below are included in B.L. Add. 48,091 and Q.C. 449, but omitted in Petyt 538/8.

Dudley Digges, Mr. Pym, and two others[51] should attend him to know what he had done in it, and to give notice that they were moved unto it by the book that Mr. Montagu had lately put forth. And then they returned answer that his Grace, being ill of the gout, did desire some time to recollect what he had done in it, being so long since [f. 122] and slipped out [of] his memory; and he would give them a good account of his care in that occasion. And about two days after,[52] his Grace not returning answer, the former messengers were again sent to his former Grace to know what he had done in it, who returned answer, which was delivered by SIR DUDLEY DIGGES, to this effect: That after such time as the House had sent to him, showing their dislike to some things that he had published in his[53] former book entitled *A New Gagg for an old Goose* which were scandalous to our religion, he[54] considered that it was a matter of great import and that it came from a great council of state. But withal he considered it came not recommended unto him also by the Lords of the Upper House, nor that it came from his Majesty, or that he had any notice of it, nor that it came recommended unto him as a high commissioner, [or unto the High Commission,][55] but only as Archbishop; wherein though he were willing to give redress, yet he knew not how safely to do it and thereupon was in some doubt what to do. At last he resolved to move his Majesty in it and to crave his leave to examine it, which [f. 122v] he accordingly did; and his Majesty gave him leave; and thereupon he wrote a letter to Mr. Montagu to come to him. He returned him answer by letter, which letter the Archbishop sent unto the House, and was there read, and

was to this effect: that he understood that he was persecuted by some vile and devilish spirits, and that he was now ill of a fever in the third fit. Therefore desired to be excused until he had strength to travel and then he would attend his Grace. Shortly after he came, and then the Archbishop related unto him that he had lately published a book which was thought to be scandalous to our religion (meaning the *Gagg*), and willed him to review and peruse it. And if there were anything that were too little, to add to it and enlarge [it]; if there were anything too much, to recall it and put it out; and if there were anything doubtful and obscure, to explain it; with grave and fatherly admonition he took then in a very good part [and] said he would do it, and so departed for that time. And from thence until May day last, which is almost a year, he never heard of him nor saw him; and then as the Archbishop was coming up to Westminster stairs, he [f. 123] presented him with his book of *Apello Caesarem,* which he had printed without his leave or privity,[56] and thereby he intimated that the House might perceive how he dealt with him. And when he received his book, he told him that he looked to have seen him and heard from him long since in another manner touching that he remembered him of, which he excused in that he had been busy in printing this book which he had now presented unto [his] Grace, and hoped that it would give him satisfaction; which, when he had read, he said he was as sorry for the publishing of it as any [member] of the House.

And upon his return the House made a committee, and sent for Mr. Montagu who attended the same.[57]

51. This was the first committee sent to the Archbishop of Canterbury on 29 June. According to the list of committee members in the Draft Journal (see above, p. 268), Pym was not appointed to that committee.
52. I.e., this day, 1 July; see above, Draft Journal.
53. I.e., Montagu's former book.
54. I.e., the Archbishop.
55. The bracketed passage is included in B.L. Add. 48,091 but omitted in Petyt 538/8 and Q.C. 449.

56. *without his liberty.* Q.C. 449.
57. Concerning the appointment of the committee on Montagu, see above, n. 17. On 4 July the committee received authority from the House to send for witnesses (see below, p. 300). For the examination of the Montagu business, recorded in Bedford MS. 197, see below, H. of C., 6 July, pp. 325–326 and n. 18. The Petyt 538/8 narrative concerning Montagu continues under 7 July, below, p. 342 (cf. above, n. 47).

V. SUBSIDY TREASURERS' ACCOUNT. HARLEIAN MS. 161, BRITISH LIBRARY, FF. 55–56v.

The three subsidies and three fifteens granted in parliament for the wars, and are thus certified by the several [*blank*] in their offices.

William Hill[58]	49,883–10–01–ob.–qz.
Richard Budd	44,810–08–06–ob.–qz.
Francis Phillipps	34,918–01–10–00–qz.
Justinian Povey	48,551–07–05–00–qz.
Sir Edmund Sawyer, Kt.	42,102–00–05–00–qz.
William Gwynne	43,575–12–10–00–qz.
Thomas Brinley	47,853–19–02–00—
	311,195–01–07–00–qz.

Discharged	Discharged by certificates of double wards' lands, Cinque Ports, and	18,862–10–01–qz.
	Fees to collectors	5,696–00–00—
Payments	To the treasurers *ut per acquit.*	270,299–04–09–qz.
Remanet	Debts depending in super and certified into the Exchequer as by	785–07–07–qz.
	Debts to be cleared by divers collectors that have not yet finished their accounts	11,552–02—
		16,337–06–07–ob.

Sum total 311,195–01–07–qz.

The total of the subsidies	The first subsidy	75,321–19–08–qz.
	The second subsidy	73,633–02–01–ob.
	The third subsidy	69,239–17–10—
		218,195–00–02—
Discharged	By certificate	15,301–10–03—
	For fees of collectors	4,801–13–00—
		20,103–03–03—
Payments	To the treasurers as appears by acquitances	186,902–09–11—
Resting	Due by divers persons certified into the Exchequer	4,392–00–00—
	Debts by collectors that have not cleared their accounts nor produced the treasurers' acquitance	6,797–07–00—
		11,189–07–00—

Sum of the discharge[d]
payments and debts is 218,195–00–02—

58. The men listed here were Revenue Auditors of the Exchequer. As is often the case with copies of seventeenth-century accounts, the figures listed do not always add up to the sum totals indicated.

Divers collectors in the county of Denbigh, Cardigan, and others have not yet accounted nor any extracts received for the same upon sight, whereof the total charge will be so much increased and the several titles of discharge, payments, and sums resting to be altered accordingly, as also the sum total of the treasurers' receipts upon knowledge had of such sums as have been paid unto them by the collectors which are hereafter mentioned, nor yet to have cleared their accounts.

The total of the 3 fifteens	The first fifteen	31,000–14–02–ob.–qz.
	The second fifteen	31,000–00–11–ob.–qz.
	The third fifteen	30,999–06–02–ob.–qz.
		93,000–01–05—
		whereof
Discharged	By writs for college lands, billets for the Cinque Ports in Kent and Sussex, and the like	3,160–19–11–ob.–qz.
	For fees of collectors	894–07–00—
		4,455–06–11–ob.–qz.
Payments	To the treasurers as has appeared by acquitances	83,390–14–10–00–qz.
Resting	Due by divers persons certified into the Exchequer	393–04–07–00–qz.
	In debts by collectors that have not cleared their accounts nor produced the treasurers' acquitance	4,754–15–00–00–qz.
		5,147–19–07–ob.—

Sum of the discharge,
payments and debts is 93,000–01–05

Upon sight of acquitances for such payments as have been made by the collectors which have not yet cleared their accounts, the sum total of the treasurers' receipts are to be altered:

	The first subsidy is	75,321–19–08–ob.
Discharged	By certificates	5,806–11–05—
	For fees of collectors	1,683–08–09—
		7,490–00–02—
Payments	To the treasurers as by acquitance	66,120–09–00–ob.
	Debts due by divers persons certified into the Exchequer	1,625–18–00—
	In debts to be cleared by the collectors	84–12–06—
		1,711–10–06—

Sum total 75,319–19–08–ob.

John Williams and Paul Perte, collectors of the subsidy of [the] King's Majesty's Household, are to account for 84–12–06 abovementioned.

The collectors of the half part of the county of Northumberland with the halmots of Norham and Eland-shire [*sic*] have not accounted, nor the liberty of the Trinity Minories near London.

	The second subsidy is	73,633–02–07–ob.
	By certificates	5,117–11–04—
	For fees of collectors	1,663–11–05—
		7,181–02–09—
Payments	To the treasurers as by acquitances	64,477–05–08–ob.
Resting	Debts due by divers persons certified	1,771–13–04—
	In debts to be cleared by the collectors	273–00–10—

Sum total 73,633–02–07–ob.

Divers collectors in the county of Wiltshire are to clear their accounts, for 215–12–08 as in the particular book delivered by Auditor Povey appears.

The collector of Holderness in the county of York is to clear his accounts for 57–08–02 as in the certificate of Auditor Brinley.

	The third subsidy is	69,239–17–10—
Discharged	By certificates	3,977–07–06—
	For fees of collectors	1,454–12–10—
		5,432–00–04—
Payments	To the treasurers as by acquitances	56,347–15–02—
Resting	Debts due by divers persons certified into the Exchequer	993–08–08—
	In debts to be cleared by the collectors	6,439–13–08—
		7,433–02–04—

Sum is 69,239–17–10

John Williams and Paul Perte, collectors for the Household, are to clear for 1,771–03–00. Walter James, collector of the Lords' subsidy, is to clear for 4,668–10–08.

	The first	31,051–14–02–ob.
Discharged	By writs, billets to the Cinque Ports, and the like	1,187–09–06–qz.
	Fees of collectors	377–02–00—
		1,494–11–06–qz.
Payments	To the treasurers as by acquitances appears	28,775–18–04–qz.

Resting	{ Debts certified into the Exchequer	126–09–02—
	{ To be cleared by collectors upon account	603–15–02—
		730–04–04—

Sum is 31,051–14–02–ob.

Sir Thomas Weston, Knight, collector of Hertfordshire, is to clear his account for 17–00–02–ob.–qz.

Robert Spente, Esquire, collector of the first fifteen in one half of Gloucester, for 586–14–11–00–qz.

	The second	31,051–00–11–ob.–qz.
Discharged	{ By writs, billets to the Cinque Ports, and the like	1,210–08–04–ob.–qz.
	{ Fees of collectors	304–00–00—
		1,514–18–04–00–qz.
Payments	To the treasurers as by their acquitances appears	29,354–11–03–ob.–qz.
Resting	{ Debts certified in the Exchequer	131–01–03–ob.–qz.
	{ To be cleared by collectors upon account	nil–00–00–00—
		131–01–03–ob.–qz.

Sum is 31,000–00–11–ob.–qz.

	The third	30,999–06–02–ob.–qz.
Discharged	{ By writs, billets to the Cinque Ports, and the like	1,163–02–00–ob.—
	{ Fees of collectors	283–05–00–ob.—
		1,446–07–00–ob.—
Payments	To the treasurers as by their acquitances appears	25,266–05–02–00–qz.
[Resting]	Debts certified into the Exchequer	135–14–02–ob.—
	To be cleared by collectors upon account	4,150–19–10–00–qz.
		4,286–14–00–ob.–qz.

Sum, 30,999–06–02–ob.–qz.

Thomas Chester, collector of the county of Gloucester, is to clear his accounts for 1,098–05–02–ob.

Sir William Whitlepoole, Knight, collector of the moiety of the county of Suffolk, for 680–18–04.

Richard Chalchroste, Esquire, for the county of Kent, [for] 1,054–07–07–ob.–qz.

Robert Fowlester, collector of the hundred of Blofield and other in Norfolk, for 1,317–08–08–00–qz.

[*Endorsed*] The account of the treasurers for the receipt of the 3 subsidies and 3 fifteens delivered to the Commons House of Parliament, *Anno* 1625.

Committee concerning **Montagu**:
  meets [*see below*]   301, *29/6
L. *2a.* An act to enable the King to
  make leases of lands parcel of
  his Highness's **Duchy of**
  Cornwall: committed   295, 299, *1/7
L. *3a.* An act for confirming of
  the copyhold estates and
  customs of the tenants of the
  manor of **Cheltenham**:
  passed   295, 299, *1/7
JOHN DELBRIDGE: concerning
  Arthur **Basset**'s case   295, *28/6
Report from the **committee of**
  privileges: on the **Yorkshire**
  election (SIR GEORGE MORE)   295, 300, 301,
                                     306; **N**, 511–
                                     516, *21/6
SIR THOMAS WENTWORTH   295, 300; **N**,
                                     513
SIR CHRISTOPHER HILDYARD   296, 300
SIR HUMPHREY MAY (Chancellor
  Duchy)   296, 301
SIR ROBERT HEATH (Solicitor)   296
WILLIAM STRODE   301
HENRY ROLLE   301
SIR EDWARD COKE   296
JOHN GLANVILLE   296, 300
SIR FRANCIS SEYMOUR   296
WILLIAM TOWSE   296
SIR EDWARD GILES   296
Petition from Sir John Savile:
  read   297, 306
Petition from Sir Richard
  Cholmley, sheriff of
  Yorkshire: read   297
SIR THOMAS HOBY   297
CHRISTOPHER WANDESFORD   297
SIR FRANCIS GOODWIN   297
SIR CLEMENT THROCKMORTON   297
JOHN LOWTHER   297
SIR EDWARD COKE   297
SIR ROBERT PHELIPS   297
Resolved upon question: the

particulars of the case by the
  sheriff and Sir Thomas
  Wentworth to be put down in
  writing and delivered to Sir
  John Savile   297, 300, 301;
                                     N, 514
Answer to the **grievances** of 1624
  to be heard and the **subsidy**
  bill to be read this afternoon
  [*see below*]   297
SIR EDWARD COKE: elects to sit for
  Norfolk   297, 300
Message from the Lords desiring
  a conference this afternoon
  on **petition concerning**
  religion (Sir John Davies and
  Sir Henry Finch) [*see below*]   297, 300, 301,
                                     *24/6
Answer given to the Lords'
  message: the House agrees to
  the conference   297, 300, 301
SIR ROBERT HATTON: elects to sit
  for Sandwich   297, 300
[*Afternoon*]
Report concerning the **oaths** of
  the **Council of War** and the
  treasurers (ROBERT CAESAR)   297, 300, *1/7
Oaths of the Council of War, etc.:
  referred to a committee   297
JOHN PYM: moves for authority to
  send for the party or
  witnesses regarding
  Montagu's book [*see above*]   297
Power given to the committee
  concerning Montagu to send
  for parties or witnesses;
  member added   298, 300
Foreman, alehouse keeper,
  brought to the bar   298, 300, *9/7;
                                     11/7
SIR THOMAS CREW (Speaker):
  charges Foreman with
  slanderous words   298

MONDAY, 4 JULY 1625

I. JOURNAL OF THE HOUSE OF COMMONS
[C.J. 801]
[p. 9] *Lunae, 4° Julii, 1° Caroli Regis*

L. 2ª. An act to enable the King's Majesty to make leases of lands parcel of his Highness's Duchy of Cornwall, or annexed to the same.

Committed to the knights and burgesses of Devon and Cornwall and all the lawyers of the House. 2 clock this[1] afternoon, in the Court of Wards.

L. 3ª. An act for the settling and confirmation of the copyhold estates and customs of the tenants in base tenure of the manor of Cheltenham.

Upon question, passed.

MR. DELBRIDGE moves the case of Mr. Basset, referred to the committee of privileges.[2]

SIR GEORGE MORE reports from the committee for privileges. 1. The case for the knights of the shire for Yorkshire.[3] That the sheriff charged: 1, that upon his view, without poll, he gave his judgment for Sir Thomas Wentworth and Sir Thomas Fairfax to be knights, where Sir John Savile most voices; 2ly, that when the poll required, he said it was only of courtesy to grant it; 3ly, that he began the poll but, having polled about 35, broke it off.

That nothing objected against Sir Thomas Wentworth or Sir Thomas Fairfax. That the sheriff being heard he, upon Saturday was sevennight, was required to answer the matter in fact, but he required to do it by counsel, yet acknowledged the poll was demanded but that it was granted ere demanded. Being demanded whether he began not the poll and broke it off, he acknowledged it, but desired by his counsel to answer to the breaking it off. That upon

Tuesday last, he, by his counsel, alleged that the day of the election, after 8 of the clock, he made proclamation and read the writ at the usual place. That the writ being read, he caused the gates being shut; he took a view of the freeholders and returning, said he thought Sir Thomas W[entworth] and Sir Thomas F[airfax] had double the voices to Sir John Savile. That he chose to take the poll at the postern gate and, having polled about 35, heard the fore gate was broken open and many freeholders gone out upon Sir John Savile's persuasions that the taking of the poll would last many days. That hereupon he broke off the poll.

Desired time for his witnesses. Some of the committee against the time because would be but a delay. [p. 10] Others, that they believed his allegation and therefore no cause for his witnesses. Others, that in justice his witnesses were to be heard who could better prove than himself who was at the polling further off. 42 committees, whereof 17 for time, the residue against it.

SIR THOMAS WENTWORTH. That he has never sought to delay his cause, only desirous to have it heard in a legal manner. 1. For the number: it will be proved fully, that without all question that the far greater number for him and Sir Thomas Fairfax. 2ly. For the quality: the return by the greatest number of men of quality than to any return these 20 years.

That on Sir John Savile's side divers out of a house where the master himself no freeholder but said they were freeholders. That his case for the poll thus: The poll demanded by Sir John Savile, with a cavil, but with no intention it should proceed. That this demand of the poll was after eleven clock. That the sheriff shut up the fore gate, went to the postern gate and, being without, the poll, by the unlawful act of Sir

---

1. *tomorrow* is crossed out in the MS. preceding *this*.
2. I.e., the privilege case of Arthur Basset. See

above, H. of C., 28 June, n. 1.
3. See above, H. of C., 21 June, n. 12.

John Savile himself, interrupted.[4] Desires this case may either be granted him or denied him: if granted, that his counsel, tomorrow, at the bar, may maintain the law to be for him; if denied, that he may be admitted to prove this case by his witnesses, which was never denied to any. That his case not like that of Cambridgeshire, where the sheriff was there demanded the poll and performed it not. 2ly, for Pontefract, the poll broken off by the parties returned.[5]

SIR CHRISTOPHER HILDYARD.[6] That about 10 of the clock he, for Sir John Savile, demanded the poll. The sheriff said it was not then time, but should have it. That Sir John Savile's company stayed/

CHANCELLOR DUCHY. Either Sir Thomas Wentworth's answer must be acknowledged true or witnesses must be heard.

[**C.J. 802**] MR. SOLICITOR, *accordant.*

SIR EDWARD COKE. 2 things considerable. Likes not the sheriff's answer that he needed not grant the poll, for bound to grant it—but not to strike these gentlemen through the sheriff's sides. 1. Whether the demand of the poll in due time—the poll the true trial, neither view nor voice can

judge it. 2ly. Whether he that demanded the poll broke it off or was the means of it. *Impotentia excusat legem.* [p. 11] That we cannot, in justice, deny them proof of this[7] matter in fact.

MR. GLANVILLE. If the poll were demanded before 11 but not granted before, then the poll not granted at all, because the time for the election past, and it like the case of Cambridgeshire, wherein the House resolved that the not polling where demanded a misdemeanor in the sheriff.[8] 2ly, that in that case also the election and return void by reason of the not granting of the poll.

In the case of Pontefract, the election not held good of Sir John Jackson, though his adversary, Sir [*blank*] Beaumont, interrupted the poll.[9]

SIR FRANCIS SEYMOUR. That the poll demanded and granted before 11. The shutting of the gate fit to exclude other freeholders who might come in and give their voices now, when the time for the election was past.

SERJEANT TOWSE. To hear witnesses to prove the matter in fact.

SIR EDWARD GILES. That Sir John Savile

---

4. For testimony concerning the fact that Sir John Savile had interrupted the polling, see the letter from John Grymesdyche to Sir Thomas Wentworth, 20 May 1625, printed in *Wentworth Papers 1597–1628*, ed. J. P. Cooper (London: Camden Society, 1973), pp. 232–234.

5. Concerning the case of Sir John Cutts in the Cambridgeshire election for the preceding parliament, see below, p. 306, and *C.J.*, I, 677–678, 729. The election was declared void in 1624 and a new writ ordered because although demanded the poll had not been proceeded in. The undersheriff was sent for to be examined by the House; his petition was read on 15 March (ibid., 686, 737); he was examined the following day, committed to the Serjeant, and ordered to make submission and acknowledgment in the county at the quarter sessions (ibid., 687, 737).

A double return was submitted for Pontefract in 1624. On 22 March (ibid., 745) the parties returned were ordered to absent themselves from the House until the election was examined by the committee of

privileges. On 1 April (ibid., 751) a petition was submitted from Pontefract and on the same day a report made from the committee. It was resolved in the House on 28 May (ibid., 714, 797) that the election was void and a new writ was to be issued. At the election the poll had been demanded on the part of Sir Richard Beaumont, one of the parties returned, but once the polling had begun it was broken off because of a disturbance caused by Beaumont's supporters (ibid., 714, and see Glanville, *Reports,* pp. 141–142). Apparently the primary grievance in this case was not with the proceedings of the polling per se but with the matter of enfranchisement, who was entitled to have a voice in the election. See also, below, H. of C., 5 July, p. 319 and n. 40.

6. Hildyard sat for Hedon-in-Holderness, Yorkshire.

7. *the.* Printed edition.

8. See above, n. 5.

9. See above, n. 5.

caused the gates to be opened, but that this was/

A petition from Sir John Savile read.

Another petition from the sheriff of York read.[10]

SIR THOMAS HOBY.[11] That witnesses must needs be heard.

MR. WANDESFORD. The question to be about the granting time for witnesses for the gentlemen returned, or for the sheriff.

SIR FRANCIS GOODWIN moves that Sir Thomas W[entworth], Sir Thomas F[airfax], and the sheriff may set down the particulars of Sir John Savile's disturbance, that the House may judge of it.

SIR CLEMENT THROCKMORTON. That the sheriff may have time for his witnesses.

MR. LOWTHER. If the House shall now judge the sheriff whether it be with him or against him this may be afterwards crossed upon an action brought by Sir John Savile for a false return.

SIR EDWARD COKE. That the poll being broken off, it may be set down by the sheriff in particular what disturbance was made by Sir John Savile. To deliver the sheriff's petition to Sir John Savile. If he grant the case in it, to judge it; if he[12] deny it, then to give the sheriff time to prove it.

SIR ROBERT PHELIPS. That the sheriff, and Sir Thomas W[entworth], and Sir Thomas F[airfax] are so joined together as the one cannot stand and the other fall.

Upon question resolved: That the case, in the sheriff's petition and Sir Thomas

Wentworth's, as he has delivered it in the House, with the particulars of the interruption and disturbance, shall be set down in writing by them and delivered to[13] Sir John Savile and, upon his answer, the House to give further direction. This to be to Sir John Savile this afternoon, and his answer to the House tomorrow morning.

[p. 12] To hear the answer to the grievances and read the subsidy this afternoon, and the Speaker to attend.

SIR EDWARD COKE elects knight of the shire for Norfolk.

Serjeant Davies and Serjeant Finch bring a message from the Lords: That they desire a conference, about 5 a clock this afternoon, in the Painted Chamber, concerning the petition lately sent unto them concerning religion. And that they intend to sit this afternoon, and desire the same committee which was last with their last committee about the fast.[14]

Answer: That the House will give a meeting to the Lords with the committee, and how/

SIR ROBERT HATTON elects for Sandwich.

Lunae, 4° Julii, 1° Caroli Regis.
Post Meridiem.

MR. CAESAR. That he has searched and finds with Mr. Saunders, the riding clerk, the oaths both for the Council of War and treasurers, which were taken by/[15]

This referred to the committees.

MR. PYM moves for authority to send for the party or witnesses concerning Montagu's book.

---

10. The petitions from Savile and from Sir Richard Cholmley, the sheriff of Yorkshire, are not extant with the records of this session.

11. *Lord Cavendish* is crossed out in the MS. preceding *Sir Thomas Hoby.*

12. *they.* Printed edition.

13. *to* is omitted in the printed edition.

14. Concerning the appointment of the committees

of both Houses, see above, H. of C., 1 July, nn. 11 and 13.

15. Robert Caesar and William Ravenscroft had been appointed on 1 July (see above, p. 283) to see if the oaths were enrolled in Chancery. Saunders, one of the Six Clerks of the Chancery (Clerks of the Enrollments), had served an earlier turn as riding clerk in 1618 (see *C.D. 1621*, III, 102–103; V, 354).

Sir H. Marten and Sir Robert Hatton to be added to the committee.[16]

Foreman brought to the bar and charged by MR. SPEAKER with the words in the petition preferred against him by Jones, concerning the bill against swearing.[17]

Richard Wakefield justifies the speaking of the words fully. William Madox affirms as much.[18]

Foreman to remain with the Serjeant till further debate.

MR. SOLICITOR. For his now Majesty's answer to the grievances.[19]

The former order for briefs renewed.[20]

SIR EDWARD COKE moves the answers may be delivered in writing and annexed to the grievances; 2ly, that when the subject complains of a thing against the law, it is no answer 'That this should be limited'; therefore, to petition the King for a fuller answer. 3ly,[21] a select committee to consider which answers not full.

MR. ALFORD. To appoint a time for this.

Mr. Solicitor delivers in the King's answer to the grievances.

[p. 13] The committee about our petition for religion went up to the Lords. Sir Edward Coke to make the report; and he to[22] intimate the joy of this House for his Majesty's presence at the fast.

L. 1ª. An act for the grant of two entire subsidies.

The bill for the subsidy to be read 2ly tomorrow morning, at 7 clock.

SIR EDWARD COKE reports from the conference: That the Lord Keeper said he had lately received a message from the King to the Lords and Commons.[23] That the King had taken into his consideration our safety, yea, more than his own. That the sickness strongly increased; that therefore, when he should hear the Commons were ready (for he[24] would not hasten us in any thing), he would put an end to this sitting.

"Many" places where no instruction, and turn it to "some".[25]

8 article. "do" countenance: who "do, may, or shall", countenance.[26]

1. Remedy.[27] That the particular of Conyers may be omitted because he already removed and punished, and the King will give further order about it.[28]

5. Re[medy]. That the King has taken

---

16. On the appointment of the committee concerning Montagu, see H. of C., 1 July, n. 17. Marten had already been named to the committee on 1 July. Both he and Hatton were part of the committee that had attended the Archbishop of Canterbury concerning Montagu on 1 July (see above, p. 282).

17. Foreman was an alehouse keeper who allegedly had slandered the House regarding its passage the previous session of *An act against swearing and cursing* (*S.R.*, 21 *Jac.* I, c. 20). See Draft Journal, below, and also see above, H. of C., 1 July, n. 7, and below, H. of C., 9 July, n. 13.

18. According to the Draft Journal, below, three witnesses testified in the case.

19. The list of grievances from the 1624 parliament and Charles's answers are printed from Bedford MS. 197 and Petyt 538/8, below, pp. 302–305 and 307–309. The list of grievances and the answers circulated as a separate and are included in several manuscript collections (e.g., Rawl. D. 974, ff. 66–67v, and S.P. 16/4:4). See also, below, n. 46.

20. See below, p. 302 and n. 50.

21. *4ly.* Printed edition.

22. *to* is omitted in the printed edition.

23. For the Lord Keeper's message from the King, see above, H. of L., 4 July, p. 84.

24. *we.* Printed edition.

25. For a copy of the completed petition concerning religion with those sentences and words italicized or annotated which at the Lords' request were resolved to be added or altered by the House of Commons, see above, H. of L., 9 August, pp. 155–160.

26. In the final petition the word order has been altered to: "do, shall, or may". See H. of L., 9 August, p. 156.

27. I.e., concerning article 1 in the section devoted to "The remedies against this contagious and dangerous disease".

28. Conyers was a recusant living and probably teaching in York. He may be the same recusant complained of in Sir Robert Phelips's report on 15 May 1621. See *C.D. 1621*, III, 262; IV, 348; V, 167. Although the reference to Conyers was deleted from the petition concerning religion, we find no corroborative evidence of specific action taken against him by King or parliament.

order that none of his own subjects recusant should serve the Queen. To turn, therefore, that petition into thanks, with request he will continue it.[29]

6. Would not have the word, "close", but would have all restrained from access to them or conference with them; and would have the like for convicted recusants imprisoned, and would have this also for all popish recusants convicted, being imprisoned for debt.

They enlarge it, that neither any foreign nor native bishop shall give orders.

8. They give way that all grants "void or voidable" shall be avoided.

13 article. That the King has taken order that none of his subjects, privileged or other, come to hear mass; to turn, therefore, our petition into thanks, with desire of continuance.

14 article. They desire the particular of Foster may be omitted because punished in part and shall be more [**C.J. 803**] when apprehended,[30] for process out against him and the Lord that protected him has renounced him.

Instead of the general commission for looking to the execution of laws against recusants they change it to a charge given by the King to his judges, justices of peace, etc., to see them executed.[31]

In the conclusion, mention of the King's promise, they desire an alteration: to give him thanks for his resolution and *desire* of the continuance of it, thanks for his many gracious promises.

[p. 14] Resolved, to agree upon a time to be intimated to the King for our recess and

for the manner of it, whether by adjournment or with a session, and a bill to continue all things *in statu quo*. This to be done 1st tomorrow morning.

The 2 first alterations, upon question, agreed.

So that for Conyers.

So that for the Queen's servants.

So the alteration in the word "close", etc.

So the next, for the addition of the word "subjects".

So for the alteration, of looking into the grants of recusants' lands "void and voidable", to be void.

So for the next, for thanks and a petition to continue.

Foster agreed to be omitted.

The special commission to be left out.

The alteration of the conclusion likewise agreed.

For the penning of these alterations:[32]

Sir Edward Coke	Sir Nathaniel Rich
Mr. Solicitor	Mr. [John] Pym
Mr. Recorder	Sir Edwin Sandys
Chancellor Duchy	Sir Francis Seymour

II. DRAFT JOURNAL, MS. 3409, H.L.R.O.

[f. 150v]   *Lunae 4 Julii 1625*

L. 2. An act to enable the King's Majesty to make leases of his Highness's Duchy of Cornwall.

Committed to the knights and burgesses of Devon and Cornwall, and all the lawyers of the House.[33] 2 clock this afternoon, Court of Wards.

L. 3. An act/[34]

Upon question, passed.

29. For the draft version of articles 5, 6, 8, 13, and 14, see H. of L., 9 August, pp. 157–159 and nn. 22–44.

30. Concerning Foster and Lord Teynham, see above, H. of C., 23 June, p. 231 and n. 25, and 28 June, p. 264 and n. 39.

31. Concerning this and the following alteration, see H. of L., 9 August, p. 160 and nn. 45 and 48.

32. *the same subcommittee* is crossed out in the MS. following the word *alterations*. Although appointed in the House, this select committee was apparently considered to be a subcommittee of the Commons' con-

ference committee originally appointed on 23 June (see above, p. 228) and therefore was sometimes referred to as a "subcommittee". Six of these eight members had formed the committee for drawing the petition concerning religion appointed on 28 June (see above, p. 260). This committee of eight met with a corresponding committee of four of the Upper House on 5 July and reported to the Commons on 6 July.

33. *tomorrow* is crossed out in the MS. preceding *2*.

34. Marginal note: "Cheltenham".

SIR GEORGE MORE reports from the committee of privileges, 1, the case of Yorkshire. Sheriff confessed that the poll was demanded and that he granted it before it was demanded. Polled about 30 or 40; said there was double the number of freeholders for Sir Thomas Wentworth and Sir Thomas Fairfax. When he was polling, word was brought that the gate was opened and that Sir John Savile had made some disturbance, and divers of the freeholders gone. Desired to have time to send for witnesses. The committee divided about this; 17 of opinion to have him to have time to send for witnesses, 25 against it.[35]

SIR THOMAS WENTWORTH. If the country be put to a new election, it will be the charge of a subsidy. Can prove directly that for Sir John Savile there came 6 or 7 out of a house that were servants and no freeholders.

[f. 151] The case is this: the poll demanded by Sir John Savile. The sheriff granted the poll. After 11 clock the sheriff began the poll and shut up the gates. The poll by Sir John Savile himself interrupted. Informed by his counsel that this a void demand of the poll, being interrupted by him that demanded it. To have his counsel heard to defend this, or else to have time to send for his witnesses.

SIR CHRISTOPHER HILDYARD. Was present at the election.[36] The poll was demanded at 10 of the clock; sheriff said it was not time, but when it was time they should have it.

MR. GLANVILLE. If the poll demanded in due time but not granted till too late, it is as if it had been denied; so that it comes home to the case of Cambridge where the poll was denied.[37]

Resolved upon question that the sheriff's case, as delivered by him in his petition, and Sir Thomas Wentworth's case, as a party interested, shall be set down and delivered to Sir John Savile this afternoon, that he may give his answer to the House tomorrow.[38]

SIR EDWARD COKE elects to serve for the county of Norfolk.

A message from the Lords by Serjeant Davies and Serjeant Finch.

The Lords signify to this House that they desire a conference, this afternoon at 5 clock, of the same committee touching the petition,[39] and to this end they purpose to sit this afternoon.

Answer: The committee of this House shall give a meeting as it is desired, and/

[f. 151v] SIR ROBERT HATTON elects to serve for Sandwich.

Lunae, 4 Julii, post meridiem

MR. CAESAR. Has, according to the command of the House, searched for the oaths of the treasurers and Council of War. Finds they were duly taken.[40]

Power given to the committee for Mr. Montagu's book to send for all those concerning that business that they think fit. Sir Henry Marten [and] Sir Robert Hatton added to the committee.[41]

The alehouse keeper brought to the bar that slandered the House.[42]

The petition against him read.

Denies those words. Withdrawn.

The witnesses called in. Richard Wakefield affirms the words. John Buckstan. William Madox affirms the words.

35. See above, nn. 3 and 4.
36. See above, n. 6.
37. See above, n. 5.
38. Marginal note: "X". See above, H. of C., 23 June, n. 9.
39. Concerning the appointment of the committees of both Houses, see above, H. of C., 1 July, nn. 11 and 13.
40. See above, n. 15.
41. See above, n. 16.
42. I.e., Foreman. See above, p. 298.

To remain in the Serjeant's hands till further order be taken with him.

MR. SOLICITOR delivers in the King's answer to the last grievances. King Charles, his answer.

The grievances read, and their several answers. To be engrossed and annexed to the petition of grievances.[43]

Our committee sent up to the Lords to confer about the petition concerning religion. Sir Edward Coke to make report, and he to intimate the joy of this House for his Majesty's presence at the fast.

[f. 152] *L. 1ª.* An act for the grant of 2 entire subsidies.

III. MS. 197, BEDFORD ESTATES, LONDON

[f. 20v] 4 *Julii* 1625.

The first part of the morning was spent in a committee about Montagu's book.[44]

SIR GEORGE MORE made a report from the committee of privilege concerning the Yorkshire case. The sheriff had confessed and Sir John Savile had sufficiently proved the poll demanded, granted, but not performed; that it was alleged that it was [f. 21] demanded after eleven of the clock, and interrupted by the misdemeanor of Sir John Savile; and they desire time for witnesses, and, if this case were admitted, to be heard by counsel.

The committee was divided, some thinking the poll so necessary a trial as no election in a case of competition could be without; and for this was vouched the case of Cambridgeshire [in] the last parliament. Others were of opinion that if the poll were demanded before eleven, and not granted

till after, it was a void grant, as in the same case of Cambridge; but if it were not demanded till after, it was a void demand, as was agreed in the case of Gloucestershire the last parliament. And although the demand and the grant were both legal, yet if the interruption were by Sir John Savile, he ought to take no benefit by his own misdemeanor, as was resolved in the case of Pontefract.[45]

MR. CHANCELLOR DUCHY. If we will go to hearing upon bill and answer, you must admit all that the defendant says to be true. So, unless Sir John Savile will agree to the case as it is propounded by Sir Thomas Wentworth, we cannot deny him witnesses.

MR. STRODE. It is not enough to allege an interruption in general, but he must assign the particular action or misdemeanor whereby the sheriff was hindered.

MR. ROLLE. It is no answer for the sheriff to say that he is interrupted; because he has the power of the county, so that it is not to be supposed that any man can interrupt him.

After very long debate it was ordered that Sir Thomas Wentworth should frame this case and deliver it to Sir John Savile to be agreed by tomorrow morning.

A message came from the Lords desiring a conference in the afternoon about the petition concerning religion; which was yielded.

[*Afternoon*]

[f. 21v] *Eodem die post meridiem.*

MR. SOLICITOR delivered his Majesty's answer to the last petition of grievance de-

---

43. Marginal note: "X".

44. Concerning the membership of the committee on Montagu, see H. of C., 1 July, n. 17. John Pym, author of the diary of which Bedford MS. 197 is a copy, was a member of the committee. On 1 July the committee had been designated to meet on 4 July at 7 A.M., before the House convened. Also, see below, H.

of C., 5 July, p. 317 and n. 26.

45. Concerning the election cases of Cambridgeshire and Pontefract in 1624, see above, n. 5. Concerning the 1624 Gloucestershire election, see *C.J.*, I, 759, and Glanville, *Reports,* pp. 99–103. These sources give no indication that the demand of the poll was an issue in the Gloucestershire case.

livered the last parliament to King James.[46]

First, against the patent for the plantation of New England.[47]

Answer. It shall be free for all the King's subjects to perform their fishing voyages upon that coast, yielding a reasonable recompense to the planters for their wood and timber; and if anything in that patent be against law it shall be amended.

2ly. Against the new corporation of Goldwiredrawers.[48]

Answer. The patent is in the Clerk of the Parliament's hand, and is not used, and his Majesty is well pleased that it be recalled by course of law, if they will not voluntarily surrender it.

3ly. Against the patent of concealments granted to Sir John Townshend.[49]

Answer. The patent is delivered to the Clerk of the Commons House and there it is and not used; and if it be thought fit to be revoked by bill, his Majesty will pass it.

4ly. Against licenses called briefs.

Answer. His Majesty has commanded none to be granted but upon certificate in open sessions; and that such certificates shall not be made but upon just cause, and that same county to be always one.

Notwithstanding this answer it was now ordered in the House that the order of the last parliament should stand, that no justices should make any such certificates.[50]

5ly. Against the letters patent of the apothecaries.[51]

[f. 22] Answer. If anything in these letters patent be amiss in the manner and form, his Majesty leaves it to the parliament to be reformed by bill, but because it concerns the life and health of his subjects, he does not think fit it should be left without government in the meantime.

6ly. Against Sir John Meldrum's patent of the lighthouse of Wintertonness.[52]

Answer. This lighthouse is useful and necessary, but if the pay[53] be too great, he wishes it may be moderated; which he refers to the advice of both Houses.

7ly. Against the abuses of Sir Simon Harvey.[54]

Answer. The particular abuses have been

---

46. Marginal note, B.L. Add. 26, 639: "Deut. 6:6". For another copy of the King's 1625 answers to the grievances, see Petyt 538/8, below, pp. 307–309. A fair copy of the 1625 answers (misplaced in the State Papers under 1624) is in S.P. 14/165:55. A quite different draft of the King's answers is in S.P. 16/4:4. Regarding the 1624 petition of grievances, see above, H. of C., 22 June, n. 7.

47. The patent referred to is that granted for the corporation of New England (18 *Jac.* I, pt. 16, MS. Cal. Pat. Rolls, f. 190v) under which Sir Ferdinando Gorges stood to benefit by a virtual monopoly over the fishing industry in that area. The patent was complained of in 1621 and 1624 (*C.D. 1621*, II, 430, 544; III, 408, 441; and *C.J.*, I, 640–641, 669, 688, 697, 777), and the issue was raised again in 1626 (ibid., 863) and 1628 (*C.D. 1628*, II, 512 n. 20). See also the references regarding the New England Plantation cited in *C.D. 1621*, VII, 413.

48. The patent specifically referred to in the petition of grievances was that of 14 June 1623 (MS. Cal. Pat. Rolls, 21 *Jac.* I, pt. 2, f. 105). Concerning the goldwiredrawers, see *C. D. 1621*, VII, 364–370. For the 1624 parliamentary activities regarding Matthias Fowle and the patent, see *C.J.*, I, 705, 726–727, 753, 765, 777, and 795.

49. The patent referred to was the commission of 5 July 1623 granted to the commissioners for defective titles (MS. Cal. Pat. Rolls, 21 *Jac.* I, pt. 8, f. 82). Concerning Sir John Townshend's earlier grants of concealed lands, see *C.D. 1621*, VII, 343–344. Concerning parliamentary activity in 1624 regarding Townshend's patent, see *C.J.*, I, 705, 777, 790, 795.

50. At the time that the House allowed the grievance against licenses called briefs, on 25 May 1624, it ordered that a separate declaration be drawn by the Clerk of the House against certificates of the justices of peace for such briefs. See *C.J.*, I, 795. For the complaints and reports regarding briefs, see ibid., 689, 788, 789, and 795.

51. For a brief history of the Apothecaries as a company separate from the Company of Grocers, see *C.D. 1621*, VII, 324–327. Regarding activities in 1624 concerning the Apothecaries' patent, see *C.J.*, I, 756, 777, 795.

52. Concerning Sir John Meldrum's patent for the Wintertonness lighthouse, see *C.D. 1621*, VII, 397–402. For activity in 1624 regarding the patent, see *C.J.*, I, 702, 706, 710, 787, 790, 794, 795.

53. *tax. C.D. 1625* (Knightley MS.).

54. Regarding the complaints against Sir Simon Harvey, Clerk Comptroller of the Household, and purveyor for the crown, see *C.J.*, I, 702, 781, 782, 787. See also, below, H. of C., 2 August, n. 27.

examined, and the compositions which were the ground of the misdemeanors are set at large.

(This was not accepted as a satisfactory answer.)

8ly. Against grants of the custody of jails to other than sheriffs.[55]

Answer. The sheriffs shall according to law have the custody of jails in those places which are in the King's hand, and all grants to the contrary left to the law.

9ly. Against the patent of surveyorship of Newcastle coals.[56]

Answer. This patent has had no countenance from his Majesty; and the validity of it is left to the law.

10ly. Against multitude of popish and seditious books.

[f. 22v] Answer. A proclamation was lately made to reform the abuses in this kind, which shall be renewed.[57]

SIR HENRY MARTEN. These books consigned to ambassadors and sold in their houses.[58]

11ly. Against the proclamation of buildings.[59]

Answer. There has much good come by the reformation of building, and such points as were formerly found inconvenient are now qualified and altered; and his Majesty is resolved to go forward with the work.

12ly. Against Doctor Anyan.[60]

Answer. When they of the college do complain to his Majesty, he will take care of them.

13ly. Concerning the instructions of the Court of Wards.[61]

Answer. His Majesty will recall the last instructions and will establish new according to the desire.

14ly. Against the Merchant Adventurers.[62]

This consists of several articles concerning trade of cloth, to which there are several answers:

First, the trade of cloth is quickened, and no complaint since the last parliament.

55. The general complaint concerning custody of jails grew out of specific grievances concerning the jails of York, Lancaster, and Worcester. *C.J.*, I, 704, 705, 708, 710–711, 788, 790, 794, 797.

56. This grievance is specifically directed against the patent of Sir Robert Sharpeigh and Alexander Hartley for the surveyorship of Newcastle coals. For 1624 activity regarding the patent, see *C.J.*, I, 685, 711, 712, 736, 795. Concerning the patent, granted in September 1623, see S.P. 14/152:58; and cf. *C.D. 1621*, VII, 429–430.

57. Regarding the 1624 complaint, see *C.J.*, I, 709 and 796. A proclamation against seditious books was issued by the King on 15 August 1624 (*S.T.C.*, no. 8736). It is printed in *Stuart Proclamations*, I, 599–600. See also, *Cal. S.P. Dom., 1623–1625*, p. 327.

58. *places. C.D. 1625* (Knightley MS.).

59. The matter of the Carpenters' petition concerning buildings and proclamations was referred to committee on 25 May 1624 (*C.J.*, I, 711, 794), and was read and allowed by the House on 26 May (ibid., 796). For a history of the grievance, see *C.D. 1621*, VII, 332–338. The latest proclamation concerning buildings had been issued by Charles on 2 May 1625. See *Stuart Proclamations*, II, 20–26.

60. Concerning Dr. Anyan, see above, H. of C., 28

June, n. 19.

61. See below, n. 107.

62. On 19 March 1624 the Company of Merchant Adventurers was ordered to bring in their patent of 28 *Eliz.* I and their account books (*C.J.*, I, 740). A report from the committee on trade was made by Sir Edwin Sandys on 3 April (ibid., 754) and the Company was then ordered to have representatives bring the account books to the meeting of the committee the following Thursday. On 14 April a report was made to the House by the committee that searched the Company books (ibid., 766–767). On 23 and 30 April and 10 May further reports on the Merchant Adventurers were made to the House (ibid., 689, 702, 773–774, 780–781, 787), and on 5 May the issues involving the Company were also debated (ibid., 698–699, 783–784). Finally, on 19 May, the Merchant Adventurers' current patent of January 1618 (MS. Cal. Pat. Rolls, 15 *Jac.* I, pt. 19, f. 161) was declared a grievance (ibid., 706, 791). See also, *C.D. 1621*, VII, 225–238, 412; and *A.P.C., 1623–1625*, pp. 268–269. For a full copy of the several articles of this grievance, see Harl. MS. 4289, ff. 180v–185v (Y.C.P.H. transcripts). See also, the grievance concerning the clothworkers, below, p. 304 and n. 70.

2ly. The many causes of the decay are removed. [1.] Dyed and dressed cloths may be vented by any other to all places except those limited to the Merchant Adventurers. 2. New manufactures by any other to any place. 3. If white cloths be not bought by the Adventurers, any other shall have leave to buy.

[f. 23] 3ly. The imposition laid by the merchant is abated and limited to a shorter time, and afterward is to be laid by.

4ly. His Majesty will write unto his ambassadors with the Archduchess and States concerning the burdens laid upon cloth in those parts.[63]

5ly. His Majesty has not time to examine the pretermitted customs, but leaves it to the next session.[64]

6ly. The fees of the Custom House shall be regulated and tables appointed.

15ly. Concerning the Company of the Merchants of the Levant.[65]

Answer. The imposition is not new, no more than as in Queen Elizabeth's time, and the Venetians offer to bear it, so they may bring in the commodities, which they

will do in English bottoms, which takes away the pretense of overcharge.

16ly. Against the patent of Benin and Guinea.[66]

Answer. This patent is delivered into the hands of the Clerk of the Parliaments, and is left to the law.

SIR HENRY MARTEN affirmed it was never allowed in the Admiralty.

17ly. Against the abuse of alnage.

Answer. The abuses of the deputy alnagers are directed to be reformed by special limitations.[67]

18ly. Concerning perpetuanas and serges.[68]

[f. 23v] Answer. The rates upon serges and perpetuanas have been complained of by the western men, and are moderated to their content.

19ly. Against the abuses of taking of prisage.[69]

Answer. Prisage shall not be taken but according to the rule of justice.

20ly. Concerning clothworkers.[70]

Answer. His Majesty leaves it to the Par-

63. Concerning the impositions placed on cloth by Isabella Clara Eugenia, Archduchess of Flanders, and by the United Provinces of the Netherlands, see C.J., I, 689, 773, 780.

64. Regarding the 1624 complaint against pretermitted customs, see C.J., I, 686, 693, 707, 764–765, 768–769, 778.

65. See below, n. 110.

66. MS.: Bynnie and Ginnye. I.e., the Africa Company. A petition against the patent of the Guinea and Benin (Binney) Company was reported to the House on 19 April 1624 (C.J., I, 771), and on 24 May the committee for trade reported, and the House resolved, the patent a grievance in the creation and execution (C.J., I, 710, 793–794). See also n. 111, below.

67. The abuses of the alnager's office are enumerated in Sir Edwin Sandys's report on 22 May 1624 (C.J., I, 709, 793). Warrants of early 1625 for assistance to be given to the deputy alnagers contained a provision that any deputy alnager who acted contrary to the meaning of the patent and statutes concerning the alnager's office should be sent to appear before the Privy Council. A.P.C., 1623–1625, pp. 444–445; A.P.C., 1625–1626, pp. 47, 88.

68. I.e., the complaint by the western merchants

that the farmers of the custom exact more than is set down in the Book of Rates for serges and perpetuanas. This grievance is included in Sandys's report of 25 May 1624 as a grievance fit to be presented to his Majesty. C.J., I, 711, 794–795. The grievance was presumably remedied by a Privy Council order of 10 September 1624. A.P.C., 1623–1625, p. 313.

69. The grievance of irregularities in the exacting of prisage on wine shipments is included in Sandys's report of 25 May 1624. C.J., I, 711, 795.

70. The clothworkers complained about not having enough work as a result of the Merchant Adventurers' avoidance of the provisions of the statute of 8 Eliz. I, c. 6, and an order of the Privy Council of 12 October 1617 (A.P.C., 1616–1617, pp. 353–355) that one out of every ten cloths exported out of the country should first be dressed. On 19 April 1624 the House resolved that the Merchant Adventurers should conform to the order of the Council or else show cause to the contrary (C.J., I, 771), and on 26 May it agreed to include the clothworkers' complaint in the petition of grievances (C.J., I, 712). See also, the petition from the Company of Clothworkers and Dyers referred from the King to the Council on 18 May 1625. A.P.C., 1625–1626, pp. 61–62.

liament House to consider what is to be done herein.

21ly. Concerning tobacco.[71]

Answer. His Majesty has prohibited all foreign tobacco, and none is to be imported but of the growth of his own dominions.

22ly. Concerning the Eastland merchants.[72]

Answer. The merchants do give way that any other may bring in necessaries for shipping and timber.

23ly. Concerning the impositions upon currants.[73]

Answer. The Venetians are contented to bear this charge so they may have the importation, and they will bring none but in English bottoms.

SIR EDWARD COKE. That the answers may be reduced to a certainty, engrossed, and annexed to the petitions. 2. When the complaint is that a grievance is against law, it is no answer to say it shall be limited. Therefore in such cases to desire a better answer. 3. To appoint a special committee to consider of these answers.

[f. 24] At a conference with the Lords the same day.

My Lord Keeper delivered a message from the King. That his Majesty took into his consideration and care our safety more than his own, the sickness strongly increasing. When he should receive word that we were ready (yet not pressing us to any haste

but such as we should think fit) he would not defer to make an end of this session by his presence, or otherwise.

Divers alterations were desired and agreed to in the petition concerning recusants.

In the 6 and 8 articles of causes, two verbal amendments.[74]

In the first remedy, the particular of Conyers left out; because removed and punished already by his Majesty's direction.[75]

In the 5 and 13 remedies, the petition turned into a thanksgiving, because the King had already given order in both cases.[76]

The sixth remedy touching close imprisonment of priests and Jesuits extended to all other recusants.

The seventh, concerning foreigners executing episcopal jurisdiction, extended to natural subjects.

The 8, concerning avoiding his Majesty's grants of recusants' lands explained by addition of these words: If they shall be void or voidable by law.

In the 14, the particular of Foster left out, a legal course being already taken for the punishing of him.[77]

[f. 24v] The 15, concerning a general commission to see the laws executed against papists left out, because the law has already trusted the judges and justices with it.[78]

In the conclusion, to the remembrance of

---

71. According to the committee report, 24 May 1624, the shortage of money in England was largely the result of the Spanish trade bringing in tobacco rather than bullion, as formerly, to the value of 100,000 *l*. a year. The House therefore petitioned the King to prohibit all imports of tobacco except that grown within the King's own dominions. *C.J.*, I, 794. By Council order, 24 May 1625, all imports of tobacco not grown in English plantations were prohibited. *A.P.C., 1625–1626*, p. 71.

72. For the points raised regarding the Eastland Company, see Sandys's report on 24 May 1624 (*C.J.*, I, 710, 793), and the copy of this grievance in John Holles's compilation, Harl. MS. 4289, ff. 190–191. The petition concerning the Eastland Company was read

and allowed on 26 May 1624. *C.J.*, I, 712, 796.

73. Marginal note in the Earl of Bedford's hand: "Lord Arundel". The 2*s*. 2*d*. imposition on currants which had been reimposed in 1619 had been farmed to Thomas Howard, Earl of Arundel, by indenture of 27 May 1620 (MS. Cal. Pat. Rolls, 18 *Jac.* I, pt. 18). Concerning the complaints against the impositions on currants, see the Levant merchants' grievance (grievance #15), below, p. 309 and n. 110).

74. See above, p. 298 and nn. 25 and 26.

75. See above, n. 28.

76. See above, n. 29.

77. See above, n. 30.

78. See above, n. 31.

the King's promise an addition made of thanks, with a desire it may be continued.

IV. PETYT 538/8, INNER TEMPLE LIBRARY

[f. 120] *Die Lunae. 27 Junii* [*sic*][79]

The report[80] of the election of the knights of Yorkshire was made by SIR GEORGE MORE. And a petition preferred by Sir John Savile was read, showing that Sir Thomas Wentworth, who was one of the knights for Yorkshire, was not duly elected. And upon debate,[81] the cause appeared to be that Sir Thomas Wentworth and Sir Thomas Fairfax, that are now in the House, knights of the shire, did join together, and Sir John Savile did also stand to be knight of the shire, and came to the sheriff [and,][82] about 10 a clock, demanded the poll. The sheriff granted it and, preparing to enter into it, and having shut up the castle gates all to one, and about 11 of the clock he entered into the poll and, having numbered some 30ta and upwards, and was in numbering of [f. 120v] the rest. Sir John Savile, having divers freeholders without the gate, to the number of 3 or 400, caused one of the gates to be opened to let in his freeholders which, being told unto the sheriff, he conceived [it] to be an interruption by Sir John Savile and thereupon broke off the poll and pronounced Sir Thomas Wentworth and Sir Thomas Fairfax knights of the shire, conceiving that by the view and care[83] they had the major voice, and returned them. And in the petition were

some 400[84] names [of] freeholders, and the petition only against Sir Richard[85] Cholmley, the sheriff, for an undue election and return. And the House proceeded against the sheriff only with an order that it should not be prejudicial to the title of Sir Thomas Wentworth until they were heard in it. And upon examination the case appeared and was agreed to be that the sheriff, conceiving that Sir John Savile had interrupted the poll by causing the postern gate to be opened so that he needed not to proceed any further in it, for that those that came after eleven a clock and were let in at the gate by Sir John Savile ought not, as he conceived, to have voice and, being mingled with others, could not be [f. 121] discerned, the sheriff broke off the poll. And for that he conceived Sir Thomas Wentworth [and] Sir Thomas Fairfax had the major voice, he pronounced them sheriffs [*sic*].[86]

Now, this being admitted of all sides to be the case, the House resolved the election to be undue because the sheriff proceeded not to the poll, which was the true and most indifferent trial.[87] And it was then also conceived by divers that the freeholders that came while they were polling came time enough to give voice, and that here was no such disturbance by Sir John Savile as might hinder the sheriff so that he could not proceed to finish the poll. And a warrant awarded for a new election, but the sheriff not punished.

Sir John Cutts his case of Cambridgeshire[88] was cited, where the sheriff being

79. The author of the original MS. of which Petyt 538/8, B.L. Add. 48,091, and Q.C. 449 are copies compiled the proceedings of 22 June and 4 and 5 July concerning the Yorkshire election into a single narrative which we have placed here on Monday, 4 July.

80. *respect.* Q.C. 449.

81. *upon due debate.* Q.C. 449.

82. The bracketed words here and below are included in B.L. Add. 48,091 and Q.C. 449 but omitted in Petyt 538/8.

83. *hue and cry.* B.L. Add. 48,091, and Q.C. 449. See above, n. 4.

84. *1400.* B.L. Add. 48,091 and Q.C. 449. Concern-

ing the figure given for the number of subscribers to the freeholders' petition, cf. above, H. of C., 22 June, p. 217 and n. 16.

85. Petyt 538/8 and Q.C. 449 erroneously give the name as *Hugh.* In B.L. Add. 48,091 the name has been correctly altered from *Hugh* to *Richard.*

86. *knights of the shire.* B.L. Add. 48,091 and Q.C. 449.

87. This resolution occurred on 5 July. See below, H. of C., 5 July, O.B.

88. *Sir John Cutts, knight of Cambridgeshire.* Q.C. 449. Concerning the Cambridgeshire case, see above, n. 5.

required to go to the poll, refused, and pronounced and returned two to be knights of the shire, and that election adjudged here to be void, and a warrant made for a new election by the Speaker, by the order of the House, etc.[89]

[Afternoon]

[f. 115v][90] It was moved to have his Majesty's answer to our petition of grievances, and also to our petition of religion, both which were ready;[91] and this to be done before such time as they entered into any debate of grieving,[92] or the manner of it, which petitions were both preferred to his late Majesty at the end of the last session of parliament and yet unanswered. And thereupon it was moved that the best manner of preferring petitions in such kind, and to have redress, is to pursue the old manner of preferring petitions, which was always wont to be in such a convenient time before the rising of the parliament that his Majesty may have time to answer the same sitting of the parliament, that so we may know was[93] his Majesty will do.

Whereof his Majesty, having notice, did answer the petition of grievances, which answer was afterwards declared by Mr. Solicitor in the House particularly to [f. 116] every grievance, after the reading thereof. The particulars whereof briefly were as follows:

1. A complaint against Sir Ferdinando Gorges's patent for sole fishing in New England, being a monopoly.[94]

His Majesty's answer: This patent shall be left to the construction of law, and the traders shall take wood (for dressing their boats) and fishes, paying for the same.

2. A complaint made against the patent made to Fowle and other for the making of gold and wire thread.[95]

Answer: This patent is in the House and has not been put in use since it was brought in, and if they yield not up their patent, it shall be repealed, or they left to the law.

3. A complaint against Sir John Townshend's patent of concealments.[96]

Answer: The patent is brought into the House and there remains; and his Majesty is pleased that neither he nor any claiming under him shall prosecute the same, and the commission whereupon it was grounded is recalled.

[f. 116v] 4. A complaint against the frequent and usual setting out of briefs published and collected in parish churches.[97]

Answer: That none should be granted hereafter but in open sessions or assizes, and that their own countries should be included as well as others.

5. A complaint against the patent that does make the Apothecaries of London to be a sole company and not to be mixed with the Grocers as anciently as they had been.[98]

Answer: This to be left to a bill to be passed in both Houses; the Apothecaries in the meantime season not [to be][99] without government.

89. In the MS. this entry is followed by Sir Francis Seymour's motion for giving one subsidy. See above, H. of C., 30 June, p. 279.

90. The following entries occur in the MS. after the account of Serjeant Hitcham's report concerning Lady Coppin's petition against Sir William Cope and the remarks concerning the case of Arthur Basset (see above, pp. 234–235). Following the chronology of the Commons Journal, we have placed the entries here on 4 July, the day on which Solicitor Heath presented the King's answers to the 1624 grievances. For the original motions for the King's answer to the 1624 petition of grievances, etc., referred to below, see above, H. of C.,

22 June, pp. 216–217 and 220.

91. read. B.L. Add. 48,091 and Q.C. 449.

92. giving. B.L. Add. 48,091 and Q.C. 449.

93. what. B.L. Add. 48,091 and Q.C. 449.

94. See above, n. 47.

95. Regarding the patent granted to Matthias Fowle, see above, n. 48.

96. See above, n. 49.

97. See above, n. 50.

98. See above, n. 51.

99. The bracketed words here and below are included in B.L. Add. 48,091 and Q.C. 449, but omitted in Petyt 538/8.

6. A complaint against Sir John Meldrum's [patent] for setting up of lights at Wintertonness and taking of 3s. 4d. a ton, whereas the lights were provided before by the Trinity House at 6d. a ton and the lighthouse made by them according to the statute of 8vo of *Eliz.*[100]

Answer: The house is needful, but if the tax be too great, to be moderated by both Houses.

[f. 117] 7. A complaint against Sir Simon Harvey for that he being his Majesty's purveyor did waste his Majesty's stock of victuals brought in and took up victuals contrary to law.[101]

Answer: The particular abuses complained of have been examined and the composition whereupon the same was grounded set at liberty.

8. A complaint that the custody of common jails were granted by letters patent to farm to others than the sheriffs, as York and Lancaster.[102]

Answer: The sheriffs are by law to have the custody of all jails, and the patents granted were left to the law.

9. A complaint against the imposition laid upon Newcastle coals by letters to Sir Robert Sharpeigh, being a native commodity, which is burdensome and unlawful.[103]

Answer: The patent has no validity from his Majesty but is left to the law; but note: there is no answer to the laying of an imposition upon a native commodity.

[f. 117v] 10. A complaint[104] against the printing and publishing of popish and seditious books, which they desire may be suppressed.

Answer: A proclamation was made in King James his time to reform abuses in this kind, which shall be renewed.

11. A complaint against the restraint of building whereby people cannot repair or amend their houses without new building the forepart with brick, which is a grievance which they desire may be repealed.[105]

Answer: There has much good come by reformation of building and divers things therein amended in his father's time, and his Majesty is resolved to go on with the work.

12. A complaint against [Dr.] Anyan, head of Corpus Christi College.[106]

Answer: If they of the College do complain unto his Majesty of him, he will take a course in it.

13. A petition of grace that divers good orders concerning wards and lunatics made and published by his late Majesty in the time that the Earl of Salisbury was Master of the Wards [f. 118] and altered by the late instructions by the Earl of Middlesex, to the great grievance and oppression of his Majesty's subjects, may be revived and the other recalled.[107]

Answer: His Majesty will recall the latter and publish the former according to your desire.

14. A complaint of the Merchant Adventurers of the decay of trade and the reasons

---

100. See above, n. 52. The statute is *S.R.*, 8 *Eliz.* I, c. 13.

101. See above, n. 54.

102. See above, n. 55.

103. See above, n. 56.

104. *complaint made.* Q.C. 449. Concerning the proclamation against seditious books, see above, n. 57.

105. See above, n. 59.

106. Concerning Dr. Anyan, see above, H. of C., 28 June, n. 19.

107. For the Instructions for the Court of Wards and Liveries promulgated in 1611 during the Mastership of Robert Cecil, Earl of Salisbury, see S.P. 14/61:6

and *Bibliotheca Lindesiana*, V, no. 1107. The petition of grievances actually called for the revival of those Instructions published in December 1618 (*S.T.C.*, no. 9239), rather than those of 1611. For the Instructions promulgated in 1622 while Lionel Cranfield, Earl of Middlesex, was Master of the Wards, see Rymer, *Foedera*, VII, pt. 4, pp. 3–8. Complaints against the alterations in the Instructions formed part of the charge against Cranfield in 1624 (see *L.J.*, III, 308, 375) and were reported as a grievance on 19 May 1624 (*C.J.*, I, 790) and allowed by the House on 25 May (ibid., 711, 795).

thereof, as impositions, etc., which they desire to be remedied.[108]

Answer: There is now no complaint of want of work by clothiers or workmen. Prices of wool rise and a bill may be drawn to stay[109] exportation; and for the pretermitted customs, his Majesty has had no time to consider of them as yet, but against the next meeting he will consider of them and then give an answer like a good, a gracious king.

15. A complaint by the Turkish merchants of impositions and extraordinary imposition laid [sic] burden laid upon currants, viz., 5s. 6d. the ton [sic], whereas of old it was but 18d. a ton.[110]

[Answer:] For the charge laid on currants, it is [f. 118v] not new but old in Queen Elizabeth's time. And the Venetians themselves offered to bring the same home in English bottoms under that burden.

16. A complaint against Sir Richard Hawkins's patent by the merchants of Guinea.[111]

Answer: This patent is left to the law.

17. A complaint against the abuse of the office of alnage in taking of money for which they ought not to take any at all, as for stuffs, and exacting more than they should where they may take, and for neglect[ing to] do their office, which happens by the deputies that execute that office.[112]

Answer: The abuses of the deputy officers are directed to be reformed by special limitation.

18. A complaint against the abuse in making of serges and Devonshire cottons, which grows by reason of the burden laid on them.[113]

Answer: The abuses of those enhancements are moderated to their good content.

19. A complaint against the enhancing and raising of prices of wine by impositions set thereon.[114]

[f. 119] Answer: The prices of wine shall not be enhanced contrary to law and justice.

20. A complaint made against[115] the clothworkers for dressing and dying of cloths.

Answer: His Majesty leaves this to the parliament to take it into their consideration.

21. A petition that no tobacco be imported but of our own growth.[116]

Answer: His Majesty is pleased that none from henceforth be imported.

22. A petition by the Eastland Company that strangers should not bring in their commodities in English bottoms.[117]

Answer: The Eastland Company does assent that strangers shall bring in those [commodities,] prout, etc.

These being read, and his Majesty's an-

108. See above, nn. 62–64.
109. expel. Q.C. 449.
110. On 24 May 1624 the committee of trade reported its opinion regarding the Levant merchants' complaint against the 5s. 6d. per cwt. impost on currants. The committee suggested that the King should be petitioned to remove the 2s. 2d. portion of the impost which had been reimposed in 1619 after being remitted in 1608. The House resolved to petition the King accordingly (C.J., I, 710, 794). For a brief history of the imposts on currants from the time of Queen Elizabeth, see C.D. 1628, III, 447 n. 10, 450 nn. 34 and 35.
111. See above, n. 66. Although Sir Richard Hawkins was a member of the Africa Company, it is unclear why his name appears here since the complaints in the House were directed against Sir William St. John and other principal patentees of the Company. The basis of the complaint was that the patent, granted in August 1618, had been given under false pretenses since Sir John Hawkins and others had traded in those areas of Africa some fifty years before the patentees professed to have "discovered" the trade.
112. See above, n. 67.
113. See above, n. 68.
114. See above, n. 69.
115. by. B.L. Add. 48,091 and Q.C. 449. Concerning the clothworkers' complaint, see above, n. 70.
116. See above, n. 71.
117. See above, n. 72.

swer thereto publicly declared, being taken in writing by Mr. Solicitor, it was ordered by the House, upon the motion of SIR EDWARD COKE, that the same should be engrossed and enrolled in the House and subscribed under each petition, to the intent that they may be perused by a [f. 119v] committee, that at our next meeting we petition his Majesty for a full answer where it is not fully answered and give thanks for that where it is fully answered; which was ordered accordingly.[118]

118. This entry is followed in the MS. by materials concerning the petition for a fast. See above, H. of C., 24 June, p. 242.

Committee concerning **Montagu**:
  meets   317,*29/6
L. 2a. An act for the grant of two
  entire **subsidies** by the
  temporalty   313, 316, *30/6
JOHN DELBRIDGE   313
Subsidy bill committed to a
  committee of the whole
  House, 2 o'clock this
  afternoon   313, 316
L. 1a. An act of a subsidy of
  tonnage and poundage (SIR
  ROBERT HEATH, Solicitor) [*see
  below*]   313, 316, *6/7;
                                          7/7; 8/7; 9/7;
                                          11/7

SIR CLEMENT THROCKMORTON:
  delivers in a petition from Sir
  Francis **Wortley**, M.P.   316
Petition from Sir Francis Wortley:
  read   313, 316
Ordered: Speaker to write a letter
  for stay of the suit in Star
  Chamber: the contempt
  referred to the committee of
  privileges   313, 316
SIR EDWARD COKE   313
Ordered: letter to be written for
  stay of suit in Chancery
  against Sir Wolstan **Dixie**,
  M.P.   313, 316
L. 1a and *L. 2a.* An act that this
  session of parliament shall
  not determine by royal assent
  to one or more acts:
  committed to committee of
  the whole House   313, 316, 317,
                                          *4/7; 6/7;
                                          7/7; 8/7; 9/7;
                                          11/7
HENRY ROLLE   317
L. 2a. An act of a subsidy of
  tonnage and poundage [*see
  above and below*]   313, 316, 317;
                                          N, 510

SIR WALTER ERLE   313, 317
SIR ROBERT PHELIPS   313, 317
SIR ROBERT HEATH (Solicitor)   314, 317
SIR EDWARD COKE   314, 318
THOMAS SHERWILL   318
Message to the Lords about the
  alterations to the **petition
  concerning religion** and
  desiring dispatch of all **bills**
  sent up to the Lords (Sir
  Edward Coke, *et al.*) [*see
  below*]   314, 316, *24/6
HENRY ROLLE: on the subsidy of
  tonnage and poundage [*see
  above*]   314
SIR FRANCIS SEYMOUR   314
ROBERT BATEMAN   314
Ordered: bill of subsidy of
  tonnage and poundage
  committed to a committee of
  the whole House   314, 316; **N**,
                                          511

Report of the Lords' answer to
  the message: Lords agree to a
  present meeting by
  subcommittee of both Houses
  for penning the alterations to
  the **petition concerning
  religion** (SIR EDWARD COKE)
  [*see above*]   314, 316
SIR GEORGE MORE: on the
  Yorkshire election   314, 316, *21/6
Dispute over whether the bar
  should be down for Sir John
  Savile's coming into the
  House   314, 316
Resolved: the bar shall not be put
  down   314
Sir John Savile: moves that
  Wentworth, Fairfax, and the
  sheriff may subscribe the case
  and avow it to be true   314, 316; **N**,
                                          514
The case subscribed by
  Wentworth and Fairfax   314, 316

TUESDAY, 5 JULY 1625

I. JOURNAL OF THE HOUSE OF COMMONS

[C.J. 803]
[p. 14] *Martis, 5° Julii, 1° Caroli Regis*

L. 2^a. An act for the grant of 2 entire subsidies.[1]

MR. DELBRIDGE. That commissioners tax men higher and lower at their pleasure, not respecting the taxations brought in by the taxation.

Committed to a committee of the whole House, 2 clock this afternoon.

L. 1^a. An act of a subsidy of tonnage and poundage.

A petition from[2] Sir Francis Wortley,[3] read.

Ordered, Mr. Speaker shall write a letter for stay of the suit in Star Chamber. The contempt referred to the committee of privileges.

SIR EDWARD COKE. That *17° E. 4*[4] informations by the Attorney General, in the King's own name, stayed by order here.

A letter to be written for stay of a suit in Chancery, for Sir W. Dixie, and a warrant to the party and he to have privilege.[5]

[L.] 1^a, [L.] 2^a. An act that this session of parliament shall not determine by his Majesty's royal assent to any act or acts of parliament.

[p. 15] Committed to a committee of the whole House, this afternoon, after the subsidy done.[6]

L. 2^a. An act of a subsidy of tonnage and poundage.

SIR W. ERLE. That the Turkish pirates come into our seas and take our ships at our doors.[7]

Pretermitted custom drawn in by this statute.[8] To commit it to a committee of the whole House.

SIR ROBERT PHELIPS. That this bill temporary till 21 *H.* 6;[9] since, granted for life. 3 additions to this bill: 1, limitation of time, to make it temporary till the payment of the last subsidy; 2, a private saving to all officers who have collected this since the last King's death, a thing much questioned *1° Jac.;*[10] 3,

---

1. *Sir Thomas Canon [illegible] for Haverfordwest* is crossed out in the MS. following the word *subsidies*. Canon was M.P. for Haverfordwest.

2. *of*. Printed edition.

3. *George Savile* is crossed out in the MS. and *Sir Francis Wortley* put in its place. We have been unable to find the petition from Sir Francis Wortley, M.P. for East Retford, or to determine the nature of the Star Chamber suit against him (see Draft Journal, below).

4. *Rot. Parl.,* 17 *E.* IV, no. 35. See also, Coke, *Fourth Inst.,* p. 24 (the marginal note incorrectly gives no. 36).

5. The letter written on the behalf of Sir Wolstan Dixie, M.P. for Leicestershire, is not extant with the manuscripts of proceedings for this session. We have been unable to determine the nature of the suit in Chancery against him.

6. *Sir Edward Coke* is crossed out in the MS. following the word *done*. Concerning the matter of an adjournment with royal assent given to bills, see above, H. of L., 6 July, n. 4.

7. There are numerous accounts of Turkish pirates on the English coast during the time of this parliament. See S.P. 16/1:68, 94; 2:33, 36; 3:76; 4:35; 5:6, 8, 23, 24, 32, 49, 55, 81, 90. See also the report concern-

ing pirates, H. of C., 11 August, below, particularly Bedford MS. 197 (pp. 459–460) and the Dyott diary (p. 468).

8. Edmund Nicholson, projector of the pretermitted customs granted in 1618, had argued that the statute of tonnage and poundage of 1 *Jac.* I (*S.R.,* 1 *Jac.* I, c. 33) allowed for the collection of customs on cloth made of wool as well as on wool itself. In its decision to petition against the pretermitted customs as a grievance in 1624, the House determined that such customs on cloth were excepted from the statute of tonnage and poundage and therefore had no legal basis. See *C.J.,* I, 693, 764–765, 768–769, 778.

9. I.e., the bill for tonnage and poundage. Tonnage of wine and poundage was granted to H. VI for life in 1453 (*Rot. Parl.,* 31 *H.* VI, no. 8; *S.R.,* 31 *H.* VI, c. 8), and was regularly granted for life to subsequent monarchs. Prior to 31 *H.* VI only H. V (*Rot. Parl.,* 3 *H.* V, no. 5) had received a grant of tonnage and poundage for more than a set number of years. See Coke, *Fourth Inst.,* p. 32

10. Although abuses by officials had been discussed during debates on a bill concerning customs officers and on the tonnage and poundage bill in King James's

a public saving that nothing in this act may be pressed against us for maintenance of impositions. To commit it.

MR. SOLICITOR moves to commit the bill to the general committee of the whole House.

SIR EDWARD COKE. Dislikes the word, "advice of the Lords".

Sir Edward Coke to desire the Lords to hasten the passage of the bills we have sent unto them.

MR. ROLLE. 1 *H*. 5, this subsidy granted but for one year; 2 *H*. 5, for 3 years.[11]

SIR FRANCIS SEYMOUR. To have this bill limited to Our Lady day next.[12]

MR. BATEMAN. No impositions nor pretermitted custom when this bill formerly passed. To have the Book of Rates surveyed.[13]

Committed to a committee of the whole House, this afternoon after the subsidy bill and that for the session done.

SIR EDWARD COKE reports from the Lords: That the Lords have appointed the committee about alteration of the petition of the House to meet presently; and have appointed 4 Lords.[14]

SIR GEORGE MORE. That Sir John Savile, though he received the case yesternight

very late, so as he could not peruse it till this morning, yet his answer ready, and desires to be heard a few words in the House upon the delivery thereof.

Dispute whether, Sir John Savile being called in, the bar should be put down.[15]

Resolved, the bar shall not be put down.

Sir John shows the case was not delivered him till this morning, yet has given an answer to make an end of this business.

Moves, Sir Thomas Wentworth, Sir Thomas Fairfax, and the sheriff may subscribe the case delivered Sir John Savile; that they may, upon their reputations, avow so much as concerns their own knowledge to be true; and that they believe the rest to be true.

Which they accordingly did.

[p. 16] Sir John Savile delivers in his answer and, required by the House, subscribes it in the same manner.

SIR THOMAS WENTWORTH. That it exceedingly imports him to make good what he has set down upon his own knowledge. Which being denied, desires liberty for his defense by counsel and witnesses.

MR. WHISTLER. Admitting the case, as Sir Thomas Wentworth, etc., have set down, yet the election not good. Is against the shutting of the gate.[16] The freeholders in-

---

first parliament (*C.J.*, I, 181, 199, 207, 232, 237, 239), no saving to the officers was incorporated in the ensuing tonnage and poundage statute. *S.R.*, 1 *Jac.* I, c. 33.

11. *Rot. Parl.*, 1 *H*. V, no. 17. According to this act the 3*s.* subsidy on wines was to be paid for one year, from the feast of St. Michael's to the feast of St. Michael's, although the rest of the act grants subsidy of tonnage and poundage for four years. In 2 *H*. V the wine subsidy and customs on cloth and foodstuffs were granted for a three year period. *Rot. Parl.*, 2 *H*. V, no. 7.

12. I.e., 25 March 1626.

13. *Sir William Strode* is crossed out in the MS. following *surveyed*.

14. For the committee of eight appointed by the Lower House to pen the alterations, see above, H. of

C., 4 July, p. 299 and n. 32. For the Lords' committee of four, see above, H. of L., 5 July, p. 89.

15. Generally the practice was that the bar was down when witnesses were brought in, but Lords and others of high rank were admitted within the bar. Hatsell, *Precedents*, II, 125–150. The resolution that the bar should not be put down was presumably a sign of respect for Savile who had been an M.P. in 1624 and several previous parliaments and was now contesting a return which was yet to be decided by the House.

Reports on the Yorkshire election case were made to the House 22 June and 5 July (see O.B.s). For a further account of the election, see below, *Negotium*, pp. 511–516.

16. See Sir George More's report, above, H. of C., 4 July, p. 295.

terested, as well as Sir John Savile, so as he, being *particeps criminis,* cannot wrong the country.

SIR GEORGE MORE. That the sheriff has misdemeaned himself. Yet doubts the election not void.

MR. SOLICITOR. That, admitting this case, Sir John Savile in the wrong. For the sheriff, having adjudged the election of Sir Thomas W[entworth] and Sir Thomas Fairfax, and returned them, this stands good till avoided by plain and good matter. If he denied the poll, good cause to avoid the election, or if he do any thing unfitting in it; but if Sir John Savile disturbed the election, and so made it impossible for the sheriff to go rightly on with the poll, then no default in the sheriff.

MR. ROLLE, *contra.* The not pursuing the poll and denying the poll all one. Sir John Savile could not waive his election, being elected;[17] therefore, his interruption made not the election and return of the other good.

Motion made for counsel to be heard, for Sir Thomas Wentworth to have counsel. The voice doubtful. The House divided; the yea went out.

Tellers for the yea:	Sir Francis Seymour
	Mr. Wandesford
For the no:	Lord Cavendish
	Sir D. Digges
With the yea:	94
	Difference: 39.
With the no:	133

A motion from Sir Thomas Wentworth, that he may be heard a few words.

Debate about it. SIR JOHN ELIOT against it.

Upon question, Sir Thomas Wentworth to be called in.

SIR THOMAS WENTWORTH opens his own case in the particulars: That the sheriff had no power when new men were let in to give them oath, whether they were present at the election or not; for a *praemunire,* if he [**C.J. 804**] had, having no power by the statute to minister that oath, and so impossible.[18] Moves for stay of the resolution of this business, being matter in law may be referred to a full House.

[p. 17] SIR H. ANDERSON moves to have it deferred till tomorrow.

SIR H. MILDMAY, *contra.*

Upon question, this business to be now determined.

MR. GLANVILLE. Adjudged, in the case of Arundel, that so many as came in during the polling had right of voices. So in the case of Gloucester.[19]

Upon question resolved, that the case concerning the election of the knights for Yorkshire, being admitted, the election of the said knights is not duly made, and a warrant for a new election.[20]

Resolved upon the question, that the sheriff shall be no further questioned concerning the election or return of the knights of Yorkshire.

17. On 2 March 1624, with regard to the Southwark election case, the House agreed that a man once chosen cannot waive his election. See *C.J.,* I, 724, and the Pym diary, Finch-Hatton MS. 50, f. 14 (Y.C.P.H. transcripts). This policy was confirmed later in the same parliament by the opinion of the committee of privileges concerning the Gloucestershire election case. See Glanville, *Reports,* p. 101.

18. Sheriffs were empowered by statute to administer an oath to electors as to whether they had 40s.

freehold. *S.R.,* 8 *H.* VI, c. 7.

19. See the reports of the 1624 cases of Arundel and Gloucester in John Glanville's *Reports,* pp. 71–75, 99–103. In the capacity of chairman of the committee of privileges in 1624 Glanville compiled and kept the reports of disputed election cases concerning that parliament.

20. *Upon a 2 question the sheriff guilty of [interlined: freely of] an [illegible] but not of a crime and not to be further punished* is crossed out in the MS. following *election.*

II. DRAFT JOURNAL, MS. 3409, H.L.R.O.

[f. 152v]   *Martis 5 Julii 1625*

L. 2ª. An act for the grant of 2 entire subsidies granted by the temporality.

Committed to a committee of the whole House, this afternoon, 2 clock, in the House.

MR. SOLICITOR delivers in the bill for tonnage and poundage.

L. 1ª. An act of a subsidy of tonnage and poundage.

SIR CLEMENT THROCKMORTON delivers in a petition from Sir Francis Wortley, a member of this House.[21] Desires the privilege of the House. Process served upon him in a suit in the Star Chamber.

Ordered, a letter shall be written by the Speaker to the Star Chamber for stay of this suit. The contempt referred to the committee of privileges.[22]

A letter to be written for stay of a suit of Sir Wolstan Dixie in the Chancery.[23]

L. 1ª. An act that this session of parliament shall not determine by his Majesty's royal assent to some especial acts.

L. 2ª. An act that this session of parliament shall not determine by his Majesty's royal assent to some especial acts.

Committed to a committee of the whole House this afternoon, after the bill of subsidy.

L. 2ª. An act of a subsidy of tonnage and poundage.

Committed to a committee of the whole House this afternoon after the other 2 bills.

[f. 153] Sir Edward Coke and the rest of the subcommittee sent up to the Lords about the alterations of the petition of religion.[24]

SIR EDWARD COKE reports from the Lords. Acquainted them that this House had agreed to all the alterations. Had appointed 4 of their House.

SIR GEORGE MORE. Sir John Savile ready to give his answer to the House.

Desires to be heard a word or 2 himself.

Sir John Savile brought in, the bar not down, after much debate.[25]

Says the case was delivered him but this morning.

Desires of the House that Sir Thomas Wentworth and Sir Thomas Fairfax and the sheriff may subscribe their names to the case and aver it to be true for so much as is upon their own knowledge, and, for the rest, that they believe it to be true.

This done by the gentlemen accordingly.

The sheriff of Yorkshire, Sir Richard Cholmley, brought in, who also subscribed the case.

Sir John Savile brought in again.

MR. SPEAKER acquainted him how that the gentlemen had freely subscribed the case.

Delivered in his answer to the case; which was read, and subscribed by Sir John Savile.

SIR THOMAS WENTWORTH. To believe neither part till the matter in fact be proved. Makes no question but he shall be able to prove it as strongly as may be. Desires he may have liberty from the House to defend himself by those weapons whereby he is opposed: counsel and witnesses.

Withdrawn.

[f. 153v] Upon question whether Sir Thomas Wentworth should be heard by counsel; the House divided.

21. See above, n. 3.
22. Marginal note: "X". On the use of this mark, see above, H. of C., 23 June, n. 9.
23. Marginal note: "X". Concerning the suit against Dixie, see above, n. 5.
24. See above, n. 14.
25. See above, n. 15.

Lord Cavendish ⎫
Sir Dudley Digges ⎬ tellers for the no
133 for the no.

Sir Francis Seymour ⎫
Mr. Wandesford ⎬ for the yea
94 for the yea.

Counsel not to be admitted.

Sir Thomas Wentworth, upon question admitted into the House to speak for himself, desires to respite this business until tomorrow.

Upon question, now to be ended.
Upon question, the election of the knights of the county of York is unduly made. A warrant to go for a new election.
Resolved upon question that the sheriff shall be no further questioned upon this return.

III. MS. 197, BEDFORD ESTATES, LONDON

[f. 24v]   5° Julii 1625.

The first part of the morning was spent in the committee for Montagu.[26]

An act for the adjournment of parliament.[27]
[f. 25] It contained that his Majesty might give his royal assent either before or after the adjournment without determining the session.

To this, exception was taken by Mr. Rolle, alleging 3 H. 6, where the Commons claim a privilege that the royal assent should be during their sitting.[28]

An act for the subsidy of tonnage and poundage.
This bill produced divers motions.

Sir Walter Erle. That the Narrow Seas may be better guarded than they have been; it being the consideration upon which this grant was first made, and that for want hereof divers ships have been of late taken upon our own shore.[29]
That it might not now pass for the King's life, till the point of the pretermitted customs be examined, which is founded upon this grant,[30] and in the meantime it might be limited for a year.

Sir Robert Phelips seconded him in both and added that it might so be passed as not to exclude the question of other impositions. Until H. the 6 time, this grant had never other than a temporary limitation.[31] Kings ever received it as a gift of the subject and were therewith contented without charging them with any other way of imposition; for if they had any such power, it were altogether unneedful to pass.
That there might be a saving for the security of those that have received these rates since the King's death, for after the death of Q. Eliz., 1° Jac., the officers were questioned in parliament for the like offense.[32]

Mr. Solicitor spoke against any change in the limitation, because it had continued so many descents and might be distasteful to the King, [f. 25v] who would be as inclinable to do matters of grace to us as any

26. Presumably this was a meeting of the same committee on Montagu that met at 7 a.m. the previous day. See H. of C., 4 July, p. 301 and n. 44.
    Following the notice of the committee on Montagu, Bedford MS. 197 contains two declarations concerning the 1624 subsidy disbursements which were part of the business of the following day (6 July). In order to maintain the chronology of business given in the C.J., the editors have inserted these declarations into the proceedings of 6 July, below.
27. I.e., an act that this session of parliament shall

not determine by his Majesty's royal assent to any act or acts of parliament. See above, n. 6.
28. We are unable to determine to what precedent Henry Rolle is referring.
29. The early grants of tonnage and poundage (see above, n. 11) had stipulated that the money was to be used for guarding the seas. Concerning ships taken along the English coasts, see above, n. 7.
30. See above, n. 8.
31. See above, n. 9.
32. See above, n. 10.

of his ancestors; yet he yielded it should be committed, and that some short proviso might be annexed to save our right in these questions.

SIR E. COKE excepted against those words, "advised by the Lords".[33] 9 *H.* 4,[34] the Lords moved for a subsidy,[35] which the Commons would not endure.

MR. SHERWILL. That there may be a proviso that the officers may receive the entries and the subsidy accordingly when they shall be tendered, which now they often refuse, both in respect of their own fees and of other impositions.

Q. What was done in my absence being at a subcommittee with the Lords for amendment of the petition according to the particulars agreed.[36]

Somewhat late in the afternoon I found the House not risen, having continued all that while in the question of the election of Yorkshire.

MR. GLANVILLE. The rules of this House not according to the rules of inferior courts. Damage against a sheriff is a recompense in ordinary actions, but not in case of the liberty of the kingdom. Fear is no justification

for a judge, sheriff, or other great officer for not doing their duty. 21 *R.* 2, the King demanded [of] the judges why he might not command the sheriff to return such of the parliament as he should name.[37] They delivered their opinions that he might. Afterward being therefore questioned, one of them answered that they should have been hanged if they had done otherwise; and yet withal confess that they deserved to be hanged for doing as they did. But if there be not a necessity of trial by the poll, then in many cases may the sheriff return whom he will. The reasons given on Sir Thomas Wentworth's behalf, he answered thus:

[f. 26] [1.] Where it is alleged that his number was the greater, which they offer to prove. In the case of Southwark (21 *Jac.*) there was a number sufficient, but because the poll was demanded and not performed, it was judged a void return.[38]

2ly. That the door was opened and divers of Sir John Savile's company let in after eleven of the clock. In the case of Arundel for a borough and of Gloucestershire for a county, it was adjudged that the burgesses and freeholders ought to be admitted at any time during the election.[39]

---

33. The C.J. records "advice" rather than "advised".

34. For the subsidy grant, see *Rot. Parl., 9 H.* IV, no. 26. Concerning the dissension between the Upper and Lower House, see Cobbett, *Parl. Hist.,* I, 307–308.

35. *moved 4 subsidies.* B.L. Add. 26,639.

36. This entry is confirmation that the Bedford MS. 197 diarist was one of the members of the committee appointed for the penning of the alterations to the petition concerning religion. See above, H. of C., 28 June, n. 50, and 4 July, n. 32.

37. In 1388 Richard II called together the sheriffs "to understand what power of men they might assure the King of to serve him against the Lords and Barons . . . and further, that where he meant to call a parliament very shortly they should so use the matter that no knight might be chosen but such as the King and his Council should name". Holinshed, *Chronicles,* II, 783. At the same time, the judges were called together to answer a set of questions which dealt with the King's authority over parliament (though none of the questions concerned the sheriffs' return of M.P.s named by the King). Robert Bealknap, Chief Justice of Common

Pleas, having been compelled along with the other judges to set his seal to answers which were favorable to the King, reportedly exclaimed, "if I had not done this, I might not have escaped your hands, so that for your pleasures and the King's I have done it, and deserved thereby death at the hands of the Lords". Ibid., 781–782. In 21 R. II (1398) another group of judges was forced to agree that the answers of 1388 were good and lawful, and the parliament of 1398, accused by opponents of having been packed by the King, passed an act confirming the questions and answers of 1388. *S.R.,* 21 *R.* II, c. 12. Articles 2 and 19 in the impeachment proceedings against Richard II condemn the King's actions with regard to the judges and his commands to the sheriffs to return his specified candidates to parliament. Cobbett, *Parl. Hist.,* I, 255–260; Howell, *S.T.,* I, 140–145. See also, the entry for Richard II in *D.N.B.*

38. For the account of the 1624 election in Southwark, see Glanville, *Reports,* pp. 7–11. Concerning Glanville's *Reports,* see above, n. 19.

39. See above, n. 19.

3ly. That the election was disturbed by the going out of Sir Thomas Wentworth's company, who (upon the speeches of Sir John Savile that the polling would last three days) made as much shift to get out of the gates unpolled as they could. Which words were as prejudicial to his own part as to the other; besides, if disturbance be a sufficient answer in any case, it should have been admitted in the case of Pontefract, where the mayor's staff was broken, but it was not then allowed, because he might have craved aid of the sheriff who has *posse comitatus*, which reason is much stronger in this case, where the sheriff himself is present. [40]

The judgment of the House was that the return was void, and a warrant to be made for a new election, yet the sheriff to be clear from any misdemeanor; both which points were determined in two distinct questions.

---

40. The reference is to the 1624 Pontefract election. See above, H. of C., 4 July, n. 5. The incident of the mayor's staff is not included in Glanville's *Reports*, or in the reports of the committee of privileges, 1 April and 28 May 1624, recorded in the *C.J.* and the 1624 diary accounts of John Holles, John Pym, or Edward Nicholas. The account of the incident may have come from Glanville's own notes; because it was not admissable evidence in the case, it was not included in the final ruling of the committee.

Meeting of the committee of the whole House: on the bill that this **session** of parliament shall not determine by royal assent to one or more acts [*see below*]   324, *5/7

Ordered: Sir William Masham may sit in the House upon promise he shall receive the communion   322

Report from the committee for penning of the alterations to the **petition concerning religion** (SIR EDWARD COKE) [*see below*]   322, *24/6

[*The completed petition concerning religion is printed on pp. 155–160*]

The alterations: read, agreed, and ordered to be engrossed   322

[*The Lords' suggested alterations to the petition concerning religion are printed on pp. 298–299 and 305–306*]

ROBERT SNELLING: moves to restrain the **players** from going into the country   322

Resolved: Sir Benjamin Rudyard to move the Lord Chamberlain to restrain the players   322, *9/7

Report from the committee of the whole: on the bill concerning this **session** of parliament (SIR ROBERT HEATH, Solicitor) [*see above and below*]   322, 325, *5/7

Amendments to the above bill: read twice; bill to be engrossed   322, 325

SIR ROBERT PHELIPS: moves that **privileges** may be continued during adjournment   322

Resolved: **committee of privileges** to consider Phelips's motion and report to the House   322

The Speaker goes out of the chair   322

The Speaker returns to the chair   322

Message to the Lords desiring them to sit this afternoon to receive the **petition concerning religion** (Sir Edward Coke) [*see above and below*]   322

Report from the committee of the whole: on the bill for the grant of two entire **subsidies** by the temporalty (SIR ROBERT HEATH, Solicitor)   322, *30/6

Amendments to the above bill: read twice; bill to be engrossed   322

Report of the Lords' response to the message: the Lords will sit this afternoon (SIR EDWARD COKE) [*see above and below*]   322

Committee of the whole House to consider the bill of a subsidy of **tonnage and poundage** this afternoon [*see below*]   322, *5/7

[*Afternoon*]

L. 2a. *An act against* **simony** *and corruption in the elections of colleges: committed*   323, *28/6

L. 3a. An act that this **session** of parliament shall not determine by royal assent to one or more acts: committed to a select committee [*see above and below*]   323

SIR ROBERT PHELIPS: moves for stay of trial against Sir Robert **Gorges**, M.P.   323

Ordered: Speaker to write a letter for stay of the trial, etc.   323

Report from the committee for considering the petition against the **imposition on wines** (SIR EDWIN SANDYS)   323, *29/6

Petition to the King against the imposition on wines: read   323

WEDNESDAY, 6 JULY 1625

I. JOURNAL OF THE HOUSE OF COMMONS

[C.J. 804]

[p. 17] *Mercurii, 6° Julii, 1° Caroli Regis*

Ordered, Sir William Masham may come and sit in the House, notwithstanding he have not received the communion, upon Sir Francis Barrington his promise he shall receive forthwith.

SIR EDWARD COKE reports from the committee for the petition of religion that they have agreed upon the petition.

The alterations read and, upon the question, agreed and ordered to be engrossed.[1]

MR. SNELLING moves that where the players being restrained here will go into the country to the danger of spreading the infection, to restrain these.[2]

Resolved, Sir Benjamin Rudyard shall, from the House, move the Lord Chamberlain to restrain these.

MR. SOLICITOR reports the bill concerning the continuance of this session.[3]

The amendments 2 read. *Engrossetur.*

SIR ROBERT PHELIPS moves that the privileges of the House may be continued during this adjournment.

Resolved, the committee of privileges shall consider hereof and, upon their report, the House will take further order.

Mr. Speaker went out of the chair.[4]

Mr. Speaker went into his chair and, upon motion, Sir Edward Coke sent up to the Lords to entreat them to sit this afternoon to agree upon the petition for religion.

MR. SOLICITOR reports the bill of subsidy, with amendments, which 2 read. *Engrossetur.*

SIR EDWARD COKE reports from the Lords that they will sit this afternoon about the petition or any thing else we shall tender.

[p. 18] The bill of tonnage and poundage to be sat upon by the committees this afternoon.

---

1. Coke apparently is reporting from the committee for penning the alterations which was appointed by the House on 4 July and met with a committee of the Lords on 5 July. See O.B.s. For the alterations, see above, H. of C., 4 July, O. B. For the finished petition, see H. of L., 9 August, pp. 155–160.

2. The theaters in London had been closed around the time of the death of James I (27 March 1625) and not reopened after his funeral because of fear of plague infection spreading in crowds. Gerald Eades Bentley, *The Jacobean and Caroline Stage* (Oxford, 1941), I, 19. Robert Snelling's remarks may have been made in response to the special license granted by King Charles on 24 June to John Heming and other players "to show and exercise publicly, or otherwise to their best commodity, when the infection of the plague shall not weekly exceed the number of forty by the certificate of the Lord Mayor of London . . . as well within these two their most usual houses called the Globe . . . and their private houses situate within the precinct of the Blackfriars within our city of London, as also within any town halls . . . or other convenient places within the liberties and freedom of any other city, university, town, or borough whatsoever within

our said realms and dominions . . .". 1 *Car.* I, pt. 1, no. 5, MS. Cal. Pat. Rolls, f. 26; the license is printed in Rymer, *Foedera*, VIII, pt. 1, pp. 87–88. According to the official register of Sir Henry Herbert, Master of the Revels, on 1 July 1625 Herbert granted a confirmation of the patent to the King's Company of players to travel for a year. Joseph Quincy Adams, ed., *The Dramatic Records of Sir Henry Herbert* (New Haven, 1917), p. 64.

Sir Benjamin Rudyard, assigned by the House to speak to the Lord Chamberlain concerning this matter, was on intimate terms with William Herbert, Earl of Pembroke, the Lord Chamberlain. *D.N.B.* For Rudyard's report from the Lord Chamberlain, who had general supervision over the Office of Revels, see below, H. of C., 9 July, p. 359.

3. I.e., An act that this session of parliament shall not determine by his Majesty's royal assent to one or more acts of parliament.

4. Apparently at this point the House went into committee. There is no extant record of the committee proceedings. Concerning matters scheduled for consideration by the committee of the whole, see below, n. 16.

Post Meridiem, eodem 6° die.

L. 2ª. An act against/[5]
Committed to

Sir Edward Coke	Sir Francis Barrington
Mr. Glanville	Sir Benjamin Rudyard
Sir Thomas Middleton	Sir William Pitt
Mr. Alford	
Sir John Stradling	
All the lawyers of the House	

And all that will come to have voice; Friday, 2 clock, Court Wards.

L. 3ª. An act that this session of parliament shall not determine by his Majesty's royal assent unto one or more acts of parliament.

After the reading of this bill doubts conceived and thereupon

Mr. Solicitor	Sir John Stradling
Mr. Glanville	Mr. Cage
Sir Robert Phelips	Mr. Alford
Sir Francis Seymour	

and all the lawyers of the House, directed to go into the Committee Chamber.[6]

SIR ROBERT PHELIPS moves for stay of a trial against Sir Robert Gorges, a member of this House.

Ordered, a letter to be written to the judges of assize, for stay, and a warrant to the parties; and Sir Robert to have privilege.[7]

SIR EDWIN SANDYS reports from the committee for the wines a petition from the House to his Majesty against the new imposition of 20 *l.* [*sic*] upon a tun, which read.[8]

That the merchants desire a present answer because they desire to know upon what conditions they may trade; for they are resolved to trade no more, except this imposition may be laid down.

Resolved, this petition shall be engrossed in parchment and be presented to his Majesty by Mr. Chancellor of the Exchequer and Mr. Solicitor.

SIR EDWIN SANDYS also reports the account given by the treasurers and Council of War, with the demands made by the country, for the expenses of the country, constables, etc.[9]

SIR EDWARD COKE. To defer the examination of these accounts.

SIR ROBERT PHELIPS, *accordant.*

[p. 19] Resolved upon question, that this House will, at our next meeting, enter into an exact and serious consideration of this account, at which time all the Council of War and treasurers are required to be present.[10]

Upon question declared, that the inten-

---

5. There is no marginal notation in the MS. to indicate the subject of this bill. Of the seventeen bills which had received a first reading in the Lower House prior to this date (6 July) but for which there is no positive record of a second reading and commitment during the 1625 parliament (see below, Table of Bills, pp. 633–637), only one, the bill against simony, first read on 28 June, is later referred to as having been formerly committed. See below, H. of C., 2 August, p. 378 and n. 2, and p. 381.

6. Upon the rare occasions when a bill was recommitted after a third reading, it was common procedure for the committee to withdraw from the House into the Committee Chamber and to report back to the House later the same day. See William Hakewill, *Modus Tenendi Parliamentum* (London, 1660), pp. 155–156. For Glanville's report from this committee, see below, p. 324.

7. We have no record of the charges on which Sir Robert Gorges was to be tried. Phelips's motion was for the traditional privilege of freedom from the prosecution of law suits against a parliament member during a session. See Hatsell, *Precedents*, I, 176–187; Elsynge, *Parliaments*, pp. 203–204.

8. For the petition to the King against the imposition of 20s. per tun, see below, pp. 326–327.

9. We do not have a copy of Sandys's report. Concerning the accounts of the treasurers and Council of War, presented to the committee of the whole on 1 July, see above, H. of C., 1 July, p. 285 and n. 32.

10. For remarks concerning the examination of these accounts, see the King's message delivered to the House by Sir John Coke on 8 July, below, H. of C., 8 July, O.B.

tion and resolution of the House was, in the act of subsidy *21° Jac.*, that all charges disbursed for the uses mentioned in that act are to be disbursed out of the subsidies and 15eens, and to be paid according to the act.[11]

MR. GLANVILLE reports a dislike of the bill for continuance of the session.[12]

L. 1ª, L. 2ª. An act for continuance of divers statutes.
Committed to
Sir Robert Phelips
Sir Edwin Sandys
Mr. [John] Glanville
Mr. [Nicholas] Hyde
and all other now in the House, presently, in the House.[13]

Mr. Speaker left the chair and Mr. Hyde had the chair at the committee.

MR. HYDE reports the said bill, with amendments; which 2 read. *Engrossetur.*

SIR EDWARD COKE reports from the Lords: That he has delivered the petition to the Lords and that the Lords have agreed of 8 of them[14] and, for the time, would presently send to the King to know his pleasure, hoping to have his answer tomorrow, wherewith they will acquaint the House as soon as they have received it.

Upon question declared, that the monies disbursed by the country and which ought, as aforesaid,[15] to have been paid out of the subsidies and 15eens, and which shall so

appear under the hands of the lord lieutenant, or 2 deputy lieutenants, or 2 justices of peace, or 2 commissioners of the subsidy, or others lawfully authorized are to be repaid out of the subsidies by warrants to be directed to the treasurers from the Council of War.

[p. 20] Resolved upon question, that his Majesty's Remembrancer and the other officers of the Exchequer shall, against our next meeting, prepare the account of the subsidies and 15eens; and that all parties who have received monies from the treasurers by warrants from the Council of War shall attend, with their accounts ready, the beginning of next session.

The Council of War to have a copy of these declarations of ours.

Upon question declared by the House, that the House conceives it fit that the monies issued for the services mentioned in the act of subsidy shall be first paid, as they were first disbursed.

A committee of the whole House to meet tomorrow morning, by 7 of the clock, about the bill of tonnage and poundage; and Mr. Speaker to be here at 8.

Mr. Solicitor, Sir Robert Phelips, and Sir Edwin Sandys to draw a preamble for this bill, against tomorrow morning.

II. MS. 197, BEDFORD ESTATES, LONDON

[f. 26]   *6ᵗᵒ Julii 1625.*

In the morning the great committee sat in the House upon the bill for adjourn-

---

11. See *S.R.,* 21 *Jac.* I, c. 33, for the provisions of the 1624 subsidy act. Concerning the repayment of the sums disbursed in the counties, see above, H. of C., 1 July, pp. 282 (and n. 8) and 285, and see the orders made later this day, below.

12. See above, n. 3. Glanville is reporting from the committee appointed to further consider this bill following its third reading earlier in the day (see above, p. 323 and n. 6). The House did not vote to pass this bill until after further debate on 7 July (see below, p. 335).

13. Apparently the House began to appoint a select

committee but then decided to adjourn directly into a committee of the whole in order to expedite the passage of the bill for continuance of statutes. See below.

14. I.e., a committee of eight Lords to join with a committee from the Commons in presenting the petition concerning religion to the King. For the appointment of the Lords' committee, see above, H. of L., 6 July, p. 98.

15. See the declaration of the House earlier this day concerning the intention of the subsidy act of 1624, above, and see above, n. 11.

ment, which, after some debate, was reported to the House and ordered to be engrossed.[16]

[*Afternoon*]

[f. 24v][17] There had been complaints from divers counties that they had sustained great charges in keeping of pressed soldiers, contrary to the express intention of the act of subsidies, wherein it was declared that all manner of charge concerning the services for which they were given should be defrayed out of those subsidies.

Wherefore it was ordered that the treasurers, out of the money remaining in their hands, shall make repayment of all such sums as have been disbursed in the several counties for any of the services mentioned in the act of subsidies, and that, upon the certificates from the deputy lieutenants, the Council of War should make warrants for the payments of all such sums as should be contained in the same certificates; which warrants should be discharged by the treasurers before any other, in such order as the money appeared to be disbursed.

[f. 26] In the afternoon Mr. Montagu was examined in the House upon divers articles.[18] The examination was long in time but short in matter; the most effectual points were these:

[f. 26v] That his first book[19] was printed by King James's special warrant, procured without his privity, as it should seem, by Dr. Lindsell and Mr. Cosin, the Bishop of Durham's chaplains, to whom he sent the book, and had, besides, the ordinary license of Dr. Worrall.[20]

That after the informations exhibited in parliament,[21] the King sent for him and spoke with him (the King that now is coming in the meantime)[22] these words: "If thou be a papist, I am a papist"; giving him leave to print somewhat in his own defense.

That my Lord of Canterbury having advised him to review his book and explain himself, and [that] he might have a fit occasion thereunto upon the coming out of the second part of the *Gagg*, the King told him he needed not to review it unless he would, and left it to his own choice whether to go to my Lord of Canterbury or not. Notwithstanding, he had done it and had provided an explication according to my Lord's direction, which he is ready to put forth if it be required.

The second[23] was printed by the King's warrant *ore tenus* at Theobalds, at which

---

16. The committee of the whole had been scheduled to consider the bill concerning this session of parliament on the afternoon of 5 July following its work on the subsidy bill and before its consideration of the bill for tonnage and poundage (see above, p. 313). However, the debate over the Yorkshire election appears to have lasted so late into the afternoon of 5 July that the business of the committee of the whole was deferred to this morning (6 July).

17. The following two paragraphs concerning the 1624 subsidy disbursements are included in the MS. among the materials for 5 July (see above, H. of C., 5 July, n. 26). We have placed them here in order to preserve the chronology of business given by the C.J.

18. The C.J. for this day includes no information regarding Montagu's attending the House. It seems likely, as Petyt MS. 538/8 indicates (above, p. 288), that the examination of the Montagu business occurred not in the House but in the select committee which had

been organized on 1 July (see above, H. of C., 1 July, n. 17), which had met on the mornings of 4 and 5 July (see O.B.s), and which, on 4 July, had been authorized by the House to send for any witnesses it thought fit (see above, p. 300). Recorder Finch reported from this committee on 7 July (see below, H. of C., 7 July, O. B.).

19. I.e., the *Gagg*, the first book of the two under discussion.

20. John Cosin and Augustine Lindsell were at this time both chaplains to Richard Neile, Bishop of Durham. *D.N.B.* Thomas Worrall was chaplain to George Monteigne, Bishop of London, and one of the "correctors" who assisted in the licensing of the press. See *C.D. 1628*, III, 151 and n. 50.

21. I.e., in the 1624 session. See *C.J.*, I, 704. See also, below, H. of C., 7 July, n. 3.

22. I.e., Charles I.

23. I.e., *Appello Caesarum*.

time, some of his opinions being proposed, the King swore, "By G[od], if this be popery, I am a papist", and when he desired leave to give public satisfaction, the King replied, "Yea, by G[od], shalt thou". Being written, he sent it to the King by my Lord of Durham,[24] and his Majesty commended it to Doctor White,[25] who gave a particular censure of every article; and that it was printed according to his approbation without alteration, my Lord of Canterbury not being made acquainted with it till afterward.

If anything be offensive to any authority supreme or subordinate to the honorable House of Commons, *indictum sit;* it was against his intention; yet he confesses his style to be too full of sharpness, [f. 27] contrary to his profession, and contrary to his disposition; but, being so traduced as he has been, desires it may be considered whether any other man would not be transported beyond moderation.

III. PETITION OF THE WINE MERCHANTS
DELIVERED AT HAMPTON COURT 8 JULY
1625.[26] RAWLINSON MS. D. 974, BODLEIAN
LIBRARY, FF. 70v–71.

To the King's most excellent Majesty,

May it please your Majesty to be informed of the grievous complaint of the merchants trading for wines: That whereas in these later times they had paid 3 *l.* the tun in duties to some of your Majesty's late progenitors and predecessors amounting to the full moiety of the value of the wines in those places where they grow and are

bought. Notwithstanding which great burden the Earl of Middlesex, late Lord Treasurer, in January in the 19th year of his late Majesty's reign procured a new imposition of [an]other 3 *l.* on the tun to be laid on all wines to continue but for one year, and this at such time as they had 2,700 tun returned and lying in the river of Thames, to the extreme wrong and oppression of the poor merchant.[27] Which imposition of 3 *l.* was afterwards reduced to 20*s.* in the port of London and 13*s.* 4*d.* in the outports upon pretense that the merchants of London had consented thereunto, which afterwards was disproved by the oaths of the merchants before the Lords.[28]

And whereas upon complaint made at the last parliament the said imposition was forborne and the merchants not pressed thereunto till Michaelmas last, at which time it was revived and set up again and the merchants enforced by seizure of their goods and other grievous vexations to enter bonds for payment of the same.[29] Upon which bonds, the merchants being unable to discharge them, divers extents have issued to the great trouble and utter impoverishing of the merchants, besides the endearing of the price of wines to all your Majesty's subjects.

Forasmuch as that pretended agreement has been disavowed upon oath and though the same had been as is pretended, yet could it no way bind the merchants of the outports who were not parties to it. And though all the merchants of the realm had consented to it, yet inasmuch as all such

24. I.e., Richard Neile.

25. Francis White, Dean of Carlisle. The book was entered in the Stationers' records 18 February 1625, "under the hands of Doctor White, Dean of Carlisle, Doctor Worrall, and Master Lownes [of the Company]". Edward Arber, *A Transcript of the Registers of the Company of Stationers of London, 1554–1640* (London, 1877), IV, 98. The *Appeal* contains an Approbation dated 15 February 1624 (1625) which states that: "I, Francis White, Doctor of Divinity and Dean of Carlisle, by the special direction and commandment of his most excellent Majesty have diligently perused and read

over this book entitled *Appello Caesarem* . . . and find nothing therein but what is agreeable to the public faith, doctrine, and discipline established in the Church of England . . .".

26. This is the petition of the House to the King. The wine merchants' petition to the House is printed above, H. of C., 29 June, pp. 269–271. For the King's answer to the petition, reported to the House on 9 July, see below, p. 359.

27. See above, H. of C., 29 June, n. 12.

28. See above, H. of C., 29 June, n. 17.

29. See above, H. of C., 29 June, nn. 18 and 19.

burdens upon the merchant do finally settle upon the whole body of the commonwealth, it could be of no validity as is proved by divers records upon complaints made upon like occasion in the time of your Majesty's progenitors.

Your humble Commons beseech your Majesty of your grace and justice to cause the said imposition of 20s. upon the tun of wine in the port of London and of 13s. 4d.

in the outports to be henceforth laid down and that as well those bonds may be delivered up and discharged and no further proceeding or prosecution at the law be had thereupon against any of the said merchants, as also that such of their goods as have been seized upon for nonpayment or not entering into bond for the payment of the said imposition of 20s. and 13s. 4d. may be restored to the merchants.

Report from the committee of the
  whole on the bill of a subsidy
  of **tonnage and poundage**
  (SIR ROBERT HEATH,
  Solicitor)   330, 336, *5/7
Amendments to the above bill:
  read twice; bill to be
  engrossed   330
SIR HENRY MARTEN: moves for
  the stay of a suit against
  himself   336
Ordered: Sir Henry **Marten** to
  have privilege; a letter to be
  sent for stay of the suit; the
  Serjeant to go for the party
  that served the subpoena   330, 336
Report from the committee
  concerning **Montagu** (SIR
  HENEAGE FINCH, Recorder)   330, 336, 342;
                                         N, 517, *29/6
CHRISTOPHER BROOKE: moves
  that a petition from Richard
  Montagu be read   333
The petition from Montagu: read   333
Resolved upon question: that
  thanks be given to the
  Archbishop of Canterbury,
  by the former committee for
  attending the Archbishop,
  for his care regarding
  Montagu's books   333, 338, 344,
                                         *1/7
Question of acquainting the
  Lords with Montagu's books
  and praying a conference
  concerning the same:
  debated   339; **N**, 518
RICHARD DYOTT   339
SIR EDWARD COKE   339
ANONYMOUS SPEECHES   339
MR. WHITAKER   339
Resolved: at the next session to
  request a conference with the
  Lords concerning Montagu's
  books   333, 344

Question of Montagu's contempt
  to the House: debated [*see
  below*]   333, 339; **N**,
                                         518
SIR EDWIN SANDYS   334
SIR FRANCIS SEYMOUR   334
Message from the Lords (Sir
  Thomas Coventry, Att.
  General, and Sir Humphrey
  Davenport) bringing: 334, 340
  the bill for the further restraint
  of **tippling** in inns, alehouses,
  etc. [*see below*]   *23/6
  and desiring:
  a **conference** on the petition of
  the **prisoners in the Fleet**
  concerning *habeas corpus*   *8/7
Addition to the bill for the
  further restraint of **tippling**:
  read three times and passed
  [*see above*]   334
Answer given to the Lords'
  message: the Commons will
  sit this afternoon and will
  send answer by messengers
  of their own (SIR THOMAS
  CREW, Speaker) [*see above*]   334
Question of **Montagu**'s contempt
  to the House: debate
  continued [*see above*]   334, 339; **N**,
                                         518
SIR HUMPHREY MAY (Chancellor
  Duchy)   334, 339
SIR HENRY MARTEN   334
SIR ROBERT PHELIPS   334
SIR NATHANIEL RICH   334
SIR EDWARD COKE   334, 340
SIR DUDLEY DIGGES   334
CHRISTOPHER SHERLAND   334
SIR ROBERT HEATH (Solicitor)   334
Resolved: that Montagu has
  committed a contempt
  against the House   334
Upon question: to respite
  punishment till the next

THURSDAY, 7 JULY 1625

I. JOURNAL OF THE HOUSE OF COMMONS

[C.J. 805]

[p. 20] *Jovis 7° Julii, 1° Caroli Regis*

MR. SOLICITOR reports the bill of subsidy of tonnage and poundage, with some amendments and alterations; which 2 read. *Engrossetur.*

A subpoena served upon Sir H. Marten, at the suit of John Melsam, telling him he knew he was a parliament/

Sir H. to have privilege. A letter for stay of the suit; and the Serjeant to go for the party that served it, to be here this afternoon.[1]

MR. RECORDER reports from the committee for Mr. Montagu:[2] 1. For the Lord Archbishop's answer, consisting of an ad-

monition and some opinion: admonition to Montagu what disturbance his 1st book had wrought both to the Church and Parliament House; advising him to survey his book.[3] That, for his opinion, my Lord told him, though there were some things which might receive a favorable interpretation, yet some other things in it were not of that nature.

That all the committee of opinion that the Lord of Canterbury had done what was fit and merited thanks of this House.

That all the committee of opinion that many things in these books which [*sic*] directly contrary to the articles established by parliament, *vizt.*, that the Church of Rome is *vera Christi ecclesia et sponsa Christi*, which contrary, as conceived, to the 19th Article; [p. 21] that the Church of Rome *eodem fundamento doctrinae et sacramentorum nititur.*[4]

But, for these points of doctrine, the

---

1. We have been unable to find further information regarding Melsam's suit against Sir Henry Marten.

2. Concerning Sir Heneage Finch, Recorder of London, as the reporter from the committee for Montagu, see above, H. of C., 1 July, n. 17.

3. For the Archbishop of Canterbury's answer to the inquiry by the committee of the House concerning the *Gagg*, see above, H. of C., 1 July, O.B. Regarding the Montagu business as a whole, see below, *Negotium*, pp. 517–519.

The arguments made against Richard Montagu in 1625 grew out of a petition submitted in 1624 by two ministers, Samuel Ward and John Yates, complaining of views expressed in Montagu's *Gagg*, published earlier the same year. Both men were Puritans and Yates had published, in 1622, *A Modell of Divinitie, catechistically composed, wherein is delivered the Matter and Methode of Religion according to the Creed . . .* (*S.T.C.*, no. 26085). *D.N.B.* John Pym, chairman of the committee concerning corruption in religion and learning, reported the petition of Ward and Yates to the House on 13 May 1624 (*C.J.*, I, 704, 788). The House sent a committee to inform the Archbishop of Canterbury (George Abbot) of the complaints against Montagu, but the session ended before any further action could be taken. Montagu proceeded, in early 1625, to publish his *Appeal* in response to the petition of Ward and Yates, referring to them in his title as "two unjust informers".

Later this day (7 July 1625) Montagu was censured for his contempt to the House and was committed to

the Serjeant, but further punishment was respited until the August session (see below, pp. 334–335). On 9 July the House received notice from the King that Montagu was his chaplain-in-ordinary and that the King would deal with the matter himself and wished Montagu enlarged (see below, p. 359). Despite the King's notice, the House continued during the August session to press its claims to jurisdiction over Montagu with regard to his contempt of the House. But Montagu, having been released on bail from the Serjeant, claimed to be ill and thereby avoided appearing before the House again (see below, H. of C., 2, 6, and 8 August, O.B.s).

He was again complained of in the parliaments of 1626 and 1628, the fullest arguments against him and his works being expressed in the latter parliament. The editors refer readers to the fully annotated accounts in *C.D. 1628*, III, 26 and 28 April (see O.B.s), and ibid., IV, 11 June (see O.B.).

4. I.e., the 39 Articles put forth by the Church of England in 1562 which were revised by Convocation and sanctioned by act of parliament in 1571 (*S.R.*, 13 *Eliz.* I, c. 12). Concerning the Articles, see Edward Harold Browne, *An Exposition of the Thirty-Nine Articles* (New York, 1870).

From Article 19: "As the church of Jerusalem, Alexandria, and Antioch have erred, so also the Church of Rome has erred, not only in their living and manner of ceremonies, but also in matters of faith".

From Article 25: "There are two sacraments ordained of Christ our Lord in the Gospel, that is to say,

committee of opinion that a conference was to be prayed with the Lords about it.

That the committee of opinion that the 2nd book[5] against the honor and dignity of this House, which the cause of sending for him.

That all the committee held this 2nd book a factious and seditious book tending manifestly to the dishonor of our late King and to the disturbance of our Church and state.

For the dishonor to the King: he, in that[6] book entitled [blank], says Arminius the first that infected Leiden with the errors and schisms/[7]

The Synod of Dort, so honored by the King, slighted by him: *Forinsecus* and partial, knows not what ends they had nor cares not.[8]

The[9] committee conceives the fire kind-led in the Low Countries by Arminius like to be kindled here likewise by this man.

He directs it to the King and calls it *Appello Caesarem*, and yet says the Pope is not[10] 'O *Antichristos*, which is contrary to that the King himself had written to all Christian princes.[11]

The Articles agreed of in Ireland and confirmed here; he delivers a point *in terminis terminantibus*, contrary to them, about justifying faith. The 38th.[12]

2nd general head, 4 particulars:

1. The committee think there is enough in this book to put a jealousy between the King and his well-affected subjects. Says there are some that desire an anarchy, means it of the Puritans, whom yet he has not defined. The committee thought fit to have it explained.

He rails at Yates and Ward and says they

---

baptism and the supper of the Lord. Those five commonly called sacraments, that is to say, confirmation, penance, orders, matrimony, and extreme unction are not to be counted for sacraments of the Gospel, being such as have grown partly of the corrupt following of the Apostles . . .".

The *Gagg*, p. 50: "In this sense, in regard of these parts, the Church is, and is esteemed, invisible. . . . *haec Ecclesia Romana . . . tamen eodem fundamento doctrinae et sacramentorum a Deo institutorum firma semper constitit. . . . Manet enim Christi Ecclesia et sponsa, quamuis multis erroribus et vitiis sponsum suum irritauerit . . .".*

5. I.e., the *Appeal.* See above, H. of C., 24 June, n. 16.

6. *the.* Printed edition.

7. Concerning the book of James I condemning Arminius, see below, n. 100.

8. The *Appeal,* pp. 69–71: "And indeed I do reverence the conveners [of the Synod of Dort] for their places, worth and learning, but I have nothing at all to do with their conclusions. . . . The Synod was *Forinsecus* and but partial. . . . What ends men had in that Synod, I know not, nor am curious to inquire; how things were carried, I as little understand or care. Whether any or all subscribed absolutely or with protestation I cannot tell. . . . I am sure it has been opposed in the Church of England".

For further remarks by Montagu concerning the Synod of Dort, see the *Appeal,* pp. 105–108. Concerning James I's support of the Synod, see below, p. 337 and n. 54.

9. The material between the words *The committee*

and *respecting Bellarmine,* below, p. 332, is written in a hand other than that of John Wright, Clerk of the House.

10. *nor.* Printed edition.

11. James's argument concerning Antichrist appears in his *A Premonition to All Most Mighty Monarchs . . .* (*S.T.C.,* no. 14401), dedicated to Emperor Rudolph II. See Charles H. McIlwain, ed., *The Political Works of James I* (Cambridge, Mass., 1918), pp. 129–133.

The *Appeal,* pp. 142–143: ". . . the Pope is Antichrist. . . . I never yet saw proof or argument brought that was persuasive, much less that was demonstrative in the case. I never yet met with argument or reason to the point but, at least to my own satisfaction, I was able to answer it".

12. The Articles of Ireland (*S.T.C.,* no. 14260) were drawn and agreed to by the Convocation of the Irish clergy held in Dublin in 1615 and were signed by Lord Deputy Chichester by order from King James in his name. See Richard Mant, *History of the Church of Ireland* (London, 1840), I, 382–388.

Article 38 of the Articles of Ireland: "A true lively, justifying faith, and the sanctifying spirit of God is not extinguished nor vanishes away in the regenerate, either finally nor totally".

The *Appeal,* p. 20: "I appeal unto their honesty, at least wise knowledge, are not my words laid down directly thus? 'For in *your* opinion, justifying faith may diminish and may be abolished and lost. Now justification being in an instant', etc. If in *their* opinion it may be lost, namely faith which justifies, then justification which is an effect of faith may also be lost . . .".

are Puritans (although they have subscribed), "Puritans in heart". He does plainly intimate that there are Puritan bishops.[13]

Committee conceived this much to tend to the disturbance of the peace of the state and Church.

Respecting[14] Bellarmine but slighting Calvin, Beza, Perkins, Whitaker, Reynolds, which a great disturbance of the peace.[15]

[p. 22] Much discountenancing, in his book, of God's word: 1. Disgracing of lectures, not lecturers; of preaching itself; yea, even of reading the Bible. 8th page, conventicles after lectures. Chew the cud[16] after lectures. For preaching: Prating, preaching, and lecturing; dictate out of their pulpits to their popular auditory;[17] handling *limbus*[18] when Yates and Ward in their pulpits.

13. On Yates and Ward, see above, n. 3. The *Appeal*, pp. 320–321: ". . . they are no Puritans: which God in goodness keep out of the Church and state, as dangerous as popery, for any thing I am able to discern the only difference being popery is for tyranny, puritanism for anarchy . . . both alike enemies unto piety".

Ibid., p. 3: ". . . unto popular irregularity, and puritanical parity, the idol of our Godly brethren. It is more than probable these informers [Yates and Ward] are of this stamp and making. I have been told, and am assured, they are two grandees of the faction".

Ibid., p. 308: ". . . so do these men [Yates and Ward], . . . Puritans in faction, and engrained in their affection that way, howsoever pretending conformity by subscription".

Ibid., p. 111: "I have learned, loved, admired . . . the discipline of the Church of England (whereunto the Puritans and schismatics themselves, at least the wiser and subtler sort of them, come off roundly . . . remaining *quod erant, quoad doctrinam, et tantum non in episcopatu puritani.* . . . I say it again, a [*sic*] never was or will be a papist, no not in heart, though many be arrant Puritans in heart that only for preferment do conform".

14. See above, n. 9.

15. I.e., Robert Bellarmine, John Calvin, Theodore de Beza, William Perkins, William Whitaker, and John Reynolds.

In addition to his numerous theological works, Cardinal Bellarmine, opposing the 1606 oath of allegiance, had written a response to James I's *Apology for the Oath of Allegiance* which was published under the name of Matthew Tortus, one of Bellarmine's chaplains. Gardiner, *History of England,* II, 31. Montagu says in the *Appeal,* pt. 2, chap. 14 (p. 209), which is devoted to salvation, that: "Neither in my opinion nor yet in Bellarmine's judgment does certainty or incertainty of salvation depend so necessarily upon merit or demerit of good works. If a man continue constant in the course of good works he is sure and certain of salvation in Bellarmine's judgment and in my opinion also, though differently". Other favorable references to Bellarmine's opinions are frequent throughout the *Appeal.*

In the *Appeal,* p. 173, Montagu speaks of "your own dictators, Calvin, Perkins, Beza", whose doctrines are discussed individually throughout Montagu's work.

Referring to William Whitaker, the *Appeal,* p. 171: "And this is the express doctrine of D. Whitaker . . . and of Calvin himself who will have men to be taught this doctrine . . .". Cf. also, ibid., pp. 87, 89, and 101.

Concerning John Reynolds, the *Appeal,* p. 287: "Now if you grant a sacrifice why deny you an altar? D. Reynolds and B. Morton have granted that though we have no proper altar yet altar and sacrifice have a mutual relation and dependence one upon the other. The name of priests is given not only unto all Christians in general, but also to the ministers of the new testament in particular by the confession of D. Reynolds out of Essay 66, 21 in his *Conference,* chap. 8, Division 4, page 470". Cf. also, the *Appeal,* p. 123.

16. MS.: *quidd.* The *Appeal,* p. 8: "I will not be put over unto classical decisions . . . unto any prophetical determinations in private conventicles after lectures".

Ibid., p. 139: "I will yet add a little more popery to the former and so leave my friends and informers to chew the cud upon it, as they do after lectures".

17. The *Appeal,* p. 49: "Every one that prates, reads, lectures, preaches, or professes must not look to have his theses, lectiones, harangues, or discourses taken as the dictates or doctrines of our Church".

Ibid., p. 15: "It may be a custom among the informers and others of that tribe to dictate to their popular auditories out of their pulpits *tanquam de tripode* . . . and the same to be received upon their bare words as divine oracles".

18. *limbus* is omitted in the printed *C.J.* The *Appeal,* p. 231 (in the chapter "*Touching Limbus Patrum*"): "It is confessed on both sides, which is most material concerning them, that being immortal in their better part after dissolution and separation they still have a being and are subsisting in *aliquo ubi;* for though the nature of a soul is not to be circumspectively in place (as Tertullian fancied) as M. Yates and M. Ward are when they are in their pulpits, yet are they confined in their proper *ubi* . . . as they speak, that is, they have not nor can have an *ubique*-subsistence but a determined and defined".

For reading the Bible says, never a saint-seeming, Bible-bearing hypocritical Puritan a better patriot than he.[19]

4. That the whole frame of this book is a great encouragement of popery: 1, in maintaining the papists to be the true church, and that they differ not from us in any fundamental point.[20] If therefore they hold us heretics, and not to be saved, and we hold the contrary of them, who will not think it safer for us to be in their church than in ours? The papists read and commend the[21] book, and commend it to others to read where they endure not the reading or having of our books.

5. That in 2 points he had done injury to this House: [1.] Knew this 1st book questioned in this House presented to the Lord of Canterbury, from whom we expected an answer. Contrary to the Lord Canterbury's admonition to print a new book worse than the other.[22] 2. Where a petition preferred by Yates and Ward to this House, so as the House possessed, he to revile them for this, reflects upon the House.[23]

Page 176: That the articles not conceived.[24]

Mr. Brooke moves a petition from Mr. Montagu, ready to be delivered, may be read.[25]

Which read.

1. Upon question resolved, thanks to be given my Lord of Canterbury for his care in the last reference to him of Mr. Montagu's book. This to be done by the former parties that were sent for and brought his answer.[26]

2. Upon question resolved, that at our next meeting to acquaint the Lords with these books, and a conference to be prayed with the Lords concerning the same.[27]

Resolved at this time only to give him a touch that, under the names of articlers and informers, Yates and Ward, he has stricken this House.

1. Upon the reference the last parliament from the Lord of Canterbury, and knowing it came from this House, and my Lord having admonished him, in one year after never came [p. 23] to my Lord of Canterbury but, after 1 year, printed this new book and

---

19. The *Appeal*, p. 43: "Comparisons are odious, yet sometimes necessary. Gall and vinegar are corrosive, but must sometime be used. There is never a saint-seeming and Bible-bearing hypocritical Puritan in the pack, a better patriot every way, than the man that has delivered such dangerous errors".

20. The *Appeal*, p.113: "I am absolutely persuaded, and shall be till I see cause to the contrary, that the Church of Rome is true, though not a sound church of Christ, as well since, as before the Council of Trent; a part of the catholic, though not the Catholic Church, which we do profess to believe in our creed: a church in which among many tares there remains some wheat. In essentials and fundamentals they agree, holding one faith, in one Lord, into whom they are inserted through one baptism".

See also, the excerpt from the *Gagg*, above, n. 4.

21. *this*. Printed edition.

22. See above, n. 3.

23. See above, n. 3.

24. I.e., the articles in the petition of Yates and Ward against Montagu. See below, p. 344.

The *Appeal*, p. 176: "For here is a charge of delivering popery and maintaining it. . . the substance in brief

of all the former suggestions; such an one as makes me believe that these informations were not gathered by any scholars or divines, but subscribed unto unadvisedly, and collected by some other at odds with his own little or frantic wits; for who can conceive that a just and unjust, a carnal and spiritual man should be the same?"

25. Montagu's petition is not among the extant manuscripts relating to the 1625 session.

26. Concerning the Archbishop's cooperation with the delegation from the 1625 parliament, see above, H. of C., 1 July, O.B. Abbot was ill when the committee first made overtures to see him (see above, H. of C., 29 June, p. 269) and desired that they wait a few days until his health improved. Although not fully recovered by 1 July he met and talked with the committee concerning his admonitions to Montagu regarding the publications of the *Gagg*.

27. Apparently because of the adjournment of proceedings on 11 July and the subsequent movement of the parliament to Oxford the Lords never conferred with the Commons in 1625 on the content of Montagu's books.

presented it then to my Lord of Canterbury.[28]

SIR EDWIN SANDYS. That this no contempt to this House. For commended[29] to
my Lord of Canterbury as a delinquent,
and then my Lord of Canterbury should
have summoned him. 2ly, his protestation
being that it was only an error and not in
contempt of this House.[30]

SIR FRANCIS SEYMOUR, *contra.*

Mr. Attorney General and Serjeant
Davenport bring from the Lords the bill of
alehouses, with addition,[31] and with a message: That they have received a petition
from the Fleet where a restraint of *habeas
corpus,* to entreat them to give order for
their liberty in this dangerous time.[32] That
they desire a conference presently about it,
in the Painted Chamber, their number
being 8.

The addition 2 read and, upon question,
refused to be engrossed, and 3ly read and
passed.

The messengers being retired and called
in, MR. SPEAKER delivers them this answer:
That we are now in a serious and weighty
business, which they conceive may hold
long; but this House will sit this afternoon
and send answer by messengers of our own.

MR. CHANCELLOR. To respite the examination of this contempt until the conference past with the Lords.[33]

SIR H. MARTEN, *accordant,* lest, intending
to punish him, we do him a good turn.

SIR ROBERT PHELIPS. To make an order
now here for taking security for his appearance the next session, and so to respite
it till our next meeting.

SIR NATHANIEL RICH. Now to judge the
contempt and then to respite the punishment.

SIR EDWARD COKE. That his traducing
Yates and Ward for petitioning this House
a contempt, [*illegible*] *lingua.*[34]

SIR D. DIGGES. That a contempt to this
House. To have him called in, and enjoined
to appear here the beginning of the next
session.

[**C.J. 806**] MR. SHERLAND. To punish him
presently.

MR. SOLICITOR. This a contempt. That
we have cognizance here of matters of religion. *Pro ecclesia Anglicana,* the 1st part of
the writ.[35] Not now to inflict a punishment
on him, which may lessen his after punishment. Moves to commit him to the Serjeant,
and, if he give security to the Serjeant for
his appearance the beginning of the[36] next
session, and so may be bailed.

[p. 24] 1. Upon question resolved, that
Mr. M[ontagu] has, *super tota materia,* committed a great contempt against this House.
2. Upon question, to respite the punish-

28. See above, n.3; and see the Archbishop of Canterbury's account of his proceedings concerning Montagu, above, pp. 285–287.
29. *commending.* Printed edition.
30. At his examination, Montagu had protested
that he had had no intention to offend the House. See
above, p. 326.
31. An act to prevent tippling in inns and alehouses
had been sent to the Upper House on 1 July. The
Lords added a provision for taverns (see below,
p. 340).
32. For the petition of the prisoners in the Fleet, see

above, H. of L.,6 July, pp. 99–100.
33. I.e., the proposed conference with the Lords on
the content of Montagu's books. See above, n. 27.
34. See above, n. 3. Each chapter in the *Appeal* begins with a paragraph of the charge against Montagu
from the "Informers", followed by commentary from
Montagu.
35. I.e., these words appear in the first part of the
writs of summons to parliament. See below, H. of C., 2
August, p. 379 and n. 15.
36. *the* is omitted in the printed edition.

ment till the next meeting and, in the meantime, to commit him to the Serjeant to be sure of his forthcoming at that time.[37]

Mr. Montagu called in to the bar, and kneeling, MR. SPEAKER pronounces his judgment accordingly.

Sir Edward Coke	Sir Henry Marten
Mr. Recorder	Sir Dudley Digges
Mr. [John] Pym	Mr. Solicitor
Sir Nathaniel Rich	Mr. Whitaker
Mr. [Christopher] Sherland	Mr. Francis Drake

to set down in writing the particulars against Mr. Montagu.

Upon question resolved, that the Lord of Canterbury shall be entreated from the House to take some such course as in his judgment he shall think fit for the suppression of these books and preventing the danger that may grow by the divulging thereof; being resolved, at their next meeting, to enter into a particular examination of such parts of the said books as tend to sedition and the general disturbance of the peace of Church and commonwealth, whereof they are already very sensible.

The engrossed petition for the merchants for the wines, read, and allowed; and to be delivered by Mr. Treasurer, Chancellor Exchequer and Duchy, and Mr. Solicitor.[38]

L. 3a. An act for continuing of divers statutes. *Obdormit,* by a general vote.

SIR THOMAS FANSHAWE reports the bill for his Majesty's making leases of the lands parcel of the Duchy of Cornwall, without amendments.

L. 3a. An act to enable the King's Majesty to make leases of lands parcel of his Highness' Duchy of Cornwall, or annexed to the same. Upon question, passed.

Upon question ordered, that information be brought to the House, against our next meeting, by all the knights of shires and burgesses in the shires where they dwell of all such places where there is no usual preaching, and also of all such benefices or stipends of ministers as are under the value of 50 *l.* per annum, and of what value the impropriations there are.

[Afternoon]

[p. 25] SIR GEORGE MORE reports from the committee for privileges for Monmouthshire [*sic*]:[39] That Mr. Wogan, before the writ for election, solicited divers for voices, threatened divers, others impressed for soldiers, divers stricken, others hindered from coming to the election.

A petition from Sir J. Perrot, read, complaining that the sheriff that made the return was no sheriff; for his commission determined by the death of the King, and not renewed by the now King.[40]

The bill for continuance of the session, amended at the board and then, upon question, passed.

The dispute, concerning Sir James Perrot's petition, renewed. No reason to suffer such misdemeanors unpunished, if proved true.

37. It was intimated to the Serjeant that he could release Montagu upon bond if he promised to appear on the first day of the next session (see below, p. 340). On 9 July the Serjeant reported that he had set Montagu at liberty upon 2,000 *l.* bail (see below, p.359). Concerning further proceedings of the House with regard to Montagu, see above, n. 3.

38. For the petition, see above, H. of C., 6 July, pp. 326–327.

39. The election in question is that of Pembrokeshire rather than Monmouthshire as is written in the C. J. No punitive action was taken by the House at this time regarding complaints against John Wogan's activities vis à vis the election.

40. An earlier petition from Perrot had been submitted by Mr. Drake on 21 June. See above, pp. 206 and 209.

Resolved, to leave all this business to the committee for privileges, as well for new examination of the misdemeanors as of the other matters contained in the 2nd petition.[41]

Mr. CHOLMLEY moves for his father, for some direction in these points: 1, whether lawful for the sheriff to minister an oath to those which shall come in as electors after 11 of the clock; 2ly, whether the sheriff may make deputies to take the oath.[42]

II. MS. 197, BEDFORD ESTATES, LONDON

[f. 27]   7° Julii 1625.

An act concerning the subsidy of tonnage and poundage.[43]

This grant related to the 27 March 1625, and was to continue until the 27 of March 1626.

Sir H. MARTEN moved for the stay of a suit against himself, and that person which served him with a subpoena might be sent for.

Which was ordered accordingly.[44]

Mr. RECORDER reported the proceedings of the committee with Mr. Montagu,[45] with their opinion of that cause, and first, concerning the first book in answer to the

Gagg.[46] That they found my Lord of Canterbury's answer to the reference made from this House in the last parliament to consist of two parts:[47] 1. An admonition to Mr. Montagu, which was grave and fatherly, that he should review, etc..[48] 2. An expression of his own judgment touching that book, which confirms us in our proceedings that we have reason to bring that book to examination. And the opinion of the committee is that his Grace has carried himself with such respect as is fit to give this House satisfaction, and deserves thanks. [f. 27v] And though there be tenets in that first book contrary to the Articles of Religion established by act of parliament,[49] yet they think fit for the present to forbear till some more seasonable time to desire a conference with the Lords that some course may be taken to repair the breaches of the Church and to prevent the like boldness of private men hereafter.

The second book[50] they conceive to be, in the manner of the putting it out, despiteful and contemptuous to my Lord of Canterbury and derogatory to the dignity of this House, and for the matter to contain divers factions[51] and seditious passages: First, to the dishonor of the King that is dead. 2ly, apparently tending to the disturbance of

41. I.e., the petition regarding Perrot's complaint that the returning sheriff had lost his office at the time of the death of King James. See below, p. 340.

42. Hugh Cholmley was speaking for his father, Sir Richard Cholmley, sheriff of Yorkshire, whose actions at the time of that county's election had been questioned (see above, H. of C., 4 and 5 July, O.B.s) and who now was preparing for the forthcoming by-election. The House resolved that he must be advised by his counsel rather than by parliament. See below, p. 342.

43. The bill was reported this day, amendments and alterations were twice read, and the bill was ordered to be engrossed. See above, p. 330.

44. See above, n. 1.

45. Regarding Sir Heneage Finch as reporter of the Montagu business, see above, H. of C., 1 July, n. 17.

46. Montagu's Gagg was written in answer to Matthew Kellison's book, The Gagge of the Reformed Gospell,

printed in 1623 (S.T.C., no. 14907).

47. See above, n. 3.

48. The following note is included at this point in the MS.: "(as before, fol. 38)". The corresponding note in the Knightley MS. (C.D. 1625, p. 47) reads: "as before, fol. 22", which refers to the folio in the Knightley MS. containing the 1 July report of the Archbishop's answer concerning Montagu. Since the "fol. 38" reference in the Bedford MS. does not correlate with the numbers of its own folios which contain the 1 July proceedings, it seems likely that it refers to a folio in the MS. from which Bedford MS. 197 was copied. This circumstance provides further evidence that Bedford MS. 197 was not copied from the Knightley MS. (see above, Introduction, p. 11).

49. See above, n. 4.

50. I.e., the Appeal.

51. factious. C.D. 1625 (Knightley MS.).

the Church and state. 3ly, offensive to the House as being against the jurisdiction and liberty of parliament.

The first point of dishonor to the King was instanced in two particulars.

1. That he labors so much to uphold the opinion of Arminius,[52] which the King so much labored to suppress:

First, by his own censure. Writing of Arminius, he says that he was the first that infected Leiden with heresy, that he was the enemy of God; and of Bertius,[53] his scholar, that he was an arrogant heretic to write a book *De Apostasia Sanctorum* and send it to my Lord of Canterbury impudently alleging it to be agreeable to the Church of England.

2ly. By procuring the Synod of Dort, sending thither four divines for England and one for Scotland, all whom consented to the decrees there made. And yet Mr. Montagu slights that synod, and goes about to elude this consent of our divines by insinuating that it [f. 28] was not absolute, but under protestation.[54] Whereas Doctor Balcanquhall,[55] examined upon this point, affirmed to the committee that the consent was upon oath and extended to all the canons excepting three concerning discipline which were excepted by protestation.

3ly. By causing the Articles of the Church of England to be sent into Ireland, under the Great Seal of England, etc., in the 38 Article—justifying faith cannot be lost, etc.; to add these words "totally and finally", which was likewise contained in the sense and intention of the Articles of England, but not so fully explained.[56]

Whereas the King by many excellent arguments proved the Pope to be Antichrist, he, in his book which yet he has dedicated to the King, presumes to write that he never saw any so much as persuasive argument in that point.[57]

The second general charge, of matters tending to the disturbance of the Church and state, was delivered in four particulars.

1. That he labors to put a jealousy between the King and his well-affected subjects by saying there is a potent prevailing faction in the kingdom, etc.;[58] and these he

---

52. Cf. the *Appeal*, pp. 3–13, where Montagu responds to the charge that views expressed in his *Gagg* savored of Arminianism. Chapters 5, 8, and 11 of part I of the *Appeal* deal with specific doctrinal points that were touched on at the Synod of Dort.

53. The editor of the Knightley text has incorrectly inserted *Vorstius* in the printed edition where *Bert* existed in the MS. (*C.D. 1625*, p. 48). Petrus Bertius (1565–1629), a student of James Arminius at the University of Leiden, besides writing several books on geography, collected the works of Arminius which were printed in Frankfurt in 1631 (*Jacobi Arminii, Opera Theologica . . .*). He also wrote a biography, *The Life and Death of James Arminius and Simon Episcopius*, published in Leiden in 1609 and translated and printed in London in 1672 (Wing, *S.T.C.*, no. B2048). Concerning James I's censure of Arminius and Bertius, see below, n. 100.

54. The Synod of Dort, which met in 1619, condemned Arminianism. James I supported the Synod by sending four English representatives: George Carleton, John Davenant, Joseph Hall, and Samuel Ward (all of whom are included in the *D.N.B.*). The Scottish representative was Walter Balcanquhall (see note below).

For Montagu's remarks concerning the Synod of Dort, see above, n. 8. On the Synod of Dort, itself, see also, Thomas Fuller, *The Church History of Britain* (London, 1837), III, 274–279; and see the account of the Synod, including extracts from the letters of John Hales and Walter Balcanquhall, printed in James Nichols, *The Works of James Arminius* (London, 1825), I, 422–515.

55. Walter Balcanquhall, Dean of Rochester. *D.N.B.* Balcanquhall was a member of the Synod of Dort and his letters from the Netherlands to Sir Dudley Carleton are collected in John Hales's *Golden Remains* (London, 1659) (Wing, *S.T.C.*, no. H269).

56. See above, n. 12.

57. See above, n. 11.

58. The *Appeal*, p. 114: "For whereas the Puritans were wont to be shrouded under the covert of the Church of England . . . M. Montagu . . . has disbanded them from their shelter . . . to the high displeasure (no doubt) and distaste of such a potent overweening faction as they are".

Ibid., p. 136: ". . . for they may be many a strong, potent, prevailing party that thus opine . . .".

See also, above, n. 13.

calls Puritans, but does not define a Puritan, and yet he says a Puritan is worse than a papist. Engrossers and regraters are defined by statute;[59] if Puritans be so bad, it were good we knew them. But Mr. Montagu leaves this uncertain, for by his opinion we may be all Puritans. Mr. Ward and Mr. Yates are Puritans, and yet these are men that subscribe and conform. 2. He says there are Puritans in heart. 3. Bishops may be Puritans, *tantum non episcopatu puritani*.[60]

[f. 28v] 2ly. In slighting those famous divines who have been great lights in this Church: Calvin, Beza, Perkins, and Whitaker.[61]

3ly. In laboring to discountenance and disgrace God's holy word, of which three instances are produced.

First, concerning lectures, not lecturers, which are always settled by authority, he has these words "prophetical determinations" in conventicles after lectures, and these, chewing the cud after lectures,[62] which is a metaphor commonly used by divines for meditation, and spoken of him by way of scorn. 2ly. Concerning preaching, he has these words: prating, preaching, and lecturing,[63] and dictates out of pulpits[64] before a popular auditory, and, the souls in *limbus patrum* not circumscribed as Mr. Yates and Mr. Ward in their pulpits.[65] 3ly. Concerning the Bible, he has these words: "Never a saint-seeming, Bible-bearing hypocritical Puritan in the pack",[66] etc.

4ly. That he gives men encouragement to persevere in popery, or to turn to it, which was thus proved: first, in that af-firming Rome to be a true church and the spouse of Christ, etc.[67] 2. In that the book was exceedingly read and commended by papists.

The third general charge, of matter offensive to the House, consisted in two points.

First, in presuming to print this second book in defense of the first before the same was examined and approved, knowing that there was a complaint against him in parliament, which stood referred by this House to my Lord of Canterbury.[68]

[f. 29] 2ly. Whereas every man that makes any complaint to the parliament is to be protected by privilege of parliament, both in his person and his fame, during the prosecution of his complaint; he, knowing Mr. Yates and Mr. Ward to be the complainants, has published in print divers reviling and scornful speeches against them contrary to that privilege.[69]

Three points were ordered upon this report.

First, that the same committee who had formerly been with my Lord of Canterbury should again repair to his Grace with thanks from the House for his pains in this business.[70]

2ly. A subcommittee was appointed to draw into writing all such articles and passages in Mr. Montagu's book as any way tended to the disturbance of the Church or state, that so the complaint might in a parliamentary manner be transferred to the Lords.[71]

3ly. That for his offense to the House he

---

59. *S.R.*, 5 & 6 *E.* VI, c. 14, *An act against regraters, forestallers, and engrossers.*

60. See above, n. 13.

61. See above, n. 15.

62. See above, n. 16.

63. See above, n. 17.

64. *quiliats. C.D. 1625* (Knightley MS.). See above, n. 17.

65. See above, n. 18.

66. See above, n. 19.

67. See above, nn. 4 and 20.

68. See above, n. 3.

69. See above, nn. 3, 24, and 34.

70. See above, n. 26.

71. For the appointment of the committee, see above, p. 335. The fact that all but two (Sherland and Whitaker) of these men already served on the committee concerning Montagu may explain the reference to them here as a "subcommittee". For debate on this and the following point, see above, pp. 334–335, and see below.

should for the present stand committed to the Serjeant, but his further punishment respited till the complaint with the Lords were adjudged.

The first of these endured[72] no debate. To the other two there was a common exception: That one parliament ought not to take notice of an offense committed against another parliament. But this was quickly suppressed, the contrary course of former parliaments upon all occasions appearing, and in particular Dr. Cowell's case was alleged, who, for a book written against one parliament, was punished in another.[73]

Those who would have diverted the second,[74] did it either by questioning the cognizance of the House in matters of religion, or by insinuating, so much as they dared, [f. 29v] a defense of Mr. Montagu's doctrine, as being popular and most common, and not yet condemned by the Church of England.

Wherein MR. DYOTT proceeded so far that he gave distaste to the House.

But the weight both of number and reasons were on the other side. Some insisted upon the general ground that the civil courts ought to have a care of the peace of the Church.

To which purpose SIR EDWARD COKE alleged *Fleta, cap. 1°*.[75]

Others, that we did not make the complaint directly for the doctrine but for the sedition.

Others, that it did sufficiently appear by the Articles what the doctrine of the English Church is, and we shall desire but justice in the execution of the law, if he have published anything contrary to those Articles.[76]

And MR. WHITAKER remembered that Barret[77] in Cambridge was forced to make a public recantation of the same points; and yet now Cambridge was so much infected as that he heard that there had been a motion for allowance of Montagu's book by the censure of the University and subscription of all graduates.

To the third, some against the charge: That for that part which concerned my Lord of Canterbury, he was his judge and might punish him himself; and touching the House, there was no offense, but only as it concerned the informers.

To this purpose, MR. C[HANCELLOR] OF THE DUCHY. That he took no pleasure in creating faults. Ill precedents are no where so dangerous as in parliament. It was no offense for him to justify himself in a cause

---

72. *induced*. B.L. Add. 26, 639.

73. John Cowell, Regius Professor of Civil Law at Cambridge, was the author of a law dictionary (*The Interpreter* [London, 1607]; *S.T.C.*, no. 5900) that defined the King as an absolute monarch and derogated the authority of parliament with regard to making laws and giving subsidies. The parliament of 1610 initiated proceedings against Cowell (Foster, *C.D. 1610*, I, xxix, 18, 24–25, 27, 180–181, 183–190; II, 33, 37–39, 48–51, 59; *C.J.*, I, 399–400, 405, 408–409; *L.J.*, II, 557, 561, 563) but dropped them when, on 25 March 1610, James I issued a proclamation suppressing the work (*Stuart Proclamations*, I, 243–245). It does not appear that Cowell's *Interpreter* was directed against a specific parliament; the book and its author were from time to time mentioned in sessions after 1610 but no proceedings were initiated against Cowell after that date. See Levack, *Civil Lawyers, sub*

Cowell.

74. I.e., the second order, above.

75. Cf. *Fleta*, Book II, chapter 1, "Of Civil Personal Actions".

76. I.e., the Articles put forth by the Church of England in 1562. See above, n. 4.

77. *Garret. C.D. 1625* (Knightley MS.). William Barret was a Cambridge divine, fellow of Caius College. His attack on the Calvinist tenets led to his being questioned by the Cambridge authorities and on 10 May 1595 he was forced to read a recantation which, in the face of further dispute with the college heads, he later retracted (the recantation along with an account of the Barret affair was printed by William Prynne in his *Anti-Arminianism* [London, 1630], pp. 59–71; *S.T.C.*, no. 20458). *D.N.B.*; McGrath, *Papists and Puritans*, pp. 322–323.

which was not judged; and to make a recantation upon my Lord Grace of Canterbury's command he was not bound.

Others against the punishment: If we should lay any upon him before, we shall thereby abate [f. 30] the eagerness of the judges in that which is the principal part of the cause; for if it be small, it will not be suitable to the dignity of the House; if great, the Lords will not think good to add any more.

And this reason prevailed so far, though not to exempt him, yet to respite the particular assignation of any punishment for his contempt to the House.

SIR E. COKE, to prove the contempt against law, did allege the last article of *Capitula Itineris: Et similiter de hiis qui vindictam*,[78] etc. And there was a revenge by the tongue or pen as well as by the hand.

Yet it was resolved he should remain in the custody of the Serjeant, with a private intimation that he might, if he thought good, take bond for his appearance the first day to the next sitting.[79]

By occasion whereof it was affirmed by SIR EDWARD COKE that the House could not take a recognizance.[80]

This debate had been a little interrupted by a message from the Lords, who sent back the bill touching alehouses with some enlargement, whereby it was likewise extended to taverners.[81]

The same messengers brought from them a petition to that House from the prisoners of the Fleet desiring some help by *habeas corpus* in respect of the infectious time, whereto their Lordships had deferred to give answer without conference with us because they heard that we had a bill depending touching that matter.[82]

[Afternoon]
Eodem die post meridiem.

[f. 30v] A report was made upon Sir James Perrot's case, who had exhibited a complaint against the election of Mr. Wogan[83] and[84] of the knights of [Pembrokeshire].[85] Two exceptions were alleged at the committee. First, of misdemeanors precedent to the election, by false rumors of Sir James Perrot's death, threatening, etc. 2ly, misdemeanors concomitant with the election, the freeholders that stood for Sir James Perrot being interrupted and refused. But neither of those two points were proved at the committee by the plaintiff.

A third exception was now propounded in the House: the disability of the sheriff to execute the writ, his commission not having been then renewed since the King's death. And it was doubted whether the proclamation which did establish all officers in the execution of their offices would enable him to this purpose.[86]

78. *S.R.*, Uncertain date, *Capitula Itineris* (the Articles of the Eyre), Concerning trespassers upon religious houses, art. 4 (*S.R.*, I, 237). Sir Edward Coke is quoting from the article: And likewise of those who have taken revenge [because that any have complained in the King's Court].

79. See above, n. 37.

80. A recognizance could be issued only from a court of record or a duly authorized magistrate. Black's *Law Dict.*

81. *taverns. C.D. 1625* (Knightley MS.).

82. For the petition of the prisoners in the Fleet, see above, H. of L., 6 July, p. 99. On 27 June the House had read twice and committed a bill to prevent the granting of writs of *habeas corpus* (see above, H. of C., 27 June, O.B.).

83. MS.: *Huggens*; *Hagens* in *C.D. 1625* (Knightley MS.).

84. *on. C.D. 1625* (Knightley MS.).

85. Both the Bedford and Knightley MSS. are blank here; the printed Knightley text includes the word *Pembrokeshire* in square brackets. See above, n. 39.

86. The proclamation referred to was issued on 28 March 1625 at the advent of the new King, and was entitled: A proclamation signifying his Majesty's pleasure that all men being in office of government at the decease of his most dear and most royal father, King James, shall so continue till his Majesty's further direction. The proclamation is printed in *Stuart Proclamations*, II, 4–6.

It was desired on the one part that the cause might be dismissed for want of proof (although Sir James alleged he had very sufficient witnesses to both points, if he might have time to bring them up), on the other part he desired judgment upon the last point.

The House—taking into consideration that this exception might extend to very many elections, and was a point of great consequence in other respects; on the other side, to give a new day after a hearing and examination of witnesses was to make a precedent for supplemental proof and be a means to delay the ending of causes—remained a while in some doubt till it was propounded: that hearing to be only *ex parte;* for the plaintiff might inform the court that he had *probabilem causam litigandi,* and so they might resolve to retain the cause; but it was never intended to be definitive, for in justice [f. 31] (whatsoever Sir James should have proved) we could not have denied the sheriff a time for defense; whereupon it was resolved that a new day peremptorily to both sides should be assigned.[87]

An act for continuing the session notwithstanding the King's royal assent.

Divers exceptions were propounded against this bill.

MR. ROLLE. That it was against the ancient course; would induce a great inconvenience by the continuing of privilege (which, as SIR H. MARTEN affirmed, the subjects in 18 found to be a worse burden than the subsidies).[88] That it would prevent the subjects in their expectation of a pardon, and all this without any fruit; for nothing is gotten at [but] the forwardness of divers bills which need not be read again, and this will be rather mischievous because the effect of these bills will be out of memory.[89]

MR. GLANVILLE. Acts are ours while we are together, but after we have passed them judges have the interpretation of them. Divers mischiefs were found in 18 which the parliament did not foresee. To recommit engrossed bills will be a dangerous precedent.

MR. SOLICITOR on the other part. That if we made it a session, the expectation of the country would be greater than if it were only an adjournment; and we shall have a more seasonable time thereafter to give them full satisfaction.

87. *admitted.* B.L. Add. 26, 639. It was resolved to leave the business of the Pembrokeshire election to the committee of privileges. See above, p. 336.

88. The MS. does not make it clear whether Marten actually spoke in the House at this point or whether Rolle was simply citing some earlier comment of Marten. The matter of adjournment was heatedly debated in 1621 and Sir Nathaniel Rich proposed that the House draw a "short bill or clause that the sessions should not end, notwithstanding the passing of such bills". Nicholas, *Proceedings and Debates in 1621,* II, 113. Concerning the 1621 summer adjournment, see above, H. of L., 6 July, n. 4; and see *C.D. 1621,* I, Index, *sub* Parliament, Adjournment of, June. Continuing privilege during an adjournment (as contrasted with a prorogation or dissolution where privilege ended sixteen days after the session was dissolved) presented problems vis à vis the inability to prosecute misdemeanors of parliament men and their servants because of their continued freedom from arrest and imprisonment and from law suits. On 20

November 1621, the first day of sitting following the summer adjournment, the attention of the Lower House had been directed to abuses of privilege through misuse of protections by members of both Houses which had "raised a universal complaint in the city and country" (*C.D. 1621,* IV, 420). See *C.J.,* I, 641; *C.D. 1621,* III, 409–410; IV, 420–421.

The question of continuing parliamentary privileges during the 1625 adjournment had been raised on 6 July by a motion from Sir Robert Phelips which was referred to the committee of privileges for consideration. See above, p. 322.

89. I.e., the pardon, traditionally granted at the close of a session, would not be issued at the time of the adjournment but rather at the final dissolution of the session, thus delaying the effect of the pardoning powers. The advantage of an adjournment over a dissolution was that the work of successive readings and debate on legislation would not be lost, i.e., the bills would carry from one meeting to the next in the state they were in at the time of the adjournment.

So the bill was passed.

MR. CHOLMLEY in behalf of his father, the sheriff of Yorkshire, desired the direction of the House in three points, whereof he doubted:[90] first, [f. 31v] whether such as come after 11 a clock may have voice? 2ly, whether he may examine the party upon oath in this or any the like case, except only that which is mentioned in the statute 8 *H.* 6, *cap.* 7?[91] 3ly, whether for better dispatch in polling, such deputies as he shall make may take these oaths.

After some debate upon these particulars, wherein there was variety of opinions, it was resolved upon the proposition of MR. LITTLETON and SIR WALTER PYE to leave the sheriff to be advised by his counsel, it not being our office, as[92] we are a court of judicature, to make or to declare the law in cases not yet in being; and if we should proceed otherwise, we shall bring orders to be in the nature of acts of parliament.

III. PETYT 538/8, INNER TEMPLE LIBRARY

[f. 123] [Thursday, 7 July 1625][93]

And upon examination of the whole justice[94] the committee agreed in opinion [which][95] was reported by Mr. Recorder, SIR HENEAGE FINCH, who did report: That

they did find in his former book he had committed an error contrary to the 19 Article established in the 13th year of the Queen Elizabeth, in that he held that *ecclesia romana est vera ecclesia et sponsa Christi.* And, contrary [f. 123v] to the 25 Article, in that he says *eodem fundamento doctrinae et sacramentorum nititur;* whereas they held 7 sacraments, and we two.[96]

And as touching the second book;[97] the opinion of the committee was that it tends much to the dishonor of his late Majesty who, writing of the religion and state of the Low Countries, shows therein that Arminius was the first, and his scholar at Leiden the second, that wrote a book most impudently in the defense and maintenance of that heresy.[98] The King showed his care to suppress the same, for which the Synod of Dort was principally called, whereto his Majesty sent four commissioners, grave and learned divines, who were presented by his Majesty's ambassador, Sir Dudley Carleton, unto that Synod, and there treated by his Majesty's appointment and direction for the suppressing of that heresy and settling of religion there according to the truth, whereon they dealt very worthily and denounced the same to be erroneous.[99] And the King, in his book against Vorstius,[100] sets forth as much, yet does he

90. See above, n. 42.

91. *S.R.,* 8 *H.* VI, c. 7, concerning elections of knights of the shires.

92. MS.: *and.* The word *as* is used in the Knightley text.

93. What follows is the continuation of the compiled narrative of the Montagu business which began under 1 July. See above, H. of C., 1 July, n. 47.

94. *business.* B.L. Add. 48,091 and Q.C. 449.

95. The words and phrases in brackets, here and below, are included in B.L. Add. 48,091 and Q.C. 449 but omitted in Petyt 538/8.

96. See above, n. 4.

97. I.e., the *Appeal.*

98. See below, n. 100.

99. See above, n. 54.

100. In 1611, after reading copies of two theological tracts written by Conrad Vorstius, who had been called to fill the place of divinity reader at the

University of Leiden vacated by the death of James Arminius, James I wrote to the States General requesting that they banish Vorstius, a "wretched heretic", from their dominions. As a narrative and explanation of his actions against Vorstius, James had published in 1612 several issues of a work entitled: *His Majesties Declaration concerning his Proceedings with the States General of the United Provinces of the Low Countreys, In the cause of D. Conradus Vorstius* (*S.T.C.,* nos. 9229–9233) in which he stated (*S.T.C.,* no. 9233, p. 15): "But before we had received this answer [of 1 October 1611] from the States, some of Vorstius's books were brought over into England, and (as it was reported) not without the knowledge and direction of the author. And about the same time one Bertius, a scholar of the late Arminius (who was the first in our age that infected Leiden with heresy) was so impudent as to send a letter unto the Archbishop of Canterbury, with a book entitled *De Apostasia Sanctorum.* And not thinking it sufficient to

not only slight the King's book, but that Synod, [f. 124] calling it forensical and partial, and knows not what particular ends they consented thereunto, nor cares.[101] And the fire being now kindled in the Low Countries was not only by this means blown[102] greater there, but broached here. And withal he affirms that the Church of England is contrary to that which they there concluded.[103]

3. A third offense [was] for dedicating it to the King and affirming that the Pope is not Antichrist; and affirming that he never saw any persuasive argument to induce him so to think whenas the King, in his book which he dedicated to the Emperor Rudolph, labored to prove the Pope to be Antichrist by most excellent arguments;[104] how is he likely to prevail in it whenas a subject of his own shall write against it.

4. A fourth offense against [the] 38th Article of Ireland: that justifying faith cannot be lost totally, nor finally, which agrees with our Church; Mr. Montagu expressed the contrary.[105]

5. A fifth offense: that there is enough in this book (if it be credited) to make a [f. 124v] breach and raise sedition between the King and his subjects in alleging that they desire an anarchy or parity in religion, which he pretended to be done by that faction of Puritans. And so through the odious name of Puritan [strikes through the sides of our religion and ranks the Puritan] with the Jesuit—the one desiring anarchy, the other a tyranny. And he has [not] only tra-

duced Yates and Ward, who were the complainants, men that have subscribed and conformed to the government of our Church, and grave preachers, but says that we have likewise Puritan bishops that were now *episcopi et tanquam episcopi* and are in heart Puritans.[106]

6. A sixth offense: the slighting of the great and reverent divines as speaking of Calvin, Beza, Perkins, Whitaker, Reynolds, etc., and of him that wrote the thesis or Dr. Prideaux, with little or no respect at all. But when he speaks of Bellarmine, he gives him attributes of worth and reputation.[107]

A 7th offense: the public disturbing and discountenancing of the preaching[108] of [God's holy word and the disgracing of] lectures.

The 8th page, branding them to make public conventicles, and abusing the professors thereof with unseemly speeches, [f. 125] viz., that there is never a saint-seeming, book-bearing hypocritical Puritan, etc., and disgracing the reading of the Bible and the preaching and professing thereof, coupling prating and preaching together, and the informers may dictate out of the pulpit, *tanquam ex tripode*.[109]

And with offense: this book is read by papists and commended and allowed of by them, as a most excellent work.

But the thing that this House looks upon is first the disturbance of the public peace and state of the Church, and the dishonor and injury done to this House.

For the first, there is too much public

---

avow the sending of such a book (the title whereof only were enough to make it worthy the fire) he was moreover so shameless as to maintain in his letter to the Archbishop that the doctrine contained in his book was agreeable with the doctrine of the Church of England". James then went on to quote a letter which he had sent to the States General on this matter, in which he refers to Arminius as an "enemy of God" and condemns the "arrogancy of these heretics".
Concerning Bertius, see above, n. 53.

101. See above, n. 8.
102. *grown*. Q.C. 449.
103. See above, n. 8.

104. See above, n. 11.
105. See above, n. 12.
106. See above nn. 13 and 58.
107. See above, n. 15. John Prideaux, who had been appointed to succeed George Abbot in 1615 as Regius Professor of Divinity at Oxford, was rector of Exeter College, a canon of Salisbury Cathedral, and vicar of Chalgrove, Oxfordshire; he is not mentioned in the other accounts nor do we find direct reference to him in the *Appeal. D.N.B.*
108. *preachers*. B.L. Add. 48,091.
109. See above, nn. 16–19.

notice taken of it and therefore that is without gainsaying; for the second, the injury done to the House consists in these two things: He confessed he had notice of the dislike of the House and the Archbishop's command to view and amend it, and did nothing but printed this second in justification of the other. Secondly, whenas Yates and Ward had once informed this House of his abuse, [f. 125v] his traducing of them and railing against them is injurious to the honor and dignity of the House and in this second book he calls them public promoters and, page the 176, he says not written by Yates and Ward but collected by some other at odds with his own brain.[110]

This report being made, it was resolved first to give thanks to the Archbishop for his grave and discreet carriage of that business, and next to move the Lords to join with us in a conference which is fit to be done touching him and his positions; disturbance of the peace and of the Church is matter for this House to inquire of, Westminster 1, *cap.* 1.[111]

And the time being short, they ordered to defer his censure until the next meeting and then to move the Lords to join with us.

In the mean season, in respect he had committed a contempt against the House, he was ordered to be brought to the bar, and there to kneel while the Speaker did deliver unto him the opinion of the House which was [f. 126] that they would not enter into any censure of him but, in respect of his great contempt committed against the House, he should stand committed to the Serjeant's ward, to the intent he may be forthcoming at their [next] meeting to know the further pleasure of the House; and withal intimated unto the Serjeant that he might take his bond for his appearance at their next meeting.[112]

And so he being called into the House to the bar accordingly had it delivered unto him by the SPEAKER, Montagu kneeling all the while on his knee. And that being done, he departed without speaking [ever a word].[113]

And about 2 days after, the King sent a message unto the House by the Solicitor.[114]

110. See above, n. 24.
111. *S.R., 3 E.* I, *Statutum Westm. Prim.,* c. 1.
112. See above, nn. 3 and 37.
113. *without speaking one word.* Q.C. 449.
114. For the King's message concerning Montagu, spoken to Solicitor Heath upon the delivery of the petition concerning religion on 8 July and reported to

the House by the Solicitor on 9 July, see below, H. of C., 9 July, O.B. In the MS. the message is not dated but is included as part of the narrative on the Montagu business. In order to preserve the chronological continuity established in the C.J., we have placed the Petyt 538/8 account of the message with the proceedings on 9 July. See below, p. 364.

HOUSE OF COMMONS
ORDER OF BUSINESS   FRIDAY, 8 JULY 1625

L. 3a. An act for the grant of two
   entire **subsidies** by the
   temporaly: passed   347, 350, *30/6

Message to the Lords sending up
   the above bill (Sir Thomas
   Edmondes, Treasurer)   347, 350, 354

Resolved: to send message to the
   Lords accepting the
   conference proposed
   yesterday on the petition
   from the **prisoners in the
   Fleet** concerning *habeas corpus*   347, 350, *7/7;
                                                9/7

Committee for a conference on
   the petition from the
   prisoners in the Fleet:
   appointed   347, *9/7

Message from the Lords bringing
   a bill for the **Earl of Dorset**
   (Sir Henry Finch and
   Richard Amherst) [*see below*]   347

Message from the King
   concerning his estate (SIR
   JOHN COKE)   347, 350, 354;
                        N, 521

SIR JOHN COKE   352; **N**, 522
SIR WILLIAM BEECHER   352; **N**, 522
EDWARD LITTLETON   352, 355
SIR EDWARD GILES   352
SIR THOMAS GRANTHAM   **N**, 522
SIR ROBERT HEATH (Solicitor)   352

Message to the Lords sending up
   the bill that this **session** of
   parliament shall not
   determine by royal assent to
   one or more acts (Lord
   Cavendish)   348, *5/7

Report from the **committee of
   privileges** concerning Arthur
   Basset (SIR GEORGE MORE)
   [*see below*]   348, 353, *28/6

ANTHONY LANGSTON: delivers a
   petition from Sir Robert
   Basset   353

Petition from Sir Robert Basset:
   read   348

EDWARD LITTLETON   348, *353*
RICHARD TAYLOR   348
HENRY ROLLE   348, *354*

Message from the Lords: the
   King will receive the petition
   concerning religion this
   afternoon (Sir Thomas
   Coventry, Att. General, and
   Sir Humphrey Davenport)   349, 354, *24/6
   [*The petition concerning religion is
   printed on pp. 155–160*]

Answer given to the Lords'
   message: Commons'
   committee will join with the
   Lords in attending the King
   accordingly   349

Committee to join with Lords in
   delivering the **petition
   concerning religion**:
   appointed; Sir Robert Heath
   (Solicitor) to report   349, 354; **N**,
                                     510

THOMAS MALET: continues
   debate concerning Arthur
   Basset [*see above*]   349, *354*

SIR HENEAGE FINCH (Recorder)   349, *354*

Upon question: Arthur Basset to
   have privilege of parliament;
   a warrant to be made to bring
   him to the House   349, 354; **N**,
                                     516

L. 3a. An act of a subsidy of
   tonnage and poundage:
   passed   349, *5/7
   [*Afternoon*]

L. 1a. and L. 2a. An act for the
   Earl of Dorset touching lands
   appointed to be sold by
   Richard, late Earl of Dorset,
   to pay his debts, etc.:
   committed [*see above*]   349, *9/7; 2/8;
                                     8/8; 9/8

SIR GEORGE MORE: concerning
   petitions for **privilege** of
   parliament   350

Ordered: More to deliver to the

FRIDAY, 8 JULY 1625

I. JOURNAL OF THE HOUSE OF COMMONS

[C.J. 806]

[p. 25] *Veneris, 8° Julii, 1° Caroli Regis*

L. 3ª. An act for the grant of 2 entire subsidies granted by the temporalty. Upon question, passed; and sent up by Mr. Treasurer.

Resolved, to send up to the Lords to accept the conference yesterday desired by Sir John Coke.[1]

[col. 1]	[col. 2]
Mr. Treasurer	Sir John Stradling
Lord Cavendish	Sir George More
Chancellor Duchy	Mr. Cholmley
Sir Nathaniel Rich[2]	Mr. [John] Rudhale
Sir Arthur Ingram	Sir Benjamin Rudyard
Sir John Coke	Sir John Hippisley
Mr. [John] Crew	Mr. [Henry] Rolle
Sir William Herbert	Sir Maurice Berkeley
Sir William Owen	

[col. 3]
Serjeant Ashley
Mr. Recorder
Sir Thomas Fanshawe
Mr. [John] Glanville
appointed for this conference.[3]

[p. 26] Mr. Serjeant Finch and Serjeant Amherst bring from the Lords a bill/[4]

SIR JOHN COKE[5] reports a commandment from his Majesty: That the King understands of our grant of 2 subsidies, which the King most graciously accepts as an argument of his subjects' love to him, accepts the manner of it, that not moved by any officers of state;[6] is very well pleased with our pressing of the accounts of the last subsidies.[7]

That the charge for the 4 regiments of the Low Countries gave the /

That the 2 subsidies now granted spent e'er received. No part of the navy charge (which is above 200,000 *l.*) out of the 3 last subsidies. The King has disbursed 46,000 *l.*

---

1. The meaning of "by Sir John Coke" is unclear. The message requesting a conference on the petition of the prisoners in the Fleet had been brought down from the Lords by Attorney General Coventry and Serjeant Davenport on 7 July. It may be that Coke was being assigned to take this message up to the Lords, but the Upper House accounts indicate that the message was actually carried up to the Lords by Lord Cavendish later in the morning along with some other matter. See above, H. of L., 8 July, O.B.

2. *Mr. Solicitor* is crossed out in the MS. following *Chancellor Duchy*, and *Mr. Alford* is crossed out in the MS. following *Sir Nathaniel Rich.*

3. Because of the presentation of the petition concerning religion this afternoon (8 July) the Lords set the time for the conference on the petition from the prisoners in the Fleet concerning *habeas corpus* for eight o'clock the following morning. See H. of L., 8 July, p. 105, and 9 July, O.B.

4. I.e., An act for the Earl of Dorset. According to the L.J. (see above, p. 104), it was Serjeant Davenport rather than Serjeant Amherst who was assigned to accompany Serjeant Finch in carrying this bill to the Lower House.

5. For an explanation regarding the Duke of Buckingham's having chosen Sir John Coke to deliver this "commandment" or message from the King (and a version of the message itself), see Eliot, *Negotium*, be-

low, pp. 520–522.

A substantial part of Coke's message is omitted in the C.J. account. We have found two fuller versions: S.P. 16/4:23 (printed in the Appendix, below, pp. 654–656), which is in Coke's hand and contains some of his own minor emendations (S.P. 16/4:24 and S.P. 16/4:25 comprise rough drafts for S.P. 16/4:23; they are in Coke's hand and contain numerous revisions); and the version included, with minor variations, in Bedford MS. 197, below, pp. 350–352, and in Eliot, *Negotium*, below, pp. 521–522. A brief report of Coke's speech is included in the 9 July letter of Thomas Locke to Sir Dudley Carleton, S.P. 16/4:29, printed in the Appendix, below, pp. 707–708.

The matter of foreign policy and finances was discussed at length in the Oxford session. See below, H. of C., 4 August, O.B., and 9 August when John Pym reported the Lord Treasurer's account of the King's estate.

6. According to the extant records Sir Francis Seymour first motioned for subsidy on 30 June (see above, p. 274); the bill was first read in the Lower House on 4 July.

7. For proceedings in the House and in the committee of the whole concerning the accounts by the Council of War and the treasurers of the receipts and disbursements of the 1624 subsidy monies, see above, H. of C., 30 June, 1 and 6 July, O.B.s.

for the army of Denmark, 20,000 *l.* a month for Mansfeld.[8] The 2 subsidies not above 160,000 *l.*[9] His ordinary revenue/

The King, when Prince, took up for the navy [20,000 *l.*];[10] the Duke, above 44,000 *l.*; other officers of state, for about 50,000 *l.*

That the estate of his Majesty, in his royal throne, the estate of religion, civil wars in France/

Bill for continuance of the session sent up by the Lord Cavendish.[11]

SIR GEORGE MORE reports from the committee for privileges Mr. Basset's case: upon mesne process imprisoned, and after chosen a burgess.[12]

Sir William Bamfield's case: imprisoned by the Lord Keeper and after chosen and enlarged here.[13] Another, called [*blank*][14] imprisoned and enlarged. Trewynard's case.[15] The substance of his petition of this information[16] proved free.

A petition from Sir Robert Basset, read.[17]

MR. LITTLETON. That Mr. Basset well elected. No common law nor statute law against it. The mesne process but an accusation, not like an execution, which the fruit of the law.[18] *18° E. I, inhonestum* to distrain for rent upon a parliament man.[19]

[p. 27] MR. TAYLOR, *contra.*

MR. ROLLE, *pro. 1° H. VII.* 12.[20]

8. King Charles I had agreed to furnish Christian IV, King of Denmark, with 30,000 *l.* a month; by the end of May 1625 Charles had paid 46,000 *l.* on account (Gardiner, *History of England,* V, 323), and, according to the Venetian ambassadors' report, by July he had paid out 56,000 *l. Cal. S.P. Venetian, 1625–1626,* p. 113. Concerning the payments to Mansfeld, see below, n. 36.

9. According to Dietz, *Public Finance,* p. 393, the two subsidies voted in 1625 netted 126,986 *l.*, being worth each about 63,000 *l.* rather than the 80,000 *l.* anticipated by the crown. In 1624 a subsidy was figured to be worth 70,000 *l.* (see *C.J.,* I, 743).

10. The bracketed figure is taken from S.P. 16/4:23. See Appendix, below, p. 656. See also Pym's report of the Lord Treasurer's account of the King's estate, below, H. of C., 9 August, p. 431, where the figures are the same. The 50,000 *l.* from "other officers of state" was advanced by Sir William Russell, Treasurer of the Navy (see above, H. of L., 9 August, p. 163 and n. 61). Concerning private support of the war effort, see Dietz, *Public Finance,* p. 222.

11. I.e., An act that this session of parliament shall not determine by royal assent to one or more acts.

12. See above, H. of C., 28 June, n. 1; and see the account of More's report in Bedford MS. 197, below, p. 353.

13. Sir William Bamfield, M.P. for Bridport, had been committed by the Lord Chancellor after the summoning of the 1614 parliament but before his election to that session. His case was brought up on 9 April 1614 (*C.J.,* I, 458) and referred to the committee of privileges. Report was made from the committee on 14 April that he should have privilege by writ of *habeas corpus* (ibid., 464). Bamfield was brought into the Commons on 16 April where the Speaker desired to know

the pleasure of the House vis à vis the case (ibid., 466); no resolution is printed in the *C.J.* but the entry for 16 April 1614 in B.L. Add. 48,101 states that Bamfield was "placed in the House" (*C.D. 1621,* VII, 629). See also Hatsell, *Precedents,* I, 133.

14. Perhaps the case of Roger Brereton (cited in Bedford MS. 197, below, as "Brewston"), M.P. for Flint, who was committed for contempt by the judges of King's Bench on 23 November 1605, fourteen days after the parliament had been prorogued. Upon resumption of the parliament Brereton petitioned the House for release; on 13 February 1606 the House ordered a writ of *habeas corpus* for Brereton; and on 15 February he was received back into the House. *C.J.,* I, 262, 267, 269; *Bowyer,* pp. 23, 35; Hatsell, *Precedents,* I, 132. William Noy (*Reports and Cases Taken in the Time of Queen Elizabeth, King James and King Charles* [London, 1669], p. 17) indicates that Brereton had been committed for making an imperfect account before the auditors.

15. See above, H. of C., 23 June, n. 35.

16. *of this information* may be crossed out in the MS. and is omitted in the printed edition.

17. We have been unable to find the petition from Sir Robert, Arthur's father, who had pressed the charges of debt against Arthur. See above, H. of C., 28 June, n. 1, and below, n. 45.

18. Mesne process signifies any writ or process issued between the commencement of the action and the suing out of execution. Black's *Law Dict.*

19. *Rot. Parl.,* 18 *E.* I, no. 192. The case is also cited in Coke's *Fourth Inst.,* p. 24, and Hatsell, *Precedents,* I, 3.

20. Presumably this is the case of Roo vs. Sadcliffe, 1 *H.* VII, Hil., *rot.* 104, printed in Hatsell, *Precedents,* I, 51–52. Sadcliffe had been arrested and imprisoned under mesne process.

Mr. Attorney and Serjeant Davenport bring from the Lords a message: That his Majesty has appointed to receive the petition from both Houses this day,[21] at 3 of the clock, at Hampton Court.

Answer: Our committee will attend accordingly.[22]

Mr. Treasurer	Mr. Solicitor[24]
Sir Sackvile Trevor	Sir Benjamin
Mr. Chancellor Duchy	Rudyard[25]
Mr. Chancellor	Sir Miles Fleetwood
Exchequer[23]	Sir Thomas Badger
Sir William Herbert	Mr. Glanville
Sir John Coke	Sir John Scudamore[26]
Lord Cavendish	
Mr. [John] Rudhale	
Sir Francis Glanville	
Sir Richard Newport	

Mr. Solicitor to make the report.

MR. MALET. Upon a mesne process the party arresting has an interest in the prisoner, but only *ad respondendum*, not *ad satisfaciendum*, as in an execution. To enlarge him. The case appeared very lamentable on the petitioner's part.

MR. RECORDER, *accordant*. That he, in execution, not eligible because he cannot come to serve the commonwealth; where he, in upon mesne process, may, upon bail, come in and serve.[27] For otherwise one

coming into a borough to be chosen may be there arrested upon mesne process, and so not eligible if this rule hold. Any man, [**C.J. 807**] arrested upon a *latitat*, is in *custodia marescalli*, so then not eligible if this rule hold.[28]

Upon question, Mr. Basset shall have the privilege of this House. A warrant to the marshal to bring him to the House tomorrow morning, 8 clock.

L. 3ª. Act for the grant of the subsidies of tonnage and poundage. Upon question, passed.

[p. 28]

Veneris, 8° Julii, 1° Caroli Regis
[*Post Meridiem*]

L. 1ª., L. 2ª. Lord Dorset's bill. Committed to

Mr. [Henry] Rolle	Mr. [John] Middleton
Mr. [Robert] Caesar	Sir Edward Giles
Sir George More	Sir Robert Hatton
Mr. More	Mr. [William] Strode
Sir Thomas Puckering	Sir Dudley Digges
Sir Francis Fulforde	Sir John Franklin
Mr. [John] Pym	Sir Gilbert Gerard
Mr. Francis Drake	Mr. [Thomas] Reynell
Mr. [John] Delbridge	Sir Francis Wortley
Mr. [Thomas] Sherwill	Sir Ferdinando Fairfax
Sir John Danvers	Sir Francis Barrington
Mr. Cholmley	Sir Thomas Middleton
Mr. [Edward] Thomas	Sir Francis Popham

21. I.e., the petition concerning religion; see above, H. of C., 28 June, O.B., and below, 9 August, O.B.
22. Bedford MS. 197, below, states that twenty members were appointed to the committee; the C.J. lists sixteen final members although five additional names are crossed out on the C.J. list (see below, nn. 23–26). The Lords originally named eight members to their corresponding committee on 6 July, but on 8 July they apparently replaced one of the original members who was absent and added another member, bringing the Lords' committee total to nine members. See above, H. of L., 6 July, pp. 96–97, 98 and n. 12, and 99, and 8 July, p. 104.
23. *Sir Thomas Grantham* is crossed out in the MS. following *Mr. Chancellor Exchequer*.
24. *Mr. Recorder* is crossed out in the MS. before *Mr. Solicitor*.
25. *Sir B. Hicks* and *Mr. Pym* are crossed out in the

MS. following *Sir Benjamin Rudyard*.
26. *Sir Thomas Puckering* is crossed out in the MS. following *Sir John Scudamore*.
27. I.e., an arrest and sentence of imprisonment would preclude immediate bail, but on a writ of mesne process (see above, n. 18) a defendant could be released on security until final sentencing.
28. See Bedford MS. 197, below. If it can be argued that the payment of bail can be made only to the sheriff, and that a defendant in all actions of the King's Bench is in the custody of the marshal of that court and therefore unable to serve the commonwealth in parliament, then the way is open "in all elections where there is competition to have arrests upon great actions of one side or other" (Bedford MS. 197, below). Granting of privilege of parliament in this case forestalled setting a precedent for such arrests.

Mr. [William] Man   Mr. [Richard] Yarwood
Mr. [John] Sackville   Mr. [George] Lowe
Mr. Whitaker   Mr. [Robert] Bateman
Mr. [Philip]   Sir Edward Hales
   Mainwaring   Sir John Eliot
Mr. [Edward] Littleton   Mr. [Samuel] Owfield
       Mr. [Nicholas]
       Eversfield

Court of Wards, tomorrow morning, 7 clock.

SIR GEORGE MORE. That he has in hands above 20 petitions about privileges.

Ordered, he shall bring them sealed up and delivered to the Clerk, with a note of the order wherein they were received.[29]

The case for Warwick to hold, if time.

All bills in committees' hands to be brought and delivered to the Clerk, upon pain of censure of the House.

II. MS. 197, BEDFORD ESTATES, LONDON

[f. 31v]   8 *Julii* 1625.

The bill of subsidy was passed and sent up to the Lords.

A conference agreed upon with the Lords concerning the petition of the prisoners for *habeas corpus*.[30]

SIR JOHN COKE.[31] By commandment from the King, to give the House true information of his Majesty's estate, as he doubts not but that we came together with true affections; and that his Majesty graciously accepts the gift which is already resolved of as a welcome and [f. 32] pledge of the love not only of this representative body, but of the whole kingdom. Yet he takes notice of our anticipation of that business, and that we fall into it without intervention of any ministers of state,[32] which he imputes to our forwardness in his service, and confidence in his favor and correspondency with us.

That his Majesty is very well satisfied in our care and diligence to examine the account, not doubting but we shall find that not a penny of it has come into the Exchequer, or diverted to any other uses but such as were intended.[33] And as the general heads cannot be excepted against, so he hopes the particular disbursements will appear to have been well and necessarily disposed, and the fruit to be as great as the expenses. There has been disbursed for Ireland to confirm the peace of that kingdom 32,000 *l.* For the navy (the preparation for the enterprise now in hand not computed) 37,000 *l.* The office of the ordnance and fees[34] 47,000 *l.* For the support of the regiments in the Low Countries 99,000 *l.* The charge of Mansfeld's army 62,000 *l.*

And because from that last business had grown some doubts, he was commanded to give a more particular account of it. His late Majesty, loving peace and hating war, when he saw how ill he had been used, that the power of the contrary party had almost overspread Christendom, and his own people discontented at his seeming backwardness in this cause, yet considering the three subsidies we had given (though a royal gift) would only enable him for a while to secure his own, and that in the end he should grow from a lingering ague to a burning fever, and by suffering the enemy

---

29. I.e., in preparation for parliament's adjournment. The bills were also to be brought to the Clerk. See below.

30. See above, n. 3.

31. See above, n. 5.

32. See above, n. 6.

33. The 1624 subsidy act (*S.R.*, 21 *Jac.* I, c. 33) explicitly spelled out the uses of the subsidy for "public service" and "not for any private end" (pt. 44), and account was to be made to the House of Commons for the spending of the money levied (pt. 39). On the proceedings of the House with regard to the accounts of the 1624 subsidy monies, see above, H. of C., 30 June, 1 and 6 July, O.B.s.

34. *forts. C.D. 1625* (Knightley MS.). "Forts" is also the word used in the *Negotium* (below, p. 521) and in the detailed account of the disbursements of the 1624 subsidy monies which is printed in *Cal. S.P. Dom., Addenda, 1625–1649*, pp. 23–27, and which substantiates the figures given here by Coke.

to enjoy that which they had gotten, [f. 32v] and by degrees to fret upon the other princes of Germany, this only would ensue, that (like Ulysses by Polyphemus)[35] he should be last devoured, he negotiated and concluded a strong confederacy with the King of France and Denmark, the state of Venice, Duke of Savoy, and Low Countries. This first appeared in the army beyond the Alps, and in Mansfeld's army.

Some fault there were in these troops while they were at Dover which cannot be excused, yet Mansfeld complains we sent him such men as would be kept under no government. But it is objected: Wherefore was Count Mansfeld, a stranger,[36] chosen to lead those troops? The answer is: That they consisted of English, French, and Dutch. If an Englishman had been appointed, the French would have been discontented; so would the English under a Frenchman. If several commanders, precedence would have bred some difficulties; therefore no man was so fit to be lieutenant as such a one as was indifferent to both.

Another objection is taken from the event of those troops. But whosoever measures things by the event is no equal judge. It is true that the change of the design caused some delay and impeachment of that good effect which was hoped; yet they have not been altogether unprofitable, for

the appearance of that army kept divers princes of Germany from declaring themselves for the Emperor.[37]

His Majesty rests not here, but has commanded to give you an account of that which is and will be spent upon the preparation now in hand. The charges of this fleet, only in the office of the navy, is above 200,000 l.;[38] in the office of the ordnance, 48,000 l.; for the land men, will be 45,000 l.; [f. 33] whereof the two subsidies which are now given will amount but to 160,000 l.[39] But this is not all. He is to pay the King of Denmark 40,000 l. to draw him into Germany, besides a monthly payment of 20,000 l., both to him and Mansfeld,[40] with which business he cannot go through without further help by parliament, or else some new way, the ordinary revenue being exhausted and overcharged with other expenses both of necessity and honor.

The King, when he was Prince, borrowed 20,000 l. for these provisions, my Lord Admiral has engaged all his estate, other ministers have furnished above 50,000 l.[41] Shall it be said that these men are left to be undone by their readiness to public service? Shall we proclaim our own poverty by losing all that is bestowed[42] upon the enterprise because we cannot go through with it? What shall we say to the honor of the King? But that is not all; even the establishment of

---

35. Homer, *The Odyssey*, 9, 364–408.

36. Count Peter Ernst von Mansfeld (1580–1626) was a vigorous supporter of the Protestant cause during the Thirty Years War. He had fought for Frederick the Elector's Rhenish provinces against General Johannes Tserklaes, Count of Tilly, for as long as Frederick's finances held out, then entered the service of the United Provinces of the Netherlands during which time he acquired English support for the subsistence of his troops. *Allgemeine Deutsche Biographie*. In April 1624 James I had promised Mansfeld 20,000 *l*. per month but then found difficulty in raising the money. Initially the Council of War had refused to supply the funds but by 24 November they relented and offered an advance of 15,000 *l*. for the cost of levying the troops and 40,000 *l*. to pay his men for two months. Gardiner, *History of England*, V, 222, 271, and

sub Mansfeld; Dietz, *Public Finance*, p. 220. The warrants for paying these amounts are listed in the account printed in *Cal. S.P. Dom., Addenda, 1625–1649*, p. 27. Concerning the condition and conduct of the soldiers at Dover, see Gardiner, ibid., V, 282–284, and Dietz, ibid., pp. 220–222.

37. *enemy. C.D. 1625* (Knightley MS.). "Enemy" is also the word used in the *Negotium*, below, p. 521.

38. *20,000. C.D. 1625* (Knightley MS.). The naval preparations were in anticipation of the expedition to Cadiz which sailed in October 1625. On war expenditures, 1624–1628, see Dietz, *Public Finance*, pp. 216–222.

39. Concerning the subsidies, see above, n. 9.

40. See above, nn. 8 and 36.

41. See above, n. 10.

42. MS.: *bestowed by*.

his Majesty in his royal throne, the peace of Christendom, the state of religion, depend upon this fleet. The adversaries deliver very insolent speeches even[43] since their taking of Breda. The French incline to a civil war; they brandle in Italy and faint as their forefathers were wont to do after the first heat of an enterprise. Our German forces have kept the Catholic League from assembling at Ulm, to the full rooting out of the Palatine and ruining of other Protestants. What have we to reunite the Princes, to encourage the French, to support the States, to oppose the princes of the Catholic League, but the reputation of Mansfeld's army, which has put them to great charge, and the expectations of his Majesty's preparations?[44]

[f. 33v] Shall it be said that by the forsaking of his subjects he has been forced to abandon religion, to seek for a dishonorable peace? It is impossible for these things to subsist but by money or credit. A present resolution for money is not expected. It remains we should give thanks to his Majesty for his care of us by engaging himself so deeply, and whereof he thought fit we should go truly informed into our countries

that so we may the better satisfy the people; and in the meantime it is requisite we should express our own affection to the business now in hand and that when we return again we are willing to relieve his Majesty in some further proportion. And whether this be fit to be kept within the walls of the House, and not by some public message to the King, or other signification, to declare our forwardness to supply the actions now begun, he humbly left to the wisdom of the House.

This motion was seconded by none but by SIR WILLIAM BEECHER, who gave this reason: that public contribution granted by public authority and spent upon public affairs never hurt the kingdom. This last year there had been greater burdens of contribution than ever before, yet we find not the stock of the kingdom decayed, for more commodity has been exported than in former years.

Those that spoke against it were MR. LITTLETON and SIR EDWARD GILES.

The disposition of the House did so fully appear that MR. SOLICITOR (desperate of bringing it to effect) took care only to lay it

---

43. *ever. C.D. 1625* (Knightley MS.).

44. This marks the end of Coke's account of the King's estate. The following paragraph is Coke's motion that the House engage itself to make a further supply to the King in the future, thereby increasing the King's credit.

An undated set of provisional instructions from the King (S.P. 16/4:26), lacking both address and endorsement, has been tentatively placed by the editors of *Cal. S.P. Dom.* with the 8 July 1625 materials. However, dating the instructions is problematical since they contain a statement implying that the times for payment of the subsidies had not yet been determined, whereas on 30 June (see above, p. 276) the House had resolved on the dates for payment. The instructions are as follows:

It remains now, seeing all events are uncertain where multitudes must resolve, that I do give you this provisional instruction by his Majesty's direction. Namely, that if you shall find the propositions of his Majesty's supply dashed after the best questions have been made which you can get means to

propound and divide the House, then you are to stand up when all those hopes are passed and say that his Majesty had likewise given you warrant to move them in his name, when you should see the utmost of that business, not to deal with any other matter before they had agreed of the times of payments of the subsidies already granted [and] given order for a bill to be drawn, because nothing does more import him than to make some provision for payment of his loans, in respect of his care to keep his word with his honest subjects, and therein much will depend upon that certainty whereat he shall be by present understanding in what time he may expect the fruit of that grant. Whereunto he has willed me to add thus much further; that although he would have been glad by some further additions to have been assured of some future comings in when so great part of these two subsidies should be employed for discharge of his loan, yet he hopes to prevent the like growing necessities by a more frugal application of his own means for his own use.

aside quietly, which he did in a short speech, that in the act of subsidies and that of tonnage and poundage we had sufficiently expressed our affections. No man ought to speak in this House but as if the King of Spain did hear us; and it is enough if we make it but appear that whensoever we meet we shall bring with us the hearts of true Englishmen.

[f. 34] SIR GEORGE MORE made a report from the committee of privilege concerning a petition delivered by Mr. Basset, being a prisoner upon mesne process at the suit of his own father who, by practice with Sir Henry Helmes,[45] had brought an action against him for a great sum, whereas indeed nothing was due, that so his friends might be afraid to bail him, and they by imprisonment might draw from him some release or other conveyance of land assured to him. And since his imprisonment he was chosen a burgess for the parliament.

The opinion of the committee is that he ought to have privilege, to which they were induced by consideration of these precedents: Sir William Bamfield, committed by my Lord Chancellor Ellesmere, afterward chosen, was released by a message.[46] Trewynard's case, 38 *H.* 8,[47] and Mr.

Brewston's, [*blank*] Eliz.,[48] who was restrained upon an action of account. And of these reasons, that upon bail he might have been released. That it does not concern him alone, but the public service.

MR. LANGSTON delivered a petition from Sir R. Basset.[49]

And the business was debated in the House and some other reasons and precedents were urged for his privilege:

If he be well elected, no doubt but he must serve, and to void the election there is neither statute nor common law; and there is great difference between an execution and a mesne process, for in that case the sheriff is liable to an escape, but not in the other.[50]

In the time of H. 3, the Earl of Cornwall was cited as he was going to parliament, and the party was fined 2,000 *l.*[51]

Before *1° Jac.* the party without remedy, and [f. 34v] therefore the case of an execution was provided;[52] but there needed not any provision for this case because the plaintiff is at no mischief, because he may bring a new action. 34 *H.* 4, in Ferrers's case, the House was divided and the party helped by bill.[53]

---

45. According to a copy of a petition from Arthur Basset to the Lords in 1621 (Harl. MS. 6799, f. 79), Sir Robert Basset, his father, and Sir Thomas Monck had corruptly paid a 1,220 *l.* bribe to Sir Henry Helmes, a favorite of Lord Chancellor Bacon, in order to obtain a Chancery decree voiding a conveyance from Sir Robert to Arthur, thereby disinheriting the latter. On 8 May 1621 a private bill for strengthening the original conveyance to Arthur was read in the Commons, but no further action was taken on the bill. *C.J.*, I, 612; *C.D. 1621*, III, 197. Concerning Arthur Basset's 1625 petition, see above, H. of C., 28 June, n. 1.

46. See above, n. 13.

47. See above, H. of C., 23 June, n. 35. Trewynard's case was heard in 36 and 37 *H.* VIII.

48. Marginal note in the E. of Bedford's hand: "q. Sir William Cope's case". The MS. cites Brewston's case in the reign of Elizabeth where probably Brereton's case is meant. See above, n. 14. Concerning Cope's case, see above, H. of C., 21 June, n. 16, and 23 June, n. 5.

49. See above, n. 17.

50. See above, nn. 18 and 27. For the names of some of the speakers in this debate, see C.J., above, p. 349.

51. *Rot. Parl.*, 18 *E.* I, no. 4. Edmund, Earl of Cornwall (he inherited the title shortly before the death of H. III), was cited in parliament-time with a process from the Archbishop of Canterbury. He later recovered damages [given in William Ryley's *Placita Parliamentaria* as 2,000 marks], from Bogo de Clare who had pronounced the citation. See also, Hatsell, *Precedents*, I, 3–6, and Elsynge, *Parliaments*, p. 198.

52. *S.R.*, 1 *Jac.* I, c. 13, *An act for new executions to be sued against any which shall hereafter be delivered out of execution by privilege of parliament, and for discharge of them out of whose custody such persons shall be delivered.* See also, Elsynge, *Parliaments*, pp. 251–252.

53. 33 & 34 *H.* VIII, the case of George Ferrers, principally recorded in Holinshed's *Chronicles*, II, 824–826, and included in Hatsell, *Precedents*, I, 53–59; Elsynge, *Parliaments*, 203.

The mesne process is but an accusation, no true debt. 1 *H.* 7, fol. 10.[54]

If in this case we do not allow privilege, we shall be sure in all elections, where there is competition, to have arrests upon great actions of one side or other. Besides, the same reason will extend as well to those who are bailed, as to other; for in the eye of the law they are in prison,[55] and the bail is only to the sheriff, therefore, the defendant in all actions in the King's Bench is said to be in *custodia marescalli,* etc.

Against his privilege:

That the law makes his body liable as well to the action as to the execution, which cannot be taken away without wrong to the subject; especially seeing the law has not provided for his relief, as in case of execution.

None of the precedents fit with this case. Trewynard was taken after he was a member of this House; Brewston, after a session of parliament, wherein he had served; Sir William Bamfield, for a contempt which might be remitted without prejudice to any.[56]

[f. 35] If this be allowed, we shall empty the prisons and fill the parliament with such members as will take more care how to shift off their own debts than to provide good laws for the commonwealth.

But the House confirmed the opinion of the committee, and that a warrant must be made to the Serjeant to fetch him out of prison and to bring him to be released at the bar.

A message came from the Lords signifying that it was the King's pleasure to receive the petition concerning religion this afternoon at three of the clock.

For which service a committee of twenty was named to join with the Lords and to wait upon his Majesty at Hampton Court.[57]

III. PETYT 538/8, INNER TEMPLE LIBRARY

[f. 126v]   [Friday, 8 July 1625]

The bill of subsidies being engrossed and sent up to the Lords, and both Houses being resolved to send to the King to give them leave to rise shortly,[58] on Friday, being the eighth of July, SIR JOHN COKE [f. 127] brought a message from his Majesty to the House (being then very thin, and scarce a grand committee for number, many being gone down and the rest expecting daily to be dismissed):

That his Majesty took notice that there had been an account given to the House of the money that they had given in the former parliament, where withal the House was not fully satisfied. And his Majesty, commending their care in looking to it so exactly, had sent him to give them not only full satisfaction therein, but also that his Majesty would give them an account of the money which they now gave him at this time, how he had laid it out before such time as he had received it. And withal told them that unless they would supply his Majesty either with more money, or credit, all this great charges that they had been at, and all the hope of this great fleet, was like to perish and come to nothing for want of money to set it forth. And he showed them that his Majesty had already laid out 32,000 *l.* for the securing of Ireland: 37,000 *l.* for the repair of the navy; 47,000 *l.* [f. 127v] for the strengthening the forts; 99,000 *l.*[59] upon the 4 English regiments in the States Country; 62,000 *l.* laid out to Count Mans-

---

54. See above, n. 20.

55. MS.: *peril.* The more accurate word *prison* is used in the *C.D. 1625* (Knightley MS.).

56. Concerning the cases cited, see above, nn. 13 and 14, and see H. of C., 23 June, n. 35.

57. The message from Lords came as an interruption of the debate on privilege. See O.B. For the committee of sixteen agreed on by the Lower House to join with the Lords' committee in attending the King, see

above, p. 349 and n. 22.

58. The resolution with the Upper House to send to the King regarding the recess was not actually agreed upon until the conference of 9 July. See H. of L., 9 July, O.B.

59. MS.: *3,900 l.* The correct figure of 99,000 *l.* is used in B.L. Add. 48,091 and Q.C. 449. See *Cal. S.P. Dom., Addenda, 1625–1649,* p. 24.

feld. Total: two hundred three score and 17,000 *l.*;[60] and 35,000 *l.* to receive.

Besides 200,000 *l.*[61] and upwards upon the navy; 48,000 *l.* upon the ordnance; 45,000 *l.* in charges of the land men, 20,000 *l.* a month to Count Mansfeld, and 46,000 *l.*[62] to bring down the King of Denmark. Total of the latter sum is 339,000 *l.*[63]

MR. LITTLETON. This speech of message which has been delivered by that worthy member of our House from his Majesty consists of three parts: first, an account of money laid out that has been received; secondly, an account of money laid out before it is received (which is that we now give); and the third, a desire to have more money given. For the first, his Majesty is sufficiently (as it seems) informed, that we have not time to enter into [it]; for the second, his Majesty shows much grace to give an account before the money be paid; but, for the last, the House being now thin, and having given so freely so lately, he thought [f. 128] this came very unseasonably; and for credit, it was such a merchant-like[64] word that he knew not what to make of it.

And so the House, showing much dislike unto it (*viva voce*), rejected it with this declaration: that their dutiful affections should never be wanting to supply his Majesty's noble designs in a fit manner and at a convenient time.[65]

60. *287,000 l.* B.L. Add. 48,091 and Q.C. 449. The sum of the figures is 277,000, or two hundred three score and 17,000 as given in Petyt 538/8.

61. MS.: *20,000 l.* B.L. Add. 48,091, Q.C. 449, and the C.J. and Bedford MS. 197, above, give 200,000 *l.*

62. *40,000 l.* in Bedford MS. 197, above; the C.J. gives 46,000 *l.*

63. This is the sum of the above expenses excluding the 20,000 *l.* monthly payment due to Mansfeld.

64. MS.: *inacute-like. Merchant-like* is given in B.L. Add. 48,091 and Q.C. 449.

65. This entry is followed in the MS. by an account of the consideration of the petition from the prisoners of the Fleet concerning *habeas corpus* which occurred on 9 July. See below, H. of C., 9 July, pp. 364–365.

L. 2a. An act for passing of
accounts of sheriffs, etc.:
committed   358, *25/6
L. 1a. An act to repeal so much of
the statute 21 *H.* VIII, c. 13,
as does restrain **spiritual
persons** to take farms   358, *11/7
Arthur **Basset** brought into the
House by the marshal   358, *28/6
L. 2a. An act for planting and
increasing of **timber and
wood**: committed   358, *29/6
WILLIAM STRODE: concerning
ending the session; and that
no new business be
entertained [*see below*]   358, *5/7
Ordered: no new business to be
received into the House   361
HENRY ROLLE: moves to send up
to the Lords the bill of
tonnage and poundage and
to intimate that all business in
the Commons has been
dispatched   358, *5/7
Ordered: Sir Robert Heath
(Solicitor) to desire a
conference with the Lords
about the time of **recess of
this session** [*see above and
below*]   358, 361, *11/7
Report from the committee on
delivering the **petition
concerning religion** to the
King (SIR ROBERT HEATH,
Solicitor): on King's response
concerning: 358, 361, 364,
365
(1) the petition concerning
religion   *24/6
(2) the matter of Richard
Montagu [*see below*]   *29/6
(3) the petition against the
imposition on wines   *29/6
(4) the **recess of this session**
[*see above and below*]
SIR THOMAS CREW (Speaker):
questions the Serjeant

concerning **Montagu** [*see
above*]   359
The Serjeant: Montagu released
on bail   359, 364
SIR NATHANIEL RICH   362
Resolved: Sir Robert Heath
(Solicitor) to acquaint the
King that the House
proceeded only for
Montagu's contempt and the
Serjeant has set him at liberty
upon bail   359, 362
SIR THOMAS MIDDLETON:
concerning payment of
charges covered by the **1624
subsidy** act   362, *6/7
SIR ROBERT PYE   362
Message from the Lords bringing
the bill that this **session** of
parliament shall not
determine by royal assent to
one or more acts; with
addition of three words (Sir
Henry Finch and Sir
Humphrey Davenport) [*see
below*]   359, *364*, *5/7
Upon question: the above bill not
to be committed   359
Upon question: the words added
to the above bill by the Clerk
and read; and the bill passed   359
Report of Lord Chamberlain's
answer concerning restraint
of **players** going into the
country (SIR BENJAMIN
RUDYARD)   359, *6/7
Ordered: thanks to be returned
from the House to the Lord
Chamberlain   359
Sir Benjamin Rudyard to signify
to the lords of the Council
the desire of the House for
an order that certain **sports**
activities be restrained during
this contagious time   359
Report from the committee on
the bill concerning **petty**

SATURDAY, 9 JULY 1625

I. JOURNAL OF THE HOUSE OF COMMONS

[C.J. 807]

[p. 29] *Sabati, 9° Julii, 1° Caroli regis*

L. 2ᵃ. An act for passing of accounts of sheriffs, escheators, collectors of subsidies, tenths, 15eens, and aids without charge or delay.

Committed to

Sir John Stradling	Mr. [Edward] Littleton
Sir Dudley Digges	Sir Arthur Ingram
Sir William Pitt	Sir Edward Giles
Sir Arthur Herris	Mr. [John] Rudhale
Mr. [Thomas]	Sir Francis Goodwin
Wentworth	Sir Francis Popham
Sir Nathaniel Napier	Sir William Owen
Mr. [Richard] Taylor	Sir Benjamin Rudyard
Mr. [Anthony]	All knights of shires
Langston	
Mr. [John] Lowther	
Mr. [John] Shuter	

The first afternoon next meeting, Court of Wards.

L. 1ᵃ. An act to repeal so much of the statute made in the 21th year of the reign of our late sovereign lord King Henry the 8, *cap. 13°*, as does restrain spiritual persons to take farms.[1]

The marshal brought in Mr. Basset,[2] and then Mr. Speaker told the marshal that the/

L. 2. An act for increase of timber and wood.

Committed to

Sir George More	Mr. [John] Middleton
Sir Francis Goodwin	Sir William Masham

Lord Cavendish	Sir William Pitt
Sir Thomas Middleton	Sir Edward Hales
Sir John Stradling	Sir Oliver Cromwell
Mr. [John] Glanville	

And all that will come to have voice, 2 clock this afternoon, Exchequer.

MR. STRODE moves to send to the King for his license to depart on Monday morning, according to his Majesty's intimation.[3] And for an order that no new matter shall be entertained, in respect of the danger of the time and thinness of the House, and only finish that we have in hand.

[p. 30] MR. ROLLE. 1, to send up the bill of tonnage and poundage, and to intimate to the Lords that we have dispatched all our businesses here.[4]

Mr. Solicitor to desire a conference with the Lords about the time of our recess. Ordered; and to intimate to them that we are ready for a recess, and that we are ready for the other conferences.

MR. SOLICITOR reports from the King concerning the petition of religion: Lord President delivered the petition, with a preface from both Houses. Thanks for his grant of the fast, and gracing it with his presence.[5] Now came to present their petition concerning religion; the penning ours.

That the King's answer: Very glad we so forward in religion. Assured us we should find him as forward as we could wish, but our petition being long could not now answer, but shortly would.[6]

That his Majesty further said he heard

---

1. *S.R.*, 21 *H*. VIII, c. 13. *An act that no spiritual persons shall take to farm of the King or any other person any lands or tenements for time of life, lives, years or at will, etc., And for pluralities of benefices, and for residence.*

2. On Basset, see above, H. of C., 28 June, n. 1.

3. At a conference on 4 July the Lords had informed the Commons that they had received a message from the King earlier that day indicating that, because of the plague, the King was willing to end the session whenever the Houses were ready. See above, pp. 298, 305.

4. According to the Upper House records Lord Cavendish carried the bill of tonnage and poundage

up to the Lords with him when he went to give notice that the Lower House was ready for conferences concerning the business of the prisoners in the Fleet and concerning the recess. See H. of L., 9 July, O.B.

5. On 28 June the King had agreed to the petition for a general fast and dates were set. See above, H. of C., 28 June, O.B., and n. 14. The two Houses held their private fasts on 2 July.

6. For the petition concerning religion and the King's answers to it, which were presented to a meeting of both Houses on 8 August 1625, see above, H. of L., 9 August, pp. 155–160.

the House was very thin; and therefore wished, till we heard further from him, we should keep together.

That the King told him Montagu [was] his servant, his chaplain-in-ordinary, and that he had taken the cause into his own hand. That he wished we should enlarge him and he would take care to give the House satisfaction in the cause.[7]

That, for the wine petition, his Majesty received it and marvelled we should now press it, because his father had set it and he continued it for the maintenance of his sister, the Queen of Bohemia.[8]

For Mr. Montagu: the Serjeant, demanded by MR. SPEAKER where Mr. Montagu was, he said he had taken bail of 2,000 *l.* for his appearance.

Resolved, Mr. Solicitor shall acquaint his Majesty that the House proceeded only for his contempt to this House; and that the Serjeant has already set him at liberty upon bail.[9]

Serjeant Finch and Serjeant Davenport bring from the Lords our bill concerning the continuance of this session with addition of three word[s] only: *vizt.,* "or[10] letters patent".

Upon question, not to be committed.

Upon 2 question, these words to be added. Which done presently [by] the Clerk;

and then 3dly read and, upon question, passed.

[p. 31] SIR BENJAMIN RUDYARD returns answer from the Lord Chamberlain, that he has given order to the Master of the Revels not to suffer any players to play in any part of England during the time of this infection.[11]

Ordered, thanks to be returned from this House to his Lordship for his care therein.

Sir Benjamin Rudyard to signify to the lords of the Council that the desire of this House is their lordships will be pleased to give a general order to restrain bearbaiting, bullbaiting, generally, and bowling alleys near London, and other like meetings dangerous in this contagious time.[12]

MR. GLANVILLE reports the bill for petty larceny, which so much altered, as newly written.

L. 1ª. An act concerning petty larceny, and punishment of the offenses therein.

LORD CAVENDISH reports from the Lords. They are ready now presently for both conferences.

The committees went presently up, with commission for the *habeas corpus,* only to hear; and to intimate to the Lords our desire of recess upon Monday morning.

---

7. There is an indication in S.P. 16/4:19, an undated State Paper (see Appendix, below, p. 654), that the King would refer doctrinal arguments regarding Montagu's books to the Convocation. Parliament had avoided theological polemics thus far and had cited Montagu for contempt only (see H. of C., 7 July, O.B.). An account of the Solicitor's exchange with the King is included in Thomas Locke's letter of 9 July to Sir Dudley Carleton, S.P. 16/4:29 (see Appendix, below, p. 708). Concerning the Montagu business, see above, H. of C., 7 July, n. 3.

8. Concerning the wine merchants' complaints, see above, H. of C., 29 June, pp. 269–271 and nn. 11–19.

9. The resolution to inform the King regarding Montagu's situation with regard to the House was an effort to clarify the concern about Montagu's enlargement raised in the King's message, above. The motion for the resolution was made by Sir Nathaniel Rich. See

Bedford MS. 197, below.

10. MS.: *our.* See *S.R.,* 1 *Car.* I, c. 7.

Letters patent had been issued during the 1542 session of parliament for the King's granting of royal assent to the bill for Catherine Howard's attainder. The session began 16 January 1542 and continued until 1 April, although royal assent by letters patent was granted for the Queen's beheading on 13 February. Coke, *Fourth Inst.,* p. 26.

Concerning the continuance of parliament following royal assent to a bill, see above, H. of L., 6 July, n. 4.

11. See above, H. of C., 6 July, n. 2.

12. We find no order of Council restraining such sports at this time. However, the Council took an active part in preventing public gatherings of all sorts, including fairs, fast services, and mustering of trained bands, in an effort to limit the spread of the plague. See *A.P.C., 1625–1626,* pp. 98, 109, 125, 127, 134, passim.

Informed that the alehouse keeper[13] committed to the Serjeant is at home and vaunts how he has escaped and triumphs over his accusers.

Resolved, he shall be brought to the House on Monday morning next; and Mr. Jordan to procure those to be then here which can prove his vaunting in this manner.

MR. JORDAN moves that divers places, *vizt.*, Clerkenwell, Pickehatch, Turnmill Street, Golden Lane, Duke Humfrey's at Blackfriars, are places of open bawdry.

Sir Robert Pye, Sir Francis Barrington, Sir William Pitt, Sir Baptist Hicks, Mr. Jordan to acquaint the Lord Chief Justice with this complaint, and to desire him to take some present order for reformation of it.

LORD CAVENDISH reports from the conference: 1, concerning the desire of recess to be upon Monday morning [**C.J. 808**] next. Lord President answered: our motion required no debate, but consent. The manner left to them.[14]

For the *habeas corpus,* that the Lords so desirous of correspondence with this House that, having a petition from the prisoners, yet would do nothing without our consent.

[p. 32] That this should not be without consent of two or three of the judges. Have sent the petition to us.[15]

MR. RUDHALE. That it was moved that this liberty might extend as well to other prisons as to the Fleet.

SIR THOMAS FANSHAWE. That the

course of these *habeas corpus* against law and, as used, an escape. For the writ bearing *Teste* in Trinity term to have the body before a judge at Serjeants Inn the beginning of Michaelmas term and, by color of this, they go all the vacation into all parts of England.[16] To give no countenance to this here. To see what done in the last plague time, and to be sure to go thither.

MR. ROLLE. This directly an escape in law; therefore not to give any way to it.

SERJEANT ASHLEY. Has known this adjudged an escape, yet would now have this liberty granted them in respect of the present occasion.

MR. TAYLOR, *contra.* Justice must be respected as well as mercy. Not to do any thing against law.

MR. LITTLETON, *accordant.* Not to make an order against law.

SIR H. MARTEN. This would be a jubilee for payment of debts. If grant it for the Fleet, then to grant it for all prisons.

MR. DUCK. Against this liberty. Not to command another's charity: the creditors may consent, not we.

MR. WHITBY. To leave this to the Lords without signification of our resolution.

MR. RECORDER. To deliver to the Lords, as the opinion of this House, that an *habeas corpus* as now used is against law, and an escape. 2ly, to deliver it to the Lords as the opinion of the House that this being an escape, a creditor consenting shall never take

---

13. I.e., Foreman. See above, H. of C., 4 July, n. 17.

14. For the manner, the members of the Upper House agreed that the Lord President should, on the behalf of both Houses, request of the King that the adjournment be on Monday, which request was granted. See H. of L., 9 and 11 July, O.B.s.

15. The prisoners imprisoned for debt were seeking release because of the increased danger of infection in the crowded prison. However, it was unlawful to grant liberty on a writ of *habeas corpus* without first obtaining the assent of the creditor. Furthermore, it was argued that the judges should be consulted con-

cerning the legality of such a release. See Rolle, *Abridgement,* "Escape", *pl.* D9. For the petition, see above, H. of L., 6 July, pp. 99–100. Also, see Secretary Conway's 31 July 1625 letter to Lord Chief Justice Crew concerning *habeas corpus* for the prisoners. *Cal. S.P. Dom., 1625–1626,* p. 77.

16. I.e., a writ of *habeas corpus* issued in Trinity term (May–June) and not returnable until the beginning of the following Michaelmas term (November) would mean release of the prisoners during the summer or vacation period when the courts were not sitting.

him more in execution; for, if he do, the prisoner may have an *audita querela*.[17] To have also a warrant from the House to refuse to consent here to any such order, nor to put it, by order, to the discretion of the judges.

Moves a bill to be drawn to that purpose.

Thanks to the Lords for their acquainting us with this, and desiring our advice. Next, that the *habeas corpus*, as used in the sense of this House, against law; for which a bill here.[18] And therefore we can give no way to it. Lord Cavendish and Mr. Recorder to report it.

[p. 33] LORD CAVENDISH reports from the Lords that he had delivered his message; to which no answer.

The House to meet at 7 clock upon Monday morning.

1, the bill for alehouses;[19] 2, for continuance of the session; 3ly, for making leases of the lands parcel of the Duchy of Cornwall; 4, for the tenants of Cheltenham, sent up by Mr. Treasurer.

Mr. [John] Glanville added to the committee for Lord Dorset's bill; Mr. [Christopher] Sherland,[20] and Mr. [Edward] Whitby; at two of the clock this afternoon, in the Court of Wards.

II. MS. 197, BEDFORD ESTATES, LONDON

[f. 35]   9° July 1625.

It was ordered that no new matter should be received into the House; and to send to the Lords to know when they would be ready to adjourn, and so upon notice from them to send to the King.

MR. SOLICITOR reported the delivery of the petition concerning religion to the King, and his Majesty's answer.

It was presented with a short introduction by my Lord President, expressing the joy and thanks of the Lords and Commons that their last petition concerning the fast was so speedily and effectually granted;[21] and that his Majesty had been pleased to grace that solemn assembly with his own royal presence.

To which the King made this return:

[f. 35v] My Lords and Gentlemen, I am very glad to see you so forward in religion. I assure you you shall find me as forward as you can wish. Your petition is long and of many parts, to which you do not expect a present answer, but you shall shortly hear from me.[22] I understand your House grows very empty and desire till you receive my further answer you will keep together.

After this, his Majesty called Mr. Solicitor aside and told him that he heard of our proceeding with Mr. Montagu, who was his chaplain-in-ordinary, and the cause he had taken into his own consideration before his appearance here. Mr. Solicitor answered that Mr. Montagu did not allege so much for himself, and that it was hardly known but to very few in the House.[23] His Majesty replied he did believe, if we had known it, we would not have proceeded in that manner. Now he wished we would set him at

---

17. I.e., a writ to obtain relief against the consequences of a judgment on account of some matter of defense or discharge arising since its rendition. Black's *Law Dict.*

18. I.e., An act to prevent the granting of writs of *habeas corpus*, read and committed on 27 June. See above, H. of C., 27 June, O.B.

19. The act for the further restraint of tippling in alehouses, passed by the Commons on 1 July and amended by the Lords, was passed by the Lower House as amended on 7 July and was now returned to the Lords for expediting.

20. *Rolle* is crossed out in the MS. preceding *Sher-*

land. Henry Rolle had been named to the committee when it was appointed on 8 July. See above, p. 349.

21. See above, n. 5.

22. See above, n. 6.

23. See above, n. 7. It appears that even Montagu did not know at this time of his appointment as the King's chaplain. On 10 July he wrote to Richard Neile, Bishop of Durham, that he hoped to get a bishopric "to take me of[f] from the Commons". *The Correspondence of John Cosin, D.D.* (Surtees Society, vol. 52; London, 1869), pp. 78–79. And William Laud recorded in his diary that on 13 July 1625 "I went into the country, to the house of my good friend Francis Windebank. In

liberty, and that he would take care to give the House satisfaction in the business. Mr. Solicitor told him the commitment was for contempt to the House. And his Majesty desired to understand the particulars, wherewith when Mr. Solicitor had acquainted him and [*sic*] smiled without any further reply.

Another petition was delivered at the same time concerning the imposition upon the wines, to which his Majesty made this answer: that he did marvel we should press that matter so much, seeing it was designed by his father to the maintenance of the Queen of Bohemia, and so continued by him; nevertheless, he would take consideration of it, and shortly give us answer.[24]

[f. 36] The Lord President did privately signify our readiness for the recess. His Majesty answered, he would take course likewise to be ready, and sent for Mr. Attorney to that purpose.

The question concerning Montagu was quickly settled according to the motion of SIR NATHANIEL RICH: that to give his Majesty satisfaction, Mr. Solicitor might inform him that it was the opinion of the Commons that the book is a seditious and seducing book, and deserves a public censure, but that we should not release him, only enter an order for the Serjeant to let him out upon bond.[25]

SIR THOMAS MIDDLETON informed the House that, whereas we had made an order that the money disbursed by the several counties for pressing and keeping of soldiers should be repaid by the treasurers before any other payments to be made by them, by the act of subsidy they could issue[26] no money but by warrant from the Council of War, and had received no warrant for the payments mentioned in the order; but for divers other services they had received directions, and could not withhold the money but with much clamor.

Which motion was further pressed by SIR ROBERT PYE in the particular of Burlamachi, who was much in debt for the King's service, and like to receive great prejudice if his payments were stopped.[27] (But nothing was done upon this motion.)

MR. JORDAN. For some punishment upon the party who stood committed for speaking words against [f. 36v] the parliament for making the bill of swearing.[28] He moved further for some course to reform the public use[29] of stews.

[Touching the later part of this motion, himself and 3 or 4 more were ordered to make known the complaint to my Lord Chief Justice, that it may please him to take some special care for the redress of these disorders.][30]

---

going thither, Richard Montagu met me by chance. I was the first who certified him of the King's favor to him". *The Works of the Most Reverend Father in God, William Laud, D.D.* (Library of Anglo-Catholic Theology, vol. 58; Oxford, 1853), III, 167–168.

24. See above, n. 8.

25. See above, n. 9.

26. *pay.* C.D. 1625 (Knightley MS.). For the order concerning the disbursements, see above, H. of C., 6 July, p. 324. For the provision in the subsidy act of 1624 that money be issued only by warrant from the Council of War, see *S.R.*, 21 Jac. I, c. 33, pt. 37.

27. Philip Burlamachi, merchant and financier, provided the crown with capital for various domestic enterprises and military expeditions between 1613 and 1631 (R. Ashton, "The Disbursing Official under the Early Stuarts", *Bulletin of the Inst. of Hist. Research*, XXX [1957], 167–174). In October 1623 Burlamachi

and Philip Jacobson were appointed sole agents for the exportation of ordnance (*A.P.C., 1623–1625*, pp. 104–105; 136–137) and in 1625 and 1626 Burlamachi was issued warrants of payment for providing arms, victuals, etc., and transport for the King's troops levied for use in Denmark and the Low Countries (*Cal. S.P. Dom., 1625–1626*, pp. 539, 546; *A.P.C., 1626*, pp. 318–319). On 10 August 1625, Sir Robert Pye delivered in a petition from Burlamachi for the payment of 7, 788 *l.* See below, p. 442 and nn. 2 and 3, and p. 447.

28. See above, n. 13.

29. *vice.* C.D. 1625 (Knightley MS.). Stews were brothels; the locations of "open bawdry" in London are cited in the C.J., above, p. 360.

30. The passage within brackets is omitted in Bedford MS. 197 but included in *C.D. 1625* (Knightley MS.). For the members appointed to acquaint the Lord Chief Justice with the problem, see C.J., above.

The LORD CAVENDISH reported a double conference with the Lords. The first touching the recess, which began on our part, wherein he made known to them that we would be ready against Monday.[31] They replied that without debate their House did fully consent with ours, and undertook, if we left it to them, to acquaint his Majesty with it.

The second began from the Lords, wherein it was declared that the House was very tender in giving their consents in any matter which was under consideration before us, but they had received a petition from the prisoners in the Fleet for *habeas corpus* in this time of infection which was full of danger; and their Lordships' opinion was that the law of necessity did plead for an answer to this petition, against which there is no law.

The petition was read in the House.[32]

SIR THOMAS FANSHAWE. *Habeas corpus* against law, and a mere escape. The *Teste* in Trinity term, the writ to bring A. B. before the judge in Michaelmas term.[33] The keeper by law is tied to the nearest way, but now they are to go whither they will. To recommend it back to the Lords to do what may be done by law, and to consider what was done the last great plague.

MR. ROLLE. The law is clear, adjudged in the King's Bench, 24 *H.* 8.[34] 4 and 5 *H.* 6 it was propounded if the state had great use of a party in prison for debt, whether he might not be taken out? The resolution was, it could not be. 13 *Eliz.*, by consent, one was [f. 37] permitted to come abroad who was in prison upon an execution for the King and a common person, and it was rolled[35] to be an escape. Therefore not to give our consent that the judges should do a thing against law. 13 *R.*

2, all kind of ease prevented, and that prisoners should not be removed from one prison to another.[36]

SERJEANT ASHLEY. To carry any man by *habeas corpus* in any other manner than the law does appoint is an escape. Therefore to consider whether in this case we may not show our respects of other men's lives without making any declaration against the law. If the prison were on fire it were no escape, and in this case the law may be interpreted by the same reason; neither is it fit, if the *habeas corpus* be allowed, that the keeper should take such fees as they usually receive.

MR. TAYLOR. There is no discretion against law.

MR. DUCK. Not to be charitable of other men's estates. If the parties will consent, they may. No minister of state can be delivered upon a privy seal, but no doubt they may be removed by warrant of the Great Seal; and if the sheriff abuse his warrant, he is punishable. But if we consent to such an order as is desired, we shall countenance that which has been complained of over the whole kingdom.

MR. WHITBY. This is no time to take away the abuse. *Necessitas inducit privilegium.* To make no answer, but leave it to the Lords.

[f. 37v] MR. RECORDER. Not to let it pass without delivering our opinion that h[abeas] *corpus* abused in such manner as they have been are against law and an escape. 2ly. If the creditors consent, it is a bar of the debt forever. 3ly. By an order to agree upon that which is against law, will be a precedent of great danger. 4ly. Not to leave to their discretion or any arbitrary course in the Lords House, which will object them to envy if it be denied, or else in the consequence prove

31. See above, n. 14.
32. See above, n. 15.
33. See above, n. 16.
34. Rolle, *Abridgement*, "Escape", *pl.* C1. We are unable to find the H. 6 case cited below.

35. *made. C.D. 1625* (Knightley MS.). Rolle, *Abridgement*, "Escape", *pl.* D8.
36. Rolle is probably citing *S.R.*, 1 *R.* II, c. 12, which limits the power of the warden to let prisoners go at large.

very hurtful if it be granted. 5ly. There rests only this way by a short bill to enact that for this time it shall be no escape.

SIR EDWIN SANDYS. There is no other way to preserve the law, and yet to show mercy, but only let the Lords know that if they frame a bill we will pass it.

LORD CAVENDISH. To give the Lords thanks for their fair proceeding with us.

SIR D. DIGGES. The time too short to redress it by law.

Ordered for the conference, with these points of direction. 1. Thanks to the Lords. 2ly. That we had received divers complaints of the abuses of *habeas corpus,* and have a bill depending for remedy.[37] 3ly. The opinion of the House that to use them as has been practiced of late, if without the creditors' consent, is an escape; if with it, a discharge.

It was doubted by the Lords (as they signified [f. 38] by a message)[38] concerning the bill for adjournment, wherein contained that the royal assent given before the adjournment should not determine the session, whether the law would intend any priority if the royal assent and adjournment should be both in a day.

The bill of drunkenness passed with the amendment inserted by the Lords to extend it to taverns as well as to other victualling houses.[39]

III. PETYT 538/8, INNER TEMPLE LIBRARY

[f. 126]   [Saturday, 9 July 1625]

[MR. SOLICITOR.][40] That he was glad we were so forward in religion and did assure us we should find him as forward as ourselves. But he thought he might have had the privilege of a parliament man for his servant, as a member of the House may for his; Montagu was his servant in ordinary, and the House had proceeded against him without taking notice of it. Whereunto the [f. 126v] Solicitor (as he said) replied that he thought none of the House knew, for he knew it not, though he were his Majesty's servant too, and withal declared (as he said), the cause of his restraint unto his Majesty, who desired to be satisfied therein. And then he delivered from his Majesty that it was his pleasure they should set him at liberty.

And the Serjeant, being called for, informed the House that the day before he was at liberty upon his bond given unto the Serjeant of 2,000 *l.* to appear at their next meeting.

And the SOLICITOR further declared from his Majesty, that he marveled we should petition him touching the imposition on wines at this time, considering the Queen of Bohemia had it for her maintenance and his father received it in his time.[41]

[f. 128] Then was the message received[42]

---

37. See above, n. 18.

38. The Lords had sent down the bill concerning this session of parliament earlier this day (9 July; see O.B.), but this point is omitted in the other accounts of that message; and no other account includes notice of another message on this matter.

39. See above, n. 19.

40. The author of the original MS. of which Petyt 538/8, B.L. Add. 48,091 and Q.C. 449 are copies included the following portion of the Solicitor's report at the end of the compiled material concerning Richard Montagu. See above, H. of C., 1 July, n. 47, and 7 July, n. 114. In order to maintain the chronology of events as outlined in the C.J. we have placed the account of

the Solicitor's report on this day (9 July).

41. This section is followed in the MS. by the account of the message from the King concerning his estate, delivered to the House by Sir John Coke on 8 July. See above, p. 354.

42. *revived.* B.L. Add. 48,091; *reviewed.* Q.C. 449. This section occurs in the MS. following the account of the 8 July message from the King. See above, H. of C., 8 July, p. 355. The first message from the Lords desiring a conference on this matter was brought down to the Lower House on 7 July, but the conference was not finally arranged until this day (9 July). See O.B.s. For the debate in the House on this subject, see C.J. and Bedford MS. 197, above.

that came from the Lords to the House to have a conference to have them join together in setting the prisoners of the King's Bench, Fleet, Marshalsea, etc., at liberty this dangerous and infectious time, as well out of compassion to them in respect of the season as out of a purpose that thereby they might compound or[43] pay their creditors; and therefore it was desired[44] they might have *habeas corpus* [returnable][45] the next term. Whereunto the Upper House was willing to consent, but upon debate our House held it against law and equity, and therefore they utterly refused to give their consents unto it, and the rather for that they had a bill in their House to the purpose,[46] whereby was declared as much. For law,[47] it is clear they are to be kept *in salva et arcta custodia*. [f. 128v] For equity or charity, that[48] ought to be of our own and not of others' [e]states. And for compassion, none were to be commiserated but those that could not in truth pay, and such could take

no benefit of this for they could not procure *habeas corpus,* wanting money; and for such as were able, and did lie in prison, not to be pitied nor aided herein. And so our House left the Lords to themselves, whereupon nothing was done by them at that time.

Upon Saturday, being the 9th of July, we had notice that his Majesty had taken into consideration the desire of both Houses and, notwithstanding his great and urgent occasions to keep us together, yet considering the danger of the time and place we sat in,[49] he was contented we should adjourn on Monday next.

And on the Thursday[50] before there came a message from his Majesty, that he took notice of the thinness of our House, which he was sorry for, and willed that none should depart that were then present. And that we should have a full answer to our petition of religion.

43. *and.* Q.C. 449.
44. *required.* Q.C. 449.
45. The bracketed word is included in B.L. Add. 48,091 and Q.C. 449 but omitted from Petyt 538/8.
46. See above, n. 18.
47. *For, by law.* Q.C. 449.
48. *and charity, it.* Q.C. 449.
49. *the time and danger of the place we sat in.* Q.C. 449.

This notice of the King's assent to the recess was not actually conveyed to the Commons until a conference on the morning of Monday, 11 July. See below, H. of C., 11 July, O.B.
50. I.e., on Saturday, 9 July. This is a part of the message delivered earlier this day (9 July) by Solicitor Heath in his report from the committee on delivering the petition concerning religion. See above.

Ordered: **Foreman**, the alehouse
  keeper, to remain in the
  custody of the Serjeant; to be
  forthcoming at the next
  meeting   368,*4/7
Warrant for Mr. **Wood** to answer
  his contempt to the House in
  not paying fees, etc.   368
L. 2a. An act to repeal so much of
  the statute 21 *H.* VIII, c. 13,
  as does restrain **spiritual**
  persons to take farms   368, *369*, *9/7
SIR NATHANIEL RICH   368, *369*
The above bill: committed   368, 370
Message from the Lords bringing
  the bill for the **subsidy** of the
  clergy (Sir George Croke and
  Sir Henry Yelverton)   368, 370
L. 1a. An act for confirmation of
  subsidies granted by the
  clergy: passed [*see below*]   368, 370; **N**,
                                          523
Message to the Lords sending up
  the above bill (Sir Edward
  Coke)   368
SIR HUMPHREY MAY (Chancellor
  Duchy): elects to serve for
  Lancaster   368
Message from the Lords desiring
  a committee of both Houses
  to meet presently concerning
  the King's answer to their
  request for a **recess** (Sir
  Thomas Coventry, Att.
  General, and Sir Humphrey
  Davenport) [*see below*]   368, 370, *9/7
Committee for conference
  concerning the recess:
  appointed   368
No business to be meddled with
  until the return of the
  committee from the
  conference   368
NATHANIEL TOMKINS: elects to
  serve for Christchurch   368
Report of the conference with the
  Lords: concerning the **recess**

(SIR EDWARD COKE) [*see
  above*]   368, 370; **N**,
                                          523
Question of sending for the
  subsidy bill: considered [*see
  below*]   368, 370; **N**,
                                          524, *30/6
Question of the bill for **tonnage
  and poundage**: considered   370, *5/7
SIR EDWARD COKE: concerning
  attendance at the next session   368, 370
SIR JOHN ELIOT   369, 370
SIR GEORGE MORE   369
Ordered: the House shall be
  called the third day of the
  next session; those absent
  shall incur censure   369, 370
Message from the Lords: that
  they have received the **royal
  assent** to bills passed this
  session and a **commission for
  the adjournment** of
  parliament, and desire
  Commons to come up and
  hear them read [*see below*] (Sir
  Thomas Coventry, Att.
  General, and Sir Humphrey
  Davenport)   369, 370; **N**,
                                          524
Answer given to the Lords'
  message: Commons will send
  answer by messengers of
  their own   369
Message from the King:
  concerning the **recess** and
  the **King's necessities** (SIR
  JOHN COKE)   369, 370
Message to Lords that the House
  will attend them to hear the
  letters patent for the royal
  assent but will not stay to
  hear the **commission for the
  adjournment** read (Sir
  Edward Coke) [*see above and
  below*]   369, 370; **N**,
                                          524
Report of the Lords' answer to

MONDAY, 11 JULY 1625

I. JOURNAL OF THE HOUSE OF COMMONS

[C. J. 808]

[p. 33] *Lunae, 11° Julii, 1° Caroli Regis*

The alehouse keeper to remain in the custody of the Serjeant, to be forthcoming against the next meeting; and the charge given the Serjeant accordingly.[1]

A warrant for Mr. Wood to answer his contempt to the House in not paying fees, for his bill, to the Speaker, Serjeant, etc.[2]

L. 2ª. An act to repeal so much of the statute made in the 21th year of the reign of our late sovereign lord King H. the 8th, *cap. 13°,* as does restrain spiritual persons to take farms.

SIR NATHANIEL RICH. To tie these to residents that shall benefit of this law. And that they take not leases of colleges, deaneries, or like.

Committed to

Sir Edward Coke	Sir William Masham
Mr. Recorder	Sir Nicholas Sanderson
Sir Nathaniel Rich	Sir A[rthur] Ingram
Sir H[enry] Marten	Mr. [Anthony]
Mr. [Henry] Rolle	Langston
Mr. [Christopher]	Mr. [John] Pym
Sherland	Sir Francis Barrington

And all that will come to have voice. Second day of the next meeting,[3] in the Exchequer Chamber.

[p. 34] Mr. Justice Croke and Mr. Justice Yelverton bring from the Lords the bill for the subsidy of the clergy.

L. 1ª. An act for confirmation of a grant of subsidies granted by the clergy.

Upon question, passed.

Sir Edward Coke sent up with this bill.

Mr. CHANCELLOR DUCHY elects for Lancaster and waives Leicester.

Mr. Attorney General and Serjeant Davenport bring from the Lords a message: That the Lords have commanded them to attend this House; that the desire of both Houses for a recess this day; that they have received his Majesty's answer, which they desire to impart to the House, for which purpose they desire a committee of both Houses, presently, in the Committee Chamber. Their number, 4.

The messengers called in, and the message accepted accordingly.

Mr. Treasurer	Sir Benjamin Rudyard
Chancellor Duchy	Mr. Solicitor
Sir Edward Coke	Mr. [Edward] Alford
Lord Cavendish	Mr. Recorder

Sir Edward Coke to report.

No business to be meddled with till their return.

MR. TOMKINS elects for Christchurch in Hampshire, and waives St. Mawes in Cornwall.

SIR EDWARD COKE reports from the conference: That the Lord President delivered that, as both House[s] petitioned the King for a recess this day, so his Majesty, respecting the paucity of the members of this House and the danger of the sickness, is pleased we shall recede this day; the particulars whereof we shall presently receive from the Lord Keeper's mouth.

The Speaker [*sic*] being, in ordinary course, now to be sent down, to be carried up by the Speaker; and it not being sent, the Serjeant/[4]

[p. 35] SIR EDWARD COKE moves, all the

---

1. On 9 July Foreman, the alehouse keeper, was ordered to be brought to the House this day. See above, H. of C., 9 July, p. 360 and n. 13.

2. We have been unable to identify Mr. Wood and the bill with which he was connected.

3. We have no record that indicates whether this committee, scheduled to meet on the second day of the new session, ever met following the adjournment.

4. Customarily the temporal subsidy bill was sent down by the Lords to the Commons to be carried up by the Speaker for presentation to the King. On the 1625 procedure for presenting the subsidy, see below, n. 8.

members of this House shall attend at the next meeting.

SIR JOHN ELIOT seconds it and moves an order that within 3 days after our next meeting the House shall be then called, and the censure of the House to pass upon all such as shall then be absent.

SIR GEORGE MORE moves we may all return after we have been with the Lords, and then make that motion.

Ordered, that the House shall be called the 3rd day of the next meeting and those which shall be then absent shall incur the censure of the House.[5]

A message from Mr. Attorney and Serjeant Davenport: That the Lords have commanded them to signify to the House that the Lords have r[eceived] a commission under the Great Seal for giving his Majesty's assent to some bills, and another commission for adjourning the parliament which they are now ready to publish if this House will come up and hear them.

Answer returned by the same messengers: We will send answer by messengers of our own.

SIR JOHN COKE. That he has received a message from the King by Mr. Secretary:[6] That the King has given way to our recess but must of necessity call us together speedily again for support of that war wherein we

have engaged him, which cannot be done without money or credit. That his proposition was [we] should declare ourselves we would not now leave him in it.

Sir Edward Coke sent up with a message: That, by the ancient precedents of this House, adjournments have been always made by ourselves.[7]

SIR EDWARD COKE reports that he delivered his message, and the Lords consented to send down the commission [**C.J. 809**] hither after they had read it there, to the end we might adjourn our own House here.

Mr. Speaker went up, attended by divers of the House, where, in his presence, the royal assent was given unto some bills;[8] and then he and the House came down.

Mr. Justice Croke and Mr. Baron Trevor brought down the commission for adjournment of this parliament. That they have there adjourned themselves, and now send it down hither; that when we have done with it here our Clerk here may deliver it to their Clerk.

MR. SPEAKER adjourned the House unto Oxford, the first day of August next.[9]

II. MS. 197, BEDFORD ESTATES, LONDON

[f. 38]   *11° Julii 1625*

An act to enable ministers to take leases. Divers cautions were desired to be applied to this bill:[10] 1. That it may not extend

---

5. See below, H. of C., 4 August, n. 5.

6. I.e., Edward, Lord Conway, Secretary of State. Sir John Coke is paraphrasing Conway's plea to the Upper House that parliament continue to support the King financially because of the heavy war expenditures. For Conway's speech, see H. of L., 11 July, pp. 116, 121.

7. The Commons informed the Lords that they would attend them to hear the royal assent to the bills but then would return to the Lower House to adjourn themselves as was customary. See H. of L., 11 July, p. 117 and n. 9.

8. For the list of the nine bills which by the King's letters patent received royal assent, see O.B.; and see below, Leg. Cit., pp. 631–632. For the printed letters

patent see H. of L., 11 July, p. 118 and n. 12. Although it was customary for the temporal subsidy to be presented from the House of Commons, apparently in 1625 the subsidy bill was annexed, along with the other bills, to the commission for the royal assent (see below, Bedford MS. 197), and could not physically be handed over by the Lower House. The Speaker gave a brief *pro forma* speech of presentation which is printed in the L.J. for this day. See H. of L., 11 July. p. 117.

9. See H. of L., 11 July, n. 6, p. 117; the commission for the adjournment is printed above, pp. 119–121.

10. See Sir Nathaniel Rich's speech in the C.J., above.

to any leases of colleges. 2ly. To any minister that shall be nonresident or have two benefices. 3ly. That they may be stinted to a certain value. 4ly. Though the interest be in them, yet they may occupy no more than will be sufficient for their house keeping, lest they become farmers.

The bill was committed; the second day of our next meeting.[11]

A message from the Lords with a bill confirming the grant of three subsidies by the clergy, which was read.

[f. 38v] It was agreed to be the custom that we ought to send for the bill of subsidy by the laity, and the Speaker to carry it up.[12] Concerning the bill for the other subsidies of tonnage and poundage then was a question made, but it was not resolved because the House was informed that the bill was not passed.[13]

A message from the Lords that the desire of both Houses has been represented to his Majesty concerning our recess, and they have received his answer, which they are willing to impart to this House, and for that purpose have appointed a committee of four to meet with a proportionable number.[14]

That conference was granted and presently dispatched, and reported by SIR EDWARD COKE to this effect:

My Lord President on the behalf of the Lords told them that, as they had joined with us in the representation of both our desires to his Majesty, so they were desirous to impart unto us the success. His Majesty, considering our danger, his own necessity, and paucity of our number, did prefer the respect of our safety before his own great

business, and was pleased there should be a recess this day; the particularities of the time and place of our meeting again, we should presently understand by my Lord Keeper.

Upon the motion of SIR EDWARD COKE, seconded by SIR JOHN ELIOT, it was ordered that the House should be called the fourth day of our next meeting, and those which should be absent to incur the censure of the House.

[f. 39] A message from the Lords that they have received his Majesty's letters patent for the royal assent, and likewise a commission for adjournment.

SIR JOHN COKE. That what he spoke yesterday was not arbitrary, but upon his Majesty's command, from whom he had now received another message by Mr. Secretary,[15] that, though out of his tender care of our health he had given way to a recess, yet his important occasions concerning his own honor and estate and the estate of Christendom do require our meeting very shortly, when he will more freely open himself to us.

Sir E. Coke sent to the Lords to let them know that the House would be ready to come up with the Speaker to the reading of the commission for his Majesty's royal assent, but at the reading of the commission for adjournment we did not think fit to be present because of our custom to adjourn ourselves in our own House.[16]

The bill of subsidy was annexed to the commission for the royal assent, as all the other bills were; and so could not be presented by the Speaker, but it was moved

11. See above, n. 3.

12. See above, nn. 4 and 8.

13. The bill for a subsidy of tonnage and poundage had passed the Lower House on 8 July but had received only its first reading (9 July) in the Upper

House.

14. For the committee of eight appointed by the Lower House, see C. J., above.

15. See above, n. 6.

16. See above, n. 8.

that he should intimate the custom in some short speech to the Lords, which (he and the Commons repairing to the Upper House) was accordingly performed.[17]

The Lord Keeper in a message from his Majesty told us that, to our petition concerning religion, [f. 39v] we should receive a more[18] particular answer, and, in the meantime, by present execution of the laws, would make a real rather than a verbal answer to our contentment and the contentment of all the kingdom.

Concerning our adjournment, he had appointed the place to be Oxford; the time, the first of August.[19]

The commission for the royal assent was read, directed to the Lords spiritual and temporal, and to the knights, citizens, and burgesses assembled in parliament.

The laws to which his Majesty gave assent were these:[20]

1. An Act/
2. An Act/
3. An Act/
4. An Act/
5. An Act/
6. An Act/
7. An Act/
8. An Act/[21]
9. An Act/[22]

[f. 40] The Lord Keeper declared further, that he had received another commission from his Majesty to adjourn the parliament to Oxford, and to the first of August.

The Speaker and the Commons return to their own House; and the SPEAKER pronounced the adjournment thus: The House does adjourn itself to Oxford upon the first day of August next.

III. PETYT 538/8, INNER TEMPLE LIBRARY

[f. 128v] [Monday, 11 July 1625]

And on Monday, being the 10th [sic] of July, according to appointment at nine a clock in the morning, we attended our Speaker to the Upper [f. 129] House, who (as the manner is) took the bill of subsidy and presented it as the free gift of the Commons.[23] And then his Majesty, by his commission under the Great Seal of England, which was read, gave authority to the Lord Keeper to give his Majesty's royal assent to divers bills, the titles whereof were in the commission.

And the Lord Keeper delivered from his Majesty how well he was pleased with our gift, and how graciously he did accept of it.

And for our petition of religion, he would give us a most real and not a verbal satisfaction therein, as fully as any of his predecessors, kings or queens of this realm, have done.

Then was the commission read that gave power to the Lord Keeper to assent unto these bills, viz.:

1. An act for the better keeping of the sabbath day, called the Lord's day, and for repressing of plays and sports on that day.[24]
2. An act that innkeepers and taverners shall be punished, as alehouse keepers,[25] for entertaining of strangers [to drink][26] in their houses.[27]

---

17. See above, n. 8.

18. *new. C.D. 1625*(Knightley MS.).

19. See H. of L., 11 July, n. 6, and p. 120.

20. For the titles of the bills, see below, Petyt 538/8, and see O.B.

21. *An act for confirmation. C.D. 1625* (Knightley MS.).

22. *An act for continuance. C.D. 1625* (Knightley MS.).

23. On the procedure concerning the presentation of the subsidy bill in 1625, see above, n. 8.

24. *S.R.*, 1 *Car.* I, c. 1. For the titles of this and the following acts, see Leg. Cit., below, pp. 631–632.

25. *as also housekeepers.* B.L. Add. 48,091 and Q.C. 449.

26. The bracketed words are included in B.L. Add. 48,091 and Q.C. 449 but omitted from Petyt 538/8.

27. *S.R.*, 1 *Car.* I, c. 4.

3. An act to enable and strengthen certain leases made by his Majesty as Prince of Wales.[28]

4. An act for the ease of pleading licenses of alienation.[29]

[f. 129v] 5. An act for confirmation of the estates made by his Majesty of copyhold lands of Cheltenham, in Gloucestershire.[30]

6. An act for confirmation of certain grants (made by his Majesty when he was Prince of Wales) of lands in Cornwall.[31]

7. An act for the giving two entire subsidies by the laity.[32]

[8. An act for the confirmation of the subsidies by the clergy.][33]

8. An act that the giving of royal assent to these acts shall not make this a session.[34]

This being done, the writ of adjournment was read,[35] whereby his Majesty, under his Great Seal, did adjourn the parliament unto the first of August, at Oxford.

And from thence the House of Commons went with their Speaker into their House again and the SPEAKER, by the consent of that House, did adjourn the same accordingly to the first of August, at Oxford.

This adjournment to Oxford, being known to the House on Monday morning before they went up, the generality was much amazed at it, and thought it to be strange dealing with them. And so the House rose, and they departed into the country to their several habitations, there dying not in all that time any man or servant (of the sickness) that was towards any parliament man.

[f. 130] *Memorandum:* That ever since the death of the late King this King did take tonnage and poundage by privy seal, which was much disliked by the House, and conceived to be against law. And the bill of [36] tonnage and poundage passed this House without any exception in as large a manner for profit as it was passed unto King James, but because it was limited but for a year from Our Lady day last,[37] and the kings and queens have used to have the same granted for life, ever since Queen Mary's time, therefore it slept in the Upper House.

[Memo: To see the statutes at large for this.][38] But the reasons that moved the House not to grant it for life, as it was in King James's time, were for that the King's Council in the parliament of 18 *Jac.* did pick out reasons of that act for the pretermitted customs and other impositions which are and were imposed on the subjects, and were very grievous unto them, and they had not

---

28. *Rot. Parl.*, 1 *Car.* I, no. 9. *An act for the enabling and confirmation of an agreement or composition made between the King's Majesty's commissioners of revenue, his Majesty then being Prince of Wales . . . of his Highness's manor of Macclesfield. . . .* The complete title of this private act is given in *S.R.*, V, 22, although the text is not printed therein.

29. *S.R.*, 1 *Car.* I, c. 3.

30. *Rot. Parl.*, 1 *Car.* I, no. 8. *An act for the settling and confirmation of copyhold estates and customs of the tenants in base tenure of the manor of Cheltenham in the county of Gloucester. . . .* The complete title of this private act is given in *S.R.*, V, 22, although the text is not printed therein.

31. *S.R.*, 1 *Car.* I, c. 2.

32. *S.R.*, 1 *Car.* I, c. 6.

33. *S.R.*, 1 *Car.* I, c. 5. This act title is omitted from Petyt 538/8 but is included in both B.L. Add. 48,091 and Q.C. 449.

34. *S.R.*, 1 *Car.* I, c. 7.

35. The commission for the adjournment was not actually read in the Upper House until after the Commons had returned to their House. See above, n. 7.

36. *against.* B.L. Add. 48,091.

37. According to the bill, the grant was to run from the beginning of Charles I's reign, 27 March 1625 (not 25 March, Lady day), to 27 March 1626. See above, p. 336. For references to the lifetime grants for previous monarchs, see the speeches following the second reading of the tonnage and poundage bill, above, H. of C., 5 July, O.B.

38. The bracketed passage is omitted from Petyt 538/8 but included in B.L. Add. 48,091 and Q.C. 449.

time to examine and redress them.[39] And
another was the immoderate[40] rate that was
set of late, which was too high; and therefore they would reduce[41] it to the rates
[f. 130v] set in Queen Mary's time, which
likewise now they had not time to do.

39. See above, H. of C., 5 July, n. 8. Concerning
complaints against the pretermitted customs in the
1621 parliament, see *C.D. 1621*, I, Index, *sub* Customs
on Cloth, pretermitted.
40. *moderate rate.* Q.C. 449. A new Book of Rates,
replacing Mary's Book of Rates of 1558, had been instituted in 1604 and rates were revised in 1608, 1610,
and 1623. The books are printed, see *S.T.C.*, nos.
7691, 7692, and 7694 respectively. See also Dietz, *Public Finance*, pp. 366–375.
41. *redress.* Q.C. 449.

HOUSE OF COMMONS
ORDER OF BUSINESS   MONDAY 1, AUGUST 1625

Four **members admitted** to the
  House notwithstanding they
  have not received
  communion   375, *2/8; 9/8;
     11/8; 12/8

L. 2a. An act against depopulation
  and **decay of farms**:
  committed   375, *20/6

SIR EDWARD COKE: moves for a
  committee to take the
  accounts of the 1624
  subsidies   375, *30/6

Resolved: a committee of the
  whole House tomorrow to
  take the accounts of the 1624
  subsidies   375

SIR EDWARD GILES: concerning a
  pardon of papists   375, 376; **N**,

   529, *6/8;
   8/8; 9/8;
   10/8; 11/8

The above pardon: read   375, 376
SIR JOHN ELIOT   **N**, 530
SIR THOMAS EDMONDES
  (Treasurer)   375; **N**, 531
NICHOLAS DUCK   375
SIR ROBERT HEATH (Solicitor)   375
SIR EDWARD COKE   375
SIR ROBERT PHELIPS   376
SIR HENRY MARTEN   376(2); **N**, 531

Ordered: a committee of the
  whole House to meet this
  afternoon; Mr. Bendbo to
  attend with the pardon   376(2); **N**, 532

MONDAY, 1 AUGUST 1625

I. JOURNAL OF THE HOUSE OF COMMONS

[C.J. 809]
[p. 36] *Lunae, 1° Augusti, 1° Caroli Regis*

Sir William Spencer, Sir William Bulstrode, Sir Robert Knollys, and [Sir] Edwin Sandys admitted into the House, notwithstanding they have not received the communion which they are, notwithstanding, to do with all speed.

L. 2ª. An act against depopulation and decay of farms, and conversion of arable into pasture.
Committed:

Sir Walter Erle   Sir Arthur Ingram
Mr. Solicitor   Sir Wolstan Dixie
Sir Francis Popham   Mr. [John] Whistler

And all that will come to have voice. Natural Philosophy Schools,[1] Thursday, next. 2 clock.

SIR EDWARD COKE moves for a committee to take the account of the 3 subsidies and 15eens.[2]

Resolved, a committee of the whole House, tomorrow, at 2 of the clock, to take this account, and all parties whom it shall concern then to attend.

SIR EDWARD GILES tenders a pardon of divers recusants; which read in the House.[3]

MR. TREASURER. That this, and some other, granted at the suit of the ambassadors of France before their return, who usually undertake that they shall depart the kingdom and not return.[4] Hopes, notwithstanding, we shall have a gracious answer for our petition for religion.

MR. DUCK.[5] That those persons who brought the pardon and delivered it on Saturday in the afternoon, so insolent that they would not consent to respite their answer till the Monday morning but request they might have a present answer, would return back and help themselves as well as they could.

MR. SOLICITOR. That this pardon had his inception before the King's answer to us for our petition for religion.[6] Moves, since these popish spirits apply themselves to foreign ambassadors, this House may take some course to prevent this.

SIR EDWARD COKE. Thinks this pardon never drawn by the King's learned counsel. *Pietate motus.* The patent [*sic*] dated the day of the warrant, if any warrant.[7] To go to the Lords.

1. During the proceedings of the session at Oxford, the Commons met in the Divinity School (see below, p. 376 and n. 12) and held their committee meetings in the chambers of the adjacent Schools Quadrangle usually occupied by the academic schools (i.e., natural philosophy, mathematics, physics, etc.). For diagrams of the rooms of the Schools Quadrangle, see Andrew Clark, *A Bodleian Guide for Visitors* (Oxford, 1906), pp. 30–32. See also, C.C.C., E257, printed in the Appendix, below, pp. 661–663.
2. On 6 July 1625 the House had resolved to consider the accounts of the 1624 subsidies upon the next meeting of parliament. See above, p. 323.
3. A copy of the pardon (in Latin) which had been issued for Alexander Baker and ten other Catholics imprisoned at Exeter is in the H.L.R.O., Main Papers, H.L., 9 August 1625. Concerning reaction to the pardon, see Russell, *Parliaments*, p. 240, n. 1. Following the reading of the pardon this day there was, according to Eliot (*Negotium*, below, pp. 530–531), a lengthy speech, possibly by Eliot himself, delivered prior to the Treasurer's speech. For further discussion of the par-

don, see H. of C., 6 August, O.B.; and see H. of L., 9 August, O.B.
4. Concerning the request of the ambassadors, see above, H. of L., 9 August, p. 153 and n. 6. In 1625 the grant of pardons at the time of the ambassadors' departure did not ameliorate the feeling of the French toward the English. Salvetti in his dispatch of 8 August (Salvetti dispatch, pp. 27–28) notes that: "The three French ambassadors have taken leave. They are dissatisfied with the obstacles thrown in their way which have prevented them arranging the household of the Queen as they wished. They are also much displeased with the position of the Catholics. . . . Such is the state of this question; the Catholics are almost without hope or comfort, and they lay the blame on the Marquis d'Effiat who was charged with their interests".
5. Nicholas Duck was Recorder and M.P. for Exeter.
6. See above, H. of L., 9 August, p. 153 and n. 5.
7. Concerning the date of the original warrant for the pardon, see the Lord Keeper's explanation, above, H. of L., 9 August, p. 154.

[p. 37] SIR ROBERT PHELIPS. No other King will, at the persuasion of any our ambassadors, release any out of the inquisition or other restraint for religion. To consider of this pardon and of all the circumstances thereof by a committee, and then to send to the Lords to know if they will join with us. To have a committee of the whole House for the debate hereof this afternoon.

SIR H. MARTEN. That we have lost more by articling these 22 years than we got by reprisals in all Queen Elizabeth's time.[8]

Ordered, a committee of the whole House to consider hereof, 2 clock this afternoon, and that Mr. Bendbo[9] shall attend this committee with this pardon, or any other of this kind lately granted.

II. MS. 197, BEDFORD ESTATES, LONDON

[f. 40] *Primo Augusti.* At Oxford.

The House met, not many in number, and very late in the forenoon; so that nothing done of any moment, only a complaint was made of a pardon given to a Jesuit and to others taken at Exeter, which pardon bore date the next day after we had received his Majesty's first answer touching

religion, and it was informed that it had been obtained by the mediation of the French ambassador.[10]

By occasion whereof SIR H. MARTEN spoke of the disadvantage which we have ever received by treaties and embassages, and that we were all now in a course of no better success employing so young men as we did.

A committee was appointed to draw a petition concerning that pardon.

III. PETYT 538/8, INNER TEMPLE LIBRARY[11]

[f. 132] [Monday, 1 August 1625]

The parliament began at Oxford the first of August according to the adjournment. The Divinity School being the place for the Lower House and the galleries over the schools for the Upper House, and Christ Church taken up for the King and his great officers, the King and Queen being[12] then at Woodstock. The House being appointed by order at London to be called on the 4th [*sic*] sitting day,[13] little was done until that day but the reading and preparing of some bills.

8. For a fuller account of Marten's speech, see *Negotium*, below, p. 531.

9. MS.: *Bembo.* On Bendbo, see above, H. of L., 11 July, n. 19. There is no account of the afternoon meeting of the committee of the whole House. The account of 6 August proceedings (see particularly Phelips's motion, p. 412) indicates that a subcommittee had been appointed to draft a petition regarding the pardon of the papists.

10. See C.J., above. Concerning the date of the pardon and the request of the ambassadors, see above, H. of L., 9 August, pp. 152–154.

11. S. R. Gardiner printed the account of the Oxford session of the parliament of 1625 given in the Harleian manuscript 5007 as an appendix to *Commons Debates 1625* (Knightley MS.). Harl. 5007 represents a fourth copy for the Oxford session of the anonymous 1625 diary also recorded in Petyt 538/8, B.L. Add. 48,091, and Q.C. 449. See above, Introduction, pp. 14–15. As with the other copies, we have collated Harl. 5007 with

Petyt 538/8 and noted the substantive variants.

12. *lying.* B.L. Add. 48,091, Q.C. 449, and Harl. 5007. At Oxford, the Lower House met in the Divinity School at the west end of the Schools Quadrangle and the Upper House met in the north side of the gallery (later known as the Picture Gallery) which formed the third story of the Schools Quadrangle. See Anthony à Wood, *The History and Antiquities of the University of Oxford* (Oxford, 1796), II, 355. Concerning the use of university rooms for the lodging of members of both Houses and the use of Christ Church by the Privy Council, see C.C.C., E257, ff. 131–132, printed in the Appendix, below, p. 661; the Council's letter of 11 July to the Vice-chancellor and heads of the colleges at Oxford, Appendix, below, p. 660; and see also, the letter of 18 July from Thomas Anyan, president of Corpus Christi College, to Sir Robert Cotton, printed in the Appendix, below, p. 718.

13. The House was to be called on the third sitting day. See below, H. of C., 4 August, n. 5.

TUESDAY, 2 AUGUST 1625

I. JOURNAL OF THE HOUSE OF COMMONS

[C.J. 809]

[p. 37] *Martis, 2° Augusti, 1° Caroli Regis*

Mr. Drewe has license for 5 or 6 days.

Mr. Fiennes and Sir Simon Weston licensed to come in before they receive the communion, which they are to receive upon Sunday next.

So for Mr. Richard Escott.

Committee for sheriff's accounts, etc., to meet at two clock this afternoon, in the Mathematic Schools. The bill to be delivered to Mr. Sherwill.[1]

Committee for the bill for the quiet of ecclesiastical persons and the preservation of rights of patrons; and all that will come, to have voice. To meet in the Committee Chamber, at 2 clock this afternoon. Delivered Sir Edward Coke.

Committee for the Earl of Dorset's bill to meet at 2 clock this afternoon, in the Physic School. Mr. Alford and the knights and burgesses of Sussex are added, and, if any letter come about it to the House, the committee may open it.

The committee for secret offices to meet at 3 clock this afternoon, in the Committee Chamber, and all that will come to have voice. Delivered Sir Edward Coke.

[p. 38] Bill against simony, formerly committed,[2] to:

[col. 1]
Mr. Treasurer
Sir Edward Coke
Sir Edmund Bacon
Sir Henry Marten
Sir Francis Seymour

[col. 2]
Mr. [John] Pym
Sir Francis Barrington
Mr. Solicitor
Sir Thomas Hatton

[col. 3]
Sir Edward Leech
Burgesses of the
University of Oxford

And all that will come to have voice; Moral Philosophy Schools, 2 clock this afternoon. Delivered to Mr. Whitaker.

Motion made, that Mr. Montagu might now appear, according to the former order.[3]

Mr. Serjeant called in, says he has taken bond of 2,000 *l.* bond, and that Mr.[4] Montagu has written to him he is sick of the stone.

He required to bring the bond and letter.

SIR EDWARD COKE. That the ancient Britons conquered by reason of want of united counsels for avoiding dangers. *Dum singuli pugnant universi vincuntur.* So it will be in divinity if every private man may put out books of divinity. This as dangerous a book as ever saw. Wishes no man may put out any book of divinity not allowed by the Convocation.

SIR W. HELE wishes a bill to that purpose.

Mr. Montagu his letter to the Serjeant read.[5]

1. When it was appointed on 9 July, this committee was ordered to meet on the first afternoon of the next session (see above, p. 358). Thomas Sherwill's name does not appear on the list of M.P.s appointed to the committee.
2. The second reading and former commitment of this bill may have occurred on 6 July. See above, H. of C., 6 July, n. 5. It is possible that the lack of a marginal note identifying the bill in the C.J. for 6 July resulted in the Clerk's losing track of the original list of committee members so that it was necessary to renominate the committee at this time (2 August). The names on the 6 July list are different from those of the 2 August list.
3. On 7 July the House had resolved to respite the punishment of Montagu until the beginning of the next session and to commit him to the Serjeant to ensure his appearance at that time. See H. of C., 7 July, pp. 334–335 and n. 37.
4. *Mr.* is omitted in the printed edition. Montagu had been suffering from "the stone" as early as 20 June. See the postscript of Montagu's letter to Cosin, 20 June 1625, printed in *The Correspondence of John Cosin, D.D.* (Surtees Society, vol. 52; London, 1869), p. 76. Concerning the bond for Montagu, see above, H. of C., 9 July, p. 359.
5. We are unable to find the letter.

SIR ROBERT PHELIPS. To send the Serjeant for him.

MR. SOLICITOR puts the House in mind of his Majesty's intimation by him before the last recess.[6] Moves to acquaint the King with the particulars and consequences of the book and doubts not but we shall have his leave to send for him.

MR. ALFORD puts the House in mind of the danger to exempt the King's servants from questioning in parliament. Moves a committee to consider both of this particular and of the general.

MR. STRODE. That our proceedings against Mr. Montagu for a contempt to the House.[7]

SIR FRANCIS SEYMOUR. Not to lose this privilege, but to desire the King to leave him for this contempt to us.

SIR G. GERARD puts the House in mind of Sir Thomas Parry, a privy councillor, whom the King desired to have left to him, but the House would not consent but put him out.[8]

MR. WENTWORTH puts the House in

mind of the Lord Chancellor and Treasurer whom the House has dealt with.[9] Montagu reproaches Bible-bearers, which the arms of this University.[10] [p. 39] To proceed to a conference with the Lords, according to the former order.[11]

SIR JOHN ELIOT. That this man remains committed by the House to the Serjeant. Therefore we cannot send for him as if he were out of prison.[12] To give the Serjeant a time to bring him in.[13]

SIR EDWARD COKE.[14] We meddle with him only for his contempt to this House, whereof we have jurisdiction. We will not meddle ourselves alone with adjudging his tenets, yet we may inform the Lords, where the bishops are, and they are to judge it. This warranted by [**C.J. 810**] the words of the writ: *defensionem ecclesiae 'Anglicanae*, which are ancient, in *H.* 4 and *H.* 5 time and before, and not brought in in *H.* 8 time.[15] Moves the Serjeant may bring in Montagu at a day to be prefixed to him.

MR. DRAKE. That this book so dangerous to the Church and state comes out *cum priv-*

---

6. See Solicitor Heath's report of the King's response concerning the Montagu business, above, H. of C., 9 July, O.B.

7. See above, H. of C., 7 July, n. 3, and p. 334.

8. Eliot (*Negotium*, below, p. 533) cites *12° Jac.* Sir Thomas Parry, Chancellor of the Duchy of Lancaster and a privy councillor, elected M.P. for Berkshire in 1614, was removed from his place by the House on 11 May (*C.J.*, I, 480) because of his interference in the 1614 Stockbridge election. The House took the action even though the King had offered to punish Parry himself. See *C.J.*, I, 477, 479, and K.S.R.L., MS E237, f. 15 (transcript Y.C.P.H.).

9. The House of Commons initiated impeachment proceedings for bribery and corruption against Sir Francis Bacon, Lord Chancellor, in 1621 (see Howell, *S.T.*, II, 1087–1120; *C.D. 1621*, I, Index, *sub* Bacon; and *L.J.*, III, 84–86, 98–101, 105–106), and in 1624 against Lionel Cranfield, Lord Treasurer, for high crimes and misdemeanors (see *L.J.*, III, 344–383; Howell, *S.T.*, II, 1183–1254; and Cobbett, *Parl. Hist.*, I, 1411–1477).

10. On Bible-bearers, see above, H. of C., 7 July, n. 19. Wentworth is voicing the traditional view that the

book in the Oxford coat of arms is a Bible. The arms of Oxford University are described as "azure, on a book open proper, leathered gules, garnished or, on the dexter side seven seals of the last between three open crowns of the same, the words '*Dominus illuminatio mea*'". *Boutell's Manual of Heraldry*, revised ed. (London, 1931), p. 126.

11. On 7 July the House had resolved, at the next session, to request a conference with the Lords concerning Montagu's books. See H. of C., 7 July, O.B.

12. See above, H. of C., 7 July, n. 3.

13. *in* is omitted in the printed edition.

14. Coke had spoken earlier this day concerning Montagu (see above) but was, contrary to the custom of the House (see Hatsell, *Precedents*, II, 103–106), permitted to speak a second time to the same issue. See Bedford MS. 197, below, p. 382.

15. The forms of several contemporary writs of summons to parliament are printed in Elsynge, *Parliaments*, pp. 67–68; and see Coke, *Fourth Inst.*, p. 9. Coke is not citing the most ancient extant writ of 49 *H.* III (Elsynge, *Parliaments*, pp. 10–11). Concerning the clergy in parliament, see ibid., pp. 25–26, 27; Coke, *Fourth Inst.*, pp. 4–5.

ilegio, which makes it accounted the doctrine of the Church of England, and so the opposers schismatics.[16] The danger to the Low Countries by Arminianism.

SIR GEORGE MORE, *accordant*.

SIR ROBERT PHELIPS puts the House in mind of the last King's last speech to both Houses: that no servant of his should be questioned.[17]

The Serjeant commanded, at his peril, to bring Mr. Montagu to the House with all convenient speed; and he to stand committed until he be discharged by the House.

Sir Robert More	Sir Benjamin Rudyard
Sir Robert Phelips	Sir Francis Seymour
Sir Simon Weston	Sir Francis Knollys
Sir John Eliot	

added to the former committee for Mr. Montagu's books.[18]

To meet on Thursday in the afternoon, 2 clock, in the Logic Schools.

Mr. Treasurer and Sir John Danvers, being burgesses for the University, presently to desire the Chancellor or, in his absence, the Vice-chancellor, to take order

that Dr. Anyan preach not tomorrow before the House.[19]

SIR NATHANIEL RICH. That the fast is not observed in divers places by reason the books not sent unto them, which the default of the bishops or their officers.[20] To send a message to the lords bishops, that this may be reformed.

SIR WILLIAM BULSTRODE affirms the same for Peterborough diocese.

[p. 40] MR. BOSWELL.[21] That the Lord Keeper has long since taken order and sent down to every parish two books, with letters to the commissaries and other officers, commanding them to see them duly executed.

SIR JOHN ELIOT. That in his country these books not come. That some particular persons have there engrossed these books, and have demanded 3*s.*, 2*s.* 6*d.*, and 2*s.* a book, for these. This so done at Plymouth.

SIR W. ERLE. That the books sold at too high a rate—10*d.* and 12*d.* a book—whereby, by computation, above 1,000 *l.* clear gains.

---

16. The *Appeal* was printed with the approbation of Francis White, Dean of Carlisle (see above, H. of C., 6 July, n. 25), but the title page does not carry the rubric *cum privilegio*. The title page of Montagu's other book complained of in this parliament, the *Gagg*, contains the rubric "Published by Authority".

17. On 29 May 1624, the final day of the 1624 parliament, in giving his assent to the act for making the lands of Lionel Cranfield, Earl of Middlesex, subject to the payment of Middlesex's debts, James I warned the Houses that "for the time to come. . . . Men shall not give informations against my officers without my leave. If there be cause, let them first complain to me, for I will not have any of my servants and officers, from the greatest Lord to the meanest scullion, complained on by any without my leave first asked. . .". D'Ewes's diary, Harl. MS. 159, ff. 135–135v (transcript Y.C.P.H.); and see also the reports of these remarks by James I in S.P. 14/165:60, 61.
Concerning Montagu's appointment as the King's chaplain-in-ordinary, see above, H. of C., 9 July, p. 361, and n. 23.

18. It is unclear whether the committee referred to

here was that appointed on 7 July for setting down in writing the particulars against Montagu (see above, p. 335) or that concerning Montagu's books which grew out of a subcommittee appointed on 24 June and which already included several of the M.P.s listed above (see H. of C., 1 July, n. 17).

19. In compliance with the proclamation of 3 July 1625 (see above, H. of L., 28 June, n. 12) a fast service was to be held on Wednesday 3 August. The Commons felt that it would be an affront to their House if Dr. Thomas Anyan, who they had complained against in the 1624 parliament (see above, H. of C., 28 June, n. 19), was allowed to preach before them at the fast. The Chancellor of Oxford was William Herbert, Earl of Pembroke; the Vice-chancellor was John Prideaux. For the Vice-chancellor's response to this request from the House, see below. We do not know who preached at the fast service in place of Anyan.

20. Concerning the books prescribing the manner of the fast services, see above, H. of L., 28 June, n. 12.

21. William Boswell, M.P. for Boston, Lincolnshire, was Lord Keeper Williams's secretary.

Sir Robert Hatton, Sir H. Marten, and Sir Thomas Hatton to acquaint my Lord of Canterbury with this neglect and, from the House, to desire he will take order to help it.

Mr. Treasurer and Sir John Danvers return answer: That the Vice-chancellor told them he had a letter from Dr. Anyan that he would not desist from preaching except he were discharged by the delegates, which thereupon he had done, and caused them to appoint another in his room.

The House adjourned till Thursday morning, 8 of the clock; and all committees appointed, to sit this afternoon.

The Serjeant's men to attend in the church to take notice of those of the House, that places may be reserved for them.

II. MS. 197, BEDFORD ESTATES, LONDON

2° Augusti 1625[22]

[f. 40] The Earl of Dorset's bill was appointed to be examined by the committee this afternoon in the Physic Schools.

Two other bills, viz., against secret offices and for restraint of h[abeas] corpus, appointed to be sat upon in the same place.

[f. 40v] The act against simony and corruption in the election of colleges, committed, was now ordered to be handled this afternoon in the Moral Schools.

The business of Mr. Montagu called upon and the last order read. The Serjeant,

commanded to bring in his prisoner, made answer that he had taken bond of him to appear the first day and had received a letter from him (which was now read) containing an excuse of his not coming because he was sick of the passion hypochondriacal.[23]

SIR EDWARD COKE spoke to the danger that grows by divisions in matters of religion, reciting the censure of Tacitus upon the old Britains, *Raro conventus ad propugnandum commune periculum; dum singuli pugnant universi vincuntur*. Finds faults with the course now used for every particular man to put out books of all sorts. Wishes that none concerning religion might be printed but such as were allowed by the Convocation.

SIR ROBERT PHELIPS insisted upon the inconveniences which spring from the usual facility of our proceedings with offenders. Wishes us to deal more roundly in this, and that he may be presently sent for by the Serjeant.

To divert with [sic], MR. SOLICITOR remembered the King's message that he was his servant, and the cause taken into his own care;[24] and advised first to send to his Majesty to acquaint him with the danger, and no doubt but we shall have leave to proceed.

Which MR. ALFORD opposed by putting us in mind of 2 or 3 late ill precedents of dismissing causes upon messages: the complaint for Ireland, in 18 [*Jac.*],[25] the business of Virginia and[26] the punishment of Sir Simon Harvey in 21 [*Jac.*].[27] All justices

---

22. In the MS. this date entry occurs on f. 40v, just before the business of Mr. Montagu, below. We have moved it up in order to maintain the chronology of events outlined in the C.J., above.

23. See above, nn. 3–5.

24. See above, n. 6.

25. On 26 April 1621 a debate in the Commons on the Irish policy resulted in the appointment of a committee to consider the matter (*C.J.*, I, 593). On 30 April James I sent a message to the House suggesting that the House leave the matter of reforming Ireland to him (ibid., 597). Despite Edward Alford's plea that it

was "a dangerous precedent to surcease upon a message", the House agreed to send a message to the King that "if he please to assume it wholly to himself, and ease us of the pains, they shall willingly submit" (ibid., 598). The King responded by message, 1 May 1621, "that he, having begun, would finish it (ibid., 600), and the issue was dropped by the Commons. See also, *C.D. 1621*, V, 118–128.

26. MS.: *as*.

27. In April 1624 the House gave up consideration of a petition regarding the Virginia Company after receiving a letter from the King urging them to press

of peace, [f. 41] all deputy lieutenants are the King's servants, and indeed no man can commit a public officer[28] but by color and opportunity of public employment and service to the King. So that, if we admit this, we shall take the way to destroy parliaments, which opinion he confirmed by a precedent, [*blank*] Eliz. in questioning Mr. Browne when the same objection was made, and overruled.[29]

SIR FRANCIS SEYMOUR added that the King ought not to take no [*sic*] notice what we do.

And SIR G. GERARD remembered the case of Sir Thomas Parry, *1° Jacobi*.[30]

MR. WENTWORTH. That for any offenses contained in his book we might proceed against him in his absence. He insisted chiefly upon the abuse of the Bible, paralleling it with that of trampling upon the Bible at Canterbury.[31] Both which, if they were not punished by authority, of private faults, would become public; and though it be at no time fit to provoke the wrath of God, yet much less at this time, when we are all, as it were, making our wills, being already under His hand. Divers great princes have been famous for their respect and honor to the Bible. Theodosius wrote out the New Testament with his own hands;[32] Alfred read over the Bible 14 times;[33] Louis the Saint,[34] being demanded where the place of his greatest honor was, did not name the place where he was crowned, but where he was made a Christian, and is commended for a diligent reader of the Bible. Queen Elizabeth, riding in state through the City, at one of the pageants was presented with a Bible, which she clapped to her heart;[35] and, as his Majesty's [piety][36] does interest him in the like honor, so no doubt but he will be very sensible of the reproach which this man has done to the Bible, when he shall be informed of it.

[f. 41v] SIR ROBERT MORE argued the question at large, touching the fallibility of grace according to the distinction of the schools of the antecedent and consequent will of God.

SIR JOHN ELIOT. Not to send for a man that by intendment should be in custody, but to command the Serjeant to bring him forth at his peril.

SIR E. COKE (having spoken before, yet being permitted contrary to the orders of the House to speak again). That the priv-

on with other matters and to leave the Virginia business to be settled by him. See *C.J.*, I, 691, 694, 775, and S.P. 14/163:71.

    Sir Simon Harvey's alleged abuses in the matter of purveyance were examined by the same parliament and were complained of in the Commons' petition of grievances. See *C.J.*, I, 696, 697, 702, 781, 782, 787; and also Cobbett, *Parl. Hist.*, I, 1493, and above, H. of C., 4 July, p. 302 and n. 54. Sir Edward Coke identified Harvey when he criticized abuses in the King's household in his speech of 5 August. See below, p. 400. James I ended the 1624 parliament with a warning that in the future none of his servants and officers should be questioned or complained of without the King's leave. See above, n. 17.

    28. *offense. C.D. 1625* (Knightley MS.).

    29. We are unable to find this precedent.

    30. See above, n. 8.

    31. Perhaps an oblique reference to the earlier description of Foster tearing the Bible in Canterbury. See

above, H. of C., 23 June, p. 231 and n. 24.

    32. We are unable to find the source of the reference to Theodosius.

    33. Presumably, King Alfred or Alured, founder of the monasteries at Winchester and Shaftsbury. Regarding his life, see Holinshed, *Chronicles*, I, 674–675; *Polydore Vergil's English History*, ed. by Sir Henry Ellis (London: Camden Society, 1846), I, 198–221.

    34. MS.: 5ᵗ. The word *saint* is used in *C.D. 1625* (Knightley MS.). King Louis IX of France, or Saint Louis. We have not found the source of the reference.

    35. During the fourth pageant of her coronation procession through the City, Queen Elizabeth was presented with a Bible which she kissed and then laid on her breast. J. E. Neale, *Queen Elizabeth I* (New York, 1957), pp. 61–62.

    36. Bedford MS. 197 is blank here, as is B.L. Add. 26,639. The word *piety* is included in *C.D. 1625* (Knightley MS.) without brackets.

ilege of the House of Commons was the heartstring of the commonwealth.[37] We are the general inquisitors, but for the point of doctrine not to judge but to transfer: *pro defensione Ecclesiae,* given as one cause of calling parliaments in all the ancient writs;[38] and when both Houses have done their duties it will come to the King at last. 18 *H.* 3, the parliament beseech the King not to pardon those who were condemned in parliament.[39] 15[40]*E.* 3, John of Gaunt and the Lord Latimer were questioned for giving the King ill counsel. No man, not John of Gaunt himself, is to be excepted. Many men (and I myself) will speak in parliament that which they dare not speak otherwise.

MR. DRAKE. Arminianism more dangerous than popery, because we are more secure of it. It is hardlier to be distinguished

and there is no law against it, though it be not only contrary to the Articles of the Church of England but of all other reformed churches, for the national Synod of Charenton was confirmed by that of Dort.[41]

It was informed that Dr. Anyan was appointed to preach tomorrow, whereupon Sir Thomas Edmondes and Sir John Brooke,[42] burgesses for the University, were sent to the Vice-chancellor, that the House [f. 42] would take as an affront that a man against whom they had received proofs of very foul crimes should be admitted to that service in their presence.

It was complained that the books of the fast were not sent into the several dioceses according to the instructions;[43] and that excessive prices were demanded for them.

37. Coke made essentially the same point on 23 June with regard to Cope's case. See above, p. 227. Concerning Coke's speaking a second time, see above, n. 14.

38. See above, n. 15.

39. Marginal note in the Earl of Bedford's hand: "No". In 1233 Henry called the barons to meet at Oxford. They several times refused his summons, complaining against the presence of Peter, Bishop of Winchester, and Peter de Rivaulx in the King's Council. The following year, 1234, a parliament convened at Westminster and again the two men were complained of. Edmund, Archbishop of Canterbury, and the prelates went to the King and told him "that if he would not consent to the conditions the Lords had already proposed to him, and agree with his faithful subjects, that he, with the bishops, would immediately excommunicate him and all his evil councillors". The Bishop of Winchester and Peter de Rivaulx were summoned before the King to answer charges against them and were banished from the court, but the following year they were pardoned and reconciled to the King's favor. Cobbett, *Parl. Hist.,* I, 14–15; and see

Matthew Paris, *Historia Anglorum* (Rolls Series, London, 1866), II, 365–372; Holinshed, *Chronicles,* II, 374–378.

40. *So. C.D. 1625* (Knightley MS.). *Rot. Parl.,* 50 *E.* III, nos. 20–29, 34. The Earl of Bedford's marginal "No" (see n. 39, above) may refer to this MS. citation which gives an incorrect regnal year. Proceedings were brought against William, Lord Latimer, and other followers of John of Gaunt, Duke of Lancaster, at the opening of parliament in April 1376.

41. The twenty-fourth national synod of the reformed churches of France met at Charenton in September 1623 and confirmed the doctrine of the Synod of Dort (1619) which had condemned Arminianism. See S. A. Laval, *A Compendious History of the Reformation and of the Reformed Churches in France . . .* (London, 1741), IV, 873–878. On the Synod of Dort, see above, H. of C., 7 July, n. 54.

42. The manuscript is incorrect; Sir John Danvers was the second burgess for the University of Oxford. Sir John Brooke sat for Great Bedwyn. Concerning the Anyan matter, see above, n. 19.

43. See above, n. 20.

L: Proceedings in House of Lords, above

SIR THOMAS CREW (Speaker): declares the King's pleasure that both Houses attend him at 9 o'clock — 385(2)

Sir Walter Pye (Attorney of Court of Wards) granted leave — 385(2)

Members given liberty to come into the House — 385

Report from the committee on the bill for the quiet of **ecclesiastical persons** (SIR EDWARD COKE) — 385(2), *23/6

Amendments to the above bill: read twice, and bill is engrossed — 385, 386

Report from the committee on the bill to prevent the granting of writs of **habeas corpus** (SIR EDWARD COKE) — 385, 386, *27/6

Amendments to the above bill: read twice, and bill is engrossed — 385, 386

Resolved: to return this forenoon after the House has attended the King — 385

The committee for the bill against the procuring of **judicial places** for money to meet Friday [5 August] — 385, *28/6

The Speaker and the House attend the King — 385, 386, 388

King's speech to both Houses — 386, 388; **L**, 132, 136; **N**, 534

Lord Conway (Secretary of State): on the state of Christendom — 386, 389; **L**, 133, 136, 137; **N**, 534

Sir John Coke — 387, 389; **L**, 133, 136, 137; **N**, 534

The Speaker and the Commons return to their House — 385, 389

Edward Littleton, justice of assize in Wales, spared for his circuit — 385

SIR EDWARD COKE: to have the heads of today's speeches to both Houses drawn up — 385

Resolved: to enter into consideration of the great business tomorrow morning — 385, 389

Resolved: all members of the House shall attend and not depart without license — 385

THURSDAY, 4 AUGUST 1625

I. JOURNAL OF THE HOUSE OF COMMONS

[C.J. 810]

[p. 41] *Jovis, 4° Augusti, 1° Caroli Regis*

MR. SPEAKER declares his Majesty's pleasure that both Houses attend him, at 9 of the clock, at Christ's Church Hall.

Mr. Attorney of the Wards has license to go his circuit.[1]

Sir Edward Dering, Sir John Trevor, Senior, Sir John Trevor, Junior, Sir H. Spilman, Mr. Mill, Mr. Jermyn, Sir Robert Crane, Sir William Spring, Sir Arnold Harbert, have liberty to come into the House.[2]

SIR EDWARD COKE reports the bill for the quiet of ecclesiastical persons and the preservation of the right of patrons, with amendments, which 2 read. *Engrossetur.*

SIR EDWARD COKE reports also the bill of *habeas corpus,* with amendments, which twice read. *Engrossetur.*

Resolved, to return again this forenoon after the House has attended his Majesty.

The committee for the bill against procuring of judicial places for money and against giving or receiving of bribes, to meet upon Friday, 2 clock, in the Physic Schools.

About 9 of the clock, Mr. Speaker, with the House, attended the King accordingly and there staying about 2 hours they returned, according to the former order.[3]

Mr. Littleton, a justice of assize in Wales, spared for his circuit.

SIR EDWARD COKE. That we have heard his Majesty, Lord Conway, and Sir John Coke. To have *capita* delivered of these things.[4]

Resolved, tomorrow morning, at 7 of the clock, to enter into consideration of the great business now propounded.

Resolved, that all the members of the House shall attend and not depart without license obtained from the House, upon pain of the censure thereof.[5]

II. MS. 197, BEDFORD ESTATES, LONDON

[f. 42]   *4to Augusti 1625.*

MR. SPEAKER acquainted the House with the King's pleasure to attend his Majesty this morning in Christ Church Hall.

SIR WALTER PYE desired leave to go keep the assizes, because his partner was dead.

SIR E. COKE reported two bills.

The first was for the quieting ecclesiastical persons and safety of patrons; the effect whereof was this: By 31 H. 8, for plu-

---

1. Sir Walter Pye was requesting leave to keep the assizes because his partner had died. See Bedford MS. 197, below.

2. These may be members who, like those listed on 1 and 2 August, were given liberty to take their seats despite the fact that they had not yet received communion in accordance with the order of 21 June (see above, H. of C., 21 June, O.B.). See the order below, 5 August, O.B., for communion on 7 August at Exeter College Chapel for all M.P.s who had not yet received it.

3. For the King's speech, see below, pp. 386 and 388, and H. of L,, 4 August, O.B.; for the speeches of Lord Conway and Sir John Coke, see below, pp. 386–388 and H. of L., 4 August, O.B., and n. 12. A report of these three speeches is included in *Negotium*, below, pp. 534–536.

4. Coke's motion was reiterated by Sir John Danvers the following day. See below, H. of C., 5 August, O.B.

5. On 11 July (see O.B.) it had been ordered that the House be called on this day, the third meeting of the new session. According to Sir Francis Nethersole (see his letter of 9 August to Sir Dudley Carleton, S.P. 16/5:30, Appendix, below, p. 710) a "proposition" was made (on 4 or 5 August) that the calling be deferred to another time because it was believed that after the call many members would leave the parliament. The resolution that M.P.s not depart without leave addressed that problem. Apparently there were still members who had not taken the communion (see above, n. 2) and therefore could not yet take their seats without special leave of the House.

ralities and dispensations, no patron can be sure from a lapse, as it [is] now interpreted.[6]

The qualification ought to be under hand and seal, but the patron can have no notice whether any man to qualify more than his number;[7] in which case that law makes the presentation and induction void, as if the incumbent had resigned or were dead. In my Lord Dyer's time, it was adjudged that it should be interpreted as dead, in which case the ordinary is not bound to give notice, as he ought in case of resignation, *indicium sequitur pejorem viam.*[8]

Ordered to be engrossed.

[f. 42v] The second was for the restraint of *habeas corpus,* wherein the committee made three alterations. [1.] To make it extend to executions upon statutes and recognizances, whereas before it reached only to judgments.

2ly. That they may be granted in the term time for 5 days, and no longer; and in the vacation *ad testificandum,* and no time allowed but to go and come.

3ly. Because the penalty is heavy, being the incurring of a *praemunire,* it was not made[9] to extend to such as shall be removed by *habeas corpus* out of county prisons.

Coram Rege a Christ Church.

Before the King's coming, the Speaker and divers of the Commons put on their hats, notwithstanding that the Lords were set, observing some difference between the ordinary meetings in the state of a committee and this where we were in the state of a House.[10]

The King, in a short speech, declared the engagement of these great affairs, wherein we did partake with him, his good acceptance of our last gift, the impossibility he had to go through with so many great affairs as were now in hand without further help. He knew it was a time of danger, and left to us to consider whether was greater, the danger of the sickness or of the reputation of the kingdom. For the great preparations he had made, though they had cost him great sums of money, yet it were better half the ships should perish in the sea than that the fleet should not now go out. He concluded with telling us that in two days we should have a particular answer to our petition for religion.[11]

[f. 43] Mr. Secretary[12] recited the difference between the state of affairs now and when the late King began first to think upon arms.

Germany was then almost wholly possessed by the force of Spain; the King's children thrust out of their inheritance; whereupon his Majesty began to consider what he could do of himself, what friends he could draw in, in France, in Germany, in Italy, for to maintain a war in Germany. A computation being made, was found would come to

---

6. *S.R.,* 21 *H.* VIII, c. 13, pts. 10–11.

7. According to *S.R.,* 21 *H.* VIII, c. 13, pt. 10, a spiritual person having several benefices before passage of the act could retain four of them.

8. 3 Dyer, *Reports,* Anonymous case, Mich., 8 & 9 *Eliz.* I, *pl.* 5.

9. *needed. C.D. 1625* (Knightley MS.).

10. At a joint meeting of both Houses (as opposed to a conference) the Speaker and other members of Commons wore their hats in the presence of the Lords. According to the Roll of Standing Orders (no. 27) and Henry Scobell's later procedural tract, during a conference it was traditional for the Lords to sit covered and the Commons to stand bare-headed. See Henry

Scobell, *Remembrance of some Methods, Orders, and Proceedings . . .* (London, 1641), chapt. 13, "Messages and Conferences". However, as early as 1606 the matter of bare-headedness presented a problem to members of the Lower House, "inconvenience and disease being found very great in the long and painful standing and being bare-headed". Hatsell, *Precedents,* IV, 26–28. Also, see below, H. of C., 8 August, n. 12.

11. The King's speech is printed below in Petyt 538/8, and see H. of L., 4 August, p. 132 and n. 2.

12. Edward, Lord Conway. Concerning other versions of Conway's and Sir John Coke's speeches, see H. of L., 4 August, n. 12.

700,000 *l.* per annum. Thereupon he began to provide his shipping. This made the princes in Germany to grow warm, France, Venice, and the Low Countries to come into a league with him. The King of France sends an army towards Italy; whereas the King of Spain and he were before about to come to a partition of the Valtellina.[13]

All this has not been done without charge. His Majesty is to contribute to the King of Denmark for the raising of an army 30,000 *l.* a month. The company for Ireland are reinforced; the supply of the Low Countries continued. The fleet has cost a great mass; there wants more, without which it cannot go to sea, and, if it should so fall out, it will discourage those princes. The time of the year is almost past, the officers are discredited by reason of the infection, all that you gave last is employed. They are disappointed of 30 or 40,000 *l.* at this instant.

The honor [and] safety of the nation and religion are at the stake if we now grow cold, and the princes of Germany will divide, the King of France come in as a party to the Catholic League, the King of Denmark make his peace with the Emperor; which difficulties his Majesty, finding an impossibility in himself to remove, has resorted to the help of his subject, which his ancestors have always found ready in the like cases.

[f. 43v] Sir John Coke was called up to the King and privately received from him some short instructions and then, returning to the middle of the hall, entered into a large discourse how the late King, at the suit of both Houses, with the cooperation of his Majesty and the Duke of Buckingham, gave his consent to break off both the treaties; and that it was then foreseen a war would ensue, there being no other means to vindi-

cate the injury received in the Palatinate, nor to moderate the greatness of the King of Spain who, proceeding in his conquest under color of the Catholic cause, will make himself a Catholic monarch, which is the title he aims at.[14]

His Majesty wisely considering the dangers of this charge, both in respect of his own people unprepared for war and long inured to peace, and in respect of the advantage which other princes might make if they should presently discover the necessity of his engagement, did forbear to show himself; but suffered himself to be entertained with new propositions of a recovery by mediation, and by degrees to be brought about to that which he intended, omitting nothing in the meantime which might settle his affairs.

The Palatinate was in possession of the enemies who divided it by consent, secured it with a great army, overran other princes contrary to those courses, called a diet to shut out all possibility for the P[rince] Palatine or his issue to be restored.

In France the King rather inclining to sheath his sword in the bowels of his own people. In the Low Countries great dangers by many armies, and the government interrupted by a new faction of Arminians.

His first care was to encourage the Low Countries by lending them 6,000 men and pay for two years upon a covenant of repayment. 2ly. To make a union with France by a match for his Majesty that now is, and to get an interest in that King by a new league. [f. 44] 3ly. To move the German princes and the King of Denmark, from whom he received a cold answer unless they should see his Majesty in the field; and, because he were very tender not to break the peace, he considered what was fit to raise such an army as might go into Germany, which by computation in parliament came to

---

13. See H. of L., 4 August, n. 15.

14. On Coke's speech, see H. of L., 4 August, n. 12. For background to the European situation, see H. of

L., 18 June, n. 5. See also Pym's report of the Lord Treasurer's speech of 8 August, below, H. of C., 9 August, O.B.

700,000 *l.*, the largess of which sum drew him to a more thrifty course, and he made a league with France, Savoy, and Venice for the raising of an army of 30,000 foot and 6,000 horse under Count Mansfeld,[15] to which he was to contribute 20,000 *l.* per month, and at the same time furnished his navy, and prepared this fleet, sent a new agent into Germany,[16] who thereupon began to take heart, and the King of Denmark was more tractable and entered into articles whereby he is to raise a great army, and the King to maintain 6,000 foot and 2,000 horse, which comes to 30,000 *l.* a month; but the fruit of this is yet under hope.

As for the enterprise of Count Mansfeld, though it have not fully answered the expectation, yet it has produced divers good effects: 1. The putting off of the diet. 2ly. The encouraging of the German princes. 3ly. The King of Denmark's taking the field. 4ly. The attempts of the French in Milan, and the peace between the King and his subjects, and the scattering of the enemy's forces in the Low Countries.

Thus it appears that his Majesty has called this parliament, not out of a formality for his coming to the crown, but to consult with you how these businesses may be proceeded in, and to let you know that what you have given he accepts graciously, but that these affairs require a further supply.

The fleet is now at sea going to the rendezvous at Plymouth, where there lie 10,000 men in pay, for which action his Majesty is deeply engaged in respect of his [f. 44v] own honor, the cause of religion, and support of his allies. He has intelligence besides of a purpose to trouble Ireland, to increase the enemy's navy[17] in the Low Countries, and to thrust over part of the army thither.

There is no less disbursed already than 400,000 *l.*; his Majesty's coffers are empty. It is fit you should consider what to do. No king loves his subjects, the laws, and religion better than he, and he is persuaded no subjects love their prince better; therefore he leaves it to your choice what to do, so as it may be put into the balance whether it be better to suffer this action to fall, or to stay a while together that you may resolve to yield him convenient help.

III. PETYT 538/8, INNER TEMPLE LIBRARY

[f. 132] [Thursday, 4 August 1625]

And on the fourth day, which was Thursday, both Houses were appointed to meet in Christ Church Hall at 9 of the clock before his Majesty, where he first himself spoke unto them showing them his wants and great necessity that he had of money to set out his fleet, etc., as follows:[18]

My Lords and you the Commons,

We all remember that from your deserts [*sic*][19] and advice my father (now with God) broke off the two treaties with Spain that were then in hand and you all foresaw that as well by the acquiring of my poor distressed brother's inheritance as our defense a war was like to succeed. And that as your counsels had led my father unto it, so your assistance in a parliamentary way to pursue it should not be wanting. The aid you gave my father by your advice was to succor [f. 133v] his allies, [for] the guarding of Ireland and the home parts with a supply of munition, repairing and the setting forth of his navy. A council thought on and appointed for the war, and treasurers for the issu-

---

15. Concerning the league with France, Venice, and Savoy, see H. of L., 4 August, n. 15. Concerning Mansfeld, see above, H. of C., 8 July, n. 36.

16. I.e., Sir Robert Anstruther. See Gardiner, *History of England*, V, 291–293, 299.

17. *army.* C.D. 1625 (Knightley MS.).

18. Concerning other versions of the King's speech, see H. of L., 4 August, n. 2. For notes on the contents of the speech, see the L.J. version, above, pp. 132–133. The text of the King's speech is omitted in B.L. Add. 48,091, Q.C. 449, and Harl. 5007.

19. The other versions of the speech give *desires.*

ing out of the money; and to bring the work of this, your advice, you gave three subsidies and as many fifteens, which was with all speed levied and by the direction of the Council of War in the preparation of this navy was disbursed. It pleased God at the very entrance of this preparation by your advice begun to call away my father to His mercy whereby I entered into the care as well of your designs as to the crown; and I did not, as princes use[d] to do for custom and for formality, reassemble you, but that by your advice and aid I might be able to proceed in that which by your counsels my father was now engaged in. Your love unto me and forwardness to further these affairs you expressed by a grant of two subsidies yet unpaid; although I must confess and assure you by myself and others upon credit they were aforehand disbursed and all far [f. 134] too short as yet to set forth the navy now preparing, as I have found of late by those of estimate, care, and skill employed about this business. Before you could be fully acquainted with these necessities it pleased God to visit the place of your assembly with a grievous plague, and to stay you in the place of danger had been great neglect of my just care, to prorogue the parliament had destroyed and cut off the entrance [sic].[20] Therefore I adjourned you to this place, then far remote and free from all infection, which since it has pleased God to visit also. Here, then, to hold you any long-

er against your desires were to express in me no care of your safeties, and to adjourn it without your further helps were to destroy the preparation made. I therefore leave the care of both in your own elections, considerations, and answers, only acquainting you with my own opinion which is that it were both far better both for your honors[21] and my own that with hazard of half the fleet it were set forth tha[n] to stay at home with assured loss of time, for much provision [f. 134v] is stayed at home. And when you shall be pleased, the particulars of all expenses laid out about this preparation my Lord Treasurer and other ministers employed about the business shall acquaint you at large.

Then spoke the Lord Conway, the King's Secretary, of the state of Christendom and the wars, how much it was advanced of late, and if we should not[22] retract, what a dishonor it would be to his Majesty and this kingdom, and a disheartening to his allies and joy to the enemies.

And then also spoke Sir John Coke, by the King's appointment, of the preparation of the navy and of the charge of it.

Which speeches being ended, our House went into their House again and then resolved to debate the same the next day and so for that time rose, it being dinner time.

20. The L.J. version gives *enterprise*.
21. MS.: *owners*.

22. *now*. B.L. Add. 48,091, Q.C. 449, and Harl. 5007.

FRIDAY, 5 AUGUST 1625

1. JOURNAL OF THE HOUSE OF COMMONS

[**C.J. 810**]

[p. 42] *Veneris, 5° Augusti, 1° Caroli Regis*

Exeter College Chapel appointed for the communicants on Sunday next.[1]

All petitions about elections to be respited till further order of the House.

MR. WHISTLER. In respect of the danger of the plague here,[2] to desire a conference with the Lords, whether they know the weight of the action in hand for the war, such as is beyond our danger.

SIR GEORGE MORE. To resolve 1st here what we think fit e'er we go to the Lords.[3]

SIR JOHN DANVERS moves the *capita* of the speeches may be set down that we may know the ground we go upon.[4]

SIR S. WESTON. To know the cause of the supply desired and the enemy against whom the preparations destined; and that the papists' estates, who contribute to our enemies, may be specially respected to supply the King.[5]

SIR FRANCIS SEYMOUR.[6]

MR. CHANCELLOR DUCHY.

MR. TREASURER. 2 subsidies, 2 15eens.[7]

SIR ROBERT PHELIPS moves a select committee to draw a petition to his Majesty comprehending the heads of all those things whereof the House shall think fit to inform his Majesty.[8]

MR. CHANCELLOR EXCHEQUER. 2 subsidies, 2 15eens; for that less will not serve for the present occasion.[9]

SIR EDWARD COKE.[10] *Necessitas: affectata, invincibilis, et improvida. Invincibilis aut inevitabilis,* breaks all laws and orders. If our necessity by improvidence, then that no cause to give. *Neutralitas nec amicos parit nec inimicos tollit. Commune periculum, commune*

---

1. A number of members had not yet taken communion. See above, pp. 375, 378, and 385, n. 2.

2. Concerning the plague, see above, H. of L., 4 August, n. 8. A fuller version of Whistler's speech is included in Bedford MS. 197, below, and in *Negotium,* below, p. 536.

3. According to the report in *Negotium,* below, p. 537, it was "alleged to be unparliamentary and improper upon a proposition from the King to seek an interpretation from the Lords, who might be as ignorant as others".

4. I.e., the heads of the speeches of the King, Lord Conway, and Sir John Coke delivered 4 August.

5. Weston is suggesting that the papists' estates be further taxed to support the war effort. According to the subsidy bill passed on 8 July, the recusants were required to pay a double subsidy. See above, p. 276, and see the subsidy act, *S.R.,* 1 *Car.* I, c. 6.

6. For the speeches of Sir Francis Seymour and Sir Humphrey May (Chancellor Duchy), see below, Bedford MS. 197, and *Negotium,* pp. 537–539.

7. A bill for two subsidies had already passed both Houses on 8 July. A fuller version (perhaps a draft) of Treasurer Edmondes's speech proposing a grant of an additional two subsidies, endorsed *Copy of my speech un[to] the parliament at Oxford,* and erroneously dated *July 1625* (S.P. 16/5:15), is printed in the Appendix,

below, p. 657.

8. For a fuller version of Phelips's speech, see below, Bedford MS. 197 and *Negotium,* pp. 540–542. Concerning the rough notes for Phelips's speech, see Russell, *Parliaments,* p. 243, n. 1.

9. See Weston's speech, Bedford MS. 197, below, and *Negotium,* pp. 543–544.

10. Fuller versions of Coke's speech are included in Bedford MS. 197, Petyt 538/8, and the Dyott notes, below. The speech apparently circulated at the time as a separate but in the proliferation of copies it underwent numerous changes of paragraph order and wording, the result being that the extant copies vary considerably in form but not content. There are copies of the circulated version of the speech in several manuscript collections (e.g., Osborn fb 155, pp. 110–112; Braye MSS. I, ff. 88v–90; Tanner MS. 72, ff. 46–47 and MS. 276, ff. 150–151; P.R.O. CRES 40/18; and Carreg-lwyd MS. 1834) as well as reports of it in printed works (Rushworth, *Hist. Collections,* I, 179; Cobbett, *Parl. Hist.,* II, 11–12). We have included in the Appendix, below, pp. 658–660, notes of Coke's speech from Carreg-lwyd MS. 1834 and the version in Tanner MS. 276 (which is the same as S.P. 16/5:16) that includes also an "addition to Sir Edward Coke's speech, and some of other men's" which we have not found in any other account.

auxilium. No King can subsist in an honorable estate without 3 abilities: 1, to maintain himself against sudden invasions; 2, to aid his allies and confederates; 3, to reward his well-deserving servants.

Medicina removens. Divers causes of the leak:[11] 1, fraud, in customs by a medium of 7 years;[12] 2, the treaty of the Spanish match;[13] 3, new-invented offices with large fees. 19 *H.* 7 and 22 *H.* 8, new offices retrenched.[14] Old unprofitable offices which the King may justly take away with law, love of the people, and his own honor. Presidents of York and Wales.[15] A president for the West refused by the west country men.[16]

Multiplicity of offices in one man. Every officer to live on his office.[17]

[p. 43] The King's household out of order. New tables[18] make the leak the greater. Upstart officers.[19]

[**C.J. 811**] The retrenching of voluntary annuities, a principal means to stop this leak. A new market of pensions, these to be stopped till the King out of debt and able to pay them.

Unnecessary charges: portage money,[20] 12*d.* in the pound.

To petition the King rather for a logic than a rhetoric hand, a straight than an open hand. 4 *H.* 4, no man to beg of the King, till he out of debt. Brangwyn.[21]

Costly diet, apparel, building increase the leak.

Medicina promovens. Multiplicity of forests and parks, now a great charge to the King, may be drawn to a great benefit to the King.

Ireland's revenue: 30,000 *l.* per annum

11. I.e., the leakage of monies away from the crown.

12. The complaint concerns the granting of the customs farm for a set annual rent for seven years. The first lease of the Great Farm, granted on 24 December 1604 was to run for seven years; following its reorganization the reconstituted Great Farm was leased again in 1621 for a period of seven years, although this time, under the influence of Lionel Cranfield, Lord Treasurer, it was conceded that the lease could be called in after a three-year period and the rents readjusted. Ashton, *Crown and the Money Market,* pp. 87, 93–94. Sir William Garway, cited in the Dyott diary, below, was one of the three holders of the first lease for the Great Farm. Ibid., p. 89.

13. In 1624 the English parliament had pressed for the dissolution of the controversial treaty with Spain, agreed to the previous year, for the marriage of Charles, then Prince of Wales, and the Infanta. See Gardiner, *History of England,* V, 43–214. See also above, H. of L., 18 June, n. 5.

14. *S.R.,* 19 *H.* VII, c. 10, pt. 3. The 22 *H.* VIII citation is incorrect and should be *S.R.,* 34 and 35 *H.* VIII, c. 21, pt. 4.

15. I.e., the president and the Council of the North and the president and the Council for Wales, both of which were innovations under Henry Eighth. The former Council was not warranted by act of parliament but was created by royal commission in 31 *H.* VIII in order to quell the disturbances relating to the suppression of the monasteries. Coke, *Fourth Inst.,* pp. 245–246. The Court of the President and Council in the Dominion and Principality of Wales was warranted by

the statute of 34 and 35 *H.* VIII, c. 26. See also, ibid., pp. 241–244.

16. According to the subsidy act, *S.R.,* 32 *H.* VIII, c. 50, a president and council had been created for the western parts having authority similar to that in the north. However this council was petitioned against by citizens of Cornwall and Devon, etc., who desired "to live under the immediate government of the King and the common law." Coke, *Fourth Inst.,* p. 246. And see Caroline A. J. Skeel, "The Council of the West", *Trans. Roy. Hist. Soc.,* 4th series, vol. IV, pp. 62–80.

17. *own office.* Printed edition.

18. I.e., free board (see Aylmer, *King's Servants,* pp. 168–169); or new rates, by which officials profited.

19. Coke specifically mentioned Sir Simon Harvey and Lionel Cranfield. See Bedford MS. 197, below. Concerning Harvey, Clerk Comptroller of the Household, see above, H. of C., 2 August, n. 27; and on Cranfield, see above, H. of C., 1 July, n. 26, and 2 August, n. 9.

20. I.e., the charges for bringing in the revenue. See Bedford MS. 197, below.

21. *S.R.,* 4 *H.* IV, c. 4. Coke claimed that the words *ex mero moto* had been added to patents since the passage of this statute which, in an old roll, was titled *Brangwyn* (Welsh for "white crow"). See Coke, 10 *Reports,* ff. 112b–113a. In 1621 he had cited this precedent, and a second one concerning King Alfred's desire for holding parliaments twice a year, and was "suspected by some malevolent persons to have devised them of his own head". *C.D. 1621,* II, 211 n. 5; V, 36, 293.

benefit to the King in E. 3 time, now a great charge.[22]

6° and 27°E. 3. The King's ordinary charge to be borne by the King's ordinary revenue.[23]

Moves a committee to set down these and such other heads as shall be offered.

MR. SOLICITOR. Wishes we may petition the King to declare the King of Spain to be our enemy, and that he has done the wrong for which he has done the wrong [*sic*]; and to secure us from the papists at home, whose hearts are with the Spaniards, and are dangerous at home while our navy is abroad. 2 subsidies, 2 5teens, payable in October and April come twelvemonth.

MR. ALFORD. Is against subsidies in reversion.[24] A committee to consider of this.

SIR GEORGE MORE. Never parliament engaged themselves. We all engaged by duty. Not to graft[25] subsidy upon subsidy in one parliament. A committee.

SIR WILLIAM STRODE. Against subsidies in reversion. A committee.

SIR FRANCIS NETHERSOLE.[26] That we engaged for recovery of the Palatinate.

SIR GEORGE GORING. A committee, and the Duke to be called to it that he may give satisfaction for any aspersions which shall be cast upon him.

II. MS. 197, BEDFORD ESTATES, LONDON

[f. 44v] 5ᵗᵒ *Augusti 1625*.

It was ordered that those who have not yet received the communion should receive upon Sunday next at Exeter College.[27]

The committees for returns and privileges was respited till further order.[28]

MR. WHISTLER, laying for his ground the King's conclusion whereby he left it to our choice whether (balancing the danger of the time with the importance of the action) we would now stay together to advise of some further supply or no; and, considering that the plague was already entered into the city, 3 of 13 parishes infected, 6 dead, and 7 or 8 sick, moved that we should first require a conference with the Lords, and if we might perceive by them this action to import the commonwealth more than our own safety, then to show ourselves willing to die for our own country. If the Lords cannot resolve us, then to resort to the King, who, as he has put them into the balance, knows best how to weigh them.

[f. 45] SIR GEORGE MORE. That the desire of a conference in this case is against privilege and order.

SIR JOHN DANVERS. Before we debate this business, to appoint a committee to set down the heads of what was spoken; because divers were not here.[29]

SIR SIMON WESTON. Causes ought to be expressed before effects. Let us first desire to know our enemy before we agree to contribute to a war. If there be a just occasion, he deserves not the privilege of a subject that will not sacrifice both his estate and his life for the public. We have amongst us enemies of the state. Let us begin with their estates who use their means to supply foreign princes.[30]

SIR FRANCIS SEYMOUR.[31] That he knew

---

22. Concerning the Irish revenues of E. III, see Holinshed, *Chronicles*, II, 824.

23. Cf. *Rot. Parl.*, 6 *E.* III, no. 3, and 27 *E.* III, no. 9.

24. I.e., Alford is against voting for new subsidies which would not become payable until after the subsidies designated in the bill which had passed the House on 8 July 1625 were collected.

25. *grant. C.D. 1625* (Knightley MS.).

26. For Eliot's description of Nethersole, see below.

Negotium, p. 548.

27. See above, n. 1.

28. The C.J., above, states only that petitions (rather than the committee) about elections should be respited.

29. *did not hear. C.D. 1625* (Knightley MS.).

30. See above, n. 5.

31. For Eliot's version of Seymour's speech, see *Negotium*, below, pp. 537–538.

no ground of this meeting unless some out of private ends seek to put dissension between the King and his people, and gave this advice out of ignorance or malice rather than out of any care of the commonwealth. His Majesty was at first well contented. If we had given more, it could not have been paid between this and April.

As for the other proposition to give the King credit by a declaration, it is a way to breed jealousy between the King and his subjects, a device of those who, knowing their own faults, seek occasions to lay blame upon us. We were told of a peace in France. Who knows not that the King is gone against the Protestants? The rumor of the flat-bottom boats we heard the last meeting.[32] We have given three subsidies and three fifteens to the Queen of Bohemia, for which she is nothing the better.[33] Nothing has been done. We know not our enemy.[34] We have set upon and consumed our own people.

Since princes must see and hear with others's eyes and ears, how happy is that King who reposes his counsel upon men of worth, and how unhappy he who relies[35] upon one or two, and they such as know better how to flatter and to beg [f. 45v] of

him than how to give him good counsel? Here give me leave to remember for the honor of Queen Elizabeth, that she governed by a grave and wise counsel and never rewarded any man but for desert; and that so sparingly, that it was out of her abundance, not taking from the subjects to give to others.

He concluded that he hoped his Majesty should be as rich in the love of his people as ever any, and doubted not, if he would deal freely with us and give us time to do somewhat for the country, but we should yield[36] to him a seasonable and bountiful supply, as it becomes us.

SIR H. MAY.[37] If the King's plate or jewels or the plate and jewels of some others, whom he hears dashed upon, could have procured money, we had not met here now. Things are turned fairly to our advantage—I will not say by whose ministry—but God had a hand in it. When the parliament gave that advice we expected a war,[38] but I thought the war would have been left upon us and the Low Countries. France and Spain were joined by marriage, and the Pope a continual mediator between them to keep them friends;[39] the Germans broken;

---

32. In a speech to a joint committee of both Houses, 1 April 1624, the Duke of Buckingham related that he had "certain information from abroad" that there were already built "100 flat-bottoms" at Dunkirk. Cobbett, *Parl. Hist.,* I, 1405. The speech was reported the same day to the Lower House by Sir Edwin Sandys. See the Pym diary, Finch-Hatton MS. 50, f. 44v (Y.C.P.H. transcript).

33. I.e., in 1624. See *S.R., 21 Jac.* I, c. 33. Support for the restitution of the Palatinate, though intentionally omitted from mention in the bill's preamble (see below, n. 134), was an underlying goal of the 1624 subsidy grant.

34. I.e., the King had not yet declared the enemy. Concerning this point, see Buckingham's response in his speech to both Houses on 8 August, above, p. 163.

35. *rests. C.D. 1625* (Knightley MS.). Cf. Prov. 11:14.

36. *that we should in love yield. C.D. 1625* (Knightley MS.).

37. In Petyt 538/8, below, the speeches of Sir

Humphrey May and Sir Thomas Edmondes are placed after that of Sir Edward Coke. See O.B.

38. I.e., the advice to break the treaties with Spain in 1624. See the preamble to *S.R., 21 Jac.* I, c. 33.

39. See the speech in *Negotium,* below, p. 538, where the words are: *France and Spain united, both in alliance and affection, and the Pope still laboring to endear them for the supportation of his cause.* The earlier rivalry between Spain and France over the Valtellina had resulted in the relinquishing of the area to the Papacy in 1623, an action viewed by contemporaries as a means of prolonging Spanish control there. The following year, 1624, the French army seized the Valtellina and held it until the treaty of Monzon was signed in 1626. However, in 1623 and early 1624 the French, although anti-Spanish, were sensitive to the religious issue and the papacy, and were reluctant to sign a treaty with England on grounds that it would "highly offend the Pope to hear they should enter into an offensive league with heretics against Catholics". Gardiner, *History of England,* V, 265–267.

the King of Denmark a wary prince, unlike to enter into any war for our sakes. Now is France separated from Spain, has sent an army into the Valtellina, another to Genoa. If Mansfeld had not gone, all those designs had stayed, all princes stood in doubt till his Majesty should do something. The next day after the news of his going, the King of France commanded his army to march. If we lose our money,[40] we lose but little; but if we lose our credit, we lose the life and soul of the state.

My Lord of Devonshire was sent into Ireland not [f. 46] by the power of his friends, but of his enemies; yet they supply him with all things needful for the honor of the state. And when the news was brought of the Spaniard landing, of the difficult seige of Kinsale, the coming down of the Irish and great hazard of that kingdom, these things coming into speech in the presence of my Lord of Salisbury, his answer was: My Lord of Devonshire cannot complain of us; he has wanted nothing from hence. If things miscarry, the blame must be somewhere else.[41]

The King's engagement is from us by undertaking our designs. I would have it in the power of this House to say: If business succeed not, blame not us, nothing has been wanting on our parts. But if we withdraw our helps, we shall furnish other men with excuses, and all the misfortune will be laid to our charge. Let us not lose this advantage to have our parts of the good, and to avoid the shame of the ill. I know we have great businesses for the commonwealth. It is not to be thought the King will lose his credit with us; but will appoint another time more fit to dispatch it if now we give him contentment; and let us remember that money given in this House and cast into the sea may do us some hurt, but if it be not given we and our posterity may rue it.

MR. TREASURER[42] brought it from the general to a particular, by moving for the addition of two subsidies and two fifteens.

SIR ROBERT PHELIPS[43] distributed that which he had to speak into four parts. First, of the cause and reason of our meeting. 2ly. Of the affairs and counsels of the kingdom for some years past. 3ly. Of the present state of the kingdom. 4ly. His opinion concerning the question.

[f. 46v] 1. That our meeting here was little less than a miracle, transcended all precedents. We met at London, where none of the King's servants but thought we had done like good subjects. The first resolution of our adjournment expressed in his Majesty's care of our health. But upon the Friday before our parting, a proposition was made by a gentleman[44] who did that yesterday which never any man did before. Did the House then think they did well? and shall

---

40. *navy. C.D. 1625* (Knightley MS.).

41. Charles Blount, Earl of Devonshire (cr. 1604), had been Lord Deputy of Ireland and held the title of Lord Mountjoy when in 1601 he commanded the English armies against the Spanish invaders at Kinsale. Although Mountjoy had been a supporter of the Earl of Essex until that Earl's rebellion, he was in 1601 receiving directions from the latter's chief rival, Robert Cecil, Secretary of State (later Earl of Salisbury). See Cecil's letter of 6 October 1601 to Mountjoy, conveying the Council's assurance that "nothing shall be wanting from hence which you shall require". *A.P.C., 1601–1604*, p. 243. On Mountjoy and Kinsale, see *D.N.B.*; J. E. Neale, *Queen Elizabeth* (New York, 1934), pp. 382–386; and the indexes of *A.P.C., 1601–1604* and *Cal. S.P. Ireland, 1601–1603*.

May, who is recounting this incident, had been in Mountjoy's service in Ireland. See *Negotium*, below, p. 539 and n. 138.

42. See above, n. 7.

43. See above, n. 8.

44. MS.: *by gentlemen*. The words in *C.D. 1625* (Knightley MS.) are *by a gentleman*. The King's message of 4 July expressed his care for the members' safety and his willingness to end the session whenever parliament was ready (see H. of L., 4 July, O.B.); on Friday, 8 July, Sir John Coke had motioned for a resolution to grant further supply following the adjournment (see above, p. 352); on 4 August, at the King's request, Coke spoke before both Houses, an action which raised questions among the members regarding procedure (see above, H. of L., 4 August, n. 12).

we now vary? A surprise had then taken us, if God had not prevented it. No new enemy, design, or danger presses. Why should we put on a new resolution? Yet he was against the opinion of those that would part, and doubted not but God had brought us hither against reason and precedent that we may do somewhat to make his Majesty glorious.

2ly. That for our sins God brought upon us the Spanish treaties from which was induced the Prince's journey, and of that the effect is this war. But all together proceed from the counsels of those who brought his Majesty in love with the deceitful face of friendship, to be seduced by the practices of that subtle, artificial, fox-like people. He remembers with comfort that he was one of those who suffered in that cause when we were under that ill planet by which some man were [*sic*] made so powerful, that we were harassed in our liberties and imprisoned in our person, from which himself was delivered without injuring the liberty of the House in words or writing, and taxed with nothing but only with speaking against the Spanish match.[45]

From this mystery of perdition we were freed by a strange counsel, the Prince's journey; [f. 47] as soon as he returned, the treaties were, in real intention, broken. He was the effective cause indeed of that whereof we were made the instrumental. Three things were then desired: 1. That the Prince would link himself in such an alliance as might agree with us in religion. 2ly. To uphold our neighbors whose safety and ours are one. 3ly. To preserve religion in the kingdom. What the Spanish articles were we know. Whether those with France be any better is doubted. There are visible articles and invisible. Those we may see, but these will be kept from us.[46]

3ly. In 7° *Jac.*, the question concerning the King's prerogative of imposing was handled in this House.[47] It was argued, debated, resolved that the subjects were free from such impositions. In 12 [*Jac.*] that question was distributed into parts; a conference desired with the Lords, and refused; which he remembers not as with any imputation of justice to the King,[48] but as a mark of the malice of his ministers.[49] All papers touching that business taken away and together with them, as much as in them lay, the liberty of the subjects were consumed in the fire.[50] In 18 [*Jac.*] we forbore

45. Phelips had been imprisoned in the Tower in January 1622 for his anti-Spanish speeches in the Commons in November and December 1621, particularly that of 3 December regarding the Spanish match. See *C.D. 1621*, II, 492–493; V, 230; VI, 221. Also, see *D.N.B.*; Gardiner, *History of England*, IV, 236–255, 266–267; Chamberlain, *Letters*, II, 418. See also 12 August, below, p. 476, where the matter of imprisonments is brought up again.

46. The French articles of marriage sworn to by Charles, Prince of Wales, were never read in parliament and, although passed by the Privy Council, were held by many to be suspect. The signing by Charles of a "private engagement" and his concomitant suspension of the recusancy laws was cause for alarm among anti-Catholics. Gardiner, *History of England*, V, 261–263, 277–279. And see above, H. of L., 9 August, n. 6; and H. of C., 23 June, n. 22.

47. See *Proceedings in Parliament 1610*, I, Index, *sub* impositions; Wallace Notestein, *The House of Commons, 1604–1610* (New Haven, 1971), pp. 361–392.

48. *injustice of the King. C.D. 1625* (Knightley MS.).

49. Following debate on 5 May 1614 the Commons appointed a committee to prepare for a conference with the Lords concerning impositions (*C.J.*, I, 472–474). Upon the report from the committee on 12 May, it was decided to divide the subject into nine parts, and conference speakers were assigned for each part (*C.J.*, I, 481–482, 486, 487, 490). On 21 May the Commons sent a message to the Lords requesting a conference with the Upper House regarding impositions and the Lords resolved to return an answer by their own messengers (*C.J.*, I, 492; *L.J.*, II, 705). On 23 May the Lords consulted with the judges and on 24 May they resolved not to meet with the Lower House on the matter of impositions (*L.J.*, II, 706, 707). A message of their negative resolution was delivered to the Commons on 26 May (*L.J.*, II, 708; *C.J.*, I, 498).

50. Following the 1614 session "Sir Samuel and Edwin Sandys, Sir Dudley Digges, Sir Roger Owen, Thomas Crew, Hakewill, and some others (I remember not) that had parts appointed them by the House in the matter of impositions were enjoined to bring in their notes and papers to be burnt". Chamberlain, *Letters*, I, 539. And see John Bruce, ed., *Liber Famelicus of Sir James Whitelocke* (London: Camden Society, 1863),

that question, and gave two subsidies for the supply of the King and Queen of Bohemia.[51] In 21 it was not stirred. Since that King's death, there is a wrong done unto us in levying the tonnage and poundage.[52] In the government there has wanted good advice. Counsels and power have been monopolized. There have been more assaults upon the liberties of the people, more pressures within this 7 or 8 years than in divers ages. These things argue God to be our enemy, and that we must first make our peace with Him, or else in vain shall we send out armadas or maintain armies abroad.

[f. 47v] 4ly. This place, Oxford, makes him remember what has been done here in former parliaments;[53] yet he is none of those that loves the disordered proceedings of parliaments. In all actions there is a mixture of good, and what was ill in our forefathers struggling with the prerogative let us avoid, but not that which was good. They looked into the disorders of the time and concluded with the King for a reformation. When kings are persuaded to do what they should not, subjects have been often transported to do what they ought not. Let us not come too near the heels of power nor yet fall too low as to suffer all things under the name of the prerogative.

Let us look into the right of the subject. He would not argue whether the fleet might go or stay, whether leagues abroad be apt to support such great actions. The match has not yet brought the French to join with us in a defensive war, or any long-er than conduces to their own ends. The French army, which they say is gone, we hear is upon return. In Germany the King of Denmark has done nothing. The best way to secure ourself is to suppress the papists here.

It seems strange it should be so hard for the King to take up 60,000 $l.$; God forgive them that have so decayed his credit! Though it be not possible the subjects should forsake their king, yet if in respect of these counsels any man make a stand, let the blame light in the right place.

To give money is the end of parliaments, but to give money upon a catch will be the shame of parliaments. It will be an honor to the King that his people be seen to have a care of the settling [f. 48] his affairs. Let the fleet go on; and let not us part till his Majesty may see an ample demonstration of our affections. Let us look into the estate and government, and, finding that which is amiss, make this parliament the reformer of the commonwealth; and, as an entrance into this, he concluded with a motion for a select committee to frame a petition to his Majesty upon such heads as may be for his honor.

SIR RICHARD WESTON[54] made a short recital of the heads of the former speech, applying to every one an answer. That concerning religion, he doubted not but the King would quickly satisfy us. What was meant by the exception against the counsels near the King, he said he understood not. The effects of the leagues did hardly yet

---

pp. 41–43. Sir Walter Chute, John Hoskins, Thomas Wentworth, and Christopher Neville were committed after the 1614 parliament, and several other M.P.s, including Sir John Savile, Sir Edward Giles, and Sir James Perrot, were restrained. See *Letters of Sir Henry Wotton to Sir Edmund Bacon* (London, 1661), pp. 32–37 (Wing, *S.T.C.*, no. W3644). See also, *A.P.C.*, *1613–1614*, pp. 456–457, 459–460, 465, 466, 467; Gardiner, *History of England*, II, 249.

51. Two subsidies were granted in 1621, *S.R.*, 18 & 19 *Jac.* I.

52. Charles I had been collecting tonnage and poundage since his father's death without the customary grant for that subsidy. Cf. above, H. of C., 5 July, pp. 313–314.

53. Several parliaments met at Oxford during the reign of Henry III. The reference here is probably to the "mad parliament" of 1258 in which the barons forced the King to agree to the formation of a council of twenty-four governors which was to hold royal authority with the objective of reforming the kingdom. Holinshed, *Chronicles*, II, 446–448.

54. For Eliot's account of Weston's speech, see *Negotium*, below, pp. 543–544.

appear, yet he insisted upon divers advantages already produced, which were the same spoken of by Sir John Coke.

There was never time so necessary wherein there should not be rumors of jealousy between the King and the people. Heretofore our meetings have been like lines in a parallel, even of equal distance. The King has learned in Spain that nothing brought his father into so much contempt as the coldness between him and his people,[55] and that the contrary cause will have the contrary effect; and, thereupon, like a happy star, led the way to the people in the last parliament, when the best laws were made that divers ages have known. Neither is he like to be behind with us since his new fortune. As our duty is descended upon him, so is his favor enlarged towards us; and the better to continue it has now other new motives, war and danger, necessity and honor.

[f. 48v] Necessity is a word we care not to hear of; we must not think he loses little if we suffer him to lose his honor. We have engaged all the princes of Christendom; they anger, they hate, they fear with us, and will they not grow cold with us? Why have we talked so much of the justice of this cause if now we will forsake it? If we do not see this day the effect of our own counsel, beyond this day we cannot counsel.

Then he related the emptiness of the late King's coffers, his debts, his anticipations, the great charges the present King has sustained since his father's death, his debt, as Prince, for this action, his late borrowing of the City upon a mortgage of lands. That the 400,000 *l.* we heard of yesterday[56] was raised by anticipation of his revenues, some till Midsummer next, some till Christmas twelvemonth. The [times][57] of a long peace and dependence upon deceivable treaties had brought things out of frame, which we might well hope in this King's time, by advice of his people, would better prosper.

Whatsoever we do hereafter, this action must be done now. When we have made his Majesty able to redeem[58] his honor, let us go to other things that will endure longer time. The affairs abroad are out of our power; there is no medium between our glory and our shame which will fall upon us, besides the loss of all our pains and what we have already done.

He concluded with a motion for two subsidies and two fifteens, and with a prayer, that, as we had given good counsel, so God would direct us in such a way that we might be able to maintain it.

[f. 49] SIR E. COKE.[59] 37 *E.* 3, when he was in the height of his glory, the Commons petition that he would command the bishops and clergy to pray for 3 things:[60] 1, for his Majesty's state; 2ly, for the peace and government of the kingdom; 3ly, for continuance of the good will between the King and his subjects; and no subsidies were then given, and yet their love continued. After this introduction he propounded two questions: 1. Whether now to give any more subsidies? 2ly. How the King may subsist without charging his people?

He delivered his opinion not to give (by the ordinance 9 *H.* 4, no man should inform the King of any man's speech in parliament, but only of the conclusions; and the title of that ordinance is against fleer-

---

55. Marginal note in the E. of Bedford's hand: "So now in France when my Lo. of Holland and Carleton went about Rochelle". The fact that Henry Rich, Earl of Holland, and Sir Dudley Carleton did not go to France until December 1625, indicates that Bedford did not annotate the account of the parliament until the winter following the close of the session.

56. See Sir John Coke's speech of 4 August, above,

p. 388; 400,000 *l.* was the amount cited as already disbursed by Charles.

57. Bedford MS. 197 is blank; the word *times* has been taken from *C.D. 1625* (Knightley MS.) where it is included without brackets.

58. *rectify.* *C.D. 1625* (Knightley MS.).

59. See above, n. 10.

60. *Rot. Parl.*, 37 *E.* III, no. 9.

ing[61] reports) and added this reason: subsidies can do no good for the present, and credit the King may have without us. Other reasons would appear in answer to those things which have been urged on the other side.

1. That we had engaged the King.

Answer. We made a protestation, which is a parliamentary way, but there is no enemy yet known. Our country does not trust us to engage them but only by act of parliament and yet, if we were engaged, we have performed it; we gave the last parliament 400,000 *l.*, now two subsidies, beside the tonnage and poundage.

2ly. The greatness of the necessity.

Answer. Necessity is a brazen wall,[62] *lex temporis;* Bracton speaks of three kinds: *affectata,* [f. 49v] *invincibilis, improvida.*[63] He cleared this from being affected, neither did he hold it invincible; but thought it rather grew by want of providence. It was never heard that Queen Elizabeth's navy did dance a pavan; so many men to be pressed, and lie so long without doing anything.

The office of Lord Admiral is the place of greatest trust and experience. That of the High Constable, Bohun had by inheritance; the Marshalship has been granted in like manner.[64] Beaumont was Lord Steward, to him and his heirs;[65] so was never any Admiral.[66] In Edward the 3rd's time, it[67] was divided into the North and South. It will be well when offices are restored to men of sufficiency. If an office be granted to an unexperienced man, it is void.[68] Such a place as this cannot be executed by deputation. The wisdom of ancient times was to put great men into places of great title, but men of parts into such places as require experience. For the most part a tradesman was Master of the Ordnance until 20 *H.* 8,[69] and since it was possessed by the nobility was never well executed.

To those answers he adjoined another reason for not giving: the affliction of the time, the cessation of trade, London shut up with the plague, the commons decayed, the woeful examples of pressing the people above their abilities. 4 *R.* 2 and 3 *H.* 7, it caused a rebellion.[70] 14 *H.* 8, one eighth of

---

61. *fleecing. C.D. 1625* (Knightley MS.). *Rot. Parl.,* 2 *H.* IV, no. 11; the citation in the text is incorrect, see the Dyott account, below, p. 407.

62. Cf. Jer. 1:18; 15:20.

63. We have been unable to find the citation in Bracton.

64. Henry de Bohun, first Earl of Hereford (1176–1220), had inherited the title of Constable of England from his father, Humphrey de Bohun (d. 1182). Concerning the inheritance of the title of Constable, see Coke, *Fourth Inst.,* p. 127, and concerning that of Marshal, see Coke, *First Inst.,* sects. 102 and 153. See also, Jacob's *Law Dict., sub* Constable; Marshal.

65. Robert de Beaumont, Earl of Leicester (1104–1168), and his heirs held the title of Lord Steward. See Coke, *Fourth Inst.,* pp. 58–59.

66. *admiral in England.* B.L. Add. 26,639. The Admiralty was an appointed office rather than a hereditary one. See Coke, *Fourth Inst.,* pp. 145–146.

67. I.e., the responsibility of the office of admiralty was divided. One admiral had the government of all the fleet from the mouth of the Thames westward, another from the mouth of the Thames northward. Coke, *Fourth Inst.,* pp. 145–146.

68. See below, p. 403 and n. 101.

69. I.e., until 1528–1529. Petyt 538/8 cites 37 *H.* VIII (1545–1546) as the date when the office was first bestowed upon a nobleman. Sir William Skeffington had been appointed Master of the Ordnance by H. VIII and held the office until 1529.

70. *Rot. Parl.,* 4 *R.* II, no. 15. This poll tax precipitated the peasant revolt of 1381 led by Wat Tyler. See Holinshed, *Chronicles,* II, 734–739; Coke, *Fourth Inst.,* p. 33.

Rot. Parl., 3 *H.* VII, no. 16. In the following year, 1489 (4 *H.* VII), complaint was made by the subsidy collectors to the Earl of Northumberland that many persons living in the bishopric of Durham and divers parts of Yorkshire refused to pay. At the crown's insistence that the money be levied regardless of public opinion the citizens rallied around John a Chamber and murdered the Earl of Northumberland and a number of his household servants. Thomas, Earl of Surrey, put down the rebellion and captured John a Chamber, who was hanged as an example to others. Holinshed, *Chronicles,* III, 492–493; Cobbett, *Parl. Hist.,* I, 457–458; Coke, *Fourth Inst.,* p. 33.

every man's estate in land, money, or plate was granted to the King, but [the Earl of Northumberland][71] was slain in the North in collecting of it; but when they complained to the King, he disclaimed it, laying it upon the Council, they put it off upon the judges, and they upon the Cardinal.[72]

Then he came to his second part, how the King [f. 50] might subsist without charging his subjects, towards which he laid this ground: That subsidies have not used to be granted for any ordinary expenses, and undertook three points. 1, to show the causes of the King's wants; 2ly, the remedies both *removent* and *promovent;* 3ly, to answer some objections and to show the ground of parliamentary proceedings.

The causes.

1. Fraud in officers; of which he gave an example of the customs, that when the farm was granted according to a medium of seven years, one man got 50,000 *l.* a year by it.[73]

2ly. The treaty of the Spanish match.

3ly. The erecting of new offices and new fees. The presidents of York and Wales put the King to a great charge.[74] The like order was made for the western men 31 *H.* 8, but they petitioned that they were well enough;[75] and there is no occasion now for the North, we being united with Scotland.

4ly. Abuses in the King's household by increasing of tables and misemploying that which comes from the subject, which must be reformed otherwise than by such men as leap from the shop to the Green Cloth; by occasion whereof he named Sir Lionel Cranfield and Sir Simon Harvey.[76]

5ly. Excess of annuities, which upon all occasions former parliaments have used to retrench.[77] All the kings since the Conquest have not been so much charged in this kind as the King now is, and by using to be bought and sold they are made perpetual.

[f. 50v] 6ly. The unnecessary charge of portage money for bringing in the revenue.

7ly. Overmuch bounty in the grant of fee farms and privy seals for money. The King's servants should be rewarded with offices and honors, not with the inheritance of the crown. 4 *H.* 4,[78] the law provided that no man should beg of the King till he were out of debt. From thence came *ex mero motu* into patents; let that now be put in execution.

8ly. Vanity and excess in costly buildings, diet, and apparel.

71. Marginal note: "*q*". The words within brackets are inserted in the manuscript in the hand of the Earl of Bedford; the same words are inserted in brackets by the editor of the printed text, *C.D. 1625* (Knightley MS.).

72. Apparently the speaker or diarist has confused matters relating to the time of H. VIII with those of 4 *H.* VII. Northumberland was murdered in 1489 (see n. 70, above). The subsidy levied in April 1523 (14 *H.* VIII) for the wars in France and Scotland seems to have created little resentment in the countryside. See Holinshed, *Chronicles,* III, 685–686; Cobbett, *Parl. Hist.,* I, 486–489; *Letters and Papers H. VIII,* III, pt. 2, 1521–1523, nos. 2956, 3024, 3282. However, Cardinal Wolsey's attempt at the end of that year to enforce payment of the subsidy monies before they were due raised opposition. Holinshed, *Chronicles,* III, 693. Cobbett, *Parl. Hist.,* I, 490. And the "Amicable Grant" of 16–17 *H.* VIII, in which Wolsey attempted to collect by commission a sixth part of every subject's estate, resulted in open rebellion in some areas. Despite Wolsey's claim that his actions had been approved by the Council and the judges, the King disavowed the commission and pardoned those who had refused to contribute. Grafton, *Chronicle,* II, 376–381; Holinshed, *Chronicles,* III, 708–710; *Letters and Papers H. VIII,* IV, pt. 3, pp. 3088–3089; Coke, *Fourth Inst.,* pp. 33–34.

73. Marginal note in the Earl of Bedford's hand: "*q*". See above, n. 12.

74. See above, n. 15.

75. See above, n. 16.

76. See above, n. 19.

77. Marginal note in the Earl of Bedford's hand: "and in being bought the [*illegible*] which was the cause of the first grant is gone in a stranger for money".

78. See above, n. 21.

From the contrary courses to these causes be deduced these remedies which he called *removent*. The remedies promovent were these:

1.[79] The improving of waste grounds. The King has 31 forests, besides parks without number, all which stands him in great charges.

2ly. The employment of good officers. The revenue of Ireland in Edward 3d's time was 30,000 *l*. per annum, and yet silver not[80] at five groats the ounce, which is now at fifteen groats.

3ly. Upon all the King's leases the rents may be raised at least a third part.

All objections of these courses will be taken away if these things be done in parliament, and out of parliament they cannot, because no man will speak so freely.

6 *E*. 3, *num*. 4, the King did undertake of his ordinary revenue to maintain his ordinary charge.[81]

27 *E*. 3, *num*. 9,[82] that he never charged the subject in 14 years for the wars in France, because he had good officers. [f. 51] 50 *E*. 3, *num*. 3; 6 *R*. 2, *num*. 16; 5 *H*. 4, *num*. 33;[83] 1 *H*. 5.[84] 11 *H*. 6, it was ordained that the ordinary charges should be defrayed by the ordinary revenue and for this reason, in 11 *H*. 6, the Lord Cromwell acquainting the parliament with the balance of the King's estate, they took order that none of the ordinary revenue should be diminished.[85] 1 *H*. 7; 11 *H*. 7,[86] the like petition[87] was made.

He concluded with a motion for a general committee, with power to make a select committee.

MR. SOLICITOR. By way of preamble, intimating that besides the common difficulties there were some particular to himself, being to act both a public and private part wherein yet he meant to show himself so indifferent as not to hold either of Cephas or of Apollo;[88] and then declaring his own opinion in the question, answered those things that had been urged to the contrary.

1. That we neither are nor can be engaged. He thought we were, unless the King should put us upon such a way as was impossible. Neither is it true that the treaties were broken before we were called upon. Indeed there was an inclination in the King that now is and he that was then at the stern fetched many sighs before he fetched it about; yet he did not hold that we were engaged to all things the King should propound, and wished we should move him to declare his enemy.

2ly. That there is no such necessity. He would not endeavor to alter his opinion who held it was *necessitas improvida*. The treasure has been exhausted in King James's time. Shall King Charles be punished? [It] shall make good that saying: "The fathers have eaten sour grapes",[89] etc. But it is not the King's [f. 51v] necessity, it is the kingdom's. Whatsoever he suffers in his honor, or otherwise, will light upon us.

3ly. The danger at home from those that

---

79. Marginal note in the Earl of Bedford's hand: "and [*illegible*] of lands".

80. *silver was then at. C.D. 1625* (Knightley MS.). Groats were first coined in the reign of Edward III, 1351. See Holinshed, *Chronicles*, II, 652. Concerning the Irish revenues of E. III, see ibid., p. 824.

81. *Rot. Parl.*, 6 *E*. III, no. 3.

82. Marginal note in the Earl of Bedford's hand: "vide the parliament of E. III, his [*illegible*] into France lest by [*illegible*] officers". Cf. *Rot. Parl.*, 27 *E*. III, no. 9.

83. *Rot. Parl.*, 50 *E*. III, no. 10; *Rot. Parl.*, 6 *R*. II,

nos. 16 and 18; *Rot. Parl.*, 5 *H*. IV, no. 33.

84. It is unclear what precedent is meant. Cf. *Rot. Parl.*, 1 *H*. V, no. 9.

85. *Rot. Parl.*, 11 & 12 *H*. VI, nos. 24 and 25. Ralph, Baron Cromwell, was Treasurer from 1433 to 1443.

86. *Rot. Parl.*, 1 *H*. VII, no. 31; *Rot. Parl.*, 11 *H*. VII, no. 37.

87. *provision. C.D. 1625* (Knightley MS.).

88. 1 Cor. 1:12.

89. Jer. 31:29.

are false-hearted amongst us. He yielded that such courses ought presently to be taken that they might not be able to do hurt.

4ly. That places are possessed by men that want experience. He confessed his obligation to the great man intended. Yet, by way of admittance, that it was so, let it be questioned; but so as not to retard the public. If he deserve blame, let the burden light upon himself, not upon the commonwealth. It is the natural order that those things be first done which are most urgent.

5ly. The present affliction of the time. Plague and famine are begun already. There is a third worse than either: the sword put into the enemy's hand, who will not be idle if we stand still. If they first disturb us in Ireland they will put us to so great a charge as we shall be able to do nothing else.

6ly. The time of the year passed for this navy. We know not the design, and therefore cannot judge of the time; but we may make it past if we stand too long in consultation of that which is to be done before it can go.

7ly. The King's estate, like a ship, has a great leak. If a ship be assailed, all must not go to mend the leak, and none to defend her. For the particular propositions delivered to this purpose he referred them to a further consideration and concluded that it was fit to give; and for the *quantum* did refer it to a second question.

MR. ALFORD. That it was never the meaning of the House to be engaged; therefore all words which might receive any such interpretation were stricken out of the preamble of the act,[90] and we ought now to be as careful to grant subsidies in reversion.

[f. 52] SIR GEORGE MORE. The business of this day is to answer his Majesty, not to inquire into the errors of former times. Parliaments have varied in the manner of their gifts—sometimes the 9th sheaf, sometimes tenths or fifteens. If the occasion now should move us to some unusual course, we shall not therein differ from our ancestors. If a word in season be precious,[91] much more a deed in season; errors in time cannot be recovered. Let us therefore do this while the opportunity requires it.

SIR WILLIAM STRODE. To spare the poor and to lay it upon the rich.

SIR FRANCIS NETHERSOLE. King James was engaged to the King and Queen of Bohemia. He took the way of treaty to fulfill that engagement. That treaty, though it could not restore all the Palatinate, yet a great part was offered. The King's resolution to leave that course was upon our promise to assist him in a parliamentary way. If we do not, we shall make the case of those princes worse than it was; we shall breed a coldness in our friends, by an opinion of our unwillingness; confidence in our enemies, by an opinion of our disability.

SIR GEORGE GORING. To appoint a committee; and that the great Lord who has been touched may come to clear himself.

III. PETYT 538/8, INNER TEMPLE LIBRARY

[f. 134v] The 4th [*sic*] of August[92]

SIR EDWARD COKE spoke. In King Edward the 3d's time, who was a valiant and a wise king, the clergy[93] did petition the King for 3 things: for the maintenance and preservation of religion, for a peaceable government, and for the continuance and increase of love between [f. 135] the King and his subjects, was that petitioned then, and is it not needful now.[94] He is afraid some ill star has ruled that has brought us hither.

---

90. See below, p. 407 and n. 134.
91. Cf. Prov. 15:23; Isa. 50:4.
92. The date is correct in Harl. 5007: *Die Veneris. 5to Augusti, 1625;* B.L. Add. 48,091 and Q.C. 449 give simply *Veneris.*
93. *parliament.* Q.C. 449.
94. *Rot. Parl.,* 37 *E.* III, no. 9.

But the place where he is now, in the Divinity School, puts him in mind not to fear any evil but to put our trust in God. For surely we have a gracious and a religious King. And are there no more precedents to this purpose? Yes, in the time of that stout and valiant King Henry the Fourth you shall find that the Commons, perceiving things to go awry, did resort unto the King by petition who rectified the same. See the records of H. 4.[95]

Two things are urged against us very strongly to give, first our engagement, secondly, the King's necessity. For the first, our engagement by the House. It was no other but if that the King would turn his[96] weapon against the right enemy, they would supply him in a parliamentary course.

And for the other argument of necessity, I find in Bracton, a father of our law, that [f. 135v] there is a threefold necessity: *necessitas affectata, inevitabilis aut invincibilis, et improvida.*[97] That this is not *affectata* in his conscience he dares acquit the King. That it is *invincibilis* or *inevitabilis*, he does not believe. God forbid that his Majesty should be put to that pinch. We have no invasions, no eighty-eights.[98] That it is *improvida* he does verily believe. And therefore he thinks that in respect that it has grown by improvidence and is not inevitable, not fit[99] to be supplied by the House.

Cannot the King as well live off his revenue as his ancestors? King Edward the 3d maintained wars in France 14 years before he had supply. Offices ought to be held and used by men of experience and understanding, of good years, judgment, and discretion, to execute such offices. Or else they were void in law, and so be our [books

and][100] law cases: *3° Eliz.,* Dyer, Skrogges's case and many other books.[101] And a kingdom can never be well governed where unskillful and unfitting men are placed in great offices and hold the great offices of the kingdom. For if they are inexperienced and unskillful themselves, they cannot execute them or make choice of fit men [f. 136] under them by reason of want of experience and judgment. Neither are young and unskillful persons to be trusted with such great offices. Besides multiplicity of offices to be held by one man is a great prejudice to the merit of honor and his Majesty's well-deserving subjects. And by this means that which was wont to be thought fit to advance divers as a reward of their good service or a token of his Majesty's favor and grace and bestowed only upon men of great desert both of king and kingdom, is now held and engrossed by one man only which is neither safe for his Majesty not profitable unto the kingdom. And whereas the king[s] might and anciently have rewarded many by one of these great offices upon one of his servants whom he found to be most fit for it and[102] another and by such means keep his revenue to himself, it is now come to pass that by engrossing of offices his Majesty's Exchequer stands charges with many pensions for the reward of service at least alleged. Nay, his ancient crown land granted away to gratify men in this kind.

The office of Admiral is the greatest office of trust about the King, for the benefit [f. 136v] of the kingdom, it being an island consisting of trade, and therefore requires a man of great experience and judgment (which he cannot attain unto in a few years), and such a one as shall have spent his time in the understanding of it.[103] And he says

---

95. See above, n. 61.

96. *the.* Q.C. 449.

97. We have been unable to find the citation in Bracton.

98. I.e., 1588, the year of the Spanish Armada.

99. *not fit* is omitted in Q.C. 449.

100. The words and phrases in brackets, here and

below, are included in B.L. Add. 48,091, Q.C. 449, and Harl. 5007, but omitted from Petyt 538/8.

101. Skrogges vs. Coleshil, 2 Dyer, *Reports,* Mich., 1 & 2 *Eliz.* I, f. 175a.

102. *more fit for it than.* B.L. Add. 48,091 and Q.C. 449.

103. See above, n. 66.

for his part were he to go to sea he had rather go with a man that had been once on[104] the seas and able to guide and manage a ship or fleet than with him that had been 10 times at the haven.

The Master of the Ordnance was anciently a tradesman until 37 *H.* 8 and then it was conferred on a nobleman and ever since it has been in the nobility and was never well governed.[105]

4° R. 2 such granting of offices wrought a great disquiet in the state. 3 *H.* 7 oppression by subsidies made [a] rebellion.[106] 14 *H.* 8, when as great taxes were laid upon northernmen by the means of the Cardinal, the Earl of Northumberland being employed in the same the people slew him; the King he laid it upon his Council, his Council on the judges, and the judges on the Cardinal, and there it rested.[107]

It has been told us that by the late King's neutrality [f. 137] the wars increased, *neutralitas nec amicos parit nec inimicos tollit,* and as the case now stands it is a good project for the parliament and a worthy action to bring the King, that he may be able to subsist of his own estate which is now in a consumption. And the ship has a great leak which may be stopped yet, but if it be not stopped in time, it will all come to nought. And subsidies never given for the ordinary but for the extraordinary expenses of the King.

No state can subsist of himself[108] in an honorable estate except it has 3 things.

First, free ability to support itself for his own necessaries and defense against any sudden invasion.

Secondly, that it must be able to aid his allies and foreign friends.

Thirdly, to reward his well-deserving servants. The ordinary to be discharged by the ordinary.

The causes of defect [are] not for want of income, but through the ill ordering of it, which grows either by wasting or surcharging it. And therefore the remedy must be accordingly. There is *medicina removens* and *medicina renovans.* He moves to have a committee to recollect the heads for memorials, which are great enemies to the revenue of the crown [f. 137v] whereof fraud is one, and instances what hurt it does in the customs. The officers bought their offices dear and they wink at the merchant. And then to make up all, there must be a medium and so the farmers grow rich. How is it else that he that was but a broken merchant lately, by farming the customs awhile, is now become worth 40 to 50,000 *l.*[109]

Another is new-invented offices with large fees. 12 *E.* 4, a complaint of the like nature for an office of Surveyor of the Brewer[s] with a large fee.[110] And old offices with new fees [and new offices with new fees] to be repealed as by the law they may be with the love of the people and honor and profit of the King. President of York to cease, president of Wales to cease;[111] they are both needless charges for the people who had rather to live under the government of the common laws. The western men had the same honor as may appear by the statute of 32 *H.* 8,[112] but they desired to be governed by the common laws and to shake off that honor. Another[113] not to monopolize offices *singula officia singulis teneantur sicut judices,* every officer to live off his office and not to beg other things.

[f. 138] If the old offices and old orders

---

104. *of.* Q.C. 449.

105. See above, n. 69.

106. See above, n. 70.

107. See above, n. 72.

108. *itself.* B.L. Add. 48,091, Q.C. 449, and Harl. 5007.

109. I.e., Sir William Garway. See above, n. 12.

110. *S.R.,* 12 *E.* IV, c. 8. For the grant of the office of Surveyor of the Brewers, see *Cal. Pat. Rolls, 1461–1467,* pp. 75–76, 456; ibid., *1467–1477,* p. 295.

111. See above, n. 15.

112. See above, n. 16.

113. MS. and B.L. Add. 48,091: *Anoteth; Another* in Harl. 5007; *And* in Q.C. 449.

were kept there would be no need of new tables and therefore Sir Simon Harvey by his will should out of his offices.[114] And voluntary annuities and pensions to be retrenched are not bought and sold, and a new market kept of them as now it is. And all unnecessary charges and portage money twelve *d.* of the pound taken away whereas they make great gain of it themselves.

And overmuch bounty is another thing that is to be restrained. For here is no friend to the King or state that seeks a fee farm or a new office. The statute of 4 *H.* 4: no man ought to beg any thing of the crown till the King be out of debt.[115] This statute is called Brangwyn, which is Welsh for a white crow. They are like a crow ever craving, and for their sins[116] they are white. In the time of want and dearth, as now it is, costly apparel, diet, and Lady Vanity is to be abandoned.

And thus much for *medicina removens.* Now for *medicina renovans.* The King has 31 forests, and parks almost without number. Every one of them is a great charge to the crown. And therefore those to be peopled, and what greater honor can be to the King than by building of churches and increasing of his people without [f. 138v] doing wrong to others to grow rich. Besides, Ireland, which is now a very plentiful and rich nation (pray God it be not monopolized), by Holinshed it appears that in King Edward the 3d's time yet it did yield clearly unto the crown 30,000 *l.* per annum and now is a great charge to the crown.[117]

His project. There is no farmer that had any lease made unto him by King James but will give half a year's rent, with all his

heart, to have the same confirmed by King Charles. And if the King will take these courses he did hope, as old as he was,[118] to live to see King Charles to be styled Charles the Great.

6 *E.* 3, *numero 4°;*[119] a[nd] 5 *E.* 3, *numero 5°.*[120] The Commons did petition the King to live off his own estate and there it is aleged that the ordinary revenue should maintain the ordinary charge. 27 *E.* 3, *numero 9°,* the King did not make a new charge to an old office.[121]

6 *E.* 1 and 1 *H.* 5[122] upon an extraordinary aid and grievance the Commons show that the King ought to keep himself within his compass.

That shop boys be not taken from their shops and placed in the office of Green Cloth.

5 *H.* 4.[123] 11 *H.* 6 *numero* 24 *et* 25,[124] the Lord Cromwell being then Treasurer acquainted the Commons with [f. 139] the King's revenue and his goings out and prayed them that the[y] would take a course to keep the King within his revenue. And in *1° H.* 7 and 11 *H.* 7 the Commons confined his Majesty to his revenue.[125]

MR. SOLICITOR first states the question and that is whether it be fit at [this] time to supply his Majesty for the setting out of the fleet, yea or no. He has 2 parts to act, one as a private man and the servant of his Majesty; the other as a public man for the public good; and for the public he speaks the best oratory that gives the best reason.

The first reason: engagement. He holds that we are engaged by our word which is to

---

114. See above, n. 19.

115. See above, n. 21.

116. *sinews.* B.L. Add. 48,091 and Q.C. 449; *finenes.* Harl. 5007.

117. See above, n. 22.

118. Coke was seventy-three years old.

119. *Rot. Parl.,* 6 *E.* III, no. 3.

120. *and 50 Edward 3, numero 5°.* Harl. 5007. *Rot. Parl.,* 50 *E.* III, no. 15.

121. See above, n. 23.

122. The first citation is incomplete in the text; we are unable to find the source of it: Q.C. 449 gives *6 E. 3;* B.L. Add. 48,091 gives *6 E. 2;* Harl. 5007 gives *6 H. 2.* For the second citation, cf. *Rot. Parl.,* 1 *H.* V, no. 9.

123. See above, n. 83.

124. MS.: *14 et 25.* See above, n. 85.

125. *Rot. Parl.,* 1 *H.* VII, no. 31; *Rot. Parl.,* 11 *H.* VII, no. 37.

be kept unless we be unable. He does not think the treaties [were] broken before our desire signified unto his Majesty in the last parliament; in[126] that it was broken by our means. But it was inclining before for the King was so in love with *pax in diebus nostris* that he could hardly be drawn to it. He does move that the King would be pleased to declare the enemies and he thinks it would much move us and he makes no doubt but it will be the same enemy we all desire: Spain. For he that was then our advocate for the breach is now our judge, and therefore more reason to harken to it and admit we were bound to supply. Some will say we are not bound to do it, hand over head. [f. 139v] That is true. But if it be necessity whether it be inevitable or improvident yet it is to be supplied. And for that the case is more but if King James had been improvident, shall not our King be relieved? And for his part he believes there is a real necessity for that the King says it. And that the necessity concerns the kingdom as well as the King for he would never sever them. Besides, the King is young and of great hope and the world takes notice of him as of his first action. And then the report of others—either they will say his heart failed him or his people failed him. Whereof the last is the worse. And he moves that we should be humble suitors to his Majesty that while the navy is abroad the falsehearted subjects might be looked unto at home and also to move him to receive[127] our petition touching religion, for the honor of God and our safety.

But there has been something spoken of great offices held by great men which reflects upon the greatest man of the king-

dom. Every man knows his great obligation to that great man but that should not make him forget his duty to this place. And when there is time for it, he will be as ready in it as any other. But there is now *unum* [f. 140] *necessarium,* this first and that after.

Fourthly, it has been objected the necessity of the time in respect of the great infection and the effects that it produced[128] throughout the kingdom: famine and want. If the laws[129] be such that it will not yield it, then he does ill; that he thinks[130] the times are not such nor the general necessity of the kingdom such as it cannot supply. Another has been objected, that the hand of the enemy is implacable and more dangerous. Therefore not to be desired, for the deferring of time disadvantage, if the cause[131] by the King of Spain's preparation against us either to be in Ireland or at home. And how dangerous it would be that the heart[132] of the war should be at home.

Another objection—that the navy can do no good, it is past time—which he cannot believe, that his Majesty will make himself ridiculous. Howsoever, let us free ourselves. But some will say peradventure it may be done safely the next year. He will not put [it] upon a peradventure so[133] jealousy and fear of relapse of other princes by our coldness. He likes the resemblance of our estate to a ship and our wants to a leak fit to be [f. 140v] stopped. But if all be mending the leak and none defending the ship, it is in danger of foreign power. How soon will it perish! And therefore he moves there may be a committee to go on for reformation and to go on with this, too, without delay. For the quantity, he propounds no new matter; and for the time to be

126. *and.* B.L. Add. 48,091 and Q.C. 449; *by.* Harl. 5007.

127. *review.* B.L. Add. 48,091 and Q.C. 449; *relieve.* Harl. 5007.

128. *and the great effect that is produced.* Q.C. 449.

129. *times.* B.L. Add. 48,091, Q.C. 449, and Harl. 5007.

130. *then he does yield; but he thinks.* B.L. Add. 48,091,

Q.C. 449, and Harl. 5007.

131. *Therefore not to be deferred, for the difference of time disadvantages the cause.* B.L. Add, 48,091, Q.C. 449, and Harl. 5007.

132. *seat.* B.L. Add. 48,091 and Harl. 5007; *heat.* Q.C. 449.

133. *for.* B.L. Add. 48,091, Q.C. 449, and Harl. 5007.

granted now, to begin after the other subsidies are ended.

MR. ALFORD. He holds we are not engaged to give for the recovery of the Palatinate; for when it was in the act of parliament, as it was first penned, it was struck out by the order of the House [as a thing unfit to engage the House] for the recovery of the Palatinate.[134] And, if possible, yet not without great charge and difficulty and not to give now, but to make unto the King an humble remonstrance of our reasons why we do not give at this time.

SIR GEORGE MORE. To give at this time, and this is not a thing to be carried with sound of voice but with sound of reason. The King's necessity, the great loss of honor, reputation, and profit by not aiding at this time make me willing to give.

SIR WILLIAM STRODE. No subsidies but an humble remonstrance.

[f. 141] SIR FRANCIS NETHERSOLE. To give, and that we are engaged.

SIR HUMPHREY MAY.[135] Moved to give in respect of the pressing necessity which is that this great design of the fleet must stay unless it be supplied by us. And withal showed that if money [could] have been taken up to set out this fleet (upon his Majesty's plate, jewels, and some of his Lords') we had not been called together now.

SIR THOMAS EDMONDES began the motion to give this day. Showed his Majesty's

wants, our engagements, and the dishonor that would ensue to the King and kingdom by relapse, and so moves to give two subsidies.

IV. DIARY OF RICHARD DYOTT, ESQ., D661/11/1/2, STAFFORDSHIRE RECORD OFFICE[136]

[f. 54v]   5 August

SIR EDWARD COKE. 37 *E.* 3, n. 9, Parliament Roll 7, the Commons petitioned King that would command bishops and clergy to pray for three things. 3, for the continuance of goodwill of his subjects. Though there were no subsidies granted then, yet goodwill continued. 2 *H.* 4, n. 11, that nothing informed the King out of the House but by direction of the House.[137] Woeful examples when greater subsidies required than people willing to pay as 4 *R.* 2; 3 *H.* 7; 14 *H.* 8.[138]

New-invented offices, large fees, 10 *E.* 4;[139] 19 *H.* 7 in print;[140] 32 *H.* 8, the western men refused to have president and council.[141] 4 *H.* 4 occasion of clause *ex mero motu.*[142] Would show how King may subsist without supply in parliament, in honor, and royal estate. His estate in a consumption, the ship [f. 54] has a leak. Subsidies not for ordinary expenses, but where *commune periculum* must be *commune auxilium.* King must have three abilities: 1, able to defend against sudden invasions; 2, to help allies; 3, to reward well-deserving subjects. *Trans in medio,* Sir William Garway got a great es-

---

134. During the debate over supply on 19–20 March 1624 the House had decided against including the recovery of the Palatinate as a fifth motive for granting the subsidies (*C.J.*, I, 740–744; the Erle diary, B.L. Add. MS. 18,597, ff. 92–101v [Y.C.P.H. transcript]). This decision was reiterated on 14 May 1624 when the House rejected Solicitor Heath's motion that the preamble to the subsidy bill be amended to include a clause concerning the Palatinate (ibid., ff. 184–184v).

135. The speeches of May and Edmondes (below) were actually given earlier in the day. See O.B.

136. Richard Dyott recorded notes for 5, 11, and 12

August 1625 in the middle of his 1624 parliamentary notebook (see Introduction for a complete description of the manuscript). The notes are spoiled by damp and consequently are difficult to read; we are indebted to Robert Ruigh for sharing with us his transcript of the Dyott diary.

137. *Rot. Parl.*, 2 *H.* IV, no. 11.

138. See above, nn. 70, 72.

139. See above p. 404 and n. 110.

140. See above, n. 14.

141. See above, n. 16.

142. See above, n. 21.

tate by it in few years.[143] New-invented of-fices. The president of York and Wales draw a great charge upon the King. It would be more acceptable to the people and more honorable [to the] King that they should cease. The western men desired to live under the common law. Would have no monopolizing of offices. King's household out of order. I could discharge the King's household for 50,000 *l.* per annum [f. 53v] if these hang-bys were taken away. Volun-tary annuities to be retrenched and so done by most kings since the Conquest. Unneces-sary charge as portage money. Overmuch bounty; would have it like logic than rhet-oric. Fee farms hurtful to King. The leak increased by costly apparel, diet, building, etc. This is my *medicina removens,* now *pro-movens:* forests in the realm, 31, every one a great charge to the King. Parks *sans* number. Turn them to tillage; build churches where trees; let men live where wild beasts. The King may hunt in every man's park; has warren in every man's ground. Would have those in remote parts disafforested and the King to preserve those only near unto his dwelling houses. [f. 53] Monopolies in Ireland. In E. 3 times Ireland yielded to the crown 30,000 *l.*, Hol-inshed, page 481.[144] No new leases made: would have them confirmed, and so he that has 20 *l.* per annum will be contented to give 30 *l.* per annum to be sure. 6 *E.* 3, n. 4,[145] ordinary revenue to support ordinary charge. 27 *E.* 3, n. 9, King never charged subjects in 14 years for war in France.[146] 50 *E.* 3, for ordinary charge, etc.[147] 6 *R.* 2, n. 18, to the same purpose.[148] 1 *H.* 5;[149] 5 *H.* 4.[150] 11 *H.* 6, came the Lord Treasurer and said to Commons, here is King's revenue, take care to balance it. 11 *H.* 6, n. 24–25. 1 *H.* 7; 11 *H.* 7.[151] *Neutralitas neque parit ami-cos neque tollit inimicos.* [f. 52v] Mises in Wales 20,000 *l.* In treasurer's hands, 36,000 *l.* Consider the other sums of money the King has received of late from his sub-jects for these occasions.

143. See above, n. 12.
144. See above, n. 22.
145. *Rot. Parl.,* 6 *E.* III, no. 3.
146. Cf. *Rot. Parl.,* 27 *E.* III, no. 9.
147. *Rot. Parl.,* 50 *E.* III, no. 15.

148. *Rot. Parl.,* 6 *R.* II, nos. 16 and 18.
149. See above, n. 84.
150. *Rot. Parl.,* 5 *H.* IV, no. 33.
151. See above, nn. 85 and 86.

MR. DRAKE: moves for a report from the Archbishop of Canterbury concerning **Montagu**   411, *1/7

Resolved: former committee for attending the Archbishop to repair to him again concerning Montagu   411

Committee on the bill for avoiding delay in **writs of partition** to meet on Monday [8 August]   411, *25/6

Committee on the bill against **exportation of wool** to meet this afternoon   411, *25/6

L. 2a. An act to minister an oath to make **true accounts** of taxes, etc.: committed   411, 414, *28/6

SIR ROBERT HEATH (Solicitor): concerning **prisoners of King's Bench**   411

Resolved: to leave the matter of the King's Bench prisoners to the Lord Chief Justice   411

L. 2a. An act concerning **petty larceny** [new]   411, 414, *23/6

WILLIAM COXE   411

SIR THOMAS FANSHAWE   411

Bill concerning petty larceny [new]: committed   411

Bill to prevent the granting of writs of *habeas corpus*: to be put to passage Monday [8 August]   411, *27/6

Bill for the quiet of **ecclesiastical persons**: to be put to passage Monday [8 August]   411, *23/6

ROBERT CAESAR: moves for privilege for a servant of Richard **Erdeswicke**, M.P.   411

Resolved: a warrant to be issued from the Speaker concerning the above privilege   411

SIR ROBERT PHELIPS: concerning the **pardon of papists**   412, 414; **N**, 548, *1/8

SIR WALTER ERLE: concerning a letter from Secretary Conway regarding Mary Estmond   412, 414, 415

The (sub)committee for drawing the petition regarding the pardon of papists to meet this afternoon   412

Secretary Conway's letter concerning Mary Estmond: read   412, 415; **N**, 549
[*The letter is printed on p. 665*]

SIR ROBERT PHELIPS   412

SIR HENRY MILDMAY   412

Resolved: Secretary Conway's letter referred to the (sub)committee for drawing the petition regarding the pardon of papists   412, 414; **N**, 549

SIR HENRY MILDMAY: concerning supply   412, 414, 416

WILLIAM CORYTON: concerning **supply** and the **state of the kingdom**   412, 416, *8/8

SIR JOHN ELIOT   412, 414, 416

SIR JOHN COKE   412, 414, 417

WILLIAM STRODE   412, 414, 417

SIR JOHN STRADLING   413, 417

SIR NATHANIEL RICH   413, 414, 417; **N**, 549

EDWARD CLARKE   413, 415, 418

Clarke interrupted by the House for speaking offensively   413, 415, 418; **N**, 549, *8/8

EDWARD CLARKE: attempts to explain his words   413, 415, 418

JOHN PYM   418

Edward Clarke is ordered to withdraw out of the House   413. 415, 418; **N**, 550

SIR FRANCIS SEYMOUR   413

SIR EDWARD GILES   413

SIR GEORGE MORE   413, 418

SIR ROBERT PHELIPS   413, 418

SATURDAY, 6 AUGUST 1625

I. JOURNAL OF THE HOUSE OF COMMONS

[C.J. 811]

[p. 44] *Sabbati, 6° Augusti, 1° Caroli Regis*

MR. DRAKE moves for a report from the Lord of Canterbury concerning Mr. Montagu his book.

Resolved, Sir D. Digges and the rest formerly appointed[1] shall repair to the Lord of Canterbury to know what his Grace has done and to make report thereof to the House upon Monday morning next.

Bill for partition, Monday next, 2 clock, Natural Philosophy Schools. Delivered Mr. Sherwill.

The bill against exportation of wools, etc., this afternoon, 2 clock, Committee Chamber.

L. 2ᵃ. An act to minister an[2] oath to make true accounts of all general and public taxes, rates, and collections. Committed to

Sir George More   Mr. Stanley
Sir Rowland St. John   Sir Edward Giles
Sir Robert Phelips   Mr. John Drake
Sir Thomas Fanshawe   Mr. [Edward] Alford
Sir Miles Fleetwood
Sir John Scudamore
Mr. [Henry] Sherfield

And all that will come to have voice; Monday, 2 clock, in the Logic Schools.

MR. SOLICITOR, in respect of the present danger of sickness, moves from the prisoners of the King's Bench, recommended by the Lord Chief Justice.[3]

Resolved, to leave this to the discretion of the Lord Chief Justice of the King's Bench; but the House will give no order in it.

L. 2ᵃ. An act concerning petty larceny and the manner of the punishment of the offenders therein.

MR. COXE. To have Southwark included.[4]

SIR THOMAS FANSHAWE. That this law inflicts punishment before indictment.

Committed to
Mr. Glanville   Mr. Edward Herbert
Sir William Strode   Knights and burgesses
Sir Alexander St. John   of London and
Mr. Recorder   Middlesex
Mr. Solicitor   All the lawyers

And all that will come to have voice, except Sir John Stradling.[5] Physic Schools, Monday, 2 clock.

Bills of *habeas corpus* and for relief of patrons,[6] to be put to passage upon Monday next, 9 clock.

[p. 45] MR. CAESAR moves for privilege for a servant of Mr. Erdeswicke.[7]

Resolved, a warrant from Mr. Speaker. The contempt respited, infection.

---

1. Concerning the committee, see above, H. of C., 1 July, p. 282 and n. 4.

2. *at.* Printed edition.

3. The matter of releasing prisoners on writs of *habeas corpus* had been discussed on 9 July. See above, H. of C., 9 July, n. 15. On 31 July Secretary Conway had written to Lord Chief Justice Crew suggesting that the prisoners of King's Bench "have the benefit of *habeas corpus*", but "leaving their petition to his consideration". *Cal. S.P. Dom., 1625–1626,* p. 77. Sir Ranulphe Crew was appointed Lord Chief Justice of the King's Bench on 26 January 1625. *D.N.B.*

4. William Coxe sat for Southwark, Surrey.

5. Stradling was apparently being denied voice at the committee because he was opposed to the body of the bill. See Stradling's speech of 25 June, above, p. 245. Concerning the procedural principle, William Hakewill states: "But he that speaketh directly against the body of the bill may not be named a committee, for he that would totally destroy will not amend". Hakewill, *Modus Tenendi Parliamentum* (London, 1660), p. 146.

6. I.e., the bill to prevent the granting of writs of *habeas corpus* and the bill for the quiet of ecclesiastical persons and the preservation of the right of patrons, both of which were reported and ordered engrossed on 4 August. See above, H. of C., 4 August, O.B.

7. We have been unable to identify Richard Erdeswicke's servant.

SIR ROBERT PHELIPS remembers the business of the pardon. Moves for the[8] draft of the petition by the subcommittee.[9]

SIR W. ERLE. A letter written from an officer of state, *vizt.*, Lord Conway, written to Mr. Drake and Mr. Gollop, 2 justices of the peace of Dorsetshire, about a gentlewoman to whom the oath of allegiance was tendered.[10]

The subcommittee for drawing the petition about the pardon to meet at 2 of the clock this afternoon, in the Committee Chamber, to prepare and finish the petition about the pardon.

The letter aforesaid read.

SIR ROBERT PHELIPS. To join this[11] with the other, in the petition.

SIR H. MILDMAY. That we called hither 1, for religion; 2, for supply of his Majesty. That our coldness in religion one of the principal causes of the grievous visitation now upon us. To add to our former petition to his Majesty[12] that he will, upon no instance, give any connivance to the papists.

Resolved, the former committee shall also take consideration of this letter.[13]

SIR H. MILDMAY. 1. We not absolutely engaged to maintain a war, but to assist and supply the King in a war. Moves, 1, to know what money will serve for the fleet; then though not by subsidy, yet by some other course (whereof there are precedents, and which being done in parliament is a parliamentary course) to raise this supply.

MR. CORYTON. A committee to consider of what fit to be done both for supply of the King and relief of the kingdom, wherein religion to have the 1st place.

SIR JOHN ELIOT. 1, to resolve whether fit to petition the King for a recess now. Moves a committee for a petition to the King to sit.[14]

SIR JOHN COKE moves the commission for the navy may be examined.[15]

MR. STRODE moves a grand committee presently to consider of the King's supply, and that all that speak may apply themselves to this: how the 2 subsidies and 15eens, payable more than one year hence,

---

8. *a.* Printed edition.

9. Phelips is concerned with the petition drafted as a result of a pardon for High Treason, dated 12 July 1625, issued for Alexander Baker, a priest, and ten others imprisoned at Exeter. See Petyt 538/8, p. 415, below, and see also the accounts on 1 August, above, pp. 375–376 and nn. 2–4. We have no account of proceedings in the committee of the whole House which was scheduled to discuss the pardon on the afternoon of 1 August; apparently it appointed a subcommittee to draft a petition to the King protesting against the pardon. See above, p. 376. For the final version of the petition concerning Baker and Mary Estmond, see H. of L., 9 August, pp. 154–155.

10. According to the other accounts Mary Estmond had had certain possessions confiscated by two justices of the peace in Dorset (Henry Drake and Roger Gollop). Among the goods taken were "an altar, copes, and other massing stuff". Bedford MS. 197, below. Estmond, committed to the custody of the constable for refusing to take the oath of allegiance, escaped and complained to the King that she was so troubled she could not bring in her harvest. Apparently she also

requested the Duke of Chevreuse to intercede on her behalf, a point which troubled parliament. Lord Conway was directed by Charles to answer her petition to the crown and order the J.P.s to restore her goods. See above, H. of L., 9 August, pp. 153–154, and below, Petyt 538/8; see also *Negotium*, pp. 548–549. For Conway's letter of 17 July to Drake and Gollop, see Appendix, below, p. 665. For the account of the Estmond case, compiled by Drake and Gollop, S.P. 16/4:152, see Appendix, below, pp. 665–666.

11. *to joint his.* Printed edition.

12. I.e., to the petition concerning religion which had been presented to the King on 8 July and which was formally answered on 8 August. See H. of L., 9 August, pp. 155–160.

13. I.e., the subcommittee mentioned above, just before the speeches by Phelips and Mildmay.

14. The version of Eliot's speech in Petyt 538/8 is considerably fuller, see below.

15. Coke was the leading Commissioner of the Navy. Concerning the commission, see below, *Negotium*, pp. 528–529 and nn. 103 and 104.

can supply the navy to go out within 14 days.

SIR JOHN STRADLING, *accordant.* And that this will breed a jealousy, that we will not give in due time without a gift now.

[p. 46] SIR NATHANIEL RICH. Not to refuse to give, but 1st to represent to the King our wants: 1, for religion—to have his Majesty's answer in full parliament, and enrolled, which then of the force of an act of parliament;[16] 2, to know the enemy against whom our war is to be made; 3, the necessity of an advised council for government of the great affairs of the kingdom; 4, the necessity of looking into the King's estate; 5, to have his Majesty's answer concerning impositions. To have a committee for these. Though this time not fit for the decision of all these points, yet to set down the heads of them and then to have the King's answer in parliament unto them. This no capitulating with the King but an ordinary parliamentary course, as 22 E. 3,[17] and that without which the commonwealth can neither supply the King, nor subsist.

MR. EDWARD CLARKE using words that there had been speeches here with invective bitterness, unseasonable for the time, there was thereupon a general acclamation, [**C.J. 812**] "To the bar".[18] At last he was heard to explain himself, which doing, he gave great-er offense. Whereupon he was ordered to withdraw himself out of the House till the same might be debated there.

SIR FRANCIS SEYMOUR. To call him to the bar and put him out of the House.

SIR EDWARD GILES. His offense great, but yet to punish him moderately.

SIR GEORGE MORE. To have him acknowledge his error at the bar.

SIR ROBERT PHELIPS. That he remain with the Serjeant till our[19] next sitting, and come in and acknowledge his error at the bar.

Ordered upon the question that Mr. Clarke shall[20] be called in to the bar and kneel while Mr. Speaker declares to him the pleasure/

Resolved also, upon question, that Mr. Speaker shall let him know that the House has taken just offense at his words, and therefore shall stand committed to the Serjeant during the pleasure of the House.

[p. 47] He was called in, and kneeling, his sentence delivered accordingly.

SIR FRANCIS SEYMOUR moves the whole House as a committee may, upon [*blank*][21] morning, debate the great business.

SIR ROBERT PHELIPS, *accordant.* At 7

---

16. For the King's answer to the petition concerning religion, see H. of L., 9 August, pp. 155–160.

17. *Rot. Parl.,* 22 E. III, no. 4.

18. In *Negotium,* below, Eliot indicates that Clarke's criticism was directed at "some passages of the former day" regarding the Duke of Buckingham. On 5 August Sir Edward Coke issued a stinging attack on the Lord Admiral by describing that office in Edward the Third's time and then noting that: "It will be well when offices are restored to men of sufficiency" (above, p. 399). Concerning Clarke, who through Buckingham's influence had served as clerk of the Council and groom of James's Bedchamber, see also below, Petyt 538/8, p. 418; *Negotium,* pp. 549–550; and S.P. 16/5:30 (9 August letter from Nethersole to Carleton printed in Appendix, below, p. 711). Prior to Clarke's remarks this day both Mildmay (below, p. 416) and Eliot (below, p. 414) attempted to vindicate the Duke's image. The incident regarding Clarke was described in a letter from Zuane Pesaro to the Doge and Senate of Venice wherein Pesaro wrote that: "One who boldly ventured to defend the Duke openly was silenced, and to keep his place in parliament had to ask pardon of the assembly on his knees". *Cal. S.P. Venetian, 1625–1626,* pp. 142–143.

19. *the.* Printed edition.

20. *stand committed to the Serjeant and there remain until Monday next during the pleasure of the House* is crossed out in the MS. following *shall.* Clarke made his submission at the bar and resumed his seat in the House on Monday morning. See below, H. of C., 8 August, O.B.

21. Monday (8 August) according to Petyt 538/8, below.

clock and Mr. Speaker to be present, and prayers may be 1st said.

Agreed.

II. MS. 197, BEDFORD ESTATES, LONDON

[f. 52]   *6ᵗᵒ Augusti 1625.*

An act for taking the account of money given to good uses.

This account was appointed to be made upon oath, before three justices of the peace.

[f. 52v] An act concerning petty larceny.

Divers exceptions were made to this bill: 1. That it alters the fundamental law, which is that no man shall be tried upon felony before indictment by the country.[22] 2ly. It will deprive the King and other lords of their escheats.

It was moved by SIR ROBERT PHELIPS that the committee might be commanded to bring in the petition concerning the pardon granted to a Jesuit and ten others taken at Exeter.[23]

SIR WALTER ERLE. Upon a search made by two justices of peace in Dorsetshire, they found in the house of one Mrs. Estmond an altar, copes, and other massing stuff. Thereupon they tendered the oath to the Mrs. of the house, which she refused and, being committed to the custody of the constable, made an escape. Complained at court; a letter was written to the justices to this effect, that they should deliver the stuff and suffer her to come quietly to her house, in regard it was harvest. This letter was signed by Secretary Conway.[24]

Referred to the former committee to be inserted with the other matter into one petition.

SIR H. MILDMAY introduced the business

of supply, concluding for two points: 1, to know what would be sufficient to set out the navy; 2ly, to grant by way of contribution, not of subsidy.

SIR JOHN ELIOT. To take off all fault from my Lord Admiral. That the matters of the navy were executed by commission.[25]

SIR JOHN COKE.[26] This tax of the Commissioners is an artificial condemning of my Lord Admiral. [f. 53] The King's navy is the most potent navy of Christendom, and if there be any thanks deserved, it is all due to my Lord Admiral.

SIR WILLIAM STRODE. How can two subsidies to be paid a year hence conduce to the going out of the navy within this fortnight?

SIR NATHANIEL RICH propounded five heads which he desired might be referred to a committee to frame into a petition, wherein the King's answer would yield a great satisfaction to the country, though they could not be all perfected now, and that answer being obtained we shall be the fitter to resolve the question of supply.

1. Concerning religion. The Israelites could not prosper so long as the execrable thing was among them. We have as little hope of success as long as popish idolatry is so common. But we already expressed the King's answer for this which he desired might be in parliament, and then it shall have the force of a law.

2ly. That we may know the enemy.

3ly. That it would please his Majesty to use grave counselors in the government of these great affairs.

4ly. That we might at our next meeting have sufficient time to look into the King's estate, that so he might be enabled to subsist of himself.

---

22. This point was made by Sir Thomas Fanshawe. See C.J., above.

23. See above, n. 9.

24. See above, n. 10.

25. Concerning the Commissioners of the Navy, see below, *Negotium,* p. 528 and n. 103.

26. See above, n. 15.

5ly. To desire his Majesty's answer concerning the impositions.

If it be objected that we shall not have time enough, the course anciently was to present the [f. 53v] heads of their petitions, and to expect an answer at the next meeting. Others may object that hereby we shall capitulate with the King. 22 *E*. 3, the Commons gave 3 fifteens upon two conditions:[27] 1, that if the war did cease, the gift might be void. 2ly, that his Majesty's answer to their petitions might be enrolled.

MR. CLARKE. Invectives with bitterness are unseasonable for this time.

Here he was stopped, commanded to explain.[28]

Which he did, but without any submission or excuse; and thereupon sent out of the House, and ordered that he should stand committed to the Serjeant till the further pleasure of the House might be known.

And being called in again to the bar, kneeling, MR. SPEAKER told him the order of the House.

III. PETYT 538/8, INNER TEMPLE LIBRARY
[f. 141]   *Die Sabathi*

It was showed by SIR WALTER ERLE that there was a letter lately written by a great person[29] unto some justices of peace in Dorsetshire to forbear the execution of law[30] against a suspect[ed] papist.

And by order of the House it, being in a member's hand of the House,[31] was produced and read. It was directed to one Mr.

Henry Drake and another justice[32] from the Lord Conway, chief Secretary of State, dated the seventeenth of July last, which was to this effect: That whereas Mary Estmond had preferred a petition unto his Majesty signifying that they had [f. 141v] taken away certain stuff of hers which he wished them to restore again unto her. And that she was so troubled [by them][33] that she could not follow her harvest to her great loss and hindrance. And took notice that they had tendered unto her the oath of allegiance, which they might forbear to press her unto till his Majesty's pleasure were further known. And in the mean season, to let her enjoy her goods and liberty without disturbance. And so he rested at their service, Edward Conway.

At the reading of this letter the House was much moved. And as well touching a pardon granted the 12th of July last unto Baker,[34] a priest, and ten others for no less than High Treason. As touching this letter, they moved to have a conference with the Lords, and had it.[35] Wherein our House desired that they would join with us in a petition to his Majesty, which they did not deny, and yet would not do it in respect of our petition lately preferred unto his Majesty touching religion. But they would move his Majesty that he should not harken any more to foreign ambassadors in the like case, and did not doubt but to prevail in it; and that the[y] would do [it][36] in the name [f. 142] of both Houses if we thought so fit. And our House approved of their motion but yet did not well relish their put off of our desire. Sir Edward Coke to the con-

27. *Rot. Parl.*, 22 *E*. III, no. 4.

28. For Clarke's explanation, see below, Petyt 538/8. See also, above, n. 18.

29. I.e., Edward, Lord Conway, Secretary of State. See above, n. 10.

30. *justice*. Q.C. 449.

31. There is no indication of which M.P., if not Erle, brought in Conway's letter.

32. According to S.P. 16/4:152 (see Appendix, below, p. 665) the letter was addressed to Henry Drake and Roger Gollop. See above, n. 10.

33. The words within brackets are included in B.L. Add. 48,091, Q.C. 449, and Harl. 5007, but omitted from Petyt 538/8.

34. *one Barker*. Harl. 5007. See above, n. 9.

35. The conference did not occur until 9 August. See H. of L., 9 August, O.B., and H. of C., 9 August, O.B.

36. The word in brackets is included in B.L. Add. 48,091 and Q.C. 449 but omitted from Petyt 538/8 and Harl. 5007.

ference carried a copy of the pardon, and the letter itself, and brought the Lords' answer.

SIR HENRY MILDMAY. In the supply two things considerable: whether we are engaged or not; secondly, whether fit or not. For the first, we are not absolutely engaged to maintain a war but engaged to assist our King against the King[37] whose money and arms have deprived the King's children and against that King that foments a faction of papists and Arminians in this state little less dangerous than a foreign invasion. And let us remember him that did us such service in Spain and in the late parliament.[38] And therefore though he may be faulty in some things yet let us not object the worst but rather excuse him in respect of the good thing he has done. We may remember how, 3 or 4 years since, we desired a war,[39] and, now we have the opportunity, to neglect it, what folly were it in us. And if our coldness shall constrain the King to conclude a disadvantageous peace, how may we all mourn. And therefore he [f. 142v] moves to know what sum of money were fitting to set out the fleet at this time. And though that it be not done by subsidies yet it may be done otherwise by parliaments and that that is done in a parliamentary course is done in parliament, and not without precedent.

MR. CORYTON. That this desire for a supply he conceives was not intimated unto us the last time at London by reason of the sickness. And he would have the King to be supplied if there be a necessity. And the King's state for his own revenue to be considered; and the kingdom looked into for impositions; and a committee to be made for these things and especially for religion.

SIR JOHN ELIOT. His care to render himself to the public and nothing private swaying with him. The labor now in this case was the proposition for money; that grounded upon a pretended necessity, that necessity enforcing a war, and the war a supply. And it has been objected that the war ensued upon the breach of the treaty [and the breach of the treaties][40] upon our advice. They give it a great sound that it extends to Denmark, Savoy, Germany, and France. He wishes he may deserve it, but if he shall deal truly he is diffident and distrustful of these things. [f. 143] And we have had no fruit yet but shame and dishonor over[41] all the world. This great preparation is now in the way, he prays it may be a prosperous going forth and a more prosperous return. At our last sitting, not a few days before our rising, the Lord Keeper from his Majesty gave thanks for our gift and tendered our safety as his own.[42] Then no necessity, and now is the necessity accrued since? None will say so. The supply demanded is grounded upon a double argument of promise and reason. Promise: that we are engaged, and he conceives that we are engaged, but he does not think that there is such a necessity as is pretended. And that he gathers out of the action itself, as it appears unto us, which those that press the necessity of it cannot but understand, and that is that our land soldiers were pressed in

---

37. I.e., against Philip IV, King of Spain.

38. I.e., the Duke of Buckingham, who stalwartly supported Charles during the Spanish negotiations and offered leadership in the previous parliament (1624). See above, H. of L., 18 June, n. 5.

39. Mildmay may be referring to the debates of 26 and 27 November 1621 when a number of M.P.s called for war against Spain. *C.J.*, I, 644–649; *C.D. 1621*, II, 445–459; III, 445–473; Gardiner, *History of England*, IV, 233–242.

40. The words within brackets are included in B.L.

Add. 48,091 and Q.C. 449 but omitted from Petyt 538/8 and Harl. 5007.

41. *to.* Q.C. 449.

42. Concern for the safety of those attending parliament was expressed in the King's message concerning ending the session presented by the Lord Keeper on 4 July (see H. of L., 4 July, O.B.); the King's thanks for the passage of the subsidy bill was included as part of the message concerning the King's estate presented by Sir John Coke on 8 July (see H. of C., 8 July, O.B.).

May last, and our seamen in April, and our victuals prepared, and all this spent with lying till this time to no purpose. If necessity, why stay they here to hinder the action, consume victual[s], and lose the season of the year? But it[43] dare in my conscience clear and vindicate that noble Lord who has had some aspersions laid upon him [f. 143v] and that if there has been any abuse in the fleet, it is not his fault; for there is a commission for the furnishing of this navy which is no new thing. It was granted or intended to be granted in the last Lord Admiral's time.[44] And therefore the commissioners, if any, faulty. We gave two subsidies two years since, 3 subsidies and 3 fifteens the last year, and two at this time.[45] Yet God forbid we should be so limited that upon whatsoever occasion we should give no more. Let us receive truly that which belongs to subjects which he thinks his Majesty will yield us, and [we should and][46] we shall do that that is fit to reduce it to some heads.

The proper resolution now is whether we shall desire to sit now for these things or to recede, and that arises out of his Majesty's gracious offers to sit now or at winter. God forbid that we should deny his Majesty supply if there be cause, and he moves that we should petition to debate these things at winter.

SIR JOHN COKE, a Commissioner of the Navy, says that there is no fault in the provision, therefore desires it may be searched into and examined and his and their credits who [f. 144] have been employed in it to stand or fall as it should appear unto the House.

MR. STRODE. The matter consists of two things, the King's desire to us and our desire to the King.[47] The King's first to be preferred.

SIR JOHN STRADLING. The King's desire is to have a present supply. And the motion that has been made for the King has been for a supply in reversion by subsidies to begin a year and a half hence. Which may not only breed a jealousy in us, whether we may meet then or not, but also a grief in us that the King should distrust us that he may not have it of us in its due time. And therefore not to give presently.

SIR NATHANIEL RICH. Some move to give and give presently, and some would not give at all, and some would give *sub modo,* and a 4th (to which he inclines) is that we should first move the King for his answer to our petition, for we can have no hope of a blessing so long as the execrable thing remains amongst us. And to have his Majesty's answer in parliament and after a parliamentary way.

And there is a necessity that his Majesty should declare the enemy to give us satisfaction and everyone may contribute his reason which may do much good. But the proper [f. 144v] design no man holds fit should be disclosed to us. And he wishes that when his Majesty does make a war it may be debated and advised by his grave council. And there is a necessity to look into the King's estate, how it may subsist of itself, which is an old parliamentary course and has always been used when as any great aid has been required of the Commons. And also to crave his Majesty's answer to the impositions. And as for that objection that the time is not now fitting, it will require a longer time than we may sit here. He thinks not

43. *I.* B.L. Add. 48,091, Q.C. 449, and Harl. 5007.

44. Concerning the Commissioners of the Navy, see below, *Negotium,* pp. 528–529 and nn. 103 and 104.

45. On 8 July a bill for two subsidies passed both Houses in the London session of the present parliament; in 1624 three subsidies and three fifteens had been granted (*S.R.,* 21 *Jac.* I, c. 33). Eliot's statement

that "we gave two subsidies two years since" refers to the 1621 grant.

46. The words within brackets are included in B.L. Add. 48,091 and Q.C. 449 but omitted from Petyt 538/8 and Harl. 5007.

47. *to him.* Q.C. 449.

so, for a committee might be named to digest into heads which might be presented unto his Majesty. And at this time to capitulate with the King, being never had the subjects more cause to do it than we have now. And is this without precedent? No. And that of the best times, even of that most renowned King Edward the 3d for he pretending to make a war, as now our King does, he did desire subsidies for[48] his subjects. And they, before they would grant it, did capitulate with him. And you shall find by the very act itself, which was in the 12th[49] year of his reign, [f. 145] that they did grant him a subsidy, and but one, and that was upon condition too, that if he did not go on with his war, the grant should cease and the same not to be levied.

MR. CLARKE. That some of this House did use particularities with bitter invectives [and unseasonable,][50] not fit for this time, and that against the officers of state in this kingdom, which he, for his part, as being advanced by him, was bound to oppose.[51]

And as he was going on he was interrupted by the House and exceptions taken that he taxed some member of the House, and in a manner the whole House and, being required to explain himself what he meant by those words, "particularities and[52] bitter invectives", he said he held that to be an invective when a man is termed by another to be incapable by reason of his years to execute his place, as was said of my Lord Admiral.

And showing some earnestness to persist in that course of speech, he was again interrupted by the House.

And MR. PYM moved to have him withdrawn [and thereupon he was withdrawn].[53]

SIR GEORGE MORE said he had the honor to serve in parliament in 23 Eliz. where, when as the bill was read against papists, Dr. Parry, being a member of this House, spoke [f. 145v] bitterly against it, for which he was sequestered.[54] And Shepherd in 18 *Jac.* for speaking against the bill of the sabbath and taxing a worthy member that then was of our House and is now of the Upper House, who brought in the bill (viz., the Lord Montagu), he was expelled the House.[55]

SIR ROBERT PHELIPS, moved with compassion for his countryman, was sorry that he has used such speeches. And he that will tax a member of this House publicly, what dares he do privately? And though we suffer by great men, yet let us not suffer of ourselves. And for another man to use his Majesty's power against him he can suffer it, and laugh at it.

Ordered to be sequestered and committed unto the Serjeant's custody until he should acknowledge his fault, make his submission, and the House take further order in it. And by order he was called in and did stay[56] while the SPEAKER[57] pronounced the

48. *from.* B.L. Add. 48,091, Q.C. 449, and Harl. 5007.

49. *22th.* B.L. Add. 48,091, Q.C. 449, and Harl. 5007. *Rot. Parl.,* 22 *E.* III, no. 4. Three fifteens were granted in 1348.

50. The words within brackets are included in B.L. Add. 48,091 and Q.C. 449 but omitted from Petyt 538/8 and Harl. 5007.

51. See above, n. 18.

52. *with.* Q.C. 449 and Harl. 5007.

53. The words within brackets are included in B.L. Add. 48,091, Q.C. 449, and Harl. 5007, but omitted from Petyt 538/8.

54. More is remembering the 1584–1585 session (27 *Eliz.* I), where he sat for the first time, as M.P. for Guildford, Surrey. *D.N.B.* Concerning William Parry, see D'Ewes, *Journal . . . Elizabeth,* pp. 340–342, 352, 355, 356; *D.N.B.*

55. I.e., the case of Thomas Shepherd, M.P. for Shaftesbury in the 1621 parliament, who was expelled from the House on 16 February for a speech he made against the sabbath bill on 15 February. See *C.J.,* I, 521–522, 524–525; *C.D. 1621,* I, Index, *sub* Shepherd.

56. *kneel.* B.L. Add. 48,091 and Q.C. 449.

57. *keeper.* Q.C. 449.

sentence against him. And so he was suspended the House.

SIR FRANCIS SEYMOUR. To have the great business debated on Monday morning by a committee of the whole House, which was assented unto.

SIR ROBERT PHELIPS. Commended the platform of Sir Nathaniel Rich and said that we were [f. 146] beholding unto him for showing us the way, which he desired we would think of again. And in the meantime to draw them into heads.

Mr. Clarke was permitted by the Serjeant to be at his chamber.

SIR MILES FLEETWOOD:
concerning **supply** and the
state of the kingdom   422, 425, *6/8
JOHN PYM   426
Report from the (sub)committee
for drawing the petition
regarding the **pardon of
papists**, etc. [*see below*]   422, 424, 426,
*1/8

The petition regarding the
pardon of papists, etc.: read,
amended, resolved   422, 424
[*The petition is printed on pp.
154–155*]
SIR ROBERT PYE: moves for
Edward **Clarke** to make his
submission at the bar   422, 424, 426,
*6/8

Agreed: Clarke to make his
submission [*see below*]   422, 424, 426
Message to the Lords desiring a
conference on religion
concerning the petition to the
King regarding the **pardon
of papists**, etc. (Lord
Cavendish) [*see above and
below*]   422, 424
Report from the committee on
the bill for the **Earl of Dorset**
(SIR ROBERT HEATH,
Solicitor)   422, *8/7
Amendments to the bill for
Dorset: read twice and
allowed   422
Committee on the bill against
simony and corruption in the
elections of colleges to meet
this afternoon   422, *28/6
Committee on the bill for
avoiding delay in **writs of
partition** to meet this
afternoon   422, *25/6
Report from the committee on
the bill against **exportation of
wool** (JOHN GLANVILLE)   422, *25/6

Amendments to the bill against
exportation of wool: read
twice; bill to be engrossed   422
Report of the Lords' answer to
the message: Lords have
appointed a committee for
conference on religion
tomorrow morning (LORD
CAVENDISH) [*see above*]   422, 424
Committee for the conference on
religion: appointed   422
Edward **Clarke** called in; makes
his submission at the bar;
withdraws [*see above*]   422, 424, 426
The House accepts Clarke's
submission; Clarke called to
bar again   422, 424, 426
SIR THOMAS CREW (Speaker):
declares House's acceptance
of Clarke's submission and
desires him to take his seat   422, 424, 426
Message from the Lords
concerning a present **meeting
of both Houses** and
requesting that Sir John Coke
be given leave to speak at the
meeting (Sir Ranulphe Crew,
L. Chief Justice, and Sir
Thomas Coventry, Att.
General) [*see below*]   423, 424, 426;
N, 551

Resolved: to send an answer to
the Lords by Commons' own
messengers   423, 426
Leave given to Sir John Coke to
speak as the King's servant at
the meeting of both Houses   423
SIR ROBERT PHELIPS   423
Resolution concerning the
manner of attending the
meeting of both Houses   423
SIR NATHANIEL RICH   425
Message to the Lords concerning
arrangements for the
meeting of both Houses (Sir

MONDAY, 8 AUGUST 1625

I. JOURNAL OF THE HOUSE OF COMMONS

[C.J. 812]
[p. 47] *Lunae, 8° Augusti, 1° Caroli Regis*

SIR M. FLEETWOOD. This time not seasonable either for supply of the navy nor for easing of the commonwealth. Not the 1st, because we cannot do here the last, for want of records, etc.

Propounds 3 wishes: 1, a gracious answer to our petition for religion, and some course for the due execution;[1] 2, that we know who is the enemy against whom our now designs intended; 3, letters of marque against the King of Spain.

Moves a committee to propound some means to give the King satisfaction that at our next meeting we will take care both for supply of the King/[2]

The committee presents the[3] petition to his Majesty concerning the pardon, etc.,[4] which 2 read and in some words amended and, upon question, resolved.

SIR ROBERT PYE moves Mr. Clarke may come and make his submission at the bar.[5]

Agreed.

Resolved, to send to the Lords to desire a conference with the Lords about matter of religion.[6] The Lord Cavendish sent with the message.

MR. SOLICITOR reports the Lord of Dorset's bill, with amendments, which twice read, and allowed.

Bill against simony, 2 clock this afternoon, in the former place.

Bill about partitions,[7] at the same time, in the former place, and all that will come to have voice.

MR. GLANVILLE reports the bill against exportation of wool, etc., with amendments, which 2 read. *Engrossetur.*

LORD CAVENDISH reports the Lords have accepted the conference, tomorrow, 8 clock, in the Painted Chamber:[8] their number, 16.
[p. 48]

Lord Cavendish	Sir John Trevor
Mr. Treasurer	Sir James Fullerton
Sir Edward Coke	Sir Robert Carr
Mr. Comptroller	Sir Andrew Corbet
Sir George More	Sir Nathaniel Rich
Sir Edward Villiers	Mr. [John] Pym
Sir Clipsby Crew	Sir Henry Marten
Mr. John Crew	Sir Thomas Cheeke
Sir Benjamin Rudyard	Sir Francis Barrington
Mr. Solicitor	Sir Gilbert Gerard
Mr. Recorder	Sir Dudley Digges
Sir Thomas Fanshawe	Sir Henry Mildmay
Sir Robert Pye	Sir Thomas Hoby
Mr. John Drake	Sir Robert Phelips
Sir Francis Seymour	Sir Thomas Puckering
Mr. William Strode	
Mr. [William] Mallory	

appointed to confer with the Lords.

Mr. Edward Clarke called in and, upon his knees at the bar, acknowledged his error very fully. He was thereupon withdrawn. He was presently called in again and, at the bar without kneeling, MR. SPEAKER told

---

1. The King's answer to the petition concerning religion was delivered this afternoon (8 August) but not reported to the House until the following morning. For the answer, see H. of L., 9 August, pp. 155–160. For a fuller account of Fleetwood's speech, see Petyt 538/8, below.

2. See Petyt 538/8, below.

3. *a.* Printed edition.

4. I.e., the petition addressed to his Majesty concerning the pardon of the papists and the letter from Lord Conway to Mary Estmond (see above, H. of C., 6 August, nn. 9 and 10). The petition is printed above,

H. of L., 9 August, pp. 154–155.

5. Edward Clarke had been censured by the House for his remarks about speeches critical of the Duke of Buckingham. See above, H. of C., 6 August, n. 18.

6. The desired conference was with regard to the pardon of the papists and Conway's letter to Mary Estmond. For the report of the conference, see above, H. of L., 9 August, O.B.; and below, H. of C., 9 August, O.B.

7. *petitions.* Printed edition.

8. Concerning the Painted Chamber, see H. of L., 2 August, n. 1.

him the House had accepted his submission, and wished him to take his place.

A message from the Lords by the Lord Chief Justice and Mr. Attorney: That the Lords have commanded them to let the House know that the King has commanded the Duke of Buckingham to deliver a message from his Majesty to both Houses; and that, because there may be use of the Lord Treasurer, Lord Conway, and Sir John Coke to deliver some things, the Lords have given consent that those of their House may speak there,[9] and desire Sir John Coke here may do the like. This to be done presently, in the Painted Chamber.

Doubt being made about the place in respect of the danger, resolved, to send answer by messengers of our own, instantly.[10]

Leave given to Sir John Coke to speak, as is desired by the said messengers from the Lords, but to speak as the King's servant, and not as a member of the House of Commons.[11]

SIR ROBERT PHELIPS moves to send to the Lords to know whether they intend a committee of the whole House, or the whole House with the Speaker because, in the one case, to be uncovered; in the other case, not.[12]

[p. 49] Resolved, the Speaker and all to go as a House and,[13] if the Lords keep bare, then to do the like; if they cover, then the Speaker and the House to do the like.

Resolved, that a message shall be to the Lords to appoint a safe place.[14] And, upon question, that the same messengers shall intimate to the Lords to explain themselves whether they intend the House should come as a House, with the Speaker, or as a committee of the whole House, without the Speaker. Sir Edward Coke the messenger.

MR. WANDESFORD moves for the 2 knights of Yorkshire who are returned (being Sir Thomas Wentworth and Sir Thomas Fairfax, the former knights returned) may come in, desiring to know the direction of the House for their taking of the oaths and receiving the communion.[15]

Resolved, they shall take the oaths before they come in but not receive the communion, having received it at the former meeting.

9. *mind* is crossed out in the MS. following *there*.
10. The House, believing the "Painted Chamber" (see H. of L., 2 August, n. 1) to be "too little and dangerous to bear so great a burden", suggested an alternative meeting place and the Lords resolved on Christ Church Hall. See Petyt 538/8, below, and see above, H. of L., 8 August, p. 147.
11. A procedural point was at issue. See above, H. of L., 4 August, n. 12.
12. The matter of wearing or not wearing hats was tied to whether the Commons went to the meeting with their Speaker in the formality of a House or whether they went simply as a committee of the whole that would subsequently report back to the House (see H. of C., 4 August, n. 10). Sir Nathaniel Rich spoke (below, p. 425) regarding the precedents in this matter. As there was initially some confusion about the manner of attendance (which was later clarified, see n. 13, below), the Commons decided at this point to follow the Lords' example regarding headcovering. Procedural matters generally seem to have suffered in the dislocation of the session. According to Lord Mon-

tagu's account (above, p. 171) a point of order was broken at the first joint conference of the Oxford session on 9 August (regarding the pardon of the papists and the case of Mary Estmond) when the Lords were seated before the Commons came, "but", he wrote, "being at Oxford, there is no precedent to be made of these small errors".
13. This resolution was passed by the Lower House before the Lords, responding to a message from Commons, explained that "the meeting of both Houses is to be understood of a committee of both Houses, and not otherwise". See H. of L., 8 August, p. 147.
14. See above, n. 10.
15. The first election for Yorkshire had been voided by the House on 5 July. See H. of C., 5 July, p. 315. Wentworth and Fairfax, who had been returned originally and received communion at the London session, were again returned in the second election and were now ordered to take the oaths of allegiance and supremacy, required of all M.P.s, before taking their seats.

A petition tendered from Captain Hart,[16] but resolved to let it stay till the House fuller.

Report by SIR EDWARD COKE that the Lords, for the place, have appointed Christ Church Hall, at 2 of the clock this afternoon, and that they intended the House without the Speaker.[17]

Answer returned to the Lords: That the time and place is accepted and that the House has licensed Sir John Coke to speak.
Sir Edward Coke, Mr. Solicitor, Mr. Recorder, Sir D. Digges, Sir Nathaniel Rich, Mr. Pym, and Sir Thomas Hoby, to make the report back.[18]

An account being required from Mr. Serjeant concerning Mr. Montagu, he informed that he had sent for him but he found him sick in his bed.

MR. SPEAKER produces a letter written to him from Mr. Montagu which, some desiring to have read, it was resolved that he, being a prisoner, ought to have petitioned and not written.[19]

II. COMMITTEE BOOK, MS. 3410, H.L.R.O.

[Afternoon]

[f. 160] *Lunae, 8° Aug. 1° Caroli Regis.*

A committee of the whole House.[20]

III. MS. 197, BEDFORD ESTATES, LONDON

[f. 53v]   *8° Augusti 1625.*

The committee brought in the petition concerning the letter and pardon, which was read.[21]
My Lord Cavendish thereupon was sent to the Lords to desire a conference, which their Lordships granted and appointed tomorrow at 8 of the clock.

SIR ROBERT PYE had informed the House that Mr. Clarke was ready at the door, humbly desiring to be admitted to make his submission.[22]

Thereupon he was called in, and at the bar made a confession of his fault, kneeling and protesting that he had rather die a thousand deaths than disturb the peace of our proceedings.

And, being sent out again, the House agreed that he should be discharged.[23] Which the SPEAKER signified unto him being again brought to the bar, but not kneeling.

A message came from the Lords that the King had commanded my Lord of Buckingham to deliver divers [f. 54] matters to both Houses; wherefore they desire our House might meet with theirs this afternoon in Christ Church Hall; and, because his Majesty had declared that he should

16. Hart's petition is printed below, H. of C., 10 August, p. 453.
17. I.e., a committee of the whole House. See above, n. 13.
18. Following the meeting of both Houses the above named seven met, agreed upon what to say, and appointed the Recorder (Sir Heneage Finch) to report the Lord Keeper's speech, the Solicitor (Sir Robert Heath) to report the Duke of Buckingham's speech, and John Pym to report the Lord Treasurer's speech. See Bedford MS. 197, below. The reports were made on 9 August (see O.B.).
19. We are unable to find the letter to the Speaker. On 2 August the Serjeant had read a letter from Montagu wherein Montagu explained his illness from "the

stone" (see above, H. of C., 2 August, p. 378 and n. 4). Nevertheless, the Serjeant was commanded to bring Montagu to the House (above, p. 380).
20. We have no evidence that the House went into committee during the morning session and therefore have deduced that this note refers to the afternoon meeting with the Lords which the Commons attended as a committee of the whole. The speeches given at this joint session were reported the following day and consequently are included in the proceedings of 9 August; see O.B.
21. See above, n. 4.
22. See above, n. 5.
23. I.e., discharged from the custody of the Serjeant and permitted to take his place in the House.

have use of Secretary Conway and Sir John Coke to assist the Duke in that service, they had given my Lord Conway leave, and prayed us to do the like for Sir John Coke.

This message bred some doubt for, if this meeting were of both Houses, the Speaker ought to go, and all the members to be covered.[24]

Some propounded to send to the Lords for an exposition of the message;[25] but that was misliked because it came from the King and it might be thought no discretion in us to desire them to expound the King's message.

SIR NATHANIEL RICH. The Speaker not to go but when the King is present in person or by commission. Anciently the Lords were wont to come down into this House to acquaint us with businesses till 2 R. 2, when they excepted against that course;[26] but afterward it was restored again till H. 6, when the Lords sent to the Commons to meet with them, which they refused, and the difference was referred to the King's pleasure, who ordered that they should not come, but with protestation that it was of favor, not of duty.[27] In 3 and 6 H. 8, divers great Lords came into this House according to the ancient manner.[28]

But the Lords, having private notice of this difficulty, sent another message declaring that their former messengers had mistaken their instructions, for their desire was that the meeting might be by the committees of both Houses, so that debate was ended.[29]

The meeting was ordered, and Sir Edward Coke, Mr. Solicitor, Mr. Recorder, Sir D. Digges, Sir Nathaniel Rich, and Mr. Pym appointed to make the report.[30]

[Afternoon]

[f. 54v] Eodem die at Christ Church.

The committees of both Houses met at Christ Church, where the Lords being all set, a little form was left at the upper end of the table for the reporters.

My Lord Keeper made the introduction; the Duke of Buckingham delivered the business; my Lord Treasurer related the state of the King's treasure.

After they had all done, the reporters went together to agree upon their report and appointed my Lord Keeper's speech to be reported by Mr. Recorder, my Lord of Buckingham's by Mr. Solicitor, my Lord Treasurer's by Mr. Pym.[31]

IV. PETYT 538/8, INNER TEMPLE LIBRARY

[f. 146]   Die Lunae

SIR MILES FLEETWOOD. This time is not fit for either[32] of the two great propositions, supply and reformation. Superstitious religion advanced by Spain and Rome and brought home and practiced among us first to be removed or else when we have war abroad we shall not have safety at home. Jehoshaphat, so long as he kept himself free from joining with the enemy of God, and gave himself to the true worship and service of God, prospered and was in great favor with God. But he no sooner joined himself unto the idolatrous nation but he lost the favor [of God][33] and fell into the

24. See above, n. 12.
25. The Upper House later clarified the matter. See above, n. 13.
26. Rot. Parl., 2 R. II, no. 23.
27. We are unable to find the H. 6 reference.
28. In both the parliaments of 3 and 6 H. 8, a delegation of Lords, led by the Lord Chancellor, went down to the Lower House to acquaint the Commons with the causes of holding the parliaments. L.J., I, 13, 21.

29. See above, n. 13.
30. Sir Thomas Hoby is included in the C.J. list, above.
31. The reports were delivered on the following day. See H. of C., 9 August, O.B.
32. MS.: neither. The word either is taken from Harl. 5007.
33. The words within brackets are omitted from Petyt 538/8 and Harl. 5007 but included in B.L. Add. 48,091 and Q.C. 449.

hands of his enemies.[34] He would have some course taken to give the King satisfaction. In the meantime he wished 3 wishes: first, that we may have the return, establishment, and execution of our petition of religion; secondly, that we may have a war declared against Spain; thirdly, concerning our satisfaction of the [f. 146v] King, to fall into a committee how we may give the King a full overture of our hearts, of our cheerfulness and readiness to supply all his good designs when we shall meet again.

MR. PYM assents to that motion.[35] And before we fall into a committee he moves to have the pardon[36] touching Baker,[37] a known Jesuit, gotten by immediate warrant from his Majesty (whereas nothing has used to pass so but for his Majesty's own special occasion), and the letter written on the behalf of Mary Estmond to be carried by some of those that are to attend the conference with the Lords and to go away presently.

And so it was ordered. And Sir Edward Coke carried the same and brought the message to be written.

SIR ROBERT PYE shows that Mr. Clarke was ready to confess his fault and make his submission and was sorry for his fault and did desire the favor of this House to come in again.

And it was ordered that he must first make his submission (which he did standing at the bar) and if that were approved, then to go forth and come in again and take his place.

And thereupon [f. 147] he was called for in and, standing at the bar, he did acknowl-

edge his error and that he was sorry for it, and did desire the favor of the House.

And then he was bid go forth, which he did.

And the House allowing of his submission, he was sent for in to take his place, and so he did.

Sir Ranulphe Crew, Chief Justice, and Mr. Attorney, brought a message from the Lords that his Majesty had sent a message to both Houses to be delivered unto them by the Lord Admiral. And that his Majesty had appointed the Lord Treasurer, the Lord Conway, and Sir John Coke to be aiding unto him, and to deliver certain things unto them. And therefore desired this House to give Sir John Coke (being a member of theirs) leave to speak, and that it might be this afternoon at two of the clock in the Painted Chamber and the whole House to be there.

Whereupon the messenger being dispatched with this answer, that they would send them an answer by messengers of their own, the House presently took into consideration that the Painted Chamber was too little and dangerous to bear so great a burden and therefore they resolved to move the Lords [f. 147v] [that it might be in Christ Church Hall, and then also to move the Lords][38] to know whether it was meant we should come with our whole House as committee or with our[39] Speaker. For if with our Speaker, then we come as court and our Speaker was to take his place, and if they were covered we were to be covered, and no report was to be made. But if as a committee, then was a report to be made

---

34. 2 Chron., chaps. 17–20.

35. I.e., the motion put forward by Fleetwood for a committee. See C.J., above. Petyt 538/8 and the related copies contain the only extant account of Pym's speech this day.

36. *petition.* B.L. Add. 48,091 and Harl. 5007; *commission.* Q.C. 449.

37. *touching A. Baker.* Q.C. 449. The priest's name was Alexander Baker. See above, H. of C., 6 August,

n. 9.

38. The words within brackets are omitted in Petyt 538/8 but included in B.L. Add. 48,091, Q.C. 449, and Harl. 5007. Concerning the weakness of the "Painted Chamber", see above, H. of L., 8 August, p. 147 and n. 6.

39. MS.: *without.* The words *with our* Speaker, which convey the correct meaning, are used in B.L. Add. 48,091, Q.C. 449, and Harl. 5007.

and we to be uncovered. And then also ordered that Sir John Coke [might speak,][40] the House disliking that he had formerly spoken without order.[41]

And accordingly, they sent away an answer by Sir Edward Coke and others. And the Lords said they intended to be the committee of the whole House and not to come with our Speaker, and liked well that it should be in Christ Church Hall.

And our House appointed Mr. Solicitor, Mr. Recorder, and Mr. Pym to report the speeches and so the House rose.[42]

[*Afternoon*]

And after, accordingly, in the afternoon at two a clock, both Houses met in Christ Church Hall. And there the Lord Keeper first began his speech in the nature of [an] exordium or introduction unto the Duke's speech which follows.[43]

[And then the Duke began his speech. And that being ended, the Lord Treasurer for the King's debts and the revenue of the crown, showed how it stood. Whereof the two first are repeated. The other was the charge of Mr. Pym. And the Lord Treasurer he showed how that the crown was indebted when he came into his office, 120,000 *l.* to the City of London and 70,000 *l.* more of late borrowed.[44] For which the customs were anticipated and his Majesty's lands at pawn for a year. 90,000 *l.* owing to the King of Denmark, 30,000 *l.* of the charge of the funeral of the late King, besides gifts to strangers and entertainment extraordinary [f. 45v]. And his late Majesty's great debts to his servants. And 20,000 *l.* a year to the Queen of Bohemia, 370,000 *l.* [*sic*][45] a year to our Queen. So that by this speech[46] it did appear that his Majesty had not means for his present expenses.][47]

---

40. The words within brackets are omitted in Petyt 538/8 but included in B.L. Add. 48,091, Q.C. 449, and Harl. 5007.

41. See H. of L., 4 August, n. 12.

42. These three men made the reports from this afternoon's meeting of both Houses on 9 August (see below, H. of C., 9 August, O.B.); the C.J. includes the names of four additional M.P.s appointed as reporters (see above, p. 424 and n. 18).

43. The account of the day's proceedings of 8 August ends in Petyt 538/8 on f. 147v with the word *follows*. This is followed on f. 148 by the account of proceedings of 11 August (see below, p. 463). For the reports of the speeches of the Lord Keeper and Duke of Buckingham given at this 8 August meeting of both Houses as recorded at the end of Petyt 538/8, see below, pp. 433–439.

The following account of the Lord Treasurer's speech, printed within brackets, is omitted in Petyt 538/8 and has been inserted in the present text from B.L. Add. 48,091. (It is also included in Q.C. 449 and Harl. 5007.)

44. For more details of the debts and expenses of the King, see the reports of the Treasurer's speech, above, H. of L., 9 August, pp. 166–168, and below, H. of C., 9 August, pp. 431–432. The figures vary considerably for several of the items.

45. *37,000 l.* Harl. 5007. This is the correct figure as given in the reports of the Treasurer's speech (see pp. 168 and 432).

46. *means.* Q.C. 449.

47. In B.L. Add. 48,091 and Q.C. 449 this paragraph is followed by a copy of the petition concerning religion and the King's answers, which is then followed by the account of the proceedings of 11 August (see below, p. 463).

James Fiennes is **admitted** to the
House notwithstanding he
has not received communion   429, *1/8

Sir Edmund Sawyer is licensed to
come into the House   429

All bill committees that are *sine die*
are to meet this afternoon   429

L. 3a. An act for the quiet of
ecclesiastical persons:
passed   429, *23/6

L. 3a. An act to prevent the
granting of writs of *habeas
corpus*   429, *27/6

Six words inserted into the above
bill by the Clerk at the board   429

The above bill to prevent the
granting of writs of *habeas
corpus:* passed   429, 430

L. 3a. An act for the **Earl of
Dorset**, touching lands
appointed to be sold by
Richard, late Earl of Dorset,
to pay his debts, etc.: passed   429, *8/7

L. 1a. **Morgan's bill** for voiding
one decree in Chancery and
confirmation of another   429

Sir Edward Coke appointed to
report the **conference on
religion** concerning a
petition to the King
regarding **pardon of papists**,
etc.   429, *1/8

Committee attends the
conference on religion   429, 430

Report of the conference on
religion (SIR EDWARD COKE)   429

Reports of the **meeting of both
Houses** yesterday in Christ
Church Hall: *8/8

SIR HENEAGE FINCH (Recorder)
reports the Lord Keeper's
speech   429, 433; **L**, 170

SIR ROBERT HEATH (Solicitor)
reports the Duke of
Buckingham's speech and the
reading of the **petition
concerning religion** and
King's answers by the
Attorney General   430, 433; **L**,
155, *24/6

[*The petition and the King's
answers are printed on pp. 155–
160*]

JOHN PYM reports the Lord
Treasurer's speech   430, 431; **L**, 166

SIR THOMAS EDMONDES
(Treasurer): concerning
supply   430, 432; **N**,
553

JOHN MAYNARD   430, 432

THOMAS MALET   430, 432; **N**,
553

SIR ROBERT PHELIPS   430, 433

SIR THOMAS HOBY   430

Resolved: committee of the whole
House to meet tomorrow
concerning question of
supply   430, 433; **N**,
553, *10/8;
11/8

TUESDAY, 9 AUGUST 1625

I. JOURNAL OF THE HOUSE OF COMMONS

[C.J. 812]

[p. 50] *Martis, 9° Augusti, 1° Caroli Regis*

Mr. Fiennes, enforced the last sabbath day to go out of town, is licensed to come into the House till he can conveniently receive the communion.[1]

Auditor Sawyer licensed to come into the House, notwithstanding the report of his house to have been in/[2]

The committed bills now *sine die* to be at 2 clock this afternoon, in the former places.

[C.J. 813] *L. 3ª.* An act for the quiet of ecclesiastical persons and preservation of the right of patrons.

Upon question, passed.

L. 3ª. An act to restrain the grant of writs of *habeas corpus*.

After the 3d reading, these words, "other than for privilege of parliament", inserted by the Clerk at the board.

Upon question, passed.

L. 3ª. The Earl of Dorset his bill. The title too long to be expressed.

Upon question, passed.

L. 1ª. Mr. Morgan's bill for avoiding one decree in Chancery, and confirmation of another.[3]

SIR EDWARD COKE being appointed to report from the conference, whereupon they went to them, being about the pardon above-mentioned, he reports from them:[4] That one of the Lords[5] demanded whether any of these papists were convicted, or not; that they said they would report to the House and send us their answer.

That the Lords would have sent another message by him but he refused, as having no authority; and therefore desired them to send it by messengers of their own.[6]

MR. RECORDER begins the report from the committee of both Houses yesterday. That 3 Lords spoke: 1, the Lord Keeper; 2, Duke Buckingham; 3, Lord Treasurer.

That Lord Keeper told them he had only to speak concerning our petition for religion, whereto the King had, last meeting,[7] given a general answer but had now given a particular and parliamentary answer to be recorded according to the usual course, in both Houses of parliament.

---

1. The last sabbath day, Sunday 7 August, had been the day set for the receiving of communion by all M.P.s who had not previously taken it. See above, 5 August, p. 393.

2. The incomplete word was probably intended to be *infected*. Sir Edmund Sawyer was M.P. for Harwich and an auditor of the Exchequer. Concerning the plague in Oxford, see above, H. of L., 4 August, n. 8.

3. No further action was taken on this bill before the end of the 1625 session. Concerning the Chancery decrees in the case between George Morgan and Richard Bowdler, *et al.*, see *C.D. 1621*, V, 318 n.1, and *C.D. 1621*, I, Index, *sub* Morgan, George; *C.J.*, I, 682, 696. For breviates prepared by Morgan giving the history of the case, see Harl. 7607, ff. 393–403.

4. Sir Edward Coke is reporting from the conference with the Lords held this morning on the matter of the papists' pardon and the Estmond case (see above, H. of C., 6 August, nn. 9 and 10). A longer report from the conference made by the Archbishop of Canterbury to the Upper House is included in the

L.J. this day (see H. of L., 9 August, O.B.). See also Lord Montagu's record of the conference, above, H. of L., 9 August, pp. 171–172.

5. We are unable to identify the Lord who raised the question.

6. Later this day the Lords sent a message by messengers of their own desiring a further conference in the afternoon concerning the proposed petition to the King regarding the pardon of papists, etc.; however the Commons had adjourned before the Lords' messengers arrived. See H. of L., 9 August, pp. 168–169.

7. I.e., in London. For the King's short response to the petition upon its presentation on 8 July, see above, Solicitor Heath's report, H. of C., 9 July, O.B. A second brief answer to the petition was given in the King's message delivered to both Houses by the Lord Keeper at the time of the adjournment, 11 July. See H. of C., 11 July, O.B. For fuller accounts of the report of the Lord Keeper's 8 August speech, see Petyt 538/8, below, and H. of L., 9 August, p. 155.

[p. 51] That the King had given the Lord Admiral direction to deliver some things, tending/

MR. SOLICITOR reports the Duke's speech:[8]

The remedies contained in our petition concerning religion, with his Majesty's particular answers to every one, read, and is well pleased that this be enrolled in parliament.[9]

That the Duke further said that the King did this, not to draw us on, but out of his own conscience and in performance of his father's last will which was that when he was married he should so respect religion here that he should marry her person and not her religion.

The Duke's preamble.

After, proceeded by questions which divided into 12 questions:

1. By what counsels the present designs begun? Response: 1, by the parliament; 2, by advice of the Council of War.

2ly. Whether the 400,000 *l.* for the navy frugally laid out? That the Duke has laid out above 44,000 *l.*, and a friend of his above[10] 50,000 *l.*

[p. 52] MR. PYM relates the Lord Treasurer's speech.[11]

MR. TREASURER. This House has 1st taken care of religion, whereunto we have now had so gracious an answer. Therefore now to descend speedily to a supply, not of his Majesty's own wants but of those of the defense of the kingdom.

MR. MAYNARD. Easy to infest the King of Spain but likes not of this vast charge, not to be supported by the kingdom. Is not for land wars, is for the seas; and there not for letters of war [*sic*][12] but for an open war. To recommend to his Majesty 1st, the means for his living gloriously at home. To desire the King to declare a war. Is against subsidies in reversion but would willingly give if he knew how. To add spurs to the seahorses by giving. Moves a general committee tomorrow.

MR. MALET. Not to stand too much upon precedents.

We have, in the act of tonnage and poundage (limited now but till *25° Martii* next) which was always from H. 6 time been given for life, varied from former precedents.[13] Moves consideration of the danger may grow by not contenting the King in his just desires this parliament.

SIR ROBERT PHELIPS moves a grand committee tomorrow, at 8 of the clock.

SIR THOMAS HOBY, *accordant.* And that that committee may take consideration what fit to be done in p/

Resolved, a committee, tomorrow, at 8 clock, to consider of both.[14]

II. MS. 197, BEDFORD ESTATES, LONDON

[f. 54v]   *9° Augusti, 1625.*

An act against *habeas corpus*, passed.

The committee met with the Lords upon a conference touching the petition con-

8. For fuller accounts of the report of the Duke's speech (the preamble and questions), see Petyt 538/8, below (and below, n. 41); and H. of L., 9 August, pp. 155–166.

9. For the petition concerning religion, with the King's answers, see H. of L., 9 August, pp. 155–160.

10. *about.* Printed edition. In the manuscript journal half of p. 51 is blank, perhaps space intentionally left for entering the remainder of the report of the Duke's speech. According to the account in the L.J., above, p. 163, the friend was Sir William Russell, Treasurer of the Navy.

11. For Pym's report of the Lord Treasurer's speech, see below, Bedford MS. 197. For other ac-

counts of the Lord Treasurer's speech, see H. of L., 9 August, p. 166 and n. 71.

12. I.e., letters of marque.

13. Regarding tonnage and poundage, see Sir Robert Phelips's speech on 5 July, above, H. of C., p. 313 and n. 9. Malet's speech, with slightly variant wording from the C.J. version, is printed in Cobbett, *Parl. Hist.*, II, 33.

14. On 10 August the committee was postponed another day because the "King's message intervening gave the business divers new considerations" (see Bedford MS. 197, below, p. 448). For the committee proceedings of 11 August, see below, H. of C., 11 August, O.B.

cerning the pardon granted to Baker,[15] etc., and my Lord Conway's letter, etc.

[f. 59v] MR. PYM reported that which was delivered by my Lord Treasurer in this manner:[16]

My Lords and Gentlemen. I am to make unto you a declaration of the King's estate, which I cannot now do so perfectly as I would, being suddenly called unto it by the King in a remote place, where I want the use of my papers, and many things are now out of my memory. What I have to say I will divide into three parts. In the first, I will show in what estate the King's revenue was left by his father. 2ly, in what estate he does now stand. 3ly, in what estate he is like to be for the future.

[f. 60] Under the first head I will declare: 1, his debts; 2ly, his anticipations; 3ly, his engagements.

The late King of famous memory was indebted to the City of London and others, for part of which the Great Seal was engaged, and for the rest the bonds of the lords of the Council, which remain forfeited, the sum of 120,000 l.[17] besides interest.

To the wardrobe and other poor men in crying debts to a great value, the certainty I cannot tell, but it is at least 40,000 l.[18]

To the King of Denmark 75,000 l., for which interest is paid.[19]

Arrears of pensions and other payments, so great a mass as I will not mention; and lastly to the household a good sum, but the certainty I do not remember.

There was anticipated upon his customs and revenue at the least 50,000 l.

His engagements were these:

To the Low Countries for the maintenance of 6,000 foot [blank].

To Count Mansfeld to maintain 10,000 men in pay, [blank].

To rig, victual, man, and furnish this great navy, the like whereof England has not set forth in man's memory, [blank].

[f. 60v] All which engagements were undertaken, as well for the defense and safety of the realm, as for the common cause of religion.

Thus was the revenue left; and now for the present state I am to note two things: first, his Majesty's own debts; 2ly, his disbursements. And here you must remember to his father's debts, anticipations, and engagements, to add two other debts of his own.

The first, when he was Prince, which he borrowed upon the security of his Council, for this navy, 20,000 l.;[20] for Count Mansfeld, 20,000 l.;[21] and for other public services, so much as in the whole is 70,000 l. Till these occasions he was little or nothing in debt; and for the discharge of this money, the land which he had when he was Prince is also assigned, but will not suffice for the payment of it.

The other debt to be added is borrowed since he was King, of the City of London, to pay the King of Denmark and for other services, 60,000 l.[22]

15. MS.: *Boles*; a traitor in *C.D. 1625* (Knightley MS.). For Sir Edward Coke's report of the conference, see the brief account in C.J., above, and see n. 4.

16. Preceding Pym's report of the Lord Treasurer's speech, Bedford MS. 197 (ff. 54v–59v) includes a report of the Lord Keeper's message and the Duke of Buckingham's speech of 8 August. The Bedford MS. 197 version of the Lord Keeper's message is similar but somewhat less complete than that included in Petyt 538/8 below; and the Bedford account of the Duke's speech is essentially the same as that in Petyt 538/8, below. Therefore, rather than print two similar versions of the message and the speech we have excised the Bedford accounts and refer the reader to the versions in Petyt 538/8. Reports of the message and the

Duke's speech, as well as the Lord Treasurer's speech, are also printed in the L.J. See H. of L., 9 August, pp. 155–168.

17. *100,000. C.D. 1625* (Knightley MS.). Concerning the debt, see H. of L., 9 August, n. 75.

18. We are unable to verify the figure from another source. See H. of L., 9 August, n. 76.

19. See H. of L., 9 August, n. 77.

20. See above, H. of C., 8 July, p. 348 and n. 10.

21. See above, H. of C., 8 July, n. 36; and see S.P. 14/181:67–68 and S.P. 14/183:55–56.

22. Charles I had borrowed 60,000 l. from the City of London in April 1625. S.P. 16/1:66; 3:9. See also Ashton, *Crown and the Money Market*, p. 127; Dietz, *Public Finance*, p. 223.

His disbursements are these:

To the King of Denmark for one month's entertainment of 6,000 foot and 1,000 horse, 30,000 *l*. For arms for those companies, 16,000 *l*.[23]

For the soldiers at Plymouth and Hull, 16,000 *l*.[24]

[f. 61] For the mourning clothes and funeral expenses, 12,000 *l*. And there remains more to be paid 16,000 *l*.[25]

The charges of the marriage, entertainment, and gifts of honor to ambassadors, 40,000 *l*. at the least.[26]

To the Queen, for her present expenses, 5,000 *l*.[27]

To the King and Queen of Bohemia this last half year, 10,000 *l*.[28]

The furnishing of the navy, 300,000 *l*., and 100,000 *l*. more is wanting, whereof 40,000 *l*. presently, and 60,000 *l*. at their return.

Now for the third, which is the state wherein the King is like to be for the future, he remains charged with all these old and new debts, and with full interest for the time before Midsummer and since, according to the statute.

He has anticipated upon the customs and revenue to be due for the year ensuing the sum of 200,000 *l*., so as we are in question how to maintain them with bread and meat.

He stands engaged:

To the King of Denmark, per mensem,[29] 30,000 *l*.

To Count Mansfeld, per mensem, 20,000 *l*.[30]

For the supply for Ireland, per mensem, 2,600 *l*.

For the army in the Low Countries, per mensem, 8,500 *l*.[31]

[f. 61v] To the Queen for her allowance and diet, per annum, 37,000 *l*.[32]

To the King and Queen of Bohemia for their allowance and diet,[33] per annum, 20,000 *l*.

Besides, other preparations for the defense of England and Ireland, and for seconding of the fleet. His lordship concluded that he had omitted divers things before his time wherewith he was not acquainted, other since, because they were not perfected; and has not cast up the total of these sums, some of them being uncertain and himself no good auditor nor having any at hand to help him.

The day was too far spent to endure any long debate.

MR. TREASURER urged the hazard of our reputation, if by our means so great an action should fail.

MR. MAYNARD spoke to the managing of the war, rather than to the supply of the King; he did not approve land service nor letters of marque but would have three points commended to his Majesty: 1, the declaration of a war; 2ly, a league offensive and defensive with the Hollanders; 3ly, the erection of a West Indian Company.

MR. MALET. That, as in the act of tonnage and poundage we had varied from

---

23. Concerning payments to the King of Denmark, see above, H. of C., 8 July, n. 8. See also the financial tables in Dietz, *Public Finance,* pp. 216–219.

24. See above, H. of L., 9 August, n. 81.

25. Concerning the expenses for James I's funeral, see above, H. of L., 9 August, n. 82.

26. Concerning the expenses for the French, see H. of L., 9 August, n. 83.

27. Concerning the Queen's expenses, see H. of L., 9 August, n. 84.

28. Concerning Elizabeth of Bohemia, see H. of L., 9 August, n. 85.

29. *per mensem* is omitted in each case in the list in *C.D. 1625* (Knightley MS.). Concerning financial arrangements with Christian IV, see above, H. of C., 8 July, n. 8.

30. Concerning commitments to Count Mansfeld, see above, H. of C., 8 July, n. 36.

31. Concerning expenses for Ireland and the Low Countries, see H. of L., 9 August, nn. 89 and 90.

32. See H. of L., 9 August, n. 84.

33. *for their allowance and diet* is omitted in *C.D. 1625* (Knightley MS.). For the allowance to the King and Queen of Bohemia, see H. of L., 9 August, n. 85.

precedent to the King's disadvantage, so in this case he would have us vary to his advantage. Parliaments never break with the King but they meet with loss.[34] *12° [Jac.]* one subsidy was propounded and denied.[35] At our first meeting in *18° [Jac.]* we gave two; the short parliament broke; and the next we gave three subsidies and three fifteens.[36] [f. 62] He concluded that we should first agree to do somewhat, and leave the proportion to another question.

SIR ROBERT PHELIPS. Though intimating his own opinion against giving, yet moved only for a committee of the whole House tomorrow morning, which was ordered accordingly.

III. PETYT 538/8, INNER TEMPLE LIBRARY

[f. 158] [Tuesday, 9 August 1625]

[MR. RECORDER reports Lord Keeper's speech.][37] My Lords and gentlemen all. It is but very little which I have to say and all that concerns a petition for and concerning religion exhibited by both Houses to his Majesty a little before the time of the last recess, to which petition his Majesty was then pleased to give a gracious answer in general and in part has effected the same.[38] Since which time on Thursday last before

both Houses his Majesty promised a new particular and, as I may term it, parliamentary answer article of article within 2 or 3 days, but the intervening of the Lord's day was the occasion it was not delivered sooner.[39]

But now his Majesty has made a very gracious and a very full and perfect answer to every branch of the petition after an ancient and parliamentary way, and delivered it to my Lord Admiral, the Duke of Buckingham, his Grace, to be done withal and recorded according to the usual course in both Houses of parliament.[40] Besides, his Majesty has given me in command to let you, my Lords and gentlemen, understand that he has given some special direction unto my Lord Admiral to deliver some other matters of great importance which may expedite the business now in agitation.

My Lord Keeper thus concluding, my Lord Buckingham's grace began thus:

[MR. SOLICITOR reports Duke of Buckingham's speech.] My Lords and gentlemen, his Majesty has laid this so great charge upon me that, looking on my own weakness, I apprehend the weight of it. But when I consider it is fit for a king to deal plainly with his people, in that respect it

---

34. Marginal note in the E. of Bedford's hand: "No".

35. On 7 June 1614, following lengthy debate on supply (12 April and 5 May, *C.J.*, I, 461–463, 472–474, 506), Nicholas Fuller proposed to "give one subsidy presently". After various other motions made the same day regarding supply and the question of remedying grievances, James I, angry at the House's refusal to pass a subsidy bill promptly, dissolved the parliament. The records of the 7 June 1614 debates are not included in the *C.J.* but are printed in Foster, *Proceedings in Parliament 1610*, II, 414–422, from Petyt 537/18, ff. 37–40; and in *C.D. 1621*, VII, 654–656.

36. A bill granting two subsidies was passed by Commons on 17 March 1621 and received the royal assent by commission on 22 March (*C.J.*, I, 561, 569); the parliament was adjourned on 4 June, reconvened on 14 November, and on 28 November the Commons agreed on one subsidy for relief of the Palatinate (*C.J.*, I, 650) but the parliament was dissolved before this

subsidy could be enacted. The three subsidies and three fifteens were enacted in 1624. *S.R.*, 21 *Jac.* I, c. 33.

37. The following reports of the 8 August speeches to both Houses by the Lord Keeper and the Duke of Buckingham occur as a separate section at the end of Petyt 538/8 (ff. 158–160v), headed: *The report of the message delivered unto both Houses of Parliament from his Majesty by the Lord Keeper, my Lord Duke of Buckingham, and the Lord Treasurer, the 8th of August 1625.* These reports are not included in B.L. Add. 48,091, Q.C. 449, or Harl. 5007. For the report of the Lord Treasurer's speech, see H. of C., 8 August, p. 427 and n. 43.

38. See above, n. 7.

39. See the King's speech, Thursday, 4 August, above, p. 386. The "intervening Lord's day" refers to Sunday, 7 August, and the communion held in Exeter College Chapel that day.

40. I.e., entered on the Parliament Roll.

falls out fit for me who have neither rhetoric nor art. In two words I will give you a full answer that all which you desire is granted, but it is fitter for your satisfaction to hear the particulars of your demands to be read and the answers unto them.

Here Mr. Attorney General, at my Lord Duke's request, read the petition and unto every remedy read the King's answer, and the like was done upon the report of the Clerk of the Commons House at the desire of the reporter.

The petition being read and the answer thereunto the reporter[41] added this of his own with the leave of the House: That his Majesty having thus delivered a gracious and a full answer unto all the parts of the petition, and for the assurance of his intention to put it into real execution having given direction that it may be recorded or otherwise ordered as we should think fittest; we ought to acknowledge his Majesty's grace and goodness with all thankfulness who has so readily and effectually granted our petition and to acknowledge the goodness and mercy of almighty God who has sent such a king and so inclined his heart (for the hearts of kings are in the hands of God) that in his young years he has expressed so much resolution unto true religion as may give an example unto the whole world. And the reporter said that as himself was persuaded in his conscience [f. 158v] that his Majesty's heart was resolved to [go] on really in the execution, so he would entreat every truehearted subject to bear the same opinion until he should find just cause to the contrary.

Then as my Lord Duke of Buckingham proceeded with his message the reporter went on with his report:

As his Majesty has taken well your putting him in mind of these things, so if you had not pressed it he would have done it himself. He does not do this to draw you on but what he has done is to discharge the duty of his conscience and of a son to his father who commanded him as his last will on his deathbed to show unto the world as soon as he was married that he did not marry her religion but her person. This the King commanded me to deliver.

And I am now, my Lords and gentlemen, to give you an account of the fleets and of all the preparations thereof.[42] The first and last time I had the honor and happiness to speak before you all in this same business.[43] I call it honor and happiness because on what I said then you granted those counsels and resolutions which have made so marvelous a change in the affairs in Christendom. And it was so happy unto me that I had the honor to be applauded by you. And now having the same heart to speak with and the same cause to speak in and the same persons to speak unto I have no doubt of the same success and approbation.

If you look upon the change of affairs that is now from the time it was then you would think it little less than a miracle, for at that time the King of Spain went conquering and was sought unto by all the world—he had mastered Germany, possessed the Palatinate, and the Valtellina. The princes of Germany were weak and unable to resist and by my master's neutrality caused by a treaty he kept all other kings and princes in awe. Whereas now the Valtellina is a liberty, the war is in Italy, the King of Denmark has an army of 17,000 foot and 6,000 horse and commissions are gone out to make them up 30,000. The King of Sweden declares himself, the princes of the union take heart, the King of

---

41. I.e., Sir Robert Heath, the King's Solicitor, who reported the Duke's speech to the House. Interposed within the Petyt 538/8 account of the Solicitor's report are reports of the Solicitor's personal observations regarding the matters at hand.

42. See H. of L., 9 August, n. 50.

43. See H. of L., 9 August, n. 51.

France is engaged with a war with the King of Spain and has given peace unto his own subjects and joined in a league with Savoy and Venice.[44]

This being the state of things then, now I hope I shall have the same construction and success I formerly had because since that time I have not had a thought nor an action but what might tend to the advancement of the business and to please your desires.

But if I should give credit or ear (which I do not) to rumor, then I might speak with some confusion fearing not to hold so good a place in your good opinions as then you gave me, whereof I have still the same ambition and hope I shall deserve it. And when I consider the integrity of my own soul and heart to the King and state I receive courage and confidence. Whereupon I make this request: that you will believe that if any among you in the discharging of their opinions and consciences say anything which may reflect upon particular persons, I shall be the last in the world to make the application to myself, being so well assured of your justice that without cause you will not fall on him that was so lately approved by you and who will never do anything that shall give cause to irritate any to have other opinion of me than of a faithful, truehearted Englishman. Being in a continual speech I cannot give you so good satisfaction in the opening of the business. I will take this order to make propositions and questions [f. 159] to myself and answer them as well as I can. I will begin with the time when the resolution was taken for breach of the treaty and alliance and give this account of my own actions.

The first question I put to myself is by what counsel this great enterprise has been undertaken and pursued hitherto.

I answer. First by the parliament.

And then he desired that the declaration made by both Houses in parliament, 23 *Martii* 1623, might be read, and said that after he would explain himself further.[45]

Mr. Attorney General read it, and that being done the Duke proceeded thus:

Here you see, my Lords and gentlemen, upon what counsel my master entered into this business. When you had given him the counsel and the means the next part was to put it to effect by setting that on work which was then proposed, which was the defense of the realm of England, the securing of the kingdom of Ireland, the assistance of our neighbors, the states of the Low Countries and United Provinces and other his Majesty's friends and allies with the setting forth of the navy royal. My master proceeded in 3 first and when he had done this much he looked into his purse and found himself unable for the navy and yet looking upon the affairs of Christendom he found that to be most necessary. Yet if then he should have named the enemy and declared the war, all his merchants' goods in Spain had been embargoed which are since drawn home.[46] The enemy had been prepared, his friends not ready to assist, his allies not so easily drawn in and so long time between the declaration and action would have made the world believe that he intended nothing.

Upon this his Majesty of famous memory being at Newmarket wrote a letter to me being at London. That looking into the affairs of Christendom he thought fit to have a royal fleet set forth, but said: I have no money in my coffers. I would have you to engage yourself and your estate and your friends to set it forward; by which means I shall seem the less engaged and other princes in hope to draw me on will the sooner come into the action.

Hereupon I went unto it with all alacrity and, knowing that all that I had [I had] re-

---

44. See H. of L., 9 August, n. 52.
45. See H. of L., 9 August, n. 53.
46. According to the L.J. report of the speech

(above, p. 163), this is part of Buckingham's answer to a second question, which is not included in the Petyt 538/8 account.

ceived from him, I could do no less. I held it a happiness that I could once say that I saw it all floating in his service which the King gave me. Then I conferred with the Council of War which were the Lord Brooke, the Lord Hervey, Sir Robert Mansell;[47] and Sir John Coke and Captain Love were also present.

We first talked of the war and then of the means. I never spoke of the business almost but with them. I never came to the town but I met with them. Either I went to them or they did me the honor as to come unto me. I never thought of alteration nor resolved of any but in their company. After, when I saw all the materials ready—ships, tackle, victuals, ordnance all prepared—then, the proportioning of times and levies, it was thought fit to communicate this with the lords of the Council for that the levies could not be but by them. I addressed myself to his Majesty and prayed him to refer it to the lords. I made the account to them with which they then remained all satisfied and said that if this were put in execution all would do well, and they were pleased to give some attributes to it.[48]

The particulars of the account his Grace referred to Sir John Coke to deliver, which in a summary manner he did, being ready, as he said, to give further particular satisfaction if the House required it.[49]

That being done the Duke proceeded and said:

[f. 159v] My Lords and gentlemen, about this time his Majesty sent me into France and then I entreated his Majesty to have a care of the business that it might be followed according to the directions agreed upon at the Council Table, and the Lord Treasurer, the Lord Chamberlain, the Lord Conway, and the Lord Brooke were named committees to see it performed.[50] This I thought fit to tell you that I might show you what great counsels this great business was carried with; and I have not made another step in them but what I have told you.

Second question I propound is whether these great sums, the 400,000 l. bestowed and to be bestowed in the navy whereby 40,000 is yet wanting to set it forth and 60,000 l. at the return be laid out in that frugal manner which is fit or not.

Answer. I answer that how much money is expended depends upon Sir John Coke's more particular account.[51] But the managing thereof was all by the proper officers in their several places. I laid out money of my own and borrowed of my friends but I made it run in the proper way as if it had come out of the Exchequer.

And here Sir John Coke, standing by, said that my Lord Duke had laid out of his own 44,000 l. and at [sic] a private friend, at his request, 50,000 l.[52]

The third question I propound is whether yet there be a considerable sum wanting to set out the fleet without which it cannot go to sea, and whether this fleet was ever intended to go forth or not.

Answer. To the first part I answer, and here you may observe a double question, there is yet wanting 40,000 l. to set out the fleet. And my master has anticipated all his revenue. He has pawned his lands, and would have pawned his plate if it would have been accepted, so that his Majesty must live in misery unless some course be taken for his supply.

For the second part of the question,

47. We are unable to find Buckingham's letter from James I. See H. of L., 9 August, n. 54. The L.J. report of the speech includes the names of Lord Conway, Lord Chichester, Lord Grandison, and Lord Carew as well. See above, H. of L., 9 August, p. 162 and n. 55.

48. See H. of L., 9 August, n. 56.

49. Apparently Sir John Coke did not give a detailed report of expenses at this time but briefly noted the country's needs and said "nothing wanted but money, and that he had all these particulars ready to be shown to the House of Commons if they should require it". See above, H. of L., p. 163.

50. See H. of L., 9 August, nn. 58 and 59.

51. See H. of L., 9 August, n. 61.

52. See above, n. 10.

whether it were intended ever to set forth the fleet or not. For my part, I know not what policy my master shall have to prepare the fleet with the charge of 400,000 *l.* only to amaze the world, to cozen his people, and put you to such hazard. What should my master gain? Would he do an act never to meet with you again? Certainly he would never have employed so great a sum of money but that he saw a necessity in the affairs of Christendom to require it and it was done with an intention to set it out with all the speed that might be.

The fourth question. But why [was] not this want of money foreseen in the first project of the whole service, but now comes to be thought upon unexpectedly and dangerously considering the sickness? At least why not before our last adjournment whereby we are drawn unto this meeting at an unseasonable time?

Answer. I answer this was foreseen but interrupted by unfortunate accidents, as the death of my gracious master of famous memory.

(And herewith the reporter observed that he spoke it fetchingly, his eyes and his tongue witnessing it, and he had good cause so to do.)

Then the funeral, which for decency could not be more hastened. Then the journey into France and the marriage which made more delays than was expected, and yet necessary. Then the parliament was called and there you heard his Majesty's declaration that there [was] now no more time for counsels but for resolutions. And when his Majesty had understood that you had given him these 2 subsidies, he conceived that they had been given only as a present for the welcome to the crown. And he intended that when you should present them unto him as he thought the manner was, at the same time to relate the business more at large to you, as afterwards he did by Sir John Coke.[53]

The fifth question. The next question I propound is who gave the counsel to meet again so suddenly when the sickness was so dangerously spread abroad in the land.

[f. 160] Answer. His Majesty commanded me to tell you that the business itself and the necessity of it gave him this counsel, else he would never have hazarded your persons nor the safety of the kingdom by the dispersing of it. And if he had been able by any means to set forth the navy without your help he would have done it and have trusted upon you for a supply afterward. But if a fault had been made why should the state, why should the action, why the affairs of Christendom suffer for it? If it be for my master's honor, which is now budding, and for your own good and the kingdom's, why should the particular mistaking of any man cause it to miscarry? I hope your wisdoms will so far pierce through it as to set it forwards.

The sixth question. The next question is why should not the King's own estate help to the business.

Answer. The answer I make is: you may judge whether it has or no. The King has chosen rather to lay out of his own estate than to press you. Whether then is there not cause to be assured that he will do more when it shall be in his power, since he has already done so much.

The seventh question. But is not the time of the year too far spent for the navy to go forth?

The answer. My master answered you it were better the fleet should go out and perish half than not to go at all.[54] For it would show want of counsel and experience in the design, want of courage to prosecute it or weakness or beggarliness as not able to go through it.

---

53. I.e., on 4 August. See above, pp. 387–388.
54. This point was initially made in the King's speech of 4 August. See above, p. 133.

But the ends propounded were three, and the time is yet seasonable for them all, which I could manifest if it were fit to publish the design which I think none of you in your wisdoms will think fit to discover.

The eighth question. I will satisfy your thoughts in other things also: whether those eight ships sent into France were set out at the charge of his Majesty out of the subsidy money and were to be employed against the Rochellers.

The answer for the first part is that they were set out at the charge of the French King; and for the other part, it is not always fit for kings to give an account of their counsels. But for this you may judge by the event.

And here the reporter entreated them to call to mind that the contract was made for six months and five of them are already past and yet no such thing has happened as has been feared.[55]

The ninth question. But you will say I was your servant to break the match with Spain but I have done as ill in making as bad conditions with France.

The answer. The contrary of this appears by his Majesty's answer given unto your petition, and it is done without breaking any public faith.[56]

The tenth question. Yea, I served you in the breach of the Spanish treaty out of particular spleen unto Count Olivares.[57]

The answer. I answer there was no cause for me to hate Olivares for that [he] made me happy. For I had out of his hands papers which I could not else recover, by which I gained a nation. I am not vindictive in my nature, neither do I love that any man should by ill means do a good action, as he

intended to serve his master and that kingdom by indirect means. I can forgive one of mine own nation but I will leave that business asleep which if it were wakened would prove a lion to devour him that was the author of it, I mean one of my own nation who did cooperate with him.[58]

[f. 160v] The eleventh question. But hitherunto you may say that I have spoken nothing but of the immense charge which the kingdom is not able to bear if it should continue, as 30,000 *l.* a month to the King of Denmark; 20,000 *l.* a month to Count Mansfeld; 8,000 *l.* the month to the Low Countries; 2,600 *l.* the month to Ireland besides the seconding of the fleet for which there are twelve more of the King's ships preparing.[59]

The answer. But make my master chief of the war and by that you shall give better assurance and assistance to his allies than if you should give them 100,000 *l.* a month. What is it for his allies to scratch with the King of Spain, that may win a battle today and lose another tomorrow, to get or lose a town by snatches and to go on with a conquest by land? The King of Spain is too strong; it is impossible to do it. But let the King, my master, be the chief of the war and make his diversion. The enemy spends the more, he must draw from other places, and this you shall give to his allies. And by this kind of war you send no coin out but what money comes from the subject returns to them again for beef, shot, etc. The kingdom is not impoverished by it and it may make good returns home.

The twelfth question. But you will say, where is the enemy?

The answer. Make the fleet ready to go out and my master gave me commandment to bid you name the enemy yourselves.

---

55. See H. of L., 9 August, n. 67.

56. I.e., in the King's answer to the petition concerning religion, delivered prior to Buckingham's speech on 8 August. For the petition and answers, see H. of L., 9 August, pp. 155–160.

57. Concerning the relationship between the Duke

of Buckingham and Count Olivares, see H. of L., 9 August, n. 69.

58. I.e., John Digby, Earl of Bristol. See H. of L., 9 August, n. 70.

59. See above, nn. 29–31, and H. of L., 9 August, n. 71.

And here the reporter made a little digression that [he] could not in this but well know his Majesty's meaning that he intended the King of Spain whom we also intended.

And the Duke proceeded and said:

Put the sword into my master's hands and he will maintain the war to your honor and the good of religion. As you issue out nothing which is lost, so you shall bring home some gain which will help to maintain the war. Make an entrance, it may afterward be maintained with profit. When the enemy is declared, demand letters of marque, none shall be denied. And I have not been so idle but I shall make propositions whither yourselves may go and have the honey of the business. Lastly, my master commanded me to pray you to have a care and regard of the season and of your own healths. If you lose time your money cannot purchase it.

Here my Lord the Duke concluded with this short apology: If in this my relation my weakness has injured the business, the King, or the affairs of Christendom, I crave your pardon. My intentions were good.

And hitherunto the reporter added this of himself: That what my Lord the Duke had concluded for his excuse, out of modesty the reporter must justly do for want of ability to perform so great a task. That he humbly craves the favor of the House assuring them that he acknowledged himself to owe a great duty to this honorable House and to owe much to the honorable person whose speech he had reported. He did assuredly believe his abilities and will to serve the King and the state, and was assured that the expression[s] he made thereof were such as did not deserve to have an ill report.

L. *1a*. An act for **naturalization** of
   Sir Daniel **Deligne**   442, 446, *11/8
L. *1a*. An act for **naturalization** of
   Samuel **Bave**   442, 446, *11/8
Message from the King
   concerning **supply**: forborne
   until the House is fuller (Sir
   Richard Weston, Chancellor
   Exchequer) [*see below*]   442
SIR NICHOLAS SANDERSON   447
SIR ROBERT PYE: delivers in a
   petition from Philip
   Burlamachi [*see below*]   447
Petition from Burlamachi: read   442
SIR ROBERT PYE   442
JOHN GLANVILLE: delivers in a
   petition from **Captain Henry
   Hart**   447, *8/8
Petition from Captain Hart: read   442, 453
   [*Hart's petition is printed on pp.
   453–454*]
SIR THOMAS HOBY: moves for a
   committee concerning the
   payment of **charges** covered
   by the **1624 subsidy** act   442, *6/7
Committee appointed, as Hoby
   moved   442
Petitions of **Burlamachi** and **Hart**
   referred to the above
   committee [*see above*]   447
Message from the King
   concerning **supply** (SIR
   RICHARD WESTON, Chancellor
   Exchequer) [*see above*]   442, 447; **N**,
   555, *11/8;
   12/8
SIR ROBERT NAUNTON (Master of
   the Wards)   443, 447; **N**,
   555
SIR THOMAS JERMYN (interrupted
   by Edward Alford)   448
EDWARD ALFORD: concerning
   committee of the whole on
   supply [*see above and below*]   443, *9/8

Resolved: first to consider the
   message from the King and
   the matter of supply in the
   House   443, 448
SIR THOMAS JERMYN   448
JOHN MAYNARD   443, 448; **N**,
   556
MR. CHOLMLEY   448
SIR SIMON WESTON   443, 448
Message from the Lords desiring
   a conference by committees
   concerning the petition
   regarding **pardon of papists**,
   etc. (Sir Thomas Coventry,
   Att. General, and Thomas
   Eden) [*see below*]   443, 449, *1/8
Answer given to the Lords'
   message: the House agrees
   for the conference
   committees to meet this
   afternoon   443
JOHN DELBRIDGE: on question of
   supply [*see above and below*]   448; **N**, 556
SIR ROBERT PHELIPS   443, 448; **N**,
   556
Message from the Lords desiring
   that Commons' committee
   for the afternoon conference
   be empowered to confer
   concerning a **collection** for
   the **distressed people of
   London** (Sir Thomas
   Coventry, Att. General, and
   Thomas Eden) [*see above*]   444, 449, *11/8
Answer given to the Lords'
   message: the Commons'
   conference committee will be
   so empowered   444, 449
SIR ROGER NORTH: on question of
   supply [*see above*]   444, 449
SIR HUMPHREY MAY (Chancellor
   Duchy)   444, 450; **N**,
   557
SIR FRANCIS SEYMOUR   444, 450

WEDNESDAY, 10 AUGUST 1625

I. JOURNAL OF THE HOUSE OF COMMONS

[C.J. 813]

[p. 52] *Mercurii, 10° Augusti, 1° Caroli Regis*

L. 1[a]. An act for naturalization of Sir D. Deligne, Knight.[1]

L. 1[a]. An act for naturalization of Samuel Bave.

Mr. Chancellor of the Exchequer delivers a message from his Majesty. Forborne till the House fuller.

A petition from Mr. Burlamachi read.[2]

SIR ROBERT PYE moves a committee to con/[3]

Another petition from Mr. Hart read.[4]

SIR THOMAS HOBY moves the knights and burgesses may meet and set down what money is disbursed by the country.

Agreed.

[p. 53]

Sir Thomas Wentworth	Sir Alexander St. John
Sir Robert Pye	Lord St. John
Sir Francis Barrington	Sir John Jephson
Sir Charles Morrison	Sir Thomas Hoby
Sir John Stradling	Sir George Goring

Sir Richard Newport
Sir Robert
   Cholmondeley
Everyone that will come to have voice; Friday, 2 clock, Arithmetic Schools.[5]

MR. CHANCELLOR. That his Majesty, having taken notice that this House intends to enter into consideration of divers heads concerning King and commonwealth has sent by him this message: That he was well pleased with their good intentions, but desired them to consider his affairs require a speedy dispatch; 2ly, the season far past, yet seasonable; 3ly, if the plague should happen in the navy, the action would be lost; 3ly [*sic*], if any here should be touched, the like would be. Therefore desires a present answer about his supply. If not, will take care of our health more than we ourselves and will make as good shift for his present occasions as he can. If will now give, gives his royal word that in winter, at what time we shall choose, we shall meet again and hold together till we have perfected all these things for the commonwealth and the King which are now in conception, and give such answer thereunto as dutiful and loving subjects may expect from a gracious and religious king. Desires us to consider that is the first request he ever made unto us.

1. The naturalization bills for both Deligne and Bave, below, were probably read a second time and committed on 11 August but they did not receive a third reading in this session. Both bills again reached the committee stage without achieving passage in the parliament of 1626 (*C.J.*, I, 857). Deligne's bill passed in 1628 (H.L.R.O., Original Act, 3 *Car.* I, no. 23) but apparently Bave's was dropped after 1626. Concerning Deligne and Bave taking the oaths of allegiance and supremacy, see below, Bedford MS. 197 and n. 28.

2. Burlamachi's petition concerning the stop of a payment to him which had been ordered by the Council of War is not extant with the proceedings for this session. We find no order of the House specifically calling for a stoppage of payments, but on 6 July (see O.B.) the House made several resolutions concerning the charges that were to be paid out of the 1624 subsidy monies. And on 9 July Sir Robert Pye moved the House in Burlamachi's behalf, but no order was made upon his motion. See above, p. 362 and n. 27. For warrants for payments to Burlamachi for the supply of

arms and soldiers in the service of Mansfeld, see *Cal. S.P. Dom., Addenda, 1625–1649*, p. 27, and *Cal. S.P. Dom., 1625–1626*, pp. 540, 565, 576. Early in the succeeding parliament, Burlamachi's petitions were ordered to be considered of by a committee of the whole House. *C.J.*, I, 822, 844; Eliot Papers (cf. H.M.C., 1 *Report, Appendix*, pp. 41–44), vol. 9, f. 68.

3. Burlamachi's petition was brought in by Sir Robert Pye (see Bedford MS. 197, below) and referred, along with Captain Hart's petition (below), to the committee listed below, appointed to meet on Friday next, i.e., 12 August, which was the day the session ended. We have no indication that either petition was further acted on in this session.

4. Hart's petition is printed below, p. 453. It was delivered this day by John Glanville and submitted to the same committee as that of Burlamachi. See above, n. 3 and below, Bedford MS. 197.

5. The parliament was dissolved by noon on Friday 12 August. We have no evidence that the committee met.

MASTER OF THE WARDS. *Qui tarde dat diu noluit.* 1. The reputation of King and kingdom in point of honor, the war, now in preparation, moving from parliament. 2. The consideration of the disastrous estate of the King's royal sister. 3. The common cause of religion in great danger abroad and suffers at home, which greatly prospered while we free from idolatry here. Many miseries upon us since connivancy at that. 4. Consideration of our confederates abroad, who will fall asunder if our King hold not them together. 5. The danger of King, Lords, and us all by the sickness by longer continuance.

[p. 54] MR. ALFORD moves the order for a committee may proceed.[6]

But the vote of the House, that this intervenient message is first to be debated in the House.

MR. MAYNARD. To decline the word "engagement", and subsidy "in reversion".[7] That the King's speech was *maximum in minimo*, the other speeches *minimum in maximo*. Moves 1 subsidy, 2 15eens.

[C.J. 814] SIR S. WESTON. To repeal now

the 2 subsidies[8] and add to them as the House shall think fit, so no subsidy shall be granted in reversion.

A message from the Lords by Mr. Attorney and Dr. Eden: That the Lords desire the committees yesterday about the petition may meet in the same place at 3 clock this afternoon, if it may stand with the conveniency of this House.[9]

Resolved accordingly, and so delivered to the same messengers.

SIR ROBERT PHELIPS. The point being now by this message reduced short to this: either to give presently, or else that in respect of our danger he will adjourn us to some other time.

The arguments for giving: honor, necessity, safety. Honorable actions grounded upon sound counsels; necessity the continual argument of supply in all parliaments. The counsels, which have put the King and this great action into this hazard, by necessity, have (whosoever they be) to answer this: 10 R. 2;[10] [blank] H. 4;[11] 28 H. 6.[12] Act of resumption passed 10 or 12 kings' reigns together.[13] France, Spain.[14]

6. I.e., the resolution made the previous day (9 August) for a committee of the whole to meet this morning which would allow for freer debate on the matter of supply. For the order, see above, p. 430. For another account of this day's proceedings, see Sir Francis Nethersole's letter of 11 August to Sir Dudley Carleton (S.P. 16/5:33) in the Appendix, below, p. 713.

7. These terms were used in the debate of 5 August. See above, p. 393.

8. I.e., the bill for two subsidies which passed both Houses on 8 July and received the royal assent on 11 July.

9. I.e., the committee appointed on 8 August for the conference on religion. See above, p. 422.

10. In 1385 (9 R. II) the Commons, displeased with Michael de la Pole's advice to the crown and continuing requests for money for the French wars, petitioned the King "that the state of his household might be looked into and examined every year . . . and what was amiss to be mended at their discretion". See Cobbett, *Parl. Hist.*, I, 183. In the following session (10 R. II) Parliament presented a remonstrance to the King stating that parliament is "where all public grievances or errors are to be redressed, and . . . that since they are

to support all public charges incumbent, they should have the supervisal how and by whom their goods and fortunes are to be expended", and the parliament proceeded to impeach Michael de la Pole. Ibid., 184–190; *Rot. Parl.*, 10 R. II, no. 7; Howell, *S.T.*, I, 91–94.

11. In 1399 (1 H. IV) the parliament accused Richard II of "ill government" and (see article 23 in the proceedings against him) of intimidating the counsel around him so "that they have not dared to speak the truth in giving their advice for the state of the King and kingdom". Howell, *S.T.*, I, 135–162; *Rot. Parl.*, 1 H. IV, nos. 10–12.

12. Phelips is citing the case of William de la Pole, Duke of Suffolk. See Bedford MS. 197, below. For the case itself, see *Rot. Parl.*, 28 H. VI, nos. 14–52; Howell, *S.T.*, I, 271–276; Cobbett, *Parl. Hist.*, I, 385–389; also cf. Hatsell, *Precedents*, IV, 66–69. Many of the precedents cited by Phelips are the same as those included in the speech that has on occasion been attributed to Sir Robert Cotton (see below, *Negotium*, n. 182).

13. See below, *Negotium*, p. 560, where it is stated that from the time of H. III to E. VI all but one king made use of acts of resumption.

14. For the points regarding France and Spain, see below, Bedford MS. 197.

Impositions 80,000 *l.* per annum; tonnage and poundage 160,000 *l.* per annum.[15]

Moves the present necessity may be supplied by some other means rather than so dangerous a precedent to be brought in. Moves Sir Robert Mansell may deliver his opinion of the designs in hand and a committee to consider of a fit answer to his Majesty why we cannot now give; and yet to give him assurance we will, in due time, supply all his honorable and well-grounded designs.

Mr. Attorney General and D. Eden bring another message from the Lords. That the Lords have commanded them to return to this House, with this addition: That the Lords desire this House will give the same committee[16] power to accept from the Lords some propositions for the relief of London and the parts adjacent.

Resolved, and so delivered to the same messengers.

SIR ROGER NORTH is now for giving, against which he was, but is now altered by his Majesty's most gracious answer to religion; 2ly, that this the King's 1st request; 3ly, the consequence of an ill parting this parliament, which would be so acceptable to the papists. [p. 55] Is for 2 15eens to the 2 subsidies.

MR. CHANCELLOR OF THE DUCHY. Not[17] to despise precedents, nor to adore them as gods. First, 2 subsidies granted in King James's first parliament, and 4 15eens within a month after; 1 subsidy more granted in the same session.[18] *Mors in olla.* If all our greatest enemies here, they would refuse to give. To give now, because we cannot else give at another time to supply.

SIR FRANCIS SEYMOUR. That the Commons of England should be called hither for supply of 40,000 *l.* shows the great necessity of the King.[19] An act of resumption of the crown land. 140,000 *l.* raised by places of honor, places of justice sold, serjeants' places sold.[20] None of the Lords to use arguments to the Commons to give, for that proper to the Lords.

MR. CHANCELLOR EXCHEQUER. To leave now our fears, jealousies, and disgusts at home, and to rely upon his Majesty's promise for our meeting to reform these things. The disorders complained of not happened in the King's time. That our King now, both in his father's time, and his own, has assured us of his desire and resolution to reform these. Moves the question whether we will give at this time or not.

SIR GUY PALMES. *Fidem qui perdit, perdere ultra nihil potest.* Moves a committee to pen

---

15. The figure cited for impositions is presumably the total expected to be collected from levies on various products. According to Sir Edward Coke's speech on 30 June (see O.B.), 160,000 *l.* was the revenue anticipated for the year from tonnage and poundage. The same sum was expected from the subsidy collection. See H. of C., 8 July, p. 348 and n. 9.

16. I.e., the conference committee which was to meet that afternoon (10 August) concerning the petition regarding pardon of papists, etc. See above, n. 9.

17. *nor.* Printed edition.

18. In the second session of the first parliament of James I two subsidies and four fifteens were agreed on by the House on 10 February 1606 and accepted by the King on 11 February. However, on 14 February, at a conference of both Houses, Thomas Sackville, Baron Buckhurst, Lord Treasurer, made a speech showing the distressed condition of the King's estate and the

need for further supply. And on 18 March following, one subsidy and two fifteens more were resolved on by the Commons. *C.J.*, I, 266–267, 271, 286; *Bowyer*, pp. 31–32, 42–45, 82–85. The total grant of three subsidies and six fifteens was then passed in a single act. *S.R.*, 3 *Jac.* I, c. 26.

19. 40,000 *l.* was the figure mentioned by Lord Conway in his speech of 4 August (see above, p. 387) and repeated by the Duke of Buckingham on 8 August (see above, p. 164) as the sum presently needed to set forth the fleet.

20. The version of Seymour's speech included in Cobbett, *Parl. Hist.*, II, 34, is worded differently: "What was become of all the money raised by the act of resumption of the crown lands? That 140,000 *l.* had been also raised by places of honor; places of justice were sold, and serjeants' places; which must come to a greater sum".

something to satisfy his Majesty that, at our next meeting, we will supply him to his content.

SIR GEORGE MORE. Precedents have always changed with the times. To give, that the 1 question; *de modo,* will speak after.

SIR THOMAS GRANTHAM. Not now to give, but thus far to engage ourselves that at our next meeting, in winter, we will respect his Majesty's occasions as shall be fitting for dutiful and loving subjects.

MR. DRAKE. The time too late for going out of the fleet; danger of enemies, foreign, domestical; infection at home, fear of a famine. Is for giving, so it be in a parliamentary manner.

SIR ROBERT PYE. For giving.

MR. MALLORY, *contra,* in respect of the precedent.

MR. CHARLES PRICE is for giving.

SIR THOMAS WENTWORTH.[21] The engagement of a former parliament binds not this. Fears the pressing of this precedent for so small a sum is to take advantage of it for greater hereafter. Is against present giving, yet most ready and willing to give in due time.

[p. 56] MR. RECORDER. Granting of subsidies in reversion, as the clergy have done, is to bind and give for our executors as they have done for their successors.[22] Dislikes

our drawing hither and wishes we may never hereafter be put upon these rocks.

Is for giving now in respect of the King's answer to religion, the rather because he has promised execution and because he said he did it not to draw us on. Yet to do this with a great caution to be entered in the House.

MR. ROLLE, *contra.* That his Majesty cannot but have credit without our grant for 40,000 *l.* If the necessity for money now so great, this our time to press for redress [of] our grievances—Turkish pirates take our ships and men, endanger our coasts; for defense whereof, they now driven to arm.[23]

SIR H. MILDMAY. That a navy appointed to secure our coasts at home as soon as this great fleet gone.

Not only the pressing of 40,000 *l.* the cause of our drawing hither, but the giving answer to our petition for religion. To give now, with a protestation never to do the like upon any necessity hereafter.

SIR W. TICHBORNE. To resolve to give, and to go to the question.

SIR ROBERT CRANE. To give now.

MR. GLANVILLE. To be wary of putting this to the question. Doubts this giving now so pressed. The money now desired not worthy of a parliament. Moves a committee to consider of a satisfactory answer to his Majesty, with some protestation without

---

21. In the collection of Wentworth papers there is one complete and one partial draft of a speech by Wentworth discussing supply and calling for the appointment of a committee to consider an answer to the King declining a present grant of further subsidies but declaring the House's willingness to entertain the question of supply at the next session. The editor of the Wentworth papers, J. P. Cooper, suggests that those undated drafts may relate to Wentworth's speech of 10 August. However, the Bedford version of the 10 August speech, below, indicates that Wentworth suggested a committee for petitions rather than for an answer to the demand for further supply. See J.

P. Cooper, ed., *Wentworth Papers 1597–1628* (London: Camden Society, 1973), pp. 236–239.

22. The bill confirming the three subsidies granted by the clergy passed the Upper House on 11 July and was assented to in the Lower House on the same day. The first payment was not to be made until 1 December 1627, the second on 1 June 1628. For the schedule of the remaining payments, see *S.R.,* 1 *Car.* I, c. 5.

23. Concerning the Turkish pirates, see above, H. of C., 5 July, n. 7, and the reports on 11 August (see below, H. of C., 11 August, O.B.).

"engagement" that we will, in due time, supply.

SIR WILLIAM SPENCER. It has been said, *bis dat qui cito dat.* If we give quickly, we may be called in again to give so again. To let the 360,000 *l.* [*sic*][24] in the treasurers' hands be paid towards the setting out of the navy.

SIR EDWARD COKE. 2 leaks to drown any ship. 1, a bottomless sieve; 2, *solum et malum consilium;* [3,] an officer should not be *cupidus alienae rei, parcus suae avarus reipublicae;* [but,] 4, *super omnia expertus—misera servitus est ubi lex incerta aut incognita. 15° H. 3,* Hubert de Burgh, Chief Justice, advised the King Magna Carta was not to hold because the King under age at the time of act.[25] Created Earl of Kent, *13°H. 3;* disgraded for this [p. 57] *15° H. 3.*

18° H. 3, Rot. Pat., n. 19°, Segrave, Chief Justice, sentenced for sole giving counsel to the King against the commonwealth.[26] *Malum consilium,* to press more subsidies when we have given 2; to bring us hither for 40,000 *l.* Offers to give rather out of his own estate 1,000 *l.* than to give any subsidy now.

SIR THOMAS HOBY desires to be satisfied what more reason to press an enlargement of two subsidies now than the 10th of July. Not now to give.

SIR ROBERT MANSELL is now against putting this to question because would have 1 negative voice.[27]

MR. WANDESFORD. A committee of the whole House to take consideration of all the business propounded in general.

SIR THOMAS PUCKERING. That this committee may hold itself to the point of the King's message.

Resolved, a committee of the whole House, at 8 of the clock tomorrow morning, to consider what return to make to his Majesty's message delivered this day.

II. MS. 197, BEDFORD ESTATES, LONDON

[f. 62]   *10° Augusti, 1625.*

Sir Daniel Deligne and Doctor Bave,[28] physician of Gloucester, came into the House to take the oaths of allegiance and supremacy, and their bills were read the second [*sic*] time for naturalization.

---

24. It seems likely that the figure intended is 36,000 *l.* In a comparable speech attributed to "Mr. Speaker" in Bedford MS. 197, the figure given is 35,000 *l.* which is described as "due to the country for levying soldiers". See below, p. 452 and n. 56.

25. Hubert de Burgh "meaning to make this a step to his ambition . . . persuaded and humored the King that he might avoid the charter of his father King John by duress . . . for that he was within age when he granted the same, whereupon the King in the 11 year of his reign, being then of full age, got one of the Great Charters and of the Forest into his hands and by the counsel principally of this Hubert, his Chief Justice, at a Council held at Oxford unjustly cancelled both the said charters . . . [Hubert] became in high favor with the King, insomuch as he was soon after . . . in the 13 year of that King, created to the highest dignity that in those times any subject had, to be an earl, viz. of Kent". Coke, *Second Inst.*, Proem (no page no.), and see also, ibid., p. 118; Cobbett, *Parl. Hist.*, I, 11–14. Hubert was created Earl of Kent in 11 *H.* III rather than 13 *H.* III as stated by Coke. Five years later, in 1232 (16 *H.* III) Hubert was stripped of his offices and imprisoned on various charges regarding his public life. *D.N.B.*; Matthew Paris, *Chronica*, III, 220–234.

26. Stephen de Segrave (d. 1241), chief justiciar, became unpopular with the magnates and bishops in 1233 for his support of the foreigners in the administration of Henry III. He was accused of giving bad counsel with regard to this matter of government personnel and in 1234 on at least two occasions his lands and estates were ransacked and burned by Richard Siward and a band of outlaws. Later that year, when Henry was reconciled to his Lords, Segrave was dismissed from his offices. We are unable to find a reference to Segrave's sentence in the printed *Calendar of Patent Rolls.* See Roger de Wendover, *The Flowers of History*, ed., Henry G. Hewlett (Rolls Series, London, 1889), III, 58, 71, 79, 88, 90, 92; *D.N.B.*

27. Traditionally subsidy votes were a unanimous expression of the House.

28. MS.: *Pavye.* See above, n. 1. By act of 7 *Jac.* I it was necessary to receive communion within one month of exhibiting a bill for naturalization and to take the oaths of allegiance and supremacy before the bill's second reading. *S.R.,* 7 *Jac.* I, c. 2. See Jacob's *Law Dict.* According to the C.J. these bills received their first reading on this day (10 August) and apparently were read a second time and committed on 11 August. See above, p. 442, and below, p. 457.

SIR NICHOLAS SANDERSON offered to speak of the great business,[29] and was not permitted, because it remained under a committee, and ought not to be spoken to in the House before a report.

SIR ROBERT PYE delivered a petition from Philip Burlamachi concerning an order from the Council of War to the treasurer for the payment of 7,788–09–00, which he could not receive by occasion of the stop made by this House.[30]

MR. GLANVILLE delivered the like petition for Captain Hart for 3,984 [l.].[31]

Both referred to a committee, to be considered of upon Friday next.

SIR RICHARD WESTON delivered a message from the King to this effect:

His Majesty has taken knowledge of your desire to reform many things tending to his particular service, and is well pleased with this your intention; but desires [f. 62v] you to take consideration of these points: That this time is fit only for such matters as are of present necessity and dispatch; that the fleet stays for your resolution, and the season of the year is near spent, though the opportunity be not yet past; that, if the plague should fall into the navy or army, all the action is lost, and if it should fall among yourselves, which God forbid, it will breed much danger and distraction, which his Majesty is loath to think upon.

His desire is that you would presently resolve whether, upon the important reasons delivered unto us, so much importing his honor, you will supply his necessity in such a proportion that he may send his navy; otherwise, if this will not move you, his Majesty will take more care of your safety than yourselves, because the sickness disperses in this town, and will do all as well as he may in such an extremity, wherein he may so much suffer. But if you will give a present

dispatch of the supply he does promise, in the word of a king, giving you that royal word which he had never yet broken, nor given cause to mistrust, that you shall meet again in the winter in a more seasonable time, and stay together till you may bring to maturity those things which were propounded; and that his Majesty will then do whatsoever belongs to a good and gracious king. This is his message, and he desires you withal to remember that it is the first request that ever he made to you.

THE MASTER OF THE WARDS, after a preamble of a reasonable length, spoke first to the manner of the giving; that it should be readily and freely, for which he gave these reasons: 1, the loss of the action, and therein of men, money, and reputation; 2ly, the danger of the sickness; 3ly, the increase of our thanks, for a kindness gotten with difficulty is so far from obliging that *satis est si tali beneficio ignoscas;* [f. 63] 4ly, that there might be a congruity between our offerings and the King's favors.

In the second place he delivered divers reasons why we should give:

1. The reputation of the King and kingdom, and of this House, being all engaged, if not by law, yet by a public declaration of our intentions. Those wars have been ever most undoubted by other nations, which have been undertaken by parliament.

2ly. The disastrous estate of the King's sister and her posterity, being a lady incomparable by the testimony of her very enemies.

3ly. The common cause of religion; the blessing we enjoyed while it was preserved, and the loss of these blessings since this coldness.

4ly. The holding together the King's allies, the most of them being tied not by unity of religion, but reason of state, which you know is easily altered.

5ly. The necessary defense of our neigh-

---

29. I.e., of supply. On 9 August (see H. of C., 9 August, O.B.) it was resolved that the question of supply should be considered in a committee of the whole

on this day (10 August).

30. See above, n. 2.

31. See above, nn. 3 and 4.

bors, whom if we suffer to be overcome, we must expect the enemy to set next upon ourselves.

6ly. The preservation of his Majesty's sacred person, the nobility, and of ourselves; which he said he put in the last place, because his Majesty had put it in the balance with all his own great affairs, which fatherly expression breeds so transcendent an obligation that we should think nothing too dear for so gracious a master.

He concluded that if all these reasons would not move us, he should apprehend it as a sad period of his discourse, and a sign of some great judgment hanging over us.

[f. 63v] SIR THOMAS JERMYN offering to speak, was interrupted by a motion to pursue the order made yesterday for a committee,[32] but it was conceived that the King's message intervening gave the business divers new considerations, which were fit still to be debated[33] in the House.

SIR THOMAS JERMYN. His opinion was to give; his reason: 1, the difficulty of recovering reputation once lost; 2ly, our security from the King's message of a fit time to do the business of the commonwealth.

MR. MAYNARD proceeded from the general to a particular of one subsidy and two fifteens, and amongst other reasons alleged this: that my Lord Admiral had showed himself by his last speech a man very capable and deserving of his offices, a logician, a rhetorician, and a charitable man.[34] Another of his reasons was this: imagine we were invaded, every man would then give; *eadem est ratio ex contrario*, now we go to invade.

MR. CHOLMLEY[35] insisted upon precedents of doing the country's business first, and not to give twice in one session.

SIR SIMON WESTON propounding a way to save this breaking of precedents by revoking the subsidies we have granted, and to make a new entire gift with some addition.

MR. DELBRIDGE opposed that heretofore we had hopes and expectations wherewith to please the country, though we gave away their money. Now there are nothing but discouragements: pardons to Jesuits,[36] the news from Rochelle, for which town we have heretofore had public fasting;[37] the interruption of the fishing trade; the losses by pirates.[38] So that, whereas we returned the last time with fasting and prayer, now we may return with sackcloth and ashes.

[f. 64] SIR ROBERT PHELIPS propounded, first, answers to the arguments for supply, then reasons against it. His answers were these:

1. That it is not for the King's honor. Reputation is a great advantage, but it is not built upon every action but upon such as have a sure ground. All wise states do in their counsels leave as little as may be to chance. If this design be not so, then is it no honor to set out that which will bring us a hazardous return.

2ly. Necessity in every parliament a pressing argument, and one of those things which can never be satisfied. If his Majesty's honor be in question and he in such necessity, they who have brought him to this strait have dishonored the King, and if they have so ill disposed of the King and the state as that he cannot furnish so small a supply, they must bear the merits of their own counsel.

Our ancestors in the like cases, when they have been pressed as we are, have taken occasion to look into the state of the commonwealth. 8 *H.* 3, a supply was demanded, the people refused it unless they might

32. The interruption was made by Edward Alford; see above, p. 443 and n. 6.

33. *delivered. C.D. 1625* (Knightley MS.).

34. See the 9 August report of Buckingham's speech of 8 August, above, H. of C., 9 August, O.B.

35. Either Hugh or William Cholmley.

36. See above, H. of C., 6 August, nn. 9 and 10.

37. We find no other evidence of a public fast for Rochelle.

38. Concerning the problem of pirates, see above, H. of C., 5 July, n. 7, and the reports on 11 August, below (O.B.).

have a confirmation of their liberties.[39] 10 *R.* 2, upon the like motion, a view and search was made into the disorders of the time.[40] In Gascoigne's story of H. 6, it is written that the Duke of Suffolk made a marriage for the King, wholly possessed the government, caused an alienation[41] of lands, did encroach upon the honor and dignity of the kingdom, etc., and that Duke, which the parliament before had an act of applause, had then, viz., H. 6, an act of censure; and when he was laid by, the reformation followed.[42]

When the Black Prince took the French King, [f. 64v] a parliament was summoned at Paris for his redemption; the Dauphin propounded assistance; they tendered their grievances; he put them off from time to time, but in the end was fain to comply with them.[43]

In Spain, when the King desired a war against the Moors, and called his people, proposing an aid by his ministers of state, the Condé de Laro stepped up and advised them to give nothing till the people were released.[44] We are the last monarchy in Christendom that retain our original right and constitutions.[45]

Either his Majesty is able to set out this fleet, or it is not fit to go at all. We ought neither to fear nor contemn an enemy. If we provide to set it out, we must provide to second it, too; for without a second it will do

nothing but stir a powerful king to invade us.

He added the safety of keeping to our precedents, the meanness of the sum required, the unfortunate counsel that brought us hither, the opening the King's necessity in such a manner as will bring us into contempt abroad, and concluded with two motions: 1, that Sir Robert Mansell might be commanded to declare his knowledge with what deliberation and counsel this design has been managed; 2ly, to appoint a committee to prepare an answer for his Majesty, and reasons why we cannot give.

By a former message the Lords had desired that the committees might meet in the afternoon at a conference concerning the petition about the pardon, etc., and now, by a second message, they prayed that the same committee might be authorized to receive something from them concerning the relief of London, which was granted.

SIR ROGER NORTH. When this was first propounded by the King's ministers, he had a resolution not to give. [f. 65] His Majesty's answer concerning religion, the extremity of the wants, that it is the King's first request, the promise of a more convenient meeting, the dangerous consequence of a bitter parting, and [*sic*] now altered him to

39. In February 1225 a fifteenth was granted to Henry III by the Council meeting at Westminster in accord with his consent to reissue the Great Charter and the Charter of the Forest. See *S.R.*, 9 *H.* III, Magna Carta; Stubbs, *Select Charters*, pp. 353–354; Cobbett, *Parl. Hist.*, I, 10–11.

40. See above, n. 10.

41. *alteration. C.D. 1625* (Knightley MS.).

42. See above, n. 12. For a more detailed account of Gascoigne's references to William de la Pole, Duke of Suffolk, see the *Negotium*, below, p. 560. Many historical incidents from the reign of Henry VI are recorded in the manuscript deposited in the library of Lincoln College, Oxford, which was written by Thomas Gascoigne and is known as his "Dictionarium Theologicum" or "Liber Veritatum". Gascoigne (1403–1458) was a theologian and was twice Chancellor of Oxford. Selected passages from Gascoigne's manu-

script have been printed under the title *Loci e Libro Veritatum* (ed. James E. Thorold Rogers, Oxford, 1881). For some of Gascoigne's comments on Suffolk's negotiation of the marriage between Henry VI and Margaret of Anjou, on the alienation of the lands of Maine, Anjou, and Normandy, and on the parliament of 1449–1450, see ibid., pp. 158, 188–190, 204–205, 219–221; see also, ibid., pp. xxvi–xxxiii, xlvi–lvi.

43. Concerning Edward, Prince of Wales, taking King John II of France prisoner after the battle of Poitiers in 1356, see Grafton, *Chronicle*, I, 391–402; Holinshed, *Chronicle*, II, 663–676.

44. We are unable to find the source of Phelips's remark.

45. Marginal note in the E. of Bedford's hand: "Lo. Carleton said in [the] Lower House and that the K. might be urged to new counsels".

consent to one subsidy and two fifteens and no more.

SIR HUMPHREY MAY. Let no man despise ancient precedents; no man adore them. Examples are powerful arguments if they be proper, but times alter; every parliament must be wise with his own wisdom. He values more a dram of wisdom fit for the present than a mountain of wisdom that was fitted for 300 years past. The first parliament of King James granted two subsidies and four fifteens and afterward, when the King's wants were opened by my Lord of Buckhurst, added one subsidy and two fifteens more.[46] Men of good affections have been known to give ill counsel; if we go this way, *mors in olla*. If all our enemies were here and had voice, would they not say give not? Let us never follow the counsel of an enemy. Give at this time, because it cannot be given at another so seasonably.

SIR FRANCIS SEYMOUR. The causes of this necessity are more fit to be opened than the necessity itself. It has not proceeded from want of great sums of money, if we consider what has been received by former grants in parliament, by prerogative, benevolences, and monopolies; but these great sums have come to private men's purses; how should so many men else be raised to so much greatness as nothing can maintain but the King's own lands? Wherefore it will be fit, both for the King's honor and necessity, that there be an act of resumption, that so he may be supplied with his own.

The King is the underline{fountain}[47] of honor, and yet that has [f. 65v] been made a merchantable commodity to be obtained by money rather than desert.[48] 140,000 *l.* is computed to have been gotten this way. Who will bring up his son in learning when money is the way of preferment? The price of a serjeant is as well known as the price of a calf; and they which buy dear must certainly sell dear. If his Majesty hear not of this by us, he shall never hear it in his bedchamber. He said he was not satisfied touching the ground of this design, and has heard nothing to believe that it proceeded from good counsel. That which was taken into consideration by the Council of War and the Lords was the proportion of money, men, and munition, not how they should be employed. There is nothing [*sic*][49] which makes him most against giving, which has not yet been observed: that a member of the Upper House, under color of a message, should press the Commons with arguments for a subsidy. That it is the King's first request moves him not much. The King's desire may be as well alleged at any time. It is unlikely he should be in such great want as not to be able to disburse 40,000 *l.*, and unfit for us, for such a sum, to deliver up the privileges of the House.[50]

MR. CHANCELLOR OF THE EXCHEQUER. It is time now to give over our distastes and disgusts; his Majesty's promise securing us of another meeting for the commonwealth. These disorders have not been in his Majesty's time, and have been such only as a long peace is apt to breed. It is our happiness to have such a King who, by the order of his own life, does assure us he will reduce all other things to a better frame; who so lives, as if he had always before him that saying of Ferdinand: "To be a king is fortune; but to be a good king is virtue".[51] What is to be desired of a king which we have not from him in effect or expectation?

Wherefore let us return his Majesty an answer with the same respect wherewith he has declared himself [f. 66] to us; that like a loving father he may not fear to meet his enemy in the face, having so many loving

---

46. See above, n. 18.

47. *fountain* is underlined in the MS. Beside the word *fountain* is a marginal note in the E. of Bedford's hand: "new [*illegible*]".

48. Marginal note in the E. of Bedford's hand:

"now money". See above, n. 20.

49. *a thing. C.D. 1625* (Knightley MS.).

50. See above, n. 19.

51. We are unable to find the source of the quotation.

sons about him. It is said that 40,000 *l.* will serve the turn. A shame to want it; more shame to deny it. If land, plate, or jewels could have procured it, we had not now been troubled. Howsoever he weighed his honor and his business, the most modest prince was loath to press his subjects in an unfit time. Would it were now seasonable to look into his estate. But neither paper nor records are at hand to build so good a work upon. He concluded with a desire to put the question: Whether supply, or no supply?

SIR GUY PALMES. For the disorders in H. 7 time, Empson and Dudley were hanged in H. 8 time.[52]

SIR GEORGE MORE. To put the question.

MR. DRAKE. That poor men under 5 *l.* might be spared.

SIR ROBERT PYE. The diseases of the state are not incurable, yet to be redressed by no means but by this House; wherein he doubted not but to acquaint the House with some things which should be useful, and was afraid of none, or did so much care for his office as to neglect his duty to the public. He confessed he had been raised by him that sits now at the helm,[53] yet he would not but these things had been spoken, hoping that Lord will make a good use of them and become an instrument of much good hereafter. And when time serves for a reformation he would speak as boldly as any man, and be as forward himself to be an instrument of it. For the present he wished we should give the King contentment, that we may not open a way to the enemies of the state to make up their own fortune by hurting the public.

SIR THOMAS WENTWORTH.[54] The word "engagement" a prejudicial word, as if we

were less forward than the last parliament. That they pretend the want [f. 66v] of 40,000 *l.*; he fears somewhat which may press us more in point of disadvantage than the sum. He is not against giving, but against this manner, to put us upon these straits to give or else to adjourn. The course of subsidies is not to be heady, but to run softly; let us first do the business of the commonwealth, appoint a committee for petitions, and afterward, for his part, he will consent to do as much for the King as any other.

MR. RECORDER expressing his good opinion of the counsels in this design, his belief that we should part fair, howsoever confessing prejudice in point of precedent, both from the time, when we can do nothing for the commonwealth, and from the place, as if we were forced to give to avoid journeys; yet concluded at this time to satisfy the King, as a part of our thankfulness to God for the satisfaction he has given to our petition of religion; and to show that precedents are our servants, not our masters, and that we will not, for so small a sum, suffer so great an action to perish.

MR. ROLLE. That there was no such necessity, and yet, if it were admitted, it was no sufficient reason, as well in respect of our other grievances, as that we shall have the hope of this navy to do good abroad that cannot keep our own coast from being infected by Turkish pirates.

SIR H. MILDMAY. There are ships appointed for guard of the coasts. The King's answer to our petition was the cause of our calling; and, since he has showed himself protector of the gospel, let us enable him to perform that protection. To put that question.

52. Sir Richard Empson and Edmund Dudley were tried for treason and beheaded in 1510. See Howell, *S.T.*, I, 283–288; *D.N.B.* Palmes's statement with reference to the Duke was probably instrumental in his being pricked for sheriff in 1626 (see Russell, *Parliaments*, p. 268).

53. Sir Robert Pye, an Auditor of the Exchequer, was a Villiers client as early as 1616. See Aylmer, *King's Servants*, pp. 308, 311; and concerning this 1625 speech, see ibid., p. 355.

54. See above, n. 21.

MR. GLANVILLE. The disputes against supply are greater in number, and weightier in reason. The wisdom of this House has not in this case used to rush so far as to a question, till it be seen to be granted; for as it will be a dishonor to the King [f. 67] if it be denied, so to pass with difficulty by numbering our voices will take away the merit from us. He has heretofore spoken against the bill of adjournment, knowing what inconveniences new courses use[d] to produce. Precedents are not to be neglected; subsidies have ever come in the last place.

It is a prerogative, questionless, for the King to call parliaments when he pleases; our ancestors that could not take that away set up this as a counter prerogative in that they had power to treat of business in their own order. In Queen Elizabeth's time there was never meeting to[55] reform grievances. To press us so hard at this time differs not much from acknowledging some kind of error in calling us hither. Before the fleet comes back we shall meet again; in the meantime it cannot be thought the King shall want credit for such a sum. He would not have it said the subject came hither and spent 7,000 *l*. a week only to grant 60 or 70,000 *l*. If we crown such counsels with success, we shall encourage those who were authors of it, and confirm their opinions that parliaments may be brought to serve turns.

He concluded for a committee for the drawing a petition, which might be accompanied with some such protestation as shall credit the King more than 60,000 *l*.

MR. SPEAKER moved that we should give the 35,000 *l*. which was due to the country for levying of soldiers, and was ready in the treasurers' hands.[56]

SIR E. COKE made a long discourse of the leak in the King's estate, of the qualities of a counsellor, of the danger to great men if they misled the King or affect to go alone against the [f. 67v] counsel of other men, and vouched the precedent of Hubert de Burgh, 9 *E*. 3,[57] of ambition, that there were no dukes between the Conquest and H. 3 time. He vouched the precedent of Segrave, *Summus Justiciarius Angliae;*[58] 50 *E*. 3, John of G[aunt] and W. Lord Latimer;[59] 11 *H*. 4;[60] 10 *H*. 6, the Duke of Suffolk.[61] That house[62] had been evil counsel: 1, to provide a navy and not to have money enough to go through with it; 2ly, to bring us from Westminster hither in the time of sickness.

Concluded not to give, upon two reasons: 1, that it was against precedent; 2ly, it cannot be levied in time for this service, and if it be anticipated, 8 *l*. per 100 *l*. will be lost. Yet for his own particular he would give 1,000 *l*. as a private man, not as a parliament man, and that willingly, notwithstanding all his crosses, and hoped those of the King's council would do as much.

---

55. *but to. C.D. 1625* (Knightley MS.).

56. The attribution of this speech to "Mr. Speaker" may be erroneous. It would be uncommon for the Speaker to make such a speech in the House (as opposed to the committee of the whole) where he usually spoke only in an official capacity as the voice of the House or on procedural matters. Similarities in the wording of this speech with that attributed to Sir William Spencer in the C.J. (see above, p. 446) suggest that "Spencer" rather than "Speaker" was intended. For resolutions of the House regarding disbursement to the counties of money in the hands of the treasurers for the 1624 subsidy, see above, H. of C., 6 July, p. 324.

57. *Hen. 3. C.D. 1625* (Knightley MS.). On de Burgh, see above, n. 25.

58. The case of Stephen de Segrave. See above, n. 26.

59. For the charges brought by parliament against William Latimer, follower of John of Gaunt, see *Rot. Parl.*, 50 *E*. III, nos. 20–29.

60. It is unclear what case is meant. In 11 *R*. II, parliament brought charges against Michael de la Pole, Earl of Suffolk, and four of his associates. *Rot. Parl.*, 11 *R*. II, pp. 229–241; Howell, *S.T.*, I, 90–123. Cf. also, above, nn. 10–11.

61. The MS. citation is incorrect; the case of William de la Pole, Duke of Suffolk, was heard in 28 *H*. VI. See above, n. 12.

62. *here. C.D. 1625* (Knightley MS.).

SIR ROBERT MANSELL. That there was no true and judicious course taken in our meeting at this time. Would have no question put, yet offered 200 *l.* of his own fortune. Then fell to justify his own proceedings: Whereas there had been speech of consultation with the Council of War,[63] he was not at any debate since February last, where some generals were propounded but nothing concluded.

When he heard the direction given for 10,000 men, he refused to deliver his opinion in the presence of Sir John Coke, being no councillor of war, nor of state.[64] Yet he thought that proportion to no purpose, being such as would rather gall the enemy than hurt him; and doubted not but to offer a proportion[65] which shall produce such effects as will procure the restitution of the Palatinate. Afterward my Lord Conway told him the resolution would admit no debate. Their advice was asked only concerning 2,000 arms. He answered, that he protested against the business itself.

This long debate ended only in this order, that the House tomorrow morning shall sit in a committee to consider what return to make to the King.

III. PETITION OF HENRY HART, ESQ. H.L.R.O., MAIN PAPERS, H.L., 25 JUNE 1625.[66]

To the honorable House of Commons in this present parliament assembled.

The humble petition of Henry Hart, Es-

quire, agent and assignee for the Right Honorable Henry, Lord Docwra, Treasurer at Wars in Ireland, humbly showing,

That where your suppliant received from the Lords and others of his Majesty's Council of War an order, directed to the treasurers specially appointed by the late act of parliament, for payment of three thousand nine hundred four score and four pounds sterling for the full six months entertainment of two hundred and thirty horsemen and two thousand two hundred and fifty footmen, with their captains and officers, sent into Ireland by his late Majesty's command in April last past for the better securing of that kingdom. And that upon your suppliant's demand of the said monies the said treasurers did absolutely refuse to satisfy the same, and still do refuse, alleging that they are restrained by this honorable House from making any more payments without further order and direction from hence. Now forasmuch as the said six months do expire before Michaelmas next and that the want of the said monies will be an occasion of disbanding those supplies whereby the kingdom of Ireland may be much weakened in these dangerous times, besides many other inconveniencies very prejudicial to his Majesty's service, those new troops being no ways able to subsist without their pay or lying upon the poor country.

The premises considered, your suppliant in most humble manner prays that you will

63. I.e., in the 8 August speech of the Duke of Buckingham. See above, p. 162. Concerning these remarks by Mansell, see also the account in Nethersole's letter to Carleton, 11 August (S.P. 16/5:33), below, Appendix, p. 714; and see Mansell's speeches of 12 August, below (O.B.).

64. I.e., when he heard the direction for 10,000 men to be employed by Count Mansfeld and maintained by England (see Pym's report [above, H. of C., 9 August, p. 431] of the Lord Treasurer's speech of the previous day [8 August]). Mansell had hesitated to discuss policy in the presence of Sir John Coke who was not then a member of the Council of War (see above, H. of L., 9 August, p. 162 and n. 55) and did not

become Secretary of State until September 1625 (see above, H. of L., 4 August, n. 12).

65. *proposition. C.D. 1625* (Knightley MS.).

66. Hart's undated petition is included in the Main Papers collection annexed to a warrant from the Council of War to the subsidy treasurers, dated 25 June 1625, directing them to pay the 3,984 *l.* owed to Lord Docwra. For a letter of 13 October 1625 authorizing the treasurers to pay to Hart the money still owed to Docwra, see *Cal. S.P. Dom., 1625–1626,* p. 550. See also, the letter from Oliver, Viscount Grandison, to Secretary Conway on Captain Hart's behalf, below, Appendix, p. 718.

be pleased to give speedy order for payment of the said monies according to the
intent and meaning of the act of parliament
and of the said Council of War. And he
shall pray, etc.

L. 2a. An act for **naturalization** *of*
Sir Daniel **Deligne**, *Knight*:
   committed   457, *10/8

L. 2a. An act for **naturalization** *of*
   Samuel **Bave**: committed   457, *10/8

Two letters concerning the
   Turkish **pirates** and Sallee:
   read (John Whitson)   457, 459, 468;
   N, 562

SIR JOHN COKE   468
SIR ROBERT MANSELL   457, 460, 468

Another letter from a captive in
   Sallee: read   457

JOHN GLANVILLE   460
THOMAS SHERWILL   460
SIR ROBERT MANSELL   460
WILLIAM WHITEWAY or JOHN
   WHITSON   457, 460
SIR EDWARD COKE   458, 460, 468
SIR WALTER ERLE   460
HENRY ROLLE   460
SIR ROBERT MANSELL   460
SIR FRANCIS SEYMOUR   458, 460; **N**,
   563
JOHN LISTER   458, 468
SIR DUDLEY DIGGES   458, 468
SIR ROBERT PHELIPS   458, 460

Resolved: a committee of the
   whole House to consider
   complaints against pirates
   this afternoon   458, 460, 468

Report of the **conference**
   yesterday with the Lords (SIR
   EDWARD COKE) on: 458, 460, 468;
   N, 563

  (1) the petition regarding
     pardon of papists, etc.   *1/8
  (2) a **collection** for the
     distressed people of London
     [*see below*]   *10/8; 12/8
SIR EDWARD COKE   461

The course propounded by the
   Lords about the petition
   regarding pardon of papists:

   agreed to be observed   459, 461; **N**,
   563

SIR NATHANIEL RICH: concerning
   enrolling and printing the
   King's answer to the **petition**
   concerning religion   459, 469, *24/6

Resolved: King's answer to
   petition concerning religion
   to be enrolled and printed   459, 461

SIR ROBERT PYE: on the
   distressed people of London
   [*see above*]   469

Business concerning the
   distressed people of London:
   committed   459, 461, 469

Giles Greene **admitted** to the
   House notwithstanding he
   has not received communion   459, *1/8

[*Committee of the Whole House:*
   Solicitor Heath in the chair]

Sir Nathaniel Rich: moves to have
   the 10 August **message from**
   the King concerning **supply**
   repeated   461, 463,*10/8

10 August message from the
   King: read (Sir Richard
   Weston, Chancellor
   Exchequer)   463; **N**, 563

Sir Richard Weston (Chancellor
   Exchequer)   463, 466
Sir Thomas Wentworth   461
William Coryton   463, 466
Sir Henry Marten   461, 463, 466,
   469; **N**, 563
Sir Francis Seymour   462, 464, 467
Sir George More   462, 465, 467,
   469
Sir Robert Heath (Solicitor)   465, 467, 470
Edward Alford   463, 465, 467,
   470
Sir Thomas Puckering   465, 467, 470
John Whistler   463, 465, 467,
   470
Sir William Strode   465, 467

THURSDAY, 11 AUGUST 1625

I. JOURNAL OF THE HOUSE OF COMMONS

[C.J. 815]
[p. 57] *Jovis, 11° Augusti, 1° Caroli Regis*

L. 1ª. [*sic*]
Committed to[1]

Sir William Bulstrode	Sir Arthur Herris
Sir Guy Palmes	Sir Thomas Fanshawe
Knights and burgesses	Mr. William Fanshawe
of Lincolnshire	Sir Thomas Cheeke
Mr. [Thomas] Reynell	Sir Miles Fleetwood
Mr. Cholmley	Sir John Stradling
Sir Francis Barrington	Mr. [Francis] Downes
Mr. [Henry]	Lord St. John
Edmondes	Mr. [Edmund] Dunch
Sir Robert Hatton	
Sir Roger James	
Sir Robert Crane	
Sir Nathaniel	
Barnardiston	

This afternoon, 4 clock, Moral Philosophy Schools.

L. 1ª. [*sic*] An act for naturalization of Samuel Bave.
Committed to the same committee, at the same time and place; the knights and burgesses of Gloucester to be added.

[p. 58] Two letters delivered in by Mr. Whitson, concerning the Turkish pirates and Sallee, read.[2]

SIR ROBERT MANSELL. That these complaints not usual heretofore. Advises to petition the King to send to the Council of War and, if they then reform it not, they will answer it with their lives.

Another letter from a captive in Sallee, read.

MR. WHITEWAY.[3] That Sir Francis Stuart, Admiral, and other ships suffered a pirate to take an English ship before their face, and the merchants going to them and acquainting them with it and desiring them to go out against them, he answered his commission was not to go on the French coast, where he conceived the pirate was, and confessed he saw the pirate[s] board the English ship, but thought they had been fishermen.[4] But, in conclusion, though he were

1. Presumably this was the second reading and commitment of the bill for Daniel Deligne's naturalization. The bills for both Bave and Deligne had been read the previous day (10 August) for the first time. It seems likely they were read again together this day and committed, although Deligne's name is omitted in the Journal and the entries for both bills cite this day as the time of the first reading of the bills rather than the second. See above, H. of C., 10 August, n. 1. The author of the MS. of which Petyt 538/8 is a copy also appears to have been confused over the status of these two bills in indicating that they had been read only once during this session. See below, p. 479.

2. For the content of the letters, see below, Bedford MS. 197 and the Dyott diary. According to James Bagg (see S.P. 16/5:6, Appendix, below, p. 719) "divers towns have written to their burgesses of the daily oppression they are subject to by the Sallee and Turkey pirates". See also S.P. 16/5:8, 23, 32; and above, H. of C., 5 July, n. 7.

3. Bedford MS. 197, below, attributes this speech to John Whitson, Alderman of Bristol and a distinguished member of the Bristol Merchant Venturers, who had delivered in the first two letters concerning the pirates (see above). Concerning Whitson,

see Patrick McGrath, *John Whitson and the Merchant Community of Bristol* (Bristol Branch of the Historical Association Local History Pamphlets, 1970). William Whiteway was a Dorchester merchant also probably knowledgeable about shipping problems and pirates.

4. In May 1625, Stuart had stayed a ship of Dunkirk in the Downs waiting further orders (S.P. 16/2:108; 3:26, 27). On 27 June, Buckingham, the Lord Admiral, following an order by the Privy Council, sent instructions to Stuart (a copy of Buckingham's letter from S.P. 16/1:48 is printed in the Appendix, below, p. 716) directing him to clear the coasts of pirates but explicitly directing him not to go so far and for so long a time as to miss the rendezvous with the rest of the fleet at Plymouth. According to Stuart's account of his efforts against the pirates (S.P. 16/5:49, Appendix, below, p. 721) he was hampered by weather and in need of a fair wind for sailing. See also an account by the mayor and others of Plymouth written to the Council on 12 August 1625 indicating that Sir Francis Stuart had set out five ships against the pirates but noting that the Turks were better sailors than the English who, unsuccessful, returned to port within a few days (S.P. 16/5:36).

offered great sums of money, or half the goods of the ship, yet refused to go out.

SIR EDWARD COKE. A committee to set down the particulars of these things, and then to go to the Lords.

SIR FRANCIS SEYMOUR. The Lord Admiral[5] has the care of these things; therefore the default must needs be in him or his agents. A committee to consider of the causes hereof and where the default.

MR. LISTER mentions the wrongs by the Dunkirke[r]s and therefore moves this committee may generally consider of the danger and means of safety of all the ports.[6]

SIR D. DIGGES. A committee.

SIR ROBERT PHELIPS, *accordant*.

Resolved, a committee of the whole House to take consideration of the matters propounded, this day, 2 clock, and they to have power to name a subcommittee.[7]

SIR EDWARD COKE reports from the conference with the Lords about the pardon. Lord Canterbury: great thanks from the Lords for our great care of religion;[8] 2ly, that they had agreed to a conference the same day we sent it, had we not been risen before expectation.

That the pardon drawn by strange importunity of the French.[9] The King could have no peace after his marriage till he had granted it. That this was in agitation long before the King's promise, [p. 59] or the date. That the Lord Keeper stayed the entering of a *recepi* for a long time, and did the best he could to stay it.[10] That an order taken in Rome, no ambassador shall come thither but attended continually by a Jesuit.[11]

That the Lords have resolved to move the King never to pardon any Jesuit or other papist til they be attainted.

For their joining in the petition they denied it not, but considering his Majesty's gracious answer to our petition for religion[12]—but considering we of both Houses were to give his Majesty thanks for it, that the effect of our now petition might be intimated to the King. This they moved us to allow of.

For the letter, written by the Lord Conway, his sincerity in religion known, but he thought the course he took would be least dangerous.[13]

That all the Lords most cheerful in the point of religion.

That the Lords propounded to acquaint the House what they had done to relieve the miserable people in and about London ready to starve by want—the principal—and gave us an order, made there by them,

---

5. I.e., the Duke of Buckingham. Lord Montagu's journal for this day (see above, p. 181) notes that in the Commons House there were "some speeches which trenched upon a great man". Eliot (*Negotium*, below, p. 563) notes that Seymour's speech was the first to accuse Buckingham directly saying, "In his person was contracted the cause of all those miseries".

6. The Dunkirkers preyed on English merchant ships in the Channel. See S.P. 16/1:42, 60; 2:10, 23, 57; 3:110; and see *Cal. S.P. Dom.*, 1625–1626, Index, *sub* "Dunkirk, and Dunkirkers". The Eliot papers (H.M.C., *1st Report, Appendix*, pp. 41–44), vol. 9, ff. 1–2, include "A declaration how the Dunkirkers may be suppressed which do so many harms upon this our coast of England".

7. *Petition for this to his Majesty. Sir Robert Phelips, Sir Robert Mansell, Sir Benjamin Rudyard, Sir Thomas Wentworth, Sir Thomas Middleton* is crossed out in the MS. following *committee*.

8. For the Archbishop's report of the conference to the Upper House, see above, H. of L., 11 August, O.B.

9. The matter of the papists' pardon and the Conway letter to Estmond being "procured at the importunity of foreign ambassadors" had been discussed at an earlier conference (9 August) and was reported in the Upper House on 9 August. See above, p. 152.

10. See the speeches of Lord Conway and the Lord Keeper in the Upper House on 9 August, above, pp. 153–154.

11. According to the account of Coke's report in Bedford MS. 197, below, this order was recited in a newly printed Italian book.

12. For the King's answer to the petition concerning religion, see H. of L., 9 August, pp. 155–160.

13. Concerning Lord Conway's letter regarding the Estmond case, see above, H. of C., 6 August, n. 10; and see Conway's speech in the Upper House on 9 August, above, p. 153.

which they have thought fit to communicate to the House.[14]

The course propounded by the Lords about our petition concerning the pardon, and letter, agreed to be observed.

SIR NATHANIEL RICH moves a committee to consider of this order and that a motion may be made to have the King's order [sic][15] enrolled in both Houses of parliament and exemplified; and that it then may be printed.

Resolved.

And that a committee:
Knights of [sic] burgesses of London and
    Middlesex
Sir Robert Pye
Sir Robert Mansell
Sir Baptist Hicks
Sir Thomas Hoby
Mr. Alford
Mr. Solicitor
And all that will come to have voice, 4 clock this afternoon, in the Grammar Schools.

Mr. Giles Greene, license to come into the House notwithstanding he have not received the communion, which he is to receive.

II. MS. 197, BEDFORD ESTATES, LONDON

[f. 68] *11° Augusti, 1625.*

Several informations were given of divers injuries done to his Majesty's subjects upon the sea and seacoasts by the pirates, Dunkirks, Rochellers. The particulars by the pirates were these.

By William Lege's letter from Sallee in Barbary, 7 *Junii* 1625: Taken in a ship of Millbrook, sold at Sallee, tormented to yield to a high ransom; of 18 other ships brought into the same place of his Majesty's subjects, 800 men captives at this time.[16] The cruelty used in cutting their ears, forcing them to eat them, burning other, and almost starving others. The excessive ransoms, 1,500, 1,000, 800, 600; the meanest, 300 ducats. Divers forced to turn Turks.

By the examination of Robert Dolling,[17] 30 July 1625: That the 23 of July, he was taken, 8 leagues from the Lands End, by a pirate of Sallee, his ship being 150 tons, and the men carried away, himself freed by the mediation of a Dutch man-of-war that came that way by chance; that 14 other pirate ships lay about Scilly[18] [and] had taken four other ships of his Majesty's dominions, whereof one was of Plymouth of 100 tons.

By a letter from John Barker of Bristol,[19] 9° August 1625: Of great spoil, within 14 days last past, upon our coasts and the coast of Brittany, and one ship of Millbrook, laden with sugar worth 9,000 *l.* at least, beside good store of plate; another ship laden with Virginia fish. That they landed on the island of Groix[20] in Brittany, and carried away about 400 people. They have taken of sundry nations, within two months, above

---

14. On 10 August the Upper House had appointed a committee to review the order made on 6 August for the collection and distribution of money for the distressed people in London and Westminster. See H. of L., 10 August, p. 174. For the order, see below, Bedford MS. 197, and above, H. of L., 6 August, p. 143.

15. I.e., the King's answer to the petition concerning religion. See below, Dyott diary.

16. We are unable to find William Lege's letter. S.P. 16/43:46 consists of an undated petition to the Duke of Buckingham from the wives of about 2,000 mariners held captive in Sallee.

17. *Deligne. C.D. 1625* (Knightley MS.). We have been unable to find a fuller record of the examination of Robert Dolling.

18. *Sallee. C.D. 1625* (Knightley MS.).

19. Probably the John Barker who had been Master of the Bristol Society of Merchant Venturers, 1617–1618, and Alderman and M.P. for Bristol in 1624. Patrick McGrath, *The Merchant Venturers of Bristol* (Bristol, 1975), pp. 21, 39; *O.R.* In October 1625 a number of Bristol merchants petitioned the Privy Council that they might have a "warrant dormant" to surprise the pirates that hid along the Severn river and preyed on Bristol merchants. In a second petition the same month the merchants requested that the crown permit ordnance made in Cardiff to be sold in Bristol and carried on the ships setting out to sea. *A.P.C., 1625–1626*, pp. 211–212.

20. MS.: *Croy.*

50 ships and 10,000[21] men; in so much as scarce any dare put to sea, to go from port to port.

That the north coasts were very much pestered with another kind of pirates, who had done a great deal of [f. 68v] mischief, and gave themselves out to be Dunkirkers.

By a letter from divers merchants of Bristol,[22] 8 July, 1625: Of divers ships of Bristol taken at Rochelle by the Mayor of Rochelle, with all their munition, victual, and other provision, and employed under Monsieur Soubise against the French King, putting the men on shore at Rochelle, without giving them any allowance.

It was alleged on behalf of my Lord of Buckingham that, upon the solicitation of my Lord Russell, Lord Lieutenant of Devonshire, he had given directions that Sir Francis Stuart, with a competent number of supplies,[23] should go against these pirates.[24]

SIR ROBERT MANSELL affirmed that if this were referred to the Council of War, they would undertake to redress it or else answer it with their lives.

MR. GLANVILLE. That the King's ships do nothing, going up and down feasting in every good port.

Which was confirmed by MR. SHERWILL, burgess for Plymouth.

SIR ROBERT MANSELL. That the directions were naught, and that all our dangers grew by our ignorant courses.[25]

MR. WHITSON.[26] That there was a barge

taken in the sight of Sir Francis Stuart, and the King's ships, which they let alone, saying they had no instructions to go upon the coasts of France.[27]

SIR E. COKE. That he had seen a notable record for the King's jurisdiction of the sea to the very coast of France.[28]

SIR WALTER ERLE. The tonnage and poundage is granted to the King in consideration of his guarding the sea.

MR. ROLLE. 25 E. 3,[29] there being the like grant, the merchants, being robbed, desired they might receive the money and they would secure themselves.

SIR ROBERT MANSELL. The defense of the kingdom is one of the considerations mentioned in the last act of subsidy.[30]

[f. 69] SIR FRANCIS SEYMOUR. Let us lay the fault where it is; the Duke of Buckingham is trusted, and it must needs be either in him or his agents.

SIR ROBERT PHELIPS. It is not fit to repose the safety of the kingdom upon those that have not parts answerable to their places.

A committee was appointed to consider of the complaints and to frame a petition upon which we might join with the Lords.

SIR E. COKE made a report of a double conference with the Lords.

The first was concerning a petition by occasion of the pardon and Secretary Conway's letter, which began from us, and the Lords made this answer: That their Lordships thought the matter of the pardon fit-

21. *1,000. C.D. 1625* (Knightley MS.).
22. We have been unable to find the letter.
23. *ships. C.D. 1625* (Knightley MS.). At the end of this sentence there is a marginal note in the Earl of Bedford's hand: "No". Francis, Lord Russell of Thornhaugh, referred to in this entry, was created Earl of Bedford in 1627.
24. Sir John Coke spoke on behalf of Buckingham. See Dyott diary, below. Concerning the directions to Stuart, see the copy of the 27 June letter from Buck-

ingham, printed in the Appendix, below, p. 716.
25. Cf. Sir John Hippisley's letter to Edward Nicholas, 8 June, wherein he complains of being weary from so often writing for a warrant to assure that the coasts be better protected. S.P. 16/3:41. See also, above, n. 4.
26. See above, n. 3.
27. See above, n. 4.
28. See Coke, *Fourth Inst.*, pp. 142–144.
29. *Rot. Parl.*, 25 E. III, no. 21.
30. *S.R.*, 21 *Jac.* I, c. 33, pt. 1.

test to be intimated to the King when we should give him thanks for his grace in the answer to our petition[31] concerning religion, the rather because they know that pardon was drawn from his Majesty by strong[32] importunity of the French ambassador; 2ly, that it was in agitation before the King's message to us; 3ly, that the Lord Keeper refused to make a *recepi,* endeavoring to stay it, but importunity did prevail.[33] By occasion of this, their Lordships spoke of an Italian book newly printed, wherein is recited an order of the Church of Rome, that no ambassador shall come into this country without a Jesuit.[34] And for conclusion of this point the Lords have engaged themselves to move the King that he will be pleased to grant no pardon to any priest before attainder.

SIR E. COKE added of himself, that this was conformable to ancient statutes, but that a wicked word of *non obstante* mars them all.

[f. 69v] To the second branch of the petition they propounded an excuse in the Lord Conway's behalf, that the King was so pressed that he could not choose but do somewhat, and that he took this course by his own private letter as least offensive.[35]

The other part of the conference moved from the Lords, and was concerning the relief of London in this time of the plague; touching which their Lordships had framed an order, in which they desired us to join (the copy whereof was now read) to this effect:[36]

That persons taxed or taxable in and about London, being not impoverished, shall bear a double proportion at least during this time of infection, and more if it be

thought requisite. And whereas divers are removed so far as no notice can be given them for supply, in the meantime it is thought expedient that the City of London be entreated, out of their Chamber, or out of the stock of London Bridge, to lend 1,000 *l.* to be paid out of this taxation, or out of a collection to be made throughout the kingdom, for which it is held necessary his Majesty's letters patent be made to some fit men to be nominated for that purpose.

It was ordered that we should join with the Lords in thanks for his Majesty's answer, and to desire the enrollment and exemplification of the same, according to old precedents. And, whereas anciently every knight of the shire was wont to have a copy, which cannot now conveniently be done, it is now desired that the answers may be printed.

The other business concerning the relief of London, etc., was committed, and the committee appointed to sit in the Physic School in the afternoon.

The House was turned into a committee.

[*Committee of the Whole House*]

[f. 70] In the great committee.

It was moved that the King's message might be repeated.

And that motion opposed by Sir Thomas Wentworth and others; but after some debate it was admitted.

Sir H. Marten. Subjects may fall into two extremes, *abrupta contumacia* and *deforme obsequium.*[37] He would advise the mean, praying that his sovereign may desire nothing but what is fit to be granted, yet if he do, he would have it denied in such a manner as

---

31. *general petition. C.D. 1625* (Knightley MS.). See above, n. 12.

32. *strange. C.D. 1625* (Knightley MS.). See above, n. 9.

33. See above, n. 10.

34. We have been unable to identify the Italian book.

35. *See more* is added following the sentence ending with the word *offensive* in *C.D. 1625* (Knightley MS.). With regard to Lord Conway's excuse, see above, H. of L., 9 August, p. 153.

36. See above, n. 14. For the full order framed by the Lords, see H. of L., 6 August, p. 143.

37. Tacitus, *Annales,* 4, 20.

may appear we take no pleasure in it; to deny the thing, not himself. The commonwealth stands in need of physic, and he likes the medicines, but doubts that August is no good season to apply them.

Tiberius was wont to say common persons are counselled by profit, princes by fame;[38] and therefore he would examine this proposition by profit.

We must take it for granted there is a necessity, and that it cannot be supplied otherwise. That admitted, he framed this dilemma: Either the money already disbursed has been well laid out and the design well grounded, or not. If well, then it is no good husbandry, by letting it fall, [to] lose both the hopes and the expenses. If ill employed and ill grounded, then, by not giving, we shall put into their mouths an excuse, drawing the blame upon us, and keeping them from being responsible. If the first, then to give is profitable *omni modo;* if the second, *aliquo modo.*

He took away divers objections thus:

1. For the proceedings have been upon no good counsel. It is not fit for us to know the design, and we cannot judge of it without knowledge, [f. 70v] alleging the example of Themistocles' project, which the Athenians commanded him to discover to Aristides.[39]

2ly. That we are infected abroad with Dunkirks and pirates, and shall be more if this fleet go. Other provision is made to prevent this, which we must trust upon.

3ly. Supply ought to be in the last place. Though the time be somewhat invested,[40] yet there is an assurance of *quid pro quo.* Remedies are ever of slower operation than diseases; there is a time designing, whereof his Majesty has assured us, when the disease may be opened and physic applied.

Besides we are not altogether without satisfaction. The answer concerning religion is worth a great deal of money. So is the taking away of this odious intolerable power of ambassadors, the Lords offering to join with us to that purpose.[41]

4ly. This should have been moved before we were put off at London. If we be wronged, we must not wrong the public. We will not break the instrument, if he be out of tune; neither is it good too narrowly to observe the obliquities of the state; and if he, at whom the exception is now taken, were the author of that obliquity, there was a time when he set the instrument in tune that was long out.

5ly. We are consumed with the plague already; if war be added, the commonwealth will hardly bear it. He will cast no aspersion upon former times, but the staff was crooked by affecting too much peace. To make it right it must be bowed another way.

We are an island and cannot subsist without trade. As trade must maintain our arms, so the reputation of our arms makes our trade safe. [f. 71] It concerns us to have a martial prince. A subsidy is quickly lost at sea. Let us take heed how we discontent a prince whom we have put into a course of war.

Sir Francis Seymour professed his former opinion against giving, but without any new reasons.[42]

Sir George More remembered a precedent, 39 *Eliz.,* when there was a subsidy given and two fifteens. The parliament sent a message to the Queen with an offer of a further supply. Her Majesty's answer was, she would search the bottom of her own coffers before she would draw any more from the subjects.[43]

38. We are unable to find the source of the reference to Tiberius.

39. Plutarch, *Lives,* Themistocles, 20.

40. *inverted. C.D. 1625* (Knightley MS.).

41. For the King's answer to the petition concerning religion, see above, pp. 155–160. Concerning the Lord's offer, see Sir Edward Coke's report of the 10

August conference, above, O.B.

42. For a fuller version of Seymour's speech, see below, Petyt 538/8.

43. In 1586 (29 *Eliz.* I) a bill passed both Houses granting a subsidy and two fifteens and tenths from the temporalty for "defense of our common mother and country" (*S.R.,* 29 *Eliz.* I, c. 8). Even before pas-

Mr. Alford. We shall meet again before any more can be paid.

Mr. Whistler. There can be no engagements. If there were, yet is there no honesty to perform it when it concerns the country that we should not.

Sir Robert Killigrew. To put the question, for it is a greater disgrace to be denied by a few than by all.[44]

III. PETYT 538/8, INNER TEMPLE LIBRARY

[f. 148]   Die Jovis

The House resolved themselves to a committee and debated the same again whether to give or not to give, Mr. Solicitor being put in the chair.

[Committee of the Whole House]

Sir Nathaniel Rich moves to have the letter or message of the King declared or repeated again by Mr. Chancellor, which the House much opposed but in the end consented unto it, and it was done by Mr. Chancellor. [And it was added by Mr. Chancellor][45] that the King did promise in the word of a king, whereof he had been and ever would be very jealous, to perform unto us what he said, viz., that we should meet again in winter and debate those businesses we had entered into, and that if we did now[46] give he would take more care of our healths than we did ourselves; and desired the House that they would take to heart what to do in it, whether to give or not or what return to make to the King.

Mr. Coryton. It has been pressed that this is the first request that the King has made to us. Secondly, that in parliament we have engaged ourselves. Thirdly, the necessity; and the great costs bestowed, like to be lost. Lastly, the disaster of [f. 148v] parting in displeasure. Yet for all these things, he cannot assent to give at this time, but hereafter.

Sir Henry Marten. We are upon a consultation and deliberation of a weighty matter between ourselves and our sovereign wherein, as Cassell says, the subjects may run into two extremes, either in affected opposition or in an ill-favored[47] flattery. For one of these he would never bring his mouth to it. And for the other, his breeding and religion has taught him to avoid it. And he says that there is a very narrow passage between the head and the body, wealth and reputation. It is no infelicity[48] for a king to have a council and[49] to harken unto them, as Galba said to Piso.[50] He does like well of all the physic that has been spoken of—*medicina removens, et medicina promovens*.[51] They were good things and there may be good use made of them, only he doubts it is not good ministering of them in the dog days and he doubts not but one day the King will make it good, that he will make his people more dear unto him than his dearest profit. Tiberius said subjects consider what is [f. 149] profitable but princes live by fame

sage of the subsidy bill the Commons were discussing the idea of offering further supply in the form of a benevolence to help offset the charges of the war in the Low Countries. Ultimately, both the Commons and Lords offered benevolences, but Elizabeth refused them. No record of Elizabeth's answer to the offers of the two Houses appears to have survived. See D'Ewes, *Journal . . . Elizabeth*, pp. 386–387, 408, 412–416; *L.J.*, II, 134, 137–138; Neale, *Elizabeth I and her Parliaments*, pp. 166–169, 175–183.

See also, Christopher Sherland's reference to the 29 *Eliz.* I precedent in his speech of 12 August, below, p. 477, and *Negotium*, below, p. 565.

44. Marginal note presumably in the Earl of Bedford's hand: "que". Possibly *lesser disgrace* is intended

in the text. Cf. the comments on this matter in the speech attributed to Sir Francis Nethersole in the Dyott diary, below, p. 470.

45. The words and phrases in brackets, here and below, are included in B.L. Add. 48,091, Q.C. 449, and Harl. 5007, but omitted from Petyt 538/8.

46. *not.* B.L. Add. 48,091 and Q.C. 449.

47. *ill-savored.* B.L. Add. 48,091, Q.C. 449, and Harl. 5007. The reference should be to Tacitus rather than Cassell. See above, n. 37.

48. *felicity.* Q.C. 449.

49. *and not.* Q.C. 449.

50. Cf. Tacitus, *Historiae*, 1, 15–17.

51. See Sir Edward Coke's speech, 5 August, above, H. of C., 5 August, O.B.

and reputation and therefore such as their fame and reputation is, such is their love and dread abroad.[52] He will examine this action for the profit and he doubts not but that he shall make it appear unto this House to be[53] profitable. He will not dispute the manner of the necessity like him that sees a man in a quagmire would needs know how he came thither before he would lend him his help to lift him out; and before the man could tell him he sank over head and ears. There is no such strong argument as by way of dilemma, either this fleet is well set out or not well set out. If well set out, shall we rather lose all the charge that has been bestowed on it than supply it with a little more? What ill husbandry were that; he knows no man would be culpable of so doing. But if ill grounded or done, we shall take upon us the fault of those that have been the instruments of it, by not supplying. For who can tell whether the victuals are good, the munition good, unless it be examined and some trial [f. 149v] made of it? And how can we examine it when we have put into their mouths this just excuse: you should have found all well if it had been set forth. But it is said we shall cast more money after and be in danger at home. Themistocles assembled the state of Athens touching a war, and told it Pericles[54] who said, Themistocles, shall we send a fleet abroad and be infested at home? He hopes the King and Council will take more care of it. But there have been objections made. First, that nothing done and that [it] is against the old orders and precedents of parliament. If he were not satisfied that we had *quid pro quo*, it should put him to a *non plus*. And for old orders and precedents, if they suit not with this time, upon good cause they were to be altered. We have made a goodly beginning touching re-

ligion, and other matters, but something else must be done or else it will come to little effect.

The exorbitant and irregular power of foreign ambassadors is fit to be looked unto, and to be restrained as in other states. If there be a fault committed and acknowledged to be a fault, let us [f. 150] not wrong the public for the private. If he (whom many men suspect) did commit the fault, remember what he did in Spain, and at the last parliament,[55] and let him not be beaten with our English proverb: What I have done well, that heard I never, but once did I ill, that I ever heard.

But it has been said it is a great deal of money that is required and a time of scarcity. He for his part was much obliged to the old King who, through his great love to peace, did bow the staff too much the one way. And as to make straight a crooked staff, it must be bowed as much the other way before it can be made straight. So though things be done amiss before they are rectified, yet there may be no fault in the governor. We are an island that consists of trade and traffic, and therefore our shipping must be maintained. This realm has lost at least a subsidy since we came hither. We ought to have a warlike king, and the wars are chargeable and troublesome. And therefore since, to my understanding, to give supply [f. 150v] is for our profit and to deny it is for our disprofit, and therefore he was for giving.

Sir Francis Seymour. It was not the meaning of the House (as he conceives) that this committee should debate whether to give or not to give, and to enter into a new debate of it and the reasons thereof, either for necessity or profit, but the order was that the House should enter into considera-

---

52. See above, n. 38.
53. *be most.* Harl. 5007.
54. Aristides is apparently meant rather than Peri-

cles. See above, p. 462 and n. 39.
55. I.e., the Duke of Buckingham. See above, H. of C., 6 August, n. 38.

tion for the manner of their answer and therefore read the order.[56] But surely for the matter of profit, whereof there has been much said to make it seem so, it may be answered in a few words: what need they insist so much upon 40,000 *l.*[57] to set it out. Nay, for to be sure of 60,000 *l.* to pay wages when they come home. It has been told us that there is 300,000 *l.*[58] already laid out in preparing the fleet. And it will be an ill voyage if the return of it should not pay that which is required of us now; the return being likely to be sooner than can possibly be received by way of subsidies. And therefore he thinks it fit to make an humble remonstrance unto his Majesty of the causes and reasons that we do not give now, with our dutiful affections upon good causes to give hereafter.

[f. 151] Sir George More. For giving. That this fleet is set out upon mature and good deliberation he presumes because the King has said it. [But surely there is no precedent for it.] The precedent of *29° Eliz.* a subsidy and 2 fifteens.[59] Popham then Speaker.

Mr. Solicitór craves leave to speak.[60] We are now in a debate what answer to make unto the King. He makes no doubt but if we were all satisfied that this action were well grounded we would give. And so he would have insinuated into the House but they should have desired to be satisfied in it from the King. Which the House utterly disliked and rejected.

Mr. Alford. For time and place it is neither fit to give nor good for the kingdom nor King. But it is a good and safe way to follow precedents and a dangerous thing to break them. We made a precedent lately and limited that that precedent should not be urged against us, and yet it has been;[61] and he is for an humble remonstrance.

Sir Thomas Puckering. Not to give but to make an humble remonstrance unto his Majesty and to show him the reasons and the danger that may ensue by our breach of liberties.

[f. 151v] Mr. Whistler. Precedents were the guides of all courts and therefore ought to be kept inviolably, and yet here is no bones made in running against and making a breach upon an army of precedents at once. Not to give.

Sir William Strode. To give at this time is the worst way and to fall to an answer will amount to an engagement, which he did not like. And therefore he would supply the King.

Sir Henry Whitehead. To give.

Sir Clement Throckmorton. [That it is a pretended necessity and therefore not to give.

Mr. Tomkins.] Not to give now. But there is another way whereby the King may be satisfied and that is there is 35,000 *l.* remaining in the treasurers' hands of the last

---

56. For the order that the committee of the whole meet "to consider what return to make to his Majesty's message", see above, p. 446.

57. MS.: *4,000.* The correct figure, 40,000 *l.*, is included in B.L. Add. 48,091, Q.C. 449, and Harl. 5007. See above, H. of C., 10 August, n. 19.

58. MS.: *3,000,000.* The correct figure, 300,000 *l.*, is included in B.L. Add. 48,091, Q.C. 449, and Harl. 5007. See above, H. of C., 9 August, p. 432.

59. See above, n. 43. Sir John Puckering, not Popham, was Speaker in 1586–1587.

60. Sir Robert Heath was in the chair for the committee, consequently it was necessary that he receive

permission from the committee to speak to the issue. See the Dyott diary, below, p. 470.

61. In passing the act for three subsidies in 1606 (see above, H. of C., 10 August, n. 18), parliament had included in the introduction to the act an explanation of the reasons for this extraordinary gift, "lest the same our doings may be drawn into precedent to the prejudice of the state of our country and our posterity" (*S.R.*, 3 *Jac.* I, c. 26). Despite this stipulation, in his speech of 10 August (see above, p. 444) Sir Humphrey May, Chancellor of the Duchy, had cited the proceedings in 1606 as a precedent for granting an additional subsidy within a single parliament.

money.[62] Let coat and conduct money for the country be unpaid and that money be converted to this use.

IV. DIARY OF SIR NATHANIEL RICH, H.L.R.O., HISTORICAL COLLECTION 143[63]

[f. 2]   11 August

[*Committee of the Whole House*]

At the committee for giving answer to the King's message.

[Sir Richard Weston.] 1. Whether we to give; 2, if not, then what answer to give the King.

Mr. Coryton. Reasons why we should give soon, these:

1. That this the first request that ever the King made, fit therefore to give [*illegible*] unto him.

2. Because we in parliament first engaged the King in this war.

3. The inevitable necessity.

4. The great costs that have been bestowed by this action not fit to be lost.

5. Fear that it may breed some discontent between the King and us.

Yet for all this not fit yet to give: 1, because the advice of the Council of War and state have not been had of this business. Moves that we may move that first.

1. Doubts that when the walls of our country be gone, to be satisfied in what case we stand for our safety.

Sir H. Marten. Tacitus says in consultations between the sovereign and subject the subject may fall into extremes.[64] Advises to contain ourselves in the middle posture, to keep between flattery and opposition. He will pray that we will guide a sovereign to

ask nothing but what is fit, a mutual relation.

2 things considerable: wealth and reputation. No infelicity that the King has such a council as will truly inform him of such things as may prevent such inconveniences in time to come. He likes the physic *medicina removens* and *promovens*. The question is whether it be good administering of it in the dog days. He will open examination only whether to give be profitable.

1 position for a ground: the King cannot supply wants. However he came into such necessity, we must help him out. No such strong reasoning as by dilemma. Either the 300,000 *l*. is well laid out or not: if well, then not fair to let it fall [to] 100,000 *l*.; or not well, and then we derive by blame from others to ourselves. [f. 2v] How shall we know whether all the provisions be well made? How shall we call them to account?

Ob[jection]: Shall we pay out more money upon any ill-grounded design?

Sol[ution]: To know this we must have the design revealed, but [*illegible*] it be to some?

Ob[jection]: Shall we neglect our own safety at home to be infested still by the Dunkirkers?

Sol[ution]: Hopes the state will look to it.

Ob[jection]: Nothing yet done. Supply should be in this place.

Sol[ution]: This so strong that if he were not satisfied we should have *quid pro quo* he would [*illegible*]. *Prout* the disease is found, the physic prepared, the time for taking it appointed.

Ob[jection]: This has the generality.

Sol[ution]: As [*illegible*] of religion will have received good assurance and that the intolerable power of foreign ambassadors

---

62. I.e., of the subsidy money granted in the previous parliament. See above, H. of C., 10 August, p. 452 and n. 56. Concerning the words in brackets, see above, n. 45.

63. Sir Nathaniel Rich's notes, "At the committee

for giving answer to the King's message", 11 August, 1625, are included on ff. 2–3v of his 1626 diary (H.L.R.O., Hist. Collect. 143). For a complete description of Rich's notes, see the Introduction, above, p. 15.

64. See above, n. 37.

shall be abated. Desires the King's message may be recorded.

We must not overthrow a great design because of the fault; not too narrowly to observe all the deliquities [*sic*] of a state. There was that time that this person did set the string of this state, and tune, that may balance actions; he was the subject of our praises and love, our strength and comfort of our hearts that we had a king that had martial meditations and warlike.

Trade cannot be maintained without reputation.

Sir F. Seymour. Thinks that not the meaning of the House to debate. Thinks it not profitable nor honorable, but that we should know the ground of it because not imparted to the Council of War, etc. We to make an ill voyage if it need 60,000 *l.* The major part is for not giving if it should be carried by voices of a few.

Answer: We give not at this time because we reserve ourselves for a fitter time then when we may enlarge ourselves.

[f. 3] Sir G. More. We must presume that the King has reasons for what he has done. We cannot inquire what they are. If a small loss may bring in gain of honor and profit/ 29 *Eliz.,* the House had given a subsidy in 2 fifteens, it had then resolved to send to the Queen to offer some further supply, but she refused.[65]

Mr. Solicitor desires leave to speak to clear a doubt.[66] If we were satisfied with our conscience that the design were good, would you not give? Moves that we would propound a way how to be satisfied.

Mr. Alford. We are all of one mind to supply. The difference is only in time and place.

Thinks not fit for kingdom that we yet give. The money cannot yet [be] paid. He will not give. From precedent by the law we are to have a parliament once a year.[67] Our love and demonstration of it will more prevail to advance the King's reputation.

Sir Thomas Puckering. He would decline; the denying of the King be a question, and to avoid multiplicity of discourses.

To supply in a parliamentary way is at the end of a parliament. The doubts are, he thinks there is no difficulty but that the fleet may go forth. Also, if the time be but now seasonable, then the preparations were too soon.

Thinks fit not to supply at this time, but when we meet we will assist.

Mr. Whistler. Precedents undervalued. Subsidy in the beginning of parliament, nay, subsidy upon subsidy. Precedents to mimic stars—to guide us. More wisdom in precedents than on the sudden we may imagine. We were offered to redeem our meeting as an engagement.

Moves we may buy out the Court of Wards.[68] Not to give.

Sir William Strode. Most unprofitable for the King that we should now give. To promise hereafter is to go to a new engagement. We would have bought this answer for religion as he would supply, too.

[f. 3v] Sir H. Whitehead. He thinks fit to give and would have it [put] to the question.

Sir Clement Throckmorton. Thinks it not an extreme case if 40,000 *l.* Moves to decline the question of giving and apply to satisfy the King.

Mr. Tomkins. To give the 3,500 *l.*[69] in the hands of the treasurer.

---

65. See above, n. 43.
66. See above, n. 60.
67. For acts for annual parliaments, see *S.R.*, 4 *E.* III, c. 14; 36 *E.* III, st. 1, c. 10.

68. Cf. the account of Whistler's speech in the Dyott diary, below.
69. The figure is correctly given as 35,000 *l.* in Petyt 538/8, above. See above, n. 62.

Mr. Sherland. Out of our way; fit to decline this dispute of giving.

V. DIARY OF RICHARD DYOTT, ESQ.,
D661/11/1/2, STAFFORDSHIRE RECORD
OFFICE

[f. 68] [Thursday, 11 August 1625]

[Letters concerning Turkish pirates:] The bay of Todos los Santos recovered by the Portuguese as news from Spain and Holland, etc.

A number of Turkish pirates upon our shore. They torture them until they turn Turks; take men and sell them. 800 Englishmen they have already; say they will have more. They are pirates of Sallee hard by Algiers but they are Algiers men too, men that rob in the name of Suleiman.

Tonnage and poundage granted to the intent to guard and defend the Narrow Seas, and merchants offered E. 3 that if they might have it [they] would defend themselves.[70] Let King be moved to take order, and no tonnage and poundage [f. 67v] granted till then. Danger if our pilots taken and employed [by] those Turks.

[SIR JOHN] COKE. That order was taken that two of King's ships taking into company 8 merchants (Sir Francis Stuart, [Sir John] Chudleigh, commanders) should scour the Channel. New instructions given by Lord Admiral. King will do all if [we] enable him.[71]

MANSELL. That such captains employed as you could not expect better fruits than these complaints. Not only care to give remedy when mischief happens, but to prevent.

Moved that the Council may be called to recoup and where the fault rests will appear.

Call likewise Sir Robert Mansell to account for Algiers voyage.[72]

[SIR EDWARD] COKE. *Hostes humani generis piratae.* Trade the life of an island. Let us search into the depth of this business and, as David says, you shall see wonders in the depth.[73] [f. 67] The sea will not be scoured by eating the King's beef. Moved that a committee to prepare the business and then desire a conference with the Lords.

LISTER. The northern coasts as much infested by the Dunkirkers.[74] Moved that the committee may as well take into consideration all the ports of the kingdom as the western.

DIGGES. Let us not too lightly censure the Council of State. Are not the coasts of Spain and France, notwithstanding their Councils, infested by these Turks? When our navy goes, if some course not taken, the Turks will come again.

Ordered that a committee for this business of whole House at 2 clock.

Report by COKE concerning pardon:

Obtained by strange importunity of France and could have no liberty till granted. It was in agitation before his answer to our petition. Lord Keeper deferred the *recepi,* [f. 66v] Court of Rome taken order that every ambassador in this kingdom must have a Jesuit attend him. They will move the King that not pardon any of them before attainted; that he may [know] his offense for cannot close his hand of mercy absolutely. They would give thanks for answer to petition of religion, intimate the substance of our petition that not give ear to unmeasurable importunity of ambassadors. Letter: Lord Conway took that course that thought least dangerous.[75]

---

70. See above, n. 29.
71. See above, n. 4.
72. I.e., the expedition under Mansell's command against the Algerine pirates in 1620–1621. S.P. 14/122:106; Gardiner, *History of England,* III, 374–375; IV, 224–225.

73. Ps. 107:24.
74. Lister, M.P. for Hull, was concerned about regions north of the English Channel. On the Dunkirkers elsewhere, see above, n. 6.
75. See above, nn. 9–13.

They acquainted us what done touching relief of the poor in London who likely to die of famine as much as plague if not relieved, etc. An order that all in the parishes of London and [f. 66] Stepney, which taxable, shall pay double taxation wheresoever they be and the Chamber of London to lend 1,000 *l.* in respect the better sort are departed thence for avoiding the contagion without making sufficient provision. The King's collection throughout the kingdom.[76]

RICH moved that the answer to religion may be enrolled and whereas used to be exemplified under Great Seal and one delivered to every knight of shire, moved that now it may be printed for the comfort and contentment of the whole realm.

SIR ROBERT PYE. That no justice of peace nor any men of value left in Westminster or thereabouts. Some course to be taken to repress disorders. The people much discontented and speak dangerously.

Committed.

[*Committee of the Whole House*]

[f. 65v] At committee for return of answer to King.

Marten. Question, whether give? If not give, what answer? Tacitus: In deliberations between king and subject the subjects may fall into two extremes: *abrupta contumacia; deforme obsequium.*[77] Advises to keep in middle posture. Like well of the physic prescribed, but question whether good in dog days. Tiberius said the people consider what profitable, but princes [look] to fame and reputation.[78] I shall examine whether profitable for us to give: 1, there is necessity; 2, cannot borrow. One fallen into a quagmire, friend came by and he said to him, "Help me out". "How came you in?"

"If I should tell you the story how I came in this body, I shall sink over head and ears". [f. 65] Shall we cast more money after evil grounded designs? Cannot judge of it, unless knew the designs, which not reasonable. Remember the story of Themistocles who had design upon Lacedaemon, would not tell it, lest prevented, but to Pericles[79] who would not be dishonest. That we leave coasts unguarded? I doubt but forts, munition, etc., so looked to that not be in danger. Why grant? Nothing done [with] subsidies granted in last place. We shall have *quid pro quo.* Body gathers strength in a month, perishes in instant. Diseases work quicker than medicine. Must have time, which granted us to reform. The answer in point of religion worth something. [f. 64v] The irregular and exorbitant power of foreign ambassadors shall be complained by us with Lords and doubt not of a good answer by King. Why granted [*sic*] being called from Westminster to Oxford? Acknowledged a fault, yet must not prejudice the public by it. If watch go wrong not break it but set it right, so [with] instrument. If he have done ill, has merited much since and set things right. Would not have the English proverb verified: If do well I hear it never, if evil hear it ever. I love not to scandalize former times, yet certain the staff of government crooked which must be bent the other way, though with cost. [f. 64] We subsist by traffic, for else not sell wool, corn, etc. And none can do that and consume foreign superfluities. We have lost a subsidy at sea since came hither. We subsist by reputation, which not without arms, which not without wages, which not without subsidies. I know my own imperfections and will not take pains to displease others. Giving for our profit; not giving to our disprofit.

Sir George More. *In principia semper praesumitur causa et ratio.* Solomon: Who

---

76. See above, n. 14.
77. See above, n. 37.
78. See above, n. 38.

79. Probably Aristides is meant. See above, p. 462 and n. 39.

shall say to king, why hast thou done it?[80] I think it well grounded. 29 Eliz., when Puckering Speaker, one subsidy and two fifteenths given. Resolved by [f. 63v] House to send to Queen and [make] offer of further supply in respect of great charge. She royally refused it being loyally offered and said would search her own coffers rather than take more money from subjects.[81]

He in the chair may speak to the question by leave, and so granted to Mr. Solicitor.[82] If were satisfied that the design were well grounded and likely to prosper, then would give. It has made a great impression in men's hearts what has been said. I desire you would think of a course how to be satisfied.

Alford. That all willing to give but differ about time and place. Whether shall give now? I think not. We are a great while in payment. There is [f. 63] a proviso in act that [it] shall not be drawn into precedent.[83] By the law a parliament ought to be every year,[84] then it may be done. Would not have the matter decided by question, for whether carry it or lose shall reap dishonor. Would have [us] think of a fair answer.

Puckering. Does not allow that no engagement, for are to supply in a parliamentary course 1st after grievances heard, etc. Nor that engagement of one parliament bound succeeding. To break the precedents of parliament which are the best evidences of privileges with a protestation that [it] shall not be brought into example, dangerous; for they may be still pressed to do against our precedents with protestation. [f. 62v] If the designs be still seasonable as Duke said, then I conclude that the preparations were too timely—4 months before the time. Would not supply but fall to remonstrance to satisfy King of our forwardness to assist him in all honor.

Whistler. Precedents undervalued by giving at beginning of parliament, in reversion, etc. The common law but custom, and custom in precedent preserved. The customs of courts at Westminster the law of kingdom. There is no engagement nor can be. Not a corporation, therefore not in law. Nor in honesty, because condition and end not performed for which given. A discredit to King not to have credit 40,000 *l.*, nor durst trust his people for so much. [f. 62] All places pay not 15ths. If King set a reasonable price on Court of Wards, will give him much more than he makes of it. Those tenures created against Scotland and Wales. The Scots are a wise and valiant people, no reason but this partition wall should be broken down.

Sir Francis Nethersole. Moves an expedient, so carry it that neither make the country seem unable nor ourselves unwilling to give, but to petition King to communicate the design to some judicious men to be nominated by both Houses in general, though not in particular, that may know whether design good, whether seasonable. Within these 14 months desired a war and [f. 61v] now I doubt not but desire it. Let us not desire the end without the means. Question: whether shall make the question give or not give, for dangerous that King lose it or to carry it by a few voices. But answer: better for King to carry it by a major part, than lose it by all. And many times has been put to the question, and fit for free people to deny or grant according to conscience, etc. And King not except at what done in reason and justice.

Solicitor. Would have no man go with a prejudicate opinion and say would have given if had known the design to be well grounded and upon good counsels. Moved that go to the King for satisfaction, or here for the discharge of him that charged, [f. 61] tomorrow morning.

80. Cf. 2 Sam. 16:10, which refers to David rather than Solomon.
81. See above, n. 43.

82. See above, p. 465 and n. 60.
83. See above, n. 61.
84. See above, n. 67.

House of Commons
Order of Business   Friday, 12 August 1625

Sir John Jackson **admitted** to the House notwithstanding he has not received communion — 472, *1/8

Report from the committee concerning a **collection** for the **distressed people of London** (SIR ROBERT PYE) — 472, *11/8

Resolved: collection for the distressed people of London to be made in the House; the collection is made — 472(2), 480

SIR ROBERT HEATH (Solicitor): concerning Mansell's remarks on the **consultations of the Council of War** — 472, 476, 480; **N**, 564

SIR ROBERT MANSELL — 473, 480
SIR JOHN COKE — 476, 480
SIR ROBERT MANSELL — 476, 480
SIR ROBERT HEATH (Solicitor) — 480
SIR ROBERT MANSELL — 480
SIR ROBERT MORE: concerning the **dissolution** of the parliament — 474
SIR ROBERT PHELIPS — 474

[*Committee of the Whole House: Solicitor Heath in the chair*]

Anonymous Speech: regarding 10 August **message from the King** concerning **supply** — 474, *10/8

Sir Robert More — 474
Sir Edward Coke — 481
Sir Francis Nethersole — 474, 481
Christopher Sherland — 474, 477, 481; **N**, 565

Sir Nicholas Sanderson — 482
Edward Alford — 475, 482

Serjeant at Arms brings news that Gentleman Usher of the Black Rod is at the door [*see below*] — 478

John Glanville: presents a draft **protestation** [*see below*] — 475, 478, 482; **N**, 567

[*The protestation is printed on p. 475*]

Anonymous Speech — 482

Sir Edward Villiers — 475
Sir Thomas Wentworth — 475, 482
John Glanville's draft protestation: passed in the committee of the whole — 475, 479, 482

[*End: Committee of the Whole House*]

Report from the committee of the whole House: on the protestation (SIR ROBERT HEATH, Solicitor) — 472, 475, 479

Upon question: the protestation to be entered in the Clerk's book and to be presented to the King — 472, 475, 479, 482

SIR THOMAS CREW (Speaker): that the Gentleman Usher of the Black Rod is at the door [*see above and below*] — 475, 479

Motion to make a declaration for the acquitting of M.P.s who were likely to be questioned for what they spoke in the House — 475; **N**, 567

SIR ROBERT PHELIPS — 476
SIR THOMAS CREW (Speaker) — 476

Message from the Lords: desiring the Lower House and their Speaker to come up to hear his Majesty's **commission for dissolving the parliament** read (James Maxwell, Gentleman Usher of the Black Rod) [*see above*] — 472, 476, 479, 482

The Speaker and the House go up to the Lords — 472, 476, 479, 483; **N**, 567

The commission is read in the Upper House and the parliament is dissolved — 472, 476, 479, 483; **N**, 567

[*The commission is printed on pp. 183–184*]

FRIDAY, 12 AUGUST 1625

I. JOURNAL OF THE HOUSE OF COMMONS

[C.J. 815]
[p. 60] *Veneris, 12° Augusti, 1° Caroli Regis*

Sir John Jackson licensed to come in and receive the communion on Sunday next.

Resolved, every knight of a shire to pay 10*s.* and every burgess, 5*s.*, according to the note delivered in by the committee for London, etc., and whosoever is absent to pay double.[1]

A protestation agreed upon by the grand committee reported to the House by MR. SOLICITOR; to be entered into the Clerk's book; and to be presented to his Majesty by all the Privy Council, and Sir J. Fullerton and Sir Robert Carr, from the House.

This, upon question, allowed, and to be entered *ut supra*, without 1 negative voice.[2]

Upon a 2nd question, the Privy Council of the House, accompanied with Sir J. Fullerton and Sir Robert Carr shall, with all convenient speed, present this to his Majesty in writing.

Mr. Maxwell, the Gentleman Usher of the Upper House, came to call the House and Speaker to come up to the Lords to hear a commission from his Majesty read to both Houses.[3]

Which was accordingly done.

II. MS. 197, BEDFORD ESTATES, LONDON

[f. 71]   *12° Augusti 1625.*

SIR ROBERT PYE reports the resolution of the committee concerning relieving the 9 out-parishes near London: That a collection should be made in the House, of every knight 10*s.* and burgess 5*s.*, which was confirmed and executed presently; and added that all such as were absent should pay double.

MR. SOLICITOR desired to give the House satisfaction concerning Sir Robert Mansell's speeches, whereby he had contradicted my Lord of Buckingham concerning the consultations,[4] and bred an ill impression in the House touching the great action now in hand.

[f. 71v] In December last it pleased the King by his letter from Newmarket to declare his pleasure to have the fleet made ready.[5] In the same month, Sir Robert Mansell, Sir John Coke, and Captain Love received commandment to meet often with my Lord of Buckingham, and Sir Robert Mansell[6] was present at least 10 or 12 times when, by examination of maps and plots, it was debated how they might best annoy the King of Spain.

The lords of the Council of War were often called. My Lord Chichester has left papers how far he agreed with them.[7] My Lord Carew is not now in town, but there

---

1. Marginal note: "The sum collected: 112 *l.* 10*s.* 4*d.*". Regarding the collection for London, see Sir Robert Pye's committee report, below, Bedford MS. 197; see also 11 August, above, pp. 458–459 and n. 14. According to the Dyott diary, below, the money was gathered "by some that went about the House".
2. Despite this order, the protestation was not entered in the C.J. For the protestation, see below, p. 475.
3. For the King's commission for dissolution, see above, H. of L., 12 August, p. 183.
4. For Buckingham's statements concerning the consultations, see the report of his 8 August speech to both Houses, above, p. 162. For Mansell's contradiction of Buckingham, see Mansell's speech of 10 August, above, p. 453. See also Mansell's second speech of 11 August, above, p. 460. For comments concerning

the Mansell-Buckingham conflict and other matters surrounding the dissolution of the parliament, see the letter of 15 August 1625 from the Earl of Kellie to the Earl of Mar, printed in H.M.C., *Mar & Kellie, Supplementary Report,* pp. 232–233.
5. See above, H. of L., 9 August, p. 162 and n. 54.
6. *Moore. C.D. 1625* (Knightley MS.).
7. Lord Chichester died on 19 February 1625 and it was rumored that he left papers relating to the debate in the Council of War. Eliot notes (*Negotium,* below, p. 564) that "the truth of the papers being uncertain, that wrought but little on the judgment of the audience". According to Sir John Coke's speech recorded in the Dyott diary, below, p. 480, the papers were in the possession of Sir Francis Onslow.

are some who can testify that he has acknowledged the pains taken in this business, and with what contentment he had been at it.[8] The Lord Hervey came in late; but my Lord Brooke and my Lord Grandison will come down and speak their knowledge to the House, if we please.

Divers places were propounded and presented to the King. It is true that Sir Robert Mansell was full of meditation upon his own devices which, though they seemed probable to himself, did not give others such satisfaction. In February he gave over upon discontent; and there be those [that] can witness that he said if he might not have his own desire, he would meddle no more with the business.[9] Afterward he never came to Council, and if he were present upon other occasions they were unwillingly to communicate those matters with him. But all things were debated and agreed upon by the Council and the officers; and

the King, from time [to time,] made acquainted with it.[10]

That it has pleased the King to propound to himself a great action; the point of the design is to be known but to a very few. But if the fleet should go away with a blast it will weaken the hands both of his friends and his subjects. [f. 72] He added that yesterday he met with Sir E[dward] Cecil who knows the design, and told him that upon his life and honor it is both very probable, and not newly thought upon, but heretofore contrived by the Prince of Orange.[11]

SIR ROBERT MANSELL.[12] That once he was made acquainted with a design, but protested against it. He consented to furnish the Newcastle ships, but in the design did oppose Captain Love,[13] though he knew not the Prince of Orange's notion.[14] But if that be the same design, thinks he should turn him. Then spoke of his cause of

---

8. According to the account in the Dyott diary, below, Sir George Goring was to testify as to Lord Carew's opinions.

9. With regard to Mansell's relationship to the Council of War, see his speech in Bedford MS. 197, 10 August, p. 453, and his speech in response to Solicitor Heath, below.

10. On the membership of the Council of War, see above, H. of L., 9 August, p. 162 and n. 55. The points in the following paragraph are attributed in the Dyott diary to the speech of Sir John Coke (see below, p. 480).

11. I.e., Prince Maurice, who died in April 1625 leaving the title to his brother Frederick Henry, who succeeded as Prince of Orange and Stadtholder. See the account in the Dyott diary, below.

The design was the plan for the projected joint English-Dutch expedition to Cadiz which sailed in October 1625. The plan was not revealed to parliament and apparently only the membership of the Council of War and a select few not on the Council were privy to the details of the design. The Salvetti dispatch of $\frac{9}{19}$ August notes that: "The destination of the fleet is a profound secret; every effort is made to keep the Spaniards in ignorance of it. The general talk—no doubt mistaken—indicates the Mediterranean, but I believe, as I have already said, that the real aim is the coast of Spain" (Salvetti dispatch, p. 29). As early as

May, Buckingham had appointed Sir Edward Cecil to command the expedition. Harl. 3638, f. 98b; see also Charles Dalton, *Life and Times of General Sir Edward Cecil.* . . . (London, 1885), II, 1–241, and John Glanville, *The Voyage to Cadiz in 1625,* ed. Alexander B. Grosart (London: Camden Society, 1883). See also S.P. 16/521:30. And see below, Appendix, pp. 740–743.

12. According to the Dyott account, below, Mansell's speech was interrupted by Sir John Coke. On 10 August Phelips had requested that Mansell might "declare his knowledge with what deliberation and counsel" the design had been managed (see above, p. 449). Later that morning Mansell described the deliberations of the Council of War to the House (see above, p. 453 and nn. 63–64). On 14 August Sir Francis Nethersole wrote that as a result of his speeches Mansell was "commanded to attend the lords of the Council here this day, where it was generally conceived that he should have received some very heavy censure", although Mansell believed all would "go well" with him. See Appendix, below, pp. 714–715 (S.P. 16/5:42). And see Gardiner, *History of England,* VI, 1. Concerning Mansell's speech, see also "An Advertisement to a Friend" (Osborn fb 155, ff. 132–133) printed in the Appendix, below, p. 667.

13. Sir Thomas Love, Captain of the *Bonaventure.*

14. *reasons. C.D. 1625* (Knightley MS.).

discontent: neglected in the proof of his own plot which he proposed to the Council. My Lord Chichester gave his opinion of it; my Lord Carew put it off, and at that time my Lord Admiral spoke with as good judgment as ever he heard. That after, when it was presented to the lords again, they rejected it, telling him he must repair to my Lord of Buckingham, who only had commission from the King to consider of new propositions.[15] But he, having received an injury from my Lord of Buckingham (by procuring a lease in reversion over his head),[16] would not go to him any more, but protested to them that if they were not in an error he was a traitor. And this was about February last.

This, he said, he spoke not concerning the present design, but that which was then propounded; and therefore desired that none of his words might hurt the King. For anything he knows, it may be, and as he thinks it is, a brave design.

It was commonly known that the King had made out his commission for dissolving the parliament; whereupon SIR ROBERT MORE moved that we should send some humble message to his Majesty desiring [f. 72v] longer respite, both for his business and the commonwealth.

This was seconded by some others that feared the evil consequence of such an abrupt parting, but opposed by SIR ROBERT PHELIPS. That rumors were no warrant for our belief, nor for such a message. We ought to go on in our business, and when we receive any such notice of the King's pleasure, to obey it. So, without further de-

bate, the House resolved itself into a committee.

[Committee of the Whole House]

In the committee.

[Anonymous.] It was moved we should fall to draw reasons of our refusal.[17]

Opposed by Sir Robert More as not seasonable, because we had not yet refused. And that we might not refuse.

Sir Francis Nethersole pressed the danger of the Imperial Diet to confirm the ban.[18]

Mr. Sherland. Against the arguments for giving: 1. That it will express our love to the King. *Amare et sapere* is so to love the King as not to neglect the commonwealth. 2ly. We shall distaste his Majesty's arguments and terror irritate more than persuade. 1 *H*. 5, the Commons desire the King he would keep his promise for execution of the laws better than heretofore. This did not[19] anger the King, but the blame rested upon them that had given him ill counsel. 3ly. To the dilemma. If the plot good, pity to lose it; if bad, not to take the fault upon ourselves; though it were good, we cannot give without wronging our successors, and if that money which is bestowed be cast away already, there is no wisdom in putting more to it. 4ly. The great necessity. But it has come into the King's estate by a postern gate, and to have avoided it, those which gave this counsel might have spared their works of magnificence. 5ly. We shall please the papists. The devil sometimes is for[20] good for an evil end.

---

15. We find no actual commission to Buckingham issued at that time. For the commission to the Council of War, see above, H. of L., 9 August, nn. 54–55.

16. See the accounts of this incident in Petyt 538/8 and the Dyott diary, below.

17. I.e., to pay further supply.

18. Nethersole was concerned with the problems of restitution of the Palatinate. See the version of his speech in the Dyott diary, below.

19. *not* is omitted in *C.D. 1625* (Knightley MS.). *Rot.*

Parl., 1 *H*. V, no. 8. According to Eliot this was Christopher Sherland's maiden speech in parliament (see below, *Negotium*, p. 565); however a brief speech by Sherland is recorded in the C.J. as early as 7 July 1625 (see above, p. 334).

20. The Earl of Bedford interlined the work *for* in the manuscript text without entirely striking through the word *against*. The word is *against* in *C.D. 1625* (Knightley MS.).

[f. 73] He proceeded to some reasons of his own. In points of prerogative or privilege we ought to hold chiefly to precedents; since King John's time never any like this, and yet there have been as great necessities. 2ly. The more easy the people are to supply, the more careless princes are of their revenue. 3ly. The doubt that subsidies may grow to a revenue, as in Spain and Naples those which were voluntary contributions are now made certain and due. 4ly. Our story mentions no levies against law which have not bred tumults and commotions; out of which in this place he derived an answer to the argument of the King's first request, in that his Majesty is wise, and better to be persuaded than a multitude in the country.

Mr. Alford propounded three heads of a declaration to the King: 1, thanks for his answer concerning religion; 2ly, for his care of our healths; 3ly, a profession of our love and affection to his Majesty.

Mr. Glanville. There are divers ways of declaring ourselves to the King, sometimes by message, by petitions, by committees, by entry of some act or protestation amongst ourselves. He doubted we had not time for any of the former, and therefore advised the latter way; and to that purpose presented the form of a protestation, ready drawn in these words:[21]

We, the knights, citizens, and burgesses of the Commons House of parliament, being the representative body of the whole commons of this realm, abundantly comforted in his Majesty's [f. 73v] late gracious answer touching religion, and his message for the care of our health, do solemnly protest and vow before God and the world, with one heart and voice, that we are resolved and do hereby declare that we will ever continue most loyal and obedient subjects to our most gracious sovereign King Charles, and that we will be ready in convenient time, and in a parliamentary way, freely and dutifully to do our uttermost endeavor to discover and reform the abuses and grievances of the realm and state; and, in the like sort, to afford all necessary supply to his most excellent Majesty, upon his present and all other his just occasions and designs; most humbly beseeching our ever dear and dread Sovereign, in his princely wisdom and goodness, to rest assured of the true and hearty affections of his poor Commons, and to esteem the same (as we conceive it is indeed) the greatest worldly reputation and security a just king can have, and to account all such as slanderers of the people's affections and enemies of the commonwealth that shall dare to say the contrary.

Sir Edward Villiers would fain have blown some life into the motion for giving.

But Sir Thomas Wentworth replied that, being now under the rod,[22] we could not with credit or safety yield; and, since we sat here, the subjects had lost a subsidy at sea.

Mr. Glanville's draft was passed in the committee.

The Speaker called to the chair, reported to the House, and passed, and ordered that a copy thereof should be presented to his Majesty [f. 74] by all the Privy Council of the House, together with Sir James Fullerton and Sir Robert Carr.

Word was brought that the Gentleman Usher in a message from the Lords attended at the door.

It was moved to make a declaration for

---

21. The declaration proposed by Glanville was passed first in committee (see below), and then by the House (see C.J., above). The version included in Bedford MS. 197 is virtually the same as that printed in Cobbett, *Parl. Hist.*, II, 37, and Rushworth, *Hist. Collec-* *tions*, I, 190–191, and included in various manuscript collections, e.g., Braye MSS. 1, f. 88; Osborn fb 155, p. 131; Tanner MS. 72, f. 45.

22. I.e., the Gentleman Usher of the Black Rod attended at the door of the House. See below.

the acquitting of those who were likely to be questioned for that which they had spoken.

SIR ROBERT PHELIPS. There has been little effect of such declarations. The last parliament, some went to the Tower, some were banished into Ireland, notwithstanding such acquittals.[23] For his part, if he were questioned, he desired no other certificate but the testimony of his conscience; in confidence whereof he would appeal from King Charles misinformed to King Charles rightly informed.

To which the SPEAKER replied, that he was one of those who were sent into Ireland; but he took it not for a banishment, he was well received when he came home, made a serjeant and the King's servant.[24]

The Gentleman Usher was called in, who signified from the Lords that they had received a commission from his Majesty, and desired the House would be pleased to come up with the Speaker to hear the same executed, which was accordingly performed, and the parliament dissolved.

III. PETYT 538/8, INNER TEMPLE LIBRARY

[f. 151v] [Friday, 12 August 1625][25]

The Speaker being in the chair, the SOLICITOR in the behalf of the Duke did desire to speak to give satisfaction unto the House that Sir Robert Mansell had been acquainted with the intention of this

fleet (and so was the rest of the Council of War).[26] And leave being had, he showed that the Duke imparted it unto him and used him, together with the rest, in all his counsel [f. 152] for the war until he refused the service himself and upon some private discontentment he said he would not attend it any longer. And thereupon after he was left out. And that it was true he made such a project as he had told which he revealed unto the rest of the[27] Council of War and it was by them utterly disliked and held a frivolous thing, yet more chargeable than this course. And the Solicitor affirmed that Captain Love was at the door that would certify that Sir Robert Mansell was made acquainted with this.

And SIR JOHN COKE, a member of this House, spoke something to it.

Whereto, SIR ROBERT MANSELL replied and justified his own project to be of far less expense and more hope of good, and affirmed that the Lord Chichester did acknowledge as much, and utterly denied that he did ever refuse the public service. But it is true that having a poor fortune which was left him of 500 *l.* per annum, the reversion being in the crown, he did desire to buy it and the Duke having notice of it, got it from him, which much moved him, and he [f. 152v] showed that his ancestors had been men of quality and served in good place in the state and yet none of them ever false. And himself, in that place which he

23. Phelips's reference is to the imprisonments that followed the parliament of 1621 despite the House's "protestation" regarding freedom of speech. William Hakewill and others were "convented" before the Council in January 1622. Three members—Sir Edward Coke, Sir Robert Phelips, and William Mallory—had been sent to the Tower in December and January, even before the dissolution of the parliament, for their activities in the parliament. John Pym had been confined to his house and Sir Dudley Digges, Sir James Perrot, and Thomas Crew (the present Speaker) were punished by being sent to Ireland as part of a commission to investigate grievances there. *Cal. S.P. Venetian, 1621–1623*, pp. 207, 372; Gardiner, *History of England,*

IV, 236–255, 260–267; Chamberlain, *Letters,* II, 418, 426–427; *A.P.C., 1621–1623,* p. 113.

24. See above note. Crew returned from Ireland in December 1622, was made Serjeant at Law in 1623 and King's Serjeant in 1625. Chamberlain, *Letters,* II, 518; *D.N.B.*

25. Petyt 538/8 and the other copies of this diary run on the following material directly after Mr. Tomkins's speech of 11 August (see above, p. 465) and do not insert "*Die Veneris*" for the proceedings of 12 August until the record of the meeting of the committee of the whole House later this morning (see below).

26. See above, n. 4.

27. *his.* Harl. 5007.

had, had been faithful and true. And he did desire to be questioned for the Algiers voyage.[28] And for this fleet, he would make it good with his life that, manned and victualed as it is, it cannot be profitable. And says that he neither desires the goodwill nor cares for the hatred of that great Lord. And yet no private cause should ever make him neglect his duty to the public. And for his part he wishes that these things might have a fair and due examination by some of both Houses. And where the fault lies, let him be punished accordingly.

But Captain Love was not called in nor Sir John Coke justified anything material against him, but the House rose.

Die Veneris

Mr. Solicitor being called to the chair and the House resolving themselves into a committee.

[Committee of the Whole House]

Mr. Sherland. The question now in debate is whether to give or not to give. [He thinks it not fit to give,][29] but before he gives his reasons he will speak [f. 153] something in answer to those reasons that have been passed for giving, and first there has been an objection made against insisting on precedents and that we should not make them our gods.[30] And though he loves precedents well, yet he will not idolize them. But precedents were the life of the parliament and therefore should be constant and certain. For as in other courts difference of precedents had been badges of worse times and of the weaker [judges],

much more would it be in this great court which makes laws for other courts. But those that speak most against them have most magnified them. For when they have deserted reason, how have they strained precedents to give some strength to their argument, as well that of 29 *Eliz.* as of *3° Jac.*[31] And yet neither of them near match this case. That of 29 *Eliz.* was only this: after such time as the subjects had given to the Queen one subsidy and two fifteens, understanding by her Majesty's Council that she was to make great preparation for a war to resist the great armada of '88, they by the Speaker [f. 153v] told the Queen that they had gone as far now for the present as they could, but if her Majesty should have occasion, they would shortly supply her again. Whereunto she graciously answered that she would first search the bottom of her own coffers before she would desire any more of them. And that of 31 *Eliz.* was after the great charge that the Queen had been at the overthrow of the Spaniard. And then was the first time that over two subsidies were given.[32] And for *3° Jacobi* two subsidies were propounded and agreed upon to be given and then upon some reasons given for his Majesty's great use they were made up three, [but all passed entirely together in one act]. And have our predecessors[33] left us free and shall we not leave our successors free? God forbid. But the law of necessity has been urged. If such a necessity as is pretended then why should not his Majesty be willing we should now[34] sit to redress the same and bring him to be able to subsist of himself as his predecessors have done, like a potent and great king?

---

28. See above, H. of C., 11 August, n. 72.

29. The words and phrases in brackets, here and below, are included in B.L. Add. 48,091, Q.C. 449, and Harl. 5007 but omitted from Petyt 538/8.

30. On 10 August, Sir Humphrey May, Chancellor of the Duchy, had spoken against adoring precedents as gods. See above, p. 444.

31. Concerning 29 *Eliz.* I, see above, H. of C., 11 August, p. 462 and n. 43; and with regard to 3 *Jac.* I,

see above, H. of C., 10 August, p. 444 and n. 18.

32. *S.R.*, 31 *Eliz.* I, c. 15, *An act for the granting of four fifteens and tenths, and two entire subsidies to our most gracious sovereign lady the Queen's most excellent Majesty.* Concerning the first grant of two subsidies, see also, Coke, *Fourth Inst.*, p. 33.

33. MS.: *precedents.* The word is given as *predecessors* in B.L. Add. 48,091, Q.C. 449, and Harl. 5007.

34. *not now.* Q.C. 449.

Besides, was there never such a necessity [f. 154] or cause for a necessity this 400 years? Surely it is likely there has been far greater causes and yet no such precedent to be found. But there has been a strong argument, *ab utile*, that it is profitable for us and therefore we should do it; *argumentum cornutum*, but[35] by way of dilemma, either it is profitable or not profitable. [If profitable, why should we not pursue. If unprofitable,] why should we take the fault from another and make it ours and thereby disable ourselves to call him to an account? By this argument the parliament should maintain all actions, for they are either good or not good. And for the calling of the actions of that great man to an account, who knows not that we can do nothing in it unless we have leave from the King, and then we may do it as well without supply as by[36] supply. And for the answering of our petition for religion, he is as glad of it as any member of the House. But who knows what will be the execution of it? Nay, have we not cause to fear the worst? And why should we not desire the King to put the laws[37] in execution against recusants which, if he would do, they might all be convicted at the next [f. 154v] sessions or assizes and then by that means his Majesty might have money to supply the sums now demanded.

H[enry] 5 was a wise, potent, and a stout King, not inferior to any since the Conquest and yet what did his subjects unto him in the first year of his reign? They had found such offense by the remissness of the execution of laws that they spoke plain language. The parliament prayed him to put the laws in execution better than his father had done,[38] which was good and wholesome counsel which, if his Majesty will be pleased to do, he may live in honor and wealth and be both loved and feared at home and abroad.

Now the House resolved to frame an humble remonstrance to his Majesty and then news was brought by the Serjeant that the Usher of the Upper House was at the door and had a message to deliver from the Lords, but before they would suffer Mr. Solicitor to depart out of the chair, since they had not the time to make a remonstrance to his Majesty, they would make a protestation expressing their dutiful affection.

And thereupon Mr. Glanville stood up and declared a short [f. 155] protestation which he had framed in writing, which the House approved.[39] And so he was required to go down and stand by the Clerk while he read it, which he did.

And then it was ordered to be entered which was to this effect:[40]

We [the] knights, citizens, and burgesses of the Commons House of parliament, being the representative body of the whole commons of this realm, abundantly comforted in his Majesty's late gracious answer touching religion, and his message for the care of our healths, do solemnly protest and vow before God and the world, with one heart and voice, that we are all resolved and do hereby declare that we will ever continue most loyal and obedient subjects unto our most gracious sovereign lord King Charles, and that we will be ready in convenient time, and in a parliamentary way, freely and dutifully to do our uttermost endeavors to discover and reform the abuses and grievances of the realm and state, and in such like sort to afford all necessary supply

---

35. *put.* Harl. 5007.
36. *with.* Q.C. 449 and Harl. 5007.
37. *cause.* Q.C. 449.
38. *Rot. Parl.*, 1 *H.* V, no. 8.
39. Glanville's draft of the protestation was read and approved first in the committee of the whole House and afterward reported to the House itself by the Solicitor (see below, and C.J., above) where it was likewise passed.

40. B.L. Add. 48,091, Q.C. 449, and Harl. 5007 contain only an abbreviated version of the following protestation.

to his most excellent Majesty, upon this present and all other his just occasions and designs. Most humbly beseeching our most dread Sovereign in his princely wisdom and [f. 155v] goodness to rest assured of the true and hearty affections of his poor commons, and to esteem the same to be (as we conceive it is indeed) the greatest worldly reputation and security that a wise king can have, and to account all such as slanderers of the people's affections and enemies to the commonwealth that shall dare say to the contrary.

Which being agreed on with this, that Mr. Chancellor of the Exechequer and[41] of the Duchy should present the same unto his Majesty.

The Solicitor quit the chair and the Speaker came to the chair.

And then the SOLICITOR reported what protestation the committee had made, which was ordered by the House [as] aforesaid.

And this done the SPEAKER gave the House notice that the Usher stayed at the door, and would know their pleasure whether he should come in or not.

And thereupon he was permitted to come in. And then the Usher, being Mr. James Maxwell, came up and delivered that the Lords had received from his Majesty a commission to dissolve the parliament and wished our House to come up to hear it.

And thereupon the Speaker and all the House went up [f. 156] presently to the Lords. And the commission directed to di-

vers Lords that were there[42] present for the dissolving of the parliament was read.

And that done, the Lord Keeper used words to this effect: The King's Majesty by his commission which you have heard read has dissolved the parliament.

And then they all came away and so the parliament ended. And the Serjeant immediately carried away his mace and delivered it up.

At this time was an act entitled An act for the quiet of ecclesiastical persons and preservation of right of patrons which recites the act of 21 *H.* 8, that where another man takes a benefice of value, not qualified, the first should be void as if he were dead. Whereas lapse may incur and the patron not in fault, therefore no lapse to incur but within 6 months after notice given unto the patron of the promotion.

Another act to restrain writs of *habeas corpus.*

Both bills engrossed and passed by the vote of the House were to be sent up.[43]

The Earl of Dorset's bill that came from the Lords agreed on for passing.[44]

The bill of bribery against the corrupt obtaining of judicial places was committed and great pains taken in it by the lawyers of the House [f. 156v], more than half gone through exactly, and left in Mr. Glanville's hands.[45]

The bill for naturalizing Sir Daniel Deligne once read.

The bill for the naturalizing of another Dutch man[46] that came with him, a bachelor in physic, likewise once read.

Memorandum. That while we were at

---

41. MS.: *one.* The word is given as *and* in B.L. Add. 48,091, Q.C. 449, and Harl. 5007.

42. *then.* Harl. 5007.

43. The act for the quiet of ecclesiastical persons and the act to prevent the granting of writs of *habeas corpus* were both read the third time and passed on 9 August. See above, H. of C., 9 August, O.B.

44. Dorset's bill passed the Lower House on 9 August.

45. The act against the procuring of judicial places for money had been committed on 29 June (see H. of C., 29 June, O.B.); the last notice of it in the House occurred on 4 August when a committee meeting was scheduled for the following day (see above, p. 385).

46. I.e., Samuel Bave. Concerning the bills for Deligne and Bave, which were apparently read twice in this session, see above, H. of C., 10 August, n. 1, and 11 August, n. 1.

Oxford, notwithstanding that the plague was dispersed in the town in six or seven places, and that divers died there while we were there, yet no parliament man died of it, nor any belonging to the House of Commons, but only Sir William Beecher's man. Whereupon, Sir William Beecher absented himself presently from the House and came not into the House after again.[47]

IV. DIARY OF RICHARD DYOTT, ESQ., D661/11/1/2, STAFFORDSHIRE RECORD OFFICE

[f. 61]   August 12

Ordered that every knight shall give 10s. at least, every burgess 5s. at least for the relief of the out-parishes of London in respect of their great distress and misery; and those that absent, double.

Some were against it because many countries infected which will need relief. Others because it was by way of taxation, and not left to every man's charity.

But because the matter is small, and that we use to give to prisons or do other works of charity at breaking up, and it is done in a parliamentary course, no inconvenience. It was gathered by some that went about the House.

Solicitor in chair, but put to make report to Speaker before should proceed.

[f. 60v] MR. SOLICITOR to the Speaker touching the design in answer to Sir Robert Mansell's charge.[48] The effect of what was offered by Mansell: That the Council for the setting forth the navy; if there be a design he not acquainted with it, though of the Council of War; such as he thought could not be successful, but would propound such a design as should be.

SIR ROBERT MANSELL. That not acquainted with the design; that not spoken with Buckingham since. First, that was averse to the course as now carried. One proportion of men and victuals. I confess I was at a running debate but nothing there resolved on. The later part I said and will maintain it. Solicitor moved not that part hence with misconceit of King's great actions. King sent letter in February for preparing navy to Lord Admiral.[49]

[f. 60] SIR JOHN COKE.[50] Mansell [was to] communicate it to them; that secret a meet often, which so often exceeded that 10 or 12 time. They reasoned it particularly by cards, maps which way [to] do most hurt to King of Spain. Lord Chichester dead, but gentleman has his papers, namely Sir Francis Onslow.[51] Lord Carew called, witness Sir George Goring, because other absent. Lord Conway ready to justify. Lord Brooke, Lord Hervey, Lord Grandison, that these councillors met often; descend to particulars, whether to such a place or such. Mansell met often with Sir John Love.[52] He was full of meditations which [f. 59v] seemed profitable to him, but after a long discourse rejected. He was of Council but gave over upon private discontent. Said if he might not obtain what he sued for he would not stir a foot in the King's service. They met, determined of all particulars, the last King [and] our King now approved it. The course propounded by Mansell was double the charge that this design. The King has undertaken a great action. If should go away with a blast in parliament,

---

47. The records of the House contain no notice of when Beecher absented himself, but Nethersole's 9 August letter to Carleton indicates Beecher's removal had occurred by that date (see Appendix, below, p. 712).

48. See above, n. 4.

49. See above, H. of L., 9 August, p. 162 and n. 54.

50. The Bedford MS. 197 and Petyt 538/8 accounts, above, attribute the following points to the speech of Solicitor Heath.

51. See above, n. 7.

52. Captain Thomas Love or Sir John Coke is meant. See Mansell's speech, below.

breed discontent in people, animate enemy.

Sir Edward Cecil knows it upon [his] [f. 59] reputation [and] life, that [design] most probable. That no new one; that [the] last Prince of Orange thought of it 9 years together, imparted it to himself [and] had attempted it if had lived.[53]

MANSELL. At disadvantage because may be questioned hereafter for what said here.[54] Admiral told me that King had disposition to set forth navy, wished us to be careful and diligent in the preparation and gave particular instructions like an admiral. The place was debated, he liked of my reasons. I met with Coke[55] many times, took order for victuals, charges that serve 20 or 40 ships as under my hand. Lord Admiral went upon Love's [f. 58v] ground. I say it will more advance Spain that [sic] my master's service. I would undertake to convert the Prince of Orange, if living; and heard my reasons. "Stay a little without, I'll call you in presently". I went away with a distaste. I was sent for again and again (being vice-admiral, understood Spain) often to by Lord Conway, gave me warning to be at the Council. It received 2 or 3 running debates. Admiral said that did affect the most that came from me, and was desired to conclude. He said in the meantime make provisions. Never heard man carry himself more judiciously. I do not flatter him, neither love him, nor hope to have cause to love him. [f. 58] Another time tendered them a paper of omissions to Council of War. They rejected it. If that be the manner of proceeding I will have no hand in it, I said. The reversion of my lease in the country bought over my head; was discontented at it, yet went next day to Admiral and offered him

my best directions in the service. For my ancestors have served and [been] trusted in this state 500 years and [I] would not strike King because Duke strikes me. He would never sit as that business requires. If he be not in an error I am a traitor. I told him so, and say so again. I never spoke against this design [f. 57v] as now prepared, but as then propounded.

SOLICITOR makes this suit, that howsoever attributes much to any yet forasmuch as King has followed other counsel let it receive no prejudice in our thoughts.

MANSELL. This design may be easy, but not so great as it should be.

[Committee of the Whole House]

Solicitor in chair.

Coke. *Potentior cum negat imperat.*[56]

[Sir Francis Nethersole.] King of Denmark in march; Emperor going to Imperial Diet in Germany where what done irrevocable, and intended to divide Palatinate and translate Elector eternally.

Sherland. It is more prejudicial to us than beneficial to King to give. 1 *H.* 5, n. 8, desired by Commons that he [f. 57] would keep his promises for the execution of laws better than his father.[57] He took it well. There has been as great necessity once within 400 years and yet no precedent of such a grant. Hav[ing] made act to prevent concurrent leases,[58] shall we grant concurrent subsidies? Dangerous lest it might be annual by degrees. I never found aid given in a new course, but commotion in people. Would have King informed of our reasons and declare how bountifully [we] will supply him hereafter. At Westminster only de-

---

53. See above, n. 11.
54. See above, n. 12.
55. I.e., Sir John Coke.
56. No other account records this speech, so the identification of the speaker is uncertain. However, it

is more likely for Sir Edward than for Sir John Coke to include a Latin tag in his speech.
57. *Rot. Parl.,* 1 *H.* V, no. 8.
58. Cf. *S.R.,* 32 *H.* VIII, c. 28; 13 *Eliz.* I, c. 10; 18 *Eliz.* I, c. 11.

sired an expression of our affections,[59] and [f. 56v] no emergent necessity since.

Sanderson. King wants money for meat, clothes, to pay servants' wages. Is driven to desperate and unthrifty bargains. Borrow upon interest, anticipates revenue. In want King calls parliament; we give freely, yet nothing to the proportion of his necessities. He calls us again, acquaints us with wants, gives gracious answer to our petition of religion, promises to meet in winter about grievances, etc.

Alford. Fisher, Bishop of Rochester, taxed Lower House with heresy; they took notice of it. So a bishop in King James's time spoke against us; we took notice of it.[60] So may take notice of this rumor of ending this session and [f. 56] apply ourselves accordingly.

Glanville. Divers ways of going to King: by petition, by Speaker, message. We used, too, to make protestation whereby all world takes notice of resolution.[61]

We being representative body of commons of this realm, abundantly comforted in/

Answer of religion and health, vow that/

Resolved to continue loyal subjects, ready in convenient time, in parliamentary way,

to discover abuses and grievances of state and realm. To afford necessary supply upon his present and all just occasions and designs and that [we] desire that his Majesty would rest assured of affections of poor commons and that the greatest strength of [a] king [is] in the love of his people [and] to account them as slanderers of people's affections and enemies to commonwealth that dare to say the contrary.

To be commended to his Majesty by all privy [councillors], honorable gentlemen of [the] House, [and] Sir James Fullerton.

[Anonymous.] Every man is resolved to give but differ in time; whether not better hereafter than now.

[Sir Thomas Wentworth.] [f. 55v] We are as it were under the rod, rumor of dissolution.

Ordered to be entered into the Clerk's book and that the Privy Council of House accompanied by Sir James Fullerton and Sir Robert Carr should present the protestation in writing to his Majesty.

The Usher of the Upper House, Mr. Maxwell, brought message from Lords that they have received a commission from King

---

59. See the message from the King delivered to the House on 8 July by Sir John Coke, above, H. of C., 8 July, O.B.

60. Alford is speaking to the issue of whether the Commons could take notice of proceedings in the Upper House without receiving official report of them by messengers from that House.

The precedent concerning the Bishop of Rochester occurred during the parliament of 1529:

Doctor John Fisher, Bishop of Rochester, said openly in the parliament chamber these words: "My Lords, you see daily what bills come hither from the Commons House and all is to the destruction of the Church, for God's sake see what a realm the Kingdom of Bohemia was, and when the Church went down, then fell the glory of the kingdom, now with the Commons is nothing but down with the Church,

and all this me seemeth is for lack of faith only".

When these words were reported to the Commons . . . they took the matter grievously, for they imagined that the Bishop esteemed them as heretics. . . .

Wherefore the Commons after long debate, determined to send the Speaker of the parliament to the King's highness with a grievous complaint.

Hall, *Chronicle*, p. 766.

In May 1614 Richard Neile, Bishop of Lincoln, criticized members of the House of Commons for striking at the root of crown prerogative by discussing the matter of impositions. See *C.J.*, I, 496–502; *L.J.*, II, 709–713; Cobbett, *Parl. Hist.*, I, 1160–1162; Gardiner, *History of England*, II, 243–246.

61. For the full protestation drafted by Glanville, see above, Bedford MS. 197.

that the Lords would have us come up to hear it.

Agreed to.

Where Lord Keeper told them they had received a commission for the dissolving of the parliament which was directed to the Privy Council, and being read, the Lord Keeper said, the parliament is dissolved.

Negotium Posterorum

Introduction

Introduction to *Negotium Posterorum*, Sir John Eliot, Vol. 3, Eliot Papers, Port Eliot.[1]

[f. 1] Strangers have observed the felicities of England by her parliaments. That and the contrary is apparent in the examples of her kings, of whom [those] whose actions had[2] concurrence with that council were always happy and successful, those that contested[3] or neglected it, unprosperous[4] and unfortunate. Of the first sort in the old times were those victorious and brave princes Edward 1, Edward 3, Henry 5,[5] that so far extended the honor of their nation in the admiration of all others, as even the name of Englishmen could do wonders of itself, taking and giving kingdoms as the subjects of their wills.[6] Of the latter were those characters of misfortune,[7] Edward 2, Richard 2, Henry 6, whose reigns were all inglorious and distracted,[8] fatal their ends. But above all, for a demonstration in this point, is that instance before these of Henry 3 who,[9] in his younger times, [f. 1v] affecting the false reasons[10] of his favorites, in opposition of the parliament involved his crown and kingdom in such misery[11] and dishonors as few times else can parallel [and] princes have seldom suffered. But after, upon the apprehension of those errors, and retracting of that course in his reconciliation and conjuncture with that great council of his people[12] (those flies of court rejected) he again recovered the lost honor unto both, restored their ancient happiness, lived and enjoyed it in a sweet[13] calmness and tranquility and, dying, left it as an inheritance to his son[14] who on that ground erected[15] the superstructure of his greatness. Henry 4, Edward 4, Henry 7, who raised their fortunes by the falls of those before them, made their errors their instructions[16] and, by complying with the parliament, what they had got with hazard, with security they retained. [f. 2] Henry 8, though otherwise rough and violent, did nothing in prejudice of that court, or if it were attempted in some particular by his ministers (as the most righteous[17] times are not without obliquities) it was soon retracted by himself, who maintained his confidence with his people, and he was not without reputation[18] with his neighbors, nor this nation in dishonor under him. That hopeful prince, his son Edward 6, in the short time he lived, having the same affiance, lessened not in the expectation of the world. But that glorious star, his sister of most ever famous memory,

---

1. Sir John Eliot's incomplete and untitled introduction to the *Negotium* is bound into volume 3 of the Eliot papers preceding the text of the *Negotium Posterorum* (see below, p. 491 and n. 1). It is numbered separately, ff. 1–10, and was at one time bound separately. Eliot did not copy the introduction in a fair hand as he did the text of the *Negotium* (see above, p. 17); consequently it is replete with interlineations and deletions. The editors have included in the footnotes below, in italics, those words and phrases which Eliot crossed out in the MS. In some cases he altered his wording twice; in these instances the editors have included the second variation in parentheses. Footnote citations to transcription differences in the "printed edition" refer to Grosart's edition of the *Negotium* [*An Apology for Socrates and Negotium Posterorum: by Sir John Eliot*, ed. Alexander B. Grosart, 2 vols. (London, 1881)].

2. *were.*

3. *neglected.*

4. *inglorious.*

5. Of *this first (last) sort were H. 6, R. 2, E. 2.*

6. *at the discretion* of their wills.

7. of *dishonor and* misfortune.

8. *unfortunate.*

9. Henry 3 *which gives a demonstration upon both* who.

10. the *counsels.*

11. the parliament *brought to the* kingdom *and himself such* misery.

12. *of the state.*

13. *great.*

14. and *when he died transmit[ted] it* to his son.

15. *directed.* Printed edition.

16. who raised *themselves by the means* of *their predecessors, in their errors saw an advantage to themselves.*

17. *sacred.*

18. *honor.*

Queen Elizabeth (for the other is not observable on this part either for her counsels or successes, her marriage and alliance leading contrary),[19] that princess who was glorious above all—all that went before her—in whom all their virtues and so their honors were contracted (for the sweetness and piety of her brother, the magnanimity of her father, the wisdom of her grandfather, [f. 2v] the fortune and valor of the rest, were all complete in her whom Mars and Apollo did present for a wonder to the world).[20]This excellent Minerva was the daughter of that Metis, that great council of the parliament was the nurse of all her actions, and such an emulation was of love between that senate and this Queen as it is questionable[21] which[22] had more affection, the parliament in observance[23] unto her, or she in indulgence to the parliament. What were the effects of this her stories do delineate: peace and prosperity at home, honor and reputation abroad, a love and observation in her friends, consternation[24] in her enemies, admiration even in all. The ambitious pride of Spain broken by her powers, the distracted French reunited by her arts, the distressed Hollanders supported by her succors, the seditious Scotch reduced[25] to the obedience of their prince, all violence and injury repealed, all usurpation and [f. 3] oppression counterwrought, the weak assisted,[26] the necessitous relieved,[27] men and money into divers[28] parts sent out, as if England had been the magazine of them all.[29] And she the

quaestor[30] that had the dispensation of these treasures, or rather the praetor and judge of all their controversies who with this magnificence abroad did not impair at home, but being good to all was most just[31] and pious to her subjects who, by a free possession of their liberties, increased in wealth and plenty, and notwithstanding that infinite of expense for support of all those charges,[32] the riches of her [Ex]chequer did improve.

This shows the importance of the parliaments and the happiness of the state, and how all the English kings have been fortunate by that council, none without it. Therefore in the description of the parliaments will be best seen the state and condition of the kingdom; in that will be emergent [f. 3v] the diseases which it suffers, sometimes propounded in their fervor and extremity for a present cure and help, sometimes in the inclination and beginning[33] before they are come to height for prevention[34] of the danger, sometimes by way of prophesy discovered as they are but in embryo and conception, both their originals and degrees came often here into[35] agitation and debate,[36] always their acts and consequences, and now and then their reasons. I speak thus of their reasons[37] because it is not always that the true case is seen. The same effect may flow from divers principles and intentions, often with states and men *aliud pretenditur aliud in mente est*, there are as the civilians have observed *causae suasoriae, causae justificae*, and

---

19. alliance *conducing to the other.*
20. Apollo *both inspired (inhabited).*
21. *doubtful.*
22. MS.: *whither.*
23. *readiness.*
24. *terror and* consternation.
25. *reclaimed.*
26. *relieved.*
27. *supplied.*
28. money *dispersed.*
29. magazine *for* all.
30. *treasurer.*
31. with *those foreign acts of greatness impaired not* at

home, but *as she was just* to all was most *pious.*
32. and notwithstanding *all expenses.*
33. in that will be emergent the diseases *of the times, sometimes propounded in the inclination to prevent them before they attain to strength,* sometimes propounded in their *danger* and extremity for a present cure and help, sometimes *for prevention,* inclination and beginning.
34. for *a [illegible].*
35. *their mob* agitation. Printed edition.
36. both their *degrees and acts with the consequence that follows them,* originals and degrees came often here into agitation and debate.
37. I *say now and then* their reasons.

both concurrent in great actions for which [f. 4] dissimulation is defined to be *politiae particulae imago*, and this[38] makes these reasons more obscure which yet in parliament come sometimes to discussion where those mysteries and secrets are unlocked, and as the dangers,[39] so the safeties are there treated of with all their incidents and concomitants, connections, adjunctions, and dependencies, what in religion or ability has relation to the kingdom, the knowledge of it moves in the agitations of the parliament which agitations therefore will be a good mirror of the times.[40]

For this, however inglorious it may seem, I have disposed my thoughts in the service of my country to compose the story of that council from the end of Queen Elizabeth. What was the condition of the kingdom when her government did leave it is well known to all men; what it is now this labor will express [f. 4v] and somewhat of the reason as it is insinuated[41] by the acts will be emergent in this work, not elsewhere so discernable, if either my pen or prospect do not fail me. Many will think, and that perhaps not lightly, the scope of this too narrow for a history, but we that take it otherwise desire their favor in our censure until they again consider it. Let them peruse the passages, observe the variety of their treaties, note their resolutions and effects, read and digest them, and then infer the judg-

ment in which we are confident they will find somewhat of delight and the rest not much unprofitable.[42]

But before we embark in this story of the parliaments it will not[43] be unnecessary in our way to take some short survey of that body, how it is composed [and] by what authority[44] it subsists.[45] For no little prejudice may be done it[46] for the opinion it receives [f. 5] *modo habendi;*[47] for the accession of her[48] powers, whatever act and exercise it have had. If it be new by concession of late times, the times that[49] change their reasons may have some color likewise to change the resolution of that grant. If the continuance have been longer and yet the grant appears (though it be much to impeach the prescription of a kingdom which for many ages recites [precedents], one being[50] admitted for the private interests[51] of men), it may be[52] some pretext that the[53] favor of one prince should not conclude the generation of successors; but if the institution be more ancient and without the introduction of such grant,[54] or that that grant of one be still confirmed by all, then all are in the faith and obligation, and the authority of that council is much more as it subsists by right and not by favor.

I know the vulgar and common tradition [f. 5v] does repute[55] that parliaments had beginning with those charters which were made by Henry 3, and that he that granted

---

38. imago *et adulationis quarta pars* and this.

39. *cure.*

40. the agitations of the parliament which *are the best glass and representation* of the times.

41. what it is now this labor will express *and somewhat of the reason, as it is insinuated by the acts, if my glass fail not (deceive me not) (if my prospect fail not) either or my pen. You/* and some what of the reason *not every day discernible* as it is insinuated.

42. Many will think, and that perhaps *more truly, this subject* too narrow for *the subject (illegible) of* a history, but we that take it otherwise desire their favor in *the* censure until they *have well perused* it. Let them peruse the passages, *read and digest* [a] variety of their treaties, note their *effects and* resolutions and effects, read and digest them, and then infer the judgment in which we are confident *there will be* somewhat *acknowledged* of

delight and the rest not *thought* unprofitable.

43. embark *for this it will not.*

44. *rights.*

45. survey *of the frame and composition of that council by which the dignity and authority may appear.*

46. prejudice *it may have.*

47. it receives *modo habendi as they (those powers) are thought to be derived (by the derivation of those powers)* modo habendi.

48. accession *to those.*

49. *again.*

50. *what* admitted.

51. *rights.*

52. *have.*

53. *successors.*

54. without *such grant of princes.*

55. *refute.* Printed edition.

those liberties to the people gave being unto parliaments, upon which foundation many arguments are laid to impair the worth of either: the weakness of that king, the greatness of his barons, the tumults of that time which made a necessity of those grants that were not taken but extorted. But truth[56] shall speak for both, how injurious is this slander,[57] how much more ancient and authentic their descent.

56. *And therefore.*

57. how injurious is this slander *which robs them.*

Negotium Posterorum[1]

King James being dead and with him the fearful security and degenerate vices of a long corrupted peace in hope and expectation laid aside, with the new King a new spirit of life and comfort possessed all men, as if the old genius of the kingdom, having with Endymion slept an age,[2] were now awaked again, moving in all the parts and members of the body to the quickening and agitation of the whole. The blood, which was the vehicle of this spirit, by divers veins was carried from the fountain of those hopes, the virtues of King Charles, to that sea of love and duty in the hearts and affections of the people. In some the consideration of his piety, his religious practice and devotion, his choice and constant preservation of that jewel in the midst of those prestigious arts of Spain, and his public professions, being from thence returned, did cause that joy and hope. Others were moved by the innate sweetness of his nature, the calm habit and composition of his mind, his exact government in the economy, the order of his house, the rule of his affairs, the disposition of his servants, being Prince, all in a great care and providence [p. 2], to the expression of his honor, and yet no thrift neglected, of which besides the order and direction, he was an example in himself.

His public industry and studies to improve his knowledge in the state and to advance that business were an indication unto others. His diligence and attendance at all councils, forwardness in all business which might render satisfaction to the subjects, as the much longed for dissolution of those treaties, the untying of those knots, the cutting of those Gordian yokes in which they were held by Spain,[3] and the preparations thereupon for revenge of all their injuries and reparation of his friends, which works were taken for a present [sign] of his virtue and a promise for the future of greater hopes to come. His exercise and recreations were not left, but some deduced their reasons even from them, both for his choice and temper.

And all having in some things their persuasion, some in all things to whom the change alone seemed fortunate, and this again endeared by reflection on the contraries; when it was thought what infelicities had been suffered, infelicities abroad, infelicities at home, in the consumption of the honor, consumption of the treasures of the kingdom, the martial powers neglected, the reputation of their wisdom in [p. 3] contempt, Mars and Apollo both forsaking them in that inextricable labyrinth of those treaties whereby religion was corrupted, justice perverted, and all this through facility and confidence, or a too much love of peace. The change which

1. The *Negotium* is printed here from the original manuscript, volume 3 of the Eliot papers in Port Eliot. We are grateful to Lord Eliot for allowing us to produce a newly edited text of the *Negotium Posterorum*. We have printed the account generally in the manner in which Sir John Eliot wrote it, incorporating only a few minor changes in form. We have paragraphed and spaced the set speeches in such a way as to make them more readily apparent to the reader and have inserted the names of the speakers within square brackets. We have also inserted dates in square brackets within the text to indicate the chronology of events and easily enable the reader to turn to the corresponding proceedings in the day-by-day accounts (above) where the annotation is fuller than in the *Negotium*. We have pro-vided complete footnotes in the *Negotium* primarily for those points not already annotated in the daily accounts, and have included a number of cross-references to previous footnotes when further elucidation of the text seemed desirable. Citations for classical references in the *Negotium* which contain Latin phrases will be found, with the translation of the Latin, in the Glossary, below. In keeping with our general editorial policy we have also modernized spelling and punctuation. For a complete description of Eliot's *Negotium Posterorum*, see the Introduction, above, pp. 17–24.

2. Apollodorus, *The Library*, I, vii, 6.

3. Concerning the breaking of the Spanish treaties, see above, H. of L., 18 June, n. 5.

was now presumed in these by the new change of persons wrought a new change of hearts—all men's affections were transferred from doubt and jealousy into hope, and all their fears and sorrows did resolve themselves to joy.

For confirmation of all these, as that which was to be the assurance of them all, and of all else that might import the happiness of the kingdom, a parliament was intimated. The summons and formalities dispatched, the elections[4] of the Commons being prepared with more than usual diligence, the emulation for the service being greater, the members chosen forthwith repaired to London to make their attendance at the time. No man would be wanting: love and ambition gave them wings. He that was first seemed happiest. Zeal and affection did so work as that circumstance was thought an advantage in the duty. To heighten the celebration of this meeting, the Queen was then [p. 4] expected out of France. The desponsories[5] being past and the ambassadors with their new mistress on their journey, the royal navy did attend her transportation on the seas. The King himself passed down to Canterbury to receive her where, the interview and nuptials being performed in a state answerable to their worths, they made their repair to London and in that first conjunction begot both love and admiration. This deferred awhile the opening of the parliament but the festivity of the time was a compensation for that want, which by prorogation was continued until the eighteenth day of June, all men in the meantime being full of joy and comfort when, as a crown to all, that solemnity was added.

[18 June 1625]

To the first ceremonies and entrance the Duke of Chevreuse and his Lady were admitted with the ambassadors and others of the French who, in honor and attendance of the Queen, had accompanied her from France. A place they had in the Lords House below the corner of the state,[6] the Queen being likewise present, all the Lords in their formalities and orders, and the Commons in great joy [p. 5] and expectation when the King, applying his speech unto the time, and both the time and that unto himself, thus gives a short character of either and in that renders the occasion of the assembly.

[The King.] My Lords and gentlemen, my natural disability to speak holds good correspondence with this time which, being designed for action, discourses will not fit it.[7] Nor is it needful in the business of this meeting that my exhortations should be long, it being begun before, in my father's days, when both I and you were severally engaged—I as your intercessor unto him, you by your advice and declaration for the work. It would be now a dishonor to us both not to give it perfection by our help, and such supply of necessaries as the importance does require. I speak not this in diffidence of your readiness but as an expression of my sense upon the public interest. I know your zeal and affection to religion, and that matchless fidelity to your king which is the ancient honor of this nation. For my part I seek [p. 6] nothing for myself but in the common happiness, for which I shall be as ready to dispose my private faculties as I doubt not of your willing-

4. *objections.* Printed edition (concerning the printed edition of the *Negotium Posterorum,* see above, p. 4).
5. Probably the preparation for Henrietta Maria's marriage to Charles is meant, which may also include her marriage by proxy before leaving France (see H. of C., 18 June, n. 4). The term *desponsories* was previously

used with regard to the earlier marriage negotiations and engagement arrangements with Spain. See *O.E.D.*
6. I.e., the chair of state. See H. of L., 18 June, n. 4. The Queen did not attend the opening of the session. See Salvetti dispatch, p. 23.
7. See H. of L., 18 June, n. 10.

ness to aid me; by which concurrence both power and reputation will be gained, and a presage and prediction to our hopes.

Both the sense and shortness of this expression were well liked, as meeting with the inclination of the time which, wearied with the long orations of King James that did inherit but the wind, was much moved at this brevity and plainness, more like to truth than art; that it drew a great applause to follow it, answerable to the opinion which it wrought, that with the manners of their ancestors they should resume their fortunes and in this turn and revolution meet the old world again.

Some time being given upon the conclusion of this speech, as the state and admiration did require, the Bishop of Lincoln, then Lord Keeper, taking his directions from the King thus seconds him, in more words, but as a paraphrase only on that text:

[The Lord Keeper.] My Lords and gentlemen, you have heard his Majesty's speech, of which I may say, as of the like it was, [p. 7] that there was *multum in parvo*, and though it contained so much as there is little left for me, yet it deserves that censure which Pliny gives of Homer upon the abundant expression of his works, that there was no word in vain.[8] All was said in that word of the engagement which concerned the business of this time. For upon that engagement of the last parliament to King James he was induced to dissolve the treaties then with Spain. That necessarily did enforce him to a war. For the war, there must be variety of preparation. To that end he contracted a league with other princes, added some forces to the States, levied an army for Count Mansfeld, armed his own ships for sea and of them provides a navy which now we may call invincible, in all to scatter the forces of his enemies in the whole circumference of their dominions, by which he became engaged to the expectation of the world, and, as a legacy, by his bequest and yours, left that engagement to his son, who now desires [p. 8] to follow it for your honors and his own. In the preparations that are past all the subsidies and fifteenths which formerly you have given are spent and much more of the revenue, for which now your further aid is craved and without which the work cannot proceed, wherein three circumstances only I will add.

The first for time, which is the great commander in all actions: for actions command not time but time, them. And, therefore, that supply that comes too late proves no supply at all. Europe is now stirred, like the pool of Bethesda by the angel, for the recovery of the honor and happiness of this nation. And if we slip the opportunity, some other may prevent us. Wherefore, it is desired we should give this meeting to this business.

The second circumstance is the manner which time does use in action, as the wings about her feet. Wherein, if you find the usual way too slack, fear not in an occasion of such consequence to resort to others fitter. All are subventions which are granted by this body, nor can it be unparliamentary [p. 9] which is resolved by parliament.

The third circumstance, and last, is the end and issue of this action which carries with it the fame and reputation of our King. For as princes sow in actions, so they shall reap in glory. And the hope and glory of our Sovereign (which is all that kings possess) he has now put on us, not in desperation as Caesar with the Romans, *jacta est alea*, but in confidence as his own motto has it, *amor civium regis munimentum*. Kings and subjects *relata simul sunt natura*, as the civilians have observed. And no sooner shall his Majesty be known a victorious prince, but

8. Pliny the Younger, *Epistolae*, V, 6, 43.

you shall be esteemed a valiant faithful people. And so to address you to this work, you are now to choose a Speaker and on Tuesday next to present him to his Majesty.

This ceremony being ended, the Commons, according to the direction that was given, retired to their House for the election of their Speaker, where a proposition being made by some privy councillors of the King,[9] members of that House, for [p. 10] Serjeant Crew, it was forthwith accepted by the rest and after some formalities, usual more than necessary, of pretended unwillingness in him and importunity in the others, with much art and rhetoric on both sides, he was led unto the chair, which in obedience he assumed, not yet in acceptation as his right.

The nomination of this man was held a good omen to the work. His former carriage in that place and the success thereof after so many nullities and breaches, making again as it were a new marriage and conjunction between the King and people, gave such satisfaction in all hope, as all men were affected with the choice. Nor wanted there in him either fitness or ability. He was a great master of the law and, in his studies, religion had a share to a great name and reputation.[10] His life and practice answered it. And his elocution was most apt for the employment he sustained; for he could express himself on all occasions of the time *pulchre et ornate,* as Quintilian makes his orator, *pro dignitate rerum, ad utilitatem temporum, cum voluptate audientium,* nature and art concurring to make him equal to the place.[11]

[20 June 1625]

[Sir Thomas Crew,] who, upon Tuesday [*sic*][12] after, being [p. 11] presented to the King and there making an apology for himself with a prayer to be excused, but not granted or allowed of, he thus submits to the burden of the service, and as his first fruits offered up this oration:

[Sir Thomas Crew.] Since it is your Majesty's pleasure to command, it is my duty to obey; *tuus o rex magne quid optes explorare labor, mihi jussa capessere fas est.*

I know a sparrow falls not to the ground without God's providence. And, as the rivers of water, so the hearts of kings are in His hands, *impellit quo voluerit.* And I am the more encouraged by the former experience of the mercy and goodness of God who, at our last meeting, made those of one House to be of one mind, and united the head and members of one body in one heart, which produced that *parliamentum felix,* crowning with honor the memory of the last public act of your dear father to all posterity, who then was pleased to ask and follow the advice of his great council in dissolving the two treaties, parted [p. 12] with some fruitful leaves from the flourishing garland of his crown for the ease and benefit of his subjects, and gave his royal assent to as many good laws as passed at any one time since the Great Charter. In which we then discerned your princely care of the public, your readiness to remove all rubs that might hinder, and your hand always at hand to help and further our desires, *et beneficium postulat officium.*

And now that God has put into your

---

9. Sir Thomas Crew was nominated by Sir Thomas Edmondes, Treasurer of the Household and privy councillor. See H. of C., 18 June, p. 193.

10. Thomas Crew had been returned for Lichfield in 1604, Bere Alston, Devonshire, in 1614, Northampton in 1621, and Aylesbury in 1624 when he was chosen Speaker. He had attended Gray's Inn where he was Lent reader in 1612. In 1621 he was part of a commission to "inquire into the state, ecclesiastical and

temporal, of Ireland". He was made one of the King's Serjeants in 1625. *D.N.B.*; Chamberlain, *Letters,* II, 606.

11. Quintilian, *Institutiones Oratoriae,* 2, 19.

12. Crew was presented to the King on Monday, 20 June. The following version of Crew's acceptance speech is nearly identical to the account in Petyt 538/8, above, pp. 198–201.

heart in your happy entrance to tread the true path of a parliamentary way, in comparison whereof all other courses are out of the way, you have to your own honor and our comfort shaken hands with your subjects and made your face to shine in the eyes of your people. Solomon, the wisest of kings, calls that land blessed whose king is the son of nobles. And blessed are those subjects whose sovereign, trained up in true religion and by lineal descent of inheritance the undoubted heir of the crown, in the prime of his strength is invested in his royal birthright by an immediate [p. 13] patent from God, with the applauses of his people.

It is God's method with his dearest children to mix crosses with comforts; but as a woman in travail forgets her sorrow for joy that a man child is born, so our grief, occasioned by the departure of our late Sovereign, is swallowed up with joy to see upon his sunset his own son arising to succeed him, of whose happy and religious reign and government we have a great expectation.

God in his eternal counsel had set the bounds of your father's days, which he could not pass, and the great husbandman best knew the time when his corn was ripe and ready to be gathered into his granary. It is He that made you, which were, as yesterday, our hopeful prince and the pledge of our future peace, to become our sovereign lord and King, and set you on your father's throne to judge the Israel of God.

The good Hezekiah was 25 years old when he began to reign; and so now writes[13] your Majesty. He did uprightly in the sight of the Lord, sanctified the House of God, had in heart [p. 14] to make a covenant with the Lord; and God magnified him in the sight of all nations and in every danger gave him deliverance. And your Majesty shall become mighty with Jotham

while you direct your way before the Lord your God.

You have a faithful and loyal people that fear and love you *et, amor civium regis munimentum.* You have a wise and understanding council to advise. Your imperial diadem shines the brighter in that it is enameled and compassed with a beautiful border of the ancient and fundamental laws of this kingdom which, as sinews, hold the body of the commonwealth together and are suitable to the nature of the people and safest for the sovereign. The ark of true religion is with you to waft you over the waves[14] of all the dangers of this life and, when you are old and full of days, to land you in the safe harbor of heaven.

David, being to go the way of all the world, gave a charge to Solomon his son to walk in the ways of God, that he might prosper in all he did. And it is our singular comforts to hear that it was the [p. 15] advice of your dear father to you at his dying to maintain the religion professed. In this we have long enjoyed the blessing of peace and gone forth in the dance of them that be joyful. In this is the truth and power of God; the other a mist of man's invention and a mystery of iniquity.

God, whom we worship according to His word, bowing down His ears to our earnest prayers, brought you back from foreign parts in a rare adventure full of peril, delivered you from the dangers of the deep, covered you under the wings of His immediate protection, suffered no man to do you harm, and wrought a marvelous light out of a fearful darkness, worthy to be written with a pen of iron and point of a diamond in all true English hearts. We then for sorrow hanged our harps upon the willows and could not sing the songs of Zion while you were in a strange land. It is lodged in the register of God's special mercies to this

---

13. So now Charles I, born in November 1600, writes his own age.

14. *waters.* Printed edition.

nation, and your Majesty may hereafter say, *forsan et haec olim meminisse juvabit.*

[p. 16] Your Majesty has the memory of the distressed Palatinate, which in our distress in the times of persecution was a sanctuary and asylum. And every good heart is sensible of the dishonor to our nation to see and suffer a confederate prince of our own religion, an immediate match with a branch of the royal blood, invaded and deforced of his ancient patrimony and inheritance in that time when there was treaty of peace and when our royal navy floated on foreign seas and was to others a wall of brass and tower of defense. Now that the scepter and sword is come into your own hands, extend it to hold up them that be helpless, that so you may be a happy instrument to close up the breaches and raise up the ruins of that desolate country. *Qui non propellit injuriam cum possit facit.* Egypt was destroyed for being a staff of reed to the house of Israel, and Meroz was cursed for not coming to help the Lord in battle against the mighty.

Lucius, a Britany king, was the first of all Europe whose [p. 17] royal diadem was brightened with the heavenly beams of Christianity. And you that are *rex totius Britaniae,* lineally descended from the royal stem of both roses, and in whose person is a union of both kingdoms, shall add happiness to your crown and state by pulling down the pride of that antichristian hierarchy and in abandoning by public edict, really executed, that wicked generation of Jesuits and seminary priests who are the sons of bitchery that blow the coals of contention, incendiaries that lie in wait to set combustion. Blood and powder are the badges of their wicked profession. Your Majesty, no doubt, in your deep wisdom does discern them and in due time will curb them and no longer suffer such locusts to eat up the good fruits of the land and to abuse the simple, lest the Church and commonwealth suffer, but send them home to their own cells not to return again.

But that I may not take away time that is so precious, especially at this time, from [p. 18] your Majesty's so many and weighty affairs, nor hinder public business, I hasten to conclusion and, according to the duty of my place by special charge and commission from the Commons House, with the warrant of ancient and approved precedents, I humbly present unto your Majesty our wonted and accustomed petitions:

1. That you would graciously give allowance of our ancient immunity for ourselves and such servants and attendants as are capable of this privilege both *eundo et redeundo* and during the time of our sitting to be free from arrests and troubles, whereby we may the better attend the public service.

2. That your Majesty would vouchsafe unto us liberty of free speech according to our ancient privilege, that by a free debate of the reasons on both sides truth may the better be discerned and matters at last by common consent happily concluded; and I doubt not but we shall confine ourselves within the limits and compass of duty and obedience.

[p. 19] 3. In regard the subject may be such and of so great moment and consequence as shall minister just cause of immediate resort for advice and redress to the oracle of your own mouth, that your Majesty would be pleased upon all needful occasions upon our humble suit, and at your fit time, to permit us access to your royal presence.

4. Lastly, that your Majesty would be graciously pleased to entertain us in your gracious and good opinion and of all our proceedings to make a benign interpretation.

There only remains that I, which by the free choice of the House and your Majesty's gracious approbation am, though unworthy, a Speaker for others, may be permitted to become an humble suitor for myself to your excellent Majesty, that you would be pleased to cover my errors and defects with the veil of gracious construction and to extend to me, your most humble servant, the first of all others that in public needs and craves it, your free and gracious pardon.

This oration of the Speaker's had this answer by [p. 20] the Keeper according to the formality of the time. The interim was little, yet awhile he seemed to study the recollection of some notes he then had taken. But that trouble was not much, nor needed at all, which, being done, he thus delivered what formerly was agreed on.[15]

[The Lord Keeper.] Mr. Speaker, his Majesty has heard you with approbation both pleading for yourself and for your country, wherein it faired with you as formerly with Gilbertus.[16] For if you had pleaded ill, which you were not wont to do, yet that could not have prejudiced the opinion of your service, which former merits have endeared. But otherwise, as you have, making known your ability by your eloquence, it confirms the reputation which you had in the judgment of his Majesty from whom I am commanded in part to make you answer.

Your speech was like that perfect body of the world, so orbicular and round that there seemed no angle in it but in such a symmetry composed, as humors well digested in the body, that there is no predominance, but in the equal temper of them all they make [p. 21] one pure complexion. Yet in that rotundity, as the later mathematicians have observed, some stops and points there may be found. That perfect body has some veins, though shadowed artificially by the skin, by which we may see the blood and spirit conveyed to the several parts and members in their spheres and by those stops and points take the commensuration of the whole, which I shall do in touching some particulars.

Somewhat of yourself you spoke and the last parliament; somewhat of his Majesty's entrance to his reign and therein of his beginning with a parliament, of his descent and blood, of his succession, of his hopes, of his deliverance out of Spain. Somewhat you spoke likewise of religion and the recommendation of that jewel to the King by the piety of his father at his dying; somewhat of the common law as the principle of this government; somewhat for the relieving of our friends; and somewhat for the repressing of our enemies, the restraint of priests and Jesuits; and lastly of those usual petitions for freedom [p. 22] of persons, liberty of speech, access upon occasion, and benign interpretation of proceedings. To which I will answer briefly. In this order and method I propound them.

First concerning yourself who say little but do much. Having once offered to his Majesty the sacrifice of your lips, and that not being accepted, then what is better [than] the offering of obedience which these first fruits do witness, being the oblation of your heart; *felix faustumque sit*, as was the issue of that parliament which concluded with King James and may be well styled happy, making a reconciliation between his Majesty and his subjects and a breach and dissolution of those treaties between his enemies and him. The hope and expectation thereupon is yet auspicious to our labors and the comfort then diffused from that garland of the crown, the King's prerogative, in the flowers that then descended, the bills of grace, cannot but yet affect us, especially if we take it from the true rise and ground, the labors and endeavors of his Majesty then here assisting us who acted [p. 23] not a little in that scene. This may assure us much of his future love to parliaments, his entrance and initiation

15. I.e., the King's response to the Speaker, traditionally delivered by the Lord Keeper.
16. Concerning Gilbertus, see H. of L., 20 June, n. 29. The wording of this paragraph of the *Negotium* is

very close to that recorded in Osborn fb 155 as the Lord Keeper's speech of approbation of the Speaker. See H. of L., 20 June, p. 37.

being such. He being then to that parliament made so happy as the soul in the body of a man, the life and glory of it, when he received such pleasure in this council as makes him still to love it.

For his entrance into government, his blood, his succession and his hopes, and that deliverance out of Spain, all speak him the son of hope and wonder. For what can give more to the satisfaction of his people than this first act of meeting and conference here with them? What can add more to the promise of his hopes than the virtue and nobility of his[17] stock, wherein he is more eminent than any prince in Christendom, having *deum in utroque parente,* as it is said, on both sides being extracted from a long descent of kings. How has his succession, in point of restitution to the kingdom, made up that breach which sorrow had enforced upon the loss of his dear father, which could not have been done by any but by him, nor by him if he had been but [p. 24] the son only of his body? Those abilities of his father's which are regnant in his soul, of which we have had experience, are a sufficient warrant for our hopes. And those hopes we have confirmed by his miraculous delivery out of Spain, which prove him as well the adopted son of God as the naturally begotten of King James. Divinity concurring with his wisdom, and giving that wisdom to him which could not be circumvented by their policy, a *noli me tangere.* I may term him one whom no human wit can deal with.

For religion, wherein, to the natural zeal and piety of his Majesty there has been added such a spur by the charge and blessing of his father, we need not doubt his tender care thereof, that principle being implanted in his heart. But as we have enjoyed under the sunshine of the gospel a long and rare felicity, so we shall still retain it under his princely providence and see our Jerusalem in prosperity all his life long.

Touching the common law, which worthily you commended as the fittest temper for this government, his Majesty is so indulgent to that [p. 25] rule as he recommends it to their studies who are professors of it to follow the ancient maxims, not resting on new cases, which are the fancies but of men, but to fetch their knowledge from the principles which were grounded first on reason and had their derivation from God's laws, in which they should want no favor from his Majesty who was most affectionate to the old, willing of reformation in the new, between which there is this difference besides their original and the time: that the conclusions of the latter are peremptory and severe, drawn from slight premises and inducements; whereas the others always have strong premises to induce them and yet such sweet conclusions as swayed by love, not force.

For the Palatinate and the restitution of our friends, Mr. Speaker, you cannot imagine how it contents his Majesty to see your care therein, by which the natural sympathy is expressed between the head and body. You, as the body, concurring with his Majesty, the head, in sense and participation of their miseries who are chief members [p. 26] of this kingdom. Nor can it be where such affections meet that the acts of Egypt, of Meroz, should be copied. Far be it here, for the honor of this nation, that it should now desert her friends, having been formerly so helpful unto strangers. And for his Majesty, I am to tell you this: that he desires not to live otherwise than in glory, and that cannot be without restitution of the Palatinate which, as it will be the whole endeavor of his Majesty, must likewise have your aids to second and supply him.

For the abandoning of those sons of Bi-

---

17. *the.* Printed edition.

chri,[18] the priests and Jesuits, which you move for, his Majesty both approves your religion and devotion and acknowledges with St. Augustine, that the poorest man on earth has as great interest in religion as the greatest prince or potentate. But, as princes were made keepers of both tables, so he desires to be trusted with this suit, which in fit time he will either grant or better it. Wherein, as his father said before him, he would be as careful and sincere as he prayed God to be merciful to him.

Lastly, Mr. Speaker, for those petitions you exhibited [p. 27] of freedom from arrests, liberty of speech, access upon occasion, and favorable construction of your actions, which are the four cornerstones of that noble building of your House, his Majesty grants them all without any bound or limitation more than your own wisdoms and modesties shall impose, not doubting but if any shall abuse this liberty which is granted, you will be more ready to punish and correct him than his Majesty to require it.

These speeches had divers censures with the hearers.[19] First by comparison and in general, wherein it was noted that the lawyer's expressions were divine, the divine's more historical and lawlike. Then in the Bishop[20] was observed, both for composition and delivery, study and affectation which the other did decline, who seemed more natural, not less eloquent. Either had those *igniculi sententiarum et flosculi ingeniorum* for his ornament. By the Bishop they were rendered to all satiety and fullness, as beauty set to sail, whereas the other made them like stars shining in the night,

admirabili quadam illuminatione sed umbram habens et recessum.

In particular of the Bishop's there were two things much observed, but with different affection and acceptance. [p. 28] The one was his insinuation to new ways and the fallacy therein used to intimate that all that is done by parliament is parliamentary, which had an ill relish and resent. The other was that passage in his answer for the privileges, terming them the cornerstones of the House; which having that expression in that presence was well liked, it being thereupon presumed in the opinion of the hearers that their future estimation should have answered it. But that discourse being formal, and no more, had not such influence on the act. States, as divines, use glosses on their texts. But, for the instant, satisfaction was pretended, and both Houses thereupon prepared them to their business.

[21 June 1625]

The Commons began with an act for observation of the sabbath and to prevent the abuses of that day which, being read for the honor of religion and to that end having the first precedence given it, further, to express the devotion of the House expecting all blessings from above.

The next thing that followed it was the desire of a communion, that all the members of that body might join and in that work of piety the better to unite them in themselves and reconcile them to their head.

[p. 29] And this religious motion was forthwith seconded by another for a day of

---

18. 2 Sam. 20:6. The reference is to St. Ambrose rather than St. Augustine in the L.J., above, p. 35. We are unable to find the source of the reference.

19. There are no remarks about these speeches included in the daily accounts of the session and we have found no comments in the extant correspondence of

the time to corroborate Eliot's statement. It is unclear whether Eliot was drawing on his memory or on letters he had access to at the time of his writing.

20. I.e., Lord Keeper John Williams, Bishop of Lincoln.

preparation to that work and a general humiliation to be made by a public fast in the kingdom, for which four reasons were assigned: 1, the miseries of the church abroad; 2, the plague and mortality at home; 3, the fleet and preparation then in hand; 4, the expectation of the parliament. To implore a blessing upon these, to deprecate the calamities of the others; which reasons were approved and the desires resolved on.

The communion was appointed for the Sunday sennight after, and a committee named to see that all performed it.

The private fast and preparation was to precede it on the Saturday.

Preachers were designed for both. And it was ordered for the general fast of the kingdom that a petition should be framed to move his Majesty therein.

Which acts of piety being resolved, they descended to the ordinary business of the House and, as the manner is, in the first place appointed a committee for their privileges, that being thought most necessary to precede, by which their powers and being did subsist. The intention of that committee, which is standing and not transient, [p. 30] has a general reflection on their rights; and, on all acts of prejudice that impeach them, to examine, to discuss them for the ease and information of the House, that there they may be punished or prevented. But the ordinary agitations which it has are for elections and returns, to rectify the obliquities therein, which are in all times many, in some more, whereof there wanted not a large proportion even in that.

Amongst others of that kind, the committee being settled, a petition was exhibited to the House against the return for Yorkshire.

The party complaining was Sir John Savile, his chief opposite then returned, Sir Thomas Wentworth; whose contestation in the country had been great, as their former emulation in that place, nor wanted they a reputation good in either, nor merit, if well exercised to support it. I mention here but that particular of Wentworth because the whole business turned on him, his colleague in that service being but passive in the work and so involved with him as what was accidental to the one was necessarily contingent to the other; for the quality and merit of their cause, the same virtue [p. 31] and the same fortune being to both.

For the present the petition was referred to the committee to be first heard and treated of.[21]

After this and some others of that kind, which had like reference from the House, an unexpected motion was delivered to decline the whole proceedings of that meeting, and to petition for an adjournment to the King. The reason pretended was the sickness, which had a great infection and increase. But most men did suppose that but the color and pretext and something more within it, which jealousy the sequel did confirm. It had its original from the north,[22] and by some other northern spirits was seconded who, after, practiced all the artifice of delay to defer the question of their knights and, since, have been declared so affected to themselves and to their own advancements that all consideration of justice and the public they postponed.

This proposition being on foot was so far pressed and followed upon the reasons and arguments given against it as the elect of Yorkshire came in particular to oppose the business propounded by the King, and for that urged the account that was behind for

---

21. Concerning the Yorkshire election, see H. of C., 21 June, n. 12. Eliot includes an additional section on the election, below, pp. 511–516.

22. See H. of C., 21 June, p. 207. William Mallory moved for the adjournment; his motion was seconded by Sir Robert Phelips and supported by Sir Thomas Wentworth and Christopher Wandesford. Mallory, Wentworth, and Wandesford served for Yorkshire constituencies. Concerning delays over settling the Yorkshire election case, see below, pp. 513–516.

the subsidies and fifteenths given [p. 32] in the former parliament, saying it was more necessary that that account were rendered than to require new aids.[23] To which it was replied, that nothing did let the account but that satisfaction might be had, and for the new demand, the time, the world, themselves might judge how far necessary it was and exceeding the terms of that comparison.

For the adjournment, it was objected to the contrary to the order of the House, which in the fast implied a resolution of their sitting, to which end was desired the public prayers of the Church to implore a blessing on their labors which, if they then declined, that act of devotion was in vain and the practice and profession were incongruous. The danger of the sickness was confessed and that balanced with the danger of the enemies, upon which David's example was induced for a direction in the case, that showed it better to fall into the righteous hands of God than into the wicked hands of men. Other reasons were added unto these, as, it being the first meeting with the King, the expectation great upon it; the reputation of much importance that should follow it, which, with the former, so swayed the sense of the House as, though new[24] names were used to [p. 33] turn it, seeking only an alteration of the place, not of the time and business, yet the motion was rejected as improper, and by some held ominous and portentous. These were the agitations of that day and the initiation of the business.

[22 June 1625]

The next (after the bill of the sabbath read again, when it received commitment) motion was made for the grand committee of the grievances, upon which there did arise a new trouble and dispute.

But before we proceed to that, I think it not unnecessary that we a little here insist upon that use and naming of committees which, being opened here, we shall the better know it elsewhere and so discern more easily, both in the execution and design, the scope and intention of those orders.

There are three grand committees consisting of the whole House, only the Speaker leaving the formality of his chair, which are permanent and standing and usually appointed in the beginning of the parliaments, for religion, grievances, and courts of justice.[25] These have their several weekly days assigned them, and take general cognizance of all [p. 34] matters, examine all complaints, send for all persons and records. All corruptions and injustices of courts, exactions of their ministers, oppressions of the people, abuses and enormities in the Church are, respectively, the subjects of their treaties. These they discuss and handle for the knowledge of the facts. And if they find them faulty, worthy a public judgment, thence they are reported to the House which thereupon proceeds to censure and determine them.

Private committees, which are transient and selected, of some few proportionable to the cause, have in their spheres and compass an equal power and interest. Those that are for bills on the second reading are designed, the first being only formal, when seldom or never they are spoken to but in point of rejection and denial, and that rarely, if there be color for the intention though there be imperfections in the draft. But at the second reading all objections do come in. The particulars both of the form and matter are then argued and debated and thereupon it passes to commitment where, by answer and reply, the discussion may be freer in the counterchange of reason and opinion (which is not admittable in

---

23. See the account of Phelips's speech in Bedford MS. 197, above, p. 210.

24. *noe*. Printed edition. Christopher Wandesford

was responsible for the new motion which was rejected. See H. of C., 21 June, O.B.

25. See H. of C., 22 June, n. 29.

the House where, to avoid [p. 35] contestation and disorder which replies and contradictions might induce, and to preserve the gravity, no man may speak in one day and to one business above once, though he would change opinion, which in committees is allowable) and therefore upon the second readings of these bills they have such reference and commitment that there they may the more punctually be considered and so come to the exacter reformation and amendment.[26]

In general, all committees are for preparation and dispatch, the judgment and conclusion is the House's. To facilitate that court in the multiplicity of her labors, these are the Argus and Briareus.[27] These committees are the sentinels upon all affairs and interests, and these dissolve the difficulties which their greatness or numbers do import.

According to these customs and reasons of the former, in this parliament it was moved likewise for the committee of the grievances, as we before observed it. Divers oppositions it received for divers interests and respects, public and private, wherein contraries did meet.[28] Some did dislike it for accident and circumstance, others simply and absolutely for itself, that it might have reflection on their errors who [p. 36] were conscious of a guilt, made these averments,[29] being obnoxious to the public; others that thought it not seasonable at that time to begin the question of those grievances, which could not then be perfected, for the more certain punishment of the offenders would have their cause reserved. Others were moved, in apprehension of the sickness, to decline that service for the dis-

mission of petitioners. Some had in contemplation the new entrance of the King, whose reign had not afforded opportunity for oppressions and should not therefore be dishonored with an aspersion of complaint. Others remembered the old grievances exhibited to King James in his last parliament, to which there had been no answer, and advised only to petition then for that.

But none of these reasons could prevail to compose the affection of the House, which to that committee for the grievances added likewise a desire of the other for religion, and therein urged the great danger and necessity upon the practice of the Jesuits, the insinuation of the priests, the exercise of the mass in despite, if not derision, of the laws, and the [p. 37] confidence and increase of papists thereupon, which plague and infection of the souls was far more to be feared than all the plagues and infections of the body. This, with the new occasion, stirred a new sense in the House and raised the arguments which did follow it to a more height and quickness, for allay whereof this catholicon, being prepared by that great artist Sir Benjamin Rudyard, was readily presented to the occasion, and in this form applied:

[SIR BENJAMIN RUDYARD.][30] Mr. Speaker, to say this is the first parliament of the King is no great matter, but that the first parliament of the King should have a temperate proceeding and propitious success is a matter of extraordinary consideration and consequence. For it is commonly seen that the same influence which governs in the beginning of an action infuses itself throughout

26. On the second reading and commitment of bills, see William Hakewill, "Orders of Passing of Bills in Parliament", B.L. Add. 8980, ff. 5–6.

27. Ovid, *Metamorphoses*, 1, 622–723; Hesiod, *Tregonea*, 1, 147–185.

28. Much of the following debate, placed by Eliot between Sir Thomas Hoby's motion for a committee of grievances and Sir Benjamin Rudyard's speech, ap-

pears in the daily accounts in speeches following that of Rudyard. See H. of C., 22 June, pp. 215–216, 220–221.

29. MS.: *avers*; *others* in the printed edition.

30. The text of Rudyard's speech included in Bedford MS. 197, above, H. of C., 22 June, p. 219, is the same, aside from some word variants, as that included in the *Negotium*.

and continues to the end, as in this particular of parliaments we have had too dear experience. Certainly the disagreement between the King, who is with God, and his people, begun and continued by mutual distastes in parliament, have been the cause almost of all [p. 38] that we can call amiss in this state. It was the King which now is who first gave the happy turn in the last, wherein I may truly say there descended more grace from the crown to the subject than in any parliament some hundreds of years before; and I may rehearse, though not object, that we also did our duties. If his Majesty when he was Prince and had but a mediating interest did us so many good offices, so many gracious favors, what may we expect now that he is King and has absolute power in his own hands? We may well trust him whom we have so well tried, especially seeing he gives us daily new arguments of his goodness and wisdom. How publicly and frequently he avows and justifies his own, the true religion, with discountenance to the false; how effectually this devotion of his works upon his life. Insomuch as I may strictly say there can hardly be found a private man of his years so free from all ill which, as it is more rare and difficult [p. 39] in the person of a king, so is it more exemplary and extensive in the operation and, no doubt, being a blessing in itself, will call down more blessings from heaven upon this kingdom for his sake.

For his wisdom, we see that in his particular actions he is naturally regular and orderly which, however some retired abstruse spirits may account but a formality, yet wise men know how much it conduces to wealth, to greatness, to government, order being indeed the very soul of outward things. Besides, his breeding has given him an advantage above all the kings in Christendom. For he has been abroad and has treated with a wise and subtle nation in a business so great as himself was the subject of it, which has not only opened and enlarged but quickened and sharpened his natural abili-

ties and made him understand his own kingdom the better. For to know a man's own country alone is but a solitary kind of knowledge in [p. 40] respect of knowing it by comparison with others.

But that which is of most use and application to us is that he has been bred in parliaments, which has made him not only to know but to favor the ways of his own subjects, whereof it becomes us always to have a grateful remembrance.

Upon these foundations, Mr. Speaker, I will humbly move this honorable House in that wherein I hope we all come hither prepared and moved in ourselves, that is to carry ourselves in this first session with sweetness, with duty, with confidence in and towards his Majesty; for which no doubt we shall respectively receive such grace, such favor, such satisfaction as the dangerousness of the time and therefore the shortness of it can possibly allow. Towards the happy effecting whereof I do further move that we may fall upon such things only as are necessary, clear, and of dispatch. And that those businesses which have in them either perplexity, difficulty, or asperity, if the House be not [p. 41] pleased altogether to omit them, yet they may be only touched by way of claim or grievance and so remitted to the next session when we shall have fitter opportunity and better leisure to debate them.

Last of all, to take off the least scruple of prejudice which misinterpretation may cast upon me, I do here solemnly protest that as heretofore I did never speak with King, Prince, or favorite of parliament business, so with our present King I never had the honor to speak forty words of any purpose whatsoever. Insomuch as what I have said I have spoken it out of the sincerity of my own heart, without any other end but the good of the commonwealth, whereof this assembly is the abridgement.

This oration in much gravity delivered, with the length and expectation that it carried, had so much of the effect as it reduced to temper the affection that was stirred. All men's intentions still went with it to observe the conclusions it would make. A great reputation was implied both in the learning and wisdom of the man. And, as [p. 42] he was in use and estimation with some great ones,[31] more was expected from him than from others, which made the satisfaction to seem less and those that were more critical to adjudge his composition more studied than exact. All men discerned in him no want of affection to be eloquent. But his expression was thought languid as the conclusion was inept, generals being fitter for discourse than in counsel or debate.

Yet so far this prevailed, or else the time by that, as the resolution was deferred to a further consideration and dispute and so the present heat declined,[32] which is observable in that House as their whole story gives it: that, wherever that mention does break off the fears or dangers in religion and the increase of popery, their affections are much stirred; and whatever is obnoxious in the state, it then is reckoned as an incident to that. For so it followed upon the agitation of that motion: first, the danger of religion was observed in some general notes of prejudice; then, by induction, it was proved in the enumeration of particulars. To that was urged the infelicities of the kingdom since that disease came in. [p. 43] This had an aggregation by a syncrisis and comparison with the days of Queen Elizabeth. To that was added the new grievances and oppressions wholly inferred and raised since the connivance with the pa-

pists: the monopolies that had been, the impositions that then were, all were reduced to this. Which I mention but to show the apprehension in that point, and the affection of that House in matter of religion.

[23 June 1625]

The next day was begun with a conference of both Houses upon the petition for the fast.[33] At the conference the Commons did present a draft of the petition and their reasons with a motion to the Lords for their concurrence in the work who, by that reverend father of the Church, the Archbishop of Canterbury, returned this answer and reply: That they approved both their intention and their reasons, and were therein ready to assist them. But withal, out of a text in Joel, gave them such a caution and advice against private undertakings of that kind as upon their return unto their House the former day was altered and some time given for expectation in that point.

[p. 44] After this the dispute of religion was resumed, wherein some introduction being made, it was thus followed for preparation and advice.

[Sir John Eliot.][34] Religion is the touchstone of all actions, the trial by which they are known, upon which all policy, all wisdom, all excellence must be grounded; and what rests not on this center can have no perfection or assurance. For what the power of man is, without God, or what, without religion, may be expected from His

---

31. Rudyard, surveyor of the Court of Wards, was a friend of William Herbert, Earl of Pembroke, Steward and Chancellor of the Household, and of numerous literary figures. *D.N.B.*; J. A. Manning, ed., *Memoirs of Sir Benjamin Rudyerd, Knt.* (London, 1841), pp. 18–23.

32. At the end of Rudyard's speech, Bedford MS. 197 (above, p. 220) states that: *The rest of the morning was spent in considering what to do rather than in doing anything.* After some debate the House resolved that they would meet as a committee the following morning to consider

the various propositions and what course to take this parliament.

33. The conference was not begun until mid-morning, after other matters of business had been dealt with in the Lower House. See above, H. of C., 23 June, O.B.

34. The following speech appears to be a fuller, more formal version of Eliot's opening speech on religion at the afternoon committee of the whole House than that recorded in the Committee Book (23 June, H. of C., p. 230).

favor, His own words and stories do sufficiently declare. Religion only it is that fortifies all policy, that crowns all wisdom, that is the grace of excellence, the glory of all power. The strength of all government is religion; for though policy might secure a kingdom against foreigners (and so I pray God this kingdom may always stand secure) and wisdom provide all necessaries for the rule and government at home; yet, if religion season not the affections of the people, the danger is as much in our own Ahithophel[35] as of Moab and all the armies [p. 45] of Philistines.[36] Religion it is that keeps the subject in obedience, as being taught by God to honor his vicegerents. A *religando* it is called, as the common obligation amongst men, the tie of all friendship and society, the bond of all office and relation writing every duty in the conscience, which is the strictest of all laws. Both the excellence and necessity hereof the heathens knew that knew not true religion, and therefore in their politics they had it always for a maxim. A shame it were for us to be therein less intelligent than they, and if we truly know it we cannot but be affectionate in this case.

Two things are considerable therein: the purity, the unity thereof; the first respecting only God, the other both God and man, for where there is division in religion as it does wrong divinity it makes distractions amongst men and so dissolves all ties and obligations, civil and natural, the observation of heaven being more powerful than either policy or blood. For the purity of religion in this place I need not speak, seeing how beautiful [p. 46] the memories of our fathers are therein made by their endeavors. For the unity, I wish posterity might say we had preserved for them that which was left to us. But a disease once entered, though it be past prevention, must have cure; and as the danger or infection be-

comes greater, the greater care and diligence must oppose it.

What divisions, what factions, nay what fractions in religion this kingdom does now suffer I need not recapitulate. What diversions, what transactions, what alienations have been made no man can be ignorant. How many members in that point have been dissected from this body (I mean the body of the land, which representatively we are) so as the body itself, though healthy, cannot but seem lame? How have those members studied to be incorporated with others? How have they threatened us, their own, not only by presumption but in greatness and given us fear,[37] more than they have taken? Blessed be that hand that has delivered us; blessed this day that gives us hope wherein the danger and infection may be stayed. For without present [p. 47] remedy the disease will scarce be curable.

To effect this the cause must first be sought from where this sickness springs, and that will be best found in the survey of the laws; for certainly it lies in the law, or execution. Either there is some defect or imperfection in the laws or their life, the execution, is remitted. For if the laws be perfect how can division enter but by a breach of them? If the execution be observed how can the laws be broken? Therefore in this does rest the cause and here must be the remedy.

To that end now my motion shall incline for a review of the laws and a special consideration in that point. That if the division have got in by imperfection of the laws, they may be amended; if by defect, that may be supplied; if, as I most do fear it, through neglect and want of execution, the power may be enforced with some great mulct and penalty on the ministers who, for that, will be more vigilant and we thereby secure.

This speech gave occasion for a general

---

35. 2 Sam. 15:12, 31, passim.
36. Cf. Judg. 3:29–31; 2 Sam. 8:1–2.

37. *far*. Printed edition.

consideration [p. 48] of the laws wherein it was confessed there was a sufficiency and fulness but the want of execution did impair it and both detract from the power and reputation of the laws. In this divers particulars were instanced, some to prevent, some to corrupt the laws.

In some there was observed to be *fraus legis*, a cozenage of the law, and that four[38] ways affected. First, by dependence on great men which were a terror to informers and without them no delinquents could be found. Secondly, by changing names and appellations, practiced both by papists, priests, and Jesuits who, by the often shift of places, so did avoid indictments. Thirdly, by procuring informations against themselves which they could press or stop, and so preventing others in the like manner, as a *supersedeas* for the peace. Fourthly, by *certioraries* removing the indictments from the countries so as no prosecutor should be found, and so no more proceeding.

And in others there was noted to be *fraus contra legem*, an abuse and cozenage of the King for [*sic*] what the law allowed him. And of this likewise there were four ways described. First, by removing of their goods into privileged and free [p. 49] places so as no forfeiture could be levied.[39] Then, by begging of such forfeitures by those about the King who intended not the punishment but favor of the papists. Thirdly, by letters procured in their behalf for stop and prohibition of proceedings. And lastly, by the pardons which too frequently were granted not only to recusants but to Jesuits. All which did hinder the execution of the laws and rendered them fruitless in that point, and were designed for causes of that disease and sickness.

Examples were cited of all these to warrant their reasons and opinions, whereof it was thought necessary there should be a true information to the King and an address and petition to reform them. For a preparation to that work the Clerk was appointed to bring in all the petitions of that kind which formerly had been made, at the next sitting, unto which the further consideration was referred.[40]

[24 June 1625]

The next day some committees of both Houses having attended on the King reported his answer to the petition for the fast, which was: that as he liked their method in beginning with devotion, so he did hope their proceedings would be answerable. That he approved of the desire [p. 50] and, after consultation with the bishops, would give it execution.

From this again, some few bills being read and that of the sabbath, upon the third reading, passed for law, the Commons resumed again the consideration of religion and in that part began where they had left it last. The former petitions were then read, which had been exhibited in 18 and 21 *Jac.*, with the protestation of the Prince made then upon the sense of his deliverance out of Spain. From which, and [from] the disputes that had been past, there was a committee then appointed to frame a new petition to the King.

[28 June 1625]

The Lords about this time having resolved upon their fast, by message did intimate their time and place to the Commons, who thereupon determined for themselves likewise to have the same day appointed. And to strengthen in this service their correspondence by the place, one church being not capable of both Houses, as the Lords did take the Abbey, they chose the

---

38. *former.* Printed edition.

39. *served.* Printed edition.

40. Although on 23 June Sir Robert Phelips proposed in the committee meeting that the former petitions against recusants be brought in, we find no other evidence of an actual order to that effect. See H. of C., 23 June, p. 231. The petitions were read in the committee of the whole House on 24 June (see H. of C., p. 242).

parish church at Westminster, in which their communions were before, and now their first of fasts.

[30 June 1625]

These points of religion thus disposed which by [p. 51] a former order of the House were to have clear precedence before all things, the proposition was admitted for supply. Some art there was to extenuate the proportion, and therefore it was begun by a gentleman of the country who,[41] unexpected to the courtiers, falling on that subject and pitching on a particular of one subsidy and fifteenth, all their rhetoric and labor could hardly thence remove it; but the inclination of the House still resorted to that principle.

Again here SIR BENJAMIN RUDYARD was employed who, but at such times and in such services, did speak never but premeditated, which had more show of memory than affection and made his words less powerful than observed. He did deduce his reason for the enlargement of the aid from the occasions and necessities of the state. These he enforced by the domestic charge of the King, the funeral of his father, the entertainment of ambassadors, the foreign expenses and engagements to Denmark, Mansfeld, and the States, besides [p. 52] his own[42] preparations then for war. All which he said required a vast supply of treasure and that must have its magazine in the people. No particular sum he instanced, which made his reasons less successful and so, in that respect, his labor was in vain.

Yet divers others followed him and in divers ways and motions. Some would have an addition of fifteenths, others of subsidies, and there were that pressed for both, but in little they prevailed. The pitch being set at first was not so easily exceeded. Yet

the *quindecima*, thought grievous to the poor, changed the proposition in that part, which was concluded in the whole for two subsidies alone.

[SIR ROBERT PHELIPS.] To endear both the proportion and the gift divers circumstances were observed of force and aggravation. First, the time, it being then but the beginning of a parliament, whereas supply was anciently a work of the conclusion. Then that the grant itself intended was of that value as not four kings of England ever had the like. Then that the condition of the people through the many violations [p. 53] of their rights in the general liberties of the kingdom, the particular privileges of that House, their burdens, their oppressions (which no times else could parallel) spoke them less able; and that complaint postponed, showed them more affectionate. Then, that there was no engagement to induce it, as many had supposed, upon the declaration of the last parliament of King James, that promise being made for supportation of a war and yet there being no knowledge of an enemy. Again, the former grant was spoken of for which there had been no reckoning.

And thereon, by way of question, it was digressed to consider what account was answerable for the many thousand men that had perished and been lost in the Palatinate and with Mansfeld; the millions of treasure that was spent, without success in profit or honor to the kingdom, which was noted not to be England's fate when God and it were friends; and for that the glories of Queen Elizabeth were instanced who, with less supplies and aids, increased herself at home, wasted her enemies abroad [p. 54] consumed Spain, raised the Low Countries, relieved[43] France. Upon all which it was desired that there might be a petition to the King to move him to consideration of those

---

41. I.e., Sir Francis Seymour.

42. I.e., Charles's. On these charges, see the report of the Lord Treasurer's account of the King's estate, above, H. of L., pp. 166–168.

43. *revived*. Printed edition.

things and to reform the government then at his entrance and beginning by the like counsel and advice; which petition and remonstrance would tell him from those reasons how affectionate was that grant. And it was added by him that so deduced it, that he was so far from augmentation as he would have no man heard to move it.

This[44] being rendered by Sir Robert Phelips with a great life and eloquence moved much in the apprehension of the House both for the settling of that question and the reflection of the times. The present poverty was felt in the general necessities of the country. The cause of that was known to be the grievances and oppressions. The loss of men, loss of honor, loss of money, the late infortunities of King James were too obvious and undoubted, as the contrary felicities of Queen Elizabeth, so as all men of themselves saw the present want of counsel, and some resolved, in time, more specially to complain it.

There was in this gentleman [p. 55] a natural grace of oratory, a moving and Nestorian way of rhetoric. A choice store he had and elegance of words, readiness and dexterity in fancy and conception, a voice and pronunciation of much sweetness. The whole expression, *profluens et canora;* but, as some judged of Cicero, by some thought in him to be *tumens et exsultans.* A redundancy and exuberance he had, and an affected cadence and delivery. But upon all occasions, at all times, *ex re nata,* he was rendered, which made his arguments as more genuine and particular, so more acceptable and persuasive. For in that place always premeditation is an error, all speech of composition and exactness being supposed *ex ore non a pectore;* and those children of the mouth only are not so much affecting as the true issues of the heart. This spell was a

charm upon the courtiers to suppress their further craving. Yet something was added by the rest for the improvement of this gift: that the recusants should pay double which, after some small lets, was likewise accorded and concluded on, whereof the acceptation and success shall be noted in their orders.

[1 July 1625]

[p. 56] That great work being done, an account was represented from the Archbishop of Canterbury of his proceedings with Montagu upon the reference of that House in the last parliament of King James which was,[45] that having convented him before him and told him of the troubles he had caused and what disturbance was grown in the Church and in the parliament by his book, he gave him this advice: Be occasion of no scandal; go home, review your book. It may be some things have slipped you, which upon second cogitations you will reform. If anything be said too much, take it away; if anything too little, add unto it; if anything be obscure, explain it; but do not wed yourself to your own opinion, and remember we must give account of our ministry to Christ. With which admonition being dismissed, it was said, he heard no more of him for a long time after till one day, going to attend upon the King, he came suddenly upon him and presented him *in cursu,* as it were, his second book. For which being shortly questioned, as the place and time permitted, of that boldness and neglect, he made a slight answer and departed.

This carriage [p. 57] and report were diversely interpreted and received. Some did wonder at the insolence of Montagu that he dared so affront the dignity of that father; for it was held no less, instead of a retraction for the former, to present a second

---

44. I.e., the speech described by Eliot in the two preceding paragraphs.

45. The Archbishop, being ill, was unable to attend the parliament House and consequently Sir Dudley

Digges took his deposition in writing and read it to the Lower House. See above, H. of C., 1 July, O.B. and n. 4. Concerning Montagu, see H. of C., 7 July, n. 3.

book in confirmation of the other for which he had been questioned, and to publish it with[out] the knowledge of the Archbishop.

Others did think it strange, the lenity of the Archbishop, that he would pass unpunished such an indignity to his place, his person likewise being injured in the fact. But those that looked more narrowly conceived one reason for both these, and both that boldness in the one and remissness of the other by command. Again the admonition given, though grave, was neither repressive nor directing, being but made in generals, and that by way of supposition and hypothesis, which hardly answered the expectation that was had. But this also was imagined the same power and[46] influence had wrought. King James was known then secretly to support him. The Archbishop did confess that he was twice with [p. 58] the King sent for in that business which, being opened, few men did after doubt by whom that scene was made. Yet it seemed strange to some that King James should so affect him, his doctrines being opposed to the decisions made at Dort, and that Synod being so honored by the King of which he assumed the patronage and so much gloried in it.[47] This man being opposite, *ex diametro*, to that, and his books likewise casting divers aspersions on the King as will hereafter be observed, many did wonder how these things could agree, which, as a secret rested upon a higher principle.

But this report being made, the House again resumed the cognizance of that matter to themselves, and referred the examinations of the books to the committee for religion.

This passed the first day of July.

[4 July 1625]

The fourth, the King's SOLICITOR did exhibit an answer to the grievances formerly complained of to King James which, because they do express much of reason of that time and the inclination of the state, we will particularly here insert them, as we have done the grievances elsewhere, noting only but the heads that were complained of for the better illustration of their answers.

[*For the grievances and answers, see above, H. of C., 4 July, pp. 301–305.*][48]

[p. 64] Divers exceptions were made at many of these answers and little satisfaction upon all. But the occasion and complaint being of former time this was accepted for the present, though the hope and expectation which was had from thenceforth did decline.

The sickness was then risen to a great infection and mortality, no part of the City did stand free. [p. 65] Divers fell dead down in the streets. All companies and places were suspected which made all men willing to remove, and those of the parliament more ready to shorten and expedite their business.

To that end the petition for religion was then speeded and imparted in a conference to the Lords, who therein concurring as the mutual act of both, it was in this form presented to the King.

[*For the petition concerning religion, see above, H. of L., 9 August, pp. 155–160.*][49]

---

46. *of.* Printed edition.

47. Concerning the Synod of Dort, 1619, see above, H. of C., 7 July, p. 331 and nn. 8 and 54.

48. The list of the heads of the grievances of 1624 and King Charles's answers to them in the *Negotium* MS. (pp. 59–64) is virtually the same as that in Bedford MS. 197 (above, pp. 301–305); therefore the editors have not reprinted it here. Concerning the list, see

above, H. of C., 4 July, n. 46.

49. The Lords this day (4 July) proposed alterations to the petition concerning religion (see H. of C., above, pp. 298–299 and 305–306) which were approved by the Commons and the petition was then presented to the King on 8 July. Eliot includes a copy of the completed petition at this point in his narrative. In order to avoid repetition the editors have excised it.

[p. 75] This petition was presented by a committee of both Houses consisting of the number of [*blank*] of the Lords and [*blank*] of the Commons,[50] who in all such special meetings and committees always observe that difference; that whatever the number be of Lords their proportion is still double it, which is a fundamental order of their House not without wisdom in the institution so appointed, not with[out] profit, practiced on all occasions and, as it was at other times, so followed now in this. The petition being delivered had no answer for the present,[51] but a benign [p. 76] gracious acceptation. The rest, as it was requisite for the state and majesty of the prince and for the weight and importance of the cause, that some time of consideration should be given it. Being referred to hope and expectation, all men were therein satisfied that the work was so accomplished, and for success, some men presumed the best.

The next thing which remained was the bill for the two subsidies that were given, which likewise being passed the House of Commons, and that intimated to the King, it produced a message from his Majesty which shortly after followed it, that gave a general hope and confidence of a speedy conclusion and recess.[52]

The message was delivered by the Lord Keeper, the King being then retired to Hampton Court from the danger of the infection, and it came as addressed to both Houses: That his Majesty received great satisfaction and contentment in their gift, both for the form and matter, it coming as an earnest of their loves. That he took into consideration their safeties, yea, more than his own in respect of the danger of the sickness still increasing. And that, when he should hear the Commons were ready, though he would not hasten them in anything, he would not defer one minute for any other reason to put an end to [p. 77] that sitting, by his presence or otherwise.

This message and the time wrought so effectually with all men, as what they desired they easily did believe, and thereupon disposed themselves presently to retire.

Their grant they saw accepted, and all things left to the discretion of the House.[53]

The business then depending was not much, new they presumed would not be received. Those few questions that remained were of no great importance and most of them but formal, so as they now conceived no necessity of their presence and that their nonattendance was dispensable. In this confidence the greatest part went off. Hardly were the Commons a fourth part of their number, and those that stayed resolved, with all the haste they could, to follow those were gone. To that end they took a survey of their business.

[5 July 1625]
In the first rank they placed the bill of tonnage and poundage, which then remained imperfect; and to this they gave the

50. Concerning the membership of the committee of both Houses, see above, H. of C., 8 July, p. 349 and n. 22.
51. A short answer to the petition was given by the King at its presentation on 8 July and was reported to Commons on 9 July; the longer, formal answer was delivered by the Duke of Buckingham at a meeting of both Houses on 8 August. See the report of the 8 August meeting, above, H. of L., 9 August, pp. 155–160.
52. The subsidy bill received its first reading in the Lower House on 4 July but was not passed by the House until 8 July, the same day that the petition concerning religion was presented to the King. Eliot's

summary of the message in the following paragraph appears to be a conflation of the King's response to the passage of the subsidy bill, reported to the House by Sir John Coke on 8 July (see above, p. 347), and of the message from the King concerning ending the session, reported to the Lords by Lord Keeper Williams on 4 July (see H. of L., 4 July, O.B.) and relayed to the Commons at the afternoon conference of 4 July (see H. of C., 4 July, pp. 298, 305).
53. Presumably Eliot is referring to the passage of the subsidy when he speaks of "their grant". See above, n. 52.

first consideration for dispatch, and so a second reading. It was drawn in the usual form, as formerly it had been in the days of King James for the like term of life, and in such latitude as to him. At which some exceptions were then made, and motions for change and alteration. Upon which [p. 78] it was referred for the better discussion and debate to the grand committee of the House, into which, the Speaker leaving his chair, they presently resolved themselves.[54]

Some did object in that the exactions of the officers and the inequality of the customs then required, and urged thereon a necessity for the merchants to have a new Book of Rates to settle and compose it, which could not be prepared in so short a time and sitting. Others alleged the pretermitted customs, grounded upon the misconstruction of that law, which ought to be examined likewise, and the laws that then remained were thought to be incapable of that work.

Therefore on these reasons they inferred a desire for a limitation in the act, and that it might but continue for one year, against which time these difficulties being resolved they might again renew it with a larger extension and continuance. Others to this added the question of impositions in the general and craved a special care not to have that excluded. The elder times were mentioned to note the former grants, wherein though there were collected a great variety and difference, yet all were within the limitation of some years; sometimes for one, sometimes for two, [p. 79] but seldom above three, and that in the best reigns and governments and to the wisest princes. Never for life till towards the end of H. 6 in whose beginnings also it had

other limitations and restraints, and for the time a less extent and latitude.

Upon which likewise it was concluded for a present alteration in that point. The King's Council opposed this with much solicitation and endeavor, and urged the distaste it might occasion having so many descents held constant in that form: all the reign of King James, all the reign of Queen Elizabeth and so to Queen Mary, E. 6, H. 8, H. 7, and beginning in that reign, not the most deserving of all others, of H. 6. The hopes and merits of the King were compared with all his ancestors and it was pressed as a prejudice therein if the grant should then be limited, having been absolute to the others. It was consented that a proviso should be added for the saving of those rights. But in other things it was craved wholly to be free, that the King might not think himself lessened in estimation. This argument was much forced for the persuasion of the House, as after it was doubted to be elsewhere made their prejudice. But it prevailed not against those other considerations that were raised, upon [p. 80] which it was concluded for a limitation and restraint.

The bill thus passed that House had its transition to the Lords, where it received like favor and dispatch but was not made a law, wanting the "*Roy le vult*", which being denied it, showed what must be looked for.[55]

[Yorkshire Election]

The next to this was the great question that was followed of the election made for Yorkshire. It had from the first day of the sitting been in continual agitation till that time. Divers examinations and debates it

54. Eliot summarizes below the issues concerning the bill of tonnage and poundage discussed in the House on the morning of 5 July (see above, H. of C., 5 July, pp. 313–314 and 317–318). For further debate on the bill, see above, H. of C., 5–7 July, O.B.s.

55. The bill for tonnage and poundage was not passed in the Lower House until 8 July (see above, H. of C., 8 July, O.B.) and was not received by the Lords until 9 July (see above, H. of L., 9 July, O.B.), when it was read once. Contrary to Eliot's remarks, the bill made no further progress in the Upper House this session.

had received in the committee,[56] several reports and motions in the House, a great disturbance it had been to the whole business of either. A fiery[57] spirit it raised almost in all the members: some in affection to the parties, who had drawn an inclination to their side, if it may be supposed in the integrity of that court; and others in dislike of the practice that was used. That by sharp arguments it had many times been handled, which from the cause had now and then some sallies on the persons and there begot distastes.

The case, in short, was this: There being a great emulation in the country for that choice, a great concourse followed [p. 81] it at the county court in York. The confusion being great, through the multitude of voices, there was no way of judgment by the cry, and the view[58] was more uncertain. The poll, which is the touchstone in such cases, was the only means of trial; which being demanded by Savile and his friends, granted by the sheriff, and followed in a part, was after interrupted and left off, and the judgment and decision made without it. This was the case in brief. Upon which it was objected that the sheriff was wholly Wentworth's; that he neglected in his favor that duty of his place to have proceeded in the poll when he discerned and saw Savile was like to carry it; that being demanded it at first, with much difficulty he admitted it, and pretended it a courtesy not a due; that contrary to all right, having assumed the judgment to himself, he pronounced the choice for Wentworth, whereas the other

had more voices, double as was pretended. This suggestion and complaint was fortified by certificate from the country under the hands of a hundred and fifty of the freeholders;[59] and seven witnesses, *viva voce*, did attest it.

Infinite had been the practices [p. 82] of the others to decline this cause and question. Divers delays were used to prevent it by the time; all the arts which northern policy could invent to gain advantage in the carriage, which by the other[60] were opposed with no less care and diligence, who, knowing those paths of subtlety, followed the hunter in his train and, being more beaten to the way, in his own traps ensnared him.

At the first hearing it was pretended by the elect[61] that the complaint was only of the sheriff, and he therefore must justify his fact. To that end was desired a time for his appearance to make his apology and defense. That being granted, fortnight was spent therein for expectation of his coming who, affecting not the service, made no haste. Being at the length convented, he answered negatively to some things, dilatorily to others, uncertainly to all; that little truth could be gathered from his words, less content and satisfaction from himself. He utterly denied Savile's pretense of voices and, on the contrary, affirmed that in his judgment the other had far more. For the difficulty in granting of the poll, he excused it by a reason of the time and said it was past eleven before the demand was made.

---

56. The matter of the Yorkshire election was reported from the committee of privileges on 22 June and 4 July and was discussed in the House on 4 July and resolved on 5 July. See H. of C., 22 June, 4 and 5 July, O.B.s. Eliot compiled all of the Commons' action on the issue, along with his own remarks, into one section, below, pp. 512–516.

57. *fierce*. Printed edition.

58. *veni*. Printed edition.

59. In the accounts of More's committee report of 22 June, the figure given for the number of subscribers to the freeholders' petition varies between 1050 and 1450. See above, H. of C., 22 June, p. 217 and

n. 16.

60. I.e., Sir John Savile, whom Wentworth refers to in one of his letters as "the old fox" (William Knowler, ed., *The Earl of Strafforde's Letters and Dispatches* [London, 1739], I, 32).

61. I.e., Sir Thomas Wentworth. Concerning arrangements for the sheriff's appearance, see above, H. of C., 22 June, pp. 217 and 218. According to More's report of 4 July, the sheriff was heard by the committee on Saturday, 25 June, and the sheriff's counsel was heard on Tuesday, 28 June. See above, H. of C., 4 July, p. 295.

For the interruption, he confessed it was done as was alleged, five and thirty [p. 83] being numbered it was proceeded in no further; but the occasion he imputed unto Savile, and that for two reasons. First, whereas for the more perfect carriage of the poll, the freeholders which were present at the reading of the writ were all drawn into the castle yard and there enclosed between the gates, those that were sworn and numbered being let out at the postern, which was done to avoid confusion and disorder and the abuse of such as might at several times present themselves and so diversely be reckoned. Savile in this proceeding breaking open one of the gates let in divers of his party that were newly come and heard not the reading of the writ who, as he thought, had no interest in the election but were a disturbance to the course and due order they were in. The second reason was that Savile, raising a report amongst the freeholders that the poll would last divers days, gave thereby such a disheartening to the company as, the gates before being opened, many did depart for fear of long attendance. Which, being known, he conceived it to be an interruption to the work, upon that left off the poll and, as in a case of much clearness, as he thought, on the behalf of Wentworth, both by the view and hearing, [p. 84] he assumed the judgment to himself; for confirmation of all which he desired a new liberty for proofs.

This again made another protraction and delay which was an advantage of some hope. The charge of the prosecutor in attendance made some satisfaction in the point. The daily increase of the sickness shortened the expectation of the sitting. All the employments of the parliament were contracted for dispatch, which promised more than usual haste and brevity and therein was implied a possibility to preserve

them. A high affection was discernible in this point; and for this only was that prodigious motion the first day.[62] So much corrupted are some hearts in the sense of their particulars as for their private humors all public interests are postponed.

This delay, being granted, brought forth nothing but another. When that liberty was expired, no witnesses appearing for the sheriff, the elect then interposes for himself. Liberty on his part was then required also for defense, and a new time for witnesses, pretending great confidence in his right; and alleging that the sheriff, being faulty in his proofs, ought not to prejudice his cause, but as the other had, so to him belonged a hearing.

[p. 85] Much trouble this occasioned in the deliberation of the House. Some did object the clearness of the proof which the other side had produced being affirmative and particular. And that the poll being demanded in due time and interrupted by the sheriff, though the major part of voices might be doubtful, was enough to void the election and return, though it concluded not another; and therefore they might with safety pass to judgment.

Others to the interruption did allege that the excuse was insufficient; for no man was compellable to be present at the election, all had free liberty to depart. Again, no power might be supposed to force an interruption on a sheriff, who had the whole power of the county; therefore in that respect there was no reason to delay.

WENTWORTH to this makes a protestation for himself, but by more heard than credited; that he affected not delay in contemplation of himself, but desired only legally to be heard, and that for the honor of the House.[63] He urged therefore, after a large narration of his cause, that it might be either granted or denied. If granted, that

62. I.e., Mallory's motion of the first day of parliament business (21 June), after the set opening speeches (18 and 20 June), to adjourn the House in

respect of the plague. See above, *Negotium*, p. 500 and n. 22, and see also, H. of C., 21 June, O.B.

63. See Wentworth's speech, H. of C., 4 July, O.B.

he might have counsel to defend it; if otherwise, that by witnesses he might prove it; which, being the common rule of justice, he expected in that court and should [p. 86] therein accordingly apply himself.

This being seconded and enforced, drew on an order for that time, that he should state his case in writing, deliver it to his adversary, and he at the next sitting to give his answer thereupon.[64] This, though desired, was no satisfaction unto Wentworth, who came unwillingly so near the determination of the question, and that but to prevent the present decision which he feared. He would fain have kept at distance upon the points of examination and defense. Delay and procrastination was his hope; many things by that might occur to work his safety; divers are the intervenients of time. The remoteness of his witnesses was a fair pretext for this, if that occasion had been granted him. But now that opportunity depending upon the discretion of his adversary, his hopes therein were lessened and what he had moved himself, himself again repented.

But the direction must be followed and the case set down in writing which, being given to Savile, he forthwith resorted to the House and there desired in some few things a hearing. Being admitted,[65] he made a short apology for himself upon the trouble of that cause, that it had so long [p. 87] been an interruption to their business. That though he had small time for consideration of the case, as it was then in writing, it being delivered him but late the night before; yet he did then accept it for conclusion of the work and to prevent their further trouble in the business. Two things only he desired: that the paper which was given him without name might by his adversary be subscribed

and that he might avow, upon his reputation in that House, so much as concerned his knowledge to be true and that the rest he thought so.

This begot new difficulties in Wentworth who then suspected the issue of his arts. Nothing he first doubted less than admission of his case, supposing the jealousy of his adversary would have made him fight at distance. But he that was his countryman and his equal, seeing the advantage readily, closed presently upon him in that grant and by concession of the case, surprised and so disarmed him. Then again he would have flown off to delay and desired his witnesses might be heard to prove the plurality of voices, which was denied him by the other.[66] But the question being stated by himself, and that depending merely upon the demand and interruption of the poll, the other was impertinent. Wherefore his protestation was required which, though unwillingly, [p. 88] was made and the House went on to judgment.

Nothing did differ in this case from what was pretended by the sheriff. The interruption objected unto Savile was but upon the rumor he gave out, or for the opening of the gate. The demand supposed unseasonable appeared otherwise by the proofs and was implicitly confessed by the practice of the sheriff. Whereon some opinions being given that did declare against him, a new motion interposed for his counsel to be heard, and so diverted that course of resolution. Much opposition was in this, the question being of fact; a great contestation it begot, even to the division of the House; upon which it being overruled and the debate resumed again, a new interruption it received by a new motion for himself once more to be heard before they went to judgment. Great labor was for this, and as

---

64. See the resolution of the House, H. of C., 4 July, O.B., that the particulars of the case be set down in writing by Wentworth and the sheriff and be delivered to Sir John Savile.

65. Sir John Savile was brought into the House on 5 July. See above, H. of C., 5 July, O.B.

66. See Wentworth's first speech of 5 July, above, H. of C., 5 July, O.B.

great care to stop it, intending but delay. Against him was objected the long time he had had from the beginning of the parliament, the often hearing he received at the committee, in the House, where his whole defense was known. That before he was withdrawn to give way to the debate, as in all such cases it was usual, he had a full liberty to express himself and his whole apology was heard. [p. 89] Nothing could be added but protraction, which would be a further injury to the House and therefore was not to be admitted or received. Upon this it was so resolved and the debate proceeded. When contrary to the fundamental orders of the House, by which no man may be present at the agitation of his own cause, Wentworth came in confidently to his place and gave occasion to him that was then speaking to make this sally on that fact and from the question then in hand to reflect upon the privilege, which thus was done for the preservation of that jewel.

[SIR JOHN ELIOT.][67] Mr. Speaker, the violation of our rights may be well excused by others when they suffer violation by ourselves. When our own members practice it, when they shall do it in contempt, in the height of scorn and injury, strangers and foreigners may be pardoned who have ignorance to plead for them; all their attempts and actions being not so prejudicial as our own.

If we admit the dishonor of ourselves, how then shall others value us? And if we admit a dishonor by our members, how [p. 90] shall we avoid it in ourselves? A greater dishonor and contempt this House has no time suffered than what does now affront it. To be excluded by a fundamental order of the House, so well known to all men, and that so lately urged by him that now does break it; to be debarred on ques-

tion, by a particular act and rule, and yet to intrude against it, what is it less than to bid defiance to your power and a farewell to your privilege? Should I compare it, it could have no parallel but that Roman's against whom Cicero does inveigh: *in senatum venit,* he comes into this senate but with a will to ruin it; for so I must interpret the intention of that act that would destroy the privilege. But did I say it was a member did it? I must retract that error in the place, or be false to the opinion which I have; for either by the election he pretends, or for this act and insolence, I cannot hold him worthy of that name, and so (involving both questions under one) as a full determination of his case, let [p. 91] us from hence expel him.

This made him presently removed and quickened the resolution of the House which, for the interruption, held the objection to be frivolous, and for the demand, it was observed that the sheriff's act confirmed it, besides the proofs that were produced, being affirmative, in the point. So, as the whole act of the sheriff was condemned and thereupon the election adjudged void which, after so much trouble and labor it had had, was the decision of that case.

It may be wondered why we have so far travailed in this question and in so small a matter made so particular a relation. But it being the occasion of greater things to come, we thought it not unnecessary the more carefully to express it, that the power and influence may be seen of such small stars and planets from whence great works, as Tacitus has observed, often receive original. Yet in the case itself, besides the art and carriage, the reason and decision are most profitable; for they do show what is the duty in like cases and how the use directs it that

---

67. The editors concur with Eliot's biographer (Forster, *Eliot,* I, 279–280) that this speech without attribution in the text was made by Eliot himself. The

C.J. verifies that Eliot spoke at this point (see above, H. of C., 5 July, p. 315).

the poll in such elections being required within the hours [p. 92] the statute does direct,[68] which is from the reading of the writ, at any time before eleven (for the printed books are falsified in that which in figures makes it *ix*, putting the *i* before the *x*, whereas the roll and original has it otherwise, the *i* being following of the *x*) the poll so demanded, no pretence or interruption may excuse it. That all that come while the election is continuing, though not present at the reading of the writ, have their free votes and suffrage, which shows the liberty of the commons in the act of such elections, and the great care of parliament to justify and preserve it, in which, yet, no man is compellable to attend.

The major part of courtiers in this question banded mainly against Wentworth, whereof he retained a memory; and others, that for pure reason did oppose him, he forgot not. The effect and operation followed after of the sense he then contracted, which from that spark did rise to a great flame and burning.

There was in that gentleman a good choice of parts, natural and acquisite, and no less opinion of them. A strong eloquence he had and a comprehension of much reason. His arguments were weighty and acute, and his descriptions exquisite. When he would move his hearers [p. 93] with the apprehension of his sense, he had both *acumina dictorum* and *ictus sententiarum* to affect them. His abilities were great both in judgment and persuasion, and as great a reputation did attend them. But those many and great virtues, as Livy says of Hannibal, as great vices paralleled,[69] or rather they were in him as Cicero notes in *Catiline, signa virtutum*, forms of virtue only, not the matter; for they seldom were directed to good ends, and when they had that color some other secret moved them. His covetousness and

ambition were both violent, as were his ways to serve them. *Neque in pecunia neque in gloria concupiscenda*, as Crassus is rendered by Paterculus, *aut modum norat aut capiebat terminum*. And those affections raised him to so much pride and choler, as any opposition did transport him, which rendered him less powerful to his adversaries, where the advantage was followed and perceived.

[Cases of Sir William Cope and Arthur Basset][70]

There were two other cases of this nature that had their determination about that time. One of Sir William Cope, who having been a member of the former parliament, in time of prorogation was arrested and taken in execution and after, by *habeas corpus* going abroad, again elected [p. 94] and returned a burgess for Banbury. The question in this was double: whether he were within the privilege of parliament in time of prorogation, and so the arrest then void; and whether, being new chosen while he was in execution, the election[71] should be good. Both ways it was negatively resolved. For the first, that the prorogation gives not privilege, as an adjournment, further than in the sixteen days after for regress. For the second, that he being in execution was not eligible because his enlargement would by law deprive the creditor of his debt. Whereupon there issued a warrant from the House for a new election to be made.

The other case was of Mr. Basset in Devonshire, who had two years been a prisoner upon original and mesne process arrested for so great a sum as no man dared to bail him, and being chosen a burgess for that parliament was admitted and set free.

I mention these cases to show their different judgments and the rules of proceeding in that House which, as they are exact to preserve the public interests, are curious

---

68. *S.R.*, 23 *H.* VI, c. 14.
69. Livy, 21, 4, 9.
70. Concerning Sir William Cope, see above, H. of

C., 21 June, n. 16; with regard to Arthur Basset, see H. of C., 28 June, n. 1.
71. *objection*. Printed edition.

also and intentive[72] for the private; justice in all being the ground on which they build, though the first stone and foundation be their privilege.

[6 July 1625]

[p. 95] Montagu at this time was attending, and called to examination in the House where, for the justification of himself, he alleged a warrant of King James for the first book he printed.[73] That being sent for by the Archbishop, the King then told him likewise he should choose whether he would go to him or no. That for his second book, he had the like warrant and authority. That upon the view of his tenets and opinions therein the King swore, if that were to be a papist so was he. Whereupon he recommended it to Dr. White who, by his censure, did approve it, as was extant with the work.

This confession being more confident than ingenuous begot new jealousies in the House; for his old patron being dead,[74] it could not be imagined he should assume that boldness of himself. Divers did wonder at it, who had filled their sails with hope, and, yet, discerned not that the winds were turned against them. But the more wise observed it as a constellation that was ominous, and therefore the more carefully did study to prevent it in the effects.

[7 July 1625]

His books to this end were considered, which had large matter of exception, besides the doctrines they implied [p. 96] (for the dispute of them, as no fit subject for the parliament, the wisdom of the Commons did decline) besides his innovations in the doctrine, which for another censure was reserved. Divers of scandal were deduced, to the dishonor of the King, the disturbance

of the state both for the Church and government, and in derogation of the parliament, for contempt of the privilege and jurisdiction of that House, and in prejudice of the whole. Instances were cited in all these.[75] And first for dishonor to the King, his upholding the opinions of Arminius was observed, which the King labored so much to suppress; which labor was apparent in three main acts and principles:

First, by his writings, in which he terms Arminius an enemy to God and Bertius, his scholar, for his book *De Apostasia Sanctorum*, a heretic. Secondly, by procuring the Synod at Dort, and favoring and approving their decrees, at which his own divines assisted. Thirdly, by sending the Articles of the Church of England into Ireland, under the Great Seal and teste; and to the 38th, of justifying faith, where it is said that it cannot be lost, adding for explanation "totally and finally", which was intended in the sense and meaning [p. 97] of the Article. By all which he endeavored the suppressing of those doctrines which the writings of Arminius would bring in. Therefore the contrary, which by Montagu was effected, inferred a dishonor to the King.

The second point of disturbance in the Church and state in four particulars was collected. First, his sowing of jealousies between the King and his good subjects, terming the Puritans (whom he defined)[76] to be a potent prevailing faction in the kingdom. Secondly, his slighting those famous divines, who have been great lights in the Church: Calvin, Beza, Perkins, Whitaker. Thirdly, his laboring to discountenance the ministry of God's word, terming the lectures, by way of irony and scorn, prophetical determinations and conventicles; preaching, prating, and the like. Fourthly, his giving encouragement to popery and a

72. *instructive*. Printed edition.
73. See H. of C., 6 July, pp. 325–326.
74. I.e., James I.
75. For the following points related by Eliot, see the Recorder's report and the subsequent debate of 7 July,

above, pp. 330–335 and 336–340, and the corresponding footnotes.
76. The other accounts of the Recorder's report state that Montagu did *not* define Puritans. See above, p. 338.

persuasion thereunto, affirming Rome to be a true church and the spouse of Christ. All which was noted to intend sedition and disturbance.

The third general, of derogation to the parliament and the jurisdiction of that House, was thus inferred. First, that being under examination and complaint there for his former book, he published the second in [p. 98] defense and maintenance of the same. And then that in that second he did scandal and revile those that did prosecute on the first, who in that respect were in the protection of that House and could not therein be calumniated without violation of the privilege.

These observations produced these motions and desires: First, that there might be a charge prepared against him out of the matter then propounded to be transmitted to the Lords. Then, that he might, in the meantime, be committed for his contempt and injury to the House, and so remain a prisoner with the Serjeant until his further punishment. These opinions, though most agreeing with the House, had yet some opposition and resistance.

It was first objected against the authority of the House, that one parliament had not cognizance of another, nor were the offenses to a former questionable, much less punishable, in a latter. But the vanity of that argument was discovered by the clear light of reason and authority; the whole course of parliament spoke against it, the practice of all times, the examples of all courts. Divers precedents were cited for illustration in the point [p. 99] which soon composed that question. Others that had an inclination to that party (for even with Christ there was one Judas in the fellowship) objected the nature of the cause and by making it seem doctrinal would exclude the jurisdic-

tion of that court, and for the doctrines likewise labored to insinuate a defense, for that they were not by any public act condemned in the censure of the Church. But these as soon were rejected and cast off by difference and distinction of the fact, in that the points insisted on were but civil—for the honor of the King, the privilege of the parliament, the peace and quiet of the state, the unity[77] and tranquility of the Church, which it was said, by Fleta, were appropriate to the secular courts and magistrates. These reasons were a satisfaction to that doubt. But further it was added, that the Articles being opposed which were confirmed by parliament, the parliament ought in duty to maintain them. Upon which it was without difficulty resolved both for the commitment and the charge. And Montagu, being called in, kneeling at the bar, had for his contempt a censure of commitment [p. 100] there pronounced. Some by way of caution had propounded a cunctation in that act, for the honor of the House, lest, contrary to their meaning, it should prove, for a punishment, a preferment. But that reason was thought lighter than the rest, which the effect and consequence proved true; and was not punic, as it was thought, but real and by a right inspection of the time; nor that by revelation, but by judgment truly taken from the meridian of the state, which had that infortunity with others to make men most obnoxious most secure, and those that were most hateful to the public, to be most honored and esteemed.[78]

Hitherto all things had succeeded to the intentions of that House. No interruptions had been raised by the influence of state. Those few public things then treated of had a free way of preparation, though some intimations had been given that their conclu-

77. *virtue.* Printed edition.

78. For an explication of these remarks by Eliot, see Forster, *Eliot,* I, 257–258. On 9 July Charles informed the House that Montagu was one of his chaplains-in-

ordinary (see above, p. 359), and in July 1628, following further parliamentary proceedings against him, Montagu was elected Bishop of Chichester.

sions would not answer it, but those had less in credit than of truth and the satisfaction was presumed to be equal to the hope. From the confidence of Montagu and that business some seeds of jealousy [p. 101] were emergent, but no more. All things else had a fair show and promise. The bill of tonnage and poundage was at rest in the custody of the Lords, and no knowledge but by divination could be had how it would speed with [them], how after with the King. The best was still expected as hope did make construction, which always has an inclination unto flattery.

But here a check came in, as distractive as unlooked for. The Duke, who was the Aeolus of that time, had cast an alteration in the air; the winds were turned, and all the former happiness must be shadowed with some new clouds and vapors he had raised. He comes from the King, who was then at Hampton Court, with a pretended order for a new motion of supply. This in all haste must be performed and his privados were all sent for to receive instruction in the point. This was about twelve a clock at night, at his own house, where, by reason of the suddenness and unseasonableness of the time, many were not present, nor such as had much judgment, they commonly being most attendant on such persons who are [p. 102] most obnoxious to their humors. These did consent in all, who studied not to counsel but to please. And so what affections he had brought, they did both heighten and confirm.

[8 July 1625]

But in the morning when it was come to others whose quality was more knowing and ingenuous they, as they apprehended it to be fatal and prodigious, so gave it demonstration to the Duke, and with all their power opposed it, adding to arguments, en-

treaties for the prevention of that evil which did imply apparently dishonor to the King, danger to him. Of this number (not to deprive any man of his due) was Sir Humphrey May, then Chancellor of the Duchy, who, having travailed with much industry in that service, but in vain, came in great haste to a gentleman whom he thought more powerful with the Duke and knew to be affectionate to the public,[79] and him he importuned to a new attempt and trial for stay or diversion of that work. It was at Westminster where he met him and near the time of the sitting of the Commons. The Duke was then at York House. The intercourse, [p. 103] it was objected, would be long. No certain period could be prescribed for conference, which in so great a difficulty was not likely to be short; so as the proposition to the parliament might be made before the discourse were ended and the travail by that means fruitless and unnecessary. But to remove this doubt the Chancellor undertook to stop the motion till he came.[80] Only he wished him to hasten his return and in his talk to intimate that stay unto the Duke.

Upon this he makes his passage and address, and coming to York House finds the Duke with his lady yet in bed. But notice being given of his coming, the Duchess rose and withdrew into her cabinet, and so he was forthwith admitted and let in. The first thing mentioned was the occasion and the fear that was contracted from that ground. The next was the honor of the King and respect unto his safety, from both which were deduced arguments of dissuasion. For the King's honor was remembered the acceptation that was made of the two subsidies which were passed and the satisfaction then professed, which the new proposition would impeach, either in truth or wisdom. [p. 104] Again the small number of

---

79. I.e., Sir John Eliot. For an explication of the following account, see Forster, *Eliot*, I, 295–300.

80. I.e., May undertook to prevent the motion for

additional supply from being made in the House until after Eliot's return from his conference with the Duke.

the Commons that remained, the rest being gone upon the confidence of that overture,[81] would render it as an ambuscade and surprise; which at no time could be honorable towards subjects, less in the entrance of the Sovereign. The rule for that was noted, *ut initia proveniant fama in ceteris est.* The necessity likewise of that honor was observed, without which no prince was great, hardly any fortunate. And on these grounds a larger superstructure was imposed as occasionally the conference did require. For his own safety many things were said, some more fit for use than for memory and report. The general disopinion was objected, which it would work to him not to have opposed it, whose power was known to all men. And that the command coming by himself would render it as his act, of which imputation what the consequence might be nothing but divinity could judge, men that are much in favor being obnoxious to much envy.

To these, answers were returned, though weak yet such as implied no yielding, that the acceptation which was made of the subsidies then granted was but in respect of [p. 105] the affection to the King, not for satisfaction to his business. That the absence of the Commons was their own fault and error, and their neglect must not prejudice the state. That the honor of the King stood upon the expectation of the fleet, whose design would vanish if it were not speedily set forth. Money there was wanting for that work, and therein the King's honor was engaged, which must outweigh all considerations for himself.

This resolution being felt, was a new way attempted to try if that might weaken it. And to that end was objected the improbability of success; and if it did succeed, the greater loss might follow it by alienation of the affections of the subjects who, being pleased, were a fountain of supply without which those streams would soon dry up. But nothing could prevail; there being divers arguments spent in that, yet the proposition must proceed without consideration of success, wherein was lodged this project, merely to be denied. This secret that treaty did discover, which drew on [p. 106] others that supported it of greater weight and moment, showing a conversion of the tide for the present. It gave that gentleman some wonder with astonishment who, with the seal of privacy, closed up those passages in silence, yet therein grounded his observations for the future that no respect of persons made him desert his country.

This labor, not misspent, had taken up much time. Two hours, at least, went into the treaty and discourse, which with the intercourse had so wasted the forenoon as there remained but little at his coming back to Westminster; where the like difficulty had been to retard the proposition for that time, it being put (not as other messages from the King into the mouth of his councillors and great officers, whereof there are never wanting in the Commons House too many) but, by a special choice, to the discretion of another as an indication of his preferment then at hand who was great, in his opinion, with that honor and employment, and labored as a woman does with child in desire to bring it forth. The success being there [p. 107] imparted, the motion did proceed, for which there wanted not some fitness in that instrument. The man so chosen was SIR JOHN COKE, raised from a low condition to that title by the Duke. To him he had been recommended by that old courtier Sir Fulke Greville, under whom he had had his education as a scholar, and so was his service and employment.[82] But his conversation being with books, and that to teach not study them, men and business

---

81. See above, p. 510.

82. Sir John Coke had been rhetoric lecturer at Cambridge, entered the service of Sir Fulke Greville in 1597, became a Commissioner of the Navy in 1618, a Master of Requests in 1622, and was knighted in 1624. *D.N.B.*

were subjects which he knew not and his expressions were more proper for a school than for a state and council.

This choice, thus fitted, thus made his entrance to that scene.

[SIR JOHN COKE.][83] That the King not doubting their affections in that meeting, and taking graciously for a testimony thereof the gift which was resolved on as a welcome pledge of the love not only of that representative body of the kingdom but of the whole (though he took notice of their anticipation in that business and that they fell into it without the intervention of any ministers of state, which he did impute to their forwardness in his service and confidence in his favor), in correspondence thereof [p. 108] had commanded him to give the House a true information of his estate, and to lay before them the necessities he was in.[84]

That there had lately been disbursed for Ireland to confirm the peace of that kingdom 32,000 l.; for the navy (the present preparations not computed) 37,000 l.; for the office of the ordnance and forts 47,000 l.; for the support of the regiments in the Low Countries 99,000 l.; for the charge of Count Mansfeld's army 62,000 l.

And because from that last business had grown some doubts, he was to give a more particular account therein. His late Majesty, loving peace and hating war, when he saw how ill he had been used, that the power of the contrary party had almost overspread[85] Christendom, and his own people discontented at his seeming backwardness in that cause, considering the three subsidies and fifteenths that were granted him (though a royal gift) would only enable him for awhile to secure his own, and that in the end he should grow from a lingering ague to a burning fever,

and by suffering his enemies to enjoy that which they had gotten make them more able by degrees to fret upon the other [p. 109] German princes, whence it would ensue that, like Ulysses with Polyphemus, he should only have the favor to be the last devoured, he negotiated and concluded a strong confederacy with the kings of France and Denmark, the state of Venice, the Duke of Savoy, and the Low Countries, which first appeared in the army beyond the Alps and with Count Mansfeld.

Some faults, he said, were to be confessed in those troops at Dover, which could not be excused, but Mansfeld complained that the men were chosen such as would be kept under no government. And if it were objected why a stranger should lead those troops, it was to be considered, that the whole army did consist of English, French, and Dutch. And if an Englishman had commanded it the French would have been discontented, and so the English if a Frenchman. And if many commanders had been made, precedence would have bred some difficulties. Therefore he that was indifferent was thought to be the fittest.

And if a further objection be taken from the event, it must be likewise considered that no success is man's, and he that measures [p. 110] things by that is no equal judge. He said also it was true that the change of the design caused some delay and impeachment of that good effect which was hoped. Yet it was not altogether unprofitable, for the appearance of that army kept divers princes of Germany from declaring themselves for the enemy. This was in general, as he said, towards the account of the three subsidies and fifteenths.

And further his Majesty had commanded him to give an account of that which would be spent upon the preparation then in hand. The charge of the fleet in the office

---

83. Concerning versions of Coke's speech, see H. of C., 8 July, n. 5.

84. See the Bedford MS. 197 account, above, p.

350. Eliot has omitted two sentences at this point.

85. *overpowered.* Printed edition.

of the navy 200,000 *l*.; in the office of the ordnance 48,000 *l*.; for the landmen it would be 45,000 *l*.; whereof the two subsidies then given would amount to but 160,000 *l*. But this not all. The King of Denmark was to have 40,000 *l*. to draw him into Germany, besides a monthly entertainment of 20,000 *l*., and as much to Count Mansfeld, which could not be supported without more help by parliament, or else some new way, the ordinary revenue being exhausted and overcharged with other expenses both of necessity and honor.

That the King [p. 111] when he was Prince borrowed 20,000 *l*. for those provisions. The Lord Admiral has engaged his estates. Other ministers have furnished above 50,000 *l*. Shall it be said that these men are left to be undone for their readiness to the public service? Shall we proclaim our own poverty by losing all that is bestowed upon this enterprise because we cannot go through with it? What shall we say to the honor of the King? But that is not all, even the establishment of his Majesty in his royal throne, the peace of Christendom, the state of religion, depend upon this fleet. The adversaries deliver very insolent speeches ever since the taking of Breda. The French incline to civil war; they brandle in Italy and faint as their forefathers were wont to do after the heat of the first enterprise. Our German forces have kept the Catholic League from assembling to the ruin of the Protestants. What have we to reunite the princes, to encourage the French, to support the States, to oppose the Catholic League, but the reputation of Mansfeld's army and the expectation of our fleet?

Shall [p. 112] it be said that being forsaken of his subjects the King has been enforced to abandon religion? To seek a dishonorable peace? It is impossible for these things to subsist but by money or credit.

Thus spoke that worthy, and then concluded with this motion: that either they would presently make an addition of supply, or pass some engagement to the King that at the next meeting they would do it, which might give him credit in the interim and so the expedition to go on.

This motion had no second but by BEECHER, a Council clerk and servant of that time. But his reason and authority being not great and all the other courtiers disaffecting it, being, in brief, opposed by a worthy gentleman of Lincolnshire, SIR THOMAS GRANTHAM,[86] who was never wanting to the service of his country, it forthwith died and perished, though from the dust thereof more troubles did spring up.

The frame and composition of that body was thought as preposterous as the soul. The immense calculations and accounts and the farfetched and impertinent relations, the positions and conclusions that were laid, all held artificial and prestigious. His [p. 113] supposition of their forsaking of the King and the King's abandoning religion was deemed both scandalous and offensive, as was that mention of new ways, which the more was noted because it had happened once before and therefore was not thought to be accidental or by chance.

But exceptions were declined through the wisdom of that time which, in the dying of that motion had satisfaction and content. There was no denial nor no question, it being never brought so far, which had almost a miracle within it; for there were hardly then threescore in the House and, of those, countrymen not the most. Any support or agitation it had had must have needs driven it to a concession, or the contrary. But, as we noted, the courtiers much disliking it—some as it came not in particular by them or that they were not preconsulted for the work; others for the danger and prejudice it imported; the rest for the suddenness and strangeness of the thing,

---

86. We have no other record that Grantham spoke on this matter.

that like a lightning broke upon them having no precogitation of the meteor; all generally abhorring it, as a constellation that was ominous—[p. 114] it vanished through its own lightness and futility, causing a reluctation in their hearts which nothing but divinity could move.

This unexpected issue to the Duke caused a new trouble and disorder. All his privados were condemned as remiss and negligent in the service. His friends were all complained of, thus to have failed his hopes. Every man was blamed but him that was most faulty. What he intended in his corrupt reason or affection, to that he would have had even the heavens themselves consenting. So unhappy are such persons through the distractions of their greatness that success the[y] think to follow the *via lactea* of their fancies, and that the rule of that, nay, of the world itself, should be by the proportion of their wills. And rather than fail therein, if the superiors be not flexible, the infernal powers shall be studied with their arts.

This was the infelicity of this man, and at this time it first opened and discovered, though not clearly but by shadows, being disordered in that purpose, which almost no man yet did know, he condemns both his fortune and his friends. But for himself nothing was [p. 115] less resolved on than that which was most necessary; no retraction of the course. That which had been, because it was done by him, must be both justified and maintained; and that justification must appear in the approbation of the work by a future prosecution that was worse.

[9 July 1625]

The House being delivered from the fear which it had contracted from that motion and the consequence that might follow it, forthwith resolved to think of nothing but recess, and the next day intimated their readiness to the Lords who, having dealt in little at this meeting, and having no business at that time, dispatched a present messenger to the King from whom they received this answer: that though his necessities were great, yet the consideration of their safeties should dispose him to dismiss them for that time, though they must shortly meet again.

That "shortly" was not then rightly understood.[87] No man did doubt that which the word intended. Most men did refer it to the winter or the spring, the conventions of that council [p. 116] being seldom nearer, or more frequent. But an effect it was of the powerful influence of the Duke, which not long after was more perspicuous and apparent. Both by that latter clause of the answer, and the rest, all men did know that their sitting was not long, and therefore sought to state their business in some order.

The chief care was for preservation of the statutes which stood upon continuance to that time. For this a short act was framed, that the royal assent should not (as was supposed by some, though precedents spoke the contrary) give a determination to that session, but that it should continue by adjournment and all things stand in the condition that they left them, so to be resumed again at the next time of meeting.[88]

This done, and the act of confirmation being passed for three subsidies then granted by the clergy, there being a little time remaining, it was spent upon a petition from the prisoners in the Fleet. They had been suitors to the Lords, in respect of the great danger of the sickness, to have liberty, by order from the parliament, by *habeas cor-*

87. See below, p. 525.

88. The bill that this session of parliament shall not determine by royal assent to one or more acts had passed the Lower House on 7 July and been sent up to the Lords on 8 July. It was amended by the Upper House, returned to the Commons on 9 July, when the amendment was voted and the altered bill passed the Lower House and was then returned to the Lords the same day.

pus to go abroad. The Lords imparted [p. 117] this motion to the Commons.

The Commons thereupon taking consideration at this leisure upon these reasons thus resolved it to be repugnant to the law. First, that it was against the intention of the writ which, commanding the keeper to bring his prisoner to a judge implies the nearest way he has, not, as the abuse went, to let him travel where he list—to hunt and hawk the whole vacation in his country and, at term again, to resort unto his prison. Then, that it was legally an escape and so the creditors should be prejudiced; for which there were divers judgments cited, and some cases demonstrative in the point, as *5ᵗᵒ H. 6* when in consideration of the state, there being special service at that time for some minister then imprisoned and the like liberty was desired, the judges, upon consultation, did deny it.[89] And before that it was noted that all kind of ease or remove from one prison to another was wholly refused, without consent and liking of the creditors. For this therefore, it being so contrary to the law and in favor of abuse, however pity did move in contemplation of the men, yet their dangers being not equal to the danger of the [p. 118] kingdom which would follow the exinanition of the laws, it was thought fit not in that particular to admit it, or that admission, at the least, not to be made by parliament.

Which opinion being signified to the Lords, they in like manner did resolve it, and so all instance ceased. This was the ninth of July being Saturday.

[11 July 1625]

On Monday there was a message to the Commons from the Lords to intimate their receipt of a commission for adjournment and another for the royal assent to the passage of some laws, for which their presence was desired in the Lords House, as it was always in such cases, there to hear them read. Upon this some short disputes arising in consideration of their privilege; they resolved them with what brevity they might and so made their passage to that end.

The first difficulty was for presenting the bill of subsidy; the usual manner being that that, having passed the Lords, should be returned again as the peculiar of the Commons; and when they attended, either for dissolution or adjournment, as their free act, to be presented by their Speaker. This being then not done, raised some jealousy in the point lest it might draw a prejudice in the future, both on their affections and those acts. But being then annexed to the commission for assent, with the other laws to pass, and that commission [p. 119] resting properly with the Lords, it was conceived that ceremony could not be, but the Speaker must supply it in an expression at the place and there receive and deliver it in their names.

The next was the consideration of the adjournment. Wherein likewise some little doubt there was for their interest in that point which having always been their own sole act and work; in admitting it by commission from the King it was then thought an innovation of the right which might induce a precedent against them and so retrench their liberty for the future. And for this purpose the difference was observed between adjournment and prorogation, as prorogation and dissolution have their odds: that the two latter, in their kinds, were in the prerogative of the King, the adjournment in the privilege only of the House.[90]

Therefore a message in that case was dispatched for accommodation with the Lords who thereupon agreed to read only in their presence the commission for assent, and in the other to leave them wholly to themselves.

---

89. Henry Rolle cited several precedents regarding the question. See above, H. of C., 9 July, nn. 34–36.

90. On the adjournment, see H. of L., 11 July, nn. 9 and 18.

All things thus settled and composed, the Commons did address themselves to hear the commission of assent, and [p. 120] being present with the Lords, and the Speaker there receiving the bill of subsidy in his hands, as it was hanging with the others to the commission that must pass them, using some rhetoric in the declaration of their right, and by their affection in the gift making an insinuation to the King in the name of all the Commons, he presented it. Which had acceptance by the Keeper, and this answer thereupon:

That the King apprehended it as a good testimony of their loves, and in correspondency of that would enlarge his favor to his subjects. That in their piety and religion he would meet them. And for their petition therein given him, the answer should be real and not verbal. That they should shortly have a particular satisfaction in that point, and in the meantime he would command a strict execution of the laws.

Whereupon the royal assent being read for the enacting of some bills, whereof the subsidy was not least in estimation and account; and the King's pleasure intimated for an adjournment unto Oxford, the attendance did dissolve and the Commons returned unto their House, no less affected with trouble than admiration.[91]

The suddenness of the time, being but the first of August, and that the eleventh of [p. 121] July, which was an exposition of that mystery, that formerly was mistaken, and an explication of the meaning of that word "shortly", and much more.[92] This, with the strangeness of the place, both unexpected and unlooked for, seemed as a prodigy to all men. The unaptness of the season for such a concourse and assembly, which was scarcely safe at any time but most dangerous then in that the epidemical infection of the plague being so universally dispersed that all persons were suspected and in jealousy, men, if they could, even flying from themselves. The houses, streets, and ways, nay, even the fields and hedges, almost in all places near London and about it (besides the miserable calamities of the City) presenting daily new spectacles of mortality.

The place also was noted as something ominous and portentous for the success it gave to the like meeting in foretimes. It raised a contemplation of the miseries which followed that unfortunate convention in the days of H. 6,[93] with the reasons and intentions that had moved it. And from the resemblance of the causes was deduced a like supposition for the effects which [p. 122] gave a fear to all men who, in their hearts, deplored the unhappiness of those princes that expose themselves to the corruption of their ministers.

To sharpen that humor and dislike, at that time happened also the infection of that place.[94] It was entered into some few houses of the town, and some of the colleges were infected. Most of the scholars were retired, and that was an aggravation to the danger which, being apprehended to the full, became an aggravation of the fear by which that fact (though a justice in the King) was thought an injury in his servants. But obedience was resolved on and through all the difficulties of the time the King's pleasure was preferred.

The Lords upon the departure of the Commons from their House, read there the commission for adjournment; so much they differ from the others in order or ob-

---

91. I.e., astonishment.

92. See above, p. 523.

93. The reference is apparently to the events of 1449–1450 when the parliament was moved temporarily away from Westminster. That assembly had impeached William de la Pole, Duke of Suffolk, on charges of corruption. Shortly afterwards occurred his murder and Jack Cade's rebellion, and subsequently the Wars of the Roses. Concerning Suffolk and the parliament of 1449–1450, see above, H. of C., 10 August, n. 42.

94. I.e., Oxford. Concerning the plague in that city, see above, H. of L., 4 August, n. 8.

servation, who,[95] having likewise the writ brought down to them, refused to read or open it, but as their own act, not varying in the circumstance, pronounced it by their Speaker that the House adjourned itself, and so dissolved that meeting.

The report of this flew presently to all parts [p. 123] and affected all men with wonder at the strangeness. London was then the constant seat of parliaments, which nowhere else had been for divers ages past, that in the vulgar sense they were incorporate to that place.[96] The time likewise seemed a miracle to those who had retired themselves, being members of that body, and heard the acceptation of their subsidies in the message from the King, the compliment that was in it for respect unto their safeties, endeared by high expressions of comparison, was also in their memories. The incongruity with that, in this alteration and adjournment, wrought much anxiety in their thoughts, and as far as fear could carry it, made a depression of their hopes.

This all men had for their entertainment in the country during that short recess. Some had but opportunity, whose habitations were remote, to make only a visit to their families and at first sight to leave them. Hardly anyone had leisure for their fit accommodation and provisions but suffered some inconvenience or defect. Their travel on the ways, their danger in the inns, and the little safety could be [p. 124] promised at the period took off all pleasure from the journey. And the occasion that did move it was more distasteful than the rest.

The satisfaction had at London was not much, the promise then far less. There in the matter of religion though there were a fair answer in the general yet Montagu was protected, and to that end made chaplain to the King.[97] In other things the answer to the grievances was but slight, and such as imported small fruit and benefit to the subject. The bill of tonnage and poundage was rejected and yet those levies made; which was held an indication of more love to the ways of power than right. The laws that had their approbation were not many and the choice of them not great. That against recusants was not passed and in all their number was but seven, whereof the subsidies of the laity and clergy made up two, so as the rest imported little to public happiness, as their following titles may express:

1. An act for punishing of divers abuses committed on the Lord's day.

2. An act to enable the King to make leases in the Duchy of Cornwall.

[p. 125] 3. An act for ease in obtaining licenses of alienation.

4. An act for restraint of alehouses and victualing houses.

5. An act for confirmation of the subsidies granted by the clergy.

6. An act for two entire subsidies granted by the temporalty.

7. An act that the session should not then determine by the royal assent to other acts.

That for religion, for so it was pretended, only did provide against bull baitings, interludes, and the like unlawful pastimes on the Sunday. And therein also, with a mixture of civil considerations and respects.

That for the Duchy had aspect but to the profit of the King, though with some shadow and pretence of advantage to the tenants.

That for alienations only looked at some small decrease of fees, and had reference but to few, and rarely of use to them.

That for restraint of alehouses was, in effect, but what had been before, for the

---

95. I.e., the Commons.

96. The last parliament to actually meet outside of London/Westminster prior to 1625 was that at Coventry in 1459. Even during the thirteenth and fourteenth centuries when parliament assembled wherever the King was in residence (including several meetings at Oxford during the reign of Henry III) Westminster was the most common meeting place. See Sir F. Maurice Powicke and E. B. Fryde, *Handbook of British Chronology* (London, 1961), pp. 492–544.

97. See above, H. of C., 7 July, n. 3.

repressing of tipplings and disorders, which both before and then were more decried than punished, as reformation is less easy than complaint.

The rest need no comment to explain them, sense without [p. 126] reason making demonstration of the subsidies; and for the other, if it had wanted midwives, much trouble had been saved,[98] which afterwards did follow that prodigious birth at Oxford.

[Oxford]

[p. 129][99] About the time of the adjournment of the parliament from London the Turks were grown very infestuous to the merchants.[100] Divers ships and vessels they had taken, with a multitude of captives drawn from them. In the west parts they had made the coasts so dangerous through their spoils as few dared put forth of their harbors; hardly in them was the security thought enough. The boldness and insolence of those pirates was beyond all comparison, no former times having been exampled with the like. Their adventure formerly on those seas was rare, almost unheard of, which made their coming then more strange. That being aggravated by their frequency and number, which their daily spoils did witness, and those much heightened by their boldness, it made a great impression on the country and possessed it with much fear; that divers alarums it received, which made divers motions in the people who, as their manner is, feigned or enlarged the cause after the apprehension of their fancies, which passing to their neighbors still affected them with more, until it had a general influence throughout [p. 130] all, even the chief

towns and strengths not privileged or exempted.

They had in some parts entered even into the mouths of the close harbors and showed themselves in them, and all the open roads they used confidently as their own. Some ships they had taken under the forts and castles. Nothing did deter them, but the whole sea seemed theirs.

In Cornwall they had landed and carried divers prisoners from the shore. All fishermen that stirred became their prey and purchase. They had gained in that summer at least twelve hundred Christians, the loss of whom caused great lamentation with their friends. This man bewailed his son, that his father, another his brother, a fourth his servant, and the like; husbands and wives, with all relations else of nature and civility did complain; besides the prejudice of the merchants, the losing of their ships, the interruption of their trade, which made a general damp on all things, commodities being not vendible where the transportation is denied; this likewise made a general cry and exclamation that no part of that country did stand free, no person but was affected with that sense.

[p. 131] Hereof a daily intelligence had been given to the ministers of the state with special addresses thereupon to implore for some relief. Divers ships were then ready of the fleet which might have been commanded to that service. They lay idle in their harbors in the Thames, at Portsmouth, and elsewhere, all their men and provisions being aboard. They were to attend the preparation of their fellows, for which generally was appointed the rendezvous at Plymouth, so as this em-

---

98. I.e., much trouble would have been saved if there had been no act for continuing the session and the session had ended on 11 July rather than been adjourned to August.

99. Page 127 of the MS. is a title page containing the entry: "Negotium Posterorum. Tomus Secundus, Liber Secundus". Page 128 of the MS. is blank. See above, Introduction, p. 17.

100. See above, H. of C., 5 July, n. 7; and see the report concerning pirates, H. of C., 11 August, above, particularly n. 6, Bedford MS. 197 (pp. 459–460) and the Dyott diary (p. 468). Also, cf. Eliot's speech on these matters in the committee of the whole House on 6 March 1626, recorded in Bulstrode Whitelocke's diary, Cambridge University Library MS. Dd. 12.20, f. 18a.

ployment would have drawn them to that place. Their countenance in the passage would have dispelled those pirates. No charge had been occasioned to the King, no waste of the provisions, no unreadiness in the ships, no disorder to the service, but rather an advantage given in all; yet nothing could be gotten, no ship might be removed, the trade and merchants were neglected, the coast was left unguarded, the country stood exposed as if in expiation of some sin it had been made a sacrifice to those monsters.

Amongst other cries and intelligences of that kind, there came one directed to a gentleman of those parts to whom it had relation by his office, being Vice Admiral of [p. 132] Devonshire,[101] that there were forty sail of Turks besides those formerly kept that coast then, in one fleet, come within the channel, and this warranted by the deposition of the master and some others of a small bark that had passed them in the night. He represents it to the King. The King resenting truly the danger of his subjects presently recommends it to his Council, commanding that gentleman to attend them who, meeting, and having the considerations laid before them of the dishonor to the King, the prejudice to the country, the necessity and facility of relief, for which some few good ships would serve, and those, being ready, importing no charge unto the King, nor hindrance to their ser-

vice, it was thereupon resolved that eight ships for that purpose should be sent which, having done that work, should await the rest at Plymouth.[102] This being settled by an order of the board was directed to the Commissioners of the Navy, certified by letters to the country, which thereupon conceived good hope and satisfaction, though the sequel did not answer it.

Those Commissioners were the men that had the great business of that time. The whole strength and [p. 133] preparation being naval, they were the masters of it. Either for that particular then in hand or any other service and design for the honor or safety of the kingdom, which consisted in those arks, their judgments and discretions must dispose it. They were first instituted, in the creation of their office under the admiralty of the Earl of Nottingham,[103] for a check and superintendance to the Admiral, that the whole kingdom stood not too much entrusted to one man. But after, through the conversion of the times, they became only subservient to the Admiral—his instruments to negotiate his ends and his objects against envy, *inani nomine*, as those ministers in Tacitus, *alienae culpae praetendebantur*. They had a great power in name but little liberty to use it, only they were an apt disguise and shadow and a common father for all faults.

I observe this the sooner to show the variety of effects which may be emergent from

---

101. I.e., Sir John Eliot.

102. Council records indicate that an order had gone out to the Commissioners of the Navy on 19 May 1625 to send out three of the King's ships to guard the western coasts against a reported fleet of pirate ships (*A.P.C., 1625–1626*, p. 59), and a further order for setting out two ships was sent to the Commissioners on 29 May (*A.P.C., 1625–1626*, pp. 79–80). It is more likely, however, that Eliot's comments relate to the letter of 27 June 1625 from Buckingham, Lord Admiral, to Sir Francis Stuart. A copy of this letter, from S.P. 16/1:48, is printed in the Appendix, below, p. 716. See also, above, H. of C., 11 August, p. 457 and n. 4, p. 460 and n. 24, and p. 468.

103. Charles Howard, first Earl of Nottingham, was

Lord High Admiral, 1585–1618. *D.N.B.* Commissioners of the Navy had been appointed on 23 June 1618 (MS. Cal. Pat. Rolls, 16 *Jac.* I, pt. 1, f. 13) to survey the expenses and investigate the condition of the navy. The report of the Commissioners (S.P. 14/100:2; 14/101) led to the resignation of Nottingham and the appointment of Buckingham as Lord Admiral, followed, on 12 February 1619, by the reappointment of the Commissioners of the Navy as a continuing body (MS. Cal. Pat. Rolls, 16 *Jac.* I, pt. 3, f. 13v). See Gardiner, *History of England*, III, 203–206. Since the latter commission terminated with the death of James I, Charles issued a new commission on 7 April 1625 (this commission is printed in Rymer, *Foedera*, VIII, pt. 1, pp. 9–12).

one cause, and how from the same root and principle both good and ill derive themselves. This office in the institution was with reason for the common good and benefit to rectify the actions [p. 134] of the Admiral (though laterally it might have some obliquity), but the execution of it after was so prestigious and corrupt as nothing more dangerous and obnoxious. The Admiral had with them a free command and liberty, whatever he but intimated they did and if complaint succeeded it the error was their own.

Of their number the first and principal was Sir John Coke, whom we mentioned before, and this was then his best honor and employment, the rest were but ciphers unto him.[104] To him that order of the Council was delivered; but he, as not subject to that authority, having greater preparations then in hand, yet not to give them perfection in their kind but to sort them to the occasion of his thoughts, and theirs from whom he had them (which likewise did afford more matter of complaint) lays it by without observance or account, so as the direction of his Majesty, the resolution of the lords, the expectation of the country were all frustrate by that means. This bred both wonder and distaste. That a private Commissioner of the Navy should presume to oppose an order of the Council, that that order being fortified by a special direction from the [p. 135] King should have no more observance in a matter so much concerning the public good and security of the kingdom, it was thought strange and fearful. Enemies at home were more doubted upon this than those pirates and enemies abroad.[105]

Which jealousy was augmented by another act and purpose that had its preparation in that time, which was for a consignment to the French of certain warlike ships, with all their apparel and munition to be delivered absolutely into their hands, which for aught was known might have been used against themselves or, as the effect did prove it, made the ruin of their friends.[106] These were seven great merchant ships and the *Vanguard* of the King's, of which we shall speak hereafter. This note being made only by the way to show the concurrence of those things: how jealousies did arise, from what root they sprang, which after branched themselves through the whole state and kingdom and in all things made expression of their fruits.

[1 August 1625]

The first bud put forth on the first day at Oxford where, according to the adjournment being met, a complaint was exhibited to the [p. 136] Commons of a pardon then granted to a Jesuit whom the town of Exeter had imprisoned.[107] Divers circumstances were observed in the aggravation of the fact. First, the insolence of the Jesuit and him that brought the pardon refusing to admit any deliberation in the point upon the presenting of the pardon, but requiring an instant answer from the mayor, and threatening him with the authorities above if he delayed the least. Then the latitude of the patent, which implied not only a pardon for the present, but in effect an indulgence more extensive for the after times to come; for as it commanded the release of his imprisonment, so it was a *supersedeas* to all officers to impeach him for the future. Then

---

104. The twelve Commissioners of the Navy (ibid., p. 9) included such influential men as Sir Richard Weston, Chancellor and Under Treasurer of the Exchequer, and Sir William Russell, Treasurer of the Navy, but it was Sir John Coke who, from the beginning, took on the active leadership of the Commissioners.

105. See the debate concerning the Turkish pirates, above, H. of C., 11 August, O.B.

106. See above, H. of L., 9 August, n. 67.

107. This complaint was tendered by Sir Edward Giles. See above, H. of C., 1 August, p. 375. Concerning the pardon, see H. of C., 1 August, n. 3.

that clause, which in all pardons is required by the statute [blank],[108] that the delinquent before his freedom and discharge in all such cases should be bound to the good behavior with good sureties, was wholly omitted and left out. Then the time likewise was observed in which that grant was made, bearing date the twelfth of [p. 137] July, the next day after the adjournment made at London when that general concession was expressed upon the petition for religion—that the answer should be real and not verbal. This being held an ill comment on that text, and an unhappy performance of that promise, which likewise was the first, it being in favor of that order which is most dangerous in religion, and for a person as obnoxious as his order.

The whole House upon the apprehension of these things assumed one face of sorrow. Wonder it wrought in some, fear generally in all. The confusion of their thoughts imposed a silence on their tongues which, having held awhile, thus at length it broke.

Seneca reports it of an emperor, that being pressed to write for the execution of a man, he used this elegy and complaint: *utinam nescirem litteras;* wishing he knew no letters, rather than to employ them to such ends.[109] I may at this time in the like sense assume the like expression for myself, *utinam nescirem loqui.* [p. 138] I would I could not speak, so there were not this occasion. But the consideration of religion, the honor of the King, the service of this place, require me to deal faithfully with my heart, having this liberty of my mouth freely to render what I do conceive and what I would desire upon the judgment of this case.

I cannot think this issued from the King or, if it did, that he rightly understood it. I cannot believe he gave his pardon to a Jesuit, and that so soon upon his promise unto us. His favor, perchance, was intended to the man, and his quality concealed by those that did procure it, who secretly of themselves might extend it to the order. It is not seldom amongst princes such things are drawn from them. They cannot read every grant that passes them, and if their leisure served, yet sometimes their confidence would decline it. Though they are princes they leave not to be men. Hearts they have still, and affections like to others. And trust will follow where love has gone before. Therefore [p. 139] I doubt this some abuse of ministers who prefer their own corruptions before religion or the King. The time perhaps is not now seasonable to question them; but yet I would have it searched to know the secrets of it. Let the Lord Keeper be examined by what warrant he did issue it, and that being known let us see who procured it.

Much may be discovered in this little, and from this evil cause some good effects may flow. The King when he shall truly be informed, may again recall his grant. It has an example with the French who, in the like, report it of St. Louis that when a murderer had petitioned him and received a promise of his pardon, as he was at his religious exercise and devotions, and coming to that in the Psalms, *beatus est qui facit justiciam in omni tempore,*[110] he revoked that promise and concession and caused the malefactor to be executed. This to a private murder that pious prince did do, how much more then may we hope it from our King upon this grand traitor to the kingdom? Infinite is the disproportion of the offenses, [p. 140] equal the piety of the princes. Therefore what justice was in that, I cannot doubt in this, when the King our saint and sovereign

108. An examination of sources on statutes reveals no such clause.

109. This speech without attribution in the *Negotium* is not recorded in the other accounts of this day's proceedings. Eliot's biographer is probably correct in attributing the speech to Eliot himself (Forster, *Eliot*, I, 332), though it is possible that the speech was never actually delivered.

110. Ps. 105(106):3.

shall rightly understand it. To that end my motion shall incline that we proceed forthwith to the examination of the fact and, that being known, then to represent it to his Majesty with our petition for some help and redress in this particular, and for a general prevention of the like.

Upon this the King's Council[111] did stand up to make an extenuation or excuse or, as some thought, to divert the disquisition that was moved for. They made an acknowledgment of the fact, and of the consequence it imported, but colored it with a necessity of the time, upon the new marriage of the Queen and her suit, with the French ambassadors assisting her. They alleged it as a custom of King James, at the departing of ambassadors, to make a gratification of that kind.[112] This, they said, was but a particular for once, and in that the danger was not much. The answer that was coming to the petition for religion they assured would give satisfaction for the general, and therefore [p. 141] desired that that scruple might resolve into a hopeful expectation for the future.

This had not the success that was intended, but the consideration of the pardon did proceed,[113] wherein it was objected against that part of the apology for ambassadors, that their intervention in such cases was one of the grievances of that time. And thereon it was observed that no other state admitted it, nor could the presence of their prince release one man in Spain.

The infelicity also of their treaties was then noted and a large discourse made on it by that learned and grave gentleman, SIR HENRY MARTEN.[114] He showed that in former times, when old ambassadors were employed whose wisdoms and experience might give a promise for their works, success did prove it not the propriety of their nation, as the Frenchmen likewise and others had observed it. That the dexterity of Englishmen was in fighting, not in treating, and by that many millions had been gained, as then exhausted by the other.[115]

He concluded in the general that there might be sought also a remedy for this, which caused a sharp reflex upon him from the envy of the state, [p. 142] those that were then in favor taking it for an aspersion on their persons, the ambassadors which had treated with the French then for the marriage of the Queen being the Duke, the Earl of Holland, and the Earl of Carlisle. The first two young and gamesome, fitter for sports than business, the other so ceremonious and affected that his judgment and reality was in doubt, and his aptness conceived more to have been *deliciarum arbiter,* as Petronius, than *arbiter regni,* or *negotius regis,* as Pallas under Nero. These did take that note of old ambassadors to have a contrary reflection upon them, which without doubt was signified; and for this, they were incensed against him, whereof he had not long after a full taste.[116]

There was in that gentleman great years,[117] great knowledge, great experience, and great abilities of nature to support them. He was a doctor of the laws, and had almost all the civil jurisdiction in his

111. The only privy councillor recorded as speaking to this issue was Sir Thomas Edmondes, Treasurer of the Household. See H. of C., 1 August, p. 375.

112. See above, H. of C., 1 August, n. 4; and H. of L., 9 August, p. 153 and n. 6.

113. See the speeches recorded in C.J., above, H. of C., 1 August, pp. 375–376.

114. Eliot's record of Marten's speech is somewhat fuller than those included in the daily accounts (see H. of C., 1 August, O.B.).

115. I.e., that gained by military ventures in Queen Elizabeth's time was since lost by diplomacy during the reign of James I. See the account of Marten's speech in C.J., above, p. 376.

116. It is not clear to what Eliot refers. Cf. below, p. 564, and Gardiner, *History of England*, VI, 42–46, 66–67.

117. Sir Henry Marten was about sixty-three years old. *D.N.B.*

hands being judge of the Admiralty, judge of the Prerogative, judge of the Arches. In the first he stood as an officer to the Duke, but the chief duty he professed was to justice, and his country. This was the first parliament he had served in, this almost his first entrance to the [p. 143] parliament;[118] this the first trial of his service, which had such a reward from the court as might have been a discouragement to some other and was not without trouble unto him. But in the House it had a good approbation and acceptance, as it did speak that truth which was written in each heart; and the general being laid up for some other opportunity, the particular was resolved on to be followed by a petition to the King. And a committee to that end appointed to prepare it.

[2 August 1625]

This was the agitation of the first day, and the next day had the like when, after the first reading of some bills, as the usual manner is before the House be full for the entertainment of the morning, the cause of Montagu was resumed and the last order read, upon which he stood committed. The Serjeant thereupon being required to bring his prisoner to the bar, answered that he had left him sick, and by a letter from him was advertised that his weakness was such as he could not travel; which, giving no satisfaction to the House that thought it an excuse, divers expressions were upon, showing a disaffection to the man. And that his letter was held dilatory [p. 144] to avoid the question of his works, which, being made an aggravation to his faults, raised the consideration of his punishment to the greater severity and height; and therefore it was urged that he should presently be sent for.

This the King's SOLICITOR did oppose by intimating a message from the King that he was a chaplain-in-ordinary to his Majesty and that his Majesty had taken that cause into his care, which would appear upon his answer to the petition for religion. Therefore he pressed for a message to the King to importune him for a remedy therein which he doubted not would be granted to the full satisfaction of their hearts, much trouble being saved and yet the work accomplished.

This was thought rather a diversion than advice and a way conducing to some new prejudice and danger, no safe retreat or issue out of that.

It was replied that answers were but words, and their satisfaction was not much where deeds did contradict them. As Montagu was said to be then a chaplain to the King it was objected, as a note for dissuasion to that way, in what time he was made so. In the beginning of the parliament he was a stranger to [p. 145] the court, received but since his question; and whether or no, on that occasion, it was doubtful, as what protection it might render.[119] Therefore that counsel of going by petition was disliked. It was said to be unparliamentary, as unsafe; but the other, *more majorum* and juridical. That extrajudicial courses to that House had been seldom fortunate and auspicious, of which some precedents were instanced, as the like remission to King James of the causes of Ireland and Virginia, *18°* of his reign, and that of Sir Simon Harvey, *21°*.[120] That all justices and deputy lieutenants in the countries, this being granted, may have the like privilege and protection. Nay it was alleged further that no man could commit a public crime or injury but by color of some public employment from the King and so all being made his servants, as that was then required, all, by the same

118. Marten was not very vocal in the London session; this appears to have been his first major speech.
119. Concerning Montagu's appointment as the King's chaplain-in-ordinary, see above, H. of C., 9 July, n. 23.
120. See H. of C., 2 August, nn. 25 and 27. These precedents were cited by Edward Alford.

reason, should be free from the jurisdiction of the parliament.

What the parliaments would be then, and what the country by such parliaments, was offered to the consideration of the House with a strong caution in that point to be careful for posterity. It was added that the [p. 146] King ought not to take knowledge of their acts before they were made public and represented by the House. That the examples of all times did warrant their intentions and all qualities of men had been subject to their questions, as the Duke of Gaunt and the Lord Latimer, 50 *E.* 3, were there impeached for giving ill counsel to the King.[121] No dukedom or greatness could exempt them from the jurisdiction of that court, and the right was still the same. The case of Sir Thomas Parry was remembered, *12° Jac.,* for whom being a councillor of state the King then by like message interposed;[122] but the privilege of the House was a direction to that time, which proceeded unto judgment, and gave sentence in the case. By these reasons was supported the resolution to proceed notwithstanding the King's message.

The vogue went generally as it was moved at first: that he should presently be sent for. But this having a little alteration in the form, for that he stood committed to the Serjeant and therefore should be taken, as in custody, and a prisoner. The Serjeant was thereupon commanded to produce him, or at his peril to answer the neglect. Some in this dispute had sallied upon [p. 147] the consideration of his books and therein took occasion to argue his opinions, descending into the subtleties of the schoolmen about the infallibility of grace, the antecedent and consequent wills of God. But their zeal being more commended than their judgment, those doctrinal points were waived as not proper subjects for that place,

and the dispute was carried only upon the consideration of his person.

This difficulty being over, a new one did arise of the same kind though differing in the form. Dr. Anyan, one of the masters of the colleges, who had likewise been questioned by that court, was appointed then to preach before both Houses the next Sunday.[123] This was thought an affront unto the parliament. The burgesses of that university were called for. These were sent to [the] Vice-chancellor to expostulate the fact. The Vice-chancellor, speaking with Anyan, returned his answer that he would not desist. But in observance to the House he after caused the delegates to meet, who discharged him from the service and named another in his stead, making with some difficulty an accommodation in that point. This showed [p. 148] likewise the spirit of that party which studied an innovation in the Church, and was taken for an indication of more danger. That boldness thought improper for such men, scholars and churchmen being not always found so confident. Still, it increased the fear and with that the jealousy grew more hot, which then appeared in sparks and after flamed more clearly.

[3 August 1625]

Both Houses here again, it being the general day appointed for the kingdom, concurred in the celebration of the fast. The outward piety seemed great and many, doubtless, had it truly in their hearts. Yet some insincerity was suspected where the practice and professions did not meet, that holiness being distrusted which has not righteousness to accompany it.

[4 August 1625]

[p. 148] The next morning, by a message from the King, both Houses were com-

121. See H. of C., 2 August, n. 40.
122. See H. of C., 2 August, n. 8.
123. Anyan, president of Corpus Christi College,

was scheduled to preach before the Houses on Wednesday (not Sunday), 3 August, at the fast service. See above, H. of C., 2 August, n. 19.

manded to attend him presently at Christ Church. Where, after some little expectation, his Majesty being come, he began with the occasion of that meeting and some short expressions of himself. Somewhat he touched of the preparation then in hand and the necessity of the work, with a remembrance of their joint and mutual engagements [p. 149] thereunto, saying that better it were half his ships should perish than that the fleet should not go forth. He urged also, in his manner, the expense that had been made, and without a further aid that there was an impossibility to proceed. Some intimation he used likewise of the gift that had been passed and his acceptance but not satisfaction in that point, concluding with a consideration of the time, how dangerous it was, and leaving it to the judgment of that council whether they would hold greater the fear of the sickness to themselves or the dishonor of their nation. Somewhat he added for the answer to the petition of religion: that within two days they should have it, which as a cordial and restorative was then given to sweeten the operation of the rest.

This was seconded by the Secretary of State, the Lord Conway who, reckoning up particulars of the charge, the same that had been formerly and afterwards were many times repeated, making an immense calculation of the treasures so exhausted, wherein, he said, there wanted some thirty or forty thousand pounds to do the work, the officers being discredited by the sickness and without [p. 150] which the fleet could not go out.

The war, he alleged, was occasioned by the parliament in the counsel which they gave for the dissolution of the treaties. In that consisted the honor of the kingdom, the safety of religion, and the general good of Christendom. If the preparations should dissolve, he said, the Germans would di-

vide, the French disband and reunite them to the Catholics, the King of Denmark retire and make his peace with the Emperor who, with the Duke of Savoy and the Venetians, were drawn by King James into the League; which difficulties being foreseen the King therefore resorted to his subjects to crave that help from them which his ancestors in like cases had received.

This was the sum of that which he delivered, being but the abstract of that which was to come. For here again were used those great abilities of Sir John Coke, on whom the weight of that burden was imposed who, though yet no public minister of the state, and a member of the Commons, was without leave from them—and that never done by any man before—in their presence made a dictator for the King.[124] And after some formality of seeming to take instructions at the present in that which he had studied long before, having the honor in the face of that assembly [p. 151] to be called up privately to the state and from thence returning, as from an oracle, inspired with a new spirit and wisdom, thus he propounds those sacred reasons he had gathered for the occasion of that time.

[Sir John Coke.] His beginning was at the end of the Spanish treaties wherein he showed that the late King at the instance of the parliament, by the cooperation of his Majesty that then was and the Duke of Buckingham (giving them that conjuncture) was drawn to break with Spain. That he thereupon, considering the troubles that must follow it, there being no other means but war for recovery of the Palatinate and to moderate the greatness of that King whose forces then possessed it and, under color of the Catholic cause and League, aspired to make himself a Catholic prince and monarch. And foreseeing the dangers of that change in respect of the quality of his

124. See H. of L., 4 August, n. 12.

people through a long peace and quiet become unapt for war, at least in much want of art and preparation, he prudently dissembled his intentions for a while that others, by the discovery of his purpose, made not advantage thereupon; and suffered himself to be entertained with mediations and entreaties and new propositions to be made him until by degrees he [p. 152] came to that which he intended, nothing being omitted in the interim that might settle his affairs.

The Palatinate he saw divided by his enemies and held, *de facto*, by their powers. A diet likewise called to invest them with the right, and to exclude all hope of restitution. In France he saw all things in combustion, and the King there inclining to sheath his sword in the bowels of his subjects rather than to turn it against others; and the Low Countries in great danger and necessity by the potency of their adversaries and the faction of the Arminians which began to make an interruption in their government and threatened them in more.

These things weighed, for an encouragement to the States he lent them 6,000 men, and pay for their entertainment for two years. And, to make the more strict conjunction with the French, sought their alliance for his son, and by that match to make the bond inviolable between them. The German princes and the King of Denmark he solicited, whose coldness was immovable until they should see his Majesty in the field. The charge for that being cast, what a land army would require, and the computation rising to 700,000 *l.* per annum, his Majesty, in contemplation [p. 153] of his people, thought of some thriftier course, and to that end drew a league between France, Savoy, Venice, the Low Countries, and himself, for the raising of 30,000 foot, and 6,000 horse, to serve under the command of Count Mansfeld, he being to contribute to that charge but 20,000 *l.* a month. This being done, and a preparation likewise of his fleet, the King of

Denmark, thereupon coming into the League, promised to raise a great army in those parts, for which the King also was to contribute 30,000 *l.* a month.

These things thus settled by King James being in preparation or in act, the fruit whereof is yet shadowed under hope, his Majesty not willing to desert it being the effect of the counsel given by parliament, by parliament he desired to follow and accomplish it. Which requiring a more charge than his treasures will supply, there being 400,000 *l.* disbursed already for the navy which is now upon the seas going towards the rendezvous at Plymouth where there be 10,000 landmen for the action which has so great an expectation in the world, there wants yet some money to supply them, some necessaries for the ships, some provisions for the men, without which neither can be serviceable.

It is the first fruits [p. 154] of our warfare, the *primitiae* of the King, wherein the hope of our allies, the interests of religion, the honor of the kingdom are engaged, which shows that this parliament was not called merely upon formality after the accession to the crown, but for the consultation of this business: that as the parliament did begin, the parliament might end it. Thus spoke that oracle.

Besides, he added that his Majesty had intelligence of a design to trouble Ireland, and an increase of the enemies' navy in the Low Countries with a purpose to thrust over part of their armies into England. But as no king was more loving to his subjects, so his Majesty was confident that no subjects were more loving to their king. And therefore he left it wholly to their choice whether, by balancing the occasions, they should think fitter upon the consideration of the time to let the action fall or to give him more relief. This was the sum of his expression, somewhat more large, but to this sense and purpose.

And further he made this postil upon that particular of Mansfeld in apology and excuse, that though it had not answered the expectation at the full, yet it had produced [p. 155] some fruits worthy of that design, as the putting off of the diet in Germany, the encouragement of the princes, the coming of the King of Denmark into the field, the attempts of the French upon Milan, the reconciliation of the French Protestants and their King, and the scattering of the enemies' forces in the Low Countries.

In which some things being more than his last discourse on the same subject did contain,[125] it was thought to be more studied not more true, nothing either of intelligence or fact having happened in that time to give it other color than his fancy. The rest being in substance but what he had said before, and a repetition in effect of his proposition made at London, had not much observation for the matter, though some passages were more noted which then did open and give discovery to the secret.

Both in the King's discourse and his, the conclusion was not judged answerable to the premises. The referring of the action at that time, advanced to so much forwardness, was not conceived agreeable with the pretended importance of the work wherein such treasures had been spent. The calculations that were made argued the necessity [p. 156] of the thing, without which infinite preparations would not be, and the *equilibrio* it was left in made it but adiaphoral. The interpretations were various which it had, according to the fancies that they came from.[126] Those that were more charitable did infer that, there being some special service first intended, the opportunity had prevented it, and so the design was lost. Those that possessed more jealousy did collect that a secret reconciliation had been made, and by some private

treaty and convention a composition and agreement of all difference. But all believed the preparation should be left—no ships nor men to be drawn further in the employment—and that the study was how to impute it to the parliament, either their counsel or denial to be an occasion to dissolve it; some color only sought for the satisfaction of the world, that whatever did occur a cause might be in readiness and, if the reason pressed it, a fair excuse at hand. But the sum moved for seemed a miracle, which had its consideration after with the Commons where the treaties and mediations that were spoken of, and that speaker's act itself, came into question and dispute;[127] and that parallel [p. 157] and conjuncture of cooperation with the King was not (though silenced) yet forgotten.

[5 August 1625]

The next day was the entrance to that scene, the remain of that[128] being reserved for meditation when, all the members of the Commons specially appointed to attend having resolved the overtures that were made, a lawyer first begins,[129] as a prologue to the act, drawing his considerations from the conclusion of the King.

[JOHN WHISTLER.] That the King having left it indifferently to their choice (balancing the importance of his service with the dangers of the time) whether they would sit to think of a new supply, or part and lose the action. He desired first that there might be a conference with the Lords to learn, if they could tell it, whether the consequence were such of the preparations then in hand, as it was more in relation to the kingdom than the safety of their lives. If so, that then he was no Englishman that would leave it; to die resolutely for their country, having

125. I.e., the speech on the King's estate, delivered by Coke on 8 July 1625. See above, H. of C., 8 July, O.B.

126. There is no record in the daily accounts of any debates or private discussions immediately following

Sir John Coke's speech.

127. See the debates of 5 August, below.

128. I.e., 4 August.

129. I.e., John Whistler. See H. of C., 5 August, O.B.

been the honor of their nation. If otherwise, that he was no friend to England that desired it, nor could they, in wisdom, give themselves as a sacrifice to their enemies. The King, he said, [p. 158] had graciously referred it unto them, and they in duty to the King ought to resolve it prudently. The greater good must be preferred. Fancy and affection must not govern in such counsels. That the probability seemed against sitting at that time; the supply which was demanded being too little for their values, less than they should spend if they continued there awhile. But the better to determine it, he wished there might be a conference with the Lords. They had like interest in the sitting, their dangers being equally involved though the supply were only the propriety of the Commons. Therefore he moved the House to go presently to them, and so by a joint advice mutually to conclude.

This introduction was not liked by those that had relation to the court, it declining wholly the course of their affections; and to that end some objections it received and some diversions followed them. It was alleged to be unparliamentary and improper upon a proposition from the King to seek an interpretation from the Lords,[130] who might be as ignorant as others, and could not judge the worth of what they knew not; nor would discretion so presume, though it might know a part, to set [p. 159] an estimate on the whole.

It was moved likewise that they should first state the propositions that were made,[131] and so by *capita* debate them; but that, leading into a labyrinth and meander where nothing but confusion could be found, was left; as that expelled the former, in the room of which another did arise

whose spirit, once up, was not so easily conjured down.

This came from SIR FRANCIS SEYMOUR who with much boldness and some asperity did deliver it, laying it for a ground upon that meeting and assembly that there could be no other end thereof than the corrupt purposes of some to put a jealousy and dissension between their Sovereign and his subjects.

The proposition he divided, and so answered that for money, which was the first part, as the King had been content with their first grant at London; if more should then be given it could not be levied till the spring when the other subsidies might be past, and against that time they might have met again.

For credit, the second part, which might be pretended by a grant, he said it was an argument to the dishonor of the King, kings having more in the general affection of their subjects than any particular declaration [p. 160] could imply, this making them but entitled to a part, the other to the whole, whatever his subjects did possess, as there was occasion for his service. It were, he said, too great a show of want and poverty in the state to suppose that small sum named,[132] which he did blush to think of, needed a parliament to procure it. Where is the old treasure of the kingdom, the reputation of the state that the times of Queen Elizabeth enjoyed when the least of many ministers of hers, if there had been occasion, could, of his own credit, have supplied a greater sum than this? And when that famous princess, never to be forgotten, having no want nor use, only in prevention of her enemies, took up at once of the Fuggers[133] then in Germany almost all the coin

130. Sir George More spoke to the problem of procedure. See H. of C., 5 August, O.B.

131. I.e., a motion by Danvers. For the names of the speakers this day, see above, H. of C., 5 August, O.B.

132. I.e., 30,000 to 40,000 *l.* needed to set forth the fleet. This sum was mentioned by Lord Conway in his speech of 4 August (see above, p. 387) and was later reiterated in Buckingham's speech to both Houses on

8 August (see above, p. 164).

133. MS.: *Foulkers.* We have not been able to determine the incident to which the text refers. On the English crown's borrowing from the Fuggers, see John W. Burgon, *The Life and Times of Sir Thomas Gresham* (London, 1839), I, 69, 82–83, 86–87, and Richard Ehrenberg, *Capital and Finance in the Age of the Renaissance,* tr. H. M. Lucas (London, 1928), pp. 116–117.

of Christendom? Where is this credit now? Where are those ministers of this age? I doubt their worth and fidelity is gone. That they are the men which bring this necessity to their master; that they have exhausted thus his treasures, spent his revenues and, being conscious of these faults, by the unnecessary preparations they have caused, now seek to color it by some others and, if they can, to lay the blame on us. [p. 161] We have been told of late of a peace in France and a reconciliation for the Protestants, but who knows not the present violence against them? And we may wish therein that our ships do not impeach them.[134] There were five[135] subsidies and three fifteenths not long since given for the Queen of Bohemia and that service, but what has she been bettered? What has been therein done worthy of that intention? No enemy is declared; nothing has been attempted but the consumption of ourselves.

Thus he said, using besides some general notes of princes, of their happiness that were counseled by men of worth and knowledge, and the contrary where they rest upon confidence of some few that can but beg or flatter. Upon which he resumed again the memory of the Queen who was munificent to her servants but from her own stores, not feeding them on the marrow of her subjects. And he concluded that he doubted not to see the like greatness in the King if he would give them leave to do somewhat for the country whereby they might be enabled and encouraged to yield him seasonable supply and from whose service no dangers could deter them.

This being another [p. 162] pitch and to another point directed than the former, some wished again for that, and in the grave thereof this other to be buried. The courtiers saw themselves encountered in

their way, and their desire of sitting then pursued, though in affection unto them, not to their end and purpose. That charge upon the ministers of state, the sally on their counsels, the parallel of the times, was no good music in their ears, with which all mention of the elders had antipathy, and the glories of that princess were like basilisks in their eyes. That note of flattery and begging also was known to have reflection on the favorites and that boldness gave suspicion yet of more. To prevent which, and the storm was like to follow it, the CHANCELLOR OF THE DUCHY did stand up and used these reasons and persuasions:

[SIR HUMPHREY MAY.] That if the plate and jewels of the King or the plate and jewels of some others, whom he heard dashed upon, could have procured money at that time, they had not met there then. Things, he said, were turned fairly to advantage, making therein an insinuation for those persons to whose merit he imputed it—not naming any but leaving it not doubted whom he meant. When the parliament did [p. 163] advise the dissolution of the treaties, he alleged a war was then expected, from which common place he argued the dangers they were in. France and Spain united, both in alliance and affection, and the Pope still laboring to endear them for the supportation of his cause. The Germans then broken by the Emperor. The King of Denmark a wary prince unlikely to engage himself in war for the benefit of others. Yet such was the conversion of the time, as France and Spain were separate. That two armies were levied by the French and one marched into the Valtellina, the other against Genoa. The Germans reunited. The Dane prepared for war. All which did follow upon the declaration of King James in the setting forth of Mansfeld. The next

---

134. The reference is apparently to the delivery of the eight English ships to the French. See above, H. of L., 9 August, p. 165 and n. 67.

135. The Bedford MS. 197 version of Seymour's

speech gives the figure of *three* subsidies. See above, H. of C., 5 August, p. 394 and n. 33. If the two subsidies of 1621 were also included, it would bring the total to five.

day after the shipping of his men at Dover, the French beginning with their armies then to march; so as the rest of the English preparations were expected, there being presumed a confidence upon that; and if that credit should be lost, besides the disadvantage of the work it would be a general loss to the honor of the nation and impeach the reputation and esteem [p. 164] which is the soul and life of every state and government.

He urged again that the King's engagement was by them and that he undertook but the designs which they propounded. And thereupon he inferred that the parliament ought not to recede; that if the success were ill, other men might be furnished with excuses and the misfortune imputed to that House for not supplying necessaries. This he enforced further with an example of those times, or next them, which he said were so precious in their memories, when the Earl of Devonshire,[136] not at his instance or his friends', was sent deputy into Ireland and, the Spanish army landing, and there joining with the rebels to the hazard of that kingdom, wherein happened that difficult siege of Kinsale, he was still furnished from the court (though by his enemies) with all things necessary for that service. And when it came into the deliberations of the Council the Earl of Salisbury, then Treasurer,[137] by way of protestation did affirm that he could not complain of them; nothing had been wanting of their help and if there were a miscarriage in the action the blame must be his [p. 165] own. From thence he drew a persuasion for the like that they should then accord to make supply, and so lay the burden upon others. He concluded with an apothegm (whereof he was never without store): that money given in that House

might be cast into the sea, and so some treasure lost; but not given, posterity might rue it, reservation in such cases being more dangerous than adventure.

The wit of this gentleman always drew the attention of the House, though his motions seldom relished it. The observation which he made upon the Earl of Devonshire was thought true, though the application were not proper, and his note but a fallacy for the time. His intelligence was known good in the passages of that scene, having been a servant to the Earl, bred under his command and with him in those troubles;[138] but his relations in other things were doubted, as his urging of the engagement was disliked, and generally his intentions had a prejudice as coming from the court. Yet some scruples he had raised by that discourse and argument. The desire and expectation of denial, which most men did believe, seemed to have a contradiction by his [p. 166] way, pressing so directly for supply, he being no stranger to the cabinet. This caused a distraction in some thoughts, that by the superficies judged the body; but those that took the dimension of all parts, in the depth thereof found another sense and meaning which was but to qualify the jealousy conceived and to divert that consideration of the counsels, which he perceived, having a sharp judgment and inspection, had so inflamed the affection of the House that no small matter could allay it; opposition being like fuel to such fires. And therefore he endeavored it by changing that supposed state of the cause that so, if possible, he might change the order in proceeding. And to endear this further, another of his fellow councillors and officers, the TREASURER OF THE HOUSEHOLD, did second him with a particular proposition for two sub-

---

136. I.e., Charles Blount, Lord Mountjoy. See H. of C., 5 August, n. 41.

137. Sir Robert Cecil, later created Earl of Salisbury, was Secretary of State, not Treasurer. See H. of C., 5 August, n. 41.

138. Humphrey May had served as gentleman usher to Lord Mountjoy, then Lord Deputy of Ireland, during the period of the Kinsale siege. See *Cal. S.P. Ireland, 1600–1601*, p. 316; *Cal. S.P. Ireland, 1601–1603*, pp. 400–401.

sidies. But that labor was in vain, the quarrel being begun; all men were apprehensive of the injury, and many did express it.

So hard it is, where public wrongs are done, to keep them from vindication or complaint. Minions may enjoy the favor of their masters, but if they once abuse it, no privilege can protect them. The subjects' [p. 167] cry will follow them, and if it prevail not upon earth, heaven will hear and help them. Justice is provided for their adversaries. Seldom they escape it here, never hereafter, but vengeance does attend them, which should make them more cautious in offending, when the offenses done are so hardly left unpunished. That meeting might have been prevented with much safety but, being met, that crime was thought unpardonable. He that was the occasion of that trouble must have his share therein, and by that means of more, till the measure of his iniquities was full, and then vengeance must surprise him like a whirlwind, and no favor or greatness may deliver him; but, as his merit, such must be his reward.

But to resume our story. The proposition of those councillors for supply had but a cold acceptance, and the intention which it carried to divert the former motions was wholly rejected and in vain. And thus those motions were pursued in a high strain of eloquence by that master of expression, SIR ROBERT PHELIPS, who, casting his motions into a quadripartite division for method and order to his speech, in more than wonted gravity to raise the expectation of his hearers, [p. 168] having composed himself, thus he propounds his sense:

[SIR ROBERT PHELIPS.] First, for the meeting (which was the first member of his division), he said it was to him not inferior to a miracle, there having been at London such satisfaction in their works as no servant of the King's, no minister of state (if they must be distinguished) but approved what they

had done; and his Majesty himself, who was more than thousands others, gave such an acknowledgment thereof as the adjournment was resolved, in counterpoise of that, for the preservation of their healths, which he did balance equally with the consideration of his own. This having been the satisfaction of that time, nothing occurring after for the change or alteration that was made, no new enemy discovered, no new design in hand, no new danger pressing it, how those new counsels should be taken, how that should seem too little which was then thought enough, how that satisfaction should be lost, and by that their favor with his Majesty, no reason, he said, could resolve him in that point, nothing but divinity could judge. That it was a strange precedent they there met when, upon the declaration of his Majesty, and his acceptance of that gift, most of their members being retired, and so few left that they could be hardly called a House, that then [p. 169] a proposition should be made, like a surprise of enemies not as an overture from friends who should deal clearly and aboveboard, not circumvent the innocent, not make such requital of their loves. This, he observed, was the action of that gentleman who, he said, did that yesterday which was never done before;[139] and for both deserved to render an account. For though the danger were avoided in the former, the attempt was not the less; and for the latter, no reason could excuse it. That those things were strange, but the adjournment and that meeting there far more, to have the whole kingdom hurried in such haste for the will and pleasure of one subject (for it could not be the King should have such mutability in himself). That that subject should presume to transfer his errors to the parliament, that the parliament should be thought a fit father for great faults, this, he professed, was beyond all example and comparison, hardly the former precedent of that place could

139. I.e., Sir John Coke. See above, H. of C., 5 August, n. 44.

be a match therein. The first danger in accession being less, the project and intention not worse, and in respect thereof, it being but justice to desire it that the success and issue, for what concerned [p. 170] those ministers, were the same. That therefore he was not of opinion with those that would not sit. That he valued not his safety with the safety and welfare of the kingdom. That God having brought them thither, as Joseph went for Egypt,[140] by that coming, though unwished for, some glorious work might be. What was not intended amongst men, providence and divinity could induce; they were to act their parts and leave the success to God.

This was his expression on that part. The next concerned the counsels of the kingdom, wherein reflecting upon the Spanish labyrinth and treaties he said that God had made it a national punishment for their sins. That by that treaty was induced that dangerous journey of their Prince, led on by the flattering counsels of those servants who had brought King James in love with the deceitful face of friendship and betrayed him to the nets of those subtle, foxlike, artificial, faithless people, as he then termed the Spaniards. He remembered what was suffered in that cause, for the opposition made in parliament *18°* of that reign when, [p. 171] he said, their liberties were harassed, their persons in restraint, of which he had borne a share by the ill influence of those planets, being taxed for nothing but speaking against that match.[141] Of which disasters being free, both in the general and particular by a cause stranger than the effect, that journey into Spain which began not to that end, that three things in the next parliament were desired and promised, but scarce kept. The first, for prevention in the future, that no more such treaties might endanger them, but the Prince to match with one of his own religion.

The second, that there might be such respect unto our neighbors, as to preserve their safeties, who were reciprocally a safety unto them. The third, to maintain the religion in the kingdom that the laws might have their life, and not delinquents be suffered to affront them. How those were kept, that, the certainty was too great. What were the Spanish articles it was known, what then the French it was doubted. That papists did still increase, their priests and Jesuits grow more bold, little being done for support of the allies, [p. 172] a professed coldness even in all; and by what counsels it was so, both truth and reason spoke.

For the present state and condition of the people, which was the third branch of his division, he deduced a demonstration from *septimo* of King James and remembered the question of imposing then on foot, and the title of prerogative therein.[142] How it was then handled in that House, argued and debated for the interests of the subject, and resolved to be their right, their inheritance to be free, and yet the fact continuing in prejudice of that liberty. How in *12°* it was resumed, distributed into parts, and a conference thereupon intended with the Lords, so by a message sought but, through the practice of some ministers, refused, and all papers after taken which had relation to that business, and the records and books which had the evidence of those liberties, burned and consumed with the liberties themselves, as far as present power could rule the judgment of posterity. Since which time, there having been a large bounty of the subject, as two subsidies *18°*, three subsidies and fifteenths given in the last parliament of King James, only with a claim for continuation in that point, and the main [p. 173] disputes declined; yet that so little had that bounty or modesty prevailed as the effect of that grievance was still on them

---

140. Gen. 39–50.
141. See above, H. of C., 5 August, n. 45.

142. On this and the following references, see H. of C., 5 August, nn. 47–52.

and, that which never was before, the tonnage and poundage, levied and collected without a grant from thence, as if right were an impertinence to states where power and force are extant. By which there had been more pressures on the people within the space of seven years then last past than almost in seven ages next before it. This, he said, for the subject, in part might show the condition he was in, what ability was left him, what affection he might have. Besides, from the consideration of the state, he said there came as small encouragement. That counsels were there monopolized, as the general liberties elsewhere. That the whole wisdom was supposed to be comprehended in one man. That he being master of the favor, was likewise master of all business. *Nihil unquam prisci et integri moris,* as Tacitus notes in the declination of the Romans, *sed exuta aequalitate omnia unius iussa aspectare.* Though there were many councillors in name, that few retained the dignity *aequales ordinis magis quam operis,* as Paterculus has it of the like, though their reputation might be somewhat yet that their [p. 174] authority was but small and their affections as much captived as their greatness.

This he did make an argument that God was not their friend. That by those abuses of favor amongst men, they had lost the favor of the Almighty. That He was become their enemy, and unless they had peace with Him, in vain it was to think of war with others. That therefore an inward preparation must precede before those outward preparations could be hopeful, the watchman waking but in vain if the Lord watch not with him.[143]

Further, he said it was a strong argument of the sickness of the state when the credit was so weak, as it was then pretended, that it could not without a parliament take up 40,000 *l.*, which was a cold persuasion then

to give when such men were so near who were the causes of it. That though it were impossible for the supposition to take place that the English should leave their king yet, in respect of this great abuse of counsels, if any man made a stand, the blame must light on those that had occasioned it, whom for security in that case, it was therefore fit, after the examples of their fathers, the parliament [p. 175] should endeavor to remove.

From thence he descended to his fourth and last particular, which was his opinion on the whole wherein, using again some touches of the former contention in that place, though not approving the disorders but commending the reformation that was sought for, he concluded for an imitation in that point. Not that he would have them tread so near the heels of majesty, yet not to suffer all things by that name. As the King was wronged in the injury of his subjects, he said it was their duty to vindicate them both. That he would not have them reason of what they understood not, whether the fleet should go or stay, not knowing the design. That the estate at home, the affairs civil and domestic were the proper objects of their cares; to settle the government of the kingdom, rectify the disorders, reform the grown[144] abuses, heal the disease thereof. That these were their business and for this he would not have them think of parting, but be suitors to his Majesty that he would give them time to sit on this great service for him, which would afford him a more ample aid and credit than many subsidies could give—the [p. 176] streams of his revenues being cleared, those scattered beams collected, his exhausted stores replenished, the fountain of his exchequer filled again, and all this with the love and satisfaction of his subjects. This he desired might be the resolution of that House, and for that address to the King a committee to prepare it.

143. Ps. 127.

144. *grave.* Printed edition.

This raised the disaffection that was moved to a greater height and sharpness. And not only the injury of that meeting was then looked at, but the whole prejudice of the time; all the misfortunes that were suffered, both foreign and domestic, were imputed to those ministers who usurped that power of greatness and by abuse of the favor of their prince drew all things to their wills. Against this prodigious greatness which, like a comet, was suspected to threaten great disasters to the kingdom, the general intention of that House began then to be inflamed and neither parting nor supply were thought considerable in the case, but the reformation that was spoken of, the restoration of the government.

To stop which stream and current another of the privy councillors stood up, SIR RICHARD WESTON, Chancellor of the Exchequer, who practiced then for others what he must after endeavor for himself, such [p. 177] being the fatality of great persons, as example of misfortunes cannot move them. This man must see in others what were the dangers of exorbitance, how Phaeton rose and fell wanting a moderation to contain him,[145] yet honor and ambition must transport him, let fortune rule the rest.

To the present purpose first he applied some short answers to that which was urged before; for religion saying that he doubted not the satisfaction would be speedy, and no more fear in that. For the counsels, he excused them with the long time of peace that had bred some errors in the state by a dependence upon treaties, which followed the inclination of King James and might then be rectified by their advice unto that King. Yet in some things he said he might justify their works and thereon mentioned the leagues that had been spoken of and the effects pretended, with the advantage under hope.

From whence he passed to positive reasons of his own, for that seeming persuasion of supply. The first was drawn from the necessities of the work, the honor of the kingdom, the restitution of their friends, the cause of religion being in it, and the general good of Christendom, all the princes as he pretended being engaged to hate and love and [p. 178] fear at once with them who, as they warmed, would cool if they had their example. The next was from the necessity of the King who by the expenses of his father had his chests emptied, his revenues all anticipated, his debts great, and for the supportation of his charge which, besides the preparation then in hand, was not little towards the funeral, ambassadors, and the like, for which he was fain to take up monies of the City upon the pawn and mortgage of his lands. Another was taken from the dangers of division if they should part abruptly. The King, he said, in Spain had observed the prejudice which his father had therein, how the homebred jealousies and distractions between his subjects and himself had brought him to contempt, which he therefore in his person had the last parliament endeavored as a happy star and planet by his sweet influence to compose, as knowing that the contrary cause must have a like contrary effect; by which parliament came more grace unto the people in the happy laws then passed than at any time before. Wherein there being so real a demonstration of his virtues, he aleged, that ought then to gain him trust, as those [p. 179] other reasons likewise drawn from the occasion and necessity, to prevail for the supply. Whatever were after done, he added, that action must be then. That

---

145. Ovid, *Metamorphoses*, 1, 750; 2, 328. Eliot may be alluding to the proceedings against Weston, then Lord Treasurer, in 1629. See W. Notestein and F. H.

Relf, *Commons Debates for 1629* (Minneapolis, 1921), pp. 170–172, 243, 265.

the affairs abroad were not to be commanded, other things might stay. The expectation of the world being upon that first action of the King, if he lost then his honor that it was no small thing he parted with, it being the honor also of the nation which had no medium between their glory and their shame. That the fruit of their former labors was in that, and if they there should leave it, both that and all their bounties were in vain; and not confirming then the counsels they had given, beyond that day there was no place for counsel.

So he concluded, and that other questions being waived that only might be spoken to, wherein he concurred with the proposition of his fellow for two subsidies and two fifteenths, rather as it was thought to join in some particular then, by instruction, for the sum. For it was noted to vary from that speech which was made before the King wherein thirty or forty thousand pounds was talked of.[146] But this perhaps was but to hasten the denial the sooner by enlarging the demand, which was considered in the replies [p. 180] that followed, with that strange clause of limitation to their counsels, wherein less being deemed of prophecy than menace, the dislike it moved was greater than the fear which, quickening still the humor that was stirred, drew this expression further from that great father of the law, SIR EDWARD COKE, who, in much observance to the House, much respect unto the cause, having consulted with his memory of the proceedings in like cases from the precedents of the ancients, made this introduction and beginning:

[SIR EDWARD COKE.] That 37 *E*. 3 when that prudent warlike king was in the exaltation of his glory, and yet the subjects suffered through the abuses of some ministers, the Commons then petitioned him to

command his bishops and clergy to pray for three things: the state and happiness of his Majesty, the peace and good government of the kingdom, and the preservation and continuance of unity[147] and love between his subjects and himself which, they then said, were all hazarded by his officers and until their remove no subventions could be made. This, he observed, was at that time without injury or distaste, and the same reason was for them, in confidence whereof, he said, he would freely speak his heart for the honor of his Sovereign, not doubting but his goodness would so take it.

After this preamble [p. 181] he made division of the question, reducing it to this: whether they should then make an addition of supply, or how otherwise to give subsistence to his Majesty. To which points he addressed his subsequent discourse, that being a superstruction on this building.

For the first he rendered his opinion not to give, because to engraft subsidies upon subsidies was not parliamentary, and what should be granted then could not be collected till the spring nor credit thereby given to the King, the affections of his subjects being beyond all grants. He added likewise the afflictions of the time, the interruption of the trade, London being shut up, the decay and poverty of the commons, upon which he cited some examples of foretimes in pressing their abilities too far, as 4 *R*. 2 and 3 *H*. 7 when rebellions did attend it. And 14 *H*. 8,[148] when the northern collectors were all slain, and so fearful an apprehension raised in the state as, to satisfy the people, the King disclaimed the fact, translating it to his councillors. The councillors from themselves did impute it to the judges, the judges to the Cardinal, which shows the danger they were in, and what effects may follow too great a load and pressure. All which he said were [p. 182] reasons against giving at that time.

---

146. See above, n. 132.
147. *virtue*. Printed edition. With regard to Coke's

speech this day, see above, H. of C., 5 August, n. 10.
148. See above, H. of C., 5 August, n. 72.

And so also he retorted that common argument of necessity against the supply of that necessity so pretended, using therein the distinction given by Bracton, of the three sorts and orders of necessity, *affectata, invincibilis, et improvida.* Of which he thought the necessity that was argued to be neither affected nor invincible but improvident and voluntary, which could be no encouragement to giving, when those that had spent the former must be masters of that store and so their supply should be but the ruin of themselves.

For other means of subsistence for the King, the second part of the division which he made, he laid this groundwork and position: that subsidies were not proper for the ordinary expense and charge, but the provision was for that in the ordinary income and revenue. That *commune periculum commune trahit auxilium,* common support and aid should be for common dangers. Lands and revenues were the proper store of princes. That so was the institution of their government, so had been the practice in foretimes. And three things he said were requisite to a king and for those there must be a constant ability in the state. The first, to defend himself against the [p. 183] invasions of his enemies; the second, to aid his confederates and allies; the third, to reward the merits of his servants, of which what wanted at that time was wanting to the King which, being there confessed, needed no arguments to prove it, but a reparation in that point was that work which would commend them. For this, he said, he would first search the causes and then propound some remedies as his reason should suggest them.

Of the causes: in the first place he ranked the fraud of officers and servants, instancing the customers, of whom one farmer, by a medium of seven years, was known to get 50,000 *l.* per annum. The second was the Spanish league and treaty, wherein was lost

and spent more than arithmetic could account, whereas from them they had always got by war. The third, the erecting of new offices with large fees and the continuance of some others that were unnecessary and unprofitable, as the presidentships of York and Wales which were a great burden to the King and no less oppression to the subject, the like whereof was intended for the west and by an order of Council so resolved 31 *H.* 8, but declined by the wisdom of that [p. 184] country which would rest upon the common law of England. Fourthly, multiplicity of offices in one man who could not serve them faithfully and by that means hindered others from preferment whose reward, if they merited, must come from the revenues of the crown, such places being possessed. Fifthly, the disorders of the household through the abuse of ministers who from a shop leapt presently to the Green Cloth, for instances therein naming Cranfield and Harvey.[149] Sixthly, excess of pensions and annuities of which he said the state had then more charge than the whole government had borne from the Conquest to that time; and that they grew into a perpetuity and continuance by being bought and sold as if there were erected a new market for such wares. Seventhly, portage for money, there being allowed twelve pence a pound out of the revenues that were gathered, whereas that service might be done without the least deduction. Eightly, the grant of fee farms and privy seals, whereas gifts and rewards should consist of offices and honors, not of the treasures or inheritance of the crown. Those he alleged were, amongst others, the causes of that want, from whence he did descend [p. 185] to the consideration of the remedies. Those he distinguished into two, *removent* and *promovent,* as physicians use in medicines.

For the *removent,* he propounded the contraries to those causes, the frauds to be corrected, treaties to be left, unnecessary

---

149. Sir Simon Harvey and Lionel Cranfield. See

H. of C., 5 August, n. 19.

offices retrenched (citing for that the precedents 19 H. 7 *et* 22 H. 8,[150] when the like was done), multiplicity of offices to be broken, abuses of the household to be rectified by the old forms and institutions, grants and annuities resumed, the sheriffs in each county to bring in the revenues to the Exchequer, and largess to be spared till the treasures did abound, as was provided by the statute 9 H. 4,[151] that no man should beg till the King were out of debt, where that clause in patents (by a special provision in the point) *ex mero motu*, did come in. These for the *removents* he propounded.

For the *promovent* he added three particulars. First, the enclosing of waste grounds, whereby there might be a large augmentation to the crown with an increase and benefit to the kingdom, the King having 31 forests, besides parks, which contain a mass of lands that then yielded nothing but a charge. Secondly, the government of Ireland to be rectified, [p. 186] which he said anciently did bring in 30,000 *l.* a year in the days of E[dward] 3 when silver was but a five groats an ounce, notwithstanding the increase therein, it then being worse than nothing. Thirdly, the King's rents to be improved which, he alleged, would bear a third part of increase, and that would be a good addition to the ordinary of revenue which ought to bear the ordinary of expense. That so 6 E. 3[152] that King did undertake it. So 50 E. 3; 6 R. 2; 5 H. 4; 1 H. 5; 11 H. 6;[153] 1 E. 4;[154] 1 H. 7, 11 H. 8,[155] it was both declared and ordained; and that in the roll 27 E. 3, *num.* 9[156] it was said that the King in fourteen years war with France did not once charge his subjects because he had good officers.

Upon all which he concluded with a desire to sit, and moved for a committee to set down those or such other heads as should be thought helpful to that service, which would give the best aid and subsistence to the King, that so they might be represented to his Majesty with a desire for time to treat and handle them according to the importance of the work.

He had by the way upon the point of improvidence observed some disorders in the Admiralty. The navy he said, which was the charge of the Lord Admiral, had not in [p. 187] the days of Queen Elizabeth danced a pavan, lying upon the water so long time in readiness without action; that that great place was not committed in old time to the trust of so great persons. Great persons had enjoyed places of great title, but by the wisdom of the elders men of sufficiency and merit were only appointed to such offices.

That tradesmen were Masters of the Ordnance till 20 H. 8, and after the nobility once possessed it, it had never been well executed. That the Admiralty in the reign of E. 3, was divided into south and north, as being in the judgment of that prince too much for one command, though then it seemed both that and many others were too little.

To which notes and arguments made by him, others by other men[157] then added, as their fancies or memories did suggest them. That there was no engagement, as it was urged. That there was no power to engage the kingdom but by act. That if there had been an engagement it was quit, the last parliament having given four hundred thousand pounds towards it besides the subsidies then granted, and yet no war proclaimed, no enemy declared. Nay, further, by induction it was argued that there [p. 188] was no necessity, and that drawn from the form of preparation. For, it was

---

150. See H. of C., 5 August, n. 14.

151. The correct citation is 4 H. IV. See H. of C., 5 August, n. 21.

152. *Rot. Parl.,* 6 E. III, no. 3.

153. See above, H. of C., 5 August, nn. 83–85.

154. The citation in the text seems to be incorrect; we are unable to find the precedent.

155. See above, H. of C., 5 August, n. 86.

156. Cf. *Rot. Parl.,* 27 E. III, no. 9.

157. *were.* Printed edition.

said, that the land soldiers were all pressed and at their rendezvous in May, the mariners in April, the victual and provisions shipped in March, whereof four months' store was spent without moving from the harbors; and the men so long under pay and entertainment, to a vast expense and charge without any service to the King, which was not convenable with the necessity then pretended, more being monthly wasted than at that time was required.

To all which, except that last, the King's SOLICITOR gave an answer, but that he balked; for to deny the argument he could not, the inference being so clear that such unnecessary preparations and expenses proved rather an excess than a necessity. To deny the particulars that made up the induction he dared not, their truth being known to all men. To grant both the induction and the inference and in the fact deny it, was as dangerous as absurd, it supposing a necessity without reason and an improvidence more shameful than the want. This therefore he declined, but to the rest replied, making first a protestation for himself, that having two capacities, one as a member of that House, the other as a servant to the King, he would without [p. 189] partiality express himself, not holding of Cephas or Apollos[158] but to the reason of the case, and in the integrity of his conscience as his judgment and opinion should direct him. For the engagement, he held that really they were bound, the dissolution of the treaties being the effect of the declaration of the parliament, and the war intended caused by the dissolution of the treaties for which the grant last made was not a satisfaction but an earnest, the obligation holding to the occasion, not the time.

For the not knowing of the enemy, he said, it was but want of ceremony to the act and at most but a dispensation for the present, not a dissolution of the bond, wherein he wished they should be suitors to the King to remove that scruple of their jealousy.[159] For the holding of places by men of no experience (acknowledging the person that was meant,[160] and his relations to him), he desired it might not be a prejudice to the public if he had been in fault; but that precedence might be given to the merit of the cause and the general first preferred, that particular coming after. For the afflictions of the time, he said, those were the powers of God and could not be prevented, nor would they excuse their not resistance of their [p. 190] enemies. Their enemies, he said, were armed, and if they sat still the others would not be idle, but either in Ireland or elsewhere make some attempt upon them which would put them to more trouble and more charge than then was sought for. And some having objected the season of the year, that the time was passed for the fleet to put to sea, and that the King's estate at home was like a leaking ship, not be ventured further until it were careened, he answered that the design was secret and therefore that the season was not known. And if a leaking ship were set upon by enemies, that all the mariners must not look to the stopping of the leak and let the ship be taken. The greater danger first must be opposed and looked to. Outward attempts are violent, inward diseases bear delay; therefore he concurred with the opinion of the councillors that it was fit to give, and that only to be the business of that time, but for the *quantum* he referred it to the House.

This was followed by some others of that kind, and opposed again by many of the contrary. The engagement was still pressed as the main argument of the court and one inferred from thence that part of the Palatinate was propounded to be restored

158. 1 Cor. 1:12.
159. I.e., to petition Charles to declare the enemy to be the King of Spain.
160. I.e., the Duke of Buckingham.

[p. 191] upon the treaty, and King James did then refuse it, changing the resolution of his course; so as if the engagement were retrenched, the war intended must be left and so the Palsgrave should have prejudice by their means, which would breed a coldness in their friends, a confidence in their enemies, the one by an opinion of unwillingness, the other of disability in the kingdom. This had as small authority as belief, it coming from a gentleman that was seldom fortunate in that place. He was a servant to the Palsgrave, secretary to his Queen, and one that had a fair education and some hope in his younger days of study; but in his exercise and practice, art had confounded nature, or time both, that mostly his affections had prejudice by his reasons.[161] That party restitution, which he spoke of, no man did credit or believe, no such effects to be emergent from those treaties, which too much had been tried. The point of the engagement was again answered, not only from the fact but from the intention of the House, wherein it was remembered that so careful they had been to avoid that rock and shelf as both in the declaration, which preceded, and in the preamble of the act, that was [p. 192] made an explanation of the former, all words and syllables were struck out that might carry an interpretation to that sense.[162]

Much time and labor being spent in those arguments and disputes, and many more intending still to speak, the House perceived the resolution was not near, and therefore left the further agitation for that time (the day being far overspent) settling it by an order to be resumed again the morrow.

All men discerned that the violence would be great. The courtiers, being fearful, grew exasperated for their friends whom they saw aimed and pointed at, and did doubt some nearer touch. The others likewise, by the opposition made more quick, in opening their grievances finding still more grievance. Their own motions warmed them and their affections were inflamed by reflection on themselves. The danger of the kingdom, their own particular dangers hazarded for the pleasure of one man raised their apprehension on these injuries and their resolutions to requite them. The neutrals were not many that had exemption from those passions and shared not in that contestation of affections. Some there were, whom fear and ignorance divided, that stood in expectation of the issue, and without reference to the cause [p. 193] resolved to be the victors. But those were few and not considerable in the question. The truth of what was urged being most obvious and apparent, those whom no private interests did move were bent wholly to complaint; those whom the court possessed were as earnest to decline it. Either part in the remainder of that day labored the strengthening of their side. Infinite was the practice used with all men to sound and gain them, wherein the courtiers did exceed. No ·promises or persuasions were too much to make one proselyte in that faith. Whom ambition had made corruptible, their offerings did allure; and what reason could not, hope did then effect.

[6 August 1625]

This being the preparation of that night, the work next day began with a remembrance of the pardon to the Jesuit[163] and a calling for the petition in that point

---

161. I.e., Sir Francis Nethersole, who had, in 1619, been appointed the English agent to the princes of the Protestant Union and secretary to Elizabeth, the Electress Palatine. *D.N.B.*

162. This point was made by Edward Alford. See above, H. of C., 5 August, p. 407 and n. 134.

163. The pardon was not the first order of business of the day. Sir Robert Phelips brought up the matter of the pardon. See H. of C., 6 August, O.B.

which, though it seemed an act of aggravation to the courtiers, was seconded by another mention of that kind that had no relation to that work but then came accidentally from the country, certified as an occurrence of the time, which wrought so powerfully on the House as did foment their jealousy, increasing [p. 194] the difficulty of atonement and making the contestation far more strong.

The particular was this.[164] Some justices of the peace in Dorsetshire having, upon suspicion or intelligence, searched a papist's house and there found an altar, copes, crucifixes, books, relics, and other popish stuff, and thereupon committed the owner of the house for refusing to take the oaths according to the law, a letter was sent them from the court, signed by the Secretary of State, requiring them forthwith to redeliver the stuff which they had taken away, and to set at liberty the party. This by those justices was certified to their friends. They, as they thought it necessary, did represent it to the House which, taking it into the number of their grievances, though they did not much dispute it, did much revolve it in the consideration of their thoughts, that at that time such countenance should be given to so great offenders of the law, that the law must be controlled in the favor of such persons and the ministers of justice, who were faithful in their offices, receive an increpation for their duties (for so the letter did imply), and that [p. 195] where religion was involved, this also went as an ingredient of the time into the matter and composition of distaste. Though the formal deliberation were referred to the committee that was appointed for the pardon, in point of remedy and redress, yet the evil was then resented and the cause not doubted to be known, which gave it an influence into the agitations of that time. Wherein five things were

first propounded to be presented to the King:[165]

[SIR NATHANIEL RICH.] For religion, to make a countermine in that against the boldness and practice of the adversaries, without which there could be no more expected from their enterprises than there happened to the Israelites while the accursed thing was with them, and for this to have the King's answer that was spoken of upon their general petition therein made, to be rendered in full parliament, that it might be recorded in both Houses to receive the quality of a law. Secondly, that if there were a real purpose for a war, the enemy might be known and some public declaration to that end. Thirdly, that a grave council might be settled to rectify the disorder of affairs. [p. 196] Fourthly, that the King's revenue might be looked into to stop the leaks in that and to restore it to its natural strength and fullness, without which they could not be without poverty in the crown, grievance and oppression in the government. Lastly, that the doubt of impositions might be cleared and an answer in that point, without which no man could say what truly was his own and so not know how to promise or to give. And to prove the demands so parliamentary and no capitulation with the King, the precedent 22 E. 3 was vouched, when like petitions were exhibited upon less reasons from that House. The necessity thereof was likewise pressed from the consideration of the kingdom, which was said to be so weak that without some help therein it could neither supply the King nor yet support itself.

Some things were said in answer unto these, and some passages of the former day were mentioned with some asperity and sharpness, wherein one CLARKE went on so far in favor of the D[uke] censoriously to

164. I.e., the case of Mary Estmond. See H. of C., 6 August, n. 10.

165. The following five heads for a petition were

proposed by Sir Nathaniel Rich. See above, H. of C., 6 August, O.B.

tax the exceptions to the Admiral as in his speech he termed them "bitter invectives".[166] At which being interrupted by a general exclamation of the House, to preserve [p. 197] their wonted gravity and the dignity of their members, he was cried unto the bar. Upon this he was withdrawn for the consideration of his punishment, that had not more expressions than new ways.

Many delivered their opinions, and most different. Some to have him excluded from that House, others forever to debar him. Some likewise did propound an imprisonment and mulct, and with variety in those both for the place and sum. Others, more favorable, moved only for an acknowledgment of his fault, and that also with some difference; some would have had it acted at the bar, others but in his place; and there wanted not that would have wholly had him pardoned and perhaps that scarcely thought him faulty. But the received opinion was that which divided between these: not to make the severity too great lest it might relish of some spleen, nor yet by lenity to impeach the justice of the House, but that the example might secure them from the like presumption in the future. Therefore his censure was to be committed to the Serjeant, and there to stand a prisoner during the pleasure of the House.

This being so resolved on, the delinquent was called [p. 198] in, who, kneeling at the bar, had that sentence there pronounced, and so the Serjeant did receive him.

This judgment, as their whole proceeding in like cases, is observable for their order. Their gravity is great in all things, this more punctually does express it. For, to avoid confusion and disturbance, on no occasion, at no time, is it lawful for a man in one day to speak to one business above once, though his opinion altered, though his reason should be changed, more than in suffrage with the general vote at last when the question is resolved by a single yea or

no. No personal touches are admitted in any argument or dispute, no cavils or exceptions, nor any member to be named; or where there is contrary and dissent may there be mention of the persons but by paraphrases and description. All bitterness is excluded from their dialect, all words of scandal and aspersion; no man may be interrupted in his speech but for transgression of that rule or breach of some other order of the House (as for the intermixing of their business, when one matter is on foot to stir another before the decision of the former, which in no case is allowable). In all [p. 199] other things, the privilege holds throughout; the business, as the person, has that freedom to pass quietly to the end; no disparity or odds makes a difference in that course; he that does first stand up has the first liberty to be heard; the meanest burgess has as much favor as the best knight or councillor, all sitting in one capacity of Commoners and in the like relation to their countries. If two rise up at once the Speaker does determine it; he that his eye saw first has the precedence given, so as no distaste or exception can be taken either for the order, or the speech.

I note this the more particularly by the way for the honor of that House. Nowhere more gravity can be found than is represented in that senate. No court has more civility in itself, nor a face of more dignity towards strangers. Nowhere more equal justice can be found nor yet, perhaps, more wisdom; but that is out of the consideration of this case which I observed only for the gravity of the House, against which that violation being made, that censure did attend it, the debate whereof prevented the greater work in hand which for that cause and interruption was deferred.

[p. 200] That gentleman being in some nearness to the Duke, this made him[167] reflect more sensibly on himself and by his neighbor's fire to think his house in danger.

166. See H. of C., 6 August, n. 18.

167. I.e., the Duke.

All his adherents told him it was an approach upon his safety. The advice he had was much to endeavor an accommodation with the parliament. The errors most insisted on were said to be excusable, if retracted; that the disorders of the navy might be imputed to the officers, that the want of counsel might be satisfied by a free admission to the Board. The greatest difficulty was conceived to rest in religion and the fleet. For the first, the jealousy being derived from his[168] protection given to Montagu; for the latter, that it had so unnecessary a preparative and expense; and yet in both that there might be a reconciliation for himself. Sending the fleet to sea and giving others the command was propounded as a remedy for the one, having these reasons to support it: that the design could not be known nor, if there wanted one, that judged by the success; and the success was answerable but by those that had the action. For the other, it was said that the leaving of Montagu [p. 201] to his punishment, and the withdrawing that protection would be a satisfaction for the present, with some public declaration in the point and a fair parting of that meeting. That the danger of the time was a great cause of the dislike; that the dislike had ushered in most of those questions that were raised; therefore, to free them from that danger would dissolve the present difficulties and facilitate the way to a future temper for agreement. That no denial could be looked for in the resolutions of the parliament nor counsels for their help, such suspicions being raised. The fleet must needs go forth to color the preparation and the return might yield something to justify the work, at least in excuse and apology for himself, by translation of the fault.

These and the like counsels were presented to the Duke which wrought an inclination for the instant that gave his friends some hope; but those that were about him gave it an alteration in the cabinet, so unhappy are great persons to be obnoxious to ill counsels, and some by every air of flattery to be moveable, [p. 202] not having constancy in themselves; of which this Duke was a full character and instance who, being uncertain to his counsels, proved unfaithful to himself. He had once determined to be guided by his friends but his parasites were more powerful to distract him from their principles, which then increased his troubles and after proved his ruin.

Yet something was changed of the form of former purposes. He then resolved that the fleet should be sent forth and presently designed another general to command it; in the rest[169] he was persuaded to make trial of some arts and by some overtures from himself to remove the harbored jealousy. So ignorant are such parasites in the knowledge of great counsels, as what in their weak judgments does seem probable they think feasible with others, not weighing the many eyes of Argus that pierce through their light cobwebs but, like to conies having scarce shadow for their ears yet taking all their bodies to be covered, so is their whole time versed in the corrupt scene of flattery, that in the end they act it on themselves.

According to that wisdom it was resolved on that the Duke should shoot in person [p. 203] some new arrows. To which end was prepared (for all things were ready at his beck) the King's answer to the petition for religion, and this to be presented by his hands as the influence of his labors, robbing his master both of the honor and the work.

[8 August 1625]

To this purpose, the next morning a message was pretended from the King for a

---

168. I.e., the Duke's. It is unclear to what Eliot is referring. Perhaps the Duke had an influence on the King's favoring Montagu with the appointment of him as royal chaplain. Buckingham, through Laud, at this time was becoming an increasingly strong supporter of Arminianism. See Roger Lockyer, *Buckingham* (London, 1981), pp. 114–115, 258–259, 305–308.

169. *west*. Printed edition.

meeting of both Houses. The occasion intimated was some general declarations from his Majesty which, being to be delivered by the Duke, the Lord Treasurer, the Lord Conway, and Sir John Coke, it was desired both of the Lords and Commons, respectively in their places, that their members might have license for that service, the former exception having been an instruction in that point.[170]

The place appointed was Christ Church Hall, which being accepted and leave given as was desired, all other things were left and every man addressed him to the place. Some doubt there was for form upon the message to the Commons, it making mention of both Houses; and in that case the Speaker must have gone, and his mace been borne before him; but if it intended the committees of the Houses, then that ceremony to be left, wherein a short intercourse being made for explanation [p. 204] in the point, and it being resolved that the committees only were intended, in that form they went to the expectation of the work.

[Afternoon]

The Lord Keeper made the entrance:[171] that whereas formerly to the petition for religion his Majesty had given a gracious answer in the general and promised likewise to make it more particular, he had then accordingly performed it to the satisfaction of their hearts, article by article resolving it, and that in the ancient way of parliaments to be recorded in both Houses, which was to be delivered by the Duke who, besides, had some other things of special importance in his charge to expedite the business in hand, which were to be propounded from his

Majesty. This, he said, he was by the King's command to intimate, which some believed and no man doubted of the meaning. That the overture should be his and the act appropriate to the Duke. All men did see it studied but a redintegration for the other, and had respect to that which was to follow from his mouth as a fomentation to an ointment, or like to pills that have some sweetness over them to make their reception the [p. 205] more easy.

But that prologue being past, the Duke then entered with his part which thus, with more hope than satisfaction, he delivered:

[Duke of Buckingham.] My Lords and gentlemen, his Majesty has this day laid so great a charge upon me that looking upon my own weakness, I apprehend the weight of it, but when I consider that it is fit for a king to deal plainly with his people, in that respect it falls fitly on me that have neither rhetoric nor art.

In two words I could give you an answer that all your desires are granted; but it will be fitter for your satisfaction to hear the particulars read of the petition you exhibited and then the answers to them.

Upon this, the petition and answer were both read. The first of which as we have formerly inserted, according to the propriety of its place, we will here also add the other, that as well their truth and substance may be seen as the use and application to that work which, having some obliquity, detracted from the expectation of the thing, the effects whereof will hereafter be observable. Only [p. 206] the answer has relation to this place, which thus was represented to the several remedies proposed.[172]

---

170. See above, H. of C., 8 August, p. 423. The "former exception" was with regard to Sir John Coke's speech to both Houses on 4 August. See H. of L., 4 August, n. 12.

171. I.e., the introductory speech at the meeting of both Houses. The meeting was held on the afternoon of 8 August. The reports of the speeches were made in each House the following morning (9 August) and are included with the daily accounts for that day. See H. of

L., 9 August, O.B.; H. of C., 9 August, O.B.

172. Eliot had included a copy of the petition concerning religion with the materials for 4 July on pp. 64–75 of his MS. See above, n. 49. Eliot's copy of the King's answers to the petition which he includes at this point in his narrative is essentially the same as that included in the Lords Journal (above, pp. 155–160); therefore we have omitted it here.

[For the King's answers to the petition concerning religion, see above, H. of L., 9 August, pp. 155–160.]

These answers being read, the Duke went on as follows.[173]

[For the Duke of Buckingham's speech, see above, H. of C., 9 August, pp. 434–439.]

After this followed the conclusion of the Treasurer, who by infinite calculations and accounts was to confound the intelligence of his hearers. His memory gave but little, but his papers spoke the rest, both which in this manner he presented:[174]

[For the Lord Treasurer's speech, see above, H. of C., 9 August, pp. 431–432.]

[p. 229] This scene thus acted and concluded, the meeting did dissolve.

[9 August 1625]

And the report thereof out of their papers, which were delivered to that end, being made readily to the Houses, amongst the Commons, where they came only to be treated of, some motions presently started up in favor of supply, thinking those overtures had captived all men's judgments, and leveled them to the pleasure of the court.

The TREASURER OF THE KING'S HOUSEHOLD first began drawing his suasory from the answer in religion; others did follow in like haste to purchase some credit by devotion. Amongst whom a lawyer, one MALET, did appear reasoning by precedents against precedents (for in all the disputes before, it being a pinching argument in point against the proposition for supply, that it was unparliamentary and unprecedented in one session to enact several grants of subsidies), therefore he replied that precedents were at the discretion of all times. That the bill of tonnage and poundage was then limited for a year, which divers ages past had been constantly for life. That that grant likewise which began it first for life was a varying from the elders that were limited, and that diversely from thence he inferred the change and alteration of all times, and that the precedent of one was not the practice of another. Therefore in that case also he persuaded to use the like liberty as their fathers, which I observe the sooner for the quality of the man—that he whose [p. 230] profession was the law, and on which ground he built all the good hopes he had, should argue against precedents which are the tables of the law and so, unlawlike, term every act a precedent, making no difference between examples and their rules. But the acceptation was according to the work and, as that reason was improper for that man, that time was thought improper for that business which, being of great importance, required greater deliberation and advice; and therefore, those motions being neglected, the debate was then put off upon more mature conceptions to be resumed next day.

In the meantime those passages were revolved that had been delivered at the meeting and divers were the apprehensions which did follow them. That the Lord Keeper, the prime officer of the kingdom, should be made subservient to the Duke (for so the act imported, being but an usher to his business) was thought preposterous and inverted. That the King's name must be a servant to his[175] ends, under color of some declaration from his Majesty, to exhibit an apology for himself, seemed as a kind of wonder. That the whole parliament should be made attendant upon him was not without a strangeness, the like [p. 231]

173. Eliot's copy of the Duke's speech, which he includes at this point in his narrative, is essentially the same as that included in Petyt 538/8; therefore we have omitted it here. See above, H. of C., 9 August, pp. 434–439.

174. Eliot's version of Pym's report of the Lord Treasurer's speech is essentially the same as that included in Bedford MS. 197; therefore, we have omitted it here. See H. of C., 9 August, pp. 431–432.

175. I.e., the Duke of Buckingham's. The following remarks of Eliot are in reference to the Duke's speech at the meeting of both Houses on 8 August.

having seldom been before. But above all, portentous, it was thought, that religion should be descended to his use and that which admits no equal or compeer to troop up with the rabble of his followers. This was thought much in him so to assume and take it, but more in those that made that concession to his power. Whatever might be promised in the words, this act of delivery did impeach it, and much of the hope and expectation in that point this form and circumstance did obliterate.

Besides, divers exceptions were emergent, some in the matter, some in the form of his discourse. Many things of arrogance were observed, as in the narrative which he made of that great change in Christendom, usurping that work unto himself which time and providence had effected, turning fortuities into glory; those things, or most of them, having no relation to his projects but in the concurrence of the time; the French preparations moving on other reasons of their own that embroiled them with the Spaniard; and the Duke of Savoy and Venetian[s] joining with them for their own interests and safeties, whose work it was, and that in contemplation of themselves, by which the Valtellina was set at liberty.

[p. 232] If the King of Denmark did declare, or Sweden, who was then scarcely heard of[176] (so envious was time unto the honor of that person whom fortune and virtue had reserved for the wonder of the world), yet it was known to be in affection to the Palsgrave, though at the instance of his friends, not induced by him or any opinion of his merit, which moved as little with the other German princes. Again, that expression, where he spoke of Olivares, that by him he had gained a nation, was so boasting and thrasonical that it seemed most ridiculous, as if nations had been the game

and play of favorites who won or lost them after their fortunes or their skills. The mention likewise of his own approbations and applauses was thought so near self-flattery as it drowned the reputation of that truth. Besides, many insolencies were obvious that had as ill acceptance, as that in the end of his narration where he summed up the whole business of that meeting, pretended to be a declaration from the King and he there calling it an account of his own actions. And that other above all, stating the preparations at his going into France, where he made, as it were, the King [p. 233] his deputy in his absence to intend the progress of that work. And that particular in his answer upon his tenth question and hypothesis intimated for his enemy at home, that he could prove a lion to devour him, all which seemed too insolent and presuming; and that as rash and indiscreet on the fourth question, where he ranks the marriage of the Queen with those he styles the unfortunate accidents of that time.[177] And many things were judged imperfect in his answers, by which many scruples more were raised than that endeavor had resolved. But specially, in the point of counsel for that meeting, so little satisfaction was conceived as the wound became the tenderer for that rubbing, and that search made the orifice more wide. For an aggravation unto this upon private disgusts amongst the courtiers, the secret was let out of the consultation thereupon and how the Keeper, with some others, when the proposition for the adjournment was first made, being but the day before it was had, with much violence opposed it to the King, with reasons both of honor and profit to persuade him, and yet were therein mastered by the Duke who, like a torrent at resistance, did [p. 234] forthwith swell against them and threat-

---

176. I.e., Gustavus (II) Adolphus, King of Sweden.
177. Eliot is referring to the tenth and fourth questions propounded by the Duke as recorded in Petyt 538/8 (and in Bedford MS. 197). See above, pp. 437

and 438. The L.J. version of the report of the Duke's speech numbers the same questions as the twelfth and the sixth respectively. See above, pp. 164 and 165.

ened with his weight their ruin for that service. This being then diffused and credited, as it was truth, cast no small prejudice both on his person and his acts. That also then began to be fomented by those opposites who, for the preservation of themselves, studied his subversion. Both could not stand together, but they must do or suffer, and the after game is not pleasant in the court. Those therefore did infuse into the humor that was stirred what gall and vinegar they might, and by their private instruments blowing the coals then kindled, added also more fuel to the fire.

[10 August 1625]

In this state comes the debate to be resumed according to the order of the Commons when, to prevent the worst, and there was reason good to doubt it, a new message was delivered from the King, but being thought an art only of diversion for that work, wanted the effect it looked for, nor was it after in their arguments distinguished from the former, but both had one joint consideration and dispute.

The message was brought by SIR RICHARD WESTON, Chancellor of the Exchequer, and to this purpose: that the King taking knowledge of their [p. 235] desires to reform many things for his service was well pleased with the intention; but desired them to take into consideration that that time was only fit for such matters as were of present necessity and dispatch. That the fleet stayed their resolution and, though the season were not past, yet it was much spent. That if the plague should fall into the navy or the army, the action were lost. That if it should fall amongst themselves it would breed much danger to the kingdom. Therefore, he desired they would presently resolve whether upon those reasons so much importing his honor they would sup-

ply his necessity for the setting forth of the fleet. Otherwise, that he would take more care for their safeties than they themselves, and would do as he might in such an extremity. But if they would give him a present dispatch for the supply, that he promised in the word of a king that they should meet again in winter and stay together till those things might be brought to maturity which were then in conception, and that he would then do whatsoever belonged to a good and gracious king; desiring them to remember that it was his first request that [p. 236] ever he made to them.

This message was seconded, without any interim of consideration first admitted, by a long composed oration of the Master of the Wards, SIR ROBERT NAUNTON, who, in his former times having been public orator for that place, the university,[178] thought it his duty then there to render some demonstrations of his skill, but found that the cold rhetoric of the schools was not that moving eloquence which does affect a parliament. His labor was more than his success and after much endeavor his work returned in vain.

[SIR ROBERT NAUNTON.] Passing a long preamble, he first spoke of the manner of the gift, and then made his persuasions for their giving, which he perchance intended for a figure,[179] others conceived to be irregular and preposterous. For the manner he propounded readiness and freeness, qualities, as he said, that would be a doubling to the gift, endear the courtesy, heighten the obligation and their thanks, using that sentence for a kindness got with difficulty, *satis esse si tali beneficio ignoscas*. For the gift, he urged divers topics to induce it: the honor of the King; the reputation of the kingdom; defense of their allies; support of the Union; preservation [p. 237] of religion;

---

178. Sir Robert Naunton had been elected fellow of Trinity Hall, Cambridge, in 1592 and was appointed public orator in 1594. *D.N.B.*

179. Marginal note: "hysterologia". I.e., the figure of speech, hysteron proteron.

the safeties of his Majesty, the nobility, and themselves which, he concluded, if they prevailed not in that case, must be esteemed a prodigious sign and omen of some great judgment near at hand.

This was followed by some others who had the same meaning and like reasons; and one insisted upon the expressions of the Admiral which the rest forbore to mention, saying that he had proved himself then capable of that place, deserving of the rest, being so well declared a logician, a rhetorician, and a charitable man, which should abate the jealousies that were had, and therefore they should give. Another[180] argued from a supposition of invasion, in which case all would give, and inferred thence that the contrary being meant, the reason of contraries should persuade them. Such was the logic of the court.

But those sophistries and sophisters, if they were worthy of that name, were not so much answered as confounded by the arguments and objections on the contrary. Wherein was alleged[181] that when formerly they had given they had hopes and expectations for the country; then there was nothing but discouragements, pardons to Jesuits, protection given to papists, [p. 238] examination of the laws, increpation of good ministers, interruptions of the trade, losses and spoils by pirates, and though complaints were often made, and means for remedy at hand, yet no relief was gotten, nor succor could be had. That the present news from Rochelle, which they had always aided (whatever was pretended), was that their ships were intended against them, and their own arms to be turned against their friends. That whereas last they went with prayer and fasting to their coun-

tries, then they might take up sackcloth and ashes in their journey. That the grievances were great which the whole kingdom suffered, and if they gave an addition of supply that would make them greater.

These and their like possessed the judgment of the House against the arguments made for giving. The scope likewise of the message was conceived, pressing the resolution to that strait, but to prevent the considerations of the state, and by a denial of supply to color the dissolution of the parliament. This was discerned and known, and against this the counterwork did trench to show the necessities of the kingdom and the ill counsels for that meeting, yet not to deny to give.

Wherein the first main overture that was made came from SIR ROBERT PHELIPS, who both did answer the [p. 239] arguments that were made, and opposed them with new reasons.

[SIR ROBERT PHELIPS.] The arguments for giving he reduced to the heads of honor and necessity, and for the first he said that the honor of a king stood not in acts of will but on designs that were grounded by advice, and a constant application of good counsels; that whatever did succeed the judgment and direction might seem good.

For the necessity, he alleged that it was the common argument in parliaments, and their experience had informed them that that necessity had been formerly but for the satisfaction of the courtiers. That if it were real then, yet that it was but occasioned by their means; their luxuries and excesses had wasted first the treasures, and then exposed the honor of the King.

From thence he descended to note some precedents of old times, some of their own,

---

180. Bedford MS. 197 (above, p. 448) attributes both the above and the following points to the speech of John Maynard, a partisan of Buckingham (*D.N.B.*). Forster (*Eliot*, II, 407) attributes the former remarks to Sir Roger North and the latter to Mr. Drake, but gives no explanation or source for these attributions. The

speeches of North and Drake given later in this day's debate (see H. of C., 10 August, O.B.) bear no resemblance to the remarks given here.

181. These points were alleged by John Delbridge. See Bedford MS. 197, above, p. 448.

some out of other nations. At home, he observed in the days of H. 3 that a supply demanded was refused until there were a confirmation of their liberties. In the reign of H. 6 likewise. When the Duke of Suffolk did engross the favor of the King, assumed the government to himself, disposed of honors, aliened the crown lands, and alone treated a marriage for that King, the like refus[al] was made till he that before had had the applause of parliament then [p. 240] received their censure; and when that point of reformation was begun, a supply did forthwith follow it. The like he said had been abroad, and that all times, all states almost, could witness it. That in France when the Black Prince had taken the French King prisoner, the estates being then convented, and the Dauphin demanding a relief for redemption of his father, the grievances of the people were exhibited; and delay being made in them, the assistance was denied until he did comply for the satisfaction of the parliament. That in Spain likewise, when for the war against the Moors a parliament was assembled at Toledo and an aid demanded for that service, the Condé de Laro did stand up and dissuaded a contribution in that case till the burdens of the people were released, which accordingly was insisted on, and that not held, with the supercilious state and nation, a breach of faith or duty. That England was the last monarchy that yet retained her liberties: let them not perish now, let not posterity complain that we have done for them worse than our fathers did for us. Their precedents are the safest steps we tread in. Let us not now forsake them, lest their fortunes forsake us. Wisdom and counsel made them happy, and the like causes will have the like effects.

Thus spoke that gentleman [p. 241] and concluded not to deny to give, but to prepare an answer to the King with a remonstrance of their reasons for the work of reformation, moving for a committee to prepare it; and Sir Robert Mansell, one of the Councillors of War, and a member of that House, to be there commanded to render his knowledge for the action, whether it did proceed by good deliberation and advice, worthy the honor of the state and such as had been pretended.

This made a level to the way, and showed the end was aimed at, which the courtiers again endeavored to divert, and to that purpose the Chancellor of the Duchy did reply upon that which he thought the most prevailing argument; and having pressed his whole faculties to that service, thus in much art delivers them:

[Sir Humphrey May.] Let no man despise the precedents of antiquity, no man adore them. Though they are venerable yet they are no gods. Examples are strong arguments, being proper, but times alter and with them, often, their reasons. Every parliament, as each man, must be wise with his own wisdom, not his father's. A dram of present wisdom is more precious than mountains of that which was practiced [p. 242] in old times. Men of good affections have been known to give ill counsels. So they may now if nothing but examples do persuade them. If we go by this way I must say, as the children of the prophets, *mors est in olla.*

Were all our enemies here, and had their voice in this assembly, would they not say, not give? Let us not therefore be guided by their rules but, leaving other things of difficulty, yield to the King's request and at this time give, because if we give not now we cannot give again.

This being so pressing and pathetical, moved more in apprehension than in judgment. Some did conceive a fear from that prophecy which he made, and from his close measuring his words by his intelligence.

But the esteem of precedents did remain with those that knew the true value of antiquity; whereof a larger collection was in store to direct the resolution in that case, which thus contained both reason and authority.

While those remained in the service of King James who were bred by Queen Elizabeth and trained in the government of that time,[182] the crown [p. 243] debts were not great, grants and commissions less complained of, trade flourished, pensions more few, and all things of moment carried by public counsel that, though there wanted something of the former, yet there was much more happiness than at this time. No honors nor judicial places set to sale, laws executed against priests, papists restrained and punished, their resort to ambassadors debarred by his Majesty's direction to his ministers and by his pen declaring his dislike of that profession. No vast expenses then in fruitless embassies and treaties, nor any transcendent power to be master of all

business, the Council Table holding her ancient dignity. Nay, so long as Somerset stood in grace and had the trust both of the Privy Seal and signet,[183] he oft would glory justly that there had passed neither to his friends nor him any large grants of lands or pensions from the King. He induced no monopolies for the grievance of the people; nor made a breach upon nobility by exposing honors unto sale, refusing [p. 244] in particular that which has since been taken, the Lord Roper's office,[184] for his barony.

The match with Spain then offered without any further toleration in religion than ambassadors were allowed, upon discovery of their falsehood was dissuaded and the King left in such distrust of Gondomar that he termed him a juggling jack and emperic.[185]

Thus stood the state when his misfortunes clouded him. Since which time we

---

182. The following is a variation of the set speech attributed by James Howell and William Cobbett to Sir Robert Cotton (see James Howell, ed., *Cottoni Posthuma* [London, 1651], pp. 270–281; Cobbett, *Parl. Hist.*, II, 14–17) and linked by later scholars with both Sir John Eliot and Sir Robert Phelips. In addition to the question of authorship, there is disagreement over whether the speech was ever actually delivered in the House and, if so, when. See Forster, *Eliot*, I, 411–422; Gardiner, *History of England*, V, 425 n. 1; Harold Hulme, *The Life of Sir John Eliot* (London, 1957), p. 92 and nn. 2–4; J. N. Ball, "Sir John Eliot at the Oxford Parliament, 1625", *Bulletin of the Inst. of Historical Research*, XXVIII (1955), 113–127; Russell, *Parliaments*, p. 243 n. 1; and Kevin Sharpe, *Sir Robert Cotton, 1586–1631* (Oxford, 1979), pp. 177–180. Separates of the speech are in Cambridge University MS. Dd. 3.87, and MS. Mm. 4.38 (ff. 95–97v); Egerton MS. 3378 (Leeds papers, vol. 55); Lansdowne 491 (ff. 138–140v); Somerset Record Office, Phelips MSS. DD/PH 216/19; S.P. 16/529:71; and Port Eliot, Eliot papers, vol. 2, ff. 19–20v, and vol. 8, ff. 18–22 (printed in Alexander B. Grosart, ed., *An Apology for Socrates and Negotium Posterorum* [London, 1881], I, 140–148).

Composition of the speech must be dated after 8 August 1625 because it contains a reference to the speech of Lord Treasurer Ley presented at the meeting of both Houses that afternoon. The speech per se does not occur in the other MS. accounts of the Oxford session, although it does combine arguments and precedents which appear in the 10 August speeches of Sir

Robert Phelips, Sir Francis Seymour (who spoke after May and before Weston, where Eliot places this speech), and Sir Edward Coke. See above, H. of C., 10 August, O.B.

For the opening section of the so-called "Cotton" version of the speech, which is omitted from the *Negotium* version, see Cobbett, *Parl. Hist.*, II, 14.

183. The signet was reported to have been given in 1612 to Robert Carr, Viscount Rochester and afterwards Earl of Somerset, and Carr became acting Keeper of the Privy Seal in June 1614 (S.P. 14/70:12, and 77:53). "Both the seals and the Lord Chamberlain's staff" were to be taken from him when he was imprisoned in 1615 (*Cal. S.P. Venetian, 1615–1617*, pp. 61, 65; and see S.P. 14/83:13).

184. I.e., the chief clerkship of the King's Bench. For a short history of the activities with regard to Roper's office, see Gardiner, *History of England*, III, 31–35; and see S.P. 14/88:9 and 90:59, and *Cal. S.P. Dom., 1611–1618*, p. 407.

185. For the wording of this section from the so-called "Cotton" version of the speech, see Cobbett, *Parl. Hist.*, II, 15. The reference is to negotiations carried on by Gondomar in 1614–1615 which were recounted by Sir Robert Cotton at a conference of committees of both Houses on 3 March 1624. At the conference Cotton stated that in 1616 King James said that "the letters from Spain which Gondomar showed him were counterfeit and that he was a juggling jack" (Finch-Hatton MS. 50 [Pym 1624 diary], ff. 15v–16 [Y.C.P.H. transcripts]).

know the treaty for the marriage was renewed, Gondomar again received and liked
of, popery heartened by admission of those
unknown conditions of connivance, the
forces in the Palatinate withdrawn upon
Spanish faith and promises, by which the
King's children lost their patrimony, and
more money has been spent in embassies
and treaties than would have kept an army
to have conquered even their Indies, our
old fast friends disheartened, and our
Sovereign that is now, exposed to more
danger than any wisdom or counsel could
admit.[186]

In like cases our predecessors have been
sedulous for relief and reparation in such
[p. 245] wrongs. The loss of the county of
Ponthieu in the time of R. 2 was laid to
Bishop Wykeham's charge for dissuading
the King from a timely aid and succor.[187]
The loss of the Duchy of Maine was a capital
crime in parliament objected to de la Pole in
the days of H. 6 for a single and unwise
treating of a marriage for that King in
France;[188] and the Palatinate was lost by a
like Spanish intercourse.

What counsel has begot such power to
foreign agents to procure liberty for papists, pardon for priests and Jesuits, and to
become solicitors at every tribunal of the
government, for the ill-affected subjects of
the kingdom, and to prevent their punish-
ments?

What grants of impositions, before
crossed, have been late passed, and complained of here in parliament, the least of
which in the time of E. 3 would have been
judged a heinous crime and capital, as well
as those of Lyons and Latimer?[189]

Parliaments have been suitors to the
[King] in the times of E. 3, H. 4, H. 6 to
bestow [p. 246] honors on some servants;
and that which was kept as the most sacred
treasure of the state now is set to sale, at
which postern more have been late admitted than all the merits of the elders have let
in these last 500 years. So tender were those
times in the preservation of that jewel that it
was made an article in the judgment of de la
Pole, that he had procured himself to be
earl, marquis, and duke of one and the self-
same place, the like titles being unques-
tioned yet with us.[190] E. 1 restrained in policy the number of those that challenged it as
due; and how the disproportion may now
sort with the reason of this state cannot be
well interpreted, when great deserts can
have no other recompense than costly rewards from the King. For now we are
taught the vile price of that which was once
inestimable.

[De]spenser was condemned in the time
of E. 2 for displacing good servants about
the King, and placing in his followers and
adherents, not leaving way, as the record of
that time says,[191] either in Church or com-

---

186. See Gardiner, *History of England*, II, 323–330;
III, 345–352; V, 107–127.

187. William Wykeham, Bishop of Winchester
(1367–1404) and Lord Chancellor (1368–1371), was
in October 1376 (50 *E*. III) charged by a great council
under the influence of John, Duke of Lancaster, with
misgovernment during his chancellorship, including
responsibility for the loss of Ponthieu in 1369. *D.N.B.;
Chron. Angliae*, pp. lxxiv–lxxviii, 106–107, 114, 126,
136, 150, 398.

188. See H. of C., 10 August, nn. 12 and 42, and
below, p. 560. The third charge against the Duke of
Suffolk concerned his promise to surrender Maine to
the French during negotiations for the marriage of
Margaret of Anjou to Henry VI of England. Cobbett,
Parl. Hist., I, 387.

189. Richard Lyons, merchant, had been accused

of deceit and extortion while a collector of subsidies,
Rot. Parl., 50 *E*. III, no. 17; and William Latimer was
tried in parliament and found guilty of giving counsel
"against the profit of the King and kingdom", *Rot.
Parl.*, 50 *E*. III, no. 28.

190. See the articles against William de la Pole,
Duke of Suffolk (*Rot. Parl.*, 28 *H*. VI, nos. 19–46;
Howell, *S.T.*, I, 271–276). Several of the articles
charged Suffolk with wrongdoing in procuring various offices and grants for himself and others (see *Rot.
Parl.*, 28 *H*. VI, nos. 31, 34, 35, 36, 41) but none deals
with his successive creations as earl (1414), marquis
(1444), and duke (1448) of Suffolk.

191. For the case against Hugh (the elder) and
Hugh (the younger) le Despenser, 15 *E*. II, see Howell,
S.T., I, 23–38; Cobbett, *Parl. Hist.*, I, 66–76.

monwealth, but to such as find with him or his dependents; and we now [p. 247] see how such offices are disposed.

It was a sad hearing the last day when the Lord Treasurer did relate the great debts, engagements, and present wants which his Majesty does sustain,[192] the noise whereof I wish may be buried in these walls lest it work courage in our enemies, disheartening to our friends. It was no small motive in the time of H. 3 to banish the King's half-brethren for procuring the King's want;[193] and Gaveston and [De]spenser for the like had the like fortune in the time of E. 2.[194] Michael de la Pole, the father of the Duke of Suffolk,[195] amongst other crimes, was adjudged for turning the subsidies that were granted not to their proper ends. And Wykeham, that great bishop, was put upon the mercy of his prince for wasting in time of peace the revenue of the crown, to the yearly oppression of the people.[196] And the like offices were objected to the ruin of the last Duke of Somerset.[197]

Too frequent are the examples in this kind that show the abuse of ministers. Such improvidence and ill counsel led H. 3 into so [p. 248] great a strait as he did pawn part of his dominions, engaged all the jewels of the crown and those of St. Edward's shrine at Westminster, not sparing, as it is said, the great crown of England.[198] But above all was that low ebb of H. 6 occasioned by his favorite, de la Pole, as it is expressed by Gascoigne in his story of that time (which I have found here since our coming to this meeting)[199] who tells that the King's revenues were so rent as he was forced to live *de talijs et quindenis populi.* That the King was grown indebted *quinquies centena millia librarum.* That that favorite, in treating a foreign marriage, had lost a foreign Duchy. That to work his ends he had caused an adjournment of the parliament *in villis et remotis partibus regni* where the people, *propter defectum hospitis et victualium,* few should attend and so enforce those few, to use that author's words, *concedere regno quae vis pessima;* and when an act of resumption was desired (that just and frequent way of reparation for the state which from the time of H. 3 to E. 6, all kings but one did exercise), [p. 249] that great man then opposed it and told the King it was *ad dedecus regis,* and so stopped it. But what succeeded in the parliament? The same author tells you that the Commons, though wearied with travail and expenses, protested that: that they would never grant an aid until the King should *actualiter resumere* all that was belonging to

192. For Pym's report of Lord Treasurer Ley's speech of 8 August, see H. of C., 9 August, pp. 431–432.

193. In the parliament of 1258 the barons forced Henry III to agree to reforms which led to the banishment of Henry's half-brothers and other Poitevins and the resumption to the crown of lands which had been granted to the aliens. Cobbett, *Parl. Hist.,* I, 28–30; Matthew Paris, *Chronica,* V, 695–704.

194. Concerning Piers Gaveston, see *Rot. Parl., 5 E.* II, no. 20 (Howell, *S.T.,* I, 21–24); regarding the Despensers, see above, n. 191.

195. See H. of C., 10 August, nn. 10 and 60.

196. The printed separate of this speech (see above, n. 182) inserts the date 50 *E.* III into the sentence following the name Wykeham. See above, n. 187. Wykeham was explicitly excepted out of the jubilee pardon, *S.R., 50 E.* III, c. 3.

197. Edward Seymour, first Earl of Hertford and Duke of Somerset (1506–1552), was the Protector. In 1549 twenty-nine charges concerning miscounsel and expenditure were drawn against him and presented to the parliament in 1550. He made a full confession and shortly thereafter was pardoned. The following year he was tried again, found guilty of felony and in 1552 beheaded. *D.N.B.;* Cobbett, *Parl. Hist.,* I, 592–593; Howell, *S.T.,* I, 509–526.

198. In 16 *H.* III (1232), Hubert de Burgh, Chief Justice of England and adviser to the King, was accused of high crimes and misdemeanors, having poorly advised H. III. See H. of C., 10 August, n. 25. For other cases of bad counsel under H. III, see H. of C., 10 August, n. 26, and see above, n. 193. Concerning H. III's building of a new shrine for St. Edward, see Matthew Paris, *Chronica,* IV, 156; V, 195.

199. Concerning Gascoigne's manuscript at Lincoln College, Oxford, see above, H. of C., 10 August, n. 42.

the crown, and that it was *magis ad dedecus regis* so to be engrossed by the counsel of one man who had brought such misery to the kingdom, such poverty to the King, on whom an act of exilement being made; the act of resumption forthwith followed it,[200] and immediately the supply.

If we should now seek a parallel for this, how it would hold to us. The revenues all wasted[201] and anticipated, as the Lord Treasurer has confessed,[202] that nothing does come from thence for the present use and maintenance, hardly anything can be looked for. The debts as excessive if not more, which we saw lately one man's arithmetic could not number.[203] What has been exhausted from the people *in talijs et quindenis* is too known in the too woeful and lamentable experience [p. 250] of late times. What was lost for the Spanish match and treaty, children can speak that were not born to see it. By whom was caused the adjournment to this place, and for what ends, there needs no prophecy to tell us. So as in all things the cases are the same if that our acts be answerable. It is true precedents are no gods,[204] yet some veneration they require. The honor of antiquity is great, though it be not an idol, and the wisdom of examples is most proper if it be well applied. What was fit at one time, all circumstances being like, cannot be said unfit, uncovenable in another. No threatenings may deter us, nor yet difficulties, from the just service of our countries. Our fathers had not a greater trust than we, their reasons and necessities were not more. Therefore, I move to pursue that remonstrance to the King and in due time we shall be ready to supply him.

This inflamed the affection of the House and pitched it wholly on the imitation of their fathers. The clear demonstrations that were made of the likeness of the times gave them like reasons who had [p. 251] like interests and freedoms. But the courtiers did not relish it, who at once forsook both their reason and their eloquence, all their hopes consisting but in prayers and some light excuses that were framed, but no defense, no more justification was once heard of, in which soft way the Chancellor of the Exchequer did discourse:

[Sir Richard Weston.] That the disorders which were spoken of were not of that King's time, but brought in under the government of his father, and such as peace and quiet had begot. That in the King that was they had the virtues of his person, the promise of his word to assure their hope of reformation if they would expect it till next meeting. Therefore, he desired those distastes might be left off and the present remonstrance that was talked of; and such an answer to be fitted for his Majesty as the gentleness of his message and sweetness of his nature did require. But finding by the inclination of the House that that way could not serve, he concluded in another for the question of supply and pressed to have a resolution in that point.

That rock was seen betimes, and therefore as speedily avoided: for the negative, the wiser sort did fear; the affirmative, all generally [p. 252] did abhor.

Therefore, in this which required little eloquence or art much was said on both sides and much contestation was upon it, wherein the new elect for Yorkshire, Sir

---

200. *Rot. Parl.*, 28 *H.* VI, no. 53.

201. MS.: *vasted.* For the final section of the so-called "Cotton" version of this speech, see Cobbett, *Parl. Hist.*, II, 17.

202. For Pym's report of Lord Treasurer Ley's speech of 8 August, see H. of C., 9 August, pp. 431–432.

203. Pym reported (above, p. 432) Lord Treasurer Ley as saying that he "has not cast up the total of these sums, some of them being uncertain and himself no good auditor nor having any at hand to help him".

204. A reference to Sir Humphrey May's speech, above, p. 557.

THOMAS WENTWORTH, by a new return then come, did so well express himself for his country as it desired that choice and allayed much of the labor to the contrary.[205]

SIR EDWARD COKE also and others that did follow him, had the same power and reason. They wholly did decline the putting of the question, wherein still some instance being made, MR. GLANVILLE, that pregnant western lawyer, did appease it, yet not by consent but resolution of the House. He pressed that as a denial were dishonorable for the King, a grant with difficulty were as disadvantageable for themselves, taking off all merit from the act and by a metamorphosis converting it to that *panis lapidosus*, of the *Ethics*. That such questions were not to be hazarded for princes, nor usually propounded in that place till the consent were manifest. That it was the prerogative of kings to call parliaments at their pleasure, but in counterpoise of that their ancestors had erected the privilege for themselves to treat of what business they should please. That to be put upon [p. 253] that question was prejudice to that liberty and the importunity therein an implicit concession of an error in the calling to that place. Should the parliament spend, as by computation it does always, 7,000 *l.* a day,[206] and that but for the grant of 40,000 *l.* in all? By crowning such counsels with success we shall give encouragement to our adversaries. Thus he declared himself and concluded for the remonstrance to the King with some form of protestation for their meanings that they did not then deny, but in due time they would supply him.

Something was added unto this by SIR ROBERT MANSELL in answer to that which was pretended for the Council who utterly disclaimed all knowledge of the action or any consultation had upon it, but said there

had been some meetings and some propositions spoken of for the navy, but no design nor enterprise and so no counsel or advice.

Upon this all color was removed from those that sought the question. No such question could seem proper where there was no reason for supply. The supply could not be hoped for in an action without counsel which, being in doubt before, then in full credit and belief, that long debate concluded for a remonstrance to the King.

[11 August 1625]

[p. 254] While the remonstrance was preparing, new complaints came in of the spoils and insolencies of the pirates and of divers cruelties which were suffered by the captives they had taken. The Turks were still roving in the west, the Dunkirks in the east; the cries came out of all parts, their losses great, their dangers more, their fears exceeding all, that no merchant dared venture on the seas, hardly they thought themselves secure enough at land. It was alleged by some that as the King's ships were stopped from going to relieve them when it was ordered by the Council, so they were then, though ready on the coasts or in the harbors near them where those rogues were most infestuous, and nothing might be done. Nay, in some cases it was proved that the merchants had been taken even in the sight of the King's ships and that the captains being importuned to relieve them refused their protection or assistance and said they were denied it by the instructions which they had. Upon which it was conceived to be more than common negligence. The Duke was thought faulty in this point, he being Admiral from whom the instructions were derived. For that he had the imputation of those [p. 255] errors

---

205. Sir Thomas Wentworth, reelected after the first Yorkshire election had been voided, had returned to the House on 8 August. See above, p. 423. For his speech this day (10 August), see above, H. of C., 10 August, O.B.

206. *9,000 l. a day.* Printed edition. This was undoubtedly a weekly rather than a daily expenditure. See H. of C., 10 August, p. 452, John Glanville's speech. The figures for the grant also vary. Ibid.

which some did then term crimes and thereupon, which formerly was forborne, he was then charged by name.

This first direct nomination of the Duke done by SIR FRANCIS SEYMOUR, took off all vizards and disguises in which their discourses had been masked. Then, in plain terms, the jealousies were expressed which hindered the satisfaction of the King. His nearness to his Majesty was too much, his greatness and exorbitance offensive, his power and practice were both doubted and disliked. In his person was contracted the cause of all those miseries. All the expressions and examples which formerly had been heard of were then applied to him. His faults and errors were the same, so was desired his punishment, and that with the rest likewise to be represented to the King.

This put new thoughts into the court how they might state their business, that though they gained not, nothing might be lost; to which end was prepared a new message from the King. Two things were then aimed at in favor of the Duke; the first an art[207] to prevent the remonstrance that was coming, with which Sir Henry Marten was entrusted; the other an answer in that point of counsel [p. 256] unto Mansell, which the King's Solicitor had in charge. And these for that work did with all diligence prepare themselves.

The next day, when those parts were to be acted, some interruption did fall in by a double conference of the Houses.[208] The first concerned the petition upon the pardon to the Jesuit, which the Lords excused only as a work of the ambassadors for whom there was an order made in Rome that none must come but with one of those familiars to attend him, which pressed their masters as importunately for their fellows as they had pressed the King. That the King's answer late delivered was a security for the future.[209] That they likewise would all move him not to give passage to the like, which they supposed might be as effectual to the end as the petition then intended, wherein they refused not to concur but said they craved only a consideration in that point. The other part was for some relief for London which they propounded to be done as by an ordinance of parliament, that in so general a calamity and distress there might be a general contribution made towards it which, being reported to the Commons, had a present confirmation [p. 257] and allowance, as in the former they also rested satisfied.

These things dispatched, the message was delivered that urged the supply again to renew the former question; which meeting as well with wonder as opposition that that question should be stirred which was before resolved on, the old artist makes his introduction from that ground,[210] and thus begins his part of the apology.

[Sir Henry Marten.] That there were two extremes which wisdom did avoid, the one *abrupta contumacia* the other *deforme obsequium,* this being base, unworthy of a man, that, both unpleasant and unsafe. That the mean only was commended, and Lepidus for that so magnified by Tacitus.[211] That he wished princes would desire nothing unfit from subjects, but if they did he would have the denial in such manner as it should seem not to their persons, but the things. He alleged that saying of Tiberius, that common men are ruled by profit, princes by fame.[212]

---

207. *act.* Printed edition.

208. The conference was on 10 August and was reported by Sir Edward Coke on 11 August following the discussion of the Turkish pirates and the remarks concerning the Duke of Buckingham. See H. of C., 11 August, O.B.

209. I.e., the King's answer to the petition concerning religion. See H. of L., 9 August, pp. 155–160.

210. I.e., Sir Henry Marten. See H. of C., 11 August, O.B.

211. Tacitus, *Annales,* 4, 20.

212. We are unable to find the source of the reference to Tiberius.

That profit therefore being more considerable with them he would that way direct his reason, framing a dilemma thereupon, that either the money disbursed on the preparations had been well spent or not. If well, that it was then no husbandry for want of a little to be added to lose so much laid out; if ill, that not giving [p. 258] would excuse those ministers that employed it. So as in the first sense, it was unprofitable *omni modo,* in the second *aliqui modo,* not to give, and therefore he wished there might be some respect of that. To dispute the necessity at that time, for the manner how it was incurred, he said would be like that act of him who seeing another in the mire that called to him for help spent so much time in questioning how he came thither that before his hand was given the other was sunk past hope. A necessity there was then that was confessed of all sides, therefore he urged that their labor ought to be how for the present to relieve it; what kind of necessity it was and how that necessity was incurred might be considered of thereafter.

From thence he descended to his more particular business and confessed in general that the kingdom was in sickness and needed physic, and that he liked the medicines that were spoken of, but doubted that those dog days were unseasonable to apply it. That having the King's assurance for a new meeting and full opportunity therein, he wished rather to defer it till that time, lest opening the wound only they should make it more incurable. Many things he propounded of that kind, but not with [p. 259] such success as was expected.

Some did imagine that an act of expiation to the court for the former trespass he had done,[213] not a will offering and what properly was his own, and in that regard gave the less credit to it. More it did lose the advocate than any way made advantage for his client whose fame was not better by that art, the others worse.

[12 August 1625]

The like fortune met the other[214] who handled that particular of the Council wherein he made a long narration and discourse how the Council had often met, as was pretended by the Duke; how Sir Robert Mansell did withdraw himself upon private reasons and distastes; how divers particulars were propounded and debated by the rest and the design in question by them all resolved on. How the Lord Chichester had left some papers that commended it; how Sir Edward Cecil, who was acquainted with the secret, and best could judge upon it, had said it was probable and an old plot of the Prince of Orange's.

Other things of this nature he produced, more coloring than conclusive. The Lord Chichester being dead and the truth of the papers being uncertain, that wrought but little on the judgment of the audience. Sir Edward Cecil, a commander for the action, could not but manife[st] [p. 260] the design, therefore was that assertion thought as invalid as the other—neither authentic for satisfaction in the proof. From the rest of the Council there came nothing, who were all living, and some there; and yet if their attestations had been brought, such a command has greatness, as some men would have doubted, though others had believed.

After this some other loose arguments being made to revive the question for supply, wherein some precedents being vouched by him that had decried them, as those of 29 and 31 *Eliz.* and 3 *Jac.*[215] wherein augmentations had been made to the grants then first resolved on, whence was inferred a persuasion for the like, a reply it

---

213. See Eliot's remarks concerning Sir Henry Marten and his speech on 1 August, above, p. 531.

214. I.e., Sir Robert Heath. For his report, see

above, H. of C., Bedford MS. 197, p. 472.

215. See H. of C., 11 August, p. 462 and n. 43, and 12 August, nn. 31 and 32.

had which was a colophon to the point, coming unexpectedly from a gentleman that had there never spoke before,[216] but by that became first known for his ability who, being a lawyer, and but young, more studied than yet practiced in the affairs of that assembly or the world, thus made his initiation to that service and his discovery unto either:

[Christopher Sherland.] Mr. Speaker, the question in debate is whether to give or no, and therein my opinion is absolute: not to give. For which before I declare my reasons I will make some [p. 261] answers to the arguments on the contrary, whereby the worth of both may more easily appear.

First, there has been an objection made against insisting on old precedents, and that we should not make them gods, which in part was answered—that they were venerable, though not idols.[217] But further, precedents are the life and rule of parliaments, no other warrant being for the parliament itself for the authorities it pretends to than the ancient use and practice which is drawn out by precedents. And should not then parliaments be careful to preserve that rule inviolable, to make it constant like itself? In other courts difference of precedents are badges of distemper and weakness in those times, much more would it be in this great court of parliament, which being the rectifier of others, should this way do itself; and if that stray or wander by which the rest are guided, who shall then rectify and reduce it? But even those that speak against them do most magnify and endear them when they [p. 262] think them useful to themselves. For when reason has forsaken them, as in the agitation of this question, how have they strained for precedents to be assistant to their arguments—as those of 29 *et* 31 *Eliz. et* 3 *Jac.*—which yet

were most different from this case and make nothing in the point? For that of 29 *Eliz.* was only thus: that after such time as the subjects had given to that good Queen of ever famous memory one subsidy and two fifteenths, understanding by her Council that she was to make great preparations for a war to resist that invincible armada in '88, they by their Speaker told the Queen that they had gone as far for that time as they could, but if she had occasion they would shortly supply her again. Whereunto she gave that answer (which I wish likewise they would register in their memories and represent it to the King), that she would first search the bottom of her coffers before she would grieve her subjects. Where now is the advantage of this precedent which so much is stood on? Nothing was done in this of that which we are pressed to. But they will suppose it [p. 263] promised; no, nor that, but rather the contrary is insinuated. They refused then to make an addition at that time and not unlikely for the reason of their privilege. That which was promised was with reference to another time and meeting, so as this confirms the insistence which we make, and does no way impeach it.

But the next, 31 of that reign, what was then added was before the act was passed and upon the excessive charge laid out for defense against the Spaniard or rather to congratulate that divine victory and deliverance, when was the first time that ever two subsidies passed at once. And for the like sum now I wish we had like occasion.

That of King James was in the same manner introduced, not when the act was passed but while it stood in the pleasure of the House; and so some others might be reckoned which sort not with our case but show what our predecessors did herein, and I do hope that we shall do the like. But

---

216. I.e., Christopher Sherland, Recorder of Northampton. The C.J. records a brief speech by Sherland as early as 7 July 1625; see above, p. 334.

217. See above, H. of C., 12 August, p. 477 and n. 30.

the law of necessity has been urged and, though answered, this more it shall receive. If there be such a necessity as is said, why should not his [p. 264] Majesty be willing that we should now redress it?

Ways have been propounded and more I know would be if that liberty were admitted, so to supply this necessity and all others and give the King subsistence, as his predecessors had before him, to be both loved and feared. Was there yet never the like necessity before this for four hundred years and more, in which we have light from parliaments? Surely there have been far greater causes than is now, and yet no such precedent can be found. But there has been a strange argument made *ab utili,* that it is profitable to give, *argumentum cornutum,* by way of dilemma to enforce it: that either the former monies spent in the preparation have been well laid out or not. If well, why should we not pursue it; if otherwise, why should we take the fault upon ourselves by refusing to add a little, and thereby be disabled to call the delinquents to account? By the reason of this argument the parliament should be bound to maintain all actions and designs; for either they are good or not, and by that rule we should give the sword unto our enemies for the ruin of ourselves. For the calling [p. 265] of the actions of that great man to question, who knows not that nothing can be done without permission of the King? And if so, it may be as well without supply as with it, it being not the manner of great princes to make merchandise of their justice.

Much has been said upon the answer of our petition for religion, and many lines drawn thence to the intention of this business as if religion were the servant, this the mistress. I am as glad of the answer in itself as any member of the House, though I am sorry to this purpose it is used. But who knows what fruit there will come from it? Nay, we have cause to fear it when the protestation is not answerable to the fact. The pardoning of Jesuits, protection given to

papists, support and countenance to Arminians even at this time shows more than common danger. Why shall we not therefore desire the King the laws may be executed on recusants? Which if he would command and that, really, to effect it, they might be all convicted at the next assize or sessions and then, by that means, there would be money to supply him with far more than is demanded.

[p. 266] Henry the Fifth was a wise and potent prince, not inferior to any since the Conquest, and yet what did his subjects unto him? In the first year of his reign they found a remissness in the execution of the laws. Upon which they spoke plain language and prayed him then, in parliament, to put the laws in execution better than his father had done. Which, though sharp, was good and wholesome counsel and followed by that King, which likewise if his Majesty will now do he may enjoy like honor and prosperity and be both loved at home and feared abroad.

There were some other arguments also used, as that it is the first request of the King. That granting it will be an expression of our loves to him; denying, a pleasing to the papists, which may as soon receive their answers. For the last, it is no reason to persuade, for the devil sometimes is consenting to good works, though for ill ends he has.

For the second, we must so love the King as we neglect not the commonwealth. We must remember the union is between them which no good subjects will divide. We must *amare et sapere,* not *depravari amore;* [p. 267] love to love always, not to perish by our love, which were not only an injury to ourselves but to the object of our love, the King.

For the first we must consider what ill effects have followed the pressures of the people, wherein our stories mention nothing but tumults and commotions; the time is dead and all commerce shut up by the sickness here at home, by the not cared for piracies and robberies abroad. The charge already laid in the two subsidies that are granted adds a great burden to the people. What more might do we know not, but his Majesty, being wise, if he fail in this request, is better to be persuaded than a multitude.

I might give other reasons against these, as that by the easiness of the subjects to supply, princes become more careless of their revenue and expense. That it may well be doubted in the frequent grant of subsidies, that they may turn in time and grow into revenue, as in Spain and Naples those which were voluntary contributions are now made due and certain; and the tonnage and poundage here with us reckoned in the ordinary, which at first was meant [p. 268] but for the guarding of the sea, and so the acts still have it. But these things need not when our own rules conclude us, which I desire we may observe, and so pass on to the remonstrance that was ordered.

This put the courtiers beyond hope, who saw no way of safety but retreat. And to that end, continual intercourse being made with intelligence to the Duke, the commission for dissolution of the parliament which was secretly prepared was forthwith delivered to the Keeper who, according to the form, was to execute and discharge it.

Some difficulties this had caused in the deliberations of the Council where it had been opposed before the King. The Keeper here again had with much earnestness declared himself, and with many reasons endeavored to dissuade it. But his power was found too weak in contestation; for the others, the faction of that party did prevail; not that it spoke more truly but more pleasantly. So was that scene contrived, that the Duke himself seemed a suitor for the contrary and on his knees did deprecate that

which he most desired. But the resolution was immovable in the King. And, as none doubted, so practiced by the other, upon which [p. 269] the opinion of the Keeper was rejected and, not long after that, himself.[218]

The commission being heard of with the Commons wrought some distraction in their minds. Those that were fearful did incline to some accommodation and respect. Those that were resolute and had hearts answerable to their heads insisted on their grievances for which, because the remonstrance was prevented by the shortness of the time, this protestation was composed as a character of their meeting:[219]

[*For the protestation, see above, H. of C., 12 August, p. 475.*]

[p. 270] This was by the pen of Mr. Glanville, who not long after had the thanks,[220] and it was forthwith read and ordered to be presented to the King by his privy councillors of that House. Which being so agreed on, and some loose motions made for clearing those by the suffrage of the House that were thought subject to distaste for their expressions in that place (some [p. 271] such overtures being made that were rejected as unnecessary, former experience having proved them to be useless and unprofitable), those things laid aside, and the Usher of the Black Rod admitted with his fatal message to the House. The Speaker left his chair, and being attended by the rest went presently to the Lords where the commission was then read, and so dissolved that parliament.

This dissolution, though thus wrought, gave not in all things satisfaction to the courtiers, though in some they had content.

218. Bishop Williams was removed from the office of Lord Keeper in October 1625. *D.N.B.*

219. The version of the protestation included in the *Negotium* is essentially the same as that included in Bedford MS. 197 and Petyt 538/8; therefore, in the interest of economy, we have omitted it here. See H. of C., 12 August, O.B.

220. Eliot may be making an ironic reference to the punishment Glanville received at the hands of Buckingham in September 1625 by being pressed into service as secretary on the Cadiz expedition. See Glanville's arguments against such employment, S.P. 16/6: 132.

That they were freed from the constellation that was over them and the dire aspect it had upon the corrupt matter of their works seemed as a happiness in part; but they still feared the influence and the future operation it might have; and, for the present, they had failed in their expectation and design.

On the other side there was not less trouble to the country, as the intelligence did disperse. That saving of their money did not please, as the demand disliked them. All men possessed their neighbors that that [p. 272] meeting was the Duke's. That he to color the folly of his enterprises had practiced to entitle[221] them to the parliament. That the parliament discovering his practice and corruption to secure himself therein, he had raised a jealousy in the King, by which that breach was made. This was believed of all; and many revolutions it did cause in minds not well composed. That sudden alteration and great change, from extremity to extremity, was more than vulgar stomachs could digest.

The great hope they had conceived to be withered in the spring cast a black face of sorrow over their whole affections. This to be done by him from whom the contrary was expected added to that an anger. Divided between these their thoughts and times were spent, while the others, not less passionate, were in study for themselves. Many things were obnoxious unto them, made them even obnoxious to themselves: the present preparation of the fleet, and the eye the world had on it, which could not be prevented or declined; the future expectation of a parliament, and the satisfaction should be given it both for the fleet [p. 273]

and them (for as they were conscious to themselves of the public injuries they had done, which they heard called upon at that meeting and could not doubt they would be forgotten in the next, so they could prophesy for the other what success should follow it, judging either by their counsels or themselves). These things therefore were a terror in their hearts running through all their motions: yet the fleet must be set out that formerly was resolved on, and the Duke was held too precious to be adventured in the voyage, whence nothing but loss and dishonor could return. However, the commission that was granted him must stand,[222] that what glory could be had (as all such expeditions afford some in their entrance and beginnings) might be added to his trophies.

And what the *exitus* might import there was another named to father it, for whom likewise a commission was dispatched of the same power and latitude, but subordinate to the other. This substitute was Sir Edward Cecil, brother to the then E. of Exeter,[223] a man whom years and experience might have squared for better purposes and employments. His whole time [p. 274] and study had been spent upon the wars. He then retained, in the service of the States, the command of a regiment of foot. His respect with them for the quality of his blood was no detraction to his merit. His carriage and deportment were not ill, his presence good, his conversation full of affability and courtship; and in his affections there was doubted nothing that was corrupt. Facility was the greatest prejudice he was subject to, which rendered him credulous and open to those that were artificial and ob-

---

221. I.e., to father his enterprises upon the parliament.

222. See the commission of 6 August 1625 to Buckingham as "Lieutenant General, Admiral, Captain General, and Governor of our said royal fleet and army . . ." with "full and absolute power and authority, the same our fleet and army, forces and supplies, to lead and conduct, as well against all and singular such

enemies to our said dear brother-in-law and sister, and to others our and their friends and allies either in defenses or offenses, or both, as you are, or from time to time shall be directed by such our private instructions . . .". Rymer, *Foedera*, VIII, pt. 1, pp. 124–126; 1 *Car.* I, pt. 9, MS. Cal. Pat. Rolls, f. 13v.

223. On Sir Edward Cecil, see H. of C., 12 August, n. 11. William Cecil was Earl of Exeter.

scure, whereby he became exposed and subservient to their wills and was drawn to tread those paths which themselves refused to walk in.

His commission styled him, in the presence of the Duke, Lord Marshal of the field (the Duke, by land and sea, being appointed general), but in his absence it did make him general, as himself, upon which there arose an adulation in the court that was not without laughter to the soldiers, the Duke for superexcellence being termed generalissimo in their dialect, and the other always general; so as this had at no time less than was his due that, as in all things else, had more.

[p. 275] This being settled for the fleet, a *consulto* likewise followed it, how to accommodate for the parliament; nor was in this the business for retraction of the errors, but for prevention of complaints. The old courses must continue without any lessening of the exorbitance, only the study was that no man might oppose it; and to that end a project was received to remove the most active of the Commons, those that had then declared themselves, charging them with the employments that might make them incapable of the parliament, presuming thereby others would be deterred and the whole ability of that House extracted with those persons so as no man should remain of knowledge or affection to contest

them. So shallow are those rivulets of the court that they think all wisdom like their murmur. Kingdoms they will measure by the analogy of their rules but in this they deceive themselves as, in all other things, the world; and as they judge of kingdoms, kingdoms may judge of them. Great is the variety in a kingdom, both of knowledge and ability. Great is the variety [p. 276] of persons and of their studies and exercises to acquire them. The forms of wisdom are as various as are men's. As one is bold and active, another will be cautious and reserved; this plots, that speaks, a third judges and discerns; and in all these some are excellent, yet appear not, while their works are done by others, but are content and happy to be shadowed in themselves, all difficulties being declined, dangers prevented, and their desires made good, yet against all, where necessity shall require, they will and are ready to stand forth. So did it prove in this, contrary to the prediction of the court; but their conclusion held proportionable to their judgment by which that project was approved, some being designed for sheriffs then at home,[224] others for other employments further off, whereby they thought themselves sufficiently secured and, in that security being settled from their resolutions in these things, they then betook themselves to other entertainments more at large.

---

224. Concerning the pricking of former Commons' leaders as sheriffs prior to the 1626 parliament, see S.P. 16/8:34; S.P. 16/10:16; William Knowler, ed., *The*

Earl of Strafforde's Letters and Dispatches (London, 1739), I, 29; and Gardiner, *History of England*, VI, 33–34. See also, above, n. 220.

Appendixes

CALENDAR OF APPENDIXES

573

REFERENCE MATERIALS AND SCHOLARLY AIDS

A. Lists of Members, H. of L.

1. By Title

The following list, based upon the lists in the MS. L.J. and the information in G.E.C[okayne]'s *Complete Peerage*, is arranged alphabetically by title (listing first the spiritual and then the temporal Lords). The given and family names of each member of the Upper House are included in parentheses. For each spiritual Lord, the date (by year) of his confirmation in office is also listed. For each temporal Lord, first the date (by year) of the creation of the current title is given, followed by the number of the creation (for example, 1st, 2d) in the history of the title, and finally the date (by year) of the accession to the title by the peer sitting in the 1625 parliament. Thus, for example, the entry for the earldom of Derby, which was a title newly created for the third time in 1485 and the one to which William Stanley acceded in 1594, appears as:

Derby, Earl of (William Stanley) 1485 3 1594.

We have not included titles held simultaneously by, but not governing the precedence of, a peer.

Spiritual	Year of confirmation
Bangor, Bishop of (Lewis Bayly)	1616
Bath and Wells, Bishop of (Arthur Lake)	1616
Bristol, Bishop of (Robert Wright)	1623
Canterbury, Archbishop of (George Abbot)	1611
Carlisle, Bishop of (Richard Senhouse)	1624
Chester, Bishop of (John Bridgeman)	1619
Chichester, Bishop of (George Carleton)	1619

Spiritual	Year of confirmation
Coventry and Lichfield, Bishop of (Thomas Morton)	1619
Durham, Bishop of (Richard Neile)	1617
Ely, Bishop of (Nicholas Felton)	1619
Exeter, Bishop of (Valentine Carey)	1621
Gloucester, Bishop of (Godfrey Goodman)	1625
Hereford, Bishop of (Francis Godwin)	1617
Lincoln, Bishop of (John Williams)	1621
Llandaff, Bishop of (Theophilus Field)	1619
London, Bishop of (George Monteigne)	1621
Norwich, Bishop of (Samuel Harsnet)	1619
Oxford, Bishop of (John Howson)	1619
Peterborough, Bishop of (Thomas Dove)	1601
Rochester, Bishop of (John Buckeridge)	1611
St. Asaph, Bishop of (John Hanmer)	1624
St. Davids, Bishop of (William Laud)	1621
Salisbury, Bishop of (John Davenant)	1621
Winchester, Bishop of (Lancelot Andrewes)	1619
Worcester, Bishop of (John Thornborough)	1617
York, Archbishop of (Tobias Matthew)	1606

Temporal	Year and number of creation		Year of accession
Abergavenny, Lord (Henry Neville)	1392	1	1622
Andover, Viscount (Thomas Howard)	1622	1	1622
Anglesey, Earl of (Christopher Villiers)	1623	1	1623

Temporal	Year and number of creation		Year of accession	Temporal	Year and number of creation		Year of accession
Arundel and Surrey, Earl of (Thomas Howard)	1138	2	1604	De La Warr, Lord (Henry West)	1570	2	1618
Arundell of Wardour, Lord (Thomas Arundell)	1605	1	1605	Denbigh, Earl of (William Feilding)	1622	1	1622
Audley, Lord (Mervin Tuchet)	1313	1	1617	Denny of Waltham, Lord (Edward Denny)	1604	1	1604
Bath, Earl of (Edward Bourchier)	1536	2	1623	Derby, Earl of (William Stanley)	1485	3	1594
Bedford, Earl of (Edward Russell)	1550	2	1585	Devonshire, Earl of (William Cavendish)	1618	5	1618
Berkeley, Lord (George Berkeley)	1421	1	1613	Dorset, Earl of (Edward Sackville)	1604	3	1624
Bolinbroke, Earl of (Oliver St. John)	1624	1	1624	Dudley, Lord (Edward Sutton)	1440	1	1586
Bridgewater, Earl of (John Egerton)	1617	2	1617	Essex, Earl of (Robert Devereux)	1572	6	1604
Bristol, Earl of (John Digby)	1622	1	1622	Eure, Lord (William Eure)	1544	1	1617
Brooke of Beauchamps Court, Lord (Fulke Greville)	1621	1	1621	Exeter, Earl of (William Cecil)	1605	1	1623
Buckingham, Duke of (George Villiers)	1623	2	1623	Grey of Groby, Lord (Henry Grey)	1603	1	1614
Cambridge, Earl of (James Hamilton)	1619	4	1625	Grey of Warke, Lord (William Grey)	1624	1	1624
Carew, Lord (George Carew)	1605	1	1605	Herbert of Chepstow, Lord (Henry Somerset)	1506	1	1604
Carey of Leppington, Lord (Robert Carey)	1622	1	1622	Hertford, Earl of (William Seymour)	1559	3	1621
Carlisle, Earl of (James Hay)	1622	2	1622	Holderness, Earl of (John Ramsey)	1621	1	1621
Clare, Earl of (John Holles)	1624	1	1624	Holland, Earl of (Henry Rich)	1624	1	1624
Colchester, Viscount (Thomas Darcy)	1621	1	1621	Howard of Walden, Lord (Theophilus Howard)	1597	1	1610
Conway of Ragley, Lord (Edward Conway)	1625	1	1625	Huntingdon, Earl of (Henry Hastings)	1529	7	1604
Cromwell, Lord (Thomas Cromwell)	1540	2	1607	Kent, Earl of (Henry Grey)	1465	5	1623
Cumberland, Earl of (Francis Clifford)	1525	1	1605	Kimbolton, Lord [see Mandeville, Viscount]			
Dacre, Lord (Richard Lennard)	1321	1	1616	Leicester, Earl of (Robert Sydney)	1618	6	1618
Danvers, Lord (Henry Danvers)	1603	1	1603	Ley of Ley, Lord (James Ley)	1624	1	1624
Darcy, Lord (John Darcy)	1548	1	1602	Lincoln, Earl of (Theophilus Clinton)	1572	9	1619
Deincourt of Sutton, Lord (Francis Leke)	1624	1	1624				

Temporal	Year and number of creation		Year of accession	Temporal	Year and number of creation		Year of accession
Mandeville, Viscount (Henry Montagu)	1620	1	1620	Saye and Sele, Viscount (William Fiennes)	1624	1	1624
Mansfield, Viscount (William Cavendish)	1620	1	1620	Scrope, Lord (Emanuel Scrope)	1371	1	1609
Montagu, Viscount (Anthony Maria Browne)	1554	1	1592	Sheffield, Lord (Edmund Sheffield)	1547	1	1568
Montagu of Boughton, Lord (Edward Montagu)	1621	1	1621	Shrewsbury, Earl of (George Talbot)	1442	2	1618
Montgomery, Earl of (Philip Herbert)	1605	1	1605	Spencer of Wormleighton, Lord (William Spencer)	1603	1	1603
Mordaunt, Lord (John Mordaunt)	1532	1	1609	Stafford, Lord (Edward Stafford)	1299	1	1603
Morley and Monteagle, Lord (Henry Parker)	1299	1	1622	Stanhope of Harrington, Lord (Charles Stanhope)	1605	1	1621
Noel of Ridlington, Lord (Edward Noel)	1617	1	1617	Stanhope of Shelford, Lord (Philip Stanhope)	1616	1	1616
North, Lord (Dudley North)	1554	1	1600	Stourton, Lord (Edward Stourton)	1448	1	1588
Northampton, Earl of (William Compton)	1618	6	1618	Suffolk, Earl of (Thomas Howard)	1603	4	1603
Northumberland, Earl of (Henry Percy)	1557	6	1585	Surrey, Earl of [see Arundel and Surrey, Earl of]			
Nottingham, Earl of (Charles Howard)	1597	6	1624	Sussex, Earl of (Robert Radcliffe)	1529	2	1593
Oxford, Earl of (Robert de Vere)	1142	1	1625				
Paget, Lord (William Paget)	1549	1	1604	Teynham, Lord (John Roper)	1616	1	1622
Pembroke, Earl of (William Herbert)	1551	9	1601	Tunbridge, Viscount (Richard Bourke)	1624	1	1624
Petre, Lord (William Petre)	1603	1	1613	Vaux, Lord (Edward Vaux)	1523	1	1595
Purbeck, Viscount (John Villiers)	1619	1	1619	Walden, Lord [see Howard of Walden, Lord]			
Robartes of Truro, Lord (Richard Robartes)	1625	1	1625	Wallingford, Viscount (William Knollys)	1616	1	1616
Rochford, Viscount (Henry Carey)	1621	2	1621	Warwick, Earl of (Robert Rich)	1618	6	1619
Russell of Thornhaugh, Lord (Francis Russell)	1603	1	1613	Wentworth, Lord (Thomas Wentworth)	1529	1	1593
Rutland, Earl of (Francis Manners)	1525	3	1612	Westmorland, Earl of (Francis Fane)	1624	2	1624
St. John, Lord (John Paulet)	1538	1	1621	Willoughby of Eresby, Lord (Robert Bertie)	1313	1	1601
Salisbury, Earl of (William Cecil)	1605	5	1612	Winchester, Marquess of (William Paulet)	1551	1	1598

Temporal	Year and number of creation		Year of accession
Windsor, Lord (Thomas Windsor)	1529	1	1605
Worcester, Earl of (Edward Somerset)	1514	5	1589
Wotton, Lord (Edward Wotton)	1603	1	1603
Zouche, Lord (Edward La Zouche)	1308	1	1569

2. By Family Name

Abbot, George
    Archbishop of Canterbury
Andrewes, Lancelot
    Bishop of Winchester
Arundell, Thomas
    Lord Arundell of Wardour

Bayly, Lewis
    Bishop of Bangor
Berkeley, George
    Lord Berkeley
Bertie, Robert
    Lord Willoughby of Eresby
Bourchier, Edward
    Earl of Bath
Bourke, Richard
    Viscount Tunbridge
Bridgeman, John
    Bishop of Chester
Browne, Anthony Maria
    Viscount Montagu
Buckeridge, John
    Bishop of Rochester

Carew, George
    Lord Carew
Carey, Henry
    Viscount Rochford
Carey, Robert
    Lord Carey of Leppington
Carey, Valentine
    Bishop of Exeter
Carleton, George
    Bishop of Chichester
Cavendish, William
    Earl of Devonshire
Cavendish, William
    Viscount Mansfield
Cecil, William
    Earl of Exeter
Cecil, William
    Earl of Salisbury
Clifford, Francis
    Earl of Cumberland
Clinton, Theophilus
    Earl of Lincoln
Compton, William
    Earl of Northampton
Conway, Edward
    Lord Conway of Ragley
Cromwell, Thomas
    Lord Cromwell

Danvers, Henry
    Lord Danvers
Darcy, John
    Lord Darcy

Darcy, Thomas
    Viscount Colchester
Davenant, John
    Bishop of Salisbury
Denny, Edward
    Lord Denny of Waltham
Devereux, Robert
    Earl of Essex
Digby, John
    Earl of Bristol
Dove, Thomas
    Bishop of Peterborough

Egerton, John
    Earl of Bridgewater
Eure, William
    Lord Eure

Fane, Francis
    Earl of Westmorland
Feilding, William
    Earl of Denbigh
Felton, Nicholas
    Bishop of Ely
Field, Theophilus
    Bishop of Llandaff
Fiennes, William
    Viscount Saye and Sele

Godwin, Francis
    Bishop of Hereford
Goodman, Godfrey
    Bishop of Gloucester
Greville, Fulke
    Lord Brooke of Beauchamps Court
Grey, Henry
    Lord Grey of Groby
Grey, Henry
    Earl of Kent
Grey, William
    Lord Grey of Warke

Hamilton, James
    Earl of Cambridge
Hanmer, John
    Bishop of St. Asaph
Harsnet, Samuel
    Bishop of Norwich
Hastings, Henry
    Earl of Huntingdon
Hay, James
    Earl of Carlisle
Herbert, Philip
    Earl of Montgomery
Herbert, William
    Earl of Pembroke
Holles, John
    Earl of Clare

Howard, Charles
Earl of Nottingham
Howard, Theophilus
Lord Howard of Walden
Howard, Thomas
Viscount Andover
Howard, Thomas
Earl of Arundel and Surrey
Howard, Thomas
Earl of Suffolk
Howson, John
Bishop of Oxford

Knollys, William
Viscount Wallingford

Lake, Arthur
Bishop of Bath and Wells
Laud, William
Bishop of St. Davids
Leke, Francis
Lord Deincourt of Sutton
Lennard, Richard
Lord Dacre
Ley, James
Lord Ley of Ley

Manners, Francis
Earl of Rutland
Matthew, Tobias
Archbishop of York
Montagu, Edward
Lord Montagu of Boughton
Montagu, Henry
Viscount Mandeville
Monteigne, George
Bishop of London
Mordaunt, John
Lord Mordaunt
Morton, Thomas
Bishop of Coventry and Lichfield

Neile, Richard
Bishop of Durham
Neville, Henry
Lord Abergavenny
Noel, Edward
Lord Noel of Ridlington
North, Dudley
Lord North

Paget, William
Lord Paget
Parker, Henry
Lord Morley and Monteagle
Paulet, John
Lord St. John
Paulet, William
Marquess of Winchester

Percy, Henry
Earl of Northumberland
Petre, William
Lord Petre

Radcliffe, Robert
Earl of Sussex
Ramsey, John
Earl of Holderness
Rich, Henry
Earl of Holland
Rich, Robert
Earl of Warwick
Robartes, Richard
Lord Robartes of Truro
Roper, John
Lord Teynham
Russell, Edward
Earl of Bedford
Russell, Francis
Lord Russell of Thornhaugh

Sackville, Edward
Earl of Dorset
St. John, Oliver
Earl of Bolingbroke
Scrope, Emanuel
Lord Scrope
Senhouse, Richard
Bishop of Carlisle
Seymour, William
Earl of Hertford
Sheffield, Edmund
Lord Sheffield
Somerset, Edward
Earl of Worcester
Somerset, Henry
Lord Herbert of Chepstow
Spencer, William
Lord Spencer of Wormleighton
Stafford, Edward
Lord Stafford
Stanhope, Charles
Lord Stanhope of Harrington
Stanhope, Philip
Lord Stanhope of Shelford
Stanley, William
Earl of Derby
Stourton, Edward
Lord Stourton
Sutton, Edward
Lord Dudley
Sydney, Robert
Earl of Leicester

Talbot, George
Earl of Shrewsbury

Thornborough, John
    Bishop of Worcester
Tuchet, Mervin
    Lord Audley

Vaux, Edward
    Lord Vaux
Vere, Robert de
    Earl of Oxford
Villiers, Christopher
    Earl of Anglesey
Villiers, George
    Duke of Buckingham
Villiers, John
    Viscount Purbeck

Wentworth, Thomas
    Lord Wentworth
West, Henry
    Lord De La Warr
Williams, John
    Bishop of Lincoln
Windsor, Thomas
    Lord Windsor
Wotton, Edward
    Lord Wotton
Wright, Robert
    Bishop of Bristol

Zouche, Edward La
    Lord Zouche

B. Proxy List, H. of L.

The following list of Lords who gave or received proxies in 1625 is arranged alphabetically by title, listing first the spiritual and then the temporal Lords. The list is compiled from the catalog on pages 1 and 2 of the MS. L.J., headed "Littorae Procuratoriae in hoc Parliamento sunt allatae", which gives the appointments of procurators (proxy holders). In the list printed below the editors include both the names of the proxy holders (procurators) and of the Lords spiritual and temporal who appointed them.

Spiritual Lords

Canterbury, Archbishop of
    procurator for: Archbp. of York
Chester, Bishop of
    appoints procurators: Bp. of Coventry and
        Lichfield
        Bp. of Llandaff
Conventry and Lichfield, Bishop of
    procurator for: Bp. of Chester
        Bp. of St. Asaph
Exeter, Bishop of
    appoints procurator: Bp. of London
Hereford, Bishop of
    appoints procurators: Bp. of Rochester
        Bp. of Oxford
        Bp. of St. Davids
Lincoln, Bishop of
    procurator for: Bp. of Salisbury
        L. Audley[1]
        E. of Westmorland
Llandaff, Bishop of
    procurator for: Bp. of Chester
        Bp. of St. Asaph
London, Bishop of
    procurator for: Bp. of Exeter
Oxford, Bishop of
    procurator for: Bp. of Hereford
Rochester, Bishop of
    procurator for: Bp. of Hereford
St. Asaph, Bishop of
    appoints procurators: Bp. of Winchester
        Bp. of Coventry and
        Lichfield
        Bp. of Llandaff

St. Davids, Bishop of
    procurator for: Bp. of Hereford
        Bp. of Worcester
Salisbury, Bishop of
    appoints procurator: Bp. of Lincoln
Worcester, Bishop of
    procurator for: Bp. of St. Asaph
    appoints procurator: Bp. of St. Davids
York, Archbishop of
    appoints procurator: Archbp. of Canterbury

Temporal Lords

Andover, Viscount
    procurator for: Visc. Wallingford
Arundel, Earl of
    procurator for: L. Arundell
Arundell, Lord
    appoints procurator: E. of Arundel
Audley, Lord
    appoints procurator: Bp. of Lincoln
Bath, Earl of
    appoints procurator: Duke of Buckingham
Bedford, Earl of
    appoints procurator: E. of Pembroke
Bristol, Earl of
    appoints procurator: E. of Pembroke
Buckingham, Duke of[2]
    procurator for: E. of Bath
        L. Carew
        Visc. Colchester
        E. of Cumberland
        E. of Exeter
        Visc. Mansfield
        L. Noel
        E. of Northumberland
        E. of Rutland
        L. St. John
        E. of Salisbury
        L. Teynham
        Visc. Tunbridge
Carew, Lord
    appoints procurator: Duke of Buckingham
Colchester, Viscount
    appoints procurator: Duke of Buckingham
Cumberland, Earl of
    appoints procurator: Duke of Buckingham
Darcy, Lord
    appoints procurator: E. of Pembroke
Deincourt, Lord
    appoints procurator: E. of Pembroke
Danvers, Lord
    procurator for: L. Denny

1. In 1626 it was ordered that "all proxies from a spiritual Lord shall be made unto a spiritual Lord, and from a temporal Lord unto a temporal Lord". *L.J.*, III, 507.

2. In the 1626 session it was ordered that thereafter "No Lord of this House shall be capable of receiving above two proxies". *L.J.*, III, 507.

Denny, Lord
    appoints procurator: L. Danvers
Derby, Earl of
    appoints procurator: E. of Pembroke
Dudley, Lord
    appoints procurator: L. Stourton
Exeter, Earl of
    appoints procurator: Duke of Buckingham
Huntingdon, Earl of
    appoints procurator: E. of Pembroke
Mansfield, Viscount
    appoints procurator: Duke of Buckingham
Mordaunt, Lord
    appoints procurator: L. Spencer
Noel, Lord
    appoints procurator: Duke of Buckingham
Northumberland, Earl of
    appoints procurator: Duke of Buckingham
Pembroke, Earl of
    procurator for: E. of Bedford
                    E. of Bristol
                    L. Darcy
                    L. Deincourt
                    E. of Derby
                    E. of Huntingdon
                    L. Sheffield
                    L. Stanhope of Shelford
                    L. Wotton
                    L. Zouche

Rutland, Earl of
    appoints procurator: Duke of Buckingham
St. John, Lord
    appoints procurator: Duke of Buckingham
Salisbury, Earl of
    appoints procurator: Duke of Buckingham
Sheffield, Lord
    appoints procurator: E. of Pembroke
Spencer, Lord
    procurator for: L. Mordaunt
Stanhope of Shelford, Lord
    appoints procurator: E. of Pembroke
Stourton, Lord
    procurator for: L. Dudley
Teynham, Lord
    appoints procurator: Duke of Buckingham
Tunbridge, Viscount
    appoints procurator: Duke of Buckingham
Wallingford, Viscount
    appoints procurator: Visc. Andover
Westmorland, Earl of
    appoints procurator: Bp. of Lincoln
Wotton, Lord
    appoints procurator: E. of Pembroke
Zouche, Lord
    appoints procurator: E. of Pembroke

C. ATTENDANCE TABLE, H. OF L.

The following table is based upon the lists of Lords present which appear at the beginning of each session's account (morning and afternoon) in the Minute Book, H.L.R.O., M.M., 1625. In the Minute Book lists the names are arranged in three columns corresponding to the three benches: bishops, earls [and viscounts], and barons. The order of the names within each column varies considerably from day to day and probably reflects the order of the Lords' entry into the House for each meeting. The lists for the three days on which the parliament was prorogued at the beginning of the 1625 session (17 and 31 May and 13 June) contain numbers next to each name which indicate the order of precedence in which the members were listed in the Lords Journal (see below). Space limitations have precluded the reproduction of the daily lists in the present volume, but the editors have compiled the attendance information into the table below. All members of the Upper House who, at any time during the 1625 parliament, were noted in the Minute Book as present in the House are listed alphabetically by title (first spiritual and then temporal Lords).[1] A "P" is entered under

each date for which a Lord was listed as present.[2]

The MS. L.J. contains a list of members of the Upper House (all spiritual and temporal Lords not otherwise disqualified) arranged by bench and by precedence at the beginning of each day's account. These MS. lists include a "pr" notation next to the name of each Lord present. A clerk transferred this attendance information to the MS. L.J. from the Minute Book lists or a similar source. Nevertheless, differences do occur between the MS. L.J. and the Minute Book data.[3] These differences are indicated in the following table through the use of symbols: an asterisk (*) is used for cases when the MS. L.J. notes a member as present on a day when he is not listed as such in the Minute Book, and a dagger (†) is used to denote cases when the MS. L.J. does *not* note a member as present who is included in the corresponding Minute Book list. Occasionally the printed *Lords Journal* does not accurately reproduce the data from the MS. L.J.; a section mark (§) is used in the table to indicate when the printed *Lords Journal* differs from the MS. L.J.

One other source of information on attendance in the House is the record of speeches.[4] Sometimes a member is re-

---

1. In addition to the members listed in the table, the Minute Book clerk recorded the name of the Bishop of St. Asaph in the lists for 17 and 31 May but then crossed it out; the MS. L.J. includes St. Asaph's name in its 18 June list, perhaps erroneously in place of the Bishop of Ely who is listed as present in the Minute Book. The MS. L.J. is probably in error in noting the Earl of Derby as present on 18 and 25 June rather than the Earl of Kent who is listed as present in the Minute Book and whose name immediately precedes Derby's in the MS. L.J. list.

Also, the King is listed as present in the House on 18 June in the Minute Book and on 18 and 20 June in the MS. L.J.

As the table shows, of the ninety-seven members who put in at least a token appearance in the House during the 1625 parliament, over forty never attended the Oxford session, while five who were never present during the London session did attend at Oxford.

2. The space is left blank when no source lists the

member as present or excused. It should be kept in mind that even those members who were not present could affect the vote of the House through the operation of the proxy system (see the Proxy List, above).

3. Many of the discrepancies apparently stem from the misreading of similar names—such as the Bishop of "Chester" for "Chichester" (as on 18 and 28 June, 1, 4, 5, and 7 July) or the Earl of "Nottingham" for "Northampton" (as on 3 August)—or the clerk's error in placing the "pr" on the name just above or below the correct name in the MS. L.J. list when transferring the attendance information (as Derby for Kent on 18 and 25 June and Andover for Rochford on 6 July P.M.).

4. Committee appointments constitute a further possible source of information concerning attendance. According to usual procedure no Lord was to be named to a committee during his absence from the House (see Henry Elsynge's "The Method of Passing Bills in Parliament", *Harleian Miscellany* [London, 1810], V, 228), so that inclusion of a Lord's name on a

corded as speaking on days when neither the Minute Book nor the MS. L.J. lists him as present. This situation is indicated in the table through the use of double daggers (‡).

In addition to the lists of Lords present, the Minute Book and the MS. L.J. contain lists of Lords excused. In the following table an "E" is entered under the date for which a Lord is listed as excused in either of the sources.[5] Since the lists of those excused are reproduced in the text of the present volume (see the Orders of Business), the editors have made no attempt to indicate in the table the discrepancies between the two manuscripts in this regard.

committee list suggests his presence in the House. However, it is unclear how closely practice followed policy in this regard, and therefore committee appointments do not provide an entirely reliable means for ascertaining attendance. For this reason, we have not included committee information in this table.

5. If a Lord is listed as both present and excused for a single meeting, the entry in the table appears as "P/E". Concerning dispensations granted to absent members, see above, pp. 44–45 and 47, and see below, Appendix II, D, 2, pp. 670–671.

Attendance Table

Spiritual	May		June										July										August											
	17	31	13	18	20 pm	22	23	25	27	28	28 pm	30	1	4	4 pm	5 pm	6	6 pm	7	8	9	11	1	2	3	4	4 pm	5	6	8	9	10	11	12
Bangor, Bp.	P		P	P	P	P	P	E	P	P	P	P	P	P	P	P	P	P	P	P	P	P	P	P	P	P				P	P	P	P	P
Bath and Wells, Bp.	P		P	P	P	P	P	P	P	P	P	P	P	P	P	P	P	P	P	P	P	P	P	P	P	P		P	P	P	P	P	P	P
Bristol, Bp.	P		P	P	P	P	P	P	P	P	P	P	P	P	P	E	P	P	P	P	P	P	P	P	P	P		E	P	P	P	P	P	P
Canterbury, Archbp.	P		P	P	P	‡	E	P	P	P	P	P	P	*	P	P	P	P	P	P	P	P	P	P	P	P		P	P	P	P	P	P	P
Carlisle, Bp.	P		P	P	P	P	P†	P	P†	P	*	P	*	*	*	*	P	P	P	P	P	P	P	P	P	P		P	P	P	*	P	P	P
Chester, Bp.	P		*					P																						*				
Chichester, Bp.	P	P	P†	P	P	P	P	P	P†	P†	P	P†	P†	P†	P†	P	P	P	P†	P	P	P	P	P	P	P		P†	P	P	P	P	P	P
Coventry and Lichfield, Bp.	P	P	P	P	P	P	P	P	P	P	P	P	P	P	P	P	P	P	P	P	P	P	P	P	P	P		P	P	P	P	P	P	P
Durham, Bp.	P		P	P	P	P	P	P	P	P	P	P	P	P	E	E	P	E	P	P	P	P	E	E	E	P								
Ely, Bp.	P		P†	P	P	P	P	P	P	P	P	P	P	P	P	P	P	P	P	P	P	P	P	E	E	P		P	P	P	P	P	P	P
Exeter, Bp.			P	P	P	P	P	P	P	E	P	E	E	P	E	P	P	E	P	P			P	E	E									
Gloucester, Bp.	P		P	P	P	P	P	P	P	P	P	P	P	P	P	P	P	P	P	P			E	E										
Hereford, Bp.	P	P		P	P	P	P	P	P	P																								
Lincoln, Bp.	P6		P	P	P	P	P	P	P	P	P	P	P	P	P	P	P	P	P	P	P	P	P	P	P	P		P	P	P	P	P	P	P
Llandaff, Bp.	P		P	P	P	P	P	P	P	P	P	P	P	P	P	P	P	P	P	P	P	P	P	P	E	P		*	P	P	P	P	P	P
London, Bp.	P		P	P	P	P	P	P	P	P	P	P	P	P	E	E	P	P	P	P	P	P	P	P	P	P		P	P	P	P	P	P	P
Norwich, Bp.			P	P	P	P	P	P	P	P†	P†	P	P	P	P								E							P	P	P	P	P
Oxford, Bp.			P	*	P	P	E	P	P														P	P	P	P		P†	P	P	P	P	P	P
Rochester, Bp.	P	P	P	P	P	P	P	P	P	P	P	P	P	P	P	P	P	P	P	P	P	E	P/E	P	P	P		P†	P	P	P	P	P	P
St. Davids, Bp.	P	P	P	P	P	P	P	P	P	P	P	P	P	P	P	P	P	P	P	P	P	P	P	P	P	P		P	P	P	P	P	P	P
Salisbury, Bp.	P		P	P	P	P	P	P	P	P	P	P	P	P	E	P	P	P	P	P	P	P	E	P	P	P		P	P	P	P	P	P	P
Winchester, Bp.			P	P	P	P	P	P	P	P	P	P	P	P	P	P	P	P	P	P	P	P				E								
Worcester, Bp.	P	P																																

6. As Lord Keeper, John Williams, Bishop of Lincoln, presided over the Upper House and was present at every meeting of the House in 1625. Although his name was sometimes omitted from the Minute Book lists, he was always noted as present in the MS. L.J. and we have inserted "P"s across from his name throughout the table.

(continued)

Temporal	May 17	May 31	June 13	June 18	June 20 pm	June 22	June 23	June 25	June 27	June 28	June 28 pm	June 30	July 1	July 4	July 4 pm	July 5	July 6	July 6 pm	July 7	July 8	July 9	July 11	Aug 1	Aug 2	Aug 3	Aug 4	Aug 4 pm	Aug 5	Aug 6	Aug 8	Aug 9	Aug 10	Aug 11	Aug 12
Andover, V.					P	P	P		P	P	E		P	P	E	P	P	*	P	P	P							P	P	P	P	P	P	P
Anglesey, E.				P		P	P	P	P	P	P	P	P	P	P	P	P		P									P	P	P	P	P	P	P
Arundel and Surrey, E.	P			P		P	*	P	P	P	P	P	P	P	P	P		P	P	P	P	P	P	P	P	P	P	P	P	P	P	P	P	P
Berkeley, L.				P		P	P	P	P	P	P	P	P†	P		P		P	P	P		P			P	P	P	P	P	P	P	P	P	P
Bolingbroke, E.	P	P		P		P	P	P	P	P	P	P	P	P	E	E		P	P	P		P	E		P	P		P	P	P	P	P	P	P
Bridgewater, E.	P			P		P	P	E	E		P												E			E			P	P	P				
Brooke, L.				P		P	P	E	E	P	P	P	P	P	E		E						P					P	P	P	P			
Buckingham, D.				P		P	P	E	E		P						P		P				P					P	P	P	P			
Cambridge, E.				P		P	P	P	P	P	P	P	P	P		P	P		P	P			P	P				P	P	P	P	P	P	P
Carey, L.				P		P	P	P	P	P	P	P	P	P	E	P	P		P			P	P		P			P	P	P	P	P	P	P
Carlisle, E.				P	*	P	P	P	P	P	P	P	P	P		P		P†	P	P		P	P					P	P	P	P	P	P	P
Clare, E.	P	P	P	P†	P	P	P	P	P	P	P†	P	P	P	P	P	P	*	P†	P	P	P		E				P	P	P	P	P	P	P
Colchester, V.				P		P	P	P	P	‡	‡																							
Conway of Ragley, L.				P		P	P	P	P	*			P	P	P	P	P	P†	P	P	P	P	P					P	P	P	P		P	
Cromwell, L.																																		P
Dacre, L.				P					*														P											
Danvers, L.	P	P		P		P	P/E	P	P	P	P	P	P	P	P†	P		P	P	P	P	P	P						P	P				
Darcy, L.	P	P		P		P	P	P	P	P	P	P	P	P	P	P	P	P	P	P	P	P	P					P	P	P	P		P	
Deincourt, L.		P		P		P	E	P	P	P	P	P	P	P	P	P	E	P	P	P		P	P	P	P	P	P	P	P	P	P	P	P	P
De La Warr, L.				P		P	P	P	P	P	P	P	P	P	P	E	E	E*	P	P			P	P	P	P	P	P	P	P	P	P	P	P
Denbigh, E.				P		P	P	P	P	P	P	P	P	P	E*									P			P	P	P	P	P	P	P	P
Denny, L.				P		P	P	P	P	P	P	P	P	P	P	P	E	E	P	P			P	P	P	P	P	P	P	P	P	P	P	P
Devonshire, E.				P		P	P	P	P	*	P	P	P	P	E*			*					P	P	P	P	P	P	P	P	P	P	P	P
Dorset, E.				P		P	P	P	P	P	P	P											P											
Dudley, L.	P	P		P	*																													
Essex, E.																																		
Eure, L.			P	P				E	E	E																								
Exeter, E.				P			E	E	E	E							E		E						P			P	P	P	P	P	P	P

Temporal	May 17	May 31	Jun 13	Jun 18	Jun 20 pm	Jun 22	Jun 23	Jun 25	Jun 27	Jun 28	Jun 28 pm	Jul 30	Jul 1	Jul 4	Jul 4 pm	Jul 5	Jul 6	Jul 6 pm	Jul 7	Jul 8	Jul 9	Jul 11	Aug 1	Aug 2	Aug 3	Aug 4	Aug 4 pm	Aug 5	Aug 6	Aug 8	Aug 9	Aug 10	Aug 11	Aug 12
Grey of Groby, L.		P	P	P	P	P		P	P	P	P	P	P	P		P	P		P†	P	P	P	P†	P	P	P	P	P	P	P	P	P	P	P
Grey of Warke, L.	P	P	P	P	P	P		P	P	P	P	P	P	P	P	P	E	E	P	P	P	P	*	P	P	P	P+7	P	P		P	P	P	P
Holderness, E.			P	P	P	P	P										E								P	P								
Holland, E.			P	P	P	P		P										E						P										
Howard, L.			P	P	P	P		P			P	P	P	P		P	E		P					P			P		P	P	P	P	P	P
Kent, E.		P	P†	P	P	P		P†	P	P	P	P	P	P																				
Leicester, E.		P	P	P	P§	P		P	P	P	P	P	P	P		E	E	E	P	P			P	P	P	P	P	P	P	P	P	P	P	P
Ley, L.			P	P	P	P		P	P	P	P	P	P	P		P	P		P															
Lincoln, E.			P	P	P	P	E	P	P	P	P	P	P	P		P	E	E	P	P			P	P	P	P	P	P	P	P	P	P	P	P
Mandeville, V.		P	P	P	P	P	P	P	P	P	P	P	P	P		P	P		P	P			P	P	P	P	P	P	P	P	P	P	P	P
Mansfield, V.			P	P	P	P	P																											
Montagu, V.		P	P																															
Montagu of Boughton, L.			P			P		P			P	P	P	P		P				P			P	P	P	P	P†	P	P	P	P	P	P	P
Montgomery, E.		P	P			P		P			P	P	P	P									P	P	P	P	P	P	P	P	P	P	P	P
Mordaunt, L.																																		
Morley and M., L.										P/E																E			P	P				
Noel, L.		P	P	P				E	P/E				P	P		P	P								E	P		P	P	P	P	P	P	P
North, L.			P	P	P	P		E	P/E			P	P	P		P	P		P	P			P	P	P	P	P	P	P	P	P	P	P	P
Northampton, E.			P	P	P	P	E	E	P		P	P	P	P		P	P		P	P			P	P	P†	P	P	P	P	P	P	P	P	P
Nottingham, E.		P	P	P	P	P		P	P	P	P	P	P	P	*	P	P		P	P	P		P	P	*	P	P	P	P	P	P	P	P	P
Paget, L.		P	P	P	P	P		P			P	P	P		*	E									E									
Pembroke, E.		P	P	P	P	P	‡	E	P	P	E	E	P	P		P§	E		E					*	E	P	P§	E						
Petre, L.		P										E	P																					
Purbeck, V.																								P†							P	P		
Robartes, L.		P	P	P	P	P	E	P	E			P	P	P		P	E		P	P			P	P	P	P	P†	P	P	P	P	P	P	P
Rochford, V.		P	P	P	P	P		P			P	P	P	P		P	P	P†	P	P§	P		P	P	P	P	P	P	P	P	P	P	E	P
Russell, L.		P	P	P	P	P		P	E														E	P	P	P	P†	P	P	P	P	P	P	P
Rutland, E.		P	P	P	P	P		E			P	P	P	P		P	P		P	P				P	P	P	P	P	P	P	P	P	P	P

7. The MS. L.J. list for 4 August P.M. does not contain notations indicating those present for any of the names in the barons' column.

Temporal	May 17	May 31	Jun 13	Jun 18	Jun 20 pm	Jun 22	Jun 23	Jun 25	Jun 27	Jun 28	Jun 28 pm	Jun 30	Jul 1	Jul 4	Jul 4 pm	Jul 5	Jul 6	Jul 6 pm	Jul 7	Jul 8	Jul 9	Jul 11	Aug 1	Aug 2	Aug 3	Aug 4	Aug 4 pm	Aug 5	Aug 6	Aug 8	Aug 9	Aug 10	Aug 11	Aug 12
St. John, L.			P	P																														
Salisbury, E.										P	P					E																		
Saye and Sele, V.		P		P	P	P	P	P	P	P				P	P	P	P	P	P	P				P				P	P	P	P	P	P	P
Scrope, L.			P	P	P	P	P	P	P	P	P		P	P	P	P	P	P	P	P	P	P												
Sheffield, L.		P	P	P	P	P	P	P	P	P	P		P	P	P	E	P	P	P	P	P	P												
Spencer, L.			P	P	P	P	P	P	P	P	P		P	P	P†								P	P	P				P					
Stanhope of H., L.	P		P	P	P	P	P	P	P	P		P⁸	P																					
Stanhope of Sh., L.						P	P	P	P	P	P	P	P	P	P	P	P		P	P			P	P	P					P	P	P		
Stourton, L.	P	P	P	P	P	P	P	P	P	P			P	P	P	P							P	P						P	P	P	P	P
Sussex, E.	P	P	P	P	P	P	P	P	P				P			E	E	E					P	P						P	P	P		
Teynham, L.				P																														
Tunbridge, V.				P																														
Vaux, L.			P	P																														
Walden (see Howard, L.)																																		
Warwick, E.			P	P	P	P	P	P	P	P	P		P	P	P	E	P	P	P	P	P	P	P	P	P	P	P	P	P	P	E	P	P	P
Wentworth, L.			P	P	P	P	P	P	P	P	P		P	P	*	P	P	P	P	P	P	P	P	P	E	E	P†	P	P	P	P	P	P	P
Westmorland, E.				P	P	P	P	P	P	P	P		P	P	*	P	P								E									
Willoughby, L.			P	P	P	P	P	P	P	P			P	P	E	P	P	P	P	P	P		P	P	P	P	E	P		P	P	P	P	P
Worcester, E.	P		P	P	P	P	P	P	P	P	P		P	P	P†	P	P†	P	P	P	P	P	P	P	P	P	*	P†	P	P	P	P	P	P

8. Lord Stanhope of Harrington is marked in the MS. L.J. as present on 30 June, although the entry in the Minute Book was simply given as "Lo. Stanhope of", without distinguishing which Lord Stanhope was intended.

D. Lists of Members, H. of C.

1. By Family Name

The following list contains the names of 487 men returned to the Lower House in 1625. Included in the list is Sir William Cope, who was returned for Banbury but sat in the House only four days before his election was declared void on 23 June. No second member was elected to serve for that constituency. Seventeen members were doubly returned; their preferred constituencies are italicized in the list. In six cases of double returns and one of a voided election no successor for the vacated place was chosen, leaving Appleby, Banbury, Cambridge University, Coventry, St. Mawes, and Westbury with a single M.P. and Caernarvon (Wales) with none.

Three persons were returned for Bridgnorth, Shropshire; on the return for that constituency the Crown Office list gives two names, Sir George Paule and George Vernon, for one vacancy. We find no evidence that the House determined the legitimacy of either candidate during the course of the session. The *O.R.* lists two returns naming four persons to represent Lostwithiel, Cornwall. On the Crown Office list no names were entered for this constituency. Sir Henry Vane, returned for both Lostwithiel and Carlisle, chose the latter, narrowing to three the field of names for Lostwithiel. The Lymington, Hampshire, return shows the name of John Button. There was a tie of ten votes each between John Mill and John More for the other seat for Lymington, but the contest was apparently not decided by the House.[1]

The total membership at the end of the session stood between 485 and 487 depending on whether the third persons for Lostwithiel, Bridgnorth, and Lymington are counted. The editors, finding no indication

in these cases of which name was eliminated, have included all of them in the list.

The manuscript materials for this parliament give little discussion of electoral proceedings aside from the contested Yorkshire election. However, it seems evident from the number of vacancies that, because of the brevity of the first session and the general apprehension regarding the length of the second, by-elections were not held, and consequently those places vacated when persons doubly elected chose to serve for other constituencies remained unfilled.

The list of members was compiled from the *O.R.*; the Crown Office list; a copy of the Crown Office list in the Hastings MSS. (Huntington Library, MS. HA. L5/B8);[2] a printed list entitled, *The Names of the Knights, Citizens, Burgesses, and Barons, 1625* (*S.T.C.*, no. 7741); the information provided by the manuscript texts of the proceedings; and the election materials printed in Appendix II, below.

For the convenience of the reader who wishes to learn additional details of the lives of many of the M.P.s, references are given to the following biographical works: *D.N.B.* (*Dictionary of National Biography*); *L.P.* (Mary Frear Keeler, *The Long Parliament, 1640–1641*); *A.C.* (John Venn and J. A. Venn, eds., *Alumni Cantabrigienses*); and *A.O.* (Joseph Foster, ed., *Alumni Oxonienses*) (the editors have designated university affiliation only in the cases where the alumni records specifically indicate parliamentary affiliation). Also useful in this regard are G. E. C[ockayne]'s *Complete Baronetage* and W. A. Shaw, *The Knights of England*.

Abbot, Maurice, Esq. (*D.N.B.*)
    Kingston-on-Hull, Yorkshire
Aglionby, Edward, Esq.
    Carlisle, Cumberland
Aldborough (Aldeburgh), Richard, Esq. (*L.P.*; *A.C.*)
    Aldborough, Yorkshire

---

1. See *O.R.*
2. Included in the Ellesmere MSS., El. 6927 (Huntington Library), is a less perfect copy of the Crown

Office list than HA. L5/B8; an uncorrected list, it provides no new information. The incomplete list in S.P. 16/2:70 also provides no additional information.

Alford, Edward, Esq.
  Colchester, Essex
Alford, William, Kt.
  Beverley, Yorkshire
Anderson, Henry, Kt. (*L.P.; A.O.*)
  Newcastle-on-Tyne, Northumberland
Annesley, Francis, Kt. and Bt. (*D.N.B.*)
  Carmarthen, Carmarthenshire, Wales
Armine, William, Bt. (*D.N.B.; L.P.; A.C.*)
  Grantham, Lincolnshire
Ashley, Francis, Kt., Serjeant at Law (*A.O.*)
  Dorchester, Dorset
Ashton, Ralph, Esq. (*L.P.; A.C.*)
  Clitheroe, Lancashire
Ashton, William, Esq.
  Hertford, Hertfordshire

Backhouse (Bakehouse), John, Esq.
  Marlow, Buckinghamshire
Bacon, Edmund, Kt. and Bt. (*A.C.*)
  SUFFOLK
Badger, Thomas, Kt.
  Stockbridge, Hampshire
Bagg, James, Esq.
  East Looe, Cornwall
Banaster, Henry, Esq., of Hackney
  Preston, Lancashire
Bancroft, Thomas, Esq.
  Castle Rising, Norfolk
Barkham, Edward, Kt. and Bt. (*A.C.*)
  Boston, Lincolnshire
Barnardiston, Nathaniel, Kt., of Ketton (*D.N.B.; L.P.*)
  Sudbury, Suffolk
Barrington, Francis, Kt. and Bt. (*A.C.*)
  ESSEX
Barrington, Thomas, Kt. (*L.P.*)
  Newtown (Isle of Wight), Hampshire
Bartlett, Walter, Esq.
  Bramber, Sussex
Basset, Arthur, Esq.
  Fowey, Cornwall
Bateman, Robert, Skinner
  London, Middlesex
Baynton (Bainton), Edward, Kt. (*L.P.; A.O.*)
  Devizes, Wiltshire
Beaumont, Richard, Kt.
  Pontefract, Yorkshire
Beecher, William, Kt. (*A.C.*)
  Dover, Cinque Port
Belasyse, Henry, Esq. (*L.P.; A.C.*)
  Thirsk, Yorkshire
Bellingham, Henry, Kt. and Bt. (*L.P.; A.C.*)
  WESTMORLAND

Bennett, Robert, Kt.
  New Windsor, Berkshire
Berkeley, Charles, Kt. (*A.O.*)
  Heytesbury, Wiltshire
Berkeley, Maurice, Kt.
  GLOUCESTERSHIRE
Bertie, Montague, Kt. (*A.C.*)
  Stamford, Lincolnshire
Bisse, Edward, Esq.
  Heytesbury, Wiltshire
Blonden (Blunden), William, Esq.
  Bishops Castle, Shropshire
Bludder, Thomas, Kt., of Reigate (*L.P.; A.C.*)
  Reigate, Surrey
Bond, Martin, Haberdasher (*D.N.B.; A.O.*)
  London, Middlesex
Borough, John, Kt.
  Horsham, Sussex
Boswell, William, Esq.[3]
  Boston, Lincolnshire
Boteler (Butler), John, Esq. (*A.C.*)
  HERTFORDSHIRE
Boteler (Butler), John, Kt. and Bt.
  HERTFORDSHIRE
Bowes, Talbot, Kt., of Streatlam
  Richmond, Yorkshire
Bowyer, Thomas, Esq. (*L.P.*)
  Bramber, Sussex
Boys, Edward, Jr., Kt. (*L.P.*)
  Christchurch, Hampshire (vice Sir Thomas Wilford)
Brandling, Francis, Kt. (*A.O.*)
  NORTHUMBERLAND
Brereton, Thomas, Esq.
  Taunton, Somerset
Bridgeman, Edward, Gent.
  Wigan, Lancashire
Brooke, Christopher, Esq., of York
  York, Yorkshire
Brooke, John, Kt. (*L.P.*)
  Great Bedwyn, Wiltshire
Brooke, Robert, Kt. (*A.C.*)
  Dunwich, Suffolk
Browne, John, Esq.
  Gloucester, Gloucestershire
Brydges (Bridges), Giles, Esq. (*A.O.*)
  HEREFORDSHIRE
Buller, Francis, Esq. (*L.P.; A.C.*)
  Saltash, Cornwall
Buller, Richard, Kt. (*L.P.*)
  Saltash, Cornwall
Bulstrode, Henry, Esq.
  BUCKINGHAMSHIRE
Bulstrode, William, Kt.
  RUTLAND

3. Possibly the same Wm. Boswell, diplomat, who is included in *D.N.B., A.O.,* and *A.C.*

Burghersh, Mildmay Fane, Lord (*D.N.B.; A.C.*)
KENT
Button, John, Esq. (*L.P.*)
Lymington, Hampshire
Bysshe, Edward, Esq., of Burstowe
Blechingley, Surrey

Caesar, Robert, Esq. (*A.O.*)
Bodmin, Cornwall
Cage, William, Esq., Alderman of Ipswich (*L.P.*)
Ipswich, Suffolk
Canon (Cannon), Thomas, Kt. (*A.O.*)
Haverfordwest, Pembrokeshire, Wales
Caple, Christopher, Esq.
Gloucester, Gloucestershire
Carew, Francis, Esq. (*A.O.*)
Haslemere, Surrey
Carew, Francis, Esq.
Helston, Cornwall
Carey, Henry, Kt. (*A.O.*)
Tregony, Cornwall
Carey, Thomas, Esq.
Helston, Cornwall
Carr, Robert, Kt.
Aylesbury, Buckinghamshire
Carvill, John, Esq. (*A.O.*)
Aldborough, Yorkshire
Cary, Philip, Kt. (*A.O.*)
Woodstock, Oxfordshire
Cavendish, William, Lord (*D.N.B.; A.O.*)
DERBYSHIRE
Cheeke, Thomas, Kt. (*L.P.; A.C.*)
Bere Alston, Devonshire
Cholmley, Hugh, Gent. (*D.N.B.; L.P.; A.C.*)
Scarborough, Yorkshire
Cholmley, William, Esq. (*A.C.*)
Great Bedwyn, Wiltshire
Cholmondeley, Robert, Bt., of Cholmondeley
(*D.N.B.; A.O.*)
CHESHIRE
Chudleigh, George, Kt. and Bt. (*D.N.B.; A.O.*)
Lostwithiel, Cornwall
Clare, Ralph, Esq. (*D.N.B.; A.O.*)
Bewdley, Worcestershire
Clarke, Edward, Esq. (*D.N.B.*)
Hythe, Cinque Port
Yarmouth (Isle of Wight), Hampshire
Clerke, Henry, Esq.
Rochester, Kent
Clifton, Gervase, K.B. and Bt. (*L.P.; A.C.*)
NOTTINGHAMSHIRE
Coke, Edward, Kt., Recorder of Coventry
(*D.N.B.; A.C.*)
NORFOLK
Coventry, Warwick

Coke, Henry, Esq. (*L.P.; A.O.*)
Chipping Wycombe, Buckinghamshire
Coke, John, Alderman
King's Lynn, Norfolk
Coke, John, Kt. (*D.N.B.; A.C.*)
St. Germans, Cornwall
Compton, Henry, K.B. (*A.O.*)
East Grinstead, Sussex
Cope, William, Kt. and Bt. of Hanwell (*A.O.*)
Banbury, Oxfordshire
[Election declared void][4]
Corbet, Andrew, Kt. (*A.O.*)
SHROPSHIRE
Corbet, John, Bt. (*A.C.*)
Great Yarmouth, Norfolk
Cornwallis, Thomas, Esq.
SUFFOLK
Coryton, William, Esq. (*D.N.B.; L.P.*)
Liskeard, Cornwall
Cotteels, Thomas, Esq.
Camelford, Cornwall
Cottington, Francis, Kt. and Bt. (*D.N.B.*)
Bossiney, Cornwall
Cotton, Robert, Kt. and Bt. (*D.N.B.; A.C.*)
Thetford, Norfolk
Cotton, Thomas, Esq. (*D.N.B.; A.C.*)
Marlow, Buckinghamshire
Morpeth, Northumberland
Courtenay, Francis, Esq.
DEVONSHIRE
Coventry, Thomas, Esq.
Droitwich, Worcestershire
Cowper (Cooper), John, Kt. and Bt.
Poole, Dorset
Coxe, William, Esq., of Southwark
Southwark, Surrey
Cradock, Matthew, Esq.
Stafford, Staffordshire
Crane, Robert, Kt., of Chilton (*L.P.*)
Sudbury, Suffolk
Cresheld (Creswell), Richard, Esq., Recorder of
Evesham (*L.P.*)
Evesham, Worcestershire
Crew, Clipsby, Kt. (*A.C.*)
Downton, Wiltshire
Crew, John, Esq. (*D.N.B.; L.P.; A.O.*)
Amersham, Buckinghamshire
Crew (Crewe), Thomas, Kt., Serjeant at Law
(*D.N.B.*)
Gatton, Surrey
Cromwell, Oliver, Kt. (*A.C.*)
HUNTINGDONSHIRE
Crow, Sackville, Esq. (*A.C.*)
Hastings, Cinque Port

4. 23 June, see Draft Journal.

Curwen, Patrick, Esq., of Workington
    (*L.P.; A.C.*)
        CUMBERLAND
Cutts (Cuts), John, Kt. (*A.C.*)
        CAMBRIDGESHIRE

Dalston, George, Kt., of Dalston (*L.P.; A.C.*)
        CUMBERLAND
Danvers, John, Kt. (*D.N.B.; A.O.*)
        Oxford University
Delbridge, John, Merchant (*A.C.*)
        Barnstaple, Devonshire
Denny, William, Esq. (*A.C.*)
        Norwich, Norfolk
Denton, Alexander, Kt. (*L.P.; A.O.*)
        Buckingham, Buckinghamshire
Dering, Edward, Kt. (*D.N.B.; L.P.; A.C.*)
        Hythe, Cinque Port
Devereux, Walter, Kt. and Bt.
        Worcester, Worcestershire
Digges, Dudley, Kt. (*D.N.B.; A.O.*)
        Tewkesbury, Gloucestershire
Digges, Richard, Serjeant at Law (*A.O.*)
        Marlborough, Wiltshire
Dixie, Wolstan, Kt.
        LEICESTERSHIRE
Doddridge, Pentecost, Merchant
        Barnstaple, Devonshire
Downes, Francis, Esq.
        Wigan, Lancashire
Dowse, Edward, Esq. (*L.P.; A.C.; A.O.*)
        Cricklade, Wiltshire
Drake, Francis, Esq.
        Amersham, Buckinghamshire
Drake, John, Esq. (*A.O.*)
        Lyme Regis, Dorset
Drewe, Robert, Esq. (*A.O.*)
        Devizes, Wiltshire
Drury, Anthony, Kt. (*A.C.*)
        NORFOLK
Duck, Nicholas, Esq., Recorder (*D.N.B.; A.O.*)
        Exeter, Devonshire
Dunch, Edmund, Esq. (*L.P.; A.O.*)
        BERKSHIRE
Dutton, John, Esq. (*L.P.; A.O.*)
        GLOUCESTERSHIRE
Dyott, Richard, Esq. (*A.O.*)
        Lichfield, Staffordshire
Dyve, Lewis, Kt., of Sherborne (*D.N.B.; A.O.*)
        Bridport, Dorset

Edmondes, Henry, Esq. (*A.O.*)
        Newton, Lancashire
Edmondes, Thomas, Kt. (*D.N.B.*)
        Oxford University
Eliot, John, Kt. (*D.N.B.; A.O.*)
        Newport, Cornwall

Erdeswicke, Richard, Esq. (*A.C.*)
        STAFFORDSHIRE
Erle (Earle), Walter, Kt. (*L.P.; A.O.*)
        DORSET
Escott, Richard, Esq., of Lincoln's Inn (*A.O.*)
        Launceston (Dunheved), Cornwall
Eversfield, Nicholas, Esq. (*A.C.*)
        Hastings, Cinque Port

Fairfax, Ferdinando, Kt. (*D.N.B.; L.P.*)
        Boroughbridge, Yorkshire
Fairfax, Thomas, Kt., of Denton (*D.N.B.; A.C.*)
        YORKSHIRE
Fairfax, Thomas, Kt., of Gilling (*A.C.*)
        Hedon-in-Holderness, Yorkshire
Fane, Mildmay (*see* Burghersh)
Fanshawe, Thomas, Esq. (*D.N.B.; L.P.*)
        Hertford, Hertfordshire
Fanshawe, Thomas, Kt. (*A.C.*)
        Lancaster, Lancashire
Fanshawe, William, Esq., Auditor for the Duchy
        of Lancaster in Northern Parts
        Clitheroe, Lancashire
Farnefold, Thomas, Kt. (*L.P.*)
        Steyning, Sussex
Fenwick, John, Kt. (*D.N.B.; L.P.*)
        NORTHUMBERLAND
Fiennes, James, Esq. (*L.P.; A.C.*)
        Banbury, Oxfordshire (vice Sir William
        Cope)
Finch, Francis, Esq. (*A.C.; A.O.*)
        Eye, Suffolk
Finch, Heneage, Kt., Recorder (*D.N.B.; A.C.*)
        London, Middlesex
Fisher, John, Esq.
        Canterbury, Kent
Fleetwood, Gerrard, Kt.
        Woodstock, Oxfordshire
Fleetwood, Miles, Kt. (*L.P.*)
        Newton, Lancashire
Fleming, Philip, Esq. (*A.O.*)
        Newport (Isle of Wight), Hampshire
Forest, Anthony, Kt.
        Wallingford, Berkshire
Fotherley, Thomas, Esq.
        Rye, Cinque Port
Francis, Edward, Kt.
        Steyning, Sussex
Franklin (Franklyn), John, Kt. (*L.P.; A.C.*)
        MIDDLESEX
Fraunceis, John, Esq. (*A.O.*)
        Tiverton, Devonshire
Freeman, Ralph, Kt.
        Winchelsea, Cinque Port
Fulforde, Francis, Kt. (*A.O.*)
        DEVONSHIRE
Fullerton, James, Kt.
        St. Mawes, Cornwall

Gawdy, Framlingham, Esq. (*D.N.B.; L.P.*)
  Thetford, Norfolk
Gerard, Gilbert, Bt. (*L.P.*)
  MIDDLESEX
Gifford, Richard, Kt.
  Stockbridge, Hampshire
Giles, Edward, Kt. (*A.O.*)
  Totnes, Devonshire
Glanville, Francis, Kt.
  Tavistock, Devonshire
Glanville, John, Esq., of Tavistock, Recorder of
  Plymouth (*D.N.B.; A.O.*)
  Plymouth, Devonshire
Glemham, Charles, Esq. (*A.O.*)
  Aldeburgh, Suffolk
Glemham, Thomas, Kt. (*D.N.B.; A.O.*)
  Aldeburgh, Suffolk
Glynne, Thomas, Esq., of Glynnllivon (*A.O.*)
  CAERNARVONSHIRE, Wales
Godfrey, Richard, Esq.
  New Romney, Cinque Port
Godolphin, Francis, Kt., of Godolphin,
  Cornwall
  St. Ives, Cornwall
Gollop, George, Alderman (*L.P.*)
  Southampton, Hampshire
Goode, Sebastian, Gent. (*A.O.*)
  Tregony, Cornwall
Goodwin, Francis, Kt.
  BUCKINGHAMSHIRE
Goodwin, Ralph, Esq., of Ludlow Castle,
  Shropshire (*L.P.; A.O.*)
  Ludlow, Shropshire
Gorges, Robert, Kt.
  Ilchester, Somerset
Goring, George, Kt. (*D.N.B.; A.C.; A.O.*)
  Lewes, Sussex
Grantham, Thomas, Kt. (*A.O.*)
  Lincoln, Lincolnshire
Greaves, Robert, Gent.
  Nottingham, Nottinghamshire
Greene, Giles, Gent. (*L.P.*)
  Weymouth and Melcombe Regis, Dorset
  (vice Sir Thomas Middleton)
Grenville, Bevil, Esq. (*D.N.B.; L.P.; A.O.*)
  – Launceston (Dunheved), Cornwall
Gresham, Thomas, Kt., of Lymsfield (*A.O.*)
  Blechingley, Surrey
Gurlyn, Thomas, Alderman
  King's Lynn, Norfolk

Haggatt, Humphrey, Esq. (*A.O.*)
  Chichester, Sussex
Hales, Edward, Kt. and Bt. (*L.P.*)
  Queenborough, Kent
Hampden, John, Esq. (*D.N.B.; L.P.; A.O.*)
  Wendover, Buckinghamshire

Hampden, Richard, Esq.
  Wendover, Buckinghamshire
Harbert, Arnold, Kt.
  Morpeth, Northumberland (vice Thomas
  Cotton, Esq.)
Hare, John, Kt.
  Aylesbury, Buckinghamshire
Harrington, William, Kt.
  Wilton, Wiltshire (vice Sir William Herbert)
Harvey, William, Kt.
  Preston, Lancashire
Harwell, Henry
  Coventry, Warwick
Hastings, Ferdinand, Lord (*A.C.*)
  LEICESTERSHIRE
Hastings, George, Kt. (*A.C.*)
  Leicester, Leicestershire
Hatton, Christopher, Esq. (*L.P.; A.C.; A.O.*)
  Peterborough, Northamptonshire
Hatton, Robert, Kt. (*L.P.*)
  Sandwich, Cinque Port
  Stafford, Staffordshire
Hatton, Thomas, Kt.
  Malmesbury, Wiltshire
Heath, Robert, Kt., Solicitor General (*D.N.B.;*
  A.C.; A.O.)
  East Grinstead, Sussex
Hele, Nicholas, Esq.
  Liskeard, Cornwall
Hele, Warwick, Kt.
  Plympton, Devonshire
Herbert, Edward, Esq. (*D.N.B.; L.P.; A.C.; A.O.*)
  Downton, Wiltshire
Herbert, George, Esq.
  Montgomery, Montgomeryshire, Wales
Herbert, William, Kt.
  MONTGOMERYSHIRE, Wales
  Wilton, Wiltshire
Herris, Arthur, Kt. (*A.C.*)
  ESSEX
  Maldon, Essex
Herris, Christopher, Esq. (*A.C.*)
  Harwich, Essex
Hewett, William, Kt.
  New Windsor, Berkshire
Hicks, Baptist, Kt. and Bt. (*D.N.B.; A.C.*)
  Tewkesbury, Gloucestershire
Hildyard (Hilliard), Christopher, Kt. (*A.C.*)
  Hedon-in-Holderness, Yorkshire
Hinton, Thomas, Kt., of Chilton Park (*A.O.*)
  Ludgershall, Wiltshire
Hippisley, John, Kt., Lieutenant of Dover Castle
  (*L.P.*)
  Dover, Cinque Port
Hirne, Thomas, Kt.
  Norwich, Norfolk

Hitcham, Robert, Kt., Serjeant at Law (*D.N.B.*; *A.O.*)
    Orford, Suffolk
Hoby, Thomas, Posthumus, Kt. (*A.O.*)
    Ripon, Yorkshire
Holles, John (*see* Houghton)
Hopton, Ralph, Esq. (*D.N.B.*; *L.P.*)
    Bath, Somerset (vice Nicholas Hyde)
Hotham, John, Kt. and Bt. (*D.N.B.*; *L.P.*)
    Beverley, Yorkshire
    Appleby, Westmorland
Houghton, John Holles, Lord, Kt. and Bt.
    East Retford, Nottinghamshire
Howard, Charles, Kt.
    Gatton, Surrey
Howard, Edward, Kt.
    Calne, Wiltshire
Howard, Robert, K.B. (*D.N.B.*; *L.P.*)
    Bishops Castle, Shropshire
Howard, William, Kt.
    Cricklade, Wiltshire
Hughes, Thomas, Esq.
    Appleby, Westmorland
Hungate, Henry, Kt. (*A.C.*)
    Camelford, Cornwall
Hungerford, Edward, Esq. (*L.P.*; *A.O.*)
    Bath, Somerset
Hutton, Richard, Esq. (*A.C.*)[5]
    Knaresborough, Yorkshire
Hyde, Nicholas,[6] Esq., Recorder (*A.O.*)
    Bristol, Gloucestershire
    Bath, Somerset
Hyde, Robert, Kt., of Charleton (*A.O.*)
    Wootton Bassett, Wiltshire

Ingram, Arthur, Kt., of York (*D.N.B.*; *L.P.*)
    York, Yorkshire

Jackson, John, Kt. (*A.O.*)
    Pontefract, Yorkshire
Jackson, Robert, Kt. (*A.O.*)
    Berwick-on-Tweed, Northumberland
James, Roger, Kt., of Reigate
    Reigate, Surrey
Jephson, John, Kt.
    Petersfield, Hampshire
Jermin, Henry, Esq.
    Bodmin, Cornwall
Jermyn, Thomas, Esq. (*L.P.*; *A.C.*)
    Leicester, Leicestershire (vice Sir
    Humphrey May)
Jermyn, Thomas, Kt. (*L.P.*; *A.C.*)
    Bury St. Edmunds, Suffolk-
Jervoise, Thomas, Kt. (*L.P.*)
    Whitchurch, Hampshire

Jones, Charles, Esq., Recorder of Beaumaris
    Beaumaris, Anglesey, Wales
Jordan, Ignatius, Esq.
    Exeter, Devonshire

Keelinge, John, Esq. (*A.O.*)
    Newcastle-under-Lyme, Staffordshire
Kendall, Nicholas, Gent., of Lanliverye (*A.O.*)
    Lostwithiel, Cornwall
Killigrew, Robert, Kt. (*D.N.B.*; *A.O.*)
    CORNWALL
Kirton, Edward, Esq. (*L.P.*; *A.O.*)
    Marlborough, Wiltshire
Knightley, Richard, Esq. (*D.N.B.*)
    NORTHAMPTONSHIRE
Knollys, Francis, Jr., Kt. (*L.P.*; *A.O.*)
    Reading, Berkshire
Knollys, Francis, Sr., Kt. (*L.P.*; *A.O.*)
    BERKSHIRE
Knollys, Robert, Kt. (*A.O.*)
    Abingdon, Berkshire

Lake, Arthur, Kt. (*A.O.*)
    Bridgwater, Somerset
Lake, Thomas, Kt. (*D.N.B.*; *A.C.*; *A.O.*)
    Wells, Somerset
Lambert, Thomas, Esq.
    Hindon, Wiltshire
Lane, Thomas, Esq. (*L.P.*)
    Chipping Wycombe, Buckinghamshire
Langston, Anthony, Esq.
    Evesham, Worcestershire
Lawley, Thomas, Esq., of Sponhill
    Much Wenlock, Shropshire
Leech, Edward, Kt.
    Derby, Derbyshire
Leigh, Francis, Jr., Kt. and Bt. (*D.N.B.*; *A.O.*)
    Warwick, Warwickshire
Leigh, Francis, Kt., of Addington (*A.C.*; *A.O.*)
    SURREY
Lestrange, Hamon, Kt. (*A.C.*)
    Castle Rising, Norfolk
Leving, Timothy, Esq. (*A.O.*)
    Derby, Derbyshire
Lewis, James, Esq., of Abertnantbychan (*A.O.*)
    CARDIGANSHIRE, Wales
Lewkenor, Richard, Esq. (*A.O.*)
    Midhurst, Sussex
Ley, Henry, Kt.
    WILTSHIRE
Lisle, Robert, Viscount
    MONMOUTHSHIRE
Lister, John, Esq. (*L.P.*; *A.O.*)
    Kingston-on-Hull, Yorkshire

5. Hutton was knighted on 17 July; see Shaw, *Knights,* II, 189.

6. The *O.R.* prints *Richard* rather than *Nicholas.*

Littleton, Edward, Esq. (*D.N.B.; A.O.*)
   Leominster, Herefordshire
   Caernarvon, Caernarvonshire
Littleton, Thomas, Kt. and Bt. (*A.O.*)
   WORCESTERSHIRE
Long, Gifford, Esq. (*A.O.*)
   Westbury, Wiltshire
Long, Walter, Esq., Common Councilman of
   Salisbury (*L.P.*)
   Salisbury, Wiltshire
   Westbury, Wiltshire
Lowe, George, Sr., Esq. (*L.P.*)
   Calne, Wiltshire
Lowther, John, Esq.
   WESTMORLAND
Lucy, Francis, Esq. (*A.O.*)
   Warwick, Warwickshire
Lucy, Thomas, Kt. (*D.N.B.; L.P.; A.O.*)
   WARWICKSHIRE
Luke, John, Kt.
   St. Albans, Hertfordshire
Luke, Oliver, Kt. (*L.P.; A.C.*)
   BEDFORDSHIRE
Luttrell, Thomas, Gent. (*A.O.*)
   Minehead, Somerset

Mainwaring, Arthur, Kt. (*A.O.*)
   Huntingdon, Huntingdonshire
Mainwaring (Manwaring), Philip, Esq. (*D.N.B.;
   A.C.*)
   Boroughbridge, Yorkshire
Mainwaringe, Edward, Esq. (*A.O.*)
   Newcastle-under-Lyme, Staffordshire
Malet, Thomas, Esq. (*D.N.B.*)
   Newtown (Isle of Wight), Hampshire
Mallory, William, Sr., Esq. (*L.P.; A.C.*)
   Ripon, Yorkshire
Man, William, Esq.
   Westminster, Middlesex
Manners, George, Kt. (*A.C.; A.O.*)
   Grantham, Lincolnshire
Mansell, Robert, Kt., Vice Admiral of England
   (*D.N.B.; A.O.*)
   GLAMORGANSHIRE, Wales
Maplisden, Edward, Gent.
   Maidstone, Kent
Marlott, William, Gent. (*L.P.*)
   Shoreham, Sussex
Marten, Henry, Kt., LL.D. (*D.N.B.; A.O.*)
   St. Germans, Cornwall
Martin, John, Gent.
   Nottingham, Nottinghamshire
Masham, William, Bt. (*L.P.; A.O.*)
   Maldon, Essex (vice Sir Arthur Herris)
Matthew, Roger, Merchant (*L.P.*)
   Dartmouth, Devonshire
May, Humphrey, Kt., Chancellor of Duchy
   of Lancaster (*D.N.B.*; A.O.)

   Lancaster, Lancashire
   Leicester, Leicestershire
Maynard, John, Esq. (*D.N.B.; A.C.*)
   Chippenham, Wiltshire
Meautys, Thomas, Esq.
   Cambridge, Cambridgeshire
Middleton (Myddelton), Hugh, Bt. (*D.N.B.*)
   Denbigh, Denbighshire, Wales
Middleton, John, Esq.
   Horsham, Sussex
Middleton (Myddelton), Thomas, Kt. (*D.N.B.*)
   London, Middlesex
Middleton (Myddelton), Thomas, Jr., Kt.
   (*D.N.B.; L.P.; A.O.*)
   DENBIGHSHIRE, Wales
   Weymouth and Melcombe Regis, Dorset
Mildmay, Henry, Kt. (*D.N.B.; L.P.; A.C.*)
   Maldon, Essex
Mill, John, Bt.
   Southampton, Hampshire
Mill, John, Esq., son of "Baronet Mill"
   Lymington, Hampshire
Mill, William, Esq.
   Arundel, Sussex
Mohun, John, Esq. (*D.N.B.; A.O.*)
   Grampound, Cornwall
Mohun, Reginald, Kt. and Bt. (*A.O.*)
   Lostwithiel, Cornwall
Mollines, Michael, Esq. (*A.O.*)
   Wallingford, Berkshire
Molyneux, Richard, Kt. and Bt. (*D.N.B.; A.O.*)
   LANCASHIRE
Monson, John, Esq. (*D.N.B.*)
   Lincoln, Lincolnshire
Montagu, Charles, Kt.
   Higham Ferrers, Northamptonshire
Montagu, Edward, Esq. (*A.C.; A.O.*)
   HUNTINGDONSHIRE
Moore, Edward, Esq.
   Liverpool, Lancashire
More (Moore), George, Kt., of Loseley (*D.N.B.;
   A.O.*)
   SURREY
More, John, Esq. (*A.O.*)
   Lymington, Hampshire
More (Moore), Poynings, Esq. (*L.P.*)
   Haslemere, Surrey
More (Moore), Robert, Kt., of Loseley (*A.O.*)
   Guildford, Surrey
Morgan, Thomas, Kt.
   Wilton, Wiltshire
Morgan, William, Kt. (*A.O.*)
   MONMOUTHSHIRE
Morrison, Charles, K.B. and Bt.
   St. Albans, Hertfordshire
Morton, Albertus, Kt. (*D.N.B.; A.C.*)
   KENT
   Cambridge University

Mychell (Michell), Barnard, Esq.
  Weymouth and Melcombe Regis, Dorset

Napier, Nathaniel, Kt. (A.O.)
  DORSET
Naunton, Robert, Kt. (D.N.B.; A.C.)
  Cambridge University
Nethersole, Francis, Kt. (D.N.B.; A.C.)
  Corfe Castle, Dorset
Newport, Richard, Kt. (D.N.B.; A.O.)
  SHROPSHIRE
North, Roger, Kt. (L.P.)
  Eye, Suffolk
Norton, Daniel, Kt.
  Portsmouth, Hampshire

Offley, John, Kt. (A.O.)
  Stafford, Staffordshire (vice Sir Robert
  Hatton)
Oglander, John, Kt. (D.N.B.; A.O.)
  Yarmouth (Isle of Wight), Hampshire
Oldisworth, Michael, Esq., of London (D.N.B.;
  L.P.; A.O.)
  Old Sarum, Wiltshire
Oliver, Richard, Esq.
  Buckingham, Buckinghamshire
Osborne, Peter, Kt. (D.N.B.; A.C.)
  Corfe Castle, Dorset
Owen, Thomas, Esq.
  Shrewsbury, Shropshire
Owen, William, Kt.
  Shrewsbury, Shropshire
Owfield (Oldfield), Samuel, Esq. (L.P.; A.C.)
  Midhurst, Sussex (vice Sir Walter
  Tichborne)
Owner, Edward, Alderman (L.P.)
  Great Yarmouth, Norfolk
Oxenbridge, Robert, Kt.
  Whitchurch, Hampshire

Palmer, Roger, Esq. (L.P.)
  Queenborough, Kent.
Palmes, Guy, Kt. (L.P.)
  RUTLAND
Paramore, Thomas, Esq.
  Lyme Regis, Dorset
Parkhurst, Robert, Jr., Gent. (L.P.; A.O.)
  Guildford, Surrey
Parkhurst, William, Kt., of London
  St. Ives, Cornwall
Paule, George, Kt. (D.N.B.)
  Bridgnorth, Shropshire
Pelham, Henry, Esq., of Gray's Inn (L.P.; A.C.)
  Great Grimsby, Lincolnshire
Pelham, Thomas, Bt., of Laughton (L.P.; A.C.)
  SUSSEX

Pepys, Talbot, Esq. (A.C.)
  Cambridge, Cambridgeshire
Percy, Algernon, Lord (D.N.B.; A.C.; A.O.)
  Chichester, Sussex
Peyton, Edward, Kt. and Bt. (D.N.B.; A.C.)
  CAMBRIDGESHIRE
Phelips, Robert, Kt. (D.N.B.)
  SOMERSET
Phelips (Phillippes), Thomas, Kt. and Bt.
  Winchester, Hampshire
Pitt, William, Kt., of Westminster
  Wareham, Dorset
Poole, Henry, Esq. (A.O.)
  Cirencester, Gloucestershire
Popham, Edward, Esq., of Huntworthy
  Bridgwater, Somerset
Popham, Francis, Kt. (D.N.B.; L.P.; A.O.)
  Chippenham, Wiltshire
Portman, Hugh, Bt. (A.O.)
  Taunton, Somerset
Powell, Lewis, Esq., of Lantfey (A.O.)
  Pembroke, Pembrokeshire, Wales
  [Cardigan, Cardiganshire, Wales][7]
Price, Charles, Esq. (L.P.)
  Radnor, Radnorshire, Wales
Price, James, Esq., of Pillith (A.O.)
  RADNORSHIRE, Wales
Price, William, Esq.
  Cardiff, Glamorganshire, Wales
Prideaux, Jonathan, Esq.
  Bossiney, Cornwall
Puckering, Thomas, Kt. and Bt. (D.N.B.)
  Tamworth, Staffordshire
Pugh, Rowland, Esq.
  Cardigan, Cardiganshire, Wales
Pye, Robert, Kt. (L.P.)
  Ludgershall, Wiltshire
Pye, Walter, Kt. (D.N.B.)
  Brecon, Breconshire, Wales
Pym, John, Esq. (D.N.B.; L.P.; A.O.)
  Tavistock, Devonshire
Pyne, Arthur, Esq.
  Weymouth and Melcombe Regis, Dorset
Pyne, John, Esq. (L.P.)
  Poole, Dorset

Rashleigh, Jonathan, Esq. (L.P.; A.O.)
  Fowey, Cornwall
Ratcliffe, John, Kt.
  LANCASHIRE
Ravenscroft, William, Esq. (A.O.)
  Flint, Flintshire, Wales
Reynell (Raynall), Thomas, Esq. (A.O.)
  Morpeth, Northumberland

7. The printed list of knights, etc., returned to this session (S.T.C., no. 7741) and HA. L5/B8 both indicate that Lewis Powell was doubly returned, although the O.R. does not.

Rich, Nathaniel, Kt. (*D.N.B.; A.C.*)
  Newport (Isle of Wight), Hampshire
Riddell, Thomas, Kt. (*D.N.B.; A.C.*)
  Newcastle-on-Tyne, Northumberland
Rivers, George, Kt.
  Lewes, Sussex
Roberts, Edward, Esq.
  Penryn, Cornwall
Rodney, Edward, Kt. (*L.P.*)
  Wells, Somerset
Rolle, Henry, Esq. (*D.N.B.; A.O.*)
  Truro, Cornwall
Rolle, Samuel, Kt. (*L.P.; A.O.*)
  Grampound, Cornwall
Rous, William, Esq. (*A.O.*)
  Truro, Cornwall
Rowse, John, Kt.
  Dunwich, Suffolk
Rudhale, John, Esq. (*A.O.*)
  HEREFORDSHIRE
Rudyard, Benjamin, Kt. (*D.N.B.;
  L.P.; A.C.; A.O.*)
  Portsmouth, Hampshire
Russell, William, Esq. (*A.O.*)
  WORCESTERSHIRE

Sackville, John, Esq. (*A.O.*)
  Rye, Cinque Port
St. Amand, John, Esq.
  Stamford, Lincolnshire
St. John, Alexander, Kt. (*A.C.*)
  Bedford, Bedfordshire
St. John, Anthony, Kt. (*A.C.*)
  CHESHIRE
St. John, Henry, Kt.
  Huntingdon, Huntingdonshire
St. John, Oliver, Lord of Bletsoe (*D.N.B.; A.C.*)
  BEDFORDSHIRE
St. John, Rowland, Kt. (*A.C.*)
  Tiverton, Devonshire
Sanderson, Nicholas, Kt. and Bt. (*A.O.*)
  LINCOLNSHIRE
Sandys, Edwin, Kt. (*D.N.B.; A.O.*)
  Penryn, Cornwall
Sandys, Henry, Esq.
  Mitchell, Cornwall
Sandys, Miles, Kt., of Brymsfield (*A.O.*)
  Cirencester, Gloucester
Saunders, John, Esq. (*A.O.*)
  Reading, Berkshire
Savage, John, Esq.
  Chester, Cheshire
Sawyer, Edmund, Kt.
  Harwich, Essex
Scudamore, John, Bt. (*D.N.B.; A.O.*)
  Hereford, Herefordshire
Selby, John, Kt.
  Berwick-on-Tweed, Northumberland

Seymour, Edward, Kt. and Bt., of Berrye Castle
  Totnes, Devonshire
Seymour, Francis, Kt. (*D.N.B.; L.P.*)
  WILTSHIRE
Sherfield, Henry, Esq., Recorder of Salisbury
  (*D.N.B.*)
  Salisbury, Wiltshire
Sherland, Christopher, Esq., Recorder of
  Northampton
  Northampton, Northamptonshire
Sherley, John, Kt., of Ifield
  SUSSEX
Sherwill, Thomas, Merchant, of Plymouth
  Plymouth, Devonshire
Shuter, John, Esq.
  Andover, Hampshire
Skeffington, Richard, Kt. (*A.C.*)
  Tamworth, Staffordshire
Slingsby, Henry, Esq. (*D.N.B.; L.P.; A.C.*)
  Knaresborough, Yorkshire
Smyth, John, Kt.
  Mitchell, Cornwall
Snelling, Robert, Esq., Alderman of Ipswich
  Ipswich, Suffolk
Speccott, Paul, Esq. (*A.O.*)
  Newport, Cornwall
Spencer, Edward, Esq. (*A.O.*)
  Brackley, Northamptonshire
Spencer, Richard, Esq. (*A.O.*)
  Northampton, Northamptonshire
Spencer, William, Kt. (*A.O.*)
  NORTHAMPTONSHIRE
Spiller, Henry, Kt.
  Arundel, Sussex
Spilman, Henry, Kt. (*A.C.*)
  Worcester, Worcestershire
Spring, William, Kt. (*A.C.*)
  Bury St. Edmunds, Suffolk
Stanhope, Henry, Esq. (*A.O.*)
  NOTTINGHAMSHIRE
Stanhope, John, Kt.
  DERBYSHIRE
Stanley, Henry, Esq.
  Thirsk, Yorkshire
Stanley, James [Lord Strange] (*D.N.B.*)
  Liverpool, Lancashire
Stanley, Thomas, Gent.
  Maidstone, Kent
Stapley, Anthony, Esq. (*D.N.B.; L.P.; A.C.*)
  Shoreham, Sussex
Stawell (Stowell), John, Esq. (*D.N.B.; L.P.; A.O.*)
  SOMERSET
Steward, Walter, Esq. (*A.C.*)
  Monmouth, Monmouthshire
Stradling, John, Kt. and Bt. (*D.N.B.; A.O.*)
  Old Sarum, Wiltshire
Strange, Lord (*see* Stanley, James)
Strangways, John, Kt. (*L.P.; A.O.*)
  Weymouth and Melcombe Regis, Dorset

Strode, John, Kt., Recorder of Bridport
    Bridport, Dorset
Strode, William, Gent. (*D.N.B.; L.P.; A.O.*)
    Bere Alston, Devonshire
Strode, William, Kt.
    Plympton, Devonshire
Suckling, John, Kt., Comptroller of the
  Household
    Yarmouth (Isle of Wight), Hampshire (vice
    Edward Clarke)

Taylor, Richard, Esq.
    Bedford, Bedfordshire
Thomas, Edward, Esq. (*L.P.*)
    West Looe, Cornwall
Thompson, William, Gent.
    Scarborough, Yorkshire
Thoroughgood, John, Esq.
    Shaftesbury, Dorset
Throckmorton, Clement, Kt. (*A.C.; A.O.*)
    WARWICKSHIRE
Thynne, Thomas, Kt.
    Hindon, Yorkshire
Tichborne, Richard, Kt.
    Winchester, Hampshire
Tichborne, Walter, Kt., of Aldercote
    Wootton Bassett, Wiltshire
    Midhurst, Sussex
Tomkins, James, Esq. (*A.O.*)
    Leominster, Herefordshire
Tomkins, Nathaniel, Esq., of Westminster
    Christchurch, Hampshire
    St. Mawes, Cornwall
Tomlins (Tomlyns), Richard, Esq., of West-
  minster (*A.O.*)
    Ludlow, Shropshire
Towse, William, Serjeant at Law
    Colchester, Essex
Trenchard, John, Esq., of Warmewell (*L.P.;*
  A.O.)
    Wareham, Dorset
Trevanion, Charles, Esq. (*A.O.*)
    CORNWALL
Trevor, John, Jr., Kt. (*D.N.B.; L.P.; A.C.*)
    FLINTSHIRE, Wales
Trevor, John, Kt.
    East Looe, Cornwall
Trevor, Sackvile, Kt.
    ANGLESEY, Wales
Twysden, Roger, Kt. (*A.C.*)
    Winchelsea, Cinque Port

Upton, John, Esq. (*L.P.; A.O.*)
    Dartmouth, Devonshire
Uvedale, William, Kt. (*L.P.; A.O.*)
    Petersfield, Hampshire

Vane, Henry, Kt. (*D.N.B.; A.C.; A.O.*)
    Carlisle, Cumberland
    Lostwithiel, Cornwall

Vaughan, Charles, Kt.
    BRECONSHIRE, Wales
Vaughan, Richard (*D.N.B.*)
    CARMARTHENSHIRE, Wales
Verney, Edmund, Kt. (*D.N.B.; L.P.; A.O.*)
    New Romney, Cinque Port
Vernon, George, Esq.
    Bridgnorth, Shropshire
Villiers, Edward, Kt. (*D.N.B.; A.C.*)
    Westminster, Middlesex

Wallop, Henry, Kt. (*L.P.; A.O.*)
    Andover, Hampshire
Wallop, Robert, Esq. (*D.N.B.; L.P.; A.O.*)
    HAMPSHIRE
Walsingham, Thomas, Jr., Kt. (*L.P.; A.C.*)
    Rochester, Kent
Wandesford, Christopher, Esq., of Kirtlington
  (*D.N.B.; A.C.*)
    Richmond, Yorkshire
Wardour, Edward, Kt. (*A.O.*)
    Malmesbury, Wiltshire
Weaver, Richard, Gent. (*L.P.*)
    Hereford, Herefordshire
Wenman, Richard, Kt.
    OXFORDSHIRE
Wenman, Thomas, Kt. (*D.N.B.; L.P.; A.O.*)
    Brackley, Northamptonshire
Wentworth, Thomas, Esq. (*A.O.*)
    Oxford, Oxfordshire
Wentworth, Thomas, Kt. and Bt., of Wentworth
  Woodhouse (*D.N.B.; A.C.*)
    YORKSHIRE
Weston, Richard, Kt. (*D.N.B.; A.C.*)
    Callington, Cornwall
Weston, Simon, Kt.
    STAFFORDSHIRE
Whistler, John, Esq. (*L.P.; A.O.*)
    Oxford, Oxfordshire
Whitaker, Lawrence, Esq. (*L.P.; A.C.; A.O.*)
    Peterborough, Northampton
Whitaker, William, Esq. (*L.P.*)
    Shaftesbury, Dorset
Whitby, Edward, Esq., Recorder of Chester
  (*A.O.*)
    Chester, Cheshire
Whitehead, Henry, Kt. (*A.O.*)
    HAMPSHIRE
Whiteway, William, Sr., Merchant
    Dorchester, Dorset
Whitmore, William, Kt.
    Bridgnorth, Shropshire
Whitson, John, Alderman (*D.N.B.*)
    Bristol, Gloucestershire
Wilde, John, Esq. (*D.N.B.; L.P.; A.C.; A.O.*)
    Droitwich, Worcestershire
Wilford, Thomas, Kt., of Ildinge
    Canterbury, Kent
    Christchurch, Hampshire

Windham (Wyndham), Edmund, Gent. (*L.P.; A.O.*)
    Minehead, Somerset
Wingfield, William, Esq.
    Lichfield, Staffordshire
Wise (Wyse), Thomas, Esq. (*L.P.; A.C.*)
    Callington, Cornwall
Withipole, William, Kt.
    Orford, Suffolk
Wogan, John, Esq., of Wiston (*L.P.; A.O.*)
    PEMBROKESHIRE, Wales
Wolrich, Thomas, Esq., of Dudmaston (*D.N.B.; A.C.*)
    Much Wenlock, Shropshire
Wolstenholme, John, Esq. (*A.C.*)
    West Looe, Cornwall
Wortley, Francis, Kt. and Bt. (*D.N.B.; A.C.*)
    East Retford, Nottinghamshire

Wotton, Henry, Kt. (*D.N.B.; A.O.*)
    Sandwich, Cinque Port
Wray, Christopher, Kt., of Ashbie (*D.N.B.; L.P.*)
    Great Grimsby, Lincolnshire
Wray, John, Kt. and Bt. (*D.N.B.; L.P.; A.C.*)
    LINCOLNSHIRE
Wraye, Edward, Esq.
    OXFORDSHIRE
Wynn, Henry, Esq.
    MERIONETHSHIRE, Wales
Wynn, Richard, Kt. (*L.P.*)
    Ilchester, Somerset

Yarwood, Richard, Esq., of Southwark
    Southwark, Surrey

2. By Constituency

The names within each constituency are listed in alphabetical order and do not indicate which of two members held the first place. Names in brackets represent those whose returns were voided and those who, having been doubly returned, chose another seat.

Abingdon, Berkshire
    Robert Knollys, Kt.
Aldborough, Yorkshire
    Richard Aldborough, Esq.
    John Carvill, Esq.
Aldeburgh, Suffolk
    Charles Glemham, Esq.
    Thomas Glemham, Kt.
Amersham, Buckinghamshire
    John Crew, Esq.
    Francis Drake, Esq.
Andover, Hampshire
    John Shuter, Esq.
    Henry Wallop, Kt.
ANGLESEY, Wales
    Sackvile Trevor, Kt.
Appleby, Westmorland
    Thomas Hughes, Esq.
    [John Hotham, Kt. and Bt.]
Arundel, Sussex,
    William Mills, Esq.
    Henry Spiller, Kt.
Aylesbury, Buckinghamshire
    Robert Carr, Kt.
    John Hare, Kt.
Banbury, Oxfordshire
    James Fiennes, Esq.
    [William Cope, Kt. and Bt.]
Barnstaple, Devonshire
    John Delbridge
    Pentecost Doddridge
Bath, Somerset
    Ralph Hopton, Esq.
    Edward Hungerford, Esq.
    [Nicholas Hyde, Esq.]
Beaumaris, Anglesey, Wales
    Charles Jones, Esq.
Bedford, Bedfordshire
    Alexander St. John, Kt.
    Richard Taylor, Esq.
BEDFORDSHIRE
    Oliver Luke, Kt.
    Oliver St. John, Lord of Bletsoe

Bere Alston, Devonshire
    Thomas Cheeke, Kt.
    William Strode, Gent.
BERKSHIRE
    Edmund Dunch, Esq.
    Francis Knollys, Sr., Kt.
Berwick-on-Tweed, Northumberland
    Robert Jackson, Kt.
    John Selby, Kt.
Beverley, Yorkshire
    William Alford, Kt.
    John Hotham, Kt. and Bt.
Bewdley, Worcestershire
    Ralph Clare, Esq.
Bishops Castle, Shropshire
    William Blonden, Esq.
    Robert Howard, K.B.
Blechingley, Surrey
    Edward Bysshe, Esq.
    Thomas Gresham, Kt.
Bodmin, Cornwall
    Robert Caesar, Esq.
    Henry Jermin, Esq.
Boroughbridge, Yorkshire
    Ferdinando Fairfax, Kt.
    Philip Mainwaring, Esq.
Bossiney, Cornwall
    Francis Cottington, Kt. and Bt.
    Jonathan Prideaux, Esq.
Boston, Lincolnshire
    Edward Barkham, Kt. and Bt.
    William Boswell, Esq.
Brackley, Northamptonshire
    Edward Spencer, Esq.
    Thomas Wenman, Kt.
Bramber, Sussex
    Walter Bartlett, Esq.
    Thomas Bowyer, Esq.
Brecon, Breconshire, Wales
    Walter Pye, Kt.
BRECONSHIRE, Wales
    Charles Vaughan, Kt.
Bridgnorth, Shropshire
    George Paule, Kt.
    George Vernon, Esq.[1]
    William Whitmore, Kt.
Bridgwater, Somerset
    Arthur Lake, Kt.
    Edward Popham, Esq.
Bridport, Dorset
    Lewis Dyve, Kt.
    John Strode, Kt.
Bristol, Gloucestershire
    Nicholas Hyde, Esq.
    John Whitson

1. The Crown Office list gives Sir George Paule and George Vernon returned for one vacancy.

Buckingham, Buckinghamshire
  Alexander Denton, Kt.
  Richard Oliver, Esq.
BUCKINGHAMSHIRE
  Henry Bulstrode, Esq.
  Francis Goodwin, Kt.
Bury St. Edmunds, Suffolk
  Thomas Jermyn, Kt.
  William Spring, Kt.
Caernarvon, Caernarvonshire, Wales
  [Edward Littleton, Esq.][2]
CAERNARVONSHIRE, Wales
  Thomas Glynne, Esq.
Callington, Cornwall
  Richard Weston, Kt.
  Thomas Wise, Esq.
Calne, Wiltshire
  Edward Howard, Kt.
  George Lowe, Sr., Esq.
Cambridge, Cambridgeshire
  Thomas Meautys, Esq.
  Talbot Pepys, Esq.
Cambridge University
  Robert Naunton, Kt.
  [Albertus Morton, Kt.]
CAMBRIDGESHIRE
  John Cutts, Kt.
  Edward Peyton, Kt. and Bt.
Camelford, Cornwall
  Thomas Cotteels, Esq.
  Henry Hungate, Kt.
Canterbury, Kent
  John Fisher, Esq.
  Thomas Wilford, Kt.
Cardiff, Glamorganshire, Wales
  William Price, Esq.
Cardigan, Cardiganshire, Wales
  Rowland Pugh, Esq.
  [Lewis Powell, Esq.]
CARDIGANSHIRE, Wales
  James Lewis, Esq.
Carlisle, Cumberland
  Edward Aglionby, Esq.
  Henry Vane, Kt.
Carmarthen, Carmarthenshire, Wales
  Francis Annesley, Kt. and Bt.
CARMARTHENSHIRE, Wales
  Richard Vaughan, Esq.
Castle Rising, Norfolk
  Thomas Bancroft, Esq.
  Hamon Lestrange, Kt.
CHESHIRE
  Robert Cholmondeley, Bt.
  Anthony St. John, Kt.

Chester, Cheshire
  John Savage, Esq.
  Edward Whitby, Esq.
Chichester, Sussex
  Humphrey Haggatt, Esq.
  Algernon, Lord Percy
Chippenham, Wiltshire
  John Maynard, Esq.
  Francis Popham, Kt.
Chipping Wycombe, Buckinghamshire
  Henry Coke, Esq.
  Thomas Lane, Esq.
Christchurch, Hampshire
  Edward Boys, Jr., Kt.
  Nathaniel Tomkins, Esq.
  [Thomas Wilford, Kt.]
Cirencester, Gloucestershire
  Henry Poole, Esq.
  Miles Sandys, Kt.
Clitheroe, Lancashire
  Ralph Ashton, Esq.
  William Fanshawe, Esq.
Colchester, Essex
  Edward Alford, Esq.
  William Towse
Corfe Castle, Dorset
  Francis Nethersole, Kt.
  Peter Osborne, Kt.
CORNWALL
  Robert Killigrew, Kt.
  Charles Trevanion, Esq.
Coventry, Warwickshire
  Henry Harwell
  [Edward Coke, Kt.]
Cricklade, Wiltshire
  Edward Dowse, Esq.
  William Howard, Kt.
CUMBERLAND
  Patrick Curwen, Esq.
  George Dalston, Kt.
Dartmouth, Devonshire
  Roger Matthew
  John Upton, Esq.
Denbigh, Denbighshire, Wales
  Hugh Middleton (Myddelton), Bt.
DENBIGHSHIRE, Wales
  Thomas Middleton (Myddelton), Jr., Kt.
Derby, Derbyshire
  Edward Leech, Kt.
  Timothy Leving, Esq.
DERBYSHIRE
  William, Lord Cavendish
  John Stanhope, Kt.

2. Littleton elected to serve for Leominster, Hereford. No other name was substituted.

Devizes, Wiltshire
    Edward Baynton, Kt.
    Robert Drewe, Esq.
DEVONSHIRE
    Francis Courtenay, Esq.
    Francis Fulforde, Kt.
Dorchester, Dorset
    Francis Ashley, Kt.
    William Whiteway, Sr.
DORSET
    Walter Erle, Kt.
    Nathaniel Napier, Kt.
Dover, Cinque Port
    William Beecher, Kt.
    John Hippisley, Kt.
Downton, Wiltshire
    Clipsby Crew, Kt.
    Edward Herbert, Esq.
Droitwich, Worcestershire
    Thomas Coventry, Esq.
    John Wilde, Esq.
Dunwich, Suffolk
    Robert Brooke, Kt.
    John Rowse, Kt.
East Grinstead, Sussex
    Henry Compton, K.B.
    Robert Heath, Kt.
East Looe, Cornwall
    James Bagg, Esq.
    John Trevor, Kt.
East Retford, Nottinghamshire
    John, Lord Houghton, Kt. and Bt.
    Francis Wortley, Kt. and Bt.
ESSEX
    Francis Barrington, Kt. and Bt.
    Arthur Herris, Kt.
Evesham, Worcestershire
    Richard Cresheld, Esq.
    Anthony Langston, Esq.
Exeter, Devonshire
    Nicholas Duck, Esq.
    Ignatius Jordan, Esq.
Eye, Suffolk
    Francis Finch, Esq.
    Roger North, Kt.
Flint, Flintshire, Wales
    William Ravenscroft, Esq.
FLINTSHIRE, Wales
    John Trevor, Jr., Kt.
Fowey, Cornwall
    Arthur Basset, Esq.
    Jonathan Rashleigh, Esq.
Gatton, Surrey
    Thomas Crew, Kt.
    Charles Howard, Kt.
GLAMORGANSHIRE, Wales
    Robert Mansell, Kt.

Gloucester, Gloucestershire
    John Browne, Esq.
    Christopher Caple, Esq.
GLOUCESTERSHIRE
    Maurice Berkeley, Kt.
    John Dutton, Esq.
Grampound, Cornwall
    John Mohun, Esq.
    Samuel Rolle, Kt.
Grantham, Lincolnshire
    William Armine, Bt.
    George Manners, Kt.
Great Bedwyn, Wiltshire
    John Brooke, Kt.
    William Cholmley, Esq.
Great Grimsby, Lincolnshire
    Henry Pelham, Esq.
    Christopher Wray, Kt.
Great Yarmouth, Norfolk
    John Corbet, Bt.
    Edward Owner
Guildford, Surrey
    Robert More, Kt.
    Robert Parkhurst, Jr., Gent.
HAMPSHIRE
    Robert Wallop, Esq.
    Henry Whitehead, Kt.
Harwich, Essex
    Christopher Herris, Esq.
    Edmund Sawyer, Kt.
Haselemere, Surrey
    Francis Carew, Esq.
    Poynings More, Esq.
Hastings, Cinque Port
    Sackville Crow, Esq.
    Nicholas Eversfield, Esq.
Haverfordwest, Pembrokeshire, Wales
    Thomas Canon, Kt.
Hedon-in-Holderness, Yorkshire
    Thomas Fairfax, Kt.
    Christopher Hildyard, Kt.
Helston, Cornwall
    Thomas Carey, Esq.
    Francis Carew, Esq.
Hereford, Herefordshire
    John Scudamore, Bt.
    Richard Weaver, Gent.
HEREFORDSHIRE
    Giles Brydges, Esq.
    John Rudhale, Esq.
Hertford, Hertfordshire
    William Ashton, Esq.
    Thomas Fanshawe, Esq.
HERTFORDSHIRE
    John Boteler, Esq.
    John Boteler, Kt. and Bt.

Heytesbury, Wiltshire
    Charles Berkeley, Kt.
    Edward Bisse, Esq.
Higham Ferrers, Northamptonshire
    Charles Montagu, Kt.
Hindon, Wiltshire
    Thomas Lambert, Esq.
    Thomas Thynne, Kt.
Horsham, Sussex
    John Borough, Kt.
    John Middleton, Esq.
Huntingdon, Huntingdonshire
    Arthur Mainwaring, Kt.
    Henry St. John, Kt.
HUNTINGDONSHIRE
    Oliver Cromwell, Kt.
    Edward Montagu, Esq.
Hythe, Cinque Port
    Edward Clarke, Esq.
    Edward Dering, Kt.
Ilchester, Somerset
    Robert Gorges, Kt.
    Richard Wynn, Kt.
Ipswich, Suffolk
    William Cage, Esq.
    Robert Snelling, Esq.
KENT
    Mildmay, Lord Burghersh
    Albertus Morton, Kt.
King's Lynn, Norfolk
    John Coke
    Thomas Gurlyn
Kingston-on-Hull, Yorkshire
    Maurice Abbot, Esq.
    John Lister, Esq.
Knaresborough, Yorkshire
    Richard Hutton, Esq.
    Henry Slingsby, Esq.
LANCASHIRE
    Richard Molyneux, Kt. and Bt.
    John Ratcliffe, Kt.
Lancaster, Lancashire
    Thomas Fanshawe, Kt.
    Humphrey May, Kt.
Launceston (Dunheved), Cornwall
    Richard Escott, Esq.
    Bevil Grenville, Esq.
Leicester, Leicestershire
    George Hastings, Kt.
    Thomas Jermyn, Esq.
    [Humphrey May, Kt.]

LEICESTERSHIRE
    Wolstan Dixie, Kt.
    Ferdinand, Lord Hastings
Leominster, Herefordshire
    Edward Littleton, Esq.
    James Tomkins, Esq.
Lewes, Sussex
    George Goring, Kt.
    George Rivers, Kt.
Lichfield, Staffordshire
    Richard Dyott, Esq.
    William Wingfield, Esq.
Lincoln, Lincolnshire
    Thomas Grantham, Kt.
    John Monson, Esq.
LINCOLNSHIRE
    Nicholas Sanderson, Kt. and Bt.
    John Wray, Kt. and Bt.
Liskeard, Cornwall
    William Coryton, Esq.
    Nicholas Hele, Esq.
Liverpool, Lancashire
    Edward Moore, Esq.
    James Stanley [Lord Strange]
London, Middlesex
    Robert Bateman
    Martin Bond
    Heneage Finch, Kt.
    Thomas Middleton (Myddelton), Kt.
Lostwithiel, Cornwall[3]
    George Chudleigh, Kt. and Bt.
    Nicholas Kendall, Gent.
    Reginald Mohun, Kt. and Bt.
    [Henry Vane, Kt.]
Ludgershall, Wiltshire
    Thomas Hinton, Kt.
    Robert Pye, Kt.
Ludlow, Shropshire
    Ralph Goodwin, Esq.
    Richard Tomlins, Esq.
Lyme Regis, Dorset
    John Drake, Esq.
    Thomas Paramore, Esq.
Lymington, Hampshire[4]
    John Button, Esq.
    John Mill, Esq.
    John More, Esq.
Maidstone, Kent
    Edward Maplisden, Gent.
    Thomas Stanley, Gent.
Maldon, Essex
    William Masham, Bt.

3. No names for Lostwithiel have been entered on the Crown Office list, the Hastings list (HA. L5/B8), or the incomplete S.P. 16/2:70 list.

4. John Button is the only name included on the Crown Office list and HA. L5/B8. We find no evidence that the contest between John Mill and John More was resolved by the Commons. A "Mr. Mill" was granted liberty to come into the House on 4 August.

Henry Mildmay, Kt.
[Arthur Herris, Kt.]
Malmesbury, Wiltshire
Thomas Hatton, Kt.[5]
Edward Wardour, Kt.
Marlborough, Wiltshire
Richard Digges
Edward Kirton, Esq.
Marlow, Buckinghamshire
John Backhouse, Esq.
Thomas Cotton, Esq.
MERIONETHSHIRE, Wales
Henry Wynn, Esq.
MIDDLESEX
John Franklin, Kt.
Gilbert Gerard, Bt.
Midhurst, Sussex
Richard Lewkenor, Esq.
Samuel Owfield, Esq.
[Walter Tichborne, Kt.]
Minehead, Somerset
Thomas Luttrell, Gent.
Edmund Windham, Gent.
Mitchell, Cornwall
Henry Sandys, Esq.
John Smyth, Kt.
Monmouth, Monmouthshire
Walter Steward, Esq.
MONMOUTHSHIRE
Robert, Viscount Lisle
William Morgan, Kt.
Montgomery, Montgomeryshire, Wales
George Herbert, Esq.
MONTGOMERYSHIRE, Wales
William Herbert, Kt.
Morpeth, Northumberland
Arnold Harbert, Kt.
Thomas Reynell, Esq.
[Thomas Cotton, Esq.]
Much Wenlock, Shropshire
Thomas Lawley, Esq.
Thomas Wolrich, Esq.
New Romney, Cinque Port
Richard Godfrey, Esq.
Edmund Verney, Kt.
New Windsor, Berkshire
Robert Bennett, Kt.
William Hewett, Kt.
Newcastle-on-Tyne, Northumberland
Henry Anderson, Kt.
Thomas Riddell, Kt.
Newcastle-under-Lyme, Staffordshire
John Keelinge, Esq.
Edward Mainwaringe, Esq.

Newport, Cornwall
John Eliot, Kt.
Paul Speccott, Esq.
Newport (Isle of Wight), Hampshire
Philip Fleming, Esq.
Nathaniel Rich, Kt.
Newton, Lancashire
Henry Edmondes, Esq.
Miles Fleetwood, Kt.
Newtown (Isle of Wight), Hampshire
Thomas Barrington, Kt.
Thomas Malet, Esq.
NORFOLK
Edward Coke, Kt.
Anthony Drury, Kt.
Northampton, Northamptonshire
Christopher Sherland, Esq.
Richard Spencer, Esq.
NORTHAMPTONSHIRE
Richard Knightley, Esq.
William Spencer, Kt.
NORTHUMBERLAND
Francis Brandling, Kt.
John Fenwick, Kt.
Norwich, Norfolk
William Denny, Esq.
Thomas Hirne, Kt.
Nottingham, Nottinghamshire
Robert Greaves, Gent.
John Martin, Gent.
NOTTINGHAMSHIRE
Gervase Clifton, K.B. and Bt.
Henry Stanhope, Esq.
Old Sarum, Wiltshire
Michael Oldisworth, Esq.
John Stradling, Kt.
Orford, Suffolk
Robert Hitcham, Kt.
William Withipole, Kt.
Oxford, Oxfordshire
Thomas Wentworth, Esq.
John Whistler, Esq.
Oxford University
John Danvers, Kt.
Thomas Edmondes, Kt.
OXFORDSHIRE
Richard Wenman, Kt.
Edward Wraye, Esq.
Pembroke, Pembrokeshire, Wales
Lewis Powell, Esq.
PEMBROKESHIRE, Wales
John Wogan, Esq.

5. Henry Moody, Kt. and Bt., is struck off the return and Hatton's name inserted. There is no evidence that Moody took a seat in the House.

Penryn, Cornwall
    Edward Roberts, Esq.
    Edwin Sandys, Kt.
Peterborough, Northamptonshire
    Christopher Hatton, Esq.
    Lawrence Whitaker, Esq.
Petersfield, Hampshire
    John Jephson, Kt.
    William Uvedale, Kt.
Plymouth, Devonshire
    John Glanville, Esq.
    Thomas Sherwill
Plympton, Devonshire
    Warwick Hele, Kt.
    William Strode, Kt.
Pontefract, Yorkshire
    Richard Beaumont, Kt.
    John Jackson, Kt.
Poole, Dorset
    John Cowper, Kt. and Bt.
    John Pyne, Esq.
Portsmouth, Hampshire
    Daniel Norton, Kt.
    Benjamin Rudyard, Kt.
Preston, Lancashire
    Henry Banaster, Esq.
    William Harvey, Kt.
Queenborough, Kent
    Edward Hales, Kt. and Bt.
    Roger Palmer, Esq.
Radnor, Radnorshire, Wales
    Charles Price, Esq.
RADNORSHIRE, Wales
    James Price, Esq.
Reading, Berkshire
    Francis Knollys, Jr., Kt.
    John Saunders, Esq.
Reigate, Surrey
    Thomas Bludder, Kt.
    Roger James, Kt.
Richmond, Yorkshire
    Talbot Bowes, Kt.
    Christopher Wandesford, Esq.
Ripon, Yorkshire
    Thomas Posthumus Hoby, Kt.
    William Mallory, Sr., Esq.
Rochester, Kent
    Henry Clerke, Esq.
    Thomas Walsingham, Jr., Kt.
RUTLAND
    William Bulstrode, Kt.
    Guy Palmes, Kt.
Rye, Cinque Port
    Thomas Fotherley, Esq.
    John Sackville, Esq.
St. Albans, Hertfordshire
    John Luke, Kt.
    Charles Morrison, Kt. and Bt.

St. Germans, Cornwall
    John Coke, Kt.
    Henry Marten, Kt.
St. Ives, Cornwall
    Francis Godolphin, Kt.
    William Parkhurst, Kt.
St. Mawes, Cornwall
    James Fullerton, Kt.
    [Nathaniel Tomkins, Esq.]
Salisbury, Wiltshire
    Walter Long, Esq.
    Henry Sherfield, Esq.
Saltash, Cornwall
    Francis Buller, Esq.
    Richard Buller, Kt.
Sandwich, Cinque Port
    Robert Hatton, Kt.
    Henry Wotton, Kt.
Scarborough, Yorkshire
    Hugh Cholmley, Gent.
    William Thompson, Gent.
Shaftesbury, Dorset
    John Thoroughgood, Esq.
    William Whitaker, Esq.
Shoreham, Sussex
    William Marlott, Gent.
    Anthony Stapley, Esq.
Shrewsbury, Shropshire
    Thomas Owen, Esq.
    William Owen, Kt.
SHROPSHIRE
    Andrew Corbet, Kt.
    Richard Newport, Kt.
SOMERSET
    Robert Phelips, Kt.
    John Stawell, Esq.
Southampton, Hampshire
    George Gollop
    John Mill, Bt.
Southwark, Surrey
    William Coxe, Esq.
    Richard Yarwood, Esq.
Stafford, Staffordshire
    Matthew Cradock, Esq.
    John Offley, Kt.
    [Robert Hatton, Kt.]
STAFFORDSHIRE
    Richard Erdeswicke, Esq.
    Simon Weston, Kt.
Stamford, Lincolnshire
    Montague Bertie, Kt.
    John St. Amand, Esq.
Steyning, Sussex
    Thomas Farnefold, Kt.
    Edward Francis, Kt.
Stockbridge, Hampshire
    Thomas Badger, Kt.
    Richard Gifford, Kt.

Sudbury, Suffolk
    Nathaniel Barnardiston, Kt.
    Robert Crane, Kt. and Bt.
SUFFOLK
    Edmund Bacon, Kt. and Bt.
    Thomas Cornwallis, Esq.
SURREY
    Francis Leigh, Kt.
    George More, Kt.
SUSSEX
    Thomas Pelham, Bt.
    John Sherley, Kt.
Tamworth, Staffordshire
    Thomas Puckering, Kt. and Bt.
    Richard Skeffington, Kt.
Taunton, Somerset
    Thomas Brereton, Esq.
    Hugh Portman, Bt.
Tavistock, Devonshire
    Francis Glanville, Kt.
    John Pym, Esq.
Tewkesbury, Gloucestershire
    Dudley Digges, Kt.
    Baptist Hicks, Kt. and Bt.
Thetford, Norfolk
    Robert Cotton, Kt. and Bt.
    Framlingham Gawdy, Esq.
Thirsk, Yorkshire
    Henry Belasyse, Esq.
    Henry Stanley, Esq.
Tiverton, Devonshire
    John Fraunceis, Esq.
    Rowland St. John, Kt.
Totnes, Devonshire
    Edward Giles, Kt.
    Edward Seymour, Kt. and Bt.
Tregony, Cornwall
    Henry Carey, Kt.
    Sebastian Goode, Gent.
Truro, Cornwall
    Henry Rolle, Esq.
    William Rous, Esq.
Wallingford, Berkshire
    Anthony Forest, Kt.
    Michael Mollines, Esq.
Wareham, Dorset
    William Pitt, Kt.
    John Trenchard, Esq.
Warwick, Warwickshire
    Francis Leigh, Jr., Kt. and Bt.
    Francis Lucy, Esq.
WARWICKSHIRE
    Thomas Lucy, Kt.
    Clement Throckmorton, Kt.
Wells, Somerset
    Thomas Lake, Kt.
    Edward Rodney, Kt.

Wendover, Buckinghamshire
    John Hampden, Esq.
    Richard Hampden, Esq.
West Looe, Cornwall
    Edward Thomas, Esq.
    John Wolstenholme, Esq.
Westbury, Wiltshire
    Gifford Long, Esq.
    [Walter Long, Esq.]
Westminster, Middlesex
    William Man, Esq.
    Edward Villiers, Kt.
WESTMORLAND
    Henry Bellingham, Kt. and Bt.
    John Lowther, Esq.
Weymouth and Melcombe Regis, Dorset
    Arthur Pyne, Esq.
    John Strangways, Kt.
    Giles Greene, Gent.
    Barnard Mychell, Esq.
    [Thomas Middleton, Jr., Kt.]
Whitchurch, Hampshire
    Thomas Jervoise, Kt.
    Robert Oxenbridge, Kt.
Wigan, Lancashire
    Edward Bridgeman, Gent.
    Francis Downes, Esq.
Wilton, Wiltshire
    William Harrington, Kt.
    Thomas Morgan, Kt.
    [William Herbert, Kt.]
WILTSHIRE
    Henry Ley, Kt.
    Francis Seymour, Kt.
Winchelsea, Cinque Port
    Ralph Freeman, Kt.
    Roger Twysden, Kt.
Winchester, Hampshire
    Thomas Phelips, Kt. and Bt.
    Richard Tichborne, Kt.
Woodstock, Oxfordshire
    Philip Cary, Kt.
    Gerrard Fleetwood, Kt.
Wootton Bassett, Wiltshire
    Robert Hyde, Kt.
    Walter Tichborne, Kt.
Worcester, Worcestershire
    Walter Devereux, Kt. and Bt.
    Henry Spilman, Kt.
WORCESTERSHIRE
    Thomas Littleton, Kt. and Bt.
    William Russell, Esq.
Yarmouth (Isle of Wight), Hampshire
    John Oglander, Kt.
    John Suckling, Kt.
    [Edward Clarke, Esq.]

York, Yorkshire
    Christopher Brooke, Esq.
    Arthur Ingram, Kt.
YORKSHIRE
    Thomas Fairfax, Kt.
    Thomas Wentworth, Kt. and Bt.

E. Lists of Officials

The following lists are arranged alphabetically, one by title of office and the other by name of the officeholder. The list by title of office is divided into four broad categories: parliament, central administration, judiciary, and London. Within each category the major offices are listed as are those minor offices mentioned in the proceedings in parliament 1625. This is not intended to serve as a complete list of officeholders but to be an aid in identifying persons connected with or referred to in parliament. Most offices outside of the London area are not included.

1. By Office

I. Parliament
  Clerk of the House of Commons
    John Wright
  Clerk of the Parliaments
    Henry Elsynge (the elder)
  Gentleman Usher of the Black Rod
    James Maxwell
  Serjeant at Arms of the House of Commons
    Edward Grimston
  Serjeant at Arms of the House of Lords
    Walter Leigh
  Speaker of the House of Commons
    Sir Thomas Crew, M.P.

II. Central Administration
  Attorney General
    Sir Thomas Conventry
  Attorney of the Court of Wards
    Sir Walter Pye, M.P.
  Attorney of the Duchy of Lancaster
    Sir Edward Moseley
  Auditor of the Duchy of Lancaster
    Sir John Trevor, M.P.
  Auditors in the Exchequer
    Thomas Brinley
    Richard Budd
    Sir Francis Gofton
    William Gwynne
    William Hill
    Francis Phillipps
    Justinian Povey
    Sir Robert Pye, M.P.
    Sir Edmund Sawyer, M.P.
  Barons of the Exchequer
    Sir Edward Bromley
    Sir John Denham

    Sir John Sotherton
    Sir Thomas Trevor
  Chancellor of the Duchy of Lancaster
    Sir Humphrey May, M.P.
  Chancellor and Under Treasurer
    of the Exchequer
    Sir Richard Weston, M.P.
  Chief Baron of the Exchequer
    Sir John Walter
  Clerk of the Crown in Chancery
    Sir Thomas Edmondes, M.P.
  Clerk of the Pells
    Sir Edward Wardour, M.P.
  Clerks of the Pipe
    Sir Henry Croke
    Anthony Rous
  Clerks of the Privy Council
    Sir William Beecher, M.P.
    John Dickenson
    Thomas Meautys, M.P.
    William Trumbull
  Clerks of the Privy Council Extraordinary
    William Boswell, M.P.
    Sir John Burgh
    Sir Dudley Carleton
    Simon Digby
    Edward Nicholas
    Lawrence Whitaker, M.P.
  Clerks of the Privy Seal
    John Packer
    Thomas Packer
  Cofferer of the Household (jointly held)
    Sir Marmaduke Darrell
    Sir Henry Vane (the elder), M.P.
  Comptroller of the Household
    Sir John Suckling, M.P.
  Earl Marshal
    Thomas Howard, Earl of Arundel and
    Surrey
  Knight Marshal
    Sir Edward Zouche
  Lieutenant of Dover Castle
    Sir John Hippisley, M.P.
  Lieutenant of the Tower
    Sir Allen Apsley
  Lord Admiral
    George Villiers, Duke of Buckingham
  Lord Chamberlain of the Household
    William Herbert, Earl of Pembroke
  Lord Chancellor, *see* Lord Keeper
  Lord Chancellor of Ireland
    Adam Loftus, Viscount Loftus of Ely
  Lord Keeper of the Great Seal
    John Williams, Bishop of Lincoln
  Lord President of the Council in the
    Marches of Wales
    William Compton, Earl of Northampton

Lord President of the Council of the North
    Emanuel, Baron Scrope
Lord President of the Privy Council
    Henry Montagu, Viscount Mandeville
Lord Privy Seal
    Edward Somerset, Earl of Worcester
Lord Steward of the Household
    William Herbert, Earl of Pembroke
Lord Treasurer
    James, Baron Ley
Lord Warden of the Cinque Ports
    George Villiers, Duke of Buckingham
Master of the Household
    Roger Palmer, M.P.
Master of the Jewel House
    Sir Henry Mildmay, M.P.
Master of the Mint
    Sir Randall Cranfield
Master of the Rolls
    Sir Julius Caesar
Master of the Court of Wards
    Sir Robert Naunton, M.P.
Masters in Chancery
    Sir Charles Caesar
    Sir Julius Caesar
    Sir Edward Clarke
    Thomas Eden, LL.D.
    Sir John Hayward
    Francis James
    Sir Edward Leech, M.P.
    John Michell
    Richard More
    Sir Peter Mutton
    Sir Robert Rich
    Sir Edward Salter
    Sir Eubule Thelwall
Masters of Requests
    Sir John Coke, M.P.
    Sir Ralph Freeman, M.P.
Master of Requests Extraordinary
    Sir William Beecher, M.P.
Receiver General and Vice Treasurer in
    Ireland
    Sir Francis Annesley, M.P.
Receiver General of the Court of Wards
    Sir Miles Fleetwood, M.P.
Remembrancer of the Exchequer
    Sir Thomas Fanshawe, M.P. for Hertford
Secretaries of State
    Edward, Baron Conway of Ragley
    Sir Albertus Morton, M.P.
Secretary for Irish Affairs
    Sir Henry Holcroft
Secretary of the Council in the North
    Sir Arthur Ingram, M.P.
Secretary to the Admiralty
    Edward Nicholas

Solicitor General
    Sir Robert Heath, M.P.
Surveyor General
    Sir Thomas Fanshawe, M.P. for Lancaster
Surveyor of the Court of Wards
    Sir Benjamin Rudyard, M.P.
Surveyor of the Ordnance (jointly held)
    Sir Thomas Bludder, M.P.
    Sir Alexander Brett
Surveyor of Victuals for the Navy
    Sir Allen Apsley
Treasurer of the Household
    Sir Thomas Edmondes, M.P.
Treasurer of the King's Chamber
    Sir William Uvedale, M.P.
Treasurer of the Navy
    Sir William Russell
Vice Admiral of England
    Sir Robert Mansell, M.P.
Vice Chamberlain to the Queen
    Sir George Goring, M.P.
Victualler of the Fleet
    James Bagg, M.P.

III. Judiciary
Admiralty
  Judge
    Sir Henry Marten, M.P.
Common Pleas
  Chief Justice
    Sir Henry Hobart
  Justices
    Sir George Croke
    Sir Francis Harvey
    Sir Richard Hutton
    Sir Henry Yelverton
King's Bench
  Chief Justice
    Sir Ranulphe Crew
  Justices
    Sir John Doddridge
    Sir William Jones
    Sir James Whitelocke
  Clerk of the Crown in King's Bench
    Sir Thomas Fanshawe, M.P. for
    Lancaster
  Chief Clerk for Enrolling Pleas (jointly
    held)
    Sir Robert Heath, M.P.
    Sir George Paule, M.P.
Prerogative Court of Canterbury
  Judge
    Sir Henry Marten, M.P.
Serjeants
  King's Serjeants
    Sir Francis Ashley, M.P.
    Sir Thomas Crew

Sir Humphrey Davenport
Sir John Davies
Sir Henry Finch
Sir Thomas Richardson
Sir Thomas Trevor
  Serjeants at Law
  Richard Amherst
  John Bramston
  Francis Crawley
  Richard Digges, M.P.
  Sir Robert Hitcham, M.P.
  John Hoskins
  Sir Egremont Thynne
  William Towse, M.P.

IV. London
  Lord Mayor of London
    Sir John Gore (October 1624 to October
      1625)
  Recorder of London
    Sir Heneage Finch, M.P.

2. By Family Name

Amherst, Richard
  Serjeant at Law
Annesley, Sir Francis, M.P.
  Receiver General and Vice Treasurer
    in Ireland
Apsley, Sir Allen
  Lieutenant of the Tower;
  Surveyor of Victuals for the Navy
Ashley, Sir Francis, M.P.
  King's Serjeant
Bagg, James, M.P.
  Victualler of the Fleet
Beecher, Sir William, M.P.
  Clerk of the Privy Council;
  Master of Requests Extraordinary
Bludder, Sir Thomas, M.P.
  Surveyor of the Ordnance
Boswell, William, M.P.
  Clerk of the Privy Council Extraordinary
Bramston, John
  Serjeant at Law
Brett, Sir Alexander
  Surveyor of the Ordnance
Brinley, Thomas
  Auditor in the Exchequer
Bromley, Sir Edward
  Baron of the Exchequer
Budd, Richard
  Auditor in the Exchequer
Burgh, Sir John
  Clerk of the Privy Council Extraordinary
Caesar, Sir Charles
  Master in Chancery

Caesar, Sir Julius
  Master in Chancery;
  Master of the Rolls
Carleton, Sir Dudley
  Clerk of the Privy Council Extraordinary
Clarke, Sir Edward
  Master in Chancery
Coke, Sir John, M.P.
  Master of Requests
Compton, William, Earl of Northampton
  Lord President of the Council in the Marches
    of Wales
Conway, Edward, Baron Conway of Ragley
  Secretary of State
Coventry, Sir Thomas
  Attorney General
Cranfield, Sir Randall
  Master of the Mint
Crawley, Francis
  Serjeant at Law
Crew, Sir Ranulphe
  Chief Justice of the King's Bench
Crew, Sir Thomas, M.P.
  Speaker of the House of Commons;
  King's Serjeant
Croke, Sir George
  Justice of the Common Pleas
Croke, Sir Henry
  Clerk of the Pipe
Darrell, Sir Marmaduke
  Cofferer of the Household (jointly with Vane)
Davenport, Sir Humphrey
  King's Serjeant
Davies, Sir John
  King's Serjeant
Denham, Sir John
  Baron of the Exchequer
Dickenson, John
  Clerk of the Privy Council
Digby, Simon
  Clerk of the Privy Council Extraordinary
Digges, Richard, M.P.
  Serjeant at Law
Doddridge, Sir John
  Justice of the King's Bench
Eden, Thomas, LL.D.
  Master in Chancery
Edmondes, Sir Thomas, M.P.
  Treasurer of the Household;
  Clerk of the Crown in Chancery
Elsynge, Henry (the elder)
  Clerk of the Parliaments
Fanshawe, Sir Thomas, M.P. for Hertford
  Remembrancer of the Exchequer
Fanshawe, Sir Thomas, M.P. for Lancaster
  Clerk of the Crown in King's Bench;
  Surveyor General

Finch, Sir Heneage, M.P.
  Recorder of London
Finch, Sir Henry
  King's Serjeant
Fleetwood, Sir Miles, M.P.
  Receiver General of the Court of Wards
Freeman, Sir Ralph, M.P.
  Master of Requests
Gofton, Sir Francis
  Auditor in the Exchequer
Gore, Sir John
  Lord Mayor of London (October 1624 to
    October 1625)
Goring, Sir George, M.P.
  Vice Chamberlain to the Queen
Grimston, Edward
  Serjeant at Arms of the House of Commons
Gwynne, William
  Auditor in the Exchequer
Harvey, Sir Francis
  Justice of the Common Pleas
Hayward, Sir John
  Master in Chancery
Heath, Sir Robert, M.P.
  Solicitor General;
  Chief Clerk for Enrolling Pleas in the King's
    Bench (jointly with Paule)
Herbert, William, Earl of Pembroke
  Lord Chamberlain of the Household;
  Lord Steward of the Household
Hill, William
  Auditor in the Exchequer
Hippisley, Sir John, M.P.
  Lieutenant of Dover Castle
Hitcham, Sir Robert, M.P.
  Serjeant at Law
Hobart, Sir Henry
  Chief Justice of Common Pleas
Holcroft, Sir Henry
  Secretary for Irish Affairs
Hoskins, John
  Serjeant at Law
Howard, Thomas, Earl of Arundel and Surrey
  Earl Marshal
Hutton, Sir Richard
  Justice of the Common Pleas
Ingram, Sir Arthur, M.P.
  Secretary of the Council in the North
James, Francis
  Master in Chancery
Jones, Sir William
  Justice of the King's Bench
Leech, Sir Edward, M.P.
  Master in Chancery
Leigh, Walter
  Serjeant at Arms of the House of Lords

Ley, James, Baron Ley
  Lord Treasurer
Loftus, Adam, Viscount Loftus of Ely
  Lord Chancellor of Ireland
Mansell, Sir Robert, M.P.
  Vice Admiral of England
Marten, Sir Henry, M.P.
  Judge of the Admiralty;
  Judge of the Prerogative Court of Canterbury
Maxwell, James
  Gentleman Usher of the Black Rod
May, Sir Humphrey, M.P.
  Chancellor of the Duchy of Lancaster
Meautys, Thomas, M.P.
  Clerk of the Privy Council
Michell, John
  Master in Chancery
Mildmay, Sir Henry, M.P.
  Master of the Jewel House
Montagu, Henry, Viscount Mandeville
  Lord President of the Privy Council
More, Richard
  Master in Chancery
Morton, Sir Albertus, M.P.
  Secretary of State
Moseley, Sir Edward
  Attorney of the Duchy of Lancaster
Mutton, Sir Peter
  Master in Chancery
Naunton, Sir Robert, M.P.
  Master of the Court of Wards
Nicholas, Edward
  Clerk Extraordinary of the Privy Council;
  Secretary to the Admiralty
Packer, John
  Clerk of the Privy Seal
Packer, Thomas
  Clerk of the Privy Seal
Palmer, Roger, M.P.
  Master of the Household
Paule, Sir George, M.P.
  Chief Clerk for Enrolling Pleas in the King's
    Bench (jointly with Heath)
Phillipps, Francis
  Auditor in the Exchequer
Povey, Justinian
  Auditor in the Exchequer
Pye, Sir Robert, M.P.
  Auditor in the Exchequer
Pye, Sir Walter, M.P.
  Attorney of the Court of Wards
Rich, Sir Robert
  Master in Chancery
Richardson, Sir Thomas
  King's Serjeant
Rous, Anthony
  Clerk of the Pipe

Rudyard, Sir Benjamin, M.P.
  Surveyor of the Court of Wards
Russell, Sir William
  Treasurer of the Navy
Salter, Sir Edward
  Master in Chancery
Sawyer, Sir Edmund, M.P.
  Auditor in the Exchequer
Scrope, Emanuel, Baron Scrope
  Lord President of the Council in the North
Somerset, Edward, Earl of Worcester
  Lord Privy Seal
Sotherton, Sir John
  Baron of the Exchequer
Suckling, Sir John, M.P.
  Comptroller of the Household
Thelwall, Sir Eubule
  Master in Chancery
Thynne, Sir Egremont
  Serjeant at Law
Towse, William, M.P.
  Serjeant at Law
Trevor, Sir John, M.P.
  Auditor of the Duchy of Lancaster
Trevor, Sir Thomas
  Baron of the Exchequer;
  King's Serjeant
Trumbull, William
  Clerk of the Privy Council

Uvedale, Sir William, M.P.
  Treasurer of the King's Chamber
Vane, Sir Henry (the elder), M.P.
  Cofferer of the Household (jointly with
    Darrell)
Villiers, George, Duke of Buckingham
  Lord Admiral;
  Lord Warden of the Cinque Ports
Walter, Sir John
  Chief Baron of the Exchequer
Wardour, Sir Edward, M.P.
  Clerk of the Pells
Weston, Sir Richard, M.P.
  Chancellor and Under Treasurer of the
    Exchequer
Whitaker, Lawrence, M.P.
  Clerk of the Privy Council Extraordinary
Whitelocke, Sir James
  Justice of the King's Bench
Williams, John, Bishop of Lincoln
  Lord Keeper of the Great Seal
Wright, John
  Clerk of the House of Commons
Yelverton, Sir Henry
  Justice of the Common Pleas
Zouche, Sir Edward
  Knight Marshal

F. GLOSSARY OF FOREIGN WORDS AND PHRASES

The Glossary provides the reader with translations of foreign words and short phrases used by the speakers in 1625. (Longer Latin passages, such as the commissions for dissolution, 11 July and 12 August, are translated in the text.)

In all cases citations to book and line number in the classics are from the *Loeb Classical Library;* Biblical quotations are from *The Holy Bible,* King James version, 1611, or when the quote appears in Latin, from the *Vulgate.* Legal writs are translated from Black's *Law Dictionary.* For legal terms, as well as writs, the reader will find lengthier definitions in Jacob's *Law Dictionary* (London, 1732) or in Rastell, *Les Termes de la Ley* (Portland, first American ed., 1812). Where Latin phrases are from statutes or cases a cross-reference following the translation is made to the section of Legal Citations (below) which will give a full reference to the legal source from which the phrase is taken.

It is important to note that the glossary translations are given in accord with the sentences in which the foreign tags occur; the translations are not meant to be read independently.

ab utili. "From the useful", i.e., on utilitarian grounds.

abrupta contumacia. "Irreconcilable opposition"; "Obstinacy". Tacitus, *Annales,* 4, 20.

accordant. "Accordant", i.e., in agreement.

actualiter resumere. "To actually recover". Gascoigne, *Loci e Libro.*

acumina dictorum. "Aptness of speech".

ad dedecus regis. "To the dishonor of the King". Gascoigne, *Loci e Libro.*

ad libitum. "During pleasure".

ad respondendum. "For answering", i.e., words used in certain writs employed for bringing a person before the court to make answer in defense in a proceeding, as in *habeas corpus ad respondendum,* etc. See Black's *Law Dict.*

ad satisfaciendum. "To satisfy", i.e., words used in the writ of *capias ad satisfaciendum,* which requires the sheriff to take the person of the defendant to satisfy the plaintiff's claim.

ad testificandum. "For testimony", i.e., a writ to bring a witness into court when he is in custody at the time of the trial, commanding the sheriff to have his body before the court to testify in the cause. Black's *Law Dict.*

ad utilitatem temporum. "For the utility of the occasion". Cf. Quintilian, *Institutiones Oratoriae,* 11, 1, 46–47.

admirabili quadam illuminatione sed umbram habens et recessum. "With a certain admirable illumination but having shadow and a background". Cf. Cicero, *De Oratore,* 3, 26, 101.

aequales ordinis magis quam operis. "Equals in position rather than in performance". Cf. V. Paterculus, *Historiae Romanae,* 1, 16, 3.

affectata. See below, *necessitas: affectata.*

agnus dei. "Lamb of God".

alienae culpae praetendebantur. "Served to cloak the faults of others". Tacitus, *Historiae,* 2, 39.

aliquo modo. "In any way".

aliud pretenditur aliud in mente est. "One thing is pretended, another is intended".

amare et sapere. "To love and be wise".

amor civium regis munimentum. "The people's love is the fortification of a king". A motto. The gold coins minted at the beginning of the reign of Charles I bore the inscription: *Amor civium regis praesidium* (The people's love is the protection of the king). See Birch, *Court and Times of Chas. I,* I, 11.

animalia solivagium. "Solitary animals". Aristotle, *De Animalibus Historiae, Lib.* 1, c. 1; *Lib.* 9, c. 4.

anno primo Caroli regis. "The first year [of the reign] of King Charles".

aquila non capit muscas. "The eagle does not stoop to catch flies". Erasmus, *Adag.* Chil. III, Cert. II, Prov. LXV.

arbiter regni. "Arbiter of the kingdom".

argumentum cornutum. "A horned argument".

audience ad audiendum errores. "A hearing for the hearing of errors".

audita querela. The name of a writ constituting the initial process in an action brought by a defendant to obtain relief against the consequences of the judgment on account of some matter of defense or discharge arising since its rendition. See Black's *Law Dict.*

aut modum norat aut capiebat terminum. "He knew no limits nor accepted any bounds". V. Paterculus, *Historiae Romanae,* 2, 46, 2.

beatus est qui facit justitiam in omni tempore. "Blessed is he who does righteousness at all times". Psalm 105(106):3.

beneficium postulat officium. "The office requires kindness".

billa eadem 3ª vice lecta et missa communibus. "The same bill is read the third time and sent to the Commons".

bis dat qui cito dat. "He gives twice who gives quickly". Proverb.

bonum publicum. "For the public good".

Cantuariam. "At Canterbury".

capita. "Heads".

Capitula itineris: Et similiter de hiis qui vindictam [fecerint]. "*Capitula Itineris* (the Articles of Eyre): And likewise of those who [have taken] revenge". *S.R.*, Uncertain Date (*S.R.*, I, 237).

causae suasoriae, causae justificae. "Persuasive causes, justifying causes".

certiorari. An original writ issuing out of Chancery or King's Bench directed in the King's name to the judges or officers of inferior courts commanding them to certify or to return the records or proceedings in a cause depending before them for the purpose of a judicial review of their action. See Black's *Law Dict.*

comitis. "Earl".

commune periculum commune (trahit) auxilium. "Common danger (draws) common aid".

concedere regno quae vis pessima. "To concede to the throne the worst things you might wish". Gascoigne, *Loci e Libro.*

conservare quam plurimus. "Preserve as well as possible".

consulto. In civil law, designedly, i.e., a design.

contra. "Against".

coram domino rege in cancellaria. "Before our lord King in Chancery", i.e., in the King's court of Chancery.

coram nomine. "In the name of the court".

coram rege. "King's court [at Christ Church]".

cum privilegio. "With privilege".

cum voluptate audientium. "With the pleasure of the audience". Cf. Quintilian, *Institutiones Oratoriae*, 11, 1, 43–45.

cupidus alienae rei, parcus suae avarus reipublicae. "Covetous of another's property, frugal of his own property and greedy for that of the state".

custodia marescalli. "Custody of the Marshal".

custos utriusque tabulae. "Guardian of both tablets".

de apostasia sanctorum. "Concerning the apostacy of the saints".

de claro. "Clearly".

de facto. "In fact".

de modo. "Of manner".

de talijs et quindenis populi. "From tallage and a fifteenth of the people". Gascoigne, *Loci e Libro.*

dedimus potestatem. "We have given powers". A writ issuing from Chancery empowering the persons named therein to perform certain acts. Black's *Law Dict.*

defensionem ecclesiae Anglicanae. "The defense of the English church".

deforme obsequium. "Ugly servility". Tacitus, *Annales*, 4, 20.

deliciarum arbiter. "Arbiter of pleasures". Cf. Tacitus, *Annales*, 16, 18.

depravari amore. "To be corrupted by love".

deus in utroque parente. "Divinity through both parents". Ovid, *Metamorphoses*, 13, 147.

dum in manibus suis excoluntur. "While they were cultivated in their [the friars'] hands".

dum singuli pugnant universi vincuntur. "While each is fighting separately all are conquered". Tacitus, *Agricola*, 12, 2–3.

eadem est ratio ex contrario. "The same reason is the opposite [situation]".

ecclesia romana est. See below, *vera Christi ecclesia.*

ejectione firmae. Ejection or ejectment of a farm. A writ or action of trespass which lay at common law where lands or tenements were let for a term of years and afterwards the lessor, reversioner, remainderman, or any stranger ejected or ousted the lessee of his term, ferme, or farm (*ipsum a firma ejecit*). See Black's *Law Dict.*

engrossetur. "Engrossed", i.e., written in a fair hand on parchment.

eodem die. "The same day".

eodem fundamento doctrinae et sacramentorum nititur. "Rests on the same foundation of doctrine and sacraments".

episcopi et tanquam episcopi. "Bishops and those like bishops".

equilibrio. "Balance".

ergo vide. "Therefore see [them]".

et beneficium. See above, *beneficium.*

et medicina. See below, *medicina.*

et 2ᵈᵃ vice lecta est eadem billa et commissa. "And the same bill is given a second reading and committed".

et similiter de hiis qui vindictam. See above, *Capitula itineris.*

eundo, (sedendo,) et redeundo. "In going, (staying,) and returning".

ex diametro. "Diametrically [opposed]".

ex mero motu. "Of his own mere motion"; "Of his own accord". Royal letters patent granted at the crown's own instance and without request made are said to be granted *ex mero motu.* See Legat's case, 10 Coke, *Reports*, ff. 112b–113a; Black's *Law Dict.*

ex ore non a pectore. "From the mouth and not from the heart".

ex parte. "On one side only".

ex praescientia operum. "From foreknowledge of the business".

ex re nata. "According to the state of affairs". Terence, *Adelphi,* 3,1,8.

excommunicatio hominis. "Excommunication of a [particular] man".

excommunicatio juris. "Excommunication on grounds of [general] law".

exitus. "Outcome".

extra regnum. "Outside of the realm".

felix faustumque sit. "Let it be happy and auspicious".

fidem qui perdit perdere ultra nihil potest. "He who loses his good faith has nothing else to lose". Proverb.

foedera infida dissolubilia. "Faithless treaties are dissoluble".

forinsecus. "Publicly"; "From without".

forsan et haec olim meminisse juvabit. "Perchance even this distress it will some day be a joy to recall". Virgil, *Aeneid,* 1, 203.

fraus contra legem. "Fraud against law".

fraus legis. "Fraud of law".

habeas corpus. "You have the body". The name given to a variety of writs having for their object to bring a party before a court or judge. See Black's *Law Dict.*

habeas corpus cum causa. "*Habeas corpus* with the cause". Another name for the writ of *habeas corpus ad faciendum et recipiendum,* which is a writ issuing in civil actions to remove the case, as well as the body of the defendant, from an inferior court to a superior court. See Black's *Law Dict.*

hoc unum necessarium. "This the one necessary [thing]".

hodie allata est a domo communi (una billa) per Thomam Edmondes, Chr., et alios, billa. "This day (one bill) for Thomas Edmondes, Knight, and others, is brought from the House of Commons, the bill . . .".

hodie allatae sunt a domo communi duae (tres, octo) billae. "This day two (three, eight) bills were brought from the House of Commons".

hodie 1ª (2da, et 3ª) vice lecta est billa (praedicta). "This day the (aforesaid) bill is given its first (second, third) reading".

hodie 2ª vice lecta est billa eadem et commissa est. "This day the same bill is read the second time and committed".

hominis. See above, *excommunicatio.*

hostes humani generis piratae. "Pirates are the enemies of the human species".

ictus sententiarum. "Force of phrase".

ideoque die hoc. "On that account this day".

idonea. "Responsible"; "Competent"; "Suitable".

igniculi sententiarum et flosculi ingeniorum. "Sparks of rhetoric and little flowers of wit".

impellit quo voluerit. "He drives them where He wishes".

impotentia excusat legem. "Inability suspends the operation of the law". Proverb.

imprimis. "First of all".

in cursu. "In progress".

in forma pauperis. "In the manner of a pauper".

in haec verba. "In these words".

in principia semper praesumitur causa et ratio. "In the beginning a cause and reason are always assumed".

in salva et arcta custodia. "In safe and close custody".

in senatum venit. "He comes into the Senate". Cicero, *Oratio in Catilinam,* 1,1,2.

in statu quo. "In the condition in which it was". See Black's *Law Dict.*

in talijs et quindenis. "On tallage and a fifteenth". Gascoigne, *Loci e Libro.*

in terminis terminantibus. "In terms of determination", i.e., in express or determinate terms.

in villis et remotis partibus regni. "In the villages and the remote parts of the kingdom". Gascoigne, *Loci e Libro.*

inani nomine. "With the empty title". Cf. Tacitus, *Historiae,* 2, 39.

indicium sequitur pejorem viam. "Disclosure follows the worse life".

indictum sit. "Let it be indicted".

inhonestum. "Shameful"; "Dishonor".

invincibilis aut inevitabilis. "Irresistable or inevitable".

ipso facto. "By the fact itself".

jacta est alea. "The die is cast". Suetonius, *De Vita Caesarum,* 1, 32.

Jove principium. "With Jove I begin". Cf. Virgil, *Eclogues,* 3, 60.

latitat. A writ issued in personal actions, so called from the emphatic word in its recital in which it was "testified that the defendant lurks [*latitat*] and wanders about". See Black's *Law Dict.*

lex sumptuaria. "A sumptuary law".

lex temporis. "The law of the time".

limbus patrum. "The limbo of the fathers". See above, H. of C., 7 July, n. 18.

magis ad dedecus regis. "More to the dishonor of the King". Gascoigne, *Loci e Libro.*

majus opprobrium. "Great contempt".

malum consilium. "Bad counsel".

malum per se. "A wrong in itself".

malum prohibitum. "A wrong [because] prohibited", i.e., not an inherently immoral wrong.

maximum in minimo. "The most in the least", i.e., [he] said the most in the fewest words.

medicina promovens. "Remedy for increasing".

medicina removens. "Remedy for removing".

medicina renovans. "Remedy for renewal".

minimum in maximo. "The least in the most", i.e., [he] said the least in the greatest number of words.

misera servitus est ubi lex incerta aut incognita. "Servitude is a wretched state where the law is uncertain and unknown". Coke, *Fourth Inst.*, p. 246.

modo habendi. "For [its] manner of being held".

modus decimandi. In ecclesiastical law, a manner of tithing. Black's *Law Dict.*

more majorum. "After the manner of our ancestors". Cf. Cicero, *Epistulae ad Atticum*, 1, 1, 4.

mors in olla. "Death in the pot". 2 Kings 4:40.

multum in parvo. "Much in a few [words]".

necessitas: affectata, invincibilis, et improvida. "Necessity: feigned, irresistable (invincible) and improvident".

necessitas compulsa. "Compelling necessity".

necessitas improvida. "Unforeseen necessity".

necessitas inducit privilegium. "Necessity gives a privilege [as to private rights]". 10 Coke, *Reports*, f. 61.

negotius regis. "Agent of the King".

nemine contradicente. "No one in opposition".

neque in pecunia neque in gloria concupiscenda. "Desiring neither money nor glory". V. Paterculus, *Historiae Romanae*, 2, 46, 2.

neutralitas nec (neque) amicos parit, nec (neque) inimicos tollit. "Neutrality neither brings forth friends nor elevates enemies".

nihil dicit. "He says nothing". The name of the judgment which may be taken as of course against a defendant who omits to plead or answer the plaintiff's declaration or complaint within the time limited. Black's *Law Dict.*

nihil unquam prisci et integri moris sed exuta aequalitate omnia unius iussa aspectare. "There was nothing of the old and pure morals but stripped of all equality all looked to the commands on one person". Cf. Tacitus, *Annales*, 1, 4.

noli me tangere. "Touch me not". John 20:17.

non intellecti nulla est curatio morbi. "There is no cure for a disease not understood".

non obstante. "Nothwithstanding". A clause frequent in statutes and letters patent importing a license from the crown to do a thing which otherwise a person would be restrained by act of parliament from doing. Black's *Law Dict.*

non plus. "Not more".

nono Augusti. "The ninth of August".

obdormit. "It sleeps".

octodecimum diem. "The eighteenth day".

omni modo. "In every way".

opus diei in die suo. "The work of the day in each day".

ore tenus. "By word of mouth". See Black's *Law Dict.*

Oxon. "Oxford".

panis lapidosus. "Stony bread". Seneca, *De Beneficiis*, 2, 7, 1; Horace, *Satires*, 1, 5, 89–91.

parcus suae avarus reipublicae. See above, *cupidus.*

parliamentum felix. "Happy parliament".

particeps criminis. A participant who shares in a crime. Black's *Law Dict.*

pax in diebus nostris. "Peace in our time".

per annum. "Yearly".

per diem. "For a day".

per dominum. "By the Lord [Steward]".

per mensem. "Monthly".

per plures. "By most"; "By the greater number".

p[er] solum. See below, *solum.*

pietate motus. "Moved by piety".

politiae particulae imago. "The image of a small part of a polity".

posse. "Power".

posse comitatus. "The power of the county". See Black's *Law Dict.*

post meridiem. "Afternoon".

potentior cum negat imperat. "When the more powerful man refuses he orders".

praemunire. An offense against the King or his government. Black's *Law Dict. Praemunire* is taken either for a writ so called, from the words therein, *Praemunire facias* or *praemonere facias*, etc., signifying to forewarn, or bid the offender take heed, or it is the offense on which the writ is granted. For a gloss on *praemunire*, see Jacob, *Law Dict.*; Coke, *Third Inst.*, pp. 119–127.

primitiae. "First fruits".

primo Eliz. "In the first year of the reign of Elizabeth".

pro. "For".

pro centum. "Per cent".

pro defensione ecclesiae. "For defense of the church".

pro dignitate rerum. "In accord with the dignity of the topic". Cf. Quintilian, *Institutiones Oratoriae*, 8, 2, 2; 12, 1, 8.

pro ecclesia Anglicana. "For the Church of England".

probabilem causam litigandi. "Probable cause of litigation".

profluens et canora. "Flowing and melodious in style". Cf. Cicero, *De Oratore*, 3, 7, 28.

promovens. "[For] increasing".

promovent. "[For] increasing".

propter defectum hospitis et victualium. "On account of a lack of lodging and food". Gascoigne, *Loci e Libro.*

prout antea. "As in the preceding".

pulchre et ornate. "Beautifully and elegantly". Cf. Quintilian, *Institutiones Oratoriae*, 8, 3–4.

quantum. "Amount".

quare impedit. "Wherefore he hinders". A writ which lies for the patron of an advowson [the right of presentation to a church or ecclesiastical benefice], where he has been disturbed in his right of patronage. See Black's *Law Dict.*

qui non propellit injuriam cum possit facit. "He who does not repel injustice at the same time makes it possible". Jenkins, *Centuries*, 271.

qui tarde dat diu noluit. "He who gives late, for a long time was unwilling".

quid pro quo. "What for what"; "Something for something".

quindecima. "Fifteenth".

quinquagesimo. "Fifty".

quinquies centena millia librarum. "Five hundred thousand pounds". Gascoigne, *Loci e Libro.*

quod uni accidit alteri potest. "What happens to one man may happen to another".

raro conventus ad propugnandum commune periculum. "Rarely an assembly for fighting common danger". Tacitus, *Agricola*, 12,2.

recepi. "To be received".

regnum Angliae. "The kingdom of England".

regnum dei. "The kingdom of God".

relata simul (sunt) natura. "[Kings and subjects] (are) related as if by nature".

religando. "A binding".

removent. "[For] removing".

retornatae sunt a domo communi quattuor billae. "Four bills were returned from the House of Commons".

retorne immediate. "Immediate return".

rex totius Brittaniae. "King of all Britain".

salus reipublicae. "The welfare of the republic".

sans. "Without".

sapiens incipit a fine. "A wise man begins with the last". 10 Coke, *Reports*, f. 25.

satis est si tali beneficio ignoscas. "It is enough if you overlook such a kindness".

schismaticus inveteratus. "Obstinate heretic".

sed exuta. See above, *nihil unquam.*

septimo. "Seventh", i.e., from the seventh year of the reign of King James.

signa virtutum. "Signs of virtues". Cf. Cicero, *Pro Caelio*, 4,12.

sine die. "Without day [appointed]".

singula officia singulis teneantur sicut judices. "A single office is held singularly as by a judge".

Sitomagus. Thetford, Norfolk.

solum et malum consilium. "Sole and bad counsel".

sub modo. "With a condition".

summus justiciarius Angliae. "Chief justice of England". See Coke, *Second Inst.*, p. 26.

super omnia expertus. "Experienced in all things".

super tota materia. "Upon all matters".

supersedeas. A writ containing a command to stay the proceedings at law. See Black's *Law Dict.*

tam pro domino rege quam pro seipso. "Both for the lord King and for himself".

tanquam ex tripode. "As from a pulpit".

tantum non episcopato puritani. "They are not Puritans only by the fact of being bishops".

teste. "Witness". The concluding clause of a writ, commencing with the word "witness". Black's *Law Dict.*

todos los diablos. "All the devils".

trans in medio. "On the other side [of the argument]".

tumens et exsultans. "Puffy and superfluous". Cf. Tacitus, *Dialogus de Oratoribus*, 18.

tuus o rex magne quid optes explorare labor mihi jussa capessere fas est. "Thy task, O King, is to search out thy desire; my duty is to do thy bidding". Cf. Virgil, *Aeneid*, 1, 77.

ubi. "Where".

unum necessarium. "One necessary [thing]".

ut initia proveniant fama in ceteris est. "As the first things succeed, fame is in the future". Cf. Tacitus, *Historiae*, 2, 20.

ut supra. "As above".

utinam nescirem litteras. "Would that I had not learned to write". Cf. Seneca, *De Clementia*, 2, 1, 3.

utinam nescirem loqui. "Would that I had not learned to speak".

velle. "Will".

venalia in Anglia. "Selling in England".

vera Christi ecclesia et sponsa Christi. "True church of Christ and bride of Christ".

vere. "Truly".

vetus querela. "An old argument".

via lactea. "Milky way". Ovid, *Metamorphoses*, 1, 168.

vide. "See".

vide postea. "See afterwards".

villis et remotis partibus regni. See above, *in villis.*

viva voce. "Orally".

G. LEGAL CITATIONS

This collection of legal citations provides complete and correct citations to all legal cases referred to by name or by date in the text, and to all statutes and rolls cited. It also includes quotations from those legal sources that are central to the debates in order that they may be readily accessible to anyone attempting to follow the arguments of the members.

The sources included in Legal Citations are (a) Cases, (b) Rolls, and (c) Statutes.

Cases

Brereton. See Noy, *Reports.*
Despenser, Hugh le. See Howell, *S.T.,* I.
Dyer, *Reports* (1794 ed.)

1 *Report*

Executors of Skewys vs. Chamond (referred to as Trewynard's case). Pasch., 36 and 37 *H.* VIII, ff. 59b–61b (*E.R.,* K.B. II, 131–135):
(f. 60a) "So we may conclude that this court of parliament is the most high court and has more privileges than any other court in the kingdom. Wherefore it seems that in every case, without any exception, every burgess is privileged, when the arrest is only at the suit of a subject. . . . And also every privilege is by prescription and every prescription which founds for the commonweal is good although it be to the prejudice of any private individual". See also Hatsell, *Precedents,* I, pp. 59–65.

2 *Report*

Skrogges vs. Coleshil. Mich., 1 and 2 *Eliz.* I, ff. 175a–175b (*E.R.,* K.B. II, 386–387):
(f.175a) "The office of Exigenter of London and other counties became vacant. . . . Queen Mary granted the office of Exigenter to one Coleshil . . . [and] granted the office of Chief Justice to Anthony Browne . . . who refused Coleshil, and admitted to it Skrogges his nephew. And now in this term there was a great contention between them for the said office; and our lady the now Queen commanded Nicholas Bacon, Knight, Keeper of the Great Seal, to examine the right and title of the said Coleshil. . . .

"[The judges] took a clear resolution after long debate and hesitation of all the premises, that the title of Coleshil was null, and that the gift of the said office by no means and at no time belongs or can belong to our lady the Queen, but is only in the disposal of the Chief Justice for the time being, as an inseparable incident belonging to the person of the said Chief and this by reason of prescription and usage. And it follows from this that our lady the Queen herself cannot be Chief Justice in the said bench".

3 *Report*

Anon. Mich., 8 and 9 *Eliz.* I, f. 255a (*E.R.,* K.B. II, 566):
(f. 255a) "A man having a benefice with cure to the value of ten pounds or more, takes another benefice with cure, and is inducted into it; now the first is void, as if it were by death or resignation, and this by statute 21 *H.* 8, [c. 13,] but the ordinary is not bound to give notice of this avoidance . . . ".

Bell vs. the Bishop of Norwich. Mich., 8 and 9 *Eliz.* I, f. 254b (*E.R.,* K.B. II, 564):
(f. 254b) Marginalia: "That the presentee is a haunter of taverns and unlawful games, which are *mala prohibita* only, is no cause for the bishop to refuse to admit him".

Gaveston, Piers. See *Rot. Parl.,* 5 *E.* II, no. 20.
Howell, *State Trials* (1816 ed.)

S.T., I
Articles of accusation against Hubert de Burgh. 23 *H.* III, pp. 13–22.
Proceedings against Hugh and Hugh le Despenser. 13 *E.* II, pp. 23–38.

Latimer, William, Lord. See *Rot. Parl.,* 50 *E.* III, nos. 20–29.
Noy, *Reports*
Brereton's case. Trin., 4 *Jac.* I, p. 17 (*E.R.,* K.B. III, 988).
Pole, Michael de la, Earl of Suffolk. See *Rot. Parl.,* 11 *R.* II, Articles 1–25.
Pole, William de la, Duke of Suffolk. See *Rot. Parl.,* 28 *H.* VI, nos. 19–46.
Rolle, *Abridgement* (1668 ed.)

"Escape", *pl.* Cl, Trin., 24 *H.* VIII. Order given to the guardians of the prisons in all of London that prisoners not go at large. (2 Dyer, *Reports*, ff. 249a–249b.)

"Escape", *pl.* D8, Mich., 12 & 13 *Eliz.* I. The King does not have power to license any man to go abroad from prison. (3 Dyer, *Reports*, ff. 296b–297a.)

Skrogges vs. Coleshil. See 2 Dyer, *Reports*.

Trewynard's case. See 1 Dyer, *Reports*.

Rolls

Parliament Rolls (*Rotuli Parliamentorum*)

18 *E.* I, no. 192 (*Rot. Parl.*, I, 61):
The case of the master of the temple wherein, as interpreted by Sir Edward Coke, "it appears that a member of the parliament shall have privilege of parliament, not only for his servants, as is aforesaid, but for his horses, etc., or other goods distrainable". Coke, *Fourth Inst.*, p. 24; Hatsell, *Precedents*, I, 3.

5 *E.* II, no. 20 (*Rot. Parl.*, I, 283):
Proceedings in parliament against Piers Gaveston who had "evilly counseled the King and had enticed him to do ill in divers manners", etc. The case is printed in Howell, *S.T.*, I, 21–24.

6 *E.* III, no. 3 (*Rot. Parl.*, II, 66):
Concerning the subsidy collection.

17 *E.* III, no. 17 (*Rot. Parl.*, II, 138):
Declaration establishing an increase in wool prices county by county.

17 *E.* III, no. 28 (*Rot. Parl.*, II, 140):
Complaint that the market towns charge subsidy on wools without the consent of the commonalty.

Response: It is the intent of our King not to charge the commonalty by the subsidy that is granted the market towns.

22 *E.* III, no. 4 (*Rot. Parl.*, II, 200–201):
The opening of parliament; concerning subsidy granted: " . . . And also that from henceforth no imposition, tallage, nor charge of tax, or other manner whatsoever, be taken by the Privy Council [of] our lord the King without their grant and assent in parliament . . . ".

25 *E.* III, no. 21 (*Rot. Parl.*, II, 229):
Request by merchants to carry their own wines.

Response: The King will advise and on this will respond in convenient manner.

27 *E.* III, no. 9 (*Rot. Parl.*, II, 248):
Things pertaining to the Staple will be under the cognizance of the mayor and ministers of the Staple.

37 *E.* III, no. 9 (*Rot. Parl.*, II, 276):
Petition from the Commons praying that the arch-

bishops, bishops, and all the clergy pray for the King's estate and for the continuance of his good-will towards the Commons.

50 *E.* III, no. 9 (*Rot. Parl.*, II, 322):
The grant of subsidy on wool, etc.

50 *E.* III, no. 10 (*Rot. Parl.*, II, 322):
Petition to the King from the Commons praying that the business of the kingdom not be passed without the assent and advice of the King's Council, that four or six such counsellors be continually in the King's Council, etc.

50 *E.* III, nos. 20–29 (*Rot. Parl.*, II, 324–326):
Charges brought by parliament against William Latimer, follower of John of Gaunt.

50 *E.* III, no. 90 (*Rot. Parl.*, II, 336):
A complaint against aliens holding benefices within the realm.

50 *E.* III, no. 96 (*Rot. Parl.*, II, 337):
A complaint against selling of benefices.

2 *R.* II, no. 23 (*Rot. Parl.*, III, 36):
The Lords reply to the Commons that it has been good custom for a small number from each House to meet together to discuss business, "sanz murmur, crye, et noise".

4 *R.* II, no. 15 (*Rot. Parl.*, III, 90):
The opening of parliament; grant of a subsidy requiring every person above fifteen years of age to pay three groats [1*s.*]. See H. of C., 5 August, n. 70.

6 *R.* II, no. 16 (*Rot. Parl.*, III, 147):
Petition to the King from the Commons praying that "without favor or singular affection" he employ only persons of great loyalty and ability to hold offices of state, and the names of such officials be shown to the parliament, and that they not be dismissed without reasonable cause.

11 *R.* II, Articles 1–25 (*Rot. Parl.*, III, 230–233):
Proceedings in parliament against Michael de la Pole, Earl of Suffolk, *et al.*, for High Treason. The case is printed in Howell, *S.T.*, I, 89–124.

1 *H.* IV, nos. 10–52 (*Rot. Parl.*, III, 416–422):
The renunciation and deposition of Richard II. For the articles of accusation against him, see Howell, *S.T.*, I, 135–162.

2 *H.* IV, no. 11 (*Rot. Parl.*, III, 456):
[Petition] to the King from the Commons concerning his hearing of matters while they are being debated and before they come to resolution.

Response: " . . . that he wishes to hear no such person, nor to give him credence before such matters be shown to the King by advice and consent of all the Commons, according to the purport of their said petition". Hatsell, *Precedents*, II, 355n.

5 *H*. IV, no. 33 (*Rot. Parl.*, III, 528–529):
Declaration of the wishes of the King read in parliament by the Archbishop of Canterbury. He is to have his household well governed, and to conform to all that is pleasing to God and agreeable and beneficial to the realm.

9 *H*. IV, no. 26 (*Rot. Parl.*, III, 612):
Grant of a subsidy of one entire tenth and fifteenth and one half tenth and fifteenth, with the accustomed subsidy for staple and other merchandises.

1 *H*. V, no. 8 (*Rot. Parl.*, IV, 4):
Request made by the Speaker on behalf of the Commons to Henry V for good government, as during the reign of his father, Henry IV.

1 *H*. V, no. 9 (*Rot. Parl.*, IV, 4):
Articles exhibited to the King by the Speaker touching the establishment of good government, provisions for resistance against enemies, etc.

1 *H*. V, no. 17 (*Rot. Parl.*, IV, 6):
Subsidy grant. See above, H. of C., 5 July, n. 11.

1 *H*. V, no. 26 (*Rot. Parl.*, IV, 9–10):
Petition to the King from the Commons regarding the payment of wages of knights and burgesses who were returned to sit in the parliament which was dissolved because of the death of H. IV on 20 March 1413. See above, H. of C., 23 June, n. 7.

2 *H*. V, no. 7 (*Rot. Parl.*, IV, 16):
Subsidy grant. See above, H. of C., 5 July, n. 11.

11 and 12 *H*. VI, no. 24 (*Rot. Parl.*, IV, 432–438):
Petition to the King from Ralph Cromwell, Lord Treasurer of England, containing articles thought by Cromwell to be "reasonable and profitable" to the King and kingdom, with a schedule of balances in the Exchequer.

11 and 12 *H*. VI, no. 25 (*Rot. Parl.*, IV, 438–439):
Petition to the King from Ralph Cromwell, Lord Treasurer of England, requesting the King "to assign and appoint a time to attend and see your books of your revenues . . . and your debts [i.e., the schedule included in no. 24, above] . . . and thereupon to appoint how . . . your yearly charges should be borne and your debts paid".

28 *H*. VI, nos. 19–46 (*Rot. Parl.*, V, 177–183):
Articles of treason and pronouncement of banishment against William de la Pole, Duke of Suffolk. The case is printed in Howell, *S.T.*, I, 271–276; cf. also Hatsell, *Precedents*, IV, 66–69.

28 *H*. VI, no. 53 (*Rot. Parl.*, V, 183–199):
Act of resumption.

31 and 32 *H*. VI, nos. 26–29 (*Rot. Parl.*, V, 239–240):

Case of Thomas Thorpe, an M.P. who stole goods from the Duke of York. Requested by the Commons to deliberate on the case, the justices determined that: " . . . if any person that is a member of this high court of parliament be arrested in such cases as be not for treason, or felony, or surety of the peace, or for a condemnation had before the parliament, it is used that all such persons should be released of such arrests and make an attorney so that they may have their freedom and liberty freely to attend upon the parliament". Hatsell, *Precedents*, I, 28–32.

17 *E*. IV, no. 35 (*Rot. Parl.*, VI, 191–192):
Petition to the King from the Commons concerning the privilege of John Atwyll. The Commons in this case claimed the privilege of not being impleaded in any personal action during the time of privilege. Hatsell, *Precedents*, I, 48–51.

1 *H*. VII, no. 31 (*Rot. Parl.*, VI, 299–303):
Schedule of payments to be made annually by the Lord Treasurer to the Treasurer of the King's Household.

3 *H*. VII, no. 16 (*Rot. Parl.*, VI, 400–401):
Subsidy grant. See above, H. of C., 5 August, n. 70.

11 *H*. VII, no. 37 (*Rot. Parl.*, VI, 497–502):
Revised schedule of payments [see *Rot. Parl.*, 1 *H*. VII, no. 31, above] to be made to the Treasurer of the King's Household.

Patent Rolls

44 *H*. III, *m.* 11, *Cal. Pat. Rolls*, H. III, 1258–1266, p. 68:
Declaration by the King to the sailors and mariners of England forbidding them to bring the King's brothers from Poitou, or any others with horses and arms, into the realm without license and the King's special mandate.

34 *Eliz*. I, pt. 15, MS. Cal. Pat. Rolls, f. 32v:
Patent to Ralph Brooke as York Herald.

2 *Jac*. I, pt. 7, MS. Cal. Pat. Rolls, f. 117:
Indenture between the crown and John Evelyn, *et al.*, concerning saltpeter.

22 *Jac*. I, pt. 1, MS. Cal. Pat. Rolls, f. 147:
Special commission to Viscount Grandison, George Lord Carew, *et al.*, to advise on such ways and means as may further advance the Low Countries, secure Ireland, and put the navy in readiness and safety.

Statutes

9 *H*. III, Magna Carta

[Uncertain date,] *Capitula Itineris* (the *Articles of the Eyre*).
Art. 4. Concerning "those who have taken revenge because that any have complained in the King's court upon the aforesaid grievances" (*S.R.*, I, 237).

10 *E.* III, st. 1.

Confirmation of former statutes; pardons not to be granted contrary to the statute of 2 *E.* III, c. 2.

25 *E.* III, st. 5.

c. 4. None shall be taken upon suggestion without lawful presentment.

27 *E.* III, st. 1.

c. 4. Cloth subsidy granted to the King.

36 *E.* III, st. 1.

c. 10. "Item, for maintenance of the said articles and statutes, and redress of divers mischiefs and grievances which daily happen, a parliament shall be holden every year, as another time [4 *E.* III, c. 14] was ordained by statute".

c. 11. Concerning subsidy and customs.

50 *E.* III, Of the pardons and graces granted by the King to the commonalty of his realm of England.

c. 3. The King's pardon to the people in the year of his jubilee; Bishop Wykeham excepted.

1 *R.* II.

c. 12. The warden of the Fleet shall not let at large prisoners in execution.

8 *R.* II.

c. 5. Pleas at common law shall not be discussed before the Constable and Marshal.

13 R. II.

c. 2. Concerning the jurisdiction of the Constable and Marshal.

c. 3. Concerning the limits of the Steward and Marshal's jurisdiction.

21 *R.* II.

c. 12. Opinions of certain judges in 11 *R.* II concerning the statute and commission 10 *R.* II.

2 *H.* IV.

c. 23. Fees of the Marshal, etc.; forfeiture of office for taking more than lawful fees.

4 *H.* IV.

c. 4. No lands, etc., to be granted by the King except to such as deserve them.

c. 17. Concerning the four orders of friars resident in England.

8 *H.* VI.

c. 7. Concerning the elections of knights of the shires, " . . And every sheriff of the realm of England shall have power by the said authority to examine upon the Evangelists every such chooser, how much he may expend by the year. And if any sheriff return knights to come to the parliament contrary to the said ordinance, the justices of Assizes . . . shall have power by the authority aforesaid thereof to inquire . . . and that the knights for the

parliament returned contrary to the said ordinance shall lose their wages".

23 *H.* VI.

c. 14. Concerning the election of knights of the shire, "And that every sheriff that makes not due election of knights to come to the parliament in convenient time, that is to say, every sheriff in his full county between the hour of eight and the hour of eleven before noon . . . shall forfeit to the King an hundred pounds . . . ".

31 *H.* VI.

c. 7. Concerning fees of those officers of the King excepted from the act of resumption, 28 *H.* VI [*Rot. Parl.*, 28 *H.* VI, no. 53].

12 *E.* IV.

c. 8. Concerning patents for searching or surveying of victuals.

1 *R.* III.

c. 15. Annulling of all letters patent made to Elizabeth, late wife of Sir John Grey.

11 *H.* VII.

c. 29. Resumption of crown lands granted by E. III and R. II to Edmund Langley, Duke of York.

c. 31. Resumption of grants made out of the manor of Woodstock.

c. 64. Conviction and attainder of William Stanley, *et al.*, and forfeiture of land seised, in the case of Perkin Warbeck.

19 *H.* VII.

c. 10, pt. 3. Grants of sinecure offices declared void.

6 *H.* VIII.

c. 25. Act of resumption.

21 *H.* VIII.

c. 13. An act that no spiritual persons shall take to farm of the King or any other person any lands or tenements for time of life, lives, years, or at will, etc. And for pluralities of benefices, and for residence.

c. 13, pt. 11. Chaplains may hold a plurality of livings.

26 *H.* VIII.

c. 1. An act concerning the King's Highness to be supreme head of the Church of England and to have authority to reform and redress all errors, heresies, and abuses in the same.

31 *H.* VIII.

c. 13. An act for dissolution of abbeys.

32 *H.* VIII.

c. 27. Act of resumption for lands in Calais, Berwick, and Wales.

34 and 35 *H.* VIII.

c. 21. An act for the confirmation of letters patent notwithstanding misnaming of anything contained in the same.

c. 21, pt. 4. Grants of certain offices with annual fees, declared to be determined if the duty ceases.

5 and 6 *E.* VI.

c. 14. An act against regraters, forestallers, and engrossers.

1 *Eliz.* I.

c. 2. An act for the uniformity of common prayer and divine service in the Church, and the administration of the sacraments.

c. 2, pt. 3. ". . . And that from and after the said feast of the nativity of St. John Baptist next coming, all and every person and persons inhabiting within this realm or any other the Queen's Majesty's dominions shall diligently and faithfully . . . endeavor themselves to resort to their parish church or chapel accustomed . . . upon pain that every person so offending shall forfeit for every such offense twelve pence . . . ".

5 *Eliz.* I.

c. 1. An act for the assurance of the Queen's Majesty's royal power over all estates and subjects within her Highness's dominions.

23 *Eliz.* I.

c. 1. An act to retain the Queen's Majesty's subjects in their due obedience.

27 *Eliz.* I.

c. 1. An act for provision to be made for the surety of the Queen's Majesty's most royal person and the continuance of the realm in peace.

29 *Eliz.* I.

c. 8. An act for the grant of one entire subsidy and two fifteens and tenths granted by the temporalty.

31 *Eliz.* I.

c. 15. An act for the granting of four fifteens and tenths, and two entire subsidies to our most gracious sovereign lady the Queen's most excellent Majesty.

35 *Eliz.* I.

c. 2. An act against popish recusants.

c. 13. An act for the grant of three entire subsidies and six fifteens and tenths, granted by the temporalty.

39 *Eliz.* I.

c. 27. An act for the grant of three subsidies and six fifteens and tenths.

43 *Eliz.* I.

c. 18. An act for the grant of four entire subsidies and eight fifteens and tenths granted by the temporalty.

1 *Jac.* I.

c. 13. An act for new executions to be sued against any which shall hereafter be delivered out of execution by privilege of parliament, and for discharge of them out of whose custody such persons shall be delivered.

c. 33. An act of a subsidy of tonnage and poundage.

3 *Jac.* I.

c. 4. An act for the better discovering and repressing of popish recusants.

c. 4, pt. 18. ". . . That if any subject of this realm . . . shall not resort or repair every Sunday to some church chapel or some other usual place appointed for common prayer and there hear divine service . . . then it shall and may be lawful to and for any one justice of peace . . . to call the said party before him and if he or she shall not make a sufficient excuse . . . that it shall be lawful for the said justice of peace to give warrant to the church-warden of the said parish . . . to levy twelve pence for every such default . . . ".

c. 5, pt. 5. ". . . That it shall and may be lawful for the King's most excellent Majesty, his heirs and successors, or for three or more of his Majesty's most honorable Privy Council . . . to give license to every such recusant to go and travel out of the compass of the said five miles for such time as in the said license shall be contained for their travelling, attending, and returning and without any other cause to be expressed within the said license . . . ".

c. 5, pt. 7. ". . . That no popish recusant convict, nor any having a wife being a popish recusant convict . . . shall exercise any public office or charge in the commonwealth but shall be utterly disabled to exercise the same by himself or by his deputy . . . ".

7 *Jac.* I.

c. 23. An act for the grant of one entire subsidy and one fifteenth and tenth granted by the temporalty.

21 *Jac.* I.

c. 20. An act against swearing and cursing.

c. 33. An act for the payment of three subsidies and three fifteens by the temporalty.

c. 34. An act for confirmation of four subsidies granted by the clergy.

1 *Car.* I.

c. 1. An act for punishing of divers abuses committed on the Lord's day, called Sunday.

c. 2. An act to enable the King to make leases of lands parcel of his Highness's Duchy of Cornwall, or annexed to the same.

c. 3. An act for the ease in the obtaining of licenses of alienation, and in the pleading of alienations with license, or of pardons of alienations without license, in the Court of Exchequer and elsewhere.

c. 4. An act for the further restraint of tippling in inns, alehouses, and other victualling houses.

c. 5. An act for the confirmation of the subsidies granted by the clergy.

c. 6. An act for the grant of two entire subsidies granted by the temporalty.

c. 7. An act that this session of parliament shall not determine by his Majesty's royal assent to this and some other acts. " . . . And to take away all doubt, whether his Majesty's royal assent unto one or more acts of parliament will not be a determination of this present session, his Majesty is well pleased that it may be enacted:

" . . . That his Majesty at his good pleasure may before the adjournment of this parliament, either in person or by his commission or letters patents as to him shall seem good, give his royal assent unto such . . . and that notwithstanding such assent to any such bills, or to this present act, this present session of parliament shall not thereby determine; but the same to be adjourned as to his Majesty shall be found requisite for the general good and welfare of this kingdom.

"And that all bills and matters whatsoever, depending in the same parliament, not fully determined or enacted before such adjournment, shall remain and continue in the same state and plight as they are or shall be the day of the said adjournment. And that all statutes and acts of parliament which are to have continuance unto the end of this present session shall be of full force after the said adjournment until this present session be fully ended and determined. And if this session shall determine by dissolution of this present parliament, then all the acts

aforesaid shall be continued until the end of the first session of the next parliament. And all statutes and acts of parliament, which before the said adjournment shall pass by his Majesty's royal assent, shall be put in execution immediately after forty days after the said adjournment, notwithstanding that by the words or letter of the said acts, or any of them, they be limited to take effect or be put in execution from or at any time after the end of this present session".

Private Acts, 1 Car. I:

1. An act for the settling and confirmation of copyhold estates and customs of the tenants in base tenure of the manor of Cheltenham in the county of Gloucester and of the manor of Ashley, otherwise called Charlton Kings, in the said county being holden of the said manor of Cheltenham according to an agreement thereof made between the King's most excellent Majesty, being then Prince of Wales, Duke of Cornwall and of York, and Earl of Chester, lord of the said manor of Cheltenham and Giles Greville, Esquire, lord of the said manor of Ashley, and the said copyholders of the said several manors.

2. An act for the enabling and confirmation of an agreement or composition made between the King's Majesty's commissioners of revenue, his Majesty then being Prince of Wales, Duke of Cornwall, and Earl of Chester, on his Majesty's behalf, and his Majesty's copyholders of his Highness's manor of Macclesfield in the county of Chester, and of a decree made in the Court of Exchequer at Chester for the perfect creation and confirmation of certain lands and tenements parcel of the said manor to be copyhold and customary lands according to the tenor of the same decree.

SUPPLEMENTARY MATERIALS

A. BILLS

1. Tables of Bills

The following tables illustrate the progress of bills in each House during the 1625 session. The bills are listed chronologically according to their first readings. In the respective columns, dates (20/6 for 20 June) are given for the first mention or introduction of the bill in each House prior to its first reading, the first and second readings of the bill, its commitment, third reading, and vote by that House, the date on which it was sent to the other House and, in the Lords' table, the date on which it was dispatched or "expedited" to the King (concerning the term *expedited,* see above, H. of L., 30 June, n. 5), and the date on which it passed for law. In each case the date in the *Sent to* column is the date of the original dispatch and not that of subsequent transfers for voting on amendments. For information on other types of activity relating to the bills (committee meetings and reports, engrossment of bills, etc.), the reader will need to consult the General Index, below, or the Orders of Business (O.B.s). The asterisks (*) in the tables denote those bills which were considered by both Houses during the 1625 session and which therefore appear in both tables. A dagger (†) in the *Introduced* column indicates that the bill originated in and was sent from the other House. An *a* is entered in the *Voted* column for bills which were "assented to" or "passed" by the House in question, and an *o* is entered for that bill which was laid to rest, *obdormit.* The boldfaced words in the bill titles will aid the reader in locating a particular bill in these tables and in the O.B.s.

A list of bills introduced in the Upper House in 1625, with notes indicating the stage of progress each bill reached, is printed in the *L.J.,* III, 490. Those bills which passed both Houses in 1625 received the royal assent at the end of the London session before the adjournment to Oxford; a list of them is included in Petyt 538/8 (see above, H. of C., 11 July, pp. 371–372). No bills received the royal assent in August at the time of the dissolution of the Oxford session.

House of Lords

	Intro-duced	1 Read	2 Read	Com-mitted	3 Read	Voted	Sent to Commons	Expe-dited	Passed for law
*For confirming of the copyhold estates and customs of the tenants of the manor of **Cheltenham**		25/6	25/6	25/6	30/6	30/6a	30/6	9/7	11/7
*To enable the King to make leases of lands parcel of his Highness's **Duchy of Cornwall**		27/6	27/6	27/6	30/6	30/6a	30/6	9/7	11/7
*For punishing abuses committed on the **Lord's day**	†	27/6	30/6	30/6		1/7a		1/7	11/7
For the making of the **arms** of the kingdom more serviceable		27/6	30/6	30/6					
For the better maintenance of **hospitals and alms-houses**		27/6	6/7	6/7					
For the better preserving of his Majesty's **revenue**		27/6	2/8	2/8					
*For explanation of a **statute of 3 Jac.** for repressing popish recusants	†	1/7	10/8	10/8					
*Concerning the manors and lands of the late Richard, **Earl of Dorset**		5/7	5/7	5/7	8/7	8/7a	8/7		
*For ease in obtaining licenses of **alienation**	†	5/7	6/7	6/7	6/7	6/7a		6/7	11/7
*For the further restraint of **tippling** in inns, ale-houses, etc.	†	5/7	5/7	5/7	6/7	6/7a		6/7	11/7
*To confirm an agreement between the King and his tenants of **Macclesfield**	†	5/7	5/7	5/7	6/7	6/7a		6/7	11/7
*For the increase of **shipping** and for free liberty of **fishing**	†	7/7	11/8	11/8					
Against forging and **counterfeiting** of the **seals** of the King's courts		7/7	11/8	11/8					
*For the grant of two entire subsidies by the **temporalty**	†	8/7	8/7		8/7	8/7a			11/7
*That this **session** of parliament shall not determine by royal assent to one or more acts	†	8/7	8/7	8/7	8/7	8/7a	8/7	9/7	11/7
*Of a subsidy of **tonnage and poundage**	†	9/7							
*For confirmation of **subsidies** granted by the **clergy**		11/7	11/7		11/7	11/7a	11/7		11/7

House of Commons

	Introduced	1 Read	2 Read	Committed	3 Read	Voted	Sent to Lords
Against depopulation and **decay of farms**		20/6	1/8	1/8			
*For punishing abuses committed on the **Lord's day**		21/6	22/6	22/6	24/6	24/6a	27/6
*To confirm an agreement between the King and his tenants of **Macclesfield**		21/6	23/6	23/6	28/6	28/6a	28/6
*For explanation of a **statute of 3 Jac.** for repressing popish recusants		23/6	23/6	23/6	28/6	28/6a	28/6
For the quiet of **ecclesiastical persons**		23/6	24/6	24/6	9/8	9/8a	
*For the further restraint of **tippling** in inns, alehouses, etc.		23/6	24/6	24/6	1/7	1/7a	1/7
For mitigation of the sentence of the greater **excommunication**		23/6	27/6	27/6			
For reversing erroneous sentences, etc., in **courts of equity**	22/6	23/6					
Concerning **petty larceny** [see new bill, below, 9/7]		23/6	25/6	25/6			
*For ease in obtaining licenses of **alienation**		23/6	25/6	25/6	1/7	1/7a	1/7
To abolish all **trials by battel**		23/6					
For restraint of assignment of **debts**		23/6	23/6	23/6			
Against **secret offices** and inquisitions	23/6	24/6	24/6	24/6			
*For the increase of **shipping** and for free liberty of **fishing**	23/6	24/6	27/6	27/6	1/7	1/7a	1/7
For the quiet of the subject against pretences of **concealments**		24/6	25/6	25/6			
For **subscription**		24/6	27/6	27/6			
For repressing **houses of bawdry**		24/6					
Concerning the granting of **administrations**	24/6	24/6					
To take away **benefit of clergy** in some cases		24/6	25/6	25/6			
For more speedy suffering of **common recoveries**		24/6					
For passing of **accounts of sheriffs**, etc.		25/6	9/7	9/7			
Against **exportation of wool**	23/6	25/6	27/6	27/6			

(continued)

House of Commons (*continued*)

	Introduced	1 Read	2 Read	Committed	3 Read	Voted	Sent to Lords
Touching **benefices appropriate**		25/6					
For avoiding delay in **writs of partition**		25/6	27/6	27/6			
Against **scandalous ministers**		25/6					
For ease of **freeholders** in the county of **York**		25/6					
For **Erith and Plumstead**		27/6	28/6	28/6			
For the free and quiet **elections** of knights and burgesses		27/6					
To prevent the granting of writs of *habeas corpus*		27/6	27/6	27/6	9/8	9/8*a*	
For the better execution of the office of **clerk of the market**	25/6	27/6					
For restraint of the transportation of **iron ordnance**		28/6					
For the breeding and bringing up of **recusants' children**		28/6					
Concerning the **privileges** of the Commons House of parliament		28/6					
For abbreviation and limitation of **Michaelmas term**	23/6	28/6					
Against the procuring of **judicial places** for money		28/6	29/6	29/6			
To minister an oath to make **true accounts** of taxes, etc.		28/6	6/8	6/8			
Against **simony** and corruption in the elections of colleges	23/6	28/6	[6/7?]	[6/7?]			
For planting and increasing of **timber and wood**		29/6	9/7	9/7			
For the maintenance of **justice and right**		29/6					
To relieve **creditors** and to reform the abuses of **sheriffs**		29/6					
*For confirming of the copyhold estates and customs of the tenants of the manor of **Cheltenham**	†30/6	1/7	1/7		4/7	4/7*a*	9/7

House of Commons (*continued*)

	Introduced	1 Read	2 Read	Committed	3 Read	Voted	Sent to Lords
*To enable the King to make leases of lands parcel of his Highness's **Duchy of Cornwall**	†30/6	1/7	4/7	4/7	7/7	7/7a	9/7
*For the grant of two entire **subsidies** by the temporalty		4/7	5/7	5/7	8/7	8/7a	8/7
*Of a subsidy of **tonnage and poundage**		5/7	5/7	5/7	8/7	8/7a	9/7
*That this **session** of parliament shall not determine by royal assent to one or more acts		5/7	5/7	5/7	6/7	7/7a	9/7
For **continuance** of divers **statutes**		6/7	6/7	6/7	7/7	7/7o	
*Concerning the manors and lands of the late Richard, **Earl of Dorset**	†	8/7	8/7	8/7	9/8	9/8a	
To repeal so much of the statute 21 H. VIII, c. 13, as does restrain **spiritual persons** to take farms		9/7	11/7	11/7			
Concerning **petty larceny** [new]		9/7	6/8	6/8			
For confirmation of **subsidies** granted by the **clergy**	†	11/7				11/7a	
Mr. Morgan's bill for voiding one decree in Chancery and confirmation of another		9/8					
For **naturalization** of Sir Daniel **Deligne**		10/8	[11/8?]	[11/8?]			
For **naturalization** of Samuel **Bave**		10/8	[11/8?]	[11/8?]			

2. Texts of Draft Bills and Letter Concerning the Bill for the Clerk of the Market

[H.L.R.O., Main Papers, H.L., 24 June 1625]

Draft of a bill for the repressing of houses of bawdry and common uncleanness.[1]

An act for the repressing of houses of bawdry and common uncleanness.

Forasmuch as we find by God's word not only in general that a land is defiled by sin and so God provoked to plague and punish it, but more specially and particularly that in one day more than 20,000 of the Israelites were swept away by the plague and pestilence for the sin of fornication and uncleanness, which plague was stayed when punishment was inflicted upon the transgressors. And for that it is too well known that there be divers houses and places of common bawdry and uncleanness in and about the City of London which is as the King's chamber, the place at or near to which is usually the assembly of the King, the head, and the 3 estates representing the whole body of the land. And for that the plague and pestilence has now lately there (as usually first it does) begun to kindle and to spread a mortal flame of wrath into divers parts of and about the City and other parts of the land. Therefore for the appeasing of God's wrath by some good endeavor to repress and redress the said occasion of God's punishment by pestilence, be it enacted by the King's Majesty, the Lords spiritual and temporal, and the Commons in this present parliament assembled, and by authority of the same: that if any person or persons shall, at any time after the end of this present session of parliament, keep, entertain, permit or admit any common bawdry in his, her, or their house or houses, edifices, or buildings or in any part thereof and be lawfully convict[ed] thereof by indictment or presentment at the sessions of the peace, or of the jail delivery of or for the county, city, town, or liberty within which such offense shall be committed shall, for the first offense, lose and forfeit, for and during the life and lives of such offender or offenders, the profits of the house, edifice, or building wherein such bawdry shall be kept or permitted. The said profits to be disposed and employed for and toward the maintenance of lame, aged, and diseased soldiers or other impotent and needy persons according to the discretion of the justices of peace or the more part of them before whom such conviction shall be. Or, in case the said offender or offenders shall have no state for 7 years or more of or in the house, room, or place abused to such uncleanness, or shall pay such a racked rent as that it shall not be worth 40s. by year over and above the same, that then every such offender shall for such offense forfeit to the uses aforesaid the sum of [blank]. And that also every offender upon the first conviction shall stand upon the pillory for the space of an hour and be with an hot iron marked and branded on the forehead with the letter B, unless for redemption from the said corporal shame and punishment, the party so to be punished shall pay to the uses aforesaid the sum of 100 marks; and that every such person being the second time convicted of the like offense shall for such second offense have his or her nose cut off and be imprisoned for the space of [blank]; and in case such person shall be at any time after 6 days after enlargement found voluntarily within [illegible] miles of the place where such offense was committed, that then every such person shall be a felon and suffer, lose, and forfeit as in case of felony.

1. This bill was given its first reading in the Commons on 24 June but progressed no further in 1625.

[H.L.R.O., Main Papers, H.L., 29 June 1625]

Last sheet of the draft of a bill for planting and increasing of timber and wood.[1]

By the owner thereof upon pain for every person to forfeit that shall not so fence and encoppice after the rates aforesaid, or shall not keep and continue the same as wood-ground in farms aforesaid, the sum of ten pounds for every acre not so encoppiced or continued, one third part thereof to our sovereign lord the King, his heirs and successors, one other part to the churchwarden of the parish where the same ground does lie, to the use of the poor there, the other part to him that will sue for the same by action of debt, bill, plaint, or information in any the courts of record at Westminster or at the general assizes and jail delivery of the said county wherein no essoin, protection, or wager of law shall be allowed. And be it further enacted that [*illegible*] such enclosing and encoppicing as aforesaid and after the end of the said three years wherein the same be used and kept in tillage as aforesaid the said 10 acres or any part thereof shall be employed to arable meadow or pasture and not kept and continued in a coppice [*illegible*] such person and persons, their heirs and assigns as [*3 words illegible*] in the same shall and may have use and enjoy their common therein as formerly they had or might have done any thing before in these presents to the contrary in anywise notwithstanding.

1. The first sheet(s) of this draft bill is not extant. The bill was given a first reading in the Commons on 29 June and was read a second time and committed on 9 July but was never reported back to the House.

[University of Nottingham MS. CL/C/360]

Letter from six gentlemen of Nottingham to Anonymous, concerning the bill for the clerk of the market, 1 August 1625, Nottingham.[1]

Noble Sir,

It being come to the knowledge of many of us, that there is at this time a bill depending in the Lower House of parliament to limit the clerk of the market, we (for ourselves and the whole country) have thought it a seasonable time to entreat your help for redress of a general enormity, long complained on but not yet reformed, which is the unreasonable and variable measures used in market towns (as the main matter of that office), which, experience of these countries have taught us to know, cannot well be remedied by cutting the measures, never so truly, without some further law than yet is made in that behalf. For reformation whereof, we have made bold to send you herewith a model for such a purpose, not with opinion to tie the wisdom of that House to any ignorant form of ours, but only to express what we desire, as conceiving that it may be fitly drawn into that bill, without the charge of a special bill, which otherwise the country would endeavor rather than endure so grievous a mischief. You cannot do a work that will more bind the country to honor you, and us to remain,

Your thankful friends,
Geo. Parkyns
Tho. Hutchinson
Ro. Sutton
Jo. [*Illegible*]
Gervas [*Illegible*]
Willmoseley

Nottingham, 1°   August 1625

1. Permission to print this letter has been granted by Lt. Col. P. T. Clifton. For notice of this or a similar letter to the knights of the shire (Henry Stanhope and Sir Gervase Clifton) from the Nottingham J.P.s, dated 7 August 1625, see H.M.C., *Various Collections*, VII, 395.

B. Materials Relating to Royal Actions

1. Prorogations and Crown Preparations for Parliament

(a) The first parliament of Charles I had been summoned to meet on 17 May 1625 but was thrice postponed, from 17 May to 31 May, again to 13 June, and then to 18 June. Private letters concerning the prorogations as well as the journal accounts of them are printed below. For other letters concerning the preparations for the parliament, see section D, 1, below, p. 669, and above, H. of L., 18 June, n. 1.

(b) 3 June 1625
Lord Keeper Williams to Secretary
Conway, S.P. 16/3:16.

May it please your Lordship,
 For fear his Majesty should have occasion to use it, I send your Lordship (at all adventures) a commission to prorogue the parliament for 4 days longer, as I have also signified in a letter to his most excellent Majesty. If there be no necessity to alter the day appointed, it may be cast away as a dead scroll, and never trouble your Lordship with the carriage. I do very much desire, until such time as I shall have undeserved it, to be esteemed, as I sincerely am,
 Your Lordship's poor
 friend and humble servant
 Jo. Lincoln C.S.
[*Postscript*] I beseech your Lordship to do me the favor as to send this enclosed to Sir George Goring.

(c) 3 June 1625
Lord Keeper Williams to Secretary
Conway, S.P. 16/3:17.

My Very Good Lord,
 I do not doubt but your Lordship has received by this time a blank for the proroguing of the parliament for some 4 days.

But because you do so direct it and that I could not guess at his Majesty's occasions I do send your Lordship, according to your directions, another prorogation with a blank which you are to fill up only with that day upon the which his Majesty shall resolve to have the parliament to hold, and the name of the place where it is dated, as also the name of the day of the month, which you may assign as you please.
 You will be pleased to pardon the clerk for his handwriting, it being in haste and this the first instrument he ever wrote in this kind. But I am sure it is right and will effect the business and the writer will keep counsel. And although the other might peradventure serve his Majesty's intendments, yet I beseech your Lordship to send me this signed because I find that a young clerk drew up the other and I am not certain (as I am of this) whether he does strictly observe all his recitals.
 I cease to be further troublesome and, with my love and true respects to your Lordship, do remain,
 Your Lordship's poor
 friend and humble servant,
 Jo. Lincoln C.S
Westminster Coll.
3 June 1625

(d) 9 June 1625
Lord Keeper Williams to Secretary
Conway, S.P. 16/3:44.

My Very Good Lord,
 Because I hear since some more certainty of the Queen's coming onward I shall desire your Lordship two days hence to be pleased to send me his Majesty's final resolution, how I shall use my power by that commission to put off the parliament, which otherwise I will do according to your last direction.
 The sickness in London does increase into a remarkable number and is very dangerously scattered, and somewhat sensibly apprehended now by the Lords and other

strangers that, by occasion of the parliament, are now about the City. But Westminster and all this side the Old Bailey (God be praised) is yet free from infection or suspicion. I thought it not amiss to give your Lordship this account, that his Majesty may betimes take it to due consideration.

May your Lordship also be pleased (if it be not yet resolved) to move his Majesty whether he will open the parliament with his crown on (being before the coronation, which is a very ancient, sacred, and weighty ceremony), or rather without it. And if so, whether in his robes, or rather (if he shall not use his crown) in his ordinary apparel, and his sword by his side. And in that case, whether the Lords shall receive his Majesty in their robes, and where, which his Majesty may signify to the Lord Chamberlain or the Earl Marshal.

I beseech your Lordship, if my Lord Duke be returned, to remember my most humble respects unto his Grace and to tell my Lord that I and others were deceived in my Lady Purbeck's defense in the High Commission, for it proves to be but modest and reserved, without any aspersion upon other parties.

I cease to be further troublesome and, recommending your Lordship to God's protection, am,

> Your Lordship's faithful
> friend and servant,
> Jo. Lincoln C.S.

Westminster Coll. this
9 of June 1625
[*Endorsed*] To the Right Honorable my very good Lord, the Lord Conway, Principal Secretary to his most excellent Majesty, at court.

(e) 13 June 1625
Lord Keeper Williams to Secretary
Conway, S.P. 16/3:62.

My Very Good Lord,

I have received your Lordship's of the 11th of this instant and according to those directions I will use only the last commission of adjournment, which puts off the parliament to Saturday next. I do also send your Lordship by this bearer not only a commission (with a blank for the day) for a further prorogation, if need should be, but withal (because with all submission to better judgments and his Majesty's resolution, I hold any further prorogation to be dangerous by reason of the sickness, and disserviceable to his Majesty because of the apprehensions made thereupon) a commission for his Majesty to authorize any 3 Lords in his absence to open the parliament, so [*illegible*] forth as to give them leave to choose their Speaker and present him, etc., that they might be more ready when his Majesty shall come in person to make his propositions unto them. Of this there are many precedents in Queen Elizabeth's time. The last of all was granted to the Lord Keeper, the Lord Archbishop of Canterbury, and the Earl of Derby. I hear her Majesty (God be pleased) is landed, so as I shall not need to doubt of our master's being here in person upon Saturday next. Yet will I not alter my resolution to send you those commissions.

Now, my very good Lord, let me once more desire your Lordship to put his Majesty in mind of the increase of the sickness and especially the most dangerous scattering thereof into all parts of the City and now into many of the suburbs. A broker has brought it (since my last unto your Lordship) hither unto us, into Westminster. The man is dead himself of the plague, as searchers say, 3 days since, but there being 6 more in his family not one of them yet has sickened. I must not also conceal from you, that in the very way and passage of his Majesty to the House of Parliament a woman was carried in a coach about midnight, very sick, into one Mansfield's house in a very suspicious manner. But the next day we returned [to] the woman (who yet lives) and have shut up the house, although Mansfield and all his family continue well and sound.

Upon all this I could have wished his Majesty had been pleased to have come no nearer this city than Greenwich, with his court. And do humbly entreat my Lord Duke (by your Lordship) to persuade his Majesty to make all his entrances into the City and the parliament in the most private manner that can be devised and to avoid, with all possible diligence, all concourse of people. And (if I might presume to descend to particulars), by water rather than by land in both his entrances. And once more I beseech your Lordship to put his Majesty in mind of thinking seriously of putting off the term and removing the parliament. For if God, for our sins, should have any secret intention to scourge us in this kind (which I hope in His mercy and goodness He will mitigate and alter), your Lordship knows best how fearful it is that the plague should find the whole kingdom convened and united in one city.

It is an extraordinary comfort to me to hear from your Lordship that his Majesty is pleased to take notice of any service of mine, who neither have nor desire any other riches or contentment in this world than to remain in his Majesty's good opinion.

I am to blame to trouble your Lordship in these times of entertainment with so long a letter. I therefore abruptly take my leave and am,

> Your Lordship's faithful,
> poor friend and servant,
> Jo. Lincoln C.S.

Westminster Coll. this
13 of June 1625
[*Postscript*] The justices of the peace about Ipswich have written letters to the Council of some poor fellows apprehended and imprisoned there for reporting the King, our master, to be dead, who God long bless and preserve. I opened them and perused the examinations; in the absence of the rest of the lords, have presumed to direct the principal reporter to be kept in prison until the assizes and left to the judges. The rest, upon bail of their good behavior, to be set at liberty, being poor people, and (it seems) all of them a little touched in their malt. But all deny the fact. If I have been too remiss, upon your Lordship's direction I will reform it.

> Your servant,
> J. L. C.S.

(f) 17, 31 May, 13 June

Journal accounts of the prorogations at the beginning of the 1625 session.

TUESDAY, 17 MAY 1625

I. JOURNAL OF THE HOUSE OF LORDS

[L.J. 432]

[p. 3] *Die Martis decimo septimo die Maii anno regni serenissima domini nostri Caroli dei gra. Angliae, Francia et Hibernia regis fidei defensoris, etc., primo*
[*List of Lords Present; see A.T.*]

Memorandum: That whereas the King's Majesty by his writs of summons bearing date at Westminster the second day of April last past appointed his parliament to begin this present day, being the seventeenth day of May in the first year of his Majesty's reign as by the same writs more plainly appears, his Majesty upon great and weighty considerations (by advice of his Privy Council) thought good to prorogue this present parliament unto the 31st day of this instant May.

Wherefore these Lords spiritual and temporal (whose names are above written), being assembled in the parliament presence and divers of the Commons being present, and prayers said, the Lord Keeper delivered unto the Clerk his Majesty's writ patent signed with his royal hand and sealed with the Great Seal of England bearing date the sixteenth of May and commanded the same to be read, the tenor whereof follows *in haec verba, vizt.*:

[*For the commission for the prorogation, see L.J., III, 432.*]

II. MINUTE BOOK, H.L.R.O., M.M., 1625

[f. 3] *Die Martis 17 die Maii 1625*
[*List of Lords Present; see A.T.*]

Prayers, etc. The Lord Keeper delivered the Clerk a writ under the broad seal to be read for the proroguing of the parliament to the *31° die* of *Maii*, which was read with a loud [voice] accordingly and by the virtue thereof it was prorogued to the said 31th.

L. Keeper. That the parliament is prorogued to the 31th of this instant.

TUESDAY, 31 MAY 1625

I. JOURNAL OF THE HOUSE OF LORDS

[**L.J. 433**]
[p. 5] *Die Martis tricesimo primo die Maii anno primo regis Caroli annoque domini 1625.*
[*List of Lords Present; see A.T.*]

Memorandum: That this day divers Lords spiritual and temporal (whose names are above written) being assembled in the parliament presence and divers other of the Commons being present and prayers said, the right honorable and reverend father in God, John, Lord Bishop of Lincoln, Lord Keeper of the Great Seal of England, delivered unto the Clerk of the Parliament his Majesty's writ patent signed with his royal hand and sealed with the Great Seal of England bearing date the one and thirtieth day of May *anno primo Caroli regis* and commanded the same to be read, the tenor of which writ follows, *vizt.:*

[*For the commission for the prorogation, see L.J., III, 433.*]

II. MINUTE BOOK, H.L.R.O., M.M., 1625

[f. 3v] *Die Martis, viz., 31° die Maii 1625.*
[*List of Lords Present; see A.T.*]

The Lord Keeper delivered the writ for the proroguing of the parliament to the 13

of June, which writ was read by the Clerk with a loud voice, part of the House of Commons being then present below the bar.

L. Keeper. My Lords, whereas his Majesty has formerly prorogued the parliament to this present day, now his Majesty for some urgent occasions, and that many of the members are now absent, has awarded this/

MONDAY, 13 JUNE 1625

I. JOURNAL OF THE HOUSE OF LORDS

[**L.J. 434**]
[p. 7] *Die Lunae decimo tertio die Junii anno primo regis Caroli anno domini 1625*
[*List of Lords Present; see A.T.*]

Memorandum: That on the thirteenth day of June, *anno primo regis Caroli*, divers Lords spiritual and temporal (whose names are above mentioned), being assembled in the parliament presence and divers of the Commons present and prayers said, the right honorable the Lord Keeper of the Great Seal of England delivered unto the Clerk his Majesty's writ patent signed with his royal hand and sealed with the Great Seal of England bearing date at Canterbury the ninth day of this instant June and commanded the same to be read, which follows *in haec verba, vizt.:*

[*For the commission for the prorogation, see L.J., III, 434.*]

II. MINUTE BOOK, H.L.R.O., M.M., 1625

[f. 4] *Die Lunae 13 die Junii 1625.*
[*List of Lords Present; see A.T.*]

Prayers.

The Lord Keeper delivered the writ for the proroguing of the parliament from this present of 13th of June to the 18th of the same month, which writ was read by the Clerk, part of the House of Commons being present.

Lord Keeper. Whereas by several writs the parliament has been put off to this present 13th of June for many urgent causes, but especially for the stay for the arrival of the Queen, which is now come and by virtue of this writ the parliament is put off from this instant to the 18th of this month.

The commission was written by the Lord Keeper with a blank for the day which was inserted by the King, viz., *octodecimum diem,* and the word *Cantuariam* was also put in by his Majesty.

Prorogued to the *18°* June.

C. Additional Materials Concerning Parliament 1625

1. Proceedings Relating to Both Houses

(a) 18 June
The prayer said at the first session of parliament, Jervoise 0.7, Hampshire Record Office.[1]

At the first session of parliament, the prayer.

O God most great and glorious which dwells in the heavens over all yet humbles thyself to behold the things that are done beneath upon the earth, and art not as one that is an idle spectator but in deed and truth the principal actor, working what it pleases thee in the armies of heaven and in the inhabitants of the earth, without error in thy judgments, without let to thy will, without cross to thy purpose. We thy people and sheep of thy pasture, thy work by creation, thy children by adoption, thy servants by covenant and saints by calling, being by thy providence assembled together to the performance of no mean service in thy presence but such as whereupon the honor of thy name, the beauty of thy church amongst us, the glory of our King, the wealth of our state, and the particular good of every private person inhabiting these late united kingdoms does depend, knowing that we can neither consider without thee which art God of wisdom nor agree without thee which art God of peace, that we can neither foresee without thee which art God of providence, nor conclude without thee which art God of counsel, that we can neither attempt nor effect anything without thee by whom all enterprises are brought to pass, do here with reverence and fear in the beginning of our consultations first look up unto thee from whom wisdom, counsel, peace, order, and happy success do come, praying thee to look down from heaven upon us with the eye of thy mercy and power and inspiration to draw near unto us with the presence of thy grace, favor, and holy direction to prepare us all with wisdom, counsel and understanding, and to be president and director of all our conferences, that those things may be propounded, conceived, allowed, and confirmed that may best please thee and most directly and soundly uphold the honor of thy name, the sincerity of thy worship, the safety of our King and peace of thy people even for thy son our Lord's sake.

And that we may not ourselves be any let to the obtaining of these our desires, either by means of any sin formerly committed by us or of any corruption yet remaining in us (for sin resting upon us calls for a curse, and corruption remaining in us cannot compass so great blessings), we humbly pray thee in his name that bore our sins in his body upon the cross to forgive our sins, in number infinite, in weight intolerable, in merit fearful, able to make an eternal separation between thee and us excluding us from all happiness and leaving us to eternal misery. Forgive then them unto us in thy mercy, Christ having suffered for them to satisfy thy justice and stand reconciled unto us in an everlasting covenant of peace, as if we had never sinned against thee, and deal graciously with us in this our own assembly as if we had never deserved to be worse dealt withal.

And with the grievousness of sin by us formerly committed heal, we pray thee, the corruptions yet remaining in us. And because our hearts by nature (since nature's corruption in the fall of our first parents) are not fit for good cogitations, create a new heart and renew a right spirit in us. Remove from us all vainglorious humor of commending our own wits, all covetous humor of advancing our private profit, all envious humor of disgracing other men's gifts, all malicious humor of hurting any man's person, and finally all froward humor of opposing ourselves against just, needful, and godly things by whomsoever propounded. Furnish us with knowledge that we may understand; with wisdom, that we may discern; and with [*illegible*] that we may prefer and set forward things worthy of our assent and furtherance. And because all good things are not of equal goodness, nor all needful things of equal necessity, let our care and zeal be wisely and equally proportioned to the degrees of things in goodness and necessity different. And therefore first make us careful of the glory of thy name, which is the high end of all thy counsels and words and ought to be the last end but first respected of all our purposes and doings. And because thy glory is best provided for where thou art rightly worshipped, and thou art rightly worshipped where the rules of holy religion are observed, and the rules of holy religion are only found in thy word, let our care be in this our great assembly to provide for the continuance of thy word and religious practice of thy worship by the ministry and means that Jesus Christ has planted in His Church.

Next after religion let the good of the kingdom move our care and seal [*sic*], which consists[2] in the safety and honor of the King and the enacting of good laws; let us be wisely careful and faithfully zealous for the person of our King whom thou, the King of kings, has in mercy set over us, religious as David and wise as Solomon, to judge our causes, to maintain our peace, and to continue and perfect that which was happily begun and set forward in the days of our late dread Sovereign now resting with thee.

And because no law can be good that is not agreeable to thy law that contains the fundamental equity of all laws, in making laws to govern the people by let us always have an eye to thy law, wisely and faithfully deriving from the moral equity thereof all possible laws applied to the curing of such evils as do arise among us, and to the continuing of peace and strengthening of every man's right without respect of persons. That neither unjust pity make us wrong the rich for the poor man's relief nor pitiless justice (which is rigor and not jus-

tice) make us wrong the poor for the rich man's pleasure. And what through thy mercy we shall here profitably enact, we pray thee that through the whole kingdom it may be truly executed that our great labors may not be disgraced with little fruit.

And take thy seat amongst us, thou which sits in the assemblies of princes and judges amongst gods. Send down thy spirit into our hearts as it was sent down upon the Apostles; give us wisdom and understanding as thou gave to Solomon; give us a tongue and utterance as the Lord Jesus promised to his Apostles, if not in such measure as those received, yet in such measure as whereby we may be fitted for the service whereunto thy providence has called us, and which thy glory, religion, the King's honor, and our country's safety requires of us.

This infusion of grace and healing of our corruptions that yet remain in us, we crave at thy hands together with forgiveness of all our former sins, that ourselves may not by any means be a hindrance to our desire for satisfying the kingdom's expectation in the holy and happy fruit of this our present assembly. Hear us we pray thee, O Father of mercy, in these our just requests, and answer us according to thy great goodness, for Jesus Christ's sake, to whom with thee and the holy cross, three persons and one God, be all praise, glory, and power from us and from all creatures now and forever. Amen.

1. In the collection of Jervoise MSS. there is an incomplete copy of the same prayer as that printed above, entitled "Prayer at the 2 session". Neither that manuscript nor the one printed here is dated, although it seems probable that the prayer was read in 1625. The reference to "our late dread Sovereign now resting" is certainly to James and not Elizabeth, who was generally referred to as the "late Queen of blessed memory". The mention of the first and second session also indicates the MS. belongs with the materials for the divided parliament of 1625. Concerning the form of parliamentary prayer, see *C.J.*, I, 150.

2. MS.: *consisting*.

(b) 18 June
The King's speech at the opening of
parliament, S.P. 16/3:88.[1]

My Lords spiritual and temporal and you
gentlemen of the House of Commons. I
may thank God that the business is now
come about at this day. I need not make any
long narration, nor use any eloquence, for I
am neither able to do it of myself, nor
stands it with my nature. It is a thing already happily begun by him that is with
God. I hope in God that you will go on as
frankly and freely as you advised him. It is
true that my father was wise (though he
might seem to be unwise) in that it was his
carefulness to see an end in no other manner than as might stand with his honor. It
pleased you to advise him to it. But after he
saw how he was abused in his confidence he
had in other states. And I need not go to
prove that, for the preparations that are
made are better able to speak it than I can do.

These preparations, both in Germany
and the preparations of the general fleet,
and the rest of the actions, which I have
only followed my father in, do sufficiently
prove the same.

My Lords, I hope you do remember that
you did help to employ me to advise my
father, so that now I cannot say that I come
hither a free man, for I am engaged before.
It is you that engaged me. It is true that I
came to the business willingly, because I am
a young man, and as a young man I came as
frankly and freely as you entreated me.

I know that you have been ever faithful
and loving to your King and so, by the grace
of God, I shall ever continue confident of it.
And shall always remember that if you will
help me at this time, at the beginning of this
action, I shall bear the same always in memory, else it will be a dishonor to me, and I
think it will be as much to you. I speak not
this out of any diffidence, but only to show
what a sense I have of my honor in it and of
yours.

I hope you will consider likewise of the
time, which I would not willingly hasten but
that there are a great number of reasons
which my Lords all know, I need not tell
them. Only I must entreat you that you consider of the shortness of time, and that I
must venture your lives if I continue you
here long, which I would be loath to do, and
you must venture the business.

I hope you will take such grave and wise
counsel as will expedite the business, and
that you will do me and yourselves honor:
you honor in showing your loves to me, and
me honor, that I may perfect a work which
my father so happily began.

So my Lords, last of all, because some
malicious men may think that I shall not be
so true a keeper and maintainer of religion
as I profess, I hope I may truly say with Paul
that I was always bred up at Gamaliel's feet,
although I confess I shall never be so impudent as to take to myself the rest.

But, my Lords, this I say, that whosoever
has known me heretofore, and shall know
me hereafter, shall find that I shall be as
willing to maintain religion as ever my father was, and so I think I have said enough
in that.

Now because, my Lords, the fashion is, as
my predecessors have done, to have my
Lord Keeper speak something for me,
therefore I have commanded my Lord
Keeper to speak something, which is more
for formality than any great matter he has
to speak to you.

1. This copy of the King's speech was enclosed with
Thomas Locke's letter to Sir Dudley Carleton, 22
June 1625.

(c) 18 June
The King's speech at the opening of
parliament, Osborn fb 155, pp. 93–94.

My Lords spiritual and temporal, and the
Commons here assembled at this. The business about which you are now gathered together, I am not myself altogether able to
declare unto you; therefore I have appoint-

ed the Lord Keeper to declare the particulars.

I am only to put you in mind of a thing that was begun in my father's lifetime, in the which I hope you will go as fairly and as speedily as you did the last session; for instance, that my father was willing to take your advice, and herein you were pleased to advise him about those things that were for his honor; and himself, seeing that he was so abused in the confidence of other states, took your advice. I need not go about to prove that, for that preparation that he then made is better able to speak than I can do; as preparations by forces abroad in Germany, and here at home, in preparing the great fleet, to the which I have added.

My Lords and gentlemen, I hope you remember how you did employ the last session in that business, and now I cannot say that I come hither as a free man, for I was then engaged. Yet it is true that I did it not unwillingly, but as I was a young man, so I did it, and that freely. And I know that therein you were faithful, and so, having proved it, I shall always remain confident. I shall only remember you that, if you are slack in helping me, it will prove to be a dishonor both to you and me. I speak this not out of any diffidence of you, but out of a sense of my own honor and yours. I hope now that you will willingly hasten, for there has been a great number of delays—I need not declare them, because most of the Lords here present know them—and that you will take such grave counsel as will expedite the business and do you and me honor in perfecting that work which my father had begun with your advice.

Last of all, some may think that I may not be so true a maintainer and keeper of the religion I profess, the which I answer that I hope I may truly say with St. Paul that I was brought up at the feet of Gamaliel, though I shall not be so arrogant as to ascribe to myself the rest. But my Lords, that I may truly say that he that has known my former actions may be assured that I will as willingly maintain true religion as ever my father did. And for the rest, my Lord Keeper shall declare to you; and as I have declared you the substance, so I have commanded him to tell you the circumstances, rather for formality than for any other matter.

(d) 4 August
Sir John Coke's speech to both Houses, S.P. 16/5:14.[1]

Being commanded by his Majesty to lay open to this honorable House the present state of his affairs, it will be requisite first to show the condition they were in at that time when the last parliament was called; the former passages having been so clearly related by the Duke of Buckingham, assisted and warranted therein by the then Prince, our now most gracious Sovereign, that it will not be necessary to look further back. Only I must call into your memories what succeeded thereupon, and how his late Majesty, of glorious memory, at the instant suit of both Houses and by the powerful cooperation of his Majesty that now is, and the Duke, gave his consent and resolution to break off the treaties then depending with Spain, both for the marriage of our Prince and for the Palatinate. And how it was then foreseen that of necessity thereupon there must a war follow, without which as we could neither recover the Palatinate nor vindicate the scorns and abuses offered to our King and country, so we should suffer the King of Spain to settle himself in his conquests, and under color of a Catholic cause advance himself to be a Catholic monarch. But withal, his late Majesty's unmatchable wisdom and sweet moderation well weighed the dangers of all sudden changes, the miseries and impieties that follow war, the minds of his subjects habituated to peace, and the great disadvantages his neighbor princes and states would cast upon him if he had overtly espoused his own quarrel and theirs. He therefore, upon mature deliberation, took a more cautious and safe course by suffering himself, for a time, to be pressed with new overtures of treaty for restoring the Palatinate, which they also cherished who favored the Spanish match, and with whom the ministers of that state could prevail. But in the meanwhile he omitted nothing which he found really expedient for the settling and fortifying of his affairs, and was contented by such degrees to be won to do things which he suffered the world to think impossible in his nature, that the wisest prince in Christendom, through so many difficulties, could not have made a fairer way. For consider how he stood. The King of Spain, by artifice or force, had now possessed the Palatinate and engaged most of the German electors and princes by making them parties to the translation both of that country and the electoral dignity. He had also seized by strong hand the estates of divers princes, and with a great army both assured his conquests and overran all those that might have any affection or memory of the liberty of Germany, leaving no marks of the union nor pretense to the freedom of conscience or of state. Nay, his party was now grown to that confidence that they projected the calling of a diet whereby, under a formal establishment of the peace of Germany, they would not only have excluded his Majesty's children from their dignities and estates but also have shut up all ways from himself to win parties or passage for recovery of their rights. And at that time the King of France was held in devotion rather to subdue and prosecute those of the religion [of] his subjects than to take arms to support the common cause. And for the Low Countries, they were then assaulted with divers strong armies and not well settled in their own government, being undermined by a party of Arminians who sided with the papists rather than with those of the reformed religion, and were fomented by such as were weary of the taxations for maintenance of the war. Through all these difficulties that wise King made his way. And considering that if the Low Countries should be won to the Spaniard there would hardly anything stand between him and his monarchy, he therefore began to conserve religion and liberty in those parts by lending them 6,000 men, paid for two years, with condition of repayment and of like assistance when there should be cause. His next endeavor was to make alliance with France, both for the importance of a meet and equal match for his son, and also by that way to get interest and draw that King (if it might be) to his party, as since is come to pass. His last and hardest act was to satisfy the world in his royal sense and resolution for vindicating his own honor, the honor of his people, and the honor and estates of his dear children; the expectation whereof had so long been asleep that it could not be revived without an army in the field. His Majesty had, indeed, solicited the princes of Germany and the Kings of Denmark and Sweden, but their answers had been cold, yet with hope that they would come to the party if his Majesty were in the field. But still his tenderness was such that he would in no sort be made the first author of taking arms. Only in case he were any way enterprised upon, he would then maintain his own honor, his people, and his kingdom both by defensive and offensive wars. And to that end he entered into the consideration of a competent army to march either directly into Germany to recover the Palatinate, or diversely into Flanders. And by computation made in parliament the charge of such an army required 700,000 *l.* a year, besides a fleet to be set forth, forts to be repaired, Ireland to be reinforced, the magazine to be furnished, and many other charges which could not be foreseen. His Majesty therefore, considering that the times would not afford means for so great undertakings, sought out an easier and more feasible way, which was by joining with the French King, the Venetians, and the Duke of Savoy to make the war at common charge. Wherein our contribution should not exceed 20,000 *l.* a month, and yet maintain an army of 30,000 foot and 5,000 horse which, under the conduct of Count Mansfeld, should attempt the recovery of the Palatinate and by diversion frustrate their enterprises of the Valtellina and Genoa. But then also did his Majesty set forward the preparations of his fleet. And when that was known abroad really to go on, and that 10,000 foot were levied in England and 5,000 horse in France, and that the exchanges of monies were made only from both countries into Holland, then the princes of Germany sent underhand to his Majesty and to the French King to require a meeting for the forming of a league and new union. And the Kings of Denmark and Sweden did not only harken more attentively to our proposition but contrived articles for bringing an army into the field, which his Majesty accepted and thereby was to contribute 16,000 *l.* towards the levying and arming of 6,000 foot and 2,000 horse and, for their payment, 30,000 *l.* a month. And thus you see, besides the fleet, two armies set on foot. What the latter will effect rests in hope. And although by God's hand the success of Count Mansfeld's troops has not altogether answered the expectation which was raised, yet there has been this fruit: that the diet of Germany is deterred and broken, that the princes of Germany look again to their interests, that the King of Denmark has put his army into the field, and that the French and the confederates pursue their engagement for recovery of the Valtellina and Genoa. Whereupon there also follows a declaration of war against the King of Spain in Milan and a peace between the King and his subjects of the religion in France, and a distraction of the enemy's forces and suspension of their enterprises in the Low Countries. And thus it appears how his Majesty has called this parliament, not for formalities concerning his coming to the crown but to acquaint his people with the

true state of his affairs, and to consult with them as well for the maintenance of his force by sea and land as for the making of good laws to establish the religion professed in our Church, and also to confirm and restore it abroad, and in the end to settle in his kingdoms good government and peace.

And though his Majesty has accepted, in most gracious part, the two subsidies which both Houses, with great freedom and unanimity have given, yet he finds it necessary to acquaint you further that the fleet is now at sea and ready to go out. Ten thousand men with their [*illegible*] captains are now at Plymouth, and their chief officers upon their dispatch. That for proceeding with effect not only his own honor is engaged, but the surety of the reformed churches abroad, the conservation of his neighbor states, and defense of his own do much rely. Great preparations and constant councils being already held in Spain both to trouble us in Ireland, to infest the coasts of England, to increase shipping and forts in Flanders, by which part of their army may be stolen over to assail us at [*illegible*]. So as howsoever the sea charges do already rise to [*blank*] and the land forces to [*blank*], besides 50,000 *l.* a month, yet of necessity this expense must be supported by your assistance with money or credit, according to your former engagement whereby he was drawn to cast himself into this condition. Wherein notwithstanding, to make the burden more supportable, his Majesty, in his princely wisdom, does resolve to cut off (as soon as may be) such charges as tend not solely to his designs. And though the navy without seconding from time to time cannot work that good effect which is desired, yet after this first fleet has laid the seas open, the experience of former times puts him in hope that the success may help to bear the charge, and that many adventurers will pursue honor and profit set before them, and that like ways may be found to raise the spirits of his people to their accustomed undertakings and to enrich the whole land at the enemy's cost if he will not condescend to that equal and Christian peace which is the end we aim at. And thus you see the ground of your calling together to this place, which was esteemed most healthful and safe. But as his Majesty believes that no king loves his people, his religion, and his laws more than he, so is he as confident in the good affection and duty of his subjects towards him. And therefore has so tender a care of your safety, as having thus made you acquainted with his necessities and with the grounds and reasons of them, he is pleased to refer the consideration of your safety and his own to yourselves, And if you shall think it fit to dissolve or adjourn and to make your meeting again at All-hallows tide, in a safe place, you may do it.

[*Endorsed*] 1625 August. Instructions for a message first appointed to be delivered in the nether House, but afterward, by commandment, delivered in the Upper House before the King, Lords, and Commons at Christ Church Hall at Oxford.

1. S.P. 16/5:14 is in Sir John Coke's handwriting.

---

2. Proceedings Relating to the Lower House

(a) 20 June
Sir Thomas Crew's acceptance speech and petition for privileges, Osborn fb 155, pp. 97–99.

Since then it is your royal pleasure to command me, so it is my duty to obey. I know that a star falls not from heaven without the providence of God and, as divisions of waters, so the hearts of kings are in His hands. I am the more confident of the mercy of God in regard of former mercies and blessings which He has showed to both the Houses of parliament in uniting all their hearts together, and to crown with honor the memorable acts of your dear father and our late dread Sovereign who was pleased to ask and take our advice in the disannulling of both the treaties and in giving his royal consent to many good and wholesome laws that passed from this throne. Wherein we desire your royal care and readiness to remove all rubs and to let your hand be ready at hand to further it.

And now God has put into your heart to tread in this way of parliaments, all which is to your honor and our comfort and will make the hearts of your royal people rejoice and be thankful. Solomon, the wisest of kings, called that land blessed, that king and people blessed, whose lives are trained up in true religion. It is the Lord's doing to put crosses on His dear children; yet it is with them as it is with a woman in travail of childbearing that for joy of a manchild delivered she forgets her former afflictions. So it is with us in the death of our late Sovereign. God in His eternal counsel did set the bounds of his life and is gone that way wherein we must all follow. Yet it has pleased God to set his own son upon his throne to judge his people.

Good Hezekiah was but 24 years old when he began to govern his people (but your Majesty has passed 24 years), who did rule his people uprightly and did sanctify the House of the Lord, and was magnified in all nations, the which you shall be if that you direct your ways unto the Lord. You have a wise, grave, and understanding council; you have a loyal and religious people which fear God, and it's the better that you are accompanied with such.

The laws of your kingdom will flourish and be upheld and will laud you in the kingdom of grace. We have long enjoyed this true religion which indeed is the truth and the power of God; the other is but a mist and man's invention. God whom we worship has brought you home from dangerous and tedious journeys, who has kept you under the wings of His mercy and has wrought great light thereby, for in those days of sorrow we hung our harps upon the willows and could not sing the song of Zion.

Your Majesty has been gracious to remember the Palatinate, the which I may truly say that in the time of our distress was a sanctuary unto us. And he is not a true member that is not sensible of those dishonors that are done both to religion and to that royal issue who [are] robbed of their ancient inheritance. For when there was treaties of peace with us they hastened with armies against them. And now seeing that they formerly were a wall of brass to us and that God has put the sword and scepter into your hands, you will be pleased to remember the distress of the Palatinate. Egypt was destroyed and cursed because that he came not out into the battle.

You that lineally descended from the streams of both, and that you and their hearts be set towards God, you shall be thrice crowned with happiness if that you set your helping hand to pull down Antichrist and abandon these Jesuits and seminaries that be the sons of Belial that blow the coals of dissension and labor with powder and blood to destroy the people of God. No doubt but your Majesty out of your wisdom sees it and will not let such locusts eat up the good fruit of the land.

But not to be too tedious, I will draw to an end. So according to our duties we do in all humbleness present ourselves to your most excellent Majesty our wonted and accustomed petitions:

That you will be pleased to afford us our ancient privileges as freedom from arrests and troubles for our own persons and our servants, that so thereby we may the better be able to attend this service. And that you will be graciously pleased to give us that ancient privilege of freedom of speech that thereby the grievances of both Houses may be known. And that you will be pleased upon due and fit times, with our humble suits, we may come to your Majesty. Lastly, during all the time of our sitting we may retain your gracious and benign opinion.

And in that by the free choice of the House, and by your Majesty's approbation, I am become their Speaker, I am an humble suitor to your excellent Majesty that all my infirmities may be censured with a gracious construction and that I, your unworthy servant, may receive your gracious acceptation.

(b) 20 June
The King's response delivered by L. Keeper Williams, Osborn fb 155, pp. 99–102.

Mr. Speaker, his Majesty has heard you with approbation and commanded me to answer some part of your speech. As great bodies, be they never so round in the compass, without all nooks to take hold upon, yet, as our later mathematicians say, there may be some points and stops. So you must give me leave to run over some of those heads distinctly: as somewhat of yourself; somewhat of the last parliament; somewhat of his Majesty's first entrance (and therein 5 circumstances: 1st, in respect of the way that was run before his Majesty; 2ly, in regard of blood; 3ly, succession after such a father; 4, future hope in regard of religious government; 5ly, deliverance by sea and land); somewhat concerning religion recommended to our King; something of the glory of his kingdom and cherishing of our friends abroad and abandoning of our foes at home; and of those 4 petitions—unity of persons, free access, benign acceptation, and freedom from arrests, which are the 4 cornerstones that hold up your House of parliament. I will answer them according to your sense and my method.

1, concerning yourself, who says but little but does much; as yielding to his Majesty, yet offers not up the sacrifice of lips but of new obedience, for obedience is better than sacrifice, *felix faustumque sit.*

2ly, concerning the last parliament: it was happily wrought by our labors and esteemed by our persons; and so nominated by you, as it was well observed therein, that the unfaithful/

[3ly,] what you said of the true religion is apparent, that it was much charged upon our King by his father, and left as a blessing upon his people. For his Majesty remembered that which I had forgot: that the last blessing that his father gave him, yet upon a motion, did recommend this true religion and his loving people to his Majesty's special care, charge, and love. And I doubt not but we shall see our Jerusalem in prosperity all his lifetime. The fruition of it has been a kind of blessing to his kingdom, not only in the life to come but even in his life by the space of 60 years and odds.

[4ly,] what you recommended to the King concerning the laws of this land, the King has not only in private, but now in public, recommended them to you and so to all them that will spend their time in the study thereof as their forefathers have done.

[5ly,] that present dishonor of that nation in the Palatinate. You cannot imagine, Mr. Speaker, how it contents his Majesty now he finds his people to be, as it were, lively members of that body, in that they have such a sympathy with their afflictions. God forbid that this kingdom, after all these prosperities, shall prove to be an Egyptian people for infidelity and cruelty. His Majesty desires not to live otherwise than in glory and reputation and you know yourselves that cannot be unless there be help in that great business of the Palatinate. And as his Majesty declares it really, so he expects of you that are his people and did set him on it, yet, upon just and grave advice, will continue him with supply.

[6ly,] in pleading for abandoning the sons of Belial, the priests and Jesuits, his Majesty returns this answer: that he does well approve of your religion and devotion and acknowledges with St. Augustine that the poorest man in all the kingdom by God has as great an interest in the religion as the greatest potentate. He is appointed by God to be the keeper and guarder of both the tables, and he desires you to trust him and his zeal, and he will be still a maintainer of the true religion. Your petition therein is granted and confesses it to be most just. Yet his Majesty desires you to remember what his blessed father said to you in this present place, desiring you to commit to him that which God had committed already—a care of the maintaining of the true religion.

[7ly,] for those usual four petitions—unity of persons, liberty in speech, free access to his Majesty, and freedom from arrests—his Majesty grants them all without any caution nor bounded with any other bounds than your own wisdoms and modesty; and knows very well if that any will abuse the same you all will be ready to inflict that punishment which his Majesty shall require. And this is all to return by way of answer.

(c) No date
A draft order to the committee concerning Richard Montagu, S.P. 16/4:18.[1]

That these honorable persons would convey the humble desire of this House to his Majesty. That whereas Mr. Montagu has lately published certain books which are conceived to contain matter seditious and tending to the disturbance of the public peace of the Church and state, which books now are questioned upon that ground in the House of Commons and that they have some informations that Mr. Montagu intends shortly to publish some other book.

That his Majesty would be graciously pleased to command, that until some order be taken concerning these books now in question, he publish no other books.

[*Endorsed*] Points required of the Lower House.

1. S.P. 16/4:8 is undated but is calendared in the S.P. Dom. under 8 July 1625.

(d) July
The King's reply concerning Montagu,
S.P. 16/4:19.

That touching the points of doctrine in
Mr. Montagu's former books, his Majesty
now refers them to the both Houses of Convocation; and that, for this interim and
hereafter, his Majesty will have his or any
other book in that argument to be perused
before it go to the press, and so well allowed
that it shall give no such scandal that may
endanger sedition or disturbance of the
public peace either of Church or state.

(e) 8 July
Sir John Coke's notes for the King's
message, S.P. 16/4:23.

[col. 1]
Subsidies a welcome: a pledge.
Our forwardness: King's confidence.
Anticipating the motion.
Accounts for 3 subsidies justified against
exceptions: for the fruit, especially Mans-
feld's army.
Late King forwarder than we.
Our subsidy enabled us but to stand upon
our guard, which would have turned *la
fièvre in* [*illegible*] *mal.*
The King made confederacy whereof
this army the first discovered. Mansfeld a fit
commander. Disorders excused.
Mortality by accident, etc., a forerunner
of the sickness.
By God's favor, the army stands on foot
to good purpose.
Account for subsidies to come.
Former allowance no part of this fleet.
The charge of the fleet double to the
subsidies.
The surcharge not to be supplied from
the ordinary.
Choose to desert the cause or supply it.
In deserting, the loss, the dishonor, the
consequence.
Kings like good chess players.
1-2-3-4 draughts.
Fleet the main [*illegible*].

[col. 2]
Enemies boast
French decline
Empire [*illegible*]
Fleet holds all in heart and distracts the
enemy. Never so fit a time. We so strong, he
so weak. All without it falls asunder.
Fleet then must proceed.
King to be enabled, with money or credit.
Credit upon promise to continue the pro-
portion of subsidies.

(f) 8 July
Report of the King's message (Sir John
Coke), S.P. 16/4:23.[1]

His Majesty, taking notice of our late resolution for the subsidies, has expressed his
most gracious acceptance thereof as a welcome to his crown and as a pledge of the
hearty affection not only of this representative body, but of his subjects in all counties
from whom we brought with us this ready
disposition. For the use that some made by
anticipating this motion before it was expected and our speedy consent without attending the ministers of state whose voices
were scarce heard, as they show that our
forwardness needed no spurs, so they testify his Majesty's royal confidence in us all,
which may encourage and comfort us in the
rest of our desires.
And his Majesty has received no less satisfaction by our diligence and care in examining the accounts of our former subsidies.
Because thereby we see plainly that no part
of those monies ever touched his Exchequer or were diverted to other uses than
were directed by ourselves. And therein the
particulars, being justified by oath, may satisfy the curiosity of the most exceptious,
that the fruit of these expenses was as much
as could reasonably be expected. For who
can doubt that two and thirty thousand
pounds disbursed for Ireland was a chief
means of keeping that kingdom in peace;
that forty-seven thousand employed upon
the forts and munition, and thirty-seven
thousand for the navy, did both strengthen

and secure our own ports; that fourscore and nineteen thousand eight hundred spent upon the regiments in the Low Countries supported our allies; and for the threescore and one thousand which paid the army of Count Mansfeld, though he that censures counsels by events leaves not God above man, yet herein consider either counsel or event and we shall find more cause of acknowledgment than complaint. For howsoever the late King, of happy memory, loved peace and hated war (a disposition to be wished and prayed for in all Christian kings), yet when by our advice the two treaties were broken off, and when he had discovered that the overspreading power which threatened all Christendom kept itself within no bounds, then even his seeming backwardness went on a faster pace than our forwardness had done. For those three subsidies, given (as we thought) with a very large hand, enabled us only to stand upon our guard, as the accounts thereof do show. But his Majesty's deep wisdom knew well that to proceed no further would but change our ague into a fever while we suffered the growing monarch to enjoy, besides all his own estates, and the returns of his treasure, both the Valtellina and the Palatinate, and to translate the Electorate, and range the Low Countries and neighbor princes under his command. He therefore found it necessary to make a balance to that power by raising a strong confederacy on the one side with France, Savoy, Venice, and the United Provinces; and on the other side with Denmark and other princes of the Empire. And this great work of his first discovered itself in that army of Count Mansfeld, which consisted of English, French, and Dutch. Wherein, if we mislike that our people were commanded by a stranger, consider whether the English would have endured to be under the French, or the French under them or, if either nation had been led by a commander of his own, how the precedency should be marshaled. And who then was so fit a head for that body as the known and esteemed lieutenant of that King under whose name they all served? Or if exceptions be taken to the disorders here at home and their perishing abroad, it cannot be denied that Count Mansfeld complained, and many counties confessed, that they sent him such men as themselves were weary of. Yet might they have mended by the discipline of his camp if some accident (which often falls out in the wars) had not changed our design and occasioned that mortality which was but the forerunner of the disease that now reigns, and against which we have no help but by fasting and prayer.

Notwithstanding, by God's favor, Mansfeld's army stands on foot and the confederacy still prevails. And his Majesty's monthly pay of 20,000 pounds both puts the enemy to the charge of many armies and interrupts the progress of that Catholic League, which now endeavors by a diet at Ulm to exclude both the Palatine and the Protestant prince from all hope of subsisting otherwise than by them. And thus, with the accounts of our monies, we see some good account of the counsels and events which should rather stir us up to pray for God's blessing upon our Prince's design than to blemish them with ill-affected apprehensions and reports.

But besides this account for the subsidies past, his Majesty is pleased to account beforehand for the subsidies to us, that howsoever the gift was free and without reservation, yet the monies may appear to be expended, with a great overplus, in the service of the kingdom, and not of the King, as some have pretended. And first, I must tell you, that the former sum allowed to the navy is no part of the charge of this fleet now at sea, and further, that this fleet will cost no less in the office of navy than near 200,000*l.*, in the office of ordnance 40,000*l.*, and for the land service above 45,000 *l.*, allowing no pay to soldiers or commanders. So as the two subsidies not exceeding 160,000 *l.* will come short of this charge above 140,000 *l.*, besides the support of the regiments, and Ireland, and the continuance of 20,000 *l.* monthly to Mansfeld, and 46,000 already paid to raise the army of Denmark. And how it may be possible to defray all their payments is now to be considered. For who can be ignorant that the ordinary revenue of the crown is already so clogged with debts and so exhausted with the late King's funerals [*sic*], the entertainments of ambassadors and strangers, the enlargement of his Majesty's household, and other expenses of necessity and honor, that there can no help be expected from thence. The choice then remaining is to call back ships and men, and so desert the cause, or to find some other way of extraordinary supply where the ordinary cannot serve. In deserting the cause, though the present loss be great, yet the dishonor and future danger will be found a great deal more. His Majesty, when he was Prince, took up for this fleet above 20,000 *l.*, the Lord Admiral 44,000 *l.*, and other good servants of the state above 50,000. And to break credit with all these is to prohibit any hereafter to engage himself for the public. And yet this dishonor at the entrance of his Majesty is of far greater consequence. For it will be made apparent that the establishing of his throne, the support of true religion, the welfare of our country, and the peace of Christendom do in a good degree depend upon the proceeding and success of this fleet. For kings, like good chess players, fortify every draught with a second, third, and fourth. Our first draught was the settling of our affairs at home; the second the four regiments sent into the Low Countries; the third the confederate armies of Italy, Denmark, and those of Count Mansfeld; and the fourth, which sustains all the rest, is the fleet. For who has not heard how they vaunt of the taking of Breda, and of the cutting the Dutch in pieces at Brazil. Besides, the French incline again to civil wars, and beyond the Alps begin to languish (like their forefathers) after the first brunt. And the northern army and princes of the Empire will readily disband,

and accept the conditions to be offered them at Ulm, if this fleet should not proceed. And if the reputation of our navy has all this while so distracted the enemy's forces that he could be nowhere strong, by the scattering of our fleet both our party will fall in summer and his forces reunite, and the Catholic League, which professes the extirpation of our religion, will find no more resistance. This fleet must then proceed, whatsoever it shall cost. And the King must be enabled with money or credit to prosecute his designs. For money, his Majesty is as tender as ever prince was not to overstrain his people, and therefore expects no more subsidies than may well be paid. All then that can be done is to cause a ground for credit by which other kings have supported their affairs. How this may be done, he that can propound the best way shall perform the best service. But if we think it safest to hold the paths of our forefathers, then let us consider well in case his Majesty shall assure us of another meeting so soon as God, in His mercy, by ceasing the plague, shall permit, and as often afterwards as we shall reasonably desire, whether if we shall not now engage ourselves to continue this proportion of subsidies for such time only as the necessity of the war shall require, we ourselves being the judges. And this [*illegible*] we are desired not suddenly to reject without a serious consideration, as well of the causes above mentioned as of the consequence of forcing his Majesty to strain some other way, which for my part I would not live to see. And therefore, again and again, I recommend the prevention thereof to the wisdom of this House. Specially, that the occasion may not rise from our denying that support to which we are engaged.

[*Endorsed*] Substance of a message sent to the Parliament House and delivered by me on Friday, [*blank*] July 1625.

1. The notes (see [e] above) and speech that comprise S.P. 16/4:23 are in Sir John Coke's handwrit-

ing. S.P. 16/4:24 and S.P. 16/4:25 comprise rough drafts of this speech, also in Coke's handwriting.

(g) 5 August
Sir Thomas Edmondes's speech, S.P. 16/5:15.

Mr. Speaker,

In perplexed councils, especially which do deeply concern the public services, it is needful that we invoke God's assistance to direct us with His spirit in the resolutions we are to take and, likewise, that in our consultations we lay aside all passion and perturbation of mind. And if ever it were behooveful so to do, then certainly most of all at this time of our meeting.

The King, our most gracious Sovereign who, before his coming to the crown, gave better proof of his true love and respective care to the commonwealth than I could yet learn that any other of his predecessors, princes of this realm, have done, has been forced by the necessity of the pressing occasions of the state to adjourn us to a speedy meeting in this place because the infection hindered us from longer continuing at London. That he might impart unto us in how great expenses he is engaged for the preparations of the royal fleet, which he is now ready to set forth for the vindicating of the honor of the state but yet wants a further supply than we have lately contributed towards that charge.

When I look upon the commonwealth in her particular parts and cast up into a total sum the great charge it has sustained within these latter years for the support of public actions, and withal take into consideration those common calamities under the which the kingdom does groan, of pestilence and fear of famine, I protest before God my very heart is grieved to propound any thing which may seem to add to these present afflictions.

Nevertheless, when I look upon the commonwealth in general, how the precious honor of it lies at this time ableeding and

must be suddenly relieved or else both King and it, and we all, must be exposed to scorn and infamy, and there cannot choose but follow a dissolution of foreign confederacies; wherefore, being warranted by the example and practice both of nature and policy wherein particulars do dispense with their private interest to serve and supply the public, I cannot but entreat this honorable House to take these things fervently into your wise considerations and to advise and determine speedily of some course to remedy the same.

And amidst these reasons of urgent necessity it may please you to remember what his Majesty's particular merit does challenge from us who, in the time when he was the child of the commonwealth, approved himself also to be the child of obedience to your desires: first, in being a means to procure you from his deceased father the many pious and beneficial laws which passed the last parliament, the like whereof have not been granted these many hundred years; secondly, in being the instrument to break off the two treaties with Spain for the which, at that time, you expressed great joy. Nevertheless, you were not satisfied in the fullness of your joy till an enemy should be declared, and that thereupon something might be done for the relieving of the distressed state of the most worthy Queen of Bohemia.

This work his Majesty has ever since most carefully studied and for that use not only all the subsidy monies have been most faithfully expended, but also very great proportions of his own revenue; and if the effects thereof have not hitherto answered our expectation, we must remember that it is no good rule to judge of counsels by their events.

But we hope that God will bless with honorable success this great enterprise which is intended by this royal fleet which, being the first of his Majesty's actions of war, shall we refuse him in so public and important a cause an extraordinary gratification, and so suffer him to be foiled and dishonored therein for want of means to pursue the same? God forbid.

Let us therefore, I beseech you, severally consider what the bonds of our duty towards so good a king, and the most pressing necessities of this action, do require from us. And let us crown our former gift with the addition of two and two fifteens subsidies more. And I hope we shall find the reward thereof in the honor and benefit which this action will procure, and in his Majesty's gracious regard of so deserving a people.

[*Endorsed*] July 1625, copy of my speech un[to] the parliament at Oxford.

(h) 5 August
Anonymous notes of Sir Edward Coke's speech, Carreg-lwyd MS. 1834 (Nat. Libr. of Wales).[1]

No king can subsist unless he be able to maintain himself: first, in a readiness to resist foreign invasions; secondly, to aid his allies; thirdly, to reward his servants.

That he be able to do this it is requisite that he live on his own means, the proper revenues of the crown. It is objected that there is a great necessity.

1. First, there is *necessitas affecta*, a voluntary necessity—of this we dare clear his Majesty.

2. Secondly, *necessitas compulsa*, a forced necessity which is that necessity now they talk of which cannot be this necessity because none invades us. We have now no '88.

But there is 3, a third necessity, *necessitas improvida*, a necessity not foreseen, and this is the necessity we now speak of.

Cannot the King now live as well off his revenues as his ancestors did off theirs? King Edward the Third maintained an army in France fourteen years before he had any supply.

To show how this necessity came and then how it may be supplied. There are two medicines: the first is *medicina removens* and the second is *medicina renovans.*

Medicina removens is for that which must be taken away and is the humor which feeds the sore and it is to [be] applied to the King's house by removing away needless officers that are erected and have tables allowed, and the many hang-bys that daily live at the court and also the tables that are newly added to ancient officers and are but needless.

1. That the officers of court live on their offices without daily begging.

2. That no Lord may have above one office.

3. That all voluntary pensions be cut off.

4. That the courtiers may be rewarded and the King not charged with stipends and pensions.

5. That all fee farms be called in that the King may make the best of his lands, for this is but a damnable course to cozen the King of his land giving him a small chief rent for it.

And because that by the act of H. 4 they can allege no consideration why they should have the King's land they have devised *ex mero moto*.

That monopolies be taken away that the subject upon all occasions may be able to give aid.

That the customs of the kingdom be employed for the defense of the kingdom and not for the maintenance of the King's house, or other private charges.

That inquiry be made how the customs and revenues of Ireland are paid for. To King Edward the 3 Ireland *de claro* was worth 30,000 *l.* by the year.

Medicina renovans is the means to aid the King. To have his revenues managed by men of understanding and by such officers as will do for the best profit, and the customs must not be let at under rates and the King infinitely deceived by the merchants.

To make profit of some of his parks and

forests which are now a great charge to him by keepers for repairing of houses and making of pales.

That understanding officers be employed in his house to reduce it to the ancient form. We mean not to join with Sir Lionel Cranfield to divide a ghost, and that Sir Simon Harvey be removed, and that shop boys be not taken from the shops and placed in the Green Cloth.

That the great offices for the defense of the kingdom be put into the hands of able men that have experience, as the Admiral's office and Mastership of the Ordnance, etc.

That all needless offices may be extinguished, as the president of Wales, North, etc.

1. MS. 1834, Carreg-lwyd deposit, is headed, "Reasons conceived by the parliament adjourned from Westminster to Oxford the 27 of July and there begun the first of August and broken off the 12 of August 1625, *anno primo Caroli Regis*". For annotation of the precedent material in these notes, see Sir Edward Coke's speech, above, H. of C., 5 August, O.B. Similar notes are included in S.P. 16/5:16 and Tanner MS. 276 (see below).

(i) 5 August
Anonymous notes of the speeches of Sir Edward Coke and three other M.P.s, Tanner MS. 276, ff. 279–281.[1]

No king can subsist unless he be able: 1, to maintain himself in readiness to resist all sudden invasions; 2, to aid his allies; 3, to reward his servants.

That he be able to do this it is requisite that he live on his own means, the proper revenues of his crown.

Objection. It is objected that there is now great necessity.

Response. I answer there is a threefold necessity: first, *necessitas affectata*—of this I dare clear his Majesty. 2, *necessitas compulsa*, the necessity they talk of cannot be this for none invades—we have no '88. But thirdly there is *necessitas improvida*, and this is the necessity now talked of. Cannot the King live as well off his revenue as his ancestors? Edward the 3 maintained wars in France 14 years before he had any supply.

To show how this necessity came and how it may be supplied. There are two medicines: the first is *medicina removens;* the second, *medicina renovans. Medicina removens* is that must take away the humor that feeds the sore and it is first to be applied to the King by removing away needless officers that are erected and have tables allowed, and the many hang-bys that daily live at the court and the tables that are newly allowed to officers but needless.

That the officers of the court do not daily beg but live on their offices.

That no Lord may have above one office. That other courtiers and well-deserving men may be rewarded with stipends and pensions.

That needless offices be taken away, as the president of Wales and the north country.

That all voluntary pensions be cut off.

To call in the fee farms, that the King may make the most of his lands. This is a damnable device to cozen the King of his lands and pay him a chief rent for it. And because of that act of Henry 4 they can allege no consideration why they should have the King's land given them. They have devised a clause *ex mero moto.*

That monopolies be taken away that the subjects may be able in all occasions to give aid.

That the customs and revenues of the kingdom be not employed for the maintenance of the King's house and other private charges but for the defense of the kingdom.

That the inquiry be made how the revenue and customs of Ireland be paid, for to Edward 3 Ireland was worth *de claro* 30,000 *l.* per annum and now it is a charge.

Medicina renovans, or the means to add to the King are:

To have his revenues managed by men of

understanding, officers that be for the best profit, and the customs must not be let at under rates and the King deceived by the merchant.

To make profit of some of his parks and forests. Whereas now they are a great charge unto him by keepers repairing of houses, making of pales, etc.

That understanding officers be employed in his house to reduce it to the ancient form, not Sir Simon Cranfield,[2] to divide a goose, and that shop boys be not taken from the shop and placed in the Green Cloth. I would have Sir Lionel Harvey removed.

That the great offices for the defense of the kingdom be put in the hands of able men that have experience, as the Admiral's office and the Mastership of the Ordnance.

Finis

Addition to Sir Edward Coke's speech, and some of other men's.

Mr. Speaker, private counsels never suit the nature of this country nor succeed well, and I remember that Aristotle, speaking against *animalia solivagium,* says that those beasts which herd together are gentle and well-natured, as deer, cattle, and divers other beasts, and every animal *solivagium* is of a cruel, fierce, and destroying nature as lions, tigers, and other ravinous beasts.[3]

[In R. 2 time John Holland, Duke of Exeter, in parliament in 20 of that King, etc., *vide* Holinshed, p. 123a,[4]] was transcendently magnified in the 13 of his reign, and in the 15 with equal disgrace disesteemed and inveighed against, inferring that there may be merit and dismerit in one person and that in a small time one after another.

IGNOTUS maintained the quantity of the gift to the King being in agitation, that since we expected and desired so much from the King in matters concerning religion, we should deal liberally with him, purchase and assay[5] his Majesty's grant to our desires.

IGNOTUS answered that the last speech not at all excited to liberality; for God forbid *venalia in Anglia*—that in England religion should be bought and sold or that the King's sincerity to the truth should be presaged vendable but rather impossible.

1. The notes of Sir Edward Coke's speech of 5 August included in Tanner MS. 276 (misdated 4 August in the MS.) are similar to those in Carreg-lwyd MS. 1834 (printed above), S.P. 16/5:16, Osborn fb 155, pp. 110–112, Braye MSS. 1, ff. 88v–90, and Tanner MS. 72, ff. 46–47. The quantity of similar manuscripts indicates the notes circulated in this form as a separate. For annotation on the precedent material in these notes, see Sir Edward Coke's speech, above, H. of C., 5 August, O.B. Tanner 276 is the only manuscript that includes the additional three speeches.
2. Marginal note in the hand of Sir Simonds D'Ewes: "These names thus mistaken on purpose in *majus opprobrium*". The reference is to Sir Lionel Cranfield and Sir Simon Harvey.
3. Aristotle, *De Animalibus Historiae, Lib.* 1, *cap.* 1; *Lib.* 9, *cap.* 4.
4. *In Edward the Second's time the Duke of Gloucester* is crossed out in the MS. and replaced by the passage printed in the present text within square brackets. The correction is in the hand of Sir Simonds D'Ewes and next to it is a marginal note, also in D'Ewes's hand: "[*Illegible*] No Duke was before [Edw.] 3 [*illegible*]". It is not clear who is being referred to in the crossed out section; Hugh le Despenser, the younger (d. 1326), sometimes called Earl of Gloucester, may be intended. *D.N.B.* D'Ewes's reference is to John Holland who was created Duke of Exeter partly as a reward for supporting the King against Thomas, Duke of Gloucester, in 1397 (20–21 *R.* II), but who in 1399 (1 *H.* IV) was called upon by parliament to justify his actions against Gloucester and was executed in 1400 for his involvement in a conspiracy to restore Richard II. Holinshed, *Chronicles,* II, 834–843; III, 7–13. *D.N.B.*
5. MS.: *easy.*

3. Miscellaneous Separate Documents

(a) 11 July
Letter: Privy Council to the Vicechancellor of Oxford and the heads of the colleges, Rawl. D. 399, Bodleian Library.[1]

After our hearty commendations,

Whereas his Majesty has been pleased to declare his resolution for the adjourning of the present parliament to Oxford, there to begin on the first of August next, we do therefore hereby will and require, and in his Majesty's name expressly charge you, to take care and speedy order that the colleges and halls there be freed from the fellows, masters of arts, and students and all the rooms and lodgings therein be reserved to the end the members of both Houses may be received and lodged with the best convenience that may be. But you are to take special care that all the rooms of Christ Church be cleared and kept for the Lords and others of his Majesty's Privy Council and such other officers whose attendance there he shall think fit to use, to which end there shall be sent an harbinger to sort out the same rooms. We expect herein such an account of your care and diligence as the obedience due to his Majesty's commandment and importance of the thing itself does require. And so we bid you heartily farewell from Whitehall, July 11, 1625.

Joan. Lincolne C.S.   Mandeville
Arundel and Surrey   E. Worcester
C. [sic] Conway   La. Winton
Tho. Edmondes

John Dickenson[2]

To the Vice-chancellor of Oxford
and the Heads of Colleges.

1. A copy of this letter is printed in *A.P.C., 1625–1626*, p. 118; a copy is also included in the Oxford University Convocation book on 13 July (Acta. Convocat. Univ. Oxon. Arch., N23, 1615–1628, f. 210v).
2. John Dickenson was a clerk of the Privy Council. The councillors whose names appear on the letter are: John Williams, Bp. of Lincoln, *Custos Sigillum;* Thomas Howard, Earl of Arundel and Surrey; Edward Viscount Conway; Thomas Edmondes; Henry Montagu, Viscount Mandeville; Edward Somerset, Earl of Worcester; Lancelot Andrewes, Bp. of Winchester.

(b) Description of preparations at Oxford and brief notes concerning the session, Corpus Christi College, E257, ff. 131–132.[1]

Memorandum: That upon the 12 or 13 of July 1625 presently after the act at Oxford was done, there was sent down a letter to the University of Oxford, namely to the Vice-chancellor and the rest of the heads of colleges and halls by some of the Privy Council, to dismiss the younger sort of scholars away from the University and all others that might possibly be spared, to the intent that the knights and burgesses of the parliament which the King had appointed to meet at Oxford, *1 Augusti,* by proclamation, together with the prelates and other of the nobility, might be the convenienter lodged in the said colleges, and especially in Christ Church for the King himself and the lords of the Council.[2] Against whose coming in the meantime the King's surveyors, workmen, and carpenters, having pulled up all the seats in the Divinity School and taken asunder the stately and solemn Doctor's chair of stone, and furnishing it all round with 5 degrees or ranks of seats up to the half of the windows, in manner of a cockpit, appointed that place for the Lower House, building a kind of terrace loft at the east end thereof, the stairs whereof went up on the north side or end. And on the other side or end, under the said terrace, there was a little room square enclosed about on boards, just on your left-hand as you enter into the east door of the Divinity School, for the west door was shut up and covered with the seats that went round about the School and the Speaker's chair also was at that end, that is to say the west end of the School.

On the south end also of the walk before the Divinity School there was another room, also enclosed with boards, for a retiring place (as it was said) for the gentlemen of the Lower House, where there was much tobacco taken.

And on the north end there was a scrivener's shop to draw writings and petitions and the like, with a way left to go to the library and through a door in the stone wall of the library yard on the east end of Exeter College and close into it leading to Exeter College place of easement, or privy, under the town wall, for the use of the Lower House.

And the door leading to the library from Exeter College garden was barricaded up.

The north side of the Gallery was taken up and appointed for the Upper House, having in the midst, as it were, a partition of boards up to the top by which there was made 2 fair and stately rooms, the inner room whereof was the Parliament House itself, at the east end whereof, toward New College, was the Chair of State. And the next room to that southward, being appointed for the King's Privy Chamber, had another Chair of State and the next to that under the tower, being severed by boards, was appointed for other uses. And the south side of the Gallery was for the grand committee; the Physic School, under that, for other committees; and the other schools were replenished with furniture belonging to the parliament use, and the under officers and attenders of the parliament lodged in them.

In Christ Church were lodged most of the lords of the Privy Council and the rest of the King's household; the Lord Keeper, then being the Bishop of Lincoln, abiding in Dr. Piers his lodging toward the street; the Archbishop of Canterbury and the Lord Treasurer lodged in Merton College; the Attorney General, Sir Thomas Coventry, in the president's lodging of Corpus Christi College,[3] in which college were also lodged 2 or 3 other knights of the Lower House of parliament. The Earl of Dorset lay in Peckwater's Inn in Dr. Hutton's lodging, subdean of Christ Church.

Upon Monday, *1 Augusti*, at the time and place appointed, both the Houses sat, and likewise on Tuesday, and some part thereof was spent in committees for matters then in hand.

Upon Wednesday was the fast, and a sermon at St. Mary's which should have been preached by Dr. Anyan, the president of Corpus Christi College, had he not been silenced by some of the Lower House the day before. Tickets also went abroad from the Vice-chancellor to all the colleges that no scholar under the degree of a doctor should repair to St. Mary's church in sermon time, because the parliament men would be there alone and in private.

Upon Thursday about 9 of the clock in the morning the King came from Woodstock to Christ Church where he made a speech to both the Houses of parliament assembled together in Christ Church Hall. That afternoon I think was spent in a committee, etc.

Upon Friday and Saturday both the Houses sat very long.

Monday and Tuesday following they sat also very long, and also upon Wednesday, there being no fast kept or sermon at St. Mary's or Carfax that day by the appointment of the parliament.

Upon Thursday also both the Houses sat very long, but in the afternoon the lords of the Council and most of the nobility went to Woodstock, being sent for by the King. And upon Friday, after they had sat from 8 in the morning until 2 in the afternoon or thereabouts, the parliament was dissolved and nothing concluded but nullities.

Thus partly by reason of the pestilence then in the city increasing, and partly through their own discord, as it was said, the same way that brought them from Thebes to Athens led them back again from Athens to Thebes, and so farewell.

The Monday following the King departed from Woodstock, coming through Oxford and so to Abington and Newbury toward New Forest.

Wednesday following the Queen came from Woodstock and followed the King the same way through Oxford.

Upon Thursday the remnant of the King's household removed from Christ Church and followed the King.

1. Corpus Christi College MS. E257 is a parchment-bound paper book with four leather strings attached to the parchment cover, two each front and back, that tie over the page edge. It contains 178 ff. of divers tracts, many of them theological disputations in Latin. There is no indication of the ownership of the book or of the authorship of the folios printed here concerning the parliament of 1625. Another copy of the account is included in C.C.C. E301.
2. For the letter, see above, p. 661; concerning the proclamation, see *Stuart Proclamations*, II, 48–49.
3. Thomas Anyan became president of Corpus Christi College on 1 June 1614. Thomas Fowler, *The History of Corpus Christi College* (Oxford, 1893), p. 379.

(c) Declared Accounts, Pipe Office: Works and Buildings, E351/3258 (RC/1537), Public Record Office, London.

Parliament House at Oxford, viz.:

Also allowed to the said accountancy for money, likewise by him issued past and defrayed for works and reparations done within the time of this account by masons, carpenters, sawyers, and other artificers, workmen, and laborers in and about the Parliament House at Oxford, at the schools and colleges there in preparing of rooms for the Upper and Lower Houses of parliament, and making sundry rooms for committees there; for performance whereof sundry emptions have been made which, with their rates, prices, and quantities together with the charges of carriages there, of wages of artificers, workmen, and laborers, taskwork, and other charges, are hereafter particularly expressed, viz.:

Emptions and provisions, viz.:

Of timber, viz., 14 lo. 14 foo. at 25s. the lo.: 17 *li*. 17s.

4er lo. 38 foo. at 26s. 8d. the lo.: 6 *li*. 7s.

5 pieces of timber for props at 18d. the piece: 7s. 6d. more

2 pieces at 2s. 8d. the piece: 5s. 4d.

and 14 pieces at 3s. the piece: 42s.

In all: 26 *li*.–18s.– 5d.

[26 *li*.–18s.–10d.][1]

Dealboards [*illegible*] 716 at 6 *li*. the hundreth:

[In all:]42 *li*.–16s.– 0d.

Oaken boards, viz., [*illegible*] 8 foo. at 8s. the hundreth: 10 *li*. 6d.

and 70 foo. at 10s. the hundreth: 7s.

In all: 10 *li*.– 7s.– 6d.

Rafters, 10 at 14d. the piece: 11s. 8d.

Firpoles, viz., 15 at 3d. the piece: 3s. 10d. [3s. 9d.];

and 53 at 8d. the piece: 35s. 4d.; [total:] 39s. 1d.

Baskets: 3s. 15d.

Brooms: 14d.

Nails of sundry sorts: 7 *li*. 18s. 8d.

Ironworks of divers kinds: 111s. 10d.

And glass and glazing at the usual rates aforesaid: 41s. 8d.

In all the said emptions and provisions [*illegible*]:

18 *li*.– 8s.– 5d.

[18 *li*.– 8s.– 4d.]

Carriages by land and water of timber, firpoles, woolpacks, tables, tressels, court cupboards, dealboards, and sundry of the said provisions:

18 *li.*– 3*s.*– 6*d.*

Wages and entertainment, viz.:

Of masons, at 20*d.* per diem: 5*s.*

Carpenters at 12*d.*, 14*d.*, 15*d.*, 16*d.*, 18*d.*, 20*d.*, and 22*d.*, the piece
per diem: 16*li.* 2*s.* 7*d. ob.*

Sawyers at 2*s.* 2*d.* the couple per diem: 4 *li.* 7*s.* 9*d.*

Laborers at 10*d.* the piece per diem: 73*s.* 9*d.*

Andrew Durdant, Clerk of the Works, for 15 days at 20*d.* per diem: 25*s.*

And Thomas Hide, purveyor, for 15 days at the like rate of 20*d.* per diem: 25*s.*

    In all the said wages and entertainments:

26 *li.*–11*s.*–10*d.*–*ob.*

[26 *li.*–19*s.*– 1*d.*–*ob.*]

Horse hire, the said Andrew Durdant, Clerk, and Thomas Ive, purveyor, for 15 days at 16*d.* the piece per diem:

[In all:] 40*s.*

Taskwork, viz.:

To Edward Robinson, painter, for laying in a brown color [on] the upper part of the partition in the Upper House by the state, cont. 5 square yards at 6*d.* the yard: 2*s.* 6*d.*

Thomas Bennett and Hugh Davies, masons, for taking down most part of the stonework of the great chair in the Divinity School (the Lower House of the parliament being to be kept there) and fitting and setting it up again after the parliament was ended in as firm manner as before it was taken down, they finding all manner of stuff and workmanship: 7 *li.*–10*s.*

And to a plasterer and three carpenters, viz., for stopping of glass in the Lower House, making up the churchyard wall at St. Hallows, which was broken down to take out timber there, and for enclosing a room with dealboards and making a table and a pair of tressels for the Clerk of the Parliament House: 8*s.* 10*d.*

In all the said taskwork: 8 *li.*–16*d.*

Reward to divers porters and laborers for carrying all the woolpacks, lined forms, tables, court cupboards, and other forms, etc., out of the Upper and Lower Parliament Houses to a barge and packing them up with straw for the better carriage of them to Oxford: 30*s.*

In all the charge of the works and reparations done and bestowed upon the Parliament House at Oxford aforesaid as by one particular paybook thereof, vouched and subscribed by the officers of the works and hereupon examined and [*illegible*] does and may appear the sum of:

155 *li.*–19*s.*–*ob.*

[154 *li.*–17*s.*–*ob.*]²

[155 *li.*– 4*s.*–7*d.*–*ob.*]³

---

1. The bracketed figures here and below represent corrected subtotals.

2. The sum total using the accountant's subtotals.

3. The sum total using the corrected subtotals.

(d) 17 July
Letter: Edward, Viscount Conway, to
Mr. Henry Drake and Mr. [Roger]
Gollop, H.L.R.O., Main Papers, H.L., 9
August 1625.

A complaint has been made to his Majesty in the behalf of Mary Estmond of Lodge
in the county of Dorset that certain stuff—
books and other things—were in June last
taken from her by you, and such further
courses taken against her for refusing to
take the oath of allegiance as she has been
constrained to fly from her house, and by
her absence suffers much prejudice in her
harvest of hay and corn, wherein humble
instance is made to his Majesty for speed in
order and relief. But before any directions
be given therein it is thought meet to receive from you a true certificate of the state
of her complaint and the manner of your
proceedings with her that such order may
be given as the cause shall require, which
certificate, I pray you, return unto me with
all speed. And in the meantime you may do
well to suffer her to return to her house and
tend her harvest business without trouble
or molestation. So, I remain,
Your very loving friend to serve you,
E. Conway
[*Endorsed*] To my very loving friends Mr.
Henry Drake and Mr. Gollop, Esquires, two
of his Majesty's justices of peace for the
county of Dorset.

––––––––––––––––

(e) 31 July
Letter: Henry Drake and Roger Gollop
to Sect. Conway, S.P. 16/4:152.

Henry Drake and Roger Gollop to Secretary Conway, 31 July 1625.
Right Honorable,
In performance of your Lordship's command, which we have received this 31th of
July, we humbly desire your Lordship to
receive this our answer unto the complaint
of Mary Estmond, widow, made unto his
Majesty.

On the twelfth day of June last, being a
sabbath day, it was rumored that the Turks
were landed in Devonshire not far from
this place, the train[ed] bands taking arms,
the common people, in great distraction,
flying from parish to parish. The constable
and divers others of the parishioners of
Chardstock, where the said Mary Estmond
dwells, gave us notice that the said Mary
Estmond had divers men's armors brought
into her house, and that great provision was
made by her for entertainment (which
made them much to fear and doubt, knowing the said Mary Estmond to be an obstinate recusant convict and dwells in a remote place, making her house to be the
common receptacle for the recusants of
these parts, of which there are not a few).
Whereupon it being late in the afternoon,
and about some six or seven miles distant
from us, command was given the constable
that he should presently (with some others
of the said parish) repair unto the said
house to search the truth of this information. And if entrance were denied him,
then to set a guard about the house until we
came the next morning. And at our coming
thither the constable informed us that he
was denied entrance, and that he and the
guard which watched perceived they had
been very busy all the night, laboring, as
they supposed, to convey the said men and
armor into their secret vats and places of
conveyance in the said house of which they
understood there were divers. But at our
entering we found no other in the said
house but only one James Fitzjames, who
confessed himself to have been a recusant
56 years, and the said Mary Estmond, her
daughter, and two women servants, which
increased our suspicion the more that the
rest were conveyed unto those secret places.
Whereupon we made diligent search but in
vain, the conveyances were so artificially
carried, until at length, two old women,
having been ancient servants unto the said
house, brought us unto a place that they
had known twenty years before for such

privy uses, wherein we found three copes for priests, crucifixes, *Agnus Dei*, and divers other relics and popish books which we caused to be brought away and, according to a statute made in the third year of our late sovereign lord King James, these relics of small value and popish books were defaced and burned. And those things of better value are reserved to be brought forth at the general sessions, there to be defaced and restored again to the owner, according to the statute.[1] We likewise tendering unto the said Fitzjames and Mary Estmond the oath of allegiance, according to a statute made in the seventh year of our said sovereign lord King James, which they refused to take,[2] and after divers persuasions by us unto them made to take the same not prevailing, we committed them, yet with this favorable direction unto the constable: that if he might think himself secure, he might give some few days respite unto the said Mary Estmond to consider of the said oath, as she had desired. And having had eight days respite in her own house, without any officer to be with her, and knowing that the said Fitzjames in the meantime had taken the said oath, yet she still remained obstinate. The constable, notwithstanding upon her deep oaths and protestations of her true imprisonment, forbore her yet a longer time; but not regarding her oaths and faithful promises she fled away and left the constable in danger, whom we bound unto the assizes, where Sir Richard Hutton, judge of this circuit, having heard the cause, bound over the said constable in 200 *l.* bond to bring in the said Mary Estmond at the next assizes, and gave him a warrant to apprehend her wheresoever he could find her within divers countries within this circuit.

And thus have we given your Lordship a true account both of the motives that drew us and of the reasons that made us thus to proceed with the said Mary Estmond, wherein we hope your Lordship will not conceive that we have done any thing but

that which appertains unto our duties and places, and according to the laws of the realm. Craving pardon of your Lordship for our tediousness, being necessarily drawn into it by the virtue of the cause, do ever rest,

> Your Lordship's humbly to be commanded,
> Hr. Drake, Roger Gollop

From [*illegible*] the 31th
of July, 1625
[*Endorsed*] To the Right Honorable our very good Lord, the Lo. Conway, Principal Secretary to the King's most excellent Majesty, these.

1. *S.R.*, 3 *Jac.* I, c. 5, pt. 15.
2. *S.R.*, 7 *Jac.* I, c. 6, pts. 1–3.

(f) August
Henry Sherfield's notes for an intended speech never delivered, 44 M 69/XXXIX. 13, Hampshire Record Office.

Reasons [*illegible*] *to give are these:*[1]
1. Precedent
2. Subsequent
3. Present *or* concomitant
1. Precedent
   1. Engagement
2. Subsequent
   1. Religion *confirmed*
   2. Request *of the King*
   3. Fear of consequences
   4. Necessity
3. Present: Weight *of the design—on that depends*
   1. *Honor of the King and navy*
   2. Reputation *of the King and navy*
   3. Profit *of the King and navy*
   4. Recovery *of the* Palatinate

Reasons *for not giving are these:*
1. Precedent
2. Subsequent
3. Present or concomitant

1. Precedent—1 former aid
    1. Smallness *of the aid demanded*
    2. Competent *aid given, etc.*
    3. Precedent dangerous
    4. Action dubious in *the* ground and [*illegible*]
2. Subsequent
    { 5. Religion *not confirmed by* execution
    { 6. Papists protected
    7. Jesuits pardoned
    8. Papists encouraged
    9. Arminians countenanced
    10. Merchants, fishermen spoiled on our coasts
    1. *Salus Reipublicae*
        1. Ships our defense
        2. Other ships not ready
        3. Counsel, *judgment of the design*
3. Present
    1. *Laws made in this parliament not countenanced*
    2. *Bonum Publicum*
        2. *Poverty of the* commonwealth
        3. Trade stopped *by the sickness*
        4. Treasury exhausted

[*Endorsed*][2] August 1625. The abstract of the grounds and plot of my speech intended to have been spoken in the parliament at Oxford touching giving or not giving more subsidy, wherein I intended to balance the reasons of either side, on which reliance had been no more having been pressed on either side. But my opinion in conclusion is not set down but intended to be proposed to the parliament.

1. The editors have translated and italicized those words which appear in French in the MS.
2. The endorsement is in Sherfield's hand.

(g) August
An Advertisement to a Friend, Osborn fb 155, ff. 132–133.

An Advertisement to a Friend.

As for parliament news, you shall understand, it broke up in discontent, for whereas they presented the grievances of the kingdom and were desirous to take into consideration the King's estate, which was then in parliament by some declared to be at a low ebb and unable by money or credit to set forth the navy without further aid of 100,000 *l.* more than has been already paid, they were commended for their due care but not permitted to go on their course, which breeds in them a jealousy of the action, whether it be really intended or no, or whether it were projected by the Duke of Buckingham for his own ends; which grew to a great question in parliament, in so much that he seemed hardly excusable. And they eager as men might be to draw the ministers of the King into due examination, that they might discover the injuries done to the King, *p[er] solum et malum consilium,* by such as lead him and make their thirst out of his revenue and, by an act of resumption, might the better enable his Majesty to subsist. Now because these good desires could not, for the present, be assented unto, but the King and his party called still for a present levy, it being contrary to all parliamentary proceedings or precedents, they concluded to give none. And the question admirably debated on both sides, whether to give or no; necessity, honor, engagement, all earnestly pressed and all wisely answered. In fine, Sir Robert Mansell standing up, being of the Council of War, began to disclaim the action of the navy: that it was not by consent of a Council of War; that they were never met but once upon it, and they only conferred of a war in general; that the Duke was advised by him to take another course for the weakening of the Spaniard, for the recovery of the Palatinate, and the honor of England, which might be accomplished with less charge, but would not attend it; that this, though chargeable, can neither be profitable nor honorable for the kingdom; and desired the next day to declare himself touching this point further but it trenched upon this rupture, notwithstanding all the Lords entreated, dissolved it, to the grief of many.

(h) 14 August 1625

A letter from Lord Keeper Williams to the King, dated 14 August 1625 and headed "Reasons to satisfy your most excellent Majesty concerning my carriage all this last parliament", is printed in Hacket, *Scrinia Reserata*, pt. II, pp. 17–18. The letter contains Williams's defense against accusations that he had followed the "popular way" and sided with the "stirring men" during the Oxford session. It includes interesting comments on some of the leading M.P.s and major legislation of that session and on the disdain with which Williams was treated by Buckingham and the King.

D. Elections and Attendance

1. Letters Concerning Preparations for the Parliament, 1625

(a) In addition to the letters printed below, see that from John Chamberlain to Sir Dudley Carleton, 23 April 1625, printed in Birch, *Court and Times of Chas. I*, I, 13–16 (Chamberlain, *Letters*, II, 611–613); Chamberlain's letter of 6 May to the same, Birch, I, 18–20 (Chamberlain, II, 614–616); the letter of Reverend Joseph Mead to Sir Martin Stuteville, 14 May 1625, Birch, I, 21. See also the letter of John Chamberlain to Sir Dudley Carleton, 21 May 1625, Chamberlain, *Letters*, II, 618–619; the same to the same, 12 June 1625, ibid., pp. 622–624, and 25 June, ibid., pp. 624–626.

Sir John Davies mentions the day for the convening of the parliament in his letter to Henry Hastings printed in *The Huntingdon Papers* (London, 1926), II, pt. 5, p. 5.

See the Salvetti dispatches, H.M.C., *11th Report, Appendix, Part I*, pp. 5, 7, 8, 17, 22, 23.

Blandford, Dorsetshire, was refused representation in 1625. See H.M.C., *12th Report, Appendix, Part I*, p. 197.

(b) [S.P. 16/1:83]

24 April 1625, Sir Francis Nethersole to Sir Dudley Carleton, The Hague.

... My Lord Conway, though he be desirous to pleasure you with a burgess-ship, yet gave no small hope save by his means when I spoke with him, but put me off to my Lord Chamberlain who came from the moor the last night, and I have been with him this day. His answer is that he has two privy councillors newly put upon him, else he could have seated you at the first hand, as he hopes he shall do yet at the second, upon some double return. And by his commandment I have entreated his secretary, Mr. Holesworth, to be your solicitor in my absence, and he has promised me to be careful of it. I shall not fail also, before my going, to speak to your other friends to the same purpose.

As I am but thus far, the bearer is come into my chamber and tells me his tide is come. I will therefore give him a brief memorial of all I had else to write, being not much in quantity and less in weight, and to commit it to his relation. Resting with the remembrance of my service to my good lady,

Your Lordship's most
humble servant,
Francis Nethersole

Hague, 24th April 1625

[*Endorsed*] 1625, Sir Fra. Nethersole, the 24 of April, by Mr. Clarke, 1625, Hague.

(c) [Downshire MS., Vol. 29, f. 175]

2 June 1625, Thomas Locke to William Trumbull.

Sir,

... We hope the parliament will hold at London for a while because the sickness decreases. I have sent you bills of this last week; the week before was 78 of the plague. We are more afraid than I hope we shall have cause, many families have removed themselves already into the country. The late presses of soldiers have ridded the City of a great many of unprofitable persons. Surely the provisions for these ships must exceed any former proportion, for there is scarce any beef to be had. I am sure in Westminster there is very small store and that exceeding dear. The furnishing of the ships with such store of cider and the casing of them with dealboards makes the western men conjecture that the voyage is for the West Indies. Sir, I hope you will excuse my boldness to trouble you with such things; with remembrances of my best love and service, I rest yours humbly at command,

Thomas Locke

---

2. Materials Concerning Upper House Attendance, 1625

(a) In addition to the documents printed below, see the Attendance Table, above, pp. 592–597, and the list of Lords excused, H. of L., 23 June, O.B. See also Henry Viscount Mandeville's letter to Lord Montagu, June 1625, in H.M.C., *Buccleuch*, I, 261, and notice of the license signed by the King to George, Earl of Shrewsbury, allowing his absence from parliament because of poor health, in H.M.C., *Various Collections*, II, 312.

(b) [S.P. 16/2:116]

The form of a license to be granted to a peer for dispensing with his personal attendance in parliament by reason of his health.

Right trusty and right well-beloved cousin, we greet you well.

Whereas we have caused our writ of summons to be directed to you (among others) to be present at our High Court of Parliament now assembled; forasmuch as we understand that by reason of your indisposition of body you cannot give your attendance at our said parliament, and thereupon have made humble suit unto us that we would be pleased to dispense with you for your absence from the same. We let you weet[1] that in regard thereof, and for divers other considerations us hereunto moving, we are pleased to give you license and by these presents do license you (our said writ of summons, or anything therein contained to the contrary notwithstanding) to be absent from this parliament. So as, nevertheless, you cause your proxy in due form of law to be sent up in convenient time, unto some such personage as may for you and in your name give his voice and consent to such matters as are to be propounded, treated, and concluded in our said parliament. And these our letters shall be your sufficient warrant and discharge in this behalf. Given under our signet at our palace of Westminster, the/

1. I.e., know.

(c) [Huntingdon Library, HA. 5501]

28 June 1625, the EARL OF HUNTINGDON to the EARL OF PEMBROKE, Dunnington.

My Lord,

Fearing lest I might incur his Majesty's displeasure by my absence since the parliament, I presume to trouble your Lordship with these lines to acquaint you with the just occasion. I had taken a house a month since, and lately the plague was so near it as I was forced to send to provide another but could not fit myself till within this two or three days, during which time the waters have been so great I could not pass with my coach. And hearing the parliament is likely to hold but for a short time, I have presumed to trouble your Lordship with my humble suit unto his Majesty to grant me that favor that my attendance may be spared. Now, which if it please his Majesty to do, I beseech your Lordship to honor me so much as to be my proxy. But if you think the motion will displease his Majesty or find the least dislike, I beseech you let me know that you think it fit for me to come and I will slack no time. But out of the hope I have by your Lordship's means to obtain the same, I have sent it you by this bearer, my servant. And so, acknowledging myself many ways bound to your Lordship for your noble favors, I rest,

Your Lordship's to do your service,
Huntingdon

Dunnington this 28th
of June 1625

(d) [S.P. 16/4:98]

21 July 1625, the EARL OF EXETER to ANONYMOUS, Burghley by Stanford.

My Lord,

Pardon me, I pray you, if I be troublesome unto you in the midst of the sea of your greater affairs to entreat you with as much speed as you can to procure me his Majesty's leave to be absent, upon urgent causes constraining me to forbear coming to the parliament now proclaimed at Oxford the first of August, having before I came down given my proxy to the most worthy the Duke of Buckingham who, I doubt not, will give your Lordship directions for the same. Yet I thought it a respect due unto your place (besides my former obligations) to make my humble suit unto you for the speedy dispatch of this bearer, the time being so short as I shall not be quiet in mind till his return. And to be unresolved in so great a point of my duty is every way prejudicial both to my stay here or my appearance there which, with myself, I recommend unto your honorable favor as,

Your faithful friend
to command,
Exeter

Burghley by Stanford
the 21 of July 1625

---

3. Materials Concerning the Elections to Parliament, 1625

Aside from the documents printed below and the references to journal articles and other works discussing various election cases in 1625, contested and otherwise, there are two books which deal with early Stuart franchises and parliamentary elections: John K. Gruenfelder, *Influence in Early Stuart Elections 1604–1640* (Columbus, Ohio, 1981), and Derek Hirst, *The Representative of the People?* (Cambridge, 1975). The editors have not specifically referred to these volumes with regard to the elections in the constituencies listed below; the references would be too numerous. Rather, they have chosen to mention the volumes here as essential research materials for anyone examining either general aspects of early seventeenth-century enfranchisement and voting patterns or specific problems within constituencies concerning electoral contests and patronage.

Aldborough, Yorkshire

See John K. Gruenfelder, "The Electoral Patronage of Sir Thomas Wentworth, Earl of Strafford, 1614–1640", *The Journal of Modern History*, 49 (1977), 570; and for a letter from Wentworth to Christopher Wandesford urging him "to secure" himself of Aldborough, see J. P. Cooper, ed., *Wentworth Papers 1597–1628* (London: Camden Society, 1973), pp. 229–230.

Anglesey, Wales

[National Library of Wales, Wynn MSS. (9060E)1326]
WILLIAM THOMAS, Sheriff, to ANONYMOUS, 16 April 1625, Quirte.[1]
Honorable Sir,

I have been informed that the writ for the electing of a knight to serve in the next parliament for this country of Anglesey was sent unto you. If it be, I desire to have it that he may be elected on Thursday next, which is the county day, lest the parliament be to begin the next county [day] following that. And so I rest at your service,

William Thomas, Sheriff
Quirte, the 16th
of April 1625

1. See also Sir Roger Mostyn's letter of 15 April to Sir John Wynn, below, *sub* Flintshire, and the general references, *sub* Wales.

Berkshire

See the letter of John Chamberlain to Sir Dudley Carleton, 6 May 1625, Chamberlain, *Letters*, II, 614–616 (S.P. 16/2:27, also printed in Birch, *Court and Times of Chas. I*, I, 18–20).

Bossiney, Cornwall

Concerning Sir Richard Weston's part in the election of Sir Francis Cottington, see Martin J. Havran, *Caroline Courtier: The Life of Lord Cottington* (New York, 1973), p. 85.

Boston, Lincolnshire

See John K. Gruenfelder, "Boston's Early Stuart Elections, 1604–1640", *Lincolnshire History and Archaeology*, 13 (1978), 48.

Brackley, Northamptonshire

[Northamptonshire Record Office, E.B. 585/1]
GEORGE SMALMAN to JOHN, EARL OF BRIDGEWATER, 26 April 1625.
Right Honorable,

May it please your Lordship, I have received your Honor's letter of the 25th April, the contents whereof, God willing, shall be effected to my best endeavors. Yesterday when I came from Brackley the writ for election of the burgesses was not come unto the mayor. I do presume upon the receipt of your Lordship's letter there will be no opposition but that, as your Honor does desire, Sir Richard Anderson shall have free election. Only 2 or 3 do desire to be free of their promises which, upon your Lordship's first letter for Mr. Spencer they had passed (as Mr. Clarke and Mr. Mayor), and I do not remember any other of the company but them two, but their voices were free for your Lordship. (I mean of those that were then present and whose hands are at the letter.) Of the passage of this business I shall, God willing, upon each occasion advertise your Lordship. I will deliver your Lordship's letter unto the mayor before Thursday night, which I am confident will be in good time.

For Ashridge: the vaults or common shores for the house are now this morning about to be opened and cleansed. My lady's little building is likewise begun upon, and I hope we shall do something to gain some passage for the vault in the waste house yard. All things here are well, and thus with my prayers to God for the increase of all honor and happiness to your Lordship and all yours in all duty do take my leave and will ever faithfully remain your Honor's servant,

George Smalman

Bridgnorth, Shropshire

For mention of the contest between Sir George Paule, client of the Duke of Buckingham, and George Vernon, see *V.C.H., Shropshire*, III, 244.

Caernarvon, Caernarvonshire, Wales

See the correspondence between Sir Peter Mutton, Sir John Wynn, and Sir William Thomas, *sub* Caernarvonshire, and also the general references, *sub* Wales.

[National Library of Wales, Wynn MSS. (9060E)1318]
EDWARD LITTLETON to SIR WILLIAM THOMAS, 12 April 1625.
Sir,

I lately received a letter from Sir Peter Mutton importing that he means to sit this parliament for the county of Caernarvon and that you and the rest of the gentlemen (he doubted not) would be content that I should sit for the town, and that he had written unto you and others to such purpose. I desire your resolution therein by this bearer, by whom the writ to the sheriff for the election is sent unto Sir Peter Mutton. If you please to think me fit for the place I should do the town such service as my understanding will enable me unto and shall acknowledge your courtesy. Howsoever I desire in this and all other places, that men be left to their free election. My wife's respect and ours to yourself and lady, I rest

Your assured loving friend,
Edward Littleton

April 12, 1625
[Illegible]

[*Postscript*] Since the sealing thereof I understand by letters from your parts that Mr. Glynne intends to stand to be knight of the shire, for that Sir Peter Mutton should not be capable thereof in regard he has no lands within the county which was a thing overruled the last parliament upon great debate, or the last but one, in Sir George Hastings's case.[1] That neither resident nor having of lands or being burgess of a town is necessary notwithstanding the statutes that seem to the contrary. I understand likewise that Mr. William Wynn desires to be burgess for Caernarvon, which is contrary to his father's resolution with Sir Peter Mutton. I should desire to know the truth in these particulars, if the electors find one more worthy or that they more affect than myself (as they may easily do) their refusal shall not break myself.

1. In 1621 Sir George Hastings was elected by the greater number of voices but the sheriff returned Sir Thomas Beaumont, believing Hastings was not a resident in the shire. After considerable debate the House proclaimed the election of Sir George Hastings good, although he had no freehold in the shire but was a renter. *C.D. 1621*, VI, 429–431.

[National Library of Wales, Wynn MSS. (9060E)1322]

SIR WILLIAM THOMAS to SIR JOHN WYNN, 14 April 1625, Caernarvon.

Honorable Sir,

I received the enclosed letter from our justice Mr. Littleton (who has received his commission for his place already) who I perceive does and is resolved to stand for the burgess-ship of the town of Caernarvon, and relies upon the resolution and promise you made Sir Peter Mutton therein. Which, being thoroughly considered with the letter you also wrote unto me to that effect, it were not convenient in my opinion to contend with them for the place, being our justice of assize and one whom Caernarvon and Conway would not willingly contradict, for then they would withdraw their favors for the assizes from that place that did oppose them, besides the special note and knowledge that no doubt they will take against such peculiar persons as will not cleave to their side. And I remember one precept of yours amongst the rest, that although a man may for his own person live within his compass, and stand at distance with his judge, yet shall he not be able to defend and protect all his friends and followers against authority. Wherefore because you have passed your goodwill and promise unto them and that my most worthy cousin Mr. William Wynn (whom I do dearly love and honor for many respects) seems belike by your best advice and counsel to surcease and to give way unto the times, I have presumed upon both your loves and wisdoms to grant my goodwill unto Mr. Justice Littleton for the burgess-ship, whom if we had opposed would have made a great faction in Pwllheli, Nevin, and Criccieth, and would have made some in Caernarvon as you know, as my neighbor, Mr. Spicer, cousin Robert Griffiths, and Sir Thomas Williams, tenants that be burgesses of the said town, and perhaps win some voices in Conway likewise, all which is not to you unknown.

The bearer that brought me the letter from Mr. Littleton delivered me the commission of the peace and *dedimus potestatem* for the swearing of the justices of peace. And although my Lord Bishop be first nominated, yet because you are *custos rotulorum* I have sent the same and the *dedimus* unto you for further to be done as you see cause. Howbeit lest my Lord Bishop happily will think it much (as also all the rest of the justice[s] of peace) to come to Gwydir or Trevor[1] to be sworn, it were not amiss in my conceit that you would send the commission forthwith and *dedimus* back again, and desire my Lord Bishop, Sir John Bodvel, and all the rest to meet at Caernarvon for that purpose.

The time for the quarter sessions ever used to be the next week after low Easter

Sunday, and I believe it is the very time that the statute does limit; and I cannot see how the same can be either summoned or kept before the justice of peace be sworn. Wherein it were expedient that you took speedy and good advice, the time being so short. If the justices were sworn, a warrant for someone might presently go forth under two of the justices of peace's hands and the quarter kept in the due time. And I do imagine that the fifteen days' warning shall not be material. And so referring all to your best consideration, with my unfeigned love unto yourself and your noble lady, I rest,

Your assured loving cousin,

W. Thomas

Caernarvon the
14th of April 1625

[*Postscript*] Spicer has laid out 12*d*. apiece for every justice of peace unto the messenger that brought the commission, etc., unto me.

[*Postscript*] This day the bearer that brought this commission brought also the writ for the electing of the knight and burgess of the parliament which, if it had come yesterday, being the county day, it had given us a bob for Mr. Thomas Glynne, whom I am told is disposed to contest with the judge. Sir Peter Mutton was here yesterday and the sheriff also, and with less than twenty men upon that sudden would have carried away the place of knightship, etc.

1. MS.: *Trevriwe*.

Caernarvonshire, Wales

[National Library of Wales, Wynn MSS. (9060E)1320]

SIR JOHN WYNN to SIR PETER MUTTON, 14 April 1625, Gwydir.

Sir,

Yesterday Richard Griffith, one of the attorneys at the Council, came hither to me, who had be[en] upon business and had been at Caernarvon the Saturday before and (among other speeches) told me that he heard it confidently reported in town that Thomas Glynne does stand for the election and would not yield the place unto you. It is like that he has the sheriff for him, and John Bodwrda and who else I know not. I remember when you were here you wrote unto him as to your assured friend and to whom besides I remember not. You see how you find him, and those whom you most trusted besides. Hereof I thought it a friend's part to give you notice that you may provide hereafter. Holding me very kindly unto you and to my good cousin your lady, do rest,

Your assured loving cousin,
John Wynn of Gwydir

Gwydir, *14° Aprilis 1625*.

[*Postscript*] He brought me also most kind commendations from Sir Thomas Chamberlain, willing him to tell me that the very last words my Lord Keeper spoke unto him were a special charge to respect me and my friends which truly he needed not, for I was ever much beholden to Sir John for his love.

[National Library of Wales, Wynn MSS. (9060E)1325]

SIR PETER MUTTON to SIR JOHN WYNN, 16 April 1625, Llewenny.[1]

Worthy Sir,

I acknowledge myself much beholding unto you for your letter and kind respects. It is true that Mr. Glynne at the last parliament told me that if any of my friends had desired the place for me he would have yielded with many protestations of his love and respect unto me; and thereupon I assured myself of his furtherance at this time and of all others that he would not have opposed. And if I had thought that he or any other would have stood against my brother Littleton and myself I would not have come upon the stage to have been a competitor with any, and thereupon I moved yourself first, and finding you to give way I did write to Sir William Thomas, my cousin, Thomas Williams, and Mr.

Thomas Glynne and to no more, expecting no opposition but thinking my brother Littleton and myself secure herein. But after the receipt of your letter this day I received another letter from Caernarvonshire that Mr. Thomas Glynne is very stiff and confident and means to stand for the place against wind and weather, so that I am sorry my name should come in question to be a competitor with him. But howsoever I acknowledge myself beholding unto you for your love and many kind respects which I have always found and hereafter I shall know my friends, etc., and so with the remembrance of my best love and service to yourself and your good lady, I shall ever remain,

Your poor kinsman and
truly well-wisher,
P. Mutton

Llewenny
16 April 1625

1. With regard to the Caernarvonshire election see also Sir Roger Mostyn's letter of 15 April to Sir John Wynn, *sub* Flintshire.

[National Library of Wales, Wynn MSS. (9060E)1329]
SIR JOHN WYNN to SIR PETER MUTTON, 17 April 1625.
Sir,

At your being here you requested me that I would not oppose you for the knight's place in the county of Caernarvon which Sir William Thomas and myself granted and are still firm for you. Thomas Glynne, to whom I saw you then wrote, opposes himself against you, might and main. You slighted then the sheriff, Sir John Bodvel, William Vaughan, John Griffith of Lleyn, Griffith Jones, and Ellis Brinker, whereof every one of them is as potent as himself if John Bodwrda be from him, who has some 3-score beggars which will give voices with him (living in Aberdaron, a corner of the country by him).

The writ for the election came to Caernarvon upon Thursday last and Sir William Thomas writes unto me that on Wednesday before, being the county day, the sheriff and Thomas Glynne were in town and might have carried it with the voice of 20 men without any opposition, wherein I do condemn you much for being so careless, thereby discrediting yourself much and those that be your friends. Now you have almost a month to labor for it, for as by computation you cannot lose it unless the defect be in yourself for want of solicitation and good handling.

Mr. Littleton (who in the new commission of the peace which I received is named Sir Edward Littleton) is sure of the burgess-ship, my son William yielding him the place. Commending me very kindly unto you and to my good cousin your lady, I rest ever your assured loving,

Cousin

[*Endorsed*] To the right worthy Sir Peter Mutton, Knight, Chief Justice of North Wales, give these.

[National Library of Wales, Wynn MSS. (9060E)1330]
SIR PETER MUTTON to SIR JOHN WYNN, 18 April 1625, Llewenny.
Worthy Sir,

I had not meddled with the matter of election but upon Mr. Littleton's letters and to draw him at this time to be of the parliament, which I conceived to be for the good of the country. And for my own part I could have been well contented to have continued my old place of burgess or not to have been at all of the parliament if I had thought that it would have been opposed by such; and in the behalf of Mr. Littleton and myself I only moved you and did write to Sir William Thomas, my cousin Thomas Williams, and Mr. Thomas Glynne, which I thought sufficient to make our desires known, thinking that no man (and especially Mr. Thomas Glynne) would not [*sic*] stand against us.

And if he do, let him take it, for I will not go a begging for it, but I do not believe but that Mr. Glynne will be better advised than to be opposite. And so I leave every man to his own humor and myself ever thankful to you for your kindness. And if it please you to have anything to London I will be your messenger, so you said within three days, for longer I shall not stay; lesser I take my journey. And this not forgetting my best respect to you and your good lady, I rest,

> Your kinsman and
> unfeigned friend,
> P. Mutton

Llewenny,
18 April 1625

[National Library of Wales, Wynn MSS. (9060E)1314]
SIR JOHN WYNN to SIR WILLIAM THOMAS, 6 April 1625, Gwydir.
My Worthy Good Cousin,

This day came Sir Peter Mutton hither out of his love to visit me as he used often to do. I thanked him for it. Being here he propounded unto me his desire and his brother Mr. Littleton['s] to be of the parliament for this next time to come—himself for the county and Mr. Littleton for the borough, desiring my goodwill and furtherance therein, thinking that if I opposed it not no other would do. I answered that you and myself were tied in that league that I could not grant them my goodwill without your's also. But if you liked of the motion (as I think you would) I would assent also. I refer myself yours to answer for both, but in my opinion they are worthy of the place, being our judges. Commending my love unto you and to your good lady, dearest ever,

> Your assured loving cousin,
> John Wynn of Gwydir

Gwydir,
6° Aprilis 1625

[National Library of Wales, Wynn MSS. (9060E)1316]
SIR WILLIAM THOMAS to SIR JOHN WYNN, 7 April 1625, Caernarvon.
Honorable Cousin,

I have received a letter from you and another from Sir Peter Mutton showing that Sir Peter had moved you for your goodwill and furtherance for the knightship and burgess-ship of the parliament for himself and his brother Mr. Justice Littleton, and that your answer was that you would not assent thereunto until you knew how I liked of that motion. Your choice I like well of for, as you do write, they are men worthy of the place. Howbeit, I have labored many of my friends already for my cousin William Wynn for the burgess-ship, though I did not explain myself so far unto the burgesses. But now I presume he will not stand in opposition with the judges, of which mind I believe you and he are of. And therefore you have given me good satisfaction in that behalf. And so with hearty thanks for the great and kind respect you ever showed me, and more especially in this wherein you did me a great deal of credit, for which you shall find me most firm and fast unto you while I live, whereof I hope you will make no doubt. Wishing you perfect health and happiness, and the like to your noble lady, and all yours, I betake us all to the protection of the Almighty, and rest,

> Your assured loving
> cousin at all assays,
> W. Thomas

Caernarvon the
7th of April 1625

[National Library of Wales, Wynn MSS. (9060E)1321]
SIR JOHN WYNN to SIR WILLIAM THOMAS, 14 April 1625, Gwydir.
My Worthy Good Cousin,

This day I received my l[ord] lieutenant's

letter, which I send here enclosed unto you, having reserved myself a copy. I know you will send Sir John Bodvel a copy, as also to the rest.

Yesterday came Richard Griffith hither, being one of the attorneys at the Council, about special business and, among other speeches that passed between us, he told me that he had been at Caernarvon on Saturday last where he heard it confidently reported that Thomas Glynne would stand for the election and that he would not yield to Sir Peter Mutton. I desire to know your opinion therein, you and I have suited ourselves like friends, and have no further to do, but I would gladly [know] who be of his part and partakers. Richard Griffith also delivered me most kind commendations for Sir Thomas Chamberlain, willing him to tell me that my L[ord] Keeper gave him charge to respect me and my friends and those were the last words which he spoke unto him when he took his farewell. Truly, said Sir Thomas, he needed not to give me any such charge for I ever loved Sir John and was much beholding unto him. Sending my love unto you and to your good lady, do rest ever,

Your assured loving cousin,
John Wynn of Gwydir

Gwydir, *14°*
Aprilis 1625

[National Library of Wales, Wynn MSS. (9060E)1334]
SIR JOHN WYNN to SIR WILLIAM THOMAS, 22 April 1625, Gwydir.
My Worthy Good Cousin,

Upon the receipt of your letter I wrote to Sir Peter Mutton (the letter whereof I send you the copy) and received this answer, whereof I send you also the copy. It seems that he thinks the valiant champion Thomas Glynne will be better advised. Whether he be or be not it is nothing to us, *stet et cudet [sic] suo domino*. Of all other things I hate

these elections—most troublesome, most unprofitable, and most thankless. Therefore I think it best to let things stand as they do, and yet I would not willingly that Thomas Glynne should carry the place, but I refer all to your consideration. I believe his place will do him little good in his estate, which I hear to be in the wane. In the mean I hear all things good and comfortable (blessed be God) from my good friends above [*illegible*] and in the country. And so with my true love to yourself and to your goody l recommend, I rest ever,

Your assured loving cousin,
[John Wynn]

Gwydir
22° Aprilis 1625

[National Library of Wales, Wynn MSS. (9060E)1341]
SIR WILLIAM THOMAS to SIR JOHN WYNN, 28 May 1625, Caernarvon.
Noble Cousin,

I finding the conveniency of this bearer, his coming unto you, I might not omit to write unto you and to certify you what I do hear from above, *vizt.*, that the coronation is deferred until September and the parliament also deferred, I know not how long. And the King is gone to Dover [*torn*] to the Queen and I believe returned before [*torn*] time. There is great pressing of men in London, [*torn*] they dare not show their faces there, but that are presently clapped up in Bridewell and other places. [The] press is likewise general throughout all England; I pray God it come not to Wales. It were not amiss that we should send for our deputations and each of us 20s. to pay for the same. For I have seen Thomas Williams, Thomas Glynne, and John Griffith send a messenger of purpose to Bewdley for their deputations. The last month what was done there I know not, but I understand they delivered 20s. apiece to pay for the same and no more, besides the bearers' charges. My cousin William Griffith received one printed in paper, and I do not love to have paper for my money in a matter of so great consequence as may be questioned thirty years hence.

I understand that the soldiers of Breda made an attempt upon two or three of Spinola his forts and won them [torn] with the loss of many men of our side. Amongst the [torn] I do hear that Sir Thomas Wynn was one, but [pr]ay God it be not so.

My brother Griffith Thomas, being desirous to live under your wing, has compounded with William Williams for his term upon your lands, that was in Cadde ap Humphrey his lands about Caernarvon; and he is the best tenant that I know in Caernarvonshire for he carries all the muck in and about the town to your ground and others in his lands, that the same will be the better many years after. The last winter storm and sea has overthrown the great stone hedge and fence which he made upon your lands between it and the sea. And now to his great cost and charges he has made it up again, which he refers to your consideration and love. But my brother tells me that the barn in Cay Gwynn is exempted out of the lease, to your own use, and now is grown to great decay as the bearer can inform you. It may be helped yet, with small changes, but if it fall down twenty [torn] will not build the like. Therefore my brother [torn] know your pleasure therein, for he is such a [torn] would have nothing fall to decay that might [torn].

I presume you have heard of all the passages [torn] of the knight of the shire long ere this. He came with all the forces of Lleyn, Evioneths, and Vchorvay, and the chief leaders were John Griffith, John Bodwrda, Henry Bodvel, and his son-in-law Griffith Madryn, Richard Vaughan, my cousin William Vaughan his son, Ellis Brinker, Robert Owen of [illegible], Humphrey Meredith, and divers other gentlemen of the better sort except Griffith

Jones. He labored as if it had been to obtain a great prize.

I pray you let me hear of all the news you have received from London by the bearer and what news I shall receive by my son which [sic] will be at home by Whitsuntide I will send you likewise.

In the meantime, praying for your healths as my own, with my true love unto yourself and your noble [torn] betake you and all yours to the protection of the Almighty.

> Your assured loving [torn]
> at your disposing,
> W. Thomas

Caernarvon the 28th
of May 1625

[National Library of Wales, Chirk Castle MS. F12.837]
ROBERT WYNN to SIR THOMAS MIDDLETON, 3 May 1625, Maes Mochnant.
Right Worthy Master,

I was determined to have spoken with my cousin Mr. William Wynn upon Thursday last but understood that he was gone to Kynnell. And thereupon I went to his son and showed him how the Thelwalls despaired of the election. If my cousin his father would remain constant unto you and do his uttermost endeavor, and [that] made known unto him withal, what a discredit it would be for him to falter therein, considering he was as deeply engaged in credit therein as yourself. Thereupon he told me that his cousin John Thelwall had been upon Easter Monday with his father and himself, and of the passages which then passed and how earnest he was with them to slacken in the business, and vowed the firmness of his father and himself to you therein to the uttermost. And I assured him in your behalf that it should not be forgotten. When occasion offered itself for requital he desired me to put you in mind to write your letter, to provide a burgess-ship in some town of England for his uncle, Sir Thomas Wynn, that he may be a member of the Parliament House, to some of your friends aboveforth, which I promised to do.

Upon Sunday last my cousin William Wynn (being come to Dyffryn Melay the night before) sent his son, my cousin John Wynn, to Gwydir to see my brother and to confer with him touching the election. And my brother and myself confirmed him in his earnestness and agreed to send abroad to their friends this week servants of theirs to labor their coming all with my cousin William Wynn; and not to labor as we do hear other gentlemen do that are on the contrary part, which labor all the same freeholders to know with which of them they will give their election, by which means many of the freeholders will stay at home for fear of displeasing any man, which makes of our part. He promised to send you the names toward the latter end of the week, and said that my cousin, Mr. John Middleton, had been with his father and himself from you since I last spoke with him.

Yesterday morning I saw some of my brother's messengers go abroad touching the business. Secondly, at night, I saw a letter written from London from an understanding gentleman to a friend of his which showed that the plague increased there. And it was talked that both the term and parliament should be kept either at Winchester or Oxford. And that our King had already given some testimony of his good and gracious government toward us by the choice of so good men to be of his cabinet council, not naming any of them, but said they were such as regarded the good of the commonwealth.

The letter mentioned further that the Duke was crazy and that he had resigned all his offices to the King, reserving only to himself his place in the Bedchamber. This is all the news I had since my going up to Caernarvonshire. I conceive the Thelwalls,

when all comes to all, will not stand for the election. My brother, Simon Thelwall, as I understand, is already gone for London. Thus, leaving you further trouble at this time, with my best wishes, do commit you to God and ever rest,

Your loving cousin and firm friend,
Robert Wynn
Maes Mochnant
May the third, 1625

Cambridge, Cambridgeshire

See Reverend Joseph Mead's letter to Sir Martin Stuteville, 9 April 1625, Birch, *Court and Times of Chas. I*, I, 5–6.

Cambridge University

Concerning the expense of electing Sir Albertus Morton, see Chamberlain, *Letters*, II, 614–616 (S.P. 16/2:27, also printed in Birch, *Court and Times of Chas. I*, I, 18–20).

Canterbury, Kent

See Chamberlain, *Letters*, II, 614–616 (S.P. 16/2:27, also printed in Birch, *Court and Times of Chas. I*, I, 18–20).

Christchurch, Kent

Sir Thomas Wilford, returned for Christchurch and Canterbury, chose to sit for Canterbury. Thomas, Lord Arundell of Wardour, supported Sir Edward Boys in the by-election in Christchurch.

[Christchurch Borough MSS., Letter, 1625]
THOMAS, LORD ARUNDELL OF WARDOUR to the MAYOR OF CHRISTCHURCH, 16 June 1625.
After my hearty commendations,

Mayor, with many thanks for choosing such burgesses as I nominated unto you, which I shall be ready to requit in any business wherein you shall have occasion to use me, I am now to let you understand that Sir Thomas Wilford, Knight, whom you were content at my motion to elect to be a burgess, is also chosen to be a burgess for the town of Canterbury, so as there will be a new writ of election sent unto you. Wherefore my earnest request unto you is that you will do me the favor as to make election of Sir Edward Boys the younger, of Fredville, in the county of Kent, Knight, for the which I shall think myself much beholden unto you and, in the meantime, I commend me kindly unto you, wishing you all happiness,

Your loving friend,
Thomas Arundell

June the 16th

Clitheroe, Lancashire

Sir Humphrey May recommended Sir Thomas Trevor for the seat, although he was not elected. See H.M.C., *14th Report, Appendix, Part IV*, p. 31.

Colchester, Essex

[Essex Record Office, Morant MSS., Vol. 43, p. 29]
SIR HENRY HOBART to the BAILIFFS OF COLCHESTER, 31 March 1625.
After my very hearty commendations;

Whereas the King's Majesty that now is has resolved to call a parliament very speedily for the which new elections must be made of knights and burgesses, wherein I am very desirous that my eldest son, Sir John Hobart, should be a burgess. My earnest desire therefore to you is that you will be pleased to make choice of him for one of your burgesses at this time. Wherein as he shall execute the same without any wages or other charge to your town, so he will be most ready to perform all the good offices of respect wherein he may any way pleasure your town either by himself or his friends upon all occasions that shall be made known unto him either by your learned counsel or any other in the behalf of your

said town. And I shall take it for a singular testimony of your respect to myself whereof I will be always mindful and rest,

Your very assured loving
friend,
Henry Hobart

Serjeants Inn the
last of March 1625

[Essex Record Office, Morant MSS., Vol. 43, p. 23]
The BAILIFFS OF COLCHESTER to SIR HENRY HOBART, Chief Justice of the Court of Common Pleas, n.d., Little St. Bartholomews.
After our right hearty commendations;

About ten days hence we received notice from Mr. Serjeant Towse that he was to deliver a letter unto us from your Lordship about the choosing of your son, Sir John Hobart, for one of our burgesses. But by reason we received no warrant for the electing of them until Friday last we could not proceed to our election until this day, whereof we gave notice to Mr. Serjeant upon Saturday last, who came this day with your letter with a full purpose and intent to have yielded his place of burgess-ship unto your son. And we and the most part of the aldermen were willing to have satisfied your request therein, and Mr. Serjeant declared himself to the whole company, how willing he was to give way to your son if it were but for this time. Yet the company, consisting of a multitude, would not anyway condescend to leave him off, alleging that it had not been known in the memory of men but our town clerk has always been one, most of them seeming to be much discontented he would be so earnest in his request; and for Mr. Alford, in respect of his long and loving service to this corporation therein, they would not consent to alter our choosing him. And therefore we assure you that ourselves and Mr. Serjeant did (both then and before) so much as lay in us. And so praying your Lordship's favor and the continuance of your love to this corporation we rest,

> Your Lordship's ever loving friends,
> Bailiffs

At Little St. Bartholomews.

[Essex Record Office, Morant MSS., Vol. 43, p. 77]
ROBERT, EARL OF SUSSEX, to BAILIFFS OF COLCHESTER, 7 April 1625.
After my very hearty commendations remembered;

Whereas our late deceased King had appointed a parliament to be held the twentieth of this instant month, but it is now disappointed by the hands of the Almighty, and now our gracious Sovereign has sent out his writ for this parliament to be held the seventeenth of May next, and for new election to be made of knights and burgesses of the shire, may it therefore please you to take into your consideration one Mr. Alexander Radcliffe who is my very near kinsman and my heir, and one that I dare commend for his judgment and discretion and ability. Let me, therefore, entreat you to elect him for one of the burgesses of Colchester and I shall ever rest myself much bound to you and your fraternity. And in doing this courtesy to him I shall ever take it as done to myself; and so desiring your speedy answer that I may provide elsewhere for him if this take not effect. And so I bid you very heartily farewell and rest,

> Your very loving friend,
> Robert, [Earl of] Sussex

From my house
at Clerkenwell this
7th of April 1625

[Essex Record Office, Morant MSS., Vol. 43, p. 25]
BAILIFF OF COLCHESTER to ROBERT, EARL OF SUSSEX, 14 April 1625.
Right Honorable,

My fellow bailiff being now in Lincolnshire I cannot acquaint him with your Honor's letter and request. For my own part, and [sic] so I doubt not but my fellow bailiff will be very willing at the time of the election of the burgesses, which as yet is uncertain for that we have not received any warrant, to acquaint the whole company that are to make that election with your Honor's letter and request. But what effect it will take is uncertain, for my fellow bailiff and myself have only our voices and how the electors will be drawn to make alteration of our former burgesses I know not. For that hitherto they have so far respected them in regard of their good and long service for this incorporation as they would not be persuaded to make choice of any other. So my humble service remembered, in all duty I rest,

> At your Honor's commandment,
> Bailiff T.

14 April 1625
[Endorsed] To the Right Honorable Robert, Earl of Sussex, at his Honor's house at Clerkenwell.

[Essex Record Office, Morant MSS., Vol. 43, p. 27]
BAILIFFS OF COLCHESTER to ROBERT, EARL OF SUSSEX, 19 April 1625.
Right Honorable,

This day being appointed for the electing of burgesses for this borough we acquainted the whole company with your Honor's request by reading your Honor's letters unto them, but they would not be persuaded to make any alteration of their ancient burgesses, and have made choice of the former, vizt., Mr. Serjeant Towse and Mr. Alford. Whereof we make bold to signify your Lordship by reason the former answer returned by your Honor's messenger was uncertain. So our humble duty remembered, we rest,

> At your Honor's commandment,
> Bailiffs

19 Aprilis 1625

[*Endorsed*] To the Right Honorable our [*illegible*] Lord Robert, Earl of Sussex, at his house at Clerkenwell.

Denbighshire, Wales

[National Library of Wales, Wynn MSS. (9060E)1315]
SIR THOMAS MIDDLETON to SIR JOHN WYNN, 7 April 1625.[1]
Worthy Cousin,

The immutability of these times does enforce these few lines. His Majesty's pleasure being made known that he will call a parliament, having a desire to do my country service I have adventured to stand to be a knight of the shire, for the better and more facile effecting whereof I desire the help and furtherance of my friends and among them yourself especially, which favor, if you please to vouchsafe me, I shall acknowledge myself (if more may be), obliged unto you, with this assurance—that you shall find me ready at all times to requite the same. The desiring your answer, with tender of my best wishes to yourself and the rest of my good cousins now present with you, I rest ever,

Your most assured cousin,
Thomas Middleton
7° April. 1625

1. See also Sir Roger Mostyn's letter of 15 April to Sir John Wynn, *sub* Flintshire.

[National Library of Wales, Wynn MSS. (9060E)1317]
SIR JOHN WYNN to SIR THOMAS MIDDLETON, 8 April 1625, Gwydir.

I am sorry, my good cousin, that I cannot satisfy your expectation at this time as you desire. For on Monday last did my cousin William Wynn of Conway send unto me for my friends' voices and mine to make his brother, Sir Thomas Wynn, knight of the shire for the county of Denbigh, which I gave him, being tied by promise to him be-

fore, since the last election there. Else I can assure you there is not anyone within the county of Denbigh that I would more freely and willingly bestow the same than on yourself. I sent my son, upon the receipt of your letter, to my cousin, John Wynn ap William, and I am told for certain that my cousin William Wynn and you shall not disagree in this business, which I was glad to hear of, being desirous that all may sort to your own content. And so with the remembrance of my best wishes to yourself and your worthy lady, I rest ever,

Your most assured
loving cousin,
[John Wynn]
Gwydir, this
8° April. 1625

Dorset

See John K. Gruenfelder, "Dorsetshire Elections, 1604–1640", *Albion,* 10, no. 1 (1978), 4.

Essex

See Chamberlain, *Letters,* II, 614–616 (S.P. 16/2:27, also printed in Birch, *Court and Times of Chas. I,* I, 18–20).

[Essex Record Office, Morant MSS., Vol. 43, p. 55]
THOMAS, VISCOUNT OF COLCHESTER, to the BAILIFFS OF COLCHESTER, 28 April 1625, St. Osyth.

I wrote unto you heretofore to desire that the voices of your freeholders at the election of knights might be cast upon Sir Francis Barrington and Sir Thomas Cheeke, as it was at the last choice of knights for the shire, but I understand by Mr. Eldreed that my letter came not to your hands. I therefore now desire that you will be pleased to deal so with your freeholders as that the voices be given to these gentlemen aforenamed according to the former choice. And this I desire the rather of you, it being at the request of my Lord of Buckingham. So I commend you to God,

Your loving friend,
Colchester

St. Osyth's, the
28th of April 1625

[*Postscript*] I am laboring (because it is a fair journey for this country) to stay the going of the freeholders if there be no contradiction which, if I shall hear there be not, I will let you understand it because I would save the travel of the country if it may be.

[Essex Record Office, Morant MSS., Vol. 43, p. 83]

ROBERT, EARL OF WARWICK, to BAILIFFS OF COLCHESTER, 29 April 1625, Leighs.

Whereas the election of the knights of the shire is to be at Braintree upon Tuesday next, being the third day of May, between the hours of 8 and 9 of the clock in the forenoon, I desire you would publish and make known unto my friends and neighbors the freeholders in the corporation that I purpose as a freeholder among them to give my voice with my cousin Sir Francis Barrington in the first place, being an ancient parliament man and a gentleman well known to them whose worth and integrity well deserves the same. And in the second place to Sir Arthur Herris whose understanding and integrity well deserves that employment, if so they shall like of it. So I kindly salute you and rest,

Your very loving friend,
Robert, [Earl of] Warwick

Leighs, this 9th of
April 1625

[Essex Record Office, Morant MSS., Vol. 43, p. 59]

THOMAS, VISCOUNT OF COLCHESTER, to the BAILIFFS OF COLCHESTER, 30 April 1625, St. Osyth.

Whereas I desired you (being moved thereunto by my Lord of Buckingham) to cast the voices of your freeholders upon Sir Francis Barrington and Sir Thomas Cheeke, I do understand now from the quarter sessions that it is agreed that Sir Thomas Cheeke does not stand for the second place. I pray you therefore let your first voice be given to Sir Francis Barrington and the second to whom you please. So I commend you to God,

Your loving friend,
Colchester

St. Osyth's, the
30th of April 1625

[Essex Record Office, Morant MSS., Vol. 43, p. 63]

THOMAS, VISCOUNT COLCHESTER, to the BAILIFFS OF COLCHESTER, 30 April 1625, St. Osyth.

Since my letter unto you dated this day I have received a letter from my Lord of Warwick this night, twelve o'clock, who desires the second place at the election be given unto Sir Arthur Herris. And because I am willing to satisfy his Lordship herein, and other the gentlemen of the country who have resolved upon this gentleman for the second place, I desire that you will be pleased to cause your friends and freeholders to give their voices accordingly, that is to Sir Francis Barrington the first place and the second to Sir Arthur Herris, and so do commend you to God and rest,

Your loving friend,
Colchester

St. Osyth's, this
night the 30th of
April 1625

Flintshire

In addition to the letters printed below, see the general references, *sub* Wales.

[Clwyd Record Office, Nawarden, D/GW/2109]

THOMAS MOSTYN to ROBERT DAVIES, 5 April 1625, Gloddaeth.

Cousin Davies,

You have heard of the death of our late King and, as I hear there is [torn] for a new parliament, I am bold [torn] your favor and your friends that [torn] supply the place for the county of Flint. I shall be ready to do the office of an honest man for my country. If you have not passed your word to another I make no doubt but you will pleasure me in this, and if the like fall out I shall be ready to requite it if it lie [in] my power. Thus, with the remembrance of my love to yourself and your bedfellow, [I] do rest,

Your assured loving cousin,
Thomas Mostyn[1]

Gloddaeth,[2] this 5th
of April 1625
[Endorsed] To the worshipful, his very loving cousin, Robert Davies, Esq., at Broighton, these.

---

1. Mostyn lost the seat to Sir John Trevor, Jr.
2. MS.: Glotheith.

[National Library of Wales, Wynn MSS. (9060E)1324]

SIR ROGER MOSTYN to SIR JOHN WYNN, 15 April 1625, Gloddaeth.

Honorable Sir,

All the news I have by my son's letter is that the funeral is to be solemnized the 10th of May, the coronation the 15th, and the parliament the 17th. Then writs of my lord's pleasure touching places in the several counties of Wales for parliament, and for my part in Flintshire it goes out according to the last choice of Sir John Trevor whereunto I, and all the friends I had, had given consent. And to make a show to seek it and fail were a greater disgrace than the benefit thereof would be to him that had it. For that in Anglesey for my son, John Mostyn, I find great opposition by Sir Sackvile[1] Trevor to whom, as I am informed, all the justices of the peace of that county have subscribed under their hands to be for him and he resolved to stand for it against all men. Taking this opportunity of the differences at Bangor, I took my journey thither to my lord and showed him the earnest desire my Lord Keeper had that my son should continue in that place, where also Mr. Richard Bulkeley of Porthamel met me. Both of them told me that Sir Sackvile had resolved to stand for it, so I conceive no means for my son to gain it unless by some late letters that came from London to Mr. William Owen of Bodyddow and others of my lord's friends both to labor and stand in it for my son, which, if I hold a likelihood that any of the justices of the peace will stand themselves and hold firm, I will not fail to put it to the plunge. The writ is come to my hands, the writs also unto me that my lord hopes that you will take a care for Caernarvonshire and Merionethshire that friends may be elected there. He directs me also to send to Sir Peter Mutton to tell him my lord's pleasure that he should absolutely stand for a place in Denbighshire and this day wrote unto him thereof, though I am assured he will not stand. For at my being with him last he showed me a letter that came from Mr. Littleton for a place in Caernarvonshire, so that they resolved, and having your consent, to stand for both the places in this county, seeing that my lord could not have su[r]er friends than they were within the House. Thereupon I replied their being of this county they possessed themselves of such places as my lord upon his word could place others there, and they, being great men, might have made choice of other places [and] so gained a stronger party in the House. But all this did not work anything with him and so I left him, and this day by my letters I [re]minded him the same. It is high time now that you should be weary of that troublesome wench, whom I will send for this day [illegible]. Sometime the next week, for aught I know, I purpose homewards. So with my hearty commendations to yourself, my mother-in-law, and all yours, I rest,

Your loving son-in-law,
Roger Mostyn

Gloddaeth,
15° Aprilis

1. MS.: *Sackefield.*

Great Yarmouth, Norfolk

For the corporation regulations for the election of burgesses, see C. J. Palmer, *History of Great Yarmouth* (Great Yarmouth, 1856), II, 204.

[Norfolk and Norwich R.O., Yarmouth Corporation MSS., ff. 323–323v]
ASSEMBLY OF COMMON COUNCIL, 27 April 1625.

At this assembly the sheriff's warrant with the copy of his Majesty's writ summoning a parliament to be held and begun on the seventeenth day of May next there included and of an election to be made of burgesses of the same parliament for this borough, being read, certain letters addressed unto Mr. Balines from divers knights and on their behalves, entreating for them to be chosen burgesses of the parliament for this borough, were also publicly read. Whereupon Mr. Balines declared what they knew or had heard in commendations of every of them.

And it was agreed and ordered upon good causes and considerations that, notwithstanding any former ordinance to the contrary, yet it should be lawful for this house to be at liberty to make their choice of burgesses for this parliament, either out of this town or within this town of their pleasures.

And it was also agreed that the choice of burgesses should be made out of [the] town, and so that which of the knights had or should have most voices should be the first burgess.

And every one of this house present being so at liberty and to give the first voice to which of the said knights, being four, they thought best. It happened that Sir John Corbet, Baronet, had the most voices, and so he was with assent of most elected the first burgess of the parliament for this borough. . . . Whereupon every man's voice passing accordingly it happened that Edward Owner . . . by the consent of this house was elected the second burgess of the parliament for the borough.

At this assembly also, to meet and confer with the said burgesses elected for the parliament to advise and give instructions to them about such matters as should be held to be dealt in by them for the general good of the town, etc., [committee members] were appointed. . . .

At this assembly [Mr. Davye] having spoken some words publicly concerning Sir John Suckling, Knight, Comptroller of his Majesty's House, and one of the Privy Council, whereto some exceptions being taken, entreated this house that the words which he had spoken, for the avoiding of misreporting, might be recorded in this assembly, which was condescended unto and thereupon recorded to be these, *videlicet:* that Sir John Suckling, being one of the officers of his Majesty's Household, it would be a question whether Sir John should incline rather to the King than to the subject, as the case might be.

Hertford, Hertfordshire

The Earl of Salisbury explained his support for William Ashton and Thomas Fanshawe in a letter written sometime before May 1625 to the Bishop of Lincoln. See H.M.C., *Salisbury*, XXII, 205.

Hertfordshire

Christopher Keightley, on behalf of the Earl of Salisbury, drafted support for the election of the Botelers. See H.M.C., *Salisbury*, XXII, 205. Sections of the Keightley letter are printed in Lawrence Stone, "The Electoral Influence of the Second Earl of

Salisbury, 1614–1668", *E.H.R.*, 71 (1956), 386. See also Chamberlain, *Letters*, II, 614–616 (S.P. 16/2:27, also printed in Birch, *Court and Times of Chas. I*, I, 18–19).

Hythe, Cinque Port

See John K. Gruenfelder, "The Lord Wardens and Elections, 1604–1628", *The Journal of British Studies*, XVI (1976), 15–16.

Kent

Sir Edwin Sandys and Edward Scott lost the Kent election to crown supporters in 1625. See the letter of Edward Boys to Edward Scott, 4 April 1625, printed in J. R. Scott, *Memorials of the Family of Scott, of Scot's-Hall* (London, 1876), p. xxvii; and see a similar letter of support to Scott from Robert Darell, ibid., pp. xxviii–xxix. The petition to the House of Commons on the behalf of Sandys and Scott describing the election as "carried with a high hand, to the great prejudice of the liberty of the said election", is also printed, ibid., p. xxvii, no. 78. See also Chamberlain, *Letters*, II, 614–616 (S.P. 16/2:27, also printed in Birch, *Court and Times of Chas. I*, I, 18–19.

[B.L., Add. 37,819, ff. 11–11v]
The DUKE OF BUCKINGHAM to SIR ROBERT JACKSON and SIR RICHARD BINGLEY, 10 April 1625, at Whitehall. (Copy)
Knowing very well the great desert of Sir Albert Morton, one of his Majesty's principal secretaries, and understanding that his name will be called on at the election of the knights of the shire for Kent which are to be chosen to serve in this approaching parliament, I thought good by this to desire you to use and employ your joint and several effectual pains and diligence to procure all your friends and tenants being freeholders, and particularly all such freeholders at or about Rochester or Chatham as have any relation to me or my office of Admiral, not only to give their voices but to procure as many of their friends as they can

possibly to assist in the election of Mr. Secretary Morton for the said place in parliament. His known worth speaks best for him, only I will add that you cannot show your affections to any man whom I more esteem, and I will promise that both you and their engagements and courtesies for him in this shall oblige me on all occasions to make you particular requitals. And so I bid you heartily farewell.
From Whitehall, 10° April 1625.
[*Endorsed*] To my very loving friends, Sir Robert Jackson, Knight, Sir Richard Bingley, Knight, and Mr. Jos[h]a [*illegible*].

[Stowe MS. 743, f. 60]
The EARL OF WESTMORLAND to SIR ANTHONY and SIR EDWARD DERING, 13 April 1625, at Mereworth Castle.
Sir,
Upon my coming to London upon Saturday last, I was earnestly importuned by my friends and divers of the principal gentlemen of this country to give my consent that my eldest son might stand to be one of the knights for this shire,[1] which I could no ways decline, considering that such their motion proceeded out of love, with assurance of your best assistance (whereof I also much presume). Be pleased therefore, I pray you, for my sake to express your good affection not only for my son, but for that noble countryman of ours, Sir Albertus Morton, his Majesty's principal secretary (who intends also to stand, for the other place), wherein your kindness shall be thankfully acknowledged by my best respects and service of them both; with the perpetual obligation of
> Your assured loving friend
> and cousin,
> Westmorland

Mereworth Castle
13° Aprilis 1625
[*Endorsed*] To the Right Honorable and my

very loving cousins, Sir Anthony and Edward Dering, Knights, at Pluckley, in haste.

1. I.e., Mildmay Fane, Lord Burghersh.

[Stowe MS. 743, f. 64]
The EARL OF DORSET to SIR EDWARD DERING, 1625.
Sir,

If you should not be assured upon all occasions wherein I might serve you to find me as ready to obey your command as I am now willing to become obliged unto you, I would not thus show you the way how to be made your debtor. There are many competitors for the knightship of your shire, and it must be the contribution of such men's favors as you are that will name the men. All cannot prevail. Let me beseech you to assist in the second place Sir Edwin Sandys, since I have heard that already you stand engaged for Sir Albertus Morton. You shall in the election of these two worthy gentlemen well serve the country and, in particular for him I recommend, time to remain,

Your most affectionate friend
and kinsman to serve you,
E. Dorset

[*Postscript*] I pray remember my best respects unto your worthy lady.
[*Endorsed*] To my noble friend, Sir Edward Dering, Knight, the younger. 1625

[Kent Archives Office, U1115, C23]
THOMAS NEBB to [*Blank*], 1625.

With my humble duty remembered unto the right worshipful, my good master and mistress, trusting in God of your good health. These are to certify unto your worship that I was at Rochester on Monday by 8 of the clock in the morning, and then Mr. Tyse was just at the Crown, taking horse to go to London to the high sheriff, and he says that he is very glad that he had the letter from you before he went and he says that he will do what he can, and he says that the writ is not out yet and the day is not till the second of May, and I hear that the Lord Burghersh has sent letters to stand for him to many gentlemen in our parts, but the clergy will do what they can on your part. Mr. Best will do what he can but he is sorry that he had word no sooner. Sir George Renharst is not at home but Mr. Lee, his lieutenant, has spoken to many of the band for your worship. I have spoken to the tenants to provide their rent, but I have not any yet, but they say that they will provide it shortly. And so I commit you to Almighty God, your obedient servant in the Lord,

Thomas Nebb

[Kent Archives Office, U1115, 015/4]
Names of freeholders who supported Sir Edwin Sandys and Edward Scott, May 1625.

We whose names are here underwritten do testify and shall be always ready to justify upon our oaths, that at the election of the knights of the shire for the county of Kent, held at Pennendon Heath 2 May 1625, we delivered up our names to the clerk at the polling, to be entered by them for the persons here undernamed, which was [*torn*] done accordingly, viz.:

For Sir Edwin Sandys, Knight:	For Edward Scott, Esquire:
Thomas Cullen	Thoms Cullen
William Burvill	William Burvill
Thomas Willsonne	Thomas Willsonne
Thomas Foche	Thomas Foche
Thomas Masshe	Thomas Masshe
Thomas Marshe	Thomas Marshe
Henry Sandys[1]	Henry Sandys

1. The name Henry Sandys has a line through it on the MS. in both lists, which may be a decorative addition to the signature or an indication that the name was deleted.

[Kent Archives Office, U1115, 015/5]
Names of freeholders who supported Sir
Edwin Sandys and Edward Scott, May
1625.

Whereas, at the last county court, the second of this present May, 1625, the election of the knights for this present parliament was referred to the poll. The appointed clerks did then publicly take our names, in writing, for one or both of the persons underwritten. In witness whereof we have hereunto set our hands, and are ready to testify the same upon our oaths.

For Sir Edwin Sandys, Knight:	For Edward Scott, Esquire:
Thomas Scott of Godmersham, the Elder	Thomas Scott of Godmersham, the Elder
Ralph Warde of Saint Dunstan's near Canterbury	Ralph Warde of Saint Dunstan's near Canterbury
Thomas Reader	Thomas Reader
John Baker	John Baker
Thomas Scott, Junior	Thomas Scott, Junior
John Yonge	John Yonge
Thomas Smith	Thomas Smith
Jacob Silver	Jacob Silver
Ralph Warde	Ralph Warde
Thomas Wanstall	Thomas Wanstall
Moyses Pearesonne	Moyses Pearesonne

Mr. Hadd of Canterbury, a barrister, and Steven Carter, draper, both freeholders in Kent, say they were polled, and for Sandys and Scott, and that if they be called unto it they will testify as much, but they have refused to underwrite their names.

[Kent Archives Office, U1115, 015/6]
Names of freeholders who supported Sir
Edwin Sandys and Edward Scott, May
1625.

We whose names are underwritten, being assembled upon the second day of May last past at the county court then held in Kent for the electing of knights for this county, were then polled by the appointment of the sheriff and did then give our

names in writing for Sir Edwin Sandys, Knight, and Mr. Edward Scott, Esquire:

Thomas Lake of [*Illegible*]
John Alphe of [*Illegible*]
Charles Greve of Hawkhurst
Richard Botfing of [*Illegible*]

Leicester, Leicestershire

In addition to the documents printed below, see John K. Gruenfelder, "The Electoral Influence of the Earls of Huntingdon, 1603–1640", *Transactions of the Leicestershire Archaeological and Historical Society*, L (1974–75), 23. In the Leicester Chamberlain's accounts there is notice of 6*s*. 8*d*. paid for gloves given to the sheriff when he made the warrant for the election; see Helen Stocks, ed., *Records of the Borough of Leicester* (Cambridge, 1923), IV, 226.

[Leicester Museum, City of Leicester
MSS., Hall Papers Bound 1623–1625,
BR II/18/15]
SIR HUMPHREY MAY to the MAYOR AND
BURGESSES OF LEICESTER, 2 April 1625.
After my hearty commendations;

Whereas you thought fit to repose so much trust in me as to make choice of me to serve for one of the burgesses of your town the last parliament, which is now dissolved by the death of our late Sovereign of blessed memory, and that it has now pleased the King to summon another parliament to be shortly held here at Westminster, I do by this my letter offer my service very willing unto you to be employed in the same place again, if you shall hold it convenient for your affairs and the affairs of the commonwealth to elect me thereunto. I shall take it very thankfully from you and esteem it as an argument of your great respect unto me and be ready to return it by any good office I may do to your corporation in general or to any particular member thereof as occasion shall be offered unto me. I commit you to the protection of God and rest,

> Your very loving friend,
> Humphrey May

Duchy House
2 April

———————

[Leicester Museum, City of Leicester MSS., Hall Papers Bound 1623–1625, BR II/18/15]
THOMAS HESILRIGE to the MAYOR OF LEICESTER, etc., 19 April 1625.
Good Mr. Mayor and the rest of your society,

My son, being willing to adapt himself for the service of this country, is desirous to become a scholar in the best school of Christendom for knowledge and experience (the Parliament House of England), a desire that every father is to further in his children. And therefore I am now justly pressed hereby to present the first request that I ever yet made to your society, that you would do me the favor and my son the grace, to bestow a burgess['s] place upon him, wherein you shall not only make him a bounden servant of your corporation but myself (for the small remainder of my aged days) an assured and faithful lover, and in all good office a ready servitor, of your society.

God leaving him and my suit to your grave considerations and yourselves to the Lord's direction and protection, I cease and rest, your very loving friend and neighbor,

> Thomas Hesilrige

Noseley, this 19 of
April 1625

———————

[Leicester Museum, City of Leicester MSS., Hall Papers Bound 1623–1625, BR II/18/15]
HENRY SHIRLEY, Sheriff, to the MAYOR AND BURGESSES OF LEICESTER, 30 April 1625.
Henry Shirley, Baronet, High Sheriff of the county aforesaid, to the Mayor, Bailiffs, and Burgesses of the Borough Leicester in my county, greeting.

Because of the advice and consent of the counsel of our sovereign lord the King for certain necessary and urgent occasions and businesses of our said sovereign lord the King, the state, and defense of this realm of England, and of his Church of England concerning, has ordained a parliament to be held at the city of Westminster, the seventeenth day of May next ensuing. And then and there with his prelates, peers, and noblemen of his Majesty's realm aforesaid to have conference. Therefore, by virtue of his Majesty's writ to me directed, I command you that proclamation being made immediately after the receipt of this my precept of the day and place aforesaid, two burgesses of your borough aforesaid, of the discreetest and most sufficient, freely and indifferently by them which at the said proclamation shall be present, according to the form of the statutes thereof made and propounded, to be chosen. And the names of those burgesses so to be chosen in certain indentures between me and you which, at the same choice, shall be present thereof, to be made. Notwithstanding such as are to be chosen be present or absent to be put into the same. And the same burgesses at the same day and place you cause to come, so as the same burgesses may have full power and sufficient authority for them and the commonalty of the borough aforesaid, severally from them to do and consent to such things which then and there of the common counsel of the said realm of England (by God's assistance) shall be ordained upon the business aforesaid. So that for default of such power or negligent choice of the burgesses aforesaid, the business of the King remain not undone in any wise. And the choice so made distinctly and openly under yourselves you do certify without delay, sending to me one part of the indentures aforesaid to these presents, annexed together with this warrant dated under the seal of my office, the 30th day of April in the first year of his Majesty's reign of England, etc., 1625.

[Leicester Museum, City of Leicester MSS., Hall Papers Bound 1623–1625, BR II/18/15]

MAYOR AND BURGESSES OF LEICESTER to SIR GEORGE HASTINGS, 3 May 1625.

Right Worshipful,

After remembrance of our loves and best respects, etc. Having received authority for the election of burgesses of parliament for this corporation, we have this day made choice of your worship to be one of our burgesses for this next ensuing parliament, which we hope your worshipful will undertake and perform. Our other burgess now chosen is Sir Humphrey May,[1] whose association in that business we doubt not but your worship will well approve of. So, not doubting of your love and good respect to this our corporation as well in this parliament as at other ensuing times, we take our leaves, resting ever,

Your worship's in all love,

Leicester, the 3d day
of May 1625

[*Endorsed*] To the Right Worshipful Sir George Hastings, Knight, these be delivered.

1. Sir Humphrey May was doubly returned and chose to sit for Lancaster.

[Leicester Museum, City of Leicester MSS., Hall Papers Bound 1623–1625, BR II/18/15]

MAYOR AND BURGESSES OF LEICESTER to SIR HUMPHREY MAY, 3 May 1625, Leicester.

Right Honorable,

After remembrance of our humble service, etc. We received your honor's letters of the second of April last whereby your honor does desire to be again one of our burgesses of the parliament, which we with all thankfulness have accepted, acknowledging ourselves much graced in that it has pleased you to undertake the same. And we have this day, with all willingness made election of your honor accordingly for the first place. We have chosen for our other burgess Sir George Hastings, Knight, who we hope your honor will well approve of. So, trusting on your honor's favor and due respect of the good of us and this corporation as well in this parliament as at all other times, we most humbly take our leaves and so leave your honor to God's blessed protection.

Your honor's in all duty
be commanded

Leicester, the
3d of May 1625

[*Endorsed*] To the Right Honorable Sir Humphrey May, Knight, Chancellor of his Majesty's Duchy of Lancaster and one of his Majesty's Privy Council, these be delivered.

[Leicester Museum, City of Leicester MSS., Hall Papers Bound 1623–1625, BR II/18/15]

SIR HUMPHREY MAY to the MAYOR AND BURGESSES OF LEICESTER, 10 July 1625.

After my hearty commendations;

I give you many thanks for your great trust reposed in me in that with so general consent you made choice of me to serve for one of the burgesses of your town this parliament. I let you know that I am likewise chosen at Lancaster and have made choice to serve for that town. I desire you to believe that it does not proceed out of any disrespect of you, for I profess you have made me so much beholding to you that I do prefer no Duchy town in my care and affection before yours of Leicester, and this you shall have care so to acknowledge when I may stead you in any of your occasions. You are now to proceed to a new election and I do most earnestly recommend to your choice in my place a near kinsman of mine,

Mr. Thomas Jermyn, a man that may prove a very useful friend unto your corporation. I know he will take it for a great courtesy from you, and I will thank you as much for your good respect showed to him as I did for myself. And so, not doubting of your good acceptance of this special recommendation of mine in the behalf of this gentleman, I commit you to the grace of God and rest,

> Your very loving friend,
> Humphrey May

Duchy [House]
this 10th July

[Leicester Museum, City of Leicester MSS., Hall Papers Bound 1623–1625, BR II/18/15]

Mayor and Burgesses of Leicester to Sir Humphrey May, 23 July 1625, Leicester. Right Honorable, our humble services remembered, etc.

We received your honor's letters whereby we understand that your honor has made choice to stand burgess for Lancaster and not for Leicester, which we are very sorry for, yet hope we shall still retain your honor's love and good respect to this our poor corporation as heretofore we have had. We have received a warrant from the sheriff for choice of another burgess and have (according to your lordship's desire by your said letters), made choice of Mr. Thomas Jermyn for our burgess, although he be altogether unknown to any of us, relying wholly upon your honor's undertaking for his worth and acceptance, which we should not have done upon any other's undertaking but your honor's, he being so mean a stranger to us all. He was first chosen a freeman of this borough and after burgess of the parliament, and it is desired that he will come to Leicester to take the oath of a freeman as others have done in like case. The indenture of his election is delivered to the undersheriff to be returned. So desiring to hear from your honor by this bearer, with hope of the continuance of your honor's favor unto us, we most humbly take our leaves, resting ever,

> Your honor's in all
> duty to be commanded,

Leicester, 23
July 1625

[*Endorsed*] To the Right Honorable Sir Humphrey May, Knight, Chancellor of the Duchy of Lancaster and one of his Majesty's most honorable Privy Council, at the Duchy House in the Strand, London, or elsewhere, these be delivered.

Leicestershire

See John K. Gruenfelder, "The Electoral Influence of the Earls of Huntingdon, 1603–1640", *Transactions of the Leicestershire Archaeological and Historical Society*, L (1974–75), 21.

[The Huntington Library, HA. 5499]
The Earl of Huntingdon to Thomas Wright, 9 April 1625, St. Albans.
Wright,

I understand the writs are gone down for the summoning of the parliament to begin the 17 of May next, and that the county court for the making the election is upon the 5th of May, and therefore I pray you to speak unto the freeholders of inheritance or for life to be there that day in the morning, by 7 of the clock at the furtherest, and to give their voices for my brother, Sir George Hastings, to be one of the knights for Leicestershire. And for the other knight, at my coming home, by the grace of God, you shall know who I desire should be the other, wherein I will be very careful to nominate such a one unto them as shall be fitting for that place to be the other, both for his religion, wisdom, and estate, and such a one as may be best accommodated to do the country service. And so desiring you to take a speedy care herein, I rest,

> Your loving master

St. Albans, this 9 of
April 1625

[*Postscript*] I would have you to speak to all the freeholders in the several towns belonging to the manor of Whitwike.

Mr. Babington the lawyer
Mr. Paulson
Mr. Stevens
Mr. Fox of Dunnington
Mr. Wright of Hucklescotte
Henry Amston

Mr. Bickerton
Mr. Budinges
Mr. Wm. Puresie
Mr. Morton
Mr. Burroues
Mr. Holt
Mr. Tisley

Lostwithiel, Cornwall

None of the records, the *O.R.*, the Hastings MS. list of returns (HA. L5/B8), nor the parliamentary accounts, indicate how the two 1625 returns for Lostwithiel were adjudicated. See W. P. Courtney, *The Parliamentary Representation of Cornwall to 1832* (London, 1889), pp. 210–211. Sir Henry Vane, a Buckingham client doubly returned, chose to sit for Carlisle. The other three, George Chudleigh, Nicholas Kendall, and Sir Reginald Mohun were active in Cornwall politics. See John K. Gruenfelder, *Influence in Early Stuart Elections 1604–1640* (Columbus, Ohio, 1981), pp. 147, 177 n. 47.

Ludlow, Shropshire

[Ludlow Corporation Minute Book, 1590–1648, 356/2/1, f. 147]
CORPORATION MINUTES, 2 May 1625.
At this day Richard Tomlins and Ralph Goodwin, Esquires, being burgesses of this corporation, are elected and chosen burgesses of the parliament to serve for this town at the parliament now next ensuing, and master bailiffs are desired in the townsmen of this town their behalf to write to the said gentlemen to give their attendance according to his Majesty's writ and proclamation.

Maidstone, Kent

The return for Edward Maplisden and Thomas Stanley is printed in W. R. James, *Charters and Other Documents . . . Maidstone* (London, 1825), pp. 119–120.

Maldon, Essex

[B.L., Add. 12,496, f. 98]
BAILIFFS OF MALDON to ANONYMOUS, 13 April 1625, Maldon.
Right Honorable, our humble duties remembered;

Having received your honor's letters concerning a place of burgess for the incorporation, we have imparted and made known the same to our brethren the aldermen and common council of our house at two several meetings before the day of election and then again in the hearing of them all and of the commons assembled (in our moot hall) at the choice, being the twelfth of this month. But those of the commonalty which are free burgesses meeting and being many in number, the greater part of the assembly (without us) prevailing, gave their voices. The first place to Sir Arthur Herris, Knight, and the second to Sir Henry Mildmay, Knight, Master of the King's Majesty's Jewel House, whereof we have thought it our duties to give speedy advertisement to your honor acknowledging that we and our township are much bounden to your honor for manifold respects for which we have will (with all readiness) to express our thankfulness so far as it lies in our power. And thus in humble wise taking our leave, we rest,

Your honor's to be commanded,
John Soan }
John Edwards } bailiffs
Maldon, this
13th of April 1625

Merionethshire, Wales

[National Library of Wales, Wynn MSS. (9060E)1312]
WILLIAM SALISBURY to SIR JOHN WYNN, 4 April 1625, Bottegir.[1]
In nomine Jesu.
Most Honored Sir,
With remembrance of my best wishes to yourself and your worthiest lady, with heartiest thanks for your manifold courtesies. After the last election of my cousin,

Mr. Henry Wynn, I promised my voice and friends to my cousin Hugh Nanney and cousin William Vaughan, those two houses having never been contrary in voices and I had their voices formerly for myself. My desire is you will be pleased to write to cousin Hugh Nanney and cousin William Vaughan, whom I assure myself (without full satisfaction to you) will grant your desire. If you please, if I should there write or travel to them or elsewhere herein upon notice from you, I shall be ready and willing to perform any kind of office and in the meantime, with my prayers for your health, I rest,

> Your very assured loving
> cousin to dispose of,
> William Salisbury

Bottegir,
this 4th of April 1625
[*Postscript*] My wife commends her service and prayers to yourself and your most honored lady with manifold thanks for many undeserved kindness[es] and courtesies to her and hers.

1. See also Sir Roger Mostyn's letter of 15 April to Sir John Wynn, *sub* Flintshire.

[National Library of Wales, Wynn MSS. (9060E)1323]
ELIOTT WYNN to SIR JOHN WYNN, 15 April 1625.
Right Worshipful,
I have lately received a letter from Mr. Salisbury of Rug wherein he wished me to certify you that Mr. Nanney and he are both joined together for their voices to my cousin Harrie Wynn to be knight of the shire for the county of Merioneth, and that you may be secure for that business if my cousin Harrie will supply the place himself; if otherwise, they desire to be freed from their promise. I cannot requite the least part of your daily goodness to me and mine but our continual prayers to God shall be for the preservation of both you and my lady together that I may never want you.

So, not forgetting my duty unto you, I take leave and rest your assured brother,

> To rest,
> Eliott Wynn

Isteratt [*sic*] the 15th
of April 1625

Middlesex

See Chamberlain, *Letters*, II, 614–616 (S.P. 16/2:27, also printed in Birch, *Court and Times of Chas. I*, I, 18–20).

Mitchell, Cornwall

[B.L., Add. 37,819, f. 11v]
The DUKE OF BUCKINGHAM to the OFFICIALS OF MITCHELL, 8 April 1625, Whitehall.[1] (Copy)
Being entreated by Sir Edwin Sandys to desire you to elect his son a burgess for this parliament to serve in the second place for your town (reserving still to me, as you have done to my predecessors, the nomination and recommendation of the first), I have not been forward to yield to his request in regard you might think that I purpose by this to gain too much ground on your liberty and freedom in that kind. But being credibly informed how hopeful and likely his son is to merit your respects, and considering how well his father has deserved of you, and his good neighborhood and readiness at all times to further the good of your town, I thought I could do no less than desire you to add to the consideration of these reasons (which you have to respect him for his father's sake) the esteem I hold of them both; and if I shall find by the success that my recommendation has added weight to the balance in your election, it shall be not only no prejudice to your privileges for the future, but a leading engagement now at the beginning of my government to encourage me with the more affection to endeavor anything that shall tend to the good of your town. And so I bid you heartily farewell.

From Whitehall, April 8th 1625.

1. Marginal note: "Letter of recommendation for a 2nd place of burgess in parliament".

New Romney, Cinque Port

See John K. Gruenfelder, "The Lord Wardens and Elections, 1604–1628", *The Journal of British Studies*, XVI (1976), 1–23.

New Windsor, Berkshire

[B.L., Add. 37,819, f. 11]
The DUKE OF BUCKINGHAM to the MAYOR and his brethren of the town of [New] Windsor, 8 April 1625, Whitehall.[1] (Copy)

As the neighborhood of the government wherewith his Majesty is pleased to trust me at [New] Windsor shall make me ready to do you and your town any good offices, so does it at this time cause me to crave your favor in a request which I trust you will not think unreasonable, which is that on my recommendations you will elect Sir William Russell, the Treasurer of his Majesty's Navy, for one of the burgesses to serve in this approaching parliament for your town. His known worth and merits speak so well for him that I shall not need to tell you what I believe of him; and being born not far from you I doubt not but you will easily grow confident that he will be very tender of the trust you shall repose in him for the good of your town. If the success shall show how powerfully my request on his behalf has wrought with you, it shall stir me up with much affection to requite your respects in any thing whereby I may approve myself yours.

Whitehall, *8° Apr.* 1625

1. Marginal note: "A letter of recommendation to a burgess's place in [New] Windsor". Sir William Russell was not elected.

Norfolk

For a brief description of the vote tally at the Norfolk election, see Katherine Paston's letter to her son William, 18 April 1625, printed in the *Norfolk Record Society* (Norfolk, 1941), XIV, 82 (no. 55).

[B.L., Egerton MS. 2715, f. 283]
GEORGE GAWDY to FRAMLINGHAM GAWDY, 10 April 1625, Shipden.
Good Sir,

I received a letter from Sir Robert Gawdy wherein he writes that the writ for the election of the knights of the shire is come down and the county day is upon Easter Monday. And he writes also that he has declared himself that he intends to stand for a voice. And he has enjoined me to give you notice of it as one of his friends upon whom he does rely. Therefore, I would entreat you, if your health would permit it, to be present at the election with such others of your friends and tenants as you have interest in or command of to do the part of a loving kinsman for him. And for the same, I know his love shall never be wanting unto you nor my poor service. I confess his letter to me does not intimate that he gives himself with any other, neither do I hear of any other that does publish himself to stand; but if you hear of any other, I shall think myself much bound unto you to let me know it by a word or two of your writing. Thus in haste, with the remembrance of my love and service unto yourself and my cousin, your wife, I rest,

Your loving kinsman to command,
George Gawdy

Shipden this Xth of April 1625

[*Endorsed*] To the Right Worshipful Mr. Framlingham Gawdy, Esquire, this be delivered at West Harling, in Norfolk.

Nottingham, Nottinghamshire

On Good Friday, 15 April 1625, the Nottingham borough council decided to choose townsmen rather than strangers in the upcoming election. See W. T. Baker, *Records of the Borough of Nottingham, 1625–1702* (London, 1900), V, 102.

Old Sarum, Wiltshire

In addition to the document printed below, see Lawrence Stone, "The Electoral

Influence of the Second Earl of Salisbury, 1614–68", *E.H.R.*, 71 (1956), 396–398.

[Hampshire Record Office, 44/M/69]
The EARL OF SALISBURY to HENRY SHERFIELD, 12 April 1625, Quickswood.
Mr. Sherfield,

To say that you can be sure of both places beforehand I will not, but I cannot but remember that I have more than once heard you say that you had so settled your lands within the borough of Old Sarum that you had half the voices (at least) at your own command for that election, so that none (as now it stands) without your consent is[1] likely to have either of those places. But now I perceive by your letter that you make it doubtful (in regard of some other voices) that if you should insist upon both for me you may be in danger to lose both and to incur the displeasure of some great ones who have sent unto you about them, and that if you should incur their displeasure by giving me satisfaction in that which now I desire you are not sure of my favor, alleging divers particulars by your letter. I thought I had given you such testimony and full satisfaction of my favor by former letters that you should not now have needed to make scruple of it, assuring you that none (much less yourself) shall suffer in any thing wherein I may help it for doing me service, and presuming only upon you, have sent to no other about it, assuring myself by your means (knowing that him who has a voice and such friends as he can make will not be wanting to give me satisfaction) to have my desire which, if I may obtain, I shall account it for a favor and respect unto me. If otherwise you have any other or better friend to pleasure with it rather than me, I must (although I make no doubt of it), leave it unto your consideration. And will ever rest,
                    Your loving friend,
                    W. Salisbury
Quickswood, 12 April 1625
[*Postscript*] Upon return of an answer of this letter by this bearer, I will presently send such names as I intend for those places.
[*Endorsed*] To my very loving friend, Henry Sherfield, Esquire, at his house in Salisbury, deliver these.

1. MS.: *as*.

Oxford, Oxfordshire

Notice of the election of Thomas Wentworth and John Whistler is included in H. E. Salter, ed., *Oxford Council Acts, 1583–1626* (Oxford, 1928), p. 330.

Pontefract, Yorkshire

See Sir Thomas Wentworth's letters to Sir John Jackson and Mr. Cowper, 6 April 1625, seeking borough support for himself but pledging to support Jackson and Sir Richard Beaumont for Pontefract if he secures the shire election. William Knowler, ed., *The Earl of Strafforde's Letters and Dispatches* (London, 1739), I, 25, 26, 27. See also Sir Richard Beaumont's letter to Wentworth (ibid., p. 27) wherein he states he would decline a seat for Pontefract. See also John K. Gruenfelder, "The Electoral Patronage of Sir Thomas Wentworth, Earl of Strafford, 1614–1640", *The Journal of Modern History*, 49 (1977), 569.

Portsmouth, Hampshire

See Violet A. Rowe, "The Influence of the Earls of Pembroke on Parliamentary Elections, 1625–41", *E.H.R.*, 50 (1935), 242–243, for a brief mention of Sir Benjamin Rudyard's election in 1625.

Queenborough, Kent

The indenture returning Sir Edward Hales and Roger Palmer is in the Kent Archives Office, Qb/Rpr/4.

[Kent Archives Office, Qb/c/137]
The EARL OF MONTGOMERY to [*Blank*], 25 April 1625, Whitehall.
After my hearty commendations;
I have just cause to make the worst con-

struction of your indiscreet and uncivil carriage towards me in slighting my letters which I directed unto you for Mr. Robert Pooley, a gent[leman] every way able to discharge a greater trust than happily might betide him from that corporation if you had made choice of him according to the tenor and meaning of my said letters. And assure yourselves since Sir Edward Hales, out of his respect to me, is content to waive acceptance of that burgess-ship, which you would enforce upon him, if in his room you choose not the said Mr. Pooley, for whom you see how much I am engaged, I shall construe[1] it as a neglect and scorn doubled upon me and shall most assuredly therefore, whensoever your occasions shall need any furtherance, be found,

> Your friend according to
> your behavior to me in this
> and in the future,
> Montgomery

Whitehall this 25th of
April 1625

1. MS.: *conster.*

Reading, Berkshire

Concerning the election of Sir Francis Knollys, Jr., and John Saunders, see the Diary of the Corporation entry 21 April 1625, J. M. Guilding, ed., *Records of the Borough of Reading* (London, 1895), II, 230–231. See also notice of the letter from William Knollys, Viscount Wallingford, to the mayor and burgesses of Reading concerning the election. Ibid.

Richmond, Yorkshire

See John K. Gruenfelder, "The Electoral Patronage of Sir Thomas Wentworth, Earl of Strafford, 1614–1640", *The Journal of Modern History*, 49 (1977), 570.

Rye, Cinque Port

In addition to the documents printed below, see John K. Gruenfelder, "The Lord Wardens and Elections, 1604–1628", *The Journal of British Studies*, XVI (1976), 15–16.

[East Sussex Record Office, Rye Corporation MSS., 47/101, 29:7]
EDWARD, EARL OF DORSET, to the MAYOR AND JURATS OF RYE, 1 April 1625, Dorset House.
After my very hearty commendations;

Whereas it has pleased our sovereign lord the King's Majesty to resolve to call a parliament in May next, to which purpose the writs of summons will speedily be brought unto you for the election of burgesses of your town, I have thought fit to recommend unto you Captain John Sackville, a worthy gentleman and a dear kinsman of mine (the rather for that he is your countryman and well known to some of you), desiring you would be pleased to elect him one of your burgesses for your town of Rye. Whereby as you shall oblige him with all care and circumspection to do his best endeavors in parliament for the good of your town and you in general, so shall every one of you in particular find him and myself ready and willing upon all occasions to give you testimony that we take this as a great courtesy and kindness from you. And so I bid you heartily farewell, and rest,

> Your very assured
> loving friend,
> E. Dorset

Dorset House the
first of April 1625

[East Sussex Record Office, Rye Corporation MSS., 47/101, 29:8]
JAMES LEY, BARON LEY OF LEY, to the MAYOR AND JURATS OF RYE, 3 April 1625, Clerkenwell.
After my very hearty commendations;

Whereas you are to make a new election of barons to serve in the parliament, which is shortly to be held. Forasmuch as Emanuel Gifford, Esquire, has heretofore served for you in that high court, and is free of your corporation, I have thought good hereby to entreat you to make choice of him again for the same purpose at this time, not only as one able and fit in all respects to serve in such an assembly, but as already understanding the state of your corporation and very well affected to do you good service without your cost and charge. But this is desired by me to be done after you have given place to such a person as shall be recommended unto you by the Duke of Buckingham, his Grace, now Lord Warden of the Cinque Ports. And if next to his Grace you shall gratify me, I shall not only take it thankfully but be ready to requite your good affection and respect showed to me herein as you shall have occasion in general or any one particular man for himself. And so I bid you farewell. From my house at Clerkenwell, the third of April, 1625.

Your very loving friend,
James Ley

[B.L., Add. MS. 37,819, f. 12]

GEORGE, DUKE OF BUCKINGHAM, to the MAYOR AND CORPORATION OF RYE, 8 April 1625, Whitehall.[1] (Copy)

The respects which you have heretofore shown my predecessors upon their recommendation of a worthy man to be by you chosen to serve in parliament as one of the burgesses of your town makes me confident that you will give me the like encouragement to be as careful of whatsoever shall concern you as they have been and, that my request may receive the better entertainment and success, I do by this recommend unto you for one of the burgesses to serve in this parliament for your town a servant of my own, Thomas Fotherley, whose sufficiency and honesty I have thoroughly experienced, and whose care and diligence in such businesses as he undertakes will, I doubt not, merit your esteem of him, wherein the relation he has to me shall double the respects you afford him, for my

sake. If you would have him sworn a freeman of your town, I pray send hither a commission to that purpose, and wherein you shall have occasion of my assistance for anything concerning the good of your town you shall find me as ready as any of my predecessors have been to affect your desires. And so I bid you heartily farewell.

From Whitehall, 8° April 1625.

1. Marginal note: "Letter of recommendation for a burgess's place in Rye". The holograph of this letter, dated 11 April, is in the East Sussex Record Office, Rye Corporation MSS., 47/101, 29:11.

[East Sussex Record Office, Rye Corporation MSS., 47/101, 29:9]
JOHN ANGELL to the MAYOR AND JURATS OF RYE, 9 April 1625, London.
Worthy Sirs,

I must ever acknowledge myself much obliged to you for that great honor you have done me in making me amongst so many worthy competitors twice your servant in the Parliament House, in which employment although it has not been possible for me to supply the necessities of your town or to answer perhaps your expectations yet, I will assure you according to the best of my foresight and judgment, I did you as faithful and effectual service as those times would give me leave. And since it has pleased God now to give occasion of calling a new parliament, your former loving and free acceptance of me does invite me once again to offer my service to you, hoping I shall not be thought more unworthy or stand less in your esteems and opinions than formerly. Howsoever you shall please to direct yourselves for your choice now, I shall desire this favor of you—that you will not think that I have had so ill breeding or so little good manners as not to have made a full and respective valuation always of your loves towards me, for which you, both in general and particular, shall always find me ready to the uttermost of my poor abilities to do you service, and so shall ever remain,

> Your faithful friend to command,
> John Angell

London, 9th
April 1625

[East Sussex Record Office, Rye
Corporation MSS., 47/101, 29:12]
EDWARD NICHOLAS to the MAYOR AND
JURATS OF RYE, 11 April 1625, Savoy.
Mr. Mayor, etc.,

I thought good, as well out of my affection to your town (with which I would gladly bring my Lord in love) as out of my well-wishings to the gentleman (Mr. Thomas Fotherley) whom my Lord has recommended to you in the first place for a burgess-ship of your town this parliament, to let you understand that he is one of my Lord's commissioners for his estate and in very great esteem with his Grace, beyond most of his Grace's servants, and ablest of any to do good offices for your town to my Lordship. Besides, he is Mr. Lieutenant's[1] brother-in-law and one whom Mr. Lieutenant holds very dear in his esteem and affection. So as the respect you give Mr. Fotherley in this election will purchase you a double esteem both from my Lord and from Sir John Hippisley, and also make me the more obliged to you also, though that cannot add any weight to the balance of the other considerations. There is nothing wherein I may do you any good offices but I will be forward to lay hold on the first opportunity to express myself.

> Your very loving friend,
> Edward Nicholas

Savoy,
11° Aprilis 1625

1. I.e., Sir John Hippisley, Lieutenant of Dover Castle.

[East Sussex Record Office, Rye
Corporation MSS., 47/101, 29:10]
GEORGE, DUKE OF BUCKINGHAM, to the
MAYOR AND JURATS OF RYE, 11 April 1625,
Whitehall.
After my hearty commendations;

Albeit I am not forward to be drawn to crave more respect than my predecessors have usually received from your town, yet being pressed by a deserving friend I could not refuse to recommend him to you to serve in the second place (this parliament) as burgess for your town (reserving howsoever the first place certain to him whom I have recommended to you for the same).[1] The gentleman's name is Sir John Franklin, and if I were not confident as well of his affections as ability to do you many good offices I would not be so earnest in my request for him in this kind. If you shall thus doubly gratify me at my first entrance into my place it shall not only not prejudice you for the future in your privileges and freedom, but stir me with the more affection to endeavor the effecting of anything wherein you shall have occasion to crave my assistance for the good of your town. And so I bid you heartily farewell. From Whitehall, 11th of April 1625.

> Your very loving friend,
> G. Buckingham

1. The Duke supported Thomas Fotherley for the first burgess. See above, his letter to the mayor and jurats, 8 April 1625. The second burgess-ship went to the Earl of Dorset's candidate, John Sackville. See above, Dorset's letter of 1 April to the mayor and jurats.

[East Sussex Record Office, Rye
Corporation MSS., 47/101, 29:13]
JOHN HALSEY to the MAYOR AND JURATS OF
RYE, 18 April 1625, London.
After my very hearty commendations, etc.;

Understanding that the time of your election of burgesses for the ensuing parliament is near at hand, and that you have more suitors than you can accommodate therewith, I make bold to commend unto your good consideration my kinsman, Mr. John Angell, of whose worth and sufficiency you may well perceive by the good and general respect the parliament has formerly had of him. And his ability to do your town pleasure (if the time prove seasonable) I know to be much better than any man that has had no experience in that high court. Wherefore if you please to confer the place of your burgess upon him, in my opinion you shall do yourselves and your town much right and oblige me, your well-willer, ever to be thankful and rest,

> Your very loving friend,
> Jo. Halsey

Old Fish Street,
London, this
18th of April 1625

Sandwich, Cinque Port

See John K. Gruenfelder, "The Lord Wardens and Elections, 1604–1628", *The Journal of British Studies*, XVI (1976), 15–16.

Scarborough, Yorkshire

Concerning the election and borough patronage, see Roy Carroll, "Yorkshire Parliamentary Boroughs in the Seventeenth Century", *Northern History*, III (1968), 77, 81–82; John K. Gruenfelder, "Yorkshire Borough Elections, 1603–1640", *The Yorkshire Archaeological Journal*, 49 (1977), 106. In 1625 a number of candidates were interested in representing Scarborough in parliament. Two letters from Francis Gargrave to the bailiffs of the town are printed in J. B. Baker, *The History of Scarbrough* (London, 1882), pp. 226–227. The first, 7 April, is to acquaint the bailiffs of Lord Sheffield's interest in nominating a burgess; the second, 1 May, is in support of Sir Edward Waterhouse. A letter from Johna. Bailey to Mr. Paul Peacock, one of the bailiffs, 1 April 1625, in support of the candidacy of Sir Clifford Slingsby is also printed in Baker, ibid., p. 224.

[Scarborough Borough MSS., General Letters, B. 1, 1597–1642]
SIR RICHARD CHOLMLEY to the BAILIFFS OF SCARBOROUGH, 13 April 1625, York.
After my very kind and hearty salutations;

Whereas by the death of his late Majesty King James the parliament then in prorogation is utterly dissolved, and that our new royal King Charles, our public and rightful acknowledged sovereign is, as I am credibly informed, resolved to call a new parliament to which there of necessity must be a new election of all the knights and burgesses of this kingdom. Having received letters lately from my son of his desire to make tender of the continuance of his service to your town rather than any other place, I have thought fitting to address unto you these letters to become in his and my behalf a suitor to yourselves and the residue of your corporation that if you shall think him worthy and me of the continuance of your favors, you will be pleased to continue his service in that kind and so to confer a place upon him. I need not say much more but, resting as confident in your affections as I am assured of my own to you, I will give you that assurance that both he and I will be no less thankful in our respects and watchfulness to anything [that] may accrue to the benefit and good of your town than formerly we have been, I will take leave and remain,

> Your most assured and
> affected friend,
> Richard Cholmley

York, the 13th
of April 1625

[Scarborough Borough MSS., General Letters, B. 1, 1597–1642]
EMANUEL, LORD SCROPE, to the BAILIFFS OF SCARBOROUGH, 14 April 1625, York.
After my hearty commendations;

I am hereby to entreat you to acquaint your borough men [*illegible*] as his Majesty's writ for election of burgesses for the parliament shall come to your hands, that you will be all pleased to make choice of Sir William Alford, one who is known to you all to be religious, discreet, and fit for the place. And I will answer you all of his willing desire to do your town any kind favor without any charge to you on his behalf. And for that the writ is not yet come and none elected, I hope your town will not deny my request and your respect therein shall be thankfully taken on my part. And so I commit you to God from the manor at York, 14 of April 1625.

Your loving friend,
Emanuel Scrope[1]

1. Emanuel, Lord Scrope, President of the Council of the North.

[Scarborough Borough MSS., General Letters, B. 1, 1597–1642]
WILLIAM THOMPSON[1] to CHRISTOPHER THOMPSON, 25 April 1625, York.
Loving father,

I had this day some occasion to visit the high sheriff, Sir Richard Cholmley, who is yet very weak and has since six week last been very sick. And having some discourse of your town he told me he made no doubt but that the town would be mindful of electing his son for a burgess, considering his respect and courtesies done for that town, which upon my own knowledge have been willingly and lovingly performed by him in behalf of the town. I told him that the town was much solicited by great ones and therefore requested him to write but, he being unable through his weakness, although he would gladly have written, called to mind the answer [the] Mr. Bailiffs had written to my Lord President, wherein they did intimate that they had chosen Sir Richard's son, though he was not named, and so his Lordship and Sir Richard did both conceive of it, in which letter there was some distaste taken by my Lord President[2] for making my Lord Sheffield his competitor and preferring him before my Lord, who is more

able to do a courtesy for the town than my Lord Sheffield (if he continue president). But the main occasion of this letter is to answer a letter here enclosed which came instantly to Sir Richard's hands as I was there, wherein he finds a great deal of ingratitude, or at least forgetfulness, in the town which does much trouble him. If he had been able to have written he would have given [the] Mr. Bailiffs satisfaction himself, but in respect of his weakness, at his entreaty, I thought fit to let you know his answer for the first part of the letter enclosed: that he and other justices should go about to undo the town it is very untrue in his particular or by any others to his knowledge, as he protests before God.

He had not heard of the state of the town but by rumors this great while, for he has laid sick here at York and so had no intelligence at all of the state of the town, but so soon as I told him what I had heard he sent presently to Whitby and other places about how to direct them to go to the markets at Scarborough. And because he would have been truly informed he sent a man upon purpose to Scarborough to desire the bailiffs to write how the sickness was in the town, for to enlarge their liberty wherein he could, which was as much as he could do, especially now in his so weak estate of sickness.

For the other part of the letter, wherein the town seems to be offended for want of their proclamation, he thus answers it: in his letter to Scarborough he certified the town that King James was dead and the new King Charles with one heart and voice acknowledged and proclaimed, and that he was proclaimed in York. Now he had not any proclamation come into his hand until 10 days after, to my knowledge, and when they did come he did of purpose omit to send to Scarborough because my Lord President and divers others did inform him that the town was as many places infected and he thought by concourse of people to his proclamation there might be some danger both to the town and country, which was more for the care and affection he had to the town than any neglect at all, and besides the preamble of his letter, though there was no mandate to have him proclaimed, it was a sufficient warrant unto the town to have proclaimed him King if the town had been free. He being the sheriff of the whole county ought to have given the town satisfaction, for they should not have received that part of the letter as from a private person. But those worthy conceits of the town have in part persuaded him they are about to shake him and his son off which, if they do, in my conceit, they do him very much wrong, but themselves more. The time is now too late for to provide another place for his son (though he might have had 2 or 3 elsewhere if he had not relied upon that). Therefore, I pray you acquaint [the] Mr. Bailiffs hereof and let them forthwith give him satisfaction by their letters in the premises, otherwise let them be assured instead of a worthy friend they will find a shrewd adversary, especially when his love and affection to the town is so ill requited. Let me have your letter also to give him satisfaction besides [the] Mr. Bailiffs. For he is exceedingly offended as ever I [have] see[n] him in my life. Thus much I thought good to certify [the] Mr. Bailiffs, desiring that they would be pleased to remember his courtesies done and not take exception in that cause. Thus in haste with my duty remembered I rest,

Your obedient son till death,
William Thompson

York, 25th *Aprilis*
1625

---

1. William Thompson owed his election for Scarborough to John Ramsey, Earl of Holderness, and his own local connections. John K. Gruenfelder, *Influence in Early Stuart Elections 1604–1640* (Columbus, Ohio, 1981), p. 119 n.100. For the letter of support from the Earl of Holderness, see J. B. Baker, *The History of Scarbrough* (London, 1882), pp. 224–225.
2. Emanuel, Lord Scrope.

[Scarborough Borough MSS., General Letters, B. 1, 1597–1642]
SIR EDWARD COKE to the BAILIFFS OF SCARBOROUGH, 25 April 1625.

May it please your worships to be advertised that whereas I have often in my meditations a long time together carried a good respect of well-wishing to this your town of Scarborough, and now time and opportunity serving whereby I may make good my former protestations, I have thought it not amiss to acquaint you with it, which is no more but this: that if your worships with the rest of the burgesses will be pleased to make choice of me to be one of your burgesses of parliament at this time for the town, I shall to the uttermost of my power endeavor and, by the means of my best friends, procure all the good I may to the same, taking my directions still from the corporation what I shall go about to effect. It may be alleged that I am yet a stranger amongst you (and yet take this withal, such a stranger); and so well know that if I were in [a] place wherein I could procure (I will not say all), but most of the Privy Council letters in the kingdom to be written in my behalf, I can but proffer you my best endeavors for this service of the town. Accept it as you please. And if you do employ me I will be fast and faithful unto you, undergoing the service at as little a charge to the town as any that shall be joined with me. Thus far I thought good to explain myself unto you, time and opportunity giving such occasion. And now, leaving the success of my suit to your advised considerations, I rest howsoever,

Yours to use in what I may,
Edward Coke

25 of April 1625

[Scarborough Borough MSS., General Letters, B. 1, 1597–1642]
RICHARD DARLEY to the BAILIFFS OF SCARBOROUGH, 1 May 1625, Buttercrambe.
Mr. Bailiffs,

I have been very desirous that Henry

Darley, my eldest son, should do his country the best service he can as a burgess of this next parliament and to that end I do most heartily entreat you if you be not formerly engaged to others that he may have your best furtherance therein. And I shall think myself much beholding to you therein and will be as ready to requite your good wills in whatsoever I shall be able to do you or the town any pleasure. And I doubt not but you shall well understand that he shall discharge the place and your trust as sufficiently as any other, and at his own charge. And so, with my love most heartily commended to you both, I shall ever rest,

Your most assured friend,
Richard Darley

Buttercrambe
this first of May 1625

———————

[Scarborough Borough MSS., General Letters, B. 1, 1597–1642]
SIR WILLIAM ALFORD to the BAILIFFS OF SCARBOROUGH, 6 May 1625, Meux.
Sir,

I received your letter the sixt[h] of this instant, wherein I find expressed the friendly inventions both of yourselves in particular and your town in general towards me for a burgess's place in this parliament, whereof I am by my neighbors of Beverley already made choice on. Accept, I pray you, the thankful acknowledgment of your well wishing, whereof now at my going to London I will acquaint my Lordship[1] of your forwardness to satisfy his desire and I make no question he will return a friendly respect for your loves to him. Myself will always remain ready to do all offices of friendship wherein you shall have cause to use me. At all times I will affectionately express myself,

Your assured friend,
William Alford

Meux, 6 of May

1. Emanuel, Lord Scrope. See above, Scrope's letter to the bailiffs, 14 April.

Somerset

For the submission of Edmund Kenne to the Privy Council and his apology for offending Sir Robert Phelips by "giving out scandalous speeches against him to hinder his election", see *A.P.C., 1625–1626*, pp. 103–104.

Thetford, Norfolk

In 1625 Sir Robert Cotton was returned for Thetford, "a seat undoubtedly in the control of Arundel". Regarding the Cotton-Howard alliance, see Kevin Sharpe, *Sir Robert Cotton, 1586–1631* (Oxford, 1979), pp. 176–177.

[B.L., Cotton MSS., Julius c. III, f. 284]
WILLIAM NORWICH, Mayor, *et al.*, to SIR ROBERT COTTON, 25 April 1625, Thetford.
Noble Sir,

Notwithstanding you are a stranger unto us, yet upon the commendation of the Right Honorable the Earl of Arundel, our most worthy Lord, we have made choice of you to be a burgess for our borough of Thetford in this next parliament, in the first place. We doubt not but our election being so free and so general as you had not one voice against you, your voice, labor, and endeavors shall not be wanting to remember the ancient and now almost ruinated borough of Thetford (which was *Sitomagus* in the Britons' time, and since a colony of the Romans). If either occasion be offered to pleasure us, or we shall have business to use your assistance in, we assure ourselves that you deserve that reputation which report (besides his Lordship's letters) has been made of you unto us. And in confidence thereof that you will answer it unto us and make it good by your actions, we remain and are bold to write ourselves what you shall ever find us,

Your loving friends ever
to be commanded,
William Norwich, Mayor
John Snelling, Coroner

John Trell
George Eless

Thetford, this
25 of April 1625

Warwick, Warwickshire

[Warwickshire R.O., Warwick Borough Muniments Minute Book 1610–1662, W. 21/6, ff. 269–279]

. . . there were other troubles and differences besides all those suits which were not only chargeable but produced much envy and contempt upon the corporation. The gentlemen who were the chief instruments herein countenancing the meaner sort of inhabitants to disregard and contemn the government of the corporation. The first was Sir Thomas Puckering who being too near a neighbor living in the priory there. . . .

. . . his natural malignity to affront the corporation and bear sway over the corporation was that they, having then for 60 years or more before constantly elected the 2 burgesses sent for that borough to the parliament, the whole corporation consisting of a bailiff and 12 principal burgesses and 12 assistant burgesses, being in the whole 25 in number, it was expected by the said Sir Thomas that they should elect him for one of their burgesses. But there being then worthy men in the corporation and the Lord Brooke, their recorder, expecting he might have the nomination, and Sir Thomas Lucy being a gentleman of an ancient family and showing more favor to the corporation than Sir Thomas Puckering who was but a stranger in the country and not so commodious by sending corn to the market for the general good of the people nor a man of such noble hospitality as that worthy family of the Lucys were. The corporation therefore rather inclined to gratify their recorder and this gentleman in the election of their burgesses in the parliament held in the first year of the reign of our sovereign lord Charles, the King's Majesty that now is. Then the said Thomas

Puckering thereupon taking displeasure that he was not elected, profanely complained in parliament that the election was unduly made and that it appertained not to the corporation alone to elect, but that it ought to be popular and that all the inhabitants had voices in the election. And hereupon the then bailiffs and others were summoned to appear before the committee for the privileges of parliament and so did at divers several times, assigned for the purposes. And upon hearing of counsel and witnesses on both sides in the Star Chamber, where the committee sat, the major part of the committee voted with the corporation observing by their proofs that they had time out of mind elected their burgesses, and so he that then sat in the chair then had prepared and intended to certify to the parliament the proofs herein to the end an order might have been conceived to have settled the election with the corporation forever in aftertimes. But before there was any opportunity for this purpose the parliament was dissolved and so all that cost and labor lost.

Weymouth and Melcombe Regis, Dorset

See Maureen Weinstock, ed., *Weymouth and Melcombe Regis Minute Book 1625–1660* (Dorset Rec. Soc., 1964), I, 7, 9. The borough and town had agreed that one of their burgesses for parliament be a resident; Giles Greene, a resident of Weymouth (Keeler, *L.P.*), was returned in a by-election to replace Sir Thomas Middleton who chose to represent Denbighshire.

Wiltshire

[S.P. 16/1:55]
SIR THOMAS THYNNE to SIR HENRY LUDLOW, 13 April 1625, Longleat.
Good Sir,

Being advised by divers my good friends to stand in the election of one of the knights of the shire for the parliament, I am bold (presuming of your love), heartily to pray you to grant me your kind assistance therein by the voices of all your friends and tenants of this county at the election at Wilton when the day shall be appointed by the sheriff for the election of knights in that behalf. Wherein, if you shall please to stand for me, I shall acknowledge your love with much thankfulness. And always remain,

Your assured loving friend,
Thomas Thynne

Longleat this 13th
of April 1625

Winchelsea, Cinque Port

[B.L., Add. MS. 37,819, f. 12]
The DUKE OF BUCKINGHAM to the MAYOR AND CORPORATION OF WINCHELSEA, 8 April 1625, Whitehall.[1] (Copy)
Understanding that amongst the respects which my predecessors, Lord Wardens of the Cinque Ports, have used to receive from your town, you have used to make election of such a sufficient man as they have recommended to you to serve in parliament for one of the burgesses of your town, I have thought good to recommend to you Sir Ralph Freeman, one of the masters of requests to his Majesty, whose work and place is such as that I am confident you will have good cause to believe that I have been careful of your good in recommending him to you. If you would have him sworn a freeman of your town, I pray send hither a commission to that purpose, and wherein there shall be any occasion, I will be no less ready to adorn the particular good of your town than forward to do what good I shall be able for the preserving of the jurisdiction and privileges of the Cinque Ports. And so I bid you heartily farewell.

From Whitehall, *8°* April 1625.

1. Marginal note: "Letter of Recommendation to Winchelsea for a burgess's place".

York, Yorkshire

[City of York House Book, 1613–1635, Vol. 34, p. 314]
Assembled from thence into the toll booth upon Ousbridge to the county court there holden, when and where Sir Arthur Ingram, Knight, and Mr. Christopher Brooke, Esquire, counsellor at law, are elected and chosen by a general and free consent to be citizens for this city for this next parliament.

Yorkshire

Letters concerning the 1625 election for Yorkshire that are part of the Wentworth/Woodhouse muniments have been edited. See William Knowler, ed., *The Earl of Strafforde's Letters and Dispatches* (London, 1739), I, 25–27, and J. P. Cooper, ed., *Wentworth Papers 1597–1628* (London: Camden Society, 1973), pp. 230–231, 232. For Fairfax letters concerning the contested election, see George Johnson, ed., *The Fairfax Correspondence* (London, 1848), I, 5–12. See also S. P. Salt, "Sir Thomas Wentworth and the Parliamentary Representation of Yorkshire, 1614–1628", *Northern History*, XVI (1980), 130–168, passim, and John K. Gruenfelder, "The Electoral Patronage of Sir Thomas Wentworth, Earl of Strafford, 1614–1640", *The Journal of Modern History*, 49 (1977), 564–566.

Wales

See the letter from Thomas Mostyn to Robert Davies, *sub* Flintshire; see also the materials cited separately above under the names of the various counties and boroughs of Wales. In addition, see the comments regarding the 1625 elections in: A. H. Dodd, "Wales in the Parliaments of Charles I", *Transactions of the Honourable Society of Cymmrodorian*, 1945, pp. 34–37; Emye Gwynne Jones, "County Politics and Electioneering 1558–1625", *Caernarvonshire Historical Society Transactions*, 1939, pp. 37–46; and John K. Gruenfelder, "The Wynns of Gwydir and Parliamentary Elections in Wales, 1604–40", *The Welsh History Review: Cylchgrawn Hanes Cymru*, 9, no. 2 (1978), 121–141.

E. General Correspondence (Newsletters)

1. Chamberlain Letters

The newsletters written by John Chamberlain, gentleman letter-writer of London, to Sir Dudley Carleton, ambassador at the Hague (1616–1625), are included in the collection of State Papers Domestic, Charles I, and are printed in full in *The Letters of John Chamberlain*, N. E. McClure, ed., 2 vols., Memoirs of the American Philosophical Society, XII (Philadelphia, 1939). Seven letters mention preparations for and proceedings in the parliament of 1625, written on 26 February, 23 April, 6, 14, and 21 May, and 12 and 25 June; they comprise pages 614–626 (volume 2) of Chamberlain's *Letters*. They are calendared in the State Papers as S.P. 14/184:47 and S.P. 16/1:80; 2:27, 55, 80; 3:60 and 91. With the exception of that for 26 February the letters are also included in Birch, *Court and Times of Chas. I*, I, 12–37, passim. However, in some instances Birch did not print the letters in their entirety but excised those passages he perceived as redundant.

2. Locke-Carleton Letters

(a) [S.P. 16/521:49]

Thomas Locke to Sir Dudley Carleton, 15 May 1625.
Right Honorable my Very Good Lord, may it please your Lordship,

I have given an account by the enclosed to the lords' colonels, as much as I can for the present, of their business, which I humbly submit to your Lordship's judgment before it be delivered. I have now received your Lordship's bill for your blacks[1] which, together with a minute for the recovery of your privy seal, I have delivered to my Lord Conway to be signed because Mr. Secretary Morton is gone into France upon Wednesday last, the 11th of this, with the Duke of Buckingham and the Earl of Montgomery and Sir George Goring. I had not then received the bill for the blacks and because

Mr. Secretary Morton was to go away before he could have gotten the King's hand to the privy seal he thought it best to refer me to my Lord Conway to give allowance for drawing the privy seal and getting the King's hand to it lest he should take it ill to be moved to get the King's hand to that which another had given order for. The King takes not his journey till the 21st of this, so that it is thought he will see the parliament begun before he goes. The sickness begins to increase here; this last week there died more by above 20 than the week before and there are nine or ten parishes more infested. I send your Lordship a letter from Mr. Barnard. And so with remembrance of my humble service rest,

Your Lordship's most humble servant,
Thomas Locke
14 May 1625
[*Postscript*] I have delivered the letter to Lord Mountjoy. Queen Mary [Henrietta Maria] is remembered in our prayers in public, with King Charles.

1. I.e., mourning clothes.

(b) [S.P. 16/3:88]

Thomas Locke to Sir Dudley Carleton, 22 June 1625, London.
Right Honorable,

My humble duty remembered to your Lordship. Your Lordship's privy seal is renewed for 4 *l.* per diem, to begin from the last of December, 1624, until which time you have been paid by the former privy seal. And for your intelligences you are paid until the first of June, 1624. There is 150 *l.* contained in the privy seal for allowance for blacks. I attended Mr. Carleton when he delivered your Lordship's letter to my Lord Treasurer, who promised to do what he could but would make no direct answers till he had spoken with Sir Robert Pye[1] to know what money there is in the

Exchequer. Sir Robert Pye is willing to do his best, but at this time he says there is small store of money. So soon as money comes in there will be order taken.

The parliament began the 18th. The King went thither by water and made a short speech, the copy whereof I have sent your Lordship. The same day the Lower House made choice of their old Speaker, Sir Thomas Crew, and the 20th they presented him to the King who came then again to the Upper House.

Yesterday was the solemnity of the declaration of the King's marriage, held in the Banqueting House at Whitehall, which was appointed to be read by my Lord Conway but for his ease was done by Sir William Beecher. The articles being read and the solemnities performed, the King conducted the Queen to her presence chamber where she dined, and the King returned to the Banqueting House where he dined with the three French ambassadors, the Duke of Chevreuse, Ville-aux-clercs, and the Marquis of Effiat. At the second course the herald came up and proclaimed the King's titles, craved a largesse, and after went to the Queen's side and did the like. When dinner was done the Queen came to the Banqueting House where the afternoon was spent in dancing.

The Upper House sat not yesterday, but the Lower House have made a beginning. They have appointed all to receive the communion upon Sunday next, and agreed to a general fast upon Saturday for themselves, and to have 3 sermons that day. The sickness is very much spread and is in 6 places in Westminster and, upon that ground chiefly, Sir Robert Phelips made a proposition to have the parliament dissolved, but his motion was utterly disliked.[2] And though it be like to be a very dangerous time, yet the parliament is like to hold so long as the term is put off, which is within 3 days of the ending of it.

This day the Dukes of Buckingham and Chevreuse dined at Nonesuch and they sup at York House where the King and Queen are to be, and within 3 or 4 days the Duke of Chevreuse and his lady take their journey for France. So I humbly take leave and rest,

Your Lordship's most
humbly at command,
Thomas Locke

22 June 1625

[*Endorsed*] To the Right Honorable Sir Dudley Carleton, Knight, Lord Ambassador for his Majesty of Great Britain with the [*illegible*] the States General at the Hague.

1. Auditor of the lower Exchequer and Scriptor Talliorum. Aylmer, *King's Servants*, p. 311.
2. Phelips seconded the motion made by William Mallory. For the speeches, see above, H. of C., 21 June, O.B.

(c) [S.P. 16/521:84]

THOMAS LOCKE to SIR DUDLEY CARLETON, 30 June 1625, London.

Right Honorable, my humble duty remembered,

I have received your Lordship's of the 18th of this with the lease. In my former I have advertised your Lordship of the passing of your privy seal with allowance of 150 *l.* for blacks. I could not well stay it any longer, neither would there have been any more allowed (unless there had been a motion made to the King about it) though the passing of the privy seals had been deferred to this time for I pressed my Lord Conway before what I could and he told me that rate was set down and that he could not exceed it. And if the privy seal had not been sued out there could no suit have been justly made to my Lord Treasurer for money which, though it be not obtained yet, I hope it will be shortly. Since my last I have spoken again to my Lord Treasurer and he has earnestly promised to remember you with the first. But at the present he complains of extraordinary scarcity. There have been divers applications about the taking of Imworth, but it is more for love of the house now at this time than desire of the land. It were better that somebody dwelt in it than otherwise.

Mr. Lampleigh gave it over because he heard that your Lordship was to come over shortly. Now there be others about it and I propose, God willing, to attend Sir Richard Harrison there within these 2 or 3 days to see if the house and land can be let together, but if the house be let yet there shall be reservation of convenient rooms for your Lordship if you come.

Yesterday the Lower House of parliament granted two subsidies to the King payable respectively in October and April.[1] It is not likely that the parliament will continue long now, for there died of the sickness this week 390, the whole number was 942 and there are 50 parishes infected. The greatest business that has been handled in parliament yet has been about recusants, which many think would have been more seasonable after the French are gone. The King stays here (as we think) to take his leave of the Duke of Chevreuse before he goe[s] to Hampton Court. His charge and [that] of the rest comes to 500 *l.* a day. I send your Lordship two letters enclosed for my Lady, and so I humbly take leave, resting

Your Lordship's most humble servant,
Thomas Locke
30 June 1625

1. On 30 June the Lower House resolved to grant two subsidies (see above, p. 276), but the subsidy bill did not pass either House until 8 July. Apparently rumors of an earlier passage circulated in the City. See Birch, *Court and Times of Chas. I*, I, 38–39.

(d) [S.P. 16/4:29]

THOMAS LOCKE to SIR DUDLEY CARLETON, 9 July 1625, London.
Right Honorable,
The last to your Lordship was of the 30 of June. I have since spoken to my Lord Trea-surer and to Sir Robert Pye about your Lordship's monies but for the present can give your Lordship small hope of receiving them, the want of monies being so great as the like has not been known. Sir Edward Barrett and Mr. Rawlins stay of purpose for want of money.[1] And since midsummer, neither Bedchamberman nor pensioner nor any other servant of the King has received any penny. All the money that is put in the Exchequer will not serve to feed the French.

The Duchess of Chevreuse being now resolved to lie in here,[2] for which purpose beer, wine, and other provisions are laid in at Richmond.

The sickness increases still more and more. The bill specified this week but 1,222, and of the sickness but 500 and odd, but by common opinion there died many more. It is not only in the City, but spares neither court nor country. Upon Sunday last, the 3 of this present, there were 3 carried out of the back part of the court at Whitehall (the King and Queen then there) sick, who all died since of the plague. The day following, the King and Queen went to Hampton Court, and we do hear that there is a French woman dead there of the sickness. The King removes from thence upon Monday next. Mr. Dudley Carleton is now there. I met with Sir Richard Harrison at Imworth 4 or 5 days since and by his direction I intend to go thither again within these two days to see certain things done, as the laying in of land lime, etc., for the building of the wall, but I perceive by Sir Richard Harrison that he desires further direction from your Lordship before he proceeds. Yet howsoever a beginning shall be made, hoping that your Lordship will be here yourself before it be so far proceeded in as that there may be doubt made.

The parliament is like to break up upon Monday next. The King left it free to the House by his pleasure, signified by Mr. Solicitor, to continue or dissolve as they should think fittest, having regard to the danger of the time and necessity of the state, promising to consent to the time that they should set down, which the House took as a gracious favor from his Majesty. And since, Sir John Coke, one of the Masters of Requests, by his Majesty's command made a long discourse and relation of the particular[s] wherein the monies of the last subsidy were expen[ded], pointing withal how these subsidies now gran[ted] should be bestowed, and tacitly inferring a kind of necessity for the continuing of the like supplies to maintain the expedition in hand and other services of the state. Which speech was seconded by some but not applauded by all nor promised for the future.

The House has received good satisfaction in the grievances preferred the last parliament. This meeting has continued but a while and yet a great deal of time has been spent in things that might have been more seasonably questioned at another time, as I have heard some of the House say. Among other things, a great deal of time has been spent about a book made by Mr. Montagu, called *Appello Caesarem*. He was committed to the custody of the Serjeant but with some secret direction that he should take bail of him to appear the next session, as he has done, but the King sent a message to the House by Mr. Solicitor concerning him, to this effect: That he was his servant and his chaplain, and that therefore he expected that the proceeding in that business should be left to him. Mr. Solicitor, to whom the King spoke in private concerning this business, told the King that for his part he had never observed (and thought the like of the rest of the House) that Mr. Montagu was his Majesty's servant. But howsoever, the answer of the House is to the King, that he is not restrained of his liberty though he go under bail. [There has been also a great controversy about the precedency of the two universities, when they shall come to be named in public acts; great part taking there was, some because they would not seem to be partial to either

side went out of the House when the matter was in question. But, in the end, Oxford got the day.][3]

One thing more I will be bold to mention because one of the gentlemen that was elected knight for Yorkshire, namely Sir Thomas Fairfax, is (is as it seems) very well affected toward[s] [*torn*] Lordship. He and Sir Thomas Wentworth having been [*torn*] by the sheriff, Sir John Savile brought th[em] before the House and indeed it is overthrown [*torn*] because the polling being demanded and [*torn*] and begun, yet the sheriff made his [*torn*] before he perfected it. About this much [*torn*] spent, and one day from 9 in the forenoon [*torn*] about nothing else.

Though the parliament be not dissolved yet, most part of both Houses are gone their ways. All ways that can be thought upon for staying the sickness, prayers and an order of fasting set forth by his Majesty's authority. The last Wednesday was the first time, and in the City trading was forborne and the day observed as much as any festival day. Fairs are forbidden and the intercourse of carriers to the City. Nor any citizen may inhabit near any of the King's houses as Windsor, Waybridge, Hampton, Oatlands, Richmond, Eaton, etc., by his Majesty's express command.

Thus craving pardon for troubling your Lordship so long, I humbly take leave and rest,

Your Lordship's most humbly at command,
Thomas Locke

9 July 1625

[*Postscript*] I send your Lordship one of the books set forth by his Majesty's authority.
[*Endorsed*] For your Lordship; Mr. Locke, the 9th of July 1625.

1. Sir Edward Barrett was appointed ambassador to France (S.P. 14/182:4; 185:73); Giles Rawlins, Agent to Savoy (ibid.).
2. The Duchess of Chevreuse gave birth to a daughter at Richmond Castle around the

end of July. See Birch, *Court and Times of Chas. I*, I, 44.

3. The square brackets around this passage are in the MS., although they were added at a later date.

3. Mead-Stuteville-Meddus Letters

The manuscript newsletters sent variously to and from Reverend Joseph Mead, Christ College, Cambridge, Sir Martin Stuteville of Suffolk, and Dr. James Meddus, rector of St. Gabriel, Fenchurch, are in the British Library, Harleian MS. 390. Twelve letters (22 April–30 July) contain reference to the parliament of 1625 and are printed in Birch, *Court and Times of Chas. I*, I, 11–44, passim.

4. Nethersole-Carleton Letters

See the letter from Sir Francis Nethersole to Sir Dudley Carleton concerning preparations for the parliament, 24 April 1625, *sub* Elections and Attendance, above, p. 669.

(a) [S.P. 16/4:61]

SIR FRANCIS NETHERSOLE to SIR DUDLEY CARLETON, 16 July 1625, London.
My Lord,

Your Lordship will understand the state of affairs here by your nephew and by Mr. Griffith, so that for the present I shall not need to write anything of them. But from Oxford, God willing, you shall hear from me at the length I use when the matter requires it, how matters go there, which, I pray God, may be more smoothly than men's fears prophesy. That the hand of God stretched out daily more and more against us by the increase of his plague in this City and the spreading thereof in the country does cause such a distraction and consternation in men's minds that the like was never seen in our age. It is observed that the number of those which died of the sickness at the beginning thereof, having been some weeks just the same as it was in the an[s]werable time of the first year of the late King,[1] is now grown the last week near a thousand greater. That makes all men that can, hasten away. Yet am I here till last week to attend the parliament and now till the next to see whether there may be any change in the adjournment thereof, of which I was in some hope these last days but shall be in no more if it be not done tomorrow at Windsor, where a kitchener of the King died of the sickness a day before his coming thither. Then I go down to drink the waters of the Wellingborough[2] till I must be at Oxford. If the fair weather we have now had one week hold longer, whereof as I write this there appears cause to doubt, and now men make hay standing up to the ankles in water. Mr. Locke has left one at his house to receive letters [ad]dressed to him, and I have left direction how such as comes for me may be sent to me. I beseech your Lordship therefore that the doubt thereof may be no occasion of your forbearing to favor me with the knowledge of what passes on that side. And so I rest,

Your Lordship's humble and faithful servant,
Francis Nethersole

London, 16th July 1625

1. There had been an outbreak of the plague in London in 1603.
2. MS.: *Wellingborne*.

(b) [S.P. 16/5:30]

SIR FRANCIS NETHERSOLE to SIR DUDLEY CARLETON, 9 August 1625, Oxford.
My Lord,

[1][In my former, which I think will go with this, I have given your Lordship an account of what passed here the two first days of this meeting of parliament.[2] The next day was spent in devotion.[3] On Thursday morning[4] the King came privately to Christ Church (I mean by privately, without state and usual solemnity at his entry into town) and, hav-

ing commanded both the Houses there to attend him, spoke to them to this purpose: That the occasion of his having called them together to this place at this time was to require their help toward the setting forth of that navy which he had put into a readiness to go to sea, with land forces likewise to go with it, but that he was not able of himself to set it out, having used all possible means both by himself and his officers to take up money; and because in hope at first to have done it, if he could have done he would not have troubled them with coming hither, but his hope therein having failed him, that he was forced to have recourse to them in confident assurance that they would not suffer this first action of his, whereon his future reputation so much depended and into which he had engaged himself by their advice, now to fall to the ground for want of means; making no doubt but that they were all of his mind which was this: that it were much better the navy should come home broken by the enemy and half lost than not gone at all, in respect of the consequences thereof, with which, as also with the whole counsel of the proceedings in this great business ever since it was undertaken by their advice, he had given charge to my Lord Conway and Sir John Coke to acquaint them particularly. And for the particular answer to their petition concerning religion he promised at the end of the last meeting, that they should have it within two days. My Lord Conway and Sir John Coke's speeches were both to the same effect, the former more brief, the latter now enlarged, and very little differing from that which the same men delivered at London, whereof I then gave a particular account, and will now therefore not repeat it. And this was all was done that day; for the Lower House, returning again to the Divinity School wherein they sit, put off the debate hereupon till next day.

The next day, on which, being the fourth of this meeting and month,[5] there should have been a call of the House, and the ex-pectation thereof had now well filled it, there was a proposition made that in respect it was to be doubted that after the call many would slip away, as then sure, it should be deferred till another time, and no certain time prefixed for it, the better to hold men here. And this thus settled, it was moved that we should fall to the business for which we were called hither, and so there was a motion made for two subsidies and two fifteenths by Mr. Treasurer of the Household, who had the good fortune to have his motion for these approved and followed the last year. But all went not now so clear. For the giving of any at all was opposed by three or four of the principal speakers who usually stand stiffest for the country and, in such a manner as they all showed a great dislike of our being called hither upon this occasion, one of them not sparing to say that he doubted whosoever gave the counsel had an intention to set the King and his people at variance, it being impossible for them to comply with this demand of his, and among other passages alleging that saying of Solomon, that in the multitude of counsellors there is health.[6] Another,[7] remembering what has heretofore passed in a parliament at this place and, after he had disallowed of the form of the proceeding then as swerving from that duty which subjects owe to their superiors, yet commending the matter was then done, and concluding that he hoped we would imitate that, and that God Almighty who, by His providence, many times disposes of things to the contrary of that which men propose, had a purpose to bring some such work to pass because He had put it into the minds of some men to counsel our calling hither, against all reason, concluding that by all means since we were here we should resolve to sit it out notwithstanding the danger of the plague and, resolving ourselves into a committee the next morning, then advise of such heads as might be the matter of an humble petition we might deliver to his Majesty for the reformation of divers abuses, as also, so the means how we might best give his Majesty satisfaction in that he desired. Another set down divers heads as he thought worthy to be taken into consideration for the enabling of the King to live, and live according to his state, upon his own revenue.[8] And among other things, thought it fit inquiry should be made how his Majesty came to be in that necessity which was now urged for a reason of our coming hither; for that without a further supply from us he was not able to set forth the fleet. From which mention of the fleet, he fell to cite old records, that the admirals in ancient time used to be men expert in sea affairs, and to allege precedents of men who by law had been put out of their offices for being unable to discharge them, though otherwise without fault. I do not tell your Lordship all was said by these men, nor by those that answered them, which were three of the best speakers of the King's learned and Privy Council,[9] for that were too long, they having spent almost all the forenoon. But this that I have written, I have written to this end because it was by a great servant of my Lord Duke of Buckingham and of the Queen, my mistress, and showed to have been spoken of his Grace, and he therefore made a motion that the committee might proceed, but that my Lord Duke might have liberty to come to it there to answer such things as could be objected against him, wherein he assured himself he would be able and ready to give the House satisfaction.[10] This was not liked by the House and as little by my Lord Duke, as I hear, although he could not be dissatisfied with him that said it, being assured of his good intention. The next day [6 August], unto which the further debate of this business had been deferred, there was not much said concerning the giving of subsidies, but there were some who had ill fortune in going about to wipe off those aspersions which they conceived had been cast on my Lord Duke. One of them let the House know that his Grace did not execute the

office of Admiral by himself, but by the certain commissioners who were to be blamed for any errors [that] might have been committed in the preparation of this fleet, which he seemed to grant.[11] And another, Mr. Clarke by name, who was once a clerk extraordinary of the Council and since a groom of his late Majesty's Bedchamber, having, it seems, a mind to say something in my Lord Duke's defense, began with taking notice and saying that there had been bitter invectives made against him the day before. Whereupon, being called to the bar, he desired to explain himself and in doing that made the business so much worse that he was presently commanded to withdraw himself and then censured to be committed to the Serjeant till the Monday following, at which time, upon his acknowledgment of his fault and submission made on his knees at the bar, he was received into the House again.

On the same Monday [8 August], being yesterday morning, there having been a message brought to us from the Lords that my Lord Duke of Buckingham had a command from his Majesty to deliver something to both Houses, and that their Lordships did therefore desire a present meeting, there was one in our House who,[12] upon this occasion, remembered precedents in very many kings' reigns, as low as Henry the 8, by which it appeared that then the Lords had not the appointment of time and place which they challenge now, but that they used many times to come down into the Lower House. This fixed another question—how we should go to this meeting; for if we went as a House, then it was said we ought to be covered there, though we use not to be at conferences, and the message was delivered in those words. This disputation cost the rest of the morning, but was at last resolved thus: that we should send to the Lords to know how they understood their message. And their Lordships explaining themselves to have meant a meeting of both the whole Houses, but in the nature of committees, the business was so accommodated and we met in the afternoon in Christ Church Hall where what passed your Lordship does receive in the adjoined papers,[13] being copies of the report [that] was made to our House thereof this day, and which took up almost all the time, for there were but five that spoke after.[14] The first that spoke moved that having now satisfaction in what we chiefly desired concerning matter of religion, we should do well to see how we could give his Majesty satisfaction in that he desired of us. The second, who was a courtier, making a long, extravagant, and impertinent speech, among other things alleged the good use of precedents and then applying this would have us make war by the precedent of Queen Elizabeth. This occasioned the next man, being a lawyer, to begin thus: That because the gentleman who spoke before had spoken like a lawyer, insisting so much upon precedent, he would change his profession and speak like a courtier, and so moved that we should give subsidies, though there were no precedent of subsidies upon subsidies given in one session of parliament. But a third [sic] rising up began that he was neither courtier nor lawyer but a plain country gentleman, and therefore as such desired we might resolve ourselves into a committee tomorrow and then debate upon the whole matter as it had been delivered and reported to us, wherein his advice was followed, and what will follow thereupon is that on which the expectations of all men are fixed but must be the subject of my next.]

On Sunday last, my Lord Duke of Buckingham had his patent of Admiral and Captain General of the Fleet, whereof if I be not deceived your Lordship shall herewith receive a copy.[15]

The sickness does so much increase both in London and in the country that there are proclamations gone forth for the removing of the Receipt of the Exchequer to Richmond and for the discharging of Bar-

tholomew and Sturbridge fairs, with others, where the plague is.[16] There are also letters written from the lords of the Council by which the public holding of the fast on the Wednesdays is discharged in all infected places, but the people are there to be exhorted to observe the same in their private houses.[17] Sir W[illiam] Beecher has had a man dead of it in this town, whereupon he, being a parliament man, is removed.

And so desiring to be excused to his Majesty for this time also, until I may see what will be the issue of this parliament, I take leave and rest,

>Your Lordship's humble servant,
>Francis Nethersole

Oxford, 9th August 1625

1. The first part of the body of the letter is enclosed in square brackets in the MS.
2. I.e., Monday and Tuesday, the first and second of August.
3. I.e., Wednesday, 3 August, the fast day.
4. I.e., 4 August.
5. The King spoke on 4 August, the day the House was to be called. See above, H. of C., 4 August, n. 5. Treasurer Edmondes's motion and the other speeches referred to below occurred on 5 August.
6. See Sir Francis Seymour's speech, H. of C., 5 August, pp. 393–394.
7. See Sir Robert Phelips's speech, H. of C., 5 August, O.B.
8. See Sir Edward Coke's speech, H. of C., 5 August, O.B.
9. See the speeches of Sir Humphrey May, Sir Thomas Edmondes, and Sir Richard Weston, H. of C., 5 August, O.B.
10. See Sir George Goring's speech, H. of C., 5 August, O.B.
11. See Sir John Eliot's speech, H. of C., 6 August, pp. 416–417.
12. See Sir Nathaniel Rich's speech, H. of C., 8 August, p. 425.
13. The reports are not included with the letter in the State Papers collection.
14. See the speeches of Sir Thomas Edmondes, John Maynard, Thomas Malet, and Sir Robert Phelips following the reports of the 8 August conference, H. of C., 9 August, O.B.
15. On the 6 August commission to the Duke of Buckingham, see above, *Negotium*, n. 222.

16. See the proclamations of 31 July and 4 August in *Stuart Proclamations*, II, 49–52.

17. See above, H. of L., 3 August, n. 2.

(c) [S.P. 16/5:33]

Sir Francis Nethersole to Sir Dudley Carleton, 11 August 1625, Oxford.

My Lord,

When we were yesterday met in the morning and ready to have turned the House into a committee, according to the order of the day before, Mr. Chancellor of the Exchequer delivered a message from his Majesty to this effect: That his Majesty taking notice of those many questions now among us whereby we were retarded from coming to a resolution in that business for which he had called us hither; and commanded him to let us understand that as the opportunity for that action he intended was not yet past, so it would be quickly if we lost any more time; and that he therefore so prayed us to give him a speedy answer, assuring us that if it were such as he hoped for to supply his present occasions we should have another session in winter, or what time soever we ourselves would appoint it, to consider of the reformation of all those things whereof we could make complaint, and that he would give free way thereunto, engaging his royal word to us for this. But that if for any considerations we should not yield to that which his occasions enforced him to require of us, he would be glad also to be speedily resolved thereof to the end that he might have the more time to think what he had to do and no longer endanger our lives to no purpose by holding us together in this place, the contagion daily spreading itself in it; concluding with this: that we would withal take into our consideration that this was the first request he had ever made to us.

Upon the occasion of this message it was ordered that the House, which should have resolved itself into a committee, should now sit as a House. And so we fell close to the business stated thus, first whether we should give his Majesty any supply at this time, if "aye", then how much, when and how; if "no", then what answer we should return his Majesty, and what reasons we should give him for our excuse. The first of these questions was excellently spoken unto on both sides. They who were for the giving of supply alleged that it concerned the King and kingdom in honor and safety; that the fleet now prepared should not stay for want of means to set it forth. They alleged the ill consequences like to ensue herein abroad by the falling back of all those princes and states who, in expectation of his Majesty's declaration by the sending out of this fleet, were either entered or entering into the same quarrel. They intimated the danger of like ill consequences at home by giving of his Majesty occasion to dislike parliaments at his first coming to the crown. They alleged as a principal inducement the great satisfaction he had given us in matter of religion and, for a greater than this, that this was the first request his Majesty had ever made to us. But they who were on the contrary alleged it was against all precedent to give either subsidies upon subsidies in one session (which one said was metal upon metal, argent upon argent) or subsidies in reversion, it having been moved that the two subsidies and fifteens might be given now but to be paid after the others formerly given. They alleged that whereas it had been delivered that a matter of 40 thousand pounds would serve to set forth the fleet, but that there would be need of 60 thousand pounds now at their coming home; that it was neither credited that his Majesty was not able to take up 40 thousand as had been said, nor a sufficient cause of calling the parliament to this place in this dangerous time for the procuring of so small and contemptible a sum; that for the other 60 thousand *l.*, we might happily have opportunity to meet again before there would be need of it. And though we should not, yet that the voyage were better be stopped than furthered if there were not likelihood that the fleet which has been said to have cost 400 thousand *l.* would bring home a return of more than 60 thousand *l.* to defray the charge which then accrues. That for the going out of the fleet, if the state of the King's debts and anticipations to such, as was delivered by my Lord Treasurer, and such as it appeared to be by our assembling here for so small a sum, it was not conceivable for us to begin a war and strike one stroke now, there being no means for us to second it with another the next year; nor so much as to defend ourselves, if it were true that there was now a necessity of anticipating subsidies to be paid appear hence toward the setting forth of this fleet. But that which moved most was that whereas my Lord Duke of Buckingham had said in his own defense that he had proceeded in the undertaking and preparation of this great action by the advice of the Council of War and of the Council of State, Sir Robert Mansell, on the contrary, moved that he [had] never been at any meeting of my Lord and of the Council of War but one in February last when there was but a running discourse held of setting forth a fleet. That my Lord Duke had never spoken to him of this business but once met at Newmarket, at which time he had showed his dislike of the action and the preparations in a high degree, and had done the like to my Lord Conway and to my Lord Treasurer when they required him, as being of the Council of War, to give warrants for monies for the land forces, which he had done but with protestation that he might not be thereby understood to consent to the design. Besides, he undertook to prove that this action now intended would not be well counselled nor likely to prosper. Thereupon, the question having been declined again, the debate was put off till this day. And this day after a long great complaint of many piracies committed on the western coasts by Turks, which one did not spare to lay to my Lord Admiral his fault, that business being referred to a committee of the whole House, we fell to the main once more, but after long debate forebore the question again. And the bold announcement of Sir Robert Mansell having been brought on the stage again, tomorrow is appointed for him to make good what he has said, and for my Lord Admiral to maintain his saying. To that, if Sir Robert fail, he is like to have an ill day of it. Howsoever, I hope it will bring it to an end of our business. And then I shall make all the haste I can to return to my simple life, asking your Lordship still in the meantime to excuse me for not writing to his Majesty. And to prepare that all my letters which have stayed one upon another be not left behind, I must abruptly end this without adding [*illegible*] but that I am ever,

> Your Lordship's most
> humble servant,
> Fra. Nethersole

Oxford, 11th August

[*Postscript*] I beseech your Lordship give me leave to include a packet I have received from Sir W. Croft to his sister, my mistress, whose hands I kiss, and your noble lady's.

(d) [S.P. 16/5:42]

Sir Francis Nethersole to Sir Dudley Carleton, 14 August 1625, Woodstock.
My Lord,

I sent your Lordship a great packet from Oxford on Thursday containing three several large letters and, in them, all had then passed in parliament there.[1] I hope it will come safe to your hands and then I am most assured there will be no further danger, though I wrote with freedom as I use to do to your Lordship. The same night [11 August] we had certain knowledge that the parliament would be dissolved the next morning, and that affected men's minds, as you imagine. All that was done the next morning before the dissolution was the making of the enclosed declaration, save that there was an answer made to what Sir Robert Mansell had averred, by Mr. Solicitor, who contradicted what the other had said in almost all. Whereupon Sir Robert explained himself and, as many men conceived, with some variation from what he had delivered the day before, but said still so much, that thereupon he was commanded to attend the lords of the Council here this day, where it was generally conceived that he should have received some very heavy censure. Yet has he been here this day and is gone away in an opinion that all shall go well with him and this matter be questioned no more.

The general and colonels of the fleet have been here also these two days, and they reckon to be going tomorrow towards Plymouth. The King goes then towards Bewley, and the Queen to Tichfield on Wednesday. The lords of the Council are all commanded to be at Southampton on Thursday next where it is said that the States' ambassador shall be treated with, if not dispatched. I am promised I shall be [dispatched] tomorrow, but with a condition to return again to court in case there should be any occasion upon Mr. Secretary Morton's return, which I hope there will not; but howsoever reckon to be at the seaside to attend a passage about 14 days hence, and long for nothing so much as to attend the Queen, my most gracious mistress, to whom, having forborne to wait thus long because I had no good news to send, I will not do it now, though it is at the worst, but restrain myself till my coming. And so kissing your Lordship's and your lady's hands, I rest ever your Lordship's humble servant,

Fra. Nethersole

Woodstock, 14th August
Sunday

1. The packet is not included in the State Papers with the Oxford letter of 11 August, printed above.

5. Pesaro Dispatches (S.P. 99)

The dispatches from Zuane Pesaro, Venetian ambassador in London, to the Doge and Senate of Venice which contain references to the parliament of 1625 are printed in *Cal. S.P. Venetian, 1625–1626*, pp. 61–147, passim. The dispatches cover the period from 30 May to 26 August (continental style); those for 4 July and 21 August contain the fullest reports of proceedings during the session as well as observations on foreign activities and preparations for the expedition to Cadiz.

6. Salvetti Dispatches (Skrine MSS.)

The dispatches from Amerigo Salvetti, appointed Tuscan Resident at the Court of Whitehall in 1616 by Cosmo de' Medici, to the Grand Duke of Florence are printed in H.M.C., *11th Report, Appendix, Part I* (Skrine MSS.). Those dispatches mentioning the first parliament of King Charles are dated 18 and 25 April, 16 and 30 May, 6 and 27 June, 4 and 11 July, and 19 August, at which time Salvetti left plague-stricken London for the country. Although only those letters listed above specifically mention the parliament, all of the dispatches dated between 11 April and 19 August (ibid., pp. 2–30) contain material relating to the Catholic question in England and the matter of preparations for sending the fleet to Spain.

F. Miscellaneous Correspondence

(1) [Egerton MS. 2715, no. 504]

Sir Thomas Hirne to Framlingham Gawdy, 20 June 1625, London.

Sir,

I do earnestly desire to speak with you about some serious business. I pray be pleased to meet me in Westminster Hall tomorrow morning about 8 a clock before we go to parliament, where and when I will expect you. So I rest,

Your assured
Thomas Hirne[1]

This 20th of
June 1625

1. Hirne and Gawdy both sat for Norfolk boroughs. We do not know whether they met for personal or parliamentary business.

(2) [Downshire MSS., Vol. 18, f. 146]

John Castle to William Trumbull, 25 June 1625.

My Noble and Dearest Friend,

. . . I have freely and largely imparted to Mr. Wooley what I knew and bid him write it unto you. He must at this time likewise supply my defectiveness in that behalf. For I shall advertise you no more than that the assembly of the House of Commons to the King's proposition for money by way shorter than parliamentary have made no other answer as yet than that as on the one part they are very willing to give his Majesty contentment therein, so on the other side they desire first to have the great penal statute touching forfeitures of 2 parts of recusants' lands to be put in execution and then they will engage themselves for supply.

A sermon made on Tuesday last (the marriage feast day) before his Majesty by Dr. Fell (which was bitterly invective against popery) and this conditional answer of the House have bred some bad impressions to the French here. And surely for my poor opinion, though both might have been good in their due time, yet to move these things in the face of the French while the great ambassador is here, and during the joy of the feast, was not so much of able judgment in the movers as out of passion and ignorance in state business.

I shall now conclude, having first from my wife, myself saluted you and your dearest Jugg with all yours, that I commit you to the protection of the blessed Trinity.

Your most faithful and
constantly assured friend
and brother to serve you,
John Castle

25 June 1625

(3) [S.P. 16/1:48]

The Duke of Buckingham to Sir Francis Stuart, 27 June 1625, York House.

After my hearty commendations;

The lords of his Majesty's Privy Council having received information by diverse complaints of particular men whose ships have been taken tha[t] not only the trade of the land is much hindered but that the inhabitants upon the western coasts are put in continual fear of the burning their hous[es], loss of their goods, and capturing their persons by a great number of Turkish pirates which have lately haunted those parts, and have thereupon give[n] directions for the sending of some ships to free both th[e] trade and country from that danger. Now for tha[t I] understand that his Majesty's ships the *Lion* and the *Rainbow* are now ready with all their provisions ab[oard] (those only excepted which are to be supplied at Plymouth), I thought it fit and do hereby requ[ire] and authorize you, Sir Francis Stuart, to go present[ly] for those parts with his Majesty's said ship the *Lion*, which you have command, and to take in your company t[he] *Rainbow* whereof Mr. John Chudleigh is captain, an[d] as many other ships of the merchants and Newcastlemen as (being pressed for his Majesty's service) are ready in the Downs or else-where to accompany you to the port of Plymouth. And in your way thither you are to inform yourself by the best means you can where any such pirates may be dis-covered and to do your best endeavor with the assistance of the said ships to take and apprehend them, or at least to clear the coasts of them. And when you are as high as Plymouth and shall there understand that the said pirates lie off, and are upon Corn-wall or Scilly, you are with a convenient number of the said ships to follow after them, so far only and so long as it may be done without absenting yourself from the rendezvous of the whole fleet when they shall make head at Plymouth, lest by your absence any prejudice may follow to the intended service, whereof you must take special care. And for your so doing, this shall be your sufficient warrant to yourself (as admiral for this particular service) and to the rest that shall attend you therein ac-cording to these instructions. And so re-quiring you to be gone with all convenient expedition, I bid you farewell.

Your very loving friend,
George Buckingham

York House
27° Junii 1625
[*Endorsed*] To my very loving friend Sir Francis Stuart, Kt., aboard his Majesty's ship the *Lion*, these.

---

(4) [S.P. 16/4:10]

SIR THOMAS CREW, Speaker of the House of Commons, to SECRETARY CONWAY, 1 July 1625, London.
Right Honorable,

My very good Lord, the warrant which I signed by order of the House is pursuant the act of parliament which extends both to the treasuries as also to the Council of War in the act mentioned. This morning an ex-cuse was made for my Lord Carew in re-gard of his indisposition of health at this time, and it was said that my Lord Viscount Grandison was at Battersea and could not have returned so soon, and I conceive it were fit that someone of the House should signify this afternoon how late your Lord-ship received notice, and that you are in a course of physic. The House sits this after-noon as a committee of the whole House, and I come not unless I be sent for, else I would not have failed to have made known the cause of your not coming at this time, and will be ever ready to do you service.

At your Lordship's
command,
Thomas Crew

July 1625
[*Endorsed*] To the Right Honorable and my very good Lord, Edward Lord Conway, Principal Secretary to the King's most ex-cellent Majesty and one of the lords of his Majesty's most honorable Privy Council, these.

---

(5) [Corporation MSS., L. 212, Kingston-upon-Hull]

JOHN LISTER to ANONYMOUS, 6 July 1625, Westminster.
After my hearty commendations;

That my last was by packet 4 days past whereby I signified unto you what had then passed, since which I have attempted the delivery of a petition touching the London trades but it so fell out by occasion of God's heavy visitation that there is no hope of re-ceiving any answer at this present, the plague having entered upon the court, being 2 or 3 dead that belonged to the King's bakehouse so as the King was forced to retire suddenly upon Monday last to Hampton Court and the Queen to Oat-lands, and all the lords that lay at Whitehall to disperse to several places so as they sit not in Council. There is a knight likewise that was every day with us at Westminster being competitor for a place in parliament, one Sir Charles Groos,[1] suddenly dead in the plague. It is feared this week's bill will be above 1,200. God in His mercy look upon us and withdraw His punishing hand. I assure [you] I was never so wary of London in all my life, yet my conscience and affection to my country will not give [me] leave to come away till I see things brought to some perfection. The subsidy bill not yet settled and the statute of tonnage and poundage for the King's customs but now presented to the House, which God knows is left very thin, being a business of the greatest importance that concerns the ports as also the new impost of wines. And if all men should do as some do, what might become of those things if none but courtiers were remaining. I hope about Tuesday next we shall make an end of this session and then I shall hasten home (God willing). The election of the knights for Yorkshire is adjudged void and a new writ to issue for a new election after a great trouble to the House of Parliament. And thus, hoping shortly to be with you, I betake you to God and rest,

> Your loving friend,
> John Lister

Westminster, *6 Julii 1625*

1. MS.: *Grosse.* Sir Charles Le Groos was defeated at the poll in the 1625 Norfolk shire election (*Norfolk Record Society*, XIV [1941], 82), but he did not die from the plague. He was M.P. for Orford, Suffolk, in 1626 and subsequent parliaments and died in 1656. *A.C.*

---

(6) A letter from Sir John Coke to Sir Robert Pye, 10 July 1625, is printed in H.M.C., *12th Report, Appendix, Part I,* p. 206.

---

(7) [Harl. MS. 7000, f. 181]

THOMAS ANYAN to SIR ROBERT COTTON, 18 July 1625, Oxford.
Noble Sir,

I shall be able to furnish yourself and your son with convenient chambers, ac-

cording to your description, but not with bedding and napery worthy of your use. You shall do therefore well to bring them with you, that you may have the more content during your abode. Here we have our commons, and constant hours of supping and dining, which, if you will not be tied unto, our cook shall provide otherwise for you. So wishing your health and happiness, I rest,

> Your very assured friend,
> Tho. Anyan

C.C.C. Ox., July 18, 1625
[*Postscript*] If you will content yourself with 4 such beds as are in those 2 chambers, they shall be reserved for you. But your linen I would have you bring with you. Your lodgings and dining room shall be without exception.
[*Endorsed*] To my noble friend Sir Robert Cotton, Knight and Baronet, at his house in Westminster, these.

---

(8) [S.P. 16/4:147]

OLIVER, VISCOUNT GRANDISON, to SECRETARY CONWAY, 30 July 1625, Battersea.
My Lord,

This bearer, Captain Hart, agent to my Lord Docwra,[1] will acquaint you with a restraint of the House of Commons laid upon the treasurers of the subsidy money for the payment of such monies as by former orders by the Council of War they were directed to pay for the supplies of horse and foot sent into Ireland which, if it be not revoked, those supplies will presently be broken, to the prejudice of his Majesty's service and the security of that kingdom.

I have written hereof to my Lord Treasurer, and pray your Lordship to procure order to those treasurers to pay those monies according to the direction of the act of parliament.

It may please your Lordship further to consider how these supplies shall be paid after Michaelmas next, which is the uttermost extent for the monies for those supplies assigned by the Council of War. For if for want of payment those supplies (the levying, arming, clothing, and transporting whereof has been so chargeable) should be discharged, much prejudice thereby may ensue to his Majesty's army and the security of that kingdom, which I beseech your Lordship (if you please) to make known to his Majesty. The residue concerning that business I leave to the relation of this bearer. And so I commend your Lordship to the safekeeping of Almighty God, and rest,

> Your Lordship's humble servant,
> [*Illegible*] Grandison

30 July 1625, Battersea

1. See the petition of Henry Hart, printed above, H. of C., 10 August, p. 453.

---

(9) [S.P. 16/5:6]

JAMES BAGG to the DUKE OF BUCKINGHAM, 2 August 1625, Plymouth.

Sir,

My last was the 27th, which humbly presented my answer to the complaint put up to your Grace against me, which I hope I have so done as to live and die in your favor, and so your servant for present.

My desire well to discharge the charge given me in the victualling of the fleet commands my unwilling stay from parliament, and there attending your Grace. Yet can I not but think myself able in the country to do your Lordship some parliament service which also may conduce to his Majesty's commodity. I hope this sitting will confirm to the King the bill of tonnage and poundage, which I wish should be offered from the House with all humbleness.

But I find from these parts divers towns have written to their burgesses of the daily oppression they are subject to by the Sallee and Turkey pirates that are even now to the number of twenty sail upon this coast. Within these six days [they] have taken a Scot and two English off the Lizard, one being of this harbor and worth five thousand pounds, which will invite those of the parliament to capitulate in passing that bill, of which I have thought it fit to advertise your Grace, hoping that some ships in special and that of the least burden which is most fittest will be provided, that it appear unto the House your Grace has ordered a remedy ere the complaint be presented.

The enclosed letter from Sir Bernard Grenville speaks that I reported to the west parts: that your Excellency had ordered some of the fleet now there to attend the coast. It gave them great satisfaction, but since Sir Francis Stuart's return from the coast the winds have kept in this harbor, have advantaged the Turks, and makes the inhabitants doubt when the fleet is gone they shall have no ships to guard the shores. This fear of theirs being cleared will sweeten all proceedings and give them the better hope of their Virginia and New Land returns, upon the safety of which their welfare and wealth much depends.

The increase of these pirates is the such that both bring them munition and buy their commodities; as now for instance, there is a ship of Mr. Peter Curtens of Middleborough passed by this place, I hope will meet with the fleet, full of Sallee commodities worth fifteen or twenty thousand pounds. I should have been happy in doing the service to your Grace to have stayed this ship if she had put into my vice admiralty, but she is passed by and unless the fleet meet her Curtens grows, by unlawful ways, rich.

Campaine,[1] the pirate, the 23th of June was at Sallee, has there made sale of the commodities taken from the *Golden Phoenix* of London. If either hostility or pardon could bring him in, the sea were well disburdened of him.

Monsieur Soubise three weeks since encountered with Hautain [who] burnt his vice admiral, sheared three other of his fleet, hurt his own ship, caused them to bear up for Blewitt, and seems to be admiral of the sea.[2] This instant here arrived from Rochelle a small ship with three men, as they call them their deputies, which are to repair unto his Majesty and intend to speed to court.

Rochelle has stayed two of our Bristol ships, and because they fear his Majesty's ship, the *Vanguard,* with other the English come thither, they stay all the English guards from sail. If I may not displease my Lord, my observations being to do you service, give me leave to say that those ships now here are already victualled, but I find the mariners out of clothes. It causes sickness, and hardly is a surgeon prepared with provisions to cure. For the *Lion,* she is not able to keep her decks free of pests without leaving fifty tons of her victuals out of her. So as Sir Francis Stuart will offer it to your Grace with a desire some victuallers be provided.

Knowing the sea is not more your Lordship's than the shore, and that it is said you shall command both, I sorrow the land men were not with more care chosen better accoutremented to do service, for if shirts, shoes, stockings, and some apparel be not made ready for them, nothing more can be feared than sickness and mortality among them.

Sir Francis Stuart desires me, that would rather come under his cover, to convey his enclosed. I disclose my boldness and my weakness unto your Excellency by my rude lines. Your favor will, I hope, pardon these faults and believe they proceed from an honest heart of your Grace's most humble, faithful, and bounden servant.

Plymouth
2d of August 1625

1. Campaine was a Dutch pirate. See *Cal. S.P. Dom., 1625–1626, sub* Campaine.
2. Hautain, Admiral of a Dutch squadron, was surprised by Soubise on 17 July; see *Cal. S.P. Venetian, 1625–1626,* p. 164n.

---

(10) A letter from Sir John Coke to Fulke Greville, Lord Brooke, 4 August 1625, is printed in H.M.C., *12th Report, Appendix, Part III,* pp. 134–135.

---

(11) [S.P. 16/5:23]

SIR RICHARD HUTTON, Justice of the Common Pleas, to LORD KEEPER WILLIAMS, 6 August 1625, Exeter.

My Very Honorable Lord,

I have presumed to send to your Lordship this petition herein enclosed,[1] presented and delivered to me by the Grand Jury of the county of Devon, now at Exeter, as a grievance whereby you may perceive that there is great cause to take some speedy course for the redress of this so great and grievous a spoil. The lamentable outcries of the wives of such as have been lately taken by the Turks and the pitiful complaints of others that have sustained great losses, even to the utter undoing of divers of them, were such as would have moved any Christian heart to commiseration. The letters that come from some that are prisoners there relating the strange and new-devised tortures that they are put unto unless they will turn Turks will grieve any Christian man to hear of. And it is written from them that the Turks do give out in speeches that they will bring as many English women thither as they have brought men; the number of the men, as it is reported, is a thousand. It is much feared that the Turkish ships are now gone to meet with the ships that come from Newfoundland which, if they do, then this country will be intolerably impoverished.

This is a matter of state and, I confess, out of my element, yet finding it a great grievance in my circuit and complained of by so many, and that it has stricken a great fear of further harm into the people of this country, I have thought it my duty to make it known to your Lordship, to the end your Lordship would be pleased either to acquaint his Majesty or the Lords and others of his Majesty's most honorable Privy Council therewith, that some such course may be taken as they in their wisdoms shall think fit.

I hope your Lordship will excuse my not attending the parliament, for I assure your Lordship my labor and extraordinary pains here in this circuit may plead for my discharge therein. The sickness is begun here at Exeter and is spread abroad very dangerously. God of His mercy withdraw this grievous punishment. And thus remembering my humble duty to your Lordship, I take my leave,

> Your Lordship's in all duty to be
> commanded,
> Richard Hutton

From Exon, this
sixth of August 1625
[*Endorsed*] To the Right Honorable and my very good Lord, John, Lord Bishop of Lincoln, Lord Keeper of the Great Seal of England, and one of his Majesty's most honorable Privy Council, give these.

1. A petition to Sir Richard Hutton from the Grand Jury of the Devon assizes complaining against the Turks follows the letter in the State Papers collection.

———————

(12) [S.P. 16/5:49]

SIR FRANCIS STUART to the DUKE OF BUCK-INGHAM, 16 August 1625, the *Lion*.
My Most Honorable Lord,

I am much grieved that these western gentlemen and merchants should inform your Grace that I have given them no help since my coming hither for securing these coasts. If their complaints were just, and that I should so abuse the trust your Grace has committed unto me, I should judge myself fitter for wapping than to command the meanest ship in the fleet.

After I had run up the channel with such ships as accompanied me from the Downs and met with many homewards bound, some from the southwards, some from the French coast, some from Ireland, and some from out the Severn, who assured us the coast was cleared of Sallee men and other pirates, the weather being thick and hawsey [*sic*], the wind high and in our teeth, we were forced back into Plymouth where we took in victuals, I being then come to our iron bound cask, the last refuge in a long voyage. Upon the first rumor of the return of the Turks, as soon as any of our ships would either sail, warp, or tow out of Catewater, I sent to sea Captain Boteler, in the *Jonathan*, with four more of the nimblest Newcastlemen in the fleet who, after ten days unprofitable and dangerous wallowing against wind and weather, were forced by stress into Falmouth, and after into Plymouth. They gave chase to six sail of Turks, who going two foot for one faster than our ships, their hulls were layed in one watch. The same day that Captain Boteler came in, Captain Edward Harvey in the *Royal Exchange*, Captain Mervin Burley in the *Mary Constance*, and three Newcastlemen more put to sea, but with little better fortune; for two of them are beaten back with foul weather into the Sound, the *Mary Constance* with such defects as may appear by an enclosed certificate under her captain's and master's hands, and one other Newcastleman with him. Captain Bond is ready in the *Sapphire*, with six ships more, with the first fair wind to set to sea, who is to join with Captain Harvey and to ply between Ushant and Cape Clear, but that they shall meet with this ship in the Sleeve, I cannot warrant, though I have given them such order according to your Grace's directions.

In lieu of those gentlemen's and merchants' complaint who came up to parliament, I had presented them with an humble petition that they would have procured an act that we might have fair winds at pleasure to perform their service, but that I doubted they would hardly find any precedent for it!

The *Lion* has been divers times loose

since taking in of our victuals to put to sea, but the wind has ever been so contrary or blown so high that we could not sail and dare not warp or tow a ship of her length out of this narrow gut the Catewater. Many of our men are fallen suddenly sick, in my opinion for want of clothes and vinegar to wash her between decks. And most of them of late, since she sprang new leaks never suspected before; for, after we had taken most of our victuals on board, she made in six hours three feet six inches in holds. Whereupon I have caused all her ordnance, victuals, and sea stores, saving her lower tier of beer (which for endangering of the casks I dare not venture on but upon mere necessity) to be taken out of her, and yet is she still a very leaky ship. Further than to see her safe I dare not meddle until I receive your Grace's commands, which I beseech you to hasten. As for my private grief in the *Nonesuch*, heretofore upon the like occasion, and now in the *Lion*, I will not trouble your Grace. But this is too ordinary a disease of the old ships which, if it be not cured by your special care may bring with it, besides dishonor, the loss both of the ships and the men that sail them.

The *Rainbow*, who has been also leaky, will be shortly ready, but being a ship of so great importance I would willingly know your Grace's pleasure whether you would have her put to sea or not against these picaroons of Sallee who, as long as they are supplied by the Flemish freebooters with men, munition, victuals, and all manner of sea stores (most whereof they have from our shore and therewithal barter with those infidels for the English and other Christians' goods). And that our Newfoundland fleet consisting of 300 sail or near upon as I am informed will not arm themselves for their defense; [they neither] choose out some few of their best ships and fit[1] them accordingly to attend and waft them nor appoint a certain time and rendezvous when and where to meet and so proceed securely on their voyage as other nations do, but go sat-

tering [*sic*] both outwards and homewards bound by twos, and threes, and single to make the best of their market, as they term it. These picaroons, I say, will ever lie hankering upon our coast, and the state will find it both chargeable and difficult to clear it or secure the Newfoundland fishermen from them unless it be directly resolved to sack Sallee—[a] sure way if easy to be performed as some report it is that are lately come from thence. In the meantime, while they are sick of this panic fear (an incurable disease in a multitude till they see the event), your Grace must expect many complaints. But by God's help, as near as I can in this particular employment wherewith your Grace has honored me, there shall be no just cause.

As for Monsieur de Soubise, his carriage and those of Rochelle, whereupon it would be necessary your Grace cast your eye, I humbly refer you to these enclosed examinations of the English and these notes under his captains' own hands, for fear of troubling you with too much letter.[2] So with the best thanks an honest heart can return for your Grace's many and great favors, and with my earnest prayers to the Almighty for your health and happiness, I kiss your hands.

Your vowed servant,
Francis Stuart

My most honored Lord these
come from on board the *Lion*
16 August 1625

1. MS.: *fitting*.
2. Included with Stuart's letter in the State Papers are depositions on the condition of the ships and the state of their supplies taken from Mervin Burley, Captain of the *Mary Constance;* Robert Cornish, Master of the *Mary Ann*, and Richard Malim, Master of the *Amity.*

---

(13) [Downshire MSS., Vol. 17, f. 134]

Sir Dudley Carleton to Anonymous, 4 September 1625, the Hague.

Sir,

With your letters of the 29 of last I received yesterday divers parliament packets, some of which I return unto you because you desire them and shall be glad to have them back when you have perused them. The rest are acts and writings in conformity to what is advertised in these letters, which for the largeness of the volume I do not send you. One is a commission for my Lord Duke of Buckingham to go in person or by deputation as chief of our great navy and land army, with power of life and death, making of knights and all other prerogatives that can be imagined for a subject, which I doubt (he not being likely to go in person) will blow the coal of envy, to which you will find by these letters he is subject, as greatness ever is.

Other news I have none, save that Sir Robert Killigrew is advertised to be the man who is to succeed me in this employment, and if he make no more finances therein than I have done, he will miss of that mark the incommodity of his estate makes him aim at.

By the last ordinary you had a large account of all our affairs and since here is no alteration. You write for a placard of defense of license. On this side here is none made. What is set out on your side we have from thence so as you may have them from Antwerp. Thus, with wonted love and good wishes I rest, your most assured to do you service,

Dudley Carleton

Hague this 4th
of 7ber 1625

---

(14) [Wynn MSS. (9060E)1371]

HENRY WYNN to SIR JOHN WYNN, 19 September 1625, Faringdon.
Sir, my humble duty remembered,

I have received your letter wherein you write for news. We are here now far from news, few or none going to and fro. I have seen a letter within these two days from Oxford which makes mention of three proclamations there in press ready to come forth. The one, commanding all officers and commanders in the fleet to repair to the charge, the second to make *cardecues* to go for nineteen pence halfpenny, the third for the abbreviation of Michaelmas term for 3 weeks.[1] The fleet, as it is thought, will be gone within this fortnight. Many suggestions there are of the design, the year being now far spent. Some speak for Portugal, the Portugals [*sic*] groaning under the Spanish yoke; others say for the Canaries which may prove to be soon, for all that have been in those parts say that this time is the fittest time of all the year. For, if they had been there now or before they had fried upon the coast of Barbary. There are there many islands and indifferent havens for the King of Spain's silver fleet always 'tis there either going or coming. And if those or some of them may be taken it will overthrow most of his West India trade, the place being so near the mouth of the Mediterranean both for the Spaniards and Genoese. And by the report of Sir Walter Aston, late ambassador in Spain, the fleet being talked of among some of their council, inquiring of what number the fleet was of, they told them so many of the fleet royal, so many merchants, and so many colliers. Inquiring what those colliers were, being told they were some about 300 ton, the least about 200 ton, and carried twelve or fourteen piece[s] of ordnance. They said that those were *todos los diablos,* which argues as much that they face those islands.

The term is uncertain where it shall be kept, yet some say at Windsor, some at St. Albans, some at Salisbury, but most conjecture that if either of the other two places be free, it is likely to be there, for the records may not be safely removed so far as Salisbury.

I saw likewise a letter with Mr. Dickenson[2] which [*sic*] lives at Faringdon, who is chief clerk of the Council, which was dated from Paris in France, which was, notwithstanding the relation lately made in parliament of the peace concluded in France, there has been of certain a great conflict at sea between the Rochellers and the French, Soubise being admiral for Rochelle, in which the Rochellers gave the overthrow. There were sunk 30 ships and 20 carried to Rochelle, so that the French were brought to that pass for want of shipping. That all those which know anything of the state of France say that there would have been a peace concluded within three weeks had not our eight ships gone from England. And now they are further from a peace than ever. For those ships, they have them absolute as is supposed, the mariners being all returned, refusing upon any terms to serve as substitutes to the French, of which there is one of the King's ships. Not long after there came here agents from the Rochellers telling the King that he was the chief of the religion, and would he give means wholly to extirpate the same in foreign parts. They received a fair answer but little else.

There are privy seals a coming forth, the ground of which is the maintaining of the wars in Ireland. There has been dispute about it at Council Board, but what I cannot learn; but now certainly they are coming forth which, if there come a parliament again, will be there questioned by what advice this comes to pass. That privy seals and subsidies come together, expressly making Ireland the ground. For it has been the last time offered in parliament that if the King would give way where it was a charge unto him, by reforming abuses, they would make it prove to him a great revenue and serve all places of defense besides.

The Turkish pirates of Algiers have taken the Isle of Lundy near Cornwall which belongs, as I am told, to Sir William Godolphin. They have done many robberies on the coast, they have continued so long that the day the parliament was dissolved there was an information made by the west countrymen that they dare not peep forth for fear of them. They draw many ships ashore. On the Isle of Wight they took men and women making of hay insomuch as they said they liked the English women so well that before they departed they would have every man one. This business, if the parliament had continued, would have gone hard against the Duke, if the King would suffer, for that concerns the Lord Admiral. For, said they, the statute of tonnage and poundage was granted, as it appears by the act itself, for the maintaining of trade by sea and securing the coasts. A number of merchants of London are quite undone, their ships pressed for this voyage, and have remained so this three quarters of year. They must continue trade or else be quite undone. They were fain to take such vessels as they could get. Being not so great nor so well manned as they were wont to be, they were most of them taken by the pirates. For it was never known afore of any Londoners taken, for they are all goodly ships of 500 ton as well manned for men and ordnance as the King's ship, that one of them was able to deal with 12 Turks, for they were the Bristol men and the west countrymen that were always taken. Some of them have petitioned the King to have leave to compound for their goods with the pirates which lay upon the coast of Ireland. It being granted and they being at charge to send a ship, but before they came the pirates were gone to Algiers. They say the English merchants in Spain were never so well used as now they are, which is thought to be in policy that when most of their commodities be there, to seize upon them or else to collude with the King to direct this fleet. Sir Albertus Morton, one of the secretaries, John Griffith's friend or master, is suddenly dead at Southampton and Sir John Coke made Secretary, who was the man that spoke before the King and both Houses in parliament. As I wrote unto you of the King, [he] is expected shortly to Woodstock. My Lord Keeper is returned from Southampton to Foxley by Windsor.

There's a speech that we shall have parliament towards the beginning of the next spring, for some say that this last parliament was not dissolved with an intent that there should come no more in haste, but to manifest the greatness of one man that hereafter they should think him as great as sure he was. And that we shall have a great many sheriffs of those which were this last time of the House. And if you think it fit, I desire to hold the same place I have done afore, and the writ for the collection of fees not to be delivered, for then the gentlemen of the country may justly except at it; and for another reason which is best known to yourself.

Our landlord Mr. Lloyd, your cousin, for he swears he is of the true blood of the Lloyd and the Bulkeley, remembers his service unto you telling me that he has been over at Gwydir[3] and that if ever he comes that way he will not fail to see you. So, praying for your health continually, I rest ever,
Your obedient son,
Henry Wynn[4]

Faringdon in Berkshire
19° Sept. 1625
[*Postscript*] Mansfeld lies near the Low Country and has no English at all with him, and his whole number does not exceed 25 hundred men which are his old sharks.

---

1. The three proclamations are printed in *Stuart Proclamations*, II, 54–59.
2. MS.: *Dickens*. John Dickenson was a clerk of the Privy Council.
3. MS.: *Gwidde*.
4. A similar but shorter letter (Wynn MSS. [9060E]1370) was written from William Wynn to his father from Faringdon, 18 September 1625.

(15) [S.P. 16/10:16]

SIR BENJAMIN RUDYARD to SIR FRANCIS NETHERSOLE, 23 November 1625, Reading.
Sir,

Your last finds me at the term in Reading from whence I can write you only such news as grows there, where there is an information exhibited in the Star Chamber by Mr. Knightley against the Lord Vaux and his brother upon occasion of Mr. Knightley's and other deputy lieutenants of Northamptonshire coming to the house of Mistress Vaux (my Lord's mother) to execute the Council's letters for disarming of papists. The house being searched and no arms found, Mistress Vaux fell into great choler, with oaths, and said that they could not be worse used except their throats should be cut, and wished that it were once come to that. Mr. Knightley reproved him for those speeches and also challenged the penalty of the statute against swearing. Whereupon they fell to further words and my Lord Vaux to blows, striking Mr. Knightley a box on the ear. And a man of Mr. Knightley's, coming to relieve his master, was knocked down with a cudgel by the Lord Vaux. This was certified to the lords, the offenders convented before his Majesty, committed to the Fleet in Reading, and a suit commenced against them for further punishment. It is not amiss that the papists begin with us, which will make them unexcusable and unpitied, how severely soever the act shall proceed against them.

The new Lord Keeper does carry himself with great modesty and judgment, gaining every man's good opinion and applause, which he is likely to hold, being a solid, steady man.[1]

The rank weeds of the parliament are rooted up, so that we may expect a plentiful harvest the next. Sir Robert Phelips is made sheriff of Somerset, Sir Francis Seymour of Wiltshire, Sir Edward Coke of Buckinghamshire, Sir Thomas Wentworth of Yorkshire, Sir Guy Palmes of Rutland, Mr. Alford of Sussex, and Sir William Fleetwood of Lancashire, *ex praescientia operum*, for he would have done as ill as the worst if he had been of the last, and will do if he should be of the next parliament. I pray God so temper the humors of our next assembly that out of it may result that inestimable harmony of agreement between the King and his people. Amen.

Your affectionate friend to do you service,
Benjamin Rudyard

Reading, 23 *9bris* 1625

1. Sir Thomas Coventry was appointed Lord Keeper on 1 November 1625.

G. Correspondence Relating to Loan of Ships to France (S.P. 16)

In the spring of 1625 the English crown contracted to loan the French King, Louis XIII, seven merchant ships and one naval vessel, the *Vanguard*. French plans for the employment of the ships were not publicized and rumors spread in England concerning the possibility of their use against the Huguenots in La Rochelle. The English merchant shippers commissioned for the scheme and the parliamentarians concerned about the country's foreign commitments viewed the design with suspicion. Not only did it generate new tensions regarding the old problem of religious alignment but because the plan was conceived and carried out in virtual secrecy almost singlehandedly by the Duke of Buckingham it bred a general distrust of the new King and his ministers.

John Pennington, Captain of the *Vanguard*, was commissioned by Buckingham to convey the merchant ships to the French King (S.P. 16/2:37). On 10 May Sir John Coke explained to Captain Pennington the stipulations of the contract made through the French ambassador, the Marquis d'Effiat, saying that no clauses in the agreement would be "strained to engage or embroil you and the ships and companies under your command in the civil wars of the French"; the ships were, he said, "to serve the French King against the foreign enemies and opposers to his honor and state" (S.P. 16/2:74). Coke's explanation of France's intentions with regard to the ships, however, did not allay Pennington's fears and as further misunderstandings developed concerning the disposition of the ships he begged to resign his commission, writing first to the Duke (S.P. 16/4:78) and then to the King directly (S.P. 16/4:132), and his seamen threatened mutiny (S.P. 16/4:78). Ultimately Captain Pennington agreed to surrender his ships (S.P. 16/5:7) although Sir Ferdinando Gorges, captain of the *Great Neptune*, refused to turn over his ship to the French (S.P. 16/5:18). In parliament at the meeting of both Houses on 8 August the Duke of Buckingham addressed the business of the contract saying that "it is not always fit for kings to give account of their counsels. Judge the King by the event" (see above, p. 165). The evasiveness of the remark exacerbated the growing distrust of the Duke and, while the parliament ended four days later having taken no action on the matter, the issue was not forgotten. In 1626 Buckingham's conduct in procuring English merchant ships for use by the French crown became Article 7 in the impeachment proceedings against him (*L.J.*, III, 621–622).

The correspondence below is from the State Papers Domestic, 1625–1626. Other letters concerning the ships are printed in H.M.C., *12th Report, Appendix, Part I* (Coke MSS.), and in S.R. Gardiner, ed., *Documents Illustrating the Impeachment of the Duke of Buckingham in 1626* (London: Camden Society, 1889), pp. 139–302.

(1) [S.P. 16/2:37]

The Duke of Buckingham to Captain Pennington, *et al.*, 8 May 1625, Whitehall.

Whereas his Majesty as well for his brotherly respect and correspondency with the French King as for other reasons to him known has been pleased, at the motion of his ambassador, to set out for his service the *Vanguard* (a principal ship of his own navy royal), and further to permit an agreement to be made with you, the captains, masters, and owners of the good ships called the *Neptune*, the *Industry*, the *Pearl*, the *Marigold*, the *Loyalty*, the *Gift*, the *Peter and John*, for the like employment in the said king's service upon such articles as are interchangeably sealed between the said ambassador and the Commissioners for the Navy on his Majesty's behalf and you (the said masters and owners) for yourselves. And his Majesty's pleasure has been sufficiently signified for the putting in readiness of all the said ships, which I doubt not is accordingly performed, the occasion of the said King's service requiring all convenient expedition. These are therefore to will and require you and every of you forthwith to call the companies aboard, which have been raised and fitted to every ship according to former instructions on that behalf; and then to take the first opportunity of wind and weather to proceed in your voyage to such a port in the dominions of France as the ambassador shall direct, and there to attend the further directions of such principal person as shall be appointed admiral of the fleet prepared for the service of the said French King. Requiring further all vice admirals and officers of the admiralty, captains of castles and forts, captains, masters, and owners of ships, mayors, sheriffs, and justices of the peace, bailiffs, constables, and all other his Majesty's officers, ministers, and loving subjects, and every of them, to give you all meet assistance and furtherances and not to hinder or interrupt you or any of your ships or company in the due performance of the service aforesaid, as they will answer the contrary at their peril. From Whitehall 8° of May 1625.

G. Buckingham[1]

To my very loving friends,
Captain Pennington, captain
of his Majesty's ship the
Vanguard, and to the captains
and masters of the seven ships
appointed for the service of
the French King, and to every
of them, and to all others
whom it may concern.

1. Below the signature are eleven cipher characters.

---

(2) [S.P. 16/2:74]

SIR JOHN COKE to CAPTAIN JOHN PENNINGTON, 10 May 1625, Whitehall.
Sir,
For your better understanding of the instructions given by the Lord Admiral, and specially of the articles of contract between the French ambassador and the Commissioners of the Navy, I am by direction to inform you: First, that no clauses therein may be strained to engage or embroil you and the ships and companies under your command in the civil wars of the French, if any happen, or against them of our religion in that kingdom or elsewhere. And secondly, that the true intention of your employment is to serve the French King against the foreign enemies and opposers of his honor and state; and the interests of both kingdoms and of the common cause of their confederacy with us at this time. And because the States of the United Provinces do herein join with us, you are for the better discharge of your duty and satisfaction to the French chiefly to insist (if you shall be pressed thereunto) upon this conjunction with them, from which you may not recede or divide in any wise. And to testify your union with their fleet you are to communicate with their admiral in your intentions and counsels, and correspond in all good offices of mutual assistance, and regulate your proceedings on both parts by this common interest in the service wherein their engagement is the same with ours. For other things you must take care to keep peace and good quarter with the French, and to advance that king's service and honor according to the trust his Majesty reposes in you to that end. And so in all your worthy endeavors, wishing you good and happy success, I rest,

Your assured friend to
serve you,
John Coke

Whitehall
May *10°* 1625
[*Endorsed*] To my noble friend, John Pennington, Esquire, Admiral of the English ships employed in the service of the French King.

---

(3) [S.P. 16/2:98]

CAPTAIN JOHN PENNINGTON to the LORD CONWAY, 27 May 1625, aboard the *Vanguard*.

Right Honorable my Very Good Lord,

I wrote to your Lordship the 22th of this instant in answer of your letter which I received but an hour before, whereby I advertised your Lordship of many things that I then wanted, of which I am since furnished with the greatest part and have now all my fleet about me being ready to take the first fair wind and weather if I have not order to the contrary. For which I humbly beseech your Lordship that I may speedily receive his Majesty's pleasure whether I shall with the first fair wind proceed on my voyage or stay for the wafting over of the Queen, according to order given me by word of mouth from Sir John Coke, one of his Majesty's Masters of Requests, and principal Commissioner of his Majesty's Navy royal. [[1]Here is also at this instant a new business fallen out wherewith I hold myself bound to acquaint your Lordship. Here is one Monsieur Raisigli,[2] Chevalier de Malta, come aboard to me and is here with me at this present, who shows me a commission from the French ambassador (the copy whereof I send your Lordship herein enclosed) by which he pretends and lays claim to have principal power and command over his Majesty's ship the *Vanguard*, wherein I serve, and all the rest of this fleet, in as ample a manner as if the Lord Admiral of France, or any other noble man of quality (whom their King shall appoint) is to have, which is contrary both to the articles of the contract and my instructions. Therefore once more I humbly beseech your Lordship that I may speedily know his Majesty's pleasure in this particular as in the former.] And also that you will be pleased to give commandment to the mayor of Dover to furnish me with two sufficient pilots for the coast of France, one for Dieppe, and the other for Havre de Grace, we being destitute of such and dare not proceed without them. Wherewith I have acquainted the mayor already by my letters but he denies to furnish me unless I will contract with them at their own rates, which I have no power to do. Thus having no other cause of stay but your Lordship's resolution concerning these three particulars, and fair wind and weather, I humbly take my leave and will remain ever,

> Your Lordship's very
> humble servant,
> J. Pennington

From aboard the *Vanguard* in
the Downs, the 27th day of
May 1625

[*Endorsed*] For his Majesty's special service. To the Right Honorable the L[ord] Conway, one of his Majesty's principal Secretaries of State and of his Majesty's most honorable Privy Council.

Haste haste post haste haste
From aboard the *Vanguard* in the
Downs this 27 of May at seven
of the clock at night.
John Pennington

1. The square brackets are as in the MS.
2. MS.: *Razilli.* See *Cal. S.P. Venetian, 1625–1626*, p. 34.

---

(4) [S.P. 16/4:40]

SIR JOHN COKE to SECRETARY CONWAY, 11 July 1625, London.

Right Honorable,

The captains, masters, and owners of the ships lately returned from the service of the French have acquainted me that the ambassador has not only protested against them as breakers of the contract, but also importuned his Majesty to put them and their ships, by his royal commandment, into the power of their people, by receiving as many French as they will send aboard. For the protest, they tell me they are ready to answer it in a legal course when it shall be pursued, and doubt not to justify their performance in every point of the contract. Besides, they will show that they are now freed from any further engagement in this service because the ambassador has broken his days of payment. And their men, without pay, will not be kept on board nor the owners supply their cables and anchors, worn and lost by staying their ships contrary to promise upon a desperate road on that coast. But that which disheartens them most is the insolent carriage of the French, who plainly have professed that they will be masters of their ships, that they will execute their martial laws upon their persons, and that they will employ both ships and men against them of our religion. For their ships, the owners say that they are their freeholds, to which they have no less right than other subjects to their houses and possessions and therefore though they ought and are ready to employ them in his Majesty's service, yet to have them put into the power of strangers, or to be required to serve with them upon other conditions than they agree unto and without sufficient security to be saved harmless, they hold it not agreeable either to precedents of former times or to the laws of this land. And therefore they appeal therein to his Majesty's justice and to his protection in their right. Then for their parts they say all: they are English free born and know the inveterate malice of the French, and therefore will not dishonor our nation and blemish in a sort their allegiance to his Majesty by putting themselves so far into French jurisdiction that they shall not have power to redeem his Majesty's honor and their own from such attempts against them, as they have cause to mistrust. And lastly, for serving against them of our religion: it is very well known that our seamen generally are most resolute in our profession, and these men have expressed it by their common petition to their admiral and otherwise by protestation, that they will rather be killed or thrown over-

board than be forced to shed the innocent blood of any Protestants in the quarrel[s] of papists. So as they will account any commandment to that end to be in a kind an imposition of martyrdom. And so the fruit to be expressed of this service on our part is the casting away of the ships and of the men and the beginning of a breach between the two nations; and on their part, our engagement against our own party and the cutting off all relation of their Protestants to us which, happily, is the chief end of pressing this business, there appearing no other they can reasonably propound. To which, if we add the discouragement of our party at home and abroad, the late murmuring against it in parliament, and the open exclaiming made in the pulpits that this taking part against our own religion is one chief cause of God's hand that now hangs over us, we can hardly balance these consequences with any interest or assistance we can have from the French, whose own engagements, without straining on our side, are the only occasions of advantage to be expected from their good will.

But because it may be objected that his Majesty was engaged by promise, and that the contract may seem to import the lending of these ships to serve the French King against whomsoever, his Majesty of England only excepted, and that with liberty to put aboard them as many French as they should think fit, though this article being framed according to the words and intention of the Venetian contract ought to be strained no further than that was to a common enemy; and though his Majesty's allies and such as are interested in his favor are duly included in the exception of the King of Great Britain, which cannot be restrained to his person alone; and though the cautions annexed in both these articles clearly free our captains from taking in more than the ships may conveniently carry with safety and health, which will include the numbers the French do press for; yet, if his Majesty, in his royal wisdom, shall think fit to write his mandative letters to the Admiral to proceed with his fleet for such service as the French King shall think fit, and to receive aboard every ship as many French as he shall appoint; yet, if the letters may be written but with this pressing clause, that if he cannot presently obey this direction by reason of any interruption whatsoever that he forthwith acquaint his Majesty therewith, that he may give order to remove it and so take away all excuse for not accomplishing the intended gratification to his dear brother, the French King. Then this clause will give time and draw from them a true declaration of their due performance of the contract, of the breach on the French part, of the shortness of their companies, of their wants of fit supplies, and of all impossibilities to perform the expected service. And if the ambassador thereupon thinks fit to prosecute his protestation he may be left to take his remedy by law, and subjects in like sort to justify their proceedings.

Wherein no exception can be taken to his Majesty who has really performed all they can require. And the issue does not answer their desire, will appear justly to fall upon themselves. And all the ill effects will be prevented, which the changing of the first intention of this service would produce. Only some care would be taken after his Majesty's letters were written that Sir Ferdinando Gorges, who attends this business and proposes to go aboard his ship to the rest of the fleet, may receive some directions for the carriage of their answers, that Captain Pennington, by the unexpected style of his Majesty's letters, may not be surprised. Which I leave to your honor's wisdom. And so having delivered my poor opinion by writing, because wanting a convenient lodging in town I am driven to my house at Tottenham, I humbly rest,

At your Honor's service,
John Coke
London, 11th July
1625

[Endorsed] To the Right Honorable Lord Conway, Principal Secretary to his Majesty, haste this.

---

(5) [S.P. 16/4:78]

CAPTAIN JOHN PENNINGTON to the DUKE OF BUCKINGHAM, 18 July 1625, aboard the *Vanguard* in Stokes Bay.
May it please your Grace,

I have even now received a letter from your Grace with strict command presently to go for Dieppe and to carry with me the rest of the merchants' ships, which I am instantly ready to obey. But having called their masters aboard and declared your Grace's pleasure therein they desired to speak with their companies, and they all absolutely deny to stir from hence before their captains come. Notwithstanding, I have read your Grace's letter unto them and made known his Majesty's pleasure, so as I must be forced either to go together by the ears with them or go without them, which I am resolved to do if their captains come not this night. Also, that your Grace will be pleased to remember I have not above 48 barrels of powder aboard, little shot, no fireworks, and never a sword, save only myself and a few gentlemen.

Furthermore, I understand that his Majesty's pleasure is that his ship wherein I serve, as also the rest of the merchants' ships, be wholly at the disposing of the most Christian King, and that they are to bring in as many of their own nation as they will and we to be wholly under their command, insomuch as the commission that I have from your Grace is totally annihilated. For my own part, it is too difficult a business for me to wade through and therefore I humbly desire that your Grace will be pleased to call me home and to send some other more able for it, who may better go upon those terms than myself, in regard they are already discontented with me for that I would not formerly yield to their desires which I thought to be wondrous unreasonable and contrary to the orders I had from his Majesty, and your Grace's commission. But now all is laid open unto them, as well for the fighting against any that they will have us, as also for governing us after the French law and indeed in making us their slaves, as they formerly told us, which for my part I hope never to be. Therefore, I humbly beseech your Grace to appoint some other for the command I now have, for that I will rather put my life upon the King's mercy at home than go upon these terms. But howsoever, I will carry the ship over according to your Grace's command, and there attend the return of this bearer and further order to whom I shall deliver over my command. Moreover, your Grace may be pleased to take notice that I have a strange uproar in my ship among my own company upon this news of going over again, I having much ado to bring them to it, though I keep all from them and make them believe we go over upon better terms than formerly. But when they shall come on the other side and find the contrary, I fear there will be something to do with them.

Thus humbly desiring your Grace's favor, and that you will be pleased to mediate for his Majesty for me for his gracious favor, that I may be called off from this service with his Majesty's favor and good liking, and to dispose of me upon any other that his Majesty or your Grace shall fit, and I shall be bound ever to remain,

> Your Grace's most humble and
> faithful servant,
> J. Pennington

From aboard the *Vanguard* in Stokes Bay, the 18th of July 1625

[*Endorsed*] To the Right Honorable my Lord Duke of Buckingham, his Grace, Lord High Admiral of England.

---

(6) [S.P. 16/4:79]

CAPTAIN JOHN PENNINGTON to LORD CONWAY, 18 July 1625, aboard the *Vanguard* in Stokes Bay.

Right Honorable, my Very Good Lord,

I have received order from my Lord Duke of Buckingham, his Grace, presently commanding me to go to Dieppe and to carry along with me the rest of the merchants' ships, which I have made known unto their masters, and they unto their companies. But in regard the captains are not here they will not stir till they come, so that I must be forced either to go together by the ears with them or to go without them; being therefore resolved to go myself, I not having power to do the other. I also understand by a warrant from your Lordship in his Majesty's name that his Majesty has left the command of these ships to his most Christian brother, the King of France, and that we are to receive so many men aboard as they think fit, and I to deliver all whatsoever to them. All which I am ready presently to obey, first for the carrying over of the ships, and then to let them do what they will with them, always hoping that it is his Majesty's pleasure that I shall return after my surrender to them, for I know that your Lordship in your grave wisdom thinks it not fit for me to continue here, having already so withstood their unreasonable demands, and so contrary to the commands of the King, my master, and my commission from my Lord Duke of Buckingham's Grace.

Therefore, I humbly beseech your good Lordship that you will be pleased to procure me his Majesty's favor that I may be called home and some other more able man for this employment put in; for I rather desire to suffer at home than to be employed where I am sure to suffer dishonor. Thus praying your good Lordship that I may have your favorable opinion and that you will believe that if I had a thousand lives, I would sacrifice them all for the honor and safety of my King and country. And thus with remembrance of my humble

service to your good Lordship, I ever
remain,

> Your Lordship's very
> humble servant,
> J. Pennington

From aboard the *Vanguard*
the 18th day of July 1625,
in Stokes Bay
[*Endorsed*] To my singular good Lord, the
Lord Conway, Principal Secretary of State
to the King's most excellent Majesty.

———————————

(7) [S.P. 16/4:83]

LORD CONWAY to CAPTAIN JOHN PEN-
NINGTON, 19 July 1625, Woking.
[¹Sir,

I have received yours of the 18th of this
present and see the perplexity that you are
in between obedience and desire to do that
which you think honorable and good. It is
almost impossible to bring the obedience to
a master opposite to his good service, and so
much is to be deferred to the wisdom and
providence of a supreme in his own service,
as the servant is to hope beyond that he sees
of a better success than he knows. My heart
bears you witness that you intend well, and
you have not only so wise and good a patron
but so happy a one, as following his directions you cannot fail of such events as will
justify you.

I have understood that the Duke, his
Grace, has employed his secretary, Mr.
Nicholas, to advise and take care with you
that this work might be conducted to the
satisfaction of the most Christian King and
to the honor of the Marquis d'Effiat, yet
with equity to his Majesty's subjects and
honor and advantage of those that command and obey in the fleet; so as if you
advise with the secretary, no doubt, you will
find out the upright way to obey.

I can by no means join with you in seeking your leave to quit that service and to
employ another in it because it must be dishonorable for you to be called from it to

employ a more sufficient, or unjust to send
another to the hazard from which you
should be preserved; and most of all, for
the evil example to admit of a disputation
between an inferior and a superior in the
very point of an execution.

You are happy that have to obey an excellent and a just King, a gracious and an honorable chief who, being well able to judge of
the goodness of your intentions, will pass by
any weakness or disadvantage that arise
from those good intentions or success and
apply to you the acceptance and reward of
what you shall deserve well in.] And in that
I shall be glad to be a witness, and both
contented and happy if I might be an instrument, being very desirous to take occasion to approve myself.

> Your affectionate friend
> to serve you,
> E. Conway

From the court at Woking
19 July 1625
[*Endorsed*] To my very loving friend, Captain Pennington, Captain of his Majesty's
good ship the *Vanguard*.

1. The square brackets are as in the MS.

———————————

(8) [S.P. 16/4:85]

The DUKE OF BUCKINGHAM to CAPTAIN
JOHN PENNINGTON, 19 July, Woking.

I have received yours of the 18th of this
present from Stokes Bay and cannot but
wonder as well as be sorry that any such
disorder should happen as the withdrawing
of the mariners from their duty and obedience, especially when a person of that
quality as the Marquis d'Effiat should be
present and have his expectation and endeavor made vain. I do require you to continue your duty and care, not only to carry
your ship and sailors to the service of the
most Christian King but also to carry the
rest of the ships according to the directions
I have given by my secretary Nicholas, who

is there to that purpose that he may witness your and each other captains', masters', and mariners' behaviors. And as the good obedience you and they shall perform in those instructions which I have given to my said secretary will procure you acceptance and estimation, so those that shall be refractory shall pass a strict examination and receive punishment accordingly.

You are therefore to have due regard to give all honor and contentment to the Marquis d'Effiat, following entirely the instructions and directions of my secretary Nicholas.

[¹I marvel of your demand, and can by no means find it reasonable that you a captain, upon the instant of your obedience required, should ask leave to withdraw yourself from this charge, which I may by no means consent unto. And therefore require you to continue it, and to confer with, and follow precisely the directions I have given to my secretary Nicholas, whom you are to believe.] And so I commit you to God.
Your very loving friend,
G. Buckingham

[*Endorsed*] To my very loving friend, Captain Pennington.

---

1. The square brackets are as in the MS.

---

(9) [S.P. 16/4:80]

The DUKE OF BUCKINGHAM to EDWARD NICHOLAS, 19 July 1625.

Upon receipt of a letter from Captain Pennington I see the disorder which has happened and am much troubled that the great respect which I desired should be given to the Marquis d'Effiat's presence, and to show affection to this business, should receive such a traverse. You know the affection I have to give the Marquis d'Effiat, for the most Christian King, satisfaction, and the directions I have given you in all events to apply yourself for the good success of that action. You are therefore,

according to the directions I have given you, to endeavor to conform those captains and ships to his will. And I having received advice lately from Lorkin¹ that the peace is concluded between the most Christian King and those of the religion, it may be the Marquis d'Effiat upon hearing the same will easily put end to all these questions, having not the use he expected. Sir Ferdinando Gorges has desired leave to go in person for the better informing and accommodating of the contracts to equity. And according to the instructions which I gave you I have referred him to advise with you, and you are to cause all the honor and contentment possible to be given to the Marquis d'Effiat for the service of the most Christian King. And by the directions I gave you, you will judge how much it will agree with my contentment. And to your care I leave it.
G. Buckingham

[*Endorsed*] To my servant Nicholas, on board the *Vanguard*. R. *19° Julii 1625*. My Lord Admiral's letter to me concerning the French business.
Woking, 19 July 1625

---

1. Thomas Lorkin, English Agent at the Court of France. *Cal. S. P. Dom., 1625–1626*, p. 154.

---

(10) [S.P. 16/4:132]

CAPTAIN JOHN PENNINGTON to the KING, 27 July 1625.
Most Sacred Majesty,

Be pleased to understand, that I being put in command of your Majesty's ship the *Vanguard*, by warrant from my Lord Admiral, for the service of the most Christian King, and thereupon received sundry instructions under his hand for the safe keeping [and] possession of the said ship during the service, which I have hitherto carefully and punctually observed; and have now lately received a warrant from my Lord Conway, dated at Hampton Court the 10th of this instant, commanding me, in your

Majesty's name, to deliver the command of this your Majesty's ship wherein I serve, with the rest of the merchants' ships (if they were in my possession) to his most Christian Majesty. This is the former part of the warrant, and then follows that I am to receive so many persons into the said ships as his Christian Majesty shall be pleased to put into them and there to be continued during the time of the contract, and that this I am to obey with the greatest moderation and discretion I can. These are the very words of the warrant which, after I had often read and in my best judgment seriously considered, I conceived (under correction) that the latter command was contradictory to the former, being by the first commanded to give up the sole command to his Christian Majesty, and by the second to receive so many aboard as it pleased his Christian Majesty to put into them during the term of the contract, which words continue me still in the possession of them. Moreover, may it please your Majesty to understand that with the said warrant I received a letter from my Lord Admiral thereby charging me to deliver over your Majesty's ship with the rest, according to the warrant, and to take security for the ships according to the true valuation. But neither out of my Lord Admiral's letter nor my Lord Conway's warrant could I perceive it to be your Majesty's intention, nor their Lordships', that I should quit your Majesty's ship to his Christian Majesty or to his ministers, howbeit I had verbal directions by my Lord Admiral's secretary for it, but that (in my opinion) was not a sufficient warrant to discharge me and my company to surrender so great a charge, and therefore dare not do it without express order from your Majesty. And for the valuing of any of your Majesty's ships (they are so precious in my estimation, and so far transcending my sphere) that I most humbly crave pardon if I be thought too curious and tender to have a hand in a matter of so great consequence.

I have used all the best means I can to give his Christian Majesty and Monsieur d'Effiat, his ambassador, content herein by offering to take aboard so many soldiers as conveniently I could, and to go upon any service that they should employ me in agreeable to your Majesty's command. But nothing would satisfy them save the possession of the ship, either by the delivery of it up into their own hands or by putting four hundred soldiers aboard with a chief commander that so they might take it when they pleased and cut all our throats as they daily threatened. And because I would not yield to either of those, his Lordship has protested against me as a rebel to your Majesty, using many other disgraceful, opprobrious, and threatening speeches tending to the taking away of my life except I would surrender the ship or receive the said commander with 400 soldiers aboard which, I refusing, not daring to do it (having received two letters, the one from my Lord Admiral, and the other from my Lord Conway, of the 19th of this month, to continue my charge), he gave me over to do what I would and utterly denied to give me any further command, though I sent expressly to offer my service to him hearing that he was yesterday to leave the town of Dieppe to go towards the court.

All my company (if it please your Majesty) exceedingly distasting those demands of theirs, weighed anchor the 25th of this present from the road of Dieppe and set sail for England, without acquainting me with it, and when I demanded their reason, they told me that they had rather be hanged at home than part with your Majesty's ship upon these terms. Yet however they did it without acquainting me, I must confess I knew of it and did connive, otherwise they should never have done it and I live, for I had rather lose my life than my reputation in my command.

I dare not trouble your Majesty with all the ways and slights that have been used to make me deliver up your Majesty's ship into their hands; but if either promises of great pensions during my life, or present sums to be laid down, or fair words or threatenings would have made me yield her up, she had been gone, and (with your Majesty's pardon) you may be confident that if they had once gotten the possession of her upon any terms, she would never have been returned. But although I be poor, I had rather live with bread and water all the days of my life than to be an actor in this business, wherein I should be a traitor to your Majesty and my country.

Thus humbly craving pardon if I have not performed your Majesty's will, and laying down my life at your sacred Majesty's feet, and praying daily for your Majesty's many and happy days, I humbly remain ever,

> Your Majesty's most humble
> and loyal subject and servant,
> J. Pennington

---

(11) [S.P. 16/4:133]

CAPTAIN JOHN PENNINGTON to SECRETARY CONWAY, 27 July 1625, aboard the *Vanguard* in the Downs.
My Honorable Good Lord,

I have received a letter and a warrant from your Lordship, the one of the 10th, the other of the 19th of this present, and have endeavored to obey your Lordship in both. I have not now time to give your Lordship a particular account of them but refer your good Lordship to my Lord Duke of Buckingham's Grace for the same. Only your Lordship may be pleased to understand that I have done my best to give content to his most Christian Majesty and his ambassador, Monsieur d'Effiat, but nothing would suffice them but the surrender of his Majesty's ship into their hands which I conceived I had not warrant for, therefore dare not do it upon pain of my head. So that I am returned with his Majesty's ship (which is all I had now under my command)

to the Downs, where I attend his Majesty's further pleasure, and ever remain,

> Your Lordship's humble and
> devoted servant,
> J. Pennington

From aboard the *Vanguard*
in the Downs the 27th day
of July 1625
[*Endorsed*] To the Right Honorable the Lord Conway, Principal Secretary of State to the King's Majesty.

---

(12) [S.P. 16/5:7]

CAPTAIN JOHN PENNINGTON to EDWARD NICHOLAS, 3 August 1625, aboard the *Vanguard*.
Sir,

I am now returned with a sufficient warrant to perform the journey my lord ambassador desires, and come ready instantly to surrender her up into his hands so soon as he pleases to provide barks to carry us off (and to cause the rest to do the like or sink by their sides). So soon as I am come to an anchor and have speech with them, I will come ashore and wait upon my Lord and acquaint him further. In the meantime, I pray remember my humble service to him and with the like to yourself, I rest,

> Your most assured loving friend,
> to serve you,
> J. Pennington

3 August, *Vanguard*
[*Endorsed*] To my noble friend Edward Nicholas, Esquire. R. *3° Aug. 1625*. Captain Pennington to me.

---

(13) [S.P. 16/5:19]

SIR FERDINANDO GORGES to the DUKE OF BUCKINGHAM, 5 August 1625, aboard the *Great Neptune* off Beachy.
May it please your Grace,

I have endeavored what lay in my power

to observe your Excellency's command and was persuaded that I had brought things to reasonable heads both for myself and the rest of the merchants in that we insisted upon three propositions. The first, to be free from the ambassador's protest; secondly, to have security for the redelivery of our ships and satisfaction of our pay; and lastly, to have sufficient warrant from our sovereign lord the King for putting our ships into the hands of strangers. The Marquis to this replied he would not budge a tittle from the contract made at Rochester between the then ambassadors and two of the merchants, which contract the merchants disclaim, and never gave (they say) their consent unto, which appears by their not signing to that the then ambassadors put to their marks. And thereupon, although we (at the road in Dieppe) acknowledged the security of Rochester very honorable, yet humbly refused it and chose rather the security of merchants, as best suiting with our ranks and qualities. But the Marquis, entering into further treaties with us, at last demanded the valuation of our ships, and thought our propositions so reasonable that he pretended to us he had sent them to Paris to receive their answer, but being thus in expectation of what we were to hear from the French court, his Majesty's ship, the *Vanguard*, came to us with a warrant from his Majesty to render herself and us to the hands of the Marquis. That it seemed most strange to us all, but particularly to myself, who have my whole estate in my ship, besides three thousand pounds I stand indebted for; so that I choose to put myself rather upon my most gracious Sovereign's pity and mercy both for my estate and life, than to give it unto strangers without any satisfaction either to my estate or credit. And it will stand more with the King's honor and my own particular safety in future times (as I conceive) that his Majesty make this an act of his own, and take my ship into his own possession, either to be

sent by his Majesty where the French desire or else to be received by the French here in England at the port where she lies. Therefore, Sir, my most humble suit unto your Grace is, that if I have done otherwise than becomed me in this business, you would be pleased to interpret it an error in my understanding, not in my affections, and mediate to his Majesty to show unto him that I think I cannot better dispose of my goods than to transfer them wholly to his Majesty's disposal, which I humbly leave to your Grace's more serious consideration to whom I desire to prove myself in all humility and service,

> Your Grace's most
> respective servant,
> Ferdinando Gorges

From aboard the
Great Neptune
off of Beachy
the 5th of
August 1625.
[*Endorsed*] To his most excellent Lord, the Duke of Buckingham, his Grace, Lord High Admiral of England, at the court, give these.

---

(14) [S.P. 16/5:18]

SIR FERDINANDO GORGES to SECRETARY CONWAY, 5 August 1625, aboard the *Great Neptune* off Beachy.
My Lord,
I doubt not but his Majesty will receive sharp informations against me from the Marquis d'Effiat, as if I had been a violent enemy to the affairs of his master. But Sir, you shall find the truth to be, I stood for the honor of my nation, and the safety and profit of myself, being engaged in that employment a matter of some twelve thousand pounds, a portion too great to be hazarded without just reason or sound consideration, at the least when it came to my own share to capitulate for myself, as at the present it

did, for now I was, at the ambassador's desire and his Majesty's command, to resign my ship and her provisions wholly to the possession of the French upon a new agreement, the first contract (made by the commissioners) being void. And upon this ground I propounded such conditions for myself and the merchants then present as were conceived to be reasonable, namely, that we would be freed from the advantages he pretended against us, by reason of his protest; and that we might be secured for the safe delivery of our ships unto us again and duly satisfied our entertainment for their employments; lastly, that we might have sufficient warrant from his Majesty for putting our ships into the hands of strangers, which we know to be a matter of no mean consequence. And howsoever reasonable these conditions were thought to be, yet his Lordship seemed to take it something tenderly, conceiving that he had sufficiently determined all those things at Rochester where there was some conferences between the three ambassadors and two of the masters of the ships, at what time their Lordships offered their own securities which, although it was honorable and becoming their greatness, yet was it not received by the masters (as they solemnly protest) as fit for the quality of merchants to accept of. Yet again his Lordship required to be punctually satisfied whether we would stand to it or not. To the which we as plainly answered, that although we esteemed it to be very honorable, yet not competent for men of our qualities to deal with, but if he pleased to give us security by merchants in Paris, to be transferred from them to merchants in London responsible, it shall satisfy us for that particular, but we likewise expected the accomplishment of the rest of our articles or otherwise we could proceed no further. But after many debatements, at the last his Lordship seemed to approve of the reasonableness of our demands, and gave me to understand by my cousin Cole (whom I have wholly employed in this business and now send to your Lordship with the rest of the particulars more at large) that he had sent them to Paris and looked for a speedy answer. So we attended in expectation thereof. In the meanwhile, Captain Pennington returned with order from his Majesty for his delivery of the *Vanguard* and her furniture into the hands of the ambassador, with like order to him to cause the merchants to do as much. Whereat, being extraordinarily perplexed for the present, and finding that the ambassador thought by that opportunity to be master of my goods, in despite of me, and to account for the same at his own will, and having it in his power to take all advantages against me (being now in possession of my ship) that the quillets of law would give him, by reason of the former protest, and assuring myself it could by no means stand with his Majesty's royal purpose to ruin his own subjects to pleasure strangers, as also conceiving a warrant directed to Captain Pennington only, to be no sufficient discharge for me if after I should be questioned legally in my own country, I resolved to put myself to his Majesty's mercy for detaining my ship, notwithstanding Captain Pennington's order in that behalf, unless the ambassador gave me the security formerly propounded, which he refused to do. And thereupon, I took the opportunity to set sail, giving his Lordship to understand (before this occasion fell out) that there was a necessity for me to go to the coasts of England with my ship, that road being unsafe to her to ride, wherein we had suffered a desperate storm, with much peril for eight and forty hours together. And that if those articles were accepted, the ship should be always ready to attend his Lordship's commands, the which I am still willing to accomplish.

Now my good Lord, if in anything thus done by me I have omitted what in duty or discretion I was bound to do, I humbly crave pardon of his most royal Majesty, to whose mercy and grace I submit myself, my life, and goods, to be disposed of according to his gracious pleasure, and for the maintenance of whose honor and happiness I will at all times readily render the same. And of thus much, I shall humbly desire your Lordship will acquaint his sacred Majesty in my behalf. And vouchsafe me that noble favor as to use the best means to excuse my errors. And for that, as for many other your honorable cares t[ak]en of me and mine, I will forever rest,

Your Lordship's humble servant,
Ferdinando Gorges

From aboard
the *Great Neptune*
off of Beachy, the
5th of August 1625.
[*Endorsed*] To the Right Honorable my very good Lord, the Lord Conway, Principal Secretary of State, at the court give these.

H. Correspondence Relating to Preparations for the Expedition to Cadiz

Preparations for the joint English-Dutch expedition to Cadiz in October 1625 began in late spring of that year and carried through the summer while parliament was in session (S.P. 16/4:99). In May, the Duke of Buckingham had chosen Sir Edward Cecil commander of the naval and land forces for the expedition and had given orders to captains and lieutenants for the pressing of mariners and levying of land troops. The scheme to attack the Spanish fort in the autumn had been revealed to the Council of War and some few privy councillors but had not been discussed openly in parliament. At the 8 August conference the Duke was as evasive about the Spanish business as he had been with regard to the ships for the French (see above and see H. of L., 9 August, p. 164). It was not until after the dissolution of the August session that the Privy Council voted to proceed with the plan (S.P. 16/5:41) and Buckingham sent instructions for the voyage to Sir Edward Cecil (S.P. 16/5:87).

Printed below are three representative documents from the collection of State Papers Domestic relating to the preparations for the expedition to Cadiz. For numerous other orders and warrants in the State Papers concerning activity preliminary to the sailing of the fleet as well as several accounts of the expedition itself, see *Cal. S.P. Dom., 1625–1626, sub* Cadiz. See also the Locke-Trumbull letter, above, section D,1(c), p. 669.

(1) [S.P. 16/4:99]
To the mayor, etc., and other officers in the towns and ports of Weymouth, Dartmouth, and Plymouth, 21 July 1625.

After our hearty commendations;

Whereas we are given to understand by the Commissioners for the Navy that divers ships appointed to serve his Majesty in the fleet now preparing are sent to take in part of their victuals at your port of Weymouth where, if they make any long stay they will not only hinder the intended service but cast a great unnecessary charge upon his Majesty. These are therefore to will and require you to use your best endeavor by a careful survey of the said victuals that none but such as are healthsome and durable may be put on board. And also to give your best direction and assistance in the speedy and safe storage thereof, and to take order that the captains, masters, and their companies be not suffered to loiter on shore as to make any stay after their provisions are taken in. And if any of the said companies offer to run away you shall do very acceptable service by causing them to be stayed and punished and by supplying their numbers as occasion shall require. Wherein what by you shall be necessarily disbursed shall upon certificate under your hands be duly repaid by the Treasurer of the Navy. And so assuring ourselves of your diligence and care in speeding away the ships which we [*illegible*] recommend unto you, we bid you farewell.
From the court at Woking
the 21 of July 1625

---

(2) [S.P. 16/5:41]
Minute of the Privy Council vote, 14 August 1625.

At the Court at Woodstock, August 14th 1625.

It being this day propounded in a full Council by his Majesty then present in Council whether, *rebus sic stantibus*, it were fit that the fleet should presently proceed in the intended expedition and be put to sea, it was, after debate had thereof, voiced at the Board and resolved, no one voice contradicting it, that the fleet should go forth with all possible expedition. And for the better and more speedy enabling his Majesty to expedite the setting out of the said fleet it was then likewise resolved that his Majesty should, by Privy Seal, desire a loan of monies from his subjects.

---

(3) [S.P. 16/5:87]

George, Duke of Buckingham, to Sir Edward Cecil, Lieutenant General and Lord Marshal of the fleet and land forces now ready to go to sea.
Instructions on the expedition set forth against Spain, 26 August 1625. Draft.

Instructions for my honorable friend Sir Edward Cecil, Knight, Lieutenant General and Lord Marshal of his Majesty's fleet and land forces now ready to go to sea.

First and above all things you shall provide that God be duly served twice a day by every ship's company, according to the usual prayers and liturgy of the Church of England.

You shall take care to have all your companies live orderly and peaceably, and to cause every captain, master, and other officer faithfully to perform the duty of his place. And if any seaman or soldier shall raise tumult or conspiracy; or commit murder, quarrel, fight, or draw weapon to that end, or be a swearer, blasphemer, drunkard, pilferer, or sleeper at his watch, or make noise, or not to betake himself to his place of rest after the watch is set; or shall not keep his cabin cleanly; or be discontented with the proportion of victuals assigned unto him, or shall spoil or waste them, or any other necessary provisions for the ships, or shall not keep clean his arms; or shall go ashore without leave; or shall be found guilty of any other crime or offense; you shall use due severity in the punishment and reformation thereof, according to the known orders and customs of the sea.

You shall require every captain to take, from time to time, just and particular accounts of the stores of all boatswains and carpenters of the ships; examining their receipts, expenses, and remains; not suffering any unnecessary waste to be made of their provisions; nor any work to be done which shall not be needful, and be directed and allowed by the said captain upon advice with his masters, boatswains, or other officers of the ship, to be necessary for the service.

You shall cause every captain to take like accounts of their pursers and stewards of their victuals and provide for the goodness and preservation thereof without waste; not suffering any suspected person to bring fresh victuals aboard, without due examination how and whence it was taken and due survey of the quality and wholesomeness thereof.

You shall require the said captains to take like accounts of their master-gunners for their shot, powder, munition, and all manner of stores contained in their indentures. And not suffer any part thereof to be sold, embezzled, or wasted, nor any piece of ordnance to be shot off without their own direction, keeping also true notes of the number and kinds that they may thereby examine their accounts which are not to be allowed in the office of the ordnance without their approbation under their hands.

You shall suffer no boats to go off for the shore or otherwise without the captain's special leave and upon necessary cause to fetch water or some other needful things, and then you shall send the boatswain, cockswain, and one quartermaster and such an orderly going as they shall make choice of and for whose good courage and speedy return they will answer.

You shall require every captain, master, and others to perform unto you due respect and obedience, not taking the wind of you at any time if they be not forced to do it, but keeping company with you as much as may be and speaking with you every morning to know your pleasure and to salute you if the time do permit and coming aboard you as often as you shall put out your flag of counsel on the starboard quarter of your ship and casting and weighing anchor, when you anchor and weigh and shall to that end shoot off a warning piece, taking care that they ride not in the wake one of another, and yet as near together as with order and safety they may, everyone keeping rank under the colors of her squadron.

If you sail by night you shall carry two lights and your vice admiral one, and shall bear such sail as the whole fleet may keep about you, everyone bearing the same course without scattering or falling foul of one another, and if misty weather or tempest shall happen to divide you, you shall give such direction that the scattered may recover the fleet in such a height as you shall assign. And if any ship spring a leak, spend a mast, or be in any distress by fire or otherwise, that they shoot off a piece or two that other ships may take warning and hasten to give help.

If any ship or pinnace shall discover any shipping at sea, they are to give notice thereof by shooting off a piece and letting fall their main topsail as many times as there be ships; and if they appear to be enemies, by shooting twice or thrice to warn the whole fleet to put in order for fight or pursuit.

If any of your fleet chance to meet any vessel from the enemy's coast they are to be directed to bring the master thereof unto you, that by them you may be informed of the enemy's state and proceedings.

But in any wise you are not to suffer any violence, wrong, or interruption to be given by any of your company to any of his Majesty's friends and allies, nor shall permit any man to go aboard them for whose fair and honest carriage you will not answer, nor shall without plain and clear proof of prohibited goods or belonging directly to the King of Spain's subjects take, seize, or stay any vessel or anything therein contained, as you will answer it at your peril.

If you meet any ship of his Majesty's allies laden with any provisions of victuals, cordage, masts, anchors, or Spanish iron you are not to take any of them without agreeing for them in friendly manner and giving your bill for payment of the same.

If you descry any fleet of enemies at sea you shall first ply to get the wind and after you the whole fleet in the due order of their squadrons shall do the like. And when you come to join battle no ship shall presume to assail the enemy's admiral or vice admiral but only you and your vice admiral, if you be able to reach them. And the other ships are to match themselves as equally as they can and to succor one another as cause shall require, not wasting their powder at small vessels or victualers nor shooting afar off, nor till they come up side to side.

You shall not suffer beds of straw nor any matter easy to take fire to be aboard in the time of fight, nor shall permit any powder to be carried up and down in open barrels or in budge-barrels, but shall command the gunners to charge all their ordnances with cartouches which may be kept covered. And for prevention of fireworks you are to cause vessels of urine to be in a readiness in every ship. And shall enjoin every ship carpenter to observe carefully in the fight if any shot chance to fall near the bilging places of the ships and ever to be ready to stop them with salt hides.

Before fight you are to cause and see all things put in order and then encourage your companies and direct them not to board the enemy's ships till the smoke of the ordnance be cleared up, nor till their men above hatches be slain or beaten off.

If any prize or ship be taken from the enemy you must give careful order that no bulk be broken up, but that the hatches be presently spiked up, that all under the overlope [sic] may be preserved for the King's use. And what is above hatches (treasure excepted) may be parted indifferently among the mariners and soldiers, and the captains also distributed with their chests and baggage according to the ancient orders of the sea.

If any of the enemy's ships be discovered to be aground in any harbor or road so as they cannot be set off but by boats, then as you begin to man your boat for that service all the rest must do the like, everyone carrying with him a boat anchor, a grapnel, and a warp. And you must also take order that the ships of least draft ride as near as may be to succor both the boats and barges when they are sent for service or to land men.

The chief intention of this voyage being the weakening and disabling of the enemy in his sea forces and trade by taking and destroying his ships, galleys, frigates, and vessels of all sorts, by spoiling his provisions in his magazines and port towns, by depriving him of seamen, mariners, and gunners, by not suffering him to gather head from any part, by intercepting his fleets either going out or returning, and by taking in and possessing some such place or places in the main of his dominions as may support and countenance our successive fleets. You shall therefore direct and govern your proceedings and services to these ends, and shall not divide your fleet or companies for any other adventure or purchase except when you find so little strength and defense upon his coasts that you may safely assail him in divers places at once. And therefore you shall circumspectly view all his coasts and look into every port, and where you find ships, galleys, or other vessels or provisions, you shall with good advice and courage, and with God's assistance, do your best to destroy them and to take and overthrow all such as shall attempt to join or consort with them.

And because all particulars for sea and land service cannot be limited with special instructions without leaving many things to the wisdom, providence, and good managing of the commanders in all such occurrences and generally in all things which are not or shall not be expressly directed, you are to use your own best judgment and discretion following the advice of such a council as is assigned unto you. That having your own experience and resolution fortified by the consent of at least the greater part of the said councillors you may give the better account of your actions, so as the success may be the more hopeful for the repressing of the ambition of that overgrowing power which has long threatened and disturbed all Christendom, and for the observing and settling of such a happy peace as both his Majesty and his late father of renowned memory have long and carefully sought after and as may tend to the honor of God, the preservation of true religion, the honor of his Majesty, and the safety of his kingdoms. You shall cause a command to be kept and shall advertise me from time to time of all your proceedings and of all things you think fit in your wisdom for me to know or make known to his Majesty. And so to God's blessing I commend your safety and good success.

From the court at Holbury
26° August 1625

Indexes

INDEX OF LEGAL CITATIONS

GENERAL INDEX

In the following index, subheadings are arranged either alphabetically or, as in the case of parliamentary business regarding bills and petitions, chronologically. Cross-references are introduced by *See* and *See also*. For Lords' attendance and excused absences, see Attendance Table.

In any heading or subheading a lower case "m" following a page number indicates that for the designated heading or subheading there are *multiple* entries on the given page. In the case of multiple entries, the reader wanting to know the exact number of such occurrences as bill readings, speeches, and committee appointments on the same page can look at the given page reference itself or the O.B. for the day in question.

We have not entered under the names of individual M.P.s references from the text which apply to them as a generic group, such as all M.P.s of a particular borough. Therefore, to determine all of the committee appointments for Robert Bateman, M.P. for London, for example, the reader must look under both "Bateman" and "London, knights and burgesses of".

H.L., 27–185; H.C., 189–483; Negotium, 487–569; Appendixes, 573–743

BARTLETTE, Thomas, bailiff, 52, 55
 discharged, 84, 85
BASSET, Arthur, M.P.
 brought into House, 358
 case of, 235, 295, 516
  petition read, 348, 353
  referred to comm. of privileges (28 Jn), 349, 354
  report on (8 Ju), 348, 353
 to have privilege, 349, 354
BASSET, Sir Robert, 348
BATEMAN, Robert, M.P.
 committee appointments, 226, 268, 350
 speeches by:
  29 Jn, 268
  5 Ju, 314
BATH, Earl of. *See* Bourchier, Edward
BATH AND WELLS, Bishop of. *See* Lake, Arthur
BATTEL, trials by
 bill to abolish
  1r, H.C., 229
BAVE, Samuel
 bill for naturalization of
  1r, H.C., 442, 446, 479
  2r(?), committed, H.C., 457
BAWDRY
 L. Chief Justice to be informed about, 360, 362
 bill for repressing houses of
  text of draft of, 638
  1r, H.C., 238
BAYLY, Lewis, Bishop of Bangor
 committee appointments, 72, 73, 74, 88, 90, 91, 95, 97m
 to dispose of fast collection, 111
 reports on Edwards's bill, 111, 113
 speeches by:
  4 Ju, 86
 to take attendance at fast, 68, 69
 takes oath of allegiance, 40
BEALKNAP, Sir Robert, Chief Justice Common Pleas (d. 1400?), 318n37
BEARBAITING, etc.
 desire for order to restrain, 359
BEAUMONT, Sir Richard, M.P.
 election of (1624), 296, 695
 election of (1625), 695
BEAUMONT, Robert de, Lord Steward (d. 1168), 399n65
BEAUMONT, Sir Thomas
 returned in 1621, 673n1
BEDFORD, Earl of. *See* Russell, Francis (d. 1641)
BEDFORD MS. 197, 11
 authorship of, 318
 dating of, 398n55
 description of, 10, 265n50

BEECHER, Sir William, M.P.
 reads marriage declaration, 706
 servant of died of plague, 480, 712
 speeches by:
  8 Ju, 352, 522
BELASYSE, Henry, M.P.
 presents bill concerning privileges, 257
BELIAL, 652, 653
BELLARMINE, Robert, 332n15, 343
BELL vs. BP. OF NORWICH
 case of (c. Eliz. I), 627
BENDBO, John, deputy to Clerk of the Crown in Chancery
 demanded fees of French ambassadors, 153
 to attend committee on papists (1 Au), 376
BENEFICES
 case of, 627, 628m
 information on, to be brought in, 335
BENEFICES APPROPRIATE
 bill touching
  1r, H.C., 245
BENEFIT OF CLERGY
 bill to take away
  1r, H.C., 239
  2r, committed, H.C., 246
BENIN. *See* Africa Company
BERKELEY, George, Baron Berkeley of Berkeley Castle
 committee appointments, 45, 48, 49, 52, 54m, 88, 89, 90, 146, 148, 149 174, 175, 176, 179, 180
 takes oath of allegiance, 46
BERKELEY, Sir Maurice, M.P.
 committee appointments, 252, 253, 347
BERKSHIRE
 election in, 671
BERTIE, Robert, Lord Willoughby of Eresby
 committee appointments, 43, 45, 46, 48, 49m, 95, 98m, 99, 127m, 139, 140, 141, 146, 148, 149, 174, 175, 176, 179, 180
 takes oath of allegiance, 46
 ushers new member, 59, 60
BERTIUS, Petrus
 student of Arminius, 337n53, 342n100, 517
BEST, Mr., 687
BETHESDA, pool of (Biblical), 30, 31, 191, 493
BEZA, Theodore de, theologian, 332n15, 338, 343, 517
BIBLE, The. *See* Scriptures
BILLS
 in H.C.
  to be delivered to Clerk, 350
 in parliament
  description of, 526–527

H.L., 27–185; H.C., 189–483; Negotium, 487–569; Appendixes, 573–743

H.L., 27–185; H.C., 189–483; Negotium, 487–569; Appendixes, 573–743

H.L., 27–185; H.C., 189–483; Negotium, 487–569; Appendixes, 573–743

H.L., 27–185; H.C., 189–483; Negotium, 487–569; Appendixes, 573–743

H.L., 27–185; H.C., 189–483; Negotium, 487–569; Appendixes, 573–743

COXE, William, M.P.
  speeches by:
    6 Au, 411
CRANE, Sir Robert, M.P.
  admitted into House, 385
  committee appointments, 206, 245, 246, 252, 253, 457
  speeches by:
    30 Jn, 275
    10 Au, 445
CRANFIELD, Lionel, Earl of Middlesex, 400, 405
  and disorders of the household, 546, 659, 660
  and Great Farm, 392n12
  impeachment proceedings against (1624), 268n3, 284n26, 379
  increased impost on wine
    complaint against (1624), 287
  Master of Court of Wards (c. 1619)
    instructions of, 308
CRASSUS, 516
CREDITORS
  bill to relieve
    1r, H.C., 269
CREW, Sir Clipsby, M.P.
  committee appointments, 252, 422
CREW, John, M.P.
  committee appointments, 252, 347, 422
  speeches by:
    28 Jn, 265
CREW, Sir Ranulphe, Chief Justice of the King's Bench
  assistant to Lords, 46, 49, 81m, 99, 174, 177m, 179m, 180m
  messenger H.L. to H.C.:
    8 Au, 147, 423, 424, 426
  returns answer from H.C.:
    8 Au, 148
  returns writ of error, 95, 97
CREW, Sir Thomas, M.P., Speaker of the House of Commons, Serjeant at Law, 34
  attribution of speech to
    10 Au, 452
  chosen Speaker (18 Jn), 191, 192, 193, 494
  experienced in law and parliament, 494n10
  leaves chair
    23 Jn, 230, 234
    24 Jn, 239
    28 Jn, 258m
    6 Ju, 322, 324
  letter to Sec'y. Conway, 717
  makes warrants for new elections, 205, 208
  nominated Speaker, 193, 494, 706
  nomination a good omen, 494
  papers of burned (1614), 396n50

presents bills for King's assent, 117, 122
sent to Ireland following 1621 session, 476n23
Speaker in 1624, 191n13, 193
speeches by:
  20 Jn (acceptance), 34, 36, 37, 196, 197, 494, 651
  25 Jn, 245
See also Privileges, H.C., customary petitions to King for; Speaker of the House of Commons
CROFT, Sir W., 714
CROKE, Sir George, Justice of the Common Pleas
  assistant to Lords, 72, 73, 74, 99, 127m, 128, 174, 175, 177, 179, 180
  brings commission of adjournment to H.C., 369
  his horse stolen, 139
  messenger H.L. to H.C.:
    11 Ju, 116, 368
  See also Pitt, Rowland
CROMWELL, Sir Oliver, M.P.
  committee appointments, 226, 257, 358
CROMWELL, Ralph, Baron Cromwell, Treasurer (c. 1433), 401, 405, 408
  petitions to *H*. VI, 629m
CROMWELL, Thomas, Baron Cromwell of Ockham
  committee appointments, 139, 140, 141
  sends proxy, 45, 47
CROUCH, Thomas, 122
  case against Edward Hayne, 95
CULPEPER, Richard, servant to L. Cromwell
  petition of
    referred to L. Keeper, 183
    referred to subcomm. of privileges, 111, 113
  discharged, 183n1
CUMBERLAND, Earl of. *See* Clifford, Francis
CURSING, etc.
  act against (1624), 631
CURTENS, Peter, of Middleborough
  regarding ship of, 719
CUSTOM HOUSE
  fees of
    to be regulated, 304
    grievance of and King's answer to (1625), 304
  rates of
    complained against (1624), 304n68
CUSTOMS
  anticipated, 427
  Great Farm of, 392n12
  pretermitted
    complained against (1621), 373n39
    complained against (1624), 304n64
    grievance of and King's answer to, 304, 308
    left to next session, 304, 308
    need for examination of, 511

H.L., 27–185; H.C., 189–483; Negotium, 487–569; Appendixes, 573–743

H.L., 27–185; H.C., 189–483; Negotium, 487–569; Appendixes, 573–743

ELIOT, Sir John, M.P., 4
  analyses of the parliament, 568–569
  committee appointments, 206, 228, 240, 350, 380
  speeches by:
    undated, 515
    22 Jn, 216
    23 Jn, 230, 504
    28 Jn, 257
    11 Ju, 369, 370
    2 Au, 379, 380, 382
    6 Au, 412, 414, 415, 711
  Vice Admiral of Devonshire
    warned of Turkish ships in channel, 528
ELIZABETH I, Queen of England, 82
  acts regarding
    continuance of peace, 631
    obedience to, 631
    royal power of, 631
    subsidies to, 631m
  assisted Low Countries, 278, 507
  clapped Bible to her heart, 382
  cleaved to God, 216, 507
  consumed Spain, 278, 488, 507
  defended herself, 278
  governed by grave and wise counsel, 394, 508
  had good credit, 537
  navy of, 399, 403, 546
  no sale of honors, etc., under, 558
  and parliamentary grievances, 452
  preserved Ireland, 278
  refused further supply, 467
  relieved France, 278, 488, 507
  rewarded men out of her abundance, 394
  subsidies granted to, 276, 279, 477
  took tonnage and poundage, 511
  was glorious above all, 488
  would search her own coffers, 462, 470, 477, 538,
    564, 565
ELIZABETH OF BOHEMIA, Electress Palatine,
    359, 362, 364, 402
  monies already paid to, 394, 538
  monthly allowance for, 168, 171, 432m
  yearly allowance for, 427
ELSYNGE, Henry, Sr., Clerk of the Parliaments
  letter of, 144n4
  marginal entries by, 7
  notes by (4 Au), 136–137
  prepared Parliament Roll, 6
  reads
    commission for dissolution, 183, 185
    commission of adjournment, 122
    King's letter patent for bills, 118, 122
  tract on bills, 146n2
  See also Clerk of the Parliaments
ELY, Bishop of. *See* Felton, Nicholas

EMANUEL, Charles, Duke of Savoy
  in confederacy, 351
  in league with France, etc., 134, 388, 649
EMPEROR of the Holy Roman Empire. *See* Ferdi-
    nand II
EMPSON, Sir Richard, 241n21, 450, 451
ENDYMION, 491
ENGLAND
  honor and safety of, at stake, 387
  an island which depends on trade, 462, 464, 469
  in league with France, Savoy, and Venice, 388, 493
  last monarchy that retained liberties, 557
  present grievances and oppressions, 508
  proverb of, 464, 469
  retains original right and constitutions, 449
  war foreseen by
    to moderate greatness of Spanish King, 387, 493
    to vindicate injury of Palatinate, 387, 388
  will not desert friends, 498
ENGLAND, Church of
  act for uniformity in, 631
  fees for nonattendance at, 631
ENGLISHMEN
  their dexterity, 531
EQUITY, COURTS OF
  bill for reversing sentences in
    1r, H.C., 228
ERDESWICKE, Richard, M.P.
  servant of
    contempt respited, 411
    motion for privilege for, 411
ERITH AND PLUMSTEAD
  bill concerning
    1r, H.C., 252
    2r, committed, H.C., 257
ERLE, Sir Walter, M.P.
  committee appointments, 205, 215, 218, 226, 228,
    230, 239, 241, 252, 253, 268, 375
  speeches by:
    5 Ju, 313, 317
    2 Au, 380
    6 Au, 412, 414, 415
    11 Au, 460
ESCOTT, Richard, M.P.
  admitted into House, 378
ESSEX, Earl of. *See* Devereux, Robert
ESSEX
  election in, 682
  knights and burgesses in
    committee appointments, 257
ESTMOND, Mary, recusant, 426
  committed to custody of constable, 412, 549
  and Conway's letters regarding, 172, 412n10, 549,
    665
    read in H.C. (6 Au), 414, 415

H.L., 27–185; H.C., 189–483; Negotium, 487–569; Appendixes, 573–743

and Drake and Gollop's letter to Conway, 665
escapes, 412
mentioned in petition to King, 154
pardon of, 172, 412n10, 549
refuses to take oath, 146n1, 412n10, 549
See also Religion, conference on
ETHICS, Aristotle, 562
EURE, William, Baron Eure of Witton
   leave to be absent, 47
   protection granted, 65n8
EVELYN, John
   indenture with the crown, 629
   patent of, 629
   petitioner to H.L.
      case recommended to L. Treasurer, 110, 113
      he remains unpaid, 110n9
EVERSFIELD, Nicholas, M.P.
   committee appointments, 350
EXCHEQUER, all officers of
   committee appointments, 238
EXCOMMUNICATION
   bill to mitigate sentence of
      1r, H.C., 228
      2r, committed, H.C., 253
EXETER, Bishop of. *See* Carey, Valentine
EXETER, Earl of. *See* Cecil, William
EXETER
   papists imprisoned at, 412
EXETER COLLEGE CHAPEL
   for communion at Oxford session, 391, 393
FAIRFAX, Captain Ferdinando, M.P.
   committee appointments, 206, 253, 349
FAIRFAX, Sir Thomas, M.P.
   election contested
      report on (4 Ju), 295, 300, 301, 306
   returned in second election, 423
   speeches by:
      30 Jn, 275
   well affected to Sir D. Carleton, 708
   See also Yorkshire, election in
FAIRS, 712
   forbidden in London, 708
FANE, Francis, Earl of Westmorland
   and the Kent election, 686
   brought into H.L., 39, 41
   committee appointments, 72, 73, 74
   created Earl, 39n2
   letter to Sir G. Manners, 133n8
   takes oath of allegiance, 40
FANE, Mildmay. *See* Burghersh, Lord
FANSHAWE, Thomas, M.P.
   election of, 685
FANSHAWE, Sir Thomas, M.P.
   committee appointments, 229, 238, 246, 257, 347, 411, 422, 457

reports by:
   7 Ju, 335
speeches by:
   23 Jn, 230
   25 Jn, 247
   9 Ju, 360, 363
   6 Au, 411
FANSHAWE, William, M.P.
   committee appointments, 457
FARINGTON, Lionell
   petitioner to H.L., 64, 68
   text of petition, 65
FARMS
   bill against depopulation and decay of
      1r, H.C., 201
      2r, committed, H.C., 375
FAST, general
   proposal for in 1624, 204n3
   See also Fast, general (July 1625); Fasts, Wednesday
FAST, general (July 1625)
   alterations in date of, 67n11
   book prescribing manner of. *See* under Fasts, Wednesday
   by warrant from King, 239
   days appointed for, 68, 69
   deferred, 241, 259
   petition for
      presented to King, 46n17
      text of, 44
   21 Jn: resolution to petition King for (H.C.), 205, 208, 211, 212, 500
      comm. to draft petition for, appointed, H.C., 205, 208, 210
   22 Jn: report from comm. to draft petition, H.C., 217, 218
      petition read and allowed, H.C., 217, 218, 221–222
   23 Jn: message H.C. to H.L. for conference, 43, 46, 228, 235
      commission for joint conference, appointed, 43, 46, 48, 228
      answer H.L. to H.C. for joint conference, 43, 46, 48
      reports on joint conference, 43, 47, 229, 233, 504
      petition read, amended, passed, H.L., 43, 44, 47
      messengers to desire access to King, appointed, H.L., 44
      report from comm. on conference, H.L., 44, 47
      report of King's answer on time for presentation of petition, 44, 48
      message H.L. to H.C. (and answer) on presentation of petition, 44, 48, 230
      engrossed petition read, allowed, H.C., 230
      H.L. comm. to receive engrossed petition, 48
   25 Jn: reports on presentation to King, 53, 54, 238, 241, 242, 243, 506

H.L., 27–185; H.C., 189–483; Negotium, 487–569; Appendixes, 573–743

H.L., 27–185; H.C., 189–483; Negotium, 487–569; Appendixes, 573–743

FISHER, Dr. John, Bishop of Rochester
  taxed H.C. with heresy, 482
FISHING, etc.
  bill for free liberty of
    1r, H.C., 238
    2r, committed, H.C., 252
    reported with amendments, H.C., 274
    engrossed, H.C., 274
    3r, passed, H.C., 282
    sent to H.L. (1 Ju), 78, 80, 282
    1r, H.L., 102m
    2r, committed, H.L., 179, 180
FITZJAMES, James, recusant, 665, 666
FLEET, the
  account of expenditures for
    8 Au (reported 9 Au), 163, 434, 436
  cost of preparation of
    for landmen, 522
    in office of navy, 521
    in office of ordnance, 522
  destination of, secret, 473n11, 481, 538, 542, 547,
    723
  for Newfoundland
    not armed for defense, 722
  King's honor rests on sailing of, 520
  lack of apparel for, 720
  resolved, should go forth, 740
  seasonable for sailing of, 165, 171, 389, 437, 547,
    654
  ships in ill repair, 722
  sum needed to set forth, 387, 438, 444n19, 450m
    465, 466, 534, 537n132, 713
  unseasonable for sailing of, 445
  whether intended to sail, 164
  See also under Navy
FLEET PRISON, prisoners in
  statute regarding warden of, 630
  6 Ju: petition of read and committed, H.L., 97, 98,
    99, 100
  7 Ju: report from comm. on, H.L., 102
    message H.L. to H.C. for joint conference on,
      102m, 334m, 340
  8 Ju: comm. for joint conference on, appointed,
    H.C., 347, 350
    answer H.C. to H.L., 104, 105, 334, 347, 350
  9 Ju: comm. on augmented, H.L., 112
    message H.C. to H.L. (and answer) for present
      conference on, 109, 112, 359, 365
    report on joint conference, 111, 360, 363, 365, 523
    judges to be consulted, 360, 363, 365
    petition of read, H.C., 363
    message H.C. to H.L., 361, 364, 365, 524
  6 Au: resolution to leave matter to L. Chief Justice,
    411
FLEET PRISON, statute regarding, 630

FLEETWOOD, Sir Gerrard, M.P.
  committee appointments, 253
FLEETWOOD, Sir Miles, M.P.
  committee appointments, 205, 226m, 228, 238,
    241, 253, 349, 411, 457
  to inform fast preachers, 205, 208
  motions for a fast, 204, 208, 210, 212
  reports by:
    27 Jn, 252
  speeches by:
    21 Jn, 204, 208, 210, 212
    8 Au, 422, 425
FLEETWOOD, Sir William
  made sheriff of Lancashire, 726
FLETA, 339, 518
FLINTSHIRE, Wales
  election in, 683
FOREMAN, alehouse keeper, 282n7
  charged at the bar, H.C., 298, 300
  in custody of Serjeant, 298, 301
  escaped from Serjeant, 360, 362
  to remain in custody of Serjeant, 368
FOREST, Sir Anthony, M.P.
  committee appointments, 229, 253m
FORSTER, John
  biographer of Eliot, 19
FOSTER, a recusant
  omitted in petition concerning religion, 299, 305
  to be punished exemplarily, 264
  reference to, 382
FOSTER, Professor E.R., 7
FOTHERLEY, Thomas, M.P.
  election of, 697, 698
FOWLE, Matthias
  holds patent for Goldwiredrawers, 302n48
FOWLESTER, Robert, Subsidy Collector, 292
FRANCE
  ambassadors of, in England
    bad impressions of, 716
    cost of maintaining, 167n83, 274, 277, 432, 507,
      656, 707
    displeased with position of Catholics, 375n4
  all things in combustion in, 535 '
  articles of marriage with, 535, 649
    not read in parliament, 369
  declines, 654
  English ships lent to
    at charge of French, 165, 438
    command of left to French King, 732
    correspondence relating to, 727–739
    design viewed with suspicion, 556, 727
    Effiat complains of English captains, 729
    for "foreign enemies", 165n67, 529, 727, 728
    French want to be masters of, 730
    plan conceived by Buckingham, 727

H.L., 27–185; H.C., 189–483; Negotium, 487–569; Appendixes, 573–743

H.L., 27–185; H.C., 189–483; Negotium, 487–569; Appendixes, 573–743

speeches by:
28 Jn, 265
HATTON, Sir Thomas, M.P.
and books for fast, 381
committee appointments, 206, 228, 246, 378
HAUTAIN, Dutch Admiral
attacked by Soubise, 719
HAWKINS, Sir Richard
member of the Africa Company, 308
HAY, James, Earl of Carlisle
negotiated French marriage treaty, 531
HAYNE, Edward, petitioner to King
to be heard next sitting, 95n1
memorandum concerning, 95, 104
writ of error
6 Ju, 95
HAYNE, Thomas, petitioner to H.L.
to be heard next session, 122
case to be arbitrated, 179, 180
members of committee for, 174, 175, 177
servant to E. of Suffolk
to have privilege, 179, 180
petition of, 116, 121, 122
See also Hayne, Edward
HEATH, Sir Robert, M.P., Solicitor General
to acquaint King about *Appeal*, 379, 381
brings in tonnage and poundage bill, 316
committee appointments, 205, 206, 207, 208, 209,
226m, 228, 238, 241, 253m, 260, 276, 299,
335, 349, 368, 375, 378, 411, 422, 459
to consider bill on session, 323
delivers King's answers to 1624 grievances
4 Ju, 298, 301m, 307
to desire conference with H.L. on recess, 358
to draw preamble to subsidy bill, 324
messenger from King to H.C.:
28 Jn, 257, 260
7 Ju, 344n114
9 Ju (petition concerning religion), 358, 361
messenger to King:
9 Ju, 359, 362
to petition King about Spain, 393, 547
to present wine merchants' petition to King, 323
regarding adjournment, 707
to report grievances of 1624, 285
to report joint conference:
8 Au, 424, 425m, 427m
reports Protestation to H.C.:
12 Au, 472
speaks privately with King, 708
takes chair, 230, 234, 341, 463, 470, 477, 480, 481
reports by:
22 Jn (general fast), 217, 218, 221
23 Jn, 230

28 Jn, 258m
6 Ju, 322m
7 Ju, 330, 341
9 Ju (petition concerning religion, etc.), 358, 361,
364
8 Au, 422
9 Au (joint meeting on religion and subsidy),
430, 433
12 Au (Protestation), 479, 564
speeches by:
21 Jn, 207, 209, 210, 213
22 Jn, 216
25 Jn, 248
4 Ju, 296, 298
5 Ju, 314, 315, 317
7 Ju, 334
8 Ju, 352
1 Au, 375
2 Au, 379, 381, 532
5 Au, 393, 401, 405, 547
6 Au, 411
9 Au, 439
11 Au, 465, 467, 470
12 Au, 472, 476, 480, 481, 714
HELE, Sir Warwick, M.P.
committee appointments, 227, 245, 246, 252, 253
speeches by:
2 Au, 378
HELMES, Sir Henry, 353
HEMING, John, 322n2
HENRIETTA MARIA, Queen of England
and accompanying Lords, 28n2
Catholic servants of, 86
chapel of, 86
cost of wedding, 432
delayed arrival of, 28n1
expected from France, 492, 640
expenses of, 168, 432m
French displeased with arrangements for, 375n4
marriage ceremony of, 706
and opening of parliament, 492
remembered in prayers, 705
stays in Woodstock, 376
yearly allowance for, 427
HENRY III, King of England (d. 1272)
declaration by, 629
"mad parliament" of, 396n50
parliament of 1234, 383
parliament of 1258, 560
pawned part of his dominions, 560
recovered lost honor, 487
supply required confirmation of liberties, 448, 557
HENRY IV, King of England (d. 1413)
dissolution of last parliament of, 227n7

H.L., 27–185; H.C., 189–483; Negotium, 487–569; Appendixes, 573–743

HUNGERFORD, Edward, M.P.
  committee appointments, 229
HUNTINGDON, Earl of. *See* Hastings, Henry
HUTCHINSON, Thomas, 639
HUTTON, Dr., subdean of Christ Church, 662
HUTTON, Sir Richard, Justice of the Common
    Pleas, 666
  assistant to Lords, 58, 60, 61, 88, 90, 91, 99
  letter to L. Keeper, 720
HYDE, Nicholas, M.P.
  chooses Bristol, 205, 208
  committee appointments, 206, 226, 241, 245, 282,
    324
  reports by:
    6 Ju, 324
HYTHE, Cinque Port
  election in, 686
IDONEA persons
  to be tried by metropolitan, 248
IMPEACHMENT, proceedings. *See* under Bacon, Sir
    Francis; Cranfield, Lionel; Latimer, William,
    Lord; Pole, Michael de la; Richard II; Villiers,
    George
IMPOSITIONS
  on currants
    grievance of and King's answer to, 305, 308
  question of, 511
  total anticipated, 444
IMPROPRIATIONS
  confirmed by law, 248
  information on to be brought in, 335
INDUSTRY (ship)
  lent to France, 727
INGRAM, Sir Arthur, M.P.
  committee appointments, 205, 226, 245, 246, 252,
    347, 358, 368, 375
  election of, 704
  to inform fast preachers, 205, 208
  speeches by:
    21 Jn, 206
INNS, etc.
  bill concerning
    to be looked up, 245
IRELAND, 137
  cost of guarding, 132, 432, 438, 521, 654, 655
  debate on (1621)
    raises procedural issue, H.C., 381, 532
  English troops for, 168n90
  intelligence report about, 388
  monies disbursed for, 350, 354
  M.P.s sent into, 476
  and payment for supplies to, 718
  privy seals for war in, 724
  rumor of a design to trouble, 535

IRON ORDNANCE
  bill against transportation of
    1r, H.C., 28 Jn, 257
ISABELLA Clara Eugenia, Archduchess of Flanders
  ambassadors of, 304
  impositions placed by, 304n63
ISRAEL, 200
ISRAELITES, 414, 549, 638
JACKSON, Sir John, M.P.
  admitted into the House, 472
  election of (1624), 296
  election of (1625), 695
JACKSON, Sir Robert
  election of, 686
JACOB (Biblical), 193
JACOBSON, Philip
  ordnance exporter, 362n27
JAILS
  custody of to other than sheriffs
    grievance of and King's answer to, 303, 308
JAMES, Sir Robert, M.P.
  committee appointments, 457
JAMES, Walter, Subsidy Collector, 291
JAMES I, King of England (d. Mar. 1625), 28
  acts regarding
    subsidy to, 631m
  borrowed for military provisions, 348, 351m
  debts to Christian IV, 167n77, 427
  desired recovery of Palatinate
    by mediation, 387
  encouraged the Low Countries, 387
  entered confederacy, 521, 655
  foreign commitments, 28n5
    and recovery of Palatinate, 29
  funeral expenses of, 167n82, 274, 277, 427, 432,
    507, 656
  gave advice to Charles, 34, 35n15, 36, 160, 170,
    196, 199, 653
  gave long orations, 493
  granted pardons, 531
  in league with France, Savoy, and Venice, 351, 388,
    535, 649
  in parliament 1624, 28n5
    answer to petition concerning religion, 79n3
    broke Spanish treaties, 121, 132, 133, 137, 198,
      387, 388, 493, 494, 534, 648, 651
    did not declare the enemy, 163, 170, 435
    had no money, 162, 435
    said his servants not to be questioned, 380
    took advice, 29, 34, 132, 190, 191, 388, 406, 494,
      534, 651
    wrote to Villiers, 162, 435
  loved peace, hated war, 521, 655
  made union with France by marriage, 387, 535

H.L., 27–185; H.C., 189–483; Negotium, 487–569; Appendixes, 573–743

H.L., 27–185; H.C., 189–483; Negotium, 487–569; Appendixes, 573–743

H.L., 27–185; H.C., 189–483; Negotium, 487–569; Appendixes, 573–743

MONTEIGNE, George (*cont.*)
  speeches by:
    28 Jn, 69
    10 Au, 174, 175
MONTGOMERY, Earl of. *See* Herbert, Philip
MONZON, treaty of (1626), 394n39
MOORE, Edward, M.P., 6
  committee appointments, 241
  speeches by:
    23 Jn, 230
    24 Jn, 239
    25 Jn, 246m
MORDAUNT, John, Baron Mordaunt
  leave to be absent, 47
MORE, Sir Edward, J.P., 92
MORE, Sir George, M.P.
  committee appointments, 205, 215, 218, 226, 228,
    229, 238m, 240, 253, 347, 349, 358, 411, 422
  motions for comm. of privileges, 205, 208
  has petitions for privileges
    order to deliver them (8 Ju), 350
  reports by:
    22 Jn, 217, 218, 221
    4 Ju, 295, 300, 301, 306
    7 Ju, 335
    8 Ju, 348, 353
  speeches by:
    21 Jn, 205m, 207, 208, 209, 210, 211
    22 Jn, 216
    23 Jn, 234
    27 Jn, 252
    30 Jn, 275
    5 Ju, 314, 315, 316, 318
    8 Ju, 350
    11 Ju, 369
    2 Au, 380
    5 Au, 391, 393m, 402, 407
    6 Au, 413, 418
    10 Au, 445, 451
    11 Au, 462, 465, 467, 469
MORE, John, M.P., 6
  election of, 598
MORE, John or Poynings, M.P.
  committee appointments, 349
MORE, Poynings, M.P., 6
MORE, Sir Robert, M.P.
  committee appointments, 253, 380
  to desire longer respite from the King, 474
  speeches by:
    2 Au, 382
    12 Au, 474
MORGAN, George
  bill for
    1r, H.C., 429

MORGAN, Sir Thomas, M.P.
  committee appointments, 245, 253, 257
MORGAN, Sir William, M.P.
  committee appointments, 206
MORLEY AND MONTEAGLE, Lord. *See* Parker,
  Henry
MORRIS, Francis, Clerk of Council of War
  to attend H.C. (1 Ju), 284
MORRISON, Sir Charles, M.P.
  committee appointments, 245, 442
MORTON, Sir Albertus, M.P., Sec'y. of State, 133n10
  dead, 724
  election of, 679, 686, 687
  in France, 705
MORTON, Thomas, Bishop of Coventry and
  Lichfield
  committee appointments, 43, 45, 47, 48, 49m, 59,
    61, 72, 73, 74, 84, 86, 89, 146, 148, 149, 174,
    175, 177, 179, 180
  speeches by:
    22 Jn, 41
    30 Jn, 73
    10 Au, 174, 175, 177
  takes oath of allegiance, 46
MOSES (Biblical), 35
MOSTYN, John, 684
MOSTYN, Sir Roger
  letter of, 684
MOSTYN, Thomas
  letter of, 684
MOUNTJOY, Lord. *See* Blount, Mountjoy
MS E237, Kenneth Spencer Research Library (Anon.
  diary)
  description of, 17
MUSCOVY COMPANY
  and case of Mary Broccas, 139–140, 141
MUSTER MASTERS, etc.
  committee appointed to draw bill for
    30 Jn, 282, 285
MUTTON, Sir Peter, 672, 673m, 674, 676, 677, 684
  letters of, 674, 675
  letters to, 674, 675
NANNEY, Hugh, 693m
NAPIER, Sir Nathaniel, M.P.
  committee appointments, 246, 358
NATURALIZATION
  bills for
    Samuel Bave, 442, 446, 457
    Sir D. Deligne, 442, 446, 457
    See also under Bave, Samuel; Deligne, Sir Daniel
NAUNTON, Sir Robert, M.P., Master of the Court of
  Wards
  committee appointments, 245, 268
  public orator of Cambridge (c. 1594), 555n178

H.L., 27–185; H.C., 189–483; Negotium, 487–569; Appendixes, 573–743

devices to avoid the law, 230
fine for absence from divine service, 231n23
letters to prohibit proceedings against, 230
remedies for increase of
  choose schoolmasters carefully, 156, 262
  confine outside of London, 159, 264
  disarm recusants, 159, 264
  enact bill to regulate nonresidency, etc., 262
  enforce fines for, 264
  enlarge preaching word of God, 157
  examine land grants of, 158, 264
  execute laws of the realm, 159
  execute recusancy laws, 158
  execute stat. of 1 *Eliz.*, 160
  fix departure of Jesuits, etc., 263
  grant commission to oversee recusancy laws, 264
  insure public education for recusants, 263
  no recusant to be prison keeper, 263
  proceed in course against Anyan, 262
  prohibit abroad, 263
  to prohibit at court, 157
  provide against education abroad, 156, 157, 263
  punish insolencies of, 159, 264
  raise livings for ministers, 262
  to remove from places of authority, 159, 264
  restore discipline of universities, 157, 262
  restore silenced ministers, 262
  take like course in Ireland, 160, 264
  that none confer orders of Rome, 158, 263
  that none hear mass, 159, 264
way to security is to supress, 397
See also Recusancy laws
PAPISTS, debate concerning, 246–250
PAPISTS, pardon of
petition regarding (text), 154–155
See also under Religion, conference on
PARCKHURST, Robert, alderman of London, etc.
petition of
  read and referred to comm. of privileges, 71, 73
PARDON
of Alexander Baker, etc.
  dispenses with law, 152, 169, 172
  no breach of King's promise, 154
  solicited by Sec'y. Conway, 153, 172
under Edward III, 630m
under Elizabeth, 153
with regard to 1625 adjournment, 340, 341n89
See also Baker, Alexander; Jesuits; Pardon, of papists
PARDON, of papists, 548
Lords refuse to join in petition regarding, 415, 563
procuring of, 230, 247, 412, 414, 415
requested by French ambassadors, 458, 461, 467
1 Au: pardon read and debated in comm. of whole,
  H.C., 375, 376, 531

6 Au: (sub)comm. to meet for drawing petition regarding pardon, 412, 412n9, 414, 415
resolved, Conway's letter referred to
  (sub)comm., 412, 414, 549
(sub)comm. to finish petition regarding, 412
8 Au: petition regarding pardon read, amended,
  agreed, H.C., 422, 424
message H.C. to H.L. (and answer) for conference, 146, 147, 148, 422, 424
comm. for conference on religion, appointed,
  H.L., 146, 147, 150
9 Au: comm. to consider pardon, 171
report on conference on religion, 152, 169, 172,
  429
proposed petition regarding pardon read, H.L.,
  154–155
10 Au: message H.L. to H.C. (and answer) for joint
  conference, 168, 171, 172, 174, 175, 443,
  449
message H.L. to H.C. (and answer) that collection for distressed of London be discussed at conference
11 Au: report from conference on religion and petition regarding pardon, 179, 180, 458, 460,
  468, 563
See also Baker, Alexander; Religion, conference on
PARHAM, John, 116, 122
petitioner to H.L.
  case to be arbitrated, 179, 180
PARKER, Henry, Lord Morley and Mounteagle
license to be absent, 47
PARKYNS, George, 639
PARLIAMENT, HOUSE OF COMMONS 1625, 3, 8
adjourn themselves, 117, 122, 369, 370, 526
against supply, 180
atmosphere of H.C. on 6 Au, 548
attend dissolution in H.L., 183, 185, 369, 370, 479,
  524, 567
attend H.L. to hear royal assent to bills, 117, 122,
  369, 370, 524
contribute to distressed of London, 472
customary petitions of, to King, 197, 200
desire recess (9 Ju), 111
divisions in
  and conference for general fast (22 Jn), 218
  and Yorkshire election (5 Ju), 315, 316, 514
doctrinal issues not in jurisdiction of, 379, 533
Grand Committees of
  custom of late, 220
  motion to relinquish, 220
  not regular under Queen Elizabeth, 220
House to be called 2nd session, 369, 370
  calling deferred, 385n5
journal of. *See* Clerk of the House of Commons

H.L., 27–185; H.C., 189–483; Negotium, 487–569; Appendixes, 573–743

H.L., 27–185; H.C., 189–483; Negotium, 487–569; Appendixes, 573–743

H.L., 27–185; H.C., 189–483; Negotium, 487–569; Appendixes, 573–743

H.L., 27–185; H.C., 189–483; Negotium, 487–569; Appendixes, 573–743

H.L., 27–185; H.C., 189–483; Negotium, 487–569; Appendixes, 573–743

H.L., 27–185; H.C., 189–483; Negotium, 487–569; Appendixes, 573–743

H.L., 27–185; H.C., 189–483; Negotium, 487–569; Appendixes, 573–743

SPAIN
  call for war against (1621), 416n39
  joined with France in marriage, 394
  kings of, 134, 161, 170
  voluntary contributions in, 567
SPAIN, King of. *See* Philip IV
SPANISH MARRIAGE TREATIES
  breaking of, 29, 35, 36, 132, 133, 137, 161, 190,
      191, 193, 435, 493, 541
  broken by Charles, Prince of Wales, 396
  cause of increase of recusants, 240
  caused suffering to opposition of, 396
  proceeded from ill-counsel, 396
  See also under Parliament (1624)
SPEAKER OF THE HOUSE OF COMMONS
  adjourns H.C. to Oxford, 369, 372
  attends at dissolution, 183, 185, 369, 371
  brings message from King (4 Au), 385m
  election and presentation of, 34, 494
  ordered copy of Protestation sent to King, 475
  petitions to King, 34, 36, 496
  receives letter from R. Montagu, 424
  regarding chairmen at committee, 234
  speeches by:
    20 Jn, 36m, 37, 494
    7 Ju, 334
  to write to stay suit for Wortley, 313, 316
  See also Crew, Sir Thomas
SPENCER, Edward, M.P.
  committee appointments, 253
SPENCER, Edward or Richard, M.P.
  committee appointments, 206
  speeches by:
    30 Jn, 276
SPENCER, Richard, M.P.
  committee appointments, 228, 241, 253, 268
SPENCER, William, Baron Spencer of Wormleighton
  committee appointments, 43, 45, 49m, 52, 54m, 59,
      61, 72m, 73m, 74m, 79, 81m, 84, 86, 127m,
      177
  to take attendance at fast, 68, 69
  takes oath of allegiance, 40, 41
SPENCER, Sir William, M.P.
  admitted into House, 375
  speeches by:
    10 Au, 446
SPENTE, Robert, Subsidy Collector, 292
SPICER, Mr., 673, 674
SPILLER, Sir Henry, M.P.
  committee appointments, 230
SPILMAN, Sir Henry, M.P.
  admitted into House, 385
SPINOLA, Ambrogio, Spanish general, 678
SPRING, Sir William, M.P.
  admitted into House, 385

STAFFORD, Edward, Baron Stafford
  license to be absent, 45, 47
STANDING ORDERS, H.L., regarding:
  adjournment of House, 104n1
  conference procedure, 171n108
  continuation of privileges, 112
  fines for absence, 40n9, 53, 54
  fines for lateness, 40, 66, 69
  hat-wearing at joint meetings, 386n10
  imprisonment of members, 110, 112
  non-members, 41, 41n13
  oath of allegiance, 39n7, 41
  privilege for servants, 58n8
  protection of peers, 58
  Roll of, read, 39, 41
  status of bishops, 39, 39n7
STANHOPE, Philip, Baron Stanhope of Shelford
  sends proxy, 45, 47
STANLEY, Henry or Thomas, M.P.
  committee appointments, 411
STANLEY, James, Lord Strange, M.P.
  committee appointments, 228, 245, 253, 268
STANLEY, Thomas, M.P.
  election of, 692
STANLEY, Sir William (d. 1495)
  and case of Perkin Warbeck, 630
STANLEY, William, Earl of Derby
  sends proxy, 45, 47
STAPLE
  organization of, 628
STAR CHAMBER
  case of Knightley vs. Lord Vaux, 725
STATUTES, 629–632
  bill for continuance of
    1r, 2r, committed, H.C., 324
    reported, amended, H.C., 324
    engrossed, H.C., 324
    3r, H.C., to sleep, 335
STEWARD, Lord. *See* Herbert, William, Earl of
  Pembroke
STEWARD, office of Lord
  inherited office, 399
STEWARD, Walter, M.P.
  committee appointments, 246, 253
STEWS (brothels), 362
STOURTON, Edward, Baron Stourton of Stourton
  committee appointments, 43, 45, 46, 48, 49m, 72,
      73, 74, 127m, 174, 175, 176, 179, 180
STRADLING, Sir John, M.P.
  committee appointments, 206, 226, 229, 238m,
      246, 252m, 253m, 323, 347, 358m, 442, 457
  to consider bill on session, 323
  denied voice on committee, 411
  granted privileges of H.C.
    proceedings against, stayed, 274

speeches by:
  23 Jn, 226m
  25 Jn, 245
  6 Au, 413, 417
STRANGWAYS, Sir John, M.P.
  committee appointments, 245, 246m, 253
STRODE, Sir John, M.P.
  presents bill on recusants' children, 257
STRODE, William, M.P.
  committee appointments, 349, 422
  speeches by:
    4 Ju, 301
    9 Ju, 358
    2 Au, 379
    6 Au, 412, 414, 417
STRODE, Sir William, M.P.
  committee appointments, 205, 215, 218, 228,
    238m, 240, 246, 252, 254, 411
  speeches by:
    21 Jn, 204, 207, 210
    30 Jn, 276
    5 Au, 393, 402, 407
    11 Au, 465, 467
STUART (Stewart), Sir Francis, an Admiral
  complains of western merchants, 721
  describes actions against pirates, 721
  no instructions for France, 460
  to pursue pirates, 457, 460, 468
STUTEVILLE, Sir Martin
  newsletters of, 679, 709
SUBSCRIPTION
  bill for
    1r, H.C., 238
    2r, committed, H.C., 253
SUBSIDIES
  debate on additional, 391–408
  gift of, accepted by King, 386, 389
  in reversion, 393m, 402m, 417, 430, 443, 445,
    544
  motions for additional, 395, 658
  regarding collection of (c. E. III), 628m
  See also under Charles I and Parliament 1625
SUBSIDIES, clerical (H.L.)
  bill for
    1r, 2r, 3r, H.L., 116, 121
    passed, H.L., 116, 121
    sent to H.C., 116, 121, 368, 370
    1r, passed, H.C., 368, 370, 523
    returned to H.L., 368
    assented to by King, 118, 372, 526
  statute regarding, 632
SUBSIDIES, Lay. *See* Subsidy (1625)
SUBSIDY (1602), 477
SUBSIDY (1604–1610), 444, 450
  subsidies granted in two sessions, 564, 565

SUBSIDY (1606), 465n61
SUBSIDY (1614)
  propounded and denied, 433
SUBSIDY (1621)
  subsidies granted in two sessions, 433
SUBSIDY (1624) (act of 21 *Jac.* I, c. 33)
  charges to be paid according to the act, 324m,
    325m
  Council of War named in, 132n4
  disbursement of, 30n11, 132n4, 161–171
  for defense of the kingdom, 460
  exhausted, 191
  for public service, 350n33
  motion to take account of (1 Au), 375
  not yet accounted for, 466, 507
  resolution concerning, 324m, 325m
  resolutions on charges concerning, 285
  stipulations of, 278n26
  treasurers named in, 132n4, 718
SUBSIDY (1625)
  assessed on real property, 275n6
  bill for
    motions for (30 Jn), H.C., 274
    comm. appointed to draw preamble for, 276
    1r, H.C., 298, 301
    2r, committed, H.C., 313, 316
    amended, 2r, engrossed, H.C., 322
    3r, H.C., 347, 350, 354, 510
    sent to H.L., 104, 347, 350, 354
    1r, 2r, 3r, H.L., 104, 106
    sent back to H.C., 106
    assented to by King, 118, 121, 372, 526
    statute regarding, 632
  can do no good, 399
  debate on, 274–279, 442–453, 461–467, 507–508
  debate on additional, 713
  King wants consideration of, 176
  motion for additional, 710
  provisional instructions for, 352n44
  recusants to pay double, 276, 279, 508, 716
  resolutions on time and amount of, 276, 279
  in reversion, 713
  value of, 348n9
SUBSIDY bill for tonnage and poundage. *See* Tonnage and Poundage
SUCKLING, Sir John, M.P., Comptroller of the
  Household
  committee appointments, 422
  remarks about, 685
SUETONIS, *De Vita Caesarum*, 191n12
SUFFOLK, Earl of. *See* Howard, Thomas
SULEIMAN, 468
SUMMONS, writs of. *See* under Writs
SURREY, J.P.s
  to receive plague orders, 80

H.L., 27–185; H.C., 189–483; Negotium, 487–569; Appendixes, 573–743

debate on, H.C., 511
reported, H.C., 330, 336
3r, passed, H.C., 349, 511
sent to H.L. (9 Ju), 109, 112, 358n4, 519
1r, H.L., 110, 112
rejected, 526
collected by Charles I, 372, 399, 542
wrong done by, 397
customs on cloth excepted from, 313n8
gift of the parliament, 279
granted for life, 372, 430, 553
granted to guard sea, 460, 468
history of grant of, 313n9, 317
immoderate rate of late, 373
received by James I, 276, 279, 511
and subsidy on wines, 314n11
1625 bill limited, 372, 511
TOWNSHEND, Sir John
holds patent of concealments, 302, 307
TOWSE, William, M.P., Serjeant at Law
and Colchester election, 680, 681
committee appointments, 253m
speeches by:
4 Ju, 296
TREASURER, Lord. *See* Ley, James, Baron Ley of
Ley
TREASURERS' Subsidy
account of 1624 collection, 285, 289–292
accounts of, reported on, H.C.
debate on, postponed, 323, 324
See also under Oaths; Subsidy (1624)
TRENT, Council of, 333n20
TRESWELL, Robert, Somerset Herald, 82n20
TREVOR, Sir John, Jr., M.P.
admitted into House, 385
and Flintshire election, 684
TREVOR, Sir John, Jr. or Sr., M.P.
committee appointments, 422
TREVOR, Sir John, Sr., M.P.
admitted into House, 385
TREVOR, Sir Sackville, M.P.
committee appointments, 349
election of, 684
TREVOR, Sir Thomas, 680
TREVOR, Sir Thomas, Baron of the Exchequer
assistant to Lords, 52, 54m, 58, 60, 61, 99m
brings commission of adjournment to H.C.,
369
messenger H.L. to H.C.
30 Jn, 275
TREWYNARD
case of (36 *H.* VIII), 233, 348, 353, 354, 627
TRINITY MINORIES
subsidy (1624) not yet accounted, 291
TRUMBULL, William
letter to, 669

TUCHET, Mervin, Baron Audley of Hely and Earl
of Castlehaven
sends proxy, 47
TUNBRIDGE, Viscount. *See* Bourke, Robert
TURKEY MERCHANTS. *See* Levant Company,
merchants of
TURKISH PIRATES. *See* Pirates, Turkish
TURKS
prisoners of
petition of wives of, 720
tortured by captors, 468, 720
TURNMILL Street
place of bawdry, 360
TYLER, Wat
led peasant revolt (1381), 399n70
TYSE, Mr., 687
ULYSSES, 351, 521
USHER, Gentleman, of the Black Rod. *See* Maxwell,
James
VALTELLINA, 394n39, 650
at liberty, 161, 434, 554
French marched into, 538
partition of, 387
possessed by Spain, 161, 434
VANE, Sir Henry, M.P.
a Villiers client, 692
chooses Carlisle, 229
Cofferer of the Household, 168n84
committee appointments, 226, 228
election of, 598
VANGUARD (ship)
captained by J. Pennington, 727
lent to France, 727
of royal navy, 529, 720, 727
See also under France
VAUGHAN, Richard, M.P.
committee appointments, 245
VAUGHAN, William, 675, 678, 693
VAUX, Mistress
case regarding, 725
VAUX, Edward, Baron Vaux of Harrowden
case against Mr. Knightley, 725
sends proxy, 47
VENICE
in confederacy, 351
VENICE, Duke of. *See* Contarini, Francesco
VERE, Sir Horace
on Council of War, 162n55
VERE, Robert de, Earl of Oxford
license to be absent, 45, 47
VERNEY, Sir Edmund, M.P.
committee appointments, 257
VERNON, George, M.P., 672
election of, 598
VICTUALS
concerning patents for (c. 1472), 630

H.L., 27–185; H.C., 189–483; Negotium, 487–569; Appendixes, 573–743

H.L., 27–185; H.C., 189–483; Negotium, 487–569; Appendixes, 573–743

WESTON, Sir Thomas, Subsidy Collector, 292
WEYMOUTH AND MELCOMBE REGIS, Dorset
  election in, 703
  letter to, 740
WHISTLER, John, M.P.
  committee appointments, 245, 375
  election of, 695
  speeches by:
    21 Jn, 205, 210
    23 Jn, 229
    5 Ju, 314
    5 Au, 391, 393, 536
    11 Au, 463, 465, 467, 470
WHITAKER, Lawrence, M.P.
  committee appointments, 206, 335
WHITAKER, Lawrence or William, M.P.
  committee appointments, 350
  and committee on bill of simony, 378
  speeches by:
    25 Jn, 249
    7 Ju, 339
WHITAKER, William, M.P.
  committee appointments, 215, 218
  speeches by:
    23 Jn, 232
WHITAKER, William, theologian, 332n15, 338, 343, 517
WHITBY, Edward, M.P.
  committee appointments, 361
  speeches by:
    9 Ju, 360, 363
WHITCHAR, George, tavern keeper, 64, 65, 68
  case referred to subcommittee of privileges, 72
  enlarged, 72, 73
  petition of (text), 74
WHITE, Francis, Dean of Carlisle, 326n25, 517
  authorized printing of *Appeal*, 380n16
WHITEHEAD, Sir Henry, M.P.
  committee appointments, 226, 239, 241, 246
  speeches by:
    23 Jn, 226, 232m
    30 Jn, 275, 278
    11 Au, 465, 467
WHITELOCKE, Bulstrode, M.P. (1626), 3
WHITELOCKE, Sir James, Justice of the King's Bench
  assistant to Lords, 46, 48, 49, 52, 54m
WHITEWAY, William, M.P.
  possible speech by:
    11 Au, 457
WHITLEPOOLE, Sir William, Subsidy Collector, 292
WHITSON, John, M.P.
  delivers letters on Turkish pirates, 457

speeches by:
  21 Jn, 204
  23 Jn, 232
  11 Au(?), 457, 460
WHOLE HOUSE
  three grand committees of
    description of, 501
    religion, grievances, courts of justice, 501
WIGHT, Isle of
  pirates on, 724
WILFORD, Sir Thomas, M.P.
  chooses Canterbury, 205, 208
  election of, 679
  speeches by:
    23 Jn, 230
WILLIAMS, Henry
  petitioner to parliament (1625), 102m
WILLIAMS, John, Bishop of Lincoln, Lord Keeper
  adjourns parliament to Oxford, 118, 119–121, 122, 371m, 525
  answers message from Commons (8 Au), 147, 148
  attempts to delay dissolution, 567
  comments on speech (20 Jn) of, 498
  committee appointments, 49, 78, 80, 84
  declares parliament dissolved, 183, 185, 479, 483, 525, 567
  to deliver King's message, 146, 148
  his letter to the King, 668
  his lodgings at Oxford, 662
  letter from Sir R. Hutton, 720
  and letter from Recorder of London, 184
  message H.L. to H.C. (fast):
    23 Jn, 43, 46
  messenger from King:
    22 Jn, 39
    4 Ju, 84, 86m, 510
    11 Ju, 117, 122, 371m
  privy councillor, 661
  received pardon of Jesuits
    stayed a *recepi*, 154, 458, 461, 468
  reports by
    1 Ju, 78, 80
    4 Ju, 85m, 86m
    8 Ju, 104
    9 Au, 155, 170, 172
  sends letters for prorogations, 640–642
  speeches by:
    18 Jn, 30, 31, 190, 192, 193, 493
    20 Jn, 34, 35, 36m, 37, 40m, 196, 497, 652
    22 Jn, 39, 40, 41m
    23 Jn, 47
    25 Jn, 52
    27 Jn, 58, 60
    28 Jn, 69

H.L., 27–185; H.C., 189–483; Negotium, 487–569; Appendixes, 573–743